Connections

Editorial Board

Year B, Volume 3

Season after Pentecost

Connections

A Lectionary Commentary for Preaching and Worship

Joel B. Green
Thomas G. Long
Luke A. Powery
Cynthia L. Rigby
Carolyn J. Sharp
General Editors

WESTMINSTER
JOHN KNOX PRESS
LOUISVILLE • KENTUCKY

© 2021 Westminster John Knox Press

First edition
Published by Westminster John Knox Press
Louisville, Kentucky

21 22 23 24 25 26 27 28 29 30—10 9 8 7 6 5 4 3 2 1

Unless otherwise indicated, Scripture quotations are from the New Revised Standard Version of the Bible, copyright © 1989 by the Division of Christian Education of the National Council of the Churches of Christ in the U.S.A., and are used by permission. Scripture quotations marked CEB are from the Common English Bible, © 2011 Common English Bible, and are used by permission. Scripture quotations marked ESV are from the *The Holy Bible, English Standard Version,* © 2001 by Crossway Bibles, a publishing ministry of Good News Publishers. Used by permission. All rights reserved. Scripture quotations marked NIV are from *The Holy Bible, New International Version.* Copyright © 1973, 1978, 1984, 2011 by Biblica, Inc.® Used by permission. All rights reserved worldwide. Scripture quotations marked NKJV are from The New King James Version. Copyright © 1979, 1980, 1982, Thomas Nelson Inc., Publishers and are used by permission. Scripture quotations marked RSV are from the Revised Standard Version of the Bible, copyright © 1946, 1952, 1971, and 1973 by the Division of Christian Education of the National Council of the Churches of Christ in the U.S.A., and are used by permission.

Excerpts from *Days and Times: Poems from the Liturgy of Living,* by Paul K. Hooker, copyright 2018, used by permission of the author. All rights reserved.

Book and cover design by Allison Taylor

Library of Congress Cataloging-in-Publication Data
Names: Long, Thomas G., 1946– editor.
Title: Connections: a lectionary commentary for preaching and worship / Joel B. Green, Thomas G. Long,
    Luke A. Powery, Cynthia L. Rigby, Carolyn J. Sharp, general editors.
Description: Louisville, Kentucky: Westminster John Knox Press, 2018– |
    Includes index. |
Identifiers: LCCN 2018006372 (print) | LCCN 2018012579 (ebook) | ISBN 9781611648874 (ebk.) |
    ISBN 9780664262433 (volume 1 : hbk. : alk. paper)
Subjects: LCSH: Lectionary preaching. | Bible—Meditations. | Common
    lectionary (1992) | Lectionaries.
Classification: LCC BV4235.L43 (ebook) | LCC BV4235.L43 C66 2018 (print) |
    DDC 251/.6—dc23
LC record available at https://lccn.loc.gov/2018006372

Connections: Year B, Volume 3
ISBN: 9780664262426 (hardback)
ISBN: 9780664264840 (paperback)
ISBN: 9781646982103 (ebook)

PRINTED IN THE UNITED STATES OF AMERICA
♾ The paper used in this publication meets the minimum requirements of the American National Standard for Information Sciences—Permanence of Paper for Printed Library Materials, ANSI Z39.48-1992.

Most Westminster John Knox Press books are available at special quantity discounts when purchased in bulk by corporations, organizations, and special-interest groups. For more information, please e-mail SpecialSales@wjkbooks.com.

Contents

LIST OF SIDEBARS   xi

PUBLISHER'S NOTE   xiii

INTRODUCING CONNECTIONS   xv

INTRODUCING THE REVISED
COMMON LECTIONARY   xvii

Trinity Sunday

Isaiah 6:1–8	2
Psalm 29	7
Romans 8:12–17	10
John 3:1–17	14

Proper 3 (Sunday between May 22 and May 28)

Hosea 2:14–20	19
Psalm 103:1–13, 22	24
2 Corinthians 3:1–6	27
Mark 2:13–22	31

Proper 4 (Sunday between May 29 and June 4)

1 Samuel 3:1–10 (11–20) and Deuteronomy 5:12–15	36
Psalm 139:1–6, 13–18 and Psalm 81:1–10	41
2 Corinthians 4:5–12	45
Mark 2:23–3:6	49

Proper 5 (Sunday between June 5 and June 11)

Genesis 3:8–15 and
   1 Samuel 8:4–11 (12–15),
   16–20 (11:14–15)
	54

Psalm 130 and Psalm 138	59
2 Corinthians 4:13–5:1	62
Mark 3:20–35	67

Proper 6 (Sunday between June 12 and June 18)

Ezekiel 17:22–24 and 1 Samuel 15:34–16:13	72
Psalm 92:1–4, 12–15 and Psalm 20	78
2 Corinthians 5:6–10 (11–13), 14–17	81
Mark 4:26–34	85

Proper 7 (Sunday between June 19 and June 25)

Job 38:1–11 and
   1 Samuel 17:(1a, 4–11,
   19–23) 32–49
	89

Psalm 107:1–3, 23–32 and Psalm 9:9–20	96
2 Corinthians 6:1–13	100
Mark 4:35–41	104

Proper 8 (Sunday between June 26 and July 2)

Lamentations 3:22–33 and 2 Samuel 1:1, 17–27	108
Psalm 30 and Psalm 130	113
2 Corinthians 8:7–15	117
Mark 5:21–43	122

Proper 9 (Sunday between July 3 and July 9)

Ezekiel 2:1–5 and 2 Samuel 5:1–5, 9–10	127
Psalm 123 and Psalm 48	132
2 Corinthians 12:2–10	135
Mark 6:1–13	140

Proper 10 (Sunday between
July 10 and July 16)

    Amos 7:7–15 and
        2 Samuel 6:1–5, 12b–19   144
    Psalm 85:8–13 and Psalm 24   149
    Ephesians 1:3–14   152
    Mark 6:14–29   157

Proper 11 (Sunday between
July 17 and July 23)

    Jeremiah 23:1–6 and
        2 Samuel 7:1–14a   162
    Psalm 23 and Psalm 89:20–37   168
    Ephesians 2:11–22   171
    Mark 6:30–34, 53–56   175

Proper 12 (Sunday between
July 24 and July 30)

    2 Kings 4:42–44 and
        2 Samuel 11:1–15   179
    Psalm 145:10–18 and
        Psalm 14   184
    Ephesians 3:14–21   187
    John 6:1–21   191

Proper 13 (Sunday between
July 31 and August 6)

    Exodus 16:2–4, 9–15 and
        2 Samuel 11:26–12:13a   196
    Psalm 78:23–29 and
        Psalm 51:1–12   201
    Ephesians 4:1–16   205
    John 6:24–35   209

Proper 14 (Sunday between
August 7 and August 13)

    1 Kings 19:4–8 and 2 Samuel
        18:5–9, 15, 31–33   214
    Psalm 34:1–8 and Psalm 130   219
    Ephesians 4:25–5:2   222
    John 6:35, 41–51   226

Proper 15 (Sunday between
August 14 and August 20)

    Proverbs 9:1–6 and 1 Kings
        2:10–12; 3:3–14   230
    Psalm 34:9–14 and Psalm 111   235
    Ephesians 5:15–20   238
    John 6:51–58   242

Proper 16 (Sunday between
August 21 and August 27)

    Joshua 24:1–2a, 14–18 and
        1 Kings 8:(1, 6, 10–11)
        22–30, 41–43   246
    Psalm 34:15–22 and Psalm 84   251
    Ephesians 6:10–20   254
    John 6:56–69   259

Proper 17 (Sunday between
August 28 and September 3)

    Song of Solomon 2:8–13 and
        Deuteronomy 4:1–2, 6–9   264
    Psalm 45:1–2, 6–9 and Psalm 15   269
    James 1:17–27   272
    Mark 7:1–8, 14–15, 21–23   277

Proper 18 (Sunday between
September 4 and September 10)

    Proverbs 22:1–2, 8–9, 22–23
        and Isaiah 35:4–7a   282
    Psalm 125 and Psalm 146   287
    James 2:1–10 (11–13), 14–17   290
    Mark 7:24–37   295

Proper 19 (Sunday between
September 11 and September 17)

    Proverbs 1:20–33 and
        Isaiah 50:4–9a   300
    Psalm 19 and Psalm 116:1–9   306
    James 3:1–12   310
    Mark 8:27–38   314

Proper 20 (Sunday between September 18 and September 24)

Proverbs 31:10–31 and Jeremiah 11:18–20	318
Psalm 1 and Psalm 54	323
James 3:13–4:3, 7–8a	326
Mark 9:30–37	331

Proper 21 (Sunday between September 25 and October 1)

Esther 7:1–6, 9–10; 9:20–22 and Numbers 11:4–6, 10–16, 24–29	335
Psalm 124 and Psalm 19:7–14	340
James 5:13–20	343
Mark 9:38–50	348

Proper 22 (Sunday between October 2 and October 8)

Job 1:1; 2:1–10 and Genesis 2:18–24	353
Psalm 26 and Psalm 8	359
Hebrews 1:1–4; 2:5–12	362
Mark 10:2–16	367

Proper 23 (Sunday between October 9 and October 15)

Job 23:1–9, 16–17 and Amos 5:6–7, 10–15	372
Psalm 22:1–15 and Psalm 90:12–17	378
Hebrews 4:12–16	381
Mark 10:17–31	385

Proper 24 (Sunday between October 16 and October 22)

Job 38:1–7 (34–41) and Isaiah 53:4–12	389
Psalm 104:1–9, 24, 35c and Psalm 91:9–16	395
Hebrews 5:1–10	398
Mark 10:35–45	402

Proper 25 (Sunday between October 23 and October 29)

Job 42:1–6, 10–17 and Jeremiah 31:7–9	407
Psalm 34:1–8 (19–22) and Psalm 126	413
Hebrews 7:23–28	416
Mark 10:46–52	420

All Saints

Isaiah 25:6–9	424
Psalm 24	428
Revelation 21:1–6a	430
John 11:32–44	435

Proper 26 (Sunday between October 30 and November 5)

Ruth 1:1–18 and Deuteronomy 6:1–9	439
Psalm 146 and Psalm 119:1–8	444
Hebrews 9:11–14	447
Mark 12:28–34	451

Proper 27 (Sunday between November 6 and November 12)

Ruth 3:1–5; 4:13–17 and 1 Kings 17:8–16	456
Psalm 127 and Psalm 146	461
Hebrews 9:24–28	464
Mark 12:38–44	468

Proper 28 (Sunday between November 13 and November 19)

1 Samuel 1:4–20 and Daniel 12:1–3	472
1 Samuel 2:1–10 and Psalm 16	478
Hebrews 10:11–14 (15–18), 19–25	482
Mark 13:1–8	487

Proper 29 (Reign of Christ)

2 Samuel 23:1–7 and
    Daniel 7:9–10, 13–14   491
Psalm 132:1–12 (13–18)
    and Psalm 93   496
Revelation 1:4b–8   500
John 18:33–37   505

CONTRIBUTORS   511
AUTHOR INDEX   515
SCRIPTURE INDEX   517
COMPREHENSIVE SCRIPTURE
INDEX FOR YEAR B   533

Sidebars

Trinity Sunday: "The Father, the Word, and Love"　　3
Bonaventure

Proper 3: "Engraved upon the Heart"　　22
Zacharius Ursinus

Proper 4: "That Insight into Spiritual Things"　　43
John Henry Newman

Proper 5: "Intoxicated with Self-Love"　　63
Johann Arndt

Proper 6: "This Kingdom of Christ"　　74
John Owen

Proper 7: "The Wise and Good Creator"　　92
Cyril of Jerusalem

Proper 8: "Waiting for God"　　115
Paul Tillich

Proper 9: "Divine Poverty"　　136
Peter Chrysologus

Proper 10: "The Countenance Divinely Human"　　158
Austin Farrer

Proper 11: "The Joy of Entire Surrender"　　164
Hannah Whitall Smith

Proper 12: "A Revolution of the Heart"　　192
Dorothy Day

Proper 13: "The Mercy of the Lord"　　203
Augustine

Proper 14: "The Essence of All Meaning"　　216
Howard Thurman

Proper 15: "Openness to the World and to God"　　234
Gerhard von Rad

Proper 16: "The Only Anchor of Our Soul"　　260
E. B. Pusey

Proper 17: "Serve the Eternal God"　　274
Menno Simons

Proper 18: "Give Birth to Praise"　　296
Ephrem the Syrian

Proper 19: "Creation's Maker and Artificer"　　309
Athanasius

Proper 20: "Lift Up Your Eyes to Heaven"　　327
Basil the Great

Proper 21: "The Remedy Which God Has Provided"　　344
John Keble

Proper 22: "Sufferings of the Soul"　　355
Teresa of Avila

Proper 23: "Our Specific and Unique Loyalty"　　376
Robert Jenson

Proper 24: "Liberation Is for All"   403
   James Cone

Proper 25: "To Converse
with God"   409
   John of the Cross

All Saints: "Let Forgiveness
of Sins Come"   431
   Ambrose

Proper 26: "The Happiness
for Which We Were Made"   452
   John Wesley

Proper 27: "Written in Love
and Loyalty"   458
   Leila Leah Bronner

Proper 28: "The Virtues of the
Living God"   476
   Philo of Alexandria

Proper 29 (Reign of Christ):
"Death Is Christ's Servant"   506
   George MacDonald

Publisher's Note

"The preaching of the Word of God is the Word of God," says the Second Helvetic Confession. While that might sound like an exalted estimation of the homiletical task, it comes with an implicit warning: "A lot is riding on this business of preaching. Get it right!"

Believing that much does indeed depend on the church's proclamation, we offer Connections: A Lectionary Commentary for Preaching and Worship. Connections embodies two complementary convictions about the study of Scripture in preparation for preaching and worship. First, to best understand an individual passage of Scripture, we should put it in conversation with the rest of the Bible. Second, since all truth is God's truth, we should bring as many "lenses" as possible to the study of Scripture, drawn from as many sources as we can find. Our prayer is that this unique combination of approaches will illumine your study and preparation, facilitating the weekly task of bringing the Word of God to the people of God.

We at Westminster John Knox Press want to thank the superb editorial team that came together to make Connections possible. At the heart of that team are our general editors: Joel B. Green, Thomas G. Long, Luke A. Powery, Cynthia L. Rigby, and Carolyn J. Sharp. These five gifted scholars and preachers have poured countless hours into brainstorming, planning, reading, editing, and supporting the project. Their passion for authentic preaching and transformative worship shows up on every page. They pushed the writers and their fellow editors, they pushed us at the press, and most especially they pushed themselves to focus always on what you, the users of this resource, genuinely need. We are grateful to Kimberley Bracken Long for her innovative vision of what commentary on the Psalm readings could accomplish, and for recruiting a talented group of liturgists and preachers to implement that vision. Rachel Toombs did an exceptional job of identifying the sidebars that accompany each worship day's commentaries. At the forefront of the work have been the members of our editorial board, who helped us identify writers, assign passages, and most especially carefully edit each commentary. They have cheerfully allowed the project to intrude on their schedules in order to make possible this contribution to the life of the church. Most especially we thank our writers, drawn from a broad diversity of backgrounds, vocations, and perspectives. The distinctive character of our commentaries required much from our writers. Their passion for the preaching ministry of the church proved them worthy of the challenge.

A project of this size does not come together without the work of excellent support staff. Above all we are indebted to project manager Joan Murchison. Joan's fingerprints are all over the book you hold in your hands; her gentle, yet unconquerable, persistence always kept it moving forward in good shape and on time. We also wish to thank Pamela Jarvis, who skillfully compiled the dozens of separate commentaries and sidebars into this single volume.

Finally, our sincere thanks to the administration, faculty, and staff of Austin Presbyterian Theological Seminary, our institutional partner in producing Connections. President Theodore J. Wardlaw and Dean David H. Jensen have been steadfast friends of the project, enthusiastically agreeing to our partnership, carefully overseeing their faculty and staff's work on it, graciously hosting our meetings, and enthusiastically using their platform to promote Connections among their students, alumni, and friends.

It is with much joy that we commend Connections to you, our readers. May God use this resource to deepen and enrich your ministry of preaching and worship.

ROBERT A. RATCLIFF
WESTMINSTER JOHN KNOX PRESS

Introducing Connections

Connections is a resource designed to help preachers generate sermons that are theologically deeper, liturgically richer, and culturally more pertinent. Based on the Revised Common Lectionary (RCL), which has wide ecumenical use, the hundreds of essays on the full array of biblical passages in the three-year cycle can be used effectively by preachers who follow the RCL, by those who follow other lectionaries, and by nonlectionary preachers alike.

The essential idea of Connections is that biblical texts display their power most fully when they are allowed to interact with a number of contexts, that is, when many connections are made between a biblical text and realities outside that text. Like the two poles of a battery, when the pole of the biblical text is connected to a different pole (another aspect of Scripture or a dimension of life outside Scripture), creative sparks fly and energy surges from pole to pole.

Two major interpretive essays, called Commentary 1 and Commentary 2, address every scriptural reading in the RCL. Commentary 1 explores preaching connections between a lectionary reading and other texts and themes within Scripture, and Commentary 2 makes preaching connections between the lectionary texts and themes in the larger culture outside of Scripture. These essays have been written by pastors, biblical scholars, theologians, and others, all of whom have a commitment to lively biblical preaching.

The writers of Commentary 1 surveyed five possible connections for their texts: the immediate literary context (the passages right around the text), the larger literary context (for example, the cycle of David stories or the passion narrative), the thematic context (such as other feeding stories, other parables, or other passages on the theme of hope), the lectionary context (the other readings for the day in the RCL), and the canonical context (other places in the whole of the Bible that display harmony, or perhaps tension, with the text at hand).

The writers of Commentary 2 surveyed six possible connections for their texts: the liturgical context (such as Advent or Easter), the ecclesial context (the life and mission of the church), the social and ethical context (justice and social responsibility), the cultural context (such as art, music, and literature), the larger expanse of human knowledge (such as science, history, and psychology), and the personal context (the life and faith of individuals).

In each essay, the writers selected from this array of possible connections, emphasizing those connections they saw as most promising for preaching. It is important to note that, even though Commentary 1 makes connections inside the Bible and Commentary 2 makes connections outside the Bible, this does not represent a division between "what the text *meant* in biblical times versus what the text *means* now." *Every* connection made with the text, whether that connection is made within the Bible or out in the larger culture, is seen as generative for preaching, and each author provokes the imagination of the preacher to see in these connections preaching possibilities for today. Connections is not a substitute for traditional scriptural commentaries, concordances, Bible dictionaries, and other interpretive tools. Rather, Connections begins with solid biblical scholarship then goes on to focus on the act of preaching and on the ultimate goal of allowing the biblical text to come alive in the sermon.

Connections addresses every biblical text in the RCL, and it takes seriously the architecture of the RCL. During the seasons of the Christian year (Advent through Epiphany and Lent through Pentecost), the RCL provides three readings and a psalm for each Sunday and feast day: (1) a first reading, usually from the Old Testament; (2) a psalm, chosen to respond to the first reading; (3) a second reading, usually from one of the New Testament epistles; and (4) a Gospel reading. The first and second readings are chosen as complements to the Gospel reading for the day.

During the time between Pentecost and Advent, however, the RCL includes an additional first reading for every Sunday. There is the usual complementary reading, chosen in relation to the Gospel reading, but there is also a "semicontinuous" reading. These semicontinuous first readings move through the books of the Old Testament more or less continuously in narrative sequence, offering the stories of the patriarchs (Year A), the kings of Israel (Year B), and the prophets (Year C). Connections covers both the complementary and the semicontinuous readings.

The architects of the RCL understand the psalms and canticles to be prayers, and they selected the psalms for each Sunday and feast as prayerful responses to the first reading for the day. Thus, the Connections essays on the psalms are different from the other essays, and they have two goals, one homiletical and the other liturgical. First, they comment on ways the psalm might offer insight into preaching the first reading. Second, they describe how the tone and content of the psalm or canticle might inform the day's worship, suggesting ways the psalm or canticle may be read, sung, or prayed.

Preachers will find in Connections many ideas and approaches to sustain lively and provocative preaching for years to come. But beyond the deep reservoir of preaching connections found in these pages, preachers will also find here a habit of mind, a way of thinking about biblical preaching. Being guided by the essays in Connections to see many connections between biblical texts and their various contexts, preachers will be stimulated to make other connections for themselves. Connections is an abundant collection of creative preaching ideas, and it is also a spur to continued creativity.

JOEL B. GREEN
THOMAS G. LONG
LUKE A. POWERY
CYNTHIA L. RIGBY
CAROLYN J. SHARP
General Editors

Introducing the Revised Common Lectionary

To derive the greatest benefit from Connections, it will help to understand the structure and purpose of the Revised Common Lectionary (RCL), around which this resource is built. The RCL is a three-year guide to Scripture readings for the Christian Sunday gathering for worship. "Lectionary" simply means a selection of texts for reading and preaching. The RCL is an adaptation of the Roman Lectionary (of 1969, slightly revised in 1981), which itself was a reworking of the medieval Western-church one-year cycle of readings. The RCL resulted from six years of consultations that included representatives from nineteen churches or denominational agencies. Every preacher uses a lectionary—whether it comes from a specific denomination or is the preacher's own choice—but the RCL is unique in that it positions the preacher's homiletical work within a web of specific, ongoing connections.

The RCL has its roots in Jewish lectionary systems and early Christian ways of reading texts to illumine the biblical meaning of a feast day or time in the church calendar. Among our earliest lectionaries are the lists of readings for Holy Week and Easter in fourth-century Jerusalem.

One of the RCL's central connections is intertextuality; multiple texts are listed for each day. This lectionary's way of reading Scripture is based on Scripture's own pattern: texts interpreting texts. In the RCL, every Sunday of the year and each special or festival day is assigned a group of texts, normally three readings and a psalm. For most of the year, the first reading is an Old Testament text, followed by a psalm, a reading from one of the epistles, and a reading from one of the Gospel accounts.

The RCL's three-year cycle centers Year A in Matthew, Year B in Mark, and Year C in Luke. It is less clear how the Gospel according to John fits in, but when preachers learn about the RCL's arrangement of the Gospels, it makes sense. John gets a place of privilege because John's Gospel account, with its high Christology, is assigned for the great feasts. Texts from John's account are also assigned for Lent, Sundays of Easter, and summer Sundays. The second-century bishop Irenaeus's insistence on four Gospels is evident in this lectionary system: John and the Synoptics are in conversation with each other. However, because the RCL pattern contains variations, an extended introduction to the RCL can help the preacher learn the reasons for texts being set next to other texts.

The Gospel reading governs each day's selections. Even though the ancient order of reading texts in the Sunday gathering positions the Gospel reading last, the preacher should know that the RCL receives the Gospel reading as the hermeneutical key.

At certain times in the calendar year, the connections between the texts are less obvious. The RCL offers two tracks for readings in the time after Pentecost (Ordinary Time/standard Sundays): the complementary and the semicontinuous. Complementary texts relate to the church year and its seasons; semicontinuous emphasis is on preaching through a biblical book. Both approaches are historic ways of choosing texts for Sunday. This commentary series includes both the complementary and the semicontinuous readings.

In the complementary track, the Old Testament reading provides an intentional tension, a deeper understanding, or a background reference for another text of the day. The Psalm is the congregation's response to the first reading, following its themes. The Epistle functions as the horizon of the church: we learn about the faith and struggles of early Christian communities. The Gospel tells us where we are in the church's time and is enlivened, as are all the texts, by these intertextual interactions. Because the semicontinuous track prioritizes the narratives of specific books, the intertextual connections are not as apparent. Connections still exist, however. Year A pairs Matthew's account with Old Testament readings from the first five books; Year B pairs Mark's account with stories of anointed kings; Year C pairs Luke's account with the prophetic books.

Historically, lectionaries came into being because they were the church's beloved texts, like the scriptural canon. Choices had to be made regarding readings in the assembly, given the limit of fifty-two Sundays and a handful of festival days. The RCL presupposes that everyone (preachers and congregants) can read these texts—even along with the daily RCL readings that are paired with the Sunday readings.

Another central connection found in the RCL is the connection between texts and church seasons or the church's year. The complementary texts make these connections most clear. The intention of the RCL is that the texts of each Sunday or feast day bring biblical meaning to where we are in time. The texts at Christmas announce the incarnation. Texts in Lent renew us to follow Christ, and texts for the fifty days of Easter proclaim God's power over death and sin and our new life in Christ. The entire church's year is a hermeneutical key for using the RCL.

Let it be clear that the connection to the church year is a connection for present-tense proclamation. We read, not to recall history, but to know how those events are true for us today. Now is the time of the Spirit of the risen Christ; now we beseech God in the face of sin and death; now we live baptized into Jesus' life and ministry. To read texts in time does not mean we remind ourselves of Jesus' biography for half of the year and then the mission of the church for the other half. Rather, we follow each Gospel's narrative order to be brought again to the meaning of Jesus' death and resurrection and his risen presence in our midst. The RCL positions the texts as our lens on our life and the life of the world in our time: who we are in Christ now, for the sake of the world.

The RCL intends to be a way of reading texts to bring us again to faith, for these texts to be how we see our lives and our gospel witness in the world. Through these connections, the preacher can find faithful, relevant ways to preach year after year.

JENNIFER L. LORD
Connections Editorial Board Member

Connections

Trinity Sunday

Isaiah 6:1–8   Romans 8:12–17
Psalm 29   John 3:1–17

Isaiah 6:1–8

¹In the year that King Uzziah died, I saw the Lord sitting on a throne, high and lofty; and the hem of his robe filled the temple. ²Seraphs were in attendance above him; each had six wings: with two they covered their faces, and with two they covered their feet, and with two they flew. ³And one called to another and said:

> "Holy, holy, holy is the LORD of hosts;
> the whole earth is full of his glory."

⁴The pivots on the thresholds shook at the voices of those who called, and the house filled with smoke. ⁵And I said: "Woe is me! I am lost, for I am a man of unclean lips, and I live among a people of unclean lips; yet my eyes have seen the King, the LORD of hosts!"

⁶Then one of the seraphs flew to me, holding a live coal that had been taken from the altar with a pair of tongs. ⁷The seraph touched my mouth with it and said: "Now that this has touched your lips, your guilt has departed and your sin is blotted out." ⁸Then I heard the voice of the Lord saying, "Whom shall I send, and who will go for us?" And I said, "Here am I; send me!"

Commentary 1: Connecting the Reading with Scripture

Isaiah 6:1–8 almost certainly originated as the account of Isaiah's call. Its placement is surprising, since one would expect Isaiah's call to appear at the beginning of the book, as in other prophetic books (see Jer. 1:4–10). Like other prophetic call narratives, it includes the divine voice and the prophetic response. Unlike the Mosaic model of call narrative found in Jeremiah 1:4–10, Isaiah responds positively, "Here am I; send me!" (Isa. 6:8). This makes the text attractive, but things are not as positive as they may seem when one reads beyond 6:8. Unfortunately, 6:1–8 is ordinarily treated in isolation from 6:9–13, a temptation reinforced by today's lection and by the frequent use of 6:1–8 in ordination services.

Why is Isaiah's call not in chapter 1, and what is the effect of its current placement? It is likely that an original form of the book of Isaiah consisted of what is now chapters 6–39. This would

mean that an original book was framed by two narrative sequences (chaps. 6–8 and 36–39), the first from the early career of Isaiah (approximately 740 to 734 BCE) and the latter from the end of Isaiah's ministry (701 BCE). At some point, an editor or editors expanded the book of Isaiah by adding chapters 1–5 and 40–66. The effect, especially as it pertains to 6:1–8, is to suggest that Isaiah's call came in the midst of pervasive disobedience on the part of Judah and its leadership. Preachers might reflect at this point on the likelihood that prophetic calls will come in the midst of a disordered and disoriented society, as was the case with Isaiah's call.

Chapters 1–5 portray Judean worship as misguided and unacceptable to God (see 1:10–20), and the nation as a whole is characterized by systemic injustice and unrighteousness (see 3:13–26; 5:1–23). Such a sorry situation sheds light on Isaiah's claim that he lives "among a

The Father, the Word, and Love

Now desire tends principally toward what moves it most; but what moves it most is what is loved most, and what is loved most is happiness. But happiness is had only in terms of the best and ultimate end. Therefore human desire seeks nothing except the highest good or what leads to or has some likeness to it. So great is the power of the highest good that nothing can be loved by a creature except out of a desire for it. Creatures, when they take the image and copy for the Truth, are deceived and in error. See, therefore, how close the soul is to God, and how, in their operations, the memory leads to eternity, the understanding to truth and the power of choice to the highest good.

These powers lead us to the most blessed Trinity itself in view of their order, origin and interrelatedness. From memory, intelligence comes forth as its offspring, since we understand when a likeness which is in the memory leaps into the eye of the intellect in the form of a word. From memory and intelligence love is breathed forth as their mutual bond. These three—the generating mind, the word and love—are in the soul as memory, understanding and will. . . . When therefore, the soul considers itself, it rises through itself as through a mirror to behold the blessed Trinity of the Father, the Word, and Love.

The image of our soul, therefore, should be clothed with the three theological virtues, by which the soul is purified, illumined, and perfected. And so the image is reformed and made like the heavenly Jerusalem. . . . The soul, therefore, believes and hopes in Jesus Christ and loves him, who is the incarnate, uncreated, and inspired Word—*the way, the truth, and the life* (John 14:6). When by faith the soul believes in Christ as the uncreated Word and Splendor of the Father, it recovers its spiritual hearing and sight; its hearing to receive the words of Christ and its sight to view the splendors of that Light. When it longs in hope to receive the inspired Word, it recovers through desire and affection the spiritual sense of smell. When it embraces in Love the Word incarnate, receiving delight from him and passing over into him through ecstatic love, it recovers its senses of taste and touch.

Bonaventure, *The Soul's Journey into God*, trans. and ed. Ewert Cousins (Mahwah, NJ: Paulist Press, 1994), 84–85.

people of unclean lips" (6:5). Perhaps even more important, the extent of Judah's unfaithfulness and disobedience documented in chapters 1–5 prepares the reader for the difficult commission that Isaiah is given in 6:9–13, and for the opposition that all who are called to prophetic resistance in such contexts can anticipate.

Even with this preparation, however, the connection between 6:8 and 6:9–13 remains difficult. It seems perverse on God's part to call Isaiah to dull people's minds, "stop their ears, and shut their eyes, so that they may not . . . turn and be healed" (6:10). The difficulty leads many to conclude that 6:9–13 was composed in retrospect to describe the actual response to Isaiah's proclamation. In any case, while the difficulty of the portrait of a God who wants to stop people's ears and shut their eyes endures, the connection between 6:8 and 6:9–10 clearly captures a persistent biblical reality: those

whom God calls to speak God's word are regularly met with powerful opposition by people who are not open to hearing, discerning, or responding faithfully. For all practical purposes, the prophetic word solidifies resistance to God and God's will! The encounter between Isaiah and Ahaz in Isaiah 7 illustrates this reality, as do thematic connections to other prophetic books.

If the connection between Isaiah 6:1–8 and 6:9–13 highlights opposition and resistance to the prophetic word, then we can identify several connections to other portions of the prophetic canon. For example, following closely upon the first version of Jeremiah's temple sermon (Jer. 7:1–15), the divine instruction to Jeremiah is this: "So you shall speak all these words to them, but they will not listen to you. You shall call to them, but they will not answer you" (Jer. 7:27).

Like Isaiah, Jeremiah has been called and must speak; but there clearly will be no faithful response. For all practical purposes, the prophetic word will have solidified the opposition. Jeremiah's "confessions," or better, "complaints," poignantly indicate that the prophetic word was roundly resisted and rejected (see Jer. 11:18–12:6; 15:10–21; 17:14–18; 18:18–23; 20:7–18).

Another instance of the prophetic word evoking and solidifying opposition is found in Amos 7. We do not have an account of Amos's call, but the vision sequence in Amos 7:1–8:3 may be related to his call. Amos's famous vision of the plumb line (Amos 7:7–9) evokes the vehement opposition of Amaziah, "the priest of Bethel" (7:10). Amaziah confronts Amos; he accuses Amos of blasphemy and treason; and then he basically issues an order for Amos's deportation. Again, the prophetic word has solidified opposition to God and God's word, as if Amos had actually intended to dull people's minds and prevent them from turning to God.

In a powerful oracle that targeted greed and systemic injustice, Micah announced judgment upon eighth-century Judah (Mic. 2:1–5). The response was immediate: "'Do not preach'— thus they preach—'one should not preach of such things; disgrace will not overtake us'" (2:6). Micah's audience was convinced God was on their side, no matter what (see 3:11). When they heard otherwise, their opposition was swift and resolute. The prophetic word again solidifies the resistance to God.

While the New Testament affirms that Jesus was more than a prophet, it also casts Jesus in the prophetic role. Hence, it is not surprising that Isaiah 6 shows up in the Gospels to characterize the response to Jesus' proclamation. In the Synoptic Gospels, Jesus alludes to Isaiah 6:9–10 to explain to his disciples that he teaches in parables so that people "may not turn again and be forgiven" (Mark 4:12; see also Matt. 13:13–15;

Luke 8:9–10). As with Isaiah 6, this seems strange, if not perverse. However, the intent of the Gospel writers may be to characterize the typical response to Jesus' proclamation and the embodiment of the realm of God. To be sure, some people responded positively, but Jesus' message and ministry were also roundly opposed. Jesus' very words and deeds solidified the resistance to God's claim and to God's will. So, Isaiah 6 became an appropriate commentary on Jesus' life and ministry.

Perhaps the most prominent homiletical direction to pursue is to affirm that God calls people to say and do things that are richly rewarding but deeply demanding. So, while accepting a prophetic call may be deeply fulfilling, one can anticipate stiff, even violent opposition. The message of Isaiah 6:1–8 and its connections were captured by Reinhold Niebuhr when he wrote the following: "If a gospel is preached without opposition it is simply not the gospel which resulted in the cross. It is not, in short, the gospel of love."[1] Because Jesus invited disciples "to take up their cross and follow me" (Mark 8:34), Isaiah 6:1–8 and its connections invite us to move beyond the priesthood of all believers to what we might call the prophethood of all believers.

Lest all this sound overly discouraging, note that the book of Isaiah makes it clear that it is not ultimately God's intent to evoke opposition. Rather, God wants people with open eyes and ears to experience the saving knowledge that the prophets proclaim (see Isa. 29:18; 32:3; 35:5; 42:16, 18–19; 43:8, all of which reverse Isa. 6:9–10). While taking up a cross may be difficult, it is the way to life (see Mark 8:35). The ultimate intent of Isaiah 6 and Jesus is not to solidify resistance, but to invite faithful discipleship.

J. CLINTON MCCANN JR.

Commentary 2: Connecting the Reading with the World

Knowing what to preach on Trinity Sunday is hard. Harder still is knowing how to preach the Trinity from the Old Testament. Inauthentic and

exegetically unsound ways to do so are legion. Fortunately, today's reading from Isaiah lends itself to faithful reflection on the triune God.

1. Reinhold Niebuhr, *Leaves from the Notebook of a Tamed Cynic* (San Francisco: Harper & Row, 1929/1956), 140.

Trinity and Mission. Call narratives like Isaiah 6 raise the daunting question of what it means to be chosen to fulfill God's purposes. In Scripture, frequently those who receive the call realize its potential to upend their lives, and so they quite understandably resist. Daunted by his call, Jeremiah objects due to his youth and inexperience in public speaking, believing he will be ineffective as a prophetic witness (Jer. 1:6). Confronted at the burning bush with God's call to deliver Israel from slavery in Egypt, Moses issues a series of increasingly desperate questions and excuses, finally pleading with God just to send someone else (Exod. 4:13). God tells Jonah to "go at once to Nineveh, that great city," to indict the Ninevites for their wickedness; Jonah heads out for Tarshish instead, with the express purpose of escaping this responsibility (Jonah 1:1–3). In light of this pattern of prophets seeking to evade their vocations, Isaiah's enthusiastic "Here am I; send me!" stands out for its willing acceptance of the divine commission (Isa. 6:8). Preachers may encourage parishioners to imitate Isaiah in being alert and ready to respond courageously when they discern God's call in their daily lives.

Whether the recipient is willing or not, the divine call lends itself to a simple summary: *Go.* Its focus is outward. God calls us to proclaim, to serve, to follow, always on behalf of others. When God calls us to move beyond ourselves, that call mirrors the life of the Trinity. The distinction between the "immanent" Trinity (the internal relationships among Father, Son, and Holy Spirit) and the "economic" Trinity (the external relationship between the triune God and the world) is contentious.[2] Yet theologians on all sides of the argument agree that the Trinity involves an unending movement of love and joy toward the created order. Out of the surplus of divine love God speaks the world into existence. At the climax of the Trinitarian narrative, God wholly joins with the sad lot of humanity in love, in order to redeem that world, as the Nicene Creed reminds us:

> For us and for our salvation
> he came down from heaven;
> he became incarnate by the Holy Spirit

> and the Virgin Mary,
> and was made human.

Finally, the incarnate and risen One promises to pour out the Holy Spirit upon his followers for the purpose of empowering their mission to the world (Acts 1:8–9). As we engage in that mission, along with Isaiah we will find ourselves joining the outward movement of God's triune love.

The Pivot Point. Two droids show up at Luke Skywalker's farm on Tatooine. A woman walks into the bar and asks the performer to play "As Time Goes By." A worried police chief says, "You're going to need a bigger boat." Plucked from the fire, a ring reveals strange words long hidden. A giant tells a young boy, "Yer a wizard, Harry." On the day of her coronation a new queen can no longer conceal her magical powers, and discovers she no longer wants to.

These movie scenes are famous because they represent *pivot points*, moments when the arc of the story starts to move in a new and definitive direction. Isaiah 6 begins at just such a moment: "In the year that King Uzziah died, I saw the Lord sitting on a throne, high and lofty." Uzziah's death marks a transition from a period of political stability to the looming Assyrian crisis. Yet it is far more about a change in God's time. This is a *kairotic* event in which the will of God can be more clearly seen and the presence of God more keenly felt. God is doing something in the life of the world, and we are called to be part of it.

The preacher should remind the congregation that divine pivot points often do not arrive with burning bushes or smoke and seraphim. When people review their lives, they often remember seemingly unremarkable but decisive moments: they glimpsed someone across a room; a friend mentioned a job posting they had seen; an encouraging word enabled the first step toward recovery from addiction. Ask them how that crucial day had begun, and they will say it was just like any other. No doubt Isaiah thought he would just pop into the temple for a minute. God the Spirit can be sneaky that way. We should be on the alert, lest God's new thing start without us.

2. See Karl Rahner, *The Trinity*, trans. Joseph Donceel (New York: Herder & Herder, 1970); Catherine Mowry Lacugna, *God for Us: The Trinity and Christian Life* (San Francisco: HarperSanFrancisco, 1993).

The Holiness of Divine Love. God's holiness is on full display in Isaiah 6. What is that holiness? To declare something "holy" originally meant to set it apart from ordinary things. Here, the term points at least partially to transcendence. Throughout Isaiah, God is known as "the Holy One of Israel." Here in the temple, the prophet encounters God, who is wholly other.

Isaiah's personal and communal confession brings a moral consideration into the story. Confronted by the presence of God, he is overcome with a sense of unworthiness, not finitude. What made him unworthy? One flawed yet frequent Christian interpretation holds that holiness equates to uprightness or blamelessness. According to this view, the contrast to Isaiah's unworthiness is God's moral purity.

Yet both Jewish and Christian traditions have discovered within the mystery of divine holiness something far richer and deeper than simple blamelessness. For example, in early Eastern Christian theology, *perfection* often stands in for holiness, as both are divine qualities in which humans can participate. The fourth-century theologian Gregory of Nyssa rejects the idea of perfection as the simple absence of flaws,

insisting instead that its essential character is change or, more specifically, growth in love of God and neighbor.[3]

The desert fathers and mothers extended this conversation by insisting that, given a choice between compassion and uprightness, they choose compassion. One time a member of a monastic community was put on trial for violating his vows. The other monks summoned Abbot Moses, famed for his holiness (that is, his uprightness), to join them in passing judgment. As they saw him approach, they noticed he was carrying a basket with holes from which sand was spilling onto the ground. When asked to explain, Moses said, "My sins are running out behind me, and I do not see them, and today I come to judge the sins of another!"[4] The accusing brothers thought they were promoting the community's holiness by protecting its good reputation. Yet by identifying with—and hence seeking to reclaim—the erring brother, Moses' action is remembered as the more holy, for it more fully expressed the gracious character of holiness refracted through the prism of divine love.

ROBERT A. RATCLIFF

3. Gregory of Nyssa, "On Perfection," in *Saint Gregory of Nyssa: Ascetical Works*, trans. Virginia Woods Callahan, The Fathers of the Church 58 (Washington, DC: Catholic University of America Press, 1967), 95–122.

4. Thomas Merton, *The Wisdom of the Desert*, rev. ed. (New York: New Directions, 1977), 40.

Psalm 29

¹Ascribe to the LORD, O heavenly beings,
   ascribe to the LORD glory and strength.
²Ascribe to the LORD the glory of his name;
   worship the LORD in holy splendor.

³The voice of the LORD is over the waters;
   the God of glory thunders,
   the LORD, over mighty waters.
⁴The voice of the LORD is powerful;
   the voice of the LORD is full of majesty.

⁵The voice of the LORD breaks the cedars;
   the LORD breaks the cedars of Lebanon.
⁶He makes Lebanon skip like a calf,
   and Sirion like a young wild ox.

⁷The voice of the LORD flashes forth flames of fire.
⁸The voice of the LORD shakes the wilderness;
   the LORD shakes the wilderness of Kadesh.

⁹The voice of the LORD causes the oaks to whirl,
   and strips the forest bare;
   and in his temple all say, "Glory!"

¹⁰The LORD sits enthroned over the flood;
   the LORD sits enthroned as king forever.
¹¹May the LORD give strength to his people!
   May the LORD bless his people with peace!

Connecting the Psalm with Scripture and Worship

Psalm 29 presents numerous points of connection with the narrative of Isaiah's vision of Yahweh in the temple (Isa. 6:1–13). Both texts picture Yahweh enthroned as a high God among a community of numinous beings. As members of the divine council, these beings attend to Yahweh with praise constantly on their lips. While the texts give glimpses of God's appearance, they also suggest that humans cannot comprehend the power of God with their eyes. Rather, the voice of God emerges as the most powerful divine attribute in each of these texts.

Psalm 29 begins with a series of imperative statements directed to *bene 'elim,* literally, "the sons of gods." This phrase refers to a divine council (see Job 1–2; Pss. 82:1; 89:6–7), numinous or "heavenly beings" that attend to Yahweh as the high God seated in their midst. The text is not clear who exactly constitutes this community. The "sons of gods" may be understood as the planets, stars, sun, and moon. All of these heavenly bodies were thought to be deities in other ancient Near Eastern religions. "The sons of gods" could also be construed as the "heavenly host" of angels, divine messengers who do the bidding of God in the world (see Ps. 103:21).

The identity of speaker(s) in these opening verses is also unclear (Ps. 29:1–2). Perhaps it is the heavenly hosts summoning themselves to bear witness to God's power. It may be that it is a human community calling out for God's praise throughout the heavens. In any case, Psalm 29 suggests that the primary function of the divine council is the exaltation of Yahweh. Three times the text calls for them to "ascribe" to Yahweh "glory" and "strength" (vv. 1–2).

This threefold ascription of Yahweh finds a close parallel to the triple declaration of God's holiness in Isaiah 6:3. In the prophet's vision (Isa. 6:1–8), Isaiah can see only the bottommost part of the divine form, the hem of Yahweh's garment that fills the temple (v. 1). Yet Isaiah can see seraphs, six-winged hybrid beings, flying around Yahweh's throne (v. 2).

Such numinous beings are often pictured in ancient Near Eastern art with their wings overshadowing other gods or people in gestures of protection. In Isaiah's vision, however, the seraphs use their wings not to protect someone else. Instead, they use their wings to protect themselves from the glory of Yahweh. God's power is so great that it overwhelms all other sources of power in the heavens and on earth. As if in response to Psalm 29:1–2, these seraphs in Isaiah 6:3 ascribe glory to Yahweh:

> And one called to another and said:
> "Holy, holy, holy is the LORD of Hosts;
> the whole earth is full of his glory."

Psalm 29 and Isaiah 6 thus give us a similar account of what happens in Yawheh's throne room. Praise resounds.

After summoning the voices of the divine council, the psalm then turns to describe the voice of Yahweh (Ps. 29:3–9). This voice (*qol*, literally "sound") is the most powerful force in the world. In the context of the psalm, thunder represents Yahweh's voice (v. 3). Thunder can be a harbinger of destruction and fire (v. 7); it also accompanies the rain that refreshes the land and brings life to the soil. Thus, for the psalmist, thunder is the perfect way to describe the complex range of Yahweh's activity in the world. Yahweh's power issues from heaven, capable of bringing forth both salvation and destruction.

The association of thunder and "the waters" in verse 3 also testifies to God's power. Like the ancient Near Eastern storm gods, Yahweh was understood to be the conqueror of the chaotic sea. Yahweh's power over that primeval force was demonstrated at creation, when Yahweh subdued the sea, bringing order into the midst of chaos. Verse 10 gives yet another picture of God's triumph over the waters of chaos; Yahweh sits enthroned over the flood. Though the sea rolls and threatens to overwhelm the land, the sea also witnesses Yahweh's power and kingship by the very fact that it stays within its borders. These waters also respond to Yahweh in the theophanic storm, becoming agitated and excited when Yahweh's voice thunders.

Yahweh's voice has an effect on everything, not just the waters. It also booms throughout the countryside (vv. 6–7). It shakes even the biggest living things, the colossal cedars of Lebanon (v. 9). No place is beyond the reach of Yahweh's voice. Everything responds to God's voice, including Yahweh's faithful in the temple. The human community in the temple thus mirrors the divine community, the *bene 'elim* (vv. 1–2). All voices glorify Yahweh, whose voice sounds throughout heaven and earth.

The psalm ends with a plea. Verses 1–10 have described the powerful voice of Yahweh, how Yahweh reaches into the world and rules it with unquestioned supremacy. Verse 11 presents the human community making a petition for divine empowerment. Such a plea recognizes that the people exist in great need of God's power. On their own, they are not powerful. They are not at peace. The community needs the blessing of a powerful God to survive and thrive in this world.

Theophanies like the ones described in Psalm 29 and Isaiah 6 overwhelm the senses, even though they grant just a glimpse of the glory of God. When heard in worship, they invite those gathered to revel in the majesty of God; bold, stirring sounds of brass, drums, and pipes are in order, or any combination of instrument that can thunder forth.

Like those in the temple, worshipers may respond in praise. There are numerous compelling choral versions of Psalm 29, as well as hymns that employ its themes. The response may come in a classic declaration such as the Gloria Patri, or a new hymn such as Paul Vasile's rousing "Glory to God, Whose Goodness Shines on Me."[1] Of course, given the pairing of Psalm 29 with Isaiah 6:1–8, the incomparable "Holy, Holy, Holy" is also a fitting congregational response, especially on Trinity Sunday.

JOEL MARCUS LEMON

---

1. See *Glory to God: The Presbyterian Hymnal* (Louisville, KY: Westminster John Knox Press, 2013), 582.

Romans 8:12–17

¹²So then, brothers and sisters, we are debtors, not to the flesh, to live according to the flesh— ¹³for if you live according to the flesh, you will die; but if by the Spirit you put to death the deeds of the body, you will live. ¹⁴For all who are led by the Spirit of God are children of God. ¹⁵For you did not receive a spirit of slavery to fall back into fear, but you have received a spirit of adoption. When we cry, "Abba! Father!" ¹⁶it is that very Spirit bearing witness with our spirit that we are children of God, ¹⁷and if children, then heirs, heirs of God and joint heirs with Christ—if, in fact, we suffer with him so that we may also be glorified with him.

Commentary 1: Connecting the Reading with Scripture

In today's lection Paul continues his discourse contrasting life in the Spirit (*pneuma*) with life lived according to the flesh (*sarx*), which begins in Romans 8:1. While this passage is often read as instructive for individual life, it is more accurately interpreted as a call to a way of living as community made possible by *pneumati theou*, the Spirit of God. Throughout Romans 8:12–17, Paul uses the plural form of "you." So, we can continue to hear Paul's exhortation to reconsider the way we live our communal life.

Today, members of a congregation are often referred to as a "church family." This language is consistent with terms Paul uses in Romans to describe common life in the Spirit. He declares those who are led by the Spirit of God to be children of God, to have received the spirit of adoption as children of God. This is no new revelation. Attending to the particulars of Paul's language can help nuance our understanding of what it means to be *family*. In 8:12, Paul says we are not debtors (*opheiletai*) to the flesh (*sarx*) and are not to live according to the flesh. A clue to interpretation lies in the word *opheiletai*, which refers to social and religious obligations or debts. In Greco-Roman culture obligations were first to gods, then to country, then to parents.[1] For Paul, this ordering of obligations is born of the flesh, the material, the distorted human world. To live life in the Spirit (*pneuma*) is to be obligated first to the one God and then to God's family constituted

by the Spirit. What, then, is the proper fealty of a Christian to their country? Which family has a primary claim upon our lives—our time, our money, our prayers, our gifts?

Paul includes within God's family all who are led by the Spirit of God. He echoes Jesus in the Synoptics: "A crowd was sitting around him; and they said to him, 'Your mother and your brothers and sisters are outside, asking for you.' And he replied, 'Who are my mother and my brothers?' And looking at those who sat around him, he said, 'Here are my mother and my brothers! Whoever does the will of God is my brother and sister and mother'" (Mark 3:32–35; see also Matt. 12:48–50; Luke 8:20–21). Doing the will of God, being led by God's Spirit: that makes one kin. Spirit ties supersede blood ties in God's family. This seems a particularly hard message for contemporary Christians to hear. The nuclear family reigns supreme in American culture. How might the church help reorder our understanding of all who have a claim on our time, love, and resources?

While Paul uses male-gendered terms throughout 8:12–15 to refer to God's children, he switches to the neuter term *tekna* in verses 16–17. This is also when Paul begins using the language of inheritance, calling the *tekna* of God heirs, heirs of God, and joint heirs with Christ. Paul employs similar language about inheritance, adoption, and children in Galatians,

---

1. Robert Jewett, *Romans: A Commentary* (Minneapolis: Fortress, 2007), 493.

but there he uses the phrase, "if a son [NRSV child] then an heir" (Gal. 4:7 RSV). By the time he writes the Letter to the Romans, Paul has adopted the more inclusive term *tekna* to refer to inheritors. By using this word, Paul signals that all God's children are entitled to God's inheritance without regard to gender. Together with Christ and without distinction among them, all God's children witness to God, inherit God's promise, suffer, and are glorified.

This new family that suffers together and together receives God's promises of a future, a hope, and a home with God is created by the Spirit. The Spirit enables the community to turn away from living out distorted patterns. The Spirit leads God's children away from fear and into life. Paul uses the word "Spirit" twenty-two times in Romans 8, more than in any other passage in all his letters.[2] It is profoundly important to recognize the life-giving, life-ordering role that the Spirit plays in our common life. The proclivity of the Spirit to enable healthy family life is also witnessed to in Galatians 5:22–26, where Paul discusses the fruit of the Spirit: love, joy, peace, patience, kindness, generosity, faithfulness, gentleness, and self-control.

Other important qualities of Spirit can be gleaned by reading this passage in conjunction with the other readings for this Sunday. Romans 8:15–16 says, "When we cry, 'Abba! Father!' it is that very Spirit bearing witness with our spirit that we are children of God." The Greek word translated here as "cry" is *krazomen*. It is an onomatopoetic term describing a raven's cry or caw. It suggests an inarticulate cry or shout full of emotion. A good contemporary illustration of *krazomen* might be the Mexican *grito*: "It is a high-pitched, sustained howl emanating from every corner of the lungs and touching the sky. Heard at family celebrations, usually to the brassy strains of mariachis, the *grito* is a primal shout, a cry for joy that moves the soul and rattles the spirit."[3] When the Spirit witnesses to God, She does not speak in a whisper. She sends up a *grito* from the depths.

While today's lections from Isaiah and Psalms do not refer to God's Spirit, they both convey the power of God vocalized. Psalm 29 says that God's voice "breaks the cedars," "flashes forth flames of fire," "shakes the wilderness," "causes the oaks to whirl, and strips the forest bare." It is powerful and full of majesty. It moves the world. In the lection from Isaiah, the prophet has a vision of being in the temple with God. In Isaiah 6:3, a six-winged seraph calls out, saying, "Holy, holy, holy is the LORD of hosts; the whole earth is full of his glory." The verb root for "call" is *qara*, which means to "call, cry, shout, or scream." Verse 4 says the posts of the threshold were shaken by the *qol*, the voice of the one who cried out.

The voice that witnesses to God is a voice that emanates power, a voice that upsets foundations, a voice akin to God's own voice. That voice and that power flows through all God's children via the Spirit. What if God's children did not hold back, but let their primal shouts loose for the world to hear? What foundations might be moved?

The lection from John 3 has a lot to say about Spirit. Jesus tells Nicodemus one must be born anew to see/perceive the reign of God. Nicodemus does not understand. Jesus explains: "No one can enter the kingdom of God without being born of water and Spirit [*pneuma*]. What is born of the flesh [*sarx*] is flesh, and what is born of the Spirit is spirit" (John 3:5–6). Not only are the children of God *led* by the Spirit; they *become* spirit. This suggests an ontological change to those who do the will of God. It is not just relationships and priorities that are transformed in the family of God, but human beings. Do we know that we *are* spirit, that God saturates our very being? Spirit is what allows us to be a family of hope and promise, a family of world-changers and love-bringers. Together, with Christ, we suffer. Together, with Christ, we cry out and move the world. Together, with Christ, we rise.

ERICA A. KNISELY

2. Roberto Pereyra, "The Holy Spirit in the Letters of Paul," *DavarLogos* 13, no. 2 (2014): 8.

3. Juan Castillo, "Échale! New App Keeps the Cherished Mexican 'Grito' Close at Hand," *NBC News*, October 1, 2015; https://www.nbcnews.com/news/latino/echale-new-app-keeps-mexican-grito-close-hand-n436966.

Commentary 2: Connecting the Reading with the World

Flesh/Spirit, debt/debtors, Spirit/children/heirs, slavery/Abba/Father, suffering/glory: double relations and correlating oppositions and connections fill this passage, offering us frames for our own thinking and acting. While our worship, churches, and communities are all part of the same web, flowing through the systems that compose our humanity, we often think in binary terms and not in correlated ways, and we act as if these spheres of life were separated. Paul's binaries expose contradictions we face in our own contexts that threaten separation, and they suggest how we might think constructively in terms of correlating oppositions and connections.

Our spirituality, for example, is often marked by a duality that opposes body and soul, or flesh and spirit. To worship in spirit too often means to worship with our mind, striving after proper knowledge of God. Our bodies are often thought to hinder our spirituality. The flesh is often portrayed as the enemy of what is holy, the source of sinful desires that lead us astray. However, when our bodies and the Spirit of God are understood and felt as living together, as one and in wholesome ways, our faith is strengthened and our desires rest in God. We start to see that the understanding that equates bodies with sin, and desires with a narrow moral code, entails guilt and shame, not freedom and responsibility. So, we are called to ponder the connection between our bodies and the presence of the Spirit.

Where is the Spirit in our bodies? Where is the body in the Spirit? We often do not know where the Spirit of God is in us. If we remind ourselves that our life was breathed into us by God, we understand that the Spirit of God is in our breathing. Breathing is a connection between mind and body. There is no distinction between body and Spirit, since we are always breathing. Our breathing has to do with the breath of God given to us when we were "fearfully and wonderfully made" (Ps. 139:14). When our bodies are celebrated as the house of the Spirit of God, we gain a connectedness that we might call a life of the Spirit, in our bodies. God's Breath/Spirit indwells our bodies. The life of the Spirit is in our bodies, and there is no life of the body outside of our Spirit.

Unless we hold on to this relation as one, forms of disassociations will make us live in disconnected realities, and we will hold on to dualisms that make us suffer, dualisms that often involve hierarchies—for example, when we think that nature is of less value than human beings. We disassociate nature and culture and think they are opposite, when they are in fact part of each other, of the same and yet different life. Moreover, this disassociation makes us think that we do not have limits and that the earth is out there to be taken, used, and exploited. If we can sustain a spirituality that holds together human beings and nature, as we consider the life of the Spirit in us, we would consider animals as having rights, ecosystems as habitats full of living creatures to be protected. In the same way, we would not use pesticides in our crops that endanger bees and our environment.

As the text says, "it is that very Spirit bearing witness with our spirit that we are children of God, and if children, then heirs, heirs of God and joint heirs with Christ—if, in fact, we suffer with him so that we may also be glorified with him" (Rom. 8:16–17). The Spirit of God bearing witness with our spirit creates the conditions for us all to become heirs of God and Christ. Thus, in the body and flesh, we must hold nature together with us as we also must hold each other's suffering.

This collective movement of belonging and mutuality is the living of God's glory enfleshed in our community. In this way, the Spirit of God in our flesh will mean honoring the earth, caring for all sentient beings, mountains, waters, and minerals. The Spirit of God in our flesh will also mean freedom to love one another, to the point of living in a community that does not cling to the spirit of the world, but holds on to the Spirit of God, who shows Godself in and through our actions and our loving of one another.

When we are connected in body and flesh, the Spirit will lead us. While some people are intolerant of others' mistakes, saying, "If they messed up, they must deal with the consequences," we will say, "We are each other's keepers," which is somewhat the same as what Paul is saying here: "For all who are led by the Spirit of God are children of God" (v. 14). Being the children of God by virtue of our baptism makes us responsible for each other's lives, no matter how badly some might go astray. In the same way, when we see the bees dying, we will promptly fight for their lives and well-being.

When we are free from disassociated ways of thinking and living of our society, we can think and act differently, discerning the ways in which everything and everyone belong together, and as a result we can live a fuller and more joyful life.

We learn with each other to be responsible for ourselves and for everyone. Then we can all feel free in the Spirit and not cling to the isolated ways of the flesh of the world. We are freed from cultural systems that say: "You are on your own." Instead, we say together: "Abba! Father!" which meant, in that time, fidelity to the God of love, in contrast to calling Caesar "father" and giving fidelity above all to Caesar.

The first Christians were engaging in civil disobedience, dismissing the "father" of that time and calling upon the presence of the living God as their Father, the one who would sustain them. Surely, in our time, we have learned to call God "Mother" and other names. When flesh and Spirit are brought together, God is understood expansively beyond the patriarchal limits of the masculine. In fact, we undo the masculine as a form of dominance. When the Spirit lives fully in our bodies we are free to call God Mother, Lover, Friend, Rock, and so much more. For the presence of life in fullness carries the many names of God.

If we have the Spirit of God bearing witness in our spirit, in our bodies, our lives can be fully renewed and constantly restored. Carrying the very breath of God in us, our spirituality finds its fullness in all bodies: the earth and sentient beings. Fully connected with God, the earth, birds, fishes, meadows, our neighbors and ourselves, we all become children of God, beloved by God, Abba. Entangled in this vast notion of grace, we find the breath of God in our communities by the way of seeing the Trinity as an ever-encompassing event of connections, connectivity, mutualities, and entanglements.

We can now engage differences and complexities because we are one and many with God and with one another. In other words, we can say that the whole is our being together in God. Now, we are better prepared to pay attention to our differences and be aware of what breaks us apart, and what divides us from the whole. Then we might understand what it means to be "glorified in God."

CLÁUDIO CARVALHAES

John 3:1–17

¹Now there was a Pharisee named Nicodemus, a leader of the Jews. ²He came to Jesus by night and said to him, "Rabbi, we know that you are a teacher who has come from God; for no one can do these signs that you do apart from the presence of God." ³Jesus answered him, "Very truly, I tell you, no one can see the kingdom of God without being born from above." ⁴Nicodemus said to him, "How can anyone be born after having grown old? Can one enter a second time into the mother's womb and be born?" ⁵Jesus answered, "Very truly, I tell you, no one can enter the kingdom of God without being born of water and Spirit. ⁶What is born of the flesh is flesh, and what is born of the Spirit is spirit. ⁷Do not be astonished that I said to you, 'You must be born from above.' ⁸The wind blows where it chooses, and you hear the sound of it, but you do not know where it comes from or where it goes. So it is with everyone who is born of the Spirit." ⁹Nicodemus said to him, "How can these things be?" ¹⁰Jesus answered him, "Are you a teacher of Israel, and yet you do not understand these things?

¹¹"Very truly, I tell you, we speak of what we know and testify to what we have seen; yet you do not receive our testimony. ¹²If I have told you about earthly things and you do not believe, how can you believe if I tell you about heavenly things? ¹³No one has ascended into heaven except the one who descended from heaven, the Son of Man. ¹⁴And just as Moses lifted up the serpent in the wilderness, so must the Son of Man be lifted up, ¹⁵that whoever believes in him may have eternal life.

¹⁶"For God so loved the world that he gave his only Son, so that everyone who believes in him may not perish but may have eternal life.

¹⁷"Indeed, God did not send the Son into the world to condemn the world, but in order that the world might be saved through him."

Commentary 1: Connecting the Reading with Scripture

Today's reading from the Gospel of John interrupts the lectionary focus on Mark, shifting our attention to the mystery of the Trinity and the transformative depths of the teachings of Jesus. The cryptic dialogue between Jesus and Nicodemus stacks up polarities between heaven and earth, perishing and eternal life, condemnation and salvation, flesh and spirit. This symbolic language is rich in images and provokes us to plumb the depths of its meanings. Precisely because of its profundity, however, such discourse does not deliver ready-made clarity. Given the depth of Jesus' teaching, it is not surprising that a major theme in John is the misunderstanding of Jesus' signs and teaching.

This encounter with Nicodemus highlights confusion over Jesus' teaching. Nicodemus acknowledges Jesus is a teacher (rabbi) who comes from God (John 3:2). Nicodemus himself is "a teacher of Israel," but he cannot fathom Jesus' words. He interprets being "born from above" into new life literally (v. 4), and so he does not understand how the status "child of God" is given to humanity. Moreover, Nicodemus has been trained to think earthly society reflects the structure and mores of heavenly society. Jesus' references to being born of Spirit, in contrast, clearly delegitimate tying the status "child of God" to such worldly distinctions. Nicodemus is conflicted, for while he accepts that the signs

Jesus performs establish that he is a teacher who has come from God, he does not understand the meaning and implications of Jesus' teaching.

Who is a child of God? The conversation between Nicodemus and Jesus revolves around this question. In the society of Jesus' and Nicodemus's day, birth cemented a person's place in society. In the society of first-century Palestine, unlike present-day North American society, achievement, work, education, or movement from one place to another rarely changed the status established at birth. Of course, even today, birth status can deliver a host of advantages or subject one to a lifetime of discrimination. We face the same challenges, if to different degrees. In Jesus' day, social status depended almost entirely on the status of the kinship group into which a person was born. Jesus of Nazareth, coming from a group with roots in Galilee, was near the bottom of the social hierarchy. A stunning reversal, obvious to John's first readers, is played out in this conversation. Nicodemus, a ruler (*archōn*) in Jerusalem, by far outranks Jesus, a peasant from Galilee. Yet Nicodemus acknowledges that Jesus comes from the "presence of God," and he accepts Jesus as *his* teacher.

This dialogue between Nicodemus and Jesus performs and displays a disruptive gospel truth. For whatever else it may mean when Jesus describes a child of God as someone who is "born from above," it means this person is born into a new family, a new kinship system, a *koinōnia* that rejects earthly hierarchies.

Paradoxically, access to this new status and quality of life comes to believers through what is considered to be *dishonorable* in Nicodemus's society: humiliation and death on a cross. Crucifixion was both a physical and a social death. As a social death, it stripped the person of social standing, making them vulnerable to verbal and physical abuse. Furthermore, hanging from the cross outside the city gates was a not-so-subtle reminder of social rejection. The paradox lies in the fact that Jesus, who "comes from the presence of God," is humiliated through death on the cross. Perhaps this status is also conferred on those who believe in him?

Nicodemus appears again later in John's Gospel in two scenes that bracket Jesus' presence on the cross. In both scenes, birth status plays an important role. It appears that Nicodemus accepted Jesus' teaching about being born again as children of God. In the first scene (7:45–52), Nicodemus appears to defend Jesus' right to a hearing, but he is put down by his fellow Pharisees, who appeal to Jesus' social origin and status in Galilee. To be born and bred in Galilee, a place considered by Judeans as "unclean," is to be part of the periphery. Jesus does not deserve a hearing because "no prophet is to arise from Galilee" (7:52).

Nicodemus appears again as a witness to the entombment of Jesus' body (19:38–42). From the worldly perspective of those who have not been born again, the process of crucifixion has progressively shamed, humiliated, and dishonored Jesus. Nicodemus, however, no longer sees through the ideological lenses of this world, for after the crucifixion Nicodemus appears with Joseph of Arimathea, treating the body of Jesus with costly spices and placing him in a rich man's tomb—all of which contradicts what the world sees as Jesus' shamed social status. Seeing with new eyes, Nicodemus honors Jesus as someone who "comes from above." These actions suggest Nicodemus was open to being taught by Jesus, for his are the actions of a person seeing with the eyes of one born again.

Although the other readings for this day were conceived and crafted in very different circumstances, they echo and enrich the images of God found in the Gospel text. In Isaiah's call narrative, God commissions him to be a bridge between heaven and earth, an essential aspect of prophetic service: "Then I heard the voice of the Lord saying, 'Whom shall I send, and who will go for us?' And I said, 'Here am I; send me!'" (Isa. 6:8). The psalm emphasizes transcendence. God is enthroned not only in the temple, as in Isaiah, but over creation, over even the chaos of the flood. Romans, too, links the powerful, transcending rule of God to the daily life of human beings. In this text, the Spirit of God is the messenger, transforming believers into children of God. God's intimate, loving care for humanity and the physical cosmos is clearly emphasized in these texts, in sharp contrast to an idea of a detached, hubristic deity—the sort that mirrors so many earthly rulers.

Images related to the Trinity also fill today's other lections: God the Mother/Father enthroned in Isaiah's vision; the wind representing the Spirit in John's Gospel; the Son talking about himself with Nicodemus. Two verses in the Gospel reading powerfully portray the *relational* character of the Trinity in *action:* "For God so loved the world that he gave his only Son" (John 3:16) and "God did not send the Son into the world to condemn the world, but in order that the world might be saved through him" (v. 17). In the Gospel of John, "'world' refers to three entities: the physical world, Israel as God's chosen [ideal] humanity, and Judeans as enemies of John's community."[1] God eternally relates lovingly to the world in all three of these senses in a positive, life-giving way that includes even enemies.

Many in our pews have a deeply held image of God that does not correspond to the idea that God loves the world and is self-giving. This is especially true, for example, of people who are part of a Christian community yet do not feel personally connected. It is also true of those who need to strive for recognition, instead of accepting that they are God's children. God is distant in such scenarios, and it is very easy to live out of a deistic frame of mind. This Sunday is an opportunity to heal and transform these distant images of the Trinity, to proclaim a gracious God who knows and loves us intimately, and to help us all glory in our status as members of one family, children of God.

RENATA FURST

Commentary 2: Connecting the Reading with the World

Henry Wadsworth Longfellow's poem "Nicodemus at Night" might be a good starting point for looking at the complex character of Nicodemus. Nicodemus is a learned man, yet he is unable to understand the truth given plainly to him by Jesus. There is a sense in which he knows this, which is why he comes to Jesus under cover of night, when "The dark houses seem / Like sepulchres, in which the sleepers lie / Wrapped in their shrouds, and for the moment dead."[2] The preacher might examine what we, like Nicodemus, do to hide our lack of knowledge. Teachers may say there is no such thing as a stupid question, but many of us are not willing to test that premise! Nicodemus, with his reputation for knowledge, is eager to learn and does not hesitate to pose his question.

The preacher might consider conversations that take place at night: campfire stories, slumber-party secrets, late-night confessions or declarations of love to a sweetheart or friend. There is something intimate and freeing about late-night conversations, where faces are half lit and background clutter fades away. Why might Nicodemus have stepped out in the dark to meet

Jesus? It might have been out of embarrassment or concern about negative consequences if he were seen consulting this radical teacher, who had just disrupted the operations of the Jerusalem temple (John 2:14–21). It might also have been motivated by a desire for a private conversation, for words half whispered, true, and life changing.

Whatever Nicodemus's reasons, we can ponder what we might learn from this approach. To what sorts of unexpected approaches might we want to be open? Which methods of evangelism make sense for particular people and particular congregations in your care?

We see Nicodemus twice more in this Gospel. In John 7, Nicodemus admonishes others to listen to Jesus before judging him. In the end, in John 19, Nicodemus provides myrrh and aloes to embalm Jesus. What began under the cover of night has become an honor that stood the test of daylight and public acknowledgment. Though Jesus called Nicodemus out for his apparent lack of understanding, Jesus did not reject him—and Nicodemus did not reject Jesus.

---

1. Bruce J. Malina and Richard L. Rohrbaugh, *Social-Science Commentary on the Gospel of John* (Minneapolis: Fortress, 1998), 246.
2. "Nicodemus at Night," in *The Complete Poetical Works of Henry Wadsworth Longfellow* (Windham, NH: Windham Press, 2013), 379.

We never find out whether Nicodemus accepted the "born again"/"born from above" proposition. We are not told whether he considered himself a follower of Jesus. We know only that he is there at the end. Perhaps Nicodemus's persistent presence is proof that those among us who have questions and doubts, who speak of our spiritual questions in the dark of night but not in front of peers, may have a place in the kingdom as well.

This lection is assigned for Trinity Sunday; here Jesus discusses all three members of the Trinity with relational language that connects them. The preacher might use this text as a springboard to theological reflection on the Trinity. Indigo Girls band member Emily Saliers (a preacher's daughter) sings, "Try making one and one and one make one, twist the shapes until everything comes undone" in her song "You and Me of the 10,000 Wars."[3] Many congregants will relate to her language. The Trinity can be hard to understand. The preacher might take this opportunity to note that perfect understanding is not prerequisite to receiving the love of the triune God to which the rest of our pericope bears witness.

John 3:16 is one of the best-known verses in the Bible. Many parishioners will be able to recite it by heart, even if they were not raised in the church. The very familiarity of the verse may limit appreciation of its radical promise. The preacher might work to make manifest to parishioners the stunning intensity of God's love for us as articulated in this verse and prominent throughout the Bible. One way of describing this love might be found in the enchanting Sam McBratney children's book *Guess How Much I Love You.*[4] Caregivers in the congregation may recognize its famous line, "I love you right up to the moon and back." Some older parents may remember the game where kids and elders would playfully and joyfully seek to best one another: "Well, I love you to the stars and back," "I love you to infinity and back," "I love you to infinity times infinity!"

The lection ends this pericope at verse 17, but after the born-again language and the beloved John 3:16, verse 17 might not get its full due. This one line—"Indeed, God did not send the Son into the world to condemn the world, but in order that the world might be saved through him"—might be used to reread the preceding passage to teach us the reason for God's sending of the Son. Jesus is sent not to condemn Nicodemus, who does not quite get it, nor to condemn the ordinary believer, whose lack of understanding or action worries them. The Son has been sent to save.

To illustrate this, the preacher can draw on stories unique to the congregation's region. National stories could include, for example, the West Nickel Mines School shooting in an Amish school, where the community, despite enduring horrific violence and the deaths of five children, did not condemn the shooter or his family, saying that was not what Jesus had been brought into this world to do. This highlights the radically gracious character of the love of God revealed in the life, works, and teachings of Jesus.

What could add to the extent of "love you to infinity times infinity"? Love that is utter and absolute apart from anything earned or deserved; love that flows despite my flaws, failures, and shortcomings; love that embraces me despite my moments of neglect, wrongdoing, ambition, and spite; love even for those so lost that they lash out in violence; love even for enemies. This is the love of Jesus, the love of God, a gracious love for one and all, a freely given love stronger than any self-condemnation, a love stronger than the hatred or bitterness that so justly flows from the injustice and abuse we have suffered from others.

As we survey daily news about our world, we realize, as did first-century Jews and Christians struggling under the oppressions of empire, that the world deserves condemnation. We realize, however, even as we identify and strive to aid those hurt by the world's injustices, that God sent the Son not to condemn the world but to save it, not to bring condemnation but to reveal gracious love. The preacher may want to clarify that this does not mean we forget the prophets

3. "You and Me of the 10,000 Wars," composed by Emily Saliers, appeared on the 1990 Indigo Girls album *Nomads, Indians, Saints* and was produced in a remastered format in 2000.
4. Sam McBratney, *Guess How Much I Love You,* 25th anniversary ed. (Somerville, MA: Candlewick, 2019).

and the prophetic aspects of Jesus' ministry, and it does not mean that we fail to name and condemn oppression and exploitation, but it does mean the prime and ultimate source of our passion is the gracious love of God, a love embracing each of us, a love for all—oppressed and oppressor, abused and exploited and those who exploit—a love through which all are born again, thanks to the work of the Son, so that we might be born again, born through the Spirit, children of God's love.

SUSAN K. OLSON

Proper 3 (Sunday between May 22 and May 28)

Hosea 2:14–20
Psalm 103:1–13, 22

2 Corinthians 3:1–6
Mark 2:13–22

Hosea 2:14–20

¹⁴Therefore, I will now allure her,
    and bring her into the wilderness,
    and speak tenderly to her.
¹⁵From there I will give her her vineyards,
    and make the Valley of Achor a door of hope.
There she shall respond as in the days of her youth,
    as at the time when she came out of the land of Egypt.

¹⁶On that day, says the LORD, you will call me, "My husband," and no longer will you call me, "My Baal." ¹⁷For I will remove the names of the Baals from her mouth, and they shall be mentioned by name no more. ¹⁸I will make for you a covenant on that day with the wild animals, the birds of the air, and the creeping things of the ground; and I will abolish the bow, the sword, and war from the land; and I will make you lie down in safety. ¹⁹And I will take you for my wife forever; I will take you for my wife in righteousness and in justice, in steadfast love, and in mercy. ²⁰I will take you for my wife in faithfulness; and you shall know the LORD.

Commentary 1: Connecting the Reading with Scripture

According to Walter Brueggemann and Tod Linafelt, Hosea 2 "is among the most important presentations of covenantal theology in all of the Old Testament."[1] Chapters 1–3 of Hosea are held together by an extended marriage metaphor. Hosea's marriage to the unfaithful Gomer is analogous to the marriage—that is, the covenant—between God and unfaithful Israel. The historical circumstances of Hosea's marriage and family life are irrecoverable, but the pertinent point is clear enough: just as Hosea's marriage and family life are in total disarray, so is the relationship between God and Israel. God's people are wedded to Baal and the ways of Baal, rather than being faithful to God and God's ways.

The names of Hosea and Gomer's children communicate the chaotic results of the infidelity—namely, divorce. The name of the daughter, Lo-ruhamah, is traditionally rendered as "Not pitied," but a better translation would be "Not motherly loved," since one of the forms of the underlying Hebrew root means "womb" (Hos. 1:6). The second son's name says it all. Lo-ammi, "Not my people," is a precise reversal of the traditional covenant formula (v. 9).

Hosea 2 is framed as a speech by these two children to their mother. The divorce is evident from the outset, "for she is not my wife, and I am not her husband." As the chapter unfolds, it is clear that Israel has wedded itself to the various manifestations of Baal, the Canaanite deity known elsewhere as the god who rode the clouds, and thus who made it rain so that the land would be productive (see esp. 2:5, 8–9, 12). Baalism represented the attempt to manipulate the means of production—making it rain—rather than to honor the ultimate Producer. This is still a temptation. Consider how frequently we attend to GNP, the Dow,

1. Walter Brueggemann and Tod Linafelt, *An Introduction to the Old Testament: The Canon and Christian Imagination*, 2nd ed. (Louisville, KY: Westminster John Knox, 2012), 247.

or other leading economic indicators, rather than thanking God for the abundant gifts that sustain our lives.

In Hosea's context, fidelity to Baal meant infidelity to God. Divorce was the result, or so it seemed. There is an abrupt shift at 2:14; and 2:14–20 is all about a reconciliation, indeed, a remarriage (vv. 19–20). In this remarriage, everything will be right, as indicated by the phrases "in righteousness" and "in justice" in 2:19. The restored relationship is founded upon "steadfast love, and . . . mercy" (v. 19). The Hebrew root underlying "mercy" is the same root in the name Lo-ruhamah.

The remarkable contrast between 2:1–13 and 2:14–20, along with explicit mention of "covenant" (2:18), is why Brueggemann and Linafelt conclude that Hosea 2 is so important, but the connection between 2:14–20 and 2:1–13 also necessitates a strong word of caution. The displeasure of the aggrieved husband, God, is expressed in violent actions toward the wife. She is stripped and exposed (2:3; cf. 2:10) and physically restrained (2:6). When we hear that the wife is suddenly wooed again in 2:14, we recognize a pattern uncomfortably close to the contemporary pattern of spousal abuse. There is a cultural chasm between ancient Israel and our time, but the imagery is potentially dangerous. In the Bible, it is almost always women who represent infidelity (e.g., Jer. 3:1–5; Ezek. 16, 23). So interpreters must be very careful, lest these texts be used against women. Some interpreters conclude the danger is so acute that these texts are irredeemable. In any case, extreme caution is in order. The point is *human* infidelity in the face of divine love and provision.

If we make this clear, then Hosea 2:14–20 can be appreciated as an extraordinary expression of divine grace in response to human sinfulness. As such, it connects to a theme not only of Hosea, but of all Scripture.

The juxtaposition of judgment (2:1–13) and promise grounded in mercy (2:14–20) is characteristic of Hosea. It begins in chapter 1, where the judgment of 1:2–9 is followed by the promise of 1:10–11; and the macrostructure of the book displays this pattern. The promise that begins in 2:14–20 extends through chapter 3, and the rest of the book proceeds as follows:

chapters 4–10: judgment; chapter 11: promise; chapters 12–13: judgment; chapter 14: promise.

The theological significance of this pattern is profound, for it communicates that God's judgment is not a matter of punishment. In short, God is not essentially retributive. Rather, God is essentially gracious; God never wills to punish. It is the people's covenant infidelity, manifest as disobedience and injustice, that in and of itself results in "punishing" consequences. God always wills to restore, to set right, to reconcile.

The need for prophets to criticize and to warn is real, because disobedience creates catastrophic results. This is demonstrated in the first passage of chapters 4–10. As 4:1–3 suggests, there are creation-wide consequences of human infidelity. The creational language of 4:3 connects back to 2:18 and makes it clear that God wills harmonious life for humans, wild animals, and birds alike. When disruption occurs, it is not God's doing; it is human malfeasance. In short, God does not will the disappearance of the one million species that may go extinct in the next few years. It will be our doing.

Hosea 11 strikingly connects to and reinforces 2:14–20. God's response to a disobedient people, here imaged as a son rather than a spouse, is not wrath but compassion (11:8–9). God promises to be "the Holy One in your midst" (v. 9). In the midst of a people whose "deeds do not permit them to return to their God" (5:4), God will have to do the turning if the relationship is to continue. God promises to do so. This is not holiness as traditionally understood, that is, separation for purity's sake. This is holiness reimagined as pure grace! There is clearly a lesson here for self-appointed guardians of purity.

The pattern of juxtaposing judgment and promise is not confined to Hosea. It occurs in virtually all the prophetic books. In this regard, the prophetic books are connected to a crucial moment in the Pentateuch—Exodus 32–34, the golden calf episode—where God's response to disobedient Israel is to forgive. The episode culminates in Exodus 34:6, God's self-revelation to Moses. Not surprisingly, two of the keywords from Exodus 34:6 occur in Hosea 2:19: "steadfast love" and "mercy." In one further connection, these two words are also the keywords in Psalm 103, the psalm for the day. Each term occurs four times; see "steadfast love" in 103:4, 8, 11, 17 and "mercy"/"merciful"/"compassion" in 103:4, 8, and 13 (twice). In narrative, in prophecy, and in song, the tradition celebrates God's amazing grace!

In an overwhelmingly graceless North American culture and in congregations populated by many who generally seem to believe that God is out to get even with sinners, we probably can never preach too often about grace. Hosea 2:14–20 and its connections afford the preacher this opportunity. Plus, in a world threatened with

ecological catastrophe, it is important to realize that our gracious God is in covenant relationship not only with us humans, but also "with the wild animals, the birds of the air, and the creeping things of the ground" (Hos. 2:18; see Gen. 9:1–17). This is at least an implicit invitation to be as expansively gracious as God is gracious (see Luke 6:36). If we fail to be so and to act accordingly, the chaotic results will not be what God wills but what we have wrought (Hos. 4:1–3).

J. CLINTON MCCANN JR.

Commentary 2: Connecting the Reading with the World

Today's first reading can be deceptive. It contains lovely, intimate words of promise, peace, and plenty from God to Israel. Hosea 2:14–20 articulates the prophetic theme of forgiveness and restoration as fully as any passage in the Hebrew Bible. The pattern of prophetic literature is to juxtapose passages like this one with others that announce divine judgment, so we can expect a stern word of warning to precede our passage's message of hope.

We may still not be prepared for the severity of Hosea 2:1–13, where words of anger rise to the level of violence. God promises to "kill [Israel] with thirst" and to take no pity on its children. Chapter 1 contains a similarly harsh message. God instructs Hosea to marry Gomer, "a wife of whoredom," who symbolizes unfaithful Israel. When they have children, God instructs Hosea to give them names of vitriolic significance, including "Lo-ruhamah" ("No compassion") and "Lo-ammi" ("No people"), for "I will no longer have pity on the house of Israel or forgive them" (Hos. 1:6) and "you are not my people and I am not your God." (v. 9). This final word of judgment directly contravenes God's covenantal promise to Israel, offered repeatedly throughout the Hebrew Bible (e.g., Exod. 6:7; Jer. 7:23; Ezek. 36:28).

When taking up difficult passages such as these in Hosea, the preacher should choose a specific interpretive strategy. One possibility

involves identifying the character through whose perspective we are meant to understand the story. In this case, there are two possibilities: Hosea and Hosea's family. While the former might seem the natural choice, the preacher would do well to consider both.

The Wounded Heart of God. From Hosea's perspective, the contrast between 2:1–13 and 2:14–20 is meant to make clear that God is not unaffected by Israel's idolatry. Medieval theologians insisted on divine impassibility, the idea that God, being utterly complete in God's own self, was not susceptible to hurt or grief on the basis of human actions. It is hard to imagine they had read Hosea. The prophet speaks for a God scarred by Israel's infidelity, because God is deeply in love with Israel. Hosea's own feelings about Gomer's rejection fuel the prophetic imagination here; he knows from wrenching personal experience the consequences within the life of God of Israel's faithless actions.

The work of Korean American theologian Andrew Sung Park can help us understand the depth of what Hosea's God is going through. In *The Wounded Heart of God*, Park brings the East Asian religious concept of *han* into conversation with Christian theology.[2] *Han* is the spiritual and psychic pain born within the human heart as a result of cruelty, hatred, or oppression. *Han* further victimizes those who suffer

2. Andrew Sung Park, *The Wounded Heart of God: The Asian Concept of Han and the Christian Doctrine of Sin* (Nashville: Abingdon, 1993).

Engraved upon the Heart

The gospel and the law agree in this, that they are both from God, and that there is something revealed in each concerning the nature, will, and works of God. There is, however, a very great difference between them:

In the revelations which they contain; or, as it respects the manner in which the revelation peculiar to each is made known. The law was engraven upon the heart of man in his creation, and is therefore known to all naturally, although no other revelation were given. "The Gentiles have the work of the law written in their hearts." (Rom. 2: 15.) The gospel is not known naturally, but is divinely revealed to the Church alone through Christ, the Mediator. For no creature could have seen or hoped for that mitigation of the law concerning satisfaction for our sins through another, if the Son of God had not revealed it. "No man knoweth the Father, but the Son, and he to whom the Son will reveal him." "Flesh and blood hath not revealed it unto thee." "The Son, who is in the bosom of the Father, he hath declared him." (Matt. 11:27; 16:17)

In the kind of doctrine, or subject peculiar to each. The law teaches us what we ought to be, and what God requires of us, but it does not give us the ability to perform it, nor does it point out the way by which we may avoid what is forbidden. But the gospel teaches us in what manner we may be made such as the law requires: for it offers unto us the promise of grace, by having the righteousness of Christ imputed to us through faith, and that in such a way as if it were properly ours, teaching us that we are just before God, through the imputation of Christ's righteousness. The law says, "Pay what thou owest." "Do this, and live." (Matt. 18:28. Luke 10:28) The gospel says, "Only believe." (Mark 5:36). . . .

They differ in their effects. The law, without the gospel, is the letter which killeth, and is the ministration of death: "For by the law is the knowledge of sin." "The law worketh wrath; and the letter killeth." (Rom. 3:20; 4:15. 2 Cor. 3:6) The outward preaching, and simple knowledge of what ought to be done, is known through the letter: for it declares our duty, and that righteousness which God requires; and, whilst it neither gives us the ability to perform it, nor points out the way through which it may be attained, it finds fault with, and condemns our righteousness. But the gospel is the ministration of life, and of the Spirit, that is, it has the operations of the Spirit united with it, and quickens those that are dead in sin, because it is through the gospel that the Holy Spirit works faith and life in the elect. "The gospel is the power of God unto salvation," etc. (Rom. 1:16).

Zacharius Ursinus, *The Commentary of Dr. Zacharius Ursinus on the Heidelberg Catechism* (Columbus, OH: Scott & Bascum, 1852), 104–5.

hurt by subjecting them to resentment, anger, and feelings of worthlessness. It is an insidious reality, in that those who carry the burden of *han* almost inevitably cause harm to others, thus extending and enlarging its cycle of hurt. While a Christian theological dimension is not part of *han*'s original meaning, Park has applied the idea of *han* to the relationship between God and humanity. Specifically, Park claims that even God experiences *han*, as God's children choose time and time again to invest their loyalty and love in that which is less than God.

This is why the preacher must approach today's reading within the context of the rest of Hosea 1–2. When YHWH speaks words of mercy and commitment to Israel in Hosea 2:14–20, we know what they cost. Human unfaithfulness has broken God's heart. In an overwhelming act of compassion, God opens up to the possibility, even the likelihood, that God's people will break that heart all over again. Hosea leaves little room for uncertainty about what the vulnerability of love means for God—who chooses to love us anyway.

The Unreliable Narrator. The problem with Hosea's perspective is that itch of recognition we experience when we read chapters 1 and 2. Both chapters vacillate between words of ugly accusation and venomous rage on the one hand,

and kind forgiveness and commitment on the other (a similar pattern happens elsewhere in the book of Hosea, esp. chap. 11). The uneasy feeling we have when Hosea gives voice to rage, then mercy, then back again, derives from its similarity to an abusive relationship, in which violent accusations of infidelity often alternate with insistent expressions of affection designed to woo the battered partner. Told from Hosea's perspective, we are meant to hear the denunciations of 2:1–13 as justified by Gomer's/Israel's behavior, while the gentle words in 2:14–20 reveal the true content of the prophet's and his deity's hearts. Yet, is that how Gomer and the children would have experienced the story line of chapters 1 and 2?

Literature has a term for storytellers like Hosea: the unreliable narrator. One of the best-known examples of this device occurs in *The Murder of Roger Ackroyd*, an Agatha Christie mystery where (spoiler alert) figuring out whodunit is rendered nearly impossible by the fact that the narrator is the murderer.[3] In a novel with an unreliable narrator, the reader must discover the truth by listening to what is not being said. In biblical passages like Hosea 1–2, we must adopt a similar strategy if we are to hear the word of God.

As we have seen, the book of Hosea magnifies the faithfulness of God by contrasting it with Israel's faithlessness. Yet if we read the book from the neglected perspective of Gomer and the children, the metaphor on which that contrast is founded—Hosea's marriage to an undeserving, faithless wife—falls apart. Once we recognize the abusive dimension of Hosea's words and actions, we realize that his assurance that he (like YHWH) will love and protect his family does not tell the whole story.

Adding Gomer's point of view to that of Hosea helps prevent the greatest misperception to which this passage might give rise: that God either does not care about abuse or condones it. Further, it helps us understand why so many people in our churches believe God cannot love them. They have heard too many preachers employ the rhetorical strategy (deriving in part from passages like ours) that insists we must first focus on our unworthiness if we want to understand God's goodness. Whether the listeners on their own, or the preachers and then the listeners, someone got stuck at the unworthiness part.

Perhaps the time has arrived for another strategy. To be sure, we are not the people we were supposed to be, but does that diminish God's love and compassion? Does not our existence still derive solely from our creator, and would we still not wish to devote our deepest gratitude to God as a result? Perhaps this week preachers might focus on God's worthiness alone, and give the human unworthiness a rest.

Elsewhere the book of Hosea moves beyond the freighted metaphor of Hosea and Gomer's marriage. Chapter 11 describes the depth of God's compassion toward Israel, that wayward yet never forsaken child. Chapter 14 pictures Israel as a garden that YHWH longs to tend and cultivate. A sermon that mentions these passages can help clarify something that chapter 2 tries (with uneven success) to proclaim: the prophet's message of God's loving forgiveness.

ROBERT A. RATCLIFF

---

3. Agatha Christie, *The Murder of Roger Ackroyd: A Hercule Poirot Mystery* (New York: William Morrow, 2011).

Psalm 103:1–13, 22

¹Bless the LORD, O my soul,
　　and all that is within me,
　　bless his holy name.
²Bless the LORD, O my soul,
　　and do not forget all his benefits—
³who forgives all your iniquity,
　　who heals all your diseases,
⁴who redeems your life from the Pit,
　　who crowns you with steadfast love and mercy,
⁵who satisfies you with good as long as you live
　　so that your youth is renewed like the eagle's.

⁶The LORD works vindication
　　and justice for all who are oppressed.
⁷He made known his ways to Moses,
　　his acts to the people of Israel.
⁸The LORD is merciful and gracious,
　　slow to anger and abounding in steadfast love.
⁹He will not always accuse,
　　nor will he keep his anger forever.
¹⁰He does not deal with us according to our sins,
　　nor repay us according to our iniquities.
¹¹For as the heavens are high above the earth,
　　so great is his steadfast love toward those who fear him;
¹²as far as the east is from the west,
　　so far he removes our transgressions from us.
¹³As a father has compassion for his children,
　　so the LORD has compassion for those who fear him.
. . . .
²²Bless the LORD, all his works,
　　in all places of his dominion.
Bless the LORD, O my soul.

Connecting the Psalm with Scripture and Worship

Psalm 103 is framed as an interior monologue in which the psalmist exhorts his soul to do two things: to bless the Lord and not to forget what God has done (Ps. 103:1–2). In the Hebrew Bible, to bless someone is simply to speak a good word about them. A blessing can be prospective, that is, a statement that expresses a desire that one's future will be filled with good things. A blessing can also be an indicative statement about the present, a positive assessment about one's character or actions. For example, one might bless someone by saying, "What you do is valuable," or "You have worth." Blessings can be also be retrospective, statements that recount the good deeds one has done in the past.

In the context of Psalm 103, retrospective blessings predominate. The psalmist looks back on all of God's benefits (v. 2), the good things that God has done. God has healed, restored, and forgiven him (vv. 3–4). Moreover, God has exalted the psalmist so that he is constantly satisfied by God's care and nourishment (vv. 4–5).

To be sure, the psalmist is not the only one to have benefited from God's actions. After announcing the ways that God has helped him, the psalmist shifts to describing God's good deeds for the community (vv. 6–18). God vindicates those who suffer oppression (v. 6). God has done so for generations, back to the time of Moses and the exodus (vv. 6–8). God also forgives those who have sinned (vv. 9–12). Even though humans break faith, God is faithful to God's promises. God makes a covenant and keeps it (vv. 7, 17–18). In short, God's forgiveness of the individual psalmist is in keeping with how God has worked throughout history.

While recounting God's gracious actions for the community, the psalmist compares God's love with that of parents for their children.

> As a father has compassion for his children,
> so the LORD has compassion for those
> who fear him. (v. 13)

While the imagery is drawn explicitly from the sphere of paternal care, the idea of maternal care is nevertheless implied. The word for "have compassion" here (*rakham*) is related to the word for womb (*rekhem*). Thus, the relationship between God and God's people is best characterized here as that between a parent and a child rather than an exclusively paternal relationship.

The metaphor of humanity as God's children (v. 13) immediately gives way to a meditation on the transitory nature of human life (vv. 14–16). While verses 14–18 are not in the lectionary, they are nevertheless essential for understanding the logic of the psalm. These verses reveal that God's care for the people is not based on human goodness or strength. In fact, the opposite is the case. The psalmist claims that God loves us because God knows who we are. God knows we are made out of dust. God loves the weak, the vulnerable, the fragile. Humans are like the grass that flourishes for a season and then fades (v. 15–16). This temporariness of human life makes the enduring love of God all the more remarkable. It extends to our children, and to our children's children (v. 17).

Modern popular psychology suggests that many problems can be addressed by adjusting one's interior monologue. Rather than harboring negative thoughts about one's self, one should say (so the conventional wisdom goes), "I'm good. I'm strong. I'm powerful. I can do anything."

The psalm, however, presents a different sort of interior monologue. Rather than blessing himself as the self-help books might suggest, the psalmist blesses God, recalling who God is and what God has done. He describes God's faithful love for the sick and the weak (v. 3), how God redeems those whose lives are in the pit (v. 4), those who are oppressed (v. 6). If our interior monologue matches the psalmist, we remember that we are among those who are in great need, and that God loves the needy. God loves us not because we are strong, but because our lives are so fleeting and because we are so frail. Acknowledging our frailty can liberate us. It can unite us with our community. It can inspire us to live with the gratitude and joy that the psalm reflects.

Psalm 103 and Hosea 2:14–20 both focus on the love and forgiveness of God in spite of our frailty and our failings. Unlike the psalm, however, the prophet employs an extended metaphor of Israel as an unfaithful wife being wooed back to God, her husband, after a period of infidelity. Its imagery draws upon concepts of love and marriage that are quite different from the cultural context of much of liberal Protestantism.

The main theme of Hosea 2:14–20 is God's love for God's people and God's eagerness to forgive. Many modern readers may find that message difficult to discern, given the patriarchal ideal that appears in the text. The immediate context of this lection is even more problematic, for it describes an adulterous woman being publicly shamed and her children punished as well (see esp. Hos. 2:2–6). By juxtaposing Psalm 103 with Hosea 2, the lectionary provides a welcome alternative for exploring the theme of God's steadfast love in spite of human frailty and folly.

Both metrical and responsorial settings of Psalm 103 may be sung in worship. This psalm has also inspired a number of popular praise choruses, including Andraé Crouch's gospel classic "Bless His Holy Name" and Matt Redmon and Jonas Myrin's soaring "10,000 Reasons (Bless the Lord)." While these can be good options, a caution is in order. Some paraphrases reinforce an individualistic spirituality that is largely discontinuous with Scripture's witness to God's saving work in the world. In Psalm 103, the psalmist's individual experience is part of a much larger pattern of God's actions with God's people. It is worthwhile to highlight the fact that Psalm 103 blesses God by recalling a wide scope of God's work in the world. God's salvation is both individual and communal.

JOEL MARCUS LEMON

Proper 3 (Sunday between May 22 and May 28)

2 Corinthians 3:1–6

[1]Are we beginning to commend ourselves again? Surely we do not need, as some do, letters of recommendation to you or from you, do we? [2]You yourselves are our letter, written on our hearts, to be known and read by all; [3]and you show that you are a letter of Christ, prepared by us, written not with ink but with the Spirit of the living God, not on tablets of stone but on tablets of human hearts.

[4]Such is the confidence that we have through Christ toward God. [5]Not that we are competent of ourselves to claim anything as coming from us; our competence is from God, [6]who has made us competent to be ministers of a new covenant, not of letter but of spirit; for the letter kills, but the Spirit gives life.

Commentary 1: Connecting the Reading with Scripture

In today's lection Paul responds to questions challenging his ministry. Where did these questions come from? The "peddlers of God's word" (2 Cor. 2:17)? Doubts arising within the congregation? We do not know, but the issues are clear: Paul is accused of being self-commending, he has no letters of recommendation, and he lacks competence. Paul responds by redirecting the Corinthians' gaze: look at yourselves.

Letters of recommendation were a necessity in the ancient world. They proved people were who they said they were. They were guarantors of identity and authorization. Why would Paul need such things? Paul had founded the church; he had revisited it; he had written to it. Paul and the Corinthians had had difficult moments, but those very difficulties had cemented the relationship.[1] He could remind the Corinthians that they knew him personally, and he could tell them, "You yourselves are our letter" (2 Cor. 3:2). They should need no further authentication.

Throughout this passage Paul stresses the idea of the truth of the gospel being written on the heart. The letter written on the heart reflects the new covenant (Jer. 31:33–34), which was also said to be written on the heart rather than engraved on stone.

The same is the case for Paul's competence. It comes from God. Paul says, in effect, "Look inward at your hearts and upward toward God to observe the effectiveness of my work."

Paul then expands upon his discussion of the new covenant. He contrasts the law, written on stone, with the Spirit, who writes upon hearts. The one is the ministry of death (referring back to 2 Cor. 2:15–16); the other is the ministry of justification. This contrast is extended to Moses, who had to veil his shining face (Exod. 34:29–35). That was the glory of the old covenant, which was transcended by the greater glory of the new. This does not mean that the Jews were rejected by God (see Rom. 11:1–2). It means that the greater glory has now been manifested.

The Corinthian correspondence contains no extended theological exposition (as does Romans), nor does it offer simply a brief greeting with short doctrinal reflections (as do 1 and 2 Thessalonians). It discusses theological issues in relation to congregational problems.

The appearance of outsiders in Corinth is one of those issues. Who are these outsiders? It is tempting to identify them with the people Paul disputes in Galatians, but observing precepts of the law, particularly over circumcision, does not seem to be the issue in Corinth.

1. See Victor Paul Furnish, *II Corinthians,* Anchor Bible 32A (New York: Doubleday, 1984), 30–48, for an analysis of Paul's correspondence with the church in Corinth.

Rather, Paul's concern is the character of the new covenant itself.

The other lections for this Sunday are Hosea 2:14–20 and Mark 2:13–22. They have a common thread: God's grace has created a new situation. The Hosea passage, which follows God's symbolic rejection of the people in chapter 1, is all expressed in the future tense. Almost every verse begins with God saying, "I will . . ." God promises to end the worship of Baal, thus purifying the people from their idolatry. God promises peace and prosperity. Above all, God promises that the people will be loved forever.

The Gospel reading from Mark, concerning the call of Levi, exemplifies these promises. The text says nothing about Levi that would indicate any merit or special qualities. All we know is that he was one of the despised tax collectors. Nevertheless, he is called and he comes. The issue is not Levi's worthiness or lack thereof. The issue is the summons of Jesus.

The reference to letters "written on human hearts" in verses 2–3 brings Jeremiah 31:33 to mind: "But this is the covenant that I will make with the house of Israel after those days, says the LORD: I will put my law within them, and I will write it on their hearts; and I will be their God, and they shall be my people." It also seems to echo Ezekiel 11:19–20: "I will give them one heart, and put a new spirit within them; I will remove the heart of stone from their flesh and give them a heart of flesh, so that they may follow my statutes and keep my ordinances and obey them. Then they shall be my people, and I will be their God" (cf. Ezek. 36:26–27). Paul has drawn the themes of a new covenant and a people with new hearts from the prophetic tradition. In that venerable tradition, obedience to the law had always been a matter of spirit as well as faithful observance of God's holy statutes.

Paul's own understanding was that the time of the law was over. It had served as a tutor until the coming of Christ, but with that coming, the tutor was no longer needed (see Gal. 3:24–25).[2] This passage from 2 Corinthians does not have this nuance. In the Corinthians passage, the Spirit gives life, but the letter—the law—simply kills.

Paul's attitude toward the law is complex; understanding it requires that we examine several passages. First, Paul never says that the law itself is bad: "So the law is holy, and the commandment is holy and just and good" (Rom. 7:12). Further, he does not hold that the law is too arduous to be performed. He was, he said, blameless as to righteousness under the law (Phil. 3:6).

The problem lay in the psychological effect of the law. The very fact that the law prohibited something made people want to do it (Rom. 7:7–8). This is the work of sin, and humans are incapable of escaping this dynamic on their own; but the Spirit, working within, sets us free. The time of the law, necessary though it was, is now over. We are in a new era.

This passage offers multiple opportunities for the preacher. One is the question of what validates one's ministry. Most working pastors have multiple credentials. These are the results of hard work and lots of time. Nevertheless their final validation is exactly what Paul says it is: a living congregation. Pastors must encourage their congregations to see themselves as the work of God, and pastors must learn to regard themselves as instruments in God's service.

A second area of preaching on this text has to do with the law. Contemporary Christians tend to regard Paul's critique of the law as a relic from another time. However, that critique applies to any law that becomes a basis of self-justification before God. Such laws are not just statutes. They can be social customs, prejudicial norms, or even ingrained habits. Pastors can explain how Paul's analysis of the way that laws can kill applies just as much to our time as it did to his. This is not a matter of old covenant versus new covenant. It is a matter of avoiding any attempt at self-justification before God.

A third homiletical possibility arises from the theme that binds the lectionary passages together: the newness of God's work. What is really new in the gospel? These passages speak of a new covenant, a new time of forgiveness,

---

2. The NRSV translates the Greek *paidagōgos* as "disciplinarian," which does not capture the sense of the Greek original. A *paidagōgos* was a slave who was both a teacher and a guardian of boys until they reached adulthood.

and renewal. That which the Bible promises still holds, no matter how grim and terrifying our present circumstances might be. Preaching good news in troubled times is a perennial obligation of the pastor.

DAVID W. JOHNSON

Commentary 2: Connecting the Reading with the World

Trust is our most fundamental social value. Families, communities, nations are built on trust. If I do not trust, I cannot have any relationships—not with a spouse, children, pastor, governor, or president. To trust is to render ourselves into somebody else's life. When we trust, we lean on somebody, we are able to give, to share, to live with and participate in various forms of relations—but to trust is so difficult.

To trust is difficult because we have all heard testimonies or had hard experiences of broken trust that have placed us and others in difficult situations. To trust is to risk vulnerability, for we have a wide range of expectations that summon different hopes that translate into forms of trust that can easily be frustrated and broken. We hire a pastor who is not doing the job we expected; we marry someone who is not turning out to be the person we had expected and trusted them to be. Of course, there may also be frustration. The pastor may find people are not responding in the ways she was promised, or a partner may say we are not proving to be whom they had trusted us to be when they entered into the covenant.

Trust is complex, and a plethora of issues defines what trust might be. Trust depends on how we were formed. Our education depends on social, spiritual, racial, sexual, and economic upbringings. To trust or to doubt or even to be scared depends on the signs we receive from life. Some white people move to the sidewalk across the street if walking toward a Black person. Some persons coming home from work cross the street to avoid crossing paths with a beggar. Some Black people freeze at the sight of a police officer. Some immigrants have issues giving out their names or addresses. We are all formed by the conditions and upbringings of our societies, and we need to be aware of both intended and unintended feelings about diverse others.

In this text, Paul is working in such a framework of trust and mistrust. Who is to be received? How should communities treat their guests? He is entertaining the possibility of receiving someone on the basis of a different sort of "letter of recommendation." For him, Christians should be living letters of recommendation, known by their fruits. Thereby, through lives of faith and works of love we can build bonds of trust. Paul challenges a culture of mistrust with a deep assurance of trust based on love.

Paul is establishing an embodied way of being, relating, and testifying in the world. He is calling for bodies that are incarnations of God's love and hospitality, for hearts fired by the gospel. When we live out incarnational love, we ourselves become Christ's letter sent to the world. Filled by the Holy Spirit, in our living we embody the gospel of Jesus Christ to each other. Local churches become communities, *koinōnias* embodying the kingdom of God. Ideally, we have such a confidence in each other that we can enjoy full trust, a trust rooted not in the person but in the God whose Spirit fills and inspires us. The gift we receive from God is the gift of just and loving community, of life under a new covenant, life under the guidance of the Spirit who gives life and sustains us in this new covenant.

This is all seriously unrealistic, right? Does not what Paul is calling for here amount to "holy irresponsibility"? Is the apostle not showing too much trust? We live in a world of sinfulness. People abuse each other, exploit each other, steal and practice all forms of violence. What are we to do, living between Paul's demand to trust and a world where suspicion, not trust, is the smart play, where naive trust is more likely to facilitate greed and exploitation than love and justice? There is no gainsaying this tension in the real world. We must be realistic, but Paul will not allow realism to breed cynicism. We need strength and street smarts to hold these poles together. We need wisdom to work with ambiguities and paradoxes, risking love and working for what is loving, while protecting against being played and exploited.

I propose we start this challenge within ourselves. Can we call ourselves letters of recommendation from God? Letters of Christ to the world? What we need is to learn how to trust God more fully. We cannot have a God that is only a language spoken from elsewhere. Rather, we must speak of God from deep within. This trust in God is deeply connected with trust in ourselves. Trust in ourselves comes only when we are affirmed by God and our people. Trust can grow; trust is a competency in itself, another fruit of the Spirit. If we find this deep trust, we can feel that we fully belong to God, in whom we find our origin and our end. As Paul says, "Our competence is from God" (2 Cor. 3:5).

Christian mystics can help us in this movement of trust. Thomas of Celano, biographer of Francis of Assisi, quotes Francis's words: "The preacher must first draw from secret prayers what he will later pour out in holy sermons; he must first grow hot within before he speaks words that are in themselves cold."[3] Catherine of Siena envisioned Jesus saying, "Dearest daughter, as I took your heart away from you the other day, now, you see, I am giving you mine, so that you can go on living with it forever."[4]

This deep connection with God causes the divisions between our trust in ourselves and our trust in God to fade away. When our trust in God is the trust in ourselves, and the trust in ourselves is the trust in God, we do not fear trusting people or even ourselves. We then have the competence to get closer to the oneness of God and the world. Moreover, this connection keeps expanding.

When our trust is a place of strength, we also learn to trust the earth. If we are all *humus*, made of the soil of the earth, we also belong to the earth, created and loved by God; the animals are as well. When we grow in this expansive competency to trust God fully, there is no separation between God, our neighbor, the earth, and the animals. Everything belongs to God and we trust in this God, who is intertwined in everything. If we see trust in God in this way, we can also trust the mountains, the birds, and the animals for they all carry the assurance of God's love. We do not see mountains' and animals' existence only for our desires. Instead, we care for each other. We belong to all, and all belong to us.

Our faith is a constant call to trust. To trust God is to go deep into God's love without reservation, fear, or caution. To trust God is to plunge into the deep waters of God's love. This love helps us connect with God's whole creation and build communities of love where people trust each other. By way of God's love and trust, we become God's trusted recommendation letter to each other, Christ's trusted letter to the world.

CLÁUDIO CARVALHAES

---

3. Brother Thomas of Celano, *The Lives of St. Francis of Assisi* (London: Methuen & Co., 1908), 295.
4. Blessed Raymond of Capua, *The Life of St. Catherine of Siena: The Classic on Her Life and Accomplishments as Recorded by Her Spiritual Director* (Charlotte, NC: TAN Books, 2009), 144.

Mark 2:13–22

[13]Jesus went out again beside the sea; the whole crowd gathered around him, and he taught them. [14]As he was walking along, he saw Levi son of Alphaeus sitting at the tax booth, and he said to him, "Follow me." And he got up and followed him.

[15]And as he sat at dinner in Levi's house, many tax collectors and sinners were also sitting with Jesus and his disciples—for there were many who followed him. [16]When the scribes of the Pharisees saw that he was eating with sinners and tax collectors, they said to his disciples, "Why does he eat with tax collectors and sinners?" [17]When Jesus heard this, he said to them, "Those who are well have no need of a physician, but those who are sick; I have come to call not the righteous but sinners."

[18]Now John's disciples and the Pharisees were fasting; and people came and said to him, "Why do John's disciples and the disciples of the Pharisees fast, but your disciples do not fast?" [19]Jesus said to them, "The wedding guests cannot fast while the bridegroom is with them, can they? As long as they have the bridegroom with them, they cannot fast. [20]The days will come when the bridegroom is taken away from them, and then they will fast on that day.

[21]"No one sews a piece of unshrunk cloth on an old cloak; otherwise, the patch pulls away from it, the new from the old, and a worse tear is made. [22]And no one puts new wine into old wineskins; otherwise, the wine will burst the skins, and the wine is lost, and so are the skins; but one puts new wine into fresh wineskins."

Commentary 1: Connecting the Reading with Scripture

"Why is Jesus not concerned about holiness?" "If Jesus wanted to live a truly holy life, would he not choose his table companions more wisely?" "If Jesus and his disciples are really interested in holiness, why do they not fast more often?" Such questions would have arisen in the minds of many of the scribes, Pharisees, and other eyewitnesses to Jesus' ministry, as they watched him eating with tax collectors and sinners, and as they saw that Jesus and his disciples ate as usual, while the Pharisees and John's disciples fasted. The social perspective of Jesus' time expected a teacher to make good use of public opinion, but Jesus was not very good at navigating the social mores of his day. Indeed, rather than consistently upholding the law, he appears regularly to trespass against it.

Usually, meals in the ancient world did not include people of different social strata. From soup kitchens to three-star Michelin restaurants, one finds much the same situation has endured to this day. When people of different social standing did dine together in the Greco-Roman world, people with different status were seated in different rooms and offered a quality of food that mirrored their rank. In addition to the question of social status, the ritual purity of the people and food at various tables would be a concern for religious leaders. Jesus' practice of eating with tax collectors and sinners consistently and starkly violated all such mores of purity and social stratification.

Tax collectors were viewed with disdain, not only in the Jewish circles surrounding Jesus, but also generally in the ancient world. Greek writers and rabbinical literature attest to the contempt in which they were held. "Rabbinic texts link tax collectors with robbers, murderers, and sinners; tax collecting appears in rabbinic lists of despised trades that no observant

Jew should practice."[1] Oppressive levels of taxation were a means used by Rome to control and plunder conquered peoples. Worse, in the Judean context tax collectors were allowed to make money by collecting a percentage of tax greater than that due Rome—even if this meant pushing people into de facto slavery or debtors' prison. Moreover, since tax collectors were typically drawn from among conquered peoples, they were acting as collaborators with Roman colonial rule. This describes Levi, a Jew who worked for the Romans as a tax collector. In the eyes of people in Jesus' world, tax collectors were vectors of social sin and ritual impurity. In fact, Jesus does not contest this identification of tax collectors as "sinners." When Jesus calls upon Levi, saying, "Follow me," Levi responds by leaving behind his job as a tax collector.

Jesus heals several people in Mark's Gospel before he calls Levi, tax collector and son of Alphaeus. Immediately before calling Levi, Jesus has been teaching (Mark 2:13), but we are not told explicitly how Levi knows Jesus. We are told that Levi responds without hesitation to Jesus' command, "Follow me." Today's reading focuses on the fact that needy, ostracized people like these "sinners" are among the people Jesus has been sent to gather and with whom he shares his meals. The text also makes clear that many responded, were healed, and readily followed Jesus. This makes it clear that holiness is found in the process of *restoring* those marginalized by sin or disease, not in relating to and dining only with the righteous. This passage, therefore, conveys a message of hope to sinners; a call to responsible holiness to all who would be truly righteous; and a call to be open to fellowship with oppressors and others living lives that are considered far from righteous.

This theme of Jesus reaching out to have fellowship with marginalized people was probably very important to Mark's original audience, who lived in a time when Christians were first being identified as a distinct religious cult after the destruction of the Second Temple in 70 CE. These *readers* may have had the experience of religious authorities considering them sinful, because as Christians they did not fully live within the law. There are also marginalized people in *the story*, whom Jesus considers to be sinful (such as Levi, an agent of Roman oppression who causes people real harm). The power of the passage is the call to have table fellowship with those whom one considers to be sinful. This is a powerful message in our current age of intolerance.

The second half of this reading focuses on the polarity between disciples who fast and those who do not. Jesus reframes the issue of the pursuit of holiness by evoking the traditional image of a wedding feast as a moment of God's grace. Should the wedding guests fast while the bridegroom is with them? Surely not. Fasting is appropriate when mourning is called for. It is a solemn form of self-deprivation during which a person looks for God's guidance. A wedding feast, by contrast, celebrates new social bonds between families of similar status and honor who are joined together through the couple's matrimonial bond. In this subsistence society, where food scarcity is common, a wedding feast is a gesture of hope and confidence that God will grace the community with abundant food in the future.

The other texts in Proper 3 enrich the interpretation of this Gospel text. In Hosea 2, written from an eighth-century-BCE perspective, God becomes a bridegroom who marries an imperfect, wayward Israel, healing and restoring her from her impurity. The wife brings dishonor to the husband, creating a situation in which the threat of famine highlights sin. The appropriate response is repentance, signified by fasting or abstention. In today's reading, however, we see Israel gradually brought back to a relationship with her husband for no other reason than the compassionate character of God, demonstrated as righteousness, justice, steadfast love, and mercy. Jesus' healing, teaching, and table fellowship, as well as his association with tax collectors and sinners, are a direct expression of this mercy. Second Corinthians 3:3 evokes this idea of transformation and acceptance in a more subtle way. Transformation is written by the Spirit on human hearts, not on stones.

When is an old custom appropriate? When is it time to innovate? When is it appropriate

---

1. Adele Yarbro Collins, *Mark: A Commentary*, Hermeneia (Minneapolis: Fortress, 2007), 194.

to follow the law? When is it appropriate to adapt to new circumstances? The comparisons between patching a new garment with old cloth and putting new wine in old wineskins address this issue using examples from everyday life that encompass the work of both men and women. Social relationships among Jesus' disciples should reflect their relationship to their Master, not the religiously accepted requirements for holiness. Fasting behavior should reflect the sorrow of mourning. Feasting is the appropriate response to the presence of God among them.

How can the meaning of fasting or feasting connect with readers/listeners today? The issue is meaning and motivation. It is possible to fast for positive reasons: to restore health to the body, express sorrow, or refocus the mind and heart on God. Similarly, it is possible to feast for negative reasons: out of gluttony, or to maintain or create a particular social status. Today's Gospel challenges listeners to think about their relationship with food, whether eating or fasting, as a response to God's presence in their midst. It also challenges people in churches to discern whether they are able to embrace the "tax collectors" and "sinners" of our world—those who share in the company of Jesus, the bridegroom who is sent as an expression of God's deep, persistent love and mercy.

RENATA FURST

Commentary 2: Connecting the Reading with the World

Falling as it does in Ordinary Time, this passage might not receive as much attention as others. That is a pity, for it contains considerable homiletical treasure. The passage illuminates both the nature of Jesus' life and the call of God upon us all. Specific subthemes about widening the table, rejection of outdated or unfair laws, and the new thing that God is doing in our midst are all viable sermon topics.

The Reverend Martin Luther King Jr. once said, "It is appalling that the most segregated hour in Christian America is eleven o'clock on Sunday morning."[2] Another highly segregated occasion is mealtime. We tend to eat most of our meals with those who match us in every demographic. Our daily bread—breakfast and lunch, at least—is ordinarily shared with family. We and our children typically sit elbow to elbow in the lunchroom with colleagues and classmates similar to us. People at our dinner parties often look a lot like us, and, again, on Sunday morning the faces around the Eucharist tend to be similar to ours. Jesus calls us to expand that table, to welcome all to join. He calls Levi, one clearly outside his social group, to become a disciple, and he joins the longer table at Levi's house.

The BBC period drama *Call the Midwife*, based on a memoir by Jennifer Worth, depicts the day-to-day lives of midwives working in London's East End. Set in the late 1950s, the series shows midwives delivering babies and tending to a variety of other medical situations in an impoverished neighborhood. In the opening episode we see newly qualified nurse Jenny Lee in her first official post. Her midwifery training had not particularly prepared her for the ways poverty manifests itself in the living conditions of her charges. Sent to perform a prenatal checkup for Conchita, a woman preparing for her twenty-fifth child, Nurse Lee arrives just as the family sits down for tea.

Conchita throws large pots of stew onto the table, and the family picks up spoons and helps themselves, eating directly from the pots. The eldest daughter urges Nurse Lee to eat, and Nurse Lee whispers that there are no plates. The daughter shrugs and tells Nurse Lee to do as she has been told. As the scene ends, we see the posh young woman in her crisp uniform dipping her spoon into the pot and eating—gingerly at first, but with more and more enthusiasm, out of the common bowl she shares with Conchita's disheveled and hungry children. This scene is

---

2. Martin Luther King Jr., quoted; http://okra.stanford.edu/transcription/document_images/Vol05Scans/17Apr1960_InterviewonMeetthe-Press.pdf.

not unlike the experience of a common meal at the Common Cathedral in Boston, and ministries modeled after it, where the homeless host the homed, and meals are shared.

Following this line of thought, congregants might be urged to consider the people with whom they are most likely to share a meal, both literally and figuratively, and to contemplate ways that their church's table might be built to be longer. Congregants (and preachers) might also be urged to look for those opportunities where they might join tables already set, similar to the experience of Jenny Lee and Conchita's family. When we consider lengthening the table, we might think only of how those with resources might share more effectively—an important sentiment, to be sure—but it is just as important to find ways to receive God's grace through others and to join tables already set.

Jesus is clearly not one to follow the letter of the law, the rules and conventions of the day. After discussing his dinner party with tax collectors and sinners, he is called to task for his disciples' failure to fast. His group is compared to the Pharisees and the disciples of John, who are, apparently, following the rules. Jesus defends his disciples' behavior by reminding them that the bridegroom is present, and therefore the wedding guests have no need to fast. There will be time for that in the future. The clever response seems to mollify his questioners, but the truth is deeper: Jesus has come to change the rules.

The Broadway musical *Matilda*,[3] based on a book by Roald Dahl, includes a delightful song where Matilda takes the listener through several classic stories with sad endings and questions why these stories were not interrupted, asking, for instance, why someone did not take the poison from Romeo's hands. "Sometimes," the precocious five-year-old sings, "you have to be a little bit naughty." While Matilda's mischief seems, at a glance, merely cute, it cuts to a deeper story. Matilda's misdeeds target adults whose behavior is clearly abusive and the rules they make, particularly those of Ms. Trunchbull, the headmistress, which are cruel and nonsensical. With "naughty" behavior, Matilda is

able to protect her peers and call into question harmful rules.

A less lighthearted example of choices made to ignore the law in favor of justice would be found in some of the stories told by the organization No More Deaths. The faith-based organization seeks to end death and suffering in the US-Mexico borderlands. Members engage in a variety of activist interventions toward these ends, including some that violate US law. One member, Scott Warren, was arrested in 2018 for providing injured migrants with food, water, and basic first-aid supplies. What is the appropriate response to laws that are unfair or cruel? How might our congregations use their faith to respond?

Another option would be to take the words of Jesus more literally and craft a sermon around what it means to be present with the bridegroom now, and how to celebrate with joy while such celebration is possible. How might our worship be more joyful? How might our lives be more joyful? How might we celebrate, despite all the challenges we see?

Jesus reminds us that patching unshrunk cloth onto an old coat is a futile endeavor. The new patch will pull away, rendering the hole bigger. Similarly, as new wine ferments, it will expand wineskins, causing old, less flexible skins to explode. In short, the new thing is powerful and growing. It deserves to stand on its own. The challenge is that some of us, as individuals and as congregations alike, get overly attached to the old. We can find it hard to let go of what has been in favor of what might be—even when that new thing is born of God's gracious love for us.

An example of new wine in new wineskins would be Enterprise Community Partners, a nonprofit that, among many other projects, has partnered with houses of worship to create low-income housing. In the mid-Atlantic region in particular, the organization works with churches and other houses of worship to sell unused land or, in some cases, to sell their entire property in order to build housing for those that might not otherwise be able to live in those

3. Tim Minchin, composer, lyricist, *Roald Dahl's Matilda: The Musical* (London: Wise Publications, 2012).

neighborhoods. As more and more churches struggle with what to do with their large buildings, for some at least, the faithful answer is to put their communities into new wineskins, so that the gospel mandate to provide for the least of these might be enlivened.

Whichever approach the preacher pursues with this Gospel lesson, the passage will serve to illuminate the signs and wonders of the Pentecost season. Surely the signs of God are evident in this passage and in our corporate lives!

SUSAN K. OLSON

Proper 4 (Sunday between May 29 and June 4)

1 Samuel 3:1–10 (11–20) and
    Deuteronomy 5:12–15
Psalm 139:1–6, 13–18 and
    Psalm 81:1–10

2 Corinthians 4:5–12
Mark 2:23–3:6

1 Samuel 3:1–10 (11–20)

[1]Now the boy Samuel was ministering to the LORD under Eli. The word of the LORD was rare in those days; visions were not widespread.

[2]At that time Eli, whose eyesight had begun to grow dim so that he could not see, was lying down in his room; [3]the lamp of God had not yet gone out, and Samuel was lying down in the temple of the LORD, where the ark of God was. [4]Then the LORD called, "Samuel! Samuel!" and he said, "Here I am!" [5]and ran to Eli, and said, "Here I am, for you called me." But he said, "I did not call; lie down again." So he went and lay down. [6]The LORD called again, "Samuel!" Samuel got up and went to Eli, and said, "Here I am, for you called me." But he said, "I did not call, my son; lie down again." [7]Now Samuel did not yet know the LORD, and the word of the LORD had not yet been revealed to him. [8]The LORD called Samuel again, a third time. And he got up and went to Eli, and said, "Here I am, for you called me." Then Eli perceived that the LORD was calling the boy. [9]Therefore Eli said to Samuel, "Go, lie down; and if he calls you, you shall say, 'Speak, LORD, for your servant is listening.'" So Samuel went and lay down in his place.

[10]Now the LORD came and stood there, calling as before, "Samuel! Samuel!" And Samuel said, "Speak, for your servant is listening." [11]Then the LORD said to Samuel, "See, I am about to do something in Israel that will make both ears of anyone who hears of it tingle. [12]On that day I will fulfill against Eli all that I have spoken concerning his house, from beginning to end. [13]For I have told him that I am about to punish his house forever, for the iniquity that he knew, because his sons were blaspheming God, and he did not restrain them. [14]Therefore I swear to the house of Eli that the iniquity of Eli's house shall not be expiated by sacrifice or offering forever."

[15]Samuel lay there until morning; then he opened the doors of the house of the LORD. Samuel was afraid to tell the vision to Eli. [16]But Eli called Samuel and said, "Samuel, my son." He said, "Here I am." [17]Eli said, "What was it that he told you? Do not hide it from me. May God do so to you and more also, if you hide anything from me of all that he told you." [18]So Samuel told him everything and hid nothing from him. Then he said, "It is the LORD; let him do what seems good to him."

[19]As Samuel grew up, the LORD was with him and let none of his words fall to the ground. [20]And all Israel from Dan to Beer-sheba knew that Samuel was a trustworthy prophet of the LORD.

Deuteronomy 5:12–15

[12]Observe the sabbath day and keep it holy, as the LORD your God commanded you. [13]Six days you shall labor and do all your work. [14]But the seventh day is a sabbath to the LORD your God; you shall not do any work—you, or your son or your daughter, or your male or female slave, or your ox or your donkey, or any of your livestock, or the resident alien in your towns, so that your male and female slave may rest as well as you. [15]Remember that you were a slave in the land of Egypt, and the LORD your God brought you out from there with a mighty hand and an outstretched arm; therefore the LORD your God commanded you to keep the sabbath day.

Commentary 1: Connecting the Reading with Scripture

The interpretive focus on 1 Samuel 3 is often exclusively on 3:1–10. Lessons derived from these verses include things like this: even children are called by God; God speaks at the most unexpected times; be sure to listen carefully for God's voice. These lessons are edifying and important. When verses 1–10 are heard in connection with verses 11–20 and in both immediate and larger contexts, it becomes clear this is not just a story for children.

When 1 Samuel 3 is heard in its entirety, it is clear that the boy Samuel was being called to do a grown-up job. The situation is critical: "The word of the LORD was rare in those days" (1 Sam. 3:1), which means there is a shortage of guidance and a lack of effective and faithful leadership. Samuel will fill the vacuum. By the end of chapter 3, Samuel is no longer "the boy . . . ministering to the LORD under Eli" (v. 1). Rather, he is "a trustworthy prophet of the LORD" (v. 20). The word of God is no longer rare, "for the LORD revealed himself to Samuel at Shiloh by the word of the LORD" (v. 21). Having been transformed by the word, Samuel is now prepared and positioned to deliver a much-needed divine word "to all Israel" (4:1).

The crisis into which Samuel is called is even clearer when we observe the connections between 1 Samuel 3 and its wider context. The preceding book of Judges has narrated an emerging crisis of leadership. Gideon is the last of the judges to achieve "rest" for the land (Judg. 8:28). Samson, the final judge, can only "begin to deliver Israel"

(13:5) from a Philistine threat that continues into 1 Samuel. The final section of the book of Judges (chaps. 17–21) is a horror story of major proportions. Leadership is entirely lacking: "In those days there was no king in Israel; all the people did what was right in their own eyes" (21:25; see also 17:6; 18:1; 19:1).

In the midst of this crisis, Samuel provides stability. Even though he himself opposed the creation of a monarchy to deal with the Philistine threat (1 Sam. 8:1–18), he would prove to be a key figure in moving Israel from disarray and near dissolution to some semblance of stability, especially with the emergence of King David. The monarchy would eventually prove to be an unfaithful institution as well, but God would raise up more prophets to deal with later crises.

The Gospel of Luke sees parallels between the birth circumstances, growth, and ministry of Samuel and Jesus. The events leading up to the births of both Samuel and Jesus are extraordinary (see 1 Sam. 1; Luke 1:26–45). Both Hannah, Samuel's mother, and Mary, Jesus' mother, sing songs in conjunction with the births of their sons—and the songs are noticeably similar (1 Sam. 2:1–10; Luke 1:46–55). Both celebrate God's incomparable deeds, carried out especially for the lowly and needy, who are exalted, while the powerful are brought low. Both Samuel and Jesus, we are told, grow physically and "in divine and human favor" (Luke 2:52; see 1 Sam. 2:26). God was revealed in and through Samuel and his word (1 Sam. 3:19–4:1), and such was certainly the case with Jesus as well.

Samuel was called to be a transitional and transformational leader. Traditionally, 1 Samuel 3 is interpreted as an invitation for us too to listen for God's call. Beyond that, however, it is also a challenge to discern what God needs us to do in our world. As Bruce Birch concludes, "We are called to become the channel for God's prophetic word to our own time."[1] In view of the persistence of poverty and hunger in the United States and the world, along with the growing gap between rich and poor, it would be appropriate to attend to Hannah's and Mary's proclamation that God exalts the lowly and brings low the powerful. While preachers may not be able to convince their parishioners to think of themselves as prophets, they may at least encourage their congregations to be a "channel for God's prophetic word to our own time."

The Ten Commandments, found in the lection from Deuteronomy, are often dismissed as outdated "thou shalt nots" that have little to do with contemporary life. Connecting them to their narrative context can help to correct this impression. The formulation of the Decalogue in Deuteronomy 5 represents a second version of the commandments (Deuteronomy means "Second Law"). This version is very close to the first version in Exodus 20:1–18.

The major difference involves Deuteronomy 5:12–15 in comparison to Exodus 20:8–11. In Exodus, deliverance from captivity and death precedes law giving. In short, the commandments are not rules to be obeyed in order to earn one's salvation or prove one's merit. Rather, they are *torah*, "instruction," offered to a liberated people so that they will be able to stay free. The lives of liberated people should look very different than life under the oppressive conditions of the Egyptian Empire. This original setting of the Decalogue remains relevant for the second version. In Deuteronomy, the people are poised to enter the land. The issue is whether they will be able to stay free as they undertake a settled existence.

While the word "Sabbath" means basically to stop, more is at stake than simply a work stoppage, although rest itself is helpful and needed. Two Sabbath connections point to what more is involved. The first mention of Sabbath in the Bible is in Genesis 2:1–4 ("rested" represents the Hebrew root), and it is the creational rationale for Sabbath observance that is featured in Exodus 20:11. Because we can assume that God does not really need to rest, Sabbath in Genesis 2:1–4 suggests taking the time to delight in and enjoy creation. God's delight in creation invites our delight in creation. The Sabbath commandment thus has an ecological reach. Sabbath observers will be creation preservers. Notably, animals are included as participants in Sabbath observance (Deut. 5:14).

Unlike Exodus 20:11, the rationale for Sabbath observance in Deuteronomy 5:15 is the remembrance of captivity in Egypt and God's liberating work. As suggested above, Exodus is the narrative setting for the first version of the Decalogue. This alone suggests that Sabbath observance is about freedom. Memorably, this includes freedom from the oppressive reality of being defined solely by work and productivity, as Israel had been defined in Egypt.

There is an earlier mention of Sabbath in the manna story in Exodus 16, where a double portion is given on the sixth day so that the people can rest on the seventh day (see esp. Exod. 16:22–30). Such reliance upon God for gracious provision of enough for everyone is a marked contrast to life in imperial Egypt. In Egypt, food had become commodified, resulting in plenty for the few and little for the many. Sabbath observance in this context means equal opportunity for all to eat.

Amid the ongoing threat of ecological catastrophe, it would be appropriate and faithful for the preacher to recover and emphasize the creational dimensions of Sabbath observance. In the midst of a production-oriented, consumerist society that encourages greed, it would be

---

1. Bruce Birch, "The First and Second Books of Samuel: Introduction, Commentary, and Reflections," in *The New Interpreter's Bible* (Nashville: Abingdon, 1998), 2:994.

appropriate and faithful to proclaim Sabbath as, in the words of Walter Brueggemann, "an *act of* *resistance*"[2] whereby we refuse, for God's sake, to be defined by production and consumption.

J. CLINTON MCCANN JR.

Commentary 2: Connecting the Reading with the World

Call stories feature prominently during the first few weeks of the season after Pentecost in Year B. On Trinity Sunday we share Isaiah's vison of YHWH in the temple, asking, "Whom shall I send?" (Isa. 6:1–8). On Proper 3, Jesus rouses Levi from his seat at the tax booth with an invitation to "follow me" (Mark 2:14). God's call of the prophet to marry Gomer in Hosea 1 creates the context for the words of divine forgiveness and mercy in Hosea 2:14–20, the first reading for Proper 3. Now on Proper 4 we hear the Lord's repeated calls to the young Samuel and witness the child's struggle to figure out exactly who is calling him. The preacher might explore this story by means of other examples of divine call in Scripture, Christian history, and theology.

Dangers of the Call. Did God speak within the biblical stories more often than today? Those tempted to reach that conclusion may be surprised to read the disclaimer that opens today's reading: "The word of the Lord was rare in those days; visions were not widespread" (1 Sam. 3:1). Might this have been partly because the call of God can be such a fraught experience, subject to misunderstanding both by recipients and their listeners? When Samuel hears God's voice, he seems to have no context within which to locate it. Even on the third call, he still thinks it has to be Eli. Would we be any less befuddled? In a classic comedy routine, the late Richard Pryor could not tell if the voice he once heard coming from a darkened alley belonged to God or a couple of guys with a baseball bat.[3]

Not knowing how to listen for the voice of God is one thing; thinking there is no need to do so is another. That is the problem confronting Swain Hammond, the protagonist in Peggy Payne's short story "The Pure in Heart."[4] A highly educated Presbyterian pastor in a university town, Hammond considers himself rational, ethical, and immune to flights of fancy (an assessment with which his congregation approvingly agrees). So, of course, when God speaks to him in a manner that Hammond cannot explain away, his whole world is upended. The worst part is his church's reaction. When Hammond feels compelled to tell them of his experience, they go through their own turmoil before eventually deciding to allow him to remain their pastor. His gratitude for their understanding curdles when he realizes they are simply humoring him. They refuse to contemplate the possibility that what he heard was the life-altering call of an undomesticated God who might just be calling them as well.

Discerning the Call. How can we be sure we are hearing the voice of God rightly? How can we know we are really being called to stake out risky ground, change our life course, or offer potentially life-altering advice? Most especially, how can we know we are hearing the authentic call of God, rather than the murmurings of our own hearts?

In our complicated world of flawed humans, the chances that God's call will definitively authenticate itself are slim. Like Swain Hammond's church, often we cannot or do not want to understand that to which God is calling us. This is where discernment comes in. We know we must test the call in order to gauge whether it comes from God, ourselves, or some other

---

2. Walter Brueggemann, *Deuteronomy*, Abingdon Old Testament Commentaries (Nashville: Abingdon, 2001), 73.
3. "Richard Pryor Meets God," www.youtube.com/watch?v=zvyaQezvmNo.
4. In C. Michael Curtis, ed., *God: Stories* (New York: Houghton Mifflin, 1998), 222–35.

source. That process of discernment is almost always rendered easier when others are involved. Without Eli, Samuel the boy never becomes Samuel the prophet and judge. Without Ananias, Saul of Tarsus never becomes the apostle Paul (Acts 9:10–18). When the wind of the Spirit blows in a person's life, it is the same Spirit who gathered the community to which that person belongs. Seeking the Spirit's leadership in that community will almost always result in a more fruitful and faithful discernment than will doing so alone. Had Hammond's congregants "test[ed] the spirits" (1 John 4:1), they likely would have perceived that their pastor was not the only person to whom God was speaking.

Scripture as Call. The church's history is full of those who, having read of God's call in Scripture, hear that same call on their own life. Antony, the founder of Christian monasticism, was only one of many to take notice of the story of the rich young man (Matt. 19:16–22) and decide that they must heed Christ's call to sell all they have and follow him. Encountering Paul's struggle in the book of Romans with the relationship between law and grace, Martin Luther felt himself led more deeply into that same struggle, emerging with a theological realization that helped spark the Protestant Reformation. Hearing a reading from Luther's commentary on that same book of Romans, John Wesley experienced God's call to a deeper joy in and assurance of his salvation.

The preacher would do well to prepare for a similar possibility on Proper 4. Somewhere in the congregation is someone who has been denying and rationalizing away an insistent tug on their life, possibly inaudible yet no less real. Hearing God's call to Samuel might be just what they need to surrender to that tug. God grant that they find a group of Christians—and a Christian preacher—willing to take the possibility seriously.

Call and Covenant. This morning's reading from Deuteronomy, in which Moses shares for the second time the Ten Commandments (specifically, the commandment to observe the Sabbath), feels like a tough homiletical nut to crack. Along with the (presumed) familiarity congregants bring with them to the subject, the Decalogue has for some time been a hot zone in our society's ceaseless culture wars. Yet the combination of the way this passage frames the commandments and the way it is conjoined in the lectionary with the story of Samuel's call offers possibilities preachers might want to consider.

When Moses brings Israel together in Deuteronomy 5, he makes clear that the covenant God has made with Israel forms the necessary context for commandments such as keeping the Sabbath holy. A community entering into a different lifestyle every seven days is what faithfulness to the covenant looks like. Contrary to the individualistic readings we often bring to the Decalogue, the life it describes makes sense only when a group of people have agreed to live that life together.

This is where the divine call comes in. God always calls people into covenant faithfulness, and that faithfulness in turn fulfills the call to witness and service. A story from the last century casts light on this interplay between call and covenant. During the 1918 influenza pandemic, the hospitals of Philadelphia were overwhelmed, especially their nursing staffs. The city's Roman Catholic archbishop issued a call to nuns in the area to leave their convents and offer volunteer nursing services. More than 2,000 of them did, providing compassionate care while risking their own lives and health.[5] Why did this group of Christians take decisive action when many others turned away in fear? Might it be that their monastic vows prepared them for a life of covenantal service, expecting to hear God's call at just such a moment as this? The preacher can remind the congregation that they too can hear that call if they open themselves to hearing it together.

ROBERT A. RATCLIFF

5. Kiley Bense, "We Should All Be More Like the Nuns of 1918," *New York Times*, March 20, 2020; https://www.nytimes.com/2020/03/20/opinion/coronavirus-nuns.html.

Proper 4 (Sunday between May 29 and June 4)

Psalm 139:1–6, 13–18

[1]O LORD, you have searched me and known me.
[2]You know when I sit down and when I rise up;
  you discern my thoughts from far away.
[3]You search out my path and my lying down,
  and are acquainted with all my ways.
[4]Even before a word is on my tongue,
  O LORD, you know it completely.
[5]You hem me in, behind and before,
  and lay your hand upon me.
[6]Such knowledge is too wonderful for me;
  it is so high that I cannot attain it.
. . . .
[13]For it was you who formed my inward parts;
  you knit me together in my mother's womb.
[14]I praise you, for I am fearfully and wonderfully made.
  Wonderful are your works;
that I know very well.
  [15]My frame was not hidden from you,
when I was being made in secret,
  intricately woven in the depths of the earth.
[16]Your eyes beheld my unformed substance.
In your book were written
  all the days that were formed for me,
  when none of them as yet existed.
[17]How weighty to me are your thoughts, O God!
  How vast is the sum of them!
[18]I try to count them—they are more than the sand;
  I come to the end—I am still with you.

Psalm 81:1–10

[1]Sing aloud to God our strength;
  shout for joy to the God of Jacob.
[2]Raise a song, sound the tambourine,
  the sweet lyre with the harp.
[3]Blow the trumpet at the new moon,
  at the full moon, on our festal day.
[4]For it is a statute for Israel,
  an ordinance of the God of Jacob.
[5]He made it a decree in Joseph,
  when he went out over the land of Egypt.

I hear a voice I had not known:
[6]"I relieved your shoulder of the burden;
  your hands were freed from the basket.

41

[7]In distress you called, and I rescued you;
  I answered you in the secret place of thunder;
  I tested you at the waters of Meribah.
[8]Hear, O my people, while I admonish you;
  O Israel, if you would but listen to me!
[9]There shall be no strange god among you;
  you shall not bow down to a foreign god.
[10]I am the LORD your God,
  who brought you up out of the land of Egypt.
  Open your mouth wide and I will fill it."

Connecting the Psalm with Scripture and Worship

Psalm 139:1–6, 13–18. The reading from 1 Samuel AND this corresponding psalm focus on God's immediate knowledge of the human condition and God's access to our thoughts and emotions. Such knowledge is mysterious, even paradoxical, for God's glory seems far removed from the mundane realities of life. Yet God attends carefully to us and intervenes when we call.

Psalm 139 provides a meditation on God's knowledge of the human condition in the context of prayer. The psalmist addresses God directly, stating who God is and what God does. In doing so, the psalm draws us into the relationship between God and the individual psalmist. When we speak the words of the psalm, we hear our own sense of wonder at God's creativity and care: "For it was you who formed my inward parts; you knit me together in my mother's womb" (Ps. 139:13).[1]

The psalm begins with a series of statements about God's knowledge and the inability of human knowledge to comprehend it (vv. 1–6). God knows every place the psalmist goes and everything the psalmist does (vv. 2–3, 5). God's knowledge extends even into the psalmist's thoughts and intentions (vv. 1–2, 4). This pervasive knowledge is possible because God's presence is inescapable (vv. 7–12). God can go anywhere, high or low (v. 8), east or west (vv. 9–10), dark or light (vv. 11–12). Nothing is beyond God's purview.

The lectionary resumes with a meditation on the actions of God (vv. 13–18). Here the psalmist focuses on the mystery of existence and the origin of human life. God's actions extend before and beyond the limits of any one lifetime (vv. 15–16). Such a realization spurs the psalmist to praise (v. 14). Yet considering the depth of these divine mysteries finally leaves the psalmist overwhelmed and unable to articulate the majesty of God's power (vv. 17–18).

The meditations on divine knowledge (vv. 1–6), divine presence (vv. 7–12), and divine action (vv. 13–18) provide the justification for the psalmist's request in the final verses (vv. 19–20), the only direct petition in the psalm. While outside the lectionary, these verses are the climax of the psalm. After extolling God's power, the psalmist finally asks God to use that power to bring about salvation from the enemies.

The statement that the wicked currently surround the psalmist (vv. 19) complicates the psalm's earlier claims about divine knowledge, presence, and action. The affirmations of God's intimate awareness of the psalmist might suggest that the psalmist is in a state of quiet confidence, resting secure in the knowledge that God is there, no matter what. Yet the last verses of the psalm reveal that the psalmist is in fact in crisis. The psalmist clings to the notion of divine presence so forcefully because the threats to the psalmist are so immediate. Survival depends on

---

1. This verse has been frequently cited as a proof text in contemporary controversies about abortion and the reproductive rights of women. When evaluating the utility of this or any proof text, it is important to keep in mind the larger context. The verse appears amid other descriptions extolling God's knowledge. The psalmist's central claim is that divine awareness and ability far surpass that of humans.

That Insight into Spiritual Things

We need not fear spiritual pride then, in following Christ's call, if we follow it as men in earnest. Earnestness has no time to compare itself with the state of other men; earnestness has too vivid a feeling of its own infirmities to be elated at itself. Earnestness is simply set on doing God's will. It simply says, "Speak, Lord, for Thy servant heareth," "Lord, what wilt Thou have me to do?" Oh that we had more of this spirit! Oh that we could take that simple view of things, as to feel that one thing which lies before us is to please God! What gain is it to please the world, to please the great, nay, even to please those whom we love, compared with this? What gain is it to be applauded, admired, courted, followed, compared with this one aim, of not being disobedient to a heavenly vision? What can this world offer comparable with that insight into spiritual things, that keen faith, that heavenly peace, that high sanctity, that everlasting righteousness, that hope of glory, which they have who in sincerity love and follow our Lord Jesus Christ?

Let us beg and pray Him day by day to reveal Himself to our souls more fully; to quicken our senses; to give us sight and hearing, taste and touch of the world to come; so to work within us that we may sincerely say, "Thou shalt guide me with Thy counsel, and after that receive me to glory. Whom have I in heaven but thee? and there is none upon earth that I desire in comparison of Thee: my flesh and my heart faileth; but God is the strength of my heart, and my portion for ever."

John Henry Newman, "Divine Calls," in *Parochial and Plain Sermons*, vol. 8 of 8 (London: Longmans, Green, Co., 1920), 31–32.

God's intervening to bring about justice and salvation (vv. 19–20).

The text of Psalm 139 often appears in affirmations of God's care. These may come in responsive calls to worship or assurances of pardon. The text is even more likely to appear in song, especially in hymns or praise choruses. The psalm is appropriate for such usages, to be sure. Yet one must be careful not to treat the text as an antidote to low self-esteem. The psalmist describes himself as "wonderfully made" (v. 14), not primarily to glorify the creation, but to glorify God the creator.

When Psalm 139 appears in worship, one should acknowledge, as the psalmist does, that the presence of God is needed because of the immediacy of injustice and oppression. Psalm 139 ends with a plea for God to act against the wicked, who pose a mortal threat to the psalmist.

The reading from 1 Samuel also confirms the idea that the divine presence is manifested in times of trouble. God appears to the young boy amid societal disarray (Judg. 19–21; 1 Sam. 3:1) and in spite of failed religious leadership (1 Sam. 2:11–17). Even though the word of God was "rare in those days" (1 Sam. 3:1), God was still making contact. God calls out to Samuel in a clear, direct, and immediate way (e.g., 1 Sam. 3:4).

Psalm 81:1–10. Along with the first reading of the day, Psalm 81 describes how a community should respond to God's saving actions. In Deuteronomy 5:12, we find the command to "observe the sabbath." This version of the Ten Commandments differs from the Sabbath rule found in Exodus 20:8–11. In Exodus, the commandment recalls the priestly account of the creation of the world (Gen. 2:2–3). The people should rest because God rested on the seventh day at the beginning of time (Exod. 20:11). In Deuteronomy 5, however, the Sabbath commandment recalls how God intervened with a "mighty hand and an outstretched arm" to bring about salvation from slavery (Deut. 5:15). The command to keep Sabbath refers not to the origins of the cosmos but to origins of a community, those whom God delivered from oppression. In Deuteronomy, God's care for God's people is the justification for everyone to rest, to take care of yourself and those whose labors support your own.

Like Deuteronomy 5:12, Psalm 81 also begins with a command, a summons for the community to respond to God's saving acts. The text begins with a call to praise God. The whole band is called into service: voices, tambourine, lyre, harp, and trumpet (Ps. 81:1–5). This call to praise God is not optional. It is a matter of law, a "statute" and an "ordinance" (vv. 4–5a) that likely refers to the command to keep the Sabbath in Deuteronomy.

The latter half of the lectionary psalm verses assumes the form of an oracle in which God speaks directly to the people (vv. 5b–10). God recounts the story of the exodus, how God relieves the burdens of the people, how God hears the cries of the people and answers them. God's action motivates the people's praise and mandates that nothing can stand between God and God's people—no other loyalties, no other gods. The psalm concludes as it began, with a command. At the beginning of the psalm the people are called to open their mouths in praise, and at the end God commands the people to "open your mouth wide" so that God may continue to care for God's people, by nourishing them and sustaining them (v. 10).

Since many Christian communities have bound Sabbath keeping to Sunday worship, musical settings of this psalm are particularly appropriate during Sunday services. Whether sung or read responsively as a call to worship, Psalm 81 highlights the importance of setting aside time to remember and celebrate what God has done. God's saving action prompts us to care for ourselves and others (Deut. 5:12–15). It prompts us to lift our voices together in praise (Ps. 81:1–5a). It prompts us to trust God now as we have done in the past (Ps. 81:5b–10). God's faithfulness continues.

JOEL MARCUS LEMON

2 Corinthians 4:5–12

[5]For we do not proclaim ourselves; we proclaim Jesus Christ as Lord and ourselves as your slaves for Jesus' sake. [6]For it is the God who said, "Let light shine out of darkness," who has shone in our hearts to give the light of the knowledge of the glory of God in the face of Jesus Christ.
[7]But we have this treasure in clay jars, so that it may be made clear that this extraordinary power belongs to God and does not come from us. [8]We are afflicted in every way, but not crushed; perplexed, but not driven to despair; [9]persecuted, but not forsaken; struck down, but not destroyed; [10]always carrying in the body the death of Jesus, so that the life of Jesus may also be made visible in our bodies. [11]For while we live, we are always being given up to death for Jesus' sake, so that the life of Jesus may be made visible in our mortal flesh. [12]So death is at work in us, but life in you.

Commentary 1: Connecting the Reading with Scripture

In this passage, Paul continues his exposition on the nature of the apostolic ministry. He does not seem to have any particular opponents in view in these verses, although 4:5, "For we do not proclaim ourselves," repeats a theme of chapter 3: Paul has no need of self-aggrandizement. But from that point, his discussion is a more general description of the life of apostles, a life marked by paradox, expressed in a series of antitheses.

This series begins with a commonplace illustration: "we have this treasure in clay jars" (2 Cor. 4:7). The "treasure" looks back to 4:1, the ministry itself. The clay jars are the apostles. The force of this metaphor might be missed today, since clay jars are not household items, but in Paul's time they were common. Clay jars had little value in themselves. Their only worth was in their use as storage receptacles. A twenty-first-century Paul might have written, "We have this treasure in tin cans."

The antitheses follow. They have a common, almost rhythmic pattern. In each pair of antitheses, the first term—"afflicted," "perplexed," "persecuted," "struck down"—describes what apostles are on their own. The second term—"not crushed," "not driven to despair," "not forsaken," "not destroyed"—demonstrates what

they become through the power of God. These comparisons are summarized and made explicit in the concluding antithesis: death is carried in the apostles' bodies in order to make life in Christ manifest. Paul concludes this selection by reminding his hearers that all this is for them, a point he emphasizes repeatedly in the subsequent parts of the letter. This is summarized by the well-known verse: "in Christ God was reconciling the world to himself, not counting their trespasses against them, and entrusting the message of reconciliation to us" (5:19). This message is not just verbal. It is displayed in the lives of the apostles: "For while we live, we are always being given up to death for Jesus' sake, so that the life of Jesus may be made visible in our mortal flesh" (4:11). The suffering itself proclaims Christ.

The antitheses in 4:8–10, moving though they are, are rather abstract. Paul does not detail any of his sufferings. Already, in 1:8–9, he has said that because of an experience in Asia he was driven to despair. Later in the letter, in 11:23–27, he details his sufferings as an apostle: he has been whipped, beaten, stoned, shipwrecked, in constant danger, and often naked and without food.[1] Paul is absolutely sincere when he says that he has been afflicted in every way. He

---

1. Many scholars regard chaps. 10–13 as a separate letter that at some point was added to chaps. 1–9.

sees his sufferings as reflecting the suffering of Christ, and consequently as a witness to Christ.

Being united with the death of Christ in order to share in the resurrection is a frequent theme in Paul's letters. In Romans 6:3–11 he associates it with baptism: to be baptized is to die with Christ in order to be raised with Christ. This also means that the body dies to sin.

The connection of the body with sin and death is a constant in Paul's letters. Death, sin, and the body are often associated with each other. They form a kind of slavery. Freedom is found in Christ. The postbaptismal life of the believer is itself a kind of resurrection, the death of both sin and death (cf. John 12:24).

The lections associated with this reading are Deuteronomy 5:12–15 and Mark 2:23–3:6. Both of these passages have to do with keeping the Sabbath. In Deuteronomy 5, keeping the Sabbath is associated with the Israelites' liberation from slavery in Egypt, whereas in the parallel in Exodus 20, the Sabbath commemorates God's rest from the work of creation. There are no exceptions or qualifications in either version of the commandment.

The Gospel reading is quite different. It tells two stories about Jesus and the Sabbath. In both stories, the Sabbath command is broken, once by the disciples and once by Jesus himself. The Pharisees here are critical of this breach of the law; in the second passage they are even watching for it. Jesus' act of healing in the synagogue on the Sabbath catalyzes the plots against him.

Uniting the three lectionary texts in a sermon would be a difficult task. The 2 Corinthians reading does not have the law in view, while in the other two passages it is prominent. If the preacher wants to discuss the law, other passages from Paul would be more appropriate. A sermon based on 2 Corinthians 4:5–12 would have to relate the lives of apostles to the death and resurrection of Christ. It also would have to convince the hearers that they are, in fact, apostles, in that they themselves are bearers of the Word. Another approach would be to apply the distinction between clay pots and treasure to contemporary life. Church members might not have any difficulty comparing themselves to clay pots, but they would have difficulty identifying the treasure that those pots contain, particularly if that treasure is associated with trial and suffering rather than achievement and success.

The presence of those whom Paul regarded as pseudoapostles forces him to catalogue his own sufferings. He does not want to boast, but he is willing to remind the Corinthians of what he has endured. Nevertheless, Paul always strikes a note of hope in the power of God to sustain him and make his ministry fruitful.

Contrast this with Jeremiah. Paul appears to have Jeremiah 1:5 in mind when he writes to the Galatians that God had set him apart before he was born (Gal. 1:15). Jeremiah suffers under the burden of being a prophet in a way that Paul apparently does not suffer in being an apostle. "My joy is gone, grief is upon me, my heart is sick," Jeremiah writes (Jer. 8:18). "For the hurt of my poor people I am hurt, I mourn, and dismay has taken hold of me" (8:21). Of course, the word that Jeremiah was instructed to declare is rather different than Paul's message. Jeremiah foretells disaster. His message is not without hope (see esp. Jer. 30–33), but that hope lies on the far side of the proclamation of guilt and suffering God has told him to proclaim.

Paul, by contrast, exudes confidence. Even when he despairs of life (see 2 Cor. 1:8), he does not despair of God. His hope is based on the resurrection of Christ, which teaches that life is present even within death (1:9). Paul could write, "For the Son of God, Jesus Christ, whom we proclaimed among you . . . was not 'Yes and No'; but in him it is always 'Yes.' For in him every one of God's promises is a 'Yes'" (1:19–20).

The tension between God's "Yes" and God's "No" can be the basis of sermons, especially when dealing with modern figures. Lottie Moon, Dietrich Bonhoeffer, and Martin Luther King all had to say both a "No" and a "Yes." The "No" was for the sake of the "Yes." It was a "No" to certain social issues—unequal status and treatment of women, Nazism, racial discrimination—that compromised or denied the "Yes" of God. Pastors must be honest about when and why God says "No," and understand that the "No" is always for the sake of the "Yes."

DAVID W. JOHNSON

Commentary 2: Connecting the Reading with the World

Every night I pray with my kids and part of our prayer goes like this: "And now, give us a good night. We are not afraid of the night, because you are the night with us, and we are the night with you. You are the darkness in us, and we are the darkness in you." I was afraid of the night when I was a kid. By associating God with the night and darkness, I want my son to know that day and night, darkness and light are parts of a whole and all belong to God. God is light and darkness as we, God's image, are also made of light and darkness.

Nonetheless, there is a part of darkness that tries to hide from the light, and that inner part of us has to do with our deep fears. This part tries hard to not see the light of God. This form of darkness tends to lead us into confusion and destruction. When Paul mentions the "light of the knowledge of the glory of God" (2 Cor. 4:6), he is talking about a light that expels any destructive darkness. To know the glory of God is to be free from confusion and self or collective destruction. Paul knew the glory of God and was able to see how God's glory could transform individuals and communities.

Under that light, Paul was a slave for Jesus, which means he first and always worked in fidelity to the gospel of Jesus, no matter the cost. Paul knew the cost in his own body. His body was marked by the bruises of the world; the scars of life covered him with sadness, frustrations, betrayals, sickness, and injustices. In Galatians 6:17 he says, "I carry the marks of Jesus branded on my body." This was not a metaphor. In 2 Corinthians 11:24–27 he relates:

> Five times I have received . . . the forty lashes minus one. Three times I was beaten with rods. Once I received a stoning. Three times I was shipwrecked; for a night and a day I was adrift at sea; on frequent journeys, in danger from rivers, danger from bandits, danger from my own people, danger from Gentiles, danger in the city, danger in the wilderness, danger at sea, danger from false brothers and sisters; in toil and hardship, through many a sleepless night, hungry and thirsty, often without food, cold and naked.

The key to Paul's endurance was to live under this light and know his light was held in and by God. He learned how to engage life *from* knowledge of that light. In our text the modifier "but not" (or "and yet," "although," "in spite of," "however") changes everything. It says Paul lived under the "light of the knowledge of the glory of God," and concretely names how God's grace is sufficient for Paul. The entire edifice of his theological reasoning hangs upon the glory and sufficiency of this light.

The transformed realities that the "but not" entails are essentially figurations of Jesus. In the light of the transfiguring reality of Jesus, oppressive, threatening, and frightening worldly realities are seen in the light of the grace of God. Thus, if I say, "I've been lonely," the *yet* of God will add, "*yet* not alone!" If you say, "I've been betrayed," the *but not* of God will continue, "*but not* destroyed!" If we say, "We have no jobs," the *however* of God will say, "*however*, God will sustain us." If we say, "The earth has been destroyed," the Spirit of God will say, "in spite of its destruction, I am the One who keeps the earth alive."

Paul's theology is deeply marked by God's modifiers, for Paul knew God was the one who modifies our lives in Jesus Christ. To live in the light is to live empowered by the Holy Spirit. It is the Holy Spirit who gives us the possibility to utter the words and know the transfiguring reality of "Jesus Christ," our "yet," "although," "but not," "however," and "in spite of" whatever goes on in our lives. These are our Christian markers.

We are a people of the *yet*, of the *but not*, of the *however*, of the *in spite of*! I will start with some possibilities, and you can create your own:

> Life is hitting us hard, YET . . .
> Somebody in my family is sick, BUT NOT . . .
> My ministry is impossible right now, HOWEVER . . .
> The world is indeed crumbling, but IN SPITE OF THAT . . .

The last word of God for us is always a redemptive "yet," "but not," "however," or "in spite of that." We are always moving in and through Jesus and the ways this holy modifier transforms us.

The ways we see the work of the Holy Spirit depend on our theologies and our interpretations of history. The condition of the possibility for God's theological modifiers to fulfill their potential has to do with the ways we see our lives in the world. In order to get into the fullness of God's modifier, we have to go deeper into our relations with those suffering.

For example, we, nonindigenous North Americans, must acknowledge the ways our official histories fail to consider indigenous people in their own sovereignty and even portray them as savage or docile. In order for the *however* of God to kick in fully and entail God's full redemption, we have to come into a new awareness of their side of the history. Once we realize that "their" history is also "our" history, including our complicity in injurious practices that have been experienced by indigenous peoples as death dealing and culture erasing, we will gain a new appreciation of the indigenous nations, we will fight for them and honor them. Only then will the *but not* of God make real sense.

We could say the same about the ways the United States has treated Black people. Unless we fully address the historical horrors with which Black people have been afflicted under slavery, Jim Crow, and ongoing dynamics of white supremacy, the *in spite of* of God will serve only those who are in power and not those trying to survive and flourish under the crushing power of racism. We could say the same for the ways this country has treated women and still keeps them from places of major power and authority, often burdening them with high pressure and lower salaries. We could also mention the poor, who are criminalized and subject to guilt and shame for not achieving economic self-sufficiency.

The *however* of God will show up powerfully only when we fully repent, Paul says in Romans 12:2: "Do not be conformed to this world, but be transformed by the renewing of your minds." When we understand that our Christian mission is messy and calls us to places where it is not easy to go, when we go after the homeless and find them a home, when we look for children without conditions to study and offer our help, when we all become responsible for those who cannot afford health insurance, when each of our communities makes a commitment to one another's full well-being, then we will become God's "however," "in spite of," "but not," and "yet." Ministering together, we can be God's modifiers in the world, making the life of Jesus "visible in our mortal flesh" (2 Cor. 4:11) as we continue the struggle until justice can kiss peace (see Ps. 85:10).

CLÁUDIO CARVALHAES

Mark 2:23–3:6

2:23One sabbath he was going through the grainfields; and as they made their way his disciples began to pluck heads of grain. 24The Pharisees said to him, "Look, why are they doing what is not lawful on the sabbath?" 25And he said to them, "Have you never read what David did when he and his companions were hungry and in need of food? 26He entered the house of God, when Abiathar was high priest, and ate the bread of the Presence, which it is not lawful for any but the priests to eat, and he gave some to his companions." 27Then he said to them, "The sabbath was made for humankind, and not humankind for the sabbath; 28so the Son of Man is lord even of the sabbath."

3:1Again he entered the synagogue, and a man was there who had a withered hand. 2They watched him to see whether he would cure him on the sabbath, so that they might accuse him. 3And he said to the man who had the withered hand, "Come forward." 4Then he said to them, "Is it lawful to do good or to do harm on the sabbath, to save life or to kill?" But they were silent. 5He looked around at them with anger; he was grieved at their hardness of heart and said to the man, "Stretch out your hand." He stretched it out, and his hand was restored. 6The Pharisees went out and immediately conspired with the Herodians against him, how to destroy him.

Commentary 1: Connecting the Reading with Scripture

What counts as "work" that violates the command about Sabbath rest? In this pericope the disciples pluck heads of grain and Jesus heals on the Sabbath. Are these violations of the Sabbath? Jesus' question summarizes the issue: "Is it lawful to do good or to do harm on the Sabbath, to save life or to kill?" (3:4). Our response to this question reveals what type of God we imagine we worship. Do we worship a God who establishes laws to be followed, no matter their concrete impact in specific circumstances? Do we worship a God who wants us to make exceptions if they are necessary to promote love, justice, and wholeness? Indeed, what is God's purpose in establishing the Sabbath?

Jesus and his disciples are going through grain fields on the Sabbath, plucking heads of grain. They are not harvesting the grain for storage or sale, but to satisfy their hunger. The Pharisees interpret this as breaking the Sabbath. Jesus does not deny that technically they are correct, but he makes clear they have failed to discern the spirit of the law. Jesus cites the example of

David, who enters the house of God and eats the bread of the Presence. Ahimelech, the priest who allows this (1 Sam. 21:1–6), and David, who instigates the action, clearly understand that the need of David and his men to eat takes priority over the technicality of the law. As Jesus says, David, a faithful ancestor, transgressed the holiness of the sanctuary by entering and eating (Mark 2:26). This establishes a criterion for understanding a violation of the Sabbath: there is no true violation of the Sabbath if one's actions meet essential needs of oneself (the disciples, David) or others (David's men, the man with the withered hand); for "the sabbath was made for humankind, and not humankind for the sabbath" (v. 27). The legalistic interpretation of Sabbath rest, of these Pharisees in particular, does not reflect the understanding of all Jews in Jesus' time, nor in ours.

Mark's Gospel records at least eleven scenes in which Jesus is challenged publicly by his opponents. Challenging Jesus publicly is an attempt to shame him by questioning his and his disciples' actions. The challenges in this passage occur during the period of Jesus' public ministry in Galilee, and they make clear that Jesus is more than a match for those who would challenge his authority to teach and heal. All three Synoptic Gospels record this healing, which takes place in a synagogue on the Sabbath. Jesus asks the man to extend his hand. The man does so and is healed. This is an unmistakable sign of God's presence, one that Jesus' opponents, a group of Pharisees, cannot contest. Legalism, a narrow view that plagues many religious traditions, is overcome by the generosity of God's love and mercy.

Unable to accept public defeat, the moment when Jesus heals the man with the withered hand marks a turning point for this faction of the Pharisees, for after this they seek to destroy Jesus by other means. Their focus is not on the meaning of the healing, but on their loss of social status. The story ends with Jesus grieving their hardness of heart. For even as eyewitnesses to a wondrous gift from God, they refuse to understand God's overwhelming concern for our well-being. They refuse to see how God's concern means that when a conflict arises between meeting human needs and meeting Sabbath requirements, the need to meet human needs takes precedence, for the Sabbath was made for our well-being.

Mark's Gospel was probably written for a community of Hellenized Jews or Christians living outside of Israel. Their physical location and social origins would have placed them on the periphery of contemporary society and on the periphery of those whom the Pharisees who challenged Jesus would have considered "righteous." As outliers, they would probably have identified with the tax collectors and sinners or the man with the withered hand in these stories. Jesus' inclusive table fellowship and concern for people's wholeness and well-being would have been a welcome source of consolation in a Gentile world that did not respect the Sabbath.

The other readings for today shed light on these two stories of challenge and response between Jesus and his opponents. Typically, the concept of "Sabbath rest" is interpreted primarily through Genesis 1, where God "rests" on the seventh day. Humans emulate their creator, and therefore "rest" and worship God. This view of God and humanity sounds as if everyone must take a break from exhaustion, but the idea of "rest" is more akin to blessing. In our day, this might look like release from the tyranny and exhaustion of the blue screen: phone, tablet, or computer. We raise our eyes from never-ending work to drink in the restfulness of the created world.

The reading from Deuteronomy 5 records the depth of meaning and the central role Sabbath plays in the faith and life of the Israelites. It focuses attention on the presence of God among them and in doing so limits the slavery of never-ending work, such as they had experienced in Egypt. Furthermore, Sabbath rest encompasses all levels of society, from Israelite males to people on the margins—women, foreigners, and their own slaves. Sabbath rest even extends to domestic animals, whom humans put to labor for their own sake. Sabbath worship was instituted not only to respect God, but also to bring rest and wholeness into the lives of all members of the community.

Sabbath rest from toil creates space to remember the character of God. Psalm 81 celebrates the response of a God who listens and removes the burdens of slavery: "I relieved your shoulder of the burden; your hands were freed from the basket. In distress you called, and I rescued you" (Ps. 81:6–7). The psalm also celebrates the fact that God not only saves, but also provides sustenance for his people: "I am the LORD your God, who brought you up out of the land of Egypt. Open your mouth wide and I will fill it." In a world where many die of hunger and in slavery, this Scripture holds out a hope or vision for a world that has not arrived at this Sabbath rest.

Regular freedom from toil for *everyone* is an alien concept in our society, where so many have to labor continuously just to make ends meet. Work is a blessing that can turn into a curse when there is no opportunity given for meaningful rest. In the world described in Deuteronomy, even creatures that provide sustenance for humankind—oxen, donkeys—are allowed to rest because all are "good" in God's eyes (Gen. 1). This is a far cry from our society, where not only scores of creatures but multitudes of humans are forced to toil continually. Even many with ample power and wealth have internalized nonstop work as a virtue.

As Jesus makes clear in this pericope, we worship a God whose goodness should incline us toward a whole, rich, and balanced life, a God who established the Sabbath for humans, not a God who would have us sacrifice humans for the sake of the Sabbath. This is a God who wants us to provide weekly Sabbath rest for all creatures, including the rich and powerful, those who are poor and desperate, and those who minister to both. Sabbath rest is not merely cessation of activity; freedom from nonstop toil restores wholeness, and thus holiness to the world. Do we provide Sabbath rest for fellow creatures? Do we provide Sabbath rest for ourselves, for those who minister and serve others?

RENATA FURST

Commentary 2: Connecting the Reading with the World

Predominant themes in this pericope include observance of the Sabbath, limits of Sabbath rules, and a theology of disability. Careful observance of the Sabbath was a critical and distinctive marker of belonging to the house of Israel. The practice was so central to Jewish identity that any challenge of it would be both immediately evident and critically important. In the preceding verses (Mark 2:1–22), Jesus continually pushes against the letter of the law by healing the paralytic man, eating with sinners, and not fasting. Jesus ups the ante when he pushes against the Sabbath rules, for Sabbath observance was very important to the house of Israel. Clearly, Jesus is doing a very new thing here. The old ways cannot be assumed.

Notably, Jesus nowhere questions the importance of the Sabbath or Sabbath keeping. This is about Sabbath only inasmuch as Sabbath is immeasurably important—therefore making any exceptions or reinterpretations a visible sign of Jesus' authority in interpreting the importance of the Sabbath.

A sermon exploring the practice and the limits that Jesus imposes could be a very useful way of beginning a conversation with a congregation about contemporary Sabbath practice and experience. Many congregants might think Sabbath keeping old-fashioned and unwarranted. Others might think it is strictly Jewish. A sermon could look at the historical observance and newer experiences of Sabbath keeping, focusing on the role Sabbath might play today in personal and communal life. What does it mean to experience Sabbath in light of contemporary lifestyles? What circumstances would warrant breaking the Sabbath?

We are people in need of rest. Many of us live in communities where response to "How are you?" is more likely to be "Stressed" or "Busy" than "Fine, thank you." We laugh when peers quip, "I'll sleep when I'm dead." We skip vacation days, come to work sick, multitask from the beach. A 2018 study of American workers showed that 47 percent did not use all their allotted paid vacation days and 21 percent left more than five days unused.[1] Sundays, once sacred days of worship and rest for Christians, are increasingly crowded with work, home responsibilities, and children's activities. We need rest but wonder how to fit it in.

MaryAnn McKibben-Dana's *Sabbath in the Suburbs* explores one family's attempt at creating and practicing Sabbath observance while balancing two careers, three young children, and the pressures of managing a household. Over the year of their experiment, the couple negotiate what Sabbath means to them, and set intentions for their family's observance. At one point, after the family's own rules trip them up, the family turns Sabbath into an adverb. They do things "Sabbathly." They might have to break their intentions with a trip to the grocery store, but by slowing the experience and being

---

1. See https://www.forbes.com/sites/victorlipman/2018/05/21/why-america-has-become-the-no-vacation-nation/#126562204c53.

mindful, they can undertake the experience Sabbathly. In the chapter "January," McKibben-Dana muses, "Maybe Sabbath is a vaccination against the breakneck speed of life."[2] Taking the vaccination metaphor further, we might be convinced, like bedtime-protesting youngsters who "do not feel tired yet," to inoculate our bodies and souls in advance of hard days ahead.

If Sabbath is made for us, where are the loopholes? Where might we do things Sabbathly instead of by a rule book? Jesus offers the answer in his statement. Sabbath is a gift to us, not a ritual we perform for God. Jesus' hungry disciples pick grain on the Sabbath, so our hunger takes priority over Sabbath rest. Jesus heals on the Sabbath, so reducing suffering takes priority over Sabbath rest (though exhausted pastors might also remember that even Jesus takes a boat to escape needy multitudes in order to find rest).

What does it mean to rest? Why is rest good and vital? When do we put our (good and appropriate) need for rest aside for the sake of other goods for ourselves or for the good of the community? Is Sabbath inherently a practice of the privileged? How do those whose lives involve running between multiple jobs or working on someone else's schedule fit into the practice of Sabbath? If economic realities prevent a traditional block of Sabbath time, how might we invite congregants to live Sabbathly? Further, how might we engage in the social justice work that brings the possibility of Sabbath rest to all?

In addition to the issue of Sabbath, the story of Jesus healing the man with the shriveled hand raises the issue of miracles and healing stories, which are tricky to preach. In almost every sanctuary, someone is praying for a miraculous healing, and someone else is mourning a healing prayer that was not answered in the way they wished. Preaching miracles and healing stories treads on fragile ground.

The preacher might consider, then, what it means to be healed, and further, what it means to be disabled or ill. Are disabled individuals broken? Mistakes? Evidence of sin? While most of us rightly recoil from such derogatory images, persons with disabilities regularly report hearing such language directed at them. One BBC article describes harmful or demeaning encounters that persons with disabilities have experienced at the hands of Christians, including being subjected to unwanted healing prayer in public places, such as the London tube.[3]

This Gospel story offers an opportunity to take on the concept of healing and God's vision for all of God's children—in whatever form their bodies and minds appear. Are not people with disabilities whole and complete as they are? It is true that the Bible is rife with stories of Jesus' miraculous healings. In Jesus' day, disability was equated with poverty and exclusion. It is often unclear what, exactly, Jesus is curing. Is the physical healing an end in itself, or is it a means to bring about justice for the person with the disability?

Many persons with disabilities consider inaccessible environments and attitudes, not their physical disabilities, to be the barriers to full participation in common life. For more insight into the theology of disability, the preacher might consider the works of Deborah Beth Creamer, Nancy Eiesland, Jennie Weiss Block, Bill Gaventa, and others who are contributing to this growing field. The Collaborative on Faith and Disability's website and events are also an excellent source of information.

It makes sense, then, to consider what purpose the actual healing in this story serves. It is, of course, a challenge *from* the Pharisees. It is also a challenge *to* the Pharisees. It gives them a technical objection upon which to base their murderous plans. Once again, Jesus demonstrates his power and authority to the Pharisees, enraging them, but probably terrifying them as well. The man with the shriveled hand did not ask to be healed, at least not as the story is narrated. He may have wanted to be healed. He may have felt complete as he was. We know nothing about what his life was like after this short object lesson, or for that matter, what it had been like before it. We do not know why

2. MaryAnn McKibben-Dana, *Sabbath in the Suburbs: A Family's Experiment with Holy Time* (St. Louis: Chalice, 2012), 69.

3. Damon Rose, "Stop Trying to 'Heal' Me," April 28, 2019; https://www.bbc.com/news/uk-48054113.

he was selected out of any number of other individuals that might have wanted or needed healing. Whether or not his hand needed to be fixed, who he is, and how he feels about this healing are all immaterial. It is not about the hand. It is about the power. The healing of the man's hand pales in comparison to the spiritual gift he receives. He has seen the power of Jesus up close, and by extension, so have we.

SUSAN K. OLSON

Proper 5 (Sunday between June 5 and June 11)

Genesis 3:8–15 and 1 Samuel 8:4–11 (12–15), 16–20 (11:14–15)
Psalm 130 and Psalm 138

2 Corinthians 4:13–5:1
Mark 3:20–35

Genesis 3:8–15

⁸They heard the sound of the LORD God walking in the garden at the time of the evening breeze, and the man and his wife hid themselves from the presence of the LORD God among the trees of the garden. ⁹But the LORD God called to the man, and said to him, "Where are you?" ¹⁰He said, "I heard the sound of you in the garden, and I was afraid, because I was naked; and I hid myself." ¹¹He said, "Who told you that you were naked? Have you eaten from the tree of which I commanded you not to eat?" ¹²The man said, "The woman whom you gave to be with me, she gave me fruit from the tree, and I ate." ¹³Then the LORD God said to the woman, "What is this that you have done?" The woman said, "The serpent tricked me, and I ate." ¹⁴The LORD God said to the serpent,

> "Because you have done this,
>   cursed are you among all animals
>   and among all wild creatures;
> upon your belly you shall go,
>   and dust you shall eat
>   all the days of your life.
> ¹⁵I will put enmity between you and the woman,
>   and between your offspring and hers;
> he will strike your head,
>   and you will strike his heel."

1 Samuel 8:4–11 (12–15), 16–20 (11:14–15)

⁸:⁴Then all the elders of Israel gathered together and came to Samuel at Ramah, ⁵and said to him, "You are old and your sons do not follow in your ways; appoint for us, then, a king to govern us, like other nations." ⁶But the thing displeased Samuel when they said, "Give us a king to govern us." Samuel prayed to the LORD, ⁷and the LORD said to Samuel, "Listen to the voice of the people in all that they say to you; for they have not rejected you, but they have rejected me from being king over them. ⁸Just as they have done to me, from the day I brought them up out of Egypt to this day, forsaking me and serving other gods, so also they are doing to you. ⁹Now then, listen to their voice; only—you shall solemnly warn them, and show them the ways of the king who shall reign over them."

¹⁰So Samuel reported all the words of the LORD to the people who were asking him for a king. ¹¹He said, "These will be the ways of the king who will reign over you: he will take your sons and appoint them to his chariots and to be his horsemen, and to run before his chariots; ¹²and he will appoint for himself commanders of thousands and commanders of fifties, and some to plow his ground and to reap his harvest, and to make his implements of war and the equipment of his

chariots. [13]He will take your daughters to be perfumers and cooks and bakers. [14]He will take the best of your fields and vineyards and olive orchards and give them to his courtiers. [15]He will take one-tenth of your grain and of your vineyards and give it to his officers and his courtiers. [16]He will take your male and female slaves, and the best of your cattle and donkeys, and put them to his work. [17]He will take one-tenth of your flocks, and you shall be his slaves. [18]And in that day you will cry out because of your king, whom you have chosen for yourselves; but the LORD will not answer you in that day."

[19]But the people refused to listen to the voice of Samuel; they said, "No! but we are determined to have a king over us, [20]so that we also may be like other nations, and that our king may govern us and go out before us and fight our battles." . . .

[11:14]Samuel said to the people, "Come, let us go to Gilgal and there renew the kingship." [15]So all the people went to Gilgal, and there they made Saul king before the LORD in Gilgal. There they sacrificed offerings of well-being before the LORD, and there Saul and all the Israelites rejoiced greatly.

Commentary 1: Connecting the Reading with Scripture

The Adam and Eve story deals more intimately with humanity and its flaws than the majestic "Seven Days of Creation" story, which presents an all-powerful being who only speaks and all is done, with Sabbath rest built into the very fabric of the created universe. Scholarship has typically dated the "Seven Day" account as postexilic (post-587 BCE) and have therefore read it in comparison with the ancient Babylonian creation stories (among others) that pit the storm god (Marduk) against the sea god (Tiamat)—a battle between storm and sea that is, without doubt, alluded to in the phrase of Genesis 1:2: "the *ruach*/storm/wind of God hovered over the face of the deep waters").

Sermons could emphasize the Hebrews' interaction with, and severe criticism of, ancient empires and their mythologies of power, especially the Babylonian traditions that emphasize cosmic warfare, rather than a single God creating in peace and, furthermore, arguably make humanity a central concern, rather than a mere "side show" of cosmic gods at war. Genesis, in fact, often critiques imperial mythologies of violence.

Our focus is the Adam and Eve story. While it may have some ancient roots, the received version of this story appears also to date from a time after the catastrophic events of the Babylonian conquest of Jerusalem in 587 BCE. This seems a reasonable conclusion based on a story

that ultimately results in an "exile" from the garden as a result of human sin. As a way of dealing with the tragedy of Babylonian conquest, this story would then fit with many other exilic and postexilic biblical texts that blame that catastrophe on the people's own sins (however troubling such a "self-blaming" theology certainly—and rightly—is for modern readers).

Ironically, however, this "self-blaming" theology (likely inspired by the preaching of Jeremiah and Ezekiel) at least offers the hope that if "we" got ourselves into this mess, then perhaps "our" repentance can move God to get us out of it. In fact, this striking "self-blaming" theology became a central theme in a later "Penitential Prayer" form that rose to prominence in postexilic literature (e.g., Dan. 9; Ezra 9; Neh. 9; cf. Bar. 1–2). These unique prayers report that the instructions and the warnings of God were clear: "From the days of our ancestors to this day we have been deep in guilt, and for our iniquities we, our kings, and our priests have been handed over to the kings of the lands, to the sword, to captivity, to plundering, and to utter shame, as is now the case" (Ezra 9:7).

This wider context may help us to understand the greater significance of the Adam and Eve story and, more importantly, the gravity of their sin. It seems reasonable to raise questions about the sin of eating forbidden fruit. Why, we may wonder, did such an apparently minor infraction result in such catastrophic consequences? The act, however, has a context in Genesis 2:

> The LORD God planted a garden in Eden . . . and there he put the man whom he had formed. Out of the ground the LORD God made to grow every tree that is pleasant to the sight and good for food, the tree of life also in the midst of the garden, and the tree of the knowledge of good and evil.
> A river flows out of Eden to water the garden. . . .
> The LORD God took the man and put him in the garden of Eden to till it and keep it. (Gen. 2:8–15)

The story features a strong emphasis on God's loving grace in all of creation. In this context, the disobedience of humanity is not merely about a piece of fruit, it is about an unbelievably short-sighted act of betrayal against God's overwhelming love—that had rather minor expectations. That seems to be the point of the simple command. The humans put their entire relationship with their Creator, *and their wonderfully favorable situation*, in doubt. Sermons could note how often we are tempted to reject acts of compassionate love from others, *and* from God.

First Samuel 8 also suggests God's strong reactions to the Israelite tribes wanting a human king. The famous passage portrays God seemingly shocked at the ingratitude!: "The LORD said to Samuel, 'Listen to the voice of the people in all that they say to you; for they have not rejected you, but they have rejected me from being king over them. Just as they have done to me, from the day I brought them up out of Egypt to this day, forsaking me and serving other gods'" (1 Sam. 8:7–8).

Once again, the context is God's care for a people. The passage seeks to remind the people of their liberation at the hands of God. In fact, the "historical" books (Joshua, Judges, 1 and 2 Samuel, 1 and 2 Kings) feature story after story of God's miraculous care. Israel's military "conquests" have not been through their own power but by God's miraculous protection: the exodus (Exod. 14); the defeat of Jericho; the victory of Gideon's tiny army in Judges 7; miraculous deliverance from Philistines in 1 Samuel 7, and so on. In the light of these acts of protection against enemies more powerful than their military, "rejecting God" seems the height of folly.

First Samuel 8 goes even further. The passage strikingly emphasizes that if the people think that they can be so strong on their own—well, then, gear up! You will have to do it yourselves now! One of my undergraduates commented on the warnings of 1 Samuel 8 by summarizing: "Sounds to me like taxes and the draft!" Precisely. Among the warnings in 1 Samuel 8 is a description of preparing a conventional army for decidedly conventional warfare—no more miraculous deliverance. In fact, occasions of "miraculous" deliverance virtually disappear. There may well be a thematic connection between Israel's later ingratitude and Adam and Eve's assumption that they can "figure out their own care and feeding," responding to God's ultimate direction: "therefore the LORD God sent him forth from the garden of Eden, to till the ground from which he was taken" (Gen. 3:23).

Pride, it seems, involves not only an overconfidence at our ability to do things by ourselves, but also an inability to appreciate the help that others have given to us. One of the most striking realities of recent economic developments in the West has been the inability of company owners and managers fully to appreciate that they did not succeed "by themselves," and therefore the union and labor movements have time and time again had to remind them of workers' value.

In our Scriptures, time and time again, the writers portray Israelite sin as a lack of gracious thanks for what was provided. In the context of political conquest and occupation (after 587 BCE), these reminders were intended to propose a change of heart and mind—toward repentance certainly, but also away from habits of overconfidence that seemed to shut off a sense of gratitude, a gratitude that can lead us away from a focus only on ourselves.

Environmental concern, for example, is often born of a renewed sense of what God has graciously provided—and what we must not endanger by our ingratitude and overconfident actions. Sermons may note that human pride discussed in biblical passages is often related to our making our own tools (swords *and* plowshares!), on which we think we can depend. Can our proud feats of engineering sometimes result in destruction of God's gracious care?

DANIEL L. SMITH-CHRISTOPHER

Commentary 2: Connecting the Reading with the World

These paired texts from Genesis 3 and 1 Samuel 8 appear to have little in common, separated by history and time, theology, and genre. Adam and Eve's confession and eventual expulsion from the garden of Eden seem unrelated and disconnected from changes in Israel's political and social organization as played out in Samuel's reluctant anointing of a king at the demand of his people. Careful attention to these two texts, however, reveals at least one common theme, providing a route for interpreting these passages for modern hearers. These iconic episodes from the Hebrew Bible, each in its own way, introduce what may be described as an onset of a great unraveling of the moral and social order.

On the one hand, Adam and Eve's acquisition of the knowledge of good and evil, by partaking of the fruit of a forbidden tree, leads to a sense of shame and embarrassment over their bodies, infusing self-awareness and distrust in all their relationships. As a consequence of their disobedience, they are punished by God, and life becomes difficult, harsh, and marked with hard labor and physical suffering. In their acts, all of humanity, indeed all of creation, unravels.

On the other hand, Samuel's warning to the people of Israel about the unintended consequences of establishing a monarchy is no contest for a population driven by frustration with leadership and insecurity, a fear of geopolitical enemies, a need for protection, and a desire to "be like other nations" (1 Sam. 8:20). Samuel's counsel and God's theocratic leadership are rejected for something more tangible, more recognizable, more secure. Israel rejects their God, and in like manner Samuel too is rejected.

Both stories inaugurate a new age, one filled with hardship, confusion, suffering, and implications for all of history. Both remind the reader that human choices have moral consequences, and that the choices humans make reveal much about those who make them.

Genesis 3:8–20 begins with Adam and Eve, now aware of their shame and vulnerability, hiding from God among the trees. What prompts the two to take cover is the sound of God out on an evening stroll. God inhabits creation and is experienced in human terms, preferring to walk when there is a cool breeze. Finally, God calls out for Adam with a question that may seem odd: "Where are you?" The mere fact that Adam is hiding must have given God pause, and the question elicits a response from Adam about his fear and shame related to his newfound nakedness. God now knows something dramatic has happened. Adam's awareness of his own nakedness betrays the couple's disobedience. In predictable fashion, the blame game begins. Adam blames Eve. Eve blames the serpent.

The habit of blaming others for bad choices we humans make is as old as the first woman and man. Modern psychology roots the human tendency to blame others for one's mistakes and bad choices in the experience of punishment and shame.[1] The power of shame to shape human behavior and self-perception is observable throughout human history and, more often than not, leads to tragic circumstances. One approach to preaching from this text is to delve into how this story speaks to human nature and illuminates the relationship between shame and blame. What is it about the knowledge of good and evil that leads one to become aware of shame and seek cover?

Preparation for preaching on Genesis 3:8–15 should address popular misconceptions and patriarchal assumptions. An uncritical reading more often than not results in interpretations of

---

1. Bernard Golden, "Seven Consequences of Blaming Others for How We Manage Our Anger," *Psychology Today* online, November 10, 2018.

the story that blame Eve for the fall and relegate her to a second-class status. Blame is not simply an action within the story but is active in widespread interpretations of the text. Indeed, the writer of 1 Timothy (1 Tim. 2:11–15) exemplifies this danger when he interprets the story in terms of the blame and due subjugation of Eve, and finds there reason for the exclusion of all women from full participation in the church. He concludes that women should not teach or have authority over men because she "was deceived and became a transgressor" (v. 14).

A careful critical reading can challenge these and other commonly held notions about these verses' meaning and purpose. As Phyllis Trible has observed, what follows disobedience is a fading of the distinction between male and female, for "they are one in hearing and hiding."[2] Adam and Eve are "equal in responsibility and in judgment, in shame and in guilt, and in redemption and in grace,"[3] and the punishment that follows is not a curse or a prescription, but a description of the consequences of a shared disobedience. Disobedient behavior and bad choices produce their own consequences for the actors and bystanders alike, and those consequences are sometimes more severe than any consequential punishment.

In 1 Samuel 8:4–11, 16–20, the elders of Israel were losing faith in the status quo of their governmental institutions. Fear and anxiety ran high. Samuel, their trusted priest and leader, was growing old, and neither of his sons came close to providing the moral or religious leadership needed to navigate the internal and external threats to the nation. If Israel was to survive, it would need what all other nations instituted, a king. A king would unify the people, provide a hierarchical structure for rule and order, and efficiently organize and employ a military capable of defending Israel against encroaching foes that

surrounded them in all directions. A king simply made sense, given the geopolitical realities of their world. Why not? Moses himself foretold the desire for a king and even granted permission for selecting a king (Deut. 17:14–15).

Frustrated, Samuel turned to God, and God instructed him to listen to the people and to warn them solemnly about the hidden costs of having a king. So, Samuel warned the people of the dangers of monarchical rule: a loss of autonomy, freedom, and ownership of material possessions. For Samuel, conditions under a king might well be akin to slavery. The irony, of course, is that it was God who delivered their ancestors from slavery and made them a free people. Fear and insecurity have a way of eroding memory, and Samuel's warning goes unheeded. The people have decided, with little regard for the cost.

Samuel's resignation to the popular will is reminiscent of a truism that every parent knows: sometimes we must learn from our own mistakes. There is no more powerful a teacher than raw experience. Failure to learn from the wisdom of experience of others stems in part from the deep need to prove oneself as the exception, free from the limitations and lessons of the past. A new king is anointed, security comes for a season, and Israel enters a new age replete with new challenges and hardships. Samuel watches from Ramah, hoping his worst fears will not be realized.

These two texts underscore moments in life marked by a sense of unraveling. In both accounts, life is filled with anxiety, disorientation, inevitability, and a recognition that the old order is crumbling. These are moments strangely familiar in our own time, and these two texts remind us that human choices have real consequences, perhaps none more significant than revealing who we are.

J. SCOTT HUDGINS

2. Phyllis Trible, "Eve and Adam: Genesis 2–3 Reread," *Andover Newton Quarterly* 13 (1973): 251–58 (256).
3. Trible, "Eve and Adam," 256.

Proper 5 (Sunday between June 5 and June 11)

Psalm 130

[1]Out of the depths I cry to you, O LORD.
   [2]Lord, hear my voice!
Let your ears be attentive
   to the voice of my supplications!

[3]If you, O LORD, should mark iniquities,
   Lord, who could stand?
[4]But there is forgiveness with you,
   so that you may be revered.

[5]I wait for the LORD, my soul waits,
   and in his word I hope;
[6]my soul waits for the Lord
   more than those who watch for the morning,
   more than those who watch for the morning.

[7]O Israel, hope in the LORD!
   For with the LORD there is steadfast love,
   and with him is great power to redeem.
[8]It is he who will redeem Israel
   from all its iniquities.

Psalm 138

[1]I give you thanks, O LORD, with my whole heart;
   before the gods I sing your praise;
[2]I bow down toward your holy temple
   and give thanks to your name for your steadfast love and your faithfulness;
   for you have exalted your name and your word
   above everything.
[3]On the day I called, you answered me,
   you increased my strength of soul.

[4]All the kings of the earth shall praise you, O LORD,
   for they have heard the words of your mouth.
[5]They shall sing of the ways of the LORD,
   for great is the glory of the LORD.
[6]For though the LORD is high, he regards the lowly;
   but the haughty he perceives from far away.

[7]Though I walk in the midst of trouble,
   you preserve me against the wrath of my enemies;
you stretch out your hand,
   and your right hand delivers me.
[8]The LORD will fulfill his purpose for me;
   your steadfast love, O LORD, endures forever.
   Do not forsake the work of your hands.

Connecting the Psalm with Scripture and Worship

Psalm 130. Psalm 130 is known as one of the Songs of Ascent or pilgrim songs that are sung on a journey toward the Jerusalem temple to attend festivals. It could have been originally an individual poem and then later included in the pilgrim songs. Verse 8 leads us to think that the psalm was recited by the poet in the liturgical context of the community, however. Though the status of the individual is not clearly indicated in the poem, some biblical scholars guess that it is the Israelite king who repents his personal and communal sins before God, seeking forgiveness and redemption (Ps. 130:7–8), while perhaps facing a national crisis.[1]

The poem has three movements. In verses 1–3, the poet cries to God for pardon from the "depth" of his heart. The tone then moves from confidence in forgiveness through repetition of the words, "wait" and "hope" in verses 4–7a, to the assurance of forgiveness grounded in God's steadfast love in verses 7b–8. The style and choice of words of the poem are masterful in expressing the human predicament of the true nature of sin and the greatness of God's gracious mercy.

This penitential tone of this psalm, along with its expression of trust in God's steadfast love, is a fitting response to the first reading for the day. Genesis 3:8–15 tells a story about the nature of sin and has traditionally been interpreted as referring to an original sin brought about by the woman. As a result, this passage has molded traditional Christian belief as sexist and patriarchal.

Feminist interpretation now helps us read the passage more critically and appropriately. The story in Genesis 3 is not a weighty accusation of original sin, but an account of the responsibility of sin shared between the man and the woman, that is, the man's "self-defense" of "his passive act of disobedience" and the woman's initiative in eating fruit from the tree of good and evil.[2] The last two verses of the passage describe the reality of sin as broken relationships between God and humanity, between the human and the nonhuman world, and between the man and the woman. As a response to the sinful situation, Psalm 130 reminds us that God's steadfast love and forgiveness are greater than our sins.

The Gospel lesson appointed for the day, Mark 3:20–35, also assures us that all our sins will be forgiven, except blasphemies against the Holy Spirit, for such sins are against God, who is the one who forgives our sins (Mark 3:29). With the psalm informing the sermon, the preacher may help listeners reflect on the sins that they have committed consciously and unconsciously, as individuals and as a community, while proclaiming the forgiveness of a loving God.

Liturgically, Psalm 130 may be heard in a number of ways. A musical setting of the psalm may be sung by the congregation or a choir, either as a part of the proclamation of Scripture or as a response to the preaching of the Word. The psalm might also be adapted for use as prayer of confession and declaration of forgiveness.

Psalm 138. Although some biblical scholars consider Psalm 138 an individual expression of thanksgiving recited by a worshiper in the temple, many contemporary commentators interpret it as a royal song of thanksgiving that must have been sung by the king during great festivals, perhaps while traveling abroad on a military journey. In the Israelite understanding of kingship, a king is not merely the political leader—the warrior, judge, and ruler—but the religious leader as well, the mediator between God and his people. As the bearer of peace, justice, wisdom, and the welfare of the nation, the king prays to God by singing this psalm in a spirit of humility.

Psalm 138 is composed of three stanzas (vv. 1–3, vv. 4–6, and vv. 7–8), in which humility is presented as a defining characteristic of the ideal king in tandem with God's character of steadfast love and faithfulness. In verses 1–3, the king worships God toward the temple with praises for God's steadfast love and faithfulness (vv. 1–2), remembering how God has answered his prayers (v. 3). In verses 4–6, the psalmist

1. Mitchell Dahood, SJ, *Psalms III: 101–150* (Garden City, NY: Doubleday & Co., 1970), 235.
2. Carol A. Newsom and Sharon H. Ringe, eds., *The Women's Bible Commentary* (London: SPCK, 1992), 14.

convinces us that in the future God shall be exalted by "all the kings of the earth" (v. 4) as the Lord of every king, since God is for and with the lowly. In verses 7–8, the king identifies himself with the lowly who need God's help and prays with the confidence that God will continue protecting him from his enemies.

Psalm 138 is selected to respond to the reading from 1 Samuel that is appointed for this day. The description of kingship in 1 Samuel 8:4–11 (12–15), 16–20 (11:14–15) stands in stark contrast to that depicted in the psalm. While Psalm 138 depicts kingship as the state that is possible only when one depends on the steadfast love and faithfulness of God, Samuel declares to the Israelites, who demand him to give them a king, that the king will not be one of humility, but one who will enslave them.

Although the Israelites, like other surrounding countries, desire kingship as protection from international threats, says Samuel, they will have to pay for that protection with heavy taxes and physical labors (1 Sam. 8:11–18). This oppressive image of the king seems to be a later insertion into the mouth of Samuel to reflect the corrupt reality of Israel's experience of kingship.[3] Against these human political realities, Psalm 138 sings of the image of the true king as one who admits God's lordship over the kings of the earth.

The Gospel reading for the day, Mark 3:20–35, echoes the theme of kingship. The entire third chapter of Mark describes the clash between human politics and the politics of God. In the kingdom of the Spirit, the people do the will of God (Mark 3:28–30, 35), while in the human kingdom, the political and religious leaders work for their vested interests (v. 22). Jesus' healing of the one with a shriveled hand in the synagogue on the Sabbath (3:1–7) is an example of the politics of God.

We live in a democratic society without a king. Yet Psalm 138 could readily be applied to our political situation. We tend to elect our political leaders based on our vested interests, without thinking about what true leadership looks like in the sight of God, and we often experience hardship as a result. By singing Psalm 138 in a liturgical context, we pray "for" us, especially when our human politics are off the rails of justice, and we join in Jesus' prayer as a community, yearning for the actualization of the politics of God on the earth, when "your kingdom [will] come, your will be done on earth as it is in heaven" (Matt. 6:10).

Many denominational hymnals include Psalm 138 in the section of the Psalter to be used as a responsive reading to the first reading. A litany of Psalm 138 can also be used for the opening prayer. The psalm suggests the singing of congregational songs that emphasize the steadfast faithfulness of God.

EUNJOO MARY KIM

3. Jonathan Kaplan, "I Samuel 8:11–18 as 'A Mirror for Princes,'" *Journal of Biblical Literature* 131, no. 4 (2012): 627.

Proper 5 (Sunday between June 5 and June 11)

2 Corinthians 4:13–5:1

^{4:13}But just as we have the same spirit of faith that is in accordance with scripture—"I believed, and so I spoke"—we also believe, and so we speak, ¹⁴because we know that the one who raised the Lord Jesus will raise us also with Jesus, and will bring us with you into his presence. ¹⁵Yes, everything is for your sake, so that grace, as it extends to more and more people, may increase thanksgiving, to the glory of God.

¹⁶So we do not lose heart. Even though our outer nature is wasting away, our inner nature is being renewed day by day. ¹⁷For this slight momentary affliction is preparing us for an eternal weight of glory beyond all measure, ¹⁸because we look not at what can be seen but at what cannot be seen; for what can be seen is temporary, but what cannot be seen is eternal.

^{5:1}For we know that if the earthly tent we live in is destroyed, we have a building from God, a house not made with hands, eternal in the heavens.

Commentary 1: Connecting the Reading with Scripture

Working with people is complicated, challenging, irritating, defeating, exhausting, and also joyous and rewarding. If one listens carefully, one can discern not only the criticisms of the Corinthians behind Paul's self-defense in 2 Corinthians 10–13, but also, in the tone of Paul's defense, his irritation and exhaustion over their verbal crucifixion of him. In terms of those who did God's work in the face of intense opposition, one is reminded of Moses, Jeremiah, Daniel, a host of other prophets, and Jesus. Irritation and exhaustion are two understandable reactions to attack, but Paul also stresses an enduring hope and vigilance: "so we do not lose heart" (2 Cor. 4:16; cf. 4:1). Ministry makes those who serve others vulnerable. There is usually tension between worldly success and lives committed to service to others. This also provides the constructive challenge of living with what Victor Paul Furnish calls "apostolic confidence."[1]

From 2 Corinthians 2:14 to 7:16 the apostle has explained, cried, defended, pleaded, and prayed about this complicated congregation. Awaiting word on how the church responds to a letter delivered by Titus (2:12–13), Paul erupts into joy, but it is not until 7:6 that we hear the good news. One almost hears Paul saying,

"They like me!" One can be both unraveled by ministry and thrilled to serve others.

Paul knows his (and our) vulnerabilities—we minister in what he calls "clay jars" (4:7). Paul experiences defeats and disappointments (4:8–12). Paul also knows whose we are (God's), who we are (children of God), and what we are called to do (new covenant mission; see 3:1–18; 4:5–6). So, Paul sees through the dismay into the glory, and his hope endures.

The OT biblical narrative (Gen. 3:8–21) does not shy away from explaining life's defeats as the consequence of human corruption and systemic, worldly evils with which we are called to struggle, working for redemption at both personal and systemic levels. Even what appears to be good can turn out to be evil, and even our own families may find themselves caught up and made complicit with corruption (Mark 3:20–35).

Paul's hope in 2 Corinthians 4:16 does not depend upon his denying his defeats (2 Cor. 4:8–12). What looks like death for him is actually life for the Corinthians (v. 12). Paul exhibits a posture of faith in the midst of ministry opposition. Paul's words "spirit of faith" could refer to the Holy Spirit (see 1 Cor. 12:9), but another view is that it refers to the enduring hope of the faithful.

1. Victor Paul Furnish, *II Corinthians*, Anchor Bible 32A (Garden City, NY: Doubleday, 1984), 277.

Intoxicated with Self-Love

The fall of Adam was disobedience to God, by which man turned away from the Divine Being to himself, and robbed God of the honor due to him alone, in that he *himself* thought to be *as God*. But while he thus labored to advance himself, he was stripped of that divine image, which the Creator has so freely conferred on him; divested of hereditary righteousness; and bereaved of that holiness with which he was originally adorned; becoming, as it regards his *understanding*, dark and blind; as to his *will*, stubborn and perverse; and as to all the powers and faculties of the soul, entirely alienated from God. This evil has infected the whole mass of mankind, by means of a fleshly generation; and has been inherited by all men. The obvious consequence arising from this is, that man is become spiritually dead and the child of wrath and damnation, until redeemed from this miserable state by Jesus Christ. Let not then any who are called Christians deceive themselves with regard to Adam's fall. Let them be cautious, how they attempt to extenuate or lessen the transgression of Adam, as though it were a small sin, a thing of little consequence, and, at the worst, but the eating of an apple. Let them rather be assured, that the guilt of Adam was that of Lucifer, namely, *he would be as God*: and that it was the same most grievous, heinous, and hateful sin in both.

This apostasy (for it was nothing less), was, at first, generated in the heart, and then made manifest by the eating of the forbidden fruit. Though man was numbered with the sons of God; though he came forth from the hands of the Almighty spotless both in body and in soul, and was the most glorious object in the creation; though, to crown all, he was not only a son, but the *delight* of God; yet not knowing how to rest satisfied with these high privileges, he attempted to invade Heaven, that he might be yet higher; and nothing less would suffice him, than to exalt himself like unto God. Hence, he conceived in his heart enmity and hatred against the Divine Being, his Creator and Father, whom had it been in his power, he was disposed utterly to undo. Who could commit a sin more detestable than this? or what greater abomination is there, that it was possible to mediate?

Hence it was, that man became inwardly like Satan himself, bearing his likeness in the heart; since both had now committed the same sin, both having rebelled against the majesty of Heaven. . . . For the devil, designing to imprint his own image upon man, fascinated him so entirely by a train of enticing and deceitful words, that man permitted him to sow that hateful seed in his soul, which is hence termed the seed of the serpent; and by which is chiefly meant, self-love, self-will, and the ambition of being as God. On this account, it is, that the Scriptures term those who are intoxicated with self-love, "a generation of vipers." Matt. 8:7. And all those who are of a proud and devilish nature, "the seed (progeny) of the serpent." So, the Almighty, addressing the serpent, says, "I will put enmity between thee and the woman, and between thy seed and her seed." Gen. 3:15.

Johann Arndt, *True Christianity: A Treatise on Sincere Repentance, True Faith, the Holy Walk of the True Christian, Etc.,* trans. A. W. Boehm (Philadelphia: Lutheran Book Store, 1868), 4–5.

Paul's enduring hope is made possible by the act of God in raising Jesus from the dead and making life eternal the final word (1 Cor. 15:1–28). This is not deluded optimism, for it is anchored in realism: the once-for-all act of God to turn death into life on Easter morning (2 Cor. 4:14).

At the heart of what Paul is saying here about a life of serving others is what Michael Gorman calls "cruciformity," a life conformed to the cross. Furnish frames what Paul is thinking here by saying ministry is "not dependent upon a curriculum vitae filled with glorious accomplishments,"[2] but a life of faithful service to others. Serving others becomes an embodiment of the life of Jesus. Jesus had been able to explain to his followers that they were to follow him in living

2. Michael J. Gorman, *Cruciformity: Paul's Narrative Spirituality of the Cross* (Grand Rapids: Eerdmans, 2001); Gorman, *Becoming the Gospel: Paul, Participation, and Mission* (Grand Rapids: Eerdmans, 2015); Furnish, *II Corinthians*, 288.

a cruciform life because the final word is not the cross but the transfiguration (Mark 8:31–9:8).

The life Paul lives, one devoted to people like the Corinthians, is a life for others, and this is a theme throughout 2 Corinthians 1–7. "Yes," he says, "everything is for your sake" (2 Cor. 4:15). For Paul, the resurrection of Jesus inspires not primarily personal ecstasy about heaven but a capacity to endure evil for the redemption of others. What is at work in this Easter posture is "grace," a power that finds a home in "more and more" (v. 15).

Paul's move from 4:15 to 4:16 is a personal reflection expressed in a pastoral manner (in terms of "we") so as to include all in the hope. Though death approaches all, he says, "our inner nature is being renewed day by day." He can minimize the body's aging process as a "wasting away," a "momentary affliction," "what can be seen," and as "temporary," in contrast to the eternal: "being renewed," "eternal weight of glory," "what cannot be seen," and the "eternal" (vv. 16–18). The tone here is one of "buoyant assurance born of divine certainties."[3] None of this should be understood in terms of a disembodied soul or a devaluing of the body, but as embodied souls or soulish bodies in Paul's Jewish sense.

Our lectionary takes us into a very difficult passage but stops at 5:1, which opens into verses about our "tent" and a "heavenly dwelling" (5:2) and being "naked" (v. 3) while desiring to be "further clothed" (v. 4), but this passage finishes with another source of Pauline hope in serving others: the internal presence of the Spirit as a guarantee (v. 5). His ministry for the Corinthians may well lead to death. In 5:1 he describes death as "the earthly tent . . . [being] destroyed,"

but he is confident, because of Easter, that "we have" not a "tent" but a "building from God, . . . not made with hands, eternal in the heavens" (v. 1). It is wise, then, to read 4:16 through 5:5 as a continuous passage, with 5:6 echoing and emphasizing anew the hope of 4:16.

In serving the wideness of others in our community, we soon encounter, especially from those suffering from diseases or tragedies or from the elderly, questions about life beyond death. They want to know if there is hope for life eternal. Paul's theology of serving others is shaped by a conviction we confess in the Nicene Creed and read about in 2 Corinthians 4–5: God raised Jesus from among the dead, and this gives us hope beyond disease, tragedy, and aging. Such hope does not mean ignoring the sinful and systemic realities of our world—it is a theology of *serving others*! It means we serve others with hope, both for others and for ourselves, rooted in the conviction central to the Christian faith: Christ has died, Christ is risen, Christ will come again.

If we rethink 2 Corinthians 2:12–7:16 in light of the criticisms leveled at the apostle in 2 Corinthians 10–13, we discover how Paul put together defeat and victory, disappointment and joy. The sufferings he experienced at the hands of critics—those who said his ministry was minimal, his success abysmal, and his skills nominal—were for him the glories of participating in the cross of Christ. When tempted to think that our service for others is insignificant, we might be drawn to think of Jesus, whose life ended on a Roman cross in utter shame and humiliation. Yet three days later a new story could be told, the story of Easter.

SCOT MCKNIGHT

Commentary 2: Connecting the Reading with the World

Ask a roomful of people, "Quick show of hands: how many of you plan to leave here younger than when you arrived?" You might hear some laughter, but no one ever raises their hand. *That* we age is never in question. *How* we age is all important. Growing older need not mean growing less

vital, enthusiastic, and engaged. Indeed, some of the youngest spirits we ever encounter may reside in some of the oldest bodies.

Classic films are rife with images of the young at heart. *Cocoon* (1985), directed by Ron Howard, is a classic example. A group of older adults

3. Murray J. Harris, *The Second Epistle to the Corinthians*, New International Greek Testament Commentary (Grand Rapids: Eerdmans, 2005), 366.

find themselves reenergized and rejuvenated by alien cocoons deposited in a nearby swimming pool. The premise of the film is not nearly as important as the imagery of adults displaying what it means to be young once more. Youth is about fun and excitement and experimentation and exploration—qualities too easily quenched later in life. The film evokes the classic comment from the film *It's a Wonderful Life*: "Aw, youth is wasted on the wrong people!" However, in big and small ways, the characters in the film have to come to grips with what it means to grow old. Youth is not all it is cracked up to be, while being older is not such a curse after all. Despite limitations and diminishing capacities, there is potentially much to value in growing older: wealth of experience, a broader perspective, and a wisdom developed over time.

This idea of inner vitality, energy, and promise existing within, while the outer nature "wastes away" or "perishes" (2 Cor. 4:16), can be as true for neighborhoods, communities, and countries as it is for individuals. Over time, focus turns from what lies ahead to what no longer functions well. Our sense of blessing decreases, as does our willingness to give thanks and appreciation. What we see with our eyes can prevent us from seeing new possibilities and opportunities.

In some places, once-thriving neighborhoods decline, and residents lament bygone days when things were fresher and newer. It sometimes takes a new set of eyes to help people view what is good and possible and exciting in existing settings. Entire nations sometimes wish to return to greatness, and they become fixated on problems and decline. How desperately we seek visionary leaders to restore hope and purpose! This is essentially the tension that Paul identifies when we see with worldly eyes rather than eyes of faith.

A central theme in many stories contrasting the older with the younger is maturity. Growing older offers no guarantee of growing wiser, kinder, more intelligent, more generous, or more ethical. On the other hand, as we age, we gain perspective that only years can bring. We experience childhood from the eyes of parenthood, celebrate successes, mourn failures, lose parents, friends, perhaps even children; there is the potential to gain maturity and insight that comes only through the passage of time.

We require a grounding and center from which to draw responses in life that are more mature, just, compassionate, and grace-filled. While our exterior may "waste away," our interior life may continue to flourish and grow, but only in a proper soil, a soil of faith in God. Aging happens naturally; maturity does not. Maturity requires hard work, important learning, gaining experience, and developing the skills of critical thinking. Without maturity, we cannot fully grasp the meaning and purpose of our lives and what impact we have on others.

It is sometimes said that the dominant culture in the United States is a "youth culture." We revere the young, the beautiful, the new, that which is bright and shiny with promise. Such an attitude is fine, as long as it does not remain superficial or unrealistic; as long as it recognizes the hard work necessary to realize promise, and the unjust obstacles or misfortune (illness, accident, war) that afflict and derail the promise of so many; as long as it does not disparage or disrespect age and the benefits that accompany graceful aging; and as long as it remembers how much about life those who are young and have known only good health and wide-open horizons cannot understand.

Many cultures greatly revere the aged. Respect is given to experience, to survival, to accomplishment, and to wisdom. The elders are sages and teachers, gurus and guides. They are not swayed much by the circumstances of the moment but keep the long view in sight. They draw from a deeper well of long and varied experience and are less likely to be swayed by fads and fancies.

A reality in our modern American context is that many of the elderly are consigned to retirement and rehabilitation facilities or nursing homes or are simply abandoned. It is incredibly difficult to maintain a sense of self-worth or value when one is displaced from one's home and essentially left alone, unvisited, and unloved. Many of our longest-living citizens are viewed as liabilities rather than assets. How we view aging and how we choose to treat others throughout the life span says a great deal about our values.

Again, what is true for individuals in our culture extends to our institutions and structures. Older can sometimes mean stuck, tired, or even irrelevant, but the opportunity for renewal, reinvention, and revival always exists. The past can function in one of two fundamental ways: as an anchor that holds us in place, or as a foundation upon which we can build.

The adage "You can't judge a book by its cover" contains a wealth of wisdom. The container can depict anything it wants, but the contents tell the real story. Children may conceal the comic book in the textbook cover, adults may dress up in elaborate costumes to disguise a variety of shapes and sizes, a fancy façade may be placed over the simplest structure, but it does not take much to discover what lies beneath or behind. Where there is depth, there is discernment. With a little digging, the truth can be revealed.

Preacher, take note. In this is a gospel message we all should heed: there is nothing to hide. Our earthen vessels are not our whole story. Who we are is defined by what we hold inside. When we are in relationship with God, we draw from a deeper center filled by the Holy Spirit. Our outer nature passes away, revealing the fruit inside, and when it is the fruit of the Spirit, what we reveal is love and joy, kindness and peace, patience and gentleness, generosity and faithfulness and self-control. We become true witnesses to the goodness and greatness of God.

We have the opportunity to proclaim that as human beings age, it is all too easy to focus on what is lost rather than what has been gained. As structures show the wear of time, it is easy to dismiss them as worthless. Old traditions can be easily demeaned as quaint or out of date. What we cannot do, or can no longer do, looms large over what we are able to do. For older people, many simple things—bending over, climbing stairs, tying a knot—become Herculean tasks. Getting out of bed in the morning can come to seem monumental, but what we cannot do should never define us. No matter how diminished we might find some capacities, we still have gifts to give and value to contribute. As the earthly recedes, the heavenly emerges.

DAN R. DICK

Proper 5 (Sunday between June 5 and June 11)

Mark 3:20–35

[20]The crowd came together again, so that they could not even eat. [21]When his family heard it, they went out to restrain him, for people were saying, "He has gone out of his mind." [22]And the scribes who came down from Jerusalem said, "He has Beelzebul, and by the ruler of the demons he casts out demons." [23]And he called them to him, and spoke to them in parables, "How can Satan cast out Satan? [24]If a kingdom is divided against itself, that kingdom cannot stand. [25]And if a house is divided against itself, that house will not be able to stand. [26]And if Satan has risen up against himself and is divided, he cannot stand, but his end has come. [27]But no one can enter a strong man's house and plunder his property without first tying up the strong man; then indeed the house can be plundered.

[28]"Truly I tell you, people will be forgiven for their sins and whatever blasphemies they utter; [29]but whoever blasphemes against the Holy Spirit can never have forgiveness, but is guilty of an eternal sin"— [30]for they had said, "He has an unclean spirit."

[31]Then his mother and his brothers came; and standing outside, they sent to him and called him. [32]A crowd was sitting around him; and they said to him, "Your mother and your brothers and sisters are outside, asking for you." [33]And he replied, "Who are my mother and my brothers?" [34]And looking at those who sat around him, he said, "Here are my mother and my brothers! [35]Whoever does the will of God is my brother and sister and mother."

Commentary 1: Connecting the Reading with Scripture

Chapter 3 of Mark opens with the well-known story of Jesus healing a man's withered hand on the Sabbath. Jesus' opponents here are Pharisees offended by Jesus' healing. Their offense angers Jesus, but the text also immediately notes that he grieves their hardness of heart (Mark 3:5). This can be read as grace that *loves* enemies even as they *remain* enemies (Matt. 5:44; Luke 6:27–36). "Love your enemies" follows Luke's withered-hand account (Luke 6:6–11). The preacher may reflect on the incredibly complicated existential dynamics such grace-qualified, righteous anger entails, a dynamic wherein one loves those whom one may fight—but only for the sake of what is loving and just for others (including oneself). Note how conceptually complex and emotionally fraught this grace-qualified anger is, in contrast to the simplistic "hate your enemies" anger dominant in Jesus' day and not only influential but overtly affirmed as rational in ours. Today the very idea of Christianity's "love your enemy" is derided by haughty but existentially and spiritually simplistic streams of modern Western rationality, precisely when such love would mitigate against caricature and extremism.

To counter anti-Semitism, preachers can caution readers against generalizing from the legalism of this group of Pharisees to all Pharisees, let alone to all Jews. Notably, Jesus' anger is precisely the righteous anger of Jewish prophets when they castigate those with means and power for prioritizing fidelity to law or ritual over fidelity to the needy (e.g., Mic. 6:6–8; Isa. 1:10–17). This concretely unfolds the meaning of Jesus' proclamation that the Sabbath was made for humans, not vice versa (Mark 2:27). Such hard-hearted legalism is most devastatingly visible today when global elites, in fidelity to the discipline of markets, impose austerity measures on whole populations. Jesus' anger over misplaced fidelity here is tightly related to the impossibility of serving both God and mammon (Matt. 6:24), to the true righteousness that distinguishes sheep from goats (Matt. 25:31–46), and to the awakening that distinguishes the Samaritan (Luke 10:25–37). All this names, in Jewish prophetic terms, what it is to "remember God."

In his teaching and in his crucifixion by state and religious authorities, Jesus stands *within* the Jewish tradition of the prophets. This is especially important to note because the attack of the "teachers of the law" (Luke 5:17), who say Jesus is out of his mind and possessed by Beelzebul (Mark 3:21–22, 30), is preceded by the report that some Pharisees and Herodians were plotting to destroy Jesus (v. 6). Historically, this has been used to generate an opposition between Christians and Jews, as if Jesus is not a Jew speaking in the line of Jewish prophets, as if Mark does not explicitly tell of Jairus, a leader of a synagogue, coming to Jesus, and of Jesus healing Jairus's daughter at his home (5:21–24, 35–43; cf. Joseph of Arimathea of the council, 15:42–46), and as if no Christians have mistaken fidelity to a form of Christianity (the confused fidelity of legalism) for fidelity to the Spirit animating Micah, Isaiah, the sheep, and the Samaritan.

Remembering all Jesus says about gracious love, a love so complex and transcendent it endures hatred and loves enemies for what is good, loving, and just, the preacher can speak against the stereotypes and extremism cultivated when anger turns into hatred. Even as Jesus is angered by and preaches against these particular Pharisees and Herodians, his anger and resistance are qualified by his love for them. Likewise, his anger toward tax collectors is qualified by his love for tax collectors (2:13–17), and his anger toward and resistance against the colonial abuses of Rome are qualified by his love for Gentile Romans (5:1–20; Jesus crossing the sea would clearly indicate to Mark's audience that Jesus' ministry extends to Jews and Gentiles).

Again, this conceptually and emotionally complex "love your enemies" dynamic displaces the enthusiasm, vengefulness, violence, and self-destructive dynamics of unqualified anger. When one also considers that Jesus is preaching and ministering in ways so threatening to the established order that his opponents are literally plotting to kill him, the remarkable quality of Jesus' uncompromising but gracious response to his opponents, and his refusal to stereotype and vilify them, becomes stunningly apparent.

Jesus' gracious spirit is precisely the Spirit highlighted in Mark's recounting of the deeds and teachings of Jesus throughout the Gospel. The Pharisees who are offended by Jesus' healing of the man on the Sabbath not only deny in their hearts but openly reject or, one might say, "blaspheme against" this Spirit. As noted above, Jesus' reaction to this blasphemy is both anger (over the suffering their hard-heartedness would cause) and grief (over their alienation from love).

Those who reject this Spirit "*can* never *have* forgiveness" (3:29). A familiar, misleading translation of this verse, "*will never be* forgiven" (e.g., NIV), has resulted in misplaced debate over an unforgivable sin, in the sense of some mysterious sin so horrible that it lies beyond the bounds of God's grace. Once someone has committed this sin, the idea goes, it is impossible that they will ever be forgiven. This "impossible . . . ever . . . forgiven" is further facilitated by the reference to "eternal life," which is easily heard in the sense of "everlasting life." All this has led to a theologically bankrupt, spiritually self-centered, and emotionally harmful idea of an unforgivable sin.

It is vital not to equate "eternal life" and "everlasting life." This is not to deny the possibility of everlasting life, but eternal life should be understood not in contrast to physical death, but in contrast to spiritual death (the death Paul talks about in Rom. 6:23), that is, in contrast to living alienated from God. "Eternal life" is not about a future reality, but about one's present, living relationship to God ("the free gift of God *is* eternal life," Rom. 6:23; cf. 6:11–14). To live eternally is to be saved, right now, to be living by grace. To live eternally is to live, right now, *forgiven* and, insofar as one is awakened to God's grace for all (for oneself and for others), to live, right now, *forgiving*.

Since this describes two elements of living in the light of the grace of God, to live forgiven and to live forgiving are two sides of *the same* coin. This is the sense in which those who do not forgive are not forgiven: not as part of some tit-for-tat dynamic, but because to live forgiven and to forgive are simultaneously part of living in the Spirit, living salvation in surrender to God's grace. It is in this sense that those who reject this Spirit "can never *have* forgiveness" (KJV is also good: "*hath* never forgiveness"). In this light—read not with the presumption that hate is the only rational response to people seeking to kill us—we can hear Jesus' statement as prophetic warning and lament over these particular Pharisees, whose hardness of heart not only contributes to the oppression of others, but also cuts them off from living forgiven, cuts them off from the grace of God.

We learn virtually nothing about Jesus' family here (Mark 3:31–35). They are obviously being manipulated by Jesus' opponents. It is impossible to know if they were willing participants or recognized the manipulation as quickly as did Jesus. Note that Jesus does not here reject love for family, but he does take this opportunity to reject the transforming of familial love into a kinship loyalty that would be privileged over the *koinōnia* created by fidelity to God, the divine *koinōnia* of gracious love that transcends all exclusivist kinship, ethnic, doctrinal, or nationalist appeals.

WILLIAM GREENWAY

Commentary 2: Connecting the Reading with the World

The Chinese sage Confucius insisted on "the rectification of names." The way social roles are named, he says, should explicitly and comprehensively determine the behaviors of those who occupy these roles. Father must *be* "real" fathers, Confucius insists, and sons must comport themselves as "true" sons—to say nothing of how rulers and subjects should mutually relate. Social order depends upon each and every member knowing their place and living up to culturally ideal norms.[1]

In such settings, those who assign the names hold the power. In human history, attempts to exercise social control by the imposition of name-rectification have been pervasive.[2] When Jesus casts out demons, he seriously disrupts the social order of his day. Thus he provokes reactions from two different directions.

His family of origin responds with apparent anxiety to external social pressure. They name Jesus as "out of his mind" (Mark 3:21), that is, out of step, his behavior out of place. How challenging it must be to face down the members of one's own family! What *kind* of a son and brother is Jesus, whose behavior seems so far beyond the boundaries of established social norms? Not a "good son." One's social identity—*who one is*—can be very difficult to disentangle from close kin. Jesus' roots are rural, peasant, uneducated. He comes carrying little in the way of social capital.

The scribes, members of "the guild"—the cadre of what might reasonably be regarded as fellow theological professionals—already have at best a tenuous relationship with Jesus. His teaching and healing demonstrate credibility, but he has none of their credentials. The perceived threat to their standing is sufficient to bring them all the way from Jerusalem in order to confront him in backwater Galilee. They put forth a hypothesis that purports to name the role of Jesus in society: not as a healer or a liberator, but as a threat; not as a servant of God, but as the lackey of a demon. In defense of this designation, they present a plausible-sounding explanation of how it might be the case: "He's one of them—a demon himself—after all, it takes one to know one. To exorcise a force so potent, you would have to derive that kind of power from the inside!"

Vocational, professional identity is deeply impacted by peer-group identity. If the religious leaders think Jesus is a demon, what are mere laypersons supposed to think—even, perhaps,

---

1. Jennifer Oldstone-Moore, *Confucianism* (New York: Oxford University Press, 2002), 54–60.
2. Resistance to such control has been evident as well. Note the sustained poetic critique offered by Lao-tzu in *Tao Te Ching*, trans. Stephen Mitchell (New York: Harper & Row, 2006).

those who thought they had experienced a healing from Jesus? His vocation, in other words, is in peril from its outset.

Jesus seems here to be akin to "a man without a country." He is a family member who does not fit the family role. He is a practicing, increasingly high-profile member of a faith community whose designated leaders accuse him not just of failing to be one of them and not being a team player, but also of being an alien intruder. How can someone so out of character be rightly named teacher?

Against this two-sided challenge, not just to his credibility but to his identity, Jesus does not attempt to defend his role as family member or teacher/healer/exorcist by providing counterevidence to the assumptions of his family or the assertions of his religious-political opponents. Rather, he undertakes his own reorienting rectification of names.

In the case of family identity, he introduces a deeply theological and radically countercultural redefinition of family: "Whoever does the will of God is my brother and sister and mother" (3:35).

Regarding vocational identity, Jesus first exposes the plausible-sounding rhetorical misidentification of himself with Beelzebul by subjecting it to exposure as an existentially self-undermining inconsistency. (Imagine a chain saw that cuts its own power cord.) Then Jesus addresses the heart of the issue, namely, that *he* is the one who can "bind the strong man," the one who has the power to name what is demonic and, in so naming, to disempower it. Such power represents a serious threat to the authority of the scribes.

Both Jesus' family and his religious critics, in the face of his disorienting words and deeds, do their best to control the narrative. Each group may do so out of deep conviction ("This *surely* is what is going on in the behavior of Jesus"). Each may also be driven by a bevy of fears for themselves, for the relative stability of a social situation that is itself beset by threat and trauma from the oppressive rule of Rome. Each may have skin in the game—self-interest to be protected or advanced by how the behavior of

Jesus can be spun. In all cases, how they want the narrative to turn out subverts the story as it is. Jesus, regardless of threats to his identity, is not about to have his mission and vocation undermined. Hence his deft, bold steps to take back the story.

Let us shift focus. The eternally unforgivable "sin against the Holy Spirit" of which Jesus warns has been the subject of consideration by scholars and a cause of consternation for many well-intentioned believers. "In a fit of temper, I blurted out: 'Curse you, Holy Spirit!' Oh, no! Am I eschatological toast?" The issue, however, is not about a slip of the tongue in a fit of frustration; rather, it has to do with the far greater danger of "talking oneself to (spiritual) death." One can put forward a false narrative to protect one's sphere of influence and control for only so long before coming to believe one's own rhetoric—not merely positing a false alternative description of facts, but embracing a universe based on one's own lies.

From that condition—wherein evil has been named as good, or wherein there is no difference to be sought or discovered between what is true and what is not—there may be no redemption possible. In that self-induced condition, how would one have facility to recognize redemption if it stood before one's face? Various writers (e.g., Charles Williams and C. S. Lewis) have taught us that whatever hell may be, the door to it is dead-bolted from the *inside*, where one has rendered oneself unable to recognize, and thus impervious to, God's relentless, never-ceasing redemption invitation. Such blasphemy cannot be forgiven, because receiving the fruits of forgiveness depends on being able to perceive one's blasphemy.

Long ago Socrates challenged the Sophists, who taught promising young Athenians to "make the weaker argument appear the stronger" for profit—even at the cost of their own self-deception.[3] Jesus, in Mark's Gospel, may be warning against a kind of spiritual sophistry that redefines illusion as reality, and reality as illusion.

So, some questions: (1) Where are we as preachers likely to be carried away by our own

---

3. See "Apology: Socrates Speaks at His Trial," in Plato, *The Last Days of Socrates*, trans. Hugh Tredennick and Harold Tarrant, Penguin Classics (New York: Penguin Books, 2003).

rhetoric, or fixated on a particular interpretational spin? (2) Where, in the vast array of media manipulation strategies inflicted on us and on our people, are we becoming unable to recognize the difference (or that there *is* a difference) between fact and fabrication? (3) Who names reality for us, and how? For whom do we name it, and how?

Mark's Jesus illustrates for preachers the vocational imperatives of countercultural perception and proclamation, and of evoking both in those with whom we minister.

DAVID J. SCHLAFER

Proper 6 (Sunday between June 12 and June 18)

Ezekiel 17:22–24 and
   1 Samuel 15:34–16:13
Psalm 92:1–4, 12–15 and Psalm 20

2 Corinthians 5:6–10 (11–13), 14–17
Mark 4:26–34

Ezekiel 17:22–24

²²Thus says the Lord GOD:
I myself will take a sprig
   from the lofty top of a cedar;
    I will set it out.
I will break off a tender one
   from the topmost of its young twigs;
I myself will plant it
   on a high and lofty mountain.
²³On the mountain height of Israel
   I will plant it,
in order that it may produce boughs and bear fruit,
   and become a noble cedar.
Under it every kind of bird will live;
   in the shade of its branches will nest
   winged creatures of every kind.
²⁴All the trees of the field shall know
   that I am the LORD.
I bring low the high tree,
   I make high the low tree;
I dry up the green tree
   and make the dry tree flourish.
I the LORD have spoken;
   I will accomplish it.

1 Samuel 15:34–16:13

^{15:34}Then Samuel went to Ramah; and Saul went up to his house in Gibeah of Saul. ³⁵Samuel did not see Saul again until the day of his death, but Samuel grieved over Saul. And the LORD was sorry that he had made Saul king over Israel.

^{16:1}The LORD said to Samuel, "How long will you grieve over Saul? I have rejected him from being king over Israel. Fill your horn with oil and set out; I will send you to Jesse the Bethlehemite, for I have provided for myself a king among his sons." ²Samuel said, "How can I go? If Saul hears of it, he will kill me." And the LORD said, "Take a heifer with you, and say, 'I have come to sacrifice to the LORD.' ³Invite Jesse to the sacrifice, and I will show you what you shall do; and you shall anoint for me the one whom I name to you." ⁴Samuel did what the LORD commanded, and came to Bethlehem. The elders of the city came to meet him trembling, and said, "Do you come peaceably?" ⁵He said, "Peaceably; I have come to sacrifice to the LORD; sanctify yourselves and come with me to the sacrifice." And he sanctified Jesse and his sons and invited them to the sacrifice.

⁶When they came, he looked on Eliab and thought, "Surely the LORD's anointed is now before the LORD." ⁷But the LORD said to Samuel, "Do not look on his appearance or on the height of his stature, because I have rejected him; for the LORD does not see as mortals see; they look on the outward appearance, but the LORD looks on the heart." ⁸Then Jesse called Abinadab, and made him pass before Samuel. He said, "Neither has the LORD chosen this one." ⁹Then Jesse made Shammah pass by. And he said, "Neither has the LORD chosen this one." ¹⁰Jesse made seven of his sons pass before Samuel, and Samuel said to Jesse, "The LORD has not chosen any of these." ¹¹Samuel said to Jesse, "Are all your sons here?" And he said, "There remains yet the youngest, but he is keeping the sheep." And Samuel said to Jesse, "Send and bring him; for we will not sit down until he comes here." ¹²He sent and brought him in. Now he was ruddy, and had beautiful eyes, and was handsome. The LORD said, "Rise and anoint him; for this is the one." ¹³Then Samuel took the horn of oil, and anointed him in the presence of his brothers; and the spirit of the LORD came mightily upon David from that day forward. Samuel then set out and went to Ramah.

Commentary 1: Connecting the Reading with Scripture

These readings give us two views on "God's responses to our crises." To begin, the prophets Ezekiel and Jeremiah give us two similar perspectives on the experience of the destruction of Jerusalem and Judah by the Babylonian Empire, and the subsequent exile of a significant number of Judeans as prisoners of war. Ezekiel was among those already exiled in 597 BCE, and is thus a prophetic figure whose texts often provide opportunities for preaching themes related to the subordinated, the minority, but especially the migrant, because Ezekiel himself represents the Hebrew people forcibly evacuated and facing new challenges in new lands. In fact, all of Ezekiel 17, from which our few verses are taken, basically reviews the conquests of Judah by Babylon and the ill-fated attempts to seek help from Egypt.

At the beginning of Ezekiel 17, the prophet refers to a tree shoot being carried to "a land of trade, set . . . in a city of merchants" (Ezek. 17:4). The "eagle," in this first case, is Babylon, carrying the king of Judah (and exiles) to Babylon, but also planting a new ruler back in Judah: The Judean ruler Jehoiachin was taken and "planted" in Babylon, while Zedekiah was "planted" back in Jerusalem. Zedekiah was tempted to side with a second "eagle," Pharaoh (v. 7). Zedekiah's attempted revolt brought down Jerusalem in 587 BCE.

In verse 22 Ezekiel finally changes the eagle imagery. Now God is the third and superior eagle who will take a "sprig" from the cedar, and plant it (back?) on Mount Zion. *What previous kings have squandered, God will restore.* The mistaken foreign policies of previous Hebrew rulers are rejected before God's direct "restoration" recounted in Ezekiel 17:22–24. In short: out with the old, in with the new!

The story in 1 Samuel 15:34–16:13 is also about God's intervention and restoration, but once again, the larger context of our reading suggests "out with the old" as well as "in with the new." The Hebrew Scriptures contain mixed reviews of kingship in Israel and Judah. First Samuel 8 contains a serious warning about asking for kings. Other texts portray the beginnings of the monarchy as a time of high hopes. So, despite such a positive beginning (outlined in 1 Sam. 9), Saul's reign is eventually doomed by his personal failures, and among these "failures" are some disturbing passages.

Just prior to our passage, before David is chosen, Saul is supposed to move against a very old enemy indeed—the Amalekites. The Amalekites are presented as an enemy from the time of the wilderness wandering (Num. 14), a bitter memory that is revived in this episode (1 Sam. 15:2). Saul is ordered to perform the "ban" against this enemy (i.e., the horrendous

This Kingdom of Christ

[Ezekiel] frequently compares the world to a field, or a forest, and the inhabitants of it to the trees therein; — an allusion exceedingly proper, considering the great variety and difference of condition both of the one and the other. The trees of the field are some high, some low; some green, some dry; some strong, some weak; some lofty, some contemptible; some fruitful, some barren; some useful, some altogether useless: so that you have all sorts of persons, high and low, of what condition, relation, or interest soever, clearly represented by the trees of the field; and these are the trees in my text.

. . . Hence, [in] verse 22 of this chapter, he calls them from their thoughtfulness about the destructions, desolations, and contentions that were amongst them in reference to their civil rule, to the consideration of that design which he was secretly and silently carrying on under all these dispensations. "I will also take of the highest branch of the high cedar, and will set it; I will crop off from the top of his young twigs a tender one, and will plant it upon an high mountain and eminent: in the mountain of the height of Israel will I plant it; and it shall bring forth boughs, and bear fruit, and be a goodly cedar: and under it shall dwell all fowl of every wing; in the shadow of the branches thereof shall they dwell." As if the Lord should say, There is a great noise in the world about setting up and plucking down of kings, in this their carnal rule; and many of you see nothing else, you will look no farther: but I also have my work in hand; my design is not bounded within these limits and outward appearances; I am setting up a King that shall have another manner of dominion and rule than these worms of the earth. . . . The setting up then of this kingdom of Christ, "who is the highest branch of the cedar," and planting it in the church, the "mountain of Israel," with the prosperity hereof, and safety of him that shall dwell therein, is the subject of ver. 22, 23.

John Owen, "The Advantage of the Kingdom of Christ in the Shaking of the Kingdoms of the World," in *The Works of John Owen*, vol. 15, ed. Thomas Russell (London: Richard Baynes, 1826), 420–22.

destruction of all living things during a conquest). However, in this episode Saul apparently allows greed to get the better of him, keeping many of the animals that were supposed to be destroyed along with the Amalekites.

When Samuel, the last judge and prophet, questions whether Saul has accomplished the bloodthirsty task as commanded, he protests against Saul's claims that "all is well," using the famous line, "What, then, is this bleating of sheep in my ears?" (v. 14). Saul appears to be condemned because he was insufficiently single-minded in carrying out the *total* annihilation of a people and their animals. To carry out what Saul was supposed to do, Samuel "hews" Agag (15:33, "in pieces," the English rather gratuitously adds in many versions). This is, therefore, among the mistakes of Saul.

As now written, the historical books describe many episodes of Saul's inexorable decline, and the first king is portrayed as growing ever more deranged and incompetent—even seeking to

kill David, whom he (rightly) perceives as a threat to his prestige and rule. It is important that our passage follows immediately from this startling description of one of Saul's "failures," just as Ezekiel's "restoration" follows a condemnation of previous rulers! In 1 Samuel 15, God is finally portrayed as saying to Samuel, "I regret that I made Saul king, for he has turned back from following me, and has not carried out my commands" (v. 11). So, "out with the old."

In our passage, then, God intervenes to renew the monarchy by naming David to save a monarchy threatened by Saul's failures. Like reading the "pro-Saul" passage of 1 Samuel 9 immediately after the "anti-king" passage of 1 Samuel 8, we have here a rejection of Saul followed immediately by what is often read as one of the "pro-David" passages in 1 Samuel. It is sometimes thought that these "pro-king" passages were older traditions, around which a later editor added the clearly "anti-king" passages, even heavily criticizing David (e.g., the Bath-sheba story, Absalom's revolt, etc.).

Later reflection on David will suggest that even he was not allowed to construct the temple because, according to the Chronicler (writing several centuries after 1 Samuel), God tells David: "you shall not build a house to my name, because you have shed so much blood in my sight on the earth" (1 Chr. 22:8). This, despite the fact that the texts portray David's battles (like Samuel's orders to Saul to wipe out the Amalekites and their animals) as having been fought *at God's command.* Do we have in Chronicles some additional pangs of conscience with regard to the monarchy?

However, matters may not be quite what they seem. Is our passage about choosing young David entirely "positive"? In this passage, Samuel is shown the new king in a most unusual manner—a kind of contest. (Does Jesse have any idea what is at stake here? Surely he knows the authority of Samuel!) Each son of Jesse is "displayed" before Samuel, but God chooses only the most unexpected—a lowly young shepherd who was not even considered "in the running," but is described in 16:12 as physically attractive: "ruddy . . . beautiful eyes . . . handsome." There are curious aspects of this. First, the report on the *physical appearance* of David is rather unexpected after God directly states (1 Sam. 16:7) that God is *not interested* in outward appearance. Secondly, we have heard this before! Like David, we were also originally introduced to Saul's father Kish, who, according to 1 Samuel 9, "had a son whose name was Saul, a handsome young man. There was not a man among the people of Israel more handsome than he." It is hard to avoid a sense of déjà vu. Thus the text rather subtly may be suggesting, Are we making another mistake here? Sermons may emphasize our constant temptation to judge by appearances, even when told not to!

If we read this story with Ezekiel 17:22–24 and then suggest that both are only about "God's intervention toward a restoration," we risk avoiding the texts previous to both our passages. The restorations involved rejections. Ezekiel 17 rejects two previous rulers before "replanting" a sprig back in Jerusalem. In 1 Samuel, young David is chosen immediately following a clear rejection of Saul.

"In with the new" invariably also meant "out with the old." The new is typically the easier part; rejecting the old is hard. What seemed to work so well in the past is hard to give up, even when clear mistakes were made. Recognizing mistakes can be the hardest part of change, because it means that "restoration" will involve new directions. Churches search for new pastors that closely resemble the previous—even when times have changed—and sometimes even ignoring clear mistakes of the past. Our two passages, however, strongly suggest that "restoration" is not the same thing as "preservation."

DANIEL L. SMITH-CHRISTOPHER

Commentary 2: Connecting the Reading with the World

Ezekiel is never one to mince words or soften the harshness of God's judgment. The poetic and visionary quality of his prophecies makes them convoluted and difficult to understand. Ezekiel's conviction about the implications of Israel's embrace of foreign gods and trust in political alliances for security, however, leaves little doubt as to why captivity had fallen on his people. Babylon is divine payback for Israel's rebellion and idolatry; Ezekiel does not let his people forget the cause of their plight.

Following a lengthy account of God's judgment, Ezekiel's tone shifts in chapter 17. Like sunlight breaking through clouds, his words of hope and promise emerge in these verses (Ezek. 17:22–24). Consistent with his use of imagery from the natural world, Ezekiel proclaims God's way forward for Israel. Exile and divine punishment give way to restoration and renewal. To illustrate his point, the prophet shares a word from God and describes what is about to happen. God appears as a planter or arborist, cutting "a sprig" from the top of a mighty cedar tree, replanting it in soil, creating the beginning of a new tree from an old one.

Ezekiel must have loved trees, and he knew something about the process of reproducing fruit trees. One method is simply to plant seeds. An alternative is to replant tender shoots from the newest growth of an older tree. The newest growth emerges at the top of an older tree. New life from an older, established tree is best suited to root and grow as a new plant. Seeds may not withstand the challenges of soil and environment, but sprigs, if able to root, are more likely to grow.

Ezekiel's description may also derive from the practice of grafting food trees in order to preserve their unique variety. Certain fruits are not simply the product of their own seeds, but are created and preserved by joining the old with the new. Grafting a scion (or tender sprig) to an older rootstock, the older tree is transformed into a new variety. In utilizing an older root system that is adapted to the soil and climate, a new scion from the top of a tree is given an environment conducive to producing a new tree and thus new fruit.

God's promise of restoration prompts listeners and preachers alike to reflect on the importance of continuity, rootedness, and purpose. Ezekiel does not proclaim a new plant disconnected from the past, but one taken from the life of the old: a new sprig planted for the purpose of growing into a stately cedar. Value is found in its purpose, not its commercial value. Its purpose is to do what cedars do: grow branches and bear fruit, creating shade where all winged creatures find a home.

Trees are physical reminders of life in the natural world, but in the final verse we are reminded that the source of life is larger than any one physical manifestation, however inspiring or beautiful. Life itself is a gift of God. Like the trees, humanity is inextricably rooted in a source that is life itself. Trees remind us of the hope of restoration.

Restoration and renewal were not on the mind of Samuel, whose long and contentious relationship with Saul ends when the two men leave one another for the last time, each heading to his respective home. Samuel is filled with resignation, and the scene in their story exudes a sense of foreboding and sadness. Samuel pleads with his people to avoid the dangers of anointing a king. But they want a leader like those of other nations. Samuel reluctantly gives them what they want. Saul becomes Israel's first king. The struggles of Samuel and Saul play out over time, their lives intertwined in constant conflict. In the end, Saul's leadership is marked by bad decisions, bad luck, and a predictable fate.

The passage describes the transition of leadership from Saul to David. A new chapter in Israel's political, religious, and social life is about to begin, but the verses before us are more than just a record of transaction, selection, and anointing. The story is imbued with human feeling, emotion, and loss. Samuel grieves over Saul. It may seem odd that one so critical of the king's choices and leadership, driven to anger and outrage in his relationship with Saul, and one so wary of monarchial rule for his people, would actually be beset with such grief. After all, Samuel could have easily rehearsed his earlier warnings and reminded the people: "I told you so." However, the prophet's life and ministry are inextricably tied to Saul. Samuel knows Saul. He has witnessed Saul's strengths and weaknesses and held a front-row seat to the tragic drama. Samuel has felt the weight of Saul's demise on behalf of their people, Israel. Samuel grieves for Israel, and for Saul.

The nature of grief, especially the deep and often conflicting emotions that emerge from its powerful foothold in human life, needs acknowledgment in these verses, and the text exhibits a tension between grief's uncontrollable presence and the potential of healing, hope, and comfort. God enters the scene with an agenda, asking what some might hear as an unanswerable question, ill-timed at best and insensitive at worst: "How long will you grieve over Saul?" (1 Sam. 16:1). For God, it is time to move on.

There is work to be done. Move on to the important task of identifying and anointing a new king. God is about the business at hand. Why not? Their protection from the Philistines and other hostile powers depends upon finding a sound and strong king. For Samuel, grief is not something one moves beyond easily or readily. Yet Samuel follows God's direction, moves forward, and perseveres. David is identified after a long search process, and he is anointed king. Once accomplished, Samuel heads home to Ramah, an indication that the past continues to haunt him. Samuel is not moving beyond grief, but with it into the future.

The grief of Samuel and the complicated, even contradictory, emotions that gather around loss are important for any preacher who utilizes this text. Grief serves as an entry point for many hearers whose own lives are burdened with the full range of feelings and beliefs surrounding loss and disappointment. Samuel's grief reveals honesty about the ambivalence that marks human relationships.

Samuel's complex relationship with Saul is captured by the colonial American painter John Singleton Copley in a painting that hangs in the Museum of Fine Arts in Boston. Titled *Saul Reproved by Samuel* (1798), the painting depicts Samuel with his arm extended and pointing toward Saul, who is surrounded by a marching column of his army. Copley's use of light penetrates the darkness and highlights both the red tunic of Saul and his humiliated, downturned face responding to the rebuke. Samuel, moving ahead of the marching column of soldiers, is contorted in his posture; he stands sideways yet moves forward, his back neither completely turned to Saul nor fully facing him. Copley's Samuel rebukes the king yet continues to march in step and move ahead in the parade.

With David's anointing, Samuel ushers in the promise of a new era of restoration and renewal for Israel. A new king emerges, and an old king is retired. A new chapter begins. As for Samuel, he returns home alone, yet forever tied to his people, to Saul, to history. In the end, the burden of Samuel is rooted in an identity inseparable from that of his people. His life is indeed more a graft than a seed. Being right does not always set one free.

J. SCOTT HUDGINS

Psalm 92:1–4, 12–15

¹It is good to give thanks to the LORD,
    to sing praises to your name, O Most High;
²to declare your steadfast love in the morning,
    and your faithfulness by night,
³to the music of the lute and the harp,
    to the melody of the lyre.
⁴For you, O LORD, have made me glad by your work;
    at the works of your hands I sing for joy.
. . . .
¹²The righteous flourish like the palm tree,
    and grow like a cedar in Lebanon.
¹³They are planted in the house of the LORD;
    they flourish in the courts of our God.
¹⁴In old age they still produce fruit;
    they are always green and full of sap,
¹⁵showing that the LORD is upright;
    he is my rock, and there is no unrighteousness in him.

Psalm 20

¹The LORD answer you in the day of trouble!
    The name of the God of Jacob protect you!
²May he send you help from the sanctuary,
    and give you support from Zion.
³May he remember all your offerings,
    and regard with favor your burnt sacrifices.

⁴May he grant you your heart's desire,
    and fulfill all your plans.
⁵May we shout for joy over your victory,
    and in the name of our God set up our banners.
May the LORD fulfill all your petitions.

⁶Now I know that the LORD will help his anointed;
    he will answer him from his holy heaven
    with mighty victories by his right hand.
⁷Some take pride in chariots, and some in horses,
    but our pride is in the name of the LORD our God.
⁸They will collapse and fall,
    but we shall rise and stand upright.

⁹Give victory to the king, O LORD;
    answer us when we call.

Connecting the Psalm with Scripture and Worship

Psalm 92:1–4, 12–15. Psalm 92 is a hymn of thanksgiving and praise for God's work, recited to music in the public worship in the temple on the Sabbath. The psalmist is identified as the king, yet the worshiping community participates in singing the song. It is noticeable that the divine name Yahweh (the LORD) appears seven times in the song, reflecting the meaning of the Sabbath, the seventh day.[1] Verses 1–4 and 12–15 include praise, thanksgiving, and benediction. While verses 1–4 are a call to worship with the joyful sound of a variety of musical instruments in praise of the saving acts of God, verses 12–15 are a climactic ending in a sapiential style with a blessing upon the righteous, following the psalmist's testimony to God's great power over his enemies (Ps. 92:5–11). The images of "the palm tree" and "a cedar in Lebanon" symbolize the fruitfulness and strength of the righteous and signify God's righteousness to the people of God. Verse 15b ("he is my rock") confirms trust in the Lord.

It is worth noting that the Mishnah, the first rabbinic literature, describes Psalm 92 as "a song for the future time, the day that shall be all Sabbat and rest in life everlasting (*Tamid* 7.4)."[2] This eschatological conception of the Sabbath connects Psalm 92 with the first reading, Ezekiel 17:22–24, which is the coda of the chapter. In the previous verses, Ezekiel prophesies the judgment of God on the Babylonian exiles. He reverses his message in verses 22–24 by announcing the good news of the restoration of the Davidic monarchy. This promise of God for the future of Israel is depicted through the same image of the cedar tree that is used in Psalm 92:12–15. In both readings, God is described as the one who is growing the cedar tree to be fruitful. God's sovereign power over the nations is the source of hope for the people of God.

The images of the palm tree and a cedar in Lebanon in Psalm 92:12–15 relate also to the Gospel reading, Mark 4:26–34, in which the kingdom of God is conveyed in the image of a full-grown tree. While the psalmist identifies the growing and flourishing tree with the life of the righteous, Jesus compares it with the kingdom of God. Both are based on the faith that God is working for justice and peace on the earth.

In our reality, where we often see the suffering of the righteous, Psalm 92 should be continuously sung as a reminder of God's promise. By singing the song, we eagerly anticipate the Sabbath, the day of rest for the righteous, and pray that it may come true soon. A hymn such as "When in Our Music God Is Glorified" reflects the tone and content of Psalm 92. Verses 12–15 of the psalm, with images of fruitful flourishing, might provide rich language for a benediction.

Psalm 20. Among various hypotheses about the historical background of Psalm 20, the prevailing opinion is that it was sung regularly at the New Year's feast, to celebrate Yahweh's kingship in conjunction with the enthronement of a new king in Jerusalem.[3] The multiple pronouns used in the psalm ("we," "I," "you," "he," and "they") indicate that it was a community ("we") song led by the priest ("I") for the king ("he" and "you") to God ("he" and "you"). Considering that Israel was a small country geographically, up against the political and military hegemony of strong neighboring countries, this psalm is a song of the powerless, united in the conviction that God protects them from their enemies ("they") through their king, who was chosen and anointed by God.

Psalm 20 comprises two stanzas. In the first stanza (Ps. 20:1–5), the community blesses the king, affirming that God will answer his prayers, protect him, accept his sacrifices, and help him succeed in his plans. In the second stanza (vv. 6–9), the priest affirms the salvation of the community by reciting that God will answer its prayers for the king and the nation (v. 6). As their response to the priest, the community reaffirms their faith and trust in God, who is the ultimate source of victory (vv. 7–9).

---

1. Carroll Stuhlmueller, "Psalms," in *Harper's Bible Commentary*, ed. James L. Mays (San Francisco: Harper & Row, 1988), 476.
2. Samuel Terrien, *The Psalms* (Grand Rapids: Eerdmans, 2003), 657.
3. Cf. Terrien, *Psalms*, 218; Artur Weiser, *The Psalms* (Philadelphia: Westminster, 1962), 206.

The reading appointed for this day, 1 Samuel 15:34–16:13, tells the story of David's anointing by Samuel. It emphasizes that God's standard for choosing the king is different from that of human beings, because the Lord does not see "the outward appearance," but "looks on the heart" (1 Sam. 16:7). What, then, does it mean to look on the heart? What does the Lord see in David's heart? The story indicates that David is far from the conventional image of the king. He is neither tall in stature nor physically proud like other warriors. Instead, he is the youngest son, the one who tends the sheep in the pastures. This implies that God looks on David's heart, that is, his humility and his compassion for the weak. In response to the first reading, Psalm 20 is a recitation that the people's king is like David, God's anointed one, chosen by God's standard and blessed by the right hand of God (Ps. 20:6b).

In the Gospel reading, Mark 4:26–34, the youngest or the smallest plays an important role in the kingdom of God. A mustard seed that is "the smallest of all the seeds on earth'" (Mark 4:31) grows to be "the greatest of all shrubs," so that "the birds of the air can make nests in its shade" (v. 32). This parable of the Mustard Seed resonates with God's way of doing things: God chooses the smallest, who walk humbly with God, and anoints them to become the agents of the kingdom, in which all people can make their homes and live harmoniously.

In general, anointing is a divinely appointed ceremony that is part of the inauguration of the king. The Bible indicates that anointing with oil or with the Holy Spirit signifies God's blessing or call on a person's life, who then humbly walks with God and participates in God's transforming work for the world. In this broad sense, Psalm 20 can be sung as a prayer for those who are the smallest, but who are called by God to become the greatest. Just as the psalmist describes the life of the anointed by singing that "[s]ome take pride in chariots, and some in horses, but our pride is in the name of the LORD" (Ps. 20:7), so those who are called by God humbly trust in the power of the Lord.

Since Psalm 20 includes the voices of the priest and of the people of the worshiping community, it can be recited as an ensemble reading. For example, in a musical setting, a worship leader could take the role of the priest by reading verses 1–4 and 6, while the congregation reads verses 5 and 7 as the ritual community. The last verse (v. 9) can be read by all together in harmony. Consider also singing a metrical or responsorial setting of the psalm as a response to the first reading.

EUNJOO MARY KIM

Proper 6 (Sunday between June 12 and June 18)

2 Corinthians 5:6–10 (11–13), 14–17

[6]So we are always confident; even though we know that while we are at home in the body we are away from the Lord— [7]for we walk by faith, not by sight. [8]Yes, we do have confidence, and we would rather be away from the body and at home with the Lord. [9]So whether we are at home or away, we make it our aim to please him. [10]For all of us must appear before the judgment seat of Christ, so that each may receive recompense for what has been done in the body, whether good or evil.

[11]Therefore, knowing the fear of the Lord, we try to persuade others; but we ourselves are well known to God, and I hope that we are also well known to your consciences. [12]We are not commending ourselves to you again, but giving you an opportunity to boast about us, so that you may be able to answer those who boast in outward appearance and not in the heart. [13]For if we are beside ourselves, it is for God; if we are in our right mind, it is for you. [14]For the love of Christ urges us on, because we are convinced that one has died for all; therefore all have died. [15]And he died for all, so that those who live might live no longer for themselves, but for him who died and was raised for them.

[16]From now on, therefore, we regard no one from a human point of view; even though we once knew Christ from a human point of view, we know him no longer in that way. [17]So if anyone is in Christ, there is a new creation: everything old has passed away; see, everything has become new!

Commentary 1: Connecting the Reading with Scripture

The apostle Paul, like some Jewish contemporaries, fellow Christians, and many in his world, did not believe death was the final word. Unlike the Platonists, Paul thought death led to resurrection into an embodied life. Unlike others, Paul believed this new, embodied, resurrection life resulted from the resurrection of Jesus. What gave Paul hope was the eschatological gift of the Spirit, which for him was evidence of the unshakable reality of the resurrection (2 Cor. 5:5).

This conviction of an embodied life after death gave the apostle a Spirit-shaped faith that could say, "So we are always confident" (v. 6). Verse 6 forms an incomplete sentence; verse 7 offers a sudden clarification; verse 8 resumes verse 6 and completes it! The term translated "confident" (from *tharreō*) means "daring, courageous, bold," even "audacious" (see 5:8; 7:16; 10:1; Heb. 13:6). Paul is expressing not arrogance but the conviction that God will not let death have the final word. That means the opposition he faces, no matter what antagonists

might do to him, will not finally be victorious. He confesses this conviction is "by faith, not by sight" (5:7). If he were to rely on external observation or the likelihood of success, he would reconsider his mission. If he were to rely on the external realities of people in Christ dying, he might rework his entire theology. However, he has an Easter-based faith.

Conviction about an embodied resurrection life beyond death gave the apostle Spirit-inspired, Easter eyes. So intimate was his relationship with the Lord that, while he could concede that "we would rather be away from the body and at home with the Lord," his eyes were fixed on pleasing the Lord (v. 9). Though his claim has been susceptible to misunderstandings, Paul is not here degrading the earthly body (see 4:16–18; 5:1–5). He is simply contrasting it to the greatness of the presence of the Lord. Earthly bodies and intimacy with God, and also resurrected bodies and perfect intimacy, are affirmed. As Ralph Martin says, while we are in the present body we are "in communion with God," but we are "nevertheless in a foreign land" as we long for and await the kingdom of God.[1] One can assure others that absence from the body is presence with the Lord, however one explains the intermediate state.[2]

Pleasing God is not about becoming a sycophant, nor should it stem from a lack of self-esteem. It is graciously relational life that expresses our love for God as we are empowered by God's love for us. Emphasis on pleasing God shaped a number of Paul's statements (Rom. 12:1–2; 14:18; Phil. 4:18; Eph. 5:10). The translation "make it our aim to please him" (v. 9) could be rendered "cherish pleasing him" or "are greatly honored to please him" or "aspire to please him." Paul knows he does not always do this, but he does always aspire to live this way.

Those who most firmly believe in divine judgment should today be the most progressive on issues of social justice. "All of us," Paul announces, "must appear before the judgment seat of Christ" (5:10; cf. 1 Cor. 3:10–15; Rom. 14:10; Matt. 25:31–46). Those who go to Corinth today can see the massive judgment seat in the center of the city. Notably, the criterion for most judgments in the Bible is behavior (though see Rom. 2:14–16; 1 Cor. 4:4–5). Judgment is not based on affirming the right tenets of faith, however important they might be. Justification is by faith, and in that regard we are made righteous through Christ (2 Cor. 5:18–19).

At the same time, this does not negate judgment about works: "so that each may receive recompense for what has been done in the body, whether good or evil" (v. 10). On the one hand, there is the significance of a final judgment so that God, who knows and sees all, can make all things right. On the other hand, our works today are judged in accord with God's desire for justice for all. Too much in our world is not right—drug and sex trafficking that destroys innocent lives, diseases for which there is not yet a cure, broken families, and systemic evils of all sorts. What we who love justice and peace

most want and for which we should work is for evil to be unmasked, unraveled, and realigned with God's goodness and righteousness.

Waiting for God's judgment, then, does not mean sitting around waiting for God to act. Rather, this kind of waiting means acting out what is said in 2 Corinthians 5:10. That is, we should do now what we know that kingdom envisions for our world. For one example, Guy Nave shows how confidence in God's final judgment played an important, society-changing role for America's slaves: "The belief that one's present reality was not the final reality, however, not only empowered slaves not to lose heart and to confidently endure, but also enabled them to reject their current reality."[3]

Confidence in God's final judgment is why Paul is confident in preaching the gospel (vv. 11–13). His motivation, which itself shaped his conviction that gave him Easter eyes, is "the love of Christ [that] urges us on" (v. 14). Debates continue about whether this is our love for Christ or Christ's love for us (the consensus), but 5:14–15 virtually announces that Christ's love is the apocalyptic act of God's gracious love in the death of Christ, a death that undoes death and turns it into life eternal. This act of God, which also includes the gracious gift of the Spirit, urges or controls or directs us to carry on in confidence. If one (Christ) died for (in the place of) all (and all means all), then all who have died in Christ have died so that the "all . . . might live no longer for themselves" but for Christ (5:15; cf. Rom. 6:3–5).

The Spirit gave Paul eyes to see through death and systemic evil into God's apocalyptic act in Christ to make all things right. That gave him a Spirit-empowered perspective. What he means by "a human point of view" or "according to the flesh" (*kata sarka*, 5:16) derives from his own conversion experience and looking at others through the lenses of death, of systemic evil, of sinfulness and sickness. A human point of view cannot get beyond the opposition to what is right and true, cannot find the courage to press

1. Ralph P. Martin, *2 Corinthians*, 2nd ed., Word Biblical Commentary 40 (Nashville: Zondervan, 2014), 266.
2. Frank J. Matera, *II Corinthians*, New Testament Library (Louisville, KY: Westminster John Knox, 2003), 124–25; Scot McKnight, *The Heaven Promise: Engaging the Bible's Truth about Life to Come* (Colorado Springs, CO: WaterBrook, 2015), 45–49.
3. Guy Nave, "2 Corinthians," in Brian K. Blount et al., eds., *True to Our Native Land: An African American New Testament Commentary* (Minneapolis: Fortress, 2007), 316.

on, and looks at humans with a cynical sneer that surrenders to hopelessness. Not Paul. He sees all humans through what God has done in Christ. He sees Christ not only as the crucified one, but as the crucified and raised king. He sees humans not as "old" creation but as "new creation," where "everything has become new" (5:17; cf. Isa. 42:9; 43:18–19; 48:6; 65:17; Gal. 6:15).

Paul's Spirit-generated eyes of faith know that "all this is from God" (5:18) and this God—in Christ—is "reconciling the world to himself" (v. 19). Whatever our mission, and wherever we might be located, we should be open to the Spirit giving us Easter eyes, so we can see beyond the evil to the goodness of God making the world new.

SCOT MCKNIGHT

Commentary 2: Connecting the Reading with the World

Christians in the modern age face serious challenges that have been around since the very inception of the faith. These challenges may be greater today than ever before. Some center around these questions: "Are you in your right mind? Are you a rational human being? Do you display good common sense? Is there consistency between what you believe and what is 'true'"?

Philosophers have wrestled for millennia with the question "What is truth?" Seldom have human beings come to a definitive and final conclusion. Most classical and modern philosophers believe there is such a thing as "absolute truth," but few have claimed to grasp it (the majority of postmodern philosophers believe that all truth is relative). Atheism and agnosticism are on the rise worldwide, yet not believing and not knowing are choices of faith just as surely as choosing to believe in a higher power or a spiritual path.[4]

It is fascinating to discover what other people think and believe, especially when such perspectives differ from our own. Some people believe in ghosts, unidentified flying objects (UFOs), extraterrestrial life forms, witches, demons, angels, a flat earth, fairies, warlocks and wizards, levitation, extrasensory perception (ESP), and a variety of superstitions (such as bad luck being caused by black cats, stepping on cracks, walking under ladders, breaking mirrors, and so on). Others believe in Bigfoot, the Loch Ness monster, yetis, that sexuality is a choice, that Elvis Presley is still alive, that cell phones cause cancer, and that Saddam Hussein was involved in the 9/11 attacks. At the same time, some do

not believe humans cause climate change, that we ever landed on the moon, that the Holocaust really happened, that evolution is true, that the earth is billions of years old, that dinosaurs ever existed, or that tobacco has harmful health effects. Each of these lists could be expanded endlessly, and it is not difficult to find people who will defend or refute anything and/or everything on such lists. Many of us may wonder, "Who in their right mind could possibly believe that?" It is difficult to set subjective filters aside and view things from an objective perspective.

Paul and other early leaders of the Christian movement faced similar questions and the challenges that accompanied them. From early days, some saw the followers of Jesus as being "filled with new wine" (Acts 2:13) and attributed the joy and energy of the faith to inebriation. According to Mark, Jesus' own family and friends questioned his sanity. Who in their right mind would talk about resurrection from the dead, cleansing of sins through water baptism and transformation through Spirit baptism, eating flesh and drinking blood, unconditional love and unmerited grace? What about traditional interpretation of the Law? What about doing things in accord with long-established traditions? Only crazy people would buy into such a topsy-turvy new paradigm.

Preachers might point out that Paul was OK with that. Addressing the dualistic Greek world, Paul was able to speak persuasively to two coexisting yet contrasting realities. One could choose to walk by sight, or one could choose to walk

4. John Gray, *Seven Types of Atheism* (New York: Farrar, Straus & Giroux, 2018).

by faith (2 Cor. 5:7). One could choose to claim an earthly home, or one could choose a heavenly home (1 Cor. 15:40; 2 Cor. 5:1; Col. 3:5–17). One could focus on exterior appearances, or one could focus on inner truth (2 Cor. 5:12).

We can look at others from a human point of view, or we can look at others as Christ sees them (1 Cor. 2:5). What seemed to some foolishness, Paul claimed was true wisdom, granted by God alone (1 Cor. 3:18; 4:10). The key to moving from a worldly, human, limited view to an expansive, spiritual, transformed view was Jesus the Christ. Once a person committed to Christ, that person became a new creation, able to think and see in new ways (2 Cor. 5:17).

Our canon of Hebrew and Christian Scriptures is the mere tip of the iceberg of all the writings, beliefs, and core tenets of the early Christian movement. From bizarre gnostic writings to widely respected and accepted writings of the Apostolic Fathers, a vast, eclectic, and complex map of Christian thought was drawn. Over time, new spiritual explorers investigated, tested, and confirmed or rejected various elements. Boundaries and borders defining "orthodoxy" (right belief) emerged. Slavery, in our Bible taken for granted as acceptable and ordained by God, is now viewed as deeply evil and unacceptable. The place, status, and roles of women, very limited in Scripture, have been greatly expanded as our understanding of gender differences has evolved. Many afflictions attributed to evil and demonic forces we now believe to be rooted in diseases or mental illness.

At no time does this mean that the Bible is wrong, but simply that our understanding and ability to interpret and apply it has progressed. For many believers, the Holy Spirit is still active in the church, and our understanding of God's will is not limited to what is written in the Bible. Revelation is an active and dynamic experience.

In a skeptical age, the tendency is to enter into argument and debate. Preachers might stress that Paul offers an alternative to persuading people to accept new thinking and practices: try it yourself. Instead of simply taking our word for it, experience it firsthand. Having a discussion about prayer is a very different experience than praying.

A biology professor and a theologian met for coffee on a regular basis, discussing and debating the reality and value of religion. The biology professor vehemently opposed organized religion, taking the position that spirituality was a delusional distraction at best. After many fruitless hours of disagreement, the theologian finally issued a challenge: apply a good and rigorous scientific method to three practices—prayer, meditation, and fasting. Engage for a month, keep a journal, reflect on what is experienced and discovered. At the end of the month, the biologist confessed that she was not ready yet to buy into religion wholesale, but she could not deny that something significant happened and that she began thinking and reflecting in a substantially different way.

This is a wonderful example of relational evangelism, reflecting the open invitation of the early church. In the minds of many, evangelism means handing out tracts and issuing a very specific invitation to accept Jesus as Savior and Lord. Relational evangelism models the earliest practices of the Christian movement by engaging people individually or in small groups, exploring together beliefs and understandings, and extending an open welcome to participate in the rituals and practices of a spiritual community.[5]

We may find ourselves in endless arguments about truth, reality, faith, religion, and the existence of God. To truly walk by faith instead of sight, to truly trust that faith in Christ has the power to transform life, and to truly believe in our hearts things that other people doubt and question, we need to let go of the desire to "win the argument" and instead extend an invitation for others to share in the experiences that have been so meaningful in our own lives. Often a lasting faith is caught more than taught. Let us live in such ways that others witness in us the fruit of the Holy Spirit (Gal. 5:22–23) and cannot wait to find out what makes such a difference in our lives.

DAN R. DICK

5. Rodney Stark, *The Rise of Christianity: How the Obscure, Marginal Jesus Movement Became the Dominant Religious Force in the Western World in a Few Centuries* (Princeton, NJ: Princeton University Press, 1996).

Mark 4:26–34

[26]He also said, "The kingdom of God is as if someone would scatter seed on the ground, [27]and would sleep and rise night and day, and the seed would sprout and grow, he does not know how. [28]The earth produces of itself, first the stalk, then the head, then the full grain in the head. [29]But when the grain is ripe, at once he goes in with his sickle, because the harvest has come."

[30]He also said, "With what can we compare the kingdom of God, or what parable will we use for it? [31]It is like a mustard seed, which, when sown upon the ground, is the smallest of all the seeds on earth; [32]yet when it is sown it grows up and becomes the greatest of all shrubs, and puts forth large branches, so that the birds of the air can make nests in its shade."

[33]With many such parables he spoke the word to them, as they were able to hear it; [34]he did not speak to them except in parables, but he explained everything in private to his disciples.

Commentary 1: Connecting the Reading with Scripture

Today's lection invites the question "Why be cryptic?" It says Jesus spoke publicly *only* in parables (Mark 4:34) and acknowledges the cryptic character of parables, saying that Jesus explained everything in private to his disciples (indicating the disciples, too, needed explanation). Why not explain everything to everyone? Why is the Teacher cryptic?

This gestures toward Mark's so-called messianic secret (v. 11). In Mark's opening chapters, Jesus from Nazareth, a backwater in imperial Rome, gains fame with blistering speed, attracting multitudes not only from Galilee, but from "Judea, Jerusalem, Idumea, beyond the Jordan, and the region around Tyre and Sidon" (3:7–8; cf. 1:45). Jesus' fame becomes so significant that Pharisees and Herodians actively conspire "to destroy him" (3:6). At the same time, he does not permit "demons" and "unclean spirits" to speak precisely because "they knew him" (1:34; 3:11–12). When the disciples ask, "Why parables?" (4:10), Jesus moves from cryptic to confounding, saying he uses parables so that people will "not perceive . . . not understand . . . not turn again and be forgiven" (4:12). All this intensifies the cognitive dissonance.

Immediately, however, we appear to be invited to relax into Mark's simple, allegorical interpretation of "the sower" (4:13–20). Allegory is inherently comforting because it involves no new understanding, merely the association of known entities (e.g., "rocky ground" equals "ones with no root"). Anyone paying attention to Jesus' explanation for using parables and his talk of new wine and fresh wineskins (2:22; cf. Matt. 9:14–17; Luke 5:33–39) will worry: "It's a trap."

The preacher may compare Jesus' spiritual genius to the Buddhist master having novices meditate endlessly upon koans such as "What is the sound of one hand clapping?" Asking "Why parables?" is like asking, "Why koans?" Mark's allegorical interpretation is like a textbook answer to the koan question: "to defeat the limits of the reasoning mind and stimulate awakening to deeper spiritual truth." Theoretically correct. However, understanding the purpose of koans theoretically is different from undergoing spiritual enlightenment through disciplined meditation upon them. Theory is vital to but different from spiritual awakening.

Consider poetry. Being able to explain the allusions, form, and so forth of a poem about losing one's parent or child is essential to understanding the poem. However, being able to explain those essential mechanisms is different from being imaginatively taken up into living the discrete experience of pain the poem contours. When dealing with spiritual matters—in contrast, say, to directions for roasting broccoli—theoretical understanding is essential but nonetheless needs in a sense to be forgotten to enable awakening to the reality invoked.

The Christian philosopher Paul Ricoeur famously coined the phrase "second naiveté" to describe this dynamic vis-à-vis Scripture. "First naiveté" remains ignorant of original context, original language, doctrinal significance, the play of one's own prejudices, and the like. Resolving first naiveté with informed understanding is essential to truly interpret a text, in contrast to unwittingly reading one's own ideas out of it. Spiritual understanding requires, on the far side of technical work, a reopening to the text, a second naiveté. Such opening to the text lies at the heart, for instance, of *lectio divina* (which is itself reliably a true reading/awakening only insofar as one has resolved first naiveté).

All this may suggest an answer to the question "Why parables?" Perhaps Jesus uses parables because they resist quick resolution, because they push us toward listening with ears that can hear, toward hearing that brings transformation and forgiveness (4:23). Perhaps Jesus is concerned over the simplistic understanding of the multitudes. Perhaps this is also why he tells the demons not to tell anyone who he is (1:34), namely, because he understands the threat of people labeling and understanding him in accord with established categories, and so never being pushed beyond theory to spiritual awakening.

In other words, perhaps parabolic teaching is a way of preventing closure at the level of the cataphatic (i.e., of preventing legalism), a way of ensuring opening to the apophatic. In this regard, we may remember James 2:19, which also distinguishes true belief in terms of a spiritual transformation that goes beyond correct knowledge that we *share* with unclean spirits—"even demons believe—and shudder." Notably, in this sense, to understand the parable of the Sower by, for instance, correctly correlating "rocky ground" with "ones with no root" is spiritually empty, understanding that looks without perceiving.

With regard to first naiveté and the two parables in today's lection, it is notable that they are two of numerous "kingdom" parables found in the Gospels (e.g., see several at Matt. 13). It may be helpful to think of each parable about the kingdom of God as adding a brushstroke or two to the fullness of our vision. The parable of the Sprouting Seed would seem to stress the miraculous character of the growth of the kingdom (the work of the Spirit?), and may suggest that just as a gardener does not create plants but facilitates their growth and delights in their fruit, so we do not design or build the kingdom but should strive to foster its emergence and to delight in its fruits (perhaps compare the fruits of the Spirit at Gal. 5:22–23).

When Jesus' listeners heard the parable of the Mustard Seed (also found at Matt. 13:31–32 and Luke 13:18–19), they would immediately have been reminded of another of today's lections, Ezekiel 17:22–24, which speaks of God taking a sprig from the top of a cedar and tending it until it becomes a "noble cedar," bearing fruit and providing homes for "winged creatures of every kind" (Ezek. 17:23). These brushstrokes seem to kindle a spirit that is alert and alive to the Spirit, even in marginal and insignificant places (like a manger), and to kindle a spirit that anticipates a kingdom providing shelter for diverse peoples and creatures.

Some have tried to mitigate the patriarchal "kingdom" with "kin-dom." Jesus, however, explicitly rejects privileging of kinship over *koinōnia* (Mark 3:31–35). There is no denying the problem with "kingdom." Indeed, it is hard to be more critical of kings and kingdoms than last week's lection from 1 Samuel, where the Lord, hostile to the very idea of kings, tells Samuel to warn the people a king will take their sons and daughters for his own purposes, will take the best fruits of their fields, and will make them into slaves (1 Sam. 8:9–20). For the prophets and Mark, monarchy is a fact of life. Invoking alternate vocabulary would have been toothless.

The clever but subversive—and therefore risky and powerful—move the prophets and Jesus make is to portray God as the paradigmatic monarch and to configure monarchy explicitly *in terms of love and justice*. So, the true king or queen is just, gracious, planter of the sprig, like the God who seeks to bless all peoples through God's own people (Gen. 12:1–3). This clearly distinguishes a true king from a tyrant, who is really no monarch at all; so it would be just to overthrow them (Calvin uses this strategy in sixteenth-century Europe).

Today in the United States—to be sure, not everywhere—we can critique monarchy and patriarchy directly, so substituting some other term for "kingdom," such as "the *koinōnia*," is wise. In sum, preachers can avoid simplistic rejection of biblical "kingdom" language, explain the faithful, subversive power of prophetic and Gospel depictions of God as king, explain the subversive impact of Jesus' depiction of the kingdom of God (in contrast to, say, the kingdom of Herod or the empire of Nero), and explain why in our context Gospel fidelity calls for new language.

WILLIAM GREENWAY

Commentary 2: Connecting the Reading with the World

When I was a small child, my father introduced me to vegetable gardening. Step by step we prepared the soil, lined out shallow furrows, positioned pea seeds, covered them over, and watered the ground. Early the next morning my father found me out in the garden scratching the ground, searching for edible peas.

Arnold Lobel, who writes a series of children's stories called *Frog and Toad*, tells a similar tale. Frog gives Toad some flower seeds to plant. He promises that Toad will have a garden "quite soon," but cautions him that gardening is "very hard work." Toad proceeds to plant the seeds, then promptly commands them: "Now seeds, start growing." They do not. Toad repeats the order more and more loudly. Frog tells Toad his seeds are not growing because Toad's shouting frightens them. He counsels Toad to "leave them alone" and let the sun and rain do their work.

Toad, however, hears only that his seeds are afraid, and undertakes a series of day-by-day moves to calm his seeds and cajole them into growing. He sets out candles at night, since they might also be afraid of the dark. He reads his seeds stories, sings them songs, quotes poems to them, plays music for them. (All these are actions that might calm *him* if he were afraid.) After many days of unremitting effort, Toad finally collapses in utter exhaustion. Frog returns for a visit to find seedlings well above ground, and Toad sound asleep. Frog awakens Toad to the news that his garden is finally growing. Toad is, of course, very pleased, but admits: "You were right, Frog. It was very hard work."[1] Indeed—hard work that has had nothing at all to do with the growing!

Children chuckle knowingly as they hear and read the story. So do adults, because it is a story for all ages, but carries a lesson that can be very hard to learn. While experience, skill, practice, and understanding in such endeavors as gardening, parenting, healing, and soul mentoring are essential, there is only so much that a farmer, a teacher, physician, therapist, community builder, parent, spouse, friend, or preacher can do to produce growth. "Produce" is a misnomer. All that any of these can do is help to prepare the possibilities for growth, to nurture and foster that growth as (or if) it happens. Such nurture and support can often consist in efforts that are "hands off"—granting, providing, and protecting the necessary growing space.

All this is in play, I think, in the parable Mark's Jesus tells. His listeners may well be anxious, apprehensive, deeply concerned over what appears to be "lack of progress" with respect to the coming to fruition of the commonwealth of God. There is, however, only so much that is theirs (or ours) to do. God's greening work is a mystery; it comes, the farmer "knows not how." Serious damage to the crop can come from trying to "make it happen" on our own.

Forces from three directions converge to exacerbate a sense of impatience among faith community members, forces that impinge from their inevitable immersion in a wider culture. (1) Omnipresent media-driven strategies of

1. Arnold Lobel, *Frog and Toad Together* (New York: Harper Trophy, 1971), 29.

consumerism conspire to create widespread cravings for instant gratification: "Anything worth having is worth having *now*; you can charge it instantly and pay later." (2) The political ideals of one tribe are often perceived only as obstacles to be summarily eradicated by an opposing tribe: "If we just defeat them in the next election, we can turn the nation around." (3) The long-endured effects of justice delayed and justice denied that so many have suffered create an understandable sense of urgency: "How many more must suffer the effects of discrimination while we continue to discuss the issue?"

The itch for immediacy, in other words, is not limited to little children. There is a Toad in all of us that keeps on urging: "We cannot just sit around and wait, we have to *do* something; God's reign may be promised, but as participants, we must not be passive." The issue here is more than just "be patient, things take time." It is that the commonwealth of God into which we are called is not under our control. Its coming is not commensurate with our felt sense of achievement. What we deem as failure does not doom God's power or intent.

Yet it is well to note that, in the parable, the farmer, while he does not know how growth takes place as he awaits its coming, is anything but passive. Sleep he may, night and day, but he does so, as it were, with one eye open. When the time is right, he is right on it. He goes in with the sickle at once.

One thing that all the growth supporters cited earlier must learn (usually by trial and error, and often different in each distinctive situation) is a sense of timing. Growth spurts and insight/awareness harvesting happen most often at teachable moments, wherein it is incumbent that just the right kind of intervention be undertaken at once—but not before. One thinks, for instance, of the movie *Good Will Hunting*, where the psychologist (played by Robin Williams) attentively awaits the dawning self-awareness of his patient (played by Matt Damon). He employs, over time, a full range of strategically introduced therapeutic techniques that challenge and evoke responses from his patient; but he does not pronounce the liberating *It's not your fault!* until the moment when the young man is able to receive it.

In working for the promised reign of God—no less than in many other growth-participation endeavors—there *are* actions to be undertaken in support of the process. Rather than exclaiming, "Look what we are doing—isn't that great?" Christians do well to be asking instead, "What does God seem to be growing, and how can we help?"

One growing parable prompts another: God's reign is like a . . . *mustard bush*? Not a cedar of Lebanon, or a giant sequoia, but an invasive plant often regarded as a weed? Perhaps the metaphor serves as a further check on strategies for church growth consciously or unconsciously charged with visions of human grandeur. Perhaps the plan of God has to do with purposes unconnected to or at cross purposes with our own. Mustard bushes proliferate in scruffy, seemingly disorderly array—and they provide resting places for flocks of birds! It can be unsettling when our designated ecclesial places and our carefully created programs produce results we were not expecting, perhaps not even wanting.

It sounds like the control issues implicitly addressed in the previous parable may present themselves in another but related form through this one. This prompts the question "Whose garden is this anyway? And what might we be unconsciously implying when we speak of 'the fruits of our labors'?"

Some questions, then, for preachers on this passage: (1) What congruence or discontinuity might there be between the energy our congregations may be investing in services, programs, projects, and causes, and that which God might be cultivating among us? (2) How can we discern, and articulate into communal awareness, the appropriate dynamic between patient sleeping and waking, and properly productive reaping and harvesting in God's garden? (3) How do we go about distinguishing *our* vision for growth from what God's might be?

"Be patient! Do not wring your hands! Do use your eyes!" Mark's Jesus seems to say. "Work with discerning diligence, as best you can, in tandem with the process of God's often unexpected, but continually unfolding commonwealth-growing givens."

DAVID J. SCHLAFER

Proper 7 (Sunday between June 19 and June 25)

Job 38:1–11 and 1 Samuel 17:(1a, 4–11,
   19–23) 32–49
Psalm 107:1–3, 23–32 and
   Psalm 9:9–20

2 Corinthians 6:1–13
Mark 4:35–41

Job 38:1–11

¹Then the LORD answered Job out of the whirlwind:

²"Who is this that darkens counsel by words without knowledge?
³Gird up your loins like a man,
   I will question you, and you shall declare to me.

⁴"Where were you when I laid the foundation of the earth?
   Tell me, if you have understanding.
⁵Who determined its measurements—surely you know!
   Or who stretched the line upon it?
⁶On what were its bases sunk,
   or who laid its cornerstone
⁷when the morning stars sang together
   and all the heavenly beings shouted for joy?

⁸"Or who shut in the sea with doors
   when it burst out from the womb?—
⁹when I made the clouds its garment,
   and thick darkness its swaddling band,
¹⁰and prescribed bounds for it,
   and set bars and doors,
¹¹and said, 'Thus far shall you come, and no farther,
   and here shall your proud waves be stopped'?"

1 Samuel 17:(1a, 4–11, 19–23) 32–49

¹Now the Philistines gathered their armies for battle. . . . ⁴And there came out from the camp of the Philistines a champion named Goliath, of Gath, whose height was six cubits and a span. ⁵He had a helmet of bronze on his head, and he was armed with a coat of mail; the weight of the coat was five thousand shekels of bronze. ⁶He had greaves of bronze on his legs and a javelin of bronze slung between his shoulders. ⁷The shaft of his spear was like a weaver's beam, and his spear's head weighed six hundred shekels of iron; and his shield-bearer went before him. ⁸He stood and shouted to the ranks of Israel, "Why have you come out to draw up for battle? Am I not a Philistine, and are you not servants of Saul? Choose a man for yourselves, and let him come down to me. ⁹If he is able to fight with me and kill me, then we will be your servants; but if I prevail against him and kill him, then you shall be our servants and serve us." ¹⁰And the Philistine said, "Today I defy the ranks of Israel! Give me a man, that we may fight together." ¹¹When Saul and all Israel heard these words of the Philistine, they were dismayed and greatly afraid. . . .

[19]Now Saul, and they, and all the men of Israel, were in the valley of Elah, fighting with the Philistines. [20]David rose early in the morning, left the sheep with a keeper, took the provisions, and went as Jesse had commanded him. He came to the encampment as the army was going forth to the battle line, shouting the war cry. [21]Israel and the Philistines drew up for battle, army against army. [22]David left the things in charge of the keeper of the baggage, ran to the ranks, and went and greeted his brothers. [23]As he talked with them, the champion, the Philistine of Gath, Goliath by name, came up out of the ranks of the Philistines, and spoke the same words as before. And David heard him. . . .

[32]David said to Saul, "Let no one's heart fail because of him; your servant will go and fight with this Philistine." [33]Saul said to David, "You are not able to go against this Philistine to fight with him; for you are just a boy, and he has been a warrior from his youth." [34]But David said to Saul, "Your servant used to keep sheep for his father; and whenever a lion or a bear came, and took a lamb from the flock, [35]I went after it and struck it down, rescuing the lamb from its mouth; and if it turned against me, I would catch it by the jaw, strike it down, and kill it. [36]Your servant has killed both lions and bears; and this uncircumcised Philistine shall be like one of them, since he has defied the armies of the living God." [37]David said, "The LORD, who saved me from the paw of the lion and from the paw of the bear, will save me from the hand of this Philistine." So Saul said to David, "Go, and may the LORD be with you!"

[38]Saul clothed David with his armor; he put a bronze helmet on his head and clothed him with a coat of mail. [39]David strapped Saul's sword over the armor, and he tried in vain to walk, for he was not used to them. Then David said to Saul, "I cannot walk with these; for I am not used to them." So David removed them. [40]Then he took his staff in his hand, and chose five smooth stones from the wadi, and put them in his shepherd's bag, in the pouch; his sling was in his hand, and he drew near to the Philistine.

[41]The Philistine came on and drew near to David, with his shield-bearer in front of him. [42]When the Philistine looked and saw David, he disdained him, for he was only a youth, ruddy and handsome in appearance. [43]The Philistine said to David, "Am I a dog, that you come to me with sticks?" And the Philistine cursed David by his gods. [44]The Philistine said to David, "Come to me, and I will give your flesh to the birds of the air and to the wild animals of the field." [45]But David said to the Philistine, "You come to me with sword and spear and javelin; but I come to you in the name of the LORD of hosts, the God of the armies of Israel, whom you have defied. [46]This very day the LORD will deliver you into my hand, and I will strike you down and cut off your head; and I will give the dead bodies of the Philistine army this very day to the birds of the air and to the wild animals of the earth, so that all the earth may know that there is a God in Israel, [47]and that all this assembly may know that the LORD does not save by sword and spear; for the battle is the LORD's and he will give you into our hand."

[48]When the Philistine drew nearer to meet David, David ran quickly toward the battle line to meet the Philistine. [49]David put his hand in his bag, took out a stone, slung it, and struck the Philistine on his forehead; the stone sank into his forehead, and he fell face down on the ground.

Commentary 1: Connecting the Reading with Scripture

The story of David and Goliath is well known. Far less well known are all the textual and historical problems related to the story, some of which have important implications for how we read these traditions. There will be plenty of opportunities in these texts for sermons emphasizing the dangers of "popular reputations" that surround famous figures, but such popular ideas often hide serious questions.

First, why does Saul not know *who David is* in this story? David was introduced to Saul in the previous chapter, and even worked for Saul! (1 Sam. 16:21–23). Second, in the wider biblical narrative, it is not at all clear *who actually killed Goliath*. In our famous story, Goliath is identified as a giant who carries a spear the size of a "weaver's beam" (17:7). However, 2 Samuel 21:19 says Goliath ("weaver's beam" and all) was killed by a certain Elhanan. Later biblical writers spotted the problem and tried to resolve it by introducing a new character in 1 Chronicles 20:5: "Lahmi," Goliath's *brother*. Was the slaying of Goliath later added among the "legendary exploits" of David? If so, why?

One reason this famous story pits young David against a Philistine champion *from Gath* becomes clear when we note David's political and military collaboration with Philistines *from Gath* (1 Sam. 27–29). Our story may well have been intended to undercut suspicions about David's potentially treasonous collaboration with an enemy of the early Israelites—a collaboration that is portrayed as *enthusiastically undertaken* by David at the time (28:2). David's story, in short, seems to engage in political spin.

Subsequent interpretive history raises other serious matters. The story clearly wants to emphasize that David had no reasonable chance of survival against Goliath. David acknowledges this when he declares that God "does not save by sword and spear; for the battle is the LORD's and he will give you into our hand" (17:47). Thus, victory resulted from the miraculous assistance of God (a theme consistent with the stories of the fall of Jericho and of Gideon defeating the Midianites with a mere three hundred incompetent soldiers). This means that the

key to David's conquest was *not* David's prowess with weapons.

Why, then, do readers from time immemorial want to discuss David's "experience" as a shepherd, and therefore his (supposed) keen abilities with a sling, and therefore (contrary to the message of the story itself) want to emphasize the importance of proper military training? We so want to say that David was "the man for the job" *because of his abilities*, and not because of his trust in a power beyond his own. The story, in short, is frequently *remilitarized* in interpretation.

I have raised suspicions that this was also a pro-David spin to distract from his previous associations with Philistines in Gath; but one could make the argument that the story is a clever *criticism* of David. For example, references to *Gath*—the very town where David collaborated with Philistines—might require a wink from the original storyteller, suggesting we are intended to remember that "the great military leader" was really successful only when trusting God's *intervening* power, rather than trusting weapons like those belonging to Goliath himself. When we take the story to be "pro-David," we may be missing an ironic gesture.

This (not very) subtle criticism of David is strengthened when the story is read in combination with the famous story of Job—and particularly the striking passage from Job on display here, which raises even more uncomfortable questions. In Job, the long-suffering main character continues to protest his innocence before God and to insist that God explain Job's innocent suffering. Job's friends, the infamous "comforters," are appalled that Job claims innocence. The book places the reader in the uncomfortable position of knowing that Job is, in fact, correct: he is not suffering through any fault of his own. Job's constant demands for an explanation are quite reasonable.

Then the unexpected happens. God *responds*. Indeed, God's response is often considered to be among the most striking and unsettling divine discourses in the Hebrew Bible. It must be remembered that Job is never reprimanded

The Wise and Good Creator

Who is the father of the rain? And who hath begotten the drops of dew? Who condensed the air into clouds, and bade them carry the waters of the rain, now *bringing golden-tinted clouds from the north,* now changing these into one uniform appearance, and again transforming them into manifold circles and other shapes? *Who can number the clouds in wisdom?* Whereof in Job it saith, And He knoweth the separations of the clouds, *and hath bent down the heaven to the earth*: and, *He who numbereth the clouds in wisdom*: and, *the cloud is not rent under Him*. For so many measures of waters lie upon the clouds, yet they are not rent: but come down with all good order upon the earth. Who *bringeth the winds out of their treasuries*? *And who*, as we said before, *is he that hath begotten the drops of dew? And out of whose womb cometh the ice*? For its substance is like water, and its strength like stone. And at one time the water becomes *snow like wool*, at another it ministers to Him *who scattereth the mist like ashes*, and at another it is changed into a stony substance; since *He governs the waters as He will*. Its nature is uniform, and its action manifold in force. Water becomes in vines *wine that maketh glad the heart of man:* and in olives *oil that maketh man's face to shine:* and is transformed also into *bread that strengtheneth man's heart*, and into fruits of all kinds which He hath created. . . .

These points my discourse has now treated at large, having left out many, yea, ten thousand other things, and especially things incorporeal and invisible, that thou mayest abhor those who blaspheme the wise and good Artificer, and from what is spoken and read, and whatever thou canst thyself discover or conceive, *from the greatness and beauty of the creatures mayest proportionably see the maker of them*, and bending the knee with godly reverence to the Maker of the worlds, the worlds, I mean, of sense and thought, both visible and invisible, thou mayest with a grateful and holy tongue, with unwearied lips and heart, praise God and say, *How wonderful are Thy works, O Lord; in wisdom hast Thou made them all*. For to Thee belongeth honour, and glory, and majesty, both now and throughout all ages. Amen.

Cyril of Jerusalem, *The Catechetical Lectures*, in *Nicene and Post-Nicene Fathers,* second series, vol. 7, ed. Philip Schaff and Henry Wace (Buffalo, NY: Christian Literature Publishing, 1895), 53–55.

for *asking questions* of God! Nor is Job accused of insolence or disrespect for demanding an answer to his questions about his unjust suffering. To the contrary, God takes the questions seriously. The answer begins with, "Are you ready to hear the answer?" "Gird up your loins" is a classic phrase that means "prepare for battle!" Thus, God initiates an intellectual "battle," a debate, but God's *opening* point is arguably God's *only* point: you are not able to understand all this. Essentially, God asks in many different ways, "If you think you are ready to know about such mysteries, then can you show me that you know the basics of creation?"

At no point does God indicate Job should never have asked his questions. Nevertheless, God makes clear that Job is in error to think he is capable of fully engaging in debate with the Creator. It is not a call from God to "know your place." It is more, "Are you in a place to know?"

The knowledge is not beyond Job's *station*, it is beyond Job's ability. Far too many readers mistake the reason for God's speech by concluding that humans do not "deserve" to know. That is never in question. Neither does God say, "Do not ask." God's answer is rather, "You are not ready, or able, to know what you ask."

Are we offended in the modern world when we acknowledge that sophisticated computers can know more than humans are capable of knowing? Are we offended by our finitude? Offended not to know as God knows? Hopefully not. Just so, we should not take offense at God's answer to Job. Reflecting on Job 38, preachers might wonder whether we humans will ever be ready for such information. Perhaps one sign that we are making progress is when the secrets of creation are not immediately used to perfect our powers of destruction. Modern Goliaths—those who believe in their own weapons—are not yet ready for more secrets of the universe.

What God chooses in the story of David and Goliath is not to make a human being a super weapon. Goliath was the super weapon, the image of human military prowess. Yet how limited is our ability to understand! The story of David and Goliath—besides being propaganda for King David's legacy (if not also a very clever joke at David's expense!)—is surely also a story revealing human foolishness at thinking we understand the success of David to be found in his honed skills.

That is not the story. Knowing what all creation is about and all its constituent details is still beyond us. We continue to search, and we are not blamed by the writer of Job for asking and trying. Rather, we are arguably blamed only when we believe we finally have it all figured out. Will we ever know all things? We must not answer too quickly. The book of Job does not condemn our frantic search for answers—only the *premature* conviction that we have "all we need to know," and the even more dangerous conviction that our knowledge is best represented by our ability to make weapons as big as a weaver's beam—rather than in our quest for understanding how we might raise each other up and build balanced, global fruitfulness, peace, and prosperity—precisely the imagery God uses to illustrate God's power in Job.

DANIEL L. SMITH-CHRISTOPHER

Commentary 2: Connecting the Reading with the World

God's response to Job is not the explanation most readers want, need, or expect. The questions raised by Job's tragic experience are insistent and inescapable: How is it possible for the righteous to experience such evil? Where is divine justice? Is personal goodness predicated on a life of blessing? Described as one "blameless and upright" (Job 1:8), Job demands an explanation from God. Finally, God has heard enough and speaks out of the whirlwind—a whirlwind that could have easily been Job's own life. God simply ignores Job's question, posing different questions altogether.

In a series of rhetorical questions emphasizing the immeasurable distance between human knowledge and divine creation, God answers: "Where were you when I laid the foundation of the earth?" (38:4). God reminds Job that God is creator of all that is: measurer and planter of the earth's foundations, maker of the songs of the morning stars, the clouds, the oceans. Recalling the majesty and power of creation, God reframes the human predicament and undercuts, at least for a moment, the outrage for personal explanation. God plays the awe card. Job's question remains unanswered.

So how might a preacher make sense of this divine speech in the context of Job's experience, or in the context of our experience, where death, loss, and meaningless tragedy invade our world, our lives, and our congregations?

One possibility is to explore the assumptions readers bring to the text concerning the nature of divine justice and motivations that guide human choices to live faithful, moral lives. Like Job, most of us desire God to be a moral accountant, a judge who maintains justice and distributes judgment fairly. Some are motivated to live moral lives out of fear, feeling that loss and tragedy are the result of a lack of goodness or faithfulness. Perhaps more subtly, we assume that prosperity and material blessings are the results of our own moral choices. With the God revealed in these verses there is no support for these assumptions—only the reality that God is far bigger, far broader, far more mysterious than humanity's capacity to know or understand.

In her review of Mark Larrimore's book *The Book of Job: A Biography*, Joan Acocella concludes her critical essay with these words:

> God's speech slaughters the moral, the what-should-be, nature of the rest of the Book of Job. It is the knife flash, the leap, the teeth. And despite, or because of, its remorselessness, it is electrifying. It is like an action movie, or a horror movie. Of course, Job is important in the story, but today he

seems the pretext, the one who is like us, and makes the argument that we would make. As for God, he makes the argument that, at least as far as nature is concerned, is true.[1]

Transitioning from a passage that leaves most more baffled than satisfied, we encounter in 1 Samuel a story familiar and morally compelling, so much so that we run the danger of overlooking details and misreading the text. How do we hear anew a text so iconic, so rehearsed in our memories?

David's improbable victory over the Philistine giant Goliath stands as a prototype of those rare but satisfying occasions when an underdog surprises everyone and takes down the more formidable, established, and highly favored opponent. The challenge for the preacher is to recast the story's obvious, well-worn truths: mustering courage in the face of insurmountable obstacles, or winning with well-honed skills and sheer determination rather than by experience, or the discovery of the power in knowing oneself and engaging in life's struggles on one's own terms. These are all lessons from the story to be sure. How have other writers and artists recast the story?

Malcolm Gladwell, in his bestselling book *David and Goliath: Underdogs, Misfits, and the Art of Battling Giants*,[2] challenges interpretations of David as the underdog and Goliath as the insurmountable obstacle. For Gladwell, the Philistines used Goliath as a ploy to intimidate the enemy and to facilitate surrender, avoiding battle altogether. According to Gladwell, at the mere sight of Goliath, "hearts failed because of him" (inferred from 1 Sam. 17:32 RSV). Saul fell for the ploy because he understood power in the form of might, strength, and intimidation.

Gladwell posits that Goliath's size resulted from a debilitating medical condition, and when heavy armor was added to his massive frame, it made him slow and sluggish. His summons to David to come to him (v. 44) was due to his immobility and bad eyesight. Goliath had to be led to the field by an attendant (v. 41), and he mistook David's weapon as a few sticks (v. 43).

David's quickness and his skill with the sling, sharpened over time in his daily work as a shepherd, eventually proved to be more powerful. For Gladwell, David began as the favorite, not the underdog. Yet for those observing from the sidelines of battle, the attribute that seemed to be the giant's source of strength turned out to be his greatest weakness. Giants are, according to Gladwell, never as strong or powerful as they seem.

Centuries earlier, David's victory over Goliath captivated the early-seventeenth-century Italian painter Michelangelo Merisi da Caravaggio. With remarkable attention to physical and emotional realism, Caravaggio painted two contrasting portraits of a victorious David holding the grotesque, decapitated head of Goliath. The first version depicts David bending over the torso of the giant, his youthful face hidden in the shadows, the light highlighting his muscular arms as he holds the sling in one hand and the bloodied head of Goliath in the other. Goliath's enormity is captured in his lifeless hand, which rests next to David's smaller foot. Caravaggio downplays any expression or personality, and instead focuses the observer's eye on muscles and sling.

A decade later, he would paint the scene with important differences. David is standing, a sword in one hand and the head of Goliath in the other. This time the light reveals David's face, expressing not celebration, but disgust, and even regret, and also the gory head of the giant, eyes and mouth wide open with a look of surprise.

What accounts for Caravaggio's interpretation? Biographers point out that the painter was often in trouble, at odds with the law. Late in his life he was on the run, accused of murder. Art historians suggest that Caravaggio painted himself in the later painting (1610), not as the hero, but as the villain. In effect, using his image as Goliath serves as a plea of guilt. As Simon Schama comments, "By offering his head in the painting, he can save himself in real life."[3]

Caravaggio, like all great artists, provokes interpreters to rethink this familiar story through the use of light, shadows, angle of vision, and

---

1. Joan Acocella, "Misery: Is There Justice in the Book of Job?" *New Yorker,* December 16, 2013.
2. Malcolm Gladwell, *David and Goliath: Underdogs, Misfits, and the Art of Battling Giants* (New York: Little, Brown & Co., 2013).
3. Simon Schama et al., "Simon Schama's Power of Art," London: BBC Video, 2007.

composition. When he superimposes his story onto the story of David and Goliath, he subverts our conventional interpretation and unveils our unexamined assumptions. Forced to wrestle with the full range of humanity, we discover that the contrast between hero and villain, victor and vanquished, vulnerability and strength, often fades in the shadows. The familiar is always more than it seems.

J. SCOTT HUDGINS

Psalm 107:1–3, 23–32

¹O give thanks to the LORD, for he is good;
   for his steadfast love endures forever.
²Let the redeemed of the LORD say so,
   those he redeemed from trouble
³and gathered in from the lands,
   from the east and from the west,
   from the north and from the south.
. . . .
²³Some went down to the sea in ships,
   doing business on the mighty waters;
²⁴they saw the deeds of the LORD,
   his wondrous works in the deep.
²⁵For he commanded and raised the stormy wind,
   which lifted up the waves of the sea.
²⁶They mounted up to heaven, they went down to the depths;
   their courage melted away in their calamity;
²⁷they reeled and staggered like drunkards,
   and were at their wits' end.
²⁸Then they cried to the LORD in their trouble,
   and he brought them out from their distress;
²⁹he made the storm be still,
   and the waves of the sea were hushed.
³⁰Then they were glad because they had quiet,
   and he brought them to their desired haven.
³¹Let them thank the LORD for his steadfast love,
   for his wonderful works to humankind.
³²Let them extol him in the congregation of the people,
   and praise him in the assembly of the elders.

Psalm 9:9–20

⁹The LORD is a stronghold for the oppressed,
   a stronghold in times of trouble.
¹⁰And those who know your name put their trust in you,
   for you, O LORD, have not forsaken those who seek you.

¹¹Sing praises to the LORD, who dwells in Zion.
   Declare his deeds among the peoples.
¹²For he who avenges blood is mindful of them;
   he does not forget the cry of the afflicted.

¹³Be gracious to me, O LORD.
   See what I suffer from those who hate me;
   you are the one who lifts me up from the gates of death,

¹⁴so that I may recount all your praises,
  and, in the gates of daughter Zion,
  rejoice in your deliverance.

¹⁵The nations have sunk in the pit that they made;
  in the net that they hid has their own foot been caught.
¹⁶The LORD has made himself known, he has executed judgment;
  the wicked are snared in the work of their own hands.   *Higgaion. Selah*

¹⁷The wicked shall depart to Sheol,
  all the nations that forget God.

¹⁸For the needy shall not always be forgotten,
  nor the hope of the poor perish forever.

¹⁹Rise up, O LORD! Do not let mortals prevail;
  let the nations be judged before you.
²⁰Put them in fear, O LORD;
  let the nations know that they are only human.   *Selah*

Connecting the Psalm with Scripture and Worship

Psalm 107:1–3, 23–32. Psalm 107 is a hymn of national thanksgiving, inviting the Israelites to return from all around the world to give thanks to God. It recites God's salvific work for them throughout their national history. Although the date of its composition is unclear, the reference to the return of Israel from the four directions of the earth (Ps. 107:3) and doing commerce in the seas (vv. 23–32) implies that the poem was originally sung during the Persian or early Hellenistic period.[1]

Psalm 107 consists of three parts: a prologue (vv. 1–3) that invites the Israelites to praise God with thanksgiving for the Lord's steadfast love; four stanzas (vv. 4–9, 10–16, 17–22, 23–32) that describe God's redeeming works for Israel; and a closing hymn (vv. 33–43) colored by Wisdom literature. The four stanzas are skillfully divided by the refrain, "Let them thank the LORD for his steadfast love, for his wonderful works to humankind" (vv. 8, 15, 21, 31). Each stanza deals with a distinct reason for gratitude, and the last stanza (vv. 23–32), which is included in the day's lectionary reading, praises God who saved those in trouble from the mighty waters of the sea.

The conventional reading of this stanza is from the contrasting view of God's salvific power and nature's destructive force, and it is customary to interpret it as saying that the God who is more powerful than the sea triumphs over it. However, the first reading, Job 38:1–11, provides a different understanding of the relationship between God and nature. It primarily emphasizes that God created nature and cares for it, as well as controls it. In particular, verses 8–11 depict the sea as a newborn infant that God cares for, rather than as God's opponent or rival, and stresses that God is the creator of the universe. As the response to Job 38:1–11, Psalm 107:23–32 is read as a reminder of God's sovereign power as the creator.

The relationship between God and nature is also described in the Gospel reading, Mark 4:35–41, in which Jesus' disciples are amazed when they witness him stilling the windstorm. Like the disciples, as well as the Israelites in Psalm 107, we are reminded of the way God created us as part of God's creation and rejoice in God's saving works for us as the creator of the universe who controls and cares for God's creatures.

1. W. Stewart McCullough et al., "The Book of Psalms," in *The New Interpreter's Bible: Psalms; Proverbs* (Nashville: Abingdon, 1955), 4:572.

Psalm 107 is a beautiful litany of thanksgiving that can be read by worshipers. The refrain after each stanza in the poem also suggests that the poem can be sung antiphonally as the response to the first reading or to the sermon.

Psalm 9:9–20. According to textual and literary criticism, Psalm 9 was originally paired with Psalm 10 in an acrostic form. The paired poems move from thanksgiving (Ps. 9) to lament (Ps. 10), and reading both poems as one makes more sense in appreciating Psalm 9. Although there are few grounds for guessing the original historical situation of Psalm 9, its literary form provides a hint that it might have been sung in liturgical ceremonies at the Jerusalem temple. The poem begins in the tone of a hymn of thanksgiving, of gladness and praise, based on the psalmist's confidence in God's righteous judgement over the nations (9:1–8), but ends in a somber and reflective tone (vv. 16–20). The two Hebrew words *Higgaion* (v. 16) and *Selah* (vv. 16, 20) are difficult to translate, but biblical scholars understand them as a call for silent reflection, accompanying musical sounds.[2]

Since Psalm 9 is a royal hymn, attributed to King David, the psalmist is assumed to be a king, and a unique representative of God's people.[3] Even though he speaks of the enemies as "my enemies" (v. 3), they are not his individual foes, but all the wicked nations (v. 17) imposing hardships on his people, identified as "the oppressed" in verse 9, the "afflicted" in verse 12, and the "needy" and "poor" in verse 18. The king testifies and rejoices that God judges his enemies and delivers his people. In this manner, the psalmist's personal salvation (v. 13) is inseparably woven into the national concern (v. 14).

Verses 9–12 recite three reasons for praise: God is "a stronghold for the oppressed" (v. 9); God has "not forsaken those who seek" him (v. 10); and God does "not forget the cry of the afflicted" (v. 12). Verses 13–14 make an urgent plea with God for the deliverance of his people from "the gates of death" (v. 13) to "the gates of daughter Zion" (v. 14). These contrasting images

of gates imply a critical situation for his people, and the present perfect tense in verses 15–16 expresses confidence in God who has meted out justice to the wicked nations. In verses 17–18, the poem turns to prophetic mode by declaring that the godless nations shall fall into ruin, while the needy and poor will be remembered by God. Verses 19–20 appeal for divine action against the wicked nations that are too arrogant to fear the Lord.

The Old Testament reading, 1 Samuel 17:(1a, 4–11, 19–23) 32–43, is a story that illustrates how God saved Israel from a wicked nation. As a powerless nation, Israel was under attack from the powerful Philistines. While King Saul and all his soldiers were deadly afraid of them, the little shepherd boy David was courageous enough to fight the giant warrior Goliath, confident that God would save him and his people from the Philistine and give him victory with his sling and pebble. The psalmist responds to this story with confidence that the God of Israel will deliver his people from powerful nations in the midst of a national crisis, just as God did with the Philistines.

The Gospel reading of Mark 4:35–41 tells another story of God's intervention in the crisis of the people of God. Jesus and his disciples were crossing the water by boat, and a great windstorm with strong waves hit while he was asleep. The disciples were so afraid as the boat was being swamped that they woke up Jesus to ask him to help. As soon as Jesus commanded the sea to be still, it immediately calmed down. This well-known passage has often been preached with an eye to individual crisis or personal fear. Yet Psalm 9 and the first reading offer a communal lens for this passage. The windstorm is like a powerful and arrogant nation's blow to people who are weak and helpless. At their urgent request, Jesus immediately delivers them from a destructive power.

For us as American Christians, especially middle- and upper-middle-class white believers, Psalm 9 may not sound like good news. It is about a God who stands for the oppressed,

2. Carroll Stuhlmueller, "Psalms," in *Harper's Bible Commentary*, ed. James L. Mays (San Francisco: Harper & Row, 1988), 438–39.
3. John H. Eaton, *Kingship and the Psalms* (Sheffield: JSOT Press, 1986), 137.

afflicted, poor, and needy of a powerless nation, and we are the citizens of the most powerful nation in the world. This situation raises some homiletical questions: Who are the listeners? What would be good news for the people of a powerful and oppressive nation? Psalm 9 is a good reminder that national security and safety come from God, not from oppressing the poor and the afflicted.

EUNJOO MARY KIM

2 Corinthians 6:1–13

[1]As we work together with him, we urge you also not to accept the grace of God in vain. [2]For he says,

> "At an acceptable time I have listened to you,
>   and on a day of salvation I have helped you."

See, now is the acceptable time; see, now is the day of salvation! [3]We are putting no obstacle in anyone's way, so that no fault may be found with our ministry, [4]but as servants of God we have commended ourselves in every way: through great endurance, in afflictions, hardships, calamities, [5]beatings, imprisonments, riots, labors, sleepless nights, hunger; [6]by purity, knowledge, patience, kindness, holiness of spirit, genuine love, [7]truthful speech, and the power of God; with the weapons of righteousness for the right hand and for the left; [8]in honor and dishonor, in ill repute and good repute. We are treated as impostors, and yet are true; [9]as unknown, and yet are well known; as dying, and see—we are alive; as punished, and yet not killed; [10]as sorrowful, yet always rejoicing; as poor, yet making many rich; as having nothing, and yet possessing everything.

[11]We have spoken frankly to you Corinthians; our heart is wide open to you. [12]There is no restriction in our affections, but only in yours. [13]In return—I speak as to children—open wide your hearts also.

Commentary 1: Connecting the Reading with Scripture

In no passage in any of Paul's letters does his vulnerability, his emotional tenuousness, his pastoral sensitivity, or his missional ambition come to the fore as in today's passage. One wonders why 2 Corinthians is not called a "pastoral" epistle. Working with others in the direction of mutual conformity to Christ (Rom. 8:29) is an emotional and psychological endeavor. At times one's emotions boil to the surface, while at other times a sheerly intellectual grasp of theology may come to the fore. In our passage, Paul's emotions are on display, and this section belongs to those passages (like 2 Cor. 1:12–2:13 and 7:2–16) where Paul is appealing to the Corinthians to be reconciled with God and himself.

Insofar as Paul's mission is pastoral theology and not abstract systematics, this part of the letter may be seen as climactic: his overarching mission in this letter is reconciliation, reconciliation among the Corinthians, with himself, and with God. Reconciliation with God entails reconciliation with Christ and reconciliation with Christ entails reconciliation with one another. Those in Christ are reconciled through Christ to God and therefore with one another. The vertical and the horizontal operate in tandem. All of 2 Corinthians 6:1–13 flows from Paul's appeal to reconciliation in 5:16–21.

Paul pleads with the Corinthians, who have fought Paul from the onset of his church work in Achaia (as one sees in 1 Cor. 1–4 and in 2 Cor. 10–13), not to "accept the grace of God in vain" (2 Cor. 6:1). This is a not-so-subtle way of saying, "Be reconciled to God by being reconciled with the gospel mission" (5:20–21). Paul contends that "now is the acceptable time" (6:2) and lists in detail how his ministry commends himself to their acceptance (the details extend from 6:3 to 6:10)! Then he admits his open vulnerability and pleads with them to become vulnerable to him (6:11–13).

One of Paul's favorite terms for his ministry companions is "coworkers" (*synergoi*; Rom. 16:3, 9, 21; 1 Cor. 3:9; 2 Cor. 8:23). The verb form of that term opens up 2 Corinthians 6, but here, he is not speaking in relation to his ministry companions or to the Corinthians. Here, Paul associates himself with God's work of reconciliation (5:16–21).[1] Paul's fear, even though he is confident (4:1, 15; 5:6, 8), is that the Corinthians, intoxicated as they are with the Roman way of life, with power mongering and displays of one's social status, might have accepted God's grace in Christ "in vain" (6:1). One is reminded of the strong appeal of Galatians 3:1–5 and even Romans 13–14. Paul knows that not affirming the resurrection renders vain one's preaching and faith (1 Cor. 15:14, 58).

So, Paul quotes Isaiah 49:8, a chapter bathed in Israel-remnant-servant imagery as a loving, faithful covenant God works to bring the exiles back home to Jerusalem. Paul sees his own mission to the Corinthians as (hopefully) accomplishing that same salvific purpose of God as he announces redemption in Christ! This appeal to Isaiah 49 is a pastorally creative and apocalyptic reading of the Bible backwards.[2] The mission of reconciliation has been fulfilled in Christ. Hence, "now is the acceptable time/day of salvation" (2 Cor. 6:2). The "now," then, is both eschatological and pastorally connected to this very moment in Paul's mission.

The apostle chooses to commend himself by turning the categories of Rome upside down in 6:4–10, which is a list of the hardships of ministry reframed by the gospel. Paul's listing breaks into at least four parts: verses 4–5, 6–7a, 7b–8a, and 8b–10. Murray Harris breaks these into outward circumstances, qualities of character, spiritual equipment, and the vicissitudes of ministry.[3] The first is about the hardships and sufferings of Paul's mission to announce to the nations the grace of God in Christ.

One has to wonder what Paul looked like after some two decades of gospel mission that had drawn forth opposition and physical violence. Broken bones and scars surely bore witness to the physical price of his mission work. Noticeably, Paul appeals to his own witness to the gospel as evidence for the gospel and as reasons for the Corinthians to respond favorably to the gospel mission. Weakness is a form of gospel power, as is made clear in 12:9–10 (the list in chapter 6 needs to be compared with the list in 11:23–33).

Paul's hardships are matched by his devotion to a life dedicated to being like Christ in purity, kindness, and love, and in truthful speech attended by God's power. Paul's approach to ministry, then, is not to claim power or to use violence against others. When Paul speaks of "weapons of righteousness," he means the power of a life conformed to the will of God revealed in Christ, the power of a life conformed to the crucifixion and resurrection of Jesus.

For Paul, this kind of life meant both "honor" (or "glory") and "dishonor," two terms that for the Corinthians described climbing the Roman path to glory (*cursus honorum*). That path was shaped by one's family, by one's wealth, by one's success in the military and sport and public eloquence. Paul rejects the *cursus honorum* because his life is shaped by the cross of Jesus. That will mean honor in relation to what is godly and dishonor in the view of his contemporaries. Paul is cutting against the Corinthians' ambitions. They want reputation and honor and fame. Paul strives for faithfulness thus he is dismissed as "impostor," "unknown," "dying," and "punished"! What matters to the Corinthians is social status; what matters to Paul is the gospel. What they see as negation, Paul sees as affirmation. What they see as bad news, Paul sees in the light of the glory of the cross. Thus, he can rejoice in sorrow, see himself as rich in the midst of poverty, and consider himself as possessing everything though he has nothing!

Second Corinthians 6:4–10 is all rhetorical criticism aimed by Paul at the Corinthians, for the world has overwhelmed their sense of gospel. This theme can be preached from every pulpit in America. We, too, are blinded by worldly ambition—by power, by reputation, by social status, and by wealth.

---

1. Victor Paul Furnish, *II Corinthians*, Anchor Bible 32A (Garden City, NY: Doubleday, 1984), 341.

2. Richard B. Hays, *Echoes of Scripture in the Letters of Paul* (New Haven, CT: Yale University Press, 1993); Hays, *Echoes of Scripture in the Gospels* (Waco, TX: Baylor University Press, 2016); Hays, *Reading Backwards: Figural Christology and the Fourfold Gospel Witness* (Waco, TX: Baylor University Press, 2014).

3. Murray J. Harris, *The Second Epistle to the Corinthians*, New International Greek Testament Commentary (Grand Rapids: Eerdmans, 2005), 466–67.

A final expression of vulnerability emerges in two forms in 6:11–13: his mouth is open ("we have spoken frankly") and his heart is widened ("our heart is wide open to you"). To "open one's mouth," a common idiom in Judaism, means to "speak from the depths of one's heart." To "open one's heart," also a common idiom, refers to Paul's desire to hear the truth from them—and he wants that truth to be their acceptance of his proclamation of the grace of God (those engaged in spiritual direction will know the reality of this proclamation as love). Paul believes the problem lies in a hard-heartedness fueled by their worldly ambitions, so his appeal is to vulnerability, for them to be as vulnerable to him as he is to them (6:13; an appeal he reiterates at 7:2). The apostle knows that Christian fellowship is formed on the basis of mutual vulnerability.

SCOT MCKNIGHT

Commentary 2: Connecting the Reading with the World

Today's lection turns upon integrity. Integrity essentially involves such qualities as trustworthiness, honor, dependability, strength of character, honesty, nobility, courage of convictions, virtue, sincerity, consistency. These are the same qualities and characteristics we expect of faithful disciples and stewards.

Today we live in a culture where suspicion and mistrust are so prevalent that many people question whether integrity even exists anymore. In surveys and interviews in which people are asked to name those they believe have integrity, they call to mind historic figures of almost mythic stature—Gandhi, Abraham Lincoln, Mother Teresa, Nelson Mandela, Franklin Roosevelt (people who were often criticized for their failings and lack of integrity when they were alive). In fact, discussions about integrity often devolve quickly into conversations about the *lack* of integrity. Sweeping generalization of those who lack integrity—business leaders, politicians, media personalities, celebrities, journalists—rouse much stronger emotional responses than lists of those we believe embody integrity. Suspicion in our contemporary context is so deep and pervasive that if a person appears too good to be true, they must have some deep, dark, despicable side hidden underneath their bright exterior.

Apparently, such suspicions were raised about Paul and the early apostolic leaders of the Christian movement. To be treated as impostors for sharing a message of grace and acceptance; to be dishonored as fakes and frauds for proclaiming forgiveness and love; to be castigated as liars and tricksters for offering salvation—these must have been difficult and trying times for people attempting to live their faith with integrity. It was challenging for early audiences to accept the gospel as a true gift freely given. Why would the apostles and evangelists endure such hardships, make such sacrifices, deny themselves comforts, and risk torment and imprisonment with no benefit or reward? The wisdom of God often appears as foolishness to humankind.

It is all too human to think the worst of others, to question their motives, second-guess their actions, and make negative assumptions about their values. Why is this so common? Central to Paul's message to the church at Corinth is that what seems impossible to mere mortals can be achieved through faith in Jesus Christ. Where ordinary people might avoid hardship and affliction, Christians are empowered by God to rise above such limitations. The heart transformed by God's grace fosters great endurance, a holiness of spirit, and a genuine love for others. It is also by God's guidance that we are able to stop believing the worst about others and find the capacity to believe only the best.

One compelling illustration of the power of faith to transform a meek and gentle soul into a champion of faith is depicted in the movie *Romero*, a film about the life and martyrdom of Archbishop Óscar Romero. Romero became a beacon and symbol of hope for the oppressed peoples of El Salvador. In one scene Father Romero attempts to enter a church under occupation by the military. They turn him away, even firing a machine gun at him as he picks up pieces of the host scattered by destruction of the altar.

Sweating and afraid, Romero leaves the church, passing by the desperate and despairing faces of the villagers. His automobile disappears in a cloud of dust. Moments later it reappears and returns to the church. The archbishop dons his robes and his stole and, with head held high, he leads the people in to reclaim the church. The soldiers stand by, bowing their heads in shame. There is no explanation for his transformation beyond the empowerment of a Holy Spirit dedicated to humble and selfless service. His witness is transforming and inspirational to friends and enemies alike.

Mother Teresa inspired millions of people and dedicated her life to serving the poor in Calcutta. Her lifetime of sacrificial service was a true incarnation of the gospel. Journalist Christopher Hitchens attempted to discredit Mother Teresa in his exposé, *The Missionary Position: Mother Teresa in Theory and Practice.*[4] The essence of Hitchens's argument is simple: Mother Teresa must have had ulterior motives for her service—fame, popularity, power, or money—because no one could give so much to so many without hope of personal gain. The book was highly criticized for its flawed central premise that there is no such thing as a selfless act. Christopher Hitchens was not alone in his skepticism. Many people find it difficult to believe that some give openly and freely to others.

Suspicion is easy, especially in a day when facts are fluid and truth is subjective. From unsubstantiated information on Wikipedia to "fake news" and Facebook pages passing as the real deal to scary scam phone calls supposedly from the IRS or one's bank, people are almost forced to be skeptical and cynical if they want to avoid being the victim of some con. Twenty-four-hour news outlets that align with particular political parties, corporate sponsors, and celebrity pundits infuse information with subtle (and not so subtle) biases, postures, and positions. Many people tune in to find confirmation for current beliefs and understanding rather than to find real information and to learn or have perspectives challenged. It becomes ever more difficult to "know what we do not know," because it is so easy to hear only what we want to hear.

Paul and the early apostles definitely brought a new message that challenged long-standing and widely held core beliefs and values. It is little wonder that they encountered the kind of resistance they discovered. Just the concept of having nothing, yet possessing everything, would have been threatening to many. While cultures and generations differ greatly in many respects, the values of money, power, and fame transcend time and place. Historically, individuals who challenge the status quo have been viewed as threats. To offer blessing to the poor and extend woe to the rich defies common sense and is about as countercultural a message as one can preach. Honoring gentleness and meekness over power, humility and contentment over fame, and simplicity and poverty over wealth seem ridiculous in cultures structured around achievement, popularity, and success, but this is the foundation upon which our Christian faith is built.

Some may resist the idea that we should be judged on the merit of our actions. Others may question why Christians should be held to a different, higher standard for our conduct. Yet this is central to our identity as followers of Jesus the Christ. "Thus you will know them by their fruits" (Matt. 7:20).

To teach unconditional love and unmerited grace, to offer forgiveness and open acceptance, and to live a life of kindness, compassion, mercy, and justice are almost certain to cause raised eyebrows and suspicious stares. Who in their right mind would voluntarily subject themselves to inconvenience, hunger, deprivation, discomfort, risk, sacrifice, and criticism, just to help another person? Perhaps that is the point. No one in their right mind would do so, but this is precisely what we are called to do as faithful Christian disciples. For those filled by God's grace and Spirit, right now is the day of salvation, and right now is the most acceptable time to put faith into action and to live a life worthy of the gospel to which we have been called. The world may continue to operate by values that praise power, wealth, and fame, but for the children of God there are things of much greater value.

DAN R. DICK

---

4. See Christopher Hitchens, *The Missionary Position: Mother Teresa in Theory and Practice* (New York: Verso, 1995).

Mark 4:35–41

[35]On that day, when evening had come, he said to them, "Let us go across to the other side." [36]And leaving the crowd behind, they took him with them in the boat, just as he was. Other boats were with him. [37]A great windstorm arose, and the waves beat into the boat, so that the boat was already being swamped. [38]But he was in the stern, asleep on the cushion; and they woke him up and said to him, "Teacher, do you not care that we are perishing?" [39]He woke up and rebuked the wind, and said to the sea, "Peace! Be still!" Then the wind ceased, and there was a dead calm. [40]He said to them, "Why are you afraid? Have you still no faith?" [41]And they were filled with great awe and said to one another, "Who then is this, that even the wind and the sea obey him?"

Commentary 1: Connecting the Reading with Scripture

"Let us go to the other side" (Mark 4:35) names Jesus' move from Capernaum to Gentile cities, signaling the inclusive *koinōnia* he envisions.[1] This mirrors the inclusiveness of Jesus' parables of the Good Samaritan (Luke 10:25–37) and of the Sheep and the Goats (Matt. 25:31–46). Who proved to be a neighbor? The one who helped, a Samaritan. What distinguishes the sheep? Not kinship relation, nationality, or religious tradition, but the one who fed, visited, clothed, and gave comfort. Also, consider Mark 3:31–35. Who are true kin of Jesus? "Whoever does the will of God."

As the unjust realities of life kick us in the face, the idea that God protects the faithful from harm is exposed as naive. Many who think they are rejecting faith are actually rejecting this pseudofaith. A lucky few can affirm this faith and believe the calming of the sea in another of today's lections, where the Lord stills a storm (Ps. 107:29; cf. Mark 6:45–52). In Jesus' day, there were many miracle workers. Special power did not settle the question of identity. Jesus' opponents do not question his power but its *source*, calling him an agent of Beelzebub (Mark 3:20–22).

This applies also to the disciples' question, "Who then is this?" (4:41). Most baffling

vis-à-vis Jesus is what is the identity of one who can calm angry seas but ends up dead on a Roman cross? Mark's audience lives in the shadow and the light of the cross. In Mark, upon Jesus' death a Roman centurion, of all people, becomes the first human to say what demons say from the beginning (1:24; 1:34): "Truly this man was God's Son!" (15:39).[2] The mystery of faith is evident when we wonder, "What did the Roman have eyes to see—not in the wake of power over storms, casting out of demons, or healings—but in Jesus' crucifixion?"

Mark says demons recognize Jesus as "the Holy One of God" (1:24) and says Jesus tells them not to tell (1:25; 3:11–12). Jesus also tells people healed not to tell (1:34; 1:43–45; 3:12; 5:43; 8:30; 9:9). This all names an important theme in Mark: miracles do not produce faith. Faith produces miracles. Accordingly, to the woman with a hemorrhage: "Daughter, your faith has made you well" (5:34; cf. healing of man with paralysis at 2:5: "When Jesus saw their faith . . ."). Mark tells us about Jesus' authority and power, but Mark also works to ensure we have the faith of that woman, faith that precedes and brings healing. Mark nowhere forthrightly defines faith. As with the woman, we are everywhere left to infer. From her we

---

1. John Donahue, "Mark," in *Harper's Bible Commentary*, ed. James L. Mays (San Francisco: Harper & Row, 1989), 990.
2. Donahue, "Mark," 985.

may conclude faith brings persistence, daring, confidence, and a sense of self-worth.

We too easily find a moral in Jesus' calming of the storm. If you have enough faith, you will have God's favor. We hard-heartedly chalk up others' misfortune to their lack of faith. Some who suffer or are persecuted may affirm this faith and, tragically, blame themselves for not having enough faith (e.g., the prosperity gospel). In these cases, we are dealing with people who have listened but not understood. The idea that "if only you have enough faith, all will be well," is naive, and crediting one's own or others' suffering to a lack of faith is confused, harmful, and tragic. Mark's audience was unlikely to make such mistakes.

Mark is written to a Jewish Christian community in imperial Rome in the tumultuous early 70s. Paul has long since been martyred. Peter has just been martyred along with many others in the persecutions of Nero (Mark is mentioned as a companion to Peter [1 Pet. 5:13]). In response to insurrection, Rome is violently crushing the Jewish state.[3] The Markan community is literally caught in a deadly storm. The disciples' question, "Teacher, do you not care that we are perishing?" (4:38), gives voice to the question of so many in Mark's community and throughout history who are suffering or persecuted and cry out, "Where are you, God? Do you not care?"

Now, within the Gospel, after baptizing Jesus, John the Baptist is arrested and disappears at Mark 1:14 (the Baptist's martyrdom is described in Matt. 14:1–12). The shadow of the cross looms from the earliest chapters of Mark (see esp. 3:6). In addition, again, Mark's audience knows that many faithful people, including John the Baptist, Peter, and Paul, have been persecuted and murdered. Obviously, any supposed connection between true faith and worldly security is confused. So, when Jesus says, "Why are you afraid? Have you still no faith?" *the faith his followers lack is not the pseudofaith that Jesus will save them from the storm.*

In Mark, the power of Jesus and of God is not in question, but as the fate of Jesus, John the Baptist, Peter, Paul, and so many other heroes of the faith makes clear, faith and God's power do not ensure worldly security. This confusion reaches its zenith in Mark in the so-called triumphal entry, where the crowds shout out their hope that Jesus will throw off Roman occupation, renew the political kingdom, and take up the mantle of David (11:10). This is an understandable hope, and Jesus certainly demonstrates and urges concrete concern for the oppressed, but nonetheless this is a vision of triumph—one to which Judas evidently remained captive (14:10–11, 43–45)—that is very different from the triumph the centurion has eyes to see on the cross.

This chapter begins with the sower. The disciples' faithless terror in the boat numbers them among those who hear the word, only to have it choked out by the cares of the world (4:18–19). Jesus sleeps—a vision of the peace delivered by faith even amid the storms of life. What if the boat is swamped and all drown? Is such a fate to be met with equanimity? No. For, as is clear throughout the Gospel, Jesus actively resists and encourages struggle against oppressive forces (he is such a concrete threat that the establishment plots to have him killed). Is such a fate to be met with faith that endures even unto death? Yes. For as Mark's readers know, true faith leads Jesus to the cross and others on that boat to martyrdom. True faith, then, is not only stronger than a most fearsome foe. It is most clearly manifest precisely as it triumphs over fear of death.

However, what of Jesus, John the Baptist, Paul, Peter, those slain by Nero, and the rest of that martyred multitude "of whom the world was not worthy" (Heb. 11:38)? The fundamental question concerns the ultimate character of reality. Resurrection of some sort becomes decisive (Matt. 28; Mark 16; Luke 24; John 20). If Jesus triumphs in fidelity but is dead, period, then the universe is ultimately tragic; what is good and loving and just is real but not ultimate. Jesus' fidelity unto death *and* resurrection, by contrast, tells a more complex but ultimately hopeful tale. Jesus' stilling of the waters testifies to the ultimate power of love (anticipating resurrection). The renewed power of the faith that flagged in the storm is not faith that God will protect us in this life, but a faith that triumphs

---

3. Donahue, "Mark," 983–84.

even unto death on a cross, a faith secure in the knowledge that "neither death . . . nor rulers . . . nor powers, nor height, nor depth . . . will be able to separate us from the love of God in Christ Jesus our Lord" (Rom. 8:38–39).

WILLIAM GREENWAY

Commentary 2: Connecting the Reading with the World

Sermons on the miracle stories of Jesus can challenge the spiritual imaginations of congregants. How might the boundaries of those imaginations need to be expanded? First, to imaginations framed within a secular scientific mind-set, miracle-story sermons can easily be dismissed as idle tales. ("That's just another version of an ancient storm god myth.") Second, to imaginations imbued with sentimental piety, miracle-story sermons can sound like a reinforcement of long-cherished religious feelings. ("Life's storms often seem overwhelming, but I must have faith that Jesus will calm them.") Third, to imaginations haunted by a sense of personal spiritual failure or a feeling of having been failed by a God in whom trust has seemed misplaced, miracle-story sermons might provoke anger, frustration, or resentment. ("Jesus did not save *my* boat; Jesus was not even *in* my boat!") Fourth, to imaginations prewired to anticipate a standard narrative trope—from "once upon a time" to "happily ever after"—miracle-story sermons can be heard as entertaining but ultimately predictable. ("After an uneventful departure, the boaters found themselves in serious trouble; but, just in time, on *that* day, Jesus woke up and saved the day; and he will do the same on *this*.")

Some listeners' imaginations may include elements from all these. Moreover, this story Mark tells of Jesus calming the sea is so familiar, listeners may think they already have a good idea just what it means. It is a challenge for preachers to make this text a challenge.

Fortunately (though dauntingly), the way Mark tells the story does not lend itself to a standard narrative trajectory moving from conflict to resolution. The fears of the disciples are not calmed by the calming of the storm. They are intensified. The Jesus in Mark's Gospel to this point has functioned as the quintessential storm chaser in his dealings with everyone he encounters.

Then, in his calming of this sea squall, Jesus creates for his disciples a storm far greater. In their journey with Jesus thus far, they have been privileged, safe observers of his healings, exorcisms, teachings, and controversies. Now they are in the thick of it, swamped up to their necks. While Jesus calms the elements with one sharp word, he names the internal, spiritual storm raging in his followers with another—a confrontational, "Why are you afraid?" Not a rhetorical question, or one that masks a condemnation, but an invitation to discernment: "Let's talk."

So, rather than getting tangled in (1) defending the scientific status of the miracle, (2) reinforcing (or undermining) anyone's religious piety, (3) trying to apologize for faith in what has been perceived as a hoax, or (4) laboring under the parameters of a standard narrative sermon structure—what if we pick up on the question Jesus poses to his disciples who, standing amid still waters, are still shaking in their sandals? What if the preacher tries to help listeners reflect upon the nature and status of their faith, to consider how that faith may be lacking, and why that is the case?

Preachers might begin by leading their listeners in specific storm naming. What are the raging waters tossing us this way and that, threatening to overwhelm us in personal relationships, jobs, our faith community, our living locality—the ecological, economic, social, and political disorders in which we are immersed? Maybe harder yet to face and name, what resentments do we experience at being left seemingly helpless in them? ("Don't you even *care,* Jesus?") Not inconceivably, and harder still, we might ask, What terrors do we not dare bring to Jesus because the very alleviating of them might render us even more terrified? ("Thank God I did not lose my job; but what am I supposed to be doing about the gnawing lack of meaning in my life?" "Her physical recovery seems miraculous—but what about our broken relationship?")

What counterfeit "fear-fixing" claims might we and our congregants be subjected to and easily seduced by? What propositions offer simplistic or agenda-driven promises of "peace, peace, when there is no peace" (Jer. 6:14)? ("If we just close our borders, we will keep out criminals who threaten our security and workers who take our jobs!")

Jesus seems to suggest, in Mark's telling of this story, that faith and fear are mutually incompatible. Is that necessarily or always so? If "the fear of the LORD is the beginning of wisdom," might there be some wisdom in the possibility of other expressions of faithful fearing? Might that lead productively to explorations as to what "faith" is anyway? Is the "trust" we have in God an unshakable presumption that God sees the world just as we do, and thus that we need take no risks of which we cannot reasonably control the outcomes?[4] Might fear as cowardice be something very different from fear as humility and awe? Might Jesus be challenging the disciples to distinguish between healthy and unhealthy fear?

This is the first of two "sea crossing" stories that Mark tells (the other is in Mark 6:45–52). Both are voyages to and from "the other side." What is Mark prompting listeners to consider in these goings back and forth? One group of scholars offers this response:

> The wind and waves in Mark's story, as cosmic forces of opposition (see Psalm 104:7), symbolize everything that impedes Jesus' attempted "boundary crossing." The enmity between Jew and Gentile was seen by most of Mark's contemporaries as the prototype of all human hostility. The separation between them was considered part of

the "natural order." Mark's harrowing sea stories suggest that the task of social reconciliation was not only difficult but virtually inconceivable.[5]

As we preachers seek to shape a challenge both grounded in this text and connected with our world, we might reflect on current tasks of social reconciliation that seem analogously inconceivable. There are storms of immigrants at national borders and stormy debates about immigration policy. Income inequality is a gathering storm. Claims of racial and sexual discrimination—and their denial—are stark indications of social upheaval. Civility is being supplanted by savagery in political and social discourse. (Consider, for instance, the mutual discounting of and increasing disdain between "coastal elites" and residents of "flyover" Middle America.) What some partisans claim as "facts," opponents dismiss as "fake news." There are few if any shared points of reference—and no neutral umpires recognized by competing player-advocates all bent on "winning." All these stress points leave us in storm-tossed social equilibrium.

How much safer to remain on our own side of the shore! Who wants to be ordered by Jesus into seas that quickly turn tumultuous? If "he is with us in the boat," why does he seem to be asleep in it? Does he not care that we, his followers, could die out here? What if the best way *out* of the storm were to stand both *with* and *for* Jesus *in* it? What might that entail in different settings?

What if storms that rage outside the boat are exacerbated by fear-storms raging inside us? What if shutdowns on the surface of the sea remove a distraction from facing those fears? How can we find faith in a salvation that is not just an idealistic version of the artist rendering of a still life (e.g., responding to angry threats with quiet clarity)? What might it mean, as Jesus does, to listen to our fears and speak into them?

DAVID J. SCHLAFER

---

4. I explore this theme in *The Shattering Sound of Amazing Grace: Disquieting Tales from Saint John's Gospel* (Cambridge, MA: Cowley, 2006).

5. Ched Myers, Marie Dennis, Joseph Nangle, Cynthia Moe-Lobeda, and Stuart Taylor, *"Say to This Mountain": Mark's Story of Discipleship* (Maryknoll, NY: Orbis, 1996), 57.

Proper 8 (Sunday between June 26 and July 2)

Lamentations 3:22–33 and
   2 Samuel 1:1, 17–27
Psalm 30 and Psalm 130

2 Corinthians 8:7–15
Mark 5:21–43

Lamentations 3:22–33

[22]The steadfast love of the LORD never ceases,
   his mercies never come to an end;
[23]they are new every morning;
   great is your faithfulness.
[24]"The LORD is my portion," says my soul,
   "therefore I will hope in him."

[25]The LORD is good to those who wait for him,
   to the soul that seeks him.
[26]It is good that one should wait quietly
   for the salvation of the LORD.
[27]It is good for one to bear
   the yoke in youth,
[28]to sit alone in silence
   when the Lord has imposed it,
[29]to put one's mouth to the dust
   (there may yet be hope),
[30]to give one's cheek to the smiter,
   and be filled with insults.

[31]For the Lord will not
   reject forever.
[32]Although he causes grief, he will have compassion
   according to the abundance of his steadfast love;
[33]for he does not willingly afflict
   or grieve anyone.

2 Samuel 1:1, 17–27

[1]After the death of Saul, when David had returned from defeating the Amalekites, David remained two days in Ziklag. . . .
   [17]David intoned this lamentation over Saul and his son Jonathan. [18](He ordered that The Song of the Bow be taught to the people of Judah; it is written in the Book of Jashar.) He said:

[19]Your glory, O Israel, lies slain upon your high places!
   How the mighty have fallen!
[20]Tell it not in Gath,
   proclaim it not in the streets of Ashkelon;
or the daughters of the Philistines will rejoice,
   the daughters of the uncircumcised will exult.

²¹You mountains of Gilboa,
　　let there be no dew or rain upon you,
　　nor bounteous fields!
For there the shield of the mighty was defiled,
　　the shield of Saul, anointed with oil no more.

²²From the blood of the slain,
　　from the fat of the mighty,
the bow of Jonathan did not turn back,
　　nor the sword of Saul return empty.

²³Saul and Jonathan, beloved and lovely!
　　In life and in death they were not divided;
they were swifter than eagles,
　　they were stronger than lions.

²⁴O daughters of Israel, weep over Saul,
　　who clothed you with crimson, in luxury,
　　who put ornaments of gold on your apparel.

²⁵How the mighty have fallen
　　in the midst of the battle!

Jonathan lies slain upon your high places.
　　²⁶I am distressed for you, my brother Jonathan;
greatly beloved were you to me;
　　your love to me was wonderful,
　　passing the love of women.

²⁷How the mighty have fallen,
　　and the weapons of war perished!

Commentary 1: Connecting the Reading with Scripture

The little book called Lamentations is a collection of poems grieving the loss of Jerusalem, its institutions, and many of its inhabitants, during the sixth century BCE. The poetic segment in 3:22–33 is in the center of the central poem of the book, which may highlight its significance. It is difficult to understand the complex poem in Lamentations 3 as the product of a single voice. It appears to be a dialogue or even a debate. The verses that precede 3:22–33 express despair. The speaker of these verses believes that God has inflicted pain and suffering upon him, and he has lost all hope. These kinds of expressions are typically omitted from lectionary readings, as they have been this week, while focus is placed upon the happier verses around them. The voice that responds to the despairing character seeks to change the attitude of that speaker, and

suggests waiting patiently for a divine shift away from punishment toward comfort. At first, this response sound callous and naive, failing to acknowledge the suffering of the first speaker.

Readers who sense an even greater degree of interruption in verses 22–24 than in the larger section may be recognizing a source of some discontinuity in the history of transmission of this text. These verses are not present in some Greek manuscripts of the Old Testament. They were likely omitted because of the similarity of the phrases at the ends of verse 21 and verse 24. The language of verses 22–24 may sound familiar, because it is laden with what sound like biblical clichés.

A look at where some of these appear in the Bible may be useful. The phrase in verse 24, "The LORD is my portion," appears in similar forms several times in Psalms (Pss. 16:5; 73:26; 119:57; 142:5). The claim that "the steadfast love of the LORD never ceases" is reminiscent of the frequent refrain, "the steadfast love of the LORD endures forever" (Pss. 100, 106, 107, and 118; 1 Chr. 16; 2 Chr. 5 and 7). These clichés in verses 22–24 connect to the phrase, "the LORD is good," in verse 25, which also appears in many other texts, some included in the lists above.

Religious clichés are a double-edged sword. They become familiar because people have found them reliable and helpful, particularly at times when life's challenges have shut down more creative ways of thinking about faith. They are like a reflex, but like reflexes they can be difficult to control and may yield unwanted results. By saying them we may be dodging our own discomfort, while doing little or nothing for the person to whom we say them.

The suffering of the earlier speaker finally finds acknowledgment in verses 29–30, and once again there is some disruption in the history of how this text has been transmitted. All or part of verse 29 is missing from some Greek manuscripts. Nobody knows exactly what it means "to put one's mouth to the dust," or how this is related to the line about hope that follows it. The puzzling nature of the verse may have led to its alteration or omission. The speaker counsels the sufferer to accept this affliction. It may be that the one hearing this advice is powerless to do anything else, but given the agony that surrounds this section of Lamentations, it sounds empty.

The name of this book comes from a word that means to cry out in pain, so how does encouraging silence fit into such a book? There is considerable tension in the little stanza of verses 31–33. The lines are difficult to translate, and the core issue seems to be whether Israel's God chooses to afflict the human(s) addressed in this part of the poem. The ambiguous answer is reminiscent of the puzzling statement about God's judgment and forgiveness in Exodus 34:6–7, which is repeated in whole or in part at many places in the Bible. The easy and callous comments often uttered to those who are suffering ignore the difference between observing that something good may come out of suffering and claiming that the benefit is the purpose of suffering and acts as adequate compensation for it.

The poem in 2 Samuel 1:17–27, which the text calls "The Song of the Bow" functions in the narrative as a lament for King Saul. David, one of Saul's potential successors, leads the people in this song, which demands attention to its political dimensions. The second half of the book called 1 Samuel presents the long conflict between Saul and David, two figures whose relationship is complex and confusing. First Samuel 31 tells the story of a wounded Saul, having lost a battle to the Philistines, taking his own life on Mount Gilboa. Second Samuel 1 opens with a messenger who has run from the battle, claiming to have killed the wounded Saul at the king's request. David orders the man executed before leading the people of Judah in the song of mourning.

It is important to see that David has a lot to gain if others choose to join him in the singing. David's chief rival for the throne is Saul's own son, Ishbaal. Note that the text gives attention to David's grief and not that of Saul's son. Clearly, David is making a play for the throne by avenging the dead king and claiming the leadership role in public mourning. This realization should send us back to the Lamentations 3 passage to ask what the speaker of verses 22–33 has to gain if the speaker of verses 1–21 accepts the invitation to join in a more hopeful song, or be silent. When the crisis of destruction and loss was over, did religious orthodoxy begin to reassert itself in order to facilitate the rebuilding of religious institutions?

Such a movement is apparent in other parts of the Old Testament. One of the most obvious is the ending of the book of Ecclesiastes. Following eleven chapters of ruminations by the character the book calls Qoheleth, often expressing the futility of life and doubts about the virtues of faithfulness, a different voice appears in 12:1–8 that reaffirms a more traditional understanding of Israelite religion, and even pretends that this is what the Qoheleth character has been saying all along. The final ten verses of the book of Job also appear to return to a simple equation of reward for faithfulness, after the long dialogue that precedes them raises painful questions about the adequacy of such a framework.

The Gospel text for this week includes a sequence of events in the life of Jesus in which religious language offers challenge, comfort, and temptation. When Jesus says things like "Your faith has made you well" (Mark 5:34), or "Do not fear, only believe" (5:36), it is easy to pull such pithy sayings out of a complex story, strip them of their rough edges, and plug them into another story, assuming they will fit naturally. When we respond to the pain or struggles of another person with tired, detached sayings like "God is in control" or "Everything happens for a reason," there is some chance it will speak to that person's need, but it may be ill fit for their situation. The reflexive repetition of platitudes shows no sign that we have listened and given careful thought to the lives into which we speak them. Seizing control of religious conversation and seeking to tame unusual or uncomfortable expression in order to replace it with the easy or the familiar is a move that should make communities of faith wary.

MARK MCENTIRE

Commentary 2: Connecting the Reading with the World

Lament. The word itself feels heavy. To lament means to mourn, to grieve, to wail in response to loss. It is often a public expression of the raw, inner pain a person feels when faced with death, destruction, dashed hopes, and devastation; lament can be an appropriate, certainly understandable, and perhaps necessary response.

One of the texts for today is from the book aptly named Lamentations, a record of the prophet Jeremiah's despair over the losses he witnessed: the ruin of a city; the dire straits this devastation caused for its inhabitants; the depths to which people went simply to survive; and the totality of this destruction with very little hope on the horizon. Lamentations leaves us with a picture of a zombie-like existence, visualized in popular films such as *Night of the Living Dead* or *The Book of Eli* and a postapocalyptic world of survival of the fittest, clips that can be used as illustrations in sermons. Lamentations evokes scenes such as these, with persons walking around the hollowed-out streets and buildings of their city in total shock, perhaps crying out, "Why?"

The second text is another story of lament, David's lament at the deaths of Saul and Jonathan (1 Sam. 31). Here, too, David's grief comes from the deep loss he experienced, "intoned" in a song. This, too, is a public expression of grief coupled with anger at the means by which Saul and Jonathan were killed. Both of these texts narrate the multiple causes of destruction and loss; the various responses that humans have, such as paralyzing grief, deep anger, resentment, and fear; and certainly the theological and moral questions raised, leaving persons to ask, "Why?"

These texts can take preachers and congregations in many directions as they hear these Scriptures read and a sermon preached that connects to the very real experience of lament and grief.

A first connection might actually be a connection to avoid: the temptation to answer the "why?" of lament. In 2 Samuel 1:19–21, David does not answer the "why" but describes what happened. Saul and Jonathan were killed in war, with Saul "falling on his sword" when he was wounded in battle (1 Sam. 31:4–6). David does not ascribe reasons to God or some abstract and unknown references to God's purposes. Even if he did, nothing would change or ameliorate his loss. He is grieving *and* angry at the means by which Saul and Jonathan died, and is giving voice to this experience, as congregants do in lamenting the loss of persons killed in the brutality of wars.

Theological reflection and interpretation on scriptural texts are influenced by cultural contexts in which we live. Those of us in contexts shaped by the hopes of scientific inquiry, and the belief that every effect has a cause that can be identified, are often pressed to find answers to the causes of lament and human suffering. The education we have received, and even the pastoral training we have undergone, pushes us in the direction of finding answers to questions and then giving these answers to others, as if this solves the existential nature of suffering.

Answers elude us but one answer to lament is lament itself, that is, allowing people to actually lament.[1] Preachers can give permission for congregants to do this as they relate the stories

---

1. See Nicholas Wolterstorff, *Lament for a Son* (Grand Rapids: Eerdmans, 1987).

of loss in these texts to the losses that members of their congregations have experienced. Loss of friends and family members, loss of homes and jobs, loss of health, among many other losses, elicit normal responses of lament.

A second connection for preaching is noting that there is no "one size fits all" form to lament. David's song of lament mourns the loss of Saul and Jonathan. However, one wonders if this might have created some inner conflict for David, knowing the troubled relationship he had with Saul, the one who was jealous of him and tried to have him killed. The way in which David lamented Saul's death is different from his more personal response to Jonathan's. David calls Israel to "weep over Saul" (2 Sam. 1:24), a more general invitation to lament. Yet his grief over Jonathan's death is more personal: "I am distressed for you, my brother Jonathan; greatly beloved were you to me" (v. 26). David lamented differently in different circumstances, as we do.

It would be important to acknowledge this in sermons, as well as in eulogies for funerals and memorial services. Often eulogies at funerals leave persons wondering, "Is this the same person *I* knew?" Congregants may still lament for people they did not particularly like without feeling they are hypocritical. Noting the different ways in which David laments these losses will connect with the different ways in which congregants lament the deaths of others without feeling guilty, when they might not be able to say, "Greatly beloved were you to me."

The third connection can be found in the prophet Jeremiah in Lamentations. The prophet is the one who experienced lament (after all, this was his city and his friends) and the one who helped others in their lament by providing a voice of hope. It is significant that these words of hope in 3:22–33 do not come at the end of the book. They come in the middle of the poems and prayers of lament expressed by Jeremiah. Jeremiah also is "bowed down" but can call to mind that the "steadfast love of the LORD never ceases" (Lam. 3:22). Jeremiah makes no promises that "time will heal" the wounds of loss but does acknowledge God's presence *in* time.

This "new every morning" promise of God's faithfulness and steadfast love is every morning of every day followed by the cycles of night. This is the ground of hope for Jeremiah, not a false optimism that tomorrow will be better, but that every morning God will be faithfully present, even as we lament. These words of hope do not make lament go away. Hope is not a tidy ending that provides "closure" to our lamenting. Hope comes in the midst of lament where it might be most needed.

A final connection is the recognition that lament is called for and necessary as a prophetic and pastoral act. Lament is a legitimate response. In other words, we *should* lament, and preachers must call congregants to do so. Walter Brueggemann in *The Prophetic Imagination* notes prophetic lament as a critique of a culture—and yes, even a church culture—that prefers unresponsiveness and becomes indifferent and apathetic. Lament is hard and painful as it names what is wrong, and even our own complicities in these wrongs, calling us to repent from our own preferred numbness and thoughtlessness.

Jeremiah is a model for this kind of prophetic lament and, for Brueggemann, is also a model for preachers. Like Jeremiah, preachers can make public lament in sermons, speaking about the realities of our world, penetrating the numbness in which we hide. Speaking truthfully about "what is" is important, yet sermons offer "an alternative perception of reality" by "letting people see their own history in light of God's freedom and his will for justice."[2] Sermons can allow persons to lament, and even call on us to do so. For all those killed in the brutalities and scorched earth of war? Lament. For racial, gender, and economic injustice? Lament. For the loss of hope and vision for a future? Lament. Even in lament, there is hope as the prophet reminds us, but perhaps only understood when we fully grasp the necessity of lament.

WYNDY CORBIN REUSCHLING

---

2. Walter Brueggemann, *The Prophetic Imagination* (Minneapolis: Fortress, 1978), 110.

Psalm 30

[1]I will extol you, O LORD, for you have drawn me up,
   and did not let my foes rejoice over me.
[2]O LORD my God, I cried to you for help,
   and you have healed me.
[3]O LORD, you brought up my soul from Sheol,
   restored me to life from among those gone down to the Pit.

[4]Sing praises to the LORD, O you his faithful ones,
   and give thanks to his holy name.
[5]For his anger is but for a moment;
   his favor is for a lifetime.
Weeping may linger for the night,
   but joy comes with the morning.

[6]As for me, I said in my prosperity,
   "I shall never be moved."
[7]By your favor, O LORD,
   you had established me as a strong mountain;
you hid your face;
   I was dismayed.

[8]To you, O LORD, I cried,
   and to the LORD I made supplication:
[9]"What profit is there in my death,
   if I go down to the Pit?
Will the dust praise you?
   Will it tell of your faithfulness?
[10]Hear, O LORD, and be gracious to me!
   O LORD, be my helper!"

[11]You have turned my mourning into dancing;
   you have taken off my sackcloth
   and clothed me with joy,
[12]so that my soul may praise you and not be silent.
   O LORD my God, I will give thanks to you forever.

Psalm 130

[1]Out of the depths I cry to you, O LORD.
   [2]Lord, hear my voice!
Let your ears be attentive
   to the voice of my supplications!

[3]If you, O LORD, should mark iniquities,
   Lord, who could stand?
[4]But there is forgiveness with you,
   so that you may be revered.

⁵I wait for the LORD, my soul waits,
   and in his word I hope;
⁶my soul waits for the Lord
   more than those who watch for the morning,
   more than those who watch for the morning.

⁷O Israel, hope in the LORD!
   For with the LORD there is steadfast love,
   and with him is great power to redeem.
⁸It is he who will redeem Israel
   from all its iniquities.

Connecting the Psalm with Scripture and Worship

Psalm 30. The alternate reading for the day is Lamentations 3:22–33, words of assurance about God's steadfast love that punctuate the lament and anguish surrounding the passage. The author knows unthinkable suffering, described in the first twenty verses of Lamentations 3, *and* the author knows the love of God. Similar to Psalm 130, with its tension between hope and lament, the Lamentations passage speaks assurances of grace into a context of the deepest desperation. The theme of the passage is hope: hope in God's mercy and love coexisting with the experience of great suffering and pain.

The reading from Lamentations 3 is forward looking: the poet (Lamentations' "strong man") is in the midst of great suffering, looking with hope for a day when the suffering will cease, "for the Lord will not reject forever" (Lam. 3:31).[1] When Psalm 30 is read in response to Lamentations 3, it offers an alternate perspective: the words of a poet who has survived suffering, looking back rather than forward. The psalmist bears witness to a relief that the author of Lamentations has not experienced, and the prayerful emotions of the two passages may be heard more clearly when read in conversation with one another. In verses 9–10, the psalmist remembers the prayers offered during great suffering, prayers that sound and feel like the words of Lamentations.

Psalm 30 bears a superscription associating it with the Feast of Dedication, a celebration marking the people of Israel's return to proper worship under the rule of the Maccabees (165 BCE) after the temple destruction. While the words of the psalm have certainly been used to celebrate Hanukkah since as early as the second century BCE, the psalm itself appears to be a much older individual song of thanksgiving.[2] The psalm is concerned primarily with praise, praise for God's deliverance. The psalmist "will extol" God (Ps. 30:1a); the Hebrew for extol (*rum*) literally means "lift up." The psalmist will lift up God's name, for God has lifted the psalmist out of great suffering (v. 1b). The psalmist takes care, however, to say that God's praise will not come only in times of prosperity. The psalmist will praise God "forever" (v. 12), and in remembering God's mercy, the psalmist says in hope, "I shall never be moved" (v. 6).

In 2015, the people of Emmanuel A.M.E. Church in Charleston, South Carolina, experienced unimaginable suffering when a young white man, whom they welcomed into their church for Bible study, murdered nine people in an attempt to start a race war. Thousands of eyes were glued to television sets and computer screens to watch the powerful funeral for Emmanuel's pastor, the Rev. Clementa Pinckney. In a powerful eulogy, Bishop John Richard Bryant repeated Psalm 30 in call-and-response style. "Weeping may endure for the night," he said, and the crowd responded, "but joy comes in the morning." Like

1. Kathleen M. O'Connor, "The Book of Lamentations," in *The New Interpreter's Bible* (Nashville: Abingdon, 1996), 6:1204.
2. J. Clinton McCann Jr., "The Book of Psalms," in *The New Interpreter's Bible* (Nashville: Abingdon, 1996), 4:795–96.

the author of Lamentations, Bishop Bryant had not yet experienced relief from his great suffering, but he offered comfort to himself and the world by leaning on the words of the psalm. If a preacher is tempted to trivialize the words of Psalm 30, to compare the assurances of the psalmist to trite phrases of shallow comfort, she/he/they would do well to remember the raw emotion and deep faith of Bishop Bryant's words.

Psalm 30 can offer language for the suffering and faith of a whole community. Adapted lines of the psalm read well as a responsive affirmation of faith after the first reading. After hearing and proclaiming the suffering and faith of the Lamentations passage, the congregation can affirm their hope together using the poetic words of the psalm:

Waiting for God

I am convinced that much of the rebellion against Christianity is due to the overt or veiled claim of Christians to possess God, and therefore, also, to the loss of this element of waiting so decisive for the prophets and the apostles. Let us not be deluded into thinking that, because they speak of waiting, they waited merely for the end, the judgment and fulfillment of all things, and not for God Who was to bring that end. They did not possess God; they waited for Him. For how can God be possessed? Is God a thing that can be grasped and known among others? Is God less than a human person? We always have to wait for a human being. Even in the most intimate communion among human beings, there is an element of *not* having and *not* knowing, and of waiting. Therefore, since God is infinitely hidden, free, and incalculable, we must wait for Him in the most absolute and radical way. He is God for us just in so far as we do *not* possess Him. The psalmist says that his whole being waits for the Lord, indicating that waiting for God is not merely a part of our relation to God, but rather the condition of that relation as a whole. We have God through *not* having Him.

Paul Tillich, *The Shaking of the Foundations* (1948; repr. Eugene, OR: Wipf & Stock, 2011), 150–51.

Reader One: We will extol you, O Lord,
Reader Two: for you have drawn us up.
Reader One: O Lord our God, we cried to you for help,
Reader Two: and you have healed us.
Reader One: Weeping may linger for the night,
Reader Two: but joy comes with the morning.
Reader One: God will turn our mourning into dancing
Reader Two: and clothe us with joy.
Reader One: O Lord our God,
Reader Two: we will give thanks to you forever.

Psalm 130. In the reading from 2 Samuel appointed for this day, readers find King David just after the battle with the Amalekites. Israel has defeated its enemy, but victory comes at the highest cost. Saul and Jonathan have been killed, and the lectionary passage reports David's lament. He rips his clothes in a sign of grief and cries out from the depth of despair. Though Israel has "won" the battle, the anguish in David's words make it clear that, in war, no one really wins.

Psalm 130 comes in response to the 2 Samuel reading, and the colorful phrasing leads the hearer to imagine King David himself crying in anguish from the pages. The prayer of the psalm rises "out of the depths," though the psalmist's deep distress seems to be concerning personal sinfulness (Ps. 130:3–4) rather than David's depths of grief and sorrow. In the 2 Samuel passage, David directs his grief to the people Israel ("*Your* glory, O Israel, is slain in high places!" 2 Sam. 1:19a) and to the land itself ("*You* mountains of Gilboa, let there be no dew or rain upon you," v. 21a). In the psalm, the poet directs the anguish to the Lord directly: "Lord, hear my voice!" (Ps. 130:1b).

Psalm 130 is the eleventh of the Songs of Ascents, short psalms likely memorized by pilgrims and/or used in religious celebrations in Jerusalem.[3] The eight short verses of this psalm

3. McCann, "The Book of Psalms," 1204.

are filled with rich liturgical language, and they can be woven throughout a worship service. The opening and closing lines read well as a call to worship:

> Reader One: Out of the depths we cry to you!
> Reader Two: O Lord, hear our voice.
> Reader One: With the Lord there is great stead-
> fast love,
> Reader Two: and with God great power to
> redeem.

Verses 3–4 beg to serve as an assurance of pardon, whether spoken by the liturgist or read responsively:

> Reader One: If you, O Lord, should mark
> iniquities, Lord, who could stand?
> Reader Two: But there is forgiveness with you,
> so that you may be revered.

The psalm is full of rich language for the intercessory prayer. On any given Sunday, it is safe to assume that the people in the pews have been "in the depths," if they are not currently there, and the psalm can carry the weight of their prayers. The opening line can be used as a spoken refrain after each intercession: (Out of the depths we cry to you. *O Lord, hear our voice!*) There are also many musical settings of the psalm, which can be woven into the prayers themselves. A choir or soloist may sing the psalm before and/or after the prayer, with humming or instrumental music played softly during the prayer itself. The sensory effect of prayers spoken over musical offerings, popular in many African American traditions, can add depth to a prayer and create space for the emotions of worshipers.

The psalm ends with a word of assurance, and the prayers should do so as well. The psalmist's audience shifts from God to Israel: "O Israel, hope in the Lord!" (Ps. 130:7a). In the midst of grief, the psalmist finds hope. In the midst of lament, the psalm praises God's power. The psalmist lives in the tension between lament and hope, and the most faithful thing a preacher or liturgist can do is invite the people of God to live there, as well.

ANNA GEORGE TRAYNHAM

2 Corinthians 8:7–15

[7]Now as you excel in everything—in faith, in speech, in knowledge, in utmost eagerness, and in our love for you—so we want you to excel also in this generous undertaking.

[8]I do not say this as a command, but I am testing the genuineness of your love against the earnestness of others. [9]For you know the generous act of our Lord Jesus Christ, that though he was rich, yet for your sakes he became poor, so that by his poverty you might become rich. [10]And in this matter I am giving my advice: it is appropriate for you who began last year not only to do something but even to desire to do something— [11]now finish doing it, so that your eagerness may be matched by completing it according to your means. [12]For if the eagerness is there, the gift is acceptable according to what one has—not according to what one does not have. [13]I do not mean that there should be relief for others and pressure on you, but it is a question of a fair balance between [14]your present abundance and their need, so that their abundance may be for your need, in order that there may be a fair balance. [15]As it is written,

"The one who had much did not have too much,
and the one who had little did not have too little."

Commentary 1: Connecting the Reading with Scripture

The immediate context of our lectionary reading is found in verse 6: Titus (2 Cor. 8:23) had been sent by Paul to the church in Corinth to follow up on the collection of an offering for "the poor among the saints" in Jerusalem (v. 10; Rom. 15:26). Reasons abound for this request: a severe famine (Acts 11:27–30), the persecution of Christian Jews at the hand of King Herod and from non-Christian Jews (Acts 8:1–3; 12:1–4). Eager to respond (Gal. 2:9–10), Paul instructed the churches to follow a systematic pattern of collection throughout the year (1 Cor. 16:1–4).

It appears, however, that the controversies that have developed (2 Cor. 1:12–7:16; 10–13) since Paul's last visit to Corinth have tempered their enthusiasm for the collection (8:11). This would explain why he seems compelled to argue for their support. There is little that gets believers to lean in more than "testimony time"—a concrete and passionate witness of the grace of God in daily life. "We want you to know, brothers and sisters," he begins, "about the grace of God" (v. 1)! With great exuberance he testifies

how God's grace stirred the otherwise severely afflicted (1 Thess. 1:6; 2:14) and extremely poor Macedonian churches to beg to share in the privilege ("grace," *charis*) of "ministry to the saints" in Jerusalem, giving "voluntarily" with overflowing "wealth of generosity" (2 Cor. 8:2–4). Paul's use of antithesis achieves its purpose; only God's grace could move a community suffused in their own pain and struggle for survival to give with "abundant joy . . . even beyond their means."

Having shared the testimony, Paul gets to the point. He is testing the "genuineness of your [the Corinthian church's] love" against the "earnestness" (*spoudē* in Gk. also means "to haste," "to move with zealous diligence") of others (i.e., the Macedonian churches, v. 8). Was Paul shaming the well-to-do Corinthian church by praising the joyful outpouring of the "poor" and "afflicted" Macedonians? Yet in his visit to the Macedonian churches (9:1–2) Paul testifies to the zeal of the Achaean churches (Corinth fell within that region). Thus, it may be more to the point that Paul is garnering enthusiasm by extolling a unified resolve of *all* the churches to take part in this act of grace. The contest here is really against their own hesitation to cross the finish line and complete what they started. How? When they entrust themselves to the Lord, God will embolden them toward the kind of genuine fellowship (*koinōnia*[1]) that bound them to the other (Gal. 3:28) through the ministry of grace-filled service (2 Cor. 8:5).

Paul's emphasis on Jesus' "generous act [grace]" points beyond the cross and the resurrection— major Pauline theological staples—to consider the status of Christ *before* and *at* the incarnation. If the Corinthians are "rich," that is, if they have experienced the grace of God's love, it is because Christ, who "was rich," for their sake "became poor" (v. 9). The meaning of "became poor" is perhaps best explained by the creed (or hymn) in Philippians 2:6–8 wherein Christ, though equal with God, chose to "strip" (or "empty," *kenōsis*) himself of his divine form (*morphē*) to take the form (*morphē*) of a slave—the lowest in the social strata—and suffer a death intended for the lowest of criminals, the cross.

Paul thus prompted the Corinthians not only to remember but to honor the grace personally and generously lavished on them by Christ (2 Cor. 8:9). Grace is love in action. It is "the gift of God for the people of God"—it has a sacramental countenance—Christ imaged in and through the people of God for the common good (2 Cor. 4:15; Phil. 2:4).

This brings us back to 2 Corinthians 8:7, Paul's list of gifts in which the Corinthians supposedly excelled at and in which they took pride (1 Cor. 1:18–25). Was Paul hinting at his earlier letter, wherein he taught that speech, knowledge, and faith without love are nothing (1 Cor. 13:1–3)? Was this a not too subtle reminder that their zeal for spiritual gifts should be guided only by an eagerness to excel in them for the "building up [of] the church" (1 Cor. 14:12)? Does not the building up of the church include excelling in this "generous undertaking [grace]"? It is doubtful that Paul's reference to excelling in these gifts would have been lost on

the Corinthians, who had previously received his exhortation to strive for the greatest gift— love—without which they are, and can gain, nothing.

Empathy usually requires humanization of suffering. Places of privilege often require a myriad of graphic pictures of children and of women and men running for their lives in order to quicken sensitivities. Paul would not need to do this, however. NT Christians experienced this reality all too well in their own lives and in the lives of loved ones. For those unfamiliar with such kinds of political, social, religious, emotional, or economic afflictions, the OT and NT lections allow us to fathom what the voices of anguish and dejection may feel, look, and sound like. "I am distressed," cries David over the death of his beloved Jonathan (2 Sam. 1:26). Later, the psalmist's despondency becomes palpable as we imagine him lifting his countenance and throwing up his hands toward the heavens calling out to God for the redemption of his people: "Out of the depths I cry to you, LORD, hear . . . my supplications!" (Ps. 130:1–2). The cries of a distinguished leader of the notorious Sanhedrin begging for the healing of his daughter, and the pain and humiliation suffered by the unclean, hemorrhaging woman (Mark 5:21–43) will be familiar reminders. The readings also help us hear what hope and overwhelming gratitude sound like (Lam. 3:32; Ps. 30:5, 11) when those in need dare to await a divine response, often through the service of the body of Christ, God's people (Phil. 4:10–20).

An important word should be said about how Paul handles the matter of the collection. The needy are not a problem to address. Not responding to the need in the spirit of *koinōnia*, however, is. Moreover, it is not a matter of giving beyond anyone's means (v. 13); it is about everyone having enough.

Paul's reference to "fair balance" challenges conformity to status quo. Underlying this challenge is a call to live out of that new and radical eschatological dimension begun by Christ, called the kingdom of God. Saints around the world, in all times and all places, express their

1. Justo L. González, *Faith & Wealth: A History of Early Christian Ideas on the Origin, Significance, and Use of Money* (New York: HarperCollins, 1990), 79–86.

citizenship in this reign through the gifts of time, talents, money, and possessions until Christ's return. In Isaiah 1:17, we hear God's admonition to "learn to do good" and in the parable of the Nations, God invites those who live out this good into God's reign (Matt. 25:31–40).

Scholars point to a variation between Paul's report—"they [the apostles] asked only one thing"—and Luke's account (Acts 15:28–29). Was the request for financial succor in *addition* to the "essentials" mentioned in Luke? Did Paul exclude those essentials in order to emphasize the oneness of the body of Christ? How would inclusion of Jewish kosher laws have helped to demonstrate the depth of the apostles' understanding of God's all-embracing grace to Jew and Gentile alike (see Acts 10:44–46 and 11:17–18)? What does it mean to be "one" church? What should "one" church look and feel like? Responses can open up varied theological avenues for preaching.

ZAIDA MALDONADO PÉREZ

Commentary 2: Connecting the Reading with the World

In 1910 in Edinburgh, 1,215 delegates representing Protestant denominations and mission agencies from all over the world met to discuss ecumenical relations, evangelism, and the promotion of Christian unity. Despite its aspirations to embody the growing confessional and geographic diversity of the global church, the World Missionary Conference was comprised mainly of Western delegates from mainstream Protestant denominations. Only nineteen delegates, eighteen from Asia and one from Africa, were from outside the West. This gathering nonetheless marked a significant moment that ushered in a new era of modern ecumenism at the cusp of changing demographics in world Christianity. When these delegates met in Scotland, more than 80 percent of the world's Christians resided in the global North. In 2010, more than 60 percent of the world's Christians resided in the global South.

One consistently challenging topic in modern ecumenism has been developing equitable cross-cultural partnerships between Christians in the global North and the global South. Although Christianity is growing in dynamic and expansive ways throughout the global South, the bulk of financial resources remains among Christians in the global North. At the World Missionary Conference in 1910, Kajinosuke Ibuka, a Japanese delegate working with US Presbyterian denominations in Japan, broached the thorny issue of how funds are managed in the mission field. He proposed a revision to the existing system, in which Western mission groups controlled the funds they raised from back home. He developed a more inclusive method of decision making that incorporated indigenous perspectives from local church leaders.[2]

In 2 Corinthians 8, Paul engages these topics of partnership and stewardship. Paul also treads carefully when addressing financial matters publicly. Paul's gentle tone reflects how it has never been easy for Christian leaders, from the first century to the present, to talk about money with their congregations. In this passage, when making his appeal to the Corinthians, Paul moves back and forth from general theological principles on stewardship to particularities about the collection for the Christian community in Jerusalem. In 8:7, Paul teaches that faithful discipleship encompasses piety, speech, knowledge, attitude, love, and material offering. In 8:8, Paul narrows his focus to the collaborative effort to raise funds for the church in Jerusalem.

He observes the collection is not a "command" with the same Greek word, *epitagē,* that appears in 1 Corinthians 7:6 in Paul's instructions for sexual relations within marriages and in 1 Timothy 1:1 on Paul's apostolic authority deriving from "the command of God." Though the collection does not rise to the mandate of a moral absolute, Paul clearly believes it possesses profound ecumenical and eschatological weight.

2. Jonathan S. Barnes, *Power and Partnership: A History of the Protestant Mission Movement* (Eugene, OR: Pickwick, 2013), 111.

At one level, Paul seeks to create a network of mutuality and unity among all the churches such that they support one another in times of crisis and need. At another level, Paul connects the relationship between the churches in Jerusalem and Corinth to his larger theological vision of the gospel of Jesus Christ for Jews and Gentiles. In Romans 15:25–27, Paul articulates how the collection for "the poor among the saints at Jerusalem" demonstrates a reciprocity in which Jews share their "spiritual blessings" with the Gentiles and the Gentiles share their "material things" with the Jews.

In 8:9–15, Paul first grounds his stewardship appeal in a theology of grace and the generosity of Jesus Christ (2 Cor. 8:9). The following five verses comprise specific advice for the Corinthians to give in proportion to their means and fulfill their pledges (vv. 10–12) and frank assessment of the differences between the Christian communities in Jerusalem and Corinth (vv. 13–14). After explaining the goal of the collection is to produce a fair balance in which one church's abundance meets the other church's needs, Paul reinforces his point in 8:15 with a reference to God's provision of manna in Exodus 16 such that every Israelite had neither too much nor too little to eat.

A strong undercurrent throughout Paul's instruction on partnership and stewardship is the complexity of first-century politics in the Greco-Roman world. Paul understood the cross-cultural tensions between a predominantly impoverished Jewish Christian community in Jerusalem and a diverse Christian community in the cosmopolitan city of Corinth facing their own divisions across differences in race, class, and gender. Paul understood the church in Corinth included members from Jewish and Gentile backgrounds, the affluent and the poor, and persons of all genders who held a plurality of beliefs and practices regarding human sexuality. Paul had to navigate the uncomfortable implications of presenting one church (Jerusalem) as holding abundant spiritual resources but lacking in material goods and the other church (Corinth) as maintaining material wealth yet needing spiritual support.

Paul's pastoral sensibilities throughout this passage illustrate his acute awareness of the complicated social and political realities within and among his congregations. Nevertheless, he does not flinch from speaking the truth in love. Paul provides the Corinthians with both general theological insights on stewardship and specific contextual applications on the importance of partnership with Jerusalem. One connection between the lectionary text and our contemporary context is the persistence of cultural, economic, political, racial, and social tensions.

We live in a world—not unlike that of the first century—fraught with sharp divisions, cultural conflicts, and competing ideologies. One of the most urgent challenges in the United States is a persistent racial wealth gap. "In 2016, white families had the highest level of both median and mean family wealth: $171,000 and $933,700, respectively. . . . Black families' median and mean net worth is less than 15 percent that of white families, at $17,600 and $138,200, respectively. Hispanic families' median and mean net worth was $20,700 and $191,200, respectively."[3]

A related obstacle in the United States is the ongoing achievement gaps in education, revealing daunting disparities in academic performance between groups of students differentiated by class, gender, ethnicity, and race. Our preaching, like that of Paul, must blend theological instruction and practical application such that the gospel of Jesus Christ provides the foundation for precise discernment that produces concrete engagement, in the forms of our time, energy, and money, to alleviate the most pressing problems in our congregations, our neighborhoods, and our world.

During the World Missionary Conference in 1910, Vedanayagam Samuel Azariah, an Indian delegate, tackled another difficult topic, race relations. Azariah believed the problems of racial discrimination against people of color impaired Christian witness and hampered ecumenical partnerships. From his experiences with the Anglican Church in India, where in 1912 he would become the first Indian to serve as a

3. https://www.federalreserve.gov/econres/notes/feds-notes/recent-trends-in-wealth-holding-by-race-and-ethnicity-evidence-from-the-survey-of-consumer-finances-20170927.htm.

bishop, Azariah criticized the superficial relationships between European mission workers and Indian Christians because of the Europeans' supercilious attitudes toward the Indians. He specifically detailed how the Europeans treated the Indians as their converts and their students, but never as their friends and their partners in ministry.

Azariah contended true cooperation would be possible only with honest communication and fair collaboration: "The exceeding riches of the glory of Christ can be fully realized not by the Englishman, the American, and the Continental alone, nor by the Japanese, the Chinese, and the Indians by themselves—but by all working together, worshipping together, and learning together the Perfect Image of our Lord and Christ."[4] Like Paul in 2 Corinthians 8, Azariah directly connected a compelling vision of Christian reciprocity and mutuality with a frank assessment of the problems and tensions in his context. In our preaching, we must also encourage our congregations toward faithful discipleship that directly connects the gifts of the church with the needs in the world.

WILLIAM YOO

---

4. V. S. Azariah, "The Problem of Co-Operation Between Foreign and Native Workers," in *World Missionary Conference, 1910* (Edinburgh: Oliphant, Anderson, & Ferrier, 1910), 306–15.

Mark 5:21–43

[21]When Jesus had crossed again in the boat to the other side, a great crowd gathered around him; and he was by the sea. [22]Then one of the leaders of the synagogue named Jairus came and, when he saw him, fell at his feet [23]and begged him repeatedly, "My little daughter is at the point of death. Come and lay your hands on her, so that she may be made well, and live." [24]So he went with him.

And a large crowd followed him and pressed in on him. [25]Now there was a woman who had been suffering from hemorrhages for twelve years. [26]She had endured much under many physicians, and had spent all that she had; and she was no better, but rather grew worse. [27]She had heard about Jesus, and came up behind him in the crowd and touched his cloak, [28]for she said, "If I but touch his clothes, I will be made well." [29]Immediately her hemorrhage stopped; and she felt in her body that she was healed of her disease. [30]Immediately aware that power had gone forth from him, Jesus turned about in the crowd and said, "Who touched my clothes?" [31]And his disciples said to him, "You see the crowd pressing in on you; how can you say, 'Who touched me?'" [32]He looked all around to see who had done it. [33]But the woman, knowing what had happened to her, came in fear and trembling, fell down before him, and told him the whole truth. [34]He said to her, "Daughter, your faith has made you well; go in peace, and be healed of your disease."

[35]While he was still speaking, some people came from the leader's house to say, "Your daughter is dead. Why trouble the teacher any further?" [36]But overhearing what they said, Jesus said to the leader of the synagogue, "Do not fear, only believe." [37]He allowed no one to follow him except Peter, James, and John, the brother of James. [38]When they came to the house of the leader of the synagogue, he saw a commotion, people weeping and wailing loudly. [39]When he had entered, he said to them, "Why do you make a commotion and weep? The child is not dead but sleeping." [40]And they laughed at him. Then he put them all outside, and took the child's father and mother and those who were with him, and went in where the child was. [41]He took her by the hand and said to her, "Talitha cum," which means, "Little girl, get up!" [42]And immediately the girl got up and began to walk about (she was twelve years of age). At this they were overcome with amazement. [43]He strictly ordered them that no one should know this, and told them to give her something to eat.

Commentary 1: Connecting the Reading with Scripture

When Jesus heals a woman by the power within him and brings a girl back to life, a series of scenes recounting his amazing deeds comes to a pinnacle. These two actions, which the narrative connects together in numerous ways, might be seen as more impressive than anything else Jesus has done throughout Mark 1–5. They stand out from other events in Mark insofar as words and intention are not required; Jesus' mere presence restores a woman's wholeness and dignity. Not even death presents a fixed barrier to him; he has the power to pull someone back from the dreaded end that eventually claims all people as its victims. In previous settings, unclean spirits and violent weather proved no match for him. Now a supposedly incurable medical condition and death itself yield to his authority. Does anything or anyone reside beyond his influence?

Whatever assails humanity's well-being—all of it appears powerless when faced with the arrival of the reign of God.

Mark is fond of intercalation, a narrative technique of connecting two stories by describing one as an interruption or a hiatus that breaks apart the description of the other (e.g., Mark 3:19a–35; 6:6b–30; 11:12–24). Intercalation invites readers to consider two stories in light of each other, to discover more through comparison and contrast than if the stories were told entirely separately. In this particular passage, the pairing of two stories offers a rich characterization of Jesus' healing ministry and the multifaceted salvation he brings. No one is out of reach.

The narrative forges connections through a collection of differences and similarities. Readers learn Jairus's name, but the woman suffering from chronic hemorrhaging remains anonymous. As a synagogue leader Jairus probably enjoys some local status and influence, while the woman has lost all her money in failed attempts to treat her condition. Assuming her hemorrhaging renders her infertile, perhaps because of a menstrual disorder or injury suffered from a previous pregnancy, the woman might find herself the object of scorn or pity from neighbors and family. In any case, her decision to approach Jesus furtively—while Jairus falls at his feet in front of a large or growing crowd—implies that she lives with some degree of shame, inflicted by others or herself. She has lived with this for twelve years, the same amount of time Jairus's daughter has been alive.

When Jesus halts his journey to Jairus's house to identify the woman who tapped into his power, their conversation has potential to restore her public dignity. Not only does her ailment disappear. Jesus makes it known that he and not some hidden sorcery caused her healing. By calling her "daughter" he openly declares his solidarity and relationship with her. To be "saved" or "made well" (*sōzō*) involves more than bodily health; in the context of the narrative it suggests a holistic sense of well-being and restoration. Of course, during the delay created when Jesus interacts with the woman in the presence of a crowd excited about witnessing what he will do for Jairus's girl, that other "daughter" succumbs to death. It looks as if he gave away her chance.

Jesus, though, makes it clear that this is no zero-sum game in which only one woman can receive a blessing from him. Both stories will end in healing, just as both stories share the question of how faith in Jesus manifests itself. Jesus identifies the woman's confident desperation as "faith" (5:34), and he urges Jairus to "continue to have faith" (v. 36, my trans.). Like other people of "faith" in Mark, these two characters need to surmount obstacles that might derail them from getting Jesus' attention (cf. 2:2–4; 9:24; 10:48).

Even though the anonymous woman and Jairus face the prospect of "fear" (5:33, 36), they must not let that become something that will eclipse their faith. Mark does not suggest that faith and fear are opposites; both of them represent ways that people might respond to dangerous circumstances or conditions that exceed humanity's ability to control (see also 4:40–41; 5:15; 6:50; 9:23, 32; 16:8). Therefore, Jesus urges Jairus not to let his fear overwhelm his belief. For "faith" or "belief" in this narrative is not about confessing correct statements about Jesus and his identity. Nor is it obedience to commands or following a pattern. It is, rather, the expression of radical trust in Jesus. It is a resolute determination born from one's sense of deep need. It is the conviction that Jesus can and will help; it refuses to take "no" for an answer.

The differences between the two connected stories expose the inadequacy of attempts to describe Jesus' ministry in one-dimensional terms. When Jesus tells people to keep the news about Jairus's daughter to themselves, an almost absurd command in light of the fact that mourners previously lamented her death in public, the story resembles other parts of Mark in which Jesus tries to keep his deeds unknown (e.g., 1:34, 44; 7:36; 8:26, 30).

On the other hand, Jesus is solely responsible for directing a crowd's attention to the woman's otherwise unseen efforts to be healed. Not every deed of power in Mark is accompanied by an injunction to secrecy (see 4:21–22; 5:19; 16:7). There is no clear pattern to what is to be concealed and what is revealed. In this scene, however, Jesus' desire to engage the woman face to face, in public scrutiny (5:30–34), ensures that everyone knows the woman is the beneficiary of Jesus' power and that she has not stolen a healing she did not deserve. The open, observed conversation between the two pulls her from the edges into the center. Without that dialogue, which serves as a kind of declaration from Jesus, she might be left in shadow, delivered from an ailment but not fully restored to wholeness.

Those who interpret this passage need to be careful not to make connections that have no basis in the passage or in other accounts of Jesus' ministry. The most important example of such an unwarranted connection has to do with matters of purity and defilement. No one, not even the Gospel's narrator, shows concern that the woman touches Jesus and that he willingly takes the hand of the recently deceased daughter. Nothing in the narrative indicates that Levitical laws about menstrual bleeding (Lev. 15:25–27) would apply among ordinary Galilean Jews in a situation like this, when the woman initiates contact with Jesus. Jesus does not break the law, nor does he risk rendering himself ritually impure by responding to those who seek him for help. These intercalated stories are not about Jesus showing disdain for Jewish religious practices that were common, for there is no evidence that such rigorous interpretations of purity laws *were commonly practiced.*[1]

Instead, these are two stories about Jesus extending wholeness and blessing to individuals who would have been considered by others to have moved out of reach of such things—past the possibility of restoration and health. Because they are those kinds of stories, they are stories that make readers consider the possibility that nothing can keep God's holiness contained.[2] No wonder Jesus is so magnetic in this Gospel, attracting people who live in desperation and yet still venture to him with a faith that insists they are not beyond his healing words and touch.

MATTHEW L. SKINNER

Commentary 2: Connecting the Reading with the World

There is so much to *explain* about this passage: how it functions as an individual literary unit with interesting narrative features and sociohistorical backdrop, how it functions within Mark's larger narrative context, and how it paints Jesus' continuing development as the border-crossing, authoritative agent of God's realm who teaches and performs miracles at every turn. Almost everyone who has preached this text before has been faced with the temptation to *explain* the text. Why not? The world behind the text and the world of the text unlock new understandings each time we come back to it.

This is particularly tempting, given the place this text is situated within the Revised Common Lectionary and the church year: the season after Pentecost. Here is the church's season for growth in discipleship. Green paraments signal our pursuit of renewed Easter-faith Pentecost living. There is hardly a better time to use our hard-won exegetical knowledge to explain one of many people's favorite Markan passages. Listeners should *understand* the rich depth of this passage!

However, there is something that does not ring quite true with preaching this passage as explanation. That stems from the fact that Mark does not necessarily write to explain Jesus. If Mark did so, he would not have written a narrative. Rather, Mark seems to want those who engage the text to *encounter* and *behold* this Jesus—more precisely in Markan parlance, to be *amazed* by this Jesus (Mark 5:42 and elsewhere). Yes, some of the literary and sociohistorical features of the text give us insight into what Mark is doing. Here, though, is a place where we might be propelled to consider when we as individuals and as church have been amazed by our personal encounters with Jesus. Not many of us will have had such dramatic encounters as Jairus and his daughter or the woman suffering hemorrhages. Still, most of us will be able to recount a moment when we encountered Jesus the Christ or when God's power became

1. Amy-Jill Levine, *The Misunderstood Jew: The Church and the Scandal of the Jewish Jesus* (San Francisco: HarperSanFrancisco, 2006), 173–77.
2. Greg Carey, *Sinners: Jesus and His Earliest Followers* (Waco, TX: Baylor University Press, 2009), 37–53.

manifest to us as individuals or as families, communities, or church.

Here is an opportunity for preachers to move beyond explaining the text to naming, sharing, and celebrating our own encounters with the restorative agent of God's inbreaking realm that Mark shows us. It might even be an opportunity for preachers or teachers to relinquish the microphone so that others can name their life-giving, restorative encounters. The preaching moment might give way to some other kind of liturgical action in which people recount these stories. Preachers and other worship leaders might follow Mark's lead: inviting others to stand, watch, and listen with amazement at God's power to act in the midst of hopelessness and despair.

However, motionless amazement can last only so long for those who follow Jesus, as we will see in the following chapter of Mark's Gospel. Those who follow Jesus will be compelled to act, assessing their own ministries in light of their restorative encounters with God's agent. A personal encounter with Jesus is incomplete without discipleship, according to Mark's Gospel. This presents an ecclesial challenge, perhaps timed well for the summer months, when some congregational ministries slow down or lie dormant, waiting for the beginning of the program year in late summer or (for those who do the work of congregational budgeting through a July-June fiscal year) early fall. The passage can present listeners with an opportunity for reflection on a congregation's ministries over the past year.

Too often our criteria for evaluating the church's ministries are formed out of budget numbers or numerical benchmarks of attendance or participation. There are standards in this passage by which we might consider our ministries to be participating effectively in Jesus' ongoing ministry to the world. First, Jesus crosses borders (5:21), not just geographical but physical and social. We do well to avoid thinking about our border crossing in a colonialist sense, but the church's ministries imitate Jesus' ministry when they carry God's healing, restorative work beyond accepted confines.

Second, Jesus confronts disease and death, that is, the deep forces that marginalize and hold people in despair. Sermons might invite reflection on how the church's ministries reach out to those who are sick, those close to death, those who are dealt death, and those who stand on the margins of society.

Third, Jesus extends the boundaries of relationality in the household of faith. Jesus recognizes the woman he heals as "daughter," like the young girl he is about to heal. In a world of fractured polarity, one of the measures of the church's mission might be how we see and relate to one another in light of the gospel. NPR highlighted a story about the 1967 "hippie anthem" entitled "Get Together" by The Youngbloods. The famous song was used in promotional materials for the National Conference of Christians and Jews, and "an early review of the song asked why it is not sung in church."[3] Like the song, this text gives us pause to think about how we see ourselves in relation to others and how our congregational and denominational ministries help us live into Jesus' enlarged vision of relationality.

On the opposite end of the spectrum from recounting stories of encounter with Jesus, the question of the emissaries of Jairus's house to Jairus in verse 35 may strike us as completely arresting: "Your daughter is dead. Why trouble the teacher any further?" Beyond a shadow of a doubt, many people come to congregational worship feeling as though their backs are against the wall. Countless human and communal scenarios present feelings of finality, unending grief, and hopelessness. As much as we might remind ourselves of God's powerful work, sometimes that seems like a dream too distant, a fantasy entirely too fantastic, to become reality. If that is the case, "Why trouble the teacher any further?" That this question remains in the text is no small gift, pastorally speaking.

Here is an opportunity for preachers and teachers not to lecture people about the necessity of faith to effect or procure change, for bootstraps are not always an option, as much as that cultural narrative persists and plagues us. Rather, in the preaching of this text there lies an

3. "'Get Together' Plays On, Long After San Francisco's Summer of Love: NPR"; https://www.npr.org/2019/04/10/711545679/get-together-youngbloods-summer-of-love-american-anthem.

opportunity for pastoral permission giving, to invite people to cry out, naming the limits that impinge upon life, and inviting listeners to live with what Joni Sancken calls "reasonable hope." This kind of hope holds room for doubt and despair and at the same time "offer[s] incremental steps toward a future."[4]

So congregational leaders might consider using this text as the opportunity to offer a worship service of healing and wholeness, either within regular congregational worship or in a service beyond it. Most denominational worship books now have liturgies for these services, and they can serve as an opportunity to encourage the people under our care to name their despair and hopelessness: an opportunity for them to "trouble the teacher" with the burdens too great to bear. This kind of service calls on the power of healing through restorative touch that we see in Jesus. The church's practices of laying on of hands and anointing with oil are vital. To come full circle, in these liturgical practices we go beyond information and explanation about Jesus and reach toward imitation of the healing encounter with Jesus that we see in this text.

RICHARD W. VOELZ

---

4. Joni S. Sancken, *Words That Heal: Preaching Hope to Wounded Souls* (Nashville: Abingdon, 2019), 14–15.

Proper 9 (Sunday between July 3 and July 9)

Ezekiel 2:1–5 and
  2 Samuel 5:1–5, 9–10
Psalm 123 and Psalm 48

2 Corinthians 12:2–10
Mark 6:1–13

Ezekiel 2:1–5

¹He said to me: O mortal, stand up on your feet, and I will speak with you. ²And when he spoke to me, a spirit entered into me and set me on my feet; and I heard him speaking to me. ³He said to me, Mortal, I am sending you to the people of Israel, to a nation of rebels who have rebelled against me; they and their ancestors have transgressed against me to this very day. ⁴The descendants are impudent and stubborn. I am sending you to them, and you shall say to them, "Thus says the Lord GOD." ⁵Whether they hear or refuse to hear (for they are a rebellious house), they shall know that there has been a prophet among them.

2 Samuel 5:1–5, 9–10

¹Then all the tribes of Israel came to David at Hebron, and said, "Look, we are your bone and flesh. ²For some time, while Saul was king over us, it was you who led out Israel and brought it in. The LORD said to you: It is you who shall be shepherd of my people Israel, you who shall be ruler over Israel." ³So all the elders of Israel came to the king at Hebron; and King David made a covenant with them at Hebron before the LORD, and they anointed David king over Israel. ⁴David was thirty years old when he began to reign, and he reigned forty years. ⁵At Hebron he reigned over Judah seven years and six months; and at Jerusalem he reigned over all Israel and Judah thirty-three years.
  . . . ⁹David occupied the stronghold, and named it the city of David. David built the city all around from the Millo inward. ¹⁰And David became greater and greater, for the LORD, the God of hosts, was with him.

Commentary 1: Connecting the Reading with Scripture

In the story of Israel as the books of Samuel tell it, 2 Samuel 5:1–5 involves a great consolidation. The disparate nature of the text and of the Israel it depicts up to this point begin to converge, and it is the power and charisma of David that drives the convergence. A casual reading of the story can lead to the conclusion that the "united monarchy" of ancient Israel was the norm, the way Israel was supposed to be. However, even such a surface-level reading

points toward only one century of this political entity, and there are reasons to think that it never existed at all.

This is one of three stories about David being anointed king (the other two are in 1 Sam. 16:1–13 and 2 Sam. 2:1–7). In similar fashion, there are three different stories about Saul becoming king of Israel (1 Sam. 8:1–9:2 + 10:17–26; 9:3–10:16; and 11:1–15 + 10:27). These stories happen in different places, in the presence of different groups of people, and at different stages in the lives of Saul and David. If there is a convergence here, then there were many versions of that story, and it creates a diagram more like an hourglass than a triangle. The unity does not last long and may be a literary mirage.

Because the lectionary has skipped 2 Samuel 4, it is easy to forget that all of this apparent peace and order, portrayed as a process of covenant making, was made possible by successfully executed acts of violence. The lectionary tells us to read 2 Samuel like 1 Chronicles. The latter has omitted these internal, Israelite acts of violence. In Chronicles and in the lectionary snippets of Samuel, the only violent act necessary to make David king is the defeat and death of Saul at the hand of the Philistines. In the full story told by 2 Samuel, however, Hebron is littered with body parts as David and the elders of Israel make their covenant there. Rechab and Baanah have assassinated David's rival Ishbaal and brought his head to David. David has responded by cutting off the hands and feet of Rechab and Baanah and putting their mutilated bodies on public display.

Like the three differing accounts of Saul being anointed king and David being anointed king, there are also three accounts of David and Saul meeting for the first time, and one of these meetings (1 Sam. 17:55–58) is facilitated by the severed head of Goliath. The juxtaposition of a story of constructing a nation with stories of tearing apart human bodies can be jarring, and it is not difficult to see why a selective presentation of texts, ancient or modern, would seek to avoid such images. Nevertheless, a more honest reckoning with the fullness of this story that we have made part of our own faith requires a full view of the scene. If there is a consolidation of institutions, then who benefits and who pays the cost?

Ezekiel 2:1–5 offers a puzzling pairing with the text from 2 Samuel. In Ezekiel 1 the prophet sees his great *merkaba* vision, the dazzling chariot of YHWH in the sky. The grand vision in Ezekiel 1–2 takes on even greater significance because Ezekiel sees it in Babylon, not in the Jerusalem temple, where such a divine encounter, like the vision in Isaiah 6, belonged. He appropriately falls on his face. When God

speaks to Ezekiel, he commands him to get up, but a spirit also enters Ezekiel and stands him up, perhaps acknowledging that the force that put him on the ground is too strong for sheer human will to overcome.

Even for modern readers the multifaced beasts and wheels within wheels can be so mesmerizing that few look away toward the other parts of the book, except for the very different vision of the valley of bones in Ezekiel 37. The story of Ezekiel here is a story of a beginning and an ending, like the story of David's anointing. The way the divine character relates to Israel changed when it became a unified nation ruled by a single king who was a divine representative. At the moment when YHWH is speaking to Ezekiel, there is no longer a king, and Jerusalem is no longer the location of the divine glory (*kabod*), which has visited Ezekiel in Babylon.

These two texts form bookends around the story of Jerusalem as ancient Israel's political and religious center and the abode of its God. In 2 Samuel 5, David stands before YHWH in Hebron, and in Ezekiel 2 the prophet stands before YHWH by the river Chebar. Between these two moments, encounters with the divine presence take place in Jerusalem. The vision in Ezekiel 1–2 is closely connected to the visions in Ezekiel 8–10 and 40–48. It is in chapters 8–10 that Ezekiel sees the divine glory rise up out of the temple in Jerusalem and fly eastward, toward those who are in exile in Babylon. YHWH must vacate the temple before it is destroyed by the Babylonian army. Ezekiel 40–48 is the prophet's vision of the new temple in a restored Jerusalem, including the return of the divine glory. The vision in Ezekiel 1–2 would seem to fit chronologically between these two, but instead it forms the dramatic opening of the book. Before showing the reader a Jerusalem with no divine presence in it, the book of Ezekiel chooses to show Babylon with a divine presence.

More recent understandings of the nature of Israel in the sixth century demand greater attention to those who were not in exile in Babylon. While the Bible might lead us to believe that the experience of exile and return was the norm for citizens of Judah in the sixth century, the historical evidence points to a different reality. The majority of the citizens of Judah would have remained in the land, but without the structure and institutions that had been at the center of their national religious life.

It is difficult to know what might have replaced the rituals of Solomon's temple during this interim. One avenue of speculation has been that the poems in the book of Lamentations may have been performed by survivors, in or near the temple ruins. If this, or something like it, was the case, then the book of Ezekiel claims that Israel's God was not present in Jerusalem to hear these painful prayers. If the exiles in Babylon possessed the traditions of Israel's religion and claimed and enjoyed the divine presence there, then of what value was the experience of those left behind? The shape of the biblical canon and the ways we choose to read

it cause certain voices to be louder and cause others to be more difficult to hear. In the competition of stories, the story of exile and return won out over a story of remaining in a defeated land, just as the story of a powerful king muffled the stories of those destroyed by the process.

The stories of Jesus and his disciples in Mark 6:1–13 also raise questions about dislocation. The response of the people in Nazareth pushes Jesus away from his hometown, and he counsels his disciples about how to respond to rejection. Displays of divine power generate conflict among those who desire the benefits. In Israel's past, efforts to become the broker of divine presence and power have not led to unity or harmony. The plot in the Gospel of Mark moves in a similar direction.

MARK MCENTIRE

Commentary 2: Connecting the Reading with the World

The two texts in the lectionary readings may appear disconnected from each other, yet when we read Ezekiel in light of the passage from 2 Samuel 5 that describes David's anointing as king of Israel, we will see a number of connections that are pertinent for preaching and for connecting these readings to the worlds of parishioners.

We enter the story of David's rise to kingship in the political and social turmoil described in the books of 1 and 2 Samuel. Competing political leaders, including Saul, Jonathan, and David, have jockeyed for power through a variety of violent means. We know of the storied history of the personal conflict between Saul and David, due to jealousy, fear, and threat. After Saul's death (1 Sam. 31), David is anointed king of Judah (2 Sam. 2:1–7). David's rise to kingship was the next step in his ascendancy to power as king over the tribe of Judah, the tribe of his lineage. It is important to note that David's reign was limited at this point to Judah. Yes, David was powerful, but his monarchy was not yet total over all of the tribes of Israel.

After the violence, chaos, and palace intrigue continued and took their toll on the stability and well-being of the nation, "all the tribes of Israel

came to David," affirming a desire that David become king over all of the tribes of Israel, based on their understanding God's promise (2 Sam. 5:1–3). One could read this request theologically, in that a messiah, a deliverer, an anointed one, would eventually come in the person of Jesus from this Davidic lineage. One can also read this text politically and see connections with how political leaders gain power in times of turmoil, uncertainty, and fear. The tribes needed a leader who could unify them and deliver them from their surrounding enemies—a leader who had been strong in battle, who had divine favor, and whose success was believed to be guaranteed because of this divine favor.

Preachers should read this text for its many layers of interpretation. No matter how this text is read, the narrator of 2 Samuel takes us to the apex of David's power. David united the tribes into one nation, moved to Jerusalem, set it up as the seat of power, naming it "the city of David," and "became greater and greater, for the LORD, the God of hosts, was with him" (v. 10).

Now read Ezekiel, this tormented prophet and visionary seeing all sorts of strange things during exile after the unified kingdom of David had been split into two, with the southern portion of kingdom exiled to Babylon, from where Ezekiel was likely prophesying. Ezekiel received his commission as a prophet to go and tell, and the message was a disturbing one: to remind the people that had been assured of God's favor through the kingship of David of their waywardness and rebellion. Ezekiel received a scroll, an unmistakable means of divine communication, and on it were the "words of lamentation and mourning and woe" (Ezek. 2:10).

Preachers will want to explore how the connections between these texts might provide connections for hearers' observations and experiences in our world. A first connection might be exploring how religion is used to justify current political arrangements and regimes by making appeals to "covenant" or "scrolls." Sociologists of religion note that religion can provide a "sacred canopy" that attempts to provide divine legitimation to a social order.[1] Appeals to a divine source, such as a covenant in David's case, or a sense of manifest destiny provide overarching legitimacy that discourages (and perhaps even punishes) challenges to regimes as though they are equivalent to challenges of divine authority.

However, others note that religion can also be "disruptive."[2] By making appeals to divine sources, such as the scroll in Ezekiel, religion also challenges the social order as transgressive and rebellious against God's purposes for human communities. Sermons can probe congregants to think of the ways they use religion and religious language when thinking about social order and political systems. Does belief in God provide justification of these systems, regardless of actions or policies, or does belief in God provide the means by which we prophetically speak about the transgressions we see?

Sermons could explore historical examples where leaders emerged in times of chaos and turmoil with messianic claims for deliverance. Certainly one of the most evil in recent memory is Hitler and his promises to restore Germany to Aryan superiority and cultural supremacy after losses in World War I. He made appeals to Christian leaders and churches and, indeed, found significant support. What a contrast to Nelson Mandela, a leader who, in the injustice and violence of apartheid in South Africa, called on people to draw on the resources of their faith to unite them around higher values of belonging, solidarity, justice, and mercy.

Sermons can explore examples of social movements and leaders that drew on the sources of faith to bring about changes reflective of God's justice and liberation, as opposed to those with their messianic, exclusive, and narcissistic aspirations. Some examples of social movements from which to gain inspiration are the early abolitionist and women's suffrage movements, the civil rights movement in the United States, the International Justice Mission, and the sanctuary movement, to name just a few. Sermons can connect persons to local initiatives in their communities that are attempting to disrupt the status quo in favor of God's commitments to justice and the well-being of all persons. Persons can be invited to share these ministries from the pulpit and invite congregants to participate.

Another connection might be found in the contrast between David and Ezekiel, the triumphant king and a mortal prophet. They provide two contrasting images of religious figures, one who had ultimate power and claims as the "Lord's anointed" (e.g., 2 Sam. 1:14, of Saul), and another with a clear sense of his own humanness, yet still a prophet. They represent what Brueggemann contrasts as the "royal consciousness" and the prophetic "pathos."[3] Preachers can help congregations reflect on the dangerous language of triumphalism, thinking there is a special calling from God that the church should be in charge and privileged above all other religious communities. The prophetic faith of Ezekiel was one that mourned for what had happened and now had a hard message of speaking truth to power.

Preachers might challenge the language of a "church triumphant" and other military metaphors used to describe the church's mission. Are we concerned about winning? Do churches feel

1. Peter Berger, *The Sacred Canopy: Elements of a Sociological Theory of Religion* (New York: Doubleday, 1967).
2. Christian Smith, *Disruptive Religion: The Force of Faith in Social Movement Activism* (New York: Routledge, 1996).
3. Walter Brueggemann, *The Prophetic Imagination* (Minneapolis: Fortress, 1978), 21–58.

as if they need to be "in charge" in order to be effective? Are we instead willing to take the risk embodied by the mortal prophet Ezekiel, one anointed by the Spirit, who was faithful to the message God gave him, with little guarantee of effectiveness? Preachers can mine the sources of church history for examples such as Perpetua and Polycarp, who did not seek to be martyrs, but whose faithfulness challenged the "royal consciousness" of imperial Rome. Modern-day examples can also be helpful, such as Archbishop Oscar Romero and the religious women killed in El Salvador, Maura Clark, Ita Ford, Dorothy Kazel, and Jean Donovan. Prophetic ministry à la Ezekiel, Perpetua, Polycarp, and others, is not a form of masochism. Instead, it is a calling that is taken on with soberness and sadness, knowing faithfulness to the message of God will come with risks.

WYNDY CORBIN REUSCHLING

Psalm 123

¹To you I lift up my eyes,
      O you who are enthroned in the heavens!
²As the eyes of servants
      look to the hand of their master,
as the eyes of a maid
      to the hand of her mistress,
so our eyes look to the LORD our God,
      until he has mercy upon us.

³Have mercy upon us, O LORD, have mercy upon us,
      for we have had more than enough of contempt.
⁴Our soul has had more than its fill
      of the scorn of those who are at ease,
      of the contempt of the proud.

Psalm 48

¹Great is the LORD and greatly to be praised
      in the city of our God.
His holy mountain, ²beautiful in elevation,
      is the joy of all the earth,
Mount Zion, in the far north,
      the city of the great King.
³Within its citadels God
      has shown himself a sure defense.

⁴Then the kings assembled,
      they came on together.
⁵As soon as they saw it, they were astounded;
      they were in panic, they took to flight;
⁶trembling took hold of them there,
      pains as of a woman in labor,
⁷as when an east wind shatters
      the ships of Tarshish.
⁸As we have heard, so have we seen
      in the city of the LORD of hosts,
in the city of our God,
      which God establishes forever.

⁹We ponder your steadfast love, O God,
      in the midst of your temple.
¹⁰Your name, O God, like your praise,
      reaches to the ends of the earth.
Your right hand is filled with victory.
      ¹¹Let Mount Zion be glad,

let the towns of Judah rejoice
  because of your judgments.

¹²Walk about Zion, go all around it,
  count its towers,
¹³consider well its ramparts;
  go through its citadels,
that you may tell the next generation
  ¹⁴that this is God,
our God forever and ever.
  He will be our guide forever.

Connecting the Psalm with Scripture and Worship

Psalm 123. The first reading is Ezekiel 2:1–5. The Lord fills the mortal with a spirit and tells him that he will be sent to the people of Israel, people who have turned against their God. The text is full of descriptors of Israel's sin: they have rebelled and transgressed (Ezek. 2:3). They are impudent and stubborn (v. 4). They "refuse to hear" and are "a rebellious house" (v. 5). The passage ends with assurance that, whether or not Israel is willing/able to hear the words of God's servant Ezekiel, "they shall know that there has been a prophet among them" (v. 5).

When read as a response to Ezekiel 2:1–5, Psalm 123 offers a prayer from the lips of Israel, the rebellious people to whom the prophet Ezekiel is sent. Whereas the people of Israel in Ezekiel 2 seem decidedly unaware of their sin, however, the speaker of Psalm 123 is conscious of a level of rebellion or suffering and prays for God's mercy. The speaker leans on God, not only for forgiveness but for life itself. Psalm 123 is one of the Songs of Ascents (Pss. 120–134). As in other Songs of Ascents, the psalmist shifts from first person singular to plural, suggesting both individual lament and the collective lament of a group. It is likely that the Songs of Ascents were sung by pilgrims on a journey to Jerusalem for a festal celebration.[1] The object of the people's complaint in the psalm comes in verse 4: "the scorn of those who are at ease [and] the contempt of the proud." The specific

lament suggests the psalm comes from a postexilic context.[2]

When the reading of the lament psalm begins, most hearers will be expecting the structure of more familiar lament psalms, such as Psalm 42: the speaker addresses God, offers a complaint, and ends with an assurance of hope in God. Psalm 123, however, has no such assurance; the song ends with the complaint of the people, as if the psalmist begins with eyes "lift[ed] up" to God and ends with eyes cast down on the reality of the people's suffering. The psalmist does not tie up the prayer with a ribbon of hope, instead leaving the hearer with the frayed ends of heartfelt lament. The psalmist sits in the complaint of the people without rushing to assurance, and the preacher should consider doing the same. The psalm is a healthy and welcome reminder that our sovereign God is with us in our suffering and our sin, even if we cannot yet see the way out.

With the mass of patriarchal language that drips from much of the Old and New Testaments, the preacher or liturgist should not miss an opportunity to "lift up" the alternate images for God found in the rich liturgical language of the psalms. Verse 2 offers parallel gender images for God: God is imagined as both master and mistress, with the people of God as servants and maids. The liturgist could choose to continue that parallel language in the prayers of

1. James L. Mays, *Psalms,* Interpretation (Louisville, KY: John Knox, 1994), 119–20.
2. J. Clinton McCann Jr., "The Book of Psalms," in *The New Interpreter's Bible* (Nashville: Abingdon, 1996), 4:1187.

intercession, alternating images for God traditionally considered masculine, ones traditionally considered feminine, and/or images that describe God beyond the framework of gender. Gender language aside, the master/servant and mistress/maid pairings clearly emphasize the sovereignty of God and the humble position of God's people.

Psalm 123 is filled with language for liturgical use, and its phrases are especially suited for a prayer of confession. The liturgist could begin the prayer with verse 1 and then offer specific prayers of confession. After each specific prayer, the people may borrow verse 3 as a corporate refrain: "Have mercy upon us, O Lord. Have mercy upon us." The language and imagery of verse 2 can be adapted and employed as an assurance of pardon:

> As the eyes of the servants look to the hand
>   of their master,
> as the eyes of a maid to the hand of her
>   mistress,
> so our eyes look to the Lord our God, who
>   has mercy upon us.

Psalm 48. Second Samuel 5:1–5, 9–10 brings us the anointing of David as king of Israel. God has made a king of the ruddy little shepherd boy, the youngest son of Jesse, and through him God will continue to guide and bless the people Israel. The text makes it clear that David's anointing as king is significant, not because of any personal attribute of the former shepherd boy himself, but because of the power of God, who is with him. King David is far from perfect, as the next chapters will make clear, but God is with him nonetheless.

At the end of the reading from 2 Samuel, the hearer is left with a celebratory feeling, a tone that is carried through and amplified in the response of Psalm 48. The psalm rings with praise as if it were a song sung at David's anointing, except that David was anointed at Hebron and the psalmist is seated at Mount Zion. The psalm is a song of Zion (see also Pss. 76, 84, 87, 122), a part of the Korahite and Elohistic collections of psalms.[3]

Psalm 48 imagines Zion as the center of the universe, the center of God's praise, and the center of God's people. In our global, pluralistic culture, that image can be problematic and may tempt the preacher to take a trail that ought not be traveled. The good news of this psalm is not that any physical place is the center of God's love. The good news is that the steadfast love of God is the center of life itself. The psalmist certainly praises God for gifts specific to Zion: the land itself, the strong military defenses, the victory in battle. It is important to notice, though, that the psalmist also praises God's steadfast love (*hesed*) and judgment. The psalmist's view of God's blessing is much more expansive than it might first appear. Jerusalem has become a physical representation of the universal reign of God: "the city of the great King" (Ps. 48:2), who reigns over all the earth. Much like the newly anointed King David, who is blessed, not because of any personal characteristic but because of God's presence with him, Zion is great, not because of the beauty of its mountain or the strength of its fortresses but because the Holy One of Israel has made it so.

It is appropriate to read or sing all of Psalm 48 in response to the 2 Samuel reading. The psalm is longer than some, but it would be a shame to lose any of the rich theological language by truncating the text.

Verses 9–10 make a powerful call to worship:

> Reader One: We ponder your steadfast love, O
>   God, in the midst of your temple.
> Reader Two: Your name, O God, like your
>   praise, reaches to the ends of the
>   earth.

The preacher or liturgist may find that verses 12–14 provide a creative framework for a charge and benediction: a chance to charge the congregation to walk about the world God has created, count the blessings, consider well the joy, go through the waters, that they may tell the next generation that this is God, our God forever and ever.

ANNA GEORGE TRAYNHAM

---

3. McCann, "The Book of Psalms," 871.

2 Corinthians 12:2–10

[2]I know a person in Christ who fourteen years ago was caught up to the third heaven—whether in the body or out of the body I do not know; God knows. [3]And I know that such a person—whether in the body or out of the body I do not know; God knows— [4]was caught up into Paradise and heard things that are not to be told, that no mortal is permitted to repeat. [5]On behalf of such a one I will boast, but on my own behalf I will not boast, except of my weaknesses. [6]But if I wish to boast, I will not be a fool, for I will be speaking the truth. But I refrain from it, so that no one may think better of me than what is seen in me or heard from me, [7]even considering the exceptional character of the revelations. Therefore, to keep me from being too elated, a thorn was given me in the flesh, a messenger of Satan to torment me, to keep me from being too elated. [8]Three times I appealed to the Lord about this, that it would leave me, [9]but he said to me, "My grace is sufficient for you, for power is made perfect in weakness." So, I will boast all the more gladly of my weaknesses, so that the power of Christ may dwell in me. [10]Therefore I am content with weaknesses, insults, hardships, persecutions, and calamities for the sake of Christ; for whenever I am weak, then I am strong.

Commentary 1: Connecting the Reading with Scripture

Paul's passionate defense of his ministry and authority climaxes in this intimately revealing chapter, full of pathos and gospel truth. Moved by "divine jealousy" for the Corinthian church he has established and loved (2 Cor. 11:2), he chides them for falling prey to the teachings peddled by "super apostles" proclaiming a "different gospel," boasting of apostolic authority above Paul's, destroying the unity of the church, and inciting a spirit of competition through their open derision of him (2 Cor. 2:17; 10:12; 11:13–14, 19–20; 12:20). These "false apostles" accuse Paul of being weak, "untrained in speech," a slanderer, and an impostor (2 Cor. 10:10; 11:6; Rom. 3:8).

Troubled by the lack of support from the Corinthian church, Paul unwillingly builds on the long list of things that should have proven his calling (2 Cor. 11:21b–30) by appealing to his experience of "revelations" in years past (12:1). His reticence to boast about his credentials explains his awkward reference to himself in the third person ("I know a person in Christ," 12:2). Paul seems to differentiate between the grace of God that allowed him such revelations and his own humanity. There is no boasting where the fount of blessing is divine grace. His repetition of being in or out of the body (vv. 2, 3) when "caught up" to the "third heaven" (understood as God's abode) and "paradise" (a place or state of conscious rest in God after death and before the Parousia) may suggest an experience of transformation or heightened spiritual self. It may simply hint at prior queries by Christians about the relation of his embodied or disembodied experience in paradise to what one might experience in the afterlife (1 Cor. 15:35).

Paul's double emphases—that only "God knows"—make the query a moot point. Any insistence is met with his inability (*exon*, 2 Cor. 12:4, "unlawful, not permitted") to express the content of the revelations. While the question of our nature after death may be something of a conundrum, the matter of our state—one of blessedness with God—is not. Already Paul has taught that in death, Christ's followers will eternally enjoy God's presence (1 Cor. 15:50–54; Rom. 8). His vision preaches to an eschatology of hope in, and through, the crucified but risen Christ.

Divine Poverty

O man, give up your resources! Divine poverty is enough for you. Put off the packs of your riches; a burdened man cannot make his way along the narrow road all the way to the work of the Lord's harvest. Come unencumbered, come free to the tasks, before you get stripped and robbed, and arrested for punishment as a worker unfaithful to all. For, as it is written: "Riches do not go along with a dying man."

Let your conscience be your wallet, let your life be your bread, in order that the true bread in your life can be Christ, who said: "I am the bread." Regard your heavenly reward as your salary. For, if in order to follow Christ a man has dispossessed himself of everything and faithfully scorned and despised what he had, he can ask a reward from Christ without any anxiety.

Peter Chrysologus, "Christ, Our Example in Manifold Ways; The Vocation of the Apostles; The Counsel of Poverty," in *Saint Peter Chrysologus Selected Sermons and Saint Valerian Homilies,* trans. George E. Ganss, *The Fathers of the Church,* vol. 17 (Washington, DC: Catholic University of America, 1953), 282.

Paul's "elation" (2 Cor. 12:7, *hyperairō*, "to be conceited, arrogant, cocky") over the "exceptional character" of his revelations was mitigated by a "thorn in the flesh" (*kolaphizō*, "a strike with a fist, a buffeting, a stake") that tormented him. Perhaps more perplexing than the identity of the painful and persistent thorn—scholars do not agree on whether this was a physical or psychological ailment—is Paul's reference to its source: a messenger from Satan. Whether or not one believes in a real Satan, his statement raises questions about the power of evil to afflict Christians. If God did not send this suffering, was God allowing it? While a theologically weighty question, Paul does not address this here. Neither does he question or blame God for his ills. Rather, he turns to the Lord in prayer.

Paul's prayer is significant for what it does and does not illustrate. One cannot ignore, for instance, that Paul begins his testimony concerning his very personal matter with the specific number of times he prayed for release: three (v. 8). Was he intending to bring to mind Jesus' own three appeals in Gethsemane and God's response (Mark 14:32–41; Matt. 26:39, 42–44)?[1] Jesus asked for the possibility of "this cup" to pass from him, adding, "Yet not what I want but what you want." Was this Paul's prayer as well? God dignified Paul with an answer ("but he said to me," 2 Cor. 12:9). The common use of the conjunction "but" instead of "and" for the Greek *kai* in verse 9 may cast an unintended negative connotation over God's response: "My grace is sufficient for you, for power is made perfect in weakness." Did Paul receive what he needed, empowering grace, but not what he wanted, healing? If Paul, like Jesus, prayed for God's will to be done in his life (Rom. 8:26, 27), it is not wrong to assume that Paul received what he needed *and* what he wanted.

How should we react to God's response when, like Jesus, we pray, "Your will be done" (Matt. 6:10)? For Paul, God's response intended "to keep [him] from being too elated" (repeated twice). That God's grace is to be sufficient in suffering is not something to bemoan. Paul's attitude of gladness confirms this (2 Cor. 12:9, 10; Rom. 8:6, 18, 31). God's grace is God's mercy (Ps. 123:2). Writing to the Romans from Corinth, Paul admonishes them to "know that all things work together for good for those who love God, who are called according to his purpose" (Rom. 8:28). If God's purpose for us is to "be conformed to the image of [God's] Son" (v. 29), it undoubtedly entails learning to surrender our will so that God's purpose for us may be fulfilled.

Human understanding of power is turned on its head. Reliance on God is our strength and our confidence (2 Cor. 2:3, 4; 12:10). "We have this treasure," says Paul, "in clay jars . . . this extraordinary power belongs to God and does not come from us" (4:7). If God's power is not something we possess, who are we to boast about it?! The crucified Christ is "the power of God and the wisdom of God" (1 Cor. 1:24; 2 Cor. 4:5; 13:4). The divine paradox is that to be

---

1. Recollection of Jesus' appeal would have been transmitted orally to Paul and the communities, since the Gospels were not yet written.

strong in Christ we must give up self-reliance and seem weak to the world. To be wise, we must become fools who forsake human "craftiness" and rely on "the message of the cross," the power of God (1 Cor. 1:18–31; 3:18; 2 Cor. 4:2; Ps. 9:11; Job 5:13). Therein lie power and authority and why Paul could boast about being "afflicted but not crushed" (2 Cor. 4:8).

Paul sets parameters for distinguishing between true and false apostles. True apostles, followers of Christ, do not commend themselves; it is the Lord that calls and commends them (2 Cor. 10:12–17; 12:12); they are merely servants working together according to God's grace (Rom. 3:5, 7–9; 2 Cor. 4:1; 5); their competence comes from God (2 Cor. 3:4–6); through their submission to God, they are continually being transformed into the image of Christ (2 Cor. 3:18; 7); they do not come to take or tear down but to build (12:14, 19); they pursue and speak the truth in love and know that "nothing is to be gained by [boasting]"

(12:1; 1 Cor. 13:1–14:1; 16:13). The lections remind us, however, that none of this exempts God's servants from contempt, even from the unexpected. The prophet Ezekiel, for instance, was met by a "rebellious house," and Jesus himself was amazed at the unbelief from those of his very hometown (Ezek. 2:1–5; Mark 6:1–13).

Although pithy, this passage preaches at many levels. Besides what has already been pointed out, one could consider the following: How might cultural norms or market-driven industries cloud our judgment concerning true servants? What does it mean to be called? What is the role of prayer? How do we understand grace when it does not look or sound like what we expect? What should be our response to God's grace? What does it mean to be strong in Christ, even though we seem weak to the world around us? How might this define our personal and corporate lives, goals, perspective, and mission in Christ?

ZAIDA MALDONADO PÉREZ

Commentary 2: Connecting the Reading with the World

This week in our liturgical calendar coincides with Independence Day, a federal holiday in the United States commemorating the signing of the Declaration of Independence on July 4, 1776. In addition to festive civic events marking the founding of the nation, many people celebrate the holiday at barbecues and picnics with their families and friends. After a day of good food, hearty conversation, and infectious laughter, people assemble at nightfall to watch wondrous displays of fireworks together in small towns and big cities across the country.

We also note that not all find joy on this holiday. Throughout US history, oppressed and vulnerable communities have experienced deep pain and frustration because of the juxtaposition of the public commemorations of national independence and their unmet demands for freedom and civil rights. On July 5, 1852, Frederick Douglass delivered a speech to an assembly of

several hundred abolitionists in Rochester, New York, highlighting how the holiday presented an opportunity for collective repentance rather than celebration. Douglass remarked, "What, to the American slave, is your Fourth of July? I answer: a day that reveals to him, more than all other days in the year, the gross injustice and cruelty to which he is the constant victim."[2] He also criticized religious hymns, prayers, and sermons that honored Independence Day but ignored the great sin and shame of slavery as hypocritical and immoral. Douglass refused to celebrate the Fourth of July until all enslaved African Americans were emancipated. Many historians contend this address was one of the greatest antislavery speeches in the United States.

In 2 Corinthians 12, Paul testifies to a powerful vision in which he encountered God in heaven and heard sacred words that could not be expressed among humans on earth (2 Cor.

---

2. Frederick Douglass, *In the Words of Frederick Douglass: Quotations from Liberty's Champion*, ed. John R. McKivigan and Heather L. Kaufman (Ithaca and London: Cornell University Press, 2012), 103.

12:4). Paul also receives a thorn in his flesh to prevent him "from being too elated," which is translated from the Greek verb *hyperairō* in 12:7 and appears in other English translations as "exalted above measure" (NKJV) and "becoming conceited" (NIV). Paul prays three times to ask God to remove the thorn, but God answers with a provision of grace and a lesson that God's power is manifest in weakness (vv. 8–9).

In its immediate context, 2 Corinthians 12:2–10 contains Paul's response to religious rivals in Corinth who are challenging him with their own competing claims based on their spiritual experiences and professed knowledge of special heavenly revelations. Thus, Paul first establishes his own authority through a recounting of his incomparable vision. He then rebukes his rivals through a boasting of his weakness, not his strength, to reinforce the message that God's power is most clearly revealed in Jesus' death and the weakness of the cross. Rather than celebrating his accomplishments, Paul chooses to elevate the insults, hardships, persecutions, and calamities that accompany his ministry.

In our contemporary context, we must discern how to utilize this passage in ways that instill humility and inspire justice. Certainly we, too, are prone to exalt ourselves above measure and become conceited when we fail to acknowledge God's grace or flail about in self-absorbed petty competitions with others. In the 1987 film *Wall Street*, the character Gordon Gekko, a cutthroat financier, illustrates the lure of self-exaltation in his declarations that greed is good for the ways it motivates people like himself to accomplish great things. *Wall Street* constructs the fictional character of Gekko as an archetype to capture the illegal, unethical, and ruthless world of finance and stock trading.

Our faith commitments do not cohere with Gekko's narcissistic pursuit of wealth by any means necessary, but we have experienced the temptation to indulge in self-exaltation and the turmoil that accompanies feelings of weakness. We grow frustrated when our pursuits of goodness and righteousness—ranging from securing employment to provide for one's family to

seeking more inclusive ministries to addressing changing neighborhood patterns—do not find success. Like Paul we ask God to remove the "thorns," such as physical ailments, difficult family members, frustrating colleagues, and character flaws we believe are preventing us from thriving. In these instances, it is appropriate to remind Christians to surrender our weaknesses to God and trust God's power will strengthen us.

At the same time, we must avoid conflating individual application and structural analysis in our preaching from this passage. Paul's vision should not be distorted to instruct oppressed persons and communities to accept discriminatory laws and unfair conditions as necessary "thorns" with divine purposes. Rather, Paul's proclamation of God's power being made perfect in weakness challenges us to enter the places of brokenness in our congregations and neighborhoods. For those of us with power and privilege, Paul's admonition on boasting is pertinent when engaging vulnerable persons and marginalized communities. In our efforts to strengthen the weak, we ought to be careful about subtly assuming postures of superiority, like the "super-apostles" Paul rebukes in 2 Corinthians 12:11, and always remember all God's children are equal recipients of God's grace.

Katie Geneva Cannon, a womanist theologian and ethicist, constructs an understanding of God's grace, grounded in the African American experience, that illumines the interpretative nuance required to preach from this passage. Cannon offers two definitions of grace that constantly and generatively interact with another. First, "grace is a divine gift of redeeming love that empowers African Americans to confront shocking, absurd, death-dealing disjunctions in life, so that when we look at our outer struggles and inner strength we see interpretive possibilities for creative change." Second, "grace is the indwelling of God's spirit that enables Christians of African descent to live conscious lives of thanksgiving, by deepening our knowledge of forgiveness given in Christ, so that even in situations of oppression we celebrate our status as beloved creatures made in God's image."[3] As

---

3. Katie Geneva Cannon, "Transformative Grace," in *Feminist and Womanist Essays in Reformed Dogmatics*, ed. Amy Plantinga Pauw and Serene Jones (Louisville, KY, and London: Westminster John Knox, 2006), 143–44.

Cannon looks back at the rich history of African American Christians, she makes an important connection between expressing gratitude for God's grace and enacting resistance against oppressive forces with God's power as interrelated rather than oppositional practices.

Several English versions of the Bible translate the Greek verb *teleō* in 2 Corinthians 12:9 as "made perfect," to delineate how God's power operates in human weakness. The preamble to the US Constitution also employs the idea of establishing justice and securing freedom in the pursuit of "a more perfect union." Yet the nation's history, as Douglass poignantly and painfully illustrated in 1852, reveals the many shortcomings and moral failings of a nation that has denied equal rights to many persons. As Christians in the United States, we are careful to respect the differences between our religious confessions and national identities. We also find connections between our Christian conviction that God's power is made perfect in weakness and our civic commitment to participating in a more perfect union.

With the presence of Independence Day during this particular week in the life of the church, preachers may ask their congregations what the Fourth of July means to them, with the recognition that answers may vary based on life experiences and social contexts. The universal message that God's grace is sufficient for all simultaneously cultivates in us a spirit of humility and challenges us to confront the evils of injustice that are harming children, communities, and creation today.

WILLIAM YOO

Mark 6:1–13

¹He left that place and came to his hometown, and his disciples followed him. ²On the sabbath he began to teach in the synagogue, and many who heard him were astounded. They said, "Where did this man get all this? What is this wisdom that has been given to him? What deeds of power are being done by his hands! ³Is not this the carpenter, the son of Mary and brother of James and Joses and Judas and Simon, and are not his sisters here with us?" And they took offense at him. ⁴Then Jesus said to them, "Prophets are not without honor, except in their hometown, and among their own kin, and in their own house." ⁵And he could do no deed of power there, except that he laid his hands on a few sick people and cured them. ⁶And he was amazed at their unbelief.

Then he went about among the villages teaching. ⁷He called the twelve and began to send them out two by two, and gave them authority over the unclean spirits. ⁸He ordered them to take nothing for their journey except a staff; no bread, no bag, no money in their belts; ⁹but to wear sandals and not to put on two tunics. ¹⁰He said to them, "Wherever you enter a house, stay there until you leave the place. ¹¹If any place will not welcome you and they refuse to hear you, as you leave, shake off the dust that is on your feet as a testimony against them." ¹²So they went out and proclaimed that all should repent. ¹³They cast out many demons, and anointed with oil many who were sick and cured them.

Commentary 1: Connecting the Reading with Scripture

Mark is a story of disruption. Beginning with the arrival of the Holy Spirit through the shredded heavens in 1:10 and ending with a tomb that used to contain a corpse, the Gospel describes the arrival of something new. Although many people in Mark fail to perceive the contours of this new thing, still it effects transformation—through altered boundary lines, transgressed norms, conflicts about authority, and the arrival of new realities that are part of what Jesus calls the reign of God.

The juxtaposition of a story about Jesus' rejection at home (Mark 6:1–6a) and one about the effects of his ministry multiplying through his followers (Mark 6:6b–13) calls attention to the transformational aspects of the good news. The message Jesus proclaims has an expansive character. It will always encounter opposition and confusion, sometimes from people who

have close connections to Jesus, but it will also find hospitable welcome in places where it brings healing and wholeness.

After recording a series of astounding deeds—calming a stormy sea, destroying a legion of demons, unintentionally healing a long-suffering woman, and bringing a dead girl back to life—the narrative follows Jesus to his hometown. There the story proceeds differently. Although those who hear him teach express amazement at his wisdom and power, as others have done previously, the distinguishing features of this scene are offense and the absence of faith.[1] Either the initial amazement expressed in 6:2 quickly fades, or it is fueled by incredulity instead of respect, because by 6:3 it is clear: "they took offense at him." The verb *skandalizō* ("to stumble, to take offense"), given its usage also in 4:17; 14:27, 29, implies a rejection, not just disappointment or

---

1. The verb for "astounded" (*ekplēssō*) appears also in Mark 1:22; 7:37; 10:26; 11:18. Mark uses different but synonymous terms in 5:20; 6:6; 12:17; 15:5, 44 (*[ek]thaumazō*); 1:27; 10:32 (*thambeō*); 2:12; 5:42; 6:51 (*existēmi*); and 5:42; 16:8 (*ekstasis*).

dishonor. Who cares what he says and does? He cannot be worth respecting or following. His family and the scribes from Jerusalem arrive at similar conclusions in 3:21–22, although their specific assessments of him differed.

Apparently, the people in Nazareth see things or know things that other audiences do not, or they find Jesus too dangerous or destructive. When they call him "the son of Mary" and refer to his siblings, they recall the statement from 3:21, saying that Jesus' family had concluded he had lost his sanity, and the scene in 3:31–35, in which his family was unable to seize him.[2] The residents of Nazareth, a village of fewer than a thousand residents, side with his family, perhaps because his kin have suffered on account of his absence. When the crowd refers to him without referring to his father, they may be emphasizing that this grown son has left a widowed mother and siblings to fend for themselves while he travels around Galilee leading a movement.

Jesus offers a mixed response to the rejection. On one hand, he is amazed by the lack of faith, even though he has experienced similar shortcomings from his own followers in 4:40. On the other hand, he describes the chilly reception in Nazareth as inevitable. He likens it to the hostility that biblical prophets received before him, as seen in passages such as Ezekiel 2:1–5.[3] Similar claims that true prophets encounter opposition appear also in Matthew 5:12; 13:57; 23:37; Luke 4:24; 6:23; 13:33–34; John 4:44; Acts 7:52; 1 Thessalonians 2:15. In Mark, Jesus speaks specifically of rejection from "kin" and "house." Mark will not refer to Jesus' family again, but will indicate that Jesus' followers constitute a new kinship group (Mark 10:29–30).

The comment about Jesus' inability to perform a "deed of power" in Nazareth, except for a few healings, is peculiar (cf. the rewording in Matt. 13:58) and amusing. Nazareth may not receive all the blessings it might have received from Jesus, but that still does not stop him from manifesting the reign of God's arrival, albeit on a smaller scale! In this story of inbreaking and opposition, the latter cannot finally halt the former.

By pairing the story of Jesus' rejection in Nazareth with the sending of the apostles, the lectionary invites comparisons. Jesus returns home; the apostles journey outward. The Nazarenes accuse Jesus of neglecting his responsibilities and relatives who need him; the apostles enter homes of strangers and bring good news.

The Bible includes several stories of charismatic leaders who seek to expand or perpetuate their influence through their helpers and successors. Moses appointed judges (Exod. 18:13–27), and God equipped many of Moses' associates to prophesy (Num. 11:16–30). Elisha received a double share of Elijah's spirit (2 Kgs. 2:1–15). Earlier in Mark, Jesus chose twelve of his followers to "be with him, and to be sent out to proclaim the message, and to have authority to cast out demons" (Mark 3:14–15). In the current passage, he equips the Twelve with "authority" and offers instructions about receiving hospitality and dealing with rejection.

Jesus' instructions reveal characteristics of the apostles' ministry. By working in pairs, their words carry greater weight (see Deut. 19:15; Matt. 18:16; John 8:17; 2 Cor. 13:1), and their partnership calls attention to a wider community to which they belong. In traveling simply, they contribute to their message's credibility and declare their confidence that God will provide for them (cf. Matt. 6:25–34). By not moving from house to house in a single village, they make it clear that they are not chasing greater comforts. When they shake an inhospitable town's dust from their feet, they completely dissociate themselves from that place's arrogance or ignorance. Just as Jesus will not be constrained by the opposition he experiences in Nazareth, likewise they should be ready to move on when necessary.

In short, the apostles' ministry is a spoken and enacted demonstration of authority, an authority they receive from Jesus Christ. Yet this transformative authority expresses itself in powerlessness, dependency, and relationships.

2. Although the NRSV renders Mark 3:21 differently, the Greek text indicates that it is Jesus' family and not unidentified "people" who decide he has "gone out of his mind."

3. Similar proverbs about truth-tellers appear in other literary settings. Note, for example, from the moral philosopher Plutarch: "The most sensible and wisest people are little cared for in their own hometowns" (*De Exilio* 604D; quoted in Joel Marcus, *Mark 1–8*, Anchor Bible 27 [New York: Doubleday, 2000], 376).

That is a familiar theme in the New Testament, especially in Paul's descriptions of both his ministry (1 Thess. 2:3–12; 1 Cor. 9:3–15) and the upside-down character of Jesus' crucifixion, in which divine power manifests itself in weakness (1 Cor. 1:18–25; see also 2 Cor. 12:8–10; 13:4; Phil. 2:1–8). The same paradoxical dynamic appears when Jesus characterizes the life of discipleship: "You know that among the Gentiles those whom they recognize as their rulers lord it over them, and their great ones are tyrants over them. But it is not so among you; but whoever wishes to become great among you must be your servant, and whoever wishes to be first among you must be slave of all. For the Son of Man came not to be served but to serve, and to give his life a ransom for many" (Mark 10:42–45). If anyone thinks that vision of self-giving is attractive or an obvious virtue, they should ask Nazareth's residents about it. Jesus' former neighbors can report how difficult it is to embrace such a vision because it does not align with conventional expectations or values.

MATTHEW L. SKINNER

Commentary 2: Connecting the Reading with the World

Following Jesus' great deeds over long-term illness, social boundaries, and death itself in the previous narrative section (Mark 5:21–43), Mark shows us a different side of Jesus' ministry in 6:1–6a as he comes back to his hometown with disciples in tow.

At a very surface reading, the turn in the narrative might mirror the reality of highs and lows in the life of the church and in our ministries. This is a theme worthy of preaching, especially in the summer season when many congregations experience a "summer slump" in attendance, and congregational energy tends to lag. There are seasons in which we find ourselves riding high in ministry, when it seems that our ministries are strong and effective, when our witness to the community and the world seemingly has the capacity to change the world. Then there are Jesus-in-Nazareth seasons: times when every faithful act seems to be thwarted by circumstance or by people—people we know and love!—who seem opposed to divine power for healing and liberation. We dare not read and preach the previous narrative (5:21–43) without this one close behind, lest we get caught in one extreme or the other. It is just as dangerous to believe the hype about our own successes as it is to focus only on the obstacles and failures that come in the path of ministry.

Let us face it: Jesus does all the right things. In fact, in Nazareth he does the things that he has done elsewhere that have been wildly successful. Those of us who engage in ministry and assess our effectiveness are quick to analyze our ministry methods and wonder if a change is warranted when success does not come. In doing so, we are tempted to dizzy ourselves with the latest fads and programming. That is not to say that we should be stuck in outdated, ineffective models of ministry. Nevertheless, perhaps in preaching this text we could take the opportunity to remind our congregations (and ourselves) about the realities of ministry, based on the shocking scene of what Jesus experiences.

Corporate myths of unending growth and ever-increasing success are not reality for the church's ministries. Sometimes we face obstacles, even when we are faithful. Sometimes our ministries encounter resistance, even when we do the right things. A sermon might point out that it is not Jesus' method in ministry that has changed, but the context and the people who are gathered. We need not vilify these people in doing so, or any other contemporary analogy to them. They are faithful people gathered for worship, seeking to live into the will of God. So even if we were Jesus, our success in ministry is never guaranteed. In an era of church decline, that seems worthy of saying from the pulpit.

Here is where the other half of the text comes in. Immediately after the somewhat failed Nazareth mission, Jesus goes back out teaching in the villages. This short transition out of Nazareth is quickly followed by Jesus' commissioning of the disciples. Do we catch that? On the heels of Jesus' first failure, he sends out disciples to proclaim the same message, to anoint, and to cure. If ever there was a tenuous, doubt-filled situation for Mark's perpetually troubled disciples, this would be it. "You want us to go and do what you do, when you have just been challenged?" Mark matter-of-factly tells us that they go according to Jesus' instructions, casting out demons and curing the sick as they go. The message for us seems simple, but no less challenging: in the face of failure, do not be swayed. When obstacles come, carry out Jesus' ministry regardless, even without a safety net (or endowment).

This passage might not only suggest *how* we are to minister in the face of challenge but also challenge us to consider *who* carries out God's work in the world. First, of course, we consider Jesus. In Nazareth, we get a mixed message about Jesus. On the one hand, the hometown crowd recognizes Jesus' "wisdom" and "deeds of power" (6:2), but they are scandalized by him (v. 3), and he can perform "no deed of power there" (v. 5). One of the powers of this narrative is that their reaction ruffles our feathers. This is good narrative design and a possible homiletical setup. As readers we relish in the hometown crowd's foolish misstep. We can take the high ground here! Whether the attribution of his parentage as "the son of Mary" is intended to be slanderous or not, there is a clear frame for Jesus by the crowd gathered in the synagogue. The reality of who Jesus is has exceeded communal expectations. Jesus' teaching and healing ministries have exposed their assumptions about him: he could not and should not be more than what they have known. As a result, their lack of faith leads to no deed of power, except for a few people being cured.

While the way Mark frames their reaction might be designed to ruffle our own feathers (he is Jesus, after all, and they should know better!), there is a double edge to this sword. The problem of the hometown gathering is not that these people misrecognize Jesus. They do not mistake him for someone else. Quite the contrary. They know who he is. The problem is that the way that they see him is too limited.

So, a sermon might use this as an opportunity to bring our congregational Christology into focus. Who is Jesus, and what picture of him emerges in our congregational ministries? How is it that we see Jesus and name him, not just in personal confession but to the world through what we do as congregations? What picture of Jesus does our community see in and through us? A sermon could serve as an interesting launching pad for conversations that focus church boards/sessions/consistories or mission councils and discussion. It might also serve as a good frame for a family conversation as well.

In our current contentious landscape, we should also consider who can be commissioned to carry on the ministry of Jesus, and what happens when we "take offense" (v. 3) at those God has commissioned to be God's agents. Notice that the Nazareth crowd's lack of faith did not have an effect just on their personal, self-interested lives. Their lack of faith blocked the path for the "deeds of power" Jesus might have performed on behalf of the entire community. Knowing Mark's narratives thus far, our imagination might run wild with possibilities for what he could have done in his hometown. He probably knew their deepest needs, and we might imagine how Jesus knew the needs of the community from early childhood, linking them to the needs in our own community.

Our individual and communal healing might be limited because of the limits we place on whom we see as fit to lead in God's mission. Our lack of faith or limited faith concerning those who would lead might make us our own worst enemies. We might stand in the way of our own healing or the healing of others because our vision for who can serve and minister is too small.

A sermon might invite listeners to consider the historical and present-day limitations we place on others to accomplish God's purposes. We might consider how individuals, congregations, and church polity have looked upon women, racial and ethnic minorities, children/youth, LGBTQ+ persons, and others who have sensed God's call to ministry. It is entirely possible that our limited view of others as viable agents of God's healing and reconciling ministry might be limiting God's healing work in the world.

RICHARD W. VOELZ

Proper 10 (Sunday between July 10 and July 16)

Amos 7:7–15 and
  2 Samuel 6:1–5, 12b–19
Psalm 85:8–13 and Psalm 24

Ephesians 1:3–14
Mark 6:14–29

Amos 7:7–15

[7]This is what he showed me: the Lord was standing beside a wall built with a plumb line, with a plumb line in his hand. [8]And the LORD said to me, "Amos, what do you see?" And I said, "A plumb line." Then the Lord said,

"See, I am setting a plumb line
  in the midst of my people Israel;
  I will never again pass them by;
[9]the high places of Isaac shall be made desolate,
  and the sanctuaries of Israel shall be laid waste,
    and I will rise against the house of Jeroboam with the sword."

[10]Then Amaziah, the priest of Bethel, sent to King Jeroboam of Israel, saying, "Amos has conspired against you in the very center of the house of Israel; the land is not able to bear all his words. [11]For thus Amos has said,

'Jeroboam shall die by the sword,
  and Israel must go into exile
  away from his land.'"

[12]And Amaziah said to Amos, "O seer, go, flee away to the land of Judah, earn your bread there, and prophesy there; [13]but never again prophesy at Bethel, for it is the king's sanctuary, and it is a temple of the kingdom." [14]Then Amos answered Amaziah, "I am no prophet, nor a prophet's son; but I am a herdsman, and a dresser of sycamore trees, [15]and the LORD took me from following the flock, and the LORD said to me, 'Go, prophesy to my people Israel.'"

2 Samuel 6:1–5, 12b–19

[1]David again gathered all the chosen men of Israel, thirty thousand. [2]David and all the people with him set out and went from Baale-judah, to bring up from there the ark of God, which is called by the name of the LORD of hosts who is enthroned on the cherubim. [3]They carried the ark of God on a new cart, and brought it out of the house of Abinadab, which was on the hill. Uzzah and Ahio, the sons of Abinadab, were driving the new cart [4]with the ark of God; and Ahio went in front of the ark. [5]David and all the house of Israel were dancing before the LORD with all their might, with songs and lyres and harps and tambourines and castanets and cymbals. . . .

[12b]So David went and brought up the ark of God from the house of Obed-edom to the city of David with rejoicing; [13]and when those who bore the ark of the LORD had gone six paces, he sacrificed an ox and a fatling. [14]David danced before the LORD with all his might; David was girded with a linen ephod. [15]So David and all

the house of Israel brought up the ark of the LORD with shouting, and with the sound of the trumpet.

¹⁶As the ark of the LORD came into the city of David, Michal daughter of Saul looked out of the window, and saw King David leaping and dancing before the LORD; and she despised him in her heart.

¹⁷They brought in the ark of the LORD, and set it in its place, inside the tent that David had pitched for it; and David offered burnt offerings and offerings of well-being before the LORD. ¹⁸When David had finished offering the burnt offerings and the offerings of well-being, he blessed the people in the name of the LORD of hosts, ¹⁹and distributed food among all the people, the whole multitude of Israel, both men and women, to each a cake of bread, a portion of meat, and a cake of raisins. Then all the people went back to their homes.

Commentary 1: Connecting the Reading with Scripture

Establishing Jerusalem as the center of Israel's story is a long process in the Bible. The city first appears by name in Joshua 10, and two chapters later, it is in a long list of cities Joshua has defeated during his invasion of Canaan, where there is nothing distinctive about it. The status of the city continues to be in flux throughout the story of settlement in Joshua, Judges, and 1 Samuel. Only as David comes into power does the city so closely tied to him in tradition come into focus.

Second Samuel 6 describes the transport of the mysterious ark of the covenant to Jerusalem. The ark has been missing from the story of Israel for some time. In 1 Samuel 4, the sons of Eli, Hophni and Phineas, had brought the ark to the site of the Israelites' loss in battle against the Philistines, between Aphek and Ebenezer. A subsequent loss led to the capture of the ark by the Philistine army. First Samuel 5–7 continues the strange story of the ark, which brings so much trouble to the Philistines that they return it to the Israelites. Some Israelites welcome the return and some do not, and the disagreement leads to a slaughter, so the ark brings suffering again. In light of this uncertainty, the ark is hidden away in a house in Kiriath-jearim. Perhaps it is no surprise that a bandit-king like David, wishing to consolidate and maximize his political power, might look to the ark again, despite the risks it holds. So Kiriath-jearim is where the new story begins, some twenty years later.

The missing piece from the lectionary reading should cause suspicion, and a glance at 2 Samuel 6:6–11 quickly reveals why. Beneath the calm surface of any story, there is always a price to be paid for the appearance of order. The lectionary, along with the version of Israel's story in Chronicles, conspires to hide the cost that the book of Samuel struggles to acknowledge. Perhaps worse, the name of the one who most directly absorbs the disorder, taking the deadly divine anger into his own body, Uzzah, is erased from memory. What might give rise to such an odd tradition? Is there a need to explain why David's initial effort to move the ark to Jerusalem fails?

The behavior of David is baffling throughout the story. He assembles an enormous cast of personnel, provides a new cart to transport the ark, and leads the people ("all the house of Israel") in an elaborate performance of song and dance as the ark makes its journey. The death of Uzzah, amid all this chaos, halts the project and makes David afraid to take the ark into his city. The most elaborate ceremony surrounding the ark up to this point in the biblical story is at the battle of Jericho in Joshua 6. In that text, the ark appears to be part of the war equipment. It is the throne upon which Israel's God sits, overseeing the battle. This seems likely to be what lies behind the decision to bring the ark to the battle in 1 Samuel 4, after a difficult loss. The ark is supposed to bring divine power, leading to victory in battle, but it failed on that occasion.

If the question the reappearance of the ark asks is whether this new king can control and utilize its power, then the answer is negative. It is perhaps David's first moment of pause in a sequence of events that has appeared so sure and confident. David is not just afraid of YHWH, but also angry at his divine sponsor. Again, the ark takes up temporary residence in a private house, where its power can be tested and measured. When the ark passes this test of safety and control after three months, the transport process resumes, this time with elaborate sacrificial rituals to accompany the procession.

Another person who pays a price in this story is the daughter of Saul and wife of David named Michal. The prior story in 2 Samuel 3 provides reason for Michal to despise David before the day of the ark's arrival, but the isolated verse in Chronicles is more likely to lead readers to conclude that the events of that day are the cause of her contempt. The story in 2 Samuel 6:20–23 provides a final interaction between David and Michal, in which she criticizes the spectacle he has created around the ark, particularly his interaction with other women. There has been much speculation about the cause of her disgust, most of which has sexist foundations. Was she jealous of the attention David received from the women in the procession? When he was dancing in the procession, had he exposed himself? The full story of Michal in 1–2 Samuel reveals that David killed members of her family and benefited from the suspicious deaths of others. One hardly needs to look for petty motives like jealousy or prudishness to find a reason for Michal to despise David.

The text in Amos 7:7–15 may be most famous for an image, a "plumb line," first produced by the King James Version, that is unlikely to be a reasonable translation. The man in 7:7 is holding something in his hand, but it seems to be merely a piece of whatever material has been used to construct the wall. The word appears nowhere else in the Hebrew Bible, and the Greek text

renders it as "adamantine." Whatever this object or substance is, 7:8–9 says clearly enough that the placement of it within the midst of Israel will have a destructive effect. The vision resembles two that precede it in 7:1–6, and one that comes after it in 8:1–3.

All of these visions point toward destruction. In the final one Amos sees a basket of fruit, and because this particular word for fruit sounds like the Hebrew word for "end," the vision is interpreted as a sign of the coming end of Israel. There is a similar vision based on a wordplay in Jeremiah 1:11–12. It is possible that Amos's vision of the man on the wall is also based on a wordplay that is lost to us because the word is too obscure.

Between the third and fourth visions of Amos, the prophet comes into conflict with a priest from Bethel named Amaziah. Bethel is a place with a long history for Israel. It is the second place to which Abraham goes in Canaan and the first place where he builds an altar (Gen. 12:8). Jacob names Bethel in Genesis 29 because it is the site of his famous dream in which he sees a ladder or ramp used by angels to ascend to and descend from heaven. It becomes one of the two sites where Jereboam son of Nebat places golden bulls in 1 Kings 12. Jerusalem and Bethel are both divine abodes, but such a designation proves to bring blessing and curse. Their holy designation is volatile, like the ark's.

Eventually, the destiny of Jerusalem becomes a symbol for the fate of all Israel. The measurement of the city's obedience (Isa. 5 and Jer. 31:37), God's punishment (Isa. 65:7 and Jer. 10:24), and the reconstruction of the city (Ezek. 40–48 and Zech. 2:2) form a common theme in the prophetic literature. The careful attention to Jerusalem provides texture for its use in the New Testament as the scene for the climax of the gospel story.

MARK MCENTIRE

Commentary 2: Connecting the Reading with the World

The lectionary texts for this Sunday again provide us with two texts that on first glance might not seem at all related. It is important to explore connections between these texts that will help congregants connect these readings to the world as they listen to the sermon. One text continues the story of David after his rise to power as the king of all of the tribes of Israel, telling of the entrance of the ark into Jerusalem. The second text comes to us from the prophet Amos, who foretold of the exile of the two kingdoms, Judah and Israel. While the story of David takes place in Jerusalem, the "city of David," Amos prophesies from his hometown of Tekoa, a small village south of Jerusalem. While David was a king, Amos was a shepherd, "no prophet, nor a prophet's son" (Amos 7:14). David had all of the accoutrements for religious celebration at his disposal: "songs and lyres and harps and tambourines and castanets and cymbals" (2 Sam. 6:5), all that was necessary for burnt offerings, and lots for food for the "multitude of Israel" (vv. 18–19). A grand city and a smaller town. A mighty king and a herder. What might be the connections between these contrasts?

A first connection might explore the significance of place. Perhaps your congregation is located in a rural area, or an area that seems distant from the grand lights of the city. Some may hold the unfortunate stereotype, reflective of our culture's attraction to power, big buildings, well-known names, and influence, that parishes and churches in small towns and rural areas are irrelevant and backwater. Yet churches in rural areas and small towns remain significant places of stability, hope, and vibrant faith, and are now receiving attention as vital places of ministry through such movements as the Rural Church Network, Rural Matters Institute, and the Small Town Churches Network.[1] Like Amos, a shepherd from the outskirts of Jerusalem called by God to prophesy a hard message to the powers that surrounded his community, churches that feel on the outskirts are called by God and remain places where God's Word is spoken and lived. Reminding congregations that their place is important, that God speaks, that God calls, that God invites them into God's work, no matter where they are, is important. Like Amos, churches that might feel that "we are only . . ." have important words from the Lord for our world today.

Second, reflecting on the richness of worship elements as David brings the ark into Jerusalem, and the danger in the absence of justice, is a concern in Amos. Second Samuel 6 provides us a picture of the majestic elements of worship, all of which add to our imaginations and sensations. There are instruments to celebrate God's presence among this people, often used in Israel's worship (cf. Ps. 150). There is dancing, this physical expression of great joy and gladness, with our bodies giving expression to the indescribable delight in being in the presence of God. Yet the narrator of 2 Samuel interrupts this celebration with a stark image: the picture of Michal, identified as the daughter of Saul, looking out a window, watching "King David leaping and dancing before the LORD" and despising "him in her heart" (2 Sam. 6:16).

While the narrator identifies Michal as Saul's daughter, reflective of how female identity and worth were shaped by male belonging, it is important to remember that Michal was one of David's wives, treated like a pawn in the conflict between Saul and David. She was given by Saul in marriage to David, and we are told "she loved David" (1 Sam. 18:20). She protected David when Saul attempted to kill him, lying to her father (1 Sam. 19:11–17), and perhaps as punishment, again Michal's father gives her away, this time to Palti (1 Sam. 25:44). However, this abusive treatment of Michal is not over, when David demands her return as a spoil of war. The scene is wrenching: she was taken from her husband Palti, one who truly loved her, who "went with her, weeping as he walked behind her all the way" until he was commanded, like a dog, to go home (2 Sam. 3:15–16).

While the narrator explains that Michal's disdain was due to David's shameful display (2 Sam. 6:20), preachers could also probe why this narrative interruption comes in the middle of the worship festivities. Was Michal's response appropriate and understandable, given the relationship between justice and worship in covenant faith?[2] She had been treated unjustly. The God to whom worship was given in this most visual way as the ark was brought into Jerusalem is the same God who expected justice,

1. For more about these organizations, see www.ruralchurchnetwork.org/; www.bgcruralmatters.com/; www.smalltownchurches.org/.
2. See Nicholas Wolterstorff, *Hearing the Call: Liturgy, Justice, Church, and World* (Grand Rapids: Eerdmans, 2011).

something that was denied to Michal by David, a leader of the worship procession.

While verse 16 might seem a disruption in this story of worship, it is one that preachers can note for possible connections. Perhaps we could interrupt worship services with visual reminders of who might be looking in on us as we worship, even putting in the windows pictures of persons who have been neglected and abused by our faith communities. Who is neglected in the lavishness of our worship practices? Are there persons whose resentment is merited because of the ways in which they have been treated? Have we justified unjust treatment by appealing to "more important" things like our worship accessories and processions? How have our own lavish worship experiences neglected God's call for justice as part of our worship?

These questions about worship and justice help preachers draw further connections with the text from Amos, this prophet who spoke the words, "Thus says the LORD," numerous times, with words directed against the lavish and unjust practices of God's people that would result in their exile. It should come as no surprise that Amaziah, the priest of Bethel (the house of God!), took issue with Amos's prophecy and sought to shut him down (Amos 7:10–12).

Perhaps by exploring the typologies of "priest" and "prophet" in Max Weber's work, we can see the tensions between this priest and this prophet and make connections with tensions churches experience today over change, renewal, mission, inclusion, and belonging.[3] In Weber's analysis, priests and prophets are often in conflict; priests desire the status quo, while prophets call communities back to covenant faith. As a corrective to these divides between priest and prophet, preachers can introduce congregants to Archbishop Oscar Romero, a prophetic priest in El Salvador, an example of how priests fulfill their prophetic function in liturgy, preaching, and social action. Archbishop Romero was murdered while presiding over the Eucharist, because of his advocacy for the poor and his criticisms of oppression and social injustice. Contra Weber's typology, Romero used his priestly office to serve a prophetic function, which preachers can do as well, as they are preaching on these texts.

Finally, we are given the image of a plumb line (vv. 7–9), which preachers can use in worship. A plumb line is a measuring device, with a weight, used to ensure that a structure is vertical and level, true to its foundation. In the context of Amos, this plumb line was measuring the commitments to justice, a foundation of covenant faith, which were found lacking in God's people. Placing a plumb at the front of a sanctuary or altar would give a visual reminder of a church's commitment to stay true to its foundation and mission in the world. What would a plumb line reveal about your house of God?

WYNDY CORBIN REUSCHLING

---

3. Max Weber, *The Sociology of Religion* (Boston: Beacon Press, 1963).

Proper 10 (Sunday between July 10 and July 16)

Psalm 85:8–13

[8]Let me hear what God the LORD will speak,
   for he will speak peace to his people,
   to his faithful, to those who turn to him in their hearts.
[9]Surely his salvation is at hand for those who fear him,
   that his glory may dwell in our land.

[10]Steadfast love and faithfulness will meet;
   righteousness and peace will kiss each other.
[11]Faithfulness will spring up from the ground,
   and righteousness will look down from the sky.
[12]The LORD will give what is good,
   and our land will yield its increase.
[13]Righteousness will go before him,
   and will make a path for his steps.

Psalm 24

[1]The earth is the LORD's and all that is in it,
   the world, and those who live in it;
[2]for he has founded it on the seas,
   and established it on the rivers.

[3]Who shall ascend the hill of the LORD?
   And who shall stand in his holy place?
[4]Those who have clean hands and pure hearts,
   who do not lift up their souls to what is false,
   and do not swear deceitfully.
[5]They will receive blessing from the LORD,
   and vindication from the God of their salvation.
[6]Such is the company of those who seek him,
   who seek the face of the God of Jacob.

[7]Lift up your heads, O gates!
   and be lifted up, O ancient doors!
   that the King of glory may come in.
[8]Who is the King of glory?
   The LORD, strong and mighty,
   the LORD, mighty in battle.
[9]Lift up your heads, O gates!
   and be lifted up, O ancient doors!
   that the King of glory may come in.
[10]Who is this King of glory?
   The LORD of hosts,
   he is the King of glory.

Connecting the Psalm with Scripture and Worship

Psalm 85:8–13. The first reading, Amos 7:7–15, tells a story of God's judgment: with the vision of the plumb line, God says to Amos that desolation is coming to the people of Israel. The text ends with what may be the defining quote for the biblical hero Amos: "I am no prophet, nor a prophet's son; but I am a herdsman, and a dresser of sycamore trees" (Amos 7:14). Like so many other Old Testament heroes, God has called the ordinary person Amos to extraordinary service among God's people. In Amos's case, his message is a universally unpopular one: Israel has forgotten their God, and God will not look upon them with favor.

Psalm 85:8–13 comes in response to the Amos story, and there is significant tension between the tone of the Amos passage and the selected verses of the psalm. Verses 1–7 of the psalm voice a corporate prayer for help: reflections on God's faithfulness in the past and pleas for God to restore Israel to salvation and favor in the present. By the beginning of the passage prescribed by the lectionary, in verse 8, the psalmist has moved from plea to assurance. A singular voice expresses confidence that God will indeed "speak peace" to the people once more. The preacher should note the difference between Amos's tone and that of the speaker in Psalm 85:8–13. The psalmist is expressing a confidence in God's mercy that the people of Israel do not yet have in Amos 7.

The verses selected in the lectionary can be a starting place for sermonizing. Are we so uncomfortable with the idea of God's judgment that we dare not read the first seven verses of Psalm 85? The preacher may be surprised to find that many in the pews will identify with the prayer of the psalmist in verses 1–7, and it is worth considering expanding the boundaries of the text if addressing it in a sermon.

Concerns about the text's boundaries aside, Psalm 85:8–13 is a powerful affirmation of faith in God's compassion. The psalm does not stop with praying for God's mercy; the psalmist goes on to state the return of God's favor as fact. God "*will* speak peace [*shalom*]" (v. 8), "salvation *is* at hand" (v. 9), "faithfulness *will* spring up" (v. 11), and so on. The semantics of the passage provide a foundation for preaching the psalm or using it in liturgy; even in a time of desperation, the psalmist shows unwavering faith in the mercy of God, sitting in the tension between confidence in God's help and awareness of present suffering. The salvation the psalmist imagines is more concrete than abstract: when God acts, the fullness of life will be restored through steadfast love, faithfulness, righteousness, and peace (v. 10), and even the land will thrive in the light of God's compassion. The psalm is "part of the liturgy of the saved community who must live in awareness that its salvation is not yet consummated."[1]

To engage the hearer in the text of the psalm, the words can be sung using a metrical or responsive setting, or read responsively. Verse 8a makes an excellent call to worship, a brief but powerful sentence that can set the tone for worship:

> Reader One: Let me hear what God the Lord will speak,
> Reader Two: for God will speak peace to God's people.

Just as the psalmist speaks assurances of God's salvation while simultaneously praying for deliverance, the modern liturgist can lean on the words of the psalm to praise God for great blessings and pray for God's help by weaving the assurances of verses 10–13 throughout the prayers of intercession.

Psalm 24. In the reading from 2 Samuel 6, worshipers hear the story of the entrance to the temple, with David's army carrying the ark of God to Jerusalem on a new cart. After all the twists and turns thus far in David's story, he has finally gotten the ark of God to the city of God, and celebration ensues. The people are not merely dancing. They are "dancing before the Lord with all their might" (v. 5)! Psalm 24 comes in response: a joyful song for a joyful day.

Psalm 24 does not simply celebrate Israel's victory. The psalmist takes care to say that the scope of God's power is much wider than the

---

1. James L. Mays, *Psalms,* Interpretation (Louisville, KY: John Knox, 1994), 277.

kingdom of David (Ps. 24:1). The shape of the psalm carries as much meaning as the words themselves. Verses 1–2 praise God's sovereignty and God's ownership of the world God created.[2] Verses 3–6 describe the righteousness of God's servant, the one to "ascend the hill of the LORD" as David has, whether literal entry to the temple of God or more general relatedness to God.[3] Verses 7–10 turn to the adoration of God, "strong and mighty," the "King of glory." Individually, each of those pieces carries theological meaning, but the order in which they are placed shines a special light on the faith and belief of the writer. First comes the sovereignty of God, which requires of the servant faithfulness, which then leads to the adoration of God. The shape of the psalm may be the shape of faith itself.

Psalm 24 bears a superscription: "Of David. A psalm." Regardless of its authorship, this psalm clearly has its origins in early liturgy, possibly liturgy for entrance to the temple gates. The refrain in verses 7–10 sings even without a musical setting. The psalm is a wealth of liturgical language, and the ten verses can be woven throughout a service of worship. Verses 1–2 make a beautiful responsive call to worship:

Reader One:	The earth is the Lord's and all that is in it,
Reader Two:	the world, and those who live in it;
Reader One:	for God has founded it on the seas,
Reader Two:	and established it on the rivers.

Verses 3–6, with their focus on the faithfulness of the servant, offer language which can be easily adapted for a responsive call to confession:

Reader One:	Who shall ascend the hill of the Lord? and who shall stand in God's holy place?
Reader Two:	Those who have clean hands and pure hearts, who do not lift up their souls to what is false.
Reader One:	They will receive blessing from the Lord, and vindication from the God of their salvation.
Reader Two:	Such is the company of those who seek the Lord, who seek the face of the God of Jacob.

Verses 7–10 make a powerful congregational affirmation after the reading of the Old Testament text or after a sermon. Since the passage divides easily between three parts, the liturgist may choose to divide the passage between the right and left side of the worship space.

Right:	Lift up your heads, O gates! and be lifted up, O ancient doors! that the King of glory may come in.
Liturgist:	Who is the King of glory?
Left:	The Lord, strong and mighty; the Lord, mighty in battle.
Right:	Lift up your heads, O gates! and be lifted up, O ancient doors! that the King of glory may come in.
Liturgist:	Who is this King of glory?
Left:	The Lord of hosts is the King of glory!

Psalm 24 carries a powerful message for the people of God. Whether resources seem scarce or abundant, the church will always need the reminder of the psalmist: the earth is the Lord's and all that is in it.

ANNA GEORGE TRAYNHAM

---

2. Mays, *Psalms*, 119–20.
3. J. Clinton McCann Jr., "The Book of Psalms," in *The New Interpreter's Bible* (Nashville: Abingdon, 1996), 4:773.

Ephesians 1:3–14

³Blessed be the God and Father of our Lord Jesus Christ, who has blessed us in Christ with every spiritual blessing in the heavenly places, ⁴just as he chose us in Christ before the foundation of the world to be holy and blameless before him in love. ⁵He destined us for adoption as his children through Jesus Christ, according to the good pleasure of his will, ⁶to the praise of his glorious grace that he freely bestowed on us in the Beloved. ⁷In him we have redemption through his blood, the forgiveness of our trespasses, according to the riches of his grace ⁸that he lavished on us. With all wisdom and insight ⁹he has made known to us the mystery of his will, according to his good pleasure that he set forth in Christ, ¹⁰as a plan for the fullness of time, to gather up all things in him, things in heaven and things on earth. ¹¹In Christ we have also obtained an inheritance, having been destined according to the purpose of him who accomplishes all things according to his counsel and will, ¹²so that we, who were the first to set our hope on Christ, might live for the praise of his glory. ¹³In him you also, when you had heard the word of truth, the gospel of your salvation, and had believed in him, were marked with the seal of the promised Holy Spirit; ¹⁴this is the pledge of our inheritance toward redemption as God's own people, to the praise of his glory.

Commentary 1: Connecting the Reading with Scripture

The contrast between last week's lectionary reading and this week's is refreshing. The thematic content moves from a posture of defense against those who challenge Paul's authority in the Corinthian church (2 Cor. 12:2–12) to exuberance over the significance of the grace of God in Christ for Jews and Gentiles alike. With the eyes of their hearts enlightened, Gentiles are invited to know "what is the hope" and "the riches of his glorious inheritance" (Eph. 1:17–19).

Although there is no scholarly consensus on the Pauline authorship of Ephesians, we know that the intended audience was mainly Gentile Christians (2:11–13)—if not in Ephesus, then in its environs (some ancient manuscripts lack 1:1). It is obvious from the contents that the writer was a Christian Jew. This is important to the overall message and purpose of Ephesians: that in and through Christ, God has unified Jewish and Gentile believers in the power of the Spirit. We have a call as members of the one body, to each other and to the world. This impartial, universal grace is for the praise of God's glory (1:6, 12, 14). The significance of

this message becomes more lucid if we understand the "we" in 1:12 to be referring to Jewish Christians, and the "you also" in 1:13 to Gentile Christians who are now equally "God's own people"—also to the "praise of his glory" (1:12, 14; 2:11–14; Rom. 3:2; Acts 2:5; 26:6; et al.).

This message, while simple, had ramifications as profound, and even scandalous, then as it does now. In Christ, there is but one new humanity; there is no "us" and "them" (Eph. 2:15–19; 4:4; Col. 1:12; Gal. 3:26–29; 1 Cor. 12:27). Those united in the one body of Christ, grounded and nourished by the "word of truth, the gospel," and sealed by the Holy Spirit, cannot be edged out!

The caring tone of the letter makes for an amenable hearing. There are no personal or hot issues that stand out in this community, as was the case for the Galatian and Corinthian churches, for instance. This is not about Judaizers, a blatant accommodation of the sinful in the church, disparaging practices, or divisions, to name a few of the issues elsewhere. The author speaks tenderly, revealing a sprightly cadence that celebrates, even as he instructs and guides the believers.

This same tone of elation and acclamation should guide the preacher's own cadence in helping to evoke, if not rekindle, the hearer's own delectation and gratitude for what can easily become old, even blasé: the grace of our new status in Christ. "Blessed be the God and Father of our Lord Jesus Christ," the writer exclaims, "who has blessed us in Christ with every spiritual blessing" (Eph. 1:3)! Through faith in Christ (2:8) believers have been "blessed" (1:3); "chosen" by him "to be holy and blameless before him in love" (v. 4); adopted as God's children (v. 5); redeemed and forgiven (v. 7); given an inheritance in Christ; and, because of Christ, marked with the seal of the promised Holy Spirit (v. 13). Christ, then, is not only the believer's "hope," he is God's "very good pleasure" for her!

This praise-full cadence, however, does not belay an urgent call for the faithful to be strengthened and equipped against the wiles of the devil (4:1, 14; 6:11–17), lest they be lured away from Christ to past lives (4:17–24). This costly grace—"through [Christ's] blood"—is not to be taken lightly (1:7); it is not entitlement, an attitude to which we might easily fall prey through ideologies of culture, class, ethnicity, or theology. "*Remember*," he enjoins twice, that "you Gentiles" were derided as "the uncircumcision" (or "the foreskin" ones!; *acrobystia* refers to the prepuce or foreskin),[1] "aliens," and "strangers to the covenants of promise, having no hope and without God" (2:11–12)! This grace, then, is the antithesis of an abject status before God; it is the reason for the new *familial* appellations in 1:3–14. Gentiles need to remember this in order to respond with gratitude.

Should perceptions of partiality linger, the writer adds that "all of us"—Jews and Gentiles, circumcised or not—were by nature "children of wrath" (2:3; Rom. 3:23–24) brought "near" through the same grace to be, and work toward, the unity of the body, God's dwelling place (Eph. 2:17, 21–22; 3:6; 4:1–6). (Note: the notion of God dwelling in *all* saints would have been foreign to Gentiles used to seeing their gods dwell in pantheons.)

The eight references to Christ in such a short section (1:3–14) may obfuscate a Trinitarian depiction of the work of redemption. The theological and liturgical ramifications of this should not be ignored. God's grace is "lavished" on us through Christ and through the Holy Spirit, who has sealed us toward redemption (note that we "*have* redemption" yet also move "*toward*" it; 1:7, 14). Thus, praise is always Trinitarian, and knowledge of who and how we are to live as the one body of Christ has the simple, yet profound *mysterium tremendum*—the revelation of the God who is three, yet in all things acts as one—as model.

Believers are not the only ones called to benefit from this grace. Through Christ, God reveals the "mystery" of the Divine: "to gather up all things in him, things in heaven and things on earth (1:10). Consequently, "knit together" and "working properly" through its gifts, the body of Christ is called to grow in Christ *and* to witness to God's redeeming grace (3:10; 4:16). If considered in light of creation's own anticipation of redemption in Colossians 1:16–20 and Romans 8:20–22, the reference to "all things," at the very least, should invoke our responsibility to care for the increasingly endangered environment on which we all depend (Gen. 1:8–31). Hence, although pithy, Ephesians 1:10 insinuates ecological and moral implications that bear upon God's call to "Love God. . . . and your neighbor as yourself" (Mark 12:30–33; Matt. 22:37–39).

The accompanying lectionary readings in 2 Samuel 6:1–5, 12b–19 and Psalms 24 and 85:8–13 share a tone of exhilaration and gratitude that may help shape dispositions. Having taken Jerusalem, David decided to bring the ark of the covenant there (cf. Heb. 9:4–5). Brimming with gratitude for God's presence and power among them in the ark, David erupted in joyful dancing and shouting before God with all the people. If the symbol of the presence of God in the ark elicited such praise, how much more grateful ought *we* be who are "built into a dwelling place for God," the "King of glory"!

David and the people knew that God's sovereign power and steadfast love for the faithful included blessing the land and its yield (Pss.

1. https://www.studylight.org/lexicons/greek/203.html.

24:4; 85:8, 12). This, too, connects back to our call to care for creation.

The call to faithfulness rooted in love is a theme that runs through the Scriptures. Faithfulness is rewarded not as a work but as active reliance on God. The "great cloud of witnesses," which goes back to Abel, persevered in faith and it was counted as "righteousness" (Gen. 22:1–18; Heb. 11; 12:1). Indeed, "steadfast love and faithfulness will meet; righteousness and peace will kiss each other" (Ps. 85:10). The exhortation to perseverance in Ephesians evokes the seer's appeal in Revelation 2:2–4 for the church to return to the love they had at first. It may be that this is just what the Holy Spirit ordered as it concerns the praise-full, thankful tone in today's reading.

ZAIDA MALDONADO PÉREZ

Commentary 2: Connecting the Reading with the World

In Greek, this text is one long sentence with several clauses and an array of vivid metaphors that elucidate the attributes of our triune God and the blessings we have received through redemption in Jesus Christ. Two prominent metaphors are "family" and "economics." The image of adoption as God's children (*huiothesia*, Eph. 1:5) is employed to illustrate our inclusion as members of God's family. Words commonly associated with financial matters are utilized in 1:11 ("inheritance") and 1:14 ("pledge") to explain what God has given to us. In its immediate context, the Greek word for "pledge" (*arrabōn*) can be found in commercial documents referring to the deposit paid by a customer to a merchant for a scheduled delivery of goods.

These two metaphors are linked in another word: *oikonomia* (1:10). The word appears as "plan" in several English translations (ESV, NLT, NRSV) and as "administration" in other English translations (NASB, Holman Christian Standard Bible), but *oikonomia* was most commonly used in the first century to denote the management of a domestic household.

Ada María Isasi-Díaz, a Cuban American theologian and ethicist, spent much of her career interrogating the ways Christian used metaphors to describe God, the church, and the world. As one of the pioneers of *mujerista* theology, Isasi-Díaz found that the idea of *familia* (family) aptly captured how Latinas in the United States exhibited their leadership and expressed their faith. Because the *familia* served as one of the core anchors for Latinx American immigrant communities in the United States, Isasi-Díaz articulates how a Christian theology centered in the idea of participating in the *familia de Dios* (God's family) could affirm, animate, and unite Latinas in their daily struggles against the forces of systemic marginalization and oppression in their congregations and larger society.

Isasi-Díaz extends her theology of the *familia de Dios* to revise a longstanding metaphor in the Christian tradition, the kingdom of God. She traces the history of the kingdom of God from its Jewish origins as a concept derived from the Egyptian and Babylonian kingships that enslaved and ruled over them to the early Christian emphasis on the transcendent eschatological promises of God's reign after the destruction of the temple in Jerusalem in 70 CE.

After the Roman emperor Constantine converted to Christianity in 313 CE, Christians increasingly understood the church as "the only access to the kingdom of God in the world to come and its most powerful symbol in this world." Isasi-Díaz replaces "kingdom" with "kin-dom" to move away from the political overtones of the former and magnify the interpersonal connections that lie at the heart of the latter. She contends the kin-dom of God "is a much more relevant and effective metaphor today to communicate what Jesus lived and died for," because it provides an inclusive and expansive picture of God's family that extends to all God's children who share a common inheritance through Christ's redemption.[2]

Despite the faithful promise of an inheritance for all in God's family, some congregations in the United States today lament their declining membership numbers and diminishing social relevance. Although Christ has provided to us the "riches of his grace" (1:7), there exists a culture of scarcity in a growing number of congregations as conversations revolve around what they are lacking.

Scholars of US religion have studied membership decline across several predominantly white mainline Protestant denominations and offered prescriptions for future sustainability. Diana Butler Bass summarizes this wide-ranging analysis in three competing visions. One approach, which she calls the neo-orthodox vision, entails congregations' retreat from direct political involvement to focus upon the spiritual formation of faithful individuals toward distinctively Christian discipleship. Another approach, the panentheist vision, encourages congregations to engage in social and political movements through partnerships with all kinds of agencies, including interfaith and secular organizations, to do good work outside of one's church. The third approach, the liberationist vision, seeks to infuse the everyday experience of worship and fellowship in congregations with explicit social-justice commitments to unashamedly reclaim the religiously motivated activism of twentieth-century pioneers like Jane Addams, Fannie Lou Hamer, Martin Luther King Jr., and Walter Rauschenbusch.[3] The preacher might want to ask the congregation which (if any) of these models applies to them.

This lection encourages congregations to begin with gratitude and remember our identity as God's children. The metaphor of family and household can be challenging in our day and age. With the rise of the "gig economy" through digital platforms, we are witnessing a plethora of independent workers who seek to meet specific yet temporary consumer needs. While potentially offering workers more flexibility and freedom, the gig economy also highlights the ongoing challenge of individualism in our capitalistic society. It can be difficult for Christians today to connect the powerful images of sharing an abundant inheritance in Christ and joining together to "live for the praise of his glory" (1:11–12) when so much of our identity is tied to our individual labor and the work each person can produce for consumers.

In the first half of the twentieth century, Protestants in the United States encountered oft-contentious divides between conservatives and progressives over matters of biblical interpretation, cultural engagement, and social witness. Amid the many disagreements and schisms, Rick Ostrander observed how different practices of prayer emerged among conservatives and progressives. Conservatives understood prayer as a means to leave the distractions and troubles of the world and receive an infusion of spiritual energy for reentry into the world. Progressives believed prayer encompassed both quiet contemplation and attention to how God was present in the world.

Ostrander provides a pair of vignettes to illustrate this contrast. In 1917, a small group of conservative women awaiting a train to return home from Cedar Lake Bible Conference in Indiana held an impromptu prayer meeting and ended up missing their train. Their pastor, E. Y. Woolley, arranged for a bus to pick them up and they arrived at their destination before the train. Woolley shared how the group was "so absorbed in their prayers that shouts, laughter and train whistles failed to move them."

William Adams Brown, a progressive theologian at Union Seminary in New York City, presented a different view of prayer in 1927. Brown recounted the example of a Christian commuting to work on a New York City train who prayed by gazing into the faces of the other passengers to see the divine image in each

---

2. Ada María Isasi-Díaz, "Identifícate con Nosotros: A Mujerista Christological Understanding," in *Jesus in the Hispanic Community: Images of Christ from Theology to Popular Religion* (Louisville, KY: Westminster John Knox, 2009), 41–44.

3. Robert P. Jones, *The End of White Christian America* (New York: Simon & Schuster, 2016), 215.

human being. Brown commended this believer for seeking after God in "a world of wonderful and ennobling things."[4] As we look back into the past and consider our present, we acknowledge Christ has given us a generous inheritance, which is evident in the rich diversity of gifts and the different ways we pray and worship within God's family. These differences within and beyond our local congregations are neither to be feared nor erased. Instead, they expand our vision of what it means to be the household of God and increase our gratitude for the inheritance we have received in Christ.

WILLIAM YOO

---

4. Rick Ostrander, "The Practice of Prayer in a Modern Age," in *Practicing Protestants: Histories of Christian Life in America, 1630–1965*, ed. Laurie F. Maffly-Kipp, Leigh E. Schmidt, and Mark Valeri (Baltimore: Johns Hopkins University Press, 2006), 194–95.

Mark 6:14–29

¹⁴King Herod heard of it, for Jesus' name had become known. Some were saying, "John the baptizer has been raised from the dead; and for this reason these powers are at work in him." ¹⁵But others said, "It is Elijah." And others said, "It is a prophet, like one of the prophets of old." ¹⁶But when Herod heard of it, he said, "John, whom I beheaded, has been raised."

¹⁷For Herod himself had sent men who arrested John, bound him, and put him in prison on account of Herodias, his brother Philip's wife, because Herod had married her. ¹⁸For John had been telling Herod, "It is not lawful for you to have your brother's wife." ¹⁹And Herodias had a grudge against him, and wanted to kill him. But she could not, ²⁰for Herod feared John, knowing that he was a righteous and holy man, and he protected him. When he heard him, he was greatly perplexed; and yet he liked to listen to him. ²¹But an opportunity came when Herod on his birthday gave a banquet for his courtiers and officers and for the leaders of Galilee. ²²When his daughter Herodias came in and danced, she pleased Herod and his guests; and the king said to the girl, "Ask me for whatever you wish, and I will give it." ²³And he solemnly swore to her, "Whatever you ask me, I will give you, even half of my kingdom." ²⁴She went out and said to her mother, "What should I ask for?" She replied, "The head of John the baptizer." ²⁵Immediately she rushed back to the king and requested, "I want you to give me at once the head of John the Baptist on a platter." ²⁶The king was deeply grieved; yet out of regard for his oaths and for the guests, he did not want to refuse her. ²⁷Immediately the king sent a soldier of the guard with orders to bring John's head. He went and beheaded him in the prison, ²⁸brought his head on a platter, and gave it to the girl. Then the girl gave it to her mother. ²⁹When his disciples heard about it, they came and took his body, and laid it in a tomb.

Commentary 1: Connecting the Reading with Scripture

This passage breaks the continuity of Mark's plot, describing action in which Jesus does not participate and letting anticipation linger concerning the outcome of the apostles' efforts at proclamation, exorcism, and healing (Mark 6:7–13, 30). Even though it interrupts, the account of John the Baptizer's morbid murder does not create a digression from the Gospel's main story. Despite any success the apostles might experience, the story of John's demise declares that the inbreaking of God's reign continues to provoke defensive and dismissive responses. Struggle, opposition, and violence answer back to those who announce God's word. Even as Amos's declarations about King Jeroboam II elicited hostility from Amaziah (Amos 7:10–13) and

John calls out Herod Antipas's sin and suffers wrath from Herodias and pathetic neglect from her husband, so will Jesus speak the truth about himself to the high priest, the priestly council, and Pilate and find himself executed as a matter of political expediency. John's death illustrates starkly what can happen to those who take up their cross and follow Jesus in the way he travels (Mark 8:34).

Although Jesus is rejected in his hometown (6:1–6a), his popularity elsewhere continues to swell. It draws attention away from the man Mark calls "King Herod," who was Herod Antipas, a son of the more famous and notorious Herod the Great. Beginning soon after his father died in 4 BCE and lasting through

The Countenance Divinely Human

God is at once infinitely remote from us and perfectly familiar to us. He is remote by what he is, he is familiar in what he does, for he identifies his thought with the thing he makes and moulds his care for it on its existence. So the mind of God becomes all things and is directly presented by what anything truly is. "He is not far from any of us, for by him we live and move and have our being" not only as souls or persons, but as animals and even as parcels of physical stuff. His will is in the drawing of our breath and in the pulses of our heart; how much more in the movement of our affection or the aspiration of our hope! Above all, he takes the form of our action when he inspires us, when we let our will be the instrument of his. To realise a union with our Creator we need not scale heaven or strip the veil from ultimate mystery; for God descends into his creature and acts humanly in mankind. He has made it our calling that we should have fellowship with himself; and so now by faith, but in heaven by sight, we are to look into the countenance divinely human and humanly divine of Christ the Lord.

Austin Farrer, *God Is Not Dead* (New York: Morehouse-Barlow Co., 1966), 127.

Jesus' lifetime, Herod Antipas ruled Galilee as a Roman client. Although this Herod appears nowhere else in Mark, he plays a larger role in Luke (Luke 13:31–33; 23:6–12). Never, in any setting, does a Gospel author depict Herod Antipas's curiosity toward Jesus in a positive or well-intentioned light.

In a narrative flashback meant to explain why Herod might think Jesus was John returned to life, Mark portrays the ruler as weak and reckless, quite unfit to hold power. The story of John the Baptizer's execution characterizes Herod in that way through his fear, his arrogant and rash vow, and his inability to do what he knows is right. Even before all of that occurs, Mark reports that John labeled him as willfully disobedient to God's law. For Herod had married a woman, Herodias, who had divorced one of Herod's half brothers (whom Mark 6:17 calls Philip). John condemns this relationship, most likely in view of Leviticus 18:16; 20:21.

Herod and Herodias respond by silencing the meddlesome prophet.

For Herodias, John's incarceration does not go far enough. When she sees an opportunity to force Herod's hand and have the prisoner executed, in about as grisly a manner as one might invent, she takes it; but she is hardly the only one to blame. The scene is macabre in every way. It intimates that the whole family—plus the rest of the nobility present, by extension—participates in vileness.

Herodias manipulates her husband and her daughter (whom other sources identify as Salome and not Herodias as in 6:22). The narrative refrains from commenting on why Herod's stepdaughter (or daughter) dances to entertain a room of powerful officials, probably mostly men. Such an act would appear beneath a prominent member of the aristocracy. The daughter's dance becomes even more potentially degrading if her performance "please[s]" Herod and his guests in erotic ways, but Mark remains very subtle about that possibility. Less morally ambiguous is what happens next, when Herodias asks her daughter to request John's severed head, and she becomes the means of transporting the bloody trophy on a serving plate to her mother.

Nothing suggests that Herod escapes blame because of Herodias's schemes and her daughter's dancing skills, whether or not one detects sexualized overtones in the scene.[1] Blaming the women for a man's lack of self-control is an all too familiar and destructive trope, but Mark steers away from that by laying chief emphasis on Herod's outright foolishness. His pledge to the daughter—offering up to half of a kingdom that is not even his to grant—is an arrogant

1. What one sees in the scene and how one characterizes the daughter often reveal much about interpreters and their gendered biases. See Janice Capel Anderson, "Feminist Criticism: The Dancing Daughter," in *Mark and Method: New Approaches in Biblical Studies*, 2nd ed., ed. Janice Capel Anderson and Stephen D. Moore (Minneapolis: Fortress, 2008), 111–43.

boast, meant to impress the other elites in attendance. Such irresponsible use of power becomes his undoing, for the preservation of his honor prevents him from breaking the promise, and killing John reveals him as a thug who eliminates God's prophet even though he knew John to be "a righteous and holy man" (v. 20). Herod exposes himself as a man with no control over himself, his words, his power, his household, and his kingdom. This scene could come across as satire if the consequences for John were not so severe and if the scene's function of foreshadowing Jesus' own death were not so tragic.

The first-century historian Flavius Josephus also mentions John's execution by Herod Antipas, although he identifies Herod's motive as concern that John's popularity could incite a political uprising.[2] Navigating among Josephus's and Mark's different accounts is historians' work, but those interpreting Mark as Scripture can see from the contrast between the two ancient accounts that Mark has no interest in assessing any political gains in Herod's deed.

Mark tells a morality tale, not about obvious topics such as the virtue of a prophet's candor or the sketchy ethics of intermarriages within the machinating Herodian family, but about an elite culture that plays by its own twisted, pernicious rules. Rome chose a pompous leader to govern Galilee, and he represents a culture fueled by power and privilege that will do anything to extend its capacity to pursue its own desires, hold onto power, trumpet its own self-importance, eliminate criticism, and resist the justice and peace that God longs to bring to fruition. John does what he has been doing since the beginning of Mark: calling for repentance (1:4; cf. 6:12). This scene illustrates what it looks like when corruption and pride make repentance impossible. Then innocent people die.

Other passages in Mark warn against taking John's death as an isolated incident. In Mark 13:9–11 Jesus tells his followers that they too will find themselves at the mercy of "councils . . . governors and kings" because of their fidelity to him. Mark includes no politically influential characters who give disciples reason to presume those officials will be sympathetic.[3] Moreover, the Herodian family's moral corruption might not be so unique. In 7:20–23 Jesus warns that people should not understand defilement as a foreign thing against which to protect themselves. Rather, defilement comes from within; "evil intentions" proceed "from the human heart." Instead of treating Herod as a unique villain, perhaps Mark urges audiences to see him as representative of the kind of moral bankruptcy that festers inside human societies, corporations, families, and institutions.

This final story about John's life casts new light on Jesus' instructions to the apostles in 6:7–11, as he prepares them for ministry. Because of John's death, their mission now looks more dangerous. In calling people to repent they may be walking on dangerous ground. A prophet's work has always been like that. Speaking truth to power requires more than one voice. It needs to be a collective effort, involving a community. John had disciples, and they care for his corpse (v. 29). With him gone, one of them will need a source of courage to speak up the next time, when the time is right.

MATTHEW L. SKINNER

Commentary 2: Connecting the Reading with the World

This passage occurs in summertime, when box office competition soars. Summer blockbuster movies clamor for our attention: action, adventure, thrillers, superheroes, and animated movies for children of all ages. In these movies, the clash between good and evil makes its way onto the big screen each and every summer. Many of us have a habit of being drawn into the intrigue and drama of the big screen during this time of year. So, this passage does not stray far from

2. Flavius Josephus, *Antiquities* 18.5.2.
3. Joseph of Arimathea may be the lone exception (Mark 15:43).

our cinematic and narrative sensibilities, the preacher might point out. Mark, here, narrates an essential chapter in the Gospel narrative that is itself a story of intrigue, shocking violence, and the struggle between good and evil.

Mark's account of the conflict between Herod's household and John the Baptist comes as an interlude between the sending of the Twelve (Mark 6:1–13) and their regathering at the feeding of the five thousand (vv. 30–44). So the narrative is a pause in the Jesus narrative, but Mark tells the story in an awkward flashback style.

Mark's narrative style notwithstanding, we do indeed get a picture of the level of disruption John's ministry had on the reigning powers. Here we see the perennial clash between imperial power that seeks personal gain through exploitation (v. 14), and the powers to restore, to heal, and to proclaim the gospel of repentance (1:1–8). Mark's references to Elijah and "the prophets of old" (6:15) could not be clearer: there is conflict between the ways of God's realm and the ways of imperial power. John and Jesus come in the line of the Hebrew prophets so obviously that they are mistaken for the prophets of the Hebrew Scriptures. Upsetting that kind of power comes with consequences that to most of us are only the stuff of cinema: John is beheaded, foreshadowing Jesus' death. So, the bottom line is clear as far as Herod is concerned: the ways of the realm of God stand in opposition to the ways of power-hungry rulers who will do anything to preserve power and prestige. When those ways come into opposition, God's agents might suffer death. Neither John nor Jesus shirks the message and responsibility of the realm of God, even unto death. The gospel *is* political, much to the chagrin of those who protest otherwise.

If there is a modern-day soundtrack to John's public call to repentance, we might hear it in theomusicologist Yara Allen's anthem "Somebody's Hurting My Brother."[4] This song has been sung by the thousands all over the United States in the past few years in gatherings of the Poor People's Campaign: National Call for Moral Revival. The song protests the damage done to marginalized communities and to the environment through public policy failures, expresses solidarity, and vocalizes the intent to work for change. It indicates that the pain, the hurt, the killing, the injustice have gone on for "far too long" and calls for an end to the silence.

On June 23, 2018, people gathered on the National Mall in Washington, DC, for the Poor People's Campaign mass rally and direct nonviolent action. The gathering and ensuing march to the US Capitol building included this song, calling on elected officials to renewed action for those who suffer by policy. This event serves as a kind of modern imitation of John's refusal to be silent, when he called Herod to account for his unlawful marriage to Herodias (6:18).

Of course, all of this was safe, relatively speaking. Within the United States, we do not expect to suffer to the degree John the Baptist did. Nevertheless, the clash of powers in the biblical narrative indicates that engaging in conflict by way of prophetic words and actions is a crucial part of the church's ministry. John called Herod, a representative of Roman power, to live in right relationship. He did so quite publicly. Even if not on the same stage or around the same particular issues, such encounters are part of our ministries as well. In word and deed, the church courageously calls the powerful to live into the shape of God's realm. This is precarious and complex work, especially for those who preach in "purple" congregations or for those whose political and ethical beliefs might not necessarily be welcome in a congregation. John shows that the mantle of carrying the message of God's reign can weigh heavy. Silence about the wrong we see at even the highest levels of human institutions might be more convenient, and silence might even preserve one's life, but silence will not do in the call to proclaim God's reign.

In another direction, an even bolder sermon could consider how we might read an unfortunate seam in the way Mark develops these characters. Herod takes relatively little blame here, coming off as somewhat of a hapless character, caught up in the pressure to please his spouse

---

4. Yara Allen, "Somebody's Hurting My Brother," at https://soundcloud.com/user-909500790/somebodys-hurting-my-brother-by-yara-allen (beginning at 4:52).

and, eventually, to fulfill the grandiose banquet promise to his daughter. Herodias, both wife and daughter, are the first women to be directly named in Mark's narrative. We have seen other narrative depictions of women previously in Mark and more will come. Jesus is referred to as the "son of Mary" in 6:3, but she is not present. Mark clearly has an interest in women and how they relate to God's reign.

While the actions of mother and daughter are certainly not worthy of praise, since they do not exhibit faithfulness to God's realm or God's agent John the Baptist, Mark develops these women characters as villains. Jean Delorme goes as far as to say that the mother "becomes John's perfect antithesis . . . she wants his head to be severed as if that would suffice to put an end to the word, as if the mouth were the word's source instead of its momentary organ."[5] This narrative rendering might be unfair. At the very least, it lets Herod off the hook. Regardless of the women's motivation (whether shame or fear of vulnerability and powerlessness), we want to be careful not to psychologize them. The truth is, these women receive the lion's share of blame over Herod, the one who holds the most power in this scenario. Mark paints Herod as "deeply grieved," while both women are attributed with acting on a bloodthirsty grudge to squash God's word in the world.

As the United States continues to struggle around issues of women's rights in significant ways, a sermon could use this text as an opportunity to lift up the ways in which women are vilified in cultural narratives, especially in ways that absolve men of their responsibility in harm. The preacher need not look far for instances of these narratives. They seem to keep repeating themselves and, in many ways, to build in intensity. Male clergy who are determined to break abusive cycles might have a particular role to play in bringing to bear Mark's theme of repentance, thinking of ways to connect the sermon to liturgies in which men, especially, confess the sin of misogyny. The sermon and liturgy could move to celebrate the roles women have played in cultural and congregational life, inviting people of all genders to live in liberative, life-giving ways both in their personal lives and communally.

RICHARD W. VOELZ

5. Jean Delorme, "John the Baptist's Head—The Word Perverted: A Reading of a Narrative (Mark 6:14–29)," *Semeia* 81 (1998): 123–24.

Proper 11 (Sunday between July 17 and July 23)

Jeremiah 23:1–6 and
  2 Samuel 7:1–14a
Psalm 23 and Psalm 89:20–37

Ephesians 2:11–22
Mark 6:30–34, 53–56

Jeremiah 23:1–6

[1]Woe to the shepherds who destroy and scatter the sheep of my pasture! says the LORD. [2]Therefore thus says the LORD, the God of Israel, concerning the shepherds who shepherd my people: It is you who have scattered my flock, and have driven them away, and you have not attended to them. So I will attend to you for your evil doings, says the LORD. [3]Then I myself will gather the remnant of my flock out of all the lands where I have driven them, and I will bring them back to their fold, and they shall be fruitful and multiply. [4]I will raise up shepherds over them who will shepherd them, and they shall not fear any longer, or be dismayed, nor shall any be missing, says the LORD.

[5]The days are surely coming, says the LORD, when I will raise up for David a righteous Branch, and he shall reign as king and deal wisely, and shall execute justice and righteousness in the land. [6]In his days Judah will be saved and Israel will live in safety. And this is the name by which he will be called: "The LORD is our righteousness."

2 Samuel 7:1–14a

[1]Now when the king was settled in his house, and the LORD had given him rest from all his enemies around him, [2]the king said to the prophet Nathan, "See now, I am living in a house of cedar, but the ark of God stays in a tent." [3]Nathan said to the king, "Go, do all that you have in mind; for the LORD is with you."

[4]But that same night the word of the LORD came to Nathan: [5]Go and tell my servant David: Thus says the LORD: Are you the one to build me a house to live in? [6]I have not lived in a house since the day I brought up the people of Israel from Egypt to this day, but I have been moving about in a tent and a tabernacle. [7]Wherever I have moved about among all the people of Israel, did I ever speak a word with any of the tribal leaders of Israel, whom I commanded to shepherd my people Israel, saying, "Why have you not built me a house of cedar?" [8]Now therefore thus you shall say to my servant David: Thus says the LORD of hosts: I took you from the pasture, from following the sheep to be prince over my people Israel; [9]and I have been with you wherever you went, and have cut off all your enemies from before you; and I will make for you a great name, like the name of the great ones of the earth. [10]And I will appoint a place for my people Israel and will plant them, so that they may live in their own place, and be disturbed no more; and evildoers shall afflict them no more, as formerly, [11]from the time that I appointed judges over my people Israel; and I will give you rest from all your enemies. Moreover the LORD declares to you that the LORD will make you a house. [12]When your days are fulfilled and you lie down with your ancestors, I will raise up your offspring after you, who shall come forth from your body, and I will establish his kingdom. [13]He shall build a house for my name, and I will establish the throne of his kingdom forever. [14]I will be a father to him, and he shall be a son to me.

Commentary 1: Connecting the Reading with Scripture

Many scholars would argue that 2 Samuel 7:1–14a represents one of the key texts in the Bible. We find two of the most important theological trends present in the Old Testament here in this reading: name theology and Zion theology. The preacher will do well to pay attention to the tension between the idealistic tendencies from the desert tradition running into the realpolitik of an urban capital of a kingdom. Jeremiah models this tension for us as he struggles with Zion theology. Jeremiah is famously one of our most challenging prophets. We even have a rarely used word in the English language taken from his name: "jeremiad," a complaint or a list of woes. Jeremiah stays true to the reputation this word implies here, as this oracle of woe opens with a blistering attack on false shepherds.

The challenge of a prophet is moving back and forth between oracles of woe and oracles of salvation. The nucleus of the book of Jeremiah is well represented by the woe of the first two verses of this oracle. The prophet Jeremiah challenges the religious orthodoxies of his time. The religious and civil leadership viewed Jerusalem as a specially blessed citadel protected by God, but Jeremiah keeps on referencing how Shiloh, which lies in ruins, was once also considered specially blessed. Now that Jerusalem has been destroyed, we see Jeremiah moving from an oracle of woe to an oracle of hope. God will still bless the scattered flock. God will restore it.

Jeremiah stands for the redemption of suffering. In the ancient world, suffering was often considered a curse from God. In Jesus' time, he was asked if the curse of disability was a result of the sin of the disabled one or their parent (John 9:2). The book of Jeremiah puts the lie to that type of thinking; suffering is not the consequence of sin or evidence of divine justice. Suffering can be a sign of faithful service to God. This still remains a challenge to the church today. It is all too easy to find the prosperity gospel being preached on TV, and examples of ministers and priests richly rewarded in this world by their congregations. Jeremiah offers the counterexample: faithfulness marked not by prosperity, but by suffering.

Much of the material before Jeremiah 23:1–6 consists of a series of personal confessions or laments in which the prophet describes the coming catastrophe on both a personal and communal level (Jer. 11–20). Verses 3–4 begin Jeremiah's hopeful response to this disaster. As much doubt as Jeremiah has cast on the supremacy of Jerusalem, he remains fiercely loyal to the city. He expresses God's communal concerns. A great desire exists to bring scattered Israel back to Jerusalem. Jeremiah will ultimately give comfort to those forced to establish new lives abroad, but here he holds out hope for the restoration of Jerusalem.

The connections of 2 Samuel 7:1–14a with the rest of the chapter should not be overlooked. Zion theology partially emanates from this chapter, because of the unconditional nature of the covenant between God and David. The key word in this chapter is "forever" (*olam*). While the word comes up repeatedly here, the only other chapter in the Bible where it appears as frequently is 1 Chronicles 17, which also describes the Davidic covenant. In relation to this, the preacher would do well to focus on the unconditional love of God. God's love is freely given; we do not have to earn it, and we do not merit it. God makes this abundantly clear to David in verse 8b: "I took you from the pasture, from following the sheep to be prince over my people Israel." This selection by God is not something David earned or was entitled to. It was pure gift.

The prophet Nathan is an important part of this chapter. He dialogues with David at the beginning of our lection, and then is the mouthpiece for God, who promises David in 2 Samuel 7:16, "Your house and your kingdom shall be made sure forever before me; your throne shall be established forever." Nathan witnesses this moment of great privilege, but he will also be there to chastise David in 2 Samuel 12, when he confronts David with the false sense of entitlement that leads him into his greatest sin. Great blessing can lead to presumption of God's forgiveness when one forgets the blessing is purely a gift. We live in a time when religious figures seem to be constantly in the news because of their sins; the dangers of entitlement and presumption are all too evident. God's loyalty to us never goes

The Joy of Entire Surrender

A shepherd and a king seem widely separated in rank, and yet, if we but understand it, their duties are the same, and their responsibilities are alike. Each is bound to care for, and protect, and bless to the utmost limit of his ability, those who are under his control; and no man is fit to be a king who is not a shepherd as well. Christians are accustomed to looking so exclusively on their side of the question, their duties and their responsibilities, that they lose sight almost altogether of God's side, and thus miss a vast amount of comfort. The responsibilities of an owner, and much more of a Creator, are greater than can be expressed. Parents feel something of this, and by a universal instinct, which is inalienable in our natures, all parents are held responsible within certain limitations, to their own consciences and to their fellow-men, for the well doing and prosperity of their children. In the same way owners of animals, or owners of property, or owners of anything, are bound to care for, and protect, and watch over that which they own, and are held responsible to repair if possible the damages which come to their possessions. Even children feel this sense of responsibility, and will go, perhaps reluctantly, to feed a bird because it is theirs, and rejoice in being released from that duty, because their property has been transferred to another owner. The position of authority and ownership, therefore, brings responsibility, and a king is bound to care for his subjects. Surely the subjects may take the comfort of this, and may rest their souls, in a glad deliverance from every anxiety, when under the care of a wise and loving Ruler. To my own mind there is immense comfort to be found in this thought. Our King is also our Owner. For, says the apostle, "Ye are not your own, but ye are bought with a price." Therefore we may safely leave the care and management of everything that concerns us, to Him, who has Himself enunciated as an inexorable law that "if any man provide not for his own, he hath denied the faith and is worse than an infidel." I feel sure, therefore, that it was not without significance that the Lord took David "from the sheepfolds, and brought him to feed His people and Israel His inheritance." He surely meant, I doubt not, to make him a type of that future King, whose control is and can be nothing but blessing to His people, because He is also their Shepherd and "careth for His sheep." I would that every one could realize the blessedness of this thought. For I feel sure that if they did, there would be no longer any delay in their surrender to this glorious Shepherd King; but like it was in Israel's case as related in I Chron. xii., there would come to our David "day by day to help Him," until there would be "a great host, like the host of God," saying, "Thine are we, David, and on thy side, thou son of Jesse." And there would be then indeed among us, as among them of old, "joy in Israel." For there are but few joys like the joy of entire surrender to the Lord Jesus Christ. The soul that has tried it knows this, and to the soul that has not, I can only say that the control of unselfish love is always lovely, even when that love is earthly, because in the nature of things love *can* choose only the best for its beloved one, and *must* pour out itself to the last drop to help and to bless that one; and that therefore the control of God, who is love; who is not merely loving, but is Love itself, must be and can be nothing but infinite and fathomless blessing.

Hannah Whitall Smith, *Old Testament Types and Teachings* (New York: Fleming H. Revell, 1878), 189–91.

away, but the danger remains that we may give up on God if we become too entitled. Congregations need to hear of the challenge of being in relationship with God as well as the consolation and hope that derives from God's promise "forever."

Second Samuel 7:9, 13 focuses on the name of God. God's name and reputation will be furthered by God's relationship with King David. Name theology can be closely related to the importance of temple complexes and other concrete signs of Israel's religious practice. The importance of name connects Israel to the other Semitic and Afro-Asiatic cultures that surround it. God's reputation will be bolstered by the success of Israel. God has created a special place for God's people, where they will be disturbed no more (v. 10). Israel has not captured the promised land; it is God who has done this thing. Special allegiance is due to God.

The preacher can challenge the congregation here to consider just how dependent they feel on God. Do we really understand that we are not responsible for our successes just as David was not responsible for his successes? We all live in a promised land. We have all inherited a life full of blessings and opportunities provided by God rather than by our own hard work. This lection is pushing us in the direction of thanksgiving rather than entitlement. God defeats our foes, God gives us good health, God provides for us. Name theology is concerned with God's reputation, which is ultimately built up or harmed by the moral lives of God's people.

Another key word in 2 Samuel 7 is *hesed*, which is translated in the NRSV as "steadfast love" (2 Sam. 7:15). This word has many meanings, and no single one of them can quite capture its meaning. There is an important sense of mercy and compassion in this word. A strong sense of relationality permeates *hesed*. We could also translate it as "solidarity." There is a feeling in this word of a God who is choosing to be with us, which is exactly what we see in Mark 6:53–56. People recognize the compassion of God in Jesus. God's compassion permeates Jesus; we hear, for example, that he is moved with compassion for the people in Mark 6:34.

In the face of massive suffering, compassion now resonates from Jeremiah's message as it switches from an oracle of woe to an oracle of salvation. This is a clear connection with Mark's Gospel for this Sunday, where we see Jesus focused on compassion in the face of many pressures (Mark 6:30). Jesus recognizes that the people were "like sheep without a shepherd" (v. 34). The second half of this Sunday's Gospel reiterates how the people recognized Jesus as the compassion of God. The model of the book of Jeremiah, with a story of the prophet's suffering and rejection, may be the closest we come in the Old Testament to a story like that of Jesus.

GARRETT GALVIN

Commentary 2: Connecting the Reading with the World

Jeremiah 23:1–6. Times of tremendous political division go hand in hand with demands for leaders who are willing to "cross the aisle" and compromise with their counterparts. People get exhausted with infighting and scandal; if they cannot find an enemy to unite *against*, they hope for a unifying leader to stand *behind*. When Jeremiah preaches his sermon about Israel's hoped-for, postexilic future, he calls to task the rulers who held (or still hold) them captive. God is not happy with shepherds who scatter the flock, and God will deal with them for their divisive ways.

The preacher may expand the connection to our cultural affinity for division. In my community, it is not unusual to see hedges, fences, and other structures that divide what is "mine" from what is "yours." In many parts of the world, homeowners cement shards of glass to the tops of their perimeter walls to dissuade burglars. Many of the patterns we see in the Western world today come from colonizers who "made order out of chaos" by clear-cutting forests, drawing lines, and creating physical boundaries.

They wanted everyone to be clear about who owned what.

We still orient our lives around ownership, and those that have much spend much more of their time worrying about how to keep it. We worry about the safety of our possessions as much as we do about ourselves. We install panic buttons, locks, security systems that we can monitor from our cellular phones. We alienate ourselves from those who are the least bit different from ourselves, and our communities become fragmented. We build walls, literal and figurative, thinking they will save us.

They will not. Our "us versus them" cultural tribes do not protect us nearly as well as we think they do. For instance, when citizens of the United States, or any country, force out or keep out immigrants, we lose out on the technological, economic, and cultural benefits they bring with them.

"Woe to the shepherds who destroy and scatter the sheep of my pasture!" God is displeased with the division in the world, but we should keep in mind that God's interest in unity in this passage is always tied to the accomplishing of justice. Justice supplants unity, and unity is possible only when everyone has their basic needs met. The preacher may want to explore ways that local needs are not being met, in order to rally the congregation to pray for and work toward a just society.

This speaks to the ways in which Christians engage in civic life, but there is also a reminder for how faith communities engage in ministry. Navigating the sacred cows of parish life can be tricky. Pieces of furniture, bulletin formats, service times . . . all sorts of things elicit the common reply, "We have always done it this way." Making small changes in a church is easy compared to the effort it takes to help a small group realize that their supposedly inclusive community has such a narrow focus that they may be leaving out entire segments of their surrounding neighborhood. Even our liturgies sometimes challenge us to divert from our normal routines: confessing sins both individual and communal, exchanging a sign of peace deliberately and out loud, sharing a meal from one loaf and one cup, to name a few. Even our congregational singing eases us into harmonious community in a way that is rarely experienced otherwise (aside from patriotic hymns during sporting events).

Jeremiah's homiletical approach hardly eases any community into harmony, and issuing "woes" is not likely to be the preferred homiletical approach for many modern preachers. However, by guiding the congregation to acknowledge who is missing from their regular worship or their social or formation events, a preacher may also guide a congregation into sharing in God's grief for the ways we are scattered. An effective sermon on this passage may energize a congregation to connect the routine aspects of the liturgy to ways they can pursue justice for all of God's children in some out-of-the-box ways: admitting complicity to societal sin, waging peace in times of angry debate and division, and breaking bread with members of the community who are tough to be around. Our liturgies teach us how to live our lives.

Our liturgies also teach us to hope. Many listeners will hear Jeremiah's words as God's promise of a particular king—Jesus, most likely. We need to avoid misappropriating Jeremiah's sermon as if it were meant for a Christian audience, yet we can point to ways that Jesus focused on unity by calling all people in (instead of calling many out). Jesus befriended tax collectors as well as fishers, he spoke with people of every gender, with Jews and Samaritans, and so on. We can remember that Jesus reminded his followers of people who lived on the outskirts of their communities by actually going to those people. We can highlight that whoever Jesus encountered saw in him a compassionate healer and selfless friend.

Followers of Jesus can be those healers and friends, continuing his work in the world as his living presence, and the preacher can inspire this in a congregation.

2 Samuel 7:1–14a. God tells the prophet Nathan to ask David if *he* is the one to build God a house to live in, pointing out that from Egypt, through the wilderness, to where they are now, God has been just fine. God wants David to do the work of discerning why exactly he wants to build a temple. Is it out of guilt? Is it out of pride?

Given God's role in bringing the people of Israel out of Egypt and toward the promised land, providing for them everything they needed to survive, it seems ridiculous that God would suddenly need a physical temple made by human hands. Throughout the Torah and into the other Hebrew Scriptures, the temple where God has been at work is within human bodies.

The preacher may want to explore the different projects in which the church engages that seem to seek to make God seem more tangible and controllable—ministry programs, buildings, and various traditions. Sometimes we create these things and then hold onto them so tightly that they become too much of the focus. Even though these projects are grounded in our participation in faith communities, they can quickly tempt us to delve into the waters of idolatry.

We need people like Nathan who raise questions about the motivations behind our ministries and programs. When a parish's primary goal becomes its own preservation, we cease to effectively serve our neighbors and lose sight of our deeper desire to reconcile our world to God. We also may forget that the house of the Lord is the one that God makes within us.

The preacher may mention the two times this year when this reading appears—Ordinary Time and Advent. In Advent, we anticipate Christ's coming into the world. During Advent, it is difficult to consider anything more than our holiday agendas. Summer months, on the other hand, offer preachers and their congregations time to rest, reflect, and have "Nathan moments" of their own—times of perspective building when self-absorbed agendas may be put aside in exchange for periods of discerning what kind of faith God may be calling us into. Ordinary Time might be an extraordinary time to plan for the coming year with a renewed focus on using the worshiping community's power to make itself busy not with institution-focused agendas but rather with ones that are focused on the mission of God.

CURTIS FARR

Psalm 23

¹The LORD is my shepherd, I shall not want.
  ²He makes me lie down in green pastures;
he leads me beside still waters;
  ³he restores my soul.
He leads me in right paths
  for his name's sake.

⁴Even though I walk through the darkest valley,
  I fear no evil;
for you are with me;
  your rod and your staff—
  they comfort me.

⁵You prepare a table before me
  in the presence of my enemies;
you anoint my head with oil;
  my cup overflows.
⁶Surely goodness and mercy shall follow me
  all the days of my life,
and I shall dwell in the house of the LORD
  my whole life long.

Psalm 89:20–37

²⁰"I have found my servant David;
  with my holy oil I have anointed him;
²¹my hand shall always remain with him;
  my arm also shall strengthen him.
²²The enemy shall not outwit him,
  the wicked shall not humble him.
²³I will crush his foes before him
  and strike down those who hate him.
²⁴My faithfulness and steadfast love shall be with him;
  and in my name his horn shall be exalted.
²⁵I will set his hand on the sea
  and his right hand on the rivers.
²⁶He shall cry to me, 'You are my Father,
  my God, and the Rock of my salvation!'
²⁷I will make him the firstborn,
  the highest of the kings of the earth.
²⁸Forever I will keep my steadfast love for him,
  and my covenant with him will stand firm.
²⁹I will establish his line forever,
  and his throne as long as the heavens endure.
³⁰If his children forsake my law
  and do not walk according to my ordinances,

³¹if they violate my statutes
    and do not keep my commandments,
³²then I will punish their transgression with the rod
    and their iniquity with scourges;
³³but I will not remove from him my steadfast love,
    or be false to my faithfulness.
³⁴I will not violate my covenant,
    or alter the word that went forth from my lips.
³⁵Once and for all I have sworn by my holiness;
    I will not lie to David.
³⁶His line shall continue forever,
    and his throne endure before me like the sun.
³⁷It shall be established forever like the moon,
    an enduring witness in the skies."

Connecting the Psalm with Scripture and Worship

Psalm 23. The six short verses of Psalm 23 may be the best-known and most frequently recited verses of the entire Psalter. They are often recited by individuals who are in any kind of difficulty; widely used in both Jewish and Christian orders of worship for funerals to comfort the grieving; and appointed in the Episcopal *Book of Common Prayer* for the ritual for Ministration to the Sick when anointing is to be included as part of the rite. Psalm 23 shows up in the Revised Common Lectionary every year on the Fourth Sunday of Easter, when the Gospel readings for each year liken Jesus to a good shepherd; on the Fourth Sunday in Lent in Year A, as a response to 1 Samuel 16:1–13, in which David is chosen over all of his brothers to be anointed as the next king; on Proper 23 of Year A, as a comment on a reading from Isaiah 25:1–9, in which the prophet assures the people that God will make a feast of all the peoples of earth, swallow up death forever, and wipe away the tears from all faces; and here, on Proper 11 of year B, where it is paired with Jeremiah 23:1–6, in which God vows to punish the false shepherds who do not take care of the people, but rather scatter and destroy the sheep of God's pasture. Even many who do not regularly attend any religious services at all can recite at least parts of the King James version from memory, so deeply embedded is it in the collective knowledge of the English-speaking world.

While the ubiquity and familiarity of this psalm make it difficult to say anything new about it, it is worthwhile to pay attention to how it speaks when read in a specific context. In today's reading from Jeremiah, God promises not only to punish the leaders who mistreat the people, but also to someday raise up as king a righteous branch of David who will bring justice and righteousness to the land. Since Psalm 23 is named as a psalm or song of David (*mizmor l'dawid*) in the Masoretic Hebrew text from which most current English translations derive, it is this explicit reference to David that connects the psalm to the prophecy. David, of course, was far from perfect, as many of the particulars of his life make clear, but as a dispenser of justice and defender of the ordinary people, he was remembered as a king after God's own heart.

This juxtaposition of Jeremiah's prophecy and the psalmist's profound trust in God's goodness speaks to every generation that feels itself oppressed by unjust rulers and tyrants. Whether the oppressors are politicians who favor the rich and powerful over those who have little, unfair bosses who live in ostentatious comfort while their employees work long hours for meager pay, or everyday domestic abusers and neighborhood bullies, God's promise to bring justice at some time in the future can sometimes feel empty.

Praying words of gratitude found in the psalm for the simple pleasures of green fields, quiet streams, and a table set with food and drink can be the antidote to fear, even when one is surrounded by enemies. The psalm is a reminder that goodness is more powerful than evil, that comfort exists even in the midst of suffering, and that God's loving-kindness does not diminish, even when everything seems headed for disaster. That does not mean that God will immediately make everything right, but rather that God is present even in the worst of times.

Psalm 89:20–37. The eighteen verses selected from Psalm 89 are a little more than a third of a much longer poem that seems to have been written directly in response to 2 Samuel 7:1–14a. This passage in the Hebrew Scriptures is presented as a historical record of David's desire to build a permanent, wooden building to house the ark in which God's presence was thought to reside. Until then, the ark had been kept in a tent, ever since its construction by the artisans Bezalel and Oholiab soon after the Israelites' escape from slavery in Egypt. Now that David has conquered his enemies, consolidated his kingdom, and had a house made of cedar built for himself and his court, he feels a little guilty that God does not also have a house to live in. However, when the prophet Nathan tells David to go ahead with his plan, God lets him know that both of them have misunderstood God's intention. In a play on words, God says, "The LORD will make you a house," referring not to a structure, but to David's heirs who "shall build a house for my name, and I will establish the throne of his kingdom forever" (2 Sam. 7:11, 13).

The psalm reflects this story. The first eighteen verses rehearse the greatness of God as creator and protector, the one who establishes and defines righteousness and justice. The verses appointed for this week reiterate that David has been anointed to rule over the people, with the assurance in verse 28 that God's steadfast love and covenant with him will stand firm forever. However, the psalmist warns, if future generations break the covenant, they will be punished severely. Even so, God promises, David's lineage "shall continue forever, and his throne endure before me like the sun. It shall be established forever like the moon, an enduring witness in the skies" (Ps. 89:36–37).

The psalm, then, is an echo of the first reading. A superscript says it was written by Ethan the Ezrahite, who is described in 1 Kings 4:31 as particularly wise. Ethan may have been a member of the court under David, Solomon, or both, and the inclusion of this psalm attributed to him attests to his importance to the Davidic line. Like Nathan, he serves as a guide and conscience for the current king and all his descendants, reminding them of their responsibilities toward God and toward the people in their care. Here, he warns them against hubris, against thinking that God's assurances of faithfulness and steadfast love are a license to do whatever they please. Rather, they are to rule with justice and mercy, to offer the people in their care the same faithfulness and steadfast love that they receive from God.

While this story and its accompanying psalm may seem to be about the anointed kings of ancient Israel, it also speaks to anyone who is in any kind of authority over others. It is easy to forget that authority and power are not absolute, but rather come with responsibility toward those over whom that authority and power are exercised. Whether one is a parent, an employer, a teacher, a summer camp counselor, or a president, it is necessary to be mindful of God's example of faithfulness and steadfast love, of justice and kindness. While many people today do not like to think about God punishing anyone for anything, the psalmist is careful to distinguish between legitimately holding those in authority to account for their actions and the withdrawal of divine love. The God pictured here is not some arbitrarily wrathful and jealous deity, but rather the protector of the powerless, the last resort of people whose lives are controlled by those who are given authority and position. This God never withdraws the divine steadfast love from anyone, this psalm seems to say, but does call people to account for how they treat one another.

DEBORAH SOKOLOVE

Ephesians 2:11–22

[11]So then, remember that at one time you Gentiles by birth, called "the uncircumcision" by those who are called "the circumcision"—a physical circumcision made in the flesh by human hands— [12]remember that you were at that time without Christ, being aliens from the commonwealth of Israel, and strangers to the covenants of promise, having no hope and without God in the world. [13]But now in Christ Jesus you who once were far off have been brought near by the blood of Christ. [14]For he is our peace; in his flesh he has made both groups into one and has broken down the dividing wall, that is, the hostility between us. [15]He has abolished the law with its commandments and ordinances, that he might create in himself one new humanity in place of the two, thus making peace, [16]and might reconcile both groups to God in one body through the cross, thus putting to death that hostility through it. [17]So he came and proclaimed peace to you who were far off and peace to those who were near; [18]for through him both of us have access in one Spirit to the Father. [19]So then you are no longer strangers and aliens, but you are citizens with the saints and also members of the household of God, [20]built upon the foundation of the apostles and prophets, with Christ Jesus himself as the cornerstone. [21]In him the whole structure is joined together and grows into a holy temple in the Lord; [22]in whom you also are built together spiritually into a dwelling place for God.

Commentary 1: Connecting the Reading with Scripture

An overarching theme in the Letter to the Ephesians is the contrast between the believer's pre-Christian past and their Christian present. The author constantly contrasts the lived reality of the Christian prior to and then after their new spiritual positioning in Christ as established in the opening verses. It is as if the writer seeks to take the reader on a voyage of self-discovery by juxtaposing the new life in Christ with their former life without God. Having already located their richly blessed position in the heavenly places in Christ (Eph. 1:3–14), prayed for their continued spiritual enlightenment and growth (1:15–23), and identified with their spiritual passage from death to life (2:1–10), the author now turns to explain the filial relationship between Gentiles and Jews seeking reconciliation (2:11–22).

Moving from the more generic spiritual experience of every believer, this passage is filled with ethnic and social tensions, which now threaten the unity of the church. What had been an insider vs. outsider debate between Jews and Gentiles has now become an in-house point of contention within the newly reconstituted people of God. In other words, it is no longer an "us vs. them" argument, but an issue of co-belonging and reconciliation, which has its roots in Genesis and points to the eschatological promises of the coming kingdom.

According to covenantal standards established by the Mosaic Law, the circumcised and the uncircumcised were physically different and therefore alienated one from the other. Literally, Gentiles were born Gentiles "in the flesh" (2:11), but Jews were made Jews through the physical act of circumcision in obedience to God's Law. Put bluntly, the uncircumcised (Gentiles) had "no hope and [were] without God in the world" (v. 12). In this scenario, the alienation of Jews and Gentiles was chalked up to divine decree.

The phrase "aliens from the commonwealth of Israel" (v. 12) denotes citizenship for the covenant people and alienation for those outside it. It is as if circumcision provided the proper documentation for belonging to God's people (Israel), whereas not having this identity badge marked one as a stranger or foreigner to God's covenant relationship. However, our text announces, the situation has changed. A new covenant has been established; a new relationship between former strangers can now be forged.

The phrase "but now in Christ" (v. 13) marks a definite transition from that which was before to a new reality that one enters through the new covenant in Jesus' blood. Whereas the old covenant created distinctions and separated the chosen people from the rest, the new covenant sought to erase divisions and break down walls. The operative factor bringing people near to God is no longer a physical act performed by human hands (i.e., circumcision), but a divine act enacted in the flesh of Jesus Christ (v. 14). Thus, the new covenant does not just primarily deal with the vertical alienation between God and humanity. It also fixes the horizontal estrangement between people.

Verse 14 clearly demarcates the cultural existence of two groups, which stood in stark opposition due to religious principles. However, now things can and should be different, because the "dividing wall" has been demolished and hostility can no longer be embraced, because the Prince of Peace has come! This is an obvious allusion to the rending of the veil in the Holy of Holies, which signaled a new beginning (Matt. 27:51). Moreover, the creation of a new humanity begins with the abolishment of the Law. It might be helpful to understand the strong language of demolishing the Law as referring to its secondary effects and not its intrinsic value. The problem was not the Law itself, but rather the religious divisions caused by the two groups it created, and the moral lines of separation between them.

Just as important, the text points to the place of reconciliation, "in his flesh" (Eph. 2:14). The two groups are made to reconcile, which they were unable to do for themselves. Rather, they are made one in the God-man Jesus Christ. Dialectically, what the Law-abiding group (Israel) and the non-Law-following group (Gentiles) were each incapable of accomplishing through obedience to the Law or any other morally ethical means, Christ accomplished in his body. On the cross, he who fulfilled all of "the law with its commandments and ordinances" (v. 15) nullified its negative effects, thus ending Israel's bondage to the Law and the alienation of those far from it. Whatever hostility resulted from the attempt or disinterest to abide by the Law was rendered null by the death of Jesus on the cross (v. 16)

The holistic image of reconciliation of Jews and Gentiles alike is beautifully portrayed in verses 17–18 as the proclamation of peace to both. John R. W. Stott summarizes this as "publishing abroad the good news of the peace he had made through the cross."[1] In the one act of the cross, those who were far off and those who were near were reconciled unto God. No special shortcut treatment for the chosen nation and no back-of-the-line stiff-arm status for Gentiles. Hearkening to the Trinitarian blessings of God in the first chapter of the letter, access to God takes on Trinitarian form: the Son provides the means and the Spirit the avenue for reconciliation with the Father (v. 18).

The rest of this passage provides helpful images for understanding the horizontal dimensions of reconciliation. If Jews and Gentiles have been reconciled with God, drawing near to God draws the two groups closer to each other. As in an equilateral triangle, despite the distance between the two groups, the nearer they each become to the Father, the closer together they are to each other. This image of togetherness and unity is further fortified by construction metaphors.

The phrases "citizens with the saints" and "members of the household of God" point to the strong bond of God's one people. No longer are we to think of Jews and Gentiles, for the two have become one. Furthermore, just as the Lord as shepherd pastored his people Israel (Ps. 23), the sheep without a shepherd would also be pastored (Mark 6:34).

The imagery of a house and a temple is significant here, for it alludes to the word of the Lord spoken to David by the prophet Nathan (2 Sam. 7:1–14a). The temple was not only a house where God dwelt, but the place God met God's people. The Gentiles, of course, were

---

1. John R. W. Stott, *The Message of Ephesians: God's New Society* (Downers Grove, IL: InterVarsity Press, 1979), 103.

allowed only in an outer court of the temple of Jerusalem, but now God's people together had become his temple (v. 21), the place where God dwells (v. 22).

Figuratively, verse 20 establishes the foundation of the new and improved temple as having the foundation of the apostles (read Jesus' disciples) and the prophets (read Old Testament authors). Significantly, Christ Jesus (the anointed/Messiah Jesus) is established as the cornerstone of the temple. As Messiah, all of the writings of the old covenant have their fulfillment in him and all of the new covenant understanding flows from him.

The architectural imagery here conveys the oneness of the structure of the newly refurbished temple. The old construction has not been laid aside completely in order to build a completely new temple. Instead, the whole structure is in the process of being built spiritually into the dwelling place of God: the church.

SAMMY G. ALFARO

Commentary 2: Connecting the Reading with the World

I live in a town north of Washington, DC. Frederick, founded in 1745, is known for its "clustered spires." On Church Street, aptly named, there are All Saints' Episcopal Church, Evangelical and Reformed United Church of Christ, Trinity Chapel, and Evangelical Lutheran Church. One block north you will find four more churches of various flavors. Their various spires punctuate the skyline and give the city its identity. They would seem to belie the testimony of the hymn "We Are One in the Spirit." The reality of our churches is too often disunity. No wonder that same hymn ends with prayers that unity be "restored."[2]

The author writing to the Christian community in Ephesus realized how divided were the members of that community. He saw the church in Ephesus was made up of a "we" and a "they." The *we*, it would seem, were the followers of Christ who had begun their journey as Jews, the circumcised (if one is male), those who came from Israel. The *they* would be those born as Gentiles, the uncircumcised. The *they* are described as those who were aliens, strangers, far off. To be a *they* was to be one without hope, to be on the outside—orphans, if you will, for the *they* had not been part of the household. The writer clearly wants the *we* and the *they* to come together.

The author reminds us that through the cross, through the blood of Jesus, the *we* and the *they* have been brought together; nevertheless it would seem that there is still a great deal of disunity. A pastor might ask their congregation: Who, in the life of our community today, do we consider the *we*, and who are the *they*? We do not always like to admit to our divisions. Name some of the many ways we are divided. Not only do we experience the us/them divide in our own church and among churches, a pastor could point out. We also experience it in our local communities, our nation, and our world. Do you reach out to other Christians? a pastor might ask. Do you reach out to your Jewish and Muslim neighbors? What about Hindu and Buddhist sisters and brothers? Do you reach out to the "Nones"?

One of the challenges of writing a commentary is that it is frozen in time. While I may be reflecting on particular issues and conflicts, those will be different if you come to this in the future. With that in mind, I will use as an example the subject of walls. As I write this commentary, the citizens of the United States are divided not by, but over the issue of, a wall. There are some who feel that, without a tall, impenetrable, continuous wall along our southern border with Mexico, American citizens cannot be kept safe. They understand walls as a way to keep the *they* away from the *we*.

Perhaps the most famous of walls is the Great Wall of China. Thirteen thousand miles long, it took more than a thousand years to build. It is certainly an amazing wall, visible from space, and portions of it remain today. It continues as

---

2. Peter Scholtes, "We Are One in the Spirit," in *Glory to God* (Louisville, KY: Westminster John Knox, 2013), 300.

a powerful symbol of identity for the people of China. However, while built to keep out invaders from the north, in the end it proved unsuccessful.

Other walls are built to keep people in. In 1961 the German Democratic Republic quickly constructed a wall that would separate the two Germanies. Yes, it was in part to keep out the West. Even more importantly, it was to keep the people of the GDR in. As the people realized what was happening, more and more tried to escape to the West. The news reports were filled with horrifying images of people throwing children out of windows beside the wall. Hundreds were successful in fleeing to a new life in the West, but many were killed.

Walls can provide security, but the author sees that a wall of hostility, mistrust, and enmity was dividing the Christians in Ephesus. He reminds that Christ Jesus "is our peace; in his flesh he has made both groups into one and has broken down the dividing wall" (Eph. 2:14). There are many images for understanding what it is like to be one in Christ. Jesus used the image of a vineyard, "I am the vine, you are the branches" (John 15:5). When we are one in Christ, we are able to flourish and produce "much fruit."

In the First Letter to the Church in Corinth, Paul uses the metaphor of the body. Even though the church has many members, "we were all baptized into one body—Jews or Greeks, slaves or free—and we were all made to drink of one Spirit" (1 Cor. 12:13). He then goes on to remind the community that although they are different—hands, eyes, feet, noses—they are still one body.

The author reminds the Ephesian community that, through the death of Jesus, they are made "one body." It is an architectural metaphor that is woven throughout the letter. He writes about dividing walls. More importantly he writes that the Jewish "we" and the Gentile "they" have been brought together and empowered by Christ to be built "into a dwelling place for God" (Eph. 2:22). He writes of structures, of foundations that are the apostles and prophets, and of the cornerstone, which is Christ.

The image of cornerstone was, for the Jewish members of the community, a messianic term. The prophet Isaiah told the people, "Therefore thus says the Lord GOD, See, I am laying in Zion a foundation stone, a tested stone, a precious cornerstone, a sure foundation" (Isa. 28:16). Jesus reminded us, "Have you never read in the scriptures: 'The stone that the builders rejected has become the cornerstone; this was the Lord's doing, and it is amazing in our eyes'?" (Matt. 21:42).

Does your church have a literal cornerstone? Those cornerstones can be a wonderful reminder of the community that built the church. I think, though, that the writer of the letter is challenging us to think not about the actual stones that are the foundation of the buildings in which we worship. Rather, he is challenging us to remember that, in Christ who is our cornerstone, we are no longer strangers and aliens who are divided by hostility. We have been made one, and in our oneness, our loving unity, we are able to reach out and break down the walls of hostility that divide our world.

Christian Führer was the pastor of Nikolai Kirche in Leipzig. In the German Democratic Republic, worship and religious activities were firmly constrained. In September 1982 he began to hold peace prayers on Monday evenings. They were not really formal services. Rather, people gathered and offered their own prayers and reflections on what it meant to live in the repressive regime. Führer was surprised how quickly the attendance grew. By early 1989 the secret police began to block the roads to the church, but the prayers continued. On the ninth of October, seventy thousand people gathered outside the church to protest for peace. Führer asked everyone to carry candles. He felt that, if they had candles, they would not throw stones at the army and police. Over the next month huge gatherings were held all over the GDR. On the ninth of November the wall fell. Christ "is our peace . . . he has broken down the dividing wall, . . . the hostility between us" (Eph. 2:14).

LUCY LIND HOGAN

Mark 6:30–34, 53–56

³⁰The apostles gathered around Jesus, and told him all that they had done and taught. ³¹He said to them, "Come away to a deserted place all by yourselves and rest a while." For many were coming and going, and they had no leisure even to eat. ³²And they went away in the boat to a deserted place by themselves. ³³Now many saw them going and recognized them, and they hurried there on foot from all the towns and arrived ahead of them. ³⁴As he went ashore, he saw a great crowd; and he had compassion for them, because they were like sheep without a shepherd; and he began to teach them many things. . . .

⁵³When they had crossed over, they came to land at Gennesaret and moored the boat. ⁵⁴When they got out of the boat, people at once recognized him, ⁵⁵and rushed about that whole region and began to bring the sick on mats to wherever they heard he was. ⁵⁶And wherever he went, into villages or cities or farms, they laid the sick in the marketplaces, and begged him that they might touch even the fringe of his cloak; and all who touched it were healed.

Commentary 1: Connecting the Reading with Scripture

Ministry is both exhilarating and exhausting. In Mark 6:7–12, Jesus *sent out* (*apostellein*) the Twelve two by two to preach the gospel, drive out demons, and heal those who were sick. In verse 30, these same *apostles* (*apostoloi*), or "sent-out ones," gather around Jesus to give a report of their mission. They tell Jesus "everything, as much as they did and as much as they taught" (my trans.). Nothing was left out of their report. The reader can sense the excitement of the Twelve in telling Jesus about every sermon they preached, every home they visited, every exorcism they performed, and every miracle they beheld.

The real test of discipleship, however, comes now. In verses 31–32, Jesus perceives the exhaustion of the Twelve and their need to recuperate after their mission, since they had not yet eaten. He invites them to a "deserted place" where they can rest. By "deserted place," Jesus likely has in mind an unpopulated area outside of the rural villages. His intent is to travel by boat on the Sea of Galilee and land in one of the coves scattered along the western shoreline between Bethsaida (Luke 9:10) and Tiberias (John 6:22–23). From there they can walk to a remote area away from the pressing crowds.

However, the popularity of Jesus as a teacher and miracle worker had already spread throughout the region (Mark 1:28) and to such a degree that people from every town ran by foot ahead of the boat to meet Jesus as he landed on shore (6:33). What happens next brings a resolution to the short story of the Twelve's failed attempt to retreat with Jesus and also introduces the following story of the feeding of the five thousand (vv. 35–44). Verse 34 functions as a hinge text between the two stories. In verse 34, when the boat lands, Jesus sees the crowds and "is moved with a deep compassion" (my trans.) for them. The affection that Jesus has for the people is a gut-wrenching sympathy (*esplanchnisthē*). He is burdened by the sight of desperate people. Jesus gives up on the retreat, and instead "he begins to teach them many things," as he has regularly done throughout his ministry (1:21; 2:13; 4:1; 6:2). Jesus feeds the crowds spiritually through his teaching (6:34) and will soon feed them materially with real bread (v. 42).

The reader may wonder what Jesus saw in the faces of people that drew such a strong emotional reaction from within him. Perhaps it was the sight of abject poverty that characterized first-century-CE Galilee that provoked Jesus.

First-century Galilee was mainly an agricultural economy with a minor fishing industry. Most lived on a humble vegetable diet, with dairy supplements, and occasionally poultry, lamb, and other meats. About 90 percent of Galilee's residents lived at the subsistence level or below it. In the ancient world, there was no middle class. The working class (*penēs*) who struggled to live at the subsistence level were often counted among Galilee's poor (*ptōchos*). They included farm families, fishermen, skilled and unskilled laborers, artisans, most merchants and traders, small shop owners and freed persons (62 percent of the population). Many farming families suffered land loss due to a poor harvest, natural calamity, and extreme taxation (Roman taxes were 20–40 percent) and consequently joined those who lived below the subsistence level among the day laborers, widows, orphans, beggars, prostitutes, bandits, and the disabled (28 percent of the population).[1] As a carpenter from Nazareth (6:3), Jesus understood the daily struggle for subsistence.

The reader is also given an Old Testament allusion to explain the source of Jesus' compassion. The multitudes in Mark's narrative are tied to an enduring Old Testament image of Israel as "sheep without a shepherd" (v. 34). The phrase evokes the long history of faithless kings and priests who neglected to lead Israel with justice and teach them to obey God's decrees with covenant fidelity (Num. 27:17; 1 Kgs. 22:17; 2 Chr. 18:16; Isa. 13:14; Ezek. 34:2–5; Zech. 10:2). Israel's leaders had failed to care for God's people spiritually and materially, and the resultant conditions of spiritual and material poverty elicited Jesus' passionate response.

In contrast to the succession of faithless rulers, there have been two leaders who stand out as faithful shepherds in Israel's history. They are the only two figures in the Old Testament who changed vocations from their previous role as literal shepherds of livestock to metaphorical shepherds of God's people: David (Ps. 78:70–72) and Moses (Isa. 63:11). Mark's Gospel presents Jesus as both the Davidic Shepherd-King and as the new Moses throughout this passage (vv. 31–34) and the subsequent episodes (i.e.,

the feeding of the five thousand in vv. 35–44 and Jesus' walking on water in vv. 45–52).

The Old Testament lections trace the prophetic promise that God would eventually send a messiah from the house of David (2 Sam 7:1–14a; Ps. 89:20–37) to shepherd God's people in a way that their past leaders did not (Jer. 23:1–3). The righteous Branch of David will reign wisely, execute justice in the land, and shepherd the people so they no longer live in fear (Jer. 23:4–5). Mark's Gospel highlights Jesus' compassion for the crowds to signal that their deplorable state as "sheep without a shepherd" has come to an end. God's Messiah has arrived. Jesus is the true Shepherd who restores and leads God's people (Ps. 23:1–6; cf. John 10:11–16; Rev. 7:17).

The Mark 6 lection takes a narrative jump from verses 31–34 to verses 53–56. It is important, however, to trace how the image of Jesus as Israel's true shepherd unfolds in the intervening episodes. In answer to the prophetic charge that the past shepherds of Israel cared only for themselves (Ezek. 34:18–19), Jesus as the Davidic shepherd-king feeds the flock of five thousand hungry people with five loaves and two fish until they are satisfied (Mark 6:42). Like Moses who fed manna to Israel in the desert, Jesus, as a new Moses, feeds bread to the crowds in a deserted place (vv. 35, 41).

The reader is then introduced to a different christological image when Jesus walks on water (vv. 45–52). Jesus' walk across the Sea of Galilee recapitulates Moses' parting of the Red Sea (Exod. 14:21–15:19) and alludes to a new, greater exodus for God's people. In this new exodus, Jesus delivers God's people not from slavery under an imperial power like Egypt or Rome (John 18:36–37), but from the forces of evil, suffering, and death (1 Cor. 15:50–57).

In verses 53–56 the same theme of the crowds who pursue Jesus is rehearsed but with greater intensity. Jesus is recognized "at once" (Mark 6:54), and the villagers "rush" toward him (v. 55). They "beg" to touch even the cloak of Jesus for healing (v. 56). The demands of crowds appear to increase. Yet in the face of human need, Jesus continues to feed people

---

1. Sakari Häkkinen, "Poverty in the First-Century Galilee," *Hervormde teologiese studies* 72, no. 4 (2016): 1–9.

spiritually and materially. While Jesus understands the importance of a strategic withdrawal from work and the need to create a sacred space for a Sabbath rest, he also remains available and flexible to the pastoral care of God's people. He models for the disciples what they themselves will have to learn as those "sent" by God and as future shepherds of God's flock. There is never a convenient time for ministry. We should expect random interruptions. Whether as ordained clergy or lay leaders, we are called to suspend our immediate plans in order to care for those in need.

MAX J. LEE

Commentary 2: Connecting the Reading with the World

You cannot begin to consider these incidents apart from what immediately precedes. John the Baptist, a distant relative of Jesus, his literal forerunner, perhaps dear friend, has been brutally executed by the faux king, Herod. In prison as a result of speaking truth to power, John's terrible death was precipitated by a frivolous promise made to a dancing girl at a royal banquet. The news must have shaken Jesus to his core. Whatever Jesus believed about his own future, John's death surely must have reminded him of harsh reality. Challenging autocratic power can be deadly.

Jesus had sent his disciples out, two by two, on their first mission venture. He gave them specific instruction on what to do, to take nothing along but sandals and one tunic, no bread, no money. They would be on their own. He assured them that they had authority to do the job. The mission was hugely successful: they had cast out demons as he instructed and healed the sick and now they had returned. They were exhausted but energized by the prospect of reporting their success to Jesus and to one another, swapping stories about what they had seen and done and experienced. Now, with his heavy burden of grief and perhaps anxiety about what lay ahead for himself and his followers, Jesus proposes a Sabbath. "Come away to a quiet place all by yourselves and rest a while" (Mark 6:31). Mark adds a delightfully suggestive anecdote: "For many were coming and going, and they had no leisure even to eat." Busy modern families understand exactly.

Sabbath is deep in Hebrew tradition, a fundamental biblical idea. God works for six days in the creation story and on the seventh day God rests. God's rest is part of the magnificent mystery of creation. Creation itself requires rest to be completed. God knows when to stop and rest. God knows how to step back, take a deep breath, and enjoy what God has created. The work of creation includes the cessation, the enjoyment. Observing Sabbath has not only disappeared from modern life; it has been replaced by incessant, nonstop work. Computers and cell phones have enabled working hours to expand to twenty-four per day. You can receive and send emails and text messages and calls, do a video conference wherever you are all day and all night. Technology allows work to follow you even on vacation anywhere in the world.

The Sabbath Jesus and his disciples need never happens. Crowds have been gathering wherever he goes. The little band has climbed into a boat and made for a quiet place along the lake shore. They have already begun to relax. Blessed rest at last—but the world, as it so often does, intercedes. A crowd of people watched them leaving. The word spreads and now the crowd is moving and by the time the boat arrives at its destination, it is not a quiet place at all. The crowd is already there to greet them, and now it is larger.

When he sees what is happening, Jesus abruptly changes the agenda. Stepping out of the boat and seeing the crowd, he suddenly feels compassion. The gathered people seem to him "like sheep without a shepherd" (v. 34). It is another rich Jewish and Hebrew biblical image: men and women, lost, wandering aimlessly, without plan or purpose, hungry for food but also for meaning and purpose. He greets them, welcomes them, speaks with them, listens to them.

My favorite part of this episode is the disciples' reaction to the sudden disappearance of the lovely promise of a quiet place, a dinner, and a good night's sleep. I understand. They do what many of us would do, what we do every day, what I do every day as I walk past the homeless man on the corner asking for money for a sandwich or a room to spend the cold night. The disciples ask Jesus to send the crowd away, so that they can return to the rest they so desperately want and need. Instead, he does the most remarkable, compassionate thing. He feeds the crowd in an act so central to who he is that it is in each of the four Gospels.

Then, instead of resting, it is back in the boat crossing the lake to Gennesaret. People rushing from the entire region are there again, this time bringing their elderly and sick dear ones, this time urgent, desperate, hungry not only for food but for healing, wholeness. Mark observes that wherever he goes now—villages, cities, farms, marketplaces—desperate people want to be close to him, to touch his robe, to be healed.

There is a built-in tension, for women and men who aspire to follow Jesus, between giving life away for others and the necessity of responsible self-care. The tension is there for everyone, but it is particularly intense for those who have answered Christ's call and who work daily for the church or other religious institutions. There are simply no built-in limits to the needs of the people we serve, not to mention institutional administrative and management responsibilities. Work is never done. Looming always is Jesus' invitation to find your life by losing it and Dietrich Bonhoeffer's "When Christ calls a man, he bids him come and die."[2]

So this episode becomes a commentary on what it means to be a Christian and to give your life away striving to obey and follow Jesus. It happens in a thousand and one decisions, small and large, every single day, about what takes commanding precedence in life. At the same time, it does raise the important question, When does self-sacrifice become unhealthy to oneself and one's family and loved ones?

Many who live out their faith by working in the church, laity and clergy, come to the unhappy realization that the never-ending demands of work result in missed one-time events in the lives of their children: recitals, basketball games, concerts. We are not the only ones sacrificing for our commitments. Families and spouses sacrifice as well. There is another commitment necessary to health and to life-giving relationships: acknowledging vocational responsibilities but also personal, family, and social responsibilities. It is possible to work hard and give life away and at the same time give life to dear ones. It can be a helpful model for others. It is okay and, in fact, responsible to miss a committee meeting to attend a daughter's volleyball game or piano recital.

Elaine Pagels observes, "Many people in antiquity spent enormous amounts of time and energy searching for ways to 'heal the heart' as countless people are doing today, expanding an enormously increasing range of clinical medications, therapeutic techniques, exercises, support groups, meditation, yoga."[3]

Not only the crowds that followed Jesus need his healing touch. Modern men, women, young people, and children also hunger for healing and wholeness. It is a good tension between giving life away to serve others and acknowledging and attending to one's own needs. This incident reminds us that the good news of God's love in Jesus Christ is for everyone: for the world and also for the women and men who have promised to give their lives to communicating and living out the gospel. It is good news for us too. The fringe of his healing cloak is available, thanks be to God, to all of us.

JOHN M. BUCHANAN

2. Dietrich Bonhoeffer, *The Cost of Discipleship* (New York: Macmillan, 1949), 79.
3. Elaine Pagels, *Why Religion, A Personal Story* (New York: Harper Collins, 2018), 207.

Proper 12 (Sunday between July 24 and July 30)

2 Kings 4:42–44 and 2 Samuel 11:1–15   Ephesians 3:14–21
Psalm 145:10–18 and Psalm 14   John 6:1–21

2 Kings 4:42–44

[42]A man came from Baal-shalishah, bringing food from the first fruits to the man of God: twenty loaves of barley and fresh ears of grain in his sack. Elisha said, "Give it to the people and let them eat." [43]But his servant said, "How can I set this before a hundred people?" So he repeated, "Give it to the people and let them eat, for thus says the LORD, 'They shall eat and have some left.'" [44]He set it before them, they ate, and had some left, according to the word of the LORD.

2 Samuel 11:1–15

[1]In the spring of the year, the time when kings go out to battle, David sent Joab with his officers and all Israel with him; they ravaged the Ammonites, and besieged Rabbah. But David remained at Jerusalem.
   [2]It happened, late one afternoon, when David rose from his couch and was walking about on the roof of the king's house, that he saw from the roof a woman bathing; the woman was very beautiful. [3]David sent someone to inquire about the woman. It was reported, "This is Bathsheba daughter of Eliam, the wife of Uriah the Hittite." [4]So David sent messengers to get her, and she came to him, and he lay with her. (Now she was purifying herself after her period.) Then she returned to her house. [5]The woman conceived; and she sent and told David, "I am pregnant."
   [6]So David sent word to Joab, "Send me Uriah the Hittite." And Joab sent Uriah to David. [7]When Uriah came to him, David asked how Joab and the people fared, and how the war was going. [8]Then David said to Uriah, "Go down to your house, and wash your feet." Uriah went out of the king's house, and there followed him a present from the king. [9]But Uriah slept at the entrance of the king's house with all the servants of his lord, and did not go down to his house. [10]When they told David, "Uriah did not go down to his house," David said to Uriah, "You have just come from a journey. Why did you not go down to your house?" [11]Uriah said to David, "The ark and Israel and Judah remain in booths; and my lord Joab and the servants of my lord are camping in the open field; shall I then go to my house, to eat and to drink, and to lie with my wife? As you live, and as your soul lives, I will not do such a thing." [12]Then David said to Uriah, "Remain here today also, and tomorrow I will send you back." So Uriah remained in Jerusalem that day. On the next day, [13]David invited him to eat and drink in his presence and made him drunk; and in the evening he went out to lie on his couch with the servants of his lord, but he did not go down to his house.
   [14]In the morning David wrote a letter to Joab, and sent it by the hand of Uriah. [15]In the letter he wrote, "Set Uriah in the forefront of the hardest fighting, and then draw back from him, so that he may be struck down and die."

Commentary 1: Connecting the Reading with Scripture

Our readings show protagonists dealing with the problem of human limitations. David refuses to respect the limitations required by God's law as he falls into self-centered behavior. Two miracles show Elisha overcoming natural limitations as he engages in other-centered behavior. Second Kings 4:38–41 has Elisha in the company of guild prophets. Elisha has his servant make some stew for the prophets, but one of the guild prophets unknowingly adds something to the stew that poisons it. Elisha quickly remedies the situation by adding some flour to the stew, and he says in 2 Kings 4:41, "Let them eat." These words will be repeated in the next three verses that constitute the lection under consideration. Our readings will offer a vivid contrast between an isolated David whose concerns seem to involve only himself, and an Elisha who is concerned that the people should eat.

A number of key words and actions stand out in the lection of 2 Samuel 11. The first verse tells us that it is the time for kings to go on war campaigns, but David is strangely absent. The author of this lection may be foreshadowing that something is amiss. David has relished the fight up to this stage; we may now be transitioning to a different part of his life. Verse 2 quickly adds to the incongruity of the opening passage, as we now see David representing the avaricious male gaze. We have seen this earlier in the Bible when Judah unknowingly sleeps with his daughter-in-law Tamar in Genesis 38. The text seems to be indicating that David has lost his discipline both on the battlefield and in his personal life. He is less worried about God and Israel, and more worried about himself.

The key word in both this lection from 2 Samuel and the chapter is *shalah*, "to send." It is used more in this chapter than any other chapter in the Old Testament. It helps paint a picture of a decadent David as he sends for both Bathsheba and Uriah. We see that Bathsheba is not without agency, as she sends a note back to David to announce her pregnancy (2 Sam. 11:5), and David's general, Joab, also has agency, as he sends Uriah to David. Uriah is the only one without agency, as he is sent around

by David (v. 6), sent away by David (v. 12), and ultimately sent to his death by David.

The other key word in 2 Samuel 11 is *shalom*, which can mean "peace" or "well-being." Yet there is a sense of foreboding here, as we find in two other passages about Abner (3:21–23) and Absalom (18:28–32). In both instances, there are inquiries about the well-being of the men, and they either die soon or are already dead. Death will also come to Uriah.

Although this material is sin-centered, the character of Uriah stands out from the crowd. All the virtues missing from David and Joab can be found in him. Whereas David's faithfulness to God and the covenant will be sorely tested here, Uriah could not be more faithful. Whereas David's personal predilections will be his undoing after so many public triumphs, Uriah's transparency and integrity between the personal and the private stand in stark contrast to David. David repeatedly tests Uriah here in this story, and this faithful man is more than up to the test. Uriah represents the perspective of virtue ethics. Rather than avoiding sin, he remains steadfast to the best of Israel's traditions.

In an age of Wikileaks, when the clay feet of public figures have become increasingly apparent, the preacher would do well to point out what a virtuous life looks like. It may not be recognized as it is lived, but posterity will tell the story. Our congregations always need overlooked heroes to follow. Uriah is a fairly minor character, but with the challenges he faces, Uriah may represent a normal congregant far better than David. Many people are pushed by bosses at work to look the other way or are rewarded for ceding to the boss's demands; Uriah offers the glorious example of following God's ways in and out of season.

The preacher can draw an important connection between 2 Kings 4:42–44 and the beginning of the chapter, which starts with the multiplication of oil (4:1–7). Both bread and oil are basic commodities and one of the essentials of life in ancient Israel. Ancient Israelites used oil as a binding agent for loaves of bread and cakes (Lev. 2:4), which served as the daily staples of their diet. The whole chapter illustrates prophetic abundance, but this theme is particularly prominent at the beginning and ending of the chapter.

Elisha would seem to be particularly motivated by a hermeneutic of generosity. He appears to realize that he is the recipient of a gift he has neither earned nor deserved. His prophetic status and perhaps the stories of how God works through him have brought him fame. He uses this fame to feed his fellow Israelites. While we hear many stories of famine in the Bible, Elisha refuses to succumb to scarcity thinking. He could hoard this grain for a rainy day (Luke 12:13–21).Instead, he models trust in God and shares his abundance with his fellow Israelites.

Second Kings 4:42–44 can also be connected to the New Testament in a number of ways. The theme of abundance comes up repeatedly in the New Testament. Elisha can be seen as a type of Christ as he lives out 2 Corinthians 8, a passage that is concerned with finding a balance between the abundance of some and the needs of others. Elisha finds that balance as he gives from his abundance to those in need. The preacher can challenge members of the congregation to consider from what mentality they approach life. Do they share from their abundance, or do they hoard, filled with worries of scarcity? Scripture invites us to follow the example of the prophet Elisha rather than his fretting servant.

The lectionary offers another wonderful connection with this lection. The promises of the Old Testament are fulfilled in the life of Christ. We can see this Gospel passage (John 6:1–21) as a complete rejection of scarcity thinking. Rather than bread and oil, Christ has bread and fish. Rather than trying like Elisha to feed a hundred men, Christ is trying to feed five thousand (v. 10). In the high Christology of John, it can be argued that Christ is not only fulfilling the promises of the Old Testament; he is also supplanting the feasts of the Old Testament, as he does this as he approaches Passover, the feast that highlights unleavened bread. Christ quickly follows this miracle with another aimed at his fretting disciples: Jesus walks on the chaotic seas, which have been swept up by a storm. We see that the fears of scarcity and chaos can all be neutralized by Jesus.

An important contrast can be drawn between the scenes of David eating with Uriah and Jesus eating with the five thousand men at the Sea of Galilee. The preacher can contrast the manipulative nature of David, who is self-centered. He eats with Uriah, but only to get him drunk, in the hope that he will forget his principles. Jesus represents the other-centered person focused on the blessings that surround him. Nowhere in this passage do we hear David giving thanks for all of his good fortune; Jesus gives thanks in John 6:11 and extends his blessing to all those who follow him. David, the self-centered person, takes what does not belong to him; Jesus, the other-centered person, gives and shares what he has.

GARRETT GALVIN

Commentary 2: Connecting the Reading with the World

Food Miracles. Anyone who does not understand biblical miracles of food multiplication has never been to a church potluck. It does not matter if your church is full of parishioners with too much money to spend or not enough. Churches of all kinds typically have the "problem" of having *too much* food rather than *not enough*. Every church kitchen ought to have plenty of take-out containers for this reason—and a healthy belief in miracles.

Faith communities experience multiplication miracles all the time, and yet they often find other ways to explain what happened, crediting effective event planning or some other human initiative. Whether food is multiplied magically or simply shared, the miracle is that everyone gets fed. Whether two lovers are drawn to each other by some force of fate or simply by chance, the miracle is that two people can find a way to love one another in an often-tragic world.

Are preachers, on Sunday morning, training their congregations to look for and interpret the miracles in their own lives? What would it look like for a preacher to spend time visiting with parishioners and drawing out examples of everyday miracles? By cultivating an awareness of the world's (and God's) abundance, a faith community might learn to model for their community what it looks like to no longer be surprised by the generous abundance in the world. The hurdle for many faith communities lies in looking past their own sacred cows, especially those ones that seem to receive unwarranted protection, to see how their traditions point to God's abundance.

The Holy Eucharist, for example, models how a few representatives from the congregation may offer oblations for the good of the whole community. What follows is a sharing of the sacrament in which we become what we consume, the body of Christ, to paraphrase Augustine. The eucharistic meal itself is a kind of miracle—declaring who we are, whose we are, and what our position as beloved children of God empowers us to do in our world. The miracle lies in what the eucharistic community does when they are dismissed into the wider world: they cross social boundaries, disrupt unjust systems, and proclaim love without borders.

We need not conjure magic to believe in miracles; all we really need is whatever we have. If we use what we have with a spirit of generosity, God will take care of the miracles.

2 Samuel 11:1–15. "You either die a hero or you live long enough to see yourself become the villain." Fictional District Attorney Harvey Dent says this in Christopher Nolan's 2008 Batman sequel *The Dark Knight*. Dent's comment reflects his own rise as a tough-on-crime public official and then his fall as an uncompromising, revenge-seeking murderer. Taken outside of the context of the film, Dent's quote illustrates how dubious hero worship can be.

The lesson we learn over and over again is that none of our heroes—be they professional athletes, actors, musicians, politicians, or activists—are saints. Movements like #MeToo and #BlackLivesMatter have sought to shine a light on ways that power leads to abuses. As we have become more prepared to take seriously the allegations made against our cultural icons, our capacity for hero worship may become more realistic.

Saints are not even saints. If we dig deep enough, we can find problematic beliefs or behaviors in any of our beloved saints. Mother Teresa, a Roman Catholic nun and founder of the Missionaries of Charity, was surrounded by controversy both during her life and when she was beatified and canonized a saint. This controversy stemmed from her strong opposition to abortion and contraception, and the conditions and procedures at her clinics for dying patients. Yet the average person would primarily know Mother Teresa as the one who said, "Not all of us can do great things, but we can do small things with great love."

Seeing heroes fall, learning that those we admire are not the perfect people we hoped they were and, perhaps, that we could become, is a difficult thing to face. When this happens too often, we might start to become purists, writing off anyone who does not meet our high standards.

King David is a hero of the Judeo-Christian faith. He was a humble shepherd and the youngest brother in his family. His kingship was unlikely, but he battled Goliath and won. He was a successful military leader and a king who established the united kingdom of Israel and Judah, which had been founded by his predecessor, Saul. His legacy becomes incredibly troublesome when he arranges to have Uriah killed in battle so that he may have Uriah's wife Bathsheba as *his* wife. What are we to glean from this story, other than a bad taste in our mouths?

David, like those who abuse their power in our time, is vulnerable to the temptations. By distancing ourselves from them, we miss their examples' relevance for our lives. What if the preacher did a little work to acknowledge the power in the room? For some congregations, this may be an exercise in identifying types of privilege not previously considered. We like to believe that everyone has the ability to pick themselves up by their bootstraps, though we fail to acknowledge that the bootstrap factory is typically only in one part of town.

For some congregations, acknowledging power might be less about looking at one's situation and focusing more on our personal gifts and skills. Power is bad only if it is used selfishly, carelessly, or maliciously. Helping people to see what kind of power they wield will help them think about how they can use that power to support their values.

The congregation itself likely possesses some power, so a congregation that has a well-articulated identity may find such an exercise helpful for engaging in ministry. Perhaps the congregation holds spiritual capital in a community, or maybe their influence is cultural. There may be opportunities for the congregation to become more involved in advocacy work. Even when it seems that fewer and fewer people pay mind to the work of the church, when a congregation from the suburbs (for instance) marches with a congregation from the inner city, people take notice. When a congregation publicly stands for something, it gets noticed.

Another DC Comics character, Lex Luthor, said in *Batman v. Superman: Dawn of Justice* that "the oldest lie is that power can be innocent." David's model shows how power corrupts, and we see in our times the many ways that we are tempted to use whatever amount of power we have to get what we believe we deserve.

How should a follower of Jesus use power?

Our liturgies give us some ideas. When we engage in confession, we admit the times we have used our power for ill as well as those times we used our power of privilege to leave things undone. When we share the peace, if we do so with hopes of reconciling with our neighbors, we have an opportunity to use our power to let go of grudges. When we conclude the Lord's Prayer with "thine is the kingdom, and the power, and the glory . . . ," we admit that the kingdom, the power, and the glory are not *ours*, which is perhaps one of the most countercultural elements of the prayer.

Followers of Jesus are called to be intentional about how they use whatever power they have and to do so always for the sake of glorifying the God who divested power in becoming human, living among us, and dying so that we might live.

CURTIS FARR

Psalm 145:10–18

¹⁰All your works shall give thanks to you, O LORD,
   and all your faithful shall bless you.
¹¹They shall speak of the glory of your kingdom,
   and tell of your power,
¹²to make known to all people your mighty deeds,
   and the glorious splendor of your kingdom.
¹³Your kingdom is an everlasting kingdom,
   and your dominion endures throughout all generations.

The LORD is faithful in all his words,
   and gracious in all his deeds.
¹⁴The LORD upholds all who are falling,
   and raises up all who are bowed down.
¹⁵The eyes of all look to you,
   and you give them their food in due season.
¹⁶You open your hand,
   satisfying the desire of every living thing.
¹⁷The LORD is just in all his ways,
   and kind in all his doings.
¹⁸The LORD is near to all who call on him,
   to all who call on him in truth.

Psalm 14

¹Fools say in their hearts, "There is no God."
   They are corrupt, they do abominable deeds;
   there is no one who does good.

²The LORD looks down from heaven on humankind
   to see if there are any who are wise,
   who seek after God.

³They have all gone astray, they are all alike perverse;
   there is no one who does good,
   no, not one.

⁴Have they no knowledge, all the evildoers
   who eat up my people as they eat bread,
   and do not call upon the LORD?

⁵There they shall be in great terror,
   for God is with the company of the righteous.
⁶You would confound the plans of the poor,
   but the LORD is their refuge.

⁷O that deliverance for Israel would come from Zion!
   When the LORD restores the fortunes of his people,
   Jacob will rejoice; Israel will be glad.

Connecting the Psalm with Scripture and Worship

Psalm 145:10–18. These few verses taken from the middle of Psalm 145 function as a joyous affirmation of God's goodness and generosity. This is demonstrated in a practical way in the reading from 2 Kings 4:42–44. Here, in the fourth of a quick series of miracle stories, Elisha feeds a hundred people with twenty loaves of barley and a few ears of grain. While this is a numerically smaller miracle than Jesus feeding five thousand people with five loaves and two fish, it is similar in that there are hungry people, someone comes with a clearly insufficient amount of food, and not only does everyone get enough to be satisfied, but there is some left over. As the prophet makes clear in verse 43, the abundance is not due his own special powers, but rather is the fulfillment of God's promise that "they shall eat and have some left." By accepting the gift of the man from Baal-shalishah and instructing his servant to give it to the hungry people before him, Elisha does what God tells him to do, and the rest is up to God.

The psalm, while not explicitly connected to Elisha, is a response to God's extravagance. Most English translations do not make clear that Psalm 145 is written as an alphabetic acrostic, in which each verse begins with the successive letter of the Hebrew alphabet. Such acrostics were prized as evidence of the poet's art, since biblical Hebrew is a language with relatively few words and its grammatical rules add identical endings to so many words that rhyme is not a particular value. Seven other psalms use this acrostic structure, as well as a few other passages in the Hebrew Bible. As biblical scholar Roelie van der Spuy points out, using alphabetic ordering to provide structure for a poem

> communicates the sense of a complete unit and wholeness, and consequently helps the process of memorization. It is a skillful and attractive way of showing that God covers everything from A to Z, *Aleph* to *Taw*. It shows both the poet's love for the Hebrew language and his poetic skills.[1]

The sense of completeness is underscored by the assertion in verse 10 that not just a few individuals or leaders but rather all of God's works give their thanks and praise, and all of God's faithful bless the Holy One. God is described in superlative words of power, glory, splendor, and eternal dominion, and God's faithfulness and graciousness in all things are remembered. Read in the context of the fulfillment of God's promise that there would be enough food for everyone, despite the apparent meagerness of the supplies, the 2 Kings passage underscores Elisha's reminder in verse 44 that the miracle was "according to the word of the LORD."

In a time when food insecurity is a daily reality in many parts of the world as well as in virtually every city, and relief organizations report that millions of people are on the brink of starvation from famine, flood, fire, and other disasters, these promises sometimes sound hollow to modern, affluent ears as well as to those who are suffering. The problems are so big and so intractable that it is easy to simply throw up one's hands and say that nothing will help.

However, it is important to remember that the psalms were written in a time and place when subsistence farming was the norm and crops often failed, leaving nothing to eat from one season to the next. Then, as today, God's promises of peace and plenty might have seemed unbelievable. Nevertheless, the psalmist insists that "The eyes of all look to you, and you give them their food in due season. You open your hand, satisfying the desire of every living thing" (Ps. 145:15–16). Just as Elisha remembers these promises and acts on them, God is near to the faithful who remember to give thanks and do their small part.

Psalm 14. The first verse of Psalm 14 has historically been used as a proof text to threaten atheists, equating lack of belief in God with abominable acts and corruption. However, a closer inspection reveals that it is a warning to those who act as though God does not care about how they use power, no matter what they

---

1. Roelie van der Spuy, "Hebrew Alphabetic Acrostics: Significance and Translation," *Old Testament Essays* 21, no. 2 (2008): 513–32.

may say about the state of their faith. While it can be read as guidance about personal morality, it is more focused on those who abuse the public trust.

It is not possible to know exactly when the psalm was written or precisely what circumstances precipitated its writing. Although it is attributed to David, it is unlikely that he wrote it. Rather, considering the yearning in the final verse for deliverance for the people of Israel and God's restoration of the people's good fortune, it seems likely that it was written during the time of exile, about four hundred years after David's reign. The perverse fool who has gone astray, then, is not David, but rather those who have taken the people captive and destroyed Jerusalem.

When read, however, alongside the harrowing story of a king who sends messengers to a woman he lusts after, demanding that she come to his palace so that he can have his way with her, it is a severe indictment of his willingness to misuse the public trust for his private pleasure. Considering his callous disregard of what Bathsheba must have been feeling, his clumsy attempts to get Uriah to break his vows of abstinence, and his casually cruel decision to put Uriah into a place where he was certain to be killed in battle, it is clear that David is the epitome of the fool who says, "There is no God." Whatever his former glory on the battlefield or as a leader, in his old age David has become corrupt, feeling entitled to have whatever or whoever he wants, just like those described in the psalm as doing no good.

In a contemporary context of extreme polarization, it is tempting to use this psalm as ammunition against whoever is currently in office, whether at the national or local level. Regardless of political persuasion, the arrogant fools of the psalm are any public figures who take advantage of privilege and position without regard to God's insistence that they use their power to help those who have none. Instead of judging the people with righteousness and justice, as described in Psalm 72, for instance, the evildoers of Psalm 14:4 "eat up the people as they eat bread." Instead of coming to the aid of widows, orphans, and others who have no means of support other than God, these selfish and self-seeking rulers confound the plans of poor people and make their lives more difficult. Instead of calling upon God for guidance and help, these God-denying fools go their own way, without any fear of consequences.

The psalmist is not explicit about what those consequences might be, either, merely saying in verse 5 that "they shall be in great terror, for God is with the company of the righteous." Perhaps it is enough to know that God is in charge and is the refuge of those who call on the divine name. Perhaps it is enough to trust that deliverance will come, and there will come a time to rejoice and be glad.

DEBORAH SOKOLOVE

Ephesians 3:14–21

¹⁴For this reason I bow my knees before the Father, ¹⁵from whom every family in heaven and on earth takes its name. ¹⁶I pray that, according to the riches of his glory, he may grant that you may be strengthened in your inner being with power through his Spirit, ¹⁷and that Christ may dwell in your hearts through faith, as you are being rooted and grounded in love. ¹⁸I pray that you may have the power to comprehend, with all the saints, what is the breadth and length and height and depth, ¹⁹and to know the love of Christ that surpasses knowledge, so that you may be filled with all the fullness of God.

²⁰Now to him who by the power at work within us is able to accomplish abundantly far more than all we can ask or imagine, ²¹to him be glory in the church and in Christ Jesus to all generations, forever and ever. Amen.

Commentary 1: Connecting the Reading with Scripture

Nestled at about the midpoint of Ephesians, this passage expands the focus on prayer not just by teaching on it, but with actual prayer. The devotional style of the author is evident throughout the letter, but especially in Ephesians 1:17–19, where prayer and instruction are mingled to develop the theme of God's power in us and for us. Similarly, this second intercessory prayer (Eph. 3:16–19) reveals the writer's desire for the readers to obtain not just head knowledge of the faith, but holistic spiritual edification and strength to live the Christian life.

The pastoral tone of the prayer is beautifully represented in the image of bowing to pray (3:14), which introduces the content. Instead of the usual Jewish custom of praying standing (Mark 11:25; Luke 18:11, 13), this verse models the importance of bending one's body in submission in prayer to God, the Father. Liturgically, the position and performance in the act of prayer is just as important as its content and purpose. As the psalmist states: "The Lord upholds all who are falling, and raises up all who are bowed down" (Ps. 145:14), signifying an attitude of humility (Jas. 4:6, 10; 1 Pet. 5:5–6).

Before words are spoken to God in supplication, one must come before God with the correct attitude, acknowledging God's supreme dominion as the universal "Father of all the families" (Eph. 3:15). As Psalm 14:2 states: "The Lord looks down from heaven on humankind to see if there are any who are wise, who seek after God." The cosmic fatherhood of God envisioned here surpasses all religious, political, ethnic, and even spatial boundaries. For whether in the spiritual or earthly realm, all families receive their names from God. For both the Christian communities who first read this epistle and us who read it today, these words have a leveling effect on familial prestige, whether political, economic, or spiritual.

Having established the correct attitude of the heart when praying, the author then moves to center on the substance of prayer. Three *hina* ("that," vv. 16, 18, 19b) clauses indicate the three integrated petitions of the author, which are offered with increasing intensity. First, the overwhelming desire expressed is for believers to be "strengthened in [their] inner being with power through his Spirit" (v. 16). Gleaning from what previously has been said about the nascent faith of the believers (1:13, 18; 2:1–2, 13), the author is preoccupied with the readers' spiritual stability; their survival and advancement in the life of faith depends on the inner strength they may receive from God's Spirit. Pointing to the abundant reservoirs of spiritual strength in the heavenly arena (i.e., "according to the riches of his glory," v. 16), the author prays for the spiritual well-being of the Ephesians.

The second integrated prayer concern intensifies the original plea by emphasizing how Christ's love grounds and roots Christian faith and practice. Throughout the epistle, the phrases "in Christ" and "in him" aim to reorient the believer's spatial consciousness by constantly reminding them of their spiritual situatedness with Christ in the heavenly places (2:6). In this prayer, that mental shift takes on a new dimension by focusing correspondingly on the dwelling of Christ in their hearts (v. 17). In other words, it is not just a matter of believers being "in Christ," but Christ abiding in them through faith; it is not just a matter of cognitive assent, but a genuine spiritual inhabitation of Christ! This simultaneous submersion in Christ and indwelling of Christ in the life of the believer consequently result in rootedness and grounding in love.

Thirdly, the intensification of the prayer request turns to the source of strength for the inner life of the believer: "the love of Christ" (v. 19). Like a bottomless reservoir that extends endlessly in every direction, so the dimensions of the love of Christ serve to illustrate its unsurpassable magnificence. As if one were thrown into the vast sea of God's endless love, the author desires the readers to comprehend the fullness of God's love by learning to swim in it. This experiential knowing of God, however, is not superficial knowledge of the Divine or entrance into the gnostic secret, but rather, as stated in the text, "to know the love of Christ that surpasses knowledge" (v. 19). Further, it is communal ("with all the saints," v. 18); the plural form of the verb emphasizes it is "so that you [all] may be filled with all the fullness of God" (v. 19). In other words, it is in the community of those who have experienced Christ's love (the church) where believers can truly experience God's unending love.

The last phrase of the prayer, referring to "the fullness of God" (v. 19), requires further explanation. Earlier in the epistle, the writer uses a similar phrase, namely, "the fullness of him" (1:23), to speak of how the church as the body of Christ represents his fullness. It is not

that the church is identical to Christ's earthly presence, but rather that the church represents Christ's presence to the world as the community of those who bear Christ. Similarly, in 3:19, the phrase "the fullness of God" refers to the corporate filling of the church. This does not mean that the church exhausts the totality of who God is, but that the church is immersed in the totality of God.

To illustrate this, the idea is not pouring the ocean's water into a cup, but immersing the cup into the vast water of the ocean. The corporate image of the church as "a dwelling place for God" (2:21–22) serves as an appropriate visual for understanding the main concept here. The church, as the temple of God, corporately becomes the spiritual edifice where God's presence is made manifest, where the fullness of his love is poured out. This does not mean that somehow it exhausts the reservoirs of God's manifest presence, as if this spiritual building could somehow house the totality of God. Nevertheless, it is in the gathered community of the church where "all the fullness of God" is experienced.

Upon penning this joyous ecclesiological truth, the author erupts in praise in light of the implications of the train of thought being developed throughout the epistle. Although believers are God's working project, the author eschatologically envisions the end product when the church will "be filled with all the fullness of God." Thus, though the readers might not realize it in the lived reality of their ordinary lives, the certainty of this future reality can be imagined because of the power of God already at work in the church (v. 20) through the resurrection of Christ.

In spite of the unfinished product believers might be sensing as they look inwardly, God is at work, and prayers on their behalf will inevitably result in a holy church without spot or blemish (5:27). There is a lot of work for God still, but God will be "able to accomplish abundantly far more than all we can ask or imagine" (3:20). This is why, though in progress, the church must rejoice and give God all the glory for the work that has been done, is being done, and is yet to be done in the lives of the saints. What is more, the church's worship of God for what he has done, is doing, and will do in Christ must resound like an echo that carries forth through every generation and unto eternity (v. 21), for which the only response must be, Amen!

SAMMY G. ALFARO

Commentary 2: Connecting the Reading with the World

What a powerful image: Paul, the imprisoned disciple of Christ, praying for his beloved family in Ephesus. He is not worried about himself. Rather, he is worried about them and, in this beautiful prayer, he offers them words of strength and encouragement.

Paul teaches the Ephesians they are one in Christ and that God loves and sustains them. It would seem, though, despite this good news, that they are losing heart. They are distressed because their brother in Christ is now a prisoner. They are afraid for and concerned about his future, and they are no doubt fearful that the same fate may befall them.

From the prison cell we hear Paul's heartfelt prayer for them. They overhear him praying that they may find strength through the Spirit. He asks that they may know the love of Christ that fills their lives and the world. He prays that they "may be filled with all the fullness of God." We should recognize that the prayer is important because it fills our hearts. Like the Ephesians, we can easily become discouraged and lose heart. Paul recognizes the importance of the church's witness as one that strengthens and encourages.

How are we, as the church, to strengthen and encourage? Following recent revelations about the abuse scandal in the Roman Catholic Church, I was speaking with a priest friend. We shared the pain he was experiencing. Then he also told me what keeps him going. A young person had recently come to speak with him about joining the church. "You want to become a Catholic? Haven't you been watching the news?" "Oh yes," the person told him, "I have, but I have also been coming to your parish. There I have experienced the love and joy of God. I want what you all have." He knew that the Spirit was empowering the congregation.

Can you invite people in the church to tell each other of those moments when they have felt the Spirit strengthen their inner being? You may invite people to point to those people and experiences in the congregation that root and ground them in the love of Christ.

It is not just news from the church that threatens to shake our faith. We live out our lives as followers of Christ in a world that challenges that faith at any turn. Paul answered God's call, for example, and found himself in prison! For Bible study classes, I often invite people to bring in news headlines and stories that are painful and discouraging, headlines that might make them question the presence of God in our world.

It was the winter of 2012, on the Friday before the Third Sunday of Advent. I already had written my sermon for Sunday morning. It was going to be a sweet sermon preparing us for Christmas, which was only nine days away. It was a sermon I never preached. That morning a young man entered an elementary school and killed twenty young children and their teachers.

I was shaken to my core, as were all of the people who gathered on Sunday. I did away with my prepared sermon. What could I say? I stepped into the pulpit and asked God to give me the words. I—we—all needed to be reminded about the "breadth and length and height and depth . . . of the love of God" (Eph. 3:19). We needed to be encouraged and strengthened through the prayer and the preaching. That morning I know that God's power at work in me was able to "accomplish abundantly far more" than I could ever have imagined. God did give me the words to speak.

Paul was one of the first prisoners for Christ. Unfortunately, he was not the last. Throughout the millennia we have told the stories of those willing to give up their lives to continue to proclaim the good news of God's unfailing love. We do not have to go back to the early church to find martyrs upon whose faith the church was built.

We continue to hear from prisoners for Christ. Paul wanted to write to the people of Ephesus to strengthen and encourage them. So, later, did another prisoner write a letter to fortify his beloved community: Martin Luther King Jr.

Early in 1963, Dr. King and the Southern Christian Leadership Conference were working to call attention to the practices of segregation and injustice in Birmingham, Alabama. When the people of God confront the powers of the empire, they can soon find themselves in prison.

While Dr. King was in jail, a group of white religious leaders published a letter in *The Birmingham News*. Their "Call for Unity" argued not for the cause of love and unity among the people of God. Rather, they sought to maintain the status quo. They thought Dr. King and his group were outsiders stirring up trouble. They should "go home."

After reading their epistle, Dr. King decided to pen his own epistle responding to their arguments. Writing, first on the April 12 issue of the newspaper containing their "Call," and then on any scrap of paper that could be smuggled to him, Dr. King wrote what has come to be called "Letter from Birmingham Jail."[1]

In his very lengthy letter, he responded to their concerns and their challenges. Were the protests unwise? Why were they not raising concerns about how the police were treating the Negro children, women, and men of Birmingham? What was his "reason" for being in Birmingham? He was there because the oppressors would not voluntarily stop the oppression. He was there to stand with his sisters and brothers who were fighting demeaning treatment and unjust laws.

Upon first reading, Dr. King seems to have addressed the letter to the white clergy of Birmingham. It was actually written to a much wider audience. It was written to the men, women, and even children who were willing to go out to the front line of the civil rights movement. It was written to remind them why they were doing what they were doing. It was written to praise their actions and courage.

What would be your prayer for your congregation, today? Where are their inner beings failing? How do they need to be strengthened and encouraged? What is causing them uncertainty and distress? Paul prays that the people will be "filled with all the fullness of God." What does it mean to be filled with the fullness of God? What does that look like? How do we experience that?

Paul did not want the people of Ephesus to "lose heart." Likewise, Dr. King did not want the people of the movement to lose heart because of all of the time he spent in jail—twenty-nine times, in fact. Dr. King knew what often becomes the fate of prisoners. Throughout his ministry and his campaigns, he spoke words of encouragement. Only four months after sitting in a jail in Birmingham, Dr. King mounted the steps of the Lincoln Memorial to declare his dream for all Americans. Then, in 1968, as he met with the striking sanitation workers on April 3, he spoke of another dream. God had taken him to the mountaintop. He had seen the promised land. So, like Paul, he ended his life with the call, "I pray therefore that you may not lose heart over my sufferings for you; they are your glory" (Eph. 3:13).

LUCY LIND HOGAN

---

1. This letter is posted by the Martin Luther King Jr. Research and Education Institute at http://okra.stanford.edu/transcription/document_images/undecided/630416-019.pdf.

John 6:1–21

¹After this Jesus went to the other side of the Sea of Galilee, also called the Sea of Tiberias. ²A large crowd kept following him, because they saw the signs that he was doing for the sick. ³Jesus went up the mountain and sat down there with his disciples. ⁴Now the Passover, the festival of the Jews, was near. ⁵When he looked up and saw a large crowd coming toward him, Jesus said to Philip, "Where are we to buy bread for these people to eat?" ⁶He said this to test him, for he himself knew what he was going to do. ⁷Philip answered him, "Six months' wages would not buy enough bread for each of them to get a little." ⁸One of his disciples, Andrew, Simon Peter's brother, said to him, ⁹"There is a boy here who has five barley loaves and two fish. But what are they among so many people?" ¹⁰Jesus said, "Make the people sit down." Now there was a great deal of grass in the place; so they sat down, about five thousand in all. ¹¹Then Jesus took the loaves, and when he had given thanks, he distributed them to those who were seated; so also the fish, as much as they wanted. ¹²When they were satisfied, he told his disciples, "Gather up the fragments left over, so that nothing may be lost." ¹³So they gathered them up, and from the fragments of the five barley loaves, left by those who had eaten, they filled twelve baskets. ¹⁴When the people saw the sign that he had done, they began to say, "This is indeed the prophet who is to come into the world."

¹⁵When Jesus realized that they were about to come and take him by force to make him king, he withdrew again to the mountain by himself.

¹⁶When evening came, his disciples went down to the sea, ¹⁷got into a boat, and started across the sea to Capernaum. It was now dark, and Jesus had not yet come to them. ¹⁸The sea became rough because a strong wind was blowing. ¹⁹When they had rowed about three or four miles, they saw Jesus walking on the sea and coming near the boat, and they were terrified. ²⁰But he said to them, "It is I; do not be afraid." ²¹Then they wanted to take him into the boat, and immediately the boat reached the land toward which they were going.

Commentary 1: Connecting the Reading with Scripture

The feeding of the five thousand (John 6:1–15) and Jesus' walking on water (vv. 16–21) are simultaneously supranatural miracles that demonstrate Jesus' divine authority over the order of creation and also theophanies that reveal Jesus' identity as the redeemer of the world. Through these miracles, the two most important biblical images of God as Creator and Redeemer are attributed to the work and person of Jesus.

The setting of the first miracle likely takes place along the northeastern hillside (v. 3) of the Sea of Galilee, more widely known in the Roman world as the Sea of Tiberias (v. 1; cf. Josephus, *Ant.* 18.36), and more provincially known in Israel as Lake Gennesaret (Luke 5:1). The feeding of the five thousand is one of the miracles found in all four Gospels (Matt. 14:13–21; Mark 6:35–44; Luke 9:10–17). John's version of the miracle is set in the narrative section that covers the entire Jewish liturgical calendar and sees Jesus as the fulfillment of every major religious feast, including the Sabbath (5:1–47), the Passover (6:1–15, 25–71), the Tabernacles Festival (7:1–52), and Hanukkah (10:22–39). The episode of the multiplication of loaves (6:1–15)

A Revolution of the Heart

The greatest challenge of the day is: how to bring about a revolution of the heart, a revolution which has to start with each one of us? When we begin to take the lowest place, to wash the feet of others, to love our neighbors with that burning love, that passion, which led to the Cross, then we can truly say, "Now I have begun."

Day after day we accept our failure, but we accept it because of our knowledge of the victory of the Cross. God has given us our vocation, as he gave it to the small boy who contributed his few loaves and fishes to help the multitude, and which Jesus multiplied so that he fed five thousand people.

Loaves and fishes! How much we owe to God in praise, honor, thanksgiving! . . .

How many times, all through my life, have I surveyed these tables full of people and wondered if the bread would go around; how many times have I noticed how one heaps his plate and the last one served has little, how one wastes his food and so deprives his brother. German George grumbles as he brings out more sticks of margarine, and refills bread plates, coffeepots, sugar bowls.

Where does it all go? Where do all the people come from? How will it all be paid for? But the miracle is that it does get paid for, sooner or later. The miracle is, also, that seldom do more people come than we can feed.

Dorothy Day, *Loaves and Fishes* (New York: Harper & Row, 1963), 210–12.

and Jesus' latter interpretation of it (vv. 25–71) all happen near the time of the Passover feast.

The Passover is a celebration of God's liberation of Israel from slavery in Egypt. In fact, the central Old Testament image that guides the interpretation of the feeding miracle is the exodus event, and especially the Lord's provision of manna to the Israelites during their forty years of wilderness wandering (Exod. 16:1–36; Ps. 78:23–25; Num. 11:4–9; Deut. 8:16; Josh. 5:12; Neh. 9:20; cf. John 6:31–35). Moses himself provides an explanation of what the daily manna symbolized for Israel: "He humbled you by letting you hunger, then by feeding you with manna . . . in order to make you understand that one does not live by bread alone, but by every word that comes from the mouth of the LORD" (Deut. 8:3). The feeding of manna is a symbol of humankind's dependence on the word of God for life. More than physical bread, life comes from being sustained by God's word.

The people who experience the feeding miracle think that Jesus is a prophetic successor of Moses (John 6:14; cf. Deut. 18:15; 1QS 9:10–11). Yet, from John's perspective, Jesus is more than who the people make him out to be. Jesus goes beyond the messianic paradigm of a new Moses who teaches God's word and gives bread to the hungry (see Mark 6:34, 41–42). Rather, Jesus does what only God can do (John 6:32). The Lord God is the source for the manna feeding, and Jesus is the source for the multiplication of loaves. Jesus authors the miracle. He is the Lord who gives spiritual food and sustains the people of God. He not only provides "bread from heaven" (vv. 31–33); he *is* the very "bread of life" (vv. 35, 48, 51), the Word of God made flesh (1:1, 14), through whom all believers find live-giving sustenance and strength (1:4; 6:51). The epistolary lection of Ephesians 3:14–21 explains that the very Spirit of Jesus is our source for knowledge, power, strength, and inner renewal.

The multiplication of loaves also provides an occasion for Jesus to test the faith of the disciples (Mark 6:37; par. Luke 9:13; Matt. 14:16) and especially Philip's (John 6:5–7). Philip does the math and calculates the impossibility of feeding five thousand "men" (*andres*, v. 10) or possibly ten thousand total people if women and children are counted. Two hundred denarii, which is about eight months of wages for the unskilled laborer, is a low estimate of how much money it would take to buy enough bread. The situation becomes even more ridiculous when Andrew, Peter's brother, suggests using a child's lunch of five pita-sized pieces of bread and two salty dried fish to feed the crowds (vv. 8–9).

Yet, when Jesus takes the loaves, gives thanks (*eucharistēsas*), and distributes them in a way that foreshadows the early church tradition on the Lord's Supper (Luke 22:17–19;

1 Cor. 11:24), the bread multiples and there is an overabundance, so all have enough to eat (John 6:11). Twelve baskets of leftover pieces (symbolic of the twelve tribes of Israel or the people of God) are saved (vv. 12–13). The left-over baskets anticipate the eschatological gathering of all God's children (11:52; 17:21–22), where none will be lost or "perish" (v. 12, *apolētai*; cf. 3:16; 10:28–29; 17:12). This miracle of supply outdoes past Old Testament equivalents like Elisha's feeding of only a hundred people with twenty barley loaves (2 Kgs. 4:42–44).

The spiritual and material care of God's flock is ultimately something miraculous that only God can do. Will the disciples of Christ be paralyzed by the impossibility of the task, or will they present what they have, however meager, and have faith that Jesus can make a miracle out of it? As we face the limitations of human agency and effort, and yet we present to God what we can, our act of faith provides a historical stage for the Lord to do the impossible. In ministry, Jesus can take what we offer him and the sum of our service, as deficient as these might be, and use them to feed the multitudes.

The next miracle features Jesus walking on water (John 6:16–21) and is set amid the unpredictable storm conditions of the sea. Because the lake lies in an inland basin some 650 feet below sea level and is surrounded by mountains up to an elevation of 4,000 feet, cool winds from the hills can sweep down into the heated desert air of the basin to create violent storms on the lake, with waves as high as six or seven feet.[1] When Jesus retreats to the mountain alone to avoid the people's attempt to make him king (v. 15),

the disciples set off in the boat toward Capernaum, perhaps in an effort to rendezvous with him (vv. 16–17). About three or four miles (lit. twenty-five to thirty *stadia*, v. 19) from shore, they are caught in a strong wind and the sea becomes frenzied (v. 18). John, however, makes it clear that the disciples are more terrified by the sight of Jesus walking toward them than by the storm itself (v. 19).

This miracle recapitulates the exodus event, where Moses leads the Israelites through the waters of the Red Sea (Exod. 14:21–15:19). The motifs of strong winds (14:21) and traveling across the sea (14:22), the fear of those who see the theophany (14:31), the admonition "Do not be afraid" (20:20), and the identification of God as "I am" (3:14) all have parallels in John's narrative.

The name of YHWH as "I am" is translated from the Hebrew by the Septuagint into Greek as *egō eimi*. Jesus uses the same designation *egō eimi* to identify himself in verse 20 to the frightened disciples, although the NRSV translates the phrase as "It is I." Jesus is the "I am" and author of a new exodus. While Moses led Israel out of slavery from Egypt, Jesus will liberate humanity from slavery to sin (John 8:34) and lead all who believe in him, Jew and Gentile alike, to a grander salvation. The identification of Jesus as "I am" also anticipates a series of seven "I am" statements in John's Gospel (6:35; 8:12; 10:7; 10:11; 11:25; 14:6; 15:1), which further reveal the divine person and character of God's Son.

MAX J. LEE

Commentary 2: Connecting the Reading with the World

Hunger and fear: two elemental human realities. In this powerful and provocative text, Jesus addresses each, feeding five thousand people and assuring his terrified disciples in the midst of a storm.

The context of the story of the feeding of the five thousand is the large crowd that is now

showing up everywhere Jesus and his disciples go. Now they are bringing their ill and infirm to him because "they saw the signs that he was doing for the sick" (John 6:2).

A sign in the Bible is an act that points to the redeeming activity of God. At the birth of Jesus an angel of the Lord tells startled shepherds:

1. John Rousseau and Rami Arav, *Jesus and His World: An Archaeological and Cultural Dictionary* (Minneapolis: Fortress, 1995), 246; Gary Burge, *John*, NIV Application Commentary (Grand Rapids: Zondervan, 2000), 192.

"This will be a sign for you: you will find a child wrapped in bands of cloth and lying in a manger" (Luke 2:12). In the Fourth Gospel, signs are often miraculous events that point to Jesus, not merely as a miracle worker, but as the Christ. Following the resurrection John summarizes: "Now Jesus did many signs in the presence of his disciples, which are not written in this book. But these are written so that you may come to believe that Jesus is the Messiah, the Son of God" (John 20:30–31).

For the writer of the Fourth Gospel, the point of this story and others is not the action itself, in this case healing the sick. Rather, the action is a "sign" pointing to Jesus. Crowds persist wherever he goes, seeking, hoping for healing but, John insists, also looking for a sign.

Literalism is not only inadequate here but distracting, as it is throughout Scripture. In designating these two incidents "signs"—Jesus feeding five thousand and then, equally astonishing, walking on water—the author of the Fourth Gospel invites readers to ponder and discern meaning rather than facticity. John wants us to dig deeper, beyond the events themselves, beyond "Did this really happen?" or "How did it happen?" to their enduring and saving truth. The story of the feeding of the five thousand is told, with slight variation, in all four Gospels. It is clearly central to who Jesus is and what he means. John tells it gorgeously with attention to aesthetics. Why does he include "there was a great deal of grass in the place" unless he wanted to introduce the idea of "abundance," lushness, the good fertility and sensuality of God's creation?

It is late in the day and people in the crowd following him are hungry. Jesus inquires where they might buy food for everyone. Philip, the literalist, patiently explains the obvious, that it would require a lot of money, much more than was available, to buy food for so many people. Almost as an aside, or to punctuate how dire the situation had become—all those people and pitiful resources—Andrew announces that the only available food is a little boy's five loaves and two fish.

Jesus' startling response? "Make the people sit down." Employing sacramental language, the writer describes Jesus giving thanks and distributing food to the hungry crowd. There is no attempt to describe what happened, just that the people were satisfied. The abundance is complete.

The dichotomy between abundance and scarcity is deep in our biblical tradition. Early in their journey through the wilderness the people of Israel complain about their hunger. When they discover the white, flaky substance on the ground in the morning and ask what it is, Moses explains that it is manna, God's gift right in front of their eyes. It is the abundance of God that requires only human imagination to pick it up and eat it. Manna cannot be hoarded. The people have to learn to trust that God's abundance will be there, new every morning.

The abundance is so complete that there are twelve baskets full after the crowd has eaten. They ate "as much as they wanted," John adds (v. 11). Eating as much as they wanted must have been a rare experience for the people in that crowd: poor, marginal, peasant people.

It is a critical issue for modern Western Christians. Walter Brueggemann introduced us to the notion of the myth of scarcity in the midst of abundance.[2] He observed that "The majority of the world's resources pour into the United States. And as we Americans grow more and more wealthy, money is becoming a kind of narcotic for us. We hardly notice our prosperity or the poverty of so many others." Brueggemann says that we believe more in the myth of scarcity than in the reality of abundance: there is not enough for everybody, so we have to get more.

This is a moral and political issue. The United States is the wealthiest nation in the history of the world. For decades the rich have become richer and the poor poorer, and everybody knows it. Recently, the very wealthy have received a significant financial bonus by way of a major tax cut, while middle-class income remains stagnant and the poor still struggle.

Jesus transformed his followers' focus on scarcity with an experience of God's abundance and the sufficiency of what they had when they offered it and shared it with the hungry.

There is a clear mandate here for his modern-day followers and his church. The church is called

---

2. Walter Brueggemann, "The Liturgy of Abundance: The Myth of Scarcity," *Christian Century* 116, no. 10 (March 24–31, 1999): 342–47.

both to feed the hungry through local food pantries and hunger initiatives, and at the same time to advocate and work, socially and politically, for a society in which no one goes to bed hungry.

Fear, as well as hunger, is basic to our humanness: fear of failing, fear of separation, fear of an uncertain future, fear of the other, and that final fear: fear of death. Fear is a potent force socially and politically and, when manipulated and exploited, can cause people and entire societies to stop thinking rationally and sacrifice freedom. History is replete with examples. Adolf Hitler brilliantly used fear of the other to fan the flames of anti-Semitism with catastrophically tragic consequences. Currently, fear of the other is prompting Americans to abandon basic values of welcome, hospitality, and human dignity and to cower behind a border wall.

In contrast, at the very heart of our faith is the admonition "Fear not." In the wilderness Moses tells the people of Israel, "It is the LORD who goes before you. He will be with you; he will not fail you or forsake you. Do not fear or be dismayed" (Deut. 31:8). During the exile the prophet assures a captive people, "Do not fear, for I have redeemed you; I have called you by name, you are mine. When you pass through the waters, I will be with you" (Isa. 43:1b–2a). To young Mary, the angel precedes the astonishing and frightening news of her mysterious pregnancy with "Do not be afraid; for see—I am bringing you good news of great joy" (Luke 2:10), and to terrified women at the empty tomb declares, "Do not be afraid. . . . He is not here; for he has been raised" (Matt. 28:5, 6).

It is the basic message of the Bible: "Do not be afraid." The storm at sea that so terrified the disciples, filled with fear for their lives, is a metaphor for threatening storms that come at and terrify every one of us: sickness, financial insecurity, unemployment, unprecedented political upheaval, and, of course, that final threat, our own mortality. To us, as to them, come the saving words of our Lord, words that free us from all fear, "It is I. Do not be afraid."

JOHN M. BUCHANAN

Proper 13 (Sunday between July 31 and August 6)

Exodus 16:2–4, 9–15 and
  2 Samuel 11:26–12:13a
Psalm 78:23–29 and Psalm 51:1–12

Ephesians 4:1–16
John 6:24–35

Exodus 16:2–4, 9–15

[2]The whole congregation of the Israelites complained against Moses and Aaron in the wilderness. [3]The Israelites said to them, "If only we had died by the hand of the LORD in the land of Egypt, when we sat by the fleshpots and ate our fill of bread; for you have brought us out into this wilderness to kill this whole assembly with hunger." [4]Then the LORD said to Moses, "I am going to rain bread from heaven for you, and each day the people shall go out and gather enough for that day. In that way I will test them, whether they will follow my instruction or not." . . . [9]Then Moses said to Aaron, "Say to the whole congregation of the Israelites, 'Draw near to the LORD, for he has heard your complaining.'" [10]And as Aaron spoke to the whole congregation of the Israelites, they looked toward the wilderness, and the glory of the LORD appeared in the cloud. [11]The LORD spoke to Moses and said, [12]"I have heard the complaining of the Israelites; say to them, 'At twilight you shall eat meat, and in the morning you shall have your fill of bread; then you shall know that I am the LORD your God.'"

[13]In the evening quails came up and covered the camp; and in the morning there was a layer of dew around the camp. [14]When the layer of dew lifted, there on the surface of the wilderness was a fine flaky substance, as fine as frost on the ground. [15]When the Israelites saw it, they said to one another, "What is it?" For they did not know what it was. Moses said to them, "It is the bread that the LORD has given you to eat."

2 Samuel 11:26–12:13a

[11:26]When the wife of Uriah heard that her husband was dead, she made lamentation for him. [27]When the mourning was over, David sent and brought her to his house, and she became his wife, and bore him a son.

But the thing that David had done displeased the LORD, [12:1]and the LORD sent Nathan to David. He came to him, and said to him, "There were two men in a certain city, the one rich and the other poor. [2]The rich man had very many flocks and herds; [3]but the poor man had nothing but one little ewe lamb, which he had bought. He brought it up, and it grew up with him and with his children; it used to eat of his meager fare, and drink from his cup, and lie in his bosom, and it was like a daughter to him. [4]Now there came a traveler to the rich man, and he was loath to take one of his own flock or herd to prepare for the wayfarer who had come to him, but he took the poor man's lamb, and prepared that for the guest who had come to him." [5]Then David's anger was greatly kindled against the man.

He said to Nathan, "As the LORD lives, the man who has done this deserves to die; [6]he shall restore the lamb fourfold, because he did this thing, and because he had no pity."

[7]Nathan said to David, "You are the man! Thus says the LORD, the God of Israel: I anointed you king over Israel, and I rescued you from the hand of Saul; [8]I gave you your master's house, and your master's wives into your bosom, and gave you the house of Israel and of Judah; and if that had been too little, I would have added as much more. [9]Why have you despised the word of the LORD, to do what is evil in his sight? You have struck down Uriah the Hittite with the sword, and have taken his wife to be your wife, and have killed him with the sword of the Ammonites. [10]Now therefore the sword shall never depart from your house, for you have despised me, and have taken the wife of Uriah the Hittite to be your wife. [11]Thus says the LORD: I will raise up trouble against you from within your own house; and I will take your wives before your eyes, and give them to your neighbor, and he shall lie with your wives in the sight of this very sun. [12]For you did it secretly; but I will do this thing before all Israel, and before the sun." [13]David said to Nathan, "I have sinned against the LORD."

Commentary 1: Connecting the Reading with Scripture

Our readings today show the danger of a cynical attitude. When we are looking for what is wrong with the world, rather than what is right, things can easily go astray. In Exodus, Israel, rather than placing their hope in the God of the present and future, is lost in nostalgia for the past. The preacher would do well to note how common this pattern is. Rather than face contemporary challenges, people focus on the past and forget all of its challenges. They romanticize it. Israel seems to forget even slavery, bondage, and the mighty acts of God; rather, they focus on Pharaoh and the security that sin can offer. We hear of the famous fleshpots of Egypt in verse 3. A negative attitude can so distort the present that even the slavery of the past can appear to be comforting in comparison with the imagined challenges of the future.

In our lection from 2 Samuel, rather than negativity, we see creativity, in the form of Nathan's use of a parable. When situations are heated or toxic, it is often more effective to use a parable in order to speak truth to power. (As we will remember, for example, Jesus uses parables strategically to navigate the politics of his ministry.) In our lection, Nathan is faced with a conundrum: How does he challenge the king without cutting off all communication? Using a parable does the trick. The king can listen to the parable

without suspecting what Nathan is doing with it. Only after King David is fully emotionally engaged does Nathan challenge him.

Prophets are often thought to be forthright and direct. Oftentimes, this is the only model of prophets portrayed in the church. We can think of bold figures who suffer greatly for the truth. While that should never be discounted, here the Bible seems to be portraying a different model of prophet. The preacher may want to point out the many different ways for a prophet to promote justice. There are times when a prophet must suffer for the truth, even if it means severing relationships, but there are other times when it is important to maintain relationships so that one can remain to fight another day.

Parables are generally thought to be more a part of Wisdom literature than prophetic literature, yet we see the prophet Nathan ably telling a parable and rebuking David without jeopardizing their relationship. The cunningness of David cannot be taken for granted, so Nathan's roundabout approach lures David into a trap that ultimately leads to his repentance and restoration. Nathan seems to enact here the advice Jesus later gives his disciples that they "be wise as serpents and innocent as doves" (Matt. 10:16b).

The most powerful lesson of this passage may concern secrecy. We live in an age where it is harder and harder to maintain secrets. While the most powerful can buy secrets or afford networks to maintain them, people are most commonly completely exposed. Here, Nathan brings to light the powerful King David's secret. Nathan tells us that God does not keep secrets, but acts in the exact opposite fashion. In verse 12, God says, through Nathan, "I will do this thing before all Israel, and before the sun." These are chilling words; yet they suggest the importance of integrity. Do we act in private as we do in public? Do we avoid hypocrisy? No one is perfect here, but this offers a chance to see the higher standards expected of God's friends.

The key word in the Exodus lection is the Hebrew verb translated as "complain" (Heb. *anan*). Some variant of this verb comes up three times in the passage. It is a very strong word in Hebrew that actually connotes rebellion more than complaint. We get a sense of a battle between two gods. Rather than simply register-ing a complaint to God, there is a sense of trea-son here. The people want a different regime. They would sooner opt out of this relationship with the living God and return to idolatry. This theme of "complaining" connects this reading with the rest of the book of Exodus, as we find the verb used in the preceding and succeeding chapters (15:24; 17:3). These three chapters fol-low perhaps the mightiest of the mighty acts of God, the crossing of the Red Sea. The preacher may want to note how quickly we can fall into cynicism if we do not actively focus on blessings and thanksgiving.

The composition of the book of Exodus is quite complicated. Although it can be very intricate, it might be easiest to talk about Priestly and non-Priestly writers being present in this book. The lectionary focuses on this pos-itive and hopeful Priestly perspective in this lec-tion, rather than on the sin-centered perspective of the non-Priestly writer. The preacher could remind the congregation that there is a positive and hopeful view of the world where humans are made in the image and likeness of God. God cares for humanity and has provided all of cre-ation for the responsible use of humanity. God provides enough. The rest of the chapter will go on to expand that the greedy manage to get only

the same as those content with their lot, as any remaining manna or quail rot the next day.

The other key word in this lection is "glory" (*kavod*), a favorite word of the Priestly writer. While it occurs only once in this passage, it occurs again in Exodus 16 and repeatedly later in the book of Exodus. The word "glory" once again betrays the hopeful perspective of the Priestly writer. Although God's majesty as represented by "glory" is usually hidden away in the temple, the glory of God can appear to the people as it does here in Exodus 16:10. The preacher may use this as an opportunity to think about how the divine presence can be seen in our world today. God's glory is not isolated in the past; this lection confirms an abundant vision of divine action in the past continuing into today.

Strong connection can be made between Exodus and John's Gospel to confirm the ongo-ing nature of divine action in biblical times. John's Gospel naturally highlights the theme of abundance, as John 6 concerns the multiplica-tion of fish and loaves. John 6:25–35 directly references this theme of manna, as Exodus 16:31 mentions manna, and offers Jesus as the fulfillment of the promises of the Old Testa-ment. The preacher must avoid all supersession-ism here, but the language of Jesus is plain as he declares in verse 35, "I am the bread of life." Exodus 3:14 offered the first time where the name of God was made known to Israel, where it is translated as "I AM WHO I AM." John 6:35a continues in that tradition, carefully modifying it. The Gospel of John also offers a very high Christology where Jesus' actions are reminiscent of the mighty acts of God.

This desire for relationship also connects 2 Samuel 12 to the Gospel reading from John. In John 6:26 we find people using Jesus for their own ends, as David used Uriah for his own ends. Jesus rejects this and challenges the people to go deeper with him. Jesus asks for faith (John 6:29). He is sent from God to give life to the world (v. 33). He promises the he is "the bread of life" in 6:35 and that if we come to him, we will never hunger or thirst. Jesus ultimately calls his disciples "friends" (15:15).

GARRETT GALVIN

Commentary 2: Connecting the Reading with the World

Exodus 16:2–4, 9–15. The grass is always greener on the other side. Moses, God's instrument of liberation for this people, receives the nonsensical complaints from the Israelites about how good they had it in captivity: "At least we had food in captivity!" Now they are wandering over unknown terrain, worried about having enough to survive.

The modern church faces a low-level anxiety regarding the future of our institution. Change is met with anxiety: "If we try this new thing, and it does not work out, we will be doomed." A preacher could explore present challenges in the life of the parish in a way that calls people into conversation that considers how God is forming them for renewed ministry. It may not be enough for churches to do what worked in the past. Communities of faith always ought to ask how God is providing for them in the present. Moses and the Israelites needed food, but their immediate challenge was in becoming a community—food insecurity was merely a window into this need.

God instructs Moses to tell the people that God will rain bread down from heaven. Each person should gather only what they need. The people gather as instructed; some collect much, and some collect a little. Even with different amounts being collected, "those who gathered much had nothing over, and those who gathered little had no shortage." Curiously, "They gathered as much as each of them needed" (Exod. 16:18).

This detail of the liberation story illumines how we strive to amass more wealth, food, and so on than we need, and protect what we have gained at all costs. Because many individuals and organizations spend so much time strategizing how to get more and preserve what they have, we cultivate incredibly anxious systems. How might a church with even a little bit of anxiety over a lack of money or volunteers hear this passage about daily bread and God's abundance? How could it change the way we engage as church together?

Moses puts on his preaching tabs here and directs them to engage in a liturgy of collecting sustenance that will benefit the community equitably. This little passage from Exodus is a precursor for liturgies like Holy Eucharist, when bread and wine are collected to be shared by the whole community. Even unofficial "liturgies," like food collections and coffee-hour refreshments, could be said to be "leftovers" of this mind-set of sharing abundance.

It may also be worthwhile to delve into the personal implications of this passage. For what reasons do people come to your church? Are they hoping merely to be part of a family? They can do that in their neighborhood. Do they want to be part of a club of do-gooders? The Rotary Club does that better. Is worship their only hour of reflection?

Christian communities gather for all of these reasons, but they also exist for the sake of helping people to shape their very lives around the cadences of prayer and the revelation of God found in Jesus Christ. How can our worship, fellowship, and other church-related activities inform and transform the rest of our lives? How does God's message of abundance speak to our vocations, our family life, the way we spend money, or what we put in our bodies? What if we became more grounded in prayer and more focused on fulfilling only our basic needs, like food, clothing, and shelter? Might we also find ourselves more in tune with our God?

2 Samuel 11:26–12:13a. This passage helps us understand the purpose of last week's, in which King David facilitated a situation by which Uriah the Hittite would die and Uriah's wife Bathsheba would become David's (2 Sam. 11:1–15). In order to help David to see the error of his ways, God sends the prophet Nathan.

When Nathan arrives on the scene, he tells a parable to make a point. Unlike Jesus' parables, Nathan's parable is a bit "on the nose"; he may as well have used character names like Blavid, Blathsheba, and Bluriah. Because of the way many people are used to hearing Scripture read aloud—often slowly and without much affect—it can be helpful for the preacher to draw attention to the ways that ancient storytelling differs from what we expect.

Nathan's parable paints the rich man as the "bad guy" and the poor man as the victim of injustice. Hearing the story, David's blood boils, and he demands that the rich man get what is coming to him. "You are the man!" Nathan exclaims. Nathan puts David in his place and explains every connection between the parable and this real-life soap-opera moment.

Parables continue to be useful to us, especially when it is hard for us to see the meaning and implications of our actions. What connections might the preacher make between the text and topical headlines?

When a major college admissions scandal emerged that implicated television stars and others, there was public outrage. How could someone bribe their way into university, taking spaces from qualified students who lack megawealthy parents? The outrage was expected, but was it justified? One schoolteacher posted a widely viewed video in response to the outrage, citing countless examples of parents who intervened in their children's work far too much. He was not surprised that those with the means would engage in unethical behavior, because he knew that people will use what power they possess to get what they believe they (or their kids) deserve.

This is generally true about how people view and use their power. Sometimes they do not even recognize that they have it, let alone that they use it in their daily life to get what they want. The preacher can explore this dynamic, especially in connection to last week's lection, in which the conflation of our agendas with God's is examined.

The troubling portion of this reading is the curse that God places on David. Many will be bothered by this and maybe even confused about how to reconcile this with the God of love. They will mistakenly assume that the God of the Hebrew Scriptures was not good enough, and that God became good only after Jesus entered the scene. Any time we preach on the Hebrew Scriptures, we must be careful about this, first asking what lesson(s) the story was meant to impart. In the story, God curses David, promising that violence will always be present in his kingdom. Furthermore, there will be trouble within his family, and his wives will sleep with other men in sight of others. The punishment fits the crime, but it also will harm more people than just David. It does not seem fair.

The preacher may remind the congregation that this is a story, and that even in the most unusual stories, there is always some wisdom to be gleaned—that violence begets violence, for instance, or that absolute power corrupts absolutely.

The end of the story includes a comically speedy and positive response from God. This passage has appropriately been removed from church seasons of penitence, like Lent, as quick forgiveness smells a lot like cheap grace. Liturgies like Holy Eucharist point us toward God's mercy and love breaking into our lives, but this reading does so to anticlimactic effect. Maybe that is the point. Maybe divine forgiveness is as absurd as it is in this story. Maybe God's mercy is as available as a handshake at the peace or the bread at Communion. Maybe all we need to *do* to experience grace is to expect it to be there.

CURTIS FARR

Proper 13 (Sunday between July 31 and August 6)

Psalm 78:23–29

[23]Yet he commanded the skies above,
   and opened the doors of heaven;
[24]he rained down on them manna to eat,
   and gave them the grain of heaven.
[25]Mortals ate of the bread of angels;
   he sent them food in abundance.
[26]He caused the east wind to blow in the heavens,
   and by his power he led out the south wind;
[27]he rained flesh upon them like dust,
   winged birds like the sand of the seas;
[28]he let them fall within their camp,
   all around their dwellings.
[29]And they ate and were well filled,
   for he gave them what they craved.

Psalm 51:1–12

[1]Have mercy on me, O God,
   according to your steadfast love;
according to your abundant mercy
   blot out my transgressions.
[2]Wash me thoroughly from my iniquity,
   and cleanse me from my sin.

[3]For I know my transgressions,
   and my sin is ever before me.
[4]Against you, you alone, have I sinned,
   and done what is evil in your sight,
so that you are justified in your sentence
   and blameless when you pass judgment.
[5]Indeed, I was born guilty,
   a sinner when my mother conceived me.

[6]You desire truth in the inward being;
   therefore teach me wisdom in my secret heart.
[7]Purge me with hyssop, and I shall be clean;
   wash me, and I shall be whiter than snow.
[8]Let me hear joy and gladness;
   let the bones that you have crushed rejoice.
[9]Hide your face from my sins,
   and blot out all my iniquities.

¹⁰Create in me a clean heart, O God,
    and put a new and right spirit within me.
¹¹Do not cast me away from your presence,
    and do not take your holy spirit from me.
¹²Restore to me the joy of your salvation,
    and sustain in me a willing spirit.

Connecting the Psalm with Scripture and Worship

Psalm 78:23–29. With seventy-two verses, Psalm 78 is the second-longest of all the psalms, although Psalm 119, the longest, has over twice as many verses. The entire poem recounts what God has done for the children of Israel from the time that God "established a decree in Jacob, and appointed a law in Israel" (Ps. 78:5) through their escape from Egypt and God's eventual choice of David to be their king. Far from a tale of triumph, the psalm instead reads as a reminder of God's repeated graciousness even when the people are ungrateful, and the eventual terrible consequences of repeatedly failing to follow God's basic instructions for living in harmony with one another and the world around them.

The seven short verses that are read along with Exodus 16:2–4 and 9–15 are a poetic retelling of God's compassionate provision of the bread of heaven, even though "the whole congregation of the Israelites" had been complaining against Moses and Aaron (and, by extension, against God). Even this brief excerpt from the psalm underscores the abrupt transition from the exultant victory songs in Exodus 15 to the complaints in Exodus 16. It reminds the reader of how quickly the people forgot that it was because God heard their complaints that they were freed from slavery in Egypt. The psalm insists that despite the clear instruction to remember, the people quickly forgot the miracle of crossing the sea safely as they escaped from Pharaoh's horsemen, or even the more recent miracle in which God changed the bitter water at Marah into a sweet, pure source of refreshment and life.

Now, just two weeks after camping at the bountiful oasis at Elim, which is described as having twelve springs of fresh water and seventy palm trees laden with dates, the people are complaining again, wishing that they had died as slaves back in Egypt rather than starving in the seemingly endless wilderness. Once again, God hears their complaints and gives them yet another miracle, this time blanketing their encampment with quails in the evening so that they could have meat for dinner; and raining down the bread of heaven in the morning for their breakfast.

For the psalmist, this pattern of God responding to the people's complaints, only for them to begin grumbling again every time they are uncomfortable, is the evidence of God's steadfast faithfulness and compassion. The language of the psalm evokes the extravagant lavishness of God's generosity, allowing human creatures to eat "the bread of angels" (v. 25), and covering the entire Israelite encampment with tasty quails that were as uncountable as dust, with "winged birds like the sand of the seas" (v. 27). Despite their constant forgetfulness and lack of trust, God gives the people the meat and bread that they crave, seemingly as soon as the words of complaint are out of their mouths.

However, Exodus 16:20 recounts that when the people insist on keeping some of the manna over for the next day, instead of trusting that God would provide more in the morning as they had been told, it becomes foul-smelling and full of worms. The implication of this in today's world, where climate change due to human burning of fossil fuels threatens death and destruction on every continent, and species extinction is happening on an unthinkable scale, is that even the most compassionate, generous God eventually runs out of patience with the greed of those who are repeatedly unwilling to live within the limits of what is given.

The Mercy of the Lord

Whoever thou art that hast sinned, and hesitatest to exercise penitence for thy sin, despairing of thy salvation, hear David groaning. To thee Nathan the prophet hath not been sent, David himself hath been sent to thee. Hear him crying, and with him cry: hear him groaning, and with him groan; hear him weeping, and mingle tears; hear him amended, and with him rejoice. If from thee sin could not be excluded, be not hope of pardon excluded. There was sent to that man Nathan the prophet, observe the king's humility. He rejected not the words of him giving admonition, he said not, Darest thou speak to me, a king? An exalted king heard a prophet, let His humble people hear Christ.

Hear therefore these words, and say thou with him: "Have pity upon me, O God, after Thy great mercy" (ver. 1). He that imploreth great mercy, confesseth great misery. Let them seek a little mercy of Thee, that have sinned in ignorance: "Have pity," he saith, "upon me, after Your great mercy." Relieve a deep wound after Thy great healing. Deep is what I have, but in the Almighty I take refuge. Of my own so deadly wound I should despair, unless I could find so great a Physician. "Have pity upon me, O God, after Thy great mercy: and after the multitude of Thy pities, blot out my iniquity." What he saith, "Blot out my iniquity," is this, "Have pity upon me, O God." And what he saith, "After the multitude of Thy pities," is this, "After Thy great mercy." Because great is the mercy, many are the mercies; and of Thy great mercy, many are Thy pityings. Thou dost regard mockers to amend them, dost regard ignorant men to teach them, dost regard men confessing to pardon. Did he this in ignorance? A certain man had done some, aye many evil things he had done; "Mercy," he saith, "I obtained, because ignorant I did it in unbelief." This David could not say, "Ignorant I did it." For he was not ignorant how very evil a thing was the touching of another's wife, and how very evil a thing was the killing of the husband, who knew not of it, and was not even angered. They obtain therefore the mercy of the Lord that have in ignorance done it; and they that have knowing done it, obtain not any mercy it may chance, but "great mercy."

Augustine, "Exposition on Psalm 51," in *Nicene and Post-Nicene Fathers,* first series, vol. 8, ed. Philip Schaff and Henry Wace (Buffalo, NY: Christian Literature Publishing, 1898), 191.

As the psalmist puts it in the verses immediately following those appointed for today, "But before they had satisfied their craving, while the food was still in their mouths, the anger of God rose against them and he killed the strongest of them, and laid low the flower of Israel" (vv. 30–31). Psalm 78 was written as a reminder and warning to later generations to learn from the mistakes of their ancestors. It is as timely today as it was on the day it was written.

Psalm 51:1–12. Tradition holds that Psalm 51 was written by David after the events recounted in 2 Samuel 11:26–12:13a, and it is read immediately following the passage in which Nathan accuses David of abusing his power as king. However, most scholars agree that the superscription making that assertion was added by scribes long after the actual writing of the psalm. Indeed, the last verse, which refers to the rebuilding of the walls of Jerusalem, must have been written in the context of the Babylonian exile, hundreds of years after David's death. Nevertheless, the long history of connecting this psalm with the story of David and Bathsheba affects any reading of it.

One of the most striking textual connections between these two texts is David's admission to Nathan, "I have sinned against the LORD," and the similar idea in verse 4 in which the psalmist cries out to God, "Against you, you alone, have I sinned, and done what is evil in your sight." Some commentators have pointed out that by concentrating on his sin against God, David has avoided acknowledging the harm that he has done to Bathsheba and Uriah and the need to make any recompense, or even an apology, to his victims. David's taking of Bathsheba by force appears much uglier than it has been portrayed in earlier generations.

In a time when women all over the world have been calling out prominent men as rapists and sexual harassers, it is no longer possible to pretend that this is a love story or that Bathsheba was either a temptress or a willing participant. David's unwillingness to acknowledge that he has harmed her as well as Uriah makes it difficult to accept his claim that his sin is only against God.

However, by reading against the traditional connection, the psalm can be allowed to stand on its own as an honest and painful expression of regret and remorse for a life lived without regard for knowing and doing God's will. Often, even when one has asked for and received forgiveness from the people who have suffered from one's misdeeds, there is a pervading need for divine forgiveness as well, in order to find absolution and renewal. While the sense of being a sinner since birth—or as the psalmist puts it in verse 5, being "born guilty, a sinner when my mother conceived me"—has been understood as the result of original sin, it might be better to call it the hyperbole of despair. The psalmist pleads for divine relief from the deep, existential awareness of having consistently fallen short of the glory of God, rather than having sinned through any particular action or inaction.

Whether read in this way, or as David's poetic lament over misusing power in order to gratify lustful desire, the psalm echoes the feeling of every person who has ever felt undeserving of God's love. The psalmist's cry in verse 10, "Create in me a clean heart, O God, and put a new and right spirit within me," is a prayer to be made new, for God to bring the penitent's heart into alignment with the heart of God. Only the willingness to allow God to be in intimate contact with the inner self can restore a sense of joy to one who is in despair, because knowing and doing God's will is the true source of lasting joy.

DEBORAH SOKOLOVE

Proper 13 (Sunday between July 31 and August 6)

Ephesians 4:1–16

¹I therefore, the prisoner in the Lord, beg you to lead a life worthy of the calling to which you have been called, ²with all humility and gentleness, with patience, bearing with one another in love, ³making every effort to maintain the unity of the Spirit in the bond of peace. ⁴There is one body and one Spirit, just as you were called to the one hope of your calling, ⁵one Lord, one faith, one baptism, ⁶one God and Father of all, who is above all and through all and in all.

⁷But each of us was given grace according to the measure of Christ's gift. ⁸Therefore it is said,

> "When he ascended on high he made captivity itself a captive;
>   he gave gifts to his people."

⁹(When it says, "He ascended," what does it mean but that he had also descended into the lower parts of the earth? ¹⁰He who descended is the same one who ascended far above all the heavens, so that he might fill all things.) ¹¹The gifts he gave were that some would be apostles, some prophets, some evangelists, some pastors and teachers, ¹²to equip the saints for the work of ministry, for building up the body of Christ, ¹³until all of us come to the unity of the faith and of the knowledge of the Son of God, to maturity, to the measure of the full stature of Christ. ¹⁴We must no longer be children, tossed to and fro and blown about by every wind of doctrine, by people's trickery, by their craftiness in deceitful scheming. ¹⁵But speaking the truth in love, we must grow up in every way into him who is the head, into Christ, ¹⁶from whom the whole body, joined and knit together by every ligament with which it is equipped, as each part is working properly, promotes the body's growth in building itself up in love.

Commentary 1: Connecting the Reading with Scripture

Like no other writing in the New Testament canon, the letter of Ephesians develops a doctrine of the church from beginning to end. The letter naturally divides in two parts, due to the distinctive content in each section: part one (chaps. 1–3) focuses on the theme of the church in Christ and part two (chaps. 4–6) on Christ in the church. Theologically, one might summarize part one as ecclesiology from above, with its God's-eye view of the church from celestial heights, and the second part as ecclesiology from below, with its terrestrial focus on the nitty-gritty of life in the church. Hinging the two parts, Ephesians 4:1–16 transitions from doctrinal explanation to practical application, from theological exposition to moral exhortation.

Verse 1 begins the transition from spiritual teaching to life application by signaling a strong plea with the word "therefore." That is, based on everything that has been previously said concerning the spiritual location of believers in "the heavenly places in Christ Jesus" (Eph. 2:6), the author urges the readers "to lead a life worthy of the *calling* to which [they] have been *called*" (4:1). The reiteration of calling in the previous phrase emphasizes the unique worth of a calling like no other, to which believers have been selected. Moreover, based on the supreme dignity of this calling, they are to approach it with humility, gentleness, patience, and, above all, familial love (v. 2). As the gathered community of believers, with a high calling, the church's goal is to safeguard "the unity of the Spirit," whose glue ("bond") is peace (v. 3).

This recurring theme of unity is developed elsewhere in the Pauline corpus, using the metaphor of the church as the one body of Christ, for example, in Romans 12:4–8 and 1 Corinthians 12:12–28. Similarly, as a strategy for maintaining unity in the church, seven pithy creedal statements are linked together, forming a triad of couplets of ones ("one body and one Spirit," "one hope" and "one Lord," and "one faith" and "one baptism," vv. 4–5), with a final all-encompassing fourfold declaration on the oneness of God (v. 6). The purposed literary effect of the creedal chain of "ones" is clear: the church is made one by the Spirit, one hope unites the church to its Lord, and unity in belief commences with baptism. Correspondingly, the church must live as one in response to God the Father of all (v. 6), for unity is the characteristic feature of the Trinitarian God.

Continuing with the theme of unity, the author moves on to concentrate on the diversity of the individual gifting of Christ's *singular* grace given to the church (v. 7). To corroborate the plurality of the singular gifts bestowed on believers by Christ, the author provides a somewhat surprising proof text from the Septuagint text (Ps. 68:18). The enigmatic allusion to the Lord's descent and ascent from and to Mount Sinai might be lost on the modern reader. In its day, though, the midrashic style of quoting the biblical text and providing an explanatory interpretation was common, even when it could creatively alter the original literal meaning of the text.

The original context of Psalms 68:18 points to the descent and ascent of Yahweh to/from Mount Sinai when Moses received the Law. However, following the midrashic conventions of the day, the author of Ephesians provides a more nuanced interpretation by identifying it as Jesus' incarnation/descent and his ascension/exaltation (vv. 8–10). Incidentally, echoes of the descent and ascension of Jesus can be seen also in the bread of life passage in John 6:25–59 with clear allusions to Exodus 16:2–15 and Psalm 78:23–29 (see esp. John 6:33, 50–51). The author's creative exegesis uses the text to lead into the gifting of the Lord Jesus at the time after his ascension, of course pointing to the outpouring of the Holy Spirit after he has sat at the right hand of the Father.

The textual connections between the feeding of Israel in the desert (Exod. 16 and Ps. 78) and the work of church leadership in equipping the saints should not be overlooked. Just as Yahweh fed his people in the desert, the fivefold ministry of the church (apostles, prophets, evangelists, pastors, and teachers, Eph. 4:11) serves "to equip the saints for the work of ministry" (v. 12).

Although one could certainly establish the distinctive features of each of the offices mentioned, the most important quality of the group is that collectively they were given to the church by Christ as a gift (v. 11). Whereas one could see the ministry offices as individual giftings in the sense of special God-given abilities or talents, the passage stresses that *they* are the gifts. The significance of this is that the church must not only acknowledge their Christ-given authority, but also their inherent value to the church as true gifts. Thus, the emphasis here is not simply on a specific grace/gift/charisma possessed by an individual whom God has gifted, but on the individual herself/himself as the gift given to the church.

The value of the gifting of these individuals is further assessed by their worth to the church in that they serve to grow to "the measure of the full stature of Christ" (v. 13). The ministerial gifts (i.e., the people themselves who minister) are valuable because they equip and build up the body of Christ (v. 12). Furthermore, their lives are gifts to the church because, through their effort, the church is becoming one in the faith and knowledge of Jesus (v. 13). The project of the maturing of the saints has been tasked on those who are gifts, and the church must value their lives and efforts. Though at times the "dirty" or "mean" work of ministry is thrust upon God's chosen leaders, the people of God should never forget their value and always continue to respect them as men and women of God who shepherd his flock by feeding them, and also, at times, by exhorting or admonishing them. The church will always need Nathans who call out sin (2 Sam. 12:1–13) and guide people in the path toward confession and restoration as we see in the life of David. As David's story of his sin and confession in Psalm 51 demonstrates, he submitted to rebuke and accepted his sins as his own fault, and did not need to kill the messenger who brought the admonishment.

The recognition that the main activity of the fivefold ministry refers to the proclamation of the Word is clearly seen in verses 14–16. The earlier issue of the maturity of the saints is now vividly pictured in a negative manner by the image of wavering infant believers who are "tossed to and fro" by the trendiest new doctrinal wind (v. 14a). Whereas immature novice Christians might easily be deceived by tricksters who have perfected the art of biblical deception through their wordy scheming (v. 14b), those who make up the fivefold ministry of the local church have been charged with growing the church into the body of Christ (v. 15). Moreover, ministers of the Word rely on truth and love to grow the whole body through an intricate operation of repairing the tears in the ligament, which combat the unity of the church.

The last verse in this section beautifully imagines the organic restorative work of the church, whose members, after being equipped and brought to a healthy working order, are able to promote the healthy growth of the greater church. This is not merely a doctrinally fine-tuned intellectual community of faith; it is the church practicing love (v. 16).

SAMMY G. ALFARO

Commentary 2: Connecting the Reading with the World

Woven throughout the Scriptures is the concept that we who follow the risen Christ live in an in-between time. We experience the tension of "already but not yet." We know how Christ is moving in and through our lives today. We also know how the story will end, what will happen to us. Christ will return. We will have life eternal at the heavenly banquet. The tension is that the glorious end is not yet here.

Already, but not yet. The first three chapters of Ephesians have been reminding us of the end of the story. It is the good news that, through the death and resurrection of Jesus Christ, we have been adopted as the children of God. We who were far off have been brought near. We have been brought into union with all of our sisters and brothers as the body of Christ. We are citizens and saints filled with the Spirit, "rooted and grounded" in the love of God. That is the "already."

However, at the same time we seem to be living in the "not yet." There is an important word in today's reading we must attend to, a word that is easily missed: "until." "The gifts he gave were . . . for building up the body of Christ, *until* all of us come to the unity of the faith and of the knowledge of the Son of God" (Eph. 4:11–13). Until—it would seem we are not yet in the full unity and knowledge of Jesus.

The author is helping us as disciples of Christ reflect on what it looks like to live between the already and the not yet. There will come a time when the tension will collapse, and we will experience full and complete unity. The whole body will finally be knit together. However, we need to live the life of the saints before that happens, in the not yet that is the here and now.

The previous reading, Ephesians 3:14–21, was the wonderful prayer for the new Christians that closes the first section of the letter. The author recognizes that his readers are worried about him as he sits in prison. He wants to let them know he is all right. He is willing to go through all of that for them because he is doing what God has called him to do. Now the letter turns to exploring how they are to live "a life worthy of the calling" (v. 1).

What are the virtues and gifts that will help them—and help us—live a worthy life? Lest readers of this letter get too excited and think they have arrived at the "already" kingdom, the author presents us with a portrait of where they are. Readers are still living in the "not yet" time. They cannot pass over to "already" too quickly. The author knows we need to be reminded that we are in the "tossed to and fro" time. We live in the "not yet" time of being tempted away from the good news. We too quickly forget whose we are.

For years many churches have been wrestling with the issue of sexual orientation. Should LGBTQ+ individuals be ordained? Should clergy be allowed to perform same-sex marriages? Several years ago the United Methodist Church called a meeting in which they could discuss, debate, and wrestle with these important questions. It quickly became clear that the decision was not going the way the leadership had hoped. Each side believed it was speaking "the truth," but neither side seemed to be speaking "in love." Each side grounded its message in the Scriptures but, after the final votes were cast, it was an angry, bitter, divided community that left the convention hall.

Where is your community experiencing tension in the body? What is causing that tension? How is your church being tossed "to and fro"?

There are two Greek conceptions of time, *chronos* and *kairos*. *Chronos* is clock time, calendar time, the passing of hours, days, weeks, months, and years. It is the time that we count, and watch pass too quickly. There are many people today who want to tell people how to live in *chronos* time. If we look on Facebook or YouTube, we will be told the best food to eat and what to avoid. I can be reminded to exercise by the watch on my wrist. They also want to sell us the perfect sheets and socks that will apparently make all of our cares disappear. In *chronos* time we are tossed to and fro, but it is where we tend to focus our attention. We ignore *kairos* time.

Kairos time is God's time. We do not count *kairos* time; rather, we live into God's appointed time. At the opening of the epistle, the author reminds us "With all wisdom and insight [God] has made known to us the mystery of his will, according to his good pleasure that he set forth in Christ, as a plan for the fullness of time [*kairos*], to gather up all things in him" (1:8–10).

The prisoner for Christ Jesus wants the church, called by God and built on the foundation of Jesus Christ's life, death, and resurrection, to "lead a life worthy of [its] calling" (4:1). How

are they to do that? How are we to do that? How are we to live in *kairos* time, God's time? I think that the author of Ephesians would probably agree that it has nothing to do with following a Keto diet or sleeping on a particular mattress. Rather, he now gives us a portrait of the full, worthy, *kairos* life. Those called to live into that life are to follow the virtues. They are humble, gentle, patient, loving, and come together in unity—but is it even possible to exhibit all of those virtues?

Speaking for myself: I know that there are days when I am able to live into three, maybe four, of those virtues. Then I run into a rude, dawdling person at the store, and there goes my patience. My children, who are now grown, will tell you that I "lost" my gentleness many an evening trying to get them to complete their homework. How are we supposed to lead that worthy life to which we are called every day? How are we to live, really, into the fullness of God?

Fortunately, God knows our weaknesses. We do not have to do it ourselves. The author reminds the members of the church that God has given wonderful gifts "to equip the saints for the work of ministry" (v. 12). There are saints, members of the church, who have been given amazing gifts that will help equip others, gifts that include offering leadership, speaking out against injustice, proclaiming the Word, encouraging, extending comfort, teaching, and mentoring. There are also other gifts not even mentioned in the letter, including, for example, plumbing and building management. All are essential for bringing the saints "to maturity" in Christ.

As you look about your community, who are the saints who have been given those gifts? Are there other gifts that God has given to the saints in your church to equip them for the ministry to which all have been called?

Finally, as we live in this "already but not yet" time, we must remember that "each of us was given grace according to the measure of Christ's gift" (v. 7). It is by God's grace that we are able to lead the worthy life, loving one another as Christ loved us.

LUCY LIND HOGAN

John 6:24–35

²⁴So when the crowd saw that neither Jesus nor his disciples were there, they themselves got into the boats and went to Capernaum looking for Jesus.

²⁵When they found him on the other side of the sea, they said to him, "Rabbi, when did you come here?" ²⁶Jesus answered them, "Very truly, I tell you, you are looking for me, not because you saw signs, but because you ate your fill of the loaves. ²⁷Do not work for the food that perishes, but for the food that endures for eternal life, which the Son of Man will give you. For it is on him that God the Father has set his seal." ²⁸Then they said to him, "What must we do to perform the works of God?" ²⁹Jesus answered them, "This is the work of God, that you believe in him whom he has sent." ³⁰So they said to him, "What sign are you going to give us then, so that we may see it and believe you? What work are you performing? ³¹Our ancestors ate the manna in the wilderness; as it is written, 'He gave them bread from heaven to eat.'" ³²Then Jesus said to them, "Very truly, I tell you, it was not Moses who gave you the bread from heaven, but it is my Father who gives you the true bread from heaven. ³³For the bread of God is that which comes down from heaven and gives life to the world." ³⁴They said to him, "Sir, give us this bread always."

³⁵Jesus said to them, "I am the bread of life. Whoever comes to me will never be hungry, and whoever believes in me will never be thirsty."

Commentary 1: Connecting the Reading with Scripture

The events in John 6 preceding Jesus' arrival at Capernaum provide an important narrative context for interpreting Jesus' discourse on "the bread from heaven" (John 6:25–35). The crowds have been following Jesus and his disciples in their mission to the towns along the western shoreline of the Sea of Galilee for the past two days. The people have just experienced the miraculous multiplication of loaves and fish (vv. 1–15). They have even made an attempt to force Jesus to become king but failed when he retreated into the hillside. That same evening, the disciples take a boat toward Capernaum (vv. 16–17), and on the way, at sea, they witness Jesus walking on water (vv. 18–21). When the people finally notice that Jesus is nowhere in the vicinity, they too head toward Capernaum (vv. 22–24). Here is where a heated exchange between Jesus and the crowds begins.

When the people catch up to Jesus, they ask him at what time he arrived (v. 25). Jesus responds in a way that confronts the motives of the questioners. With a double "Amen!" ("very truly," NRSV), Jesus accuses the crowds of seeking him not for the signs he performed but for physical bread they received (v. 26). "Signs" (*sēmeia*) have a technical meaning in the Gospel of John and refer to those miracles that specifically reveal an aspect of Jesus' messianic and divine identity. It becomes apparent in the unfolding episode that the crowds have no idea who Jesus truly is. Therefore, though they experienced something miraculous with the multiplication of bread, they nevertheless missed the sign.

Jesus challenges three misconceptions held by the crowds that keep them in a state of unbelief. First, the crowds misunderstand the significance of the multiplication of bread. Jesus exhorts them to focus not on material loaves, which perish, but on spiritual food, which lasts forever (v. 27). Their worldview is too earthly, temporal, and mundane. Jesus' reproof of the crowds is reminiscent of what he says to Peter at Caesarea Philippi: "You do not have in mind the things of God but only human things" (Mark 8:33, my trans.). Until the crowds start seeing the world with spiritual eyes, they will always misunderstand who Jesus is and what he does. Their vision needs to align with God's purposes to usher in an eternal kingdom that not only feeds the body but also heals the soul, transforms the mind, renews the spirit, and liberates the whole self from sin's tyranny (cf. John 18:36; 1 Thess. 5:23).

Second, the crowd misunderstands the works *they* must do. It is not exactly clear what the people mean when they ask, "What should we do so that we *work the works* of God?" (v. 28; my trans.; in the Greek text both the verb and the noun for "work," that is, *ergozomai* and *ergon*, are used). They could refer to the works of the Law required of every pious Jew in covenant fidelity with God. Perhaps they refer to specific works that might trigger the arrival of God's kingdom, since they have already tried on one occasion to anoint Jesus as king (v. 15). The Roman historian Josephus records a messianic pretender named Theudas who claimed he could part the Jordan River. He rallied many followers, but his revolution failed (Josephus, *Ant.* 20.97–98; cf. Acts 5:36). It might be the crowds were asking about the kind of works they should perform if Jesus was Israel's true prophet. Should they band together as a revolutionary movement? What works should they work out?

However, Jesus' kingdom cannot be commandeered by violence. It is inaugurated as an act of God through his Son's atoning death. Whatever their definition of work, Jesus corrects it. He redirects their attention to the one thing they must do: believe. The true work of God is to believe in the one whom the Father has sent (v. 29), that is, the true Son upon whom God places his royal seal (*esphragisen*) of authenticity (v. 27).

Believing is a central recurring theme in John's Gospel (e.g., 1:12; 3:16; 20:31). Believing (*pisteuein*) means entrusting oneself completely to someone or some cause. It is an abiding trust in, and allegiance to, Christ. The crowds are shocked that Jesus would ask such a total commitment from them, and so they demand an additional sign or proof of his messianic credentials before they can believe (v. 30; cf. Matt. 16:1–4; Mark 8:11–12; Luke 11:16).

Their request for a sign spurs a debate between Jesus and the crowds concerning the provision of manna for Israel in the desert, which is referenced by the Old Testament lections (Exod. 16:2–4, 9–15; Ps. 78:23–29). The debate centers on Jewish interpretations concerning the symbolic importance of manna (Wis. 16:20; *2 Bar.* 29:8; *Midr. Mek. Exod.* 26:25; 38:4; *Midr. Rab. Eccl.* 1:9; *Midr. Tanḥ. Beshalaḥ* 21:1; Josephus, *Ant.* 3.32; Philo, *Mut.* 258–60).[1] In the Jewish exegetical tradition, manna represents spiritual food and heavenly nourishment. It is a metaphor for consuming and living out the Torah. By consuming heavenly food and wisdom, that is, by faithfully obeying the Law of Moses, Israel sought to experience eternal life and God's sustaining presence. An excerpt from *Midrash Tanḥuma Beshalaḥ* 21:1 provides a succinct example of this rabbinic interpretation:

> And Moses said unto Aaron: "Take a jar and put an omerful [2 liters] of manna therein" (Exod. 6:33). . . . Rabbi Eliezer was of the opinion that it was put there for the Messianic era, for a time about which the prophet Jeremiah said to Israel: "Why do you not devote yourself to the Torah?" And they replied: "If we do, how shall we obtain our sustenance? . . ." "Your fathers occupied themselves with the Law, and see how they were fed; concern yourselves with the Law, and I [the Lord] shall feed you from this jar."[2]

1. Raymond Brown, *The Gospel according to John I–XII* (New York: Doubleday, 1966), 264–66; Craig Keener, *The Gospel of John: A Commentary*, vol. 1 of 2 (Peabody, MA: Hendrickson, 2003), 679–82.

2. Eng. trans. from Samuel A. Berman, *Midrash Tanhuma-Yelammedenu: An English Translation of Genesis and Exodus from the Printed Version of Tanhuma-Yelammedenu with an Introduction, Notes, and Indexes* (Hoboken, NJ: KTAV, 1996), 440. https://www.sefaria.org/Midrash_Tanchuma%2C_Beshalach.21.1?lang=bi&with=all&lang2=en

Eating manna was not only a symbol of Israel's dependence on God's word for life (Deut. 8:3) but a promise that anticipates a new messianic age. The messiah to come would inaugurate a new exodus and reopen the heavens for a new manna to feed God's people. The crowds might possibly be wondering if Jesus is the new Moses through whom a messianic kingdom would come. They seek further verification from him.

The people, however, wrongly think the source of manna during the forty years of wilderness wandering is Moses (John 6:31). This is the third misconception that Jesus seeks to correct. Jesus tells them it is not Moses but God who feeds Israel with bread from heaven (v. 32).

If God, not Moses, was the one who first fed manna to Israel, Jesus, through his miraculous feeding of the five thousand, has done what only God can do. He is more than a new Moses. Jesus is the divine source for the heavenly bread. Sharing the Godhead of God, Jesus as God gives heavenly bread and new life (v. 33). As the Word of God, Jesus is the bread of life who satisfies humankind's spiritual hunger and thirst (v. 35; cf. 4:9–15). The only proper response to Jesus' divine claim is to consume it and believe. Tragically the people will reject the Word and consequently reject life itself (v. 36–71).

MAX J. LEE

Commentary 2: Connecting the Reading with the World

"What is it we want when we can't stop wanting?"[3] poet Christian Wiman asks in his book *He Held Radical Light: The Art of Faith, the Faith of Art.* A devastating diagnosis of potentially terminal cancer raised profound questions of the meaning and purpose of life for Wiman and led him to a reconsideration of Christian theology and Christian faith. It also prompted him to probe his own experience of deep spiritual hunger.

According to Jesus, hunger for bread represents a deeper, spiritual hunger. It is the theme of an exchange between Jesus and a crowd of hungry people who have been following him for days. The author of the Fourth Gospel describes the crowd that follows Jesus as relentless, determined, driven. They are not about to be distracted or discouraged. Their hunger is deep, palpable.

The text, John 6:24–35, is part of a larger, defining narrative: Jesus miraculously transforming a pittance, five loaves of bread and two fish, into abundance so generous that it feeds five thousand people to their fill, with twelve baskets left over. Then he appears walking on water to his terrified disciples in a small boat in

a raging storm. "It is I," he assures them. "Do not be afraid" (John 6:20).

The crowd closely watches Jesus' every move. When they notice that he is not in the boat with his disciples, they commandeer another boat and sail to Capernaum, where they finally find him again. The crowd is determined and still hungry. Jesus uses the occasion to lead them into the deeper water of wanting. They have followed him across the sea, not because of the signs they experienced, but because of the bread. They ate their fill and now they want more. Patiently, Jesus points out that bread is as temporary as the feeling of satisfying fullness they experience after eating. Hunger returns quickly, always, but there is bread that does *not* spoil or lose its capacity to satisfy, bread that endures forever. This is bread that will satisfy their deepest, most persistent hunger, their relentless wanting.

Then comes the sublime dialogue: the crowd, "Sir, give us this bread always"; Jesus, "I am the bread of life. Whoever comes to me will never be hungry, and whoever believes in me will never be thirsty" (v. 35). This is bread that satisfies ultimate hunger. He is the bread that sustains always, without limits, bread that lasts, the bread of life.

---

3. Christian Wiman, *He Held Radical Light: The Art of Faith, the Faith of Art* (New York: Farrar, Straus & Giroux, 2018), 7.

It is what the poet means by the question, "What is it we want when we can't stop wanting?" It is what everyone experiences sooner or later. It is deep in us. To be human is to long for more than daily life provides. To be human is to yearn for meaning, ultimacy, salvation. That hungry yearning inspires poets, artists, musicians to dig deep and reach high and to write and paint and compose. That hunger drives scientists to experiment and explore the unknown. That longing for something more is the source of human restless creativity and accomplishment. It is one of the things that defines us as human. It is created in us by God.

Alternative answers are plentiful. Sometimes political ideology proposes that it is the answer to our hunger. Sometimes authoritarian ideology forces the issue. Early Marxism taught that the hunger for God goes away, once people learn that religion is an opiate, an unnecessary addiction. When the hunger persisted, Communist dictators tried to crush it, jailing clergy, tearing down churches, and turning them into concert halls.

The former Soviet Union scorned religion, laughed at it, and, when the world was not watching, persecuted it. The state even censured literature and music that seemed to be expressing deep human longing, persistent human hunger. Composers, poets, and playwrights were warned, criticized in the state press, arrested, and exiled. The Stalinist press sharply criticized composer Dmitry Shostakovich's music for being unharmonious. Popular composers were ordered to write joyful, uplifting music, not music that expresses longing, wanting, hunger. Fascism offers its ideology of race and radical nationalism as the answer to ultimate hunger and in the process imitates the rituals and accoutrements of religion: processions and banners and hymns and huge worshipful rallies of the faithful.

Closer to home, our own market economy, powered by highly sophisticated advertising, promises fulfillment and happiness and tells us that the answer to our relentless hunger is purchasing the right automobile or clothing or jewelry, drinking the right scotch, visiting the right resorts, travel locations, and luxury cruises.

The bold and countercultural claim of Jesus is that all of it is like bread that becomes stale and ultimately spoils. There is only one thing that ultimately satisfies our deep hunger. Furthermore, the theologians intriguingly suggest that God is responsible for the hunger in us. Augustine wrote the provocative truth: "Thou hast made us for thyself, O Lord, and our hearts are restless until they rest in thee."[4]

The Reformers taught that faith itself is a gift of God, that God not only creates hunger for God in us, but also gives us the ability to believe, to have faith and trust in God. Testimony is both ancient and modern. The reality of hunger itself suggests that there is food to satisfy that hunger.

The late Joseph Sittler, a Lutheran theologian and professor of theology at the Divinity School of the University of Chicago, wrote, "Hunger unabated is a kind of testimony to the reality of food. To want to have may become a strange kind of having."[5]

Trust your hunger. Trust your hunger for God as you know and trust your hunger for food. Both hungers are deeply part of our humanity and who we are. "Do not work for the food that perishes," Jesus said, "but for the food that endures for eternal life, which the Son of Man will give you" (v. 27). We need bread, but we equally need the "bread of life."

A provocative modern witness is Sara Miles in her book *Take This Bread: The Spiritual Memoir of a Twenty-First-Century Christian*. "One early, cloudy morning, when I was forty-six, I walked into a church, ate a piece of bread, took a sip of wine. . . . I'd led a thoroughly secular life, at best indifferent to religion, more often appalled at its fundamentalist crusades. This was my first communion."[6]

Bread opened the door to faith and a call to discipleship for Sara Miles. She organized a feeding program in her new church that has grown and now feeds hundreds of the hungry and needy poor weekly. She recalls how she had read the story about Jesus seeing the hungry

4. Augustine, *The Confessions of St. Augustine* (New York: Pocket Books, 1957), 1.
5. Joseph Sittler, "The View from Mount Nebo," in *The Care of the Earth and Other University Sermons* (Philadelphia: Fortress Press, 1964), 87.
6. Sara Miles, *Take This Bread, The Spiritual Memoir of a Twenty-First-Century Christian* (New York: Ballantine Books, 2007), prologue, p. xi.

crowd and telling his surprised disciples to give them something to eat.

In the sacrament of the Lord's Supper, we are reminded not only of our physical hunger but our deeper hunger for wholeness, for redemption, for the bread of life. We eat bread and drink wine together and confess our hunger and our trust that Jesus Christ, the love of God incarnate, not only nurtures our hunger, but also meets it with his own unconditional love, the bread of life. He is the bread.

JOHN M. BUCHANAN

Proper 14 (Sunday between August 7 and August 13)

1 Kings 19:4–8 and 2 Samuel 18:5–9, Ephesians 4:25–5:2
   15, 31–33 John 6:35, 41–51
Psalm 34:1–8 and Psalm 130

1 Kings 19:4–8

⁴But [Elijah] himself went a day's journey into the wilderness, and came and sat down under a solitary broom tree. He asked that he might die: "It is enough; now, O LORD, take away my life, for I am no better than my ancestors." ⁵Then he lay down under the broom tree and fell asleep. Suddenly an angel touched him and said to him, "Get up and eat." ⁶He looked, and there at his head was a cake baked on hot stones, and a jar of water. He ate and drank, and lay down again. ⁷The angel of the LORD came a second time, touched him, and said, "Get up and eat, otherwise the journey will be too much for you." ⁸He got up, and ate and drank; then he went in the strength of that food forty days and forty nights to Horeb the mount of God.

2 Samuel 18:5–9, 15, 31–33

⁵The king ordered Joab and Abishai and Ittai, saying, "Deal gently for my sake with the young man Absalom." And all the people heard when the king gave orders to all the commanders concerning Absalom.
   ⁶So the army went out into the field against Israel; and the battle was fought in the forest of Ephraim. ⁷The men of Israel were defeated there by the servants of David, and the slaughter there was great on that day, twenty thousand men. ⁸The battle spread over the face of all the country; and the forest claimed more victims that day than the sword.
   ⁹Absalom happened to meet the servants of David. Absalom was riding on his mule, and the mule went under the thick branches of a great oak. His head caught fast in the oak, and he was left hanging between heaven and earth, while the mule that was under him went on. . . . ¹⁵And ten young men, Joab's armor-bearers, surrounded Absalom and struck him, and killed him. . . .
   ³¹Then the Cushite came; and the Cushite said, "Good tidings for my lord the king! For the LORD has vindicated you this day, delivering you from the power of all who rose up against you." ³²The king said to the Cushite, "Is it well with the young man Absalom?" The Cushite answered, "May the enemies of my lord the king, and all who rise up to do you harm, be like that young man."
   ³³The king was deeply moved, and went up to the chamber over the gate, and wept; and as he went, he said, "O my son Absalom, my son, my son Absalom! Would I had died instead of you, O Absalom, my son, my son!"

Commentary 1: Connecting the Reading with Scripture

These two stories can be said to narrate both the effects of war and hostility on a very personal level. This is no more evident than in the account of Elijah under the broom tree, where we encounter an utterly depressed, burnt-out prophet. This is most certainly not the fiery champion of God who defeated the prophets of Baal (1 Kgs. 18:20–40), who saw fire coming down from heaven in response to his passionate prayers (18:38), and who outran the chariot of Ahab (18:46). This is a man who is fearful, fleeing for his life to Beer-sheba, which is as far away as possible, as evident in the saying, "from Dan to Beer-sheba."[1] Even at this farthest end of being far away, Elijah goes away even further, leaving his servant behind in Beer-sheba to travel a day's journey into the wilderness, where he goes to lie down under a lonely broom tree (19:3–5).

It is a sad picture. Sadder still is his lament to God in verse 4: "Enough, now." He implores God to see his misery, lamenting that what he currently is experiencing is much too much for any person to endure. Elijah had lost his will to live and prays to God to take his life and so end his misery.

In our second story, we encounter yet another story of conflict that had escalated out of control. King David was challenged by his son Absalom in a family feud that, according to 2 Samuel 19:5, had threatened the life of David, in addition to "the lives of [his] sons and [his] daughters, and the lives of [his] wives and [his] concubines." This feud led to a most brutal battle in the forest of Ephraim, resulting in the massacre of twenty thousand men. In vivid terms, the widespread effects of this war are portrayed as the battle rages on all across the country, with the forest being said to play an active partner in war, "claim[ing] more victims that day than the sword" (18:8). One of these victims is David's own son, Absalom. Caught with his hair in one of the trees, Absalom dies at the hand of David's fiercely loyal general Joab, who violently pierces

Absalom's heart with three spears, leaving it to his armor-bearers to finish the job (vv. 14–15).

This act of violence is followed by a dramatic race to go inform the king (vv. 16–29). Two men—Ahimaaz, son of Zadok, and a Cushite—try to outrun one another to go tell the king paradoxical news: he has won the war, but he has lost his son. Both Ahimaaz and the Cushite focus on the good news in their respective messages to the king, celebrating the fact that the king has been vindicated, that the king has been delivered from his enemies. However, it is the Cushite—the ethnic outsider who perhaps has known his share of pain and exclusion—who ends up revealing to David the greatest pain any father may feel: the enemy who is dead is the young man, Absalom (v. 32).

The reader is furthermore transported to the inner chambers of the king, where we are offered an intimate look into a father's grief. In a profound manner, 18:33 captures the effects upon David of losing his son; David, who is said to be "deeply moved" (NRSV) or "shaken" (NIV), bitterly weeps as he is walking up to his chamber. Repeating five times the designation, "My son," he cries out for all to hear: "O my son Absalom, my son, my son Absalom! Would I had died instead of you, O Absalom, my son, my son!"

In this story, we thus are shown a snapshot of the grief of one father over his dead son. We should not forget, though, that this dramatic account is but one story of loss on this particular day. There were twenty thousand other sons, fathers, brothers, husbands, friends who were all brutally murdered in the Ephraim forest. In some sense, this story of one father's grief draws our attention to many other wasted lives that are lost to the horrors of senseless personal feuds and vendettas that can devastate an entire community.

In this regard, Judith Butler rightly reminds us that without some sort of obituary by means of "which life becomes, or fails to become, a publically grievable life," it may be considered to be

---

1. This phrase is used nine times in the OT to describe the geographical span of Israel. See Judg. 20:1; 1 Sam. 3:20; 2 Sam. 3:10; 17:11; 24:2, 15; 1 Kgs. 4:25; 1 Chr. 21:2; and 2 Chr. 30:5.

The Essence of All Meaning

Behold the miracle! Love has no awareness of merit or demerit—it has no scale by which its portion may be weighed or measured. It does not seek to balance giving and receiving. Love loves; that is its nature. But this does not mean that love is blind, naive, or pretentious. It does not mean that love holds its object securely in its grasp. . . . Here is not traffic in sentimentality, no catering to weakness or to strength. Instead there is a robust vitality that quickens the roots of personality creating an unfolding of the self that redefines, reshapes and makes all things new. Thus the experience is so fundamental in quality that the individual knows that what is happening to him can outlast all things without itself being dissipated or lost.

Whence comes this power which seems to be the point of referral for all experience and the essence of all meaning? No created thing, no single unit of life can be the source of such fullness and completeness. For in the experience itself a man is caught and held by something so much more than he can ever think or be that there is but one word by which its meaning can be encompassed—God.

Howard Thurman, *Mysticism and the Experience of Love* (Wallingford, PA: Pendle Hill, 1961), 22–23.

For all fathers and mothers and anyone who has ever suffered the traumatic effects of losing a loved one, the second part of the pericope in 1 Kings 19:4–8 may offer a word of hope. God's presence is powerfully captured in an angel who gently touches Elijah, telling him to get up and eat the freshly baked bread and drink some water in the middle of the wilderness, far removed from everyone. In response to this act of kindness, Elijah eats and drinks and goes to sleep again. A second time, the angel comes and prods Elijah to eat and drink so as to build up his energy. As the angel says in 19:7, "Otherwise the journey will be too much for you."

We see in the example of Elijah how this traumatized individual, utterly exhausted by a battle that included having to flee for his life, is helped in his grief by means of acts of compassion and care. There, when he finds himself under the broom tree, God's provision of sustenance by means of a messenger helps Elijah to grow stronger, so that he can go on "in the strength of that food" for forty days and forty nights.

However, there seems to be no such respite for the grieving father in 2 Samuel 19, as the king is exhorted by his general Joab to "man up," get up out of his chambers, and go meet the despondent troops, something that David ends up doing in verse 8. In conversation with 1 Kings 19, we may wish that this grieving father would have been afforded the same kind of compassionate care experienced by the prophet Elijah as narrated in the first of our lectionary readings this week.

"not quite a life" and hence "not worth a note. It is already the unburied, if not the unburiable."[2] Thus, by means of this vivid portrait of a father's immense sorrow about the violence that killed his son and threatened to destroy the entire community, we are urged to remember that there are many more fathers, not to mention mothers, whose grief is beyond measure.

Moreover, the effects of this loss continue well into the next chapter, when it is repeatedly shown that the king is weeping and mourning for his son (19:1–2). In verse 4, David repeats once more his heartfelt lament from the previous chapter: "O my son Absalom, O Absalom, my son, my son!" Here, we can sense a resonant echo of Elijah's lamentations under the broom tree, as the king lies in his chamber, utterly depressed, refusing to eat and drink. He finally finds refuge in sleep as he is overwhelmed by sorrow.

L. JULIANA CLAASSENS

---

2. Judith Butler, *Precarious Life: The Powers of Mourning and Violence* (London: Verso, 2004), 34.

Commentary 2: Connecting the Reading with the World

Anybody in leadership—and perhaps especially Christian leadership—knows that there is a fine line between success and failure. The OT lections set down for today concern two quite different men: Elijah and David. One is a prophet and one a king; one is remembered as a great warrior and one a polarizing prophet on the margins. We know much about the web of David's relationships, while we know next to nothing about Elijah beyond his prophetic actions. Yet for all their differences, each tasted failure in success and success in failure.

1 Kings 19:4–8. These verses are best understood in the context of 1 Kings 19 as a whole. The start of the chapter finds Elijah flushed with the successes of chapter 18. The prophets of Baal have been spectacularly beaten (setting aside for the moment the problem of the prophet slaughtering them), the drought over the land has broken, and Elijah has fled for his life from Jezebel. Adrenaline is pumping.

Now comes the letdown. Elijah's experience will be familiar to many in leadership, however small or great their sphere of influence. Whatever label we might want to put on it, I read four particular aspects of that experience of debilitating letdown after great achievement or blessing: fear, a sense of unworthiness, loneliness, and a loss of perspective. Often these things follow success. For Elijah, it is a naked fear for his life (1 Kgs. 19:3, 10). Accompanying this is his expressed sense of unworthiness: "I am no better than my ancestors" (v. 4). He feels profoundly alone: "only I am left" (v. 10). This very sense of aloneness betrays also his loss of perspective. These will all be familiar currency for many hearers of today's sermon. Success often opens the door to a sense of worthlessness that is paradoxically self-centered at the same time. We see this here in Elijah.

Although he felt alone, God had not left him. In this chapter we might also isolate three aspects of God's response to the despairing, self-absorbed prophet. First, a *mal'ak* of the Lord came to Elijah (vv. 5–7). The term that NRSV translates as "angel" could as easily be translated

"messenger" or even "prophet," according to context. Whatever the nature of the figure who came to him, he or she was experienced by Elijah as a sustaining agent of the Lord. For the moment, that was enough, and the sustenance provided by the "angel" got him to Horeb (v. 8). Congregants may at this point be able to think of "agents of God" in some form who have stepped in at critical moments and helped them take the next step on a difficult journey. At the same time, if this passage is read in the context of a Eucharist, a link could be drawn between the cake and water supplied by the angel (vv. 6–7) and Jesus as "the bread of life" (John 6:35), the sustainer for difficult journeys.

As we read on in the chapter, we find that Elijah's difficulties are not yet over. Despite the miraculous journey to Horeb, he still feels abandoned. God patiently comes to Elijah again, this time not in the pyrotechnics of nature but in "a sound of sheer silence" (the Hebrew is evocative, and may be translated "the sound of finely ground silence," v. 12). In that silence somehow God speaks, and Elijah learns that he is not alone after all; there remain "seven thousand in Israel" who "have not bowed to Baal" (v. 18). Those hearing the sermon today might be similarly encouraged to live on the lookout for the restoring sound of God's silence in the midst of despair.

God also provides a third response to Elijah's sense of failure in the wake of success. In the midst of some political instruction, God directs him to begin succession planning by appointing Elisha. So the chapter ends with a disciple for Elijah (v. 21); he is no longer alone.

As members of a eucharistic community gathered in Christ, neither need we be alone in our work.

2 Samuel 18:5–9, 15, 31–33. Around ideas of success and failure, events in this reading present a somewhat different scenario. Rather than the letdown and loss of perspective of Elijah, they entail the grief that so often accompanies achievement. Events in this reading cannot properly be interpreted outside of a brief telling of the sprawling saga of David's family and tensions around his succession. In the telling, it becomes clear that David's experience of grief in the midst of success relates to the complex interaction of faithfulness and frailty that characterize his life.

Today's lesson includes the tail end of David's son Absalom's brief and very nearly successful attempt to usurp his father. His rebellion is best understood in the context of David's dysfunctional family relationships, particularly the ambitious Absalom's response to the rape of his sister Tamar by his half brother Amnon (2 Sam. 13). This outrage set in train events culminating in 2 Samuel 18. Absalom was, not surprisingly, embittered both by Amnon's actions against his half sister and by the king's inaction. His arranged murder of Amnon (13:23–29) was likely motivated both by that offense and by the opportunity to eliminate another claimant to the throne, although the narrator leaves Absalom's motivation to the reader to decide.

Now Absalom is dead, killed by David's longtime henchman Joab (18:14–15). David appears at this point to be paralyzed by the clash of his paternal feelings and the political imperatives facing him. Joab, thinking of the politics, not for the first time, has acted in what he sees as the best interests of the king (see 14:1). On the news of Absalom's death, David the father is incapacitated by grief (18:33). It takes Joab to confront him with the responsibility to focus on the political responsibilities of David the king (19:5–8).

This is a story filled with the idiosyncrasies of human nature, especially on display in the vexed question of who should tell David that his son Absalom was dead. Joab sent an unnamed Cushite, despite the desperation of Ahimaaz to bear the tidings, presumably in the hope of some reward for bearing good news (vv. 19–23). Ahimaaz beats the Cushite to the king, but when he hears David's hopeful question that Absalom has been spared, quickly backs off and pretends to know nothing (vv. 29–30). David's initial feelings of grief are then exacerbated by the way in which he is given the news by the unwitting Cushite, for whom the possibility that David might be grieving a son—not merely rejoicing in the death of an enemy—completely escapes him (vv. 31–32).

Many of the congregation hearing this reading will themselves have struggled with personal and professional success that have come at the cost of family relationships and will know how difficult it is to come to some kind of resolution of these matters. We feel the unbearable pain and unresolved guilt in David's cry, "Would I had died instead of you, O Absalom, my son, my son!" (v. 33).

In the liturgical setting of today's readings, Psalm 130 may be employed as a response to the type of agony experienced by David and by all of us who see those we love pay a price of our own responsibilities. With the aid of that psalm we may cry from the depths of our pain (Ps. 130:1) and learn perhaps to wait and "watch [in hope] for the morning" (Ps. 130:6)—and then to rest in the one whose "steadfast love" (v. 7) holds all things together.

TIM MEADOWCROFT

Proper 14 (Sunday between August 7 and August 13)

Psalm 34:1–8

¹I will bless the LORD at all times;
   his praise shall continually be in my mouth.
²My soul makes its boast in the LORD;
   let the humble hear and be glad.
³O magnify the LORD with me,
   and let us exalt his name together.

⁴I sought the LORD, and he answered me,
   and delivered me from all my fears.
⁵Look to him, and be radiant;
   so your faces shall never be ashamed.
⁶This poor soul cried, and was heard by the LORD,
   and was saved from every trouble.
⁷The angel of the LORD encamps
   around those who fear him, and delivers them.
⁸O taste and see that the LORD is good;
   happy are those who take refuge in him.

Psalm 130

¹Out of the depths I cry to you, O LORD.
   ²Lord, hear my voice!
Let your ears be attentive
   to the voice of my supplications!

³If you, O LORD, should mark iniquities,
   Lord, who could stand?
⁴But there is forgiveness with you,
   so that you may be revered.

⁵I wait for the LORD, my soul waits,
   and in his word I hope;
⁶my soul waits for the Lord
   more than those who watch for the morning,
   more than those who watch for the morning.

⁷O Israel, hope in the LORD!
   For with the LORD there is steadfast love,
   and with him is great power to redeem.
⁸It is he who will redeem Israel
   from all its iniquities.

Connecting the Psalm with Scripture and Worship

Psalm 34:1–8. In these first eight verses of Psalm 34, the psalmist begins by vowing perpetual praise to God. Such praise can be tasted; it will be "in my mouth," the psalmist says (Ps. 34:1). Perhaps this is an anticipation of the well-loved invitation we find in verse 8: "O taste and see that the LORD is good." By the second verse it becomes clear that Psalm 34 is no private soliloquy—the psalmist has an audience in mind. It is "the humble" who are instructed to hear this blessing, praising, and boasting "in the Lord" and rejoice in it. They are not only to listen but also to participate, joining their voices with the psalmist (v. 3). Verses 4–8 interweave the psalmist's testimony of deliverance with related advice and encouragement, directed, again, to the humble, the God-fearers.

While there are no specifics, the psalmist describes a dramatic rescue, not just from any one trouble, but from *all* troubles, *all* fears. The psalmist called on God and God acted. On this basis, hearers are encouraged to do the same. They will be heard and they will be helped, not left in the shame of abandonment. In verse 7, the psalmist shows what this looks like: the angel of the Lord surrounds God-fearers, rescuing them. A divinely appointed bodyguard is right there, keeping watch.

These are big promises, and for some of us this confidence sets off alarm bells. The psalmist had a powerful experience. Whatever the bad stuff was, it did not prevail. Is this always the case for people who fear, trust, and love God? The psalmist is exuberant and undaunted here, as people sometimes are when they have survived an ordeal. You do not believe me? Try it. "O taste and see that the LORD is good; happy are those who take refuge in him." We are not invited to respond to testimony with logical arguments but by calling on God ourselves and seeing what happens. Is skepticism that God will save us from every trouble so easily dismissed?

In contrast, Elijah has plenty of doubts in the reading from 1 Kings, in spite of the fact that he has just tasted and seen the Lord's deliverance for himself. Yahweh answered Elijah's prayers

in spectacular fashion on Mount Carmel, and rain finally met long-parched earth. Nonetheless, Elijah is undone by Jezebel's threat. In this text, the "angel of the LORD" is not just a poetic way of describing God's providential care. Elijah sees the angel. The angel touches Elijah. It says things. It, apparently, knows how to bake.

Psalm 34:1–8 offers an interesting conversation partner for the preacher grappling with Elijah's depression and God's intervention. Because of its testimonial character, these opening verses from Psalm 34 work well when read expressively by a lector, and verse 8, of course, can serve as an effective invitation to the Lord's Supper. The responsive setting of the first part of Psalm 34 by James Moore, "Taste and See," features a very singable refrain for the congregation.[1]

Psalm 130. Psalm 130 comes with a descriptor: it is a "Song of Ascents"; that is, it is part of a group of psalms suitable for use by those on a pilgrimage. This makes sense when you consider the ways Psalm 130 is brimming with passion but scant on detail. Because much is left vague, seekers of all sorts can (and have) taken up this prayer as their own. The famous opening line: "Out of the depths I cry to you, O LORD," does not tell us anything about the nature of the "depths" beyond what we can deduce from verses 3–4. Whatever this desperate situation is, only God's forgiveness can alleviate it, and forgiveness is what is sought. For this reason, scholars often classify Psalm 130 as penitential, though it is clearly a lament as well.

Like many psalms, the structure includes some abrupt shifts. The psalmist begs God to listen in verses 1–2, but then takes a surprising turn, reminding God that everyone is equally incapable of meeting divine standards. If God held human beings to account, "who could stand?" (Ps. 130:3)—but you are a God who forgives, the psalmist continues. Verse 4 may suggest that God's forgiveness is what enables sinful people to worship at all, to bear the presence of the Holy.

Verses 5–6 mark another change of direction. The first half of the psalm is addressed to God,

1. See *Glory to God* (Louisville, KY: Westminster John Knox, 2013), 520.

but now the pray-er turns inward; the psalmist declares intentions, confesses faith, and vows to keep watch. "Waiting" for the Lord is bound up with hope in God's "word" in verse 5, though what this means is not explained. The beautiful repeated phrase "more than those who watch for the morning" may refer to the expectation voiced elsewhere in the book of Psalms, that God's deliverance comes with the dawn.

The final stanza of the psalm changes course again, moving from introspective declaration to exhortation, urging all of Israel to hope in the God of steadfastness and power who will redeem the people from sin (vv. 7–8). Given this confident ending, some have argued that Psalm 130 is a psalm of thanksgiving, in spite of its opening lamentation. Perhaps it is not necessary to decide. Lament is tangled with confession and eventually chased by thanksgiving—not a bad description of the life of faith.

The story of Absalom's death in 2 Samuel 18 is also a complex of emotions. Although the narrative has been simplified by trimming some verses, there is still plenty of drama to go around. The heartbeat of the text is David's reaction to the news that his plan to protect his traitorous son had failed. As the story continues, it becomes clear that David's comrades-in-arms are baffled by his lament for his son. David should be celebrating that his underdog army had thwarted a powerful upstart, family ties notwithstanding.

With its mingling of lament and penitence, Psalm 130 can help the preacher resist the temptation to cast David as a model parent or find in his anguish over Absalom a parable of divine forgiveness. Of course, there are cases to be made for these interpretations: parents should love children no matter what they do. God does forgive traitors. Nevertheless, perhaps something deeper is buried in David's lament. Is he mourning only the death of his son, or is it the whole situation that haunts him, the reality that human beings practice so much violence, so much mercilessness? Psalm 130's acknowledgment that all have fallen short of what God requires may inoculate the preacher from the veneration of David, but the preacher can still empathize with David in his grief. He is not a perfect father, or king, or human being. He is not only caught in, but contributes to, the tenacious web of human cruelty.

Psalm 130 is ripe for use in the context of the confession/assurance of pardon sequence. Verses 1–6 can serve as a call to confession, with verses 7–8 taken up as part of the assurance of pardon. There are also some lovely settings of Psalm 130 for congregational singing, particularly "For You, My God, I Wait" with a melody by David Ward.[2] This could be an effective bridge between the reading of the 2 Samuel text and the sermon, or sung as a response to the preaching of the Word.

ANGELA DIENHART HANCOCK

---

2. See *Psalms for All Seasons: A Complete Psalter for Worship* (Grand Rapids: Calvin Institute of Christian Worship, Faith Alive Christian Resources, and Brazos Press, 2012), 130G.

Ephesians 4:25–5:2

⁴:²⁵So then, putting away falsehood, let all of us speak the truth to our neighbors, for we are members of one another. ²⁶Be angry but do not sin; do not let the sun go down on your anger, ²⁷and do not make room for the devil. ²⁸Thieves must give up stealing; rather let them labor and work honestly with their own hands, so as to have something to share with the needy. ²⁹Let no evil talk come out of your mouths, but only what is useful for building up, as there is need, so that your words may give grace to those who hear. ³⁰And do not grieve the Holy Spirit of God, with which you were marked with a seal for the day of redemption. ³¹Put away from you all bitterness and wrath and anger and wrangling and slander, together with all malice, ³²and be kind to one another, tenderhearted, forgiving one another, as God in Christ has forgiven you. ⁵:¹Therefore be imitators of God, as beloved children, ²and live in love, as Christ loved us and gave himself up for us, a fragrant offering and sacrifice to God.

Commentary 1: Connecting the Reading with Scripture

Though the passage's focus is the manner of future living, the vision for the future is layered on an older foundation. The passage calls for a future marked by the past. Even while they engage the hoped-for potential the writer suggests, readers should keep in mind God's past promises from which that future arises.

The passage itself is noteworthy for its specificity. The writer exhorts with a moral focus by calling for honest and gracious talk, appropriately timed and modulated levels of anger, proper use of one's hands (honest labor to share with the needy), and encouragement of others. It is not clear why these particular specifics arise, as opposed to others. For example, was the author particularly aware of problems with theft (Eph. 4:28)? What is clear, however, is the reasons *why* the author calls the audience to these actions: God's love, sacrifice, and the forgiveness that has come through Jesus Christ. The demands for particular ways of living arise from the particular gift of God in Christ. Because they were "marked with a seal for the day of redemption," they can live honest, caring lives (v. 30). In sum, the passage calls for a life of imitating and living into a new reality as modeled by the love of God. Because they are "beloved

children" of God, certain demands have been placed upon them. These demands, however, flow from what has happened already. So, future living is a result of past action of God and not merely in anticipation of future judgment.

In the lectionary cycle, our text continues many weeks drawn from the Letter to the Ephesians. This week, however, marks a shift from the writer's theological teachings (chaps. 1–3) to ethical exhortations (chaps. 4–6). The shift is marked by the word "therefore" (4:1), and that pivot is important to note when reading the second half of the book. As my NT professor often asked, "What's the 'therefore' there for?" In this case, our pericope should be considered in light of the book's opening three chapters, in which the writer sermonizes about the blessings of God, salvation by grace through faith, and how Christ broke down the wall between Jews and Gentiles. Our passage follows a section in which the phrase "no longer" is used twice. Our passage anticipates a new way of living, an active shift to how the promises of God demand a very practical response. Indeed, the preceding verses juxtapose old and new, former and renewed self. Clothed with a new self, even the likeness of God (4:24), the text exhorts its audience to live into new practices of emotional regulation, generosity, and kindness.

As the book continues, Ephesians contrasts this new way of living with the former "living in darkness" (5:8–11). Indeed, hearers are now to "live as children of light" (v. 8). Importantly, the comprehensive nature of this new way of living is striking. Life in the light makes claims on social and familial relationships, business practices, household order, sexual practices, and even appropriate vocabulary.

As Ephesians wrestles with the implications of this new way of living, the social and cultural contexts of the time loom large. Many scholars argue that the letter is not written to one specific congregation but was an epistle intended to be read and passed along to many communities. Perhaps, given this general audience and in light of the tensions between Jews and Gentiles that are clearly at play in the context, the text focuses on how Christ breaks down the dividing wall between Jew and Gentile, freeing them to live as God's beloved children together. Importantly, then, the ethical injunctions of the passage apply to all. There are not separate instructions for different groups. Because of Christ, together they— and we—are all called to a new way of living.

Given the shift from theological language to more practical implications for living, the preacher may emphasize the practical nature of the other lections for the day. In John 6, Jesus describes himself as the "bread of life." Those fed by him will not be hungry or thirsty; indeed, they will live forever. Yet we know that living into this reality is a significant challenge. Even when we taste and see God's goodness, we may struggle to live out that goodness in our lives. The Ephesians lection details what, practically, it might look like to live into the promise of life in Christ.

In another lection, Psalm 34, we find a hymn of praise, testifying to the deliverance found in God. It could be read as a form of testimony, exalting God because of what God has done. The pairing of this passage with Ephesians allows for the question of how one's very practical ethical decisions may testify to what God has already done. In other words, while it is well and good when our "soul makes its boast in the LORD" (Ps.

34:2), Ephesians 4 reminds us that the words from our mouths and the actions of our hands also matter alongside the praise of our soul.

More broadly, the injunction to imitate God is a theme that connects various parts of Scripture, perhaps particularly portions of the New Testament calling for the imitation of Christ. In the middle of the Sermon on the Mount, Jesus exhorts his audience to "be perfect, therefore, as your heavenly Father is perfect" (Matt. 5:48). In the Letter to the Philippians, Paul introduces the Christ hymn (Phil. 2:5–11) with the invitation to "let the same mind be in you that was in Christ Jesus" (v. 5).

So, too, the juxtaposition of light and darkness, forces of evil and forces for good, is reflected in much of Scripture. In Ephesians, human existence seems to be beset by demonic forces at work in the world. The battle among these forces is more explicit in some areas than others. For example, 1 John engages light/dark language very specifically: "whoever says, 'I am in the light,' while hating a brother or sister, is still in the darkness" (1 John 2:9). So, too, the conclusion of 1 Thessalonians makes the reality clear: "But you, beloved, are not in darkness, . . . for you are all children of light and children of the day; we are not of the night or of darkness" (1 Thess. 5:4–5). The notion that resistance is required underlies much of this lightness and darkness framework. The way of Christ's light is visible, and Christ has dominion over "thrones or dominions or rulers or powers" (Col. 1:16), yet the struggle to consistently live in the light marks the call to discipleship.

A sermon on this passage, therefore, might draw upon the challenge and opportunity of faith's ethical mandates. Even when these are framed correctly as a response to the gift of Christ, living in love is a tall task. The question of *why* we ought to live in this way—speaking truth, giving generously—may present fruitful directions for the preacher. While "good works" on earth are sometimes framed as a way to get into heaven, this passage, even with its specific call to right actions, is predicated on the assumption that "God in Christ has forgiven you" (Eph. 4:32). Further, a sermon could explore the implications of this way of ethical living. Outcomes may include evangelism, healthy relationships, and, depending on the hearer's vocational setting, success or failure at work. If this range seems too wide, a preacher could instead engage a single, particular aspect of faithful living from the list presented.

ADAM J. COPELAND

Commentary 2: Connecting the Reading with the World

The author of Ephesians makes an important move toward ethics in chapter 4. After recounting God's plan, including God "gather[ing] up all things" (Eph. 1:10), offering forgiveness (2:4), and entrusting the church to proclaim and embody the message to all creation (3:10), the author begins this section on the ethical response of the church. Although the church certainly faces disagreement over many points of theology, the most contentious current battles come in the broad area of ethics, that is, how we decide what our faithful response to God's grace is. This letter does not take an explicit stand on contemporary hot-button issues but endorses values and personal/ecclesial characteristics that underlie the church's proper ethical reflection and praxis (see, e.g., 4:2, 15–16, 22–24).

For Ephesians, at the top of the list of values is truth. If the first casualty of war is truth, that aphorism applies equally to church fights at all levels. Whether the falsehoods come in the form of spreading rumors within a local church, posting outrageous whoppers on social media, or engaging in propaganda at the denominational level, the church too often does not protect the truth. The call to truthfulness here invites reflection on why we lie. Too often, especially within the church, we lie in order to win an argument, fight, or dispute. We attack the character of the one with whom we disagree. We distort the position of our opponent. We do these things willfully and consciously, yet consider ourselves the honest ones. Even though rhetoricians warn us that ad hominem arguments, which attack the person, not the idea, are wrong, we use them because they work in one way. The end justifies the means.

The rationale for speaking the truth in Ephesians 4 draws on the relationship between love and trust within the church: "we are members of one another" (4:25). We tend to see only those who agree with us as "members" of the same group. This verse pushes the church to find ways in which disagreeing factions can see each other as "members of one another." If the message of the church truly spreads to the cosmos itself (3:10), our witness should be that we can disagree without stooping to dishonesty. The world, if not the cosmos, needs the witness that the truth matters, even in the midst of intense disagreement. In a world where fact-checkers work overtime, the church should make the commitment to seek the truth, even if we must concede some ground to those with whom we disagree.

The next verse taps into an emotional response to deception. Verse 26 introduces anger to the equation but does not expound on how we should understand it. Whatever the cause of anger, it can wreak destruction on multiple levels. The passage mentions anger both here and in verse 31. Everybody feels anger on occasion, but for some people anger creates real problems. No one can avoid feeling angry, but we must find healthy ways to manage it, to control it, to harness it. Anger can destroy a marriage, a family, a Sunday school class, a church. Just as lying can serve as a useful but destructive tool, so can anger. We can use anger to control others, to get our way, to win an argument, or at least to bully the other person into silence. Unhealthy anger often arises from deep hurt within a person. When I served as a chaplain intern in a psychiatric hospital, the staff had an aphorism: it is easier to feel the anger than the hurt. Anger can mask feelings of helplessness and grief. Displaying anger can make a person feel tough, when inside the person feels vulnerable.

Explosive or too frequent anger can indicate a need for intervention, although such persons often resist intervention, because they use their anger as a weapon. In a group setting, one person's anger can feed on the anger of others.

Sermons may have limited ability to enable people to recognize their problems with anger. Many angry people see not their inability to control their anger but only the cause of their anger. Focusing on the cause shields them from seeing their reaction. Probably, few sermons deal directly and in depth with anger. The church needs such sermons, as fraught with danger as they are, because anger can cause much destruction. The preacher should tread carefully, but it is a path upon which the preacher should venture.

Besides prevarication and anger, the passage also points to a number of vices, any one of which can weaken the church. Although NT admonitions about working hard have been used politically as an excuse to unravel the social safety net, the passage undercuts that type of exegetical manipulation. Working hard serves, in part, to provide resources to share with those in need. The passage encourages honesty and diligence. The Greek phrase translated "evil talk" (*logos sapros*) has some suggestive dimensions. In other contexts, the term *sapros* could mean "rotten," as in rotten food. Certainly, every church has experienced backbiting, negativity, complaints, and other forms of "rotten talk." Some people tear down others to build themselves up.

Bitterness presents a complex problem. We think we gain something by nursing bitterness, even though we can see and feel its unhealthy side, often making us miserable. Bitterness often arises out of the unfairness and tragedy of life. We respond in bitterness to betrayal, bad luck, regrets, missed opportunities. We hold on to the bitterness because we cannot make life treat us in an evenhanded way. By raising the issue of grieving the Holy Spirit, Ephesians lifts the discussion out of the psychological and a focus on group dynamics. Unchecked anger, bitterness, snark, and malice do more than hurt the individuals and others within the church. These traits and actions also affect the Spirit, who empowers and animates the church. Our psychological baggage does more than cause conflict within the church. Our neediness and lack of self-control bring grief and sorrow to the Godhead.

The author of Ephesians falls into the "trap" that catches many preachers. The passage spends several verses talking about the negative attitudes and behaviors we ought to avoid. Then, the reader sees only a few words about the positive side of Christian ethics, the life of faith. The external behaviors the author advocates seem straightforward enough: kindness, forgiveness, love. All of the Christian virtues that come in 4:32–5:2 sound simple on the surface. Nevertheless, each one requires attention and God's help to carry out. The Holy Spirit enables us to live out these virtues. We often have to make a conscious effort to love, even if we can decide what love means in a particular situation. We often have to fight through many feelings in order to love. Even when we cannot call up the feelings, we can act in kindness. The actions of kindness can help to elicit love when we cannot muster it any other way. Each episode of forgiveness carries its own complication. We may forgive but still end a relationship. We may forgive but recognize the need to protect ourselves. We may have to practice forgiveness more than once for a particular person, a particular misdeed. We may have to forgive persons who do not admit the harm they have caused us. The passage teaches that love, kindness, and forgiveness do not arise only within us as individuals. The church seeks to become a community that practices these virtues, even though we now fall far short. We do this with God's example and help.

CHARLES L. AARON JR.

John 6:35, 41–51

³⁵Jesus said to them, "I am the bread of life. Whoever comes to me will never be hungry, and whoever believes in me will never be thirsty. . . ."

⁴¹Then the Jews began to complain about him because he said, "I am the bread that came down from heaven." ⁴²They were saying, "Is not this Jesus, the son of Joseph, whose father and mother we know? How can he now say, 'I have come down from heaven'?" ⁴³Jesus answered them, "Do not complain among yourselves. ⁴⁴No one can come to me unless drawn by the Father who sent me; and I will raise that person up on the last day. ⁴⁵It is written in the prophets, 'And they shall all be taught by God.' Everyone who has heard and learned from the Father comes to me. ⁴⁶Not that anyone has seen the Father except the one who is from God; he has seen the Father. ⁴⁷Very truly, I tell you, whoever believes has eternal life. ⁴⁸I am the bread of life. ⁴⁹Your ancestors ate the manna in the wilderness, and they died. ⁵⁰This is the bread that comes down from heaven, so that one may eat of it and not die. ⁵¹I am the living bread that came down from heaven. Whoever eats of this bread will live forever; and the bread that I will give for the life of the world is my flesh."

Commentary 1: Connecting the Reading with Scripture

This reading is part of the larger section in John's Gospel sometimes called the Book of Signs, in which Jesus performs various miraculous feats with symbolic import. Each sign, including the feeding of the five thousand in this chapter, is to be interpreted through the lens of John 20:30: "But these [signs] are written so that you may come to believe that Jesus is the Messiah, the Son of God, and that through believing you may have life in his name."

These acts of Jesus are more than miracles designed to benefit the recipient; they are intended to point people to Jesus, convince them to believe in Jesus, and receive from Jesus life in his name. John's Gospel is no mere on-location reporter of the ministry of Jesus. John is also a theological commentator, an expositor of the truths and meaning beyond the events he is narrating.

Recorded in all four Gospels, the feeding story is the fourth of John's list of seven signs, a kind of pivotal linchpin to what he wants to proclaim about Jesus. The story not only contains all the theological features of the other signs; it is also

the most visceral, physical, and tangible of all the signs of Jesus in this section of John. It speaks of hunger and nourishment, bread and flesh, blood and wine, the basic necessities of human survival.

In so doing, John creates a critical convergence between divine and earthly reality, in which Jesus comes to meet our spiritual needs in real, earthly terms. One cannot help but read John 6 in light of the Gospel's prologue in John 1. The Word has become flesh (chap. 1), and now that flesh will be broken as the bread of life (chap. 6). That life that is the light of all people (chap. 1) will be offered so that others may live (chap. 6). The Word that has come to dwell among us (chap. 1) will call us to abide in him, and we can thereby be in relationship to the Father (chap. 6).

Given the significance of signs in John's Gospel and of this sign in particular, it should be no surprise then that the lectionary spends five weeks in this chapter alone and that Propers 14–16 even overlap parts of these texts. Believing in Jesus as the bread of life, whose flesh and blood provide us the means of true life and abiding in God, is a critical part of Johannine theology, Christian belief, and sacramental practice.

To further draw the reader's attention to the meaning of the feeding story, John incorporates some familiar OT tropes and archetypes and draws a clear connection to two predominant narratives in Jewish history: the exodus and the exile.

Consider first the setting of the story. The feeding takes place "on the other side" of the Sea of Galilee, such that to follow Jesus, the people have to cross a large body of water in order to find him. This echoes the Israelites' crossing of the Red Sea in Exodus 14. Even after the people are fed by Jesus, this pericope opens with the people grumbling at Jesus, a nod to the murmuring of the Israelites against Moses in Exodus 16. The clearest connection to the exodus is made by Jesus himself, who reminds the people that just as the Israelites received manna from God in the wilderness, he has been sent by God to be their nourishment.

Of these three references to the exodus, it is the grumbling of the people on which John chooses to do further theological reflection. Whereas the Israelites grumbled against Moses because they were physically hungry, longing for Egypt, and resenting their current state of disillusionment, the people in John 6 are angry at Jesus for a different reason. They are incredulous about the claims Jesus has been making about his divine identity and purpose. In 6:42, they reiterate his earthly biography, his human ancestry, and express disbelief at the possibility that he can be anything more than a human being. "How can he now say, 'I have come down from heaven'?" they say.

Jesus' response is telling. Unlike Moses, who had to intercede before God on behalf of the grumbling Israelites, Jesus tells them that he is in fact God's divine presence among them. To be in his presence is to be drawn into God's presence by God's power (John 6:44); not only should his divine personhood go unquestioned, it need not be feared. In fact, it ought to be revered and worshiped.

To emphasize that last point, Jesus refers to the second of the two major narratives in Israelite history: the return from exile. In verse 45, he paraphrases the great prophet Isaiah from Isaiah 54:13: "All your children shall be taught by the LORD, and great shall be the prosperity of your children."

Just as God was directly leading the Israelites back to their homeland after years in Babylonian exile without the need of a liberating figure like Moses, Jesus is directly leading the people to new life through belief in his name. He is more than his human biography, just as the bread is more than earthly food. He is calling the people to look past the earthliness of the signs they can see with their eyes and believe that to which the signs are pointing: his divinity, his messianic purpose, and his invitation to them for new life.

A sermon based on this text might get to the heart of a person's perception of the life of faith and how a person might perceive what Jesus means to them. First, it might center on our penchant toward grumbling and complaining when it comes to who Jesus is. The people's disappointment in Jesus' words may have stemmed from their earlier efforts to crown him king and leader of their political opposition party (v. 15). How might we veer away from an anthropocentric view of Jesus, in which we expect him to relate to us on our terms, and mitigate the inevitable disappointment and complaint that ensue? The sermon might therefore focus on the opening words of Jesus' response, "Do not complain among yourselves" (v. 43).

Second, a sermon might challenge us to draw deeper into a *relationship* with Jesus, not just *knowing about him*. Just as the people's view of Jesus is too small, confining him by their preconceived notions of who he may be, how might this text invite us to gain a fuller understanding of Jesus? Not just as someone to get to know but someone in whose life we are called to fully participate? How might the Christian faith be not just a set of propositions but a way of life in which we are called into deeper commitment?

Finally, a sermon on this text might invite us to recall God's saving activity in our personal histories. Just as John recounts God's deliverance in the exodus and the exile, how might this text renew our gratitude for God's prevenient grace?

Jesus portrays himself as more than a liberating leader in the style of Moses; he names himself as the very presence of God, a bread from heaven that people are not simply to admire. They are being drawn into union with him, to eat of his body, and thereby be in union with the God who created them. To do so is to gain new life, to "eat and never die."

MAGREY R. DEVEGA

Commentary 2: Connecting the Reading with the World

This chapter spins outward from Jesus feeding five thousand hungry people until all were satisfied: "from the fragments of the five barley loaves, left by those who had eaten, they filled twelve baskets." (Evidently, the people had eaten all the fish!) For five weeks, churches that follow the lectionary are reading through this sixth chapter of John. People will hear about bread until the end of August. By then, many preachers may run out of things to say about bread, which could explain why so many clergy go on vacation in August!

Today's reading marks the midpoint in this chapter and begins by repeating a verse from last week's Gospel: "I am the bread of life. Whoever comes to me will never be hungry, and whoever believes in me will never be thirsty" (John 6:35). This is an assuring word of hope, but there is a hint of danger in the verses that follow. We may wish John had stopped after Jesus said, "I am the bread of life." Something shifts after that verse, something that alerts us to one of the dangers of John's Gospel. "The crowd" that ate on the hillside and followed Jesus around the sea becomes "the Jews" for the rest of this chapter.

This is the first time in John that the people of Galilee have been referred to as "the Jews." As this chapter unfolds, we hear a change in language: "The Jews began to complain about him because he said, 'I am the bread that came down from heaven'" (v. 41). A bit later, Jesus says to them, "Your ancestors ate the manna in the wilderness, and they died" (v. 49).

Your ancestors? Why did Jesus not say, "Our ancestors . . ."? After all, Jesus was a Jew, his disciples were Jews, most of the women who followed him were Jews, including his mother, Mary. Jesus appears to be standing over against "the Jews" as though he were not one of them.

"Your ancestors ate the manna in the wilderness, and they died." Manna here seems to become a death-sign in contrast to Jesus, the life-sign.

This is John the evangelist speaking. By the time John wrote his account of Jesus' life, the split had widened between Jews who believed Jesus was the Messiah and those who did not. There was yet no distinct separation between "Jews" (who were a diverse group) and "Christians" (who did not yet exist as a separate religion). The animosity between Jesus-believing Jews and non-Jesus-believing Jews leaked back into the Gospel of John. Jesus' enemies are not only Pharisees or particular Jewish leaders; they are "the Jews." This opposition builds until the last days of Jesus' life. As John tells the passion story—the Gospel often read on Good Friday—the Jews seem responsible for Jesus' death (19:7, 12, 14–16).

Good Friday is a difficult time to preach a sermon about John's use of the phrase "the Jews." Today would be a good time. Why should we do this? Because NT texts, including John, have fertilized the soil where anti-Semitism has flourished. Mary Boys's book *Redeeming Our Sacred Story* traces this tragic history and offers new ways of telling the story without demeaning and damning Jews. She begins with NT texts, then traces what happened in the centuries after those texts were written. In the medieval period, "Jews were portrayed as less than human, as usurers, bribers, and secret killers who needed the blood of Christian children for their Passover rituals."[1] In next week's Gospel, Jesus will say, "Those who eat my flesh and drink my blood have eternal life" (6:54). Was there any connection between the blood of Christian children and drinking the blood of Jesus?

Jewish people were driven out of many countries, and the Christ-killer charge followed them

---

1. Mary C. Boys, *Redeeming Our Sacred Story: The Death of Jesus and Relations between Jews and Christians* (New York: Paulist, 2013), 138.

wherever they moved. From 1923 to 1945, the German tabloid *Der Stürmer* kept the Christ-killer charge alive. On Easter Sunday 1933, that paper featured a sketch of a Nazi soldier and a German woman gazing at the crucified Jesus, a church steeple visible in the background. The caption read:

> The Jews nailed Christ onto the cross and thought he was dead. He is risen. They nailed Germany to the cross and thought it was dead, and it is risen, more glorious than ever before.[2]

Germany was defeated in that war, but anti-Semitism was not. Jews have been blamed not only for killing Jesus but for controlling the economy, culture, and the media. Media have sometimes added fuel to anti-Semitic flames.

Mel Gibson's movie *The Passion of the Christ* was released in 2004. When the movie premiered, reporters interviewed people outside theaters. In one news broadcast, a woman exiting the theater told the reporter, "Now we know who killed Jesus." That movie made $612 million worldwide, the highest grossing Christian film ever made. It is likely that more people saw the movie than read the NT.

Years after that movie appeared in theaters, anti-Semitism has increased in the United States. In August 2017, white nationalists rallied at the University of Virginia under the theme "Unite the Right." They chanted, "Jews will not replace us," as they marched with torches reminiscent of KKK rallies. Hateful words turned to tragic violence on October 27, 2018, at a synagogue in Pittsburgh. A gunman murdered eleven worshipers and wounded six more, an act that mocked the synagogue's name, "Tree of Life." Not only did he want to kill Jews, but he was also angry about the congregation's work to resettle refugees. Exactly six months after the killings at Tree of Life, a gunman disrupted services at Congregation Chabad in Poway, California, on the last day of Passover. He killed one and wounded three, including the rabbi. The gunman had posted a message online that Jews were ruining the world—not so different from the caption that ran at the bottom of *Der Stürmer's* front page: "The Jews are our misfortune."

After the first synagogue attack, Sara Bloomfield, director of the US Holocaust Memorial Museum, issued a statement: "Moving forward this must serve as yet another wake-up call that antisemitism is a growing and deadly menace. . . . All Americans must unequivocally condemn it and confront it in wherever it appears."[3] Surely that call includes those of us who preach. John the evangelist had no way of knowing that six million Jews would perish in the Holocaust or that worshipers would be gunned down in synagogues in more recent history. We live on this side of the Holocaust. When we hear John say, "The Jews began to complain about [Jesus]," we hear with a tragic history and a violent present in our ears.

Jews and Christians are yearning for the bread of life alongside each other, not in the same way, but yearning still. The prophet Isaiah called the people of Israel to abundant life: "Ho, everyone who thirsts, come to the waters; and you that have no money, come, buy and eat! . . . Why do you spend your money for that which is not bread, and your labor for that which does not satisfy?" (Isa. 55:1a, 2).

There is plenty of bread to go around.

BARBARA K. LUNDBLAD

2. Boys, *Redeeming Our Sacred Story*, 143.

3. Shannon Van Sant and James Doubek, "California Synagogue Shooting Investigated As a Hate Crime After 1 Killed, 3 Injured," n.p.; https://www.npr.org/2019/04/27/717849871/injuries-reported-in-shooting-at-california-synagogue.

Proper 15 (Sunday between August 14 and August 20)

Proverbs 9:1–6 and 1 Kings 2:10–12;   Ephesians 5:15–20
   3:3–14   John 6:51–58
Psalm 34:9–14 and Psalm 111

Proverbs 9:1–6

¹Wisdom has built her house,
    she has hewn her seven pillars.
²She has slaughtered her animals, she has mixed her wine,
    she has also set her table.
³She has sent out her servant-girls, she calls
    from the highest places in the town,
⁴"You that are simple, turn in here!"
    To those without sense she says,
⁵"Come, eat of my bread
    and drink of the wine I have mixed.
⁶Lay aside immaturity, and live,
    and walk in the way of insight."

1 Kings 2:10–12; 3:3–14

2:10Then David slept with his ancestors, and was buried in the city of David. ¹¹The time that David reigned over Israel was forty years; he reigned seven years in Hebron, and thirty-three years in Jerusalem. ¹²So Solomon sat on the throne of his father David; and his kingdom was firmly established. . . .

3:3Solomon loved the LORD, walking in the statutes of his father David; only, he sacrificed and offered incense at the high places. ⁴The king went to Gibeon to sacrifice there, for that was the principal high place; Solomon used to offer a thousand burnt offerings on that altar. ⁵At Gibeon the LORD appeared to Solomon in a dream by night; and God said, "Ask what I should give you." ⁶And Solomon said, "You have shown great and steadfast love to your servant my father David, because he walked before you in faithfulness, in righteousness, and in uprightness of heart toward you; and you have kept for him this great and steadfast love, and have given him a son to sit on his throne today. ⁷And now, O LORD my God, you have made your servant king in place of my father David, although I am only a little child; I do not know how to go out or come in. ⁸And your servant is in the midst of the people whom you have chosen, a great people, so numerous they cannot be numbered or counted. ⁹Give your servant therefore an understanding mind to govern your people, able to discern between good and evil; for who can govern this your great people?"

¹⁰It pleased the Lord that Solomon had asked this. ¹¹God said to him, "Because you have asked this, and have not asked for yourself long life or riches, or for the life of your enemies, but have asked for yourself understanding to discern what is right, ¹²I now do according to your word. Indeed I give you a wise and

discerning mind; no one like you has been before you and no one like you shall arise after you. [13]I give you also what you have not asked, both riches and honor all your life; no other king shall compare with you. [14]If you will walk in my ways, keeping my statutes and my commandments, as your father David walked, then I will lengthen your life."

Commentary 1: Connecting the Reading with Scripture

In the first of this week's two lectionary readings, Wisdom in Proverbs 9:1–6 builds her house, firmly established with seven sturdy pillars. In this well-founded home, Wisdom emerges as the hostess par excellence. She offers bread and wine to her guests. In compelling fashion, Proverbs images this bread and wine as a rich symbol of abundant life and of what it means to become wise and "walk in the way of insight" (Prov. 9:6).

Wisdom's call goes out everywhere, calling from the highest places to whoever has ears to hear to come join the feast and thus grow in wisdom and understanding (vv. 3–6). However, we should not miss that 9:1–6, as well as the second lectionary reading for this week (a selection of verses from 1 Kgs. 2–3), both reflect the lives of the upper class. So in Proverbs 9:3, Wisdom is said to have servant girls whom she sends out to deliver her invitation all across the city. Moreover, Wisdom's feast consists of the most luxurious foods, including an abundance of meat and wine that rightly can be described as affluent people's food, that is, the food regularly gracing the tables of kings. Such ties to luxury and privilege likely resonated in a sociocultural context that tended to associate wisdom with the educated, male elite.

We might wonder if much has changed in the intervening years. Think, for instance, of James 2:1–7, where followers of Jesus have to be reminded to turn their eyes to the poor, even as we are tempted to privilege the wealthy. In addition, and probably offering the strongest link to our second lectionary text, Proverbs 8:15 teaches that it is by means of *Wisdom* that *kings* reign. At least, this is how they ought to reign!

In 1 Kings 2:10–12, the royal succession is firmly established as Solomon takes his place on the throne of his father David, who had ruled for forty years. In subsequent chapters, we will see how Solomon quite literally will be building a house, as well as a temple where God will dwell and which will serve, like the pillared house built by Wisdom, as a space for stability and order in the community (1 Kgs. 8:13).

The lectionary then continues with 3:3–14, in which 1 Kings describes just how much this newly inaugurated king is ruling by means of Wisdom as spelled out in Proverbs 8:15. King Solomon is said to love the Lord God (cf. Prov. 9:6) and to walk in the statutes of his father, David. This is evident in the way King Solomon sacrifices: in the right place and in the right manner (1 Kgs. 3:3–4).

In Solomon's dream, this theme of walking in the ways of his father, David, who himself walked in the ways of God by exhibiting faithfulness, righteousness, and an upright heart (v. 6), is further explicated. Continuing the theme of kings ruling by means of Wisdom, the one thing Solomon asks of God is to be able to govern with wisdom, to have insight and understanding, to discern between good and evil (v. 9). Aligning with one of Wisdom literature's basic tenets that doing good is rewarded by a long life, riches, and honor (Prov. 3:2, 16–18; 8:18; 16:31), God goes on to promise Solomon that he will be given all these things if he continues to walk in God's ways, which means keeping the statutes and commandments just as his father David had done (1 Kgs. 3:14).

It is quite interesting that this pericope also ends with King Solomon offering a feast to his servants in addition to the burnt offerings and peace offerings dedicated to God. In this way, the king's identification with Wisdom, who offers her own feast in Proverbs 9:1–6, has been accomplished on a symbolic level.

When reading together two lectionary texts that make such a compelling connection between wisdom, food, governance, and prosperity, it is important to keep the following critical perspectives in mind. First, as mentioned before, we should interrogate the notion of class when reading this text. We can and should ask where all the luxury goods that adorn the feasts of both Wisdom and King Solomon came from. The frightening vision of 1 Samuel 8 about the propensity of all kings to extract wealth from peasants and employ forced labor to build their great building projects should not be forgotten. The rich food that is generously provided by both the king and Wisdom comes at a cost to the poor and the powerless. A full account of these texts must weigh these costs.

Second, the picture of the king ruling by means of wisdom could be read as a declaration of what truly ought to be the hallmark of a good king. As in Psalm 72, the ideal king's reign should be marked by understanding and discernment as he is called to reign in generosity and justice. Such a wise king ought to ensure that the poor and needy will be cared for (Ps. 72:4, 12–14), for it is the widow and orphan and the poor and the foreigner that are most in need of food, clothing, and justice (Deut. 10:18).

Thus, as we read about the houses that both King Solomon and Wisdom have built, we rightly wonder whether this sanctuary will be open to all or only to the powerful and the privileged. Will this temple actually be turned into a site of injustice that continues to exclude the marginalized? A great example of the significance of this question is evident in the intrabiblical struggle to undo the exclusionary laws of Deuteronomy 23:1–3 that prohibit eunuchs, Moabites, Ammonites, and children born from incestuous acts to become part of the congregation of God. In addition, we can find a critique of exclusion as Isaiah exhorts the importance of "maintain[ing] justice, and do[ing] what is right" (Isa. 56:1) and challenges the community by prophesying that those eunuchs and foreigners who walk in the ways of the Lord are welcome in "[God's] house [that] shall be called a house of prayer for all peoples" (vv. 4–7).

Thus, reading against the grain of the elite, educated, male audience likely envisioned by 1 Kings and Proverbs alike, we can affirm that Wisdom's call does indeed go out broadly, to the entire city, reaching to the farthest corners, where the poorest of the poor and the most excluded of the excluded reside. A truly good and just king who reigns with Wisdom will do no less.

Finally, the metaphor of Wisdom as host is continued in the NT in the form of Jesus as the Wisdom of God who frequently provides food and drink (e.g., Matt. 14:15–21; Mark 6:35–44; Luke 9:10–17; John 6:5–15). Jesus' generous provision of food documented throughout the Gospels culminates in the event of the Last Supper (Matt. 26:26–29; Mark 14:22–25; Luke 22:17–20), in which bread and wine serve as a powerful means of what Jane Webster has described as *Ingesting Jesus*, the title of her book on food and drink imagery in the Gospel of John.[1] In this regard, it is important to underscore that the Jesus who is Host, the very Wisdom of God (1 Cor. 1:24), crosses borders and invites all to join the feast. Indeed, Jesus as the Wisdom of God is on the side of the poor and needy and desolate. Jesus, the Wisdom of God, ultimately calls us to change how we think about not just Solomon when he asks to rule by means of wisdom but also every king since.

L. JULIANA CLAASSENS

Commentary 2: Connecting the Reading with the World

These readings bring a strong focus on wisdom, inviting the liturgist to make the theme of "living well" a centerpiece of today's service. Both of the psalms reflect it with their focus on "the fear of the LORD" (Pss. 34:9; 111:10). The exhortation of the Letter to the Ephesians to "be careful then how you live" (Eph. 5:15) encapsulates the call to wisdom; care is to be exercised around

---

1. Jane S. Webster, *Ingesting Jesus: Eating and Drinking in the Gospel of John* (Atlanta: Society of Biblical Literature, 2003).

being "wise" rather than "unwise." The author of the letter then applies this distinction to personal behavior and the worshiping life of the believer. The OT readings take a broader view of what constitutes wise and unwise living, and in the case of the writer of our Proverbs reading, centers it on the "fear of the LORD." The Proverbs reading paints a poetic picture of wisdom, or "living carefully," while the reading from 1 Kings invites reflection on what that might look like in one life.

Proverbs 9:1–6. These verses are part of a beautiful cameo on wisdom presented in chapter 9 as a whole and as a culmination to the first eight chapters of Proverbs; as such they are best applied in the context of the cameo as a whole. The central section of the chapter (Prov. 9:7–12) highlights and instances the organizing concept of the book of Proverbs, that the key to wisdom is the "fear of the LORD" (v. 10).

This is framed by contrasting pictures of the wise woman (vv. 1–6) and the foolish woman (vv. 13–18) as personifications of wisdom and folly. The character of Wisdom is evident in the metaphor. It lives in a magnificent house (v. 1). Wisdom's preparation for the great banquet is immaculate: the food and wine are prepared and their presentation carefully arranged (v. 2). Then the guests are invited "from the highest places" (v. 3). Since the highest place in a town is typically the site of a temple, this implies that Wisdom's house is a place of worship around which people gather. This invitation from the highest places is not to the elite but to "the simple" and "those without sense" (v. 4). The word translated as "simple" is from the same root as "immaturity" (v. 6). Neither term is a negative one; rather, both are more indicative of those who have not yet grown into the choice between Wisdom and Folly. "Those without sense" are literally "those who lack heart," which implies those whose will at this point is indecisive.

The wisdom values of this reading are lifted into sharp relief by verses 13–18, which are evidently intended to form a contrast with Woman Wisdom. Unlike her, Woman Folly has done no preparations for guests. She sits outside at the "high places of the town" (v. 14), seeking to distract the immature—the "simple" and "those

without sense"—on their way to the "highest places" (v. 3). She has no substance to offer and that which she has is stolen; she offers only secrecy and the temporary thrill of breaking the rules (v. 17). Ultimately, her way leads only to the place of the dead.

A sensitive handling of this passage must face contemporary gender sensitivities. The fact is that the preservation of the son from loose women is a key organizing metaphor in the book of Proverbs, and women may wonder where they find themselves in that taxonomy, especially since they are somewhat typecast by Proverbs into a "virgin or whore" binary. It is important to acknowledge the pain that this causes many, with thanks that the one who fulfills wisdom consistently breaks down this binary. Today's epistle reading stops just short of the egalitarian instruction to men and women to "be subject to one another" (Eph. 5:21).

Beyond that, the Proverbs passage is disconcertingly relevant to a time of polarized views, manipulation of information, and the triumph of style over substance. It is a reminder to worshipers to discern well the "stolen water" and "bread eaten in secret" (v. 17) of public and published life, and a challenge to imbibe our thinking at the table set by Wisdom. It also calls those who have influence to use it to "turn the simple" toward wisdom and not death.

1 Kings 2:10–12; 3:3–14. From an exalted reflection on wisdom and folly, personalized as two types of women, we turn to one particular man facing a choice. Would he look for the easy pickings of Woman Folly or the better prepared, and perhaps less exciting, fare of Woman Wisdom? The opening verses of chapter 3 are David's final charge to his son Solomon. Effectively, David hands over the unfinished business of his convoluted reign. Rather than instructing him in the way of wisdom in the face of this complexity, he seems content with the hopeful, "You are a wise man; you will know what to do" (1 Kgs. 2:9)! Now suddenly Solomon is in charge.

The remainder of chapter 2 describes the realpolitik required of a new king. This in itself is a pointer to wisdom as something that is hard won and achieved in the heat of daily

Openness to the World and to God

Israel's wise men began with the conviction that there is an order in things, and they therefore pushed their students into the fight between making and losing sense. Only a fool will dispense, to his own disadvantage, with trying to overhear those regulations that support life. But the fight is not won with the will to knowledge only. All knowledge about the world and man begins with knowledge about God. The fear of the Lord, knowledge about God, is the beginning of all wisdom. It is never true that the world refuses when we ask it about God and his rule. On the contrary, it becomes at once both quite real and mysterious only in light of this question. I see the actual achievement of these wise men in their awareness, with wide-awake common sense, that this world is governed through and through by God. Only when one begins with that awareness, i.e., from this openness to the world and to God, will one understand one of the most profound of Israel's insights: the truly wise person is only the one who thinks himself not wise. To think of oneself as wise is a sure sign of foolishness.

Gerhard von Rad, *God at Work in Israel*, trans. John H. Marks (Nashville: Abingdon, 1980), 181–82.

choices and compromises, often having to tidy up messes in the hope of achieving something better—the very stuff, in fact, of most people in paid employment who are hearing the word of God this Sunday. Wisdom founded in the fear of God is for the hurly-burly of daily life on all seven days of the week.

Then Solomon turns to God to ask for the wisdom that his father David assumed he already had. The prayer and subsequent dream (3:3–14) is almost textbook Proverbs 9. Wisdom is sought in the highest place and in the context of worship. Solomon seeks the understanding and discernment that Woman Wisdom offers those who feast at her table. God promises this wisdom as long as Solomon walks in God's ways (v. 14). Then he receives the "wise and discerning mind" (v. 12) that the Wise Woman of Proverbs 9 offers the simple and immature. The feast Solomon then puts on for all his servants is perhaps an unconscious reflection of Solomon's sense of having been well fed by wisdom (v. 15).

Given the gendered portrayal of wisdom that we are seeing, the opening and closing of 1 Kings 3, which frame Solomon's dream and answered prayer, are telling. Famously, Solomon's first test of God's wisdom is the case of two women arguing over the surviving child (vv. 16–23). By offering to cut the child in two, Solomon flushes out the real mother, the one willing to sacrifice herself for her child. Are these two women perhaps microcosms of Woman Wisdom and Woman Folly? One seeks the highest good, while the other is content with a counterfeit: style over substance, the very choices that Solomon will face throughout his life.

Ominously, chapter 3 opens with Solomon's marriage to the daughter of Pharaoh (v. 1). NRSV calls it a "marriage alliance," reflecting the Hebrew text, which focuses on Solomon's becoming Pharaoh's son-in-law, rather than on the marriage itself. There is little possibility that this was a love match, and so the seeds of Solomon's later failures are sown. Solomon's distraction by many foreign women is spelled out in stark detail in 1 Kings 11:1–8; he becomes distracted by the false pleasures promised by Woman Folly of Proverbs 9.

Taking care not to imply in any way that men's distractions are women's fault, the preacher today could challenge congregants who face regular and overwhelming choices, not to settle for the easy and the stolen and the gratifying. The hard way is often the best way. By losing sight of that, Solomon lost a kingdom for his successors (1 Kgs. 11:12).

TIM MEADOWCROFT

Proper 15 (Sunday between August 14 and August 20)

Psalm 34:9–14

[9]O fear the LORD, you his holy ones,
   for those who fear him have no want.
[10]The young lions suffer want and hunger,
   but those who seek the LORD lack no good thing.

[11]Come, O children, listen to me;
   I will teach you the fear of the LORD.
[12]Which of you desires life,
   and covets many days to enjoy good?
[13]Keep your tongue from evil,
   and your lips from speaking deceit.
[14]Depart from evil, and do good;
   seek peace, and pursue it.

Psalm 111

[1]Praise the LORD!
I will give thanks to the LORD with my whole heart,
   in the company of the upright, in the congregation.
[2]Great are the works of the LORD,
   studied by all who delight in them.
[3]Full of honor and majesty is his work,
   and his righteousness endures forever.
[4]He has gained renown by his wonderful deeds;
   the LORD is gracious and merciful.
[5]He provides food for those who fear him;
   he is ever mindful of his covenant.
[6]He has shown his people the power of his works,
   in giving them the heritage of the nations.
[7]The works of his hands are faithful and just;
   all his precepts are trustworthy.
[8]They are established forever and ever,
   to be performed with faithfulness and uprightness.
[9]He sent redemption to his people;
   he has commanded his covenant forever.
   Holy and awesome is his name.
[10]The fear of the LORD is the beginning of wisdom;
   all those who practice it have a good understanding.
   His praise endures forever.

Connecting the Psalm with Scripture and Worship

Psalm 34:9–14. "The fear of the LORD" is a theme in Psalm 34:9–14. In its opening verses, the psalm features testimony intermingled with instruction, but in this portion, instruction takes center stage. Verse 9 admonishes the "holy ones" to fear God, but surely, if they are "holy ones" do they not already fear God? Perhaps this highlights the way that "fearing" is not a state of being or an idea but a practice, a relationship, something in motion. At any rate the psalmist believes some dimension of it can be taught (Ps. 34:11). This is one place in the psalm where advice is given that indicates what it looks like to fear the Lord: do not use words to do bad things, run away from evil, do good, chase after peace. These are broad categories, though, and the psalmist does not unpack them further.

Perhaps most interesting is the pedagogical approach of the psalmist/teacher in this section, framing this instruction with a question, Which of you wants to live? The assumption is that deep, enduring, satisfying existence is bound up with fear of the Lord, and manifests itself in honest speech, righteous paths, good works, and a hunger for peace.

Psalm 34 can sound like some sort of prosperity gospel, indeed; verse 10 declares that lions go hungry but those who seek God will have everything they need. It helps to keep in mind that Psalm 34 is written by one who has experienced a recent deliverance, and those high expectations shape the whole. This section of the psalm is a summons to "holy ones," to "children," to fear the Lord, thus discovering not just a way of life but the way that means life.

Proverbs 9:1–6 is also an invitation to come, taste, see, and live. Wisdom in this text is an architect, a stonemason, a butcher, a vintner, a hostess, and a boss. She is throwing a lavish party for "the simple," that is, those who by virtue of youth or stubbornness have not yet committed themselves to the practice of the fear of the Lord. Note that only a few verses after this reading ends, we encounter the foundational conviction of the book of Proverbs: "The fear

of the LORD is the beginning of wisdom" (Prov. 9:10). In verse 5, Wisdom invites the uncommitted to "taste and see," that is, to experience the satisfaction of this way for themselves. This resonates with the approach of Psalm 34, which also has a "taste and see" motif (Ps. 34:8).

Proverbs 9:1–6 reads like a parable, and its lack of specificity is both a challenge and an opportunity for the contemporary preacher. A sermon on Proverbs 9:1–6 might include something of a roll call of some of the other times in Scripture when invitations to "come and live" have gone out, and this section of Psalm 34 (perhaps including v. 8) would work beautifully among them.

Psalm 34 is assigned to be read in sections over the course of three Sundays (Proper 14–16), but if the opening portion is not read the previous week, it would provide a helpful introduction to include it in the reading. For contexts where responsorial psalms are the norm, there is a tuneful setting of Psalm 34 that features verses 9–22, using the familiar cadences of verse 8 ("Taste and see the goodness of the Lord") as the refrain.[1]

Psalm 111. The singer of Psalm 111 is overflowing with gratitude. Unlike many other such thanksgiving psalms, however, this one is not the testimony of an individual who was delivered from some personal danger, toil, or snare and lived to sing about it. Rather, Psalm 111 thanks God for the things God has done in relation to the people of Israel in the context of covenant relationship. It is a public recounting of those wonder-inducing deeds "in the company of the upright, in the congregation" (Ps. 111:1). Embedded in verse 2 is the rationale for the recitation of actions already well known: God's works are "studied" by those who celebrate them. Public repetition, command performances, are part of what it means to praise God.

The bulk of the psalm (vv. 3–9) declares all the ways God's actions are Halleluiah worthy and names God's interventions on Israel's

---

1. The psalm tone is ST. MEINRAD VIII, with refrain by Robert E. Kreutz. See *The Psalter: Psalms and Canticles for Singing* (Louisville, KY: Westminster John Knox, 1993), 33.

behalf. It should be noted that the latter is done with a certain subtlety, at least for readers far removed in time and space. The exodus narrative is in the deep background, and so the mention of food evokes manna in the wilderness, the "heritage of the nations" (v. 6) the land of promise, and so forth. A world of stories lies behind the psalmist's list.

The final verse of the psalm is something of a surprise, turning from the listing and praising to offer some advice to the congregation. Whatever it means to "fear" the Lord, it is not just emotional or intellectual, but lived, practiced. It is participation in a ceaseless tradition of remembrance and worship, the rhythms of obedience and praise. This participation, the psalmist says, is the "beginning of wisdom," its incubator, we might say.

The reading from 1 Kings also has the beginning of wisdom in view. The text depicts a Solomon who practices the fear of the Lord: obeying the law, making numerous sacrifices, speaking to God with appropriate humility. It is worth noting that Solomon's address, just like Psalm 111, includes the recitation of the things God has done; in his case, it is a description of the things God did for his father David, things that culminated in Solomon's ascension to the throne. God responds to Solomon's "fear" by giving him the wisdom he requests (along with a bunch of other goodies). Solomon test-drives this gift soon after with resounding success.

Those who know the full arc of Solomon's story know that he will not always be wise. What are we to make of this? Psalm 111 might help the preacher think through this conundrum. The psalm is clear that wisdom is not something humans possess, but something that is given. It grows out of the practice of "fear of the LORD," that is, the practice of attention to God's work and God's precepts. It emerges in this intense relationship and cannot be separated from it. In the 1 Kings text, Solomon does practice fear, and from that fear, by God's initiative, wisdom begins. However, there will come a time when Solomon does not fear, is not attentive to the things of God, does not participate in the rhythms of obedience and praise. When that happens, wisdom fades. Psalm 111 (along with Solomon's whole story), can help the preacher explore the ways that the categories "wise" and "foolish" are not static but fluid.

Because the allusions to the exodus narrative are subtle in Psalm 111, it might be illuminating to project a series of relevant images while the text is read in worship, evoking the deep music beneath the surface. The psalm also works well if read by a number of lectors scattered throughout the worship space, each taking a line. All can then join together in unison on verse 10. The adventurous might also experiment with the very last phrase of verse 10 ("His praise endures forever"), having each lector repeat it a few times, staggering the entrances to give the effect of something that reverberates, and then gradually letting this cacophony fade into the next element of worship.

ANGELA DIENHART HANCOCK

Ephesians 5:15–20

[15]Be careful then how you live, not as unwise people but as wise, [16]making the most of the time, because the days are evil. [17]So do not be foolish, but understand what the will of the Lord is. [18]Do not get drunk with wine, for that is debauchery; but be filled with the Spirit, [19]as you sing psalms and hymns and spiritual songs among yourselves, singing and making melody to the Lord in your hearts, [20]giving thanks to God the Father at all times and for everything in the name of our Lord Jesus Christ.

Commentary 1: Connecting the Reading with Scripture

For the writer of Ephesians, faith looks a certain way. Indeed, discipleship leads to specific ethical actions that engage the *hows* of living. As always, these ethical implications are centered in theological claims, even as they emphasize the practice—including the words, actions, even songs—of faithful living.

From the beginning of chapter 5, the writer suggests a series of action-based titles that the community should take on. They should "be imitators of God, as beloved children" (Eph. 5:1). Further, they are to live as "children of light" (v. 8). Scholars believe the short hymn quotation in verse 14 is a reference to baptism, when the believer takes on the identity of the risen Christ. It is important, therefore, to understand the moral injunctions of the passage as tied to self-identity, particularly identity in Christ. They are not merely ethical suggestions but theological claims that implicate the identity of the believer, who then acts in a way reflective of this self-identification. In other words, those who identify as Christ's are claimed by him, while at the same time believers claim a way of right and faithful living in response.

For example, a list of ethical acts makes up several verses of the passage. These are often contrasted so the reader understands what life they are called from and to what life they should go (e.g., unwise vs. wise, foolish vs. understanding God's will, drunk with wine vs. being filled with the Spirit). The practical nature of the faith here is clear. Following Christ requires a wisdom reflected in acts of mind, body, and soul. It is a life in contrast to the lives of those who have not followed Christ.

More broadly, and like much of the book, this passage also reflects the sense that human reality is experienced in a world beset by demonic beings and evil, unseen forces. In other words, the life of ethical action takes place in a conflicted cosmic reality. For the writer, these demonic forces are real, present, even prevalent. So, to rally against them, the author emphasizes a Christian way of being. These forces affect what we might understand as deeply personal acts, such as drinking and sexual activity. Yet they also implicate how the broader community of the faithful interact: what spiritual songs they sing, in what ways their families and households reflect Christ's sovereignty, and how the whole body of believers is knit together.

In a devotional, Eugene Peterson and Peter Santucci pen a prayer reflecting on this passage that summarizes the sentiment well:

> Instead of careless, unthinking lives, we want to understand what you, our Master, want. What we really want is to drink your Spirit, huge draughts of your Spirit. We want hearts so full that they spill over in worship as we sing praises over everything, taking any excuse for a song to you our Father in the name of our Master, Jesus Christ.[1]

---

1. Eugene H. Peterson and Peter Santucci, *Practice Resurrection: Study Guide* (Grand Rapids: Eerdmans, 2010), 54.

Indeed, being "filled with the Spirit" is a theme of the passage and draws to mind the work of the Spirit throughout Scripture (v. 18). Here an insightful connection may be made to the Pentecost story of Acts 2. In it, those gathered were "filled with the Holy Spirit" (Acts 2:4), mirroring the text of Ephesians. Interestingly, in Acts some thought the result of the Spirit's work was drunkenness, before Peter explained the reality of God's powerful vision. Ephesians, as well, contrasts the danger of actual drunkenness with the power of the Spirit to accompany the singing of songs of thanks to God.

Further, the passage's emphasis on right living certainly recalls the wisdom tradition of the OT. Our author puts it like this: "Be careful then how you live, not as unwise people but as wise" (Eph. 5:15). The contrast between foolishness and wisdom may recall multiple notions of wisdom and its sharp contrast to folly, including Proverbs 5–7. The path of wisdom is one of upright living, sobriety, and reflection on the graciousness of God.

Given that verse 15 follows the quotation of the baptismal hymn, scriptural connections to baptism are also relevant. Romans 13:14 alludes to baptism when it exhorts readers to "put on the Lord Jesus Christ," and the preceding verses read very similarly to our passage in that they emphasize right living, avoiding works of darkness, and particularly the dangers of debauchery. Clearly, the image of baptism is meant to draw to mind right and faithful living, centering the hearers in their true identity.

More specifically, the lection engages two faith-related themes that appear throughout Ephesians. On the one hand, faith brings peace. As we read throughout the first few chapters of the letter, we see that, for the writer of Ephesians, Jesus Christ has created a "new humanity . . . thus making peace" (2:15). In Christ, those who were once strangers have become joined together as citizens of God. This reality comes with a sense of placidness, opening up a new reality of hope and identity in God.

On the other hand, faith also brings conflict. The writer repeatedly acknowledges the ongoing conflict with the forces of darkness, the push and pull of the foolish (both people and ways), and the conflict that arises among those who engage in debauchery, slander, lying, lust, and more. A sermon on this passage might acknowledge this push and pull in the lives of modern believers, appreciating both the forces of darkness present today, even as hope in Christ continues to reign.

For the preacher, the week's readings offer unusually clear potential for engagement with other lections. In the OT lesson from 1 Kings 2, God instructs Solomon in a dream about the ways he might lead. God is pleased that Solomon has asked not for riches but for wisdom, and God grants Solomon a "wise and discerning mind" (1 Kgs. 3:12). As in the Ephesians passage, the subject of how to respond to God's gifts with appropriate daily tasks and vocation is at the heart of the matter. A sermon engaging the theme of wisdom might draw upon both passages. Similarly, it might prove most wise to connect Ephesians' call to "sing psalms and hymns and spiritual songs" (Eph. 5:19) with the singing of a psalm.

An additional preaching theme may be to interrogate how the act of Christian worship supports faithful living. The passage picks up, after all, following an early baptismal hymn. The Gospel lection for the day considers Jesus as the bread of life. Further, the preacher may seek to contrast the wine of the Lord's Supper with the wine of debauchery referenced in the text. Further, the call to sing, having been filled with the Spirit, certainly raises many possibilities for worship and liturgical connections.

Finally, the preacher may seek to address questions of moral living. Doing so, of course, is never an easy task. What ethical choices should the preacher engage? What standards of moral living are better left untouched? I do not have an answer for these questions, but what does remain clear is the *why* behind the ethics. The why is God, or particularly God revealed through the power of salvation in Jesus Christ. Eugene Peterson makes that connection between theology and practice in this way: "The primary way in which we participate in who God is in all the particularities of our actual living, deeply, personally, and inextricably in relationship, is the way of the Holy Spirit."[2]

ADAM J. COPELAND

---

2. Eugene H. Peterson, *Practice Resurrection: A Conversation on Growing Up in Christ* (repr., Grand Rapids: Eerdmans, 2013), 204.

Commentary 2: Connecting the Reading with the World

I hope that this commentary series continues to be influential long after the term has faded from popular slang, but at the time of writing, activists encourage those who care about justice to "stay woke." In verse 14, just before our reading begins, the author of Ephesians calls the church to a similar status. The rest of this reading gives important suggestions for staying "woke." In both cases, the term refers to remaining alert to injustice, oppression, resistance to the divine will. That resistance may take the form of racism, anti-immigrant bias, ignoring systemic causes of poverty, or any of a number of injustices. Staying "woke" implies seeing below the surface to the underlying causes of social problems.

The admonition to "stay woke" calls the reader to "be careful." Much of Ephesians promotes a high ecclesiology. The church has important work to do (Eph. 3:10), so the church must use its time well and stay aware of the lurking dangers. Even small things can distract the church from its mission. Discerning those dangers requires wisdom. The Wisdom literature of the Bible often sets up a divide between wise and foolish (see Prov. 14:1–3). Ephesians employs this same divide. The contemporary church can begin to see the need for wisdom by reflecting on the considerable effort that has been expended seeking to convince the public not to text and drive, a clearly foolish action. In such a society (and one could cite many other examples), the church must model wisdom.

The church might regard some of the components of wisdom as maturity, discernment, character, and self-control. This understanding of wisdom contrasts and critiques the temptation of the church toward indulgence and triumphalism. Wisdom grows in the soil of struggle and the acceptance of limitations. Such wisdom is not constricted by the size of the church. The wisdom to which Ephesians calls the church includes recognizing when a social norm or public policy slips into foolishness. Like mass incarceration, some policies are self-defeating, costing money *and* hurting families. The terms "wise" and "foolish" can operate on the individual or the collective level. When foolishness manifests on the collective level, the church's role of making known God's will includes pointing toward wisdom. For personal growth, economic policy, international relations, environmental health, and other large issues, the church can model wisdom. A wise person and a wise society alike recognize that they cannot always get their way, that they must empathize with others, that they must evaluate policies for outcome and for fairness. Ephesians has already made as strong a statement as one can find in the NT that works do not effect salvation (2:9) but developing wisdom and using time productively strengthen the church for its mission.

If we are honest, some of us will admit that we do not gravitate to sermons on the message of this passage about not getting drunk with wine. At least within mainline denominations, some of us fear that a sermon on drinking will lead to parishioners labeling us a "stick in the mud." Yet an examination of the misery caused by various kinds of abuse of alcohol reveals a mountain of devastation. From the simple embarrassment of an office party and the occasional hangover to arguments within a marriage and the graver consequences of sexual assault and automobile deaths, alcohol can cause significant damage. Alcohol may not cause all of the problems by itself, but alcohol makes them all worse and serves as a catalyst to much agony.

If we expand on the words of the text to talk about illegal drugs as well as alcohol, the situation grows even more complex. American drug use profits the gangs and cartels who provide these products. The violence perpetrated among those gangs and their forceful recruitment of young men fuel much of the desperation that leads to asylum seeking at the southern border. The preacher can thus address drinking and drugs in a number of ways. The preacher can affirm that addiction is a disease that requires comprehensive treatment. The preacher can name the disease, offer support to family members, and promote treatment. The preacher can speak about the emptiness that often causes people to seek solace in substances. The preacher can inculcate the maturity that recognizes when drinking has become a problem.

The response by some in your churches will likely include much resistance. Family members of alcoholics and addicts and even of those who drink to mask their pain know the tenacity of denial. Yet the preacher cannot shirk this duty. The preacher may endure ridicule, but the topic matters. In order to preach on alcohol or drugs, the preacher must gain solid information. Seeking the facts about alcohol and drug abuse falls under the passage's call to wisdom. Sermons on substance abuse must be well-researched, so that the preacher does not speak naively about complex topics. At the time of writing, opioid addiction is rampant in many American communities. This situation involves physician-written prescriptions for pain, as well as underground production. The preacher must do her homework, but the problem deserves a careful effort. The preacher should also address the needs of youth and young adults on drinking and drug use. While avoiding scolding, the preacher can challenge the party culture of college life and young adults that encourages drinking to excess. The church can offer hope in place of despair, community in place of isolation, and healing for the underlying pain that leads to substance abuse.

The reading ends with positive steps. One might wonder how well a word from the church about substituting singing for drinking might go over, especially at a college party. Nevertheless, singing is part of church. Singing benefits people and groups on physical, emotional, and spiritual levels. Hearing an upbeat song can lift our spirits. Individual singing has some health and cognitive benefits. Contemporary research into music therapy indicates that "musical interventions can help reduce chronic pain, help stroke patients regain speech, increase social engagement in children with autism and help patients with acquired brain injury or Parkinson's disease improve their gait."[3] Ephesians considers singing to be a means of opening the church to the presence of the Spirit. One may not always be able to support such a claim with scientific research, but the witness of the church knows its truth.

What the preacher can say about music and singing applies also to the words that close out the reading on gratitude. Contemporary Christians know from experience that gratitude can transform a disposition. As with music, the behavioral sciences have researched gratitude. One cannot measure gratitude itself, but researchers have measured the effects of such actions as journal writing on emotional health. These studies suggest that on an individual level, actions intended to express gratitude increased optimism and even the likelihood of exercise. Within a marriage, expressing gratitude can improve communication and empathy of each partner for the other.[4]

Ephesians considers singing and gratitude as more than physical and emotional therapy, even though those aspects are important. Ephesians considers these conscious actions as ways to improve the health of the church, as it makes the most of the time by living into its role within God's cosmic mission. The church can affirm the therapeutic benefits of singing and gratitude but can also place those benefits within the understanding of Ephesians that the church proclaims its message even up to heaven.

CHARLES L. AARON JR.

3. Matthew Bambach, "Therapeutic Benefits of Music Being Used to Treat Alzheimer's, Addiction, and Depression," *The Globe and Mail*, n.p. https://www.theglobeandmail.com/life/health-and-fitness/health/the-power-of-music-to-heal/article18914499/.
4. Harvard Health Publishing, "In Praise of Gratitude," n.p. https://www.health.harvard.edu/newsletter_article/in-praise-of-gratitude.

John 6:51–58

[51]"I am the living bread that came down from heaven. Whoever eats of this bread will live forever; and the bread that I will give for the life of the world is my flesh." [52]The Jews then disputed among themselves, saying, "How can this man give us his flesh to eat?" [53]So Jesus said to them, "Very truly, I tell you, unless you eat the flesh of the Son of Man and drink his blood, you have no life in you. [54]Those who eat my flesh and drink my blood have eternal life, and I will raise them up on the last day; [55]for my flesh is true food and my blood is true drink. [56]Those who eat my flesh and drink my blood abide in me, and I in them. [57]Just as the living Father sent me, and I live because of the Father, so whoever eats me will live because of me. [58]This is the bread that came down from heaven, not like that which your ancestors ate, and they died. But the one who eats this bread will live forever."

Commentary 1: Connecting the Reading with Scripture

Whereas last Sunday's Gospel reading featured the people grumbling against Jesus, in this text the people are arguing among themselves. They were debating how to reconcile Jesus' claims about his divine identity with his human appearance. The question, "How can this man give us his flesh to eat?" is not only a reasonable one; it is one that has been a matter of fierce debate throughout the formative centuries of Christian belief and doctrine.

This kind of theological reflection in John is one of the many distinguishing features of this Gospel that sets it apart from the Synoptics. He is both historian and theologian, both play-by-play announcer and color commentator. He not only wants to record the events; he wants to point beyond them to reveal their deeper meaning.

Many times, he does this by having the key characters in the narrative ask questions: "How can anyone be born after having grown old? Can one enter a second time into the mother's womb and be born?" asks Nicodemus in 3:4. "Sir, you have no bucket, and the well is deep. Where do you get that living water?" asks the Samaritan woman in 4:11.

"What is truth?" asks Pilate in 18:38.

As John moves through his exposition of the signs that Jesus performs, he uses questions to invite the reader to think deeply about what these signs mean. For John, theological reflection is grounded in the courage and clarity to ask the right questions, especially those for which there are no readily apparent answers.

The ability to ask the right questions is critical in the quest for wisdom. That premise is a connecting thread among all the lectionary texts for this Sunday. First Kings 2 is the story of the transition from David to Solomon, a narrative in which God tests Solomon, gauging his ability to ask the right question. "Ask what I should give you," the Lord says (1 Kgs. 3:5). Solomon's request for "an understanding mind" to govern the people, the ability to discern between good and evil, is pleasing to God.

The text from Proverbs is an illumination of Wisdom, in which those who are "simple" and "without sense" are invited to partake of Wisdom's bread and wine, a metaphor that serves as a compelling connection to the invitation Jesus makes of the disciples.

In the Ephesians text, Paul encourages the church to live as wise rather than unwise people, not as foolish ones but as those who understand the will of the Lord. To do so, Paul calls them to be filled with the Spirit, rather than getting drunk on the wine of the world's inferior wisdom.

A sermon on these texts might focus on how to live a life based on asking the questions that really matter and on an openness to God for the answers that only God can provide.

In John 6:53–54, Jesus responds to the people's question but not in a way they are expecting. He chooses not to answer the "how" of their question, that is, the mechanics of how one is to eat of his body or drink of his blood. His is a response similar to the ones he gives Nicodemus, the Samaritan women, and others, who are more fixated on physical, rational explanations for "being born again" and "drinking everlasting water."

For Jesus, those are not the best, most beneficial, questions to ask. Instead, Jesus is more focused on the "why." He shifts the framework of their questions to explain to them not how the sign works but the truth that the sign reveals. That is the right question to ask.

Partaking of the body and blood of Jesus, participating fully in his life, will have three benefits according to John's Jesus: (1) the acquisition of eternal life (6:54a), (2) being raised with Jesus (v. 54b), and (3) receiving "true" food and drink.

Eternal Life. The promise of eternal life is a predominant theme throughout John's Gospel, so it should be no surprise that it is part of Jesus' interpretation of the feeding of the multitude. It is consistent with what he tells Nicodemus about the benefits of believing in Christ, such that one does not perish but has eternal life (3:16). It is also consistent with what he tells the Samaritan woman about "the spring of water gushing up to eternal life" (4:14). He explains many of his other "I am" statements by connecting them to the promise of eternal life, including "I am the good shepherd" (10:27–28) and "I am the resurrection and the life" (11:25). For Jesus, the ability to ask the right questions and to be open to God's answers, as irrational as it might seem, is not just a matter of intellectual curiosity. It is a matter of life and death, the alternative between the kind of life God wants us to live here and now and the kind of life devoid of meaning in which "you have no life in you" (6:53).

Raised Up on the Last Day. To partake of Jesus' body and blood is to participate in his story of death and resurrection. The sacramental and eucharistic connections to this text are clear. Though John's depiction of the Last Supper does not contain the institutional words "took," "blessed," "broke," and "gave" that are common to the Synoptic Gospels and Paul's letters, it still offers a compelling and nuanced eucharistic theology. To receive Communion is to gratefully surrender one's life into the story of God's salvation in Jesus. It involves our willingness to die to ourselves, so that in being raised to new life in Christ, we can live in great thanksgiving for what God has done in Christ.

True Food and True Drink. The acquisition of God's truth is a key theme running throughout the Johannine literature. It is not merely about gaining intellectual knowledge. It is about having the ability to see spiritual truths beyond the physical signs that point to them. It is about being able to see the activity of the Spirit and the promises of God despite the darkness, thirst, and hunger of the world. For John, truth is not just an ethical distinction between right and wrong or knowledge and ignorance. Truth is the ability to see the world as God wants us to see it and experience the power to live accordingly. That is why, for John, truth and love are so intertwined, especially in the Johannine epistles. "Little children," 1 John 3:18 reads, "let us love, not in word or speech, but in truth and action. And by this we will know that we are from the truth and will reassure our hearts before him."

A sermon based on this text might invite the congregation to ponder the kinds of questions they implicitly ask to govern their lives. Are our "life questions" based on the world's wisdom, in which we are fixated on the physical, earthly standards of fame, wealth, and self-preservation? Do our questions instead pursue God's truth, which calls us to love one another? Do our questions focus on life as our human nature prefers to live it? Do they instead point us to life as God intends it, in which we are raised to new life in Christ?

MAGREY R. DEVEGA

Commentary 2: Connecting the Reading with the World

Again this week, the Gospel reading begins by repeating a verse from the week before: "I am the living bread that comes down from heaven. Whoever eats of this bread will live forever; and the bread that I will give for the life of the world is my flesh" (John 6:51). The last words—"my flesh"—set up the controversy in the verses that follow. Scholars disagree about whether these verses were a later addition to the text, but no matter who wins this debate, the church has been reading these verses as part of John 6 for centuries. It is not hard to understand why some would like to delete them all together.

Preacher and listeners are likely to echo the question asked in verse 52: "How can this man give us his flesh to eat?" Regular churchgoers have become so accustomed to hearing "The body of Christ given for you" and "The blood of Christ shed for you" that the strangeness has worn off. Today's Gospel brings the strangeness back into focus. Many people outside the church—and perhaps many within—can relate to a small sign that has traveled around Facebook. The sign pictures a mother with her grade-school-age son. She is looking down at him, responding to something he must have said to her:

> "No, sweetheart. Jesus rose from the dead, but he's not a zombie.
> And drinking his blood every Sunday doesn't make us vampires.
> Let's go get ice cream!"

That is, let us change the subject. It is not surprising that this boy would imagine Jesus as a zombie or that drinking blood would remind him of vampires. Television, movies, and video games have probably shaped his worldview more than the Bible. The biblical text itself, though, elicits a question the young boy might ask: "How can this man give us his flesh to eat?" After all, Jesus is standing right there talking to the people who ask the question. In the verse immediately after today's reading, we learn that Jesus is teaching in the synagogue at Capernaum.

The controversy about bread and flesh is taking place within Jesus' religious community.

The controversies about bread and flesh carried over into communities of believers long after that day in Capernaum. The church has been asking questions about the bread for centuries. Is Christ present *in* the bread? If so, how? Does the bread become something other than bread? Can we eat bread with those who do not believe what we believe about the bread? These questions continue to divide Roman Catholics and Protestants, as well as Protestants from each other. It is at the Table where the bread is broken that our churches have been most broken, cut off from one another, suspicious, and judgmental. After years of walking on the long, difficult road of ecumenical dialogues, Lutheran and Reformed churches finally reached an agreement for "full communion" in 1997. One of the background documents that led to this agreement dealt with how Christ is present in the sacrament:

> Both Lutheran and Reformed churches affirm that Christ himself is host at the table. Both churches affirm that Christ himself is truly present and received in the Supper. Neither communion professes to explain how this is so.[1]

"How can this man give us his flesh to eat?" These ecumenical dialogues did not answer that question. These traditions believe Christ is present. Neither can explain how, but the eating and drinking are important: "Those who eat my flesh and drink my blood abide in me, and I in them" (v. 56). The very physicality of eating and drinking is important. If we neglect these embodied acts in Communion or devalue the body by stressing only the symbolic, we diminish the reality of Jesus' presence in ordinary things and ordinary actions.

A few years ago a woman named Sara Miles walked into a church and has never been the same since. She talks about that day in her book *Take This Bread:*

---

1. James E. Andrews, *Invitation to Action: The Lutheran-Reformed Dialogue, Series III, 1981–1983* (Minneapolis: Fortress, 1984), 14.

One early, cloudy morning when I was forty-six, I walked into a church, ate a piece of bread, took a sip of wine. A routine Sunday activity for tens of millions of Americans—except that up until that moment I'd led a thoroughly secular life, at best indifferent to religion, more often appalled by its fundamentalist crusades. This was my first communion. It changed everything. . . . The mysterious sacrament turned out to be not a symbolic wafer at all but actual food—indeed, the bread of life. . . . I took communion, I passed the bread to others, and then I kept going.[2]

Indeed she did! She kept going to that very church, St. Gregory's in San Francisco, and distributed groceries to hungry people. On Sunday, people gather around the altar to eat the bread and share the cup. During the week, Sara and her friends pass out food from the same altar where she first tasted the bread. Within a few years, she and the people who had received food started nearly a dozen food pantries in the poorest parts of their city.

Was it really that moment of tasting the bread that changed her after all those years disdaining church? There was something about the physical reality of eating that made a difference. Sara Miles describes her conversion this way: "I discovered a religion rooted in the most ordinary yet subversive practice: a dinner table where everyone is welcome. . . . And so I became a Christian, claiming a faith that many of my fellow believers want to exclude me from; following a God my unbelieving friends see as archaic superstition."[3]

Sharing Communion may not seem subversive, but for Miles and others, that ordinary eating signaled a different way of living. Several years ago, my friend Jon Nelson, a Lutheran pastor in Seattle, was arrested for protesting the deployment of Trident nuclear submarines. Jon and others were particularly outraged when one of these submarines was christened *USS Corpus Christi*. Though that Trident was named for the city in Texas, the name is Latin for the "Body of Christ." Jon joined others in their speedboats to stop the mighty Trident from entering Puget Sound. Of course, their little boats could not stop the powerful Trident. The coast guard rounded them up and maneuvered their boats to shore. Jon was arrested because he had done this sort of thing before.

While he was in jail, several friends came to visit. One of the pastors in the group brought a loaf of bread and a small plastic container of wine, so they could share Communion. They knew a glass bottle would never be allowed, and they did not even consider bringing a knife to cut the bread! Nevertheless prison authorities confiscated the bread and the wine as *contraband*. Jon's friends were distressed, for they so wanted to share Communion with him in prison. When they told Jon what had happened, he broke into an enormous grin: "Communion as contraband!" he laughed, "That's it, isn't it? Communion as contraband, threatening to the powers who think they own the world."

The Eucharist is a moral and mystical meal, a subversive and sustaining presence. Jesus longed for his followers to know that he would abide with them forever. He would become part of them as surely as the bread they ate and the wine they drank. How that was possible Jesus never explained, but the promise to abide was as real as the taste of bread in their mouths.

BARBARA K. LUNDBLAD

2. Sara Miles, *Take This Bread: The Spiritual Memoir of a Twenty-First-Century Christian* (New York: Ballantine Books, 2007), xi.
3. Miles, *Take This Bread*, xiii.

Proper 16 (Sunday between August 21 and August 27)

Joshua 24:1–2a, 14–18 and
  1 Kings 8:(1, 6, 10–11) 22–30, 41–43
Psalm 34:15–22 and Psalm 84

Ephesians 6:10–20
John 6:56–69

Joshua 24:1–2a, 14–18

¹Then Joshua gathered all the tribes of Israel to Shechem, and summoned the elders, the heads, the judges, and the officers of Israel; and they presented themselves before God. ²And Joshua said to all the people, "Thus says the LORD, the God of Israel: Long ago your ancestors—Terah and his sons Abraham and Nahor—lived beyond the Euphrates and served other gods. . . .

¹⁴"Now therefore revere the LORD, and serve him in sincerity and in faithfulness; put away the gods that your ancestors served beyond the River and in Egypt, and serve the LORD. ¹⁵Now if you are unwilling to serve the LORD, choose this day whom you will serve, whether the gods your ancestors served in the region beyond the River or the gods of the Amorites in whose land you are living; but as for me and my household, we will serve the LORD." ¹⁶Then the people answered, "Far be it from us that we should forsake the LORD to serve other gods; ¹⁷for it is the LORD our God who brought us and our ancestors up from the land of Egypt, out of the house of slavery, and who did those great signs in our sight. He protected us along all the way that we went, and among all the peoples through whom we passed; ¹⁸and the LORD drove out before us all the peoples, the Amorites who lived in the land. Therefore we also will serve the LORD, for he is our God."

1 Kings 8:(1, 6, 10–11) 22–30, 41–43

¹Then Solomon assembled the elders of Israel and all the heads of the tribes, the leaders of the ancestral houses of the Israelites, before King Solomon in Jerusalem, to bring up the ark of the covenant of the LORD out of the city of David, which is Zion. . . . ⁶Then the priests brought the ark of the covenant of the LORD to its place, in the inner sanctuary of the house, in the most holy place, underneath the wings of the cherubim. . . . ¹⁰And when the priests came out of the holy place, a cloud filled the house of the LORD, ¹¹so that the priests could not stand to minister because of the cloud; for the glory of the LORD filled the house of the LORD. . . .

²²Then Solomon stood before the altar of the LORD in the presence of all the assembly of Israel, and spread out his hands to heaven. ²³He said, "O LORD, God of Israel, there is no God like you in heaven above or on earth beneath, keeping covenant and steadfast love for your servants who walk before you with all their heart, ²⁴the covenant that you kept for your servant my father David as you declared to him; you promised with your mouth and have this day fulfilled with your hand. ²⁵Therefore, O LORD, God of Israel, keep for your servant my father David that which you promised him, saying, 'There shall never fail you a successor before me to sit on the throne of Israel, if only your children look to their way,

to walk before me as you have walked before me.' [26]Therefore, O God of Israel, let your word be confirmed, which you promised to your servant my father David.

[27]"But will God indeed dwell on the earth? Even heaven and the highest heaven cannot contain you, much less this house that I have built! [28]Regard your servant's prayer and his plea, O LORD my God, heeding the cry and the prayer that your servant prays to you today; [29]that your eyes may be open night and day toward this house, the place of which you said, 'My name shall be there,' that you may heed the prayer that your servant prays toward this place. [30]Hear the plea of your servant and of your people Israel when they pray toward this place; O hear in heaven your dwelling place; heed and forgive. . . .

[41]"Likewise when a foreigner, who is not of your people Israel, comes from a distant land because of your name [42]—for they shall hear of your great name, your mighty hand, and your outstretched arm—when a foreigner comes and prays toward this house, [43]then hear in heaven your dwelling place, and do according to all that the foreigner calls to you, so that all the peoples of the earth may know your name and fear you, as do your people Israel, and so that they may know that your name has been invoked on this house that I have built."

Commentary 1: Connecting the Reading with Scripture

Joshua 24 is couched as a moment of decision. Gathering all the tribes of Israel at Shechem, Joshua offers the people and their leaders a history lesson regarding their journey with God, all the way back from when their ancestor Abraham was led by God to the land of Canaan. In the section preceding this week's lectionary reading (Josh. 24:3–13), Joshua's history lesson centers on a number of active verbs associated with God, who is said to take, lead, give, send, bring, plague, rescue, destroy, and drive out—all to the benefit of the people of Israel. As a result of these divine actions, the people of Israel are now able to live in a land for which they did not labor, dwell in houses that they did not build, and harvest gardens that they did not plant (v. 13).

Joshua evokes these memories of divine action to form the context for the pivotal decision posed to the people in verses 14–18. Will they serve the Lord God alone? Will they exhibit complete obedience and not follow other gods? Underlying this decision is the central question, Do the people accept Joshua's version of their past, a history punctuated by God's activity?

How does this theologized version of history shape the way they will live in the years to come?

A helpful category to explain what is happening here is the notion of "cultural trauma," which, according to Ron Eyerman, is at work when a community experiences the dissolution of "collective identity." At this threshold moment in time, what is desperately needed is "a re-narration of the myths and beliefs which ground that collective."[1] Much like Joshua and the elders speaking to the people in chapter 24, one could say that "carrier groups" such as public intellectuals, preachers, authors, artists, and—in a contemporary society—mass media play a vital role in the process of interpreting traumatic events so as to help reestablish collective identity.

By means of "public reflection and discourse," the cultural trauma experienced by a group is "understood, explained and made coherent"; in this way, the group agrees upon a way to explain their past trauma in a way that leads to a unified approach to living life in future.[2] The newly narrated past creates the possibilities of a new future.

1. Ron Eyerman, "Social Theory and Trauma," *Acta Sociologica* 56, no. 1 (2013): 49.
2. Ron Eyerman, "The Past in the Present: Culture and the Transmission of Memory," *Acta Sociologica* 47, no. 2 (2004): 12.

In 24:16–18, this theoretical perspective is evident in the way that the people reclaim the version of events outlined by Joshua in the previous section. In one of the earliest confessions of faith in the OT, they confess that it is God who brought them and their ancestors out of Egypt, out of the house of slavery. It is God who protected them during their sojourn in the wilderness and who drove out the people of the land before them. In light of this agreed-upon version of the evidently traumatic events that this group of people had lived through, they accept the interpretative framework offered by Joshua and thus reestablish their collective identity as a people who serve the one Lord God.

This moment of decision in Joshua 24 runs over into the second lectionary text for this week, selections of 1 Kings 8 that narrate the procession of the ark of the covenant to its new home as overseen by King Solomon and the leaders of Israel. The sanctuary that Solomon built and the incalculable number of sacrifices that the king offered up to God (1 Kgs. 8:5) serve as a clear example of just how serious the people of Israel took their decision to serve the God of Israel. Reiterating the standardized narrative of God bringing the people of Israel out of Egypt, King Solomon's prayer at the dedication of the temple is deeply rooted in the covenant reaffirmed in Joshua 24, when Joshua called upon the people to serve the Lord their God.

This sanctuary, this "exalted house, a place for [the divine] to dwell in forever" that Solomon built (1 Kgs. 8:13) is furthermore the culmination of the covenant promise made to King David that someone from the line of David would forever sit on the throne in Jerusalem (2 Sam. 7:12–16). In Solomon's prayer at the dedication of the temple, the king thus once again reasserts the royal ideology that Jerusalem is the chosen city and that his father David and his descendants after him were the chosen kings (1 Kgs. 8:16).

It is significant, though, that in his prayer Solomon hopes that this temple serves as a house of prayer where people can come and bring their deepest joys *and* greatest sorrows before God, a mode of praise and lament modeled regularly in the psalms. In his dedication, the king implores God to "hear the plea of [God's] servant and of [God's] people Israel when they pray toward this place" (1 Kgs. 8:30).

The temple is thus a space where people come to rejoice and give thanks for a good harvest, for deliverance from enemies, for peace and safety and security. The temple is also there when people suffer from illness; from famine, drought, and pestilence; from fear of what enemies could do and have done. All these tragedies, whether great or small, are to be brought before the Lord, who heeds all prayers.

Yet a question remains: whose house is this in the end? That is, who exactly is welcome in this house of prayer? This issue is deeply contested in the Hebrew Bible itself, with laws in Deuteronomy 23:1–3 quite explicitly excluding, for example, Moabites, Ammonites, and children born out of incest. Yet other texts exclude from the sanctuary women who are menstruating or recovering from childbirth (Lev. 12:2, 4–5, 7–8; 15:19–30), along with anyone who suffers from any sort of ailment or disability (21:16–23).

Such exclusionary debates are not exclusive to the texts of the OT. In the history of my own Dutch Reformed Church in South Africa, we find a shocking example of exclusion from the house of God because of skin color in a profound act of inhospitality and faithlessness. Even more, in one of the early precursors of apartheid in South Africa, the DRC synod voted in 1857 to offer separate occasions for serving Communion to Black and white church members. To make matters worse, the church justified this racist decision by pointing "to the weakness of some."[3]

It is very telling how this very human tendency to exclude—this very human drive to keep the house clean and ordered and pure and free of foreigners, barbarians, and all those who are considered to be other or inferior—is already foreseen and countered in 1 Kings 8:41–43, when this temple is explicitly named a house of prayer for the foreigner. In King Solomon's prayer, it is significant that he implores

---

3. Robert Vosloo, "Christianity and Apartheid in South Africa," in *The Routledge Companion to Christianity in Africa*, ed. Elias Kifon Bongmba (New York: Routledge-Taylor & Francis, 2016), 403.

that when a foreigner comes and prays in this house, God, dwelling in heaven, would hear their prayers too. By elevating countervoices, such as these, the human inclination to exclude whoever seemingly does not fit my own narrow vision of who belongs might be tamped down in a perhaps small but significant fashion.

L. JULIANA CLAASSENS

Commentary 2: Connecting the Reading with the World

Our readings draw us to think about new stages and fresh starts. Often those new stages and fresh starts confront people with stark choices. The readings also bring the promise of God that we are not alone, and the opportunity to remind listeners that new stages and fresh starts are also the occasion of rejoicing. Psalms 34 and 84 give voice to celebration of the work of God among God's people, and Ephesians 6 catalogues the assistance of God for God's redeemed servants (Ps. 34:22) as they obey the call. The reading from Joshua occurs at the end of the long process of coming into the land, while the reading from 1 Kings is from a later time when the people of Israel reflected on the significance of their newly built temple and set themselves to move on to a new episode in their life as a covenant people. These readings might be a chance for a local congregation to celebrate together milestones and commitments in their own common life.

Joshua 24:1–2a, 14–18. It is the end of the long process of finding a stake in the land that God promised the people long ago. Joshua has led the people over the Jordan and through to this moment when the Lord gave "rest to Israel from all their enemies" (Josh. 23:1); now it is time for Joshua to depart. I wonder if Joshua felt echoes of that much earlier time when Moses, his own task complete, commissioned Joshua himself to lead the people over the Jordan and into a new life. Neither Joshua nor Moses had much choice in the matter of laying down their leadership, as they looked toward a more settled period. Nevertheless, both took steps to prepare their succession, Moses by equipping Joshua (Deut. 34:9) and Joshua by reaffirming the people in their commitments. Joshua succeeded less well than Moses, as we witness in the chaos of Judges. In any case, worshipers could be reminded of the importance of discerning

when their contribution is over, and it is time to get out of the way. Many leaders, some of whom will be in the pews (or perhaps up front!) today, fail to recognize when that time has come. One of the hardest aspects of leadership is confronting that moment, and few do it well.

Transition moments involve two things. First, Joshua looked back. He remembered back to the call of Abraham from "beyond the Euphrates" (Josh. 24:2), through the Egypt experience and the exodus, and on to the recent struggle of the people to establish themselves in the new land. God has been with them throughout. The earliest inhabitants of my country, the Maori of New Zealand, have a proverb that they use often: *ka mua, ka muri*, roughly translated "walking backwards into the future." As with many ancient peoples, including I suspect the Hebrews, the future is best known in the past. The first step in dealing with new circumstances is to look back to what has been achieved and what God has done.

Joshua's second move was to commit to the same allegiances that had carried their ancestors this far, to serve in the future the God who delivered and led them in the past. There are hints, though, that it may not have been as simple as that. The advice to turn from "the gods your ancestors served" (v. 15) is telling. Does it imply that the ancient gods dating back to Abraham's time have never been entirely abandoned, that a commitment to ancient understandings remained a struggle for the Israelites? Had they never completely shaken off the ancient gods? One could easily imagine that when they encountered the Canaanite pantheon, it was tempting to get involved with their gods too.

Few hearing the preaching today are likely to be animist polytheists. However, almost all will work with a backup system that enables them not to have to trust God completely. It is easy to say, "We also will serve the LORD, for he is our God" (v. 18); it is much harder to practice that completely. This reading challenges hearers and their faith communities to ask themselves what they rely on instead of God: pensions, insurance schemes, career structures, political leaders, money? The list is endless. In terms of the Gospel reading, What it is that we find offensive in the message of Jesus (John 6:60–61)?

1 Kings 8:(1, 6, 10–11) 22–30, 41–43. Many years have now passed since Joshua's farewell speech. The people since then have undergone a long chaotic period as their identity gradually emerged on what was once Canaanite soil. They have gone from a very loose set of affiliations among tribes to something like a nation-state. The promise made to Joshua to serve the Lord has been kept—occasionally. The presence of God among the people remained focused on the mobile tabernacle, which had been stationed at Shiloh for a long period. Now they are securely united under a king and have a magnificent temple, finally a permanent home fit to house the ark as a sign of God's enduring presence in their midst (1 Kgs. 8:11). Perhaps there can now be "rest" (v. 56).

Solomon's prayer focuses on the temple where God is met and where the covenant is maintained in regular worship. Each of his seven major petitions (vv. 31–46), only portions of which the lectionary has selected, is a sermon in its own right, but the lectionary selection of verses 41–43, the reference to the foreigners, draws the reader back to verses 27–30, in which Solomon reflects a fundamental paradox. The king's prayer makes clear that the temple is regarded as what the Celts are often credited with calling a "thin space," a place where the barrier between God and the people is especially thin and God is accessible in a particular way. Transactions with God took place in a unique way at the temple.

Yet, as Solomon's question in verse 27 ("But will God indeed dwell on the earth?") implies, the temple is also representative; it is a reminder that God cannot be contained by the temple. This tension dogged the faith of Israel, and too often they collapsed the paradox into a kind of domestication of God. Yet the commitment to the inclusion of foreigners (vv. 41–43) denotes a recognition that the people of God are destined to become much more than an exclusive group who gather around one particular building. Like Solomon's ancient people, the church has had constantly to relearn this lesson: that the institution can never be an end in itself but is always a sign of something more. At this point in his career, Solomon seems to understand this. He appears subsequently to have forgotten it, and unlike Joshua and Moses before him, ends up sowing the seeds of a divided kingdom rather than providing a healthy transition.

The challenge of Solomon's prayer for the congregation today is to appreciate the fact that their place of worship provides a "thin space" in which to meet God. The place is not an end in itself. At times of celebration and renewed commitment in congregational life, it is good to thank God for institutional achievement, while at the same time recommitting to a gathering around a new covenant. For Christians, that covenant is now Jesus. For a eucharistic service, the Gospel reading is a timely reminder that we gather around the body and blood of Jesus himself, expressed for us today in the shared bread and wine (John 6:56–58).

TIM MEADOWCROFT

Proper 16 (Sunday between August 21 and August 27)

Psalm 34:15–22

¹⁵The eyes of the LORD are on the righteous,
 and his ears are open to their cry.
¹⁶The face of the LORD is against evildoers,
 to cut off the remembrance of them from the earth.
¹⁷When the righteous cry for help, the LORD hears,
 and rescues them from all their troubles.
¹⁸The LORD is near to the brokenhearted,
 and saves the crushed in spirit.

¹⁹Many are the afflictions of the righteous,
 but the LORD rescues them from them all.
²⁰He keeps all their bones;
 not one of them will be broken.
²¹Evil brings death to the wicked,
 and those who hate the righteous will be condemned.
²²The LORD redeems the life of his servants;
 none of those who take refuge in him will be condemned.

Psalm 84

¹How lovely is your dwelling place,
 O LORD of hosts!
²My soul longs, indeed it faints
 for the courts of the LORD;
my heart and my flesh sing for joy
 to the living God.

³Even the sparrow finds a home,
 and the swallow a nest for herself,
 where she may lay her young,
at your altars, O LORD of hosts,
 my King and my God.
⁴Happy are those who live in your house,
 ever singing your praise.

⁵Happy are those whose strength is in you,
 in whose heart are the highways to Zion.
⁶As they go through the valley of Baca
 they make it a place of springs;
 the early rain also covers it with pools.
⁷They go from strength to strength;
 the God of gods will be seen in Zion.

⁸O LORD God of hosts, hear my prayer;
 give ear, O God of Jacob!
⁹Behold our shield, O God;
 look on the face of your anointed.

¹⁰For a day in your courts is better
   than a thousand elsewhere.
I would rather be a doorkeeper in the house of my God
   than live in the tents of wickedness.
¹¹For the LORD God is a sun and shield;
   he bestows favor and honor.
No good thing does the LORD withhold
   from those who walk uprightly.
¹²O LORD of hosts,
   happy is everyone who trusts in you.

Connecting the Psalm with Scripture and Worship

Psalm 34:15–22. The last eight verses of this psalm are included in the alternate readings for the day. For those dropping in on the psalm at this point, it is important to remember that it begins with the testimony of someone who experienced life-changing deliverance from an unnamed peril. The psalmist is full of gratitude and hope, and from that perspective seeks to instruct others, inviting them to "taste and see" that God will do the same for them, if they live in the ways fitting for God-fearers.

In the final section of the psalm (Ps. 34:15–22), that "if" becomes central. There are extravagant promises for the righteous, the brokenhearted, and the crushed in spirit, and dire predictions about the fate of evildoers, the wicked, and those who hate the righteous. The starkness of this contrast might rightly make us uneasy—can people really be reduced to one of these or the other? Perhaps a bigger puzzle is the content of these declarations. According to the psalmist, righteous people will be rescued from every trouble and will never break a baby toe, much less a hip. Bad people will die (and be forgotten).

Read this text aloud in a congregation, and many people will start thinking of specific examples that contradict these claims. Lots of faithful people wait for rescue and suffer injury. Lots of mean-spirited people flourish. Even the psalmist seems to recognize the obvious in verse 19, acknowledging that "many are the afflictions of the righteous." Whatever it means that God-fearers want for nothing, it does not mean they will not suffer. Is there an eschatological horizon that might illuminate this further? If

so, the psalmist does not name it explicitly. The tensions remain, simmering.

The reading from Joshua 24 also deals in some stark contrasts. With all the tribes gathered together, Joshua preaches a sermon in which he voices God's claim on the people and then pressures them to make a decision about whom they will fear going forward: Yahweh, or one of the many local gods on offer. Many a preacher has suggested that the choice should have been obvious. Surely it was not that obvious, or Joshua's sermon would be unnecessary. In choosing Yahweh, the people echo the rationale Joshua (speaking as God) gives them. They choose Yahweh because of the things God has done for Israel in the past, for the ways God delivered and protected, culminating in the "possession" of the land. However, the people depicted in the text, as well as the people for whom this text was written, surely know that the story from Abraham to exodus to promised land was not without its troubles. They are in the land God had given, yes, but precariously.

The little chink in the otherwise deliriously confident armor of Joshua—the affirmation that the righteous will suffer—can help the preacher sink into the complexity of the "choice" presented in the Joshua 24 excerpt. There is life for those who choose Yahweh, and there are many reasons to affirm that. There are also death, jealousy, anger, vulnerability, suffering, struggle, and mystery.

In the context of worship, Psalm 34:15–22 might be read by an expressive lector, but it is wise to preface the reading with a few lines of introduction, explaining the way these verses grow out of the testimony of someone who has just experienced God's intervention. The very brave might consider pairing the reading with projected images that challenge some of its more radical claims about the protection of the crushed in spirit and the ruin of the hate-filled, but only if these issues will be explored in the sermon (or elsewhere in the service).

Psalm 84. Psalm 84 practically sings itself. It is a psalm of longing and conviction, the perfect text for a pilgrim to have on her lips as she makes her way up Mount Zion to the temple. Though this "dwelling place" is certainly admired by the psalmist—for its loveliness, for its hospitality to feathered things and wanderers—it is not the house but the living God who is the ultimate object of adoration (Ps. 84:2). The first of three beatitudes refers to those who "live" in God's house, worshiping all the time, the second to those who seek refuge there, and enjoy God's protection en route (vv. 5–7). The idea of "dwelling" in the house of the Lord is a common trope in the psalms (see, e.g., Ps. 23:6). What does it mean to live with God, in God's house? The psalmist likely had the resident priests in mind, but some commentators argue that the psalm also alludes to the temple as a place of asylum for those in need. The house of the Lord offers life in life-crushing situations, because the Lord of life is present there.

Verses 8 and 9 are something of an interruption, with the psalmist asking God to listen and "behold," that is, bless, the reigning king. Then verse 10 marks a return to the heartbeat of the psalm. Better to be even briefly on the threshold of the place where God is present than to spend years at the hub of a godless establishment. God is protector and provider for those who seek the paths of righteousness in verse 11, and a final beatitude concludes the psalm.

The 1 Kings passage is also concerned with God's promises in relation to the temple. In 1 Kings 8:1–66 we find a description of the festal liturgy at the time the temple is dedicated, and Solomon's extensive prayer on the occasion. Understandably, the lectionary omits many of the details as well as a large swath of the prayer. What remains includes the opening of Solomon's prayer, in which he praises God for keeping God's covenant promises to Israel and to David in particular, asking that God continue to confirm this "word" and to listen to all who pray in, and "toward," the temple (vv. 22–30). Interestingly, the lection then jumps over several specific petitions regarding God's response to the prayers of the people of Israel in various circumstances (particularly in relation to the effects of sin) to alight on Solomon's request on behalf of "foreigners" who come and pray "toward this house," asking that God might likewise hear and respond to their pleas (vv. 41–43).

For the preacher, this hospitable stance toward outsiders in need might be a place of fruitful interaction with Psalm 84. A preacher might connect this portion of Solomon's prayer to the psalm, with its allusions to the temple as a place of refuge for those coming from afar. With the plight of immigrants and refugees meeting us with every newsfeed, the contemporary relevance is not difficult to see.

The poetry and passion of Psalm 84 have attracted the attention of numerous composers and songwriters over the centuries, and there are many musical possibilities from which to choose for use in worship. Among the many metrical hymns, standouts include "How Lovely, Lord" (Merle's Tune)[1] and "How Lovely Is Thy Dwelling Place" (Brother James' Air).[2] There are also excellent responsorial versions with chanted verses and a congregational refrain.

ANGELA DIENHART HANCOCK

---

1. See *Glory to God* (Louisville, KY: Westminster John Knox, 2013), 402.
2. See *Psalms for All Seasons: A Complete Psalter for Worship* (Grand Rapids: Calvin Institute of Christian Worship, Faith Alive Christian Resources, and Brazos, 2012), 84E.

Ephesians 6:10–20

[10]Finally, be strong in the Lord and in the strength of his power. [11]Put on the whole armor of God, so that you may be able to stand against the wiles of the devil. [12]For our struggle is not against enemies of blood and flesh, but against the rulers, against the authorities, against the cosmic powers of this present darkness, against the spiritual forces of evil in the heavenly places. [13]Therefore take up the whole armor of God, so that you may be able to withstand on that evil day, and having done everything, to stand firm. [14]Stand therefore, and fasten the belt of truth around your waist, and put on the breastplate of righteousness. [15]As shoes for your feet put on whatever will make you ready to proclaim the gospel of peace. [16]With all of these, take the shield of faith, with which you will be able to quench all the flaming arrows of the evil one. [17]Take the helmet of salvation, and the sword of the Spirit, which is the word of God.

[18]Pray in the Spirit at all times in every prayer and supplication. To that end keep alert and always persevere in supplication for all the saints. [19]Pray also for me, so that when I speak, a message may be given to me to make known with boldness the mystery of the gospel, [20]for which I am an ambassador in chains. Pray that I may declare it boldly, as I must speak.

Commentary 1: Connecting the Reading with Scripture

At times, we can overplay language concerning battle or war as we seek clarifying metaphors for faithful living. Others of us might seek to avoid violent language altogether. Whether it feels comfortable or not to us, in the case of this passage, the battle metaphor is simply impossible to avoid. Therefore, readers should consider the language in its fullness, not reading into it more than is there, while appreciating the armor of God metaphor as written. Readers who do so will find a powerful message addressing how to stand firm in the face of trial.

Our passage appears near the end of the letter and functions as a sort of transitional hinge, a final extended appeal before the closing salutations. It directly follows a detailed discussion—not included in the lectionary—of rules for household relationships, particularly governing wives and husbands, children, and slaves. Congregations that include the epistle reading every week in worship should note that this reading is the culmination of seven weeks of excerpts from Ephesians. Even so, these final verses of the letter function fairly well on their own, so preachers who have not drawn from Ephesians over the previous weeks may embrace the opportunity to engage the epistle at its end.

The entire book of Ephesians may be thought of as a sort of instruction book. The first half is composed mostly of instructional theory (what we call "theology"), while the second half explains practical steps. The practical steps of this passage, interestingly, rely on an extended metaphor to aid hearers in their practical engagement. Yet the theory is still mixed in with the practical, so interpreters should hesitate to make too many connections to actual armor, given that the metaphor never loses its connection to theology.

In other words, the writer is giving spiritual guidance, not military strategy, and the language of the latter should not be confused with the goal of the former. To that point, readers should not overlook the fact that the only weapon named—that is, the only tool for offensive action—is "the sword of the Spirit, which is the word of God" (Eph. 6:17). The Spirit—and God's sovereignty—is the ultimate power on which the writer relies. There is no safety in fighting back with human strength or ingenuity. Only in God can salvation be found. Indeed, the believer can already taste victory even as the battle wages, thanks to the power of God. Victory, however, is spiritual, and not the result of actual physical confrontation.

Context always matters, but perhaps especially for this reading. It is important to appreciate the context of the ongoing spiritual battle experienced by the writer and writer's community. The passage gives instructions for ways to endure and remain faithful amid the battle. Note, however, that the author makes clear the battle is not against human bodies. Neither is the battle a traditional war. Instead, the spiritual battle is particularly "against the rulers, against the authorities, against the cosmic powers of this present darkness, against the spiritual forces of evil in the heavenly places" (v. 12). These forces have human, material implications, so it is not as if human bodies are unaffected. Yet the battle is not a physical war in the traditional sense.

These heavenly forces seem linked to the juxtaposition of light and darkness earlier in the book (5:8–9). While the forces of the devil are clearly at play and need to be contended with, the important point is that they can be contained. Indeed, these forces should always be understood within the context of the book's introduction, where the writer proclaims God's power at work in Christ, soaring in the "heavenly places, far above all rule and authority and power and dominion, and above every name that is named, not only in this age but also in the age to come" (1:21). So, while a battle is raging and the hearers of the letter must be prepared, there is clarity as to who ultimately wins. Indeed, connections to the heavenly realm occur throughout Ephesians (1:22–23; 2:6; 3:10).

For more contemporary readers, it may be difficult to connect to such language. Preachers would be wise to admit as much. Yet, perhaps surprisingly, Dietrich Bonhoeffer's writing may

be instructive here. To the earlier point that these spiritual battles have an effect on physical bodies, Bonhoeffer wonders, "How can one close one's eyes at the fact that the demons themselves have taken over the rule of the world, that it is the powers of darkness who have here made an awful conspiracy."[1] Given our limitations, we should take care when ascribing any singular item or issue to the "powers of darkness," yet Bonhoeffer's words are instructive in their call to living with our eyes wide open to the awful work of the powers.

Considering the other lections for the day yields fruitful connections. For those wishing to emphasize the armor of God angle, Psalm 84 will serve as a helpful companion. In it, the psalmist, too, proclaims the wisdom and power that come with reliance on God alone, "for the LORD God is a sun and shield" (Ps. 84:11). Perhaps, given the somewhat open-ended nature of the Ephesians passage, Psalm 84 may be used to acknowledge that the spiritual battle is always ongoing *and* that a sense of contentedness ultimately awaits those who rely on the Lord. As the psalm proclaims, "happy is everyone who trusts in you" (v. 12). While the Gospel passage in John 6:56–69 does not use similar battle language exactly, it does raise the question of spiritual battles among and within the disciples. Indeed, "because of this many of his disciples turned back and no longer went about with him" (John 6:66). Though as the beginning of Ephesians makes clear, God in Christ has won, there is still quite the ongoing earthly challenge raging. Just as some of the disciples struggled to understand the work of the God in Christ through the Spirit, so, too, did the audience of Ephesians. Surely, contemporary readers can expect our own challenges.

Indeed, much of the NT addresses ways early Christ followers should prepare for conflict. In this context, Ephesians is clear with regard to the required response: stand firm. This injunction is echoed in other Pauline writings (e.g., 1 Thess. 5:6–8; 1 Cor. 15:58; 16:13; Rom. 13:11–14). That the theme is common may alleviate concerns of preachers hesitant to engage the battle metaphor.

---

1. Quoted in Charles L. Campbell, *The Word before the Powers: An Ethic of Preaching*, 1st ed. (Louisville, KY: Westminster John Knox, 2002), 6.

Speaking of preaching, several directions emerge from the passage. Charles Campbell's work on preaching before the powers invites preachers not to shy away from the spiritual context of the passage. Campbell writes, "The ethical context of preaching is the activity of the principalities and powers. . . . [T]he principalities and powers of the world remain aggressive actors that shape human life today and provide the context of Christian preaching."[2] Relatedly, Campbell's work particularly explores the nonviolent nature of faithful resistance. In a world beset by violence, the "sword of the Spirit"—the Word—upends early expectations. Sermons might explore ways the Christian life pushes back through faithful, even surprising, acts of discipleship. The lection provides an opportunity for preachers to engage the strange message of the gospel, resting in the promise that the ultimate victory has already been won.

ADAM J. COPELAND

Commentary 2: Connecting the Reading with the World

Ephesians closes in a powerful way, depicting a cosmic battle and the weapons needed by the church for the fight. Popular Christian culture has elevated this passage to iconic status, sometimes literally. One can go online to order "action figures" and statues decked out in the "armor of God." Children can don the armor of God for Halloween. What can the contemporary church make of this passage with its talk of "cosmic powers" and the "spiritual forces of evil in the heavenly places"? Such ideas arise not just here in Ephesians but throughout the NT. Very early in the Gospel of Mark, Jesus vanquishes an "unclean spirit" that has taken possession of a man and confronts Jesus in the synagogue at Capernaum (Mark 1:21–28). John refers to "the ruler of this world," who must be driven out (John 12:31). Preachers and leaders in the church must discern some way to understand this language and these ideas.

Contemporary thinkers have considered several possibilities. This talk may simply represent prescientific explanations for such things as mental illness and the evil in the world. One can see how a schizophrenic person might appear "possessed" to those who lived before the advent of modern medicine. These explanations, however, do not do justice to the extensive influence that the NT assumes for these "powers." Second, other Christians might give too much credence to such language. News reports often recount a child dying during an "exorcism" to cleanse the child of illness, a chronic condition, or rebellious behavior. A third possibility regards this language as a metaphor for the intractability, insensibility, and enormity of evil. Does not the Holocaust seem beyond the evil that one could expect just of human nature?

Well-informed, critical thinkers have also tried to take seriously the language of spirits, powers, and the demonic in the NT. Can contemporary thinkers imagine an evil antecedent to human evil? Does the irrationality of racism, genocide, or sex trafficking suggest an evil greater than human greed, desire for power, and cruelty? The church can affirm the insight of the NT into evil as a power that influences human behavior without holding an exorcism for every case of influenza or every at-risk youth.

Such powerful evil is still present in our midst. Here, I will be pointing to an article that deals with the sensitive topic of domestic violence. An investigative report into misogyny in Latin America revealed the shocking brutality of both gang violence and domestic abuse in Honduras. Husbands have amputated the limbs of their spouses with machetes. Those who try to intervene or report the problem disappear. One case in particular might generate discussion about the text. Rose Castellano fled to a women's shelter after a gruesome assault by her husband. Her four-year-old son, Jose Daniel, ran into the

2. Campbell, *The Word*, 2.

street to seek help. Ms. Castellano and her husband followed. The husband put a gun to Ms. Castellano's forehead. He then fired four shots into the ground at the feet of his wife and son. Ms. Castellano reported, "I saw a demon in his eyes." What exactly did Ms. Castellano see? We are likely familiar with the look in the eyes of an enraged person. Did Ms. Castellano see only the natural result of pure fury? Did she see an evil greater than human evil? Even if the language of demons and "powers" functions only as a metaphor, it can function as a helpful, instructive, revelatory metaphor.[3]

If the wild glow in the eyes of an enraged person might seem "demonic," such a look does not provide evidence of the existence of an evil antecedent to human evil. What gives opportunity for serious reflection comes in examining the persistence of larger social evils. One researcher on racism comments, "All systems of oppression are adaptive; they can withstand and adjust to challenges and still maintain inequality."[4] In one sense, racism and all forms of oppression are abstractions; that is, racism itself is not a singular, conscious entity. It cannot analyze what opposes it; it cannot strategize. It continues to evolve and sustain its existence, nevertheless. Racism continues to thrive generation to generation. Though some forms of racism are not as blatant and overt as they were decades ago, their subtler, covert forms continue to inflict damage, while resisting attempts clearly to identify them.

One might describe this change as evolution, adapting in order to survive. The social sciences can help explain the mechanisms of racism and oppression. The church should not quarrel with these insights. The church should not discount social science research and claim "cosmic powers" as the sole cause of racism. Nevertheless, the persistence and adaptability of systems of oppression seem to be evils that stretch beyond the human capacity to create and sustain them. Once again, those who consider the language of cosmic powers in the NT as metaphor may be correct.

Nevertheless, the ability of abstract systems to survive and evolve makes it an insightful metaphor. If this language does describe some ontological reality, the church cannot speak of it precisely, in ways that clear up all questions and doubts. The NT itself says little about the origins of these powers. The writers simply assume they exist and that they are somehow part of the creation as it now stands. The church can point with theological insight to examples of evil that seem to defy rational explanations.

Even if the church claims that it can legitimately talk of evil antecedent to human evil that somehow exerts an influence on human sin, such an acknowledgment does not absolve those involved and implicated in such human evil from responsibility. People choose to participate in oppressive behavior and then to ignore its deadly impact. People actively and passively cooperate with evil, even if we can discuss "powers" that influence that evil.

The language of Ephesians describes a battle, complete with protective gear. Those on the front lines of ministries that oppose contemporary evils like sex trafficking might claim that they find their work a fight. The protective gear of Ephesians does not simply guard the individual human heart against temptation. The armor recommended in Ephesians enables the church to fight against the structures of evil and oppression. These oppressive structures seem imposing in their size and complexity. Even if many in the church cannot accept the talk of "powers," the church cannot escape the severity of the conflict and the endurance needed for even the slowest of progress. The church needs the protective armor both for the active battle and to counteract despair for the long haul.

Our passage moves the discussion of truth, righteousness, faith, and salvation from the realm of individual piety and into the fight against injustice and oppression. These qualities matter as much as strategies and fund-raising. Praying in the Spirit serves not just for individual faith development but as part of the

3. Sonia Nazario, "Someone Is Always Trying to Kill You," *New York Times,* April 5, 2019; https://www.nytimes.com/interactive/2019/04/05/opinion/honduras-women-murders.html.
4. Robin Diangelo, *White Fragility: Why It's So Hard for White People to Talk about Racism* (Boston: Beacon, 2018), 40.

fight that the church must engage against evil that transcends what an individual can combat alone. Truth counteracts the lies and misinformation that exist everywhere. Righteousness builds relationships that sustain and enable the work. The gospel of peace presents a vision of what God wills for creation. Faith keeps at least some energy going in the face of setbacks and defeats. Salvation includes the healing and personal growth that inspires the battle. The Spirit and the Word of God animate and guide the battle against the evil of the world.

CHARLES L. AARON JR.

Proper 16 (Sunday between August 21 and August 27)

John 6:56–69

56"Those who eat my flesh and drink my blood abide in me, and I in them. 57Just as the living Father sent me, and I live because of the Father, so whoever eats me will live because of me. 58This is the bread that came down from heaven, not like that which your ancestors ate, and they died. But the one who eats this bread will live forever." 59He said these things while he was teaching in the synagogue at Capernaum.

60When many of his disciples heard it, they said, "This teaching is difficult; who can accept it?" 61But Jesus, being aware that his disciples were complaining about it, said to them, "Does this offend you? 62Then what if you were to see the Son of Man ascending to where he was before? 63It is the spirit that gives life; the flesh is useless. The words that I have spoken to you are spirit and life. 64But among you there are some who do not believe." For Jesus knew from the first who were the ones that did not believe, and who was the one that would betray him. 65And he said, "For this reason I have told you that no one can come to me unless it is granted by the Father."

66Because of this many of his disciples turned back and no longer went about with him. 67So Jesus asked the twelve, "Do you also wish to go away?" 68Simon Peter answered him, "Lord, to whom can we go? You have the words of eternal life. 69We have come to believe and know that you are the Holy One of God."

Commentary 1: Connecting the Reading with Scripture

The opening verse of our text contains the word "abide," a key concept in John's Gospel and one of its most recurring themes: Jesus, full of grace and truth, has come to abide with us. It is a theme introduced in John's prologue, in which the Word made flesh has come to dwell among us. It is developed most fully in John 15 with the vine and branches metaphor, in which Jesus calls his disciples to "abide in me as I abide in you" (John 15:4). The Greek verb *menō,* translated as "abide," "dwell," or "remain," occurs thirty-four times in John, three times more often than in the three Synoptic Gospels combined.

Why is the idea of *abiding* so important to John? Perhaps because he seems most interested in exploring the mystery and complexity of the incarnation, the convergence of spirit and flesh in the person of Jesus. In Christ, we see the fullness of God's divinity expressed in the fullness of Jesus' humanity. John understands *abiding* as a kind of covalent bond between two distinct realities, human and divine, the fusion of which

compromises neither and offers hope for the world.

The significance of *abiding* for John is more than just an intellectual enterprise, more than just understanding the doctrine of the incarnation. It is also a key to transformation; it is an important part of Jesus' invitation to the disciples to participate in the life of faith. He offers himself to be the means through which we can *abide* in God, so that God can *abide* in us. The work of Jesus means that we, too, can live at the intersection of the human and the divine, whenever we "eat of his flesh" and "drink of his blood." In reconciling us to God, Jesus enables us to live fully into what it means to be human, as God is most fully lived out in us.

This is a highly nuanced, complicated theological exposition that John is offering here, one that is puzzling to consider. It should be no surprise, then, that in John 6:60, the disciples are practically asking this question on our behalf: "This teaching is difficult; who can accept it?"

The Only Anchor of Our Soul

The Holy Supper is not a gazing up into heaven after Christ. No thoughts of Christ, however holy; no longings after Him, however sanctified; no wish to be with Him, however purified; no thoughts on His Cross and Passion and Previous Death, however devout; no devotion of self to Him; no acknowledgement of Him as our Priest, Prophet, King, and God; no setting Him up in our hearts as (as with the Father and the Holy Ghost) the One Object of our love; no reliance upon Him as the only Anchor of our soul, however real, come up to the truth. We ought to meditate on Him, long for Him, desire to be with Him, rely on Him, devote ourselves to Him, pledge ourselves to obey Him, and do what we have pledged. We should look for His coming, avow Him, be ready in all things, in suffering as in joy, to be partakers with Him, partakers of His Cross, and Death, and Burial. All this we should be at all times, but all this does not yet make us yet partakers of Him, for man cannot make himself a partaker of Him; He must give Himself. As He gave Himself to death upon the Cross for our sins, so in the Holy Eucharist must He, if we are partakers of Him, give Himself to us. We have of Him only what He giveth.

E. B. Pusey, "Holy Communion—Privileges," in *Parochial Sermons* (London: Walter Smith, 1886), 351–52.

We would agree that this kind of thinking is not easy to get our minds around.

Nor should it be surprising that there is such a struggle in this passage. We remember that this Gospel reading is the culmination of a five-week lectionary tour of John 6, and we notice that the presence of conflict is a continuing thread among the Sundays. Whereas the Gospel text from Proper 14 contained the grumbling of the people against Jesus and Proper 15 contained the people arguing among themselves, the lection this week contains the deepest kind of conflict: the disciples struggle with what it means to believe.

Jesus tests the depth of the disciples' struggle with the question "Does this offend you?" (6:61). In other words, does this cause offense to your senses, your rationale, your reason? To what degree does one need evidence in order to believe? Jesus asks, "Then what if you were to see the Son of Man ascending to where he was before?" (v. 62). What kind of physical proof would mitigate their disbelief? It is an odd question, given that the Jesus in John's Gospel is replete with signs and wonders that prove his identity and mission.

It is in this moment that we discover an important facet of belief for John: God makes belief possible, but humans are still required to accept it. Belief comes at the intersection of God's grace and human free will. Again, the divine and the human intertwine. Both parts of the statement are necessary; neither is more important than the other.

First, God provides the basis for belief. Jesus performs the signs and wonders. The Spirit gives life, as the flesh is useless (v. 63). No one comes to Jesus unless they are granted to do so by the Father (v. 65). This is not simply a case for predestination, as it is only one part of the equation. Humans still have both the capacity and responsibility to choose to believe, evidenced by those who chose to fall away from Jesus (v. 66). Even though Jesus was aware of those who would fall away and those who would remain with him (v. 64), he still asked Peter and the disciples what choice they would make: "Do you also wish to go away?" It is this final exchange between Jesus and Peter that we might consider to be the climax of the whole chapter. "To whom can we go?" Peter asks (v. 68). He is pondering alternatives to following Jesus and concludes that all of them are insufficient. None of them fulfill the promise of eternal life and truth. No other option can provide that which comes through abiding in Christ.

The other lectionary texts underscore Peter's conclusion. Paul portrays the armor of God to the Ephesians as an effective counter to the rulers, authorities, "cosmic powers of this present darkness," and "the spiritual forces of evil in the heavenly places" (Eph. 6:12). Like Peter, Paul concludes this to be a binary choice, between believing in Christ on the one hand, or ascribing to the forces of darkness in the world on the other. Joshua says it plainly: "Choose this day whom you will serve" (Josh. 24:15). The Israelites could either follow the way and will of the Lord who delivered them from Pharaoh, or they could choose to worship the gods of the Amorites. Both Joshua and Peter come to parallel conclusions: "As for me and my household, we will serve the LORD" and "You have the words of eternal life. We have come to believe and know that you are the Holy One of God" (John 6:68, 69).

A sermon on these texts might conclude with an invitation for a congregation to make such a choice with similar resolve. Will we choose to follow Jesus or be among those who "turned back and no longer went about with him" (v. 66)? Will we abide in Jesus or be drawn to any of a number of alternatives in the world that may offer short-term satisfaction but offer no long-term redemption?

Will we choose to put on the armor of God as a disciplined daily practice, or will we allow ourselves to be vulnerable to the powers of this world that would distract us and draw us into a life that leads to death? Will we choose the way of faithfulness, granted to us by the grace of a God who freed us from slavery to sin and led us through a wilderness of darkness and sorrow? This day, whom shall we choose to serve?

Ultimately, a sermon might lead a congregation to affirm with wholehearted commitment: "As for me and my house, we will serve the Lord." The sign of the feeding of the five thousand points to the choice that we have as to which kind of spiritual bread we will eat. On the one hand is the world's bread, which, like the manna in the wilderness, is only temporarily filling and cannot be stored for future purposes. On the other hand is the bread that comes to us in the body and blood of Christ, a spiritual nourishment that comes at the intersection of infinite and the finite, which can help us "live forever" (Luke 6:58).

MAGREY R. DEVEGA

Commentary 2: Connecting the Reading with the World

After spending four weeks in the sixth chapter of John, people may have had their fill of bread! Jesus' teaching has elicited several complaints up to this point; now it is the disciples' turn: "This teaching is difficult; who can accept it?" (John 6:60). It is not completely clear what they found difficult. Was it that Jesus called people to eat his flesh or that he said that he came down from heaven? Probably both. Jesus' answer seems directed at the latter, for he talks about the Son of Man "ascending to where he was before" (v. 62). Those who hear Jesus today are likely to share the disciples' response: "This teaching is difficult; who can accept it?" If Jesus turns to us and asks, "Does this offend you?" (v. 61), we are likely to respond, "Yes!"

Perhaps we, too, will go away like those who turned back after they heard Jesus' teachings. Some did not turn back; some stayed, including Simon Peter. "Lord, to whom can we go? You have the words of eternal life" (v. 68). These words have become part of the liturgy in some churches. In many Lutheran congregations, people rise to sing these words to welcome the Gospel: "Alleluia! Lord, to whom shall we go? You have the words of eternal life. Alleluia! Alleluia!"

Why do some stay—or come back? Years ago, I got a phone call from a man I had never met, a man named Paul. He had heard a sermon I preached on *The Protestant Hour* radio program and asked where he could get a copy of my sermon. Of course, I was flattered, as most preachers are when someone wants a copy of a sermon. This is especially true when you preach on the radio, and you are not sure if anybody is listening. I told him where he could get the booklet of sermons, and a couple weeks later, he wrote me a letter:

> When I came to the moment where they recognized Jesus, I broke into uncontrollable sobbing. After I regained my composure, I came back to finish the story, and the same thing happened again. What on earth was happening to me? After an hour of sitting and wondering,

I went back to finish the story. . . . Since then, I have gone through the necessary motions of life, but my head and my heart are full of the same questions, endlessly repeated—what has happened? What is happening? What must I do?

I would like to claim that my sermon created this life-changing moment, but I am sure that something else was going on. That sermon was almost a word-for-word retelling of the story of Jesus' encounter with two disciples on the road to Emmaus. It was the gospel that touched this man. It was Jesus who met him in the story. He went on to tell me a bit about his life, how he had grown up in a Christian home and studied the Bible as a youngster. Then he had found it harder and harder to reconcile the Jesus story with a lifetime of study and teaching. In his words, he had decided that Jesus was a "charismatic lunatic." Now years later, this retired professor had been caught off guard by Jesus. He dared to look again at the Jesus he did not believe in. He had packed Jesus away as a childhood memory he had outgrown. Now Jesus had interrupted his settled worldview. It may be as disruptive to consider the possibility of believing as it is to consider the possibility of doubt. Either way, nothing is ever quite the same again.

Poet Stephen Dunn paints a picture of parents who had no intention of following Jesus or being part of any church. In his poem "At the Smithville Methodist Church," he introduces us to parents who sent their daughter to vacation Bible school. She liked her friends and the songs they sang, but when she came home with a "Jesus Saves" button, they decided to have a talk. What could they say? It had been years since they believed, and they thought their children would think of Jesus as they might think about Abraham Lincoln or Thomas Jefferson. They also began to realize that they did not have any story for their daughter—or maybe even for themselves. From what the poem reveals, they cared deeply for their daughter. They were

rational people. They trusted history and science. One of them admitted aloud,

You can't say to your child
"Evolution loves you." . . .
I didn't have a wonderful story. . . .[1]

At the end of the poem, they went to parents' night at the church. They looked at the art projects all spread out "like appetizers." They were a bit embarrassed or uncomfortable when the children jumped up and down for Jesus. The last lines take place on the drive home, with their daughter still jumping up and down for Jesus: "There was nothing to do / but drive, ride it out, sing along / in silence."[2] The reader is left wondering why the driver was singing along in silence. Was she longing for a story of her own? Was he rethinking why Jesus had no place in his life? The poet leaves us with the questions.

Perhaps Jesus is too particular for those parents or for many people in this pluralistic world. When I was a pastor in New York City, there was a garden outside our church building. Whenever I was working in the garden, neighbors would soon stop by to chat. He or she would often end our conversation by saying something like, "Well, Reverend, we all have the same God, don't we?"—which could be translated, "You will not see me in church Sunday." God could be a bit more general than Jesus.

"You have the words of eternal life." Is this too particular? In an address titled "Must Jesus Christ Be a Holy Terror?" theologian Carter Heyward is honest about the danger of using Jesus' name as a weapon against other religions. She is critical and suspicious of much in the Christian tradition. Yet she also sees danger in denying the particularity of Jesus:

Christian faith must, I believe, point directly and particularly to the human life, faith and teachings of Jesus as Christ, rather than simply to a free-floating symbol of what is valuable to us. For symbols do not, in fact, float freely, but rather are reflections of what

---

1. Stephen Dunn, *New and Selected Poems 1974–1994* (New York: W. W. Norton, 1994), 183–84.
2. Dunn, *New and Selected Poems*, 184.

we value in our life together. When Christians lose sight of the particular message and mission of Jesus, we open the door to the making of anyone or anything into our "Christ."[3]

"Lord, to whom can we go? You have the words of eternal life. We have come to believe and know that you are the Holy One of God." Simon Peter kept asking and answering that question for the rest of his life. Perhaps that is why John's Gospel ends twice. The last two verses of chapter 20 are a clear ending. Then chapter 21 starts all over again, perhaps in order to give Simon Peter a chance to reaffirm his belief as he shares Jesus' meal of bread and fish.

Perhaps the end of the story is not the end for us either. There is always another chapter.

BARBARA K. LUNDBLAD

3. Carter Heyward, *Our Passion for Justice: Images of Power, Sexuality, and Liberation* (New York: Pilgrim, 1984), 220.

Proper 17 (Sunday between August 28 and September 3)

Song of Solomon 2:8–13 and
  Deuteronomy 4:1–2, 6–9
Psalm 45:1–2, 6–9 and Psalm 15

James 1:17–27
Mark 7:1–8, 14–15, 21–23

Song of Solomon 2:8–13

8The voice of my beloved!
    Look, he comes,
leaping upon the mountains,
    bounding over the hills.
9My beloved is like a gazelle
    or a young stag.
Look, there he stands
    behind our wall,
gazing in at the windows,
    looking through the lattice.
10My beloved speaks and says to me:
"Arise, my love, my fair one,
    and come away;
11for now the winter is past,
    the rain is over and gone.
12The flowers appear on the earth;
    the time of singing has come,
and the voice of the turtledove
    is heard in our land.
13The fig tree puts forth its figs,
    and the vines are in blossom;
    they give forth fragrance.
Arise, my love, my fair one,
    and come away."

Deuteronomy 4:1–2, 6–9

1So now, Israel, give heed to the statutes and ordinances that I am teaching you to observe, so that you may live to enter and occupy the land that the LORD, the God of your ancestors, is giving you. 2You must neither add anything to what I command you nor take away anything from it, but keep the commandments of the LORD your God with which I am charging you. . . .

6You must observe them diligently, for this will show your wisdom and discernment to the peoples, who, when they hear all these statutes, will say, "Surely this great nation is a wise and discerning people!" 7For what other great nation has a god so near to it as the LORD our God is whenever we call to him? 8And what other great nation has statutes and ordinances as just as this entire law that I am setting before you today?

[9]But take care and watch yourselves closely, so as neither to forget the things that your eyes have seen nor to let them slip from your mind all the days of your life; make them known to your children and your children's children.

Commentary 1: Connecting the Reading with Scripture

The passage for this Sunday from the Song of Songs, also known as the Song of Solomon, with its language of leaping gazelles and sprouting fig trees, seems rather out of place in Scripture and therefore a bit of a misfit for the lectionary. Indeed, the book begins by calling forth a kiss from the protagonist's lover: "Let him kiss me with the kisses of his mouth" (Song 1:2). As is evident, the Song of Songs, with its erotic imagery and lack of mention of God or Israel, sounds more like love poetry than what we conceive of as sacred text. Indeed, modern readers who start reading the Song of Songs are not the only ones that are surprised to discover that this text is in the Bible. The book was so much of an outlier that some rabbis in the first century CE also wondered why it was included in the canon.

This problem of its "sacrality," in part, was resolved by the argument that this text was allegorical. The Song of Songs, according to ancient Jewish readers, was indeed about love—that is, the love between God and Israel. Not to be outdone, Christian readers also said that the Song of Songs was about love, but the love that God had for the church. That being said, the presence of a single passage from Song of Songs in the lectionary still speaks to a certain level of discomfort and confusion about this book. Especially unclear is how this text can and should be used in ecclesial and worship settings.

Most modern interpreters view the Song of Songs as an anthology of erotic or love poetry that was composed over a span of time, possibly between the mid-tenth century BCE and about the fourth or fifth century BCE. The book consists of lyric poetry that celebrates and describes the sexual relationship between a woman, who is described as "black, but comely" (1:5 KJV), and who is the main speaker and protagonist of this text, and her male lover. Though shocking to modern sensibilities, this text parallels other ancient erotic poetry from Mesopotamia and Egypt.

The dominance of the female voice is significant and telling. In the passage for this Sunday, the female protagonist is depicted as openly admiring her lover, who she compares to a gazelle or a young stag that "comes, leaping upon the mountains, bounding over the hills" (2:8). Even more shocking, this young lover comes to the protagonist to encourage her to come away with him for a tryst, telling her that nature with its fruiting fig trees and blossoming, fragrant vines are loudly and clearly declaring that the time is ripe for love and love making (2:13). As is evident, lush, fecund images from nature are utilized to suggest and bring out the erotic undertones. Perhaps it was because of the nature imagery that this text is linked in Judaism to the celebration of Passover, which was originally an agricultural festival.

Many of us will likely find the sexual nature of the Song of Songs a bit uncomfortable. The dominant female voice that so freely expresses sexual desire is now deemed something shocking and embarrassing to many of us, more so than it was to ancient readers/listeners of the past. This says something particular about us and our latent assumptions and biases. It appears that we have been taught to divorce sexuality and religion, an idea that directly contradicts much of what we find in Hebrew biblical text, which adamantly is centered around the reproductive abilities of Israel's ancestors and Israel's God, Yahweh. In the ancient world, the sacred was frequently intertwined with fecundity and reproduction, especially as expressed in the natural world, of which human beings were a part.

Our discomfort, especially with the free expression of female desires and sexuality that is evident in the Song of Songs, likely also stems from the sexism that is latent in our society and in the church. For most of its history, society and the church were led by men and interpreted and understood from the perspective of men. A possible sermon topic that emerges from this passage from the Song of Songs is an examination of and perhaps deconstruction of these latent fears, repression, and biases, especially about sexuality, in the church and in society. In this, the presence of this feminine perspective in the Scriptures is important, as it lends support to the idea that the expression of sexuality, especially from the perspective of women, is not something to be dismissed or silenced as ungodly.

The second Old Testament text for this Sunday, which comes from Deuteronomy 4:1–2, 6–9, and which celebrates God's giving of the law to Israel, also initially appears misplaced. Its connection to the love-filled Song of Songs seems murky at best. However, both Deuteronomy and the Song of Songs center on love. While Song of Songs is centered on erotic and sexual love between two lovers, Deuteronomy is about love as a political and legal concept, centered on and expressed by the election of Israel and its covenant with God. It is important to remember that love in the Hebrew Scriptures is conceived differently from how we think of it now, as a kind of an emotion or feeling. Rather, love in the Hebrew biblical text, especially as discussed in Deuteronomy, was centered on political loyalty, service, and fulfillment of Israel's covenant or contract with God. In short, in the Hebrew Bible, love was not devoid of feeling, but it also entailed action, the doing of the laws or instructions given by God to Israel.

With this conception of love in mind, we can now make sense of this passage from Deuteronomy. The giving of the law of God to Israel was a demonstration of God's love for God's nation. It meant that Israel was special and unique and beloved by God: "what other great nation has statutes and ordinances as just as this entire law that I [Moses] am setting before you today?" (Deut. 4:8). The people's fulfillment of the law—following God's commands and instructions—was the main way that the people demonstrated and expressed love for their God and acknowledged that this God cared for and loved them back. This is why the writer of Deuteronomy encourages the audience to follow the law diligently (vv. 2, 6). Like the Song of Songs, Deuteronomy—the book of the "second law"— is therefore also very much about love.

This understanding of love makes a good deal of sense. A love that consists merely of feeling is insubstantial and hollow. Rather, love is shown and made evident in action; indeed, it is inseparable from action. This idea is reaffirmed in the passage from James, which is also assigned for this Sunday. James urges his audience to "be doers of the word, and not merely hearers who deceive themselves" (Jas. 1:22). He goes further: "But those who look into the perfect law, the law of liberty, and persevere, being not hearers who forget but doers who act—they will be blessed in their doing" (v. 25).

If love, especially one's love of God and God's love for us, is not just a feeling but consists of actions, key ideas emerge as possible topics for a sermon: How has God shown us, the church, God's love? How can we show love to each other, to God, and to the world? What are the actions that display and indicate that love is present? What actions done in the name of love have been shown to not really be love at all?

SONG-MI SUZIE PARK

Commentary 2: Connecting the Reading with the World

Seemingly, the two Old Testament texts before us are rather disparate. The one exudes the language of relational intimacy, while the other exhorts hearers to attend carefully to divine guidelines for human behavior. There is, however, something that unites them—namely, a shared interest in the things that make for human flourishing.

It is no accident that the Christian mystics, like Bernard of Clairvaux, were drawn to the Song of Solomon. While the Song of Solomon may rightly be regarded as a celebration of the joy of human love and intimacy, it has just as often been interpreted as an inspired allegory of the human quest for a love-union with God—as an invitation to experience an exquisite foretaste of future union with God, the eternal dance of reciprocating delight. In a world geared to human achieving, increasingly transactional relationships, and a disturbing commodification of persons, the Song of Solomon is a reminder of the reality, in Jewish philosopher Martin Buber's summation, that "[a]ll real living is meeting."[1] In the end, communion rather than the wielding of power is what matters and endures.

It is certainly a bold move to compare God to a young stag, as the mystics' hermeneutic clearly implies. Yet it is also eminently fitting. The stag's leaping and bounding over the mountains convey the energy and vitality of the source of life itself. This vitalizing God *comes to us* in order to invite us to *come with him*. According to the mystics' interpretation, it amounts to an invitation to a "with God" life, one in which the vitality of God is contagious.

So much modern evangelism looks and feels like marketing. Caught up in ubiquitous cultural values, many Christians and churches have accepted unreflectively the premise that the church is on earth to sell its religion, and that to do so persuasively requires that Christians highlight all its benefits (its takeaways, if you will) for discriminating consumers. In contrast, the Christian mystics bear witness that our highest end is actually relational and communal, to experience the ecstasy of self-forgetful love—in Charles Wesley's hymnal phrase, to become "lost in wonder, love, and praise."[2]

Moreover, we can perceive in the repeated plea here to "come away" (vv. 10 and 13) the necessary relinquishment of what the lover presently has. Coming away involves some leaving behind. As with the Genesis ideal for marriage, one must, in the language of the Authorized Version, leave in order to cleave (Gen. 2:24).

The poet sets this invitation against a springtime landscape. The scene is filled with sights, smells, and sounds of new life. Anticipation is in the air; newness and adventure beckon. The poet's use of such evocative imagery is surely

intentional. Like all effective communicators, this writer grasps that any invitation, if it is to be compelling, must go beyond mere statement. It must also become emotionally meaningful. The lover's desire must become strong enough to overcome any lingering instinct to settle for the safety of the familiar.

It is tempting to disdain such an invitation to a vibrant inner spiritual life. It may appear to the jaundiced eye as a flaky or intellectually weak proposition. The preacher can help us know again that great minds and wise voices of the past should give us pause. Roman Catholic theologian Karl Rahner, for example, predicted that "the Christian of the future will be a mystic or he or she will not exist at all."[3]

This second text, from Deuteronomy, seemingly breathes a very different air. Here the focus is upon the law divinely revealed to the children of Israel, through Moses, on Mount Sinai. The imagery here is legal, forensic, judicial. The statutes and ordinances under consideration were given to benefit the people of God. They laid out a sure pathway to human flourishing in the midst of many hazards and risks.

The preacher might rehearse how the trajectory of Western culture has always been energized by the human aspiration toward freedom. In recent times, the concept of law is viewed with intensifying suspicion. It is commonly regarded now as a socially constructed weapon of the powerful to undermine the libertarian freedoms of less-advantaged individuals. From such a perspective, human laws rarely possess moral legitimacy. There is considerable truth to such analysis, but in such a cultural environment, is the classic call to trust and obey divine law obsolete?

The pivotal discovery of every spiritual searcher is that God and God's prescribed ways are *good for us*. This is the linchpin issue, the necessary epiphany, that determines the voluntary alignment of a life. Christians rightly seek to discern the enduring moral principles that inform the contextually conditioned expressions

1. Martin Buber, *I and Thou*, 2nd ed. (New York: Charles Scribner's Sons, 1958), 11.
2. Charles Wesley, "Love Divine, All Loves Excelling" (1747).
3. Karl Rahner, *The Practice of Faith* (New York: Crossroad, 1983), 22.

of divine law in Scripture. Then, once these are recognized, they are to be followed in the confidence that they were shaped by a benevolent Creator for the blessing of God's creatures and children. The true fear of the Lord is not ultimately fear of punishment, but fear of willfully missing out on all that God's benevolent heart has planned. This is another great paradox of the Christian experience: that submission does not result in confinement but leads rather to expansiveness and fulfillment.

Notice also that the emphasis of the writer here is on *remembering* and not forgetting this great legacy of wisdom for living. By implication, humans are prone to forgetfulness. Things easily slip from our minds (Deut. 4:9). So, it requires intentionality, determination, and diligence to remember and not to forget the proven pathway of life. This is not just for our own benefit, but for the sake of generations to come. The preacher may help us recall that first remembering, and then winsomely rehearsing what is true and good, is also essential to the successful intergenerational transfer of faith and morals.

There is such a thing as historical amnesia, forgetting the past. It is pandemic today. Modern culture has become so exclusively fixated on the notion of progress, and of leaning into the future, that as a society we often become indifferent to, and forgetful of, our roots. The risks associated with such forgetfulness are considerable, not least because we find our identity in what has already happened. We can move forward only by extrapolating from the past and following the trajectory of such historical realities into the uncharted future.

The preacher can guide us to see that one of the great responsibilities, therefore, of individual Christians, as for each and every constructive historian, is *retrieval*. We must be neither slaves to nostalgia nor iconoclastic practitioners of what has been memorably described as "chronological snobbery." Rather, we must "test everything [and] hold fast to what is good" (1 Thess. 5:21). We must selectively appropriate from the riches of the past what can be brought meaningfully to bear on contemporary challenges and opportunities.

Remembering is one of the greatest spiritual disciplines of all. Human beings have unique capacities to recall and to anticipate. We are able to reach beyond the present moment to encompass the past and anticipate the future. This power to transcend time in our consciousness is part of human dignity. Likewise, the church at its best is a community of tradition and hope.

GLEN G. SCORGIE

Psalm 45:1–2, 6–9

¹My heart overflows with a goodly theme;
   I address my verses to the king;
   my tongue is like the pen of a ready scribe.

²You are the most handsome of men;
   grace is poured upon your lips;
   therefore God has blessed you forever.
. . . .
⁶Your throne, O God, endures forever and ever.
   Your royal scepter is a scepter of equity;
    ⁷you love righteousness and hate wickedness.
Therefore God, your God, has anointed you
   with the oil of gladness beyond your companions;
    ⁸your robes are all fragrant with myrrh and aloes and cassia.
From ivory palaces stringed instruments make you glad;
    ⁹daughters of kings are among your ladies of honor;
   at your right hand stands the queen in gold of Ophir.

Psalm 15

¹O LORD, who may abide in your tent?
   Who may dwell on your holy hill?

²Those who walk blamelessly, and do what is right,
   and speak the truth from their heart;
³who do not slander with their tongue,
   and do no evil to their friends,
   nor take up a reproach against their neighbors;
⁴in whose eyes the wicked are despised,
   but who honor those who fear the LORD;
who stand by their oath even to their hurt;
⁵who do not lend money at interest,
   and do not take a bribe against the innocent.

Those who do these things shall never be moved.

Connecting the Psalm with Scripture and Worship

Psalm 45:1–2, 6–9. This song, likely composed for a royal wedding in ancient Israel, honors the king, "the most handsome of men," at his marriage. The psalmist opens with words of praise, describing the king as not only attractive, but righteous and dreaded in battle (Ps. 45:3–5). Verse 6 shifts to honor God, whose throne "endures forever." The reader might wonder, however, What is the relationship between the king and God? It seems that the king himself is being addressed *as God*, the only time such an identification occurs in Hebrew Scriptures, though deification of royalty was well known among Israel's neighbors. In the next verse, king and God are again distinguished: the ruler is beloved by God, anointed and closely associated with God's own righteousness, but not identical with God. At the close of verse 9, the king stands beside the queen, who is richly clad in the "gold of Ophir," the couple poised to enter the palace for their wedding.

These psalm verses from the semicontinuous lectionary cycle follow the Old Testament reading from Song of Solomon 2:8–13. Both texts focus on the human love-pair. Both texts allude to the sensuous "fragrance" associated with love or the beloved (Song 2:13; Ps. 45:8). Both describe music sounding (in Ps. 45:8, from stringed instruments; in Song 2:12, the "time of singing" and the "voice of the turtledove"). The mood in both is celebratory, rejoicing at the joining of two people.

The psalm differs from the Old Testament reading, however, in two important ways. First, the setting for the psalm is explicitly a wedding, while the Song consists of love poetry (although it is often used at weddings). Thus, the psalm's context is public and ceremonial, while the Song is intimate and personal. Second, in the psalm, the bridegroom is a king, so that the psalm is as much about royal power as about human love. The text focuses on Israel's ruler, to whom the queen is supposed to bow down (Ps. 45:11). The Song, by contrast, focuses on the mutual desire of the man and the woman for each other, with the lectionary text including both of their voices. Preachers and worship leaders do well to notice these differences, particularly the gendered power differential in the psalm, in considering how to include it in worship.

Though worship leaders need to exercise care in employing the psalm in worship without interpretation, it could offer an opportunity to reflect on the nature of appropriate political authority. After all, the king here is glorified in relation to God, whose righteousness this king reflects. This serves as a subtle reminder that political powers are called to serve God's cause

of truth and justice. When they do not do so, Christians rightly challenge their authority.

Alternatively, a brave preacher might choose to develop a sermon focusing on the Song of Songs, drawing from the long tradition of Christian bridal mysticism that interprets the "beloved" as Jesus the Messiah. If the preacher does this, Psalm 45 could enter the picture as a surprising praise of Jesus' beauty (think, for instance, about singing the hymn "Fairest Lord Jesus" in connection with this text). To imagine Jesus as handsome and fragrant may shock us, given the hardships of his life, his suffering, and his cruel death. Yet precisely this kind of shock may helpfully unsettle our assumptions, opening us to think in fresh ways about what it means to love Jesus, even as Jesus unsettles our assumptions about what it means to be "king."

Psalm 15. This brief psalm, from the complementary lectionary cycle, asks who is worthy to abide in God's sanctuary. It may have originated as a liturgy for those seeking admission to the temple. The answer is simple (though not easy): the ones who "dwell on [God's] holy hill" are those who "walk blamelessly," who speak the truth, who do no evil, who stand by their oath, "who do not lend money at interest, and do not take a bribe against the innocent" (Ps. 15:5). In other words, the ones who enter the temple are those who keep the law.

We might pause here. Does good behavior earn a place in God's presence? Although verses 2–5 seem to offer a list of requirements for behaviors that qualify one to enter the temple, the beginning and end of the psalm subtly complicate such an assumption. To begin with, the first verb in verse 1, often translated as "abide," literally means "sojourn, be a resident alien."[1] In other words, all who dwell in God's tent do so as sojourners, which tempers any hint of presumption. One can come before God only because of God's gracious permission.

Furthermore, the last line of the psalm does not actually answer the opening questions directly. To the questions "who may abide? . . . who may dwell . . . ?" we might expect the psalmist to conclude, "the people who do these things

---

1. J. Clinton McCann Jr., "Psalms," in *The New Interpreter's Bible* (Nashville: Abingdon, 1996), 4:733.

are worthy to abide in the God's tent." Yet that is not what the psalmist says. Instead, the conclusion, "Those who do these things shall never be moved," describes the character of those whose lives are already planted in God's abiding presence. It is not because of their behavior that they are granted admission; it is because they are rooted in God's presence that they show God's own gracious, steadfast character. These people shall not be moved.[2]

Such a theme pairs well with the appointed reading from Deuteronomy, in which Moses calls Israel to "keep the commandments of the LORD your God with which I am charging you" (Deut. 4:2). In both cases, moral behavior brings reward: in the psalm, it brings entrance to the temple, and in Deuteronomy, it brings entrance to the promised land. Both Psalm 15 and Deuteronomy portray obedience to the law as leading to stability and endurance. "Those who do these things shall never be moved" (Ps. 15:5). Yet in both cases, the good behavior does not arise independently of God; the actions described by Psalm 15, like the laws given in Deuteronomy, display what it looks like when people live in covenant relationship with God, displaying faithfulness to the one who has promised to be faithful to them.

The psalm is consistent also with the epistle reading for this day. James urges his readers in 1:22 to "be doers of the word," living by the implanted word of truth, which shows itself in their actions of mercy and perseverance. In this way, the writer of James makes explicit the relational view of God's word/law and human activity that is implicit in the psalm and Deuteronomy. A sermon on the living character of God's law/word that empowers works of justice and mercy might helpfully draw from all three of these texts.

Aside from reading and preaching, the psalm might also be integrated into other portions of worship. Consider using a refrain drawn from the spiritual "Like a Tree That's Planted by the Water, We Shall Not Be Moved." This psalm could also be a response to the declaration of forgiveness, affirming that those who have been forgiven by God will live in a way consistent with God's forgiving grace. The opening could also be part of a call to worship, and the responses could be shared by multiple voices, of many ages, perhaps using pictures drawn or tableaus to portray the various ways that people who dwell in God's presence behave.

MARTHA L. MOORE-KEISH

---

2. McCann, "Psalms," 733.

James 1:17–27

¹⁷Every generous act of giving, with every perfect gift, is from above, coming down from the Father of lights, with whom there is no variation or shadow due to change. ¹⁸In fulfillment of his own purpose he gave us birth by the word of truth, so that we would become a kind of first fruits of his creatures.

¹⁹You must understand this, my beloved: let everyone be quick to listen, slow to speak, slow to anger; ²⁰for your anger does not produce God's righteousness. ²¹Therefore rid yourselves of all sordidness and rank growth of wickedness, and welcome with meekness the implanted word that has the power to save your souls.

²²But be doers of the word, and not merely hearers who deceive themselves. ²³For if any are hearers of the word and not doers, they are like those who look at themselves in a mirror; ²⁴for they look at themselves and, on going away, immediately forget what they were like. ²⁵But those who look into the perfect law, the law of liberty, and persevere, being not hearers who forget but doers who act— they will be blessed in their doing.

²⁶If any think they are religious, and do not bridle their tongues but deceive their hearts, their religion is worthless. ²⁷Religion that is pure and undefiled before God, the Father, is this: to care for orphans and widows in their distress, and to keep oneself unstained by the world.

Commentary 1: Connecting the Reading with Scripture

The Letter of James is addressed "to the twelve tribes in the Dispersion" (Jas. 1:1). If read as a biblical trope, the letter's implied audience is God's covenant people ("twelve tribes") who reside as marginal outsiders ("the Dispersion") in a "world of iniquity" (3:6; cf. 1:27; 4:4). There they experience "trials of any kind" (1:2). The most relevant details of James's résumé are found in the NT itself. As a character of Acts, for example, it is he who exercises his pastoral authority by extending Peter's testimony that God purifies "hearts" through grace by faith (Acts 15:7–11) to include a code of purity practices that embody a community's devotion to God and one another (Acts 15:20; cf. 15:29; 21:25).

This watershed exchange between James and Peter at the Jerusalem council anticipates the powerful vision of Christian existence that James describes in terms of "pure and undefiled" practices (Jas. 1:27). The social imaginary of a community of outsiders engages its hardships as spiritual tests that threaten its allegiance to God (vv. 12, 27). While more mature sisters and brothers pass these tests with "nothing but joy" (v. 2), the struggle to interpret them against the horizon of God's new creation where nothing is lacked (vv. 4, 12) is more challenging for those who are easily "deceived" (v. 16). They fail to embrace the wisdom of God, supposing that God lures them into sin to undermine their hope of promised blessings (vv. 12–15). James issues a response to this theological deception by encouraging the community to think their trials are spiritual tests that present the prospect of a "crown of [eternal] life" (v. 12; cf. Rev. 5:4). This soul-saving choice to love God rather than doubt God's "word of truth" is the pivot point of this letter (vv. 16–21).

The community's confidence in the truth and redemptive effect of God's word is based upon its divine source: God invariably gives good gifts to God's people (v. 17). Whether or not God's word will issue in a redemptive result, however, depends largely on the manner of its reception from "wise and understanding" teachers (3:13) who "implant" it (1:21) within the community to sow the "first fruits" of God's new creation (1:18). Not only must the community first purify itself from the "sordid" manners and evil intentions (v. 21) learned from the surrounding world (v. 27); it must then receive this saving word as God's gift and so from a posture of "meekness" (v. 21).

Yet the mere reception of God's word of truth is not the same as performing it. The community must also become prompt "doers of the word" (v. 22). This exhortation gives expression to what is of decisive importance for this letter's moral vision: a faith that is not practiced is worthless (cf. 2:14–17). Not only are believers deceived when they say that a generous God tempts people to sin (1:16); they are also deceived when they foolishly think that an orthodox faith, even when firmly professed, is sufficient for their salvation (2:18–20). In the next chapter James repeatedly contends that a genuine faith—a covenant-keeping faith—requires faithful actions; friendship with God depends upon it (2:23).

The shape of these faithful actions is outlined by a most important aphorism of James: the proverbial rubric of three purity practices, "quick to listen, slow to speak, and slow to anger" (1:19). This single rubric brings to focus the obedient performances of God's "word of truth" that orders not only the community's devotion to God but also its care for one another. In this regard, each purity practice is picked up and developed in the letter's main body in two interpenetrating ways. First, each envisions a practice of God's word embodied as a "pure and undefiled" response in faithfulness to God (v. 27). In this sense, each practice is prophetic in that its performance publicly testifies to a core truth of God's word. Second, each practice is demonstrable as a redemptive response to some social crisis that threatens the community's own well-being. That is, God's word not only communicates the good news of God's salvation from sin and death (5:20); it

also directs the salvation of needy others from their distress (1:27).

The initial purity practice mentioned in 1:19, "quick to listen," is picked up and elaborated in 1:22–27. Both Jewish and Jesus traditions underscore the synergism between listening and obeying. James makes this point by telling a parable: consider the foolish person who "looked" carefully into a mirror only then to turn away, forgetting what they saw. Likewise, the person who looks into God's word as a reflection of truth about themselves—God's vision of what they really look like—but then foolishly fails to act upon what is illumined there is "deceived" (v. 22). The deception in this case is to suppose that a saving practice features a low bar of just listening to God's word rather than actually doing it. "Quick listening" promptly *does* God's will, without which one is not purified of sin.

Moreover, God's word is obeyed because it is "the perfect law of liberty" (v. 25). Although this catchphrase has been variously understood by its interpreters, most find the first predicate, "perfect," allusive of Psalm 19:7's affirmation that "the law [*torah*] of the LORD is perfect" because it "revive[s] the soul . . . making wise the simple." Such an affirmation agrees with James, which speaks of a word that saves souls (v. 21) of those who humbly receive its truth (v. 18). James's prior use of the word "perfection" (*teleios*) characterizes both the ends of human existence that lacks for nothing (v. 4) and also stipulates the means for doing so: God generously provides "every perfect gift" necessary for salvation (v. 17). In this sense, then, the "law" to which the community quickly listens is "perfect," not because its words are without error, but because it produces a redemptive result for those who practice it. In a world of unending report cards of the perfect life measured by well-paying careers and attractive appearances, James reminds us that a perfectionism suitable for God's people is measured by obedience to God's word.

A second predicate presents a more controversial claim: this is a law that *liberates*, which seems to undercut Paul's belief that a believer is liberated *from* the law rather than *by* it. While

Serve the Eternal God

Therefore, dearly beloved brethren and sisters in the Lord, reject not the chastening and instruction of your affectionate Father, but receive, with abundant joy, the exhortation of his sincere affection, giving thanks, that through his paternal favor he has chosen you in Christ Jesus, as the children of his love, taught and called you by the word of his power, enlightened you with the Holy Spirit, that through the salutary influence of the cross of Christ, you may restore to health your poor, weak, mortal flesh, which is subject to so many loathsome, infectious diseases of concupiscence, and wean it entirely from the pleasures and enjoyments of the world; that you may be made partakers of the cross of Christ, and rendered conformable unto his death, and, by this means, attain unto the resurrection of the dead; as Paul, in a certain place instructs, saying, "We are troubled on every side, yet not distressed; we are perplexed, but not in despair; persecuted, but not forsaken; cast down, but not destroyed; always bearing about in the body the dying of the Lord Jesus, that the life also of Jesus might be made manifest in our body," 2 Cor. 4:8, 10. But we who live, surrender ourselves daily unto death for Jesus' sake, that the life also of Jesus might be made manifest in our mortal flesh.

Behold, for this reason, he teaches, admonishes, rebukes, threatens and chastises that we should deny ungodliness and worldly lusts; die entirely unto the world, flesh and the devil; seek our treasure, portion and inheritance in heaven, alone. Love and believe the true, living and eternal God, looking in patience for that blessed hope, and the glorious appearing of our Lord and Savior Jesus Christ, who gave himself for us, that he might redeem us from all iniquity, and purify unto himself a peculiar people, serving him in righteousness and godliness all the days of our life.

And for the same reason James says, "My brethren, count it all joy when ye fall into divers temptations; knowing this, that the trying of your faith worketh patience. But let patience have her perfect work, that ye may be perfect and entire, wanting nothing," James 1:2, 4, for as gold, in passing through the fire, is severed from the dross and becomes more and more refined, so the susceptible man of God is subdued, purified, and refined, in the fiery furnace of affliction, that he may enhance the everlasting praise and glory of Christ and the Father, and may out of a pure heart, without hinderance, fear, love, honor, thank, and serve the same eternal God.

Menno Simons, "A Consoling Admonition Concerning the Sufferings, Oppressions and Persecutions of the Saints," in *The Complete Works of Menno Simons* (Elkhart, IN: John F. Funk and Brother, 1871), 207.

Paul opposes the belief that the mere doing of the *torah* marks out the identity of a religion that is "pure and undefiled before God," he does contend that the "law of Christ"—that is, the *torah* as interpreted and practiced by Jesus (see Matt. 5:17–20)—liberates the needy from their burdens (see Gal. 6:2). Given the frequent allusions to Leviticus in James, it is perhaps more plausible that this combination of "law" and "liberty" echoes a cluster of themes found in *torah*'s legislation of a jubilee year (Lev. 25:1–13), especially liberty from financial debts owed by the indigent poor. Such an economic practice helped shape the prophetic typology of "new creation" in which the disparity between rich and poor would end.

James illustrates the wisdom of obeying God's law of liberty by contrasting two imaginary congregations differently appraised by God (Jas. 1:26–27). The community who "hears the word but are not doers" deludes itself by supposing that a mere profession of God's word without its practice is approved by God. By contrast, the "religion that is pure and undefiled before God" is marked by care for the poor and powerless without being contaminated by the world (v. 27). Here then is the metric that measures the spiritual maturity of the covenant-keeping congregation: does it actively care for and journey with the least, last, lost, and the lame in its midst who struggle to find their way in the world?

ROBERT W. WALL

Commentary 2: Connecting the Reading with the World

James 1:17–27 concludes a section where James emphasizes that God does not tempt us (Jas. 1:13) but rather gives only good gifts (v. 17). Since God is constant, unlike even the celestial bodies that appear stable but change with the seasons and even die over time, we can trust God's character to remain faithful. Such faithfulness is in direct contrast to our own desires (vv. 14–16), which lead us into temptation and sin. There is hope in that God has given birth to us (v. 18) and implanted wisdom in us (v. 21) so that we are empowered to live differently. It is this call to respond to this new life that James focuses on in 1:19–27.

James begins with advice from the wisdom tradition of Scripture: "be quick to listen, slow to speak, and slow to anger" (v. 19). James then dissociates human anger from God's justice (v. 20). This claim raises two points, one personal and one social. On a personal level, we run into danger when we become convinced that our anger outstrips God's justice. On a social level, James is not talking about situations where lament, including anger, is the appropriate faithful response. He addresses those situations later in the letter (5:1–6). Here, James is describing the kind of reactionary speech and anger that occurs without deep, active listening or reflection. Such speech and anger, done quickly, creates violence in communal life. It does not come from the "implanted word," associated with wisdom and the gospel.

In fact, much of the rest of the letter indicates the violence that the community is doing with their quick speech and ineffective listening: not listening well enough to follow the law (1:22–27), speaking quickly in partiality (2:1–10), and speaking quickly in ways that curse (3:5b–6, 8–12) and perpetuate their "cravings" (4:1–2). Being slow to speak is directly contrasted with being deceived by our desires (1:16, 26): those who do one will not do the other. James does not tell us never to speak or become angry, but rather to be slow in those reactions, to prioritize honoring our relationships with all people (2:1–10) by listening and then acting accordingly based on what we hear (1:22–27; 2:14–17).

From James's perspective, this is not just good advice. James argues that such actions are for the well-being of the community that has been birthed by God (1:18) and blessed with divine gifts of wisdom (v. 17). Therefore, seeking the well-being of the community should be part of our motivation to follow his teaching. Nevertheless, because advice from James can sound like advice given from a parent or elder, we are not always inclined to follow it, even if we know it is best. To avoid this, James provides additional motivation to follow his advice.

In this section, James offers two other important motivators.[1] The first is theological: James is asking the church to imitate the God they worship. James describes God as one who does not change (v. 17). For example, instead of being divided, like having faith but not living it, God is marked by integrity. James asks the church not to forget who they are (v. 24), but rather to be shaped by the wisdom God has planted in their hearts, calling them to be a people who not only hear the word but do it (v. 22).

The second motivation is personal: James tells the congregation that they will "be blessed" as they live out this law of love (v. 25). This blessing, as in Jesus' Beatitudes (Matt. 5:1–13), promises joy in unexpected and counterintuitive places. It does not mean that acting in accordance with the law of love (Jas. 1:27) will be easy. Rather, it affirms that God will bless the action and the one who does it. Alternately, James wants believers to realize that there is a personal cost to not following God's law. We become those who deceive not just others but ourselves, characterized by a sordid soul (v. 21). Our priorities not only illustrate the way we have been formed in our faith, but they also become part of the formation of faith itself. To become the people God has called us to be, this faith, this hearing of the law, must be embodied.

It is hard to miss how important the lack of an embodied faith, or the distance between what Christians say and what we do, has been in recent years, especially for younger generations. When asked about the church, the first word

---

1. Elsa Tamez, *The Scandalous Message of James: Faith without Works Is Dead* (New York: Crossroad, 1990), 29, 49.

college students think of often is "hypocrite." Indeed, the Gospel of Matthew's condemnation of hypocrites shares a lot with James's condemnation of those who know or say the right things but who do not do them. This is why understanding James's implicit motivations for believers is important. Still, even understanding those motivations is not enough. From the perspective of skeptical congregation members, or the "nones" who have left Christianity, a church that does not practice what it preaches is, functionally, not a church.

Like much of James, however, we often find it easy to see where *others* have failed in this, be it other congregations, other "types" of Christians, or other organizations. It is much harder to see where *we* have failed to live out the faith to which God has called us (Matt. 7:3–5). James's solution to this is "looking into," or meditating on, the "law of liberty" (Jas. 1:25). James contrasts this with the analogy to the mirror: the person does not use the mirror to adjust their looks, but rather forgets whatever they saw in it. Perhaps they were in a hurry, or were distracted, or were not concerned to learn anything from looking. This is contrasted with the type of "looking" that James recommends for the law. Instead of being rushed, distracted, or self-assured, James tells his hearers to be prepared to be so changed that not only their thoughts but also their actions will be transformed by the grace of God through the gift of wisdom, here identified with the "law of liberty." In this way,

the people of God are asked to consider how they look deeply into this law, embodied by the life and death of Jesus, to be proclaimed by the church in both word and deed.

Sometimes, when we look around in the world and mourn the state of things, we find ourselves lamenting and wishing for a better time. For some of us, that better time may have been in the past, joined together with particular memories. For others, that time is future, joined together with particular hopes. For those who find their longing in reminiscing, singer/songwriter Josh Ritter's song "All Some Kind of Dream" (2019) provides some reflection. In this song, Ritter does mourn the state of the world, from his perspective. For every problem he states, whether the distance between neighbors, the refugee crisis, or fighting for justice, he asks if there was not a time when things were better. The song also asks hearers to reflect on whether such reminiscences tell the whole story. Did we ever actually live as our ideals, or as our faith, calls us to? What needs confession, repentance, and change? These are questions that go to the core of our identity. Our corporate worship offers regular opportunities for such examination, truth-telling, and transformation, if we are willing to "look at [ourselves] in the mirror" (v. 23) seriously and thoughtfully. James asks us not to live in the past or the future, but rather in the present. Faith needs to be embodied here and now.

LAURA SWEAT HOLMES

Mark 7:1–8, 14–15, 21–23

¹Now when the Pharisees and some of the scribes who had come from Jerusalem gathered around him, ²they noticed that some of his disciples were eating with defiled hands, that is, without washing them. ³(For the Pharisees, and all the Jews, do not eat unless they thoroughly wash their hands, thus observing the tradition of the elders; ⁴and they do not eat anything from the market unless they wash it; and there are also many other traditions that they observe, the washing of cups, pots, and bronze kettles.) ⁵So the Pharisees and the scribes asked him, "Why do your disciples not live according to the tradition of the elders, but eat with defiled hands?" ⁶He said to them, "Isaiah prophesied rightly about you hypocrites, as it is written,

'This people honors me with their lips,
    but their hearts are far from me;
⁷in vain do they worship me,
    teaching human precepts as doctrines.'

⁸You abandon the commandment of God and hold to human tradition." . . .

¹⁴Then he called the crowd again and said to them, "Listen to me, all of you, and understand: ¹⁵there is nothing outside a person that by going in can defile, but the things that come out are what defile." . . .

²¹"For it is from within, from the human heart, that evil intentions come: fornication, theft, murder, ²²adultery, avarice, wickedness, deceit, licentiousness, envy, slander, pride, folly. ²³All these evil things come from within, and they defile a person."

Commentary 1: Connecting the Reading with Scripture

It is likely clear even to the casual reader of the Gospels that this passage takes the form of a controversy story. In such a story, we see a person or group of people ask Jesus a question that is a veiled challenge to his authority or an attempt to trap him. Jesus answers the question in a way that his askers do not expect, demonstrating in the process their duplicity and the folly of their attempt to undermine him.

A fractured text such as this one is often an indication of issues the lectionary does not want to have to deal with. In the present text, the first omitted section (Mark 7:9–13) relieves the preacher from having to explain the meaning of the word "Corban," a term meaning "sacrifice." The second (vv. 17–20) helps the preacher avoid a long digression into the nature of the kosher laws—not to mention omitting the reference

to the latrine (tactfully translated "sewer" in the NRSV). While the omission of verse 17 obscures the shift of audience from the crowds to the disciples, the message of the passage is otherwise intact, so this commentary will focus on the lectionary text.

The reader of Mark's Gospel will, by this point, be familiar with the scribes and Pharisees as hostile to Jesus' ministry, as demonstrated by previous controversy stories. The Pharisees have thus far criticized Jesus' eating with tax collectors and sinners (2:15–17) and the disciples' plucking grain on the Sabbath (2:23–27), and the Pharisees' fasting provokes people to critique the disciples for not also fasting (2:18–20). The scribes figure in a controversy story inside a healing story (2:1–12), in which they (silently) accuse Jesus of blasphemy for forgiving the sins of the paralyzed man. When Jesus pronounces another rebuke on the occasion of his next Sabbath healing (3:1–6), we hear that the Pharisees enter into a conspiracy to destroy him.

The present passage, however, is the first time that Mark's narrator provides additional information about the Pharisees, and in so doing implies that his intended audience is likely to be unfamiliar with Jewish ritual washing practices. Jesus' questioners are concerned about being sure that God's people are not "defiled." While we might read this text as being about cleanliness and avoidance of dangerous germs, we need to remember that ritual purity, or the absence of defilement, was not cleanliness per se; indeed, a ritual bath might be taken in a stagnant and smelly *mikvah*! The conversation here is not about health practices but something much more significant: the right way to honor God in all aspects of one's life.

Although first-century Jews agreed on the necessity of following God, they disagreed on how best to do so. The priestly families in Jerusalem, for example, saw the maintenance of temple practice as the best way to keep the divine commandments—even if they had to cooperate with the Roman authorities in order to be able to do so. Zealots believed that it was impossible to follow God's will as long as Rome held the land as colonies, and so made it their first priority to overthrow the Roman overlords. Pharisees, whose main strength was in areas away from Jerusalem, sought to adapt the ancient laws in such ways that they could be kept in vastly altered political and social circumstances. Being ritually clean was, according to biblical law, a requirement for entering the temple—hardly a daily concern for, say, Galileans. The Pharisees' "innovation" was to try to live by purity laws in their daily lives, and because they believed that this honored God, they understandably encouraged others to do so, albeit with mixed results (the narrator's "all the Jews" in v. 3 is exaggeration).

Jesus and the Pharisees, then, engage in an intra-Jewish debate on how best to keep God's law. Jesus quotes Isaiah 29:13 in verses 6–7, the second time that Mark's Gospel cites Isaiah, although the passage represented in 1:2–3 as from "the prophet Isaiah" is a combination of

Malachi 3:1 and Isaiah 40:3. Jesus no doubt recognizes that the Pharisees seek to follow God's commandments, but he wants them to consider a different way of doing so. Neither Jesus nor the Pharisees nor their original audience would have seen debate about how to keep God's law as being adversarial; on the contrary, vigorous discussion and disagreement were seen as essential to greater understanding. In his own day, Jesus might have been challenged for not being educated in the right schools or being connected to the right traditions, but not simply for the fact that he engaged in debate about the best way to serve God.

Although Jesus goes on (vv. 9–13) to talk about placing tradition above God's commandment, the Isaiah quotation, along with the notion of defilement, serves to help pivot away from a contrast between Scripture and tradition and toward a contrast between "in" and "out." When the Gospel writer recounts Jesus' pronouncement in verses 14–15, it is with one eye to controversies in the early church, in which somewhat different questions regarding food are straining relations among congregations (see 1 Cor. 8–10). Jesus says in one sentence what takes Paul three chapters: food does not defile a human being if it is (purportedly) ritually "tainted."

Jesus does not stop at clarifying dietary practice; his main point is much more incisive. Jesus offers to his disciples a list of "evil intentions," a form that would have been familiar both to Mark's Christian readers and to others in the Greco-Roman world. Often referred to as "vice lists," they were a common teaching tool since the classical Greek period, and the foundation for discussion of philosophy and ethics. In the New Testament we see similar lists at 1 Corinthians 6:9–10; Galatians 5:19–21; Colossians 3:5–8; and 2 Timothy 3:2–5, among others.

Notably, while Jesus characterizes these as "the evil things [that] come from within" (Mark 7:23), what they seem to share is a character of acquisitiveness, a desire for inappropriate "taking in." Whether offenses against others' property (such as theft, avarice, and deceit) or others' persons (such as fornication, murder, and slander), these vices point to a way of living that obtains by evil means, even if what is consumed is ethically neutral. Contemporary interpreters might do well to pivot away from the apparently individualistic nature of the vices listed and consider how, for example, overconsumption of consumer goods, even if those goods are in themselves ethically neutral, ensnares us in a web of exploitation of those most vulnerable.

If we come to the present text with the caricature of the Pharisees as hypocritical dictators of Jewish law in mind, we are likely to have our prejudices affirmed. All the more important, then, that we acknowledge the multilayered nature of Mark's narration and the multiple purposes it serves. Just as Jesus' comments that food cannot defile are recounted with an eye to first-century Gentile Christian issues, Mark tells the story of Jesus' controversies with the Pharisees through the lens of later-first-century tensions between Jews and the emerging church. Yet our tendency to read this text as a condemnation of hypocritical Pharisees may be more dangerous than simply a misunderstanding of early-first-century Jewish history. Jesus critiques the Pharisees for elevating their pet concerns over divine commands, and thus failing to turn their attention inward to what they may be doing to ignore rather than uphold God's law. If we make scapegoats out of the Pharisees, we are committing the same sin: failing to attend to what evils may come from within ourselves.

SANDRA HACK POLASKI

Commentary 2: Connecting the Reading with the World

Purity codes in the traditional Jewish practices of Jesus' day strike many Christian believers as odd. They can seem legalistic and anachronistic to people not deeply familiar with ancient Israelite culture and its practices; but purity codes of that particular time and place bear some similarities to some contemporary expectations on cleanliness and propriety. All hospitals have hand sanitizers bolted to the walls of patient rooms; many churches do this as well. Churches also carefully distinguish between gluten-free Communion bread and regular wheat-based bread. Cultures around the world have varied expectations on what to eat and when to eat it. A sermon that points out that "purity codes" in some form or another continue to operate in multiple cultures today may help congregations to correct this old misunderstanding.

So, the fact that the disciples lived in a religious context of purity codes is not so unusual. What is unusual is that Jesus saw clearly that, in this particular case, the insistence on purity codes was a cover-up for self-righteousness. Jesus certainly did not dismiss traditional religious practices that had shaped him from his childhood. However, in this incident he revealed that the protests of some Pharisees and scribes were an entry point to a much deeper question, namely, "What separates a person from God?" According to traditional understandings of dietary laws, this question was answered with an insistence that contact with impure objects is what separates a person from God. Jesus said, "No. Rather, what separates a person from God is a hateful heart, bad intentions, and hypocrisy." In other words, it is not what goes into the body that causes impurity; it is what comes out of the heart. What comes out of a heart diseased with hate and arrogance is the whole list of vices in verses 21 and 22. Clearly, a damaged heart produces an exponential trail of devastation.

The analogy that Jesus uses is striking. He takes sharp issue with the traditional Jewish notion that some foods are defiling foods. Jesus says that food simply goes into the stomach and passes through the body and that this does not have the power to defile the person and alienate them from God. Defilement comes not from the stomach but from the heart.

The apostle Peter needed to learn this basic rule as well. The story of the sheet coming down from heaven in Acts 10 underscores the point that Jesus makes in Mark 7. When Peter learns this lesson, it frees him to see the universal reach of the good news of Jesus Christ; no one is excluded; all are welcome; God's covenant faithfulness includes the Gentiles. In this brief story from Mark 7, Jesus is setting the foundations for the early church's shocking realization that God's gracious reach extends to all the world.

This basic rule that Jesus uncovered to his disciples and his accusers has striking and immediate implications for Christian persons today. The implications ripple out from the personal to the congregational to the communal to the political and global.

Consider the context of worship. If the preacher and congregation take seriously Jesus' insight that what comes from the heart is what defiles a person and alienates them from God, then the congregation will take seriously the prayer of confession. Far from being an expendable liturgical moment, as some churches unfortunately have assumed, the prayer of confession invites the congregation to deep self-awareness. It invites worshipers to consider honestly the attitudes and habits of their hearts that might be alienating them from God and others.

The Lord's Supper also leads to personal and congregational self-awareness of what motivates and animates the heart. At the Table, we realize that we have the capacity to be like Judas. After all, Jesus shared his meal with his betrayer. The former archbishop of Canterbury, Rowan Williams, once said that the Lord's Supper "reminds us of the need for honest repentance—of the need to confront our capacity to betray and forget the gift we have been given."[1] When the Lord's Supper is received with honesty, self-awareness, and repentance, it draws the worshipers into gratitude for the world and for each other. Again, Rowan Williams says that "it changes how we see one another (as we learn to see our neighbor as God's guest)."[2] The Lord's Supper has, through the power of the Holy Spirit, the capacity to change how we see creation, how we see other people, how we see ourselves.

When Jesus rejects the assumption that food is what defiles us, he hints at the tragic reality that true defilement is not something that is taken into the body and then passes quickly out. Defilement lurks in the heart. It is tenacious and hard to root out. It puts on multiple masks and disguises. This defilement shows up in a depressing variety of forms, as indicated in

verses 21 and 22. John Siegenthaler, who served as an advisor to Attorney General Robert Kennedy during the civil rights movement, mused late in his life how puzzled and dismayed he was about the deep attitudes of racial prejudice he struggled to overcome. He said, in a documentary, "I just don't know what was in my heart. I don't know what was in the hearts of my father and mother."[3] It bothered him, as he looked back on his life, how tenacious prejudice is and how hard it is to eradicate.

Another place of connection is the troubled arena of national and global politics. It is no surprise to any preacher and any congregation that fierce emotions abound in this arena. Many preachers dread addressing political issues from the pulpit; they know full well that they will be criticized no matter what they say. Nevertheless, vague generalities concerning profound human issues are not an option for the faithful preacher. Jesus made clear in this story that what alienates people from God are the murky and tangled motivations of the heart. These motivations, in political discourse, can include bias, ignorance, judgment, and blame. They can include racism, sexism, and national chauvinism. They can include hatred and revenge. These are the heart diseases that defile us, disable our ministries, and undermine human flourishing. The preacher must name these heart diseases.

Excavating the deepest failures of our hearts is no small task. This is due to our persistent resistance to self-awareness and to the sheer tenacity and extended reach of heart corruptions. The legacy of trauma in an individual has lifelong consequences. Likewise, the legacy of national or corporate trauma stretches for decades and generations. The preacher has the challenge of calling the congregation to the kind of heart awareness that is usually plastered over with defensiveness and self-justifications.

Understanding and acknowledging the distortions of the heart, both personally and corporately, is a painful and difficult challenge. We resist it with all our might. It was terribly difficult

1. Rowan Williams, *Being Christian: Baptism, Bible, Eucharist, Prayer* (Grand Rapids: Eerdmans, 2014), 52, 53.
2. Williams, *Being Christian*, 51.
3. "Freedom Riders," *American Experience*, season 23, #12, directed by Stanley Nelson, PBS, 2011, film.

for Christian white slave owners to acknowledge the wrong of enslavement in the American South in the nineteenth century. It was painfully difficult for the architects and defenders of apartheid in South Africa to truly listen to their victims in the Truth and Reconciliation Commission in the 1990s. This text in Mark 7, in an original context of dietary practices, invites hearers today to consider what actually is in their heart that alienates them from God.

LEANNE VAN DYK

Proper 18 (Sunday between September 4 and September 10)

Proverbs 22:1–2, 8–9, 22–23
and Isaiah 35:4–7a
Psalm 125 and Psalm 146

James 2:1–10 (11–13), 14–17
Mark 7:24–37

Proverbs 22:1–2, 8–9, 22–23

[1]A good name is to be chosen rather than great riches,
and favor is better than silver or gold.
[2]The rich and the poor have this in common:
the LORD is the maker of them all.

. . . .

[8]Whoever sows injustice will reap calamity,
and the rod of anger will fail.
[9]Those who are generous are blessed,
for they share their bread with the poor.

. . . .

[22]Do not rob the poor because they are poor,
or crush the afflicted at the gate;
[23]for the LORD pleads their cause
and despoils of life those who despoil them.

Isaiah 35:4–7a

[4]Say to those who are of a fearful heart,
"Be strong, do not fear!
Here is your God.
He will come with vengeance,
with terrible recompense.
He will come and save you."

[5]Then the eyes of the blind shall be opened,
and the ears of the deaf unstopped;
[6]then the lame shall leap like a deer,
and the tongue of the speechless sing for joy.
For waters shall break forth in the wilderness,
and streams in the desert;
[7]the burning sand shall become a pool,
and the thirsty ground springs of water.

Commentary 1: Connecting the Reading with Scripture

The passages assigned for this Sunday offer hope to the poor, marginalized, and suffering. Both Isaiah 35:4–7a and Psalm 125 encourage the fearful and the downtrodden to trust the Lord. The eternal protection of God is reaffirmed in Psalm 146:1–10, which states that the reign of the God of Israel "who executes justice for the oppressed, who gives food to the hungry," who "watches over the strangers," and "upholds the orphan and the widow" is perpetual. This sentiment is echoed in Proverbs 22 and James 2, which assert that piety and wisdom are not just about faith or belief (Jas. 2:17) but about one's treatment of the poor and the afflicted who are under God's watch and care. Finally, care of the afflicted is given dramatic enactment with the healing of the deaf man and the daughter of the Syrophoenician woman who boldly engages Jesus in Mark 7.

Befitting the theme of this Sunday, the verses from Proverbs 22 discuss the care of the poor and the nature of injustice. The chapter from which these verses are taken consists of collection of various sayings, all supposedly associated with Solomon (Prov. 10:1–22:6). Whether Solomon was the real author is difficult to ascertain. Likely, these proverbs were linked to Solomon because of his connection to sapiential traditions.

Why and how Solomon came to be so closely connected to wisdom—so much so that several chapters of Proverbs are attributed to this figure—is intriguingly unclear. This association between Solomon and wisdom might have stemmed purely from propagandistic reasons— that is, to assert the greatness of Solomon by portraying him as renowned for his wisdom. Indeed, Ashurbanipal, king of Assyria, boasted of his scribal education and was famous for his collection of texts in Nineveh. This link between Solomon and wisdom, as some have speculated, might also have stemmed from this king's support or patronage of sapiential schools.

Proverbs 22 itself is an anthology within a larger anthology called the book of Proverbs. The book of Proverbs consists of a collection, or anthology, of different instructions, sayings, advice, and poetic units. As a result of this anthology-like aspect of Proverbs, the book as a whole is difficult to date, and various sections within the corpus are dated differently. Though it is impossible to know for sure, it is possible that Proverbs 22, as part of the sayings of Solomon, stemmed from the time period of this king. Proverbs, alongside Job, Ecclesiastes, and Song of Solomon, is a wisdom book, which in the Jewish ordering of the Hebrew biblical books is placed in the final section of the Bible called the Writings (*Ketuvim*). This last section consisted of texts that were likely the last to be canonized.

The particular sayings chosen from Proverbs 22 for this Sunday center on the treatment of the poor and issues concerning wealth. The passage begins with the statement that a good name is better than money or riches. One's name in the Hebrew Bible is not simply a designation but denotes one's reputation, fame, or essential essence. The name can also mean something that lives on after your death as a kind of memorial (Deut. 25:6). Hence, this verse might imply, echoing the sentiments in Ecclesiastes 3:20 and 9:2, that all of us are equal in that we all die, whether rich or poor—an idea that is affirmed in the next verse, which states that the Lord is the maker of both the rich and the poor (Prov. 22:2). Not only are we all equal in the eyes of God, no matter our wealth, but we all share the same fate; we cannot take our riches with us. Therefore, Proverbs urges, we should pay attention to the things that are more permanent, not to things that are fleeting like wealth—an idea worthy of reminder from the pulpit.

Because God is the master of everyone, the other verses from Proverbs 22 suggest that God is taking care to watch and observe the treatment of those that are less powerful. Proverbs 22:8–9, for example, reminds readers that one who "sows injustice will reap calamity" (v. 8), while, in contrast, those who "share their bread with the poor" will be blessed (v. 9). These sentiments of God's desire for the care of the poor are confirmed in verses 22–23, which directly command that one "not rob the poor . . . or crush the afflicted at the gate" (v. 22). This advice is laced with threat. The Lord, the writer of Proverbs states, "despoils of life those who despoil them," that is, the poor (v. 23).

Similar sentiments are also found in the second passage for this Sunday from Isaiah 35:4–7a, which, though part of the earliest preexilic part of the book of Isaiah, First Isaiah (Isa. 1–39), appears to have been inserted later, possibly during the time of the exile. Isaiah 35:4–7a is a lyrical and hopeful passage that promises reversals and divine aid for the hopeless, the suffering, and the fearful hearted (Isa. 35:4). God promises through Isaiah that the eyes and ears of the blind and deaf will be opened, the lame will leap like a hare, and the mute will sing with joy (vv. 5–6).

These reversals are likened to revivification of flora and fauna in the dry, parched desert, which suddenly overflows with life-giving water in the form of streams, pools, and springs (v. 7a). The image of the life that springs forth from this sudden inundation of water is akin to a resurrection, which is fitting, as God promises at the end of Isaiah 35 (v. 10), that Israel, likely exiled and therefore seemingly dead, will again be revived when God comes and saves it (v. 4).

The sentiments found in Proverbs and Isaiah—to care for the poor, that God is on the side of the suffering and the fearful—initially seem like easy ideas to extol at the pulpit, especially in a world of increasing wealth inequality. Yet the execution of these sentiments, especially when laced with the threat that God will despoil those who despoil the poor, is difficult and unclear in the modern world. Are partaking

in the stock market or buying cheap clothing or items made in another country with unknown labor laws akin to despoiling the poor that Proverbs warns against? Hence, one potential topic of discussion at the pulpit might be on the difficulties of caring for the poor and suffering in an increasingly complicated world.

Indeed, it is not just the world that is complicated but the biblical text as well. For example, when we consider verses in Proverbs and Isaiah that were excluded from the lectionary readings, some challenging ideas are evident. Proverbs 22:15, for example, encourages corporal punishment for children, while Proverbs 22:4, in an echo of the prosperity gospel, seems to promise unequivocally that those who are humble and fearful will be awarded by God with riches, honor, and life (22:4). These are problematic verses that support behavior and ideas that many of us now find uncomfortable.

The excluded verses therefore challenge us to ask important questions about the reading and interpretation of Scripture. What should we do with biblical passages that convey sentiments that we now consider sexist, racist, illegal, or even just impolite? Should we ignore such passages, and how much decontextualization should be allowed? In short, the larger context of the texts from Proverbs and Isaiah encourages us to examine ourselves as readers and interpreters, so that we can respect the ancient context of our canonical texts, while discerning in it a message that is fitting and necessary for the people of God today.

SONG-MI SUZIE PARK

Commentary 2: Connecting the Reading with the World

We have come to understand the book of Proverbs as Wisdom literature, as a repository of wise ways to navigate life. It may feel, therefore, mildly surprising to come across these verses from chapter 22 that speak for the poor with the sort of passionate advocacy we typically associate with the prophets and with Jesus himself. Here in these six terse verses we have, in fact, a distillation of moral imperatives that permeate the rest of the Scriptures.

The writer of these proverbs presupposes a chronic problem: that wealth and the social clout associated with it end up being unevenly distributed in society. Human nature being what it is, such inequitable conditions are always ripe for abuse. If the scenario is allowed to play out unchallenged, the weaker will only become more disadvantaged and oppressed by those who are stronger and more privileged than their victims.

From a purely Darwinian perspective, such developments are inevitable, and how they play out are a matter of no moral consequence. However, this is not so from a biblical perspective: the rich and the poor, the oppressed and their oppressors, are all creatures of the same Maker (Prov. 22:2). Therefore, everyone must one day give an account of how they have treated their neighbors and sought to live in alignment with their Maker's just intentions.

Perhaps the most decisive claim made here is that the Creator God champions the cause of those who have been victimized by human systems that enable increasingly asymmetrical distributions of wealth and power. The implicit explanation is that the Creator's heart desires that the dynamics of human society should reflect, rather than obscure, the *equal* dignity and worth of all God's image-bearers. Christians should wince whenever they hear anyone's "net worth" calculated in a dollar amount. One of the chief functions of a culture is to tell its members what they ought to value most. The church, as an alternative culture, must practice and commend a different calculus in estimating the worth of human beings, and God's other creatures as well.

What does it mean to know God? To acquire information about God is useful and necessary, but there is more than this to knowing God in the biblical sense. To experience the presence of God, to have some personal acquaintance with the presence of the Divine, is an important addition to, and upgrade on, this first, intellectual way of knowing God.

Scripture teaches a third and even higher sense in which we can know God. This is to participate in the divine disposition, to have our hearts beat in sync with the heart of God. "He judged the cause of the poor and needy," wrote the prophet Jeremiah, then adding rhetorically, "Is not this to know me? says the Lord" (Jer. 22:16). To know God, which is surely the loftiest of Christian aspirations, involves apprehending God intellectually and experientially, but also and ultimately to care about what God cares about.

This insight into the heart of God points Christians in the direction of a generous "third way," beyond the polarizing rhetoric of competing political camps. In our personal voting patterns, in the management of our workplace budgets, in deciding whom we invite to join our boards and why, and in our everyday contributions to church decision-making, those who know their God will consistently regard all persons more highly than they regard ruthless loyalty to financial advantage and further aggregation of power.

The passage from Isaiah is part of a grand vision of a blessed future for God's people. The prophet sees rejoicing and splendor and provision and peace ahead. At the very center of this promised future is the splendor of God's own self (Isa. 35:2), radiating outward to the farthest corners of the scene. It is a splendid example of the so-called optimistic eschatology of the Judeo-Christian tradition, the declaration that in the end, and despite all foreboding, shorter-term indicators to the contrary, God's goodness and justice will eventually prevail. The last word in human history shall be *shalom*.

It is noteworthy that the disclosure of this vision has a very practical and pastoral purpose. Our text begins, "Say to those who are of a fearful heart, 'Be strong, do not fear!'" (v. 4a). The purpose of the vision is to counter and correct a disposition of fear in the hearts of Isaiah's hearers. It is little wonder that people were fearful. Just glancing forward and back from the text we discover encroaching armies and reports of calamities everywhere. The circumstances were chaotic, uncertain, and ominous.

Fear is a powerful human emotion. It shows up in almost all psychology-generated lists of the most basic human emotional responses to life. In its essence, it is triggered by the anticipation of a negative or threatening possibility. It is very much tied to the perception of future vulnerability. In his famous ode "To a Mouse" (1785), the Scottish poet Robbie Burns rued his capacity to anticipate the future.

> Still thou art blest, compared wi' me!
> The present only toucheth thee:
> But och! I backward cast my e'e,
>   On prospects drear!
> An' forward, tho' I canna see
>   I guess an' fear.[1]

---

1. "To a Mouse," in *The Poems of Robert Burns* (New York: Thomas Y. Crowell & Co., 1900), 38.

Fear can be a healthy response to a genuine threat. Even then, it is best experienced occasionally rather than perpetually. It is quite another thing when fear becomes a chronic disposition, a habituated pattern of response to the totality of life. Twentieth-century theologian Reinhold Niebuhr diagnosed the human condition as driven by anxiety, which he depicted as a kind of low-grade fear triggered by consciousness of our mortality, and the frailty of our existence. When real and present dangers compound our life situation, chronic anxiety can spike into full-blown fear. We are living in a surreal time in which unprecedented prosperity for some is combined with a pervasive fear of what the future holds for all.

The biblical author here, however, seeks to defuse such a disposition of fear because of its dispiriting impact on those overwhelmed by it. "Be strong, do not fear!" (v. 4a). Fear weakens by intimidating. It erodes resilience. It makes cowards of us all. Then what we fear can become a self-fulfilling prophecy. Our demoralized passivity can actually hasten the scenario we most dread.

The healing antidote to such downward spirals is hope, the confident and sustaining anticipation of a positive future. There is good reason why it remains one of the three great Christian virtues, alongside faith and love (1 Cor. 13:13). Hope keeps us leaning into the future, rather than recoiling from it. Here it rests on an assurance of God's coming intervention in history. Admittedly, the future God promises looks as improbable as it appears wonderful. It will be characterized by dramatic reversals, wholesale turnarounds in the fortunes of the most disadvantaged, and fruitfulness in the most unpromising of situations. Water will gush forth where presently we see only burning sand.

Believing this makes us strong. Being *able* to believe it is, of course, the great challenge. Mysteriously, inexplicably, faith can and often does emerge as a natural response to the hearing of the inspired word of assurance. So, the church must keep declaring it, again and again, to those who are fearful in heart. As it does, it must count on the witness of the Spirit to make the divine promise emotionally meaningful, in ways that alter the default settings of the psyche.

GLEN G. SCORGIE

Proper 18 (Sunday between September 4 and September 10)

Psalm 125

[1]Those who trust in the LORD are like Mount Zion,
  which cannot be moved, but abides forever.
[2]As the mountains surround Jerusalem,
  so the LORD surrounds his people,
  from this time on and forevermore.
[3]For the scepter of wickedness shall not rest
  on the land allotted to the righteous,
so that the righteous might not stretch out
  their hands to do wrong.
[4]Do good, O LORD, to those who are good,
  and to those who are upright in their hearts.
[5]But those who turn aside to their own crooked ways
  the LORD will lead away with evildoers.
  Peace be upon Israel!

Psalm 146

[1]Praise the LORD!
Praise the LORD, O my soul!
[2]I will praise the LORD as long as I live;
  I will sing praises to my God all my life long.

[3]Do not put your trust in princes,
  in mortals, in whom there is no help.
[4]When their breath departs, they return to the earth;
  on that very day their plans perish.

[5]Happy are those whose help is the God of Jacob,
  whose hope is in the LORD their God,
[6]who made heaven and earth,
  the sea, and all that is in them;
who keeps faith forever;
  [7]who executes justice for the oppressed;
  who gives food to the hungry.

The LORD sets the prisoners free;
  [8]the LORD opens the eyes of the blind.
The LORD lifts up those who are bowed down;
  the LORD loves the righteous.
[9]The LORD watches over the strangers;
  he upholds the orphan and the widow,
  but the way of the wicked he brings to ruin.

[10]The LORD will reign forever,
  your God, O Zion, for all generations.
Praise the LORD!

Connecting the Psalm with Scripture and Worship

Psalm 125. This psalm, one of the "Songs of Ascents" (Pss. 120–134), likely originated in the Israelite experience of making pilgrimages to Jerusalem. The references to Mount Zion and the mountains surrounding Jerusalem (Ps. 125:1, 2) suggest the specific geography that pilgrims will see as they approach the city, and "the land allotted to the righteous" (v. 3) will remind the travelers of the blessing of the entire land around them as they journey. The content of the psalm affirms God's faithful protection in all circumstances ("the LORD surrounds his people, from this time on and forevermore," v. 2) and asks that it continue ("Do good, O LORD, to those who are good," v. 4).

The psalmist describes the people in relationship to the Lord as righteous (v. 3), good, and upright in their hearts (v. 4). Unlike some biblical texts, this is not an exhortation to good behavior, but simply a description of people who trust in the Lord (v. 1). Those who are on the journey, joining their voices in this song, simply will be steadfast. Like Psalm 15 (which is appointed for the previous week), Psalm 125 emphasizes that those who trust in God will not be moved.

Verse 3, in describing the "scepter of wickedness" on the land, has led many to conclude that this psalm comes from the postexilic period, when foreign rulers had authority in the land, tempting the people to adopt their ways and "do wrong." In response, the psalmist asserts that such "wicked" power is not ultimate, but that God as protector of the people will "lead away" evildoers and those who follow them. Overall, the psalm shows a basic contrast between earthly rulers, who wield the "scepter of wickedness" now, and God, whose righteous protection will finally triumph.

In the semicontinuous lectionary cycle, this psalm responds to Proverbs 22:1–2, 8–9, 22–23. The passages share similar themes of God's faithfulness in caring for people: the poor in Proverbs 22:23 and the good/righteous in Psalm 125:4. In addition, Psalm 125, like Proverbs 22, emphasizes that righteous behavior will be rewarded, and wicked behavior will have bad consequences (Prov. 22:8–9; Ps. 125:3–5). The

threat of punishment in both passages is compared to a stick, presumably raised to strike the offender: "the rod of anger" (Prov. 22:8) and the "scepter of wickedness" (Ps. 125:3) ("rod" and "scepter" are the same word in Hebrew). Proverbs 22 is more interested in the just and generous treatment of "the poor" (a term that recurs four times in eight verses), while Psalm 125 focuses more on categories of righteousness and wickedness, but they share confidence that God's righteousness will prevail.

In addition to hearing this psalm as a response to the Old Testament reading, it could function well adapted as a call to worship (esp. vv. 1–2), perhaps as a responsive reading in procession, evoking the original setting of the psalm.

One complication in liturgical use of the psalm is the final prayer, "Peace be upon Israel!" (v. 5), in a day when Israel is not only an ancient identity but also a modern nation-state. Any use of this prayer needs to avoid both anti-Judaism (in rejecting such language) and uncritical endorsement of all policies of any particular Israeli government (in simply offering such a prayer without interpretation). Yet surely, now as then, we can and should pray for the peace of Israel and all its inhabitants. More, this prayer can be heard as a plea not only for one part of the world, but for all peoples and nations, including our own. It is a prayer that God's peace will prevail despite all those who may wield "scepters of wickedness."

Psalm 146. This psalm is the first of the final praise psalms in the Psalter (Pss. 146–150), all of which begin and end with "Praise the LORD!" (*Hallelu-ya*). The psalmist here summons all to praise and then affirms, "I will sing praises to my God all my life long" (Ps. 146:2). The causes for praise are manifold: God's creation and enduring faithfulness (v. 6); executing justice, feeding the hungry, and setting the prisoners free (v. 7); opening the eyes of the blind and caring for all the vulnerable, including strangers, widows, orphans, and those who are bowed down (vv. 8–9). "The righteous" might sound like an outlier in this list of the vulnerable, but this assumes that those who reflect God's righteousness will suffer for it, so they are in fact among the vulnerable. The overall tone is exultant, focusing on the goodness of the "God of Jacob," who has done such marvelous things.

There are notes of contrast, as the psalmist acknowledges the fleeting power of princes (v. 3) and "the wicked" (v. 9). Yet these threats to God's reign are only temporary; the princes "return to the earth" and "their plans perish" (v. 4), while God brings "the way of the wicked" to ruin. Those who hear and sing the psalm are reminded that they should not put their trust (or their fear) in such powers, for it is God, and not they, who will reign forever.

Verse 5 affirms that the one who trusts in God rather than human powers is "happy" or "blessed." This echoes Psalms 1 and 2, thus bookending the entire Psalter and reiterating the central message that God alone is sovereign and worthy of praise, and that those whose lives are rooted in God will be truly happy.

Throughout this psalm the focus on God's care for the oppressed echoes Isaiah's focus on God's saving justice for the oppressed, heard in the first reading of the day. In both cases, the eyes of the blind are opened (Ps. 146:8; Isa. 35:5). Other categories of the vulnerable are different, but the overall emphasis is the same: God will save those who are crushed or ignored by the world. This theme also connects with James's concern for the poor and oppressed in the reading from James 2:1–10, 14–17.

Furthermore, the psalm anticipates Jesus' care for the oppressed. In the passage from Mark appointed for this day, Jesus encounters the Syrophoenician woman and heals a man who has both speech and hearing disabilities. The psalm praises God "who gives food to the hungry" (Ps. 146:7), and the Syrophoenician woman challenges Jesus with another feeding metaphor: "Sir, even the dogs under the table eat the children's crumbs" (Mark 7:28). Indeed, a sermon on the encounter between Jesus and this multiply oppressed woman might engage Psalm 146 deeply, as the woman urges Jesus to truly embody the power of God in executing justice for the oppressed, setting free the prisoner (her daughter who is possessed by an unclean spirit), and watching over the stranger and those who are bowed down. Has she herself been overhearing Psalm 146, and is she now calling Jesus to put it into practice?

In addition to reading and preaching, a congregation might engage this Hallelujah psalm liturgically. Imagine using the opening verses at the beginning of worship, perhaps alternating spoken phrases with a sung "Alleluia." Imagine adapting the phrases from verses 6–9, the central section naming God's saving acts, for intercessory prayer. The prayer leader, for instance, might affirm with the psalmist: "The Lord sets the prisoners free," and then offer prayers for all those now in prison, then moving in similar fashion through the remaining affirmations. Alternatively, a prayer leader might invite members of the congregation to offer free prayers of their own in response to each of the phrases naming God's acts of saving justice.

MARTHA L. MOORE-KEISH

James 2:1–10 (11–13), 14–17

¹My brothers and sisters, do you with your acts of favoritism really believe in our glorious Lord Jesus Christ? ²For if a person with gold rings and in fine clothes comes into your assembly, and if a poor person in dirty clothes also comes in, ³and if you take notice of the one wearing the fine clothes and say, "Have a seat here, please," while to the one who is poor you say, "Stand there," or, "Sit at my feet," ⁴have you not made distinctions among yourselves, and become judges with evil thoughts? ⁵Listen, my beloved brothers and sisters. Has not God chosen the poor in the world to be rich in faith and to be heirs of the kingdom that he has promised to those who love him? ⁶But you have dishonored the poor. Is it not the rich who oppress you? Is it not they who drag you into court? ⁷Is it not they who blaspheme the excellent name that was invoked over you?

⁸You do well if you really fulfill the royal law according to the scripture, "You shall love your neighbor as yourself." ⁹But if you show partiality, you commit sin and are convicted by the law as transgressors. ¹⁰For whoever keeps the whole law but fails in one point has become accountable for all of it. ¹¹For the one who said, "You shall not commit adultery," also said, "You shall not murder." Now if you do not commit adultery but if you murder, you have become a transgressor of the law. ¹²So speak and so act as those who are to be judged by the law of liberty. ¹³For judgment will be without mercy to anyone who has shown no mercy; mercy triumphs over judgment.

¹⁴What good is it, my brothers and sisters, if you say you have faith but do not have works? Can faith save you? ¹⁵If a brother or sister is naked and lacks daily food, ¹⁶and one of you says to them, "Go in peace; keep warm and eat your fill," and yet you do not supply their bodily needs, what is the good of that? ¹⁷So faith by itself, if it has no works, is dead.

Commentary 1: Connecting the Reading with Scripture

The Letter of James addresses a Diaspora congregation whose allegiance to God is tested by "trials of various kinds" (Jas. 1:1–2 ESV). Instead of blaming God for what they lack in material goods (v. 13), which is the fool's deception (v. 16), James encourages believers to ask a generous God for wisdom (vv. 5–6)—a "word of truth" that God gives any who ask (vv. 17–19). When humbly received, God's word is able to save the faithful from inward sin (see 1:14–15). In particular, the community that quickly receives and "looks into" God's word as "the perfect law" (v. 25) liberates its members from inward sin and also the community's most vulnerable members—its "widows and orphans"—from their experiences of "distress" (v. 27).

James applies this opening discourse on Christian existence to a social crisis that tests the community's devotion to God—a God who has elected the poor to be rich in faith and heirs of God's coming reign (2:5). Jesus is introduced in 2:1 as the normative personification of a community that testifies to its friendship with God by its loving responses to poor and powerless members (vv. 2-3). Those who practice mercy toward their neighbors in obedience to God's royal rule have reason to anticipate their reception of divine mercy in the coming age (see 2:8–13). Implicit throughout James are the contrasting destinies of communities who care for the community's poor in obedience to God's "royal law of love" (v. 8) and those who favor rich outsiders to the neglect of their own poor members (vv. 2–4). God targets them for a merciless judgment (v. 13) on a terrifying "day of slaughter" (see 5:4–6).

Today's lesson provides a catalogue of evidences God attends to when determining whether or not to give mercy to a people. In doing so, James upends the secular wisdom that money makes might. Preaching James should issue a strong reminder that the mission of God's people should identify with the faithful poor as heirs of the coming kingdom.

In response to James's witness to God's preferential option for the poor, readers may note a connection between the injustice and disgrace the poor experience in the law courts at the hands of the oppressive rich (vv. 6–7) and the rich farmers who unjustly withhold wages due their poor field hands (5:4–6). These extravagant case studies in James explore the link between a community's tacit participation in acts of social injustice, especially toward their own members, and the favoritism of the community's leaders who "take notice" of the rich (2:2–3), while sounding pious platitudes about the poor, without then actively supplying them with the material goods they need (2:14–17). Following the gospel of OT prophets, James asserts that God desires works of obedience rather than a religion of the mouth (see 1:26).

James is concerned about the consequences of human speech within a community's life. In a digital world, where blogging and tweets often divide a community, preaching James should issue a reminder that our language, whether verbal or digital, should embody God's love in a way that heals a community rather than fracturing it.

The title James uses for "our glorious Lord Jesus Christ" (2:1) is robust. In a single expression, James puts Jesus forward as the Messiah (Christ) whose incarnation ("glorious," cf. Ezek. 1:29) confirms his exalted role in God's victory over sin and death ("Lord," cf. Phil. 2:6–11). Jesus is introduced by James at this particular point to underscore his messianic ministry to the poor (see Luke 14:4–14; 18:1–8). Jesus provides a prophetic example for the community, whose favored treatment of the rich is considered law breaking and may even imperil its future with God (cf. 2:9–13).

The prohibition not to "deny the faithfulness of our Lord Jesus Christ" (2:1 CEB) shares a striking resemblance to Paul's positive use of the phrase when characterizing Jesus' death as an act of faithfulness to God and the means by which God's promise of salvation is fulfilled (so Rom. 3:22; Gal. 3:22). In both cases, the genitive relationship between faith and Jesus Christ is subjective and refers to Jesus' faithfulness to God, rather than to the community's faith in him. In this case, James implicates Jesus' ministry among the poor as exemplary of a community's obedience of God's "royal (=kingly) law," which therefore demands that it care for its most needy members (see Lev. 19:18; Gal. 5:14). To obey this law is to "do well" in God's eyes (Jas. 2:8).

Christlike faithfulness, then, is demonstrated by acts that align with God's preferential option for the faithful poor (v. 5), rather than with the actions and dispositions of those who favor the rich and famous (vv. 2–4). A community that transgresses God's law of love (v. 8) and sins by marginalizing the poor is no different from those who commit murder and adultery (v. 11)—transgressions of biblical proportion that all believers would agree are covenant breaking.

James's use of the adjective "royal" (*basilikos*) to underwrite the Levitical demand to love neighbors links it to the letter's radical understanding of divine election: "God has chosen the poor . . . to be heirs of the kingdom [*basileia*]" (v. 5). Any who profess the lordship of Jesus but then engage in acts that privilege the wealthy of the community at the expense of its poor members fail God. The consequences of doing so are starkly stated: the apocalypse of God's judgment will be without mercy to those who show no mercy to their poor neighbors (v. 13).

James reprises the earlier use of "law of liberty" (1:25; 2:12), not only to indicate God's metric for distributing divine blessing, but also to expose the duplicity of a community that says one thing but does its opposite. James coins a word for such duplicity: "double-minded" (lit. "two-souled," 1:8; 4:8; see 3:9). God's kingdom is not a place for the double-minded but welcomes those with a track record of showing mercy to others.

The subtext of the letter's deliberative discourse against favoring the rich over the poor is now made crystal clear in 2:14–17: those who profess to follow Jesus and say they obey God's rule of law as he did, but then provide no material help to their own members who are naked and hungry, but rather pass the peace of the Lord to them in pious benediction (2:16), practice a "dead" faith (vv. 14, 17). The repetition of the rhetorical question, "What good is it?" (vv. 14, 16), presumes two outcomes. Of course, such neglect offers no help to those who desperately need it. It also is of no benefit eschatologically when what a community says and does is measured by the law of liberty, which demands acts of mercy toward the poor neighbor. This second outcome anticipates the merciless judgment of God.

The claim that "faith by itself, if it has no works, is dead" (v. 17) is elaborated and illustrated by the remainder of James 2. Besides the example of Jesus, two other biblical figures, Abraham and Rahab, are mentioned, along with "the demons," to underwrite the dispositions and practices of a "religion that is pure and undefiled before God" (1:27). Their examples assert that the mere profession of orthodox faith does not save anyone if it is not demonstrated by works of mercy. The professed faith of the demons whose evil works oppose God is contrasted with the faith of both Abraham and Rahab, patriarch and prostitute, to secure two of James's most pressing claims: not only must what a community believes about God be "brought to completion by the works" regulated by God's "law of liberty" (2:22), but a community's friendship with God, and the covenant blessings implicated by such a friendship, is forged by a faith that is embodied in works of love (vv. 23–26).

ROBERT W. WALL

Commentary 2: Connecting the Reading with the World

James 2 continues the main points of his argument from chapter 1. He focuses on the dangers of speech, both how speech can be misused to show favoritism, and how even faithful speech is insufficient for an embodied and practiced faith.

In James 1, the author has highlighted how our speech can be deceptive, deceiving us into forgetting our own identity (Jas. 1:24–25) or encouraging us to give into dangerous desires (v. 15). Such speech makes our faith "worthless" (v. 26). In the next section, James stresses that speech can have negative consequences even in the service of something good, like hospitality. The congregation James has in mind seems to be known for offering hospitality to visitors, and they do so in part through speech. Of course, speech is one important way to convey to visitors that they are welcome, whether in a home, in a space of worship, or in a public venue. However, there are also ways that spoken and unspoken speech reinforces social hierarchies. In one example, James says the congregation encourages those who are wealthy to enjoy seats of honor, while those who are impoverished ("filthy clothes") are ostracized or subordinated (2:2–3).

It is easy to see that such discrimination is wrong. There are consistent critiques of the dangers of money in politics, for example. We are often concerned about how money provides access to some, and how money can enable a lack of accountability for unethical dealings (2:6). It is so easy to see how money is a problem "over there." The preacher can help listeners understand James's insistence that our internalization of "worldly" (1:27) economic values, as opposed to the values of the kingdom of God (2:8), shapes even the ways that we welcome people into the life of the worshiping community.

Perhaps this is in part because James indicates that the problem here is not just what we say, though that is a central piece of his argument. It is also how we "take notice" (2:3) of things. Preachers could ask, What draws our attention? What influences have shaped our vision? North American cultures have often valued the cult of celebrity, celebrating those who have money and influence and access. Social-media platforms have encouraged this and helped it intersect with our everyday lives. These experiences shape our vision to value, envy, or laud such constructed lives, while knowing little about the actual lives people live.

James's recommendation is twofold: first, we are to remind ourselves that God has "chosen the poor" (2:5), and second, we are to be "quick to listen" to the "word of truth" that has given us a new identity in Christ (1:18–19; 2:1), to live out "the royal law." James says that we can fulfill "the royal law"—the law of the kingdom of God—if we love our neighbors as ourselves (2:8). Showing partiality prevents us from loving our neighbors, both rich and poor (2:9). The rich, as recipients of favoritism, become formed into the kind of people who expect such power and access, while the poor receive the message that they are not wanted, needed, or loved.

Furthermore, showing partiality may have shaped whom we see as our neighbors. The formative influences of both God's identity and the shape of God's instruction through the Scriptures should help us see how God's vision and calling on our lives are wholly different from the values perpetuated by society.

If the danger of speech in terms of hospitality is in what we say and to whom we direct that speech, James next returns (1:22, 25) to a different danger of speech. Here, we say something well-meaning, but it is empty because there is no action attached to it. James identifies this problem with the same kind of language he uses in chapter 1. Even faithful speech without action is like hearing the word of God and then forgetting it, instead of acting upon it. James specifically offers the example of wishing someone in need well, instead of blessing them and then providing for their needs (2:15–16).

The individualization ("a brother or sister") of this text makes it provocatively incisive. Who among us in Christian communities has not passed by one in need without even speaking, or spoken without acting? Of course, there are many debates about the best and most effective ways to help those in need. James keeps us on our toes by highlighting the importance of doing something tangible and immediate, not just saying kind words.

This teaching about speech is analogous to the debates about the use of the phrase "thoughts and prayers," offered after many tragedies but especially after mass shootings in the United States. The critique of this phrase is not that offering thoughts and prayers in themselves is wrong or unhelpful. Rather, the repeated offering of "thoughts and prayers" may feel empty to survivors who see no action. James might say, in this context, that prayer that does not lead to responsible, faithful action is foolish, or even dead (5:14–15). In his example, James does not offer prescriptions on how his audience might "supply [the] bodily needs" of the person who "is naked and lacks daily food" (2:15–16). The congregation (2:14) as a whole should simply act in faithful ways to supply them. This is exactly what is meant by loving one's neighbor (2:8).

James's ultimate point about faith, speech, and action is also his most famous: a faith that is only spoken (2:14) but not enacted (2:17) is no faith at all. James's first example of this (2:15–16) echoes Jesus' parable of the sheep and the goats from Matthew 25:31–46. However, this theme is also present in Paul's letter to the churches in Galatia. Here, Paul tells the churches that the "whole law" can be summarized in the commandment to love one's neighbor (Gal. 5:14; see Jas. 2:8) and that the Spirit produces in us fruit that includes love. Furthermore, Paul encourages the church to "bear one another's burdens," thereby fulfilling "the law of Christ" (Gal. 6:2). It is this care for one another, for their neighbors, that both Paul and James challenge the church toward.

James highlights two Old Testament examples to illustrate his meaning (2:18–26). Both are exemplars known for their hospitality (Gen. 18 and Josh. 2), which seems notable, given James's teaching on hospitality (Jas. 2:1–7; see Heb. 13:2). Furthermore, Abraham's faithfulness is shown through his unimaginable willingness to offer back to God his son Isaac, the literal embodiment of God's promises to him. We know Abraham had faith, not because of what he said, but because of what he did. It seems unsurprising that James would choose Abraham as an exemplar of faith; he is often described as such in the New Testament (e.g., Gal. 3:6–9; Rom. 4:1–3, 9–12; Heb. 11:8–19). Rahab, on the other hand, is a surprising example of faith in action. As a Canaanite/Gentile woman, she is notable for her spoken confession of faith in the

God of Israel (Josh. 2:8–14). James focuses on the fact that this spoken faith in God was followed by her faithfulness to the Israelite spies, sheltering them and aiding them in their escape.

In such examples, James encourages us to explore where we find our own models of embodied faith. The fact that James uses both expected and unexpected models, for whom the offering of indiscriminate hospitality—love of neighbor or love of those we do not yet know to call neighbors—was essential to their practice of faith, points us toward the places that we might see and be such models of enacted faith.

LAURA SWEAT HOLMES

Mark 7:24–37

24From there he set out and went away to the region of Tyre. He entered a house and did not want anyone to know he was there. Yet he could not escape notice, 25but a woman whose little daughter had an unclean spirit immediately heard about him, and she came and bowed down at his feet. 26Now the woman was a Gentile, of Syrophoenician origin. She begged him to cast the demon out of her daughter. 27He said to her, "Let the children be fed first, for it is not fair to take the children's food and throw it to the dogs." 28But she answered him, "Sir, even the dogs under the table eat the children's crumbs." 29Then he said to her, "For saying that, you may go—the demon has left your daughter." 30So she went home, found the child lying on the bed, and the demon gone.

31Then he returned from the region of Tyre, and went by way of Sidon towards the Sea of Galilee, in the region of the Decapolis. 32They brought to him a deaf man who had an impediment in his speech; and they begged him to lay his hand on him. 33He took him aside in private, away from the crowd, and put his fingers into his ears, and he spat and touched his tongue. 34Then looking up to heaven, he sighed and said to him, "Ephphatha," that is, "Be opened." 35And immediately his ears were opened, his tongue was released, and he spoke plainly. 36Then Jesus ordered them to tell no one; but the more he ordered them, the more zealously they proclaimed it. 37They were astounded beyond measure, saying, "He has done everything well; he even makes the deaf to hear and the mute to speak."

Commentary 1: Connecting the Reading with Scripture

The lectionary passage encompasses two healing stories, each with a different focus. Each of these is rich in itself, and the preacher may understandably want to focus on one or the other. We may also choose to reflect on the choice of the creators of the lectionary in listing them together, and ultimately of the Gospel writer in placing them side by side. The thread that draws these two stories together is speaking: a man who cannot speak, and a woman who does.

Jesus travels into the edge of Gentile territory in these two pericopes, first in Tyre and then in the Decapolis. It is not Jesus' first encounter with Gentiles in the Gospel of Mark (in 5:1–20 he heals the Gerasene demoniac), but this excursion is more deliberate, and the narrator clues us in that Jesus' purpose is retreat rather than ministry. In the first part of Mark, we frequently hear that Jesus is besieged by people seeking teaching and healing (Mark 1:32–33, 37, 45;

2:2; 3:7–10, 20; 4:1; 5:21, 24; 6:31, 33–34, 54–56), and references to his being unable to eat and being pressed by the great crowd prepare the reader to sympathize with Jesus when he "entered a house and did not want anyone to know he was there." Yet Jesus' presence is, as often in Mark, a secret that cannot be kept: "he could not escape notice" (7:24).

The story of the Syrophoenician woman is unlike any other in Mark's Gospel, and yet it bears parallels with many other Markan accounts of Jesus' ministry. Like Jairus, the woman comes to Jesus because of the illness of her "little daughter" (5:23; 7:25). Like many of those whom Jesus heals, the little girl has "an unclean spirit." Like the woman with a hemorrhage, the Syrophoenician approaches Jesus without invitation. When the conversation with Jesus turns to a feeding metaphor, her retort recalls that those to whom Jesus gave bread and fish "ate and were

Give Birth to Praise

Glory be to Him Who received from us that He might give to us; that through that which is ours we might more abundantly receive of that which is His! Yea, through that Mediator, mankind was able to receive life from its helper, as through a Mediator it had received in the beginning death from its slayer. Thou art He Who didst make for Thyself the body as a servant, that through it Thou mightest give to them that desire Thee, all that they desire. Moreover in Thee were made visible the hidden wishes of them that slew (Thee) and buried (Thee); through this, that Thou clothedst Thyself in a body. For taking occasion by that body of Thine, Thy slayers slew Thee, and were slain by Thee; and taking occasion by Thy body, Thy buriers buried Thee, and were raised up with Thee. That Power Which may not be handled came down and clothed itself in members that may be touched; that the needy may draw near to Him, that in touching His [humanity] they may discern His Godhead. For that dumb man (whom the Lord healed) with the fingers of the body, discerned that He had approached his ears and touched his tongue; nay, with his fingers that may be touched, he touched Godhead, that may not be touched; when it was loosing the string of his tongue, and opening the clogged doors of his ears. For the Architect of the body and Artificer of the flesh came to him, and with His gentle voice pierced without pain his thickened ears. And his mouth which was closed up, that it could not give birth to a word, gave birth to praise to Him Who made its barrenness fruitful in the birth of words. He, then, Who gave to Adam that he should speak at once without teaching, Himself gave to the dumb that they should speak easily, tongues that are learned with difficulty.

Ephrem the Syrian, "On Our Lord," in *Nicene and Post-Nicene Fathers,* second series, vol. 13, ed. Philip Schaff and Henry Wace (Buffalo, NY: Christian Literature Publishing, 1898), 309.

filled" (6:42). The astute reader will remember that there was plenty left over.

The conversation between Jesus and the unnamed woman unnerves some readers and delights others. Many have preferred to read it as a test, with Jesus as the teacher: if the woman can come up with the right response (and she does), then she passes the exam and Jesus will grant her request. Yet the way the story is narrated points in another direction. Jesus does not go to Tyre to perform healings; his privacy is invaded by a Gentile—and a Gentile woman at that. His response is to defend Jewish honor. His comment to her reflects both his fatigue and his dedication to his mission to the Jews. It is as frosty and unhospitable as it sounds.

The woman, though, is no more deterred by Jesus' hostility than Jairus or the woman with the hemorrhage was deterred by the crowds surrounding Jesus. Jesus has in effect called her a dog—a biting insult, since dogs in first-century Palestine were seen as scavengers rather than pampered pets. She replies with wit and even humor. Little dogs have a way of getting themselves let into the house, and children apparently have never been able to resist feeding them under the table. If she is offended by Jesus' comment making her a second-class human being, she counters by refusing to be placed in the role of a victim. If this is the system, then she will subvert it. She is determined that her voice be heard.

On this reading, it is the Syrophoenician woman who becomes, for the moment, the teacher. This is a reversal of the controversy stories, in which Jesus gets the best of the Pharisees, and it is her response that undercuts the presumption of Jesus' comment. He acknowledges that she has gained the upper hand and heals the daughter, not expressly due to her mother's faith, but "because of this word you have said" (7:29, my trans.). Her audacity in speaking out shames the very conventionality that would label her behavior as shameful. Not only Mark's readers but even Jesus himself now knows that God's reign has dawned among the Gentiles.

The specific way we valorize or commend the Syrophoenician woman to our own communities may require careful pastoral discernment. Contemporary congregations are likely to be "multi-" in various ways: race, socioeconomic status, gender identity, sexuality, age, political perspective, and the list goes on. The proclaimer is likely to be on the culturally favored side of many of these differences and faces the challenge of speaking as an ally about a story of a person who neither has nor seeks an ally. Finally, this is a story of one individual both acquiescing to and challenging a particular social structure in ways that may not be an appropriate model for every person or every circumstance.

After a woman who speaks audaciously, Jesus next encounters a man who is unable to speak clearly at all. He is deaf, and his speech unintelligible. The lectionary text from Isaiah gives us, in effect, a script for this healing: "Then . . . the ears of the deaf [shall be] unstopped; . . . the tongue of the speechless [shall] sing for joy" (Isa. 35:5–6). This story has some parallels to the healing of the paralytic in 2:1–12, in that companions of the man (here, an unspecified "they") bring him to Jesus and request healing on his behalf. For the first time in the Gospel of Mark, Jesus does not cure simply by word or touch, but must perform rituals to effect healing. He does not perform in front of the crowd, but heals the man in private—although we as readers, with the benefit of Mark's narrator, are permitted all the details, including that Jesus puts his fingers in the man's ears as if literally to "unstop" them. (The Greek word meaning "spit," incidentally, is the onomatopoeic *ptyō*.)

Jesus' word of healing is presented in Aramaic, "Ephphatha," and translated for the reader, "Be opened." Jesus' Aramaic healing words have appeared previously in Mark's Gospel when he says to Jairus's daughter, "Talitha cum" (Mark 5:41). In both these instances, Jesus heals in private, and the verbatim recording of Jesus' words contributes to the intimacy of these scenes:. the little girl whose hand Jesus takes and raises her from her bed, and the deaf man who feels Jesus' hands in his ears and Jesus' spit on his tongue.

Jesus does not express hesitancy or fatigue with this man's healing, unless his "sighing" or the need to perform rituals of healing points to the fact that healing has become a greater burden for him. These healings, as evidenced by the Isaiah text, are part of Jesus' work of bringing about God's reign in the world. Yet the end of this passage is somehow unsettling, even in its very familiarity. As we have seen many times before, Jesus orders the healed man and the ones who brought him not to tell, and once again Jesus' command is flouted.

As readers of Mark's Gospel, we know, from Jesus, that "there is nothing hidden, except to be disclosed; nor is anything secret, except to come to light" (4:22); yet the tension, here, remains ominous. Although the unspecified "they" praise Jesus for having "done everything well" (7:37), we will see in the very next verses that Jesus' own disciples still do not understand what he most wants them to know. Jesus is a healer—but more than a healer. That "more" is what the rest of the Gospel will reveal.

SANDRA HACK POLASKI

Commentary 2: Connecting the Reading with the World

Jesus' encounter with some leaders of the Jewish people in the first part of this chapter (Mark 7:1–23) about what defiles a person is clearly a conversation intended for Jewish community members who understood the issue of purity codes. The encounters of Jesus with the Syrophoenician woman and the deaf-mute man are quite different; they are encounters with Gentiles, with persons outside the Jewish community. This big change of context

is signaled in the text with the phrase in verse 24, "From there he set out and went away to the region of Tyre." Tyre was a city up north in Sidon, quite a journey by foot for Jesus and his disciples. Here a local woman sought him out and urgently asked for healing for her seriously ill daughter. The exchange between them raises multiple interpretations. Hardly any other Gospel story triggers more sharp reactions than this one.

Some readers object strongly to Jesus' tone and words to the woman. He was being rude and dismissive and patronizing! Other readers, trying to shield Jesus from such an accusation, suggest he was joking. Still others wonder if Jesus was exhausted from his long and arduous journey and was depleted emotionally. These are all very different readings of this story, but they share one thing in common: they assume that Jesus was the one in a position of authority over a defenseless woman of Tyre. This is not an unreasonable understanding; women certainly had low cultural status at this time. It is plausible to imagine that that this unnamed woman crept into the house where Jesus was staying and tried to get his attention out of sheer desperation. It may even be that she was a widow and was even lower on the socioeconomic scale. If this was her situation, Jesus' sharp words to her strike us as truly unconscionable.

An alternate proposal turns the story upside down. It may be that this woman was one of the power brokers of Tyre, one of the economic and political elite. Under Roman occupation, Tyre's leaders acted as political pawns to extract goods and services from the regions further south, where Jewish communities clustered. It may be that this woman did not creep in the back door of the house, hoping to see Jesus, but that she entered boldly, accustomed to her place of privilege. Yes, she longed for healing for her daughter. Yes, she sought help from Jesus, this healer whose reputation preceded him. However, if she was from the upper class, she assumed a position of power over Jesus.

If this was the case, Jesus' sharp words to her would be understood quite differently. According to this possibility, Jesus confronted her unjust economic advantage with blunt words. One commentary on Mark suggests that perhaps Jesus was saying, in effect, "First, let the poor people in Jewish rural areas be satisfied. For it is not good to take poor people's food and throw it to the rich Gentiles in the cities."[1] A postcolonialist scholar, Poling Sun, suggests that Jesus' initial offensive words "could be grasped as an act of resistance to yet one more appropriation of the resources of the oppressed by the powerful."[2]

The socioeconomic location of the Syrophoenician woman, elite upper class or oppressed lower class, does not alter the sheer audacity of her retort to Jesus. Either way, she spoke up boldly on behalf of her child and refused to accept the rebuff of Jesus. She was convinced that grace and mercy extended to her as well, and she was there to claim it.

One immediate connection of this story to our personal and ecclesial lives is the model of this audacious prayer. Our prayers are often meager and tepid. We pray in the subjunctive, using phrases that express our wishes and suggest possible actions to God. Sometimes our prayers do not convey confidence or urgency. It must quickly be said that such prayers do have some solid theology behind them! We do not know the mind of God. We are unaware of God's particular providential plans. A prayer that sighs out, "Not my will, but yours be done" was prayed by none other than Jesus himself. The Syrophoenician woman models a no-holds-barred form of prayer that might instruct our personal and congregational prayers. This Gentile woman argued with Jesus; should our prayers be more argumentative, more filled with lament?

It is certainly the case that prayers of lament are powerful avenues toward hope and healing and, eventually, even praise. The psalms are filled with lament and earnest pleas to God, but these same psalms frequently flow into an ocean of gratitude. Psalm 30, for example, includes words that the Syrophoenician woman could have said, "O LORD my God, I cried to you," but then ends with, "O LORD my God, I will give thanks to you forever." The deep pastoral connections of honest lament and renewed hope seen in Scripture can be echoed in prayers and hymns that evoke those connections.

Another clear link to our ecclesial communities is the challenge to follow the pattern of Jesus in engaging the "other." In the Gospel of Mark, only after Jesus deeply engaged with "othered" people, those who lived outside the bounds of his familiar culture, did he begin his

1. John R. Donahue and Daniel J. Harrington, *Gospel of Mark* (Collegeville, MN: Liturgical Press, 2005), 75.
2. Poling Sun, "Naming the Dog: Another Asian Reading of Mark 7:24–30," *Review and Expositor* 107 (Summer, 2010): 43.

pattern of healing the sick and feeding the multitudes. Encountering the "other" seemed, in Mark, to change Jesus, to expand his horizons and enlarge his empathy. Similarly, our congregations are enlarged and deepened by authentic encounters with the "other."

It must be admitted, however, that many congregations participate in a sort of faux engagement with the "other." Mission trips are a model that might actually perpetuate dominant paradigms of privilege. Pastoral leaders must be clear about how to respectfully and authentically engage others and enlarge capacity for empathy and service. Wise congregations will be willing to talk deeply and honestly about this issue of genuine encounter with other cultures and peoples.

The healing of the man with hearing and speaking disorders, which follows immediately after the account of the Syrophoenician woman, is an example of Jesus deeply engaging those outside his familiar circle. The region of the Decapolis was, like Tyre, a Gentile region, heavily influenced by Roman occupation. Yet when concerned friends brought the deaf-mute man to him, Jesus did not turn away. In fact, he healed him with striking intimacy and touch, and the community "zealously proclaimed" the news, as the text says. One can hardly help wonder if zealous proclamation characterizes the response of many of our churches to the grace and mercy of God.

The implications for the mission of the church are clear in both these stories in Mark 7. The church is called to extend itself far beyond the cozy boundaries of familiarity. Furthermore, the church must listen carefully to the voices of those at the margins. Often, it is the powerless who are the teachers. The Syrophoenician woman, even if she was part of the elite class, nevertheless taught Jesus. The man with hearing and speaking disorders encountered Jesus with silence; he left speaking and his community left in enthusiastic proclamation. In our own context and time, our proclamation and service must avoid the temptations of a closed system of certainty. Rather, we must be open to those strangers and foreigners, those "others" who will teach us new insights, infect us with fresh joy, and renew us with eager praise.

LEANNE VAN DYK

Proper 19 (Sunday between September 11 and September 17)

Proverbs 1:20–33 and Isaiah 50:4–9a   James 3:1–12
Psalm 19 and Psalm 116:1–9   Mark 8:27–38

Proverbs 1:20–33

²⁰Wisdom cries out in the street;
 in the squares she raises her voice.
²¹At the busiest corner she cries out;
 at the entrance of the city gates she speaks:
²²"How long, O simple ones, will you love being simple?
How long will scoffers delight in their scoffing
 and fools hate knowledge?
²³Give heed to my reproof;
I will pour out my thoughts to you;
 I will make my words known to you.
²⁴Because I have called and you refused,
 have stretched out my hand and no one heeded,
²⁵and because you have ignored all my counsel
 and would have none of my reproof,
²⁶I also will laugh at your calamity;
 I will mock when panic strikes you,
²⁷when panic strikes you like a storm,
 and your calamity comes like a whirlwind,
 when distress and anguish come upon you.
²⁸Then they will call upon me, but I will not answer;
 they will seek me diligently, but will not find me.
²⁹Because they hated knowledge
 and did not choose the fear of the LORD,
³⁰would have none of my counsel,
 and despised all my reproof,
³¹therefore they shall eat the fruit of their way
 and be sated with their own devices.
³²For waywardness kills the simple,
 and the complacency of fools destroys them;
³³but those who listen to me will be secure
 and will live at ease, without dread of disaster."

Isaiah 50:4–9a

⁴The Lord GOD has given me
 the tongue of a teacher,
that I may know how to sustain
 the weary with a word.

Morning by morning he wakens—
 wakens my ear
 to listen as those who are taught.
⁵The Lord GOD has opened my ear,
 and I was not rebellious,
 I did not turn backward.
⁶I gave my back to those who struck me,
 and my cheeks to those who pulled out the beard;
I did not hide my face
 from insult and spitting.

⁷The Lord GOD helps me;
 therefore I have not been disgraced;
therefore I have set my face like flint,
 and I know that I shall not be put to shame;
 ⁸he who vindicates me is near.
Who will contend with me?
 Let us stand up together.
Who are my adversaries?
 Let them confront me.
⁹It is the Lord GOD who helps me;
 who will declare me guilty?
All of them will wear out like a garment;
 the moth will eat them up.

Commentary 1: Connecting the Reading with Scripture

All the passages for this Sunday center on the teaching and knowledge of wisdom, which is imagined as inseparable from God. The passages from Proverbs 1 and the Wisdom of Solomon both envision wisdom as a female partner, prophet, or reflection of God. Psalm 19 describes how wisdom, which is equated with God's law and precepts and is evident in nature, will assuredly lead to a great reward for God's servant (Ps. 19:11). This servant is imagined in Isaiah 50:4–9a as a Suffering Servant who teaches wisdom through the endurance of suffering. Continuing this theme, James 3:1–12 warns that teachers will be judged more harshly; while Mark 8:27–36 portrays Jesus as the ultimate innocent, suffering teacher of wisdom. The passages for this Sunday thereby link teaching and knowledge of wisdom with the suffering endured by God's servant.

Proverbs 1, from which the passage for this Sunday is taken, begins the book of Proverbs, which consists of a collection of sayings on wisdom and foolishness, and instructions on how to live a good and pious life. The first section of this book, Proverbs 1–9, which is dated to the postexilic period, contains advice to a young male neophyte, addressed as "my son," on the need to obtain Wisdom, who is imagined as a worthy woman (Prov. 1:2–6). Wisdom is contrasted to Folly, who at points is imagined as a strange, that is, foreign, seductress bent on adultery (Prov. 7). Proverbs, at points, therefore functions as an advice book on how and why young men should find the right woman, Wisdom, instead of the wrong woman, the Strange Woman or Folly, who will lead them to their disaster. Thus, Proverbs is very much presented from a male point of view.

The masculine point of view raises questions about the biblical text that are worthy of exploration at the pulpit. Namely, how does the overwhelmingly masculine viewpoint that is present in this text impact our reading and interpretation of the Bible? Does imagining Wisdom as a woman uphold stereotypes of women as more moral than men? If so, what are responsible ways to counter-read respectfully literature that we hold as sacred?

The section from Proverbs 1:20–33 assigned for this Sunday follows the feminine depiction of Wisdom as a passionate street preacher or prophet, a depiction of Wisdom that is reiterated in Proverbs 8:1–11. In public places crowded with people, such as the streets, the markets, or at the entrance to the gates, she loudly shames the passersby: "How long, O simple ones, will you love being simple? How long will . . . fools hate knowledge" (1:22). That Wisdom is presented as crying out in well-populated, public places shows the prevalence of wisdom. She is omnipresent, but only to those willing to open their eyes and ears long enough to notice her presence and give heed to her call.

Indeed, this idea of the omnipresence of wisdom is echoed in Psalm 19:1–14, another passage assigned for this Sunday, which describes how nature clearly declares knowledge and wisdom, which is paralleled to the fear of and obedience to God. This idea that wisdom is intimately linked to God is found in several places in Proverbs. For example, Proverbs 8:22–31 imagines Wisdom as a kind of consort or goddess who alongside God created the universe. Moreover, Proverbs 1:7, among other verses (8:13; 9:10; 10:27; 14:27; 15:33; 22:4), declares that the fear of God is the beginning of wisdom. Fear entails not just feelings of being scared but having reverence for the magnitude and power of God, which is manifest in obeying God's commandments. These verses, therefore, directly link wisdom with following God's laws.

Hence, in Proverbs, wisdom, intelligence, and obedience to God's commands are all interlinked and synonymous as are their opposites: foolishness, the lack of intelligence, and disobedience or disregard of God's commands. Not only are wisdom and lack of wisdom clear and binary, but in the universe of Proverbs, this binarism extends to the workings of the universe. According to Proverbs, if you are wise and pious, good things will happen; if you are opposite, that is, unwise and impious, then bad things, such as hardships and suffering, will follow (1:33; 2:7–8; 2:21; 3:23–26, 33; 10:29–30; 11:4–5, 21).

In such a fair and ordered universe, the ethical and religious actions of the individual are depicted as wholly determinant of the outcome. Understandably, as a result, Wisdom is portrayed as rather unsympathetic to those who suffer hardship: "Because I have called and you refused to listen, . . . I will laugh at your calamity; I will mock when panic strikes you" (1:24, 26). If hardships are the inevitable result of the sufferer who chose to be unwise, then it was entirely the sufferer's fault and, hence, there is little need for sympathy or understanding.

This ordered vision of the universe promoted by Proverbs is undeniably problematic. By putting the blame for suffering entirely on the sufferer, it assumes a universe at odds with the one that we inhabit. In our world, bad things happen to good and pious people—and vice versa—all the time. Indeed, it is frequently the case that it is the innocent, the blameless, and the powerless who suffer the most through no fault of their own. The message of Proverbs, therefore, needs to be tempered by other Wisdom texts in the Bible, such as Ecclesiastes and Job, which challenge and deconstruct the problematic and unrealistic vision of the universe laid out in Proverbs.

The other passages assigned for this Sunday also help to recontextualize Proverbs and reframe its interpretation. This is precisely what happens when Proverbs 1 is juxtaposed to the song of the Suffering Servant in Isaiah 50:4–9a. This passage is one of the four Servant Songs or the Songs of the Suffering Servant (Isa. 42:1–4; 49:1–6; 50:4–9a; 52:13–53:12) found in Deutero- or Second Isaiah (Isa. 40–55), which describes an anonymous character known as the Suffering Servant. At times identified with Jesus in Christian traditions, it is more likely that the Suffering Servant referred to either an unknown individual or to the nation of Israel, which had been exiled, destroyed, and oppressed.

While Proverbs 1 posits a wholly fair universe in which Wisdom is unsympathetic to the cries of the sufferer, Isaiah 50 portrays the opposite: an innocent and wise teacher figure—"the Lord GOD has given me the tongue of a teacher" (50:4) who, despite being innocent, suffers needlessly. While the reference to a teacher links this passage to the depiction of the scorning teacher-preacher Wisdom in Proverbs 1, Isaiah 50 wholly undermines and deconstructs the message conveyed in Proverbs, that wisdom and piety will necessarily lead to a good life. Instead, Isaiah 50 shows that pious servants of God, though obedient to God, do not always get the treatment they deserve. Instead, at times, in this unfair world, they are shamed, struck, insulted, and spit upon. Then their only hope is to wait patiently for God, who they know with certainty will vindicate and help them (vv. 7–9).

Who are today's equivalents of the Suffering Servant? Who now suffer, are struck, and are shamed for doing and speaking God's truth to the world? What does being wise mean, and what actions does it entail in a universe that continues to shame and hurt the innocent? Moreover, what is the wisdom that is being proclaimed by nature and the world around us, and what is it telling us to do? How do we open our eyes and ears and listen and attend to this voice of wisdom that is speaking all around us?

SONG-MI SUZIE PARK

Commentary 2: Connecting the Reading with the World

The Proverbs text is an ode to wisdom that sets the tone for the rest of the book. The premise of Proverbs is that following wisdom's pathway is key to human flourishing and to navigating life successfully. Wisdom loves the truth and embraces it. It submits to, rather than denies or resists, every faithful portrayal of reality, regardless of its source. Wisdom also aligns itself with the moral and spiritual principles that undergird creation and move history positively forward.

The incarnation quintessentially embodied such wisdom in time and space, when the eternal Son "became for us wisdom from God" (1 Cor. 1:30). At that moment, the personification of wisdom moved from being a literary device, as here in Proverbs, to a historical reality. Sixth-century Christians, like so many who were fascinated with this biblical portrayal of Jesus Christ, chose to name the greatest church in Christendom Hagia Sophia (lit., Holy Wisdom).

This particular text, however, is not so much about wisdom per se. It is more about the maddening *rejection* of wisdom. It amounts to the cry of a wounded lover, mourning the foolish rebuffs that she has received, and wincing in anticipation of the consequences of such folly for her beloved.

We are living in surreal days, when wisdom seems alarmingly disdained, and modern-day scoffers find delight in sneering at inconvenient facts. Partisan groups craft their own preferred narratives and theories, without any particular interest in aligning their thoughts and pronouncements with hard evidence. The looming crisis is that without a shared commitment to truth and wisdom, the very possibility of public conversation and consensus begins to break down. Under such conditions, how is it even possible to reason together?

This text underscores the fact that there are moral and spiritual preconditions to acquiring wisdom. Wisdom will not be heard, even if she raises her voice and sets up in the busiest intersections (Prov. 1:20–21), unless her hearers are *inclined* to listen to her. Unfortunately, as this text declares, people can actually "hate knowledge." They can "love being simple," and find delight in scoffing, that is, in preemptively dismissing Wisdom's claims (v. 22). Such a predisposition will lead to catastrophe.

Consider, for example, the persistence of climate-change skepticism today. For a long time, environmental leaders assumed, optimistically, that if only the scientific evidence for climate peril was adequately disseminated, people would sensibly agree to necessary changes. As it turns out, the environmentalists were naive. As George Marshall has pointed out, in his *Don't Even Think about It*,[1] the obstacles to embracing climate wisdom lie deep in the contrarian

---

1. George Marshall, *Don't Even Think about It: Why Our Brains Are Wired to Ignore Climate Change* (New York: Bloomsbury, 2014).

human psyche, and are shaped there by what people fear, and by what they, therefore, choose to deny or avoid.

We are creatures of desire, and ultimately it is not what we know, but what we care about most, that really matters. Building on venerable insights of Augustine and other thinkers, theologian James K. A. Smith, in *Desiring the Kingdom* and elsewhere, reminds us that the chief function of Christian worship is "the pedagogy of desire."[2] At its best, worship directs the adoring gazes of worshipers upward to the divine source of all goodness, beauty, and *truth*. It shows us and teaches us, by means of an illuminating vision, what is most deserving of our courageous allegiance. In facilitating this, worship becomes a subversive and morally transforming activity. Ultimately, trust in God and love for the truth are what overcomes fear and folly.

If our Proverbs text describes persons who are resistant to wisdom's call, Isaiah 50 depicts those who are sensitive and responsive to the divine voice. The contrast between the two is striking and so are the consequences for each. The scoffer's pathway leads to catastrophe, while the attentive listener experiences ultimate vindication (Isa. 50:8).

Prayer is the Christian's experiential lifeline to God. The chief forms of prayer that Christians practice are petition and intercession. We ask God for things we need or want or, with a bit more muted self-interest, appeal to God on behalf of others we know to be in need. Prayer becomes an oddly asymmetrical form of communication when limited to these forms. For prayer to be truly the language of relationship, it should involve speaking *and listening*— communicating our thoughts to God, but also allowing God to speak into our attentive, receptive hearts. Much of the recent interest in Christian spiritual formation has been directed toward the resuscitation of the lost arts of meditation, mindfulness, waiting in silence and solitude, and general receptivity. In the language of the child Samuel, the waiting believer prays: "Speak, for your servant is listening" (1 Sam. 3:10). It is fascinating to note the similarity between this image of a divinely awakened or

opened ear (Isa. 50:4–5) and the contemporary colloquial idiom of becoming "woke." Both refer to a heightened consciousness of truth and its social implications.

We are reticent to listen very much to the voice of God, including when it is mediated through conscience. One reason is that the message we hear may call for some form of inconvenient, even risky, obedience from us. None of us is wired to relinquish our precious self-determination easily. We recoil from threats to our autonomy. From this text, we get the impression that the devout listener in view was confronted with a daunting assignment, one that would incline timid persons to cut and run, but this particular hearer "was not rebellious [and] did not turn backward" (v. 5).

The chapter goes on to describe the suffering that ensued. Later on, of course, the Gospel writers treat these words as prophetic anticipations of the sufferings of Christ. From this, we can infer at least two things. The first is that the voice of God does not always invite us to enjoy still waters and renewing comforts; at times, it can call us to endure some challenging things, and submit to difficult treatment for the sake of a worthy goal. Walter Rauschenbusch, the father of the early-twentieth-century social gospel movement, observed that evangelism must involve more than an invitation to get something for free. Otherwise, it is simply an appeal to selfishness at a higher level. Today, the prosperity gospel markets the faith as an easy way to score unsullied health and wealth simply by punching in the secret passwords of faith.

The second insight this text affords, once the New Testament witness is factored in, is that Jesus Christ is the exemplar of this path of purposive vocation, which often runs through, rather than around, the gauntlet of suffering. To "set my face like flint" (v. 7) anticipates Jesus' own "setting his face" toward Jerusalem (Luke 9:51), despite his full awareness of the hostility that awaits him there.

One of the standard complaints of liberation theology is that traditional Christian spirituality has too often legitimized pointless, masochistic suffering and treated passivity as a

---

2. James K. A. Smith, *Desiring the Kingdom: Worship, Worldview, and Cultural Formation* (Grand Rapids: Baker, 2009), esp. 24–25.

virtue. Liberation theology's call for resistance to injustice is rooted in a vision of human dignity and worth. It is significant, in this light, that the prophet's suffering does not culminate in personal disgrace, or end in shame. Despite his suffering, the prophet is not diminished; his dignity is ultimately enhanced rather than reduced by the fires of adversity. The God who calls is the God who also sustains, and ultimately vindicates God's listening, obedient friends.

GLEN G. SCORGIE

Psalm 19

¹The heavens are telling the glory of God;
    and the firmament proclaims his handiwork.
²Day to day pours forth speech,
    and night to night declares knowledge.
³There is no speech, nor are there words;
    their voice is not heard;
⁴yet their voice goes out through all the earth,
    and their words to the end of the world.

In the heavens he has set a tent for the sun,
⁵which comes out like a bridegroom from his wedding canopy,
    and like a strong man runs its course with joy.
⁶Its rising is from the end of the heavens,
    and its circuit to the end of them;
    and nothing is hid from its heat.

⁷The law of the LORD is perfect,
    reviving the soul;
the decrees of the LORD are sure,
    making wise the simple;
⁸the precepts of the LORD are right,
    rejoicing the heart;
the commandment of the LORD is clear,
    enlightening the eyes;
⁹the fear of the LORD is pure,
    enduring forever;
the ordinances of the LORD are true
    and righteous altogether.
¹⁰More to be desired are they than gold,
    even much fine gold;
sweeter also than honey,
    and drippings of the honeycomb.

¹¹Moreover by them is your servant warned;
    in keeping them there is great reward.
¹²But who can detect their errors?
    Clear me from hidden faults.
¹³Keep back your servant also from the insolent;
    do not let them have dominion over me.
Then I shall be blameless,
    and innocent of great transgression.

¹⁴Let the words of my mouth and the meditation of my heart
    be acceptable to you,
    O LORD, my rock and my redeemer.

Psalm 116:1–9

¹I love the LORD, because he has heard
    my voice and my supplications.
²Because he inclined his ear to me,
    therefore I will call on him as long as I live.
³The snares of death encompassed me;
    the pangs of Sheol laid hold on me;
    I suffered distress and anguish.
⁴Then I called on the name of the LORD:
    "O LORD, I pray, save my life!"

⁵Gracious is the LORD, and righteous;
    our God is merciful.
⁶The LORD protects the simple;
    when I was brought low, he saved me.
⁷Return, O my soul, to your rest,
    for the LORD has dealt bountifully with you.

⁸For you have delivered my soul from death,
    my eyes from tears,
    my feet from stumbling.
⁹I walk before the LORD
    in the land of the living.

Connecting the Psalm with Scripture and Worship

Psalm 19. This psalm, familiar to many people because of the Haydn setting, "The Heavens Are Telling," celebrates God's glory in creation (Ps. 19:1–6) and in the gift of the law (vv. 7–13). It concludes with a verse that has been much used as a prayer before preaching: "Let the words of my mouth and the meditation of my heart be acceptable to you, O LORD, my rock and my redeemer" (v. 14). In other ancient Near Eastern cultures, the sun was worshiped as a god, but here the sun is a creature that gives glory to God, who made it. The whole creation is given a voice to praise God, as the heavens "tell," the firmament "proclaims," days "pour forth speech," and night "declares." When one reads or sings these opening verses, it is hard to avoid the sense of being part of a cosmic chorus of creation, all singing praise to the one who made heaven and earth.

For contemporary readers, the connection of creation and law in this psalm may seem odd. "Creation" tends to stimulate our imaginations with scenes of expansiveness, generativity, and (increasingly) vulnerability. "Law," by contrast, evokes images of punishment, constriction, and control. Not so for the psalmist. The law here gives life (v. 7), joy, and light (v. 8). The commandments entice the psalmist with desire, as he compares the law to gold and to dripping honey. This itself is already a helpful challenge for us to rethink God's law as a life-giving gift, as generative as creation, as sensuous as honey.

Together, creation and the law teach us how we are to live: in praise of God and oriented toward God's glory. The God glorified here does not remain aloof; in verses 12–13, the psalmist acknowledges that there will be errors and faults that need to be forgiven. "Clear me from hidden faults," pleads the speaker. With God's help and protection, "I shall be blameless, and innocent of great transgression." In other words, the psalmist cannot keep the law perfectly apart from God's intervening grace—and God does forgive. The psalm concludes with a call to God as "my rock and my redeemer." "Redeemer" is a common translation of *go'el*, used elsewhere in Hebrew Scriptures to name the next of kin responsible to buy back a family member from slavery (see, e.g. Lev. 25:47–49 and Ruth 4:1–4). As Clinton McCann observes, the implication of the whole psalm is astonishing: "The God who set the sun on its course is the same God the psalmist has experienced personally as 'my next of kin'!"[1]

This psalm from the semicontinuous lectionary track responds to the passage from Proverbs, which portrays Woman Wisdom crying out against those who refuse to listen to her teaching, pointing out the dire consequences of failing to pursue wisdom. Those who do listen to her teachings, however, will "be secure and will live at ease, without dread of disaster" (Prov. 1:33). Both Psalm 19 and Proverbs 1 call the listener to heed wisdom/*torah*/law in order to flourish. The psalm focuses more on the positive effects of the law, while Proverbs 1 focuses on the negative consequences of failing to listen. Engaging these texts together illuminates the overlap of "law" (*torah*) and "wisdom," terms that we tend to separate, but which the ancient Israelites understood as similar ways of naming the divine teaching that leads to life.

In worship, this psalm offers a good opportunity for singing, whether Haydn or another setting. Verses 1–6 could also function well as an opening call to worship, perhaps with images of the heavens created by members of the congregation or printed or projected for visual engagement. Verses 7–11 could be used as a response to a declaration of forgiveness, affirming the goodness of God's *torah* that nourishes us like honey. These verses also work well as either an introduction to Scripture reading, or as a response.

Psalm 116:1–9. This psalm offers a heartfelt prayer of thanksgiving to God for deliverance. In verse 3, the writer describes suffering as being "encompassed" (NRSV) or "entangled" (NIV) by "snares of death," as if she is caught in a net and unable to break free. Later the psalmist compares suffering to being unable to walk steadily; he praises God because "you have delivered . . . my feet from stumbling. I walk

before the LORD in the land of the living" (Ps. 116:8–9). Whatever the particular distress, God has heard the cry of the sufferer and has saved them. As a result, beyond just offering thanks, the psalmist professes love for God, because of salvation from death: "I love the LORD, because he has heard my voice and my supplications" (v. 1). The psalms rarely speak about loving God (but see Pss. 5:11; 31:23; 40:16), but here the psalmist's adoration of God is profound, leading to lifelong commitment to keep calling on the name of the Lord (v. 2) and proclaiming God's saving love to others.

The lectionary pairs this psalm with verses from Isaiah 50. Here, the prophet speaks in the voice of the Suffering Servant, who is both teacher and student of God's word. In response to God's word, the Servant in Isaiah submits to insult and injury (Isa. 50:6), but affirms that God helps even in that unjust treatment (vv. 7, 9). Isaiah's confidence in God's help resonates with the psalmist's testimony: "The LORD protects the simple; when I was brought low, he saved me" (Ps. 116:6). A sermon on Isaiah might well draw on the psalm to focus on the real suffering that comes to those who listen closely to God's word, coupled with the confidence that God does not abandon those who are suffering. Death and suffering never have the last word with God, according to both Isaiah and the psalmist.

This good news is embodied in Jesus' life, death, and resurrection, anticipated in the Gospel reading from Mark 8 appointed for this day. Many preachers will opt to focus on this text, with its well-known question, "Who do you say that I am?" Jesus' stern words about the suffering that he will endure, followed by the promise that after three days he will rise again (Mark 8:31), connects well with this psalm as well as Isaiah. A preacher might invite the congregation to hear the psalm in the voice of Jesus crying out for deliverance, together with the affirmation that God did—and does—hear the plea of the suffering.

In addition to drawing on the psalm for preaching, the psalm lends itself to use in prayer. "I Love the Lord, Who Heard My Cry"

---

1. J. Clinton McCann Jr., "Psalms," in *The New Interpreter's Bible* (Nashville: Abingdon, 1996), 4:753.

Creation's Maker and Artificer

But perhaps those who have advanced beyond these things, and who stand in awe of Creation, being put to shame by these exposures of abominations, will join in repudiating what is readily condemned and refuted on all hands, but will think that they have a well-grounded and unanswerable opinion, namely, the worship of the universe and of the parts of the universe. For they will boast that they worship and serve, not mere stocks and stones and forms of men and irrational birds and creeping things and beasts, but the sun and moon and all the heavenly universe, and the earth again, and the entire realm of water: and they will say that none can shew that these at any rate are not of divine nature, since it is evident to all, that they lack neither life nor reason, but transcend even the nature of mankind, inasmuch as the one inhabit the heavens, the other the earth. It is worth while then to look into and examine these points also; for here, too, our argument will find that its proof against them holds true. But before we look, or begin our demonstration, it suffices that Creation almost raises its voice against them, and points to God as its Maker and Artificer, Who reigns over Creation and over all things, even the Father of our Lord Jesus Christ; Whom the would-be philosophers turn from to worship and deify the Creation which proceeded from Him, which yet itself worships and confesses the Lord Whom they deny on its account. For if men are thus awestruck at the parts of Creation and think that they are gods, they might well be rebuked by the mutual dependence of those parts; which moreover makes known, and witnesses to, the Father of the Word, Who is the Lord and Maker of these parts also, by the unbroken law of their obedience to Him, as the divine law also says: "The heavens declare the glory of God, and the firmament sheweth His handiwork." But the proof of all this is not obscure, but is clear enough in all conscience to those the eyes of whose understanding are not wholly disabled. For if a man take the parts of Creation separately, and consider each by itself,—as for example the sun by itself alone, and the moon apart, and again earth and air, and heat and cold, and the essence of wet and of dry, separating them from their mutual conjunction,—he will certainly find that not one is sufficient for itself but all are in need of one another's assistance, and subsist by their mutual help. . . . How then can these things be gods, seeing that they need one another's assistance? Or how is it proper to ask anything of them when they too ask help for themselves one from another? For if it is an admitted truth about God that He stands in need of nothing, but is self-sufficient and self-contained, and that in Him all things have their being, and that He ministers to all rather than they to Him, how is it right to proclaim as gods the sun and moon and other parts of creation, which are of no such kind, but which even stand in need of one another's help?

Athanasius, *Contra Gentes, Nicene and Post-Nicene Fathers*, second series, vol. 4, ed. Philip Schaff and Henry Wace (Buffalo, NY: Christian Literature Publishing, 1892), 18.

by Richard Smallwood is a moving setting of the opening verses, which can be an effective refrain to lead into prayer or repeated in response to a series of petitions.

In Jewish practice, this psalm is used as part of the Passover liturgy, and in that setting the suffering recalls the exodus narrative and God's deliverance of Israel from bondage in Egypt. Christians have long used this psalm in connection with Jesus' final meal with his disciples, which the Synoptic Gospels portray as a Passover meal, and which is particularly remembered on Maundy Thursday. In that context, the "snares of death" and "pangs of Sheol" (v. 3) are connected with Jesus' approaching betrayal, torture, and crucifixion. In light of the Christian proclamation of Easter, the psalmist's proclamation here takes on new meaning: "I walk before the LORD in the land of the living" (v. 9).

MARTHA L. MOORE-KEISH

James 3:1–12

¹Not many of you should become teachers, my brothers and sisters, for you know that we who teach will be judged with greater strictness. ²For all of us make many mistakes. Anyone who makes no mistakes in speaking is perfect, able to keep the whole body in check with a bridle. ³If we put bits into the mouths of horses to make them obey us, we guide their whole bodies. ⁴Or look at ships: though they are so large that it takes strong winds to drive them, yet they are guided by a very small rudder wherever the will of the pilot directs. ⁵So also the tongue is a small member, yet it boasts of great exploits.

How great a forest is set ablaze by a small fire! ⁶And the tongue is a fire. The tongue is placed among our members as a world of iniquity; it stains the whole body, sets on fire the cycle of nature, and is itself set on fire by hell. ⁷For every species of beast and bird, of reptile and sea creature, can be tamed and has been tamed by the human species, ⁸but no one can tame the tongue—a restless evil, full of deadly poison. ⁹With it we bless the Lord and Father, and with it we curse those who are made in the likeness of God. ¹⁰From the same mouth come blessing and cursing. My brothers and sisters, this ought not to be so. ¹¹Does a spring pour forth from the same opening both fresh and brackish water? ¹²Can a fig tree, my brothers and sisters, yield olives, or a grapevine figs? No more can salt water yield fresh.

Commentary 1: Connecting the Reading with Scripture

The opening exhortation of the Letter of James addresses a Diaspora community whose various trials occasion a testing of faith in God. Rather than waver in its confession that God is generous with "good gifts," James encourages readers to receive with humility and act upon God's "word of truth," exemplified by the "glorious Lord Jesus Christ" and "implanted" in their midst to save them from inward sin and the community's poorest members from neglect.

Central to this spiritual test is the possibility of failing to walk the talk of Christian discipleship. Repeatedly James notes the disjunction between what believers "say" they believe and how they embody these claims in their relationships with others. The "worthless religion" is one characterized by the "unbridled tongue" (Jas. 1:26) or the faith that is as good as dead is characterized by pious confession without a complement of charitable works (2:14–17). Nowhere in Scripture is this deadly contradiction between a professed but inactive faith

more vigorously exposed than in today's lesson, where a badge of the "religion that is pure and undefiled before God" (1:27) is to be "slow [i.e., careful] to speak" (1:19–20). Slow speech envisages a redemptive manner of speech characterized by the covenant-keeping virtues catalogued in James 3:17 and slows the slanderous and duplicitous chatter that can threaten a community's life with God and with one another. It encourages a discipleship that talks the walk.

This lesson's theme is directed especially at teachers of wisdom (3:1), whose "wise and understanding" speech is most evident and crucial in nurturing the community's life with God (3:13–16). After all, teachers' role is to "implant" the saving word within the community's soul (1:21) to harvest the first fruits of God's new creation (1:18). Already, the difficulty of the teacher's task is indicated by the repeated use of "many": not "many" should become teachers because we all make "many" mistakes and only the "perfect" teacher avoids God's "strict judgment"—a hyperbole that sounds a cautionary note for preachers to choose their words very carefully!

James's earlier use of "making mistakes" (lit. "to stumble"; NRSV 2:10, "fails in one point") concerned obeying the whole Torah, especially the "royal" command to love others (2:8); here, it is used of teachers who may use words to lead others astray. The subtext in both cases is the deception that partial obedience of God's law or teaching only a partial truth is sufficient to maintain a community's life with God, when in fact the "whole body" must be kept.

James uses four illustrations to underscore the difficulty the community's teachers face in controlling what they say. The first (3:3) repeats the "bridling" image of 3:2 to make the analogy plain: the "tongue" (or power of speech) is to the teacher what the "bit" is to the horse: both are physically small objects that direct and determine good ends of the larger whole. Implicit in this analogy, of course, is that these objects, whether bit or tongue, are directed by the instructions given them by the rider or teacher.

The second illustration (3:4–5a) is similar to the first; both are proverbs about giving direction to right the course. Two new elements are added that underscore the difficulty in doing so: pilots follow a careful plan of navigation (*boulomai*) to direct a ship's rudder to safe harbor through the dangers of "strong winds." This, too, is an analogy of a teacher's speech that guides the direction of the whole community toward its proper ends in God, especially when faced by "strong winds"—"trials of any kind" (1:2)—that test their love of neighbors (2:8) and friendship with God (2:23).

The third illustration (3:5b–6) makes clear the subtext of this lesson. Preachers who are unable to control their tongues and boast of great exploits, rather than speak in ways that edify the whole congregation, have the power to redirect its course from its proper ends in loving God and neighbors toward the dangers lurking in a "world of iniquity" that ultimately ends in the destructive fires of gehenna (3:6).

In this illustration, the fiery role of the tongue is performed by a forest fire: while the congregation plays the kindling, the fire destroys. Fire is a familiar trope of divine judgment: the peril

imagined is divine judgment concentrated by the threat of gehenna, a trope borrowed from Jesus' tradition for the fiery destination of the unfaithful wicked (see Mark 9:43–47). The connection between James's definition of the social manners of a religion blessed by God as "unstained [*aspilos*] by the world" (1:27) and the effect of unedifying speech as "staining [*spiloō*] the whole body" (3:6) is crucial to make. Sharply put, James teaches that the community's accommodation of a world of unrighteousness (=injustice) imperils its future with God.

The final illustration (3:7–8) continues the theme of 3:6. In this case, James draws an analogy between a zoo of domesticated animals (3:7) and the tongue that is impossible to tame with destructive results (3:8). The hyperbole of this analogy intensifies James's larger point about the tongue's potential for good and for evil.

This zoological image brings to full development this lesson's arresting theme. What began with the illustration of a rider's ability to direct a horse by a small bit, which commends the teacher's capacity to direct the power of speech to good ends, here concludes in a pessimistic manner by comparing one's ability to do so with an untamed animal. The wisdom of "slow to speak," which is thematic of this letter, fully recognizes the teacher's power to lead a community into the saving word of truth, but is also alert to the dangers of abusive speech that redirects this same community's movement away from God toward gehenna.

The preacher may note that the increasing peril these four illustrations depict underscores the ever-increasing difficulty of controlling the effects of what we say. The philosophers of antiquity taught that the virtue of self-control was something more caught, not taught. It was a habit cultivated by a disciplined assessment of gains made and setbacks experienced. Controlling what we say is a habit formed by spiritual discipline.

The shift to the first-person plural signals a more practical part of James's thematic development, which applies the wisdom of controlled speech to intramural conflicts within the community. This passage deals with what is publicly said about God and about one's neighbor: to bless God in worship is defeated whenever one curses their neighbors who are made in God's image (see Gen. 1:26–27). According to this theo-logic, the congregation's preacher may be guilty of duplicity (3:9–10), a peril already noted by James (1:5–8), if their doxology is blunted by their slanderous speech or idle gossip about another.

The triad of illustrations (3:11–12), which draws the principle of consistency from nature (spring, plant, water), alludes to the creation story to remind readers that God made the human species in God's image. The principle of consistency, then, extends from creaturely existence to human speech—a point made by the parallelism between the phrase "from the same mouth comes . . ." (3:10a) and "from the same

opening flows . . ." (3:11a). The implication is clear: the first fruits of a new creation are harvested only when what is planted and watered by the tongue is consistent with God's word of truth (1:18, 21).

The sobering notes sounded by James in this lesson may have a quieting effect on pastors who resist prophetic preaching for fear of alienating congregations, even though they may clearly require correction or redirection. The principal exhortation of this lesson is not to rid sermons of challenging social and spiritual commentary but to keep their proclamation set on God's way of wisdom.

ROBERT W. WALL

Commentary 2: Connecting the Reading with the World

This section of James 3 focuses on speech, using the metaphor of the tongue. This expands James's teaching from earlier in the letter: "If any think they are religious, and do not bridle their tongues but deceive their hearts, their religion is worthless" (Jas. 1:26). James uses the metaphor of "bridling" one's tongue to highlight the tongue's influence and power, its dangers, and what resources the Christian community should use to focus on its control.

James introduces his comments on the tongue by talking about "we who teach" (3:1). He singles out teachers not because of specific advice about pedagogy or instruction, but because of the influence that teachers have on those they teach. With this influence comes greater responsibility, and therefore they are to be "judged with greater strictness" (3:1; see Matt. 18:1–7). James challenges teachers to watch what they say in two different capacities: they should practice what they teach, and they should be confident that what they are teaching is true (3:13). Given that influence is James's main point, it is important to broaden his instruction beyond those who are professional teachers. Much of James's instruction highlights how control over the tongue is something that everyone needs, regardless of profession (vv. 2, 8).

For those in positions of influence (whether professional, social, or familial), James reminds us that our words have great power. Just as the tongue, though small, can control the actions of the body (vv. 3–4), so "mistakes" in speech, which we all make (v. 2), affect the body of Christ. These spoken mistakes might be gossip, lying, or bullying, but they all seek to wield influence over others, using the power of the tongue to direct in ways that are not life-giving or aligned with God's will in Christ. Before considering these ways that the tongue can go wrong, it is worth remembering James's suggestion for avoiding these mistakes, as noted in James 1–2: practicing integrity. Whatever we say, we do. We do not let our teaching, instruction, or influence outstrip our action. It is a high standard. If we will not do it, we should not teach it.

Considering the dangers of speech, James is concerned about the power of the tongue to say things that are not true. He describes the tongue as a fire that can consume a whole forest (vv. 5b–6). One of the ways in which false speech can multiply is through psychological effects. Based on psychological research beginning in the 1970s, scientists have found that people are more likely to believe information if it is familiar to them.[1] Therefore, all it takes

1. Lynn Hasher, David Goldstein, and Thomas Toppino, "Frequency and the Conference of Referential Validity," *Journal of Verbal Learning and Verbal Behavior* 16 (1977): 107–12.

for our brains to accept that something is true, or at least possibly true, is for us to encounter the statement more than once. This is true even if participants possess knowledge that runs counter to the repeated statements.[2] This process is called "illusory truth." Something has the illusion of truth, whether or not it is verified, because we are familiar with it.

Therefore, if those with influence communicate false statements multiple times—even if they qualify or dispute them—we are more likely to believe the original false statement. This puts a large degree of responsibility on those who have influence when they speak, to speak with integrity, living out what they say and speaking only what they know to be true. Preachers can call their congregants to reflect on how they, and those in their spheres of influence, have experienced or promoted false speech, and how to be people of integrity, and guard against it.

Another way in which speech is dangerous and can inflame communities like a forest fire is through the effects of bullying, among both children and adults. Bullying is an umbrella term that includes any repeated use of force or speech by an individual or a group of people with power to cause hurt to or harm others who are vulnerable and feel helpless to respond. While such tactics are nothing new, the augmentation of the effects of bullying in online spaces, especially among young adults, has been particularly concerning in recent years.[3] Online spaces heighten the effects of bullying because of the seemingly omnipresent reach of the internet. There is no time when it is not active, and there are no spaces where one can hide. The ripple effects of online bullying and its persistence (files on the internet are difficult to delete) have created a context in which speech really does seem to have the same tangibly destructive effects as a forest fire. Speech is never just speech; it shapes our views of ourselves and our world.

James is remarkably realistic about how much humans, on our own, can do to control our tongues. He calls the tongue "a world of iniquity" (v. 6), "a restless evil, full of deadly poison" (v. 8). Like Paul, James sees speech as one of the core ways in which we sin (3:2; see Rom. 3:9–20). James does not recommend that we cut out our tongues or stop speaking (see Matt. 18:8–9). If we did, we would not be able to "bless the Lord" (Jas. 3:9). However, we should not be so willing to "curse those who are made in the likeness of God" (v. 9). James uses a lot of imagery from the story of creation in Genesis 1 to develop this argument. James's point is that as those who are created by God we should act accordingly. God's speech in creation was good, both in its content and its effect (e.g., Gen. 1:3–4). So should ours be.

James then concludes with two points: one about identity, and one about integrity. In terms of identity, he claims that not only are we, as teachers, created in the image of God; so are all others. It is not only that we need to come to terms with our own identity, but also that we need to ensure that we prioritize the identity of others. This is particularly true in contexts that encourage false speech, suppositions, or bullying. Encouraging empathy toward others by keeping their identity as children of God at the forefront can help check our speech. This is a responsibility of the community as a whole, not just of individuals. Identity formation is community formation. For James, speech can destroy a community, as a fire can destroy a forest and anyone who lives in or near it. Speech and its corresponding actions can also convey the blessing of God who created us and gives us life.

James also highlights how we should speak and act with integrity. He claims that no one can be what they are not created to be, any more than a fig tree can produce olives or a salty spring can produce fresh water. Therefore, James encourages, if God has given us wisdom from above, then we can only bless and be a people of integrity (vv. 17–18). Otherwise, we are denying our identity as the people God has created and redeemed us to be. This blessing produces "a harvest" of righteousness and justice (*dikaiosynē*) and peace (v. 18).

LAURA SWEAT HOLMES

2. Lisa K. Fazio, Nadia M. Brashier, B. Keith Payne, and Elizabeth J. Marsh, "Knowledge Does Not Protect Against Illusory Truth," *Journal of Experimental Psychology* 144, no. 5 (2015): 993–1002.

3. Emily Bazelon, *Sticks and Stones: Defeating the Culture of Bullying and Rediscovering the Power and Character of Empathy* (New York: Random House, 2013).

Mark 8:27–38

²⁷Jesus went on with his disciples to the villages of Caesarea Philippi; and on the way he asked his disciples, "Who do people say that I am?" ²⁸And they answered him, "John the Baptist; and others, Elijah; and still others, one of the prophets." ²⁹He asked them, "But who do you say that I am?" Peter answered him, "You are the Messiah." ³⁰And he sternly ordered them not to tell anyone about him.

³¹Then he began to teach them that the Son of Man must undergo great suffering, and be rejected by the elders, the chief priests, and the scribes, and be killed, and after three days rise again. ³²He said all this quite openly. And Peter took him aside and began to rebuke him. ³³But turning and looking at his disciples, he rebuked Peter and said, "Get behind me, Satan! For you are setting your mind not on divine things but on human things."

³⁴He called the crowd with his disciples, and said to them, "If any want to become my followers, let them deny themselves and take up their cross and follow me. ³⁵For those who want to save their life will lose it, and those who lose their life for my sake, and for the sake of the gospel, will save it. ³⁶For what will it profit them to gain the whole world and forfeit their life? ³⁷Indeed, what can they give in return for their life? ³⁸Those who are ashamed of me and of my words in this adulterous and sinful generation, of them the Son of Man will also be ashamed when he comes in the glory of his Father with the holy angels."

Commentary 1: Connecting the Reading with Scripture

Peter's confession at Caesarea Philippi is found in all three Synoptic Gospels, and readers of the New Testament are likely to be more familiar with Matthew's version, with Jesus' grand pronouncement that "upon this rock I will build my church," than with the version here in Mark. Rather than reading this text as lacking or incomplete, we need to think carefully about the way Mark tells this story.

Interpreters often identify this passage as the center or turning point of Mark's Gospel. Heretofore Jesus has been teaching and healing throughout Galilee and the surrounding areas, but from this point he will be journeying inexorably toward Jerusalem, the place of his impending suffering and death. He will teach his disciples about these things, as we see in verse 31, but over and over again they will misunderstand and even deny that it is necessary for Jesus to suffer.

At the beginning of our passage, Jesus and his disciples are in "the villages of Caesarea Philippi," on the edges of the region of Galilee, and they have a discussion as they are "on the way"—a seemingly benign phrase that carries enormous symbolic meaning. Discipleship happens "on the way," as Jesus' followers listen and observe and gain greater understanding. The group is "on the way" to Jerusalem, although they may refuse to recognize it.

"Who do people say that I am?" Readers of the Gospel of Mark have known since the very beginning that they are reading "the good news of Jesus Christ, the Son of God" (Mark 1:1), although thus far in the story world the only ones who have affirmed it are the heavenly voice (1:11) and the demons (1:24, 34; 3:11; 5:7). Resonant, too, is the story of Moses at the burning bush in Exodus 3, in which God reveals the divine name to Moses as "I AM" or "I AM WHO I AM" (Exod. 3:14).

The disciples' report of the "people's" views of Jesus corresponds to previous narratives. When Herod hears of Jesus' teaching, we learn that "some were saying, 'John the baptizer has been raised,'" while "others said, 'It is Elijah.' And others said, 'It is a prophet, like one of the prophets of old'" (Mark 6:14–15). Jesus seems to expect a different answer from his disciples, and Peter provides it, the first such confession from a human being in Mark's Gospel: "You are the Messiah."

Finally! Peter is right! These hardheaded disciples finally get it! But if so, why does Jesus repeat the familiar order not to spread the news? The "messianic secret" motif is by this point in the story very familiar to readers of Mark. We know that Jesus exercises power over demons, not permitting them to speak (1:34). When those who are healed flout his command not to tell, Jesus is besieged by crowds (1:45). At the seaside he needs a boat so that he will not be crushed by the crowds (3:9). He redirects the attention of the Gerasene demoniac to God's goodness and mercy rather than his own healing power (5:19). When Peter offers the "right answer," though, and Jesus repeats the command not to tell, we sense that something else is at work.

At this turning point in Mark's story, Jesus begins to lay out a vision of what is to come that is so contrary to the disciples' expectations that we as readers begin to understand why understanding Jesus as Messiah may be inadequate. "Messiah" is the English form of the Hebrew word meaning "anointed one"; the Greek equivalent is *Christos*, which comes into English as "Christ." The anointed one of God is a leader, a powerful figure, a savior, sent by God to rescue God's people. Although a messiah was generally understood to be one of God's chosen people, such as a priest, king, or prophet, Jews recognized that God could work even through unwilling means to accomplish divine purposes. The Persian ruler Cyrus is called a "messiah" in Isaiah 45:1 because his conquest of the Babylonians paves the way for Jewish exiles to return to their native land and rebuild the temple.

By contrast, Jesus begins to speak of his own future, briefly encapsulating the events of his passion (8:31), using the much more ambiguous term "Son of Man" (or "Human One"). In so doing, he lifts the imagery from a historical to an apocalyptic plane, referencing not Israel's story

but the visions of Daniel in the divine throne room. In the "night visions" of Daniel 7:13–14, "one like a son of man" (NRSV "human being") appears before the Ancient One. In context and at first glance, the title seems entirely descriptive. This being, unlike other beings in Daniel's vision, does not have eagle's wings or three tusks or four heads; it looks like an ordinary human being. The term "son of man" is, in one sense, a declaration of anonymity; rather than being, for example, the "son of Amoz" (Isa. 1:1, designating paternity) or "son of a prophet" (Amos 7:14, designating membership in a guild), the "son of man" is, very simply, human. We might use the term "Nobody" or "Everyman."

Yet the Son of Man/human being in Daniel comes "with the clouds of heaven" and immediately gains a very special status:

> To him was given dominion
> and glory and kingship,
> that all peoples, nations, and languages
> should serve him.
> His dominion is an everlasting dominion
> that shall not pass away,
> and his kingship is one
> that shall never be destroyed.
> Dan. 7:14

Jesus presents himself as this enigmatic figure in order to lay out the path that lies ahead of him, and the disciples cannot accept this challenge to their view of the Messiah. Peter, who has just earned the readers' favor by giving the right answer, now "rebukes" Jesus—the same term used when Jesus casts out demons (Mark 1:25). Jesus rebukes Peter in return, calling him "Satan." Having gained knowledge of Jesus as Messiah is inadequate; from this point forward in Mark's Gospel, Jesus will teach the disciples the rest of what they need to learn.

For the last section of our passage, the audience shifts from Jesus' disciples to include "the crowds" as well; this, apparently, is not a teaching to be kept secret. Jesus' three-part command to deny self, take up the cross, and follow him is clearly a challenge to political power, since crucifixion was a punishment for enemies of the Roman state, and those about to be crucified typically carried their own instruments of torture to the site of their deaths. Those who read this text in the early centuries of the church could be reassured that the persecution and martyrdom many congregations were experiencing were part of the central paradox of life in death, gain in loss, that is the way of Christ.

Three pitfalls loom for the interpreter of this text. The first, and most common, is to so spiritualize the text that it loses all political implications. The second is to decide that unless one is being offensive, one is not Christian. The third, and perhaps most insidious, is to assume that one's "minority" views or the ones that are opposed by "society" are the elements of one's belief that most mark a person as Christian. The contemporary preacher lives in a very different "adulterous and sinful generation" than the first- and second-century audience of this text, but the challenge of this central paradox of faith persists.

SANDRA HACK POLASKI

Commentary 2: Connecting the Reading with the World

When Jesus asked his disciples that famous question, "Who do people say that I am?" he and his disciples were in Gentile territory, to the north and east of the Jordan River. They had been there for some time; we do not know the exact time frame, but Jesus had engaged in works of healing and feeding and teaching and traveling from town to town, from the northwestern city of Tyre to the cluster of towns in the Decapolis just east of the Sea of Galilee and then to the northeastern town of Caesarea Philippi. Some Jewish leaders were apparently in the crowd that followed Jesus, but, for the most part, Jesus interacted with those outside the Jewish community. One day, Jesus polled his disciples on what the word on the street was concerning him. Not surprisingly, they reported that everyone had a different opinion. Then, as now, attitudes and beliefs about Jesus ranged widely.

In some congregations, this simple observation will be a surprise. Some communities have deep assumptions that their language and ideas of God are universal. However, often the God-talk of Christian communities is highly coded language; it is insider language that bears the weight and freight of culture, language that signals who is in and who is out. The simple observation that "outsiders" also have their own understanding of who Jesus is and what he means today can encourage some congregations to expand their curiosity and broaden their scope of interest.

Peter's bold answer to Jesus' next question, "But who do you say that I am?" marks him as an early hero of faith and proclamation. It is a stirring scene, but Peter's moment of glory is fleeting. In the very next conversation, he argues with Jesus and attempts to correct Jesus' self-understanding. Peter's notions of Messiah clash with Jesus' notions of Messiah, and Peter is quite sure he is right. When Peter hears Jesus describe the hard and painful calling he has taken up as the Son of Man, Peter tries to impose his own expectations, "No, Lord, that cannot possibly be right!" This early disciple attempted to correct his teacher, and we continue to do so today.

Again, the connection to a congregation is clear. Like Peter, we may believe that Jesus is the Christ, but we may be completely mistaken about what that actually means. The name of Jesus has been used as a sponsor for wars and purges and persecutions and prejudices and oppressions in every conceivable way for hundreds of years. In many contexts, the people who perpetrated these outrages—and we certainly are on that list—confessed Jesus as Messiah but were shockingly mistaken about what that means.

It is a constant challenge to every Christian community to relinquish their preconceptions of who the Messiah is. Each age and each community have their "favorite Jesus," but such favorites can be idolatrous or even demonic. John Calvin once famously observed that the human heart is a "factory of idols"; we even make an idol of our preferred Messiah. We would much rather write Jesus' job description for our convenience than follow him when he calls.

False messiahs can quickly become the true gods of a faith community. Many Christian churches in Nazi Germany constructed a messiah associated only with the pure Aryan race. Many Christian churches in apartheid South Africa constructed a messiah that endorsed racial segregation and oppression. The temptation of constructing false and idolatrous messiahs is very real. The challenge of preaching is to unmask false messiahs not only in other communities but also in one's own.

After Jesus decisively corrects Peter, he goes on to enumerate the requirements of true discipleship. Jesus clearly includes everyone in his statement. In fact, one can assume that he includes even the Gentiles. The text says that he "called the crowd with his disciples." Perhaps one connection to our context today is that the Christian church should engage the public square more boldly. Perhaps the church should "think out loud" in the presence of other faith communities. This would seem to follow the pattern of Jesus himself.

So, when Jesus says, "If *any* want to become my followers, let them deny themselves and take up their cross and follow me," he includes everyone. Yet this command has often been wrongly applied only to certain persons, such as women and enslaved persons. For hundreds of years in America, enslaved Africans were taught to deny themselves and endure their lot in life because God commanded it. Old catechisms exist that instructed enslaved persons to take up their cross as God's plan. One includes this question and answer: "Q. How are you to show your love to your master and mistress? A. I am never to lie to them, to steal from them, nor speak bad words about them; but always to do as they bid me."[1] Another such document includes this instruction: "Was Paul a good man? *Yes, he was a holy saint.* What did he do? *He sent back a runaway slave.* What was his advice, and that of the other apostle, to the slave? *To abide in their calling, and be obedient to their masters.*"[2]

For even longer, women have been taught that their proper calling is self-denial. In recent decades, feminist theology has insisted that profound damage has been done to women and communities in the name of a patriarchal interpretation of Jesus' words. This command of Jesus cannot be used as a warrant to oppress or enslave. Rather, it is a comprehensive command to mutually serve, to advocate, to persist, and to pursue justice.

The pursuit of justice is comprehensive because the wounds of injustice impact everything; because our brokenness is so deep and wide, our obedience to the command of Jesus must also be deep and wide.

It is the peculiar task of the preacher to name the deep wounds in persons and communities that result from injustice and also to map the pathway forward into practices and commitments that restore *shalom*. Prophetic preaching that names idolatries in ways that can be heard, pastoral care that discerns wisely both comfort and confrontation, engagement and action in the public square are all tasks of the pastoral leader.

Idolatries run very deep in individual hearts and corporate communities. One strategy for the preacher that connects with Jesus' sharp rebuke of Peter in this story is to explore a range of titles for Jesus. Traditional titles for Jesus often lean heavily on authoritarian power dynamics. Titles such as King and Lord lean heavily toward political and military imagery. We are perhaps at a time when we need to express Jesus' person and work in expanded ways. The preacher who presents a portrait of Jesus, for example, as a counselor and guide will open up new imaginative spaces for the congregation. Global cultures also have rich resources for images of Jesus. Some African cultures present titles like Ancestor or Brother or Elder.

This text is filled with hard and enigmatic words. The sharp rebuke to Peter is a warning to communities of faith that destructive notions of God damage communities and deform minds and hearts. Jesus' exposition on taking up the cross makes clear that old, constructed patterns of power and privilege do not display true discipleship and will not be endorsed by God and the angels in the day of glory.

LEANNE VAN DYK

1. "Catechism, To Be Taught Orally to Those Who Cannot Read; Designed Especially for the Instruction of the Slaves," from "Documenting the American South," University of North Carolina at Chapel Hill; https://unc.edu/imls/catechisms/catechsl.html.

2. "Pro-Slavery Catechism," *The National Era*, July 8, 1847; www.accessible-archives.com/2016/06/pro-slavery-catechism.

Proper 20 (Sunday between September 18 and September 24)

Proverbs 31:10–31 and
   Jeremiah 11:18–20
Psalm 1 and Psalm 54

James 3:13–4:3, 7–8a
Mark 9:30–37

Proverbs 31:10–31

¹⁰A capable wife who can find?
   She is far more precious than jewels.
¹¹The heart of her husband trusts in her,
   and he will have no lack of gain.
¹²She does him good, and not harm,
   all the days of her life.
¹³She seeks wool and flax,
   and works with willing hands.
¹⁴She is like the ships of the merchant,
   she brings her food from far away.
¹⁵She rises while it is still night
   and provides food for her household
   and tasks for her servant-girls.
¹⁶She considers a field and buys it;
   with the fruit of her hands she plants a vineyard.
¹⁷She girds herself with strength,
   and makes her arms strong.
¹⁸She perceives that her merchandise is profitable.
   Her lamp does not go out at night.
¹⁹She puts her hands to the distaff,
   and her hands hold the spindle.
²⁰She opens her hand to the poor,
   and reaches out her hands to the needy.
²¹She is not afraid for her household when it snows,
   for all her household are clothed in crimson.
²²She makes herself coverings;
   her clothing is fine linen and purple.
²³Her husband is known in the city gates,
   taking his seat among the elders of the land.
²⁴She makes linen garments and sells them;
   she supplies the merchant with sashes.
²⁵Strength and dignity are her clothing,
   and she laughs at the time to come.
²⁶She opens her mouth with wisdom,
   and the teaching of kindness is on her tongue.
²⁷She looks well to the ways of her household,
   and does not eat the bread of idleness.
²⁸Her children rise up and call her happy;
   her husband too, and he praises her:
²⁹"Many women have done excellently,
   but you surpass them all."

³⁰Charm is deceitful, and beauty is vain,
　　but a woman who fears the LORD is to be praised.
³¹Give her a share in the fruit of her hands,
　　and let her works praise her in the city gates.

Jeremiah 11:18–20

¹⁸It was the LORD who made it known to me, and I knew;
　　then you showed me their evil deeds.
¹⁹But I was like a gentle lamb
　　led to the slaughter.
And I did not know it was against me
　　that they devised schemes, saying,
"Let us destroy the tree with its fruit,
　　let us cut him off from the land of the living,
　　so that his name will no longer be remembered!"
²⁰But you, O LORD of hosts, who judge righteously,
　　who try the heart and the mind,
let me see your retribution upon them,
　　for to you I have committed my cause.

Commentary 1: Connecting the Reading with Scripture

Proverbs 31:10–31. Who *is* this woman? Does she exist in our world, or is she someone's fantasy dream? Is her example possible to follow, or is it a measure by which all women must fall short? The history of interpretation includes both conclusions. What can be said is that there is no cultural one-size-fits-all for gender roles; breaking rules or norms is sometimes not a bad thing. Important questions remain: What does *she* want? Has she been consulted in this? Does she consider herself lucky or little better than a slave?

According to the beginning of chapter 31, the mother of King Lemuel (about whom we know nothing other than his appearance here) is giving sage instructions for his finding an appropriate wife. Part of this lection can be seen as a counterweight to the negative views of women sprinkled throughout Proverbs. There is the merely foolish woman of 9:13, for example. Then there is the contentious wife who makes several appearances: 19:13; 21:9; 21:19; 27:15, and elsewhere. Most especially, a contrast is made through large swaths of the book between Lady Wisdom and Dame Folly.

Two chiastic structures have their concluding portions here. Wisdom is personified as a woman beginning in chapter 2. Perhaps the specificity of chapter 31's woman is companion to chapter 2's, as if to say the characteristics attached to the abstraction "wisdom" can also be found in individuals such as the one described in this final chapter. Additionally, the "beginning of wisdom" is familiarly defined as "the fear of the LORD" in 1:7. The penultimate verse of the book uses this same descriptor as the final encomium of this wife (Prov. 31:30).

This woman is not merely an *'ishah* (woman/wife) but an *eshet hayil,* variously translated as "worthy" or "valorous" woman. The adjective is used primarily with men, often as "worthy" or "able" (Gen. 47:6; Exod. 18:21) or "men of valor" (Josh. 8:3; Judg. 3:29; 20:44, 46). This description is spoken about one other biblical woman (Ruth 3:11), by a man who himself is described by the same adjective in Ruth 2:1. It is spoken to a poor, widowed, foreign woman, and is thus a great contrast to the woman described in our text. The preacher can help us see that the terms used with two such different woman open the possibility that any woman can be valorous, worthy, or able.

This individual is shown doing things usually considered outside the sphere of biblical women, such as buying and selling goods and even, surprisingly, land. She is indefatigable, rising before everyone else and working into the night by candlelight. Clearly, she belongs to the upper stratum economically, for she has servants of her own. She provides well for her own family and servants and also for the poor, embodying in verse 20 the command of Deuteronomy 15:11 to "open [one's] hands wide to the needy."

Men are sometimes said to need to rein in "their" women lest they, the men, be shamed (see Esth. 1:15–22). This man, however, takes his place among the elders at the gate—not in spite of his wife but in large part because of her. He does have the generosity to praise her publicly (Prov. 31:28–29).

Whether or not she represents one individual, she is an idealized figure. The preacher can help us take a closer look at what is being praised so highly. It is basically domestic work: securing food, making clothing, taking care of the members of the household. She may be more extravagant with her purple and scarlet garments than the woman who shops at Goodwill, but they are both doing important and often overlooked work.[1]

Jeremiah 11:18–20. Jeremiah 11 begins a section of the book with many interwoven laments (often termed "confessions") and announcements of judgment. The prophet, the people, and the Lord all lament. Jeremiah is trying to be faithful to his call from God and yet faces opposition from every direction, including his own neighbors and extended family. With knowledge that our book of Jeremiah was put into the form we now have during the exile, the question arises as to the objective of recording such laments to and for a people who have lived

through catastrophes themselves. The preacher might highlight at least this: by recognizing grief, by acknowledging what needs to be lamented, accompanied by a word of hope from God, a people may find a way through.

The prophet Jeremiah is "of the priests . . . in Anathoth" (Jer. 1:1). This note conveys more than merely geographical information. In the days of confusion and contention surrounding King David's death, when several of his sons competed for the kingship, the priest Abiathar backed Adonijah. Upon his succession to the throne, Solomon apparently had no qualms about executing military men who had supported rivals but hesitated to order the killing of a priest. Thus, Abiathar was merely exiled to the town of Anathoth, a few miles from Jerusalem. Since the Levites had been given no arable land in the great division when Israel crossed the Jordan after their wilderness wanderings, priests supported themselves and their families largely from the grain and animals brought for sacrifices. With access to the temple in Jerusalem blocked, Abiathar, though still a priest, was cut off from his livelihood (see 1 Kgs. 1:5–2:35).

What is fascinating, and germane to understanding this pericope, is to see how long the family holds on to this identification as "the priests of Anathoth." Solomon became king approximately 1000 BCE, and Jeremiah 1:2 places the beginning of Jeremiah's ministry in the thirteenth year of King Josiah, a good three and a half centuries later. The double identity is important: priest and of Anathoth.

We are not told straight out, but the inference pointed to by that double identification is that this family continued to think of themselves as a priestly family and that they would bear a grudge against the Jerusalem establishment. Jeremiah's public pronouncements up to this point have spared neither Jerusalem nor the priestly class. The men of his hometown are not pleased with his oracles and have plotted to kill him, which is clear in the verse following this pericope (Jer. 11:21). The charge against him could be called a lack of patriotism. Jeremiah is preaching loyalty to God as a greater good than loyalty to self or

1. See Kate Raworth, *Donut Economics* (White River Junction, VT: Chelsea Green Publishing, 2017) for a clear explication of how our general economic thinking usually leaves out so much that is important.

king or nation, even when God's contemporary word is warning of punishment under a foreign power. This seems a natural place the preacher might help the congregation wrestle with competing calls for loyalty. Being faithful is not the same as being unfailingly optimistic, nor does faithfulness to God require unquestioning subservience to the Deity.

Jeremiah's knowledge of the plot, of the danger he is in, comes in some manner from God. Having heard about it, he lays out his innocence and his concerns before God. "Let me see your vengeance" (NIV, KJV; NRSV "retribution"), he says. Jeremiah does not try to pretend any

reaction that is "nice" or "religious"—but look carefully. "Let me see your vengeance" is quite different from "strengthen me to go kill them." This is a conversation with God, rather than gathering up a militia of his own or even a coterie of bodyguards.

The combination of facing dangerous external reality along with internal qualms and calling upon God's strength, rather than relying on whatever brute force one can muster, is modeled here by Jeremiah. The preacher might find local contemporary examples the congregation would recognize.

REBECCA ABTS WRIGHT

Commentary 2: Connecting the Reading with the World

A capable wife and a lamenting prophet: the lectionary offers two human profiles to explore this Sunday. Proverbs 31, oft read at the funeral of a beloved matriarch, details the qualities of a near impossibly perfect partner: industrious, entrepreneurial, generous, strong, dignified, kind. Indeed, as the writer of Proverbs notes, who can find such a person? Her capacities seem superhero-like. Then, in Jeremiah 11, this brief outburst of the prophet's pain, he describes himself as a lamb led to slaughter, as his faithfulness to his calling will get him killed, even as he proclaims his trust in the Lord. Jeremiah's qualities seem well beyond average human attainment too. So, what connects these biblical people to the ones in our contemporary pews?

Taking each text in turn, the preacher could do an exploration of what fearing the Lord enables one to do and be, or how a sense of call motivates, or what a life lived not solely or mostly for oneself looks like. These roads could offer needed connecting points to those living in a post-#MeToo world populated more with self-aggrandizing politicians than weeping prophets.

Proverbs 31 poses challenges in a cultural context where gender roles grow increasingly fluid and binary language of husband and wife comes across in some contexts as antiquated at best and tone-deaf at worst. Naming the large chasm of culture allows the preacher to acknowledge the discomfort some hearers will no doubt feel when this text is read, while

also not dismissing the word of the Lord to be found in these verses. After all, in some ways the capable wife described in Proverbs 31 does not fit with the norms of *her* day. Nowhere is she praised for being a mother, for example. In fact, she is a business woman whose spheres of influence go well beyond the walls of her home.

One avenue for preaching could explore the truth that a God-fearing person expands traditional roles and expectations, because loyalty to the Lord and divine call trump any cultural limitations and human judgments. Consider the people of faith who have broken assumed unbreakable boundaries in service to a higher calling. From Joan of Arc to the freedom riders of the civil rights movement, those who fear the Lord do not cow to norms imposed by mere mortals.

Those who chafe at the language of "capable wife" in this text might be challenged to expand their understanding of this passage through the lens of what it means for a person to fear the Lord, rather than capitulate to the limits of historical laws or human expectations. What if the preacher asked hearers to consider the capable wife as one who first and foremost fears the Lord and from there explore what a life lived with God as our ultimate judge looks like? Characteristics like kind, generous, bold, in tune to the needs of others, would surely follow. Other qualities, like physical beauty, perpetual youth, and the ability to charm, so prized by culture, might fall away.

Another reading of Proverbs 31 could invite worshipers to remember that this text is part of Wisdom literature, and the capable wife reflects divine wisdom. Rather than a text that diminishes the feminine, Proverbs 31 recognizes that God is not bound by gender, encompassing male and female. The preacher could take the opportunity to wrestle with gender stereotypes of both God and people, asking hearers to question their assumptions about both. How do we limit God and others by our narrow beliefs about what is appropriate or biblical or divinely ordained? A look at church history calls forth many examples, from who can be ordained to ministry to what kind of music should be used in worship. If the wisdom of God imbues both business practices and personal relationships, evident in the town square and around the kitchen table, where do we see it, unbound by our expectations, today? Preachers, like the writer of Proverbs, should notice, name, praise, and commend the wisdom of the Lord wherever they see it.

Jeremiah, for all his weeping and complaint, fears and trusts the Lord. Jeremiah, confident in his call and correctness, calls upon the Lord to bring his vindication and give those who seek his demise their divine comeuppance. Surely, such sentiments should not be spoken lightly. In fact, preachers ought to caution the community of faith, themselves included, about being too sure of knowing the mind of God. History proves Jeremiah right, but often history reveals that human ways are decidedly not God's ways.

Nonetheless, Jeremiah's lament resonates with all those seeking to do God's will in a world fraught with evil, injustice, and suffering. Doing the work of the Lord, as Jesus plainly states, brings pushback from earthly powers, unpopularity, and even death. The stakes for prophets then and people of faith now are high, and this snippet from Jeremiah demands that the preacher name the risks of discipleship and ask those gathered if they have considered the costs.

Jeremiah refuses to let believers off the hook from the reality that following God's call demands our life, our all. Confidence in God compels risk even through cries of lament and anguish. Preachers could lift up well-known examples ranging from Bonhoeffer to Martin Luther King Jr. Even more relatable than those luminaries of the faith are lesser known prophets who took a stand for justice and sought to do the will of God in their own time and place. Every community, every congregation, has their Jeremiahs. Preachers could do some research, ask longtime congregants, and find out who they are, in order to tell their stories, lament and all. Church and town histories reveal the people of faith, confident in God's power, willing to risk their safety and security, who trusted that ultimately God would bring vindication and therefore they would persevere in fulfilling their call, regardless of the consequences. The question the preacher must raise is this: are we willing to do likewise in our own lives?

Each of the Old Testament readings appointed for this week highlights what a life lived in fear of the Lord looks like. Regardless of cultural or historical context, those who seek to fulfill the Lord's call stand out. They refuse to be bound by human norms if God requires them to do and be otherwise. God's judgment and vindication alone matter. Their focus on the Divine moves them beyond themselves and their own self-interests. In the case of the capable wife, wisdom reveals itself in kindness, generosity, hard work, and care for the vulnerable. The prophet Jeremiah laments, grieves, holds none of his distress or disillusion back from God, and yet persists in fulfilling his call, trusting that the God who told him to pluck up and to plant, will be faithful.

As distant as the capable wife and the weeping prophet may seem, their examples of what fear of and faith in God look like compel the preacher to ask how our own lives, individually and corporately, reflect our loyalty to the Lord who calls, equips, and sends us into the world. Where is the wisdom of God evident, and how are we not just pointing to it and praising it, but enacting it? What boundaries are we to break for the sake of doing God's will? What are we willing to risk in order to proclaim and enact God's word? Who are the divinely capable and the bravely prophetic not just in our history, but in our midst, and how do we emulate them? The stakes are high, but God is trustworthy.

JILL DUFFIELD

Proper 20 (Sunday between September 18 and September 24)

Psalm 1

¹Happy are those
　who do not follow the advice of the wicked,
or take the path that sinners tread,
　or sit in the seat of scoffers;
²but their delight is in the law of the LORD,
　and on his law they meditate day and night.
³They are like trees
　planted by streams of water,
which yield their fruit in its season,
　and their leaves do not wither.
In all that they do, they prosper.

⁴The wicked are not so,
　but are like chaff that the wind drives away.
⁵Therefore the wicked will not stand in the judgment,
　nor sinners in the congregation of the righteous;
⁶for the LORD watches over the way of the righteous,
　but the way of the wicked will perish.

Psalm 54

¹Save me, O God, by your name,
　and vindicate me by your might.
²Hear my prayer, O God;
　give ear to the words of my mouth.

³For the insolent have risen against me,
　the ruthless seek my life;
　they do not set God before them.

⁴But surely, God is my helper;
　the Lord is the upholder of my life.
⁵He will repay my enemies for their evil.
　In your faithfulness, put an end to them.

⁶With a freewill offering I will sacrifice to you;
　I will give thanks to your name, O LORD, for it is good.
⁷For he has delivered me from every trouble,
　and my eye has looked in triumph on my enemies.

Connecting the Psalm with Scripture and Worship

Psalm 1. This psalm, which opens the whole Psalter, is a beatitude declaring that those who follow God's law live happy and prosperous lives. The opening words, "Happy are those . . . ," set the tone of the entire Psalter, echoing the themes of Wisdom literature and encouraging a life of faithful and fruitful obedience. Those who are happy "delight in the law" and meditate on it "day and night" (Ps. 1:2), unlike those who willfully ignore God's law and take their own ill-considered paths.

The psalm presents a stark contrast between "the wicked," who will ultimately perish, and the righteous, who are like "trees planted by streams of water, which yield their fruit in its season, and their leaves do not wither" (v. 3). The wicked are those who refuse to be instructed by God; they go off on their own way, unconcerned with the welfare of others, pursuing their own desires instead of justice. Eventually, they will be blown away like dust, inconsequential, forgotten, gone forever.

Those who will prosper, however, are those who are continually open to God's teaching. They seek to follow the ways of the Lord. They take delight in the way God instructs them to live. They do not wither away, but they discover that life is full of vitality and joy.

One beauty of Psalm 1 is that it is not simply a finger-wagging command to do this and not do that. At the heart of the psalm (v. 3) is a gorgeous image of trees, filled with luscious fruit, their roots reaching deep into rich soil where they are constantly fed by living streams. The psalm portrays a life full of joy and continual blessing. To live any other way is to miss the flourishing beauty and abundance of the good life.

Proverbs 31:10–31. Psalm 1 is chosen to respond to Proverbs 31:10–31, which constitutes the end of the book of Proverbs. This passage, subtitled in the NRSV "Ode to a Capable Wife," describes the ideal woman as industrious, obedient to her husband, and perpetually caring for her family, while running her own business, weaving her own cloth, running a vineyard, and cooking all the meals. She works day and night, and somehow also manages to care for the poor, dispense wisdom, and teach kindness.

Although this text is sometimes used to describe what an "ideal woman" is like, the extraordinary woman described at the close of Proverbs—whom some scholars name the Woman of Substance—may be understood as a composite picture of a number of real women, not just one woman. These are likely women of means, who are admirable in their own right and a credit to their husbands.[1] At the same time, however, this portrait hearkens back to the personification of wisdom as a woman—sometimes called Woman Wisdom—in Proverbs 1–9. Woman Wisdom speaks out publicly, warning those who will not listen to her teachings that they will not survive and assuring those who do listen that they will live in security. Wisdom is to be sought; there is nothing more precious. She is a tree of life, and "those who hold her fast are called happy" (Prov. 3:18).

The woman depicted in Proverbs 31:10–31 then is perhaps more than simply a description of a wonderfully adept woman, but an earthly picture of divine wisdom. It is by wisdom that God creates the world (3:19–20). Wisdom teaches the way of the Lord; "she is more precious than jewels, and nothing you desire can compare with her" (3:15). To embrace wisdom is to live a long life and enjoy God's blessings.

Psalm 1 is a fitting response to Proverbs 31:10–31. After hearing a description of divine wisdom as depicted in the life of a gifted and capable woman, worshipers respond with the words of the first Psalm. A responsorial setting, such as Juan Espinosa's "Feliz la gente/How Blest the People," or a metrical setting, such as David Gambrell's "How Happy Are the Saints of God," allows the people to sing with the psalmist and reinforce their desire to follow the ways of the Lord. These words serve as a fine prelude to both the epistle and Gospel readings appointed for this day, both of which compare earthly and divine wisdom.

---

1. Christine Roy Yoder, "The Woman of Substance: A Socioeconomic Reading of Proverbs 31:10–31," *Journal of Biblical Literature* 222, no. 3 (2003): 446.

Psalm 54. This brief psalm is a plea to God for salvation and vindication. The life of the psalmist is in danger, and the psalmist's enemies are not God-fearers. Yet the psalmist expresses confidence that God will not only save his life but punish those who seek to harm him. The superscription of the psalm refers to an episode in the life of David (1 Sam. 23), indicating that the editor of the Psalter saw a connection between the psalm and that particular story from Israel's history. Contemporary hearers, however, can easily place the words in their own mouths; such a prayer for help is not only a historical artifact. It may be read as an individual prayer or as a communal lament.

The enemies in this psalm are "the insolent" and "the ruthless," people who do harm to others. Again, this might be interpreted on an individual level or a corporate one. Whoever is threatening the psalmist's life is out to do no good; whatever they are up to, the psalmist considers it to be evil. The prayer for vindication, then, is not a plea for revenge, but a plea for justice. The expression of confidence in God's salvific power reflects the psalmist's conviction that God will, indeed, make things right when all is said and done.

Psalm 54 is spoken as a response to Jeremiah 11:18–20, three verses that constitute Jeremiah's own prayer in the face of danger. God has just commanded Jeremiah to deliver a message of condemnation against Judah, for they have not been faithful to their covenant with God.

Jeremiah responds by acknowledging God's complaint against the people, but confesses that he feels like a lamb being led to slaughter; he knows there is a plot brewing against him. The people are not going to take kindly to his prophesying, and he is afraid for his life. Yet Jeremiah expresses his trust in God to protect him, "for to you I have committed my cause" (Jer. 11:20).

The first reading from Jeremiah and the accompanying Psalm 54 are part of the complementary set of readings provided by the Revised Common Lectionary. One can hear the resonances between Jeremiah's words and Mark's account of Jesus as he predicts that the Son of Man will be betrayed and killed. Danger lurks in the shadows.

In singing or reading Psalm 54, contemporary worshipers remember their ancestors in the faith who faced the threats of people doing evil. Their voices echo the pleas of the psalmist, and David, and Jeremiah. Yet they also voice the promise of vindication—God will prevail. Those who do harm to others and seek to destroy will be themselves destroyed. The evil that pervades our society and our world will one day be no more. God will raise Jesus from the dead, conquering all that hurts and kills. Although a service of worship may begin in lament, naming the evils of the day and pleading for God's help, it ends with a confident declaration of the justice that is to come.

KIMBERLY BRACKEN LONG

James 3:13–4:3, 7–8a

3:13Who is wise and understanding among you? Show by your good life that your works are done with gentleness born of wisdom. 14But if you have bitter envy and selfish ambition in your hearts, do not be boastful and false to the truth. 15Such wisdom does not come down from above, but is earthly, unspiritual, devilish. 16For where there is envy and selfish ambition, there will also be disorder and wickedness of every kind. 17But the wisdom from above is first pure, then peaceable, gentle, willing to yield, full of mercy and good fruits, without a trace of partiality or hypocrisy. 18And a harvest of righteousness is sown in peace for those who make peace.

4:1Those conflicts and disputes among you, where do they come from? Do they not come from your cravings that are at war within you? 2You want something and do not have it; so you commit murder. And you covet something and cannot obtain it; so you engage in disputes and conflicts. You do not have, because you do not ask. 3You ask and do not receive, because you ask wrongly, in order to spend what you get on your pleasures. . . . 7Submit yourselves therefore to God. Resist the devil, and he will flee from you. 8Draw near to God, and he will draw near to you.

Commentary 1: Connecting the Reading with Scripture

The theme of wisdom is prominent in James. It appears four times, three in this passage and once in 1:5, where the writer says that if anyone lacks wisdom, this person should ask God for it, and it should be given. The example for this is of course Solomon (see 2 Chr. 1:7–12a). He is the model of every wisdom-seeker in the Bible. Fear of God is the source of true wisdom (Ps. 111:10; Prov. 9:10; Job 28:28; Sir. 1:14), and God will give it to those who seek it (Prov. 2:6–15).

The asking should be done in faith, like Solomon's request; otherwise God will not grant the petition. So, from the very beginning, by making a connection between faith and wisdom, understood as the art of living meaningfully, this letter prepares the reader for its main theme, namely, the relationship between faith and works, or faith and praxis. However, we should be aware that James uses faith (*pistis*) with two different meanings: trust in God (Jas. 1:6), and a set of theological beliefs, such as that God is one (2:19). Therefore, careful attention to the context needs to be exercised, lest we misunderstand the author's message.

By affirming that wisdom is an essential condition of a perfect and complete human existence (1:4), the author is drawing from the wisdom tradition where *sophia* is personified as a feminine concept and associated with the lifegiving cycle (Prov. 1–9; 16:22). In terms of style, James seems also to be imitating the Wisdom of Solomon, which uses diatribe as a rhetorical device. Our passage is a clear example of this.

In 3:13 the connection between faith and wisdom is made clear: works, that is, ethical living, are born of faith/wisdom. To be wise is not to be enlightened, but to know how to live ethically. This is wisdom from above, from God, and it is described with eight qualities: pure, peaceable, gentle, willing to yield, full of mercy, full of good fruits, without a trace of partiality or hypocrisy (3:17). Another way of translating these qualities could be innocent, peaceful, tolerant, obedient, full of compassion, with good fruits, nonjudgmental (or impartial), without hypocrisy.

There is another kind of wisdom that is earthly, unspiritual, and devilish (3:15), completely opposite to the one from above. Its distinguishing characteristics are envy, selfish

Lift Up Your Eyes to Heaven

If you have any hope of salvation; if you have the least thought of God, or any desire for good things to come; if you have any fear of the chastisements reserved for the impenitent, awake without delay, lift up your eyes to heaven, come to your senses, cease from your wickedness, shake off the stupor that enwraps you, make a stand against the foe who has struck you down. Make an effort to rise from the ground. Remember the good Shepherd who will follow and rescue you. Though it be but two legs or a lobe of an ear, spring back from the beast that has wounded you. Remember the mercies of God and how He cures with oil and wine. Do not despair of salvation. Recall your recollection of how it is written in the Scriptures that he who is falling rises and he who turns away returns; the wounded is healed, the prey of beasts escapes; he who owns his sin is not rejected. The Lord willeth not the death of a sinner but rather that he should turn and live. Do not despise, like the wicked in the pit of evil. There is a time of endurance, a time of long suffering, a time of healing, a time of correction. Have you stumbled? Arise. Have you sinned? Cease. Do not stand in the way of sinners, but spring away. When you are converted and groan you shall be saved. Out of labour comes health, out of sweat salvation. Beware lest, from your wish to keep certain obligations, you break the obligations to God which you professed before many witnesses. Pray do not hesitate to come to me for any earthly considerations. When I have recovered my dead I shall lament, I shall tend him, I will weep "because of the spoiling of the daughter of my people." All are ready to welcome you, all will share your efforts. Do not sink back. Remember the days of old. There is salvation; there is amendment. Be of good cheer; do not despair. It is not a law condemning to death without pity, but mercy remitting punishment and awaiting improvement. The doors are not yet shut; the bridegroom hears; sin is not the master. Make another effort, do not hesitate, have pity on yourself and on all of us in Jesus Christ our Lord, to Whom be glory and might now and for ever and ever. Amen.

Basil the Great, "Letter to a Lapsed Monk (Letter XLIV)," in *Nicene and Post-Nicene Fathers,* second series, vol. 8, ed. Philip Schaff and Henry Wace (Buffalo, NY: Christian Literature Publishing, 1895), 147.

ambition, disorder, and wickedness (v. 16). The author seems to suggest that some in his community subscribe to this type of wisdom and even boast about it (v. 14). The apostle Paul also distinguishes between human and divine wisdom (1 Cor. 1:18–25) when he writes about the crucified Christ being the power and wisdom of God. God's wisdom has nothing to do with knowledge, for it is an act, an event that reflects God's heart full of compassion and mercy and love. It is action, not mere thinking; practice, not mere theory.

Asking something from God and not receiving it for lack of faith (Jas. 1:6) or for asking wrongly (4:3) is one of the themes of this letter. There can be two reasons for asking: for wisdom (1:5), or for spending on one's passions (4:3). In the first case, faith is required (1:6–8), in the second, the right motivation. Asking to spend on one's pleasures or asking without faith does not procure favor from God (1:8; 4:3). Every good thing a believer has comes from God (1:17), and the only way to enjoy the blessings of God is to submit to God, to draw near to God, so that God may draw near to us (4:7–8a).

The community to which the author is writing is obviously experiencing a difficult time. They are having problems interacting with each other. The text refers to these problems as disorder, wickedness, conflicts, and disputes, all of them produced by envy and selfish ambition. Envy surfaces in the context of this community that is marked by social differences (2:1–7) and engages gossip and slander (3:1–12). Envy is the desire to have what others have, whether this be material things, in which case it is called coveting (4:2), or the desire for power, which is always exclusive and self-centered (3:14, 16; 4:3). James's community is suffering from an excessive desire for power, causing a deep crisis.

This disorientation is described by the language of the marriage covenant; an adulterous relationship with the world means a betrayal of or enmity with God (4:4). Portraying God as a jealous husband, the author summons the believers to submit to God. The verb is *hypotassō*, which is used in the NT to depict the relationship between husbands and wives (Eph. 5:22; Col. 3:18; Titus 2:5; 1 Pet. 3:1). The believers then should submit, that is, obey God as a wife obeys her husband. In 4:7, the sexual connotations are even greater. The devil is portrayed as a potential lover who needs to be resisted in order for him to stop seducing the community, which then should draw near to God in an intimate relationship that will be reciprocated by God drawing near to the believers.

In the OT, this idea of drawing near to God is used in connection with priestly service (Exod. 19:22; 34:30; Lev. 10:3) and in the NT figuratively as the spiritual service of Christians (Matt. 15:8; Heb. 7:19; Jas. 4:8).[1] Still the sexual connotations are present, especially when seen in the larger context of the Hebrew Bible, where the relationship between Yahweh and Israel is described in terms of a marriage (Ezek. 16:1–17; Hos. 2; Isa. 54:4–8). For example, 4:5 expresses the idea that God yearns jealously for or over the spirit that God has made dwell in us, whether this be the human spirit or the Holy Spirit, something the text does not clarify.

Certain concepts are difficult to understand in this passage. First, what does the author mean by murdering (*phoneuete*)? It cannot be understood literally, can it? There are many other ways in which one can "kill" a person, that is, deprive them of life—socially, psychologically, and the like. In James, the social murder of those of lower classes by the affluent seems to be the case. In 4:2, the parallelism between murder and disputes and conflicts suggests that the author sees the disputes among his community as a kind of murder. Since these disputes seem to be triggered by envy and jealousy, they point at an attitude very different from that of Jesus. He addressed the divisions between his disciples with the example of a child, whom he placed among them as an example of how they should relate to each other, not on the basis of power but on the basis of mutual service (Mark 9:30–37).

When divisions occur in our congregations today on the basis of social class, political preferences, education, and culture, among other things, we demonstrate how little we know of the true knowledge, that which comes from God. Conversely, acting according to true knowledge, we invest our lives in the lives of others, disregarding our petty desires for power.

OSVALDO D. VENA

Commentary 2: Connecting the Reading with the World

It is difficult to imagine a biblical text any more pertinent to the current social and political climate of the United States, and indeed of the world. No one need tell us that we live in deeply polarized societies, a fact made all the more apparent and immediate by social media (esp. Facebook!). People of all persuasions publish their convictions, suspicions, and insinuations via the internet, and international debates ensue. Those debates often degenerate into ugly diatribes within minutes.

Preachers can help us see how James, the New Testament's most obvious example of

Wisdom literature, implores its readers to take a different tack. Words may be cheap (Jas. 2:15–16), but they are nonetheless very often destructive of others (3:5–12); by contrast, *works* "done with gentleness born of wisdom" are the fruit of the good life (3:13). In a world in which mudslinging and character assassination are all the rage, such lives seem difficult to come by.

If only it could be different in our churches! We know that too often it is not. It may be helpful to remember that the larger setting for this passage is a wisdom-styled meditation on the role of being a teacher within the

---

1. William F. Arndt and F. Wilbur Gingrich, *A Greek-English Lexicon of the NT and Other Early Christian Literature* (Chicago/London: University of Chicago Press, 1957), 213.

church—prefaced by the warning "Not many of you should become teachers" (3:1). Why? Because the tongue is so difficult to tame, and even teachers (and preachers!) can yield to the allure of "boast[ing] of great exploits" (3:5). The same strident spirit of competitiveness and divisiveness that has come to characterize contemporary secular societies is all too often evident in and among our churches. Thus, James warns, there are "conflicts and disputes among you" (4:1), and of course the plural "you" in question is a Christian congregation.

Hence the question that opens our passage, "Who is wise and understanding among you?" is intended first of all to thin out the crop, so to speak, of potential teachers and congregational leaders. Not everyone who desires to teach actually lives with the requisite wisdom. It is critical to note that "wise and understanding" in this case is not first of all a matter of intellectual giftedness; it is a matter of a life well lived in "gentleness born of wisdom" (3:13). This is "wisdom from above"—divine wisdom, reflecting the very nature of God—and so is "pure, then peaceable, gentle, willing to yield, full of mercy and good fruits, without a trace of partiality or hypocrisy" (v. 17).

Our current political climate is not conducive to such virtues, but again, perhaps we ought not to look too far beyond our own congregations and our own pastoral leadership. This is why it is wise of denominational structures to utilize appropriate tools to measure, and to encourage, emotional stability and growth in those engaged in the ordination process. We note that James warns against "envy and selfish ambition" twice within our passage (vv. 14, 16) and, again, the immediate problem is with those who are jockeying for position and influence within the church as teachers. The end result? "Disorder and wickedness of every kind" (v. 16). We have all witnessed, far too often, the carnage left behind by an ego-driven pastor, teacher, or professor. The preacher would do well to pay attention to how this happens in all aspects of society and name those pertinent to the congregation.

James insists that we, particularly we who have indeed answered the call to preach and to teach within our churches, must engage in the hard work of introspection. Whence do our "conflicts and disputes" arise? "Do they not come from your cravings that are at war within you?" (4:1). Perhaps we would rather not acknowledge those cravings: perhaps for power, for status, for wealth, for praise, for security, for leisure, and, all too often, at the expense of others. "You covet something and cannot obtain it," and most assuredly our world economies are now driven largely by creating false needs through manipulative advertising. "Such wisdom does not come down from above" (v. 15). The inevitable disappointment of seeking (and even attaining) false goods, James warns, leads to "disputes and conflicts" (4:1–2). Let us again appreciate that James is diagnosing a problem already evident in the earliest generation of Christian congregations; of course, Paul addressed the same issue (1 Cor. 3:1–17). Two millennia later, we still find ourselves too often mired in those same conflicts.

"You do not have" all those things we crave because we "ask wrongly, in order to spend what you get on your pleasures" (4:2, 3). James had already counseled his readers regarding the appropriate request of God: "If any of you is lacking in wisdom, ask God, who gives to all generously and ungrudgingly" (1:5). Hence, we come full circle: we engage in disputes and conflicts because we "covet something and cannot obtain it" (4:2); we covet these worldly "goods" because we do not live in "the wisdom from above" (3:17); we do not so live because we have not asked divine wisdom to be imparted to us (1:5). We prefer to seek after other, likely more immediately pleasing, goods. Far too often our churches merely mirror the world's conflicts rooted in insatiable desire, perhaps even simply the desire to maintain our standard of living at the expense of the world's poor (2:5–7). New Testament scholar Robert Wall writes insightfully, "A good and gracious God (cf. 1:5, 17) simply does not respond to petitions motivated by self-centered commitments; such prayer is idolatrous, even blasphemous, because it renders God as mere provider of pleasure rather than as sovereign covenant partner."[2] Preachers

2. Robert W. Wall, *Community of the Wise: The Letter of James* (Valley Forge, PA: Trinity Press, 1997), 198.

could help congregations see ways that, at times, our prayers (and sermons?!) fall short of what God desires.

God as one who satisfies our desires—as inviting as such a deity may appear in an era of megachurches and prosperity preaching—is not the God to whom we are to submit, nor to whom we are encouraged to draw near (4:7, 8). The God to whom James bears witness is the God of wisdom, indeed the God who is wisdom. This wisdom gives birth to gentleness in our lives toward others (3:13). It surely is not the wisdom of this age, at least as exemplified in our current political discourse.

Finally, it is striking that James describes the wisdom from above as "peaceable, gentle, willing to yield" (3:17). Given the difficulty of finding such wisdom at work in our Christian congregations, perhaps it is far too much to expect it of our political leaders in the United States and elsewhere. Nonetheless, few would dispute the fact that in the contemporary world of political diatribe (the word "discourse" seems distant from current reality), the depth of division, suspicion, and hatred has reached new lows. The fault lines have wreaked havoc in far too many of our churches. How far short we fall from a wisdom that is "peaceable, gentle, willing to yield"! Sometimes, though, this wisdom may confront us from an unexpected source. In the recent Werner Herzog documentary *Meeting Gorbachev*, the former leader of the Soviet Union says, "There are those who don't understand the importance of cooperation. There should be no place for such people in politics." James would add, and no place for such people in the church—especially in church leadership.

MICHAEL LODAHL

Mark 9:30–37

30They went on from there and passed through Galilee. He did not want anyone to know it; 31for he was teaching his disciples, saying to them, "The Son of Man is to be betrayed into human hands, and they will kill him, and three days after being killed, he will rise again." 32But they did not understand what he was saying and were afraid to ask him.

33Then they came to Capernaum; and when he was in the house he asked them, "What were you arguing about on the way?" 34But they were silent, for on the way they had argued with one another who was the greatest. 35He sat down, called the twelve, and said to them, "Whoever wants to be first must be last of all and servant of all." 36Then he took a little child and put it among them; and taking it in his arms, he said to them, 37"Whoever welcomes one such child in my name welcomes me, and whoever welcomes me welcomes not me but the one who sent me."

Commentary 1: Connecting the Reading with Scripture

The Gospel passage for today features the second passion prediction of Jesus. In all three passion predictions recorded by Mark, and later copied by Matthew and Luke, we find a similar pattern: announcement, misunderstanding, and explanation. First, Jesus announces his imminent death to his disciples as they travel on their way to Jerusalem; second, the disciples have trouble understanding Jesus' admonishment; third, Jesus translates the message about his death in terms of discipleship. With this particular triad of predictions and teachings, one wonders, Did Jesus emphasize this message three times? Was it Mark who collected many versions of this encounter and summarized it with this threefold pattern? Either way, the emphatic repetition in Mark highlights the centrality of the message. These stories hold many preaching possibilities.

If we focus on Jesus' words about his upcoming passion, we notice how they go from the broad to the specific. First, he will suffer and be rejected (Mark 8:31); second, he will be betrayed (9:31); and third, he will experience mocking, spitting, and flogging (10:34). The preacher could focus on this sequence in order to talk about the consequences of Jesus' radical ministry; we can all consider ways our lived faith may upset the status quo and bring about our suffering as we persevere in discipleship. There are certainly places around our world where Christians are a minority and suffer religious persecution for their faith.

Preachers can also identify how these three predictions function as a summary of the intensification of negative responses to Jesus' life and ministry throughout this Gospel. Additionally, three of today's other readings (Wisdom of Solomon, Jeremiah, and Psalm 54) illustrate precisely how Jesus' followers, those who "have knowledge of God" (Wis. 2:13), who "have committed" their cause to the Lord (Jer. 11:20), and say, "God is my helper" (Ps. 54:4), will be rejected and persecuted, for they are an inconvenience for the unrighteous, whose evil actions they expose. Regardless of the consequences, giving our life for others is Jesus' instruction to his followers—yesterday, today and tomorrow—"For the Son of Man did not come to be served but to serve, and to give his life a ransom for many" (Mark 10:45).

The preacher may linger over some of the details of this account. Notably, the disciples act out when Jesus speaks of death. They change the topic and start talking among themselves about who is the greatest of the group. When Jesus asks about their conversation, they keep silent about their trivial arguments. The good teacher, aware of their thoughts, guides them toward what matters and away from concern about power and positions of privilege. Jesus answers their question: greatness comes from serving.

The preacher could explore the meaning of greatness according to the gospel versus the meaning of greatness in our current culture of consumerism and greed. This involves serving and caring for the vulnerable ones of society, for those who cannot return the favor, for those like children. Greatness comes from welcoming the marginalized of society. In doing these things, we welcome not only Jesus but God, by receiving and serving the most vulnerable ones.

As we connect this story to the whole of Mark 9, we notice that the evangelist continues to employ certain patterns. Jesus offers a revelation and a call, and the disciples react with confusion and failure to respond. In Mark 9:2–10, Jesus reveals himself to Peter, James, and John; he transfigures himself in front of them at the top of a mountain. Overwhelmed, Peter quickly declares that they should camp there, but Jesus directs them toward the waiting crowd. As they descend, Jesus orders them not to tell anyone about this experience until after he has risen from the dead. They obey and keep the story to themselves, mainly because they do not understand what he means by rising from the dead. They obey out of confusion, not out of understanding. The patterns of misunderstanding, avoidance, and misdirection continue.

This is not the first time Jesus announces his impending death nor the first time the disciples seem to ignore this announcement and the commitment that Jesus is calling them to embrace. Earlier, Jesus foretells his death (8:31–33), with more detail than in 9:30, and Peter rebukes him. Judging by Jesus' reaction, (calling Peter "Satan"), we imagine Peter tried to dissuade Jesus from talking about death or directed him instead into making plans for their future places of honor in a material kingdom. Perhaps this story is repeated several times as a genuine call to discipleship for all believers, including us.

In Mark 10:32–34, we find the third passion prediction. Sounding as if preparing them for a final exam, Jesus tells his disciples that they are all going on to Jerusalem, that the people will kill him, but after three days he will rise again. Still James and John ask to sit on Jesus' right and left in his glory. When the others hear the request, they get angry with James and John; we might presume this is because they did not have the chance to make the same request first. Jesus gathers them and once more tells them they are not to fight for power, that whoever wishes to be great among them should be servant of all, just as he has come to serve and give his life for many. Once again, Jesus instructs his disciples to serve others and give their lives in service for others.

The preacher can find an abundance of textual material detailing the cost of discipleship in our Gospel reading and the surrounding narrative material. Again and again, the disciples travel with Jesus, hear his predictions and instructions, and fail to comprehend. Is not the same true for us in our time? We are the ones who know that his predictions came true. We have received all that was handed on to us. Yet still we argue about greatness and fail to follow him along the path of service to the least of these.

The other readings for this Sunday offer us examples of service, of living a life for God. The capable woman of Proverbs 31:10–31 shows us what it means to live a life for the Lord as she gives her life in service to others. In Psalm 1, we find the counterpart of the life of the man who fears the Lord and lives a righteous life. Three of the passages remind us that the life of the righteous will not be an easy life. There will be jealousy and anger from those who feel accused and threatened by the life of the righteous. All three passages give us some light on what it means to follow Jesus and how Jesus was handed over to be killed (Wis. 1:16–2:1, 12–22), what it means to commit our cause to the Lord and like a gentle lamb be led to the slaughter. In Psalm 54, we are reminded that God is helper and the Lord is the upholder of life, even when Jesus is suffering at the hands of adversaries. The final text from James comes as an admonition, echoing Jesus' words of keeping our eyes on what counts: mercifulness, peacemaking, generosity, true wisdom from above, discipleship, resisting evil, and submitting ourselves to God (Jas. 3:13–4:3, 7–8a). The call is clear: Jesus' disciples should follow a path of commitment to God and service to the least of these. Let us not forget, real greatness comes from serving and welcoming the powerless.

LETICIA A. GUARDIOLA-SÁENZ

Commentary 2: Connecting the Reading with the World

This text states that while Jesus and his disciples were passing through Galilee, he did not want anyone to know where he was, because he was teaching his disciples. Previous parts of the story describe his many acts of healing people who were afflicted with various illnesses, which in his day invariably drew much attention, as countless others with disabilities longed for healing and eagerly followed anyone reputed to be a healer.

Since the author of Mark's Gospel began with the claim that Jesus was the Messiah, the Son of God, Jesus had much work to do in explaining the meaning of his messianic mission to those close to him, because it differed so much from the traditional teachings that the expected Messiah would restore Israel's monarchy and its expansive influence.

Most teachers can easily understand the difficulty Jesus must have faced in teaching his disciples a new understanding of his messianic mission. Few things can be more difficult than that of changing fixed opinions on any subject, especially one as important as Jewish messianic expectations.

Since all such understandings threatened the security of the political and religious authorities of his day, Jesus knew the importance of preparing his disciples in advance. He also knew that his association with John the Baptist, who had baptized him and later was beheaded by Herod, evidenced the dangerous nature of his mission. Thus, all the more reason for keeping his activities and location secret.

In teaching his disciples the true meaning of his mission, he was probably not fully surprised by their lack of understanding, even though their ignorance sometimes provoked his anger, and that may have made it difficult for them to raise questions, lest they be viewed as stupid and unworthy to be among his closest friends. Nonetheless, he clearly told them what was about to happen, namely, that he would be betrayed, killed, and raised from the dead. Since such a declaration contradicted all the traditional understandings, it provided an ideal moment to raise any number of questions. Yet they were afraid to do so and, hence, chose to remain in ignorance.

Certainly a key dimension of all learning is to ask questions, which requires courage to risk embarrassment by revealing one's vulnerability in the presence of others. By not asking questions we live into a lie by giving the impression that we understand when we do not. Unfortunately, the disciples fell into that trap.

Now, immediately after Jesus told the disciples about his pending betrayal, death, and resurrection, readers are shocked by the next part of the story. When he was in the house at Capernaum, he inquired about their conversation that he had overheard along the way. The narrator states that they became quiet because they had been arguing about who was the greatest among them. Sadly, instead of commiserating with one another about the sad news he had shared with them about his pending death, they began arguing about who would gain higher status afterwards. In other words, they were discussing which one of them would assume leadership.

Once again, they must have been surprised by his response. He told them that anyone who wants to be first must be the very last and the servant of them all. That had to be the reverse of everything they had ever heard. Jesus was actually giving primacy to the exact contrary of their viewpoints by saying that the greatest among them must be the servant of them all. Such a reversal of their ordinary thought must have shocked them as much as it has shocked all future readers over the centuries.

In order to make his point even clearer, Jesus took a child in his embrace and said that whoever welcomes the child welcomes him, and whoever welcomes him welcomes the one who sent him. Since children had no social status whatsoever in ancient Israel, he was clearly stating a reversal of the social order by making the least first and the first last. In other words, his messianic kingdom would establish a new social ethic by reversing the social and political fortunes of the dispossessed and restoring health to those who were sick and disabled, as well as dignity and value to children, women, and the outcasts.

Jesus' act of elevating a child to the center of his teaching about who would be the greatest in the kingdom reverberated in the twentieth-century civil rights movement when both Black children and Black women played a crucial role in dismantling Jim Crow segregation throughout this nation.

First, the 1954 Supreme Court decision *Brown v. Board of Education* that provided the legal foundation for the civil rights movement was set in motion by Reverend Oliver Brown of Topeka, Missouri, who tried to register his daughter, Linda, in the all-white elementary school in that city. The consequent overthrow of the 1896 *Plessy v. Ferguson* decision, which had upheld the *separate but equal* doctrine for more than a half century, immortalized Linda Brown's name in the historic record of the American legal system.

Second, another child icon in the twentieth-century civil rights movement was the fourteen-year-old Emmett Till from Chicago, who was spending the summer of 1955 with his grandparents in Money, Mississippi. By playing a childish prank on the white woman store owner in the presence of his peers, he jokingly intended to demonstrate his urban sense of manliness to his rural peers by saying, "'Bye, babe," as they left the store after buying some candy. That night he was taken from his grandparents' home by the Ku Klux Klan, mercilessly tortured, killed, and thrown into the Tallahatchie River. His mother insisted on an open casket, and the photo of his unrecognizable mutilated body was published by *Jet* magazine. Shocked mourners, passing by the casket, saw the horror of his body alongside the photo of a handsome young boy sporting a hat. Nothing could have been more effective in showing the world the brutality of Jim Crow segregation. Emmett Till's death as a young boy elevated his memory to a status that has inspired all future generations to seek, secure, and celebrate racial justice.

In the days of racial segregation, Black children shared the status of being among the least important people in the nation with that of Black women, whose immense suffering has extended from the days of slavery to the present era. Yet the civil rights movement that changed America was begun with the courageous act of a Black woman, Rosa Parks, who refused to give up her seat to a white man on a bus in Montgomery, Alabama. That act was the impetus for the Montgomery bus boycott that lasted for thirteen months and launched the civil rights movement that ushered in the Civil Rights Act of 1964 and the Voters Rights Act of 1965.

Since children in the United States cannot register to vote until they are eighteen, their voice on public issues is not counted. Yet one of the most impressive national demonstrations occurred in Washington, DC, on March 24, 2018, following the February 18, 2018, killing of seventeen students and wounding of seventeen others at the Marjory Stoneman Douglas High School in Parkland, Florida. Much to the surprise of most, those high school children organized and executed an extraordinary "March for Our Lives," aimed at persuading the lawmakers in Washington, DC, about the urgent need for effective legislation to stop such brutal attacks on our schools. Thus, preachers would do well to heed the moral lessons that many children have been trying to teach their elders for quite some time.

PETER J. PARIS

Proper 21 (Sunday between September 25 and October 1)

Esther 7:1–6, 9–10; 9:20–22 and
    Numbers 11:4–6, 10–16, 24–29
Psalm 124 and Psalm 19:7–14

James 5:13–20
Mark 9:38–50

Esther 7:1–6, 9–10; 9:20–22

7:1So the king and Haman went in to feast with Queen Esther. 2On the second day, as they were drinking wine, the king again said to Esther, "What is your petition, Queen Esther? It shall be granted you. And what is your request? Even to the half of my kingdom, it shall be fulfilled." 3Then Queen Esther answered, "If I have won your favor, O king, and if it pleases the king, let my life be given me—that is my petition—and the lives of my people—that is my request. 4For we have been sold, I and my people, to be destroyed, to be killed, and to be annihilated. If we had been sold merely as slaves, men and women, I would have held my peace; but no enemy can compensate for this damage to the king." 5Then King Ahasuerus said to Queen Esther, "Who is he, and where is he, who has presumed to do this?" 6Esther said, "A foe and enemy, this wicked Haman!" Then Haman was terrified before the king and the queen. . . . 9Then Harbona, one of the eunuchs in attendance on the king, said, "Look, the very gallows that Haman has prepared for Mordecai, whose word saved the king, stands at Haman's house, fifty cubits high." And the king said, "Hang him on that." 10So they hanged Haman on the gallows that he had prepared for Mordecai. Then the anger of the king abated. . . .

9:20Mordecai recorded these things, and sent letters to all the Jews who were in all the provinces of King Ahasuerus, both near and far, 21enjoining them that they should keep the fourteenth day of the month Adar and also the fifteenth day of the same month, year by year, 22as the days on which the Jews gained relief from their enemies, and as the month that had been turned for them from sorrow into gladness and from mourning into a holiday; that they should make them days of feasting and gladness, days for sending gifts of food to one another and presents to the poor.

Numbers 11:4–6, 10–16, 24–29

4The rabble among them had a strong craving; and the Israelites also wept again, and said, "If only we had meat to eat! 5We remember the fish we used to eat in Egypt for nothing, the cucumbers, the melons, the leeks, the onions, and the garlic; 6but now our strength is dried up, and there is nothing at all but this manna to look at." . . .

10Moses heard the people weeping throughout their families, all at the entrances of their tents. Then the LORD became very angry, and Moses was displeased. 11So Moses said to the LORD, "Why have you treated your servant so badly? Why have I not found favor in your sight, that you lay the burden of all this people on me? 12Did I conceive all this people? Did I give birth to them, that you should say to me, 'Carry them in your bosom, as a nurse carries a sucking child,' to the land that you promised on oath to their ancestors? [13]Where am I to get meat to give to all this people? For they come weeping to me and say, 'Give us meat to eat!' [14]I am not able to carry all this people alone, for they are too heavy for me. [15]If this is the way you are going to treat me, put me to death at once—if I have found favor in your sight—and do not let me see my misery."

[16]So the LORD said to Moses, "Gather for me seventy of the elders of Israel, whom you know to be the elders of the people and officers over them; bring them to the tent of meeting, and have them take their place there with you." . . .

[24]So Moses went out and told the people the words of the LORD; and he gathered seventy elders of the people, and placed them all around the tent. [25]Then the LORD came down in the cloud and spoke to him, and took some of the spirit that was on him and put it on the seventy elders; and when the spirit rested upon them, they prophesied. But they did not do so again.

[26]Two men remained in the camp, one named Eldad, and the other named Medad, and the spirit rested on them; they were among those registered, but they had not gone out to the tent, and so they prophesied in the camp. [27]And a young man ran and told Moses, "Eldad and Medad are prophesying in the camp." [28]And Joshua son of Nun, the assistant of Moses, one of his chosen men, said, "My lord Moses, stop them!" [29]But Moses said to him, "Are you jealous for my sake? Would that all the LORD's people were prophets, and that the LORD would put his spirit on them!"

Commentary 1: Connecting the Reading with Scripture

Esther 7:1–6, 9–10; 9:20–22. Esther is a clear antithesis of the valiant woman from last week's Proverbs text and her whirlwind of productive activity. Esther is queen because she won a beauty contest. There is no indication that she has any royal duties, any hobbies, any activities of any sort. Still, she puts herself at great risk to save her people. After an edict has been proclaimed calling for the extermination of all Jews in the realm, she cleverly asks King Ahasuerus for the safety of her people in a way that does not disclose her own Jewish identity until he has agreed to her request. She risks everything when she could have kept quiet and been safe herself, at least for a time.

Today's cut-and-paste version of Esther is all we hear from this book in the entire three-year lectionary cycle. If the complete story were more familiar to the standard Christian congregation, this would be less troublesome. However, it is not, and so the circumstance needs to be considered. A minor matter is that there is no mention of God in the whole book. (This apparently was enough of a major matter to some members of the ancient community that

the Septuagint [Greek Old Testament] includes additional verses that make up for this lack. These additions can be found in the Apocrypha under the title Additions to Esther.)

Today's pericope is a sanitized version in which the disturbing parts have been carefully excised. Not only is there is a great deal of violence in Esther; there is much celebration of that violence. Preachers should be aware of the content of the entire book, especially in a world and in a culture with "open carry" and some churches having Blessing of the Firearms services. Not only the mass killings at the end but also the casual elimination of Haman, the book's archvillain, in 7:9–10 should be disquieting.

At various times in their history Israelites lived as captives in a foreign land; other times, they were in their own land but under the domination of others. The Old Testament includes a thread of what might be called "literature from the underside." Several texts that were composed or edited during the exile make fun of the overlords in a circumspect way, even though it is highly unlikely that any Babylonian or Persian ruler lampooned therein would ever read them.

King Ahasuerus is assumed to be all powerful, and yet the best penalty he and his counselors can come up with to punish Queen Vashti for refusing to parade herself in front of the king's banquet guests is to forbid her ever to be in his presence again (Esth. 1:12–22). Not only Ahasuerus but also the monarchs in the book of Daniel can apparently promulgate any law or decree they choose, but then there is said to be no way it can be either altered or rescinded. The unnamed Pharaoh of Exodus 1 apparently thinks that the way to reduce a population is to reduce the number of males rather than limiting the females. Any lowly chicken farmer could have educated him on population reduction.

Laughing at the foibles and lack of common sense of those presumably their "betters" could be spirit-raising and spirit-sustaining. It also left room for individuals such as Mordecai and Esther (as well as Joseph and Daniel and others) to find the interstitial openings through which they could survive and even thrive as a people. Using today's pericope as an example, the preacher might want to dwell on how, with courage and tenacity and community, being faithful to God is possible in any location under any political regime.

Numbers 11:4–6, 10–16, 24–29. We have been here before. The Israelites are in the wilderness, fussing against Moses and complaining about food. Moses is complaining to God about the burden of being responsible for the whole crowd. (That may be the origin of the place's name; the Hebrew for "burden" sounds quite like Massah.)

They are said to want "meat" rather than "food." Is this a major point of the episode? When what we have is enough but we want more or better or fancier, should we simply be satisfied with enough? The first time the people complain about lacking potable water (Exod. 15:22–26) is alright because they have not yet seen God's provision. Now that they have experienced God's faithful sustenance, their complaining is illegitimate.

The grumbling leaders are referred to as "riffraff" with wordplay carried on throughout the chapter. The root also means "gather," whether gather to fuss or gather to lead. The "riffraff"

are, here, contrasted with the "Israelites," but the latter, too, are susceptible to complaints and grumbling. Robert Alter comments on the "selective memory" in verse 5. The diet of Egypt that they now long for sounds rich. Their saying it was "for free" forgets that they had been slaves. The preacher might use this text, with local examples, to help us see there are tradeoffs when going from one situation to another, and that selective memory can be a trap.

Moses also complains, asking what he may think is a rhetorical question: "Where shall I get meat to feed all these people?" The question is echoed in feeding stories in the Gospels (Matt. 14:15; 15:33; Mark 6:33–44; Luke 9:12ff.; John 6:5ff.), albeit with the reversal of Jesus' asking the question.

Preachers can help congregations see that often the issue is not in asking a question in itself but, rather, in the attitude behind the query. The asking can go too far. This sort of asking assumes God/Jesus is as limited as any human—or any human's imagination. It assumes that "if I cannot see an obvious solution, there is no solution possible." Preachers may be able to find contemporary examples in their own settings to be appropriate illustrations.

God's first response to Moses' plaint seems to ignore the issue of food altogether; rather, provision is made for shared governance. (Notice, though, that the matter of food is revisited in some lectionary-omitted verses.)

The sharing of God's spirit with the seventy chosen elders is carried out in the presence of all the people; "transparency" we might call it today. Even this does not meet with universal approbation. Eldad and Medad famously stay within the camp instead of going to the tent of meeting. A lad tells Joshua, who tattles the indignity of their separation to Moses. Moses is having none of it.

God's spirit, and the sharing thereof, is not dependent upon our ways. (Cf. also, for example, the early church's experience of baptism, and that when Paul and others came upon them, some knew only the "baptism of John" [Acts 19:1–7], and others received the Holy Spirit before baptism. You can almost hear the latter-day Eldads and Medads calling out, "Hey, Paul, they did not do it right!")

That the seventy elders prophesy is a public demonstration of their having received a portion of the shared authoritative spirit of God. After one demonstration, there is no need for it to be repeated. These men are set apart for administration; Moses retains the role of prophet. "The 'gathering' of the leaders to share the spirit is the antithesis of the mob of riffraff that assembles to express in complaint the dictates of the belly, not the spirit."[1]

We are back to where we began, with the wrangle between fractious complaint and gratitude for enough.

REBECCA ABTS WRIGHT

Commentary 2: Connecting the Reading with the World

Leadership entails a multitude of burdens and stressors. Inevitably, the leader's actions garner anger, complaining, or admonishments to make different decisions than the ones made. Sometimes being the leader means putting one's self in harm's way, even risking death. Such was the case for Moses and Esther, two of the main characters in this week's Old Testament readings. When we meet Moses in Numbers, Pharaoh's army no longer poses a threat. Now God's own people present the obstacles to getting to the promised land. They long for the fleshpots of Egypt, tire of the sameness of the daily bland manna, and wish Moses and God would come up with a better, more palatable plan.

The people weep, the Lord is very angry, and Moses is displeased. Unhappiness abounds among the chosen and holy this week. Moses goes on a rant against God, unleashing his frustration and exasperation. Moses lets God know that, ultimately, these stiff-necked, ungrateful, grumbling people are *God's* responsibility, not *his*. God gets the message and calls in reinforcements for Moses, visiting not just Moses, but the seventy elders, distributing the divine Spirit upon them all. When Joshua gets wind of a few of these new prophets speaking, he asks Moses to shut them down, but Moses affirms the fact that God's call resides with more than one person.

Moses, leader exemplary, cannot carry the weight of all the people, with their physical, spiritual, and psychological needs. No one leads alone, at least not well or for long. The Bible is no self-help or best-practices book, but it does invite preachers to teach and proclaim a theology of sound life together. The text from Numbers points preachers to examine how congregations operate: Is a small group always making decisions? Is one person responsible for far too much? Are the voices of those who object to certain norms and practices honored and heard? Is there room for new prophetic voices?

Alternatively, this story could allow preachers to explore our responses to God's provisions. Often people of faith lament what was, selectively remembering the good old days, rather than give thanks for current gifts and the promise of what is and what will be accomplished. What manna are we weeping about, when we should, in fact, rejoice that God feeds us daily? Lamenting what was and complaining about what is make absolutely everyone miserable. Every leader, even Moses, must have help tending to the needs of God's people.

The preacher would do well to remember Moses' meltdown, as it contains important biblical and theological truths. First, ultimately these people do belong to God, and God is responsible for them. The burden of leadership, while great, is not the leader's alone to bear. Second, baring our deepest needs and frustrations to God is faithful. The people weep openly, Moses laments his fate. God hears our petition, whether said corporately in worship or voiced inaudibly in private. Our cries of pain or joy to God do not go unheard or unheeded. God listens and responds. Preaching that simple, yet profound message gives hope, grants courage, and feeds the faithful no less than manna, or meat, in the desert.

The readings from Esther offer another lens through which to view biblical and faithful

---

1. Robert Alter, *The Hebrew Bible*, vol. 1 (New York: W. W. Norton, 2019), 517.

leadership. Again, however, leadership does not happen apart from community. Mordecai recognizes the power of Esther's role and her unique position to advocate on behalf of her people. Esther acts within her sphere of influence as queen. She calculates the when, where, and what of approaching the king. Everything about this story points to the complexity of working for justice and the risk such work requires.

The preacher could take Esther's story as a parable for how people of faith today might stand up to power and use their influence on behalf of the most vulnerable. A fruitful approach could invite hearers to consider the various characters in the text and ask where they place themselves. Are they the elder mentor, encouraging younger leaders to take their place and use their gifts for good? Are they Esther, uniquely positioned to speak and sway those in power? Are they, or we collectively, Haman? This last question may be difficult to ask, but it is nonetheless necessary. A brief glimpse at history reveals that people of faith have long been not just complicit, but perpetrators of exploitation, injustice, and evil.

The preacher could employ this part of the book of Esther to wrestle with how and when God vindicates the oppressed. A word of caution might be lifted about feeling too satisfied with Haman's poetic demise. Vengeance is God's, even as God's followers are called to advocate for the vulnerable, even at the risk of their comfort, status, and, yes, lives. While the story of Esther is ancient, in every time and place, people of faith feel compelled to put themselves in peril for the sake of those who cannot stand up for themselves.

A sermon that tells Esther's story alongside the stories of more contemporary examples of those who have done likewise in their context would make the connection between the biblical story and our own. A well-known example is that of German industrialist Oskar Schindler, who used his power and wealth to save many Jews from the Holocaust, documented in the movie *Schindler's List*. However, mining local histories and even church meeting minutes might unearth brave, faithful leaders, the communities that nurtured them, and the people they helped much closer to home, and perhaps more relatable. The preacher might share their own heroes in the faith who have shaped and inspired her.

One community of faith, while doing research for a milestone anniversary, discovered ancestors in the pews and pulpit who heeded Martin Luther King Jr.'s call for clergy to come march in Selma. They also found ardent segregationists who vowed to leave the church if African Americans were welcomed into the sanctuary. Every community contains within it Mordecai, Esther, and Haman. Perhaps each of us contains them all in any given moment. The preacher could call hearers to examine the complex reality of both our call to work for justice, our reluctance to do so, and, sometimes, our participation in evil.

The preacher should encourage those gathered to look for and name those in their midst with the gifts and ability to help the vulnerable, step out in courage, and call out evil not only in others, but among and in themselves. The preacher should also be mindful that in their pews are those in the position of power, and note that King Ahasuerus did in fact listen to Esther, rather than Haman.

While Moses and Esther may seem outliers to our modern ears, using their stories to plumb the possibilities for faithful, biblical leadership in the current context would prove rich and helpful. Communities shape and raise leaders, share responsibilities, and keep one another accountable. Each person has gifts and influence to be used in service to God and for the sake of the vulnerable. In every time and place, God calls, equips, and sends people to care for God's people. Leadership is challenging, but no leader is tasked with doing everything alone. Ultimately, God provides for God's people, vindicates the oppressed, and judges those who exploit the vulnerable. Given the certainty of God's provision and power, the preacher must challenge the faithful to act bravely, prophesy boldly, and trust that weeping may last for a season, but joy, like manna and meat, comes in the morning.

JILL DUFFIELD

Psalm 124

¹If it had not been the LORD who was on our side
    —let Israel now say—
²if it had not been the LORD who was on our side,
    when our enemies attacked us,
³then they would have swallowed us up alive,
    when their anger was kindled against us;
⁴then the flood would have swept us away,
    the torrent would have gone over us;
⁵then over us would have gone
    the raging waters.

⁶Blessed be the LORD,
    who has not given us
    as prey to their teeth.
⁷We have escaped like a bird
    from the snare of the fowlers;
the snare is broken,
    and we have escaped.

⁸Our help is in the name of the LORD,
    who made heaven and earth.

Psalm 19:7–14

⁷The law of the LORD is perfect,
    reviving the soul;
the decrees of the LORD are sure,
    making wise the simple;
⁸the precepts of the LORD are right,
    rejoicing the heart;
the commandment of the LORD is clear,
    enlightening the eyes;
⁹the fear of the LORD is pure,
    enduring forever;
the ordinances of the LORD are true
    and righteous altogether.
¹⁰More to be desired are they than gold,
    even much fine gold;
sweeter also than honey,
    and drippings of the honeycomb.

¹¹Moreover by them is your servant warned;
    in keeping them there is great reward.
¹²But who can detect their errors?
    Clear me from hidden faults.

¹³Keep back your servant also from the insolent;
   do not let them have dominion over me.
Then I shall be blameless,
   and innocent of great transgression.

¹⁴Let the words of my mouth and the meditation of my heart
   be acceptable to you,
   O LORD, my rock and my redeemer.

Connecting the Psalm with Scripture and Worship

Psalm 124. The architects of the Revised Common Lectionary chose the ecstatic psalm that is Psalm 124 as a response to the first reading, the conclusion of the story of Esther. Esther is a biblical narrative that serves as an origin story for the Jewish festival of Purim. The story is one of intrigue and foiled plots, and Esther is hailed as a heroine who saves her people from genocide. Psalm 124, with its exuberant expressions of thanksgiving, is a fitting reply to the story.

The psalm begins with call and response. "If it had not been the LORD who was on our side," begins the song leader, who then exhorts the people to join in: "let Israel now say . . ." With that, a rapid-fire antiphony launches: "when" enemies acted, "then" they would have prevailed, except that God rescued Israel.

The second half of the psalm erupts in thanksgiving. "Blessed be the LORD," the people cry, for they have escaped. They have escaped the trap that was set for them. The final, eighth, verse of the psalm is an affirmation of faith that has become part of the contemporary liturgical repertoire: "Our help is in the name of the LORD, who made heaven and earth."

Psalm 124 invites a celebratory tone in worship, one borne of a long history with a just and faithful God. Verse 8 is a fitting opening to worship: "Our help is in the name of the Lord, who made heaven and earth." John Calvin began services in Strasburg and Geneva with these words, and they have been used in Reformed communities ever since. Those same words might also be used as a refrain during intercessory prayers,

repeated by the assembly after each intercession is spoken.

If the psalm is read aloud, its form lends itself to being spoken antiphonally, alternating between a leader and the worshiping body or between the two halves of the assembly. "When our enemies attacked us," one side begins; "then they would have swallowed us up alive," responds the other, and so on. One voice might then emerge to speak verses 6–7, announcing the people's escape. Then the entire assembly joins to proclaim, with confidence, "Our help is in the name of the Lord, who made heaven and earth."

Both Psalm 124 and the Esther story invite contemporary worshipers to give their own testimony. "If it had not been the Lord who was on our side," might easily be the first phrase of any number of stories of personal or communal experience in which God has brought about salvation, reconciliation, or justice. Although some free-church traditions may be more comfortable with such a practice, it is certainly possible—and even commendable—for churches with more formal liturgical patterns to incorporate testimony into worship. God is still at work in this world, in our communities, and in our own lives, and we encourage one another by telling each other's stories.

Psalm 124 also serves as a crucial reminder that it is the grace of God that sustains and empowers. As Clinton McCann points out, "to profess that God is our fundamental help means to profess that we are not sufficient to create and secure our own lives and futures."[1] This goes

---

1. J. Clinton McCann Jr., "The Book of Psalms," *The New Interpreter's Bible* (Nashville: Abingdon, 1996), 4:1191.

against the prevailing opinion that we make our way through the world by our own strength. To name such a truth—that we are dependent on the God who was faithful in the past, holds the future, and guides the present—is to free ourselves from anxiety and guilt and to tether ourselves to hope in the coming reign of God.

Psalm 19:7–14. This psalm is chosen as a response to the first reading, Numbers 11:4–6, 10–16, and 24–29. In the passage from Numbers, the Israelites bemoan their lack of a decent diet. God has given them miraculous food in the desert, but they are sick of manna. All they can think about is the food they left behind in Egypt: fish and cucumbers and melons, leeks and garlic and onions—and meat! Give us meat!

God is angry about the people's complaining, and Moses is fed up with it too. He goes off on his own rant, directed at God, griping that God has given him too great a burden in expecting him to take care of all these people. Once again, God deigns to meet Moses' needs, directing him to gather seventy elders. These seventy are endowed with God's own spirit, that they may share in the work.

After hearing the reading from Numbers, worshipers are invited to sing or speak the words of Psalm 19. At first, it may seem like there is no connection at all. As the psalm progresses, however, the claim becomes clear: to walk with God is better than the finest food, "sweeter than honey, and the drippings of the honeycomb" (Ps. 19:10). God's laws and decrees are best understood as God's teaching or instruction. Just as the sun gives life to the earth (vv. 4b–6), God's *torah* gives life to all who depend on divine guidance.[2] God's exhortations revive the soul and imbue wisdom; they bring joy and illumination. Those who follow God's ways are so greatly rewarded that God's law is to be desired more than the purest gold. For this reason, the psalmist asks for God's protection from any who would lead him astray.

The psalm ends with words that have often served as a prayer for preachers about to launch into a sermon: "Let the words of my mouth and the meditation of my heart be acceptable to you, O Lord, my rock and my redeemer" (v. 14). These are not just a preacher's words, however. These words are the prayer of anyone who would choose the sort of life that God waits to bestow, a life that reflects the very glory of God that is described in the opening of the psalm (vv. 1–6). What is at stake here is more than obedience to a set of rules, but rather a dependence on the living and life-giving God. To sing or speak the words of Psalm 19 is to declare a desire to be in relationship with the God of all creation.

Liturgically, Psalm 19 is a fitting response to the first reading. Verses 7–10 (or some part of that) may also be spoken after a declaration of forgiveness, as an expression of Calvin's third use of the law. After confessing sin corporately, and being assured of God's mercy, the people affirm that it is God's commandments that lead to a fruitful and fulfilling life. Psalm 19 may also serve well as a prayer of commitment after the preaching of the gospel.

In Mark 9:38–50, Jesus admonishes his listeners to take care not to stumble or lead others astray. Voicing the words of the psalm after hearing such an exhortation would give the worshiping assembly an opportunity to reaffirm its commitment to live the Christian life. Composers have provided the church with a number of metrical and responsorial settings of Psalm 19. *Psalms for All Seasons* includes six different settings that may be sung and/or spoken in a variety of ways.[3]

KIMBERLY BRACKEN LONG

---

2. McCann, "The Book of Psalms," 752.
3. *Psalms for All Seasons: A Complete Psalter for Worship* (Grand Rapids: Faith Alive Christian Resources, 2012).

James 5:13–20

[13]Are any among you suffering? They should pray. Are any cheerful? They should sing songs of praise. [14]Are any among you sick? They should call for the elders of the church and have them pray over them, anointing them with oil in the name of the Lord. [15]The prayer of faith will save the sick, and the Lord will raise them up; and anyone who has committed sins will be forgiven. [16]Therefore confess your sins to one another, and pray for one another, so that you may be healed. The prayer of the righteous is powerful and effective. [17]Elijah was a human being like us, and he prayed fervently that it might not rain, and for three years and six months it did not rain on the earth. [18]Then he prayed again, and the heaven gave rain and the earth yielded its harvest.

[19]My brothers and sisters, if anyone among you wanders from the truth and is brought back by another, [20]you should know that whoever brings back a sinner from wandering will save the sinner's soul from death and will cover a multitude of sins.

Commentary 1: Connecting the Reading with Scripture

There are three general themes in this section of James that reveal conditions in that community: suffering, sickness, and sin. There are three specific community activities that respond to these conditions: prayer, singing, and anointing.

The first condition is suffering (*kakopatheō*). The word can mean "to suffer misfortune" (2 Tim. 2:9), or "to bear hardships patiently" (2 Tim. 4:5). In the present context it probably refers to the hardships produced by the oppression of the rich (Jas. 5:1–6). How do you deal with this kind of suffering? You pray, either for relief from it or for the endurance to survive it until the coming of the Lord (5:7–8), where the rich will be judged (5:3–4).[1]

Another way of dealing with suffering is by being cheerful *(euthymeo)* and singing. The word can also mean "to take courage in spite of suffering hardship" (Acts 27:22, 25), which is likely the meaning here. While some pray for deliverance, others assume that they will be delivered and praise God in advance, because they know God is compassionate and merciful (Jas. 5:11). They also know that the last days are approaching, when their oppressors, the

rich, will be judged (5:1–6), so patient waiting is required (5:7, 10). It is not clear what kind of praise is meant here, but it could be either a psalm or an early Christian hymn.

The second condition, sickness (*astheneō*), refers to bodily weakness. When this happens to members of the community, they should call for the elders of the church (*ekklēsia*), who will then pray over them and anoint them with oil. Healing is assured if the prayer is done with faith, the same way wisdom is given if asked (prayed) in faith (1:5–6). Forgiveness of sins is offered, should the person have sinned. Notice the conditional aspect of the action conveyed by the expression "and if he has committed sins." James does not seem to connect sickness with sin, as other authors in the Bible do (Deut. 28:1–68; Prov. 11:19; 13:13–23; 1 Cor. 11:29–30; though not John 9:1–3). For him, there can be a person in the congregation whose sickness is not related to sin.

The healing is produced by the intercessory prayer of the elders. It is praying for one another (Jas. 5:16) that brings healing, regardless of the faith of the individual (here it is not required,

---

1. Luke Timothy Johnson, *The Letter of James,* Anchor Bible 37A (New York: Doubleday, 1995), 329.

The Remedy Which God Has Provided

Effectual charity, then, to the souls of men; the real, practical conversion of a sinner from the error of his ways, is one of the methods appointed in the Gospel for healing the wounds made by sin in Christian souls. It has some kind of virtue in covering, i.e. in hiding and veiling over, the backslidings even of Christian people; heavy as those backslidings are, and severe as are the warnings of Holy Scripture on their consequences. Yet the conversion of souls has in it some kind of power to obtain of God that infinite mercy, that He will pass over those sins, and account them as if they had never been. "He will cast them," as the prophet says, "behind His back:" He will remember them, as the Prayer book says, no more.

And this, not because of any power or virtue or holiness which our labours and fruits in that kind have in themselves, but because they are a principal way ordained by Him for our laying hold of the Cross, and applying the Blood of Christ, the sovereign remedy, to the disorders of our own souls. It will avail for our pardon, in the same kind of sense as confession of our sins will, if hearty and sincere: or the prayers of the Church and of good Christians in our behalf: or as fasting and weeping and mourning, with which we are invited to turn to the Lord our God: or as alms, and shewing mercy to the poor, by which a great king of old was instructed to break off his iniquities: or as charity in general, which as S. Peter teaches, in the same words as S. James, will surely cover our multitude of sins. The holy writers in all such places as these mean no doubt to teach Christian people, that all these are so many parts of the remedy which God has provided for the sin and backslidings even of Christians: they are means, the sincere use of which will help greatly, each in its way, towards our obtaining the benefit of Christ's Cross: and yet all the while whatever pardon and salvation it may please the All-Merciful to bestow upon us comes from that Cross and from it alone. There is the Fountain opened for sin and for uncleanness: the good works and penitential rules of Christians are healing, because they help us in some mysterious way to lay hold of that Cross: to sprinkle ourselves with that Fountain: in that way they cover sins, and break off iniquities, and obtain pardon: therefore the Apostles and Prophets and the Church of God in recommending them as remedies to the sinner do by no means make void faith and the Cross, but rather bring them home to the consciences and daily lives of every one of us.

Let us not then doubt, but earnestly believe, that the conversion and amendment of other men's sin and unbelief, practiced as a part of repentance, will truly help towards obtaining forgiveness: will hide even in God's sight, a multitude of sins: provided, of course, that those sins be truly repented of and forsaken: for otherwise the doing good to others in order to obtain leave to sin ourselves, would be the worst kind of pharisaical hypocrisy.

John Keble, "Effectual Care for Other's Souls, One Chief Means of Healing Our Own," in *Sermons for the Christian Year,* vol. 11 (Oxford: James Parker and Co., 1880), 157–59.

but see 1:5–6, where the prayer of faith is required from the individual who is asking for wisdom, a very different matter than healing). The word for healing (*sōzō*) is the same word used for spiritual salvation in John 3:17 and physical deliverance in Acts 27:20. It has multiple meanings, though we tend to see only its spiritual connotations.

The same thing happens with the word for raising up (*egeirō*). It can mean resurrection (1 Cor. 15:15), waking up (Mark 4:27), or healing (John 5:8). Does James mean then healing or salvation? Probably both, but the primary meaning seems to be healing, the same way that the primary meaning of raising seems to be to restore to an active life and not so much to the resurrection, which may have been intended also, since the context of the whole chapter points to the fast-approaching eschatological end (Jas. 5:8–9).

The healing process outlined here is threefold: they summon the elders who pray for the sick person and then anoint them in the name of the Lord. The person is to be healed, not cured as we may assume, the distinction being one between the ancient conception of sickness as disease, which affects the whole community, and the modern understanding of it as illness, which affects only the individual and is cured by medicine. Healing in this context means social restoration and not so much individual well-being. The elders, figures of authority in the community, rather than doctors (see Mark 5:26), are called to enact the healing.

The anointing is to be done with oil, which was used in the Greco-Roman world for many different purposes (cosmetic, gymnastic, religious, medicinal). Here it is being used liturgically, even sacramentally, because it is done in the name of the Lord, and its purpose may have been to make visible, palpable, the presence of the Spirit. In 2:26, it is said that "the body without the spirit is dead," meaning that a person without the spirit is like a corpse. There is something in each of us that makes us human, namely, the spirit of life breathed by God at the beginning of creation (Gen. 2:7). In the act of healing, the Spirit is invoked through the symbolism of oil and the sick person is restored to life.

The forgiveness of sins comes as an afterthought. Was it to follow or to precede the healing? Was it a consequence or a prerequisite for it? Did it occur simultaneously with it? In Mark 2:1–12, there is a healing that is preceded by the forgiveness of sins, suggesting that sin and sickness are connected, and that one has to be removed before the other (i.e., first forgiveness, then healing). James seems to differ, for he clearly—or not so clearly—says that forgiveness follows, not precedes, the healing, which makes it difficult to understand verse 16, which proposes a different order: confessions of sins, prayer, and healing! For us, contemporary readers who value orderly and logical argumentation, James's rhetoric throws us off, for it has been suggested, "James addresses sickness, sin, health, and forgiveness together."[2]

The mention of a righteous person in verse 16 harks back to verse 6 and refers to those being oppressed by the rich. It also connects this person with the prophet Elijah, who is presented as a model of the effectiveness of a righteous person's prayer, having great power (*energoumenē*), a word that carries the idea of energy, precisely what the sick person is lacking.

In verses 19–20, restoring the sinner in order to save his soul points at people inside the community who have wandered from the truth. It refers back to the double-minded individual of 1:8, unstable in all his ways. The word for "way" (*hodos*) is a technical term that refers to the way of salvation.[3] The concern is not with evangelism but with the restoration of a person into the life of the community, similar to the way a sick person is nurtured back into a healthy community life.

Among the many applications that this passage may elicit in us, we want to highlight three:

Medical science and alternative ways of healing, such as faith, can work in tandem. While it is dangerous to refuse medical treatment in the name of religious convictions, it is very appropriate, and nowadays even suggested by physicians, to combine both of them.

Connecting sin and sickness should be avoided at all costs. This is especially true when it comes to AIDS and sexually transmitted diseases. It is very dangerous to apply first-century sexual mores to our present world, for what was then explained religiously can now be explained scientifically.

Lastly, bringing people back to the church may be as important as getting new people into it. Church growth, the salient feature of many churches today, need not outshine restorative ministries, but both can be held in a creative and healthy balance.

OSVALDO D. VENA

---

2. William F. Brosend II, *James and Jude*, New Cambridge Bible Commentary 3 (Cambridge, UK: Cambridge University Press, 2004), 161.

3. Brosend II, *James and Jude*, 161.

Commentary 2: Connecting the Reading with the World

James encourages Christian believers to be people who pray. Whether in trying times or happy, we are called to lift up our hearts and voices to God (Jas. 5:13). This counsel raises some interesting questions.

Preachers can lead listeners through questions about prayer. What happens when we pray? Does God need our prayers? If not, is prayer simply for our own benefit, a kind of self-therapy? James seems to assume a connection between physical illness and unforgiven sin. What sort of connection is this? Is illness to be viewed as a direct result of sin? Further, James mentions the role of elders anointing the sick with oil and praying for them; what is the oil for, and why should it be thought important? Any attempt to answer such questions will inevitably spawn a new batch of queries.

The preacher might explore ways that in contemporary Western culture it has become a truism that there are profound interconnections between emotional and physical well-being. Prayer as a kind of self-therapy is widely accepted. Authors like Caroline Myss and Larry Dossey have spawned a cottage industry of books exploring these interconnections. There is something to be said for this.

It is not impossible that ancient prayer practices in many different religious traditions have developed, over time, in response to a discovery that there is some kind of healing energy that can flow not simply among different facets of an individual's life, but actually among people. Indeed, popular films, such as *Avatar* and the *Star Wars* saga, suggest that these interconnections exist well beyond human relations, to include the more-than-human world as well. Perhaps Christian prayers for healing have historically provided avenues or conduits for some kind of life-energy that can be shared among people to positive effect.

This possibility does not in itself mitigate against Christian faith and teaching, since our belief in God obviously includes our confidence that this God to whom we pray is the Creator of all things. This includes the rich, complex interconnections among those things. Thus, preachers can help us see that scriptural injunctions to pray such as these in our James passage can be understood to be divine encouragement to us to participate redemptively in the energies of an interconnected world (see Phil. 1:19).

Probably the theological tradition that has most extensively explored this potential interpretation of prayer has been process thought. Marjorie Hewitt Suchocki, for example, writes of prayer, "Suppose that prayer is our openness to the God who pervades the universe and therefore ourselves, and that prayer is also this God's openness to us. . . . This would make prayer essential to God as well as to ourselves. What if prayer increases the effectiveness of God's work in the world?"[4]

Beyond the potential contribution of process theologies to a theology of prayer, we ought to be attentive to the theological implications of intercessory prayer as described and encouraged in this James passage. Why is "the prayer of the righteous . . . powerful and effective" (5:16)? Why would God desire that we pray for one another? Is it a way in which the Spirit labors to intertwine our lives more deeply in the body of Christ? Surely the God we worship is not a deity who needs to have the divine arm twisted!

Yet, putting it more positively, perhaps the preacher could help us understand Scripture's encouragement that we pray for one another as a way in which God enlists us to participate more fully in God's love and desire for the well-being of all people. No one doubts that praying for another should never be a substitute action for doing something practically for the other when the opportunity arises; clearly, there are times when our prayers for others can be a goad to action. Even so, this does not eliminate the possibility that God in mysterious, covenantal love has chosen to make our prayers for one another part of the very ways in which God acts healingly in the world and in our communities of faith.

All of the above, however, presumably would hold true without the need for "the elders of the

4. Marjorie Hewitt Suchocki, *In God's Presence: Theological Reflections on Prayer* (St. Louis: Chalice Press, 1996), 18.

church . . . anointing them with oil in the name of the Lord" (Jas. 5:14). This raises new questions: Why the elders? Why the oil? Is this magic?

No. The preacher can help us understand that we would rightly identify these as means of grace, that is, ways in which God has chosen wisely to channel the life-giving energy of the divine Spirit to people, especially to those in deep need (5:13). Within the context of James, elders would be people who have sought and received divine wisdom, and so would be in a position, presumably, of being able to ask God rightly rather than wrongly (4:3). Olive oil traditionally was considered to possess healing effects already, but there was also at least some slim precedent in the early church's memory of Jesus' disciples (Mark 6:13). While the symbolic power of oil as instantiating the healing presence of God's Spirit should not be overlooked, perhaps it is as much the very materiality of the oil being applied by the human hands of others that communicates the healing love of God. William Temple is justly remembered for his claim that Christianity is "the most avowedly materialist of all the great religions."[5] Anointing the sick with oil lies precisely in line with this sentiment.

The preacher can help us learn about one other means of grace mentioned by James, and that is mutual confession of sins. Mutual confession leads to praying for one another, "so that you may be healed" (Jas. 5:16). James has already documented the destructive effects of anger (1:19–21), favoritism (2:1–13), envy and selfish ambition (3:14–16), conflicts and disputes (4:1–2, 11–12), and love of riches (5:1–6). There is plenty to confess! Rather than hiding or rationalizing our faults and downfalls, James calls us to be honest with one another regarding our transgressions. Confessing to one another, and listening to one another's confessions and admissions of struggle and failure, create bonds of empathy and compassion. In such bonds, forgiveness is forged. Mutual confession, accordingly, is another means of divine grace, another gift of God's healing and loving presence in the church.

If indeed there is communal healing through these means of grace—wise elders, anointing with oil, mutual confession and forgiveness—then it is not surprising that James ends with a note of concern for those who have strayed outside of the healing circle. When our lives have become intertwined by prayer, confession, forgiveness, and human touch, we cannot and should not easily dismiss the wanderer. We will feel their absence. Here, once more we encounter a God who longs to labor in and through us. Indeed, there is no explicit mention of God here: "whoever brings back a sinner from wandering will save the sinner's soul from death and will cover a multitude of sins" (5:20); but surely this is divine labor. God is present and active, we believe, in and through the church as a wisdom community that seeks God, lives by the law of liberty, practices pure and undefiled religion, shows no favoritism, speaks slowly and carefully, and lovingly seeks out those who have gone astray. May our churches be such communities as this!

MICHAEL LODAHL

---

5. William Temple, *Nature, God and Man* (London: Macmillan, 1935), 478.

Mark 9:38–50

³⁸John said to him, "Teacher, we saw someone casting out demons in your name, and we tried to stop him, because he was not following us." ³⁹But Jesus said, "Do not stop him; for no one who does a deed of power in my name will be able soon afterward to speak evil of me. ⁴⁰Whoever is not against us is for us. ⁴¹For truly I tell you, whoever gives you a cup of water to drink because you bear the name of Christ will by no means lose the reward.

⁴²"If any of you put a stumbling block before one of these little ones who believe in me, it would be better for you if a great millstone were hung around your neck and you were thrown into the sea. ⁴³If your hand causes you to stumble, cut it off; it is better for you to enter life maimed than to have two hands and to go to hell, to the unquenchable fire. ⁴⁵And if your foot causes you to stumble, cut it off; it is better for you to enter life lame than to have two feet and to be thrown into hell. ⁴⁷And if your eye causes you to stumble, tear it out; it is better for you to enter the kingdom of God with one eye than to have two eyes and to be thrown into hell, ⁴⁸where their worm never dies, and the fire is never quenched.

⁴⁹"For everyone will be salted with fire. ⁵⁰Salt is good; but if salt has lost its saltiness, how can you season it? Have salt in yourselves, and be at peace with one another."

Commentary 1: Connecting the Reading with Scripture

"Teacher!" Rudely interrupting Jesus' teaching, John ironically exemplifies a central theme weaving through the community's journey to Jerusalem (Mark 8:27–10:52): the disciples repeatedly fail to understand what Jesus says about God's reign and God's anointed one.

Three times (8:31; 9:31; 10:33–34), Jesus predicts his death and resurrection; each time, the disciples resist this teaching. Instead, they grapple with fantasies of status (9:34; 10:35ff.). Indeed, in his anxiety over the unnamed exorcist, John's tongue makes a Freudian slip: "he was not following *us*." John seems to have forgotten that the teacher, not the students, is the focus of following. Preachers can encourage empathy among contemporary disciples, exploring how the church has demonstrated a similar lapse in memory.

Jesus' rebuke, summarized by 9:40 ("Whoever is not against us is for us"), deconstructs John's assumptions with three clauses, each framed by the article *gar*. Reading Jesus' response as one sentence can evoke the force of his frustration: "Do not stop him, *because* no one who does a deed of power in my name will be able soon afterward to speak evil of me, *because* whoever is not against is for us, *because* truly I tell you whoever gives you a cup of water to drink because you bear the name of Christ will by no means lose the reward" (9:39–41). If welcoming children and offering water in Jesus' name are graced actions, how much more is healing the afflicted!

Preachers may have forgotten that in 9:36 Jesus took a little child in his arms. Philip Ruge-Jones wisely notes, "We have no indication that Jesus has set aside the child."[1] This is the second of three occasions on the road to Jerusalem (see 9:36–37; 10:13–14) where Jesus blesses children. John's tattletale action interrupts his teacher's encouragement to welcome the presence of God in children; when Jesus resumes his speech about "these little ones who believe

1. Philip Ruge-Jones, "Commentary on Mark 9:38–50," *Working Preacher*, September 30, 2018; https://www.workingpreacher.org/preaching.aspx?commentary_id=3787.

in me," he is not speaking abstractly. Preachers might make this point by miming a child bouncing in their arms, as Ruge-Jones does in his dramatic portrayal of Mark's Gospel.[2]

Four times Jesus warns against that which causes people to stumble, trip, or take offense. The verb *skandalizō* gives English "scandalize," offering itself to preachers' imagination. Note two other, surprising instances of the same verb in Mark: hearers of God's word who are not deeply rooted "fall away" when persecution arises (4:17); and, on the night of his arrest, Jesus tells his disciples that they will "become deserters" (14:27). Very real trouble lies ahead for God's anointed and those who follow him; Jesus' startling words about severing limbs are meant to deter disciples from fracturing the community of the faithful with manufactured trouble. Such undue scandal always comes at the expense of the church's witness to Christ.

Preachers do well to encourage their communities to examine any practices (individual or communal) that may unintentionally hinder neighbors from receiving the life-giving embrace of Jesus. Perhaps the congregation recalls similar words from Jesus' Sermon on the Mount (Matt. 5:27–30, Sixth Sunday after Epiphany, Year A). If so, how have they grown in their teacher's grace? Like John, do we find it difficult to grasp what Jesus teaches?

Allusions to the unquenchable fires of hell serve Jesus' rhetorical purposes; less likely do they support the contemporary preachers' task. However, the enigmatic promise in 9:49, "Everyone will be salted with fire," holds out hope. "Salt is good," Jesus reassures his listeners, thus moving the metaphor "fire" from the source domain of destruction and punishment (e.g., Jer. 4:4; 2 Thess. 1:8; Rev. 20:10) to the domain of purification and holiness (e.g., Isa. 6:6–7; Ezek. 1:13; Acts 2:3). Preachers should note that this shift does not render fire less intimidating, as the prophet Joel (Joel 2:30–31) and the apostle Paul (1 Cor. 3:13) can attest.

By linking fire with salt—whose source domain includes cooking, food preservation, and disinfecting—Jesus speaks about God's redemptive power. When God's reign holds sway over history, all that is good will be preserved for life eternal. Jesus makes a similar point in the metaphor of the vine and its branches (John 15:1–8, Fifth Sunday of Easter, Year B): God the vinegrower not only removes fruitless branches, but by Jesus' word prunes branches to promote further growth. God's ultimate intentions are oriented toward restoring creation's goodness (see Mark 10:9, Proper 22, Year B) rather than penalizing its brokenness.

Preachers have at least two options for interpreting the middle clause of 9:50. In one reading, Jesus invokes salt losing its saltiness as an absurd idea. In this case, the directive "Have salt in yourselves" affirms the inherent capacity of Jesus' disciples—hard of heart though they (we) may be—to follow in his ways. Another reading suggests that the salt commonly available to impoverished households may have contained bitter minerals improperly separated from sodium chloride (NaCl, table salt). In this case, Jesus returns to his teachings about self-discipline: "Have salt in yourselves," that is, cut away anything that hinders life in God's reign.

In any case, Jesus clarifies the saying: "Be at peace with one another." This line ends the episode that began at 9:30, neatly summarizing Jesus' intent for the disciples' communal life. Do not argue over who is the greatest. Be at peace. Do not set yourself against your allies. Be at peace. Do not let your behaviors scandalize believers, especially children. Be at peace.

How might preachers connect this portion of Mark with the other readings suggested for Proper 21?

If the Gospel is paired with the semicontinuous Old Testament reading from Esther (7:1–6, 9–10; 9:20–22), preachers may build on the theme of allies. In vilifying the Jewish people, Haman appears to be "for" the king's interests. Esther's self-revelation and exposing of Haman's destructive plot demonstrates that she is a true ally to the king and to her people. Through Esther's courage, God "salts" the royal household "with fire," thwarting Haman's scandalous intentions and ensuring peace for the nation.

---

2. Ruge-Jones's storytelling performance of Mark is available on YouTube.com at the Ankos Films channel. Ruge-Jones presents each chapter as a whole; preachers should listen for how Mark 9 flows together.

If the Gospel is paired with the complementary Old Testament reading from Numbers 11:4–6, 10–16, 24–29, preachers may note several points of resonance. Like the disciples, the Israelites are not focused on following God's servant. The people's lack of gratitude scandalizes Moses, yet God redirects him to trust God's power (also, the use of children as a negative image contrasts to Jesus' positive view). Ultimately, God's spirit empowers prophetic leadership among seventy elders; ministry in the Lord's name is the work of many people, like the unnamed exorcist (and the disciples, as Mark 6:12–13 notes).

In the Gospel's conversation with the epistle reading from James (Jas. 5:13–20), preachers can find examples of communal living that reflect Jesus' desire for the disciples. Acts of prayer and anointing the sick demonstrate servant leadership; elders in the church do not share the disciples' preoccupation with status or competition. Confessing sin to one's neighbor, praying for one another, and reaching out to those who have sinned—those who have fallen away or those who have caused others to stumble—are practices that maintain salt in the church, preserving peace and wholeness.

In the final analysis, preaching Mark 9:38–50 raises questions about the congregation's own journey of discipleship. How the community welcomes children, perceives outsiders, works to clear away scandal from their path, and seeks peace are all areas of concern that Jesus urges us to explore. Communities that consider these matters seriously prepare themselves to follow Jesus to Jerusalem and beyond, undeterred by the scandal of the cross, witnessing to the saving power of God's anointed.

BENJAMIN P. MASTERS

Commentary 2: Connecting the Reading with the World

Much of Jesus' teaching occurred in the midst of his daily activities with the disciples. Frequently, it took the form of correcting them. On this occasion, John seems to be disturbed by a recent incident. He told Jesus that they discovered a man driving out demons in his name, and they told him to stop. Jesus responded by saying, "Do not stop him. . . . For no one who does a miracle in my name can in the next moment say anything bad about me, for whoever is not against us is for us" (Mark 9:39 NIV). He then continued by saying that "anyone who gives you a cup of water in my name . . . will certainly not lose their reward" (v. 41 NIV).

In a somewhat disconnected way Jesus proceeded to teach them some additional things about discipleship. He said that if anyone causes one of the little ones to sin, it would be better if they be thrown into the sea with a millstone round their neck. In other words, there would be no forgiveness for anyone who harmed the "little ones," whether they be children or newcomers to the faith, whom he often referred to by the same designation.

Jesus went on to speak about the virtue of discipleship by likening it to the action of a person with a bad arm, leg, or eye for whom it would be better to amputate any such body part and live maimed, than to sin with both of them and thereby enter the eternal destiny of death and decay (hell, Gk. *gehenna*), namely, the burial place where dead bodies were constantly being burned in the ravine outside the city of Jerusalem. Preachers can help us renew our understanding that discipleship implies the art of living in peace with one's neighbors and doing what is good for them, rather than cultivating the spirit of rivalry and hostility.

The preacher could help us see this teaching as also a positive message for those who are maimed or disabled either by birth or circumstance. Rather than spending a lifetime feeling sorry for themselves or envying others, they can, with appropriate assistance from others, undertake an active life despite their disability and thereby overcome the limitations posed by such disabilities. For example, Ludwig van Beethoven was able to exercise his musical genius, despite his progressive disability of deafness. My roommate in seminary was totally blind. Yet, with the help of readers and the use of braille, he was able to attain both undergraduate and seminary degrees and had a lifelong vocation as a pastor in my native province of Nova Scotia.

In the early 1960s Eunice Shriver, the sister of President John F. Kennedy, envisioned a special program for children and adults with intellectual deficiencies that in 1968 culminated in the first Special Olympics games in Chicago. This is now a global event supported by governments and thousands of benefactors for the purpose of developing physical fitness, courage, and pride of accomplishment in millions of people who, more likely than not, would have led meaningless lives otherwise. Most important, the extraordinary development of their skills and talents has won the admiration of the world at large.

Today, numerous laws have been passed in support of those with special needs. Public buildings are required to be accessible for them, as are public schools for children of all ages. Consequently, employment agencies can no longer discriminate against them as they once did. Colleges and universities now have programs in disability studies that cover a wide range of subjects. All of these accomplishments and many more have been inspired by the values implicit in Jesus' teachings concerning true discipleship, which can be exemplified sometimes by those who themselves have special needs.

Everyone knows the function of salt in preserving the freshness of foods and enhancing their taste. Growing up on the eastern seacoast of Canada with a plentiful supply of fish, I vividly recall the barrels of salted cod, herring, and mackerel that seemed ubiquitous. Clearly, Jesus' disciples had no problem understanding what Jesus meant by saying that every sacrifice shall be salted, because that would have been a necessary condition for its preservation while en route to the temple. Thus, he used salt as a metaphor for discipleship, along with the warning that salt is good as long as it retains its quality. If it loses that quality, though, it is no longer any good. Accordingly, he warns his disciples not to lose the quality of their discipleship by quarreling, but to live in peace with one another. Thus, the preacher can help us evaluate our congregation's saltiness.

Now, a clear sign of discipleship is doing what is necessary and good to protect the so-called "little ones" about whom Jesus was so concerned in this passage and others. In my judgment, there can be no better example of that concern and care than the rescue activity of the Huguenot pastor and teacher Andre Trocmé in the village of Le Chambon-sur-Lignon in Vichy France, who during World War II helped save over three thousand Jewish children from the Nazi Holocaust. Though it is a story of love and courage in the midst of one of the world's most horrific crimes against humanity, its final outcome caused both joy and sorrow for the parents of the rescued children. Because they had been separated from one another for such a long time, the children could no longer speak their native German or communicate with their parents, whom many of them had forgotten.

In our day, the separation of immigrant children at the Mexican border by the United States government raises many questions about the abuse of migrants seeking asylum and their children, issues that are not likely to be resolved fully for many years to come. Similar sorrow attends those immigrants who came into the United States undocumented, either as infants or small children, grew up in this country, and now face the threat of being deported to a country that they do not know and whose language they do not speak. These children are often referred to by the acronym DACA (Deferred Action for Childhood Arrival).

The world is only recently learning about the thousands of children who have been sexually abused over the years by Roman Catholic priests whose actions the church's authorities concealed by a variety of clever strategies. This horrific story of ecclesial conspiracy gained much public attention after the 2015 Academy Award–winning best picture *Spotlight*, which provided a vivid account of an investigation by the *Boston Globe* into the conspiracy of concealment by the archdiocese of Boston.[3]

Suffice it to say, this movie brought the issue of the sexual abuse of children to national prominence. Its impact eventually reached the Vatican and forced the Vatican to undertake its own investigation into the church's internal governance procedures on such matters.

3. Tom McCarthy, dir., *Spotlight* (2015, United States: Open Road Films, LLC), film.

Increasing numbers of archbishops, bishops, and priests have been tried and found guilty of such abuses. The Roman Catholic Church has spent hundreds of millions of dollars worldwide in settlement costs and its investigations are still ongoing.

None of this implies, however, that the issue of child sexual abuse is limited to the Roman Catholic Church. Nothing could be further from the truth. One takeaway from this story, however, is that no institution in our society should be above the law and free to govern itself on all issues. Rather, preachers would do well to tell their congregations that legal abuses within the privacy of the home or the church should be rightful matters of civil and criminal law, as well as a clear mandate for true discipleship.

PETER J. PARIS

Proper 22 (Sunday between October 2 and October 8)

Job 1:1; 2:1–10 and Genesis 2:18–24   Hebrews 1:1–4; 2:5–12
Psalm 26 and Psalm 8   Mark 10:2–16

Job 1:1; 2:1–10

¹:¹There was once a man in the land of Uz whose name was Job. That man was blameless and upright, one who feared God and turned away from evil. . . .

²:¹One day the heavenly beings came to present themselves before the LORD, and Satan also came among them to present himself before the LORD. ²The LORD said to Satan, "Where have you come from?" Satan answered the LORD, "From going to and fro on the earth, and from walking up and down on it." ³The LORD said to Satan, "Have you considered my servant Job? There is no one like him on the earth, a blameless and upright man who fears God and turns away from evil. He still persists in his integrity, although you incited me against him, to destroy him for no reason." ⁴Then Satan answered the LORD, "Skin for skin! All that people have they will give to save their lives. ⁵But stretch out your hand now and touch his bone and his flesh, and he will curse you to your face." ⁶The LORD said to Satan, "Very well, he is in your power; only spare his life."

⁷So Satan went out from the presence of the LORD, and inflicted loathsome sores on Job from the sole of his foot to the crown of his head. ⁸Job took a potsherd with which to scrape himself, and sat among the ashes.

⁹Then his wife said to him, "Do you still persist in your integrity? Curse God, and die." ¹⁰But he said to her, "You speak as any foolish woman would speak. Shall we receive the good at the hand of God, and not receive the bad?" In all this Job did not sin with his lips.

Genesis 2:18–24

¹⁸Then the LORD God said, "It is not good that the man should be alone; I will make him a helper as his partner." ¹⁹So out of the ground the LORD God formed every animal of the field and every bird of the air, and brought them to the man to see what he would call them; and whatever the man called every living creature, that was its name. ²⁰The man gave names to all cattle, and to the birds of the air, and to every animal of the field; but for the man there was not found a helper as his partner. ²¹So the LORD God caused a deep sleep to fall upon the man, and he slept; then he took one of his ribs and closed up its place with flesh. ²²And the rib that the LORD God had taken from the man he made into a woman and brought her to the man. ²³Then the man said,

"This at last is bone of my bones
    and flesh of my flesh;
this one shall be called Woman,
    for out of Man this one was taken."

²⁴Therefore a man leaves his father and his mother and clings to his wife, and they become one flesh.

Commentary 1: Connecting the Reading with Scripture

Job 1:1; 2:1–10. We are here in the realm of fable, of truth rather than fact. Job 1:1 is a biblical Hebrew equivalent of "long ago and far away." Just as fairy tales can tell the truth, as elementary schools in the United States still celebrate George Washington as the hatchet-carrying boy who "cannot tell a lie," and, most significantly, as Jesus taught often by way of parables, the book of Job tackles deep theological issues through the medium of fable.

The Adversary ("Satan," Job 2:1) is not the devil, at least not the devil we know from Dante and Milton. The word is a title, a job description, one whose responsibility is to ask the hard or embarrassing questions.

It is imperative to read the prose prologue (chaps. 1 and 2) as a parable, a literary setup for the theological dialogues that follow. If these chapters are taken as fact, we are left with a portrait of a monstrous God who is willing to have people slaughtered to win a narcissistic bet. The question at the heart of Job is emphatically *not* "Why do good people suffer?" Everyone who lives in this world knows there is innocent suffering. The question is rather, "Given the world as we know it, in which there is innocent suffering, does God know or care? Is it possible to be faithful in such a world? Should one even attempt to be faithful?" The final chapter will answer all of these questions in the affirmative, without attempting an explanation that will answer all human questions.

The assumption was—and often still is—that much suffering is punishment for sin. This is the same question the disciples ask in John 9:2. Jesus totally shuts down the punishment explanation in verse 3. The question is still heard in the common query, "What have I done to deserve this?" The preacher might remind the congregation that God's faithfulness is not measured in sending punishments for all our sins.

No, this prologue has to be "fiction," because Job is presented as "blameless and upright" (Job 1:1, 8, 22; 2:10), lest the dialogues become sidetracked into a calculus of sin. Job is the "pure" example, to allow the theological positions to be argued in the next thirty-plus chapters. Yes, there are verses that state plainly, if we do good and live by the covenant, there will be good results. Also, if we do evil and abandon the covenant, there will be bad results. However, it is not legitimate to argue the other way around, that good results prove covenant faithfulness or bad results prove sinful living. Job's friends believe the simple equation. Part of Job's anguish at the start is that he does too. When his friends tell him to repent, he does not argue sinlessness, but, rather, that he does not know his sin and thus does not know how to repent.

For three weeks we have had texts with women: the idealized, talented, hardworking wife in Proverbs, the courageous Esther, and now the slandered grieving wife and mother. The treatment of Job's wife through centuries of commentaries and sermons is another example of human perverseness. Preachers might suggest we stop being so hard on her (2:10) and others in devastating situations when we too often blame them for their plight. She, too, has lost all her children. Whether Job's wife is thinking that his pain can be eased only by death and that his cursing God would call down that death swiftly, or whether she is being sarcastic, she has not abandoned him as his words rebuff her. She does not throw the accusations the friends will hurl at him; she is not under the thrall of the assumption that Job has brought all this calamity upon himself (and his children, servants, flocks, and herds). She is the only person who offers Job grace.

Genesis 2:18–24. Genesis 2:18 has the first notice in Scripture of something "not good." The 'adam's (human being) being alone needs to be solved. So, God makes land animals and birds, bringing them to be named, to be put under human dominion, but none of them solves the aloneness problem. (What is simply stated in the first creation narrative ["have dominion," Gen. 1:28] is here represented by the act of naming.) Finally, God takes a portion of the 'adam (human being) and fashions an 'ishah (woman).

The vagaries of both the lectionary and the Hebrew/English interface require an aside on

Sufferings of the Soul

Now, though the soul acknowledges itself to be miserable, and though it is painful to us to see ourselves as we are, and though we have most deep convictions of our own wickedness,— deep as those spoken of just now, and really felt,—yet true humility is not attended with trouble. . . . That other humility, which is the work of Satan, furnishes no light for any good work; it pictures God as bringing upon everything fire and sword; it dwells upon His justice; and the soul's faith in the mercy of God— for the power of the devil does not reach so far as to destroy faith—is of such a nature as to give me no consolation: on the contrary, the consideration of mercies so great helps to increase the pain, because I look upon myself as bound to render greater service.

This invention of Satan is one of the most painful, subtle, and crafty that I have known him to possess; I should therefore like to warn you, my father, of it, in order that, if Satan should tempt you herein, you may have some light, and be aware of his devices, if your understanding should be left at liberty: because you must not suppose that learning and knowledge are of any use here; for though I have none of them myself, yet now that I have escaped out of his hands I see clearly that this is folly. What I understood by it is this: that it is our Lord's pleasure to give him leave and license, as He gave him of old to tempt Job; though in my case, because of my wretchedness, the temptation is not so sharp.

It happened to me to be tempted once in this way. . . . The trial then lasted only till the day of the feast itself. But, on other occasions, it continued one, two, and even three weeks and—I know not—perhaps longer. But I was specially liable to it during the Holy Weeks, when it was my habit to make prayer my joy. Then the devil seizes on my understanding in a moment; and occasionally, by means of things so trivial that I should laugh at them at any other time, he makes it stumble over anything he likes. The soul, laid in fetters, loses all control over itself, and all power of thinking of anything but the absurdities he puts before it, which, being more or less unsubstantial, inconsistent, and disconnected, serve only to stifle the soul, so that it has no power over itself; and accordingly—so it seems to me—the devils make a football of it, and the soul is unable to escape out of their hands. It is impossible to describe the sufferings of the soul in this state. It goes about in quest of relief, and God suffers it to find none. The light of reason, in the freedom of its will, remains, but it is not clear; it seems to me as if its eyes were covered with a veil. As a person who, having travelled often by a particular road, knows, though it be night and dark, by his past experience of it, where he may stumble, and where he ought to be on his guard against that risk, because he has seen the place by day, so the soul avoids offending God: it seems to go on by habit—that is, if we put out of sight the fact that our Lord holds it by the hand, which is the true explanation of the matter.

Teresa of Avila, *The Life of St. Teresa of Jesus, of the Order of Our Lady of Carmel,* trans. David Lewis (London: Thomas Baker, 1904), 262–64.

nomenclature. Not until verse 23 is there a male human being as distinct from a female human being. At the beginning of chapter 2, God takes some soil and fashions a creature (2:7). In Hebrew, this is an *'adam* formed from the *'admah* (ground). The relationship can be hinted at in English: a *human* is constructed from the *humus.* Despite it being spelled like a masculine name, this *'adam* is a human being without regard to gender. We can say "human

being" to keep that point, but too often Bible translators choose the word "man" instead. Similar to *'adam /'admah* pair in verse 7, there is a close linguistic relationship between the words used in verse 23b in both Hebrew and English: the woman (*'ishah*) is taken from the man (*'ish*).

What is necessary to erase the "not good"-ness of the aloneness? A "suitable helper" is called for. The word translated "helper" is significant. It appears in the OT more than sixty times in both noun and verb forms, most often in the book of Psalms. In the majority of cases, it refers to God. This is an indication that the "helper" is more than an assistant human being; a helper cannot be just someone on whom one can put all the difficult or distasteful drudge work. A helper is what does for us what we cannot do by and for ourselves. When I want to put a rarely used platter on the top shelf, the step stool is my helper. When I want to open the new bottle of vinegar, my daughter is my helper. In the case of the first human, the problem is not just one of strength but of an appropriate sort of companionship or, as Robert Alter translates, "a sustainer beside him."[1] Yes, some of the animals will be found to be companionable, but still not quite what is needed.

What is needed is not just a helper, but a suitable helper and a suitable helper for the *'adam*. We have inherited the term "helpmeet" from the KJV, but having lost an old meaning of "meet" ("suitable, appropriate"), have also lost the notion of correspondence or coordination; we then have assumed the new creature is to be a helper in terms of being secondary in importance to the first creature. We also tend to commingle separate texts, reading some of Genesis 3:16b into this text, for instance, and positing males as divinely established to be in positions of authority over females.

The preacher could remind us that God's poetry addressing serpent, woman, and man in chapter 3 *follows* the humans' disobedience; it is presented as a result of sin and not original divine intention. At the end of today's pericope (v. 24b), there is a harmony, a congruence, a *meet* relationship between the two that will indeed be broken by the disobedience of both of them, one by commission, the other by omission. Still, the original appearance of male and female is one of mutual gift and mutual blessing. Our calling as Christians is not to perpetuate a pernicious result of sin.

REBECCA ABTS WRIGHT

Commentary 2: Connecting the Reading with the World

The preacher receives from the lectionary two rich texts to mine this week, both with challenges, whatever the preacher's context. God and Satan discuss righteous Job. God gives Job's fate over to Satan, asking only that Job's life be spared, but all other manner of torment kept on the table. The Genesis text continues the creation narrative with the Lord declaring that is it not good for man to be alone, bringing forth a multitude of creatures, culminating with the creation of a woman from the man's rib, each named by the man. The preacher could explore large themes in these stories, themes such as providence and suffering or the role of women in church and culture from the first woman to Job's wife, who advises her husband to "curse God and die." Certainly, the preacher could take on contemporary topics around creation care through the Genesis text, and the human struggle with theodicy never loses its resonance. Exploring how much free will we humans

exercise or how much participation we have in God's creation could prove fruitful too. Each text offers its own avenue to wrestle with these big questions.

Perhaps the preacher could lay out one of those big questions and then examine it in a variety of ways. Taking this story from Job, for example, and declaring that on this Sunday the topic will be: Where is God when we suffer? The preacher could begin with a discussion of the origins of evil, looking at classic theological explanations such as evil as an absence of good and asking, How does that definition fit with this text from the book of Job? Where does that definition fall short? Evil seems more active than passive in the form of Satan trolling the earth in search of someone to inflict with harm.

What do the preacher's hearers believe about evil? Satan? What does it mean to pray week in and week out, "And lead us not into temptation, but deliver us from evil"? The Westminster

---

1. Robert Alter, *The Hebrew Bible,* vol. 1 (New York: W. W. Norton, 2019), 14.

Shorter Catechism says, "[W]e pray that God would either keep us from being tempted to sin or support and deliver us when we are tempted." Does Job's unwillingness to curse God reveal the very righteousness that got him targeted for Satan's cruelty? What of those people of faith who succumb to railing against God when life's trials become overwhelming? Psalms of lament indicate that such a reaction is not off-limits. A sermon on this text from the alternative perspective of Job's wife could address the many people who are not as stalwart or stoic as Job and yet no less faithful.

Offering examples of those who lament and doubt, as well as those who remain steadfast, gives hearers the ability to consider those trying times in their own lives and the role their faith plays in both offering comfort and raising ultimate questions. The preacher could note that a life of discipleship contains seasons of obedience despite feeling forsaken and times of cursing God in utter confusion. God remains present through them all.

The dialogue between Satan and God and the subsequent one between Job and his wife could be applied by the preacher not just to individuals' circumstances, but to those seemingly intractable, painful issues in communities and the world. Why does racism persist? What about war? Poverty? The devastation of natural disasters? If the answer is "sin" or "evil" or even "Satan," what are believers to do in response? Curse God and die? Remain stoic in faith and wait for divine intervention? The appointed passage for Job does not reveal the answers to these questions, but it does provide a jumping-off point to explore them. These verses demand that the preacher take the problems of evil and suffering seriously and invite hearers into an honest struggle with what faithful responses to these realities look like. No platitudes allowed. Raw vulnerability like that exhibited by Job's wife is absolutely warranted and, if not the last word, surely part of the conversation.

What then of this Genesis text? It, too, provides an avenue to think carefully about big questions. How are human beings invited to participate in God's creating power? The ability to name is no small privilege in the Old Testament or now. Names matter. A quick look at street names in any town tells a story of what is important to the people there, or at least what was and is deemed important by those who had or have the authority to grant those names. Names have meaning. Family names, namesakes, all communicate the values of those giving them. The preacher could use this Genesis text to examine the names present in the church itself, such as Sunday school classes named for past parishioners, named rooms, and endowed lecture series. What do these names communicate about the values of the congregation? What about street names around the church building? In the town? A truthful look at what story, and whose story, those names tell could be an avenue for the preacher and congregation to consider what kind of community is being created, or not, as a result. Do these stories jibe with God's salvation narrative of goodness and God's image, or not?

Another big question that could be tackled through this Genesis text is one of stewardship of creation. If God grants humans the power to name, how then will they care for that which has been entrusted to them? Given the current state of our globe, the preacher ought to take every opportunity to preach about the role human beings play in either caring for or destroying that which God created and called good.

Yet another big question this text brings to the surface is the relationship between human beings. If we are flesh of one another's flesh, how then do we treat one another? In an era when large scale, systematic abuse is being exposed in almost every profession, in our culture as a whole and in the church, this Genesis text reminds believers that we belong to one another, are gifts from God to each other, and therefore ought to be loved and respected, not exploited and used. This is so not just for male and female couples, but for all of humanity, which these two first humans represent.

Preaching about big questions requires humility on the part of the preacher. No one sermon can address every angle of issues that permeate our daily lives and persist over a lifetime. The preacher would do well to state this truth up front, offering the opportunity for ongoing conversations in a variety of settings. Few things are worse than a sermon on a big question that offers small, pat, or neat answers. Both of these texts provide avenues to begin needed discussions about theodicy, evil, sin, providence, creation, the relationship between God and humans, and the relation of human beings with one another. Each text could be material for an entire series of sermons, taking one big question at a time. Preachers who remind their hearers that believers in all times and places face these big questions, and confess that they, too, are not immune to doubt or even lament, make themselves vulnerable and, in so doing, model for the congregation that God welcomes Job, Job's wife, and every creature under heaven, calling each and every one good.

JILL DUFFIELD

Psalm 26

[1]Vindicate me, O LORD,
    for I have walked in my integrity,
    and I have trusted in the LORD without wavering.
[2]Prove me, O LORD, and try me;
    test my heart and mind.
[3]For your steadfast love is before my eyes,
    and I walk in faithfulness to you.

[4]I do not sit with the worthless,
    nor do I consort with hypocrites;
[5]I hate the company of evildoers,
    and will not sit with the wicked.

[6]I wash my hands in innocence,
    and go around your altar, O LORD,
[7]singing aloud a song of thanksgiving,
    and telling all your wondrous deeds.

[8]O LORD, I love the house in which you dwell,
    and the place where your glory abides.
[9]Do not sweep me away with sinners,
    nor my life with the bloodthirsty,
[10]those in whose hands are evil devices,
    and whose right hands are full of bribes.

[11]But as for me, I walk in my integrity;
    redeem me, and be gracious to me.
[12]My foot stands on level ground;
    in the great congregation I will bless the LORD.

Psalm 8

[1]O LORD, our Sovereign,
    how majestic is your name in all the earth!

You have set your glory above the heavens.
    [2]Out of the mouths of babes and infants
you have founded a bulwark because of your foes,
    to silence the enemy and the avenger.

[3]When I look at your heavens, the work of your fingers,
    the moon and the stars that you have established;
[4]what are human beings that you are mindful of them,
    mortals that you care for them?

[5]Yet you have made them a little lower than God,
    and crowned them with glory and honor.

[6]You have given them dominion over the works of your hands;
     you have put all things under their feet,
[7]all sheep and oxen,
     and also the beasts of the field,
[8]the birds of the air, and the fish of the sea,
     whatever passes along the paths of the seas.

[9]O LORD, our Sovereign,
     how majestic is your name in all the earth!

Connecting the Psalm with Scripture and Worship

Psalm 26. For those following the semicontinuous track of the Revised Common Lectionary, this day begins a series of Sundays when the story of Job is heard. The first reading, Job 1:1; 2:1–10, introduces worshipers to the man Job, who is "blameless and upright" (Job 1:1), and the contest between God and Satan to prove that even Job can be made to curse God, if he is made miserable enough. This saga of Job is not a historical account, but a vehicle for considering one of the deepest questions of human existence, the problem of theodicy.

The architects of the lectionary offer Psalm 26 as a response to this introduction to the story of Job. Indeed, one can imagine Job himself uttering these very words. The psalmist asserts his integrity and claims that his trust in God is unwavering. As Clinton McCann explains, the Hebrew word that is translated as "my integrity" and "blameless life" (*tōm*) "does not indicate personal achievement or sinlessness," but "indicates complete devotion or total orientation of one's life to God."[1] The psalmist is faithful in worship as well, participating in cultic rituals, singing praises, and proclaiming God's "wondrous deeds" to all who would listen (Ps. 26:6–7). The psalmist then asks God to be gracious, to redeem him, to protect him from "sinners," "the bloodthirsty," and those who do evil of any kind (vv. 9–10).

Psalm 26 is a prayer for justice ("vindicate me," v. 1), prayed by one who professes unwavering loyalty to God. It is the kind of prayer that is directed at God when an innocent person has been accused without warrant, or when one is pleading that God will restore one's life to its previous state.[2] Here again, we can see Job's story reflected in these words. A preacher who focuses on the Job narrative might incorporate a portion of the psalm in a sermon, perhaps inviting her listeners to voice it as a prayer, as an illustration of Job's steadfastness. While Job's wife, understandably, is ready to curse God, Job is unmoving in his trust in the God he has always glorified.

It may seem at first glance that the author of Psalm 26 is overly sure of his own righteousness. Yet this prayer does not assume that the one who voices it is sinless; rather, it is an expression of one's intention to continue in a life of faithfulness, one's desire to live in a trusting relationship with the God she loves. To sing or speak this psalm in worship is to join the psalmist—and so many others who pray the psalms—in seeking God's help in restoring justice, to affirm one's trust in God in difficult circumstances, and to declare one's dependence in a trustworthy God, a God who is at the center of one's life.

This tone of utmost trust might imbue an entire service of worship, from opening sentences ("O LORD, I love the house in which you dwell, and the place where your glory abides," v. 8) to closing charge ("Your steadfast love is before my eyes, and I walk in faithfulness to you," v. 3). While there are but a few musical settings of Psalm 26, several classic hymns reflect the psalm's confidence in God and dedication to God's faithfulness in troubling times. "Jesus Calls Us,"

---

1. J. Clinton McCann Jr., "The Book of Psalms," in *The New Interpreter's Bible* (Nashville: Abingdon, 1996), 4:782.
2. James L. Mays, *Psalms* (Louisville, KY: Westminster John Knox, 1994), 128.

"O Jesus, I Have Promised," and "O Master, Let Me Walk with Thee" enable worshipers to express their intention to follow Christ and their need for his companionship and empowerment, as does the African American spiritual "Lead Me, Guide Me." "Goodness Is Stronger Than Evil," with its text by Desmond Tutu, acknowledges the reality of injustice while proclaiming faith in God's final victory, as does "O God, Who Gives Us Life," written by Carl Daw.

Psalm 8. Psalm 8 is an expression of pure wonder. With awe, the psalmist sings a song of praise to the God whose glory cannot be contained. She extols the beauty of heaven and earth and marvels that God has entrusted creation to human beings. Not only does God create a gorgeous, generative world; God establishes justice as its foundation (Ps. 8:2). In the midst of this world—and indeed, right in the middle of this psalm—human beings appear. The psalmist's awe is obvious here as well: how can humans, who are so small when compared to the vastness of the cosmos, mean anything at all to God? Yet God entrusts this amazing creation to these fragile human beings.

Psalm 8 is chosen, appropriately, as a response to the end of the second creation account, Genesis 2:18–24. Here, God forms every living being, seeking to provide a companion for the first human, finally creating another human being who is "bone of my bones and flesh of my flesh" (Gen. 2:23). After hearing the Genesis text, worshipers are invited to offer their own song of praise and awe as they sing Psalm 8, marveling at their seemingly insignificant place in the cosmos while acknowledging the surprising realization that God considers them just "a little lower" than divine beings.

It should be noted that the author of Hebrews quotes Psalm 8 in the epistle reading appointed for this day (Heb. 2:6). Here, it is Jesus who was "for a little while made lower than the angels" before suffering and dying "so that by the grace of God he might taste death for everyone" (2:9). If worshipers express awe at God's remarkable generosity in the psalm, their wonderment and reverence only deepen before the knowledge that God incarnate took on human flesh in order to die and be raised for their sakes.

Psalm 8 informs preaching and worship on this day in several ways. In an era of twenty-four-hour news cycles, it seems less and less common to simply pause in wonder. This day could be one of respite, in which the assembled congregation considers the mystery and beauty of creation, the gift of our existence, and our relationship with God the creator. This day may be an opportunity to focus on the utter glory and majesty of God, to take time to consider the wonder and splendor of the God who made us.

This day might also be a time to acknowledge our interdependence with the rest of the created order. Both the creation account and Psalm 8, each in its own way, imply that human beings are superior to other created beings and have the power to use (and abuse) the earth, its waters, and its air. Yet both texts also make clear that we are among the created; we may be "a little lower than God" (Ps. 8:5), but we are not God. A service of worship on this day might make clear that being given "dominion over the works of your hands" (v. 6) does not give us license to abuse creation, but that we are entrusted with the stewardship of it.

It is no wonder that composers have responded to the poetry of Psalm 8 by fashioning musical settings. The marvelous collection *Psalms for All Seasons* includes six settings in a wide range of musical styles, from an eighteenth-century German chorale to a sprightly Scottish tune to a chorus by American gospel artist Richard Smallwood.[3] Whatever vehicle is chosen to proclaim Psalm 8, these words help give voice to our own astonishment before the glory of God.

KIMBERLY BRACKEN LONG

---

3. *Psalms for All Seasons: A Complete Psalter for Worship* (Grand Rapids: Faith Alive Christian Resources, 2012).

Hebrews 1:1–4; 2:5–12

^{1:1}Long ago God spoke to our ancestors in many and various ways by the prophets, ²but in these last days he has spoken to us by a Son, whom he appointed heir of all things, through whom he also created the worlds. ³He is the reflection of God's glory and the exact imprint of God's very being, and he sustains all things by his powerful word. When he had made purification for sins, he sat down at the right hand of the Majesty on high, ⁴having become as much superior to angels as the name he has inherited is more excellent than theirs. . . .

^{2:5}Now God did not subject the coming world, about which we are speaking, to angels. ⁶But someone has testified somewhere,

"What are human beings that you are mindful of them,
    or mortals, that you care for them?
⁷You have made them for a little while lower than the angels;
    you have crowned them with glory and honor,
⁸subjecting all things under their feet."

Now in subjecting all things to them, God left nothing outside their control. As it is, we do not yet see everything in subjection to them, ⁹but we do see Jesus, who for a little while was made lower than the angels, now crowned with glory and honor because of the suffering of death, so that by the grace of God he might taste death for everyone.

¹⁰It was fitting that God, for whom and through whom all things exist, in bringing many children to glory, should make the pioneer of their salvation perfect through sufferings. ¹¹For the one who sanctifies and those who are sanctified all have one Father. For this reason Jesus is not ashamed to call them brothers and sisters, ¹²saying,

"I will proclaim your name to my brothers and sisters,
    in the midst of the congregation I will praise you."

Commentary 1: Connecting the Reading with Scripture

This passage is rich with christological themes. By the time this book was written, perhaps between 60 and 90 CE, early theological speculations concerning Jesus had already begun, starting with Paul in the early 50s. The Letter to the Hebrews—not a letter really, but more like an early Christian sermon (see Heb. 13:22)—was written to encourage a group of believers who had suffered for their faith in the past (10:32–34) but who were now in danger of lapsing in their Christian commitment (2:3; 6:4–6; 10:35; 12:25). They are assured that their suffering is not in vain, for God works through human suffering, as shown in the example of

Jesus (2:10, 18), who is presented as God's Son, the only one worthy of worshiping.

If this document was written after the destruction of the temple in 70 CE, then many of its assertions can be explained by this event. The replacement of the temple's temporary sacrifices by Jesus' permanent one (chap. 9) and his eternal priesthood as compared to the Levitical priesthood are examples. Added to that is the contrast between heavenly realities as ideal and the earthly ones as their reflection. This is a Platonic idea that is also seen in the writings of Philo of Alexandria. Hebrews was shaped by this type of Platonic-influenced Hellenistic

Judaism. This philosophy lends itself naturally to the ideology of replacement or supersession that permeates the whole book. This illustrates the beginning of anti-Jewish sentiments in the early church.

In 1:1–4, God is said to have spoken in the past (a reference to the first covenant with Israel) by the prophets (an indirect way of speaking), but that in these last days (not a reference to the readers' time but to the eschatological times) God has spoken directly through God's Son, Jesus. Included in these four verses are many themes that will be developed later in the body of the work. From the author's point of view, Jesus is the heir of all things, the agent and sustainer of creation, the image of God that reflects perfectly God's nature, redeemer, priest, and exalted Son of God in heaven. The preacher finds no shortage of christological themes in this book.

Behind the portrayal of Jesus as agent in creation there lies the Wisdom tradition where *sophia* is personified as God's helper in creating the world (Prov. 8:22–31; Sir. 1:4; Wis. 7:22; 9:9). The idea of Jesus' exaltation to heaven as God's Son may be a counternarrative to the depiction of Titus, Vespasian's son, ascending into heaven at his death, which can still be seen in the Arch of Titus at Rome.[1] According to the author of Hebrews, Jesus, not Titus, is the true Son of God, who because of his sacrifice for humankind has been given all authority.

While Jesus is being portrayed as Son of God in 1:1–4, he is portrayed as human in 2:5–12. Quoting from Psalm 8:4–6 in the Septuagint (LXX), the author argues that humans, though made a little lower than angels, were given by God the authority to subject everything (*ta panta*) in creation. Nothing has been left outside their control. However, this has not happened yet. So, what is it that has happened?

Instead of humans' having gained the status that God bestowed on them in creation, Jesus, God's Son, has acquired that status by means of his sacrifice on behalf of the human race. He shared the human condition for a while, so he could taste death as a mortal being (angels, unlike humans, cannot be crucified). Jesus had to share in the human nature "for a little while" in order to become the sanctifier who, together with those being sanctified, that is, made holy, may acknowledge the supreme and only authority of the Father (2:11). Therefore, Jesus and the believers are brothers, *adelphoi* (NRSV, "brothers and sisters"). Here we have an important christological reminder: Jesus is our sibling, our equal in many ways. He is someone who invites us to participate in the construction of God's reign as codisciples of God.[2]

Jesus partakes of human nature (2:14) and through death and resurrection takes away the fear of death, which is the most basic fear of all humans. The mentioning of the superiority of Jesus to angels may be due to the fact that some people would have understood him as an angel similar to Michael or Raphael[3] and would then worship them (see Col. 2:18). Jesus is superior to angels because while they are only ministering spirits (Heb. 1:14), he is God's Son. They serve (v. 7); Jesus reigns (v. 8). So, even the angels should worship the Son (v. 6). Another possibility for the mention of angels is to affirm the superiority of Christianity to Judaism. The law, says the author, was given by angels (2:2). Christ is the direct word of God to humans, so the law is superseded. This will be a major part of the argument in the book proper.

The message of Hebrews is theocentric, even though it is all about Jesus Christ, God's Son. The communication between God and humans is described in terms of speech: God spoke. This is the third book in the Bible that starts with a prologue on creation by God's word: Genesis 1:1–31; John 1:1–5; and here Hebrews 1:1–4. While in Genesis there is no agent that helps God in the creation of the world (God alone does it through his word), in John and in Hebrews, following the wisdom tradition, God creates through the agency of God's Son, Jesus Christ.

When preaching from these passages, there are some things that we may want to consider. First,

---

1. Warren Carter and Amy-Jill Levine, *The New Testament: Methods and Meanings* (Nashville: Abingdon, 2013), 267.
2. For a detailed study of this idea, see Michael Lodahl, *Jesus, Disciple of the Kingdom* (Eugene, OR: Pickwick Publications, 2014).
3. Amy-Jill Levine and Marc Zvi Brettler, eds., *The Jewish Annotated New Testament* (New York: Oxford University Press, 2011), 407.

understand the context. At this time the Christian community was a minority group struggling to make sense of who Jesus was. It represents the beginning, not the end, of the debates that culminated with the developed christological affirmations of the Councils of Nicaea (325 CE) and Chalcedon (451 CE). It shows an embattled community responding theologically to its historically conditioned situation.

Because of that, its conclusions, for example the theology of replacement or supersessionism that pervades the whole document, may be problematic for some modern audiences. In an age of pluralism and religious dialogue, the book of Hebrews sounds like a terrorist text, full of unwanted toxicity. We need to read it with a hermeneutic of suspicion that will liberate it from the chains of Christian exclusivism with which orthodox interpretations have bound it.

Second, God's words cannot be owned in exclusivity. Some people will claim to have the monopoly of that speech and so lock themselves up in sectarian and/or nationalistic groups. This can only hurt society, as has been painfully demonstrated throughout the history of the world. Rather, we should acknowledge that God's initiative in communicating with humans can be seen in all religious traditions, rendering them equally valid. More important, this self-revelation of God still goes on. God still speaks; we just have to open our ears.

OSVALDO D. VENA

Commentary 2: Connecting the Reading with the World

The Letter to the Hebrews—which reads much more like a passionate sermon—opens with one of the most dramatic christological passages in the New Testament. The first claim this document makes about Jesus is that God "has spoken to us" through him (Heb. 1:2). The verb tense suggests not simply that God spoke in the past through Jesus, but that this divine speech continues to echo strongly into the present; what God has spoken in Christ is, in effect, still ringing in our ears.

The importance of this idea cannot be overemphasized, given the significant number of Christians who, when hearing terms like "revelation" or "word of God," tend first to think of the Bible. The Bible itself—the New Testament, that is—insists that God's ultimate revelation is the person of Jesus. The perfect accompaniment to this opening passage in Hebrews is John 1:1–14, where we read that the divine Word, God's speech through which all things came into being, became *flesh*—creaturely existence as fragile, frail, and vulnerable—and lived among us as the first-century Jew Jesus. This is an astounding claim!

It is not difficult, at first glance, to connect the claim in this reading with the world. God created all things through the speaking of the Word, "*Let there be . . .*" If this divine speech truly did become incarnate as a human being in a particular time and place (the scandal of particularity), then Hebrews can boldly proclaim that Jesus the Son is the one "through whom [God] also created the worlds"; indeed, he is said to "sustain all things by his powerful word" (1:2, 3). Preachers can help congregations adopt, indeed celebrate, a Christic vision of the universe. This implies that what we encounter in the Gospels, regarding the words and deeds of Jesus, provides us an important clue about the nature and goal of God's creative activity throughout the unimaginable expanses of the universe. Indeed, since Jesus is "the reflection of God's glory and the exact imprint of God's very being" (1:3), his words and deeds provide us also the most critical clues about God, period.

This seems a hard lesson for the church to learn. Preachers can help us see that we all too often allow all sorts of other notions or images of God to provide templates for our theological imagination. These may include the "In God We Trust" on US currency, or the God of "God bless America" as US presidents (and perhaps other national leaders) apparently feel required to recite, or perhaps the common (and commonly unexamined) platitude "God is in control."

Whoever or whatever such deities might be, they seem to bear little resemblance to this Son who "taste[d] death for everyone" (2:9).

Karl Barth faced this issue squarely during the Confessing Church's opposition to Adolf Hitler and the Nazi program. The Nazis appealed to nationalistic interests to try to create a "German Church" and "German Christianity" that would support Hitler's rule and policies. Under Barth's strong theological guidance, the 1934 Barmen Declaration insisted instead that "Jesus Christ, as he is attested for us in Holy Scripture, is the one Word of God which we have to hear and which we have to trust and obey in life and in death."[4]

The fact that so many German Christians happily embraced Hitler for restoring law and order, cleaning up the streets, boosting the German economy, and uplifting German pride (dare we say that he was "making Germany great again"?) should give us pause—not in order to condemn them from a hindsight position of moral superiority, but to acknowledge that the situation is not so different today. Too many people in our churches (whether mainline or evangelical) have uncritically internalized a nationalistic (verging toward militaristic) version of Christianity that is a far cry from "Jesus Christ, . . . the one Word of God."

It would be impossible to miss the author's concern that his audience is fixated on angelology to the detriment of their attention to Jesus; angels are mentioned, somewhat demeaningly, in the last verse of the first passage (1:4) as well as the first verse of the second passage (2:5), and in virtually all of the material in between! Hebrews offers no support or solace to contemporary, popular fascination with angelic beings, an interest that certainly continues to thrive in New Age literature.

New Testament scholar Robert Jewett encourages a deeper engagement with the implications of angelic fascination as criticized by Hebrews: "This ascription of functional ultimacy to angels seems to offer a rather sophisticated way to avoid outright idolatry. It is similar to the modern ascription of ultimacy to the forces of economics or history, the institutions of government or business, or the methods of technological manipulation."[5] Hebrews, then, calls us away from the penultimate powers and principalities—whether embodied in political systems, popular entertainments, denominational loyalties, economism, for only a few possibilities—and beckons to us to "see Jesus" (2:9) as the very "pioneer and perfecter of our faith" (12:2).

If the opening passage of Hebrews (1:1–4) emphasizes the divine nature of the Son, the second part of the reading gives important recognition to Jesus' human nature. Hebrews connects Jesus' identity and destiny to Psalm 8, which asks the question, "What is *'adam* [man, humanity] that you [God] are mindful of him, or *ben 'adam* [humanity's offspring] that you care for him?" (Ps. 8:4). In the psalm, this question is a parallel couplet, asking the same question two different ways. Our author understandably gravitates to the phrase *ben 'Adam* ("son of man") to make a christological connection. Perhaps the most important contemporary concern is that Psalm 8 initially is a reaffirmation of the human vocation described in Genesis 1, where *'adam* as "male and female," that is, all human beings, are created and called to be God's "image," reflecting God's purposes and care for all creatures.[6] There is a crucial ecological ethic implied in Genesis 1 and Psalm 8; is that ethic diminished or obscured by redirecting its meaning toward Jesus?

It need not be. Reading Psalm 8 in the light of Christ can be a powerful way of acknowledging the Christian confidence that Jesus is the True Human, "the last Adam" (1 Cor. 15:45), the ultimate unveiling not only of divine nature, but of human nature as well. Jesus fulfills the calling of the True Human by offering himself fully for the sake of creation's redemption, "now crowned with glory and honor because of the suffering of death" (Heb. 2:9).

Jesus, however, does not replace us or relieve us of our vocation as God's representative

---

4. "The Theological Declaration of Barmen," 8.11, as found in *The Book of Confessions* (Louisville, KY: Office of the General Assembly of the Presbyterian Church (U.S.A), 1999), 249.

5. Robert Jewett, *Letter to Pilgrims: A Commentary on the Epistle to the Hebrews* (New York: Pilgrim, 1981), 27.

6. See Michael Lodahl, *Renewal in Love: Living Holy Lives in God's Good Creation* (Kansas City: Beacon Hill Press of Kansas City, 2015).

caregivers toward creation; rather, he represents us, faithfully *re-presenting* what it means to be a human being whose faithful obedience "images" or reflects God. "For this reason," we might adapt Hebrews, "Jesus is not ashamed to call [us] brothers and sisters" (2:11), since through him God is "bringing many children to glory" (2:10), the very glory with which God has crowned humanity in the act of creation!

MICHAEL LODAHL

Mark 10:2–16

²Some Pharisees came, and to test him they asked, "Is it lawful for a man to divorce his wife?" ³He answered them, "What did Moses command you?" ⁴They said, "Moses allowed a man to write a certificate of dismissal and to divorce her." ⁵But Jesus said to them, "Because of your hardness of heart he wrote this commandment for you. ⁶But from the beginning of creation, 'God made them male and female.' ⁷'For this reason a man shall leave his father and mother and be joined to his wife, ⁸and the two shall become one flesh.' So they are no longer two, but one flesh. ⁹Therefore what God has joined together, let no one separate."

¹⁰Then in the house the disciples asked him again about this matter. ¹¹He said to them, "Whoever divorces his wife and marries another commits adultery against her; ¹²and if she divorces her husband and marries another, she commits adultery."

¹³People were bringing little children to him in order that he might touch them; and the disciples spoke sternly to them. ¹⁴But when Jesus saw this, he was indignant and said to them, "Let the little children come to me; do not stop them; for it is to such as these that the kingdom of God belongs. ¹⁵Truly I tell you, whoever does not receive the kingdom of God as a little child will never enter it." ¹⁶And he took them up in his arms, laid his hands on them, and blessed them.

Commentary 1: Connecting the Reading with Scripture

One of the tactics of adversarial people is to point fingers at other persons' faults so theirs will remain hidden. Such is the encounter that this Gospel reading witnesses. The Pharisees are not really interested in preserving marriages; their question about divorce is just a plot to test Jesus on a very public debate—Herod's divorce condemned by John the Baptist (Mark 6:17–29)— in hopes of getting him in trouble with Herod himself. Jesus turns the tables on their inquiry, and the Pharisees' hardness of heart is exposed. They knew the answer to the question they used to challenge him: divorce was legal. Jesus, instead, stresses that divorce is not the ideal ending of a marriage.

When considering the theme of marriage and divorce in Scripture, specific texts come to mind, especially in light of this Gospel lection. Certainly the preacher could think about Deuteronomy 24:1–4, which requires a husband to give a certificate of divorce to his ex-wife. This document recognized the vulnerability of a divorced woman, permitting her to move to a different household, giving her legitimacy and the legal validation she needed to be able to survive. The preacher may want to explore the details of the narrative in Genesis 2:18–24, which Jesus recalls in his statement "God made them male and female" (Mark 10:6), to appreciate Jesus' emphasis on such a poetic story of the creation of humanity and marriage. The man, like all the animals he names in the story, was created from the dust of the ground, but the woman was created from the flesh of the man, not as a by-product or to show dependency, but to make them equal, from the same flesh and bones, to make them one flesh, equal human companions.

Preachers could explore how Jesus uses this text to explain that divorce is not a male's prerogative, that men and women are equal partners in the marriage, equally responsible for holding together what God has joined, and potentially equally capable of filing for divorce, if the hardness of their hearts brings them to that point. Additionally, this Genesis text grounds the importance of married relations; legal divorce is not an excuse to jump in and out of marriages at will.

In our text, once Jesus and the disciples go home and have, therefore, moved from the public into the private and intimate space of their family, the disciples ask Jesus to say more about his early encounter with the Pharisees. He ignores their self-serving question regarding the Pharisees and addresses what concerns him the most: the people who are involved in the divorce (rather than the technicalities of laws regarding marriage and divorce). Jesus' reply does not justify adultery.

Rather, he redirects their and our focus to the relationships of the people involved. Instead of continuing a debate of the legal views regarding what circumstances constitute reasons for divorce, Jesus invites the hearers to consider what God intended in creation. Men and women are equally condemned if they are trying to get a divorce simply to marry someone else, when there is no fault in the person they are divorcing; they are at fault if the divorce is compelled by nothing more than the capricious desire of the man or woman for someone else.

Perhaps this is behind John the Baptist's recriminations of Herod Antipas regarding his union with Herodias (6:14–29). Building on this theme of the relationships, the preacher may also point to Mark 10:28–31. In this text there is speech about leaving the household, mothers, fathers, sisters and brothers, and children for the sake of Jesus, yet we do not hear that wives and husbands are to be left behind for the sake of ministry.

According to Jesus' words, we could see marriage as a call to equality, as an ideal situation of commitment to one another that should be such that none should break them apart, since God has joined them together. At the same time, we know that this phrase has become a cliché, an automatic formula that is commonly used in marriage ceremonies, perhaps suggesting that newlyweds are magically

protected against divorce. The preacher might explore ways we confirm that God is bringing two people together rather than simple desire or impulse.

It is no coincidence that the next story Mark presents concerns children and their importance in God's kin-dom.[1] Perhaps this was a way of affirming the family in order to protect children and women from abandonment, challenging listeners with commitment, so those vulnerable within the union could be protected. The preacher could explore the concept of family as a commitment for keeping the weak protected and included as part of the kin-dom as a way of expressing the ruling of God in our lives.

When we look for the connections of this text with the prior stories, the preacher can help us see how the evangelist has led us along a particular path, that of care for the vulnerable ones, especially the care of little children. We are cautioned not to make the little ones stumble or lose their faith (9:42); we have been charged to welcome a child and in doing so, welcome Jesus, and God who sent him (9:37); we have seen fathers and mothers so moved by their love for their sons and daughters that they seek out Jesus to request healing for their children (5:23; 7:25; 9:17). Now we encounter people bringing little children to Jesus that he might touch them and give them healing and blessings (10:13).

Then, just when we think the disciples have learned the lessons of such care, we see them fail once more. They reject the children, and they reject those who are bringing the children, thinking that they are protecting Jesus from being disrupted. Jesus' indignation rises, and he orders the disciples to bring back the children. He wishes to teach them once and for all the central truth about the kin-dom of God; it belongs to the little ones (10:14). If they cannot receive a little child like these, they will not receive the kin-dom (10:15). The preacher can help us know again: what does it mean to receive a child? Jesus says that to welcome a child is to become a servant; it is to become

---

1. Concept used by Latina theologian Ada María Isasi-Díaz to avoid "kingdom" because it is sexist, elitist, and hierarchical. She says, "When the fullness of God becomes a day-to-day reality in the world at large, we will all be sisters and brothers—kin to each other" (*En la Lucha/In the Struggle* [Minneapolis: Fortress, 1993], ix).

a caregiver for the vulnerable; it is to care for the one who cannot take care of herself; it is to live our life in service to others. That is how we receive the kingdom.

The preacher might note that the most common passage referenced for this scene, concerning the kingdom and the little children, is the more well-known version of Matthew 18:3–4, which seems to emphasize humility: "Truly I tell you, unless you change and become like children, you will never enter the kingdom of heaven. Whoever becomes humble like this child is the greatest in the kingdom of heaven." While humbleness is important, entering the kin-dom is even more so about taking care of the children, caring for the vulnerable ones, and giving them a family. It is about living our lives in service of others, especially the neediest among us.

LETICIA A. GUARDIOLA-SÁENZ

Commentary 2: Connecting the Reading with the World

The Pharisees were members of a Jewish group that frequently clashed with Jesus over traditional thought and practice. Consequently, they often sought to entrap him into saying something contrary to their official teaching. One day they asked him if it is lawful for a man to divorce his wife. Fully aware of their intent, Jesus responded by asking them another question, namely, Moses' teaching on the subject. When they said that Moses taught that a man could divorce his wife with a letter of divorcement, Jesus commented that was because of the hardness of their hearts. He then proceeded to put the subject in a larger theological context by saying that, at the beginning of creation, God made man and woman so that the man could leave his father and mother and cleave to his wife and they could become one flesh. Accordingly, they would no longer be two but one. He concluded with the words that have been repeated at wedding ceremonies for many centuries: "Those whom God has joined together let no one put asunder" (*Book of Common Prayer* [2000], 428, from Mark 10:9).

Later in the house, Jesus' disciples inquired further about his thinking on the subject. He then stated unequivocally that any man who divorces his wife and marries another commits adultery with her, and similarly any woman who divorces her husband and remarries.

Two things can be said about this passage: First, Jesus sets forth an understanding of marriage as an ideal institution that is not established as a contractual arrangement between two families, as was common practice in those days, but as mingling the blood of two people so that they become one and are no longer two. Under such conditions, the action cannot be reversed. Hence, if any man divorces his wife and marries another, he invariably commits adultery with the woman and vice versa for any woman who does similarly, because in each case, their first marriage was indissoluble. Thus, the focus on divorce seems to be on the act of remarrying. Nothing is said about the possibility of one or the other divorcing and not remarrying. The silence on that matter could imply that such a situation would pose no problem.

Now, contrary to all patriarchal practices, Jesus speaks not only of men divorcing their wives but also of women divorcing their husbands. In that regard, his teaching implies the principle of gender equality, which was certainly a radical notion at that time.

For many centuries, the Christian church had either upheld Mark's absolute prohibition of divorce or permitted Mathew's allowance of divorce in the case of adultery as the one exception (Matt. 19:9). It taught that since the Gospel of Mark focuses entirely on the character of the kingdom Jesus was bent on establishing, his ethics concerning divorce in that kingdom were an ideal and not intended as a normative policy for either ordinary civil or ecclesiastical practice. In other words, the writer is discussing the subject of marriage and divorce in the context of the kingdom of God, not that of the present age.

The only way one can relate to Jesus' teaching on divorce in Mark's Gospel is to say that it fails to do justice to the lived reality of modern-day human beings, who often choose their marital partners with all the limitations implicit in being young, limitations that fail to recognize serious potential conflicts resulting from character flaws, personality changes, the impact of economic and social stresses, cultural differences, and/or the development of bad habits that sometimes lead to some type of addiction. Any or all of these conditions can lead to the physical or mental abuse of one or both partners. All such conditions are on full display in the many family courtrooms throughout this nation every day of the week.

Additionally, while divorce does rescue many from having to endure bad marriages, more often than not, the mother and children are left with fewer economic resources with which to live. Further, those children who truly love both parents are often traumatized by the experience of separation, which can have enduring psychological consequences for the rest of their lives.

Since the last quarter of the twentieth century, divorce has become widespread throughout the United States. The intoxicating culture of fame and fortune that permeates the world of professional entertainment is saturated with multiple divorces that greatly complicate family relationships as children strive to relate to many strands of siblings bearing different surnames and living in different homes. Celebrative occasions of birthdays, graduations, and weddings are constantly marred by the anxiety produced by the potential and sometimes actual blowups.

During the first five or six decades of the twentieth century, divorce required proof of adultery. Thus, those who sought a divorce often paid out huge amounts of money to hire thugs to follow their partner in order to catch him or her in a compromising situation. The publicity surrounding such practices added shame and embarrassment to the social stigma that had long been associated with divorce.

The 1979 movie *Kramer vs. Kramer* played a major role in sensitizing the public to look more favorably on the issue of divorce.[2] The film won five Academy Awards, including the best actor award for Dustin Hoffman and the best actress award for Meryl Streep. Though somewhat outdated in not having weighed the psychological impact of divorce or allowing the child to speak during the custody battle, the film's excellence lies both in its refusal to take sides in the conflict or to provide easy answers. Its empathic realism, coupled with the excellent acting of Hoffman and Streep, has given it enduring value up to the present day.

In our day, smart phones, the internet, and social media are immensely helpful resources for exploring all dimensions of this difficult subject. Most important, much of that help can be gained in the privacy of one's own home. Any question about any part of the process can be investigated on the internet free of charge, including that of assessing the merits of specific counselors, psychologists, attorneys, financial advisors, and so on, before meeting any of them in person. Countless books, lectures, panel discussions, personal testimonies are among the numerous available resources.

Finally, since the subject of divorce is a negative topic, its study is similar to the study of disease. One studies the latter not for its own sake, but in order to understand health and its preservation. Similarly, one should study the reasons for divorce in order to understand good marriages and how they can be preserved and even enhanced. Since marriages comprise two people desirous of building a life together, the maintenance of mutual respect and continuous communication are two necessary ingredients. They are the salt that keeps the relationship fresh. When they diminish, the relationship does likewise.

Since 40 to 50 percent of all first marriages in the United States end in divorce, much careful attention should be devoted to the issue long before couples begin thinking about getting married. Voluntary structured programs focusing on young people and their future marriages should be available for students in high schools, junior and four-year colleges, churches, synagogues, temples, mosques, and all social

---

2. Robert Benson, dir., *Kramer vs. Kramer* (United States: Columbia Pictures, 1979), film.

organizations that they frequent. In every such situation, student evaluation of the program is necessary, as well as their input. It is important that all such programs deal adequately with the questions young people have, because many may feel uneasy about asking them, since many emerge out of their personal experiences. Thus, the design of such programs requires the expertise of psychologists and pastoral-care specialists.

PETER J. PARIS

Proper 23 (Sunday between October 9 and October 15)

Job 23:1–9, 16–17 and
    Amos 5:6–7, 10–15
Psalm 22:1–15 and Psalm 90:12–17

Hebrews 4:12–16
Mark 10:17–31

Job 23:1–9, 16–17

¹Then Job answered:

²"Today also my complaint is bitter;
    his hand is heavy despite my groaning.
³Oh, that I knew where I might find him,
    that I might come even to his dwelling!
⁴I would lay my case before him,
    and fill my mouth with arguments.
⁵I would learn what he would answer me,
    and understand what he would say to me.
⁶Would he contend with me in the greatness of his power?
    No; but he would give heed to me.
⁷There an upright person could reason with him,
    and I should be acquitted forever by my judge.

⁸"If I go forward, he is not there;
    or backward, I cannot perceive him;
⁹on the left he hides, and I cannot behold him;
    I turn to the right, but I cannot see him.
. . . .
¹⁶God has made my heart faint;
    the Almighty has terrified me;
¹⁷If only I could vanish in darkness,
    and thick darkness would cover my face!"

Amos 5:6–7, 10–15

⁶Seek the LORD and live,
    or he will break out against the house of Joseph like fire,
    and it will devour Bethel, with no one to quench it.
⁷Ah, you that turn justice to wormwood,
    and bring righteousness to the ground!
. . . .
¹⁰They hate the one who reproves in the gate,
    and they abhor the one who speaks the truth.
¹¹Therefore because you trample on the poor
    and take from them levies of grain,
you have built houses of hewn stone,
    but you shall not live in them;

you have planted pleasant vineyards,
　　but you shall not drink their wine.
¹²For I know how many are your transgressions,
　　and how great are your sins—
you who afflict the righteous, who take a bribe,
　　and push aside the needy in the gate.
¹³Therefore the prudent will keep silent in such a time;
　　for it is an evil time.

¹⁴Seek good and not evil,
　　that you may live;
and so the LORD, the God of hosts, will be with you,
　　just as you have said.
¹⁵Hate evil and love good,
　　and establish justice in the gate;
it may be that the LORD, the God of hosts,
　　will be gracious to the remnant of Joseph.

Commentary 1: Connecting the Reading with Scripture

Job 23:1–9, 16–17. Job 23 forms a literary unit with chapter 24, together comprising a speech by Job that responds to a preceding speech by his so–called friend Eliphaz the Temanite (Job 22). A brief speech by the friend Bildad the Shuhite follows Job's (chap. 25). This dialogic structure governs the book's largest section (chaps. 3–31), in which Job delivers nine speeches, Eliphaz three, Bildad three, and Zophar the Naamathite two. Speeches by Job open and close the dialogue (see 3:1; 31:40–32:1) and respond to each of the friends' speeches in turn. At times, they talk past one another; at times, they agree with, criticize, or refute one another. The multi-voiced poetic text resists reduction to one moral message, yielding what Carol Newsom has called "a contest of moral imaginations" that simultaneously affirms and denies each answer to the conundrums of human suffering and divine justice,[1] even as it repeatedly privileges the experience and voice of the one who suffers.

In the preceding speech, Eliphaz accused Job of great wickedness, specifically of depriving others of clothing, water, food, and land (22:5–9). He blamed the victim, Job, for his own suffering (vv. 10–11) and urged him to "return" to God (v. 23). Job addressed these charges in a

later speech (29:12–16; 31). Here, however, Job focuses on the deity: Job would indeed turn to God, if only he could find God (23:3).

Indeed, the elusiveness of God—and by extension, of God's justice—is the guiding theme of 23:1–9 (cf. 11:7; 13:24; 37:23). It is both God's presence and God's logic that Job finds impossible to pin down. Job is eager to confront God (23:3), to present the case for his innocence (vv. 4, 7), and to learn and understand God's reasoning (v. 5). Job's body holds the record of his experience and becomes a point of reference in his search for God, but his faculties of movement, cognition, and sight do not equip him to find a God who hides or to discern what logic guides this God's decisions and actions (vv. 8–9). Job's frustrated search for God will thus be matched later in the book by a poetic meditation on the search for wisdom (chap. 28): "Where shall wisdom be found, and where is the place of understanding?" (28:12; cf. 38:19–24). Just as Job twice complains that he cannot see God (23:9; cf. 35:14), so the poet will declare that wisdom "is hidden from the eyes of all living" (28:21).

The lectionary pairs Job 23 with Psalm 22, wherein the psalmist grapples with the felt

1. Carol Newsom, *The Book of Job: A Contest of Moral Imaginations* (Oxford: Oxford University Press, 2003).

absence and silence of God in a time of great personal anguish (Ps. 22:1–2). The psalmist received the same advice Eliphaz gave to Job: "Commit your cause to the LORD" (v. 8). While the psalm moves through complaint (vv. 1–2, 6–8, 12–18) and trust (vv. 3–5, 9–10) to petition (vv. 11, 19–21) and praise (vv. 22–31), Job's speech takes a different turn. Job acknowledges that he *has* felt God's presence (23:15), but it did not comfort him. Rather, it terrified him (vv. 15–16) so much that it is now Job who would hide (v. 17). Nor does the continuation of Job's speech in chapter 24 match the psalmist's confidence that God will save the afflicted. Rather, Job has observed a world where orphans go naked (24:9–10) and where God ignores the cries of the dying (v. 12) but grants long life and security to the wicked (vv. 21–23). Job's countertestimony will not have the last word in the book but will ultimately summon forth God's own response (chaps. 38–41; 42:7–8).

Amos 5:6–7, 10–15. Amos 5:1–17 exhibits a concentric structure (A-B-C-D-C'-B'-A') in which praise of the creating and destroying God (D: 5:8–9) erupts from the midst of a critique of injustice that promises retaliation against those who hoard resources for themselves and corrupt the systems of justice (C: v. 7; C': vv. 10–13). Exhortation frames this critique with a hope that Israel may yet seek that which leads to life (B: vv. 4–6; B': vv. 14–15). This hope of life is framed in turn by songs of death, beginning with a funeral dirge the prophet sings over a personified, fallen Israel (A: vv. 1–3) and concluding with a future scene of wailing and mourning in city and field alike (A': vv. 16–17).[2]

Within this broader unit, the lectionary passage narrows the hearer's focus to the elements of critique and exhortation. The lectionary's temporary muting of funeral songs and doxology does not deny the deadly consequences of economic injustice nor the sovereignty of God. Rather, it emphasizes that if there is no justice, there will be no life.

A futility curse occupies the center of the lectionary passage (v. 11). The form of futility curse has parallels elsewhere in the Old Testament, with its most detailed articulation among the covenant curses of Deuteronomy 28 (esp. Deut. 28:30–44; cf. vv. 48–68; other parallels include Zeph. 1:13, Hag. 1:5–6, and reversals in Amos 9:14 and Isa. 62:8–9). The form is this: whatever or whoever you have prized, or labored for, or believed was yours, you will not retain nor reap the reward. Invasion, exile, pestilence, drought, and economic reversal will transform bounty into barrenness.

Amos 5:11 is likely the earliest biblical occurrence of the futility curse. By comparison with other occurrences, it also has a distinctive feature: the houses "you shall not live in" are not the modest, mud-brick domiciles of Israel's villages. They are dwellings of the powerful, crafted by stonemasons to display strength and wealth (see Amos 3:15; 6:4). Neither are the vineyards whose wine "you shall not drink" ordinary vineyards; they are "vineyards of desire." The noun "desire" shares its root (*ḥ-m-d*) with the verb "to covet," familiar from the Decalogue's prohibition of coveting what belongs to another (Exod. 20:17; Deut. 5:21). In analyzing Amos 5:11, Marvin Chaney describes a process whereby "multipurpose land" would be "convert[ed] into vineyards" to produce "wine . . . desired by the elite." As a result, "many freeholding villagers lost their land and were ruined."[3]

Amos speaks into the reality of widening socioeconomic disparity within eighth-century Israel. Policies that favored the wealthy and disenfranchised the poor led to increasing centralization of resources, including the land and its yield, in the hands of a few. Israel's elites had thus already rendered futile the labor of the lower classes (see Amos 2:6–8; 8:4–6). Amos both promises change and urges his hearers to use their positions of power not for their own gain but to "establish justice in the gate" (5:15).

The question the young man asks Jesus in this week's Gospel passage, "What must I do

---

2. See especially J. De Waard, "The Chiastic Structure of Amos V 1–17," *Vetus Testamentum* 27, no. 2 (1977): 170–77; Göran Eidevall, *Amos: A New Translation with Introduction and Commentary*, Anchor Yale Bible 24G (New Haven, CT: Yale University Press, 2017), 152.

3. Marvin Chaney, *Peasants, Prophets, and Political Economy: The Hebrew Bible and Social Analysis* (Eugene, OR: Cascade, 2017), 163.

to inherit eternal life?" (Mark 10:17), echoes Amos's exhortation to "seek good and not evil, that you may live" (Amos 5:14; cf. 5:6). Jesus, like Amos, links life with God to economic justice for the poor (Mark 10:21; Amos 5:14).

ANATHEA E. PORTIER-YOUNG

Commentary 2: Connecting the Reading with the World

In Amos 5:6–7, 10–15, those who chose to ignore the Law and its ideals of truth, justice, and mercy were bringing judgment on the entire "house of Joseph." Injustice was rampant, not as a result of God's absence, but because of the many sins of the northern kingdom's landowners, who were using unfair practices against smaller rural landowners to accumulate more and more land.

What Amos found among the house of Joseph was an illusory, mock practice of justice and truth and an outright disregard and abhorrence of its pursuit among those who should have been most familiar with God's brand of justice. The descendants of Joseph, one of the biblical narrative's most merciful characters, diluted justice and distorted its practice. The seeds of bitterness were sown among the victims of these distortions of justice.

Similarly, we have witnessed modern democratic nations—many with high ideals of freedom, liberty, and equal rights for all written into their founding documents or codified in law—establish systems of justice that are incongruent with their expressed national precepts. The resulting injustices have led to an erosion of individual and economic rights and eventual social unrest. We recall, for example, the United Kingdom's occupation and rule of India, the colonization of Afrikaners in South Africa, and the United States' slavery and Jim Crow laws.

In recent memory, we have the maltreatment of migrants seeking "justice in the gate" (Amos 5:15) along the US border. These migrants have been turned away or imprisoned, or have seen their families divided—mothers and fathers from their children—as they seek economic opportunity, safety from wars of violence, and relief from poverty. At the gates of America's borders it is difficult to find our expressed ideals of life, liberty, and the pursuit of happiness.

The northern kingdom had an identity linked to their covenant with the Lord. Their God is not indifferent or aloof, but angered by injustice. God watches God's people and promises to wield righteous judgment if the people do not change their ways (Amos 5:11, 12, 15).

Without the presence of justice in the places where it should be most easily accessible, life itself disappears. The pursuit of those seeking justice becomes an abiding source of bitterness, turning justice into "wormwood" (v. 7). Mercy and justice can no longer be found; instead, what are found are obstacles to a life of freedom, peace, and prosperity.

While the judicial malpractitioners expect their actions of "trampling on the poor" and collecting "levies of grain" (v. 11) to lead to riches and enhanced lives, Amos delivers the message that God has other plans. The physical markers of their ill-gotten abundance will not enrich their lives. The Lord will ensure that the benefits of their fine houses and vineyards lead them *away* from life. Without houses that can be lived in, or vineyards where fruit provides food, comfort, and drink, those at the city gates will become like those they have tossed aside: empty, lacking, starved, bitter, and seeking mercy.

Amos reminds the people that the righteous practice of justice is not out of reach. To seek justice is to seek life is to seek God. The precursors to the establishment of justice in the gate are an active hatred of evil and love of good, a justice of observable mercy, not mere words or ideals. There is a pathway back to justice. The first steps require one to love good wherever it may be found and to reject evil outright. Amos insists that this is the only way back to a life worth living—a life in the presence of God. To enter into God's presence, one must not remain among the "prudent" who "keep silent" (v. 13).

Our Specific and Unique Loyalty

Israel had been accustomed to prophets—that is, persons who claimed to have been sent by the Lord to speak the will of God in the lives of the people of Israel. I put it in this awkward fashion because Israel's prophets did not just tell the people of Israel the will of God. They came to enforce it. In about the middle of the eighth century and continuing then through the seventh century, and through the time of exile and for a time after the exile, a movement among the prophets arose proclaiming something religiously unprecedented: Israel's own God, they proclaimed, was responsible for their exile! . . . [T]hese prophets insisted that the Lord God of Israel is so much God that even when his own people are undone, he is the one who has undone them. Now why had the Lord done this? The prophets involved in this movement said there were two reasons: one was the prevalence of injustice in the lives of Israelites. The lives of Israel, according to the prophets at least, were permeated with violence, false witness, adultery, theft, and so on. And second, idolatry. That is to say, if indeed the Lord was the specific God of this specific people, then they owed him their specific and unique loyalty. In fact, throughout their whole history until the exile, the people of Israel were characteristically quite happy to worship the Lord God so long as there were other gods to worship too.

Robert Jenson, *A Theology in Outline: Can These Bones Live?* (New York: Oxford University Press USA, 2016), 22–23.

Silence is kept only to avoid the experience of suffering that may come if one speaks against wrongdoing. Turning away from injustice and saying nothing in an "evil time" leads to a perpetuation of, and an increase in, suffering; one's avoidance and complacency become accessories to injustice and evil. Amos chooses to enter into unjust suffering.

What does the righteous pursuit of God's justice look like for an individual in times when God seems absent or hard to find? What does it look like when an individual is faithfully seeking to live in the presence of God? Should the pursuer of justice remain motionless, paralyzed by the pain of injustice? Does the search for justice in such cases take on a different shape? What actions should guide the pursuit of justice when it is difficult to obtain? Where should one look for justice?

Job offers a surprising perspective on those times when God is silent and injustice overwhelms us. He goes directly and defiantly to the source—to God in "his dwelling" (Job 23:3b)—to gain a just verdict for his complaint.

Modern examples of justice-seeking remind us that momentum for justice movements often comes in surprising ways and from unusual places. Many movements are led by individuals who are willing to pursue justice at the source, using new forms for achieving it. Mahatma Gandhi entered the halls of British imperial power after creating homespun clothes and marching to the sea for salt. Labor leader César Chávez sought higher wages with the United Farm Workers through activism and campaigns in the lawmaking halls of the United States. Nelson Mandela used his prison cell as the bullhorn for his calls for justice in the South African fight against apartheid. Martin Luther King challenged the power of Jim Crow[4] laws enforcing racial segregation through peaceful marches, the first of which was over the Edmund Pettus Bridge in Selma, Alabama.

The powers that be, of course, have the ability to ignore the protests, hedge their bets, and wait for things to settle down. Fortunately, history tells a different story in these instances, though the extent to which the injustices of poverty, unfair wages, white supremacy, and imperial power have been lessened is a dangling and prescient question.

There is a different power at play in Job. Job keeps his understanding of God rooted in the hope that God is just and will always listen and

---

4. The term "Jim Crow" originally served as a derisive term for a Black man in the post–Civil War South.

offer mercy and restoration. If God is not just and merciful, can justice and mercy exist in the cosmos?

In what places is justice conspicuously absent? How might our churches become places of refuge and action on behalf of those who are seeking justice? How does the church vigorously seek justice, filling the void where justice is not present? What are some creative and surprising ways churches might make justice known in unforeseen places? What actions might we take that would create justice outside of the regular channels?

Civil right activists, Gandhi, Chavez, King, and Mandela knew that their cries for justice would eventually be heard. They understood that "the arc of the universe is long and it bends towards justice," as King shared in his baccalaureate sermon at Wesleyan University in 1964.[5] Job knows this too. If only Job *could* "vanish in darkness" (Job 23:17); but, as this verse indicates, he *cannot* escape God's justice, because he knows his shouts of despair and anguish will be answered by God in time (v. 7).

BRADY BANKS

---

5. A paraphrase from a sermon titled "Of Justice and the Conscience," by abolitionist Theodore Parker, published in 1853. The full text of King's baccalaureate sermon is archived at Wesleyan University Library Special Collections and Archives-Media Collection, Middletown, CT.

Proper 23 (Sunday between October 9 and October 15)

Psalm 22:1–15

[1]My God, my God, why have you forsaken me?
  Why are you so far from helping me, from the words of my groaning?
[2]O my God, I cry by day, but you do not answer;
  and by night, but find no rest.

[3]Yet you are holy,
  enthroned on the praises of Israel.
[4]In you our ancestors trusted;
  they trusted, and you delivered them.
[5]To you they cried, and were saved;
  in you they trusted, and were not put to shame.

[6]But I am a worm, and not human;
  scorned by others, and despised by the people.
[7]All who see me mock at me;
  they make mouths at me, they shake their heads;
[8]"Commit your cause to the LORD; let him deliver—
  let him rescue the one in whom he delights!"

[9]Yet it was you who took me from the womb;
  you kept me safe on my mother's breast.
[10]On you I was cast from my birth,
  and since my mother bore me you have been my God.
[11]Do not be far from me,
  for trouble is near
  and there is no one to help.

[12]Many bulls encircle me,
  strong bulls of Bashan surround me;
[13]they open wide their mouths at me,
  like a ravening and roaring lion.

[14]I am poured out like water,
  and all my bones are out of joint;
my heart is like wax;
  it is melted within my breast;
[15]my mouth is dried up like a potsherd,
  and my tongue sticks to my jaws;
  you lay me in the dust of death.

Psalm 90:12–17

[12]So teach us to count our days
  that we may gain a wise heart.

[13]Turn, O LORD! How long?
  Have compassion on your servants!

¹⁴Satisfy us in the morning with your steadfast love,
  so that we may rejoice and be glad all our days.
¹⁵Make us glad as many days as you have afflicted us,
  and as many years as we have seen evil.
¹⁶Let your work be manifest to your servants,
  and your glorious power to their children.
¹⁷Let the favor of the Lord our God be upon us,
  and prosper for us the work of our hands—
  O prosper the work of our hands!

Connecting the Psalm with Scripture and Worship

Psalm 22:1–15. Psalms of lament and psalms of praise are often interwoven in the Psalter. Psalm 22 begins with a cry of distress: "My God, my God, why have you forsaken me?" (Ps. 22:1), then changes to an expression of trust: "Yet you are holy, enthroned on the praises of Israel. In you our ancestors trusted; and you delivered them" (vv. 3–4). The psalm then returns to lament, "But I am a worm" (v. 6), then to trust, "Yet it was you who took me from the womb; you kept me safe on my mother's breast" (v. 9), and back again to lament, "you lay me in the dust of death" (v. 15).

"The simultaneity of complaint and praise," is interpreted by biblical scholars as "an expression of the perennial reality of the life of faith."[1] This pattern is interrupted by a lone prayer of petition: "Do not be far from me, for trouble is near and there is no one to help" (v. 11), revealing a deep relationship in which the psalmist's cry is not for blessings, but only for Yahweh's presence. This call for divine presence echoes throughout the psalms. Like the psalms on either side—with praise for "the joy of your presence" (21:6) and trust that "even though I walk through the darkest valley, I fear no evil; for you are with me" (23:4)—Psalm 22 expresses the Israelites' persistent longing to behold the face of God.

This yearning for God's presence is palpable in the reading from Job, whose contemptuous response to Eliphaz reveals his problem with God's absence: "Oh, that I knew where I might find him" (Job 23:3). Yet God remains elusive:

"If I go forward, he is not there; or backward, I cannot perceive him; on the left he hides, and I cannot behold him; I turn to the right, but I cannot see him" (vv. 8–9).

The lessons from Job and the psalm shed light on times of despair that are part of the journey of faith and give voice to the question of God's absence. To answer the question, the preacher can turn to the other readings, which assure us of God's presence. In Hebrews, the presence of Jesus as the great high priest allows the author to issue an invitation for all: "Let us therefore approach the throne of grace with boldness, so that we may receive mercy and find grace to help in time of need" (Heb. 4:16). In the Gospel lesson, Jesus invites a man to give up his possessions and "follow me" (Mark 10:21). When he cannot, the crowd asks, "Then who can be saved?" (v. 26). Jesus answers, "For mortals it is impossible, but not for God; for God all things are possible" (v. 27). Indeed, it is only through God's sacrificial love that we are saved.

Psalm 22 has an obvious connection to the Gospel story, as Jesus uttered the same words from the cross: "My God, my God, why have you forsaken me?" (Mark 15:34). "By telling the story of Jesus using Psalm 22, the Gospel writers affirm that in Jesus' faithful suffering, as in the psalmist's faithful suffering, God was present."[2] The preacher can tie the Scripture readings together by reminding people that the God who suffered for us is powerfully present with us, even and especially in the midst of our suffering. This is a cause for praise.

---

1. J. Clinton McCann Jr., "The Book of Psalms," in *The New Interpreter's Bible* (Nashville: Abingdon, 1996), 4:646.
2. McCann, "The Book of Psalms," 766.

This relationship between lament and praise can be enacted liturgically. As a call to worship, the congregation can sing "Surely the Presence of the Lord Is in This Place" and as a response after the final blessing, "God Be with You Till We Meet Again." Worshipers might also sing hymns that express lament, such as "Lord, Why Have You Forsaken Me"; trust, as in "There Is a Place of Quiet Rest"; and thanksgiving for God's presence, as heard in "God Is Here."

Psalm 22 allows us to hold our deepest lament and highest praise in holy harmony.

Psalm 90:12–17. The nearly fifty psalms preceding Psalm 90 capture the laments of people who have lost their land, temple, and monarchy. In a strange place and uncertain time, they are crying out. With the unique superscript, "A Prayer of Moses, the man of God," Psalm 90 is a fitting response from the man who led their ancestors to the promised land to remind people of God's faithfulness. It begins with a strong affirmation of holy place: "Lord, you have been our dwelling place in all generations" (Ps. 90:1) and holy time: "from everlasting to everlasting, you are God" (v. 2). The selected pericope begins with a prayer of pleasure, "So teach us to count our days that we may gain a wise heart" (v. 12), but moves quickly to a petition, "Satisfy us in the morning with your steadfast love, so that we may rejoice and be glad all our days" (v. 14). Moses reminds the people that just as God answered the prayers of the Israelites in the wilderness and fed them with manna (Exod. 16), so we can depend on God to nourish us with new mercies, giving us strength and hope. The psalmist continues with prayers for God to "make us glad" (Ps. 90:15), "let your work be manifest" (v. 16), and "let the favor of the Lord our God be upon us" (v. 17). Only one is repeated: "prosper for us the work of our hands—O prosper the work of our hands" (v. 17). This emphasis on the work is evident in the Amos reading, with its repeated calls to active engagement: "seek the Lord and live" (Amos 5:6), "seek good and not evil, so that you may live, and so the Lord, the God of hosts, will be with you" (v. 14), "hate evil and love good. . . . the Lord will be gracious" (v. 15). The psalm's focus on "prospering the work of our hands" is echoed in Amos's call to "seek the Lord." Both express confidence that our efforts will be used and blessed for God's purpose, so that our time in this place becomes meaningful.

From the pulpit, a message of the redemptive power of God that transcends time and yet is grounded in our time would speak a word people need to hear. A preacher might focus on the ways that our work—whether teaching Sunday school, rocking a child in the nursery, singing a solo, serving a meal at a homeless shelter, or visiting a hospital or jail—shows that we seek to do good, and we pray that God will bless our efforts to be the hands of Christ on earth. Realizing "how hard it will be for those who have wealth to enter the kingdom of God" (Mark 10:23), Jesus calls people to follow, not with clenched fists, but with open hands and hearts.

Liturgically, this psalm provides a call to worship with the words "Satisfy us in the morning with your steadfast love, so we may rejoice and be glad (in this day and) all our days." It also offers words of response, in "Prosper the work of our hands," that can be expressed in singing a hymn such as "What Does the Lord Require of You?" The theme of the psalm can be reinforced by singing "O God, Our Help in Ages Past," "Take My Life," or "The Church's One Foundation."

Psalm 90 is both a reassuring reminder of God's faithful presence and a rousing call to use our gifts to change the world for good.

DONNA GIVER-JOHNSTON

Hebrews 4:12–16

[12]Indeed, the word of God is living and active, sharper than any two-edged sword, piercing until it divides soul from spirit, joints from marrow; it is able to judge the thoughts and intentions of the heart. [13]And before him no creature is hidden, but all are naked and laid bare to the eyes of the one to whom we must render an account.

[14]Since, then, we have a great high priest who has passed through the heavens, Jesus, the Son of God, let us hold fast to our confession. [15]For we do not have a high priest who is unable to sympathize with our weaknesses, but we have one who in every respect has been tested as we are, yet without sin. [16]Let us therefore approach the throne of grace with boldness, so that we may receive mercy and find grace to help in time of need.

Commentary 1: Connecting the Reading with Scripture

The theme of rest is introduced in the fourth chapter of Hebrews and carries throughout the homily. Rest is a goal, a promise for believers. The prospect of rest for a persecuted and weary group was likely a welcome message. The writer of Hebrews not only reminds the audience of the good news that has been proclaimed to them; he also instructs that rest remains available to the faithful and obedient. While the promise of rest is good news, this word of exhortation (Heb. 13:22) emphasizes the need to remain obedient and faithful until the very end to obtain this reward.

The exhortation in this passage, and of the homily as a whole, is to hold firmly to the confession of faith. Jesus is the affirmation of this faith. He is both the object and subject, an exemplar for others to emulate. There is no need to hide in the presence of an omnipresent God. On the contrary, the good news is that faith in Jesus Christ ignites boldness, even as the word of God strips us of all our pretenses and removes anything that covers our truest self. When we are weak and weary, there is a place we can go to—the throne of grace where we are met by a sympathetic high priest who extends mercy. Hebrews beckons the believer to draw close to God, particularly in their time of need.

One way to draw close to God is by studying the word of God. The writer of Hebrews describes the word of God as living and active. The Gospel of John similarly describes the word as living: "And the Word became flesh and *lived* among us, and we have seen his glory, the glory as of a father's only son, full of grace and truth" (John 1:14, italics mine). While the Gospel writer declares Jesus to be the very Word of God, the writer of Hebrews illuminates another aspect: the word of God also functions as a judge. In the Gospel of John, the Word became flesh; here, the word pierces the flesh. The word of God is similarly described as a sword of the Spirit in Ephesians 6:17. Describing the word as a sharp, two-edged sword means that the word not only interprets the law as a judge; it also exposes one's innermost being. It cuts both ways, both executing judgment and extending mercy. This sword gets to the heart of the matter.

Nothing is hidden before God (Rom. 8:27; 1 Cor. 4:5; and 1 Thess. 2:4). One's intentions and the thoughts of the heart are brought to the light. The word of God strips one down, layer by layer, dividing and separating until the innermost condition is visible. We are exposed before the one to whom we must give an account for our deeds and our intentions. The emphasis, here, is on both our actions and the reasoning behind our actions. This exposure of naked truth results in a kind of vulnerability that brings to mind the narrative of Adam and Eve in Genesis 2:25: "The man and his wife were both naked, and were *not* ashamed" (italics mine). The revelation is for humanity; sin opens *our* eyes to our nakedness. Yet we must learn that vulnerability and shame are not synonymous, because all of creation is naked before God.

To be "laid bare to the eyes" of God reminds us that God is a God who sees. Hagar's identification of God as "El-roi," the God who sees, affirms this assertion: "So she named the LORD who spoke to her, 'You are El-roi'; for she said, 'Have I really seen God and remained alive after seeing him?'" (Gen. 16:13). It is a two-way exchange; God sees and is revealed. Hagar is seen by God and sees God.

Like Hagar, the audience of this homily is experiencing trials that are testing their faith. God sees and responds. Recognizing that God sees us should not be met solely with fear and trepidation. One should also have a sense of eager anticipation, knowing that the God who sees is also the God who reveals Godself and responds with mercy and grace. When Moses asks to see God, God responds: "I will make all my goodness pass before you, and will proclaim before you the name, 'The LORD'; and I will be gracious to whom I will be gracious, and will show mercy on whom I will show mercy" (Exod. 33:19). The revelation of God is accompanied by the manifestation of God's goodness, grace, and mercy. Judgment is one aspect of the sword. It is important to recognize that the word of God is also compassionate. The word of God is, indeed, two-edged.

The expectation that grace and mercy are available in time of need and vulnerability is bolstered by the fact that Jesus serves as a great high priest (introduced earlier in the text in Heb. 2:17 and 3:1). As our high priest, Jesus is not disappointed or saddened by our weakness but empathizes with it, having experienced it himself. Weakness is mentioned three more times in this homily (Heb. 5:2; 7:28; and 11:34).

Paul also emphasizes weakness, concluding that God's "grace is sufficient for you, for power is made perfect in weakness." Consequently, Paul opted to "boast all the more gladly of my weaknesses, so that the power of Christ may dwell in me. Therefore I am content with weaknesses, insults, hardships, persecutions, and calamities for the sake of Christ; for whenever I am weak, then I am strong" (2 Cor. 12:9–10). Weakness is not a permanent condition for the believer. Paul describes it as transactional. Weakness can result in the revelation of God's power. The audience, and by extension we, should find assurance in having an empathetic high priest. This is one way that Jesus' priesthood is distinctive.

Jesus' priesthood is unique in that he is a priest who has been tested but has never sinned. Just as Jesus' faith was met with opposition, believers, too, can anticipate challenges to their faith. However, such tests should not result in the loss of faith. Rather, it is the confession of one's faith that enables believers *boldly* to approach God in pursuit of grace and mercy. Jesus breached the boundaries between heaven and earth to be seated at the right hand of God the Father and forever to intercede on behalf of believers (see Heb. 12:2).

Jesus has cleared the path, and the believer needs only to walk it. The believers' prayers can pierce heaven and be embraced by a high priest who made a once-and-for-all offering on behalf of all our sins (see Heb. 10:14). Jesus, as the Son of God, is uniquely qualified as a high priest. The writer of Hebrews is teaching his audience that they, too, are uniquely positioned; having Jesus as a high priest provides unprecedented access to the throne of grace. What makes these confessors unique from all others who have to stand before the judgment of God? They have an intercessor who has made straight their path to the one who can offer them assistance in their time of need.

The writer of Hebrews seems well aware of the potential power contained in words. His rhetorical prowess is evidence of this. Understanding the word of God as sharp, active, and living, reminds believers that their confession, words, and steadfast faith have the potential to bring about their desired rest. They can find respite, even in difficult times, knowing that they have access to a gracious and merciful God.

JENNIFER T. KAALUND

Commentary 2: Connecting the Reading with the World

Several decades ago, I was with a group of Christian educators in western Tennessee for several days of retreat and reflection. We began each day in worship, sitting in an oval in the meeting room of the conference center. The person leading us stood in our midst toward one end of the oval and was reading a psalm aloud. It felt as though the psalm were addressing us, taking up our experiences into its words. As the reading continued, and without warning, my mind's eye seemed to zoom out and hover like a drone viewing this scene from above. It struck me in that instant that, from an outsider-looking-in perspective, this all could seem very strange, even odd. Here we were, a couple dozen reasonably sane people listening to a reading from an ancient text! You know, a scene out of a fantasy or a science-fiction film.

The scene was more meaning-laden than that. Tolkien-esque, perhaps. Somewhat monastic, but happening right now among a group of ordinaries. We listened as the ancient text spoke to our pains and struggles, anticipated our hopes and dreams, tugged on us for loyalty to a divine voice, and guided our wills and actions—almost like a cultish coven, but not. It was something more profound. The ancient text was speaking into being what now is our reality and welcoming that which is yet to come.

The preacher of this text might point out to the congregation that, earlier in the chapter where our text is to be found, the author was assuming something like the experience I have described. The first-century reader is placed before an ancient text (Ps. 95). The text echoes God's ancient promise of entering his Sabbath rest. "Today," the author reads on, "if you hear his voice, do not harden your hearts." It is presumed that the "today" was the author's and the hearer's own day. You, the author says, are in the "today" of which the ancient text speaks. The promised Sabbath rest remains to be entered! What we read here in an ancient text (to us), is that text's reading of a still more ancient text (to that day's readers). In both cases, the ancient text speaks now, about now.

It is against this backdrop that the author gathers together a masterful description of what the word of God is like (Heb. 4:12–13). Scalpel and laserlike, coming as it does in the ancient texts, the word of God is living and active (now!). It is incisive; it divides what is indivisible. It discriminates the thoughts and intentions of the heart and lays them bare. No hiding or confusion is left. Everything is made clear.

These lofty statements about the word of God in Hebrews 4, then, do not supply an affirmation about the Bible that is merely theoretical. The teachings of this text, rather, have on-the-ground application to our day-to-day lives. They lead us to reckon with what the living and active word of God does, now, as the ancients reckoned with it then (their now).

In the general climate of present-day life, listening to ancient texts in this way does seem very odd, if not naive. The secularized spirit of the age has little place for it in its imagination. Certainly, it values all sorts of ancient texts as providing historical and philosophical information and perspective, perhaps even entertainment. It does so, though, not in the way that welcomes them as the schema for understanding life and its destiny or for guiding personal choices and patterns of life. It is not viewed as divine word.

Perhaps it is Canadian theologian-philosopher Charles Taylor who has put his finger on the nature of the secularized spirit of the age in his helpful book *A Secular Age*.[1] Engaging the debate about what, exactly, is the dynamic of secularization that has become so prevalent in the current age, he suggests that the normal depictions of the waning of religion in Western industrial societies, or the displacement of religion to a more marginal role in public life, are insufficient for grasping the nature of the shift that has been underway. He offers another explanation. Five hundred years ago, he says, we lived in a society in which a belief in a God, such as the one described in the Bible, was so presumed that it would have been hard, if not

---

1. Charles Taylor, *A Secular Age* (Boston: Harvard University Press, 1992).

virtually impossible, *not* to believe in such a God. Today, five hundred years later, we share in a society in which belief in such a God is not at all presumed and is in fact very difficult to hold. In other words, there has been a major shift over time in the societal "conditions of belief." In such a social order, reading an ancient text in the way Christians continue to do would indeed seem odd, or strange, or worse.

What has been borne along in the Christian tradition of the worship of God has been just this: listening to the ancient texts. Living in the recognition of what is set forth in Hebrews 4:12–13 about the nature and functional reality of the "word of God," is a move against the grain of general thinking. Yet it remains an intrinsic practice for the formation of the people of God. All are invited to join in the practice.

The other thread that runs through the church's liturgy is the prayers of the people. The word and the prayers are continuously intertwined. The liturgy is a dialogue, a dance, of listening and speaking. God speaks, and we listen. In response, we speak, and God listens—and so on. Recognizing such a dance in the history of Christian worship makes it all the more remarkable to find in Hebrews 4 a dynamic, if unpredictable, union of these two threads. Immediately, once the nature of the word of God has been depicted, the author exhorts the readers, "let us hold fast to our confession" and "let us therefore approach the throne of grace with boldness" (4:14–16).

Why is it that this brief text so starkly places these two threads together? Regarding the first thread, it affirms that the word of God "judges" thoughts and intentions of the heart and all creatures are "naked and laid bare" before the eyes of "the one to whom we must render an account" (vv. 12–13). That is what implicates the need for the second thread, "Let us therefore approach the throne of grace . . . so that we may receive mercy and find grace to help in time of need" (v. 16). Whenever the word of God pierces and judges, it leaves us in need of mercy and grace. Hearing and praying are bound together.

Why must we make that move? How dare we do so? Because, the author says, "we have a great high priest . . . , Jesus, the Son of God" (4:14; cf. 2:17 and 3:1). He also was addressed by the ancient texts and faced the same tests of loyalty that we face, "yet without sin" (cf. Luke 4:1–13). He sympathizes with our weaknesses. He leads us to pray in boldness at a throne unlike any we have ever known—not a throne of "Games," of power and revenge, of vindictive violence. It is that most unusual of thrones: a throne of grace. A throne you run to when overcome by disappointment, failure, shame, or guilt. A throne where you find mercy and help.

GEORGE R. HUNSBERGER

Mark 10:17–31

[17]As he was setting out on a journey, a man ran up and knelt before him, and asked him, "Good Teacher, what must I do to inherit eternal life?" [18]Jesus said to him, "Why do you call me good? No one is good but God alone. [19]You know the commandments: 'You shall not murder; You shall not commit adultery; You shall not steal; You shall not bear false witness; You shall not defraud; Honor your father and mother.'" [20]He said to him, "Teacher, I have kept all these since my youth." [21]Jesus, looking at him, loved him and said, "You lack one thing; go, sell what you own, and give the money to the poor, and you will have treasure in heaven; then come, follow me." [22]When he heard this, he was shocked and went away grieving, for he had many possessions.

[23]Then Jesus looked around and said to his disciples, "How hard it will be for those who have wealth to enter the kingdom of God!" [24]And the disciples were perplexed at these words. But Jesus said to them again, "Children, how hard it is to enter the kingdom of God! [25]It is easier for a camel to go through the eye of a needle than for someone who is rich to enter the kingdom of God." [26]They were greatly astounded and said to one another, "Then who can be saved?" [27]Jesus looked at them and said, "For mortals it is impossible, but not for God; for God all things are possible."

[28]Peter began to say to him, "Look, we have left everything and followed you." [29]Jesus said, "Truly I tell you, there is no one who has left house or brothers or sisters or mother or father or children or fields, for my sake and for the sake of the good news, [30]who will not receive a hundredfold now in this age—houses, brothers and sisters, mothers and children, and fields, with persecutions—and in the age to come eternal life. [31]But many who are first will be last, and the last will be first."

Commentary 1: Connecting the Reading with Scripture

Mark 10 is part of a transitional section in this Gospel. Many scholars group chapters 8:22–10:52 together, since they begin and end with the healing of a blind man (Mark 8:22–26; 10:46–52). This section also records Jesus' travel with his disciples on the road to Jerusalem, where he will experience rejection, crucifixion, and, as promised by him, his resurrection (10:34). As is customary in Mark, Jesus traveled rapidly from place to place. His journey took him throughout Galilee (8:22–9:50), then southward to the region of "Judea beyond the Jordan" (10:1–31) on a road "up to Jerusalem" (10:32–45) and Jericho (10:46–52), teaching and healing along the way. In spite of Jesus' repeated teachings about his identity and the importance of serving one another, no one seemed to understand.

As he traveled, Jesus was confronted by a variety of people wanting to see him. One of them was the wealthy man we read about in this week's lectionary. Unlike the children in 10:13–16 and blind Bartimaeus in 10:46–52, this man, literally the "*one*" (Gk. *heis*, v. 17), was not prevented from approaching Jesus. We know only that this man ran toward Jesus and, kneeling before him, perhaps gasping, asked, "Good Teacher, what must I do to inherit eternal life?" (10:17). His hurried approach could communicate an earnest desire for knowledge and, more importantly, an anxiety about eternal life.

The man's presence interrupted Jesus' travel, yet Jesus delayed in order to talk with him. Jesus' disciples, so keen to disrupt the children's approach the day before, did not prevent this one from advancing. The man's easy access to Jesus is in stark contrast to the struggle the children, and those caring for them, faced (10:13–16). This flies in the face of our own biases inside and outside church settings. Although readers may be tempted to think the disciples have learned their lesson that Jesus is no respecter of persons, later exchanges demonstrate otherwise. In 10:46–52, the disciples attempt to keep blind Bartimaeus from interrupting Jesus' journey into Jerusalem. Jesus' indignant response to favoring the rich over the poor (10:14, 49) resonates with the lectionary reading in Amos 5:11–13, 24.

The confused disciples questioned Jesus (10:23–31), repeatedly misunderstanding his message about the coming passion and his vision of a new reign where "the one who wishes to be first must be last of all and servant of all" (9:35; 10:43–44). The series of characters in Mark 10:13–52 is preceded by a confrontation from another corner: a group of Pharisees who queried Jesus with the goal of "testing" rather than learning from him (10:2–9).

In contrast to these characters, the wealthy man showed submission and respect before Jesus. Unlike the Pharisees, he did not want to test Jesus; he wanted to learn what he needed to do "to inherit eternal life." Nevertheless, Jesus did not seem impressed. Jesus questioned the man's decision to call him "good," since the only *one* (Gk. *heis*) who is "good" is God (Deut. 6:4–5), and he reminded him of the commandments. On the surface, Jesus' list of commandments seems to contrast the one he gave a scribe in Mark 12:28–34. In this later passage, Jesus quoted first from Deuteronomy 6:5, which emphasizes utter devotion to God, and then from Leviticus 19:18, where God calls for "lov[ing] your neighbor as yourself." A closer look, however, reveals Mark 10 to be in harmony with the list in Mark 12:28–34. Jesus alludes to Deuteronomy 6:4 in Mark 10:18 with the reminder that "no one is good but God alone" (Gk. *heis*). As in Mark 12, Jesus first establishes God's unique goodness and worth before listing additional commandments about loving others (10:19; 12:31). For Jesus, as

for Old Testament prophets, believers ought to live in ways that reflect God's identity.

Once again, the wealthy man seemed to answer aptly: "Teacher, I have kept all these since my youth." Jesus, however, was again unimpressed. Instead, he showed his love by speaking truthfully to the man: "You lack *one thing*" (Gk. *hen*) (v. 21). Despite keeping God's commandments, this certain "one" was still missing "one thing," perhaps the most important *one* of all. Jesus' command for the man to sell all his possessions and give the money to the poor shocked and grieved the man, who was once eager to hear Jesus' words. He had too many things to give up. The comfort and status that his money afforded him was impossible for him to surrender (10:26–27)!

The lectionary sets the wealthy man in Mark 10 alongside another rich man, Job. The man in Mark 10 feared the loss of his many possessions. Job, on the other hand, had experienced losing everything, and he was angry. In Job 23, he complained against God, emphasizing his righteousness in contrast to what he deemed to be God's unjust treatment of him. "I would lay my case before him, and fill my mouth with arguments. I would learn what he would answer me, and understand what he would say to me" (Job 23:4–5). Like the man in Mark 10, Job was running up to his Lord, confident in his own righteousness, and he, too, was not ready to hear the answer he would receive (40:3–5).

Jesus' words in Mark 10:21 may sound harsh to contemporary ears, especially those of us affluent enough not to struggle to eat and have a roof over our heads. Although it is tempting to make Jesus' words more palatable, Mark challenges us to consider Jesus' responses and imitate him. Even though the rich man is earnest and knows his commandments, his focus is on the wrong thing, *his* life. Jesus admonished that "if any want to become my followers, let them deny themselves . . . and follow me. For those who want to save their life will lose it, and those who lose their life for my sake, and for the sake of the gospel, will save it" (Mark 8:34–35). The wealthy man is at an impasse; he wants to save his life without losing it first (10:17–22).

The disciples were perplexed by Jesus' words and questioned him (10:23–31). "Then who can be saved?" they asked. Jesus responded to them just as God did to Job; salvation is God's doing from God's own righteousness, rather than something people can gain on their own (Job 38:1–40:2). "For mortals it is impossible, but not for God; for God all things are possible" (Mark 10:27).

Peter's question in 10:28 reveals that he (and the disciples), once again, had not understood: "we have left everything and followed you!" Peter insisted that, unlike the rich man who walked away, *he* (and the disciples) had earned their reward. Even though there is some truth to Peter's words—they had left their families and old livelihood behind (1:16–20)—they are not unblemished. Peter reprimanded Jesus concerning his passion predictions (8:31–34) and the

disciples jockeyed to be the "first" or the greatest (9:33–35; 10:35–45) among them. In contrast to the wealthy man who walked away *and* the disciples who remained with him, the only character in Mark 10 who really understood is Bartimaeus, who threw off his cloak and followed Jesus into Jerusalem (10:50–52). The last one in this chapter becomes the first (10:31).

For preaching, one may have hearers explore with which character they identify most and why. What constitutes our individual and/or communal impasse to following Jesus? Does it lie in our treatment of others? In a desire for security, prestige? Regardless, Jesus continues to beckon us to follow his example.

ALICIA D. MYERS

Commentary 2: Connecting the Reading with the World

This Gospel lesson invites us to pay attention to and honor our Jewish roots while also challenging us to live into the world in a new way. Jesus speaks to the young man as a Jewish teacher. His first instructions to the young man are to follow the commandments that God has given the Israelites through Moses. Though we clearly know that Jesus was a Jew, often we do not highlight that fact in our sermons and teachings. Yet it is clear, from the very beginning of his ministry, when he read from Isaiah 61:1–2 (Luke 4:14–21) and declared the prophecy fulfilled, right to the very last night of his life, when he celebrated the Passover with his disciples (Matt. 26:17–19; Mark 14:12–16; Luke 22:7–13), that Jesus was a devout Jew. Not to consider this is to miss a central part both of who Jesus is and who we are called to be.

Like the young man, we are called to know the commandments and to recognize them as foundational to our life as Christians. It is tempting to place the commandments in public places for people to see, for instance. This misses the point: knowing them is not enough. Jesus expects us to live by them. It is after the young man asserted that he had indeed lived by them that Jesus looked at him and "loved him." That the young man was living the life of a devout

Jew calls forth love from Jesus, another devout Jew. This is one of the readings that connects our faith and beliefs as Christians to the faith and beliefs of those of the Jewish faith. To take this knowledge seriously is also to take up the task of inviting our congregations into a deeper consideration of the church's beginnings as a Jewish sect. What might it ask us to explore about our core beliefs, our relationship with present-day Jews, and our understanding of both religious and civil history?

It is revealing that the commandments Jesus highlighted include one that is not one of the ten. We know that Jesus knows his commandments, so it is not a mistake that he includes "thou shalt not defraud" with the other five. While this commandment is not one of the ten, it is, nevertheless, one that is often repeated in the Hebrew Scripture—not to cheat, especially the widow and orphan (Lev. 6:2; 19:13; 19:35; Amos 8:4–7; and Isa. 10:1–2).

That Jesus chooses to highlight not to defraud others is important because he is speaking to a wealthy young man. Be aware of how you make and maintain your wealth, is the message. This message was important in Jesus' time, as we see in the results of Jesus' interaction with Zacchaeus, the tax collector (Luke 19:1–10).

Those with power and influence would cheat and cause the poor and the weak to pay more than the fair price for goods and services. Thus, Jesus added the admonition against defrauding to the core commandments to emphasize that how wealth is accumulated is important.

That message is just as important in our time. We seem to be enthralled by wealth, as evidenced by the popularity of TV shows like *Lifestyles of the Rich and Famous, The Real Housewives*, and so on. Such shows do not provoke us to examine wealth's sources; they simply encourage us to be impressed by it. As we see the gap between the rich and the not-rich widening, how wealth is achieved and maintained should be a challenge we raise with our congregations and with ourselves. What would a world look like where we really lived into the commandments that Jesus required of the young man?

In working with this reading, we may be tempted to concentrate on the young man's wealth. After all, Jesus told him to sell all that he owned, give the money to the poor, and follow him (v. 21). Later, explaining his statement to the startled disciples, Jesus went further by saying that it is "easier for a camel to go through the eye of a needle than for someone who is rich to enter the kingdom of God" (Mark 10:25). Focusing on the perils of wealth may indeed offer a challenge to the hearers. However, since few of us believe ourselves as wealthy as we imagine the young man to be, we may end up feeling more relieved than challenged. The gospel, then, can be heard as a warning for only the very rich.

However, if we consider the rest of Jesus' words to his disciples, it is clear that Jesus was asking more of him than just to give up his money. Jesus was inviting him to give up what held him back from loving God completely. It was not wealth per se that was the young man's problem; it was his attachment to his possessions. He could not imagine a life without his possessions. He could not also imagine his worth without them. Jesus offered him a life without the security of things and with the assurance of what the young man said he wanted—eternal life.

If, as Christians, we claim that our aim is to be found worthy to live eternally with God, then the preacher may pose Jesus' challenge differently. If not on riches, on what other objects might we be centering our trust? What physical or nonphysical "things of the world" stop us from giving God our whole heart and make it hard for us to follow Jesus? What request from God would leave us shocked and grieving? Why?

Jesus is talking about the things that enthrall us to the point that we cannot fully accept God's sovereignty. From the very beginning of his ministry, when Jesus called the disciples, he made it clear that he needed them to drop everything and follow him. Peter reminded him that he was talking to those who had heeded his call (v. 28). Of what could Jesus assure them? Jesus stated what he promises his followers. Just as he added to the commandments highlighted for the wealthy young man, Jesus added a promise that did not seem to fit: the promise of persecution (v. 30). In the previous two chapters (chaps. 8 and 9), Jesus foretold his death and does so, again, immediately following our reading (10:32–34). This addition of the promise of persecution to the promises of family and wealth merits our attention.

How might we understand the message both of abundance and persecution that Jesus was trying to convey to the disciples? The reading begins with Jesus the devout Jew and ends with Jesus' promising the hard results of truly following him. It foretells the character of the life of the early church, whose members found family in one another, even as they faced persecution from the authorities.

Jesus offers several challenges we can take up as we preach the good news to our communities. Are we creating family as members of Christ's body? If we are accepted in places of power and recognized as part of the status quo, are we truly walking the new way of Jesus? If we are not being persecuted, does it mean we are failing fully to live out our faith? Are we showing the world what it means to trust God and love one another as brothers, sisters, mothers, fathers, and children? Are we honoring our Jewish roots and living out our call as a new community?

NONTOMBI NAOMI TUTU

Proper 24 (Sunday between October 16 and October 22)

Job 38:1–7 (34–41) and Isaiah 53:4–12
Psalm 104:1–9, 24, 35c and
   Psalm 91:9–16

Hebrews 5:1–10
Mark 10:35–45

Job 38:1–7 (34–41)

¹Then the LORD answered Job out of the whirlwind:

²"Who is this that darkens counsel by words without knowledge?
³Gird up your loins like a man,
   I will question you, and you shall declare to me.

⁴"Where were you when I laid the foundation of the earth?
   Tell me, if you have understanding.
⁵Who determined its measurements—surely you know!
   Or who stretched the line upon it?
⁶On what were its bases sunk,
   or who laid its cornerstone
⁷when the morning stars sang together
   and all the heavenly beings shouted for joy?
. . . .
³⁴"Can you lift up your voice to the clouds,
   so that a flood of waters may cover you?
³⁵Can you send forth lightnings, so that they may go
   and say to you, 'Here we are'?
³⁶Who has put wisdom in the inward parts,
   or given understanding to the mind?
³⁷Who has the wisdom to number the clouds?
   Or who can tilt the waterskins of the heavens,
³⁸when the dust runs into a mass
   and the clods cling together?

³⁹"Can you hunt the prey for the lion,
   or satisfy the appetite of the young lions,
⁴⁰when they crouch in their dens,
   or lie in wait in their covert?
⁴¹Who provides for the raven its prey,
   when its young ones cry to God,
   and wander about for lack of food?"

Isaiah 53:4–12

⁴Surely he has borne our infirmities
    and carried our diseases;
yet we accounted him stricken,
    struck down by God, and afflicted.
⁵But he was wounded for our transgressions,
    crushed for our iniquities;
upon him was the punishment that made us whole,
    and by his bruises we are healed.
⁶All we like sheep have gone astray;
    we have all turned to our own way,
and the LORD has laid on him
    the iniquity of us all.

⁷He was oppressed, and he was afflicted,
    yet he did not open his mouth;
like a lamb that is led to the slaughter,
    and like a sheep that before its shearers is silent,
    so he did not open his mouth.
⁸By a perversion of justice he was taken away.
    Who could have imagined his future?
For he was cut off from the land of the living,
    stricken for the transgression of my people.
⁹They made his grave with the wicked
    and his tomb with the rich,
although he had done no violence,
    and there was no deceit in his mouth.

¹⁰Yet it was the will of the LORD to crush him with pain.
When you make his life an offering for sin,
    he shall see his offspring, and shall prolong his days;
through him the will of the LORD shall prosper.
    ¹¹Out of his anguish he shall see light;
he shall find satisfaction through his knowledge.
    The righteous one, my servant, shall make many righteous,
    and he shall bear their iniquities.
¹²Therefore I will allot him a portion with the great,
    and he shall divide the spoil with the strong;
because he poured out himself to death,
    and was numbered with the transgressors;
yet he bore the sin of many,
    and made intercession for the transgressors.

Commentary 1: Connecting the Reading with Scripture

Job 38:1–7 (34–41). God's appearance from the midst of the whirlwind has been heavily anticipated throughout the book of Job's poetic dialogues. In those dialogues, Job and his friends debated the reasons for Job's suffering, framing Job's case within a broader debate about how the world works. They imagined that if God would only speak, God would reconcile for them the evidence of Job's experiences with the systems in which they believed. To this end, Zophar exclaimed, "O that God would speak, and . . . tell you the secrets of wisdom!" (Job 11:5–6a). Job responded, "I would speak to the Almighty, and I desire to argue my case with God" (13:3). Later he urged, "Let the Almighty answer me!" (31:35; cf. 23:3–5). Yet when the Almighty does speak, the answer seems to have little to do with the case Job hoped to argue.

God's first speech from the whirlwind (38:1–40:2) both bypasses the particulars of Job's case and confounds the more generalized, systematic notions of justice seemingly shared by Job and his friends. God decenters Job and humankind and instead highlights aspects of creation beyond human knowing and power. The speech emphasizes the limits of human understanding, the gulf between humans and God, and the wild freedom of the world God has created.

God's opening challenge to Job turns the tables on God's human interlocutor, demanding that Job answer God rather than the other way around (38:3). A series of rhetorical questions follows. The five questions in verses 4–7 focus on God's work in creation. God's first question to Job, "Where were you when I laid the foundation of the earth?" anticipates a negation: "I was not there." "I did not exist then." From there, God makes it clear to Job that there were others who *did* witness and celebrate God's primordial, architectural handiwork (v. 7) and perhaps even participated in it, as does Wisdom in the book of Proverbs (Prov. 8:22–31). Those witnesses and participants were not human.

This decentering of humankind continues in the poem's personification of stars (Job 38:7), sea (vv. 8–11), dawn (vv. 12–13), light and darkness (vv. 19–20), and lightning (v. 35), whereby it portrays a living and dynamic universe that responds to God's actions and voice. Job's voice commands no comparable obedience. Similarly, God's creation is populated with nonhuman creatures whose needs Job cannot satisfy, but who rely on God and their own species for sustenance (vv. 39–41). Humans may be important to humans and to God, but they do not direct the operations of the cosmos and are not necessary for its functioning.

A corollary to humanity's decentering is the limit of human knowledge. The nouns "knowledge," "wisdom," "understanding," and verbal forms from the same roots present a thematically unified cluster of keywords throughout chapter 38 (38:2, 4, 5, 18, 21, 33, 36–37; cf. 39:1–2, 17, 26). God emphasizes Job's lack of knowledge and understanding by reading to Job the chapter headings from the tomes of creation but withholding each chapter's content.

The theme of hidden knowledge resonates strongly with the book's beginning. There, a scene played out in heaven that shaped events on earth. In the process, certain narrative details were made known to the reader that remained hidden from the book's human characters. Most important of these is that Job was innocent, and God authorized his suffering in order to determine whether a human would serve God "for nothing."

In the present chapter, God implies that Job and the friends do not have enough information to resolve their disputes. While God will later affirm that Job (alone among the story's human characters) spoke rightly of God (42:7), God's tempestuous and dizzying interrogation so humbles Job that he soon chooses silence (40:4–5).

Isaiah 53:4–12. This week's lectionary passages from Job and Isaiah each raise and respond to questions about theodicy, or the justice of God. Their combined witness confounds simplistic explanations of human suffering.

Isaiah 53:4–12 contains the middle and final stanzas of a longer poem that begins in Isaiah 52:13. The longer poetic unit focuses on the role and fate of an unnamed individual who is called "my servant" (52:13; 53:11) and "righteous one" (53:11).

In the Old Testament Scriptures, when God is the identified speaker, the title "my servant" designates an individual or group whom God has chosen, commissioned, or sent and with whom God has a special relationship. In descending order of frequency, the term is applied to royal figures, prophets, and God's people. David is the individual most commonly called "my servant" (2 Sam. 3:18; 7:5, 8; 1 Kgs. 11:13, 32, 34, 36, 38; 14:8; 2 Kgs. 19:34; 20:6; 1 Chr. 17:4, 7;

Ps. 89:3, 20; Isa. 37:35; Jer. 33:21, 22, 26; Ezek. 34:23, 24; 37:25); his descendant Zerubbabel also merits the title (Hag. 2:23; cf. Zech. 3:8), as does, more surprisingly, the Babylonian king Nebuchadnezzar (Jer. 25:9; 27:6; 43:10). Elsewhere, the title is used of God's prophets, both as a group (2 Kgs. 9:7; 17:13; Jer. 7:25; 26:5; 29:19; 35:15; 44:4; Ezek. 38:17; Zech. 1:6) and as individuals (Moses: Num. 12:7, 8; Josh. 1:2, 7; 2 Kgs. 21:8; Isa. 20:3). The next most frequent usage of the title is in conjunction with the names Jacob, Israel, and Jeshurun, whereby God's chosen people as a group are designated God's servant (Isa. 41:8–9; 44:1–2, 21; 45:4; 49:3; Jer. 30:10; 46:27, 28; Ezek. 28:25; 37:25; cf. Isa. 65:8, 9, 13, 14). In six instances, God also uses the title "my servant" to describe Job (Job 1:8; 2:3; 42:7, 8 [3x]). Each of these uses of the title "my servant" has important links to the interpretation of Isaiah 53:4–12.

Within the book of Isaiah, the longer poetic unit 52:13–53:12 is the longest of four poems commonly referred to as the Servant Songs. The other three Servant Songs are contained in Isaiah 42:1–4; 49:1–6; and 50:4–7. Since the work of Bernhard Duhm, scholars have frequently studied these poems as a thematically interrelated collection that may even have existed independently before being integrated into the book of Isaiah.[1]

Interpreters have variously identified the servant(s), unnamed in three of the four poems, with one or more anonymous prophets, the chosen people (cf. Isa. 49:3), or a royal messiah.

The history of inner-biblical interpretation of Isaiah 52:13–53:12 affirms both collective and individual interpretations, opening up multiple possibilities for preaching on Isaiah 53:4–12. In the second century BCE, a group of "wise teachers" likely responsible for composing much of the book of Daniel, understood their own witness and teaching, by which they would "lead many to righteousness" (Dan. 12:3; cf. Isa. 53:11), as a recapitulation of the role of the Servant in Isaiah 53:4–12. They anticipated that they would die martyrs' deaths during persecution (Dan. 11:33) and, like the Servant of Isaiah 53:4–12, believed that their suffering would help to atone for the sins of their people (Dan. 11:35).[2] A few centuries later, followers of Jesus found a fulfillment of the poem's prophetic testimony in the suffering and death of Jesus (e.g., Matt. 8:17; Acts 8:32–33; 1 Pet. 2:21–25). The lectionary pairing with Mark 10:35–45 draws these interpretive threads together, grounding the servanthood of Jesus' disciples in Jesus' own willingness to "give his life a ransom for many" (Mark 10:45).

ANATHEA E. PORTIER-YOUNG

Commentary 2: Connecting the Reading with the World

Job 38:1–7 (34–41). There are a number of popular modern theorists who have introduced theoretical science to the masses, successfully interpreting complicated concepts in common language everyone can understand. Among them are string theorist Brian Greene, futurist and theoretical physicist Michio Kaku, and Hayden Planetarium astrophysicist Neil deGrasse Tyson. These theorists and many others excavate the mysteries of the universe, delivering mind-blowing explanations of the beginnings and mechanics of our cosmos. Each of them has a gift for communicating

the vastness of our universe and the correlating smallness of humankind. However, the progenitor of all modern popularizers of science is astronomer, professor, and author Carl Sagan. He possessed a prodigious skill for explaining the intricacies of scientific truth and providing new vistas for thinking about interstellar space. He also knew how to make his case for the smallness of humankind in creation.

In his book *Pale Blue Dot*, Sagan brings devastating news for anyone with a human-centered worldview. Sagan describes a photograph taken by the Voyager 1 spacecraft that appears to be

---

1. Bernhard Duhm, *Das Buch Jesaia* (Göttingen: Vandenhoeck & Ruprecht, 1892).
2. Anathea Portier-Young, *Apocalypse against Empire: Theologies of Resistance in Early Judaism* (Grand Rapids: Eerdmans, 2011), 272–76.

a canvas of solid black. He goes on to tell his reader that the photo was taken from 4 billion miles away from our planet. Then he points out a faint, barely detectable object reflecting the sun's light. It is earth: small, feeble; seemingly insignificant. Yet this is the place where human thought, experience, and action occur. His description pushes the reader to embrace a diminished sense of the status of the human person in the context of the vast universe. On a spectrum—from quantum mechanics to the theory of relativity and everything in between—humankind is a small matter when it comes to the cosmos. Sagan's take on our earthly smallness leaves readers undoubtedly humbled, deconstructed, and, perhaps, even defeated.

In the book of Job, humankind receives a more nuanced understanding of our place in the world. God listens to us in spite of our relative smallness. In chapter 38:1–7 and subsequently in verses 34–41, God acts almost like a rapper in a freestyle rap battle between two rappers, face to face, on stage under the lights and peering eyes of freestyle hip-hop connoisseurs. Job has expressed his defiance and bewilderment at God, so now it is God's turn to respond. Job has asked God some hard questions, shaking his fist at the Lord and searching for God in God's absence. God comes prepared with a few lyrical retorts as a response to Job's constant probing and pestering. Like American rappers Eminem in a rap battle from the movie *Eight Mile*, or Rakim and KRS-ONE on *Yo! MTV Raps* "Back in the day," the hip-hop artist's goal is to deliver verse with a better flow, a better argument for why their skills are superior. Blow by lyrical blow, the rapper works to diminish their foe's reputation and beef up their own.

God steps to the cosmic microphone with a bruising question: "Who is this that darkens counsel by words without knowledge?" (Job 38:2). The crowd—and reader—shout, "Ooooooh!" Then God warns Job to get ready for this battle: "Gird up your loins like a man, I will question you, and you shall declare to me" (v. 3). It is time to listen up to God's claim to be the greatest. God was here from the beginning; "Where were you when I laid the foundation of the earth?" (v. 4). Job has no control over the stars; "Can you bind the chains of the Pleiades,

or loose the cords of Orion?" (v. 31). Who even gave Job the ability to understand anything at all? God did! (v. 36). God provides sustenance for the mightiest of creatures; who can "satisfy the appetite of young lions?" (v. 39) and, who cares for the raven's young "when its young ones cry to God and wander about for lack of food?" (v. 41). Yeah, that's me: G-O-D. Mic drop. Job leaves humbled, bewildered, deconstructed, and maybe even a wee bit defeated.

Take heart, dear friend Job. God *spoke* to you, even when you could not find or perceive God (23:8–9). God speaks to us too, despite our smallness. Why God speaks to us and responds to our indignation draws us into the mystery of God's desire for relationship with us. God is deeply involved in Job's experience. What might this say about each and every human's importance to God? Pass the mic. Preach.

Isaiah 53:4–12. The reality and experience of suffering troubles the typically calm waters of spiritual experience. In fact, avoiding suffering at all costs can sometimes become the sole focus and goal of spiritual practice.

Many Christians have developed a bad habit of rushing through the Songs of the Suffering Servant in chapters 52 and 53 of Isaiah, hastily determining that this passage is solely a prophetic exposition of Jesus' passion on his way to the cross. The resemblances to Jesus' suffering are certainly present, and they are intriguing. Still, if the reader bravely sets aside the resemblances, new paths of spiritual understanding may open up.

What does it look like for a faithful person to enter into suffering? What are the essential elements of suffering in this narrative? What do these narratives have to say about the practice—dare one say—of the spiritual discipline of suffering for the individual and the church?

The Hebrew Bible depicts many forms of suffering. Frequently, the forms of suffering are levied as divine retribution for sinful behavior. It is unwanted and something akin to misery. Isaiah tweaks these familiar forms and gives suffering a subtle and profound significance. Isaiah 53 takes the reader by the hand and guides them into the troubled waters, away from retributive understandings of suffering. Suffering becomes a righteous and redemptive practice—but in what way? A review of the Suffering Servant's actions can assist in extracting the subtleties.

Isaiah's Suffering Servant (1) bears our infirmities and carries our diseases (v. 4), (2) is wounded for our transgressions, crushed by our iniquities (v. 5), and (3) takes on all iniquity laid on him by the Lord while humankind goes "our own way" (v. 6). This brand of suffering is one of active *taking on*, of *bearing*, of *woundedness*. The Lord actively gives the Servant over to suffering. While the Servant is "oppressed," "afflicted," and "led to the slaughter," this "perversion of justice" will lead him to "see light . . . [and] find satisfaction through his knowledge" (vv. 7–11). The impression here is that the kind of suffering we see in Isaiah 53 can become a blessing; it becomes suffering on behalf of and in the place of those who are already suffering, and it leads

to a deeper understanding and more abundant spiritual reward (v. 12).

Where might we find examples of this kind of suffering in recent memory? Perhaps we recall stories about Mother Teresa and her work among the sick, destitute, and orphans in Calcutta as she bore the infirmities of those around her. We may reach back to the examples of mendicant monks, like Francis of Assisi, who took on poverty to grow closer to God.

Are there those in your community who chose to bear infirmities in the course of their service to God, who became wounded when others would not, who stayed the course while others went their way? Explore the stories of those who have taken a step out, who gladly accepted suffering as part of their ministries, because they knew it was necessary to lead your community to a better understanding of God's abundance.

BRADY BANKS

Proper 24 (Sunday between October 16 and October 22)

Psalm 104:1–9, 24, 35c

[1]Bless the LORD, O my soul.
    O LORD my God, you are very great.
You are clothed with honor and majesty,
    [2]wrapped in light as with a garment.
You stretch out the heavens like a tent,
    [3]you set the beams of your chambers on the waters,
you make the clouds your chariot,
    you ride on the wings of the wind,
[4]you make the winds your messengers,
    fire and flame your ministers.

[5]You set the earth on its foundations,
    so that it shall never be shaken.
[6]You cover it with the deep as with a garment;
    the waters stood above the mountains.
[7]At your rebuke they flee;
    at the sound of your thunder they take to flight.
[8]They rose up to the mountains, ran down to the valleys
    to the place that you appointed for them.
[9]You set a boundary that they may not pass,
    so that they might not again cover the earth.
. . . .
[24]O LORD, how manifold are your works!
    In wisdom you have made them all;
    the earth is full of your creatures.
. . . .
[35c]Praise the LORD!

Psalm 91:9–16

[9]Because you have made the LORD your refuge,
    the Most High your dwelling place,
[10]no evil shall befall you,
    no scourge come near your tent.

[11]For he will command his angels concerning you
    to guard you in all your ways.
[12]On their hands they will bear you up,
    so that you will not dash your foot against a stone.
[13]You will tread on the lion and the adder,
    the young lion and the serpent you will trample under foot.

[14]Those who love me, I will deliver;
    I will protect those who know my name.

> [15]When they call to me, I will answer them;
>   I will be with them in trouble,
>   I will rescue them and honor them.
> [16]With long life I will satisfy them,
>   and show them my salvation.

Connecting the Psalm with Scripture and Worship

Psalm 104:1–9, 24, 35c. Psalm 104 recounts the creation story, not as a detailed explanation, but as a celebration of the goodness and abundance of creation. Beginning with the invocation, "Bless the LORD, O my soul" (Ps. 104:1), this psalm is a rousing doxology of the God who "stretched out the heavens . . . and made the clouds your chariot, . . . the winds your messengers" (vv. 1–4), who "set the earth on its foundations. . . . You cover it with the deep as with a garment" (vv. 5–6), and created all things on the earth, including plants, trees, animals, and people (vv. 10–23). This God is worthy of awe. "O LORD, how manifold are your works!" cries the psalmist. "In wisdom you have made them all; the earth is full of your creatures" (v. 24). The Creator provides a stable world, in which even the powers of watery chaos are kept under control—"You set a boundary that they may not pass, so that they might not again cover the earth" (v. 9). The psalmist joyfully declares that everything derives from and depends on God. For the first time in the Psalter, the psalmist ends in a triumphant: "Praise the LORD!" (v. 35c).

The limits of the lectionary preserve the celebratory tone of Psalm 104 as well as the balanced relationship between creation and its Creator. The message of the psalm seems clear: Go forth and give thanks for the beauty of God's creation. Sing "All Creatures of Our God and King" and "All Things Bright and Beautiful," and encourage people to spend time in nature. Yet the melancholic note struck in the first part of verse 35—"let sinners be consumed from the earth, and let the wicked be no more"—signals

that perhaps more is going on here. As Walter Brueggemann notes, "There is an obvious move to our own ecological crisis, even if the lectionary does not want to acknowledge it here."[1]

Long before we knew about global warming, claims J. Clinton McCann, the writer of Psalm 104 was an environmentalist, who "knew about the intricate interconnectedness and subtle interdependence of air, soil, water, plants, and animals, including humans." As God's creatures, we all must be stewards of the earth, motivated by the belief that "everything we do has an effect on God's world and thus on God."[2]

This focus on divine creation and design is evident in the reading from Job, whose challenge is answered with a reminder of God's sovereignty: "Where were you when I laid the foundation of the earth?" (Job 38:4). In the Gospel reading, Jesus calls us to our rightful place: "whoever wishes to become great among you must be your servant" (Mark 10:43). We humans are created to care for God's creation and serve God's purpose.

A sermon might focus on creation as God's continuous renewing of the earth, in which all creatures have to take part. Call your hearers to action, urging them to carpool, recycle, turn off lights, conserve water, reduce waste, and use renewable energy. The hymn "God of the Sparrow" invites singers to ask how we save, how we care. "God, You Spin the Whirling Planets" allows people to affirm God's continuing creative work. At the baptismal font, one can pour water visibly and audibly, while speaking words of renewal and promise. At the Lord's Table, the presider can give thanks for the fruit of the vine

---

1. Walter Brueggemann, "Exegetical Perspective on Psalm 104," in *Feasting on the Word, Year B, Volume 4* (Louisville, KY: Westminster John Knox, 2009), 181.
2. J. Clinton McCann Jr., "The Book of Psalms," in *The New Interpreter's Bible* (Nashville: Abingdon, 1996), 4:1099.

and the wheat of the earth that are blessed to be the gifts of God for the people of God.

Reading the entirety of Psalm 104 responsively allows worshipers to celebrate the magnificent blessing of creation, while committing to preserving the earth.

Psalm 91:9–16. Classified as a psalm of trust, Psalm 91 professes confidence in God as a refuge and a dwelling place, in which "no evil shall befall you, no scourge come near" (Ps. 91:9–10). The psalmist is confident that God is a protector who will "command his angels concerning you to guard you in all your ways" (v. 11). This psalm affirms the value of trusting God at all times, because whether one is in need of a "safe place" (vv. 9–10) or a "safe journey" (vv. 11–13), God's protection is unswerving and sure. There is nothing that can harm those who love God.

Psalm 91 has the power to sustain believers who profess their faith in a loving God. While the first thirteen verses are spoken in a human voice, the psalmist rightly gives the last word to God, the ultimate source of our trust, who promises, "I will deliver, I will protect" (v. 14); "I will answer them, I will be with them in trouble, I will rescue them" (v. 15); "I will satisfy them, and show them my salvation" (v. 16).

The language of this psalm emboldens deep trust and abiding faith. Yet those who speak and hear this psalm dare not assume that divine protection means a life without trouble or danger. By putting this psalm in conversation with the other readings, preachers and worship leaders allow it to be considered against the whole witness of Scripture. Isaiah reminds us of the Suffering Servant: "out of his anguish he shall see light" (Isa. 53:11). Jesus asks his disciples who want to sit at the right hand of God, "Are

you able to drink the cup that I drink?" (Mark 10:38). In Hebrews, as the Son of God, Jesus "learned obedience through what he suffered, and . . . became the source of eternal salvation for all who obey him" (Heb. 5:8–9). God promises to protect the faithful but does not guarantee a life of ease.

The call of the preacher is to honestly present a life of faith that includes both brightly lit mountains and deep dark valleys, trusting that a God who suffered on the cross and defeated death for us and for our salvation is worthy of our trust in times of both blessing and suffering. The psalm's references to refuge, dwelling place, and protection might lead a preacher to wonder with her listeners about contemporary situations. Where is God's protection, for instance, for the refugee or immigrant child without a parent? As Christians, what is our response? The psalm also offers an opportunity for testimony, when worshipers give witness to times when God was a refuge who provided deliverance from trouble.

Psalm 91 can be sung as a choral anthem or as a congregational song. "On Eagles' Wings," "Leaning on the Everlasting Arms," and "It Is Well with My Soul" are all appropriate choices. This psalm may also inspire a corporate confession of faith that inspires trust, such as the Brief Statement of Faith found in the *Book of Confessions* of the Presbyterian Church (U.S.A.): "In life and in death we belong to God. . . . We trust in the one triune God, the Holy One of Israel, whom alone we worship and serve. . . . With believers in every time and place, we rejoice that nothing in life or in death can separate us from the love of God in Christ Jesus our Lord."[3]

Psalm 91 provides a solid foundation of faith in a God who alone is worthy of our trust.

DONNA GIVER-JOHNSTON

3. "A Brief Statement of Faith," in *The Constitution of the Presbyterian Church (U.S.A.)*, Part I: *Book of Confessions* (Louisville, KY: Office of the General Assembly, Presbyterian Church (U.S.A.), 2016), 311–12.

Hebrews 5:1–10

[1]Every high priest chosen from among mortals is put in charge of things pertaining to God on their behalf, to offer gifts and sacrifices for sins. [2]He is able to deal gently with the ignorant and wayward, since he himself is subject to weakness; [3]and because of this he must offer sacrifice for his own sins as well as for those of the people. [4]And one does not presume to take this honor, but takes it only when called by God, just as Aaron was.

[5]So also Christ did not glorify himself in becoming a high priest, but was appointed by the one who said to him,

"You are my Son,
today I have begotten you";

[6]as he says also in another place,

"You are a priest forever,
according to the order of Melchizedek."

[7]In the days of his flesh, Jesus offered up prayers and supplications, with loud cries and tears, to the one who was able to save him from death, and he was heard because of his reverent submission. [8]Although he was a Son, he learned obedience through what he suffered; [9]and having been made perfect, he became the source of eternal salvation for all who obey him, [10]having been designated by God a high priest according to the order of Melchizedek.

Commentary 1: Connecting the Reading with Scripture

The letter is considered by scholars to be in the form of a homily. As all good preachers do, the author incorporates metaphors with which his listeners are familiar, in order to enhance the effectiveness of his message. The central metaphor he develops is that of Jesus as high priest.

Priests were a part of the culture in the first-century Mediterranean world. In antiquity, Greek, Roman, Egyptian, and Jewish priests played an important role in the devotional life of the people, serving as intermediaries between the gods and humans. They were a bridge. Hebrews, however, is the only canonical text where Jesus is referred to as a high priest. The author clearly believes the use of the metaphor conveys something distinctive about who Jesus is and what he accomplishes on our behalf.

In this lection, the author is deepening the metaphor introduced earlier in the text (Heb. 2:17; 3:1; 4:14–15). While it is an honor to

serve as a priest, with the office comes a great deal of responsibility. Priests offer gifts and sacrifices to the gods on behalf of the people and for themselves. The priests can relate to the people because they, too, are subject to weakness. This commonality, however, should inspire the priest to deal gently with people. Surrounded by weakness (the people's and their own), priests are obligated (*opheilei*) to offer sacrifices. In light of this obligation, one does not so much take on the role of the priest as one responds to the call (*kaloumenos*) to be a priest. That is, one is bound by their commitment, their duty. Jesus, however, is designated (*prosagoreutheis*, 5:10) a high priest. This is the first distinction that is made between Jesus and other high priests. Jesus is appointed by God, not chosen from among mortals.

By comparing the Levitical priesthood (see the call and description of Aaron and his sons' priesthood in Exod. 28–29; Lev. 8–9; and Num. 17–18) to the circumstances of Jesus' priesthood, the writer contends that Jesus' priesthood is, in fact, unusual. Firstly, Jesus was not called but appointed by God through the declaration: "You are my Son, today I have begotten you. . . . You are a priest forever, according to the order of [King] Melchizedek" (vv. 5, 6). In Psalm 2:7, the pronouncement of the anointed one as the Son of God describes the promises of an eternal king who has been set apart from earthly rulers. Furthermore, this lord, according to Psalm 110:4 and affirmed in Hebrews 8:1, sits at the right hand of the Lord (Ps. 110:1). In this position, Jesus functions as a high priest. The writer is identifying Jesus as the priestly, kingly ruler described in these psalms.

What does it mean to say that Jesus is a priest of a distinctive order, that of King Melchizedek? Melchizedek is mentioned only twice outside of Hebrews (Gen. 14:18; Ps. 110:4) and three times in Hebrews (Heb. 5:6, 10; 6:20; 7:1, 10, 11, 15, 17). He is described as a "priest of God Most High." Typically, priests were descendants of Aaron who followed in the Levitical line. Certainly, they were worshipers of the one God of Israel. Melchizedek, however, worshiped a Canaanite deity. Jesus was "of the order of Melchizedek" in the sense that he, like Melchizedek, did not fit the profile of a priest and yet he was appointed as a priest by God the Father, even as Melchizedek was recognized as a priest by Abram. Neither sought to have this role for his own glory (5:5).

Genesis 14 describes a brief encounter between Abram and Melchizedek (Gen. 14:17–21). In this interaction, Abram gives a tithe to Melchizedek, and the king blesses Abram for being victorious in battle. A biblical figure who signifies the inauguration of not only a new covenant, but also a new understanding of the Divine (see Gen. 12 and 17), Abram is the progenitor of the faith. Like Melchizedek, Jesus is the priest of God Most High. Like Abram, Jesus is the forerunner of our faith (see Heb. 6:20), and through Jesus all are blessed. Jesus is the promise fulfilled, the anointed one, the kingly high priest of the heavenly tabernacle, and God's Son.

As the begotten (*gegennēka*, v. 5) Son of God (see Heb. 1:5 for a similar description), Jesus is

uniquely positioned in the heavens at the right hand of God. Jesus is also described as the begotten Son of God in Acts 13:32–33, where the writer proclaims: "And we bring you the good news that what God promised to our ancestors he has fulfilled for us, their children, by raising Jesus; as also it is written in the second psalm, 'You are my Son; today I have begotten you.'" The good news is that Jesus lives and reigns. The Gospel of John describes Jesus as the *only* begotten Son (*monogenē*) and affirms that those who believe in Jesus will have everlasting life (John 3:16). As the Son of God, the high priest seated at the right hand of God, Jesus is the promise fulfilled; he is the source for eternal salvation.

Enveloped between the repetition of Melchizedek in chapter 5 of Hebrews (Heb. 5:6 and 10), the writer describes Jesus' humanity: "Jesus offered up prayers and supplications, with loud cries and tears, to the one who was able to save him from death" (v. 7). As listeners are implored to imitate Jesus, they, too, should offer up prayers to the one who can save them (see Heb. 6:12). All priests present a way to salvation; however, Jesus *becomes* the way of eternal salvation. The suffering of Jesus and his explicit humanity, emphasized by "in the days of his flesh," connect him to the suffering of the listeners to this homily. Jesus' suffering results in perfection. As such, the audience, too, can anticipate their wholeness despite their current suffering.

Perfection is a theme repeated throughout this sermon (see Heb. 2:10; 7:28; 9:11). Perfection (*teleiōtheis*), at its etymological root, is concerned with time. At an appointed time, things or people will be finished or completed. Perfection is a state of wholeness and, here, is also associated with the concept of perseverance. One must endure in order to experience perfection; that is, one must remain faithful until the end, even when it is difficult to do so. Obedience is also necessary for perfection.

The time emphasized in the homily is today. The writer states: "Again he sets a certain day—'today'—saying . . . , 'Today, if you hear his voice, do not harden your hearts'" (Heb. 4:7). Quoting from Psalm 95:8, the reference is to the ancestors at Meribah (see Deut. 1:26–38). This narrative reminds the audience that the Lord went before the children of Israel fighting their battles, and yet they did not obey. The writer of Hebrews presents Jesus as the Lord who has gone ahead of the believer. The believer need only choose today to follow him wholeheartedly.

Later in this homily, Jesus is described as the pioneer and perfecter of our faith (Heb. 12:2). Throughout his earthly life, Jesus demonstrated how to remain obedient even while crying out to God to save him. Jesus is the source of eternal salvation for all. The writer of Hebrews is making the case for the audience to continue to believe the gospel that they had been taught in the face of opposition. In this text, the exhortation to endure until the end is undergirded by the knowledge of Jesus' serving as a high priest of an eternal order. He continues to plead for those who are obedient and remain faithful.

JENNIFER T. KAALUND

Commentary 2: Connecting the Reading with the World

It would be worth asking the question: Who are the priests and priestesses in today's world? To whom do we tend to go to seek connection with a higher power or inner strength? To whom do we go to release our inner potential or readjust life patterns that interfere with that potential? Who informs our hope for a preferred future, or assuages our fears that it will never come about? To whom might we go to find absolution or restitution for misdeeds or ill-spoken words? Where do we seek life beyond shame, or certainty beyond conjecture, or stability beyond awkwardness? Who can weave together the social fabric of broken relationships or our inwardly fractured selves?

Where, and to whom, do people you know go for help when facing such things as personal or family brokenness, failures of character, shame and guilt? Naming such people, groups, or agencies opens up an important set of connections to the Hebrews text for the day. The self-help literature, the psychological counselors, the pop-culture gurus, and the recovery programs all attend in one way or another to the way the text describes Israel's priesthood. Like the priests of ancient Israel, do not today's priests and priestesses offer, in some sense, redemption for the guilty, restoration for the broken, and hope for the despairing? Do they not, at their best, "deal gently with the ignorant and wayward," recognizing that they themselves are "subject to weakness" (Heb. 5:2)? Do they not model in themselves the patterns of redemptive action they commend to others?

The panoply of contemporary priestlike agencies connects with and helps interpret this Hebrews text in at least these five ways. First, people in today's postindustrial, secular society still seek the kinds of help that were in view in the divinely established priesthood of Israel. At the very least, a comparison between ancient and contemporary priests and priestesses suggests that the human condition to which the priests of Israel responded is very much with us today. The fact that contemporary people seek help with the same problems suggests that the description of the priesthood in the text is far from irrelevant, much as it may feel ancient and remote for some upon a first read. It is not remote to a contemporary audience's experience, and neither is it for those in the church and in the wider society. It is timely.

Second, today's priests and priestesses, whether religious, quasi-religious, or entirely secular, may have much to offer. Insofar as they in some sense have a healthy grasp of the nature of the human person and human community, they can help people navigate the circumstances of life. Even when they function without an explicit sense that God may be in the picture as an active agent, they may be fulfilling some of the purposes of God. The sending into the world of God's Spirit—the Spirit of Christ—gives us reason to hope and expect as much.

Third, this text speaks into this set of connections by way of contrast. In the midst of the author's depiction of the commission of the high priest, there is a feature that moves considerably beyond what modern society's priests and priestesses are likely to provide. The high priest is "put in charge of things pertaining to God" (v. 1). The role of the priest is thus given a fixed location in the perspective and desires of the God of Israel, the living God who is the maker of all things. That includes the human person. Healing human brokenness is hardly complete without the healing of the fundamental brokenness, a broken intimacy with God.

The phrase "things pertaining to God" (v. 1) invites us to see as incomplete any priestly activity that omits or neglects the living, divine agent whose presence—amid all the ranges of human experiences—is essential for true healing of human brokenness. The language of "sins" and "sacrifices" (v. 1) cannot make full sense apart from human relatedness to the Divine.

Fourth, Jesus is introduced within this matrix. Jesus is presented as a high priest like others in the ancient institution of Israel (v. 5). Unlike others, however, his work far exceeds the intent and function of the priesthood. The point of the text is not that other priests—whether in ancient Israel or contemporary society—are not useful and important. Rather, it shows them to be limited. Jesus is a priest beyond all other priests.

Jesus was not self-appointed. Israel's priests, likewise, did not take the honor to themselves. They were "appointed" and "called" to the priesthood, as was their forefather Aaron. Jesus, of course, was not of the tribe of Levi or the priestly line of Aaron. Like Aaron, Jesus was "appointed" (v. 5) and "designated by God" to be a high priest, though more directly, not depending on bloodline. By God's decree, he was made "a priest forever, according to the order of Melchizedek" (v. 6). (According to Gen. 14:18–20, Melchizedek was the king of Salem to whom Aaron's forefather, Abraham, had paid tithes.)

Jesus cannot be dismissed for lack of a priestly genealogy; nor may self-appointed priests (like perhaps some of today's would-be priests and priestesses) presume upon themselves the priestly honor. Someone of larger scope has come among us. This Jesus, whom the author has already introduced as God's Son

(Heb. 1:2–3), has taken on our humanity and "in the days of his flesh" (5:7) "learned obedience through what he suffered" (v. 8). In his prayers and in his sacrificial death, he fulfilled his priesthood. Like Israel's priests, he knows our pains; unlike them, he was made perfect in his suffering and had no need to make sacrifice for his own sins, nor to repeat the sacrifices over and over again. His one sacrifice is sufficient. By divine designation, he becomes "the source of eternal salvation" (v. 9).

Fifth, we find here our identity as the church. The prayers of Jesus that are mentioned in the text (v. 7) are undoubtedly those uttered on the way to his death. As John attests in chapter 17 of his Gospel, those prayers on the eve of his death include intercession for his followers and the whole world. The church has traditionally called that chapter-long prayer the high-priestly prayer of Jesus, underscoring an understanding that intercession lies at the heart of a priestly vocation. It is to such a vocation that the Spirit has called the church, the community of the followers of Jesus. This vocation is made clear in the surrounding New Testament literature. Jesus has "made us a kingdom, priests to his God and Father" (Rev. 1:4–6). In 1 Peter we are called "a holy nation, a royal priesthood" (1 Pet. 2:9). Empathy with the weak and prayers of intercession on their behalf are at the heart of our vocation, as they were for Jesus.

I know a church, not a large one, although a very old one. They are a lively bunch. They have gained a reputation in their small New Jersey town. It frequently happens that when a couple of townspeople might be in conversation and one shares a serious concern about their life, their family, or their job, the other will suggest that they should go to "those people over there at that church. . . . They will pray for you." This is as worthy a reputation for a Christian community as I have ever witnessed!

GEORGE R. HUNSBERGER

Mark 10:35–45

[35]James and John, the sons of Zebedee, came forward to him and said to him, "Teacher, we want you to do for us whatever we ask of you." [36]And he said to them, "What is it you want me to do for you?" [37]And they said to him, "Grant us to sit, one at your right hand and one at your left, in your glory." [38]But Jesus said to them, "You do not know what you are asking. Are you able to drink the cup that I drink, or be baptized with the baptism that I am baptized with?" [39]They replied, "We are able." Then Jesus said to them, "The cup that I drink you will drink; and with the baptism with which I am baptized, you will be baptized; [40]but to sit at my right hand or at my left is not mine to grant, but it is for those for whom it has been prepared."

[41]When the ten heard this, they began to be angry with James and John. [42]So Jesus called them and said to them, "You know that among the Gentiles those whom they recognize as their rulers lord it over them, and their great ones are tyrants over them. [43]But it is not so among you; but whoever wishes to become great among you must be your servant, [44]and whoever wishes to be first among you must be slave of all. [45]For the Son of Man came not to be served but to serve, and to give his life a ransom for many."

Commentary 1: Connecting the Reading with Scripture

Mark 10:35–45 recalls a conversation between Jesus and two of his disciples, James and John, the sons of Zebedee. The mention of Zebedee in 10:35 reminds the audience of the sacrifice of James and John in following Jesus, a statement that resonates with Peter's comment in 10:28: "We have left everything and have followed you." In response to Peter, Jesus promised that whoever leaves behind their families, households, and properties for his sake and the sake of the "good news," will receive back a hundredfold for their sacrifice (Mark 10:29–30). It seems that James and John were ready to start cashing in when they approached Jesus with their request to grant them "to sit, one at your right hand and one at your left, in your glory" (vv. 35–37).

"Teacher, we want for you to do whatever we should ask you," they said to Jesus (v. 35). Their opening designation, "teacher," at once highlights the irony of their request: Jesus, you are our teacher, but we want you to do what we want! Their approach was savvier than that of the wealthy man who walked away grieving after asking Jesus what he must do to inherit eternal life (vv. 17–31). Having learned from that experience, James and John did not call Jesus "Good Teacher" (vv. 17–18) and hedged their bets: "if we can get Jesus to agree to do whatever we want first, then we can ask for whatever we want!" This is a classic rhetorical move that anyone who spends much time with children knows well.

The disciples' bold and childish request continues a theme that runs through Mark 8–10, namely, a description of what people want. The verb for "want" (*thelō*) shows up ten times in these two chapters, often as a contrast between our "want" for what we think is best for us and our lack of "want" for the work or sacrifice it takes to participate in it. For example, as part of his reprimand for Peter's rebuking his first passion prediction, Jesus told his disciples: "If any *want* to become my followers, let them deny themselves and take up their cross and follow me. For those who *want* to save their life will lose it, and those who lose their life for my sake, and the sake of the gospel, will save it" (8:31–35; cf. 10:32–34).

Following Jesus, therefore, does not mean glory and high places in a worldly kingdom; that is human thinking (8:31). Following Jesus means leaving behind what the world tells us to value in order to see what and who is truly good (10:18). The world reacts harshly to such a readjustment of values; that is why Jesus is rejected and killed and why his followers—those who really follow him—suffer similar fates.

Jesus coaxed the real "want" from James and John (10:36–37). Eagerly they asked, "*Grant us* to sit, at your right and one at your left, in your glory!" The Teacher responded, "You do not know what you are asking." James and John not only misjudged what Jesus' glory would look like (15:22–27); they also misjudged their own preparation to follow him. "Are you able to drink the cup that I drink, or to be baptized with the baptism that I am baptized with?" Aware of the rest of the narrative on Jesus' trial and crucifixion, we know their answer should have been "No," but James and John said, "We are able!" (10:38–39). Their readiness was based on *their* understanding of glory, not *God's*. That glory requires a complete readjustment of values that none of the disciples *wanted* to do just yet. In fact, when the other disciples learned of the boldness of James and John, they "began to be angry" toward them (v. 41; NIV "indignant"). It seems that they were angry—not because of the audacity of the request—but because they did not think of asking Jesus first! Once more we find Jesus having to talk to the disciples about their "wants" (vv. 42–45).

In 10:42–45, Jesus laid bare the disciples' true desire: they wanted to be in charge. They wanted special places in his coming kingdom; but they were not yet ready for what that entails. The "high places" they wanted correspond to human ways of thinking, and bring life to no one. In contrast, Jesus chose to give up what he wanted in order to do what the Father wanted. Having fallen upon his knees in Gethsemane, Jesus cried out in prayer: "Abba, Father, for you all things are possible; remove this cup from me; yet, not what *I want*, but what *you want*" (14:36; cf. Pilate's questions in 15:9, 12).

Jesus' prayer shows us what it looks like to lose one's life *and* to save it; it means surrendering our wants for God's and, in so doing, showing our trust and faith in God when it really counts. Whoever *wants* to be first must be a slave of all (10:44; cf. 9:35; 10:43). In Mark's Gospel, Jesus suffered the fate of a slave: beaten and crucified as a revolutionary, he was an example displayed by the Romans to scare anyone who should dare challenge their human ways of thinking.

Liberation Is for All

To be a "slave of all" is to recognize that the struggle of liberation is for all. This recognition does not make one submissive to unjust powers, but humble before Jesus Christ who is the Lord of all. His presence in our midst requires that we subordinate our personal interests to the coming liberation for all. Those who see God's coming liberation breaking into the present must live as if the future is already present in their midst. They must bear witness to humanity's liberation by freeing the present from the past and for the future. This means fighting for the inauguration of liberation in our social existence, creating new levels of human relationship in society. The struggle for liberation is the service the people of God render for all, even those who are responsible for the structure of slavery.

The assertion that liberation is for all does not mean that all will regard God's coming realm of freedom as good news. Even some oppressed people, having "made" it in the oppressors' world, will not always welcome the freedom that the liberation struggle inaugurates. Their mental enslavement to their few crumbs from the master's table often negates their desire to share in the freedom of humanity. Therefore, though oppressed, they do not share the consciousness that arises from the dialectic of oppression and liberation in the political praxis of the people. They thus must be liberated in spite of and against themselves.

James Cone, *God of the Oppressed* (New York: Orbis, 1997), 138–39.

There is already plenty in this short section on which to preach, but it is worth noting the other lectionary texts connected to it, especially Job 38. In the previous lectionary passage, Job expressed his desire to speak with God, to show God how God had wronged him, and to experience justice (Job 23:1–9, 16–17). Job's request is similar to that of the wealthy man in Mark 10:17–31 and is also a good comparison to that of James and John (Mark 10:35–45). Like these disciples, Job realized that he really did not know what it was he was asking God. In fact, that is what God told him, speaking from the "whirlwind" in Job 38. Like James and John, Job overestimated his abilities and the veracity of his perspective. Psalm 104 emphasizes God's greatness and wisdom as Creator and provider, therefore calling our thoughts—indeed our wants—to be pleasing unto God (Ps. 104:34).

The lectionary readings for this week remind us of something we often forget: only God is God. Jesus reminded the rich man of this in Mark 10:17–18 and his disciples in 10:35–45. Like these disciples, we can easily succumb to our own human ways of thinking; we need God to disrupt and save us from these selfish patterns. Although we think we can secure our salvation through our own morality (I've kept all these commandments since I was a kid!) or ambition (Put me on the right and my brother on the left!), these requests amount to the same thing: left to our own devices, we all really want to be God. Such a desire not only brings our own destruction; it brings suffering to the many we crush beneath us as we fearfully hold on to what we believe is "life."

Instead, Jesus says, if we really want to live, we need to let go. We need to leave these ideas behind and accept the life that God desires to give us, instead of the lives we fashion for ourselves. We need to remember that God alone is God and to surrender to what he wants, no matter what. Such surrender does not mean we will not fear or not want another fate. Even Jesus cried out, "Take this cup from me!" Nevertheless, he followed that request with, "Not what I want, but what you want." May we do the same.

ALICIA D. MYERS

Commentary 2: Connecting the Reading with the World

Whenever I read the Gospel lessons in which the disciples figure, I am so grateful. I am grateful because I feel assured that if Jesus chose this group to be his closest companions, there is nothing but hope for the rest of us. Whenever they are given the chance to prove that they are worthy companions for the one who comes to offer salvation, they always choose the wrong path, the wrong question, the wrong answer. We cannot help but wonder how it is that they spend so much time in close proximity to Jesus and yet seem to insist on refusing to "get it." Over and over they misunderstand Jesus' teachings, seeing and hearing only what they choose. Their ignorance and misunderstanding of who Jesus is and the work he has come into the world to accomplish are what give me hope for us and our world.

The disciples believe the Messiah they have been promised will free Israel from Roman rule. The Messiah they have been waiting for will reestablish Israel as a powerful nation and will rule Israel as was promised by the prophets (e.g., Isa. 11:10–12; Jer. 23:5–8; and Zech. 8:7–8). The disciples refuse to give up their ideas about the kind or manner of salvation the Messiah would bring, even when Jesus repeatedly tells and shows them that the kingdom he offers in no way resembles the kingdoms of this world.

In this reading, we find the disciples, once again, laying claim to something Jesus has never said he is offering. James's and John's approach, "Teacher, we want you to do for us whatever we ask of you" (Mark 10:35), is so direct that it would be comical, were it not meant to be taken seriously by Jesus. After all, who says, "You have to say yes to whatever we ask," except for little children hoping to get their parents to agree to ice cream before their vegetables? Yet, here are James and John requesting with all seriousness that they be assured seats of privilege in Jesus' kingdom—one that he has repeatedly told them upends the ways of earthly kingdoms. From his birth in a stable in Bethlehem to his teachings and his life, Jesus shows that his reign is not that of a conquering, majestic emperor or king. He has come to show the world that God resides with, and has compassion for, the marginalized of humanity. One would think that this would be obvious to his disciples, who were themselves among the poor, the marginalized, and the oppressed, and not among the religious or political elite.

James and John subscribe to the dream of Jesus' kingdom as a reversal of what they know. Such a reversal would move them from the margins of society to a place of power in the world that Jesus, as they understood it, would establish. They cannot relinquish the ways of earthly kingdoms, wherein the conquerors take for themselves the wealth and the power of the conquered. The anger with which the other disciples respond upon hearing of their request may suggest that James and John were not alone in hoping that, as Jesus' companions, they would attain status and power when he established his reign.

We can look back at the disciples and wonder how they could have misunderstood Jesus' teachings and his call. We can insert ourselves into the readings and imagine what better disciples we would have been in their place. In hindsight, we can shake our heads at their inability to hear that the good news Jesus was offering was not the assurance of wealth and power as the world understands wealth and power.

However, we should not be too quick to assume we have a better understanding than did the disciples of the gospel and the life, death, and resurrection of Jesus. We, too, try to make the kingdom of God look like the kingdoms of this world. How often do we claim God is responsible for our political victories? How many times do we hear and believe claims that God blesses with wealth and health those who honor God best? What do we think we are saying when we claim that our overcoming of illness or a difficulty in life is due to God's blessing us?

In many ways we actually take the request that James and John made a step further. We do not simply ask Jesus to place us at his right and left. We claim that we already occupy those privileged places. When we claim that our victories are a result of God's blessings, are we not saying that God has chosen to elevate our needs, dreams, and wants over and above those of others? Are we not saying God has found us worthy of a place of honor and that what happens in this world, in this life, is a measure of how faithful God has found us to be?

The prosperity gospel that teaches that God blesses with wealth and power those whom God loves is not only wrong; it is a complete reversal of what Jesus tries to teach his followers in this and in other passages. It says that Jesus is wrong when he says that the community he came to build is the opposite of the society that exists and that, unlike "the rulers of the Gentiles" (v. 42), those who follow him cannot aspire to be rulers or tyrants but must accept the call to serve.

While the movement that Jesus started has spread to the four corners of the earth, we have managed to grow the movement without using the teachings of Jesus to change the world. We who call ourselves Christians must look beyond our prayer and worship to see how Jesus lives in us. We must look at whether the lives we lead align with the example and lessons Jesus gave us. Rather than pointing a finger, the preacher may raise questions that invite the listener to reflect upon how their own lives align with the kingdom of God as Jesus lived it.

Are we, for instance, truly working toward the kingdom that Jesus proclaimed? Are we upending the hierarchy of the Gentiles and modeling a society in which we show our greatness by our willingness to serve? Are we those who live with Jesus on the margins of society, uplifting the poor and oppressed, or are we simply trying to make sure that we sit in the seats of power and privilege? How does the work we do in the world resemble the work that Jesus spoke about and modeled in his life? Are we indeed those who challenge systems that oppress by fighting against the powers and principalities that dehumanize children of God because of their race, gender, religion, sexual orientation, or class? Can we hold up to the world the picture of a different way of living in the world that honors and values the image of God in all of God's children? Will we choose a path that makes it clear that we are not in awe of wealth and worldly status, because that is not what God calls us to value? Do we strive for a new kind of kingdom where the last will be first (Mark 10:44; Matt. 20:16)? Are we, rather, followers of the preresurrection disciples claiming that our proximity to Jesus assures us places of power and privilege? If our claim is to a Jesus who bestows worldly power, then we have less understanding and belief in Jesus than James, John, and the other ten as they squabbled over his kingdom's thrones.

NONTOMBI NAOMI TUTU

Proper 25 (Sunday between October 23 and October 29)

Job 42:1–6, 10–17 and
   Jeremiah 31:7–9
Psalm 34:1–8 (19–22) and Psalm 126

Hebrews 7:23–28
Mark 10:46–52

Job 42:1–6, 10–17

¹Then Job answered the Lord:

²"I know that you can do all things,
   and that no purpose of yours can be thwarted.
³'Who is this that hides counsel without knowledge?'
Therefore I have uttered what I did not understand,
   things too wonderful for me, which I did not know.
⁴'Hear, and I will speak;
   I will question you, and you declare to me.'
⁵I had heard of you by the hearing of the ear,
   but now my eye sees you;
⁶therefore I despise myself,
   and repent in dust and ashes."

. . . .

¹⁰And the Lord restored the fortunes of Job when he had prayed for his friends; and the Lord gave Job twice as much as he had before. ¹¹Then there came to him all his brothers and sisters and all who had known him before, and they ate bread with him in his house; they showed him sympathy and comforted him for all the evil that the Lord had brought upon him; and each of them gave him a piece of money and a gold ring. ¹²The Lord blessed the latter days of Job more than his beginning; and he had fourteen thousand sheep, six thousand camels, a thousand yoke of oxen, and a thousand donkeys. ¹³He also had seven sons and three daughters. ¹⁴He named the first Jemimah, the second Keziah, and the third Keren-happuch. ¹⁵In all the land there were no women so beautiful as Job's daughters; and their father gave them an inheritance along with their brothers. ¹⁶After this Job lived one hundred and forty years, and saw his children, and his children's children, four generations. ¹⁷And Job died, old and full of days.

Jeremiah 31:7–9

⁷For thus says the Lord:

Sing aloud with gladness for Jacob,
   and raise shouts for the chief of the nations;
proclaim, give praise, and say,
   "Save, O Lord, your people,
   the remnant of Israel."
⁸See, I am going to bring them from the land of the north,

and gather them from the farthest parts of the earth.
among them the blind and the lame,
    those with child and those in labor, together;
    a great company, they shall return here.
⁹With weeping they shall come,
    and with consolations I will lead them back,
I will let them walk by brooks of water,
    in a straight path in which they shall not stumble;
for I have become a father to Israel,
    and Ephraim is my firstborn.

Commentary 1: Connecting the Reading with Scriptures

Job 42:1–6, 10–17. Job's speech in 42:1–6 is the second of two replies to God's speeches from the whirlwind (Job 38–39; 40:6–41:34). Combined, the two divine speeches demarcate the limitations of human knowing, doing, and ordering; they decenter human experience and desire, and indicate the wondrous breadth and play of the world God has made and governs. Job's first reply declines to answer God's flurry of questions and instead emphasizes his own smallness in the face of the vast, mysterious cosmos God has described (40:3–5).

In the second reply, Job twice paraphrases God's own words: 42:3a paraphrases 38:2, and 42:4b paraphrases 38:3b and 40:7b. Job's repeated alternation of divine question/imperative and human response recapitulates within the structure of his speech the macrostructure of the broader unit (38:1–42:6). It thus offers Job's distillation of and conclusion from this series of exchanges: in the end, it is not really about Leviathan, or ostriches, or singing stars. It is about God. Whatever Job had known about God previously was hearsay, not admissible in court. While Job had previously complained that he could not see God, no matter which direction he searched (23:8–9), now he has indeed seen God (42:5). The testimony of his eyes generates a profound reversal (v. 6).

The nature of Job's reversal is debatable, as the Hebrew text in 42:6 allows for multiple meanings.[1] The Hebrew verb *'em'as,* which NRSV translates "I despise myself," is not reflexive and has no object in Hebrew. Its possible meanings range from repudiation (of Job's case? of previously held beliefs or statements? of things others have said?) to melting (cf. Job 7:5). The second verb, *wenihamti,* which NRSV translates "repent," denotes a reversal in heart or mind. Such reversal might entail being comforted in the face of loss (e.g., Jer. 31:15), altering a plan (Exod. 13:17; 32:12; Jonah 3:10; 4:2), or regretting a past action (Gen. 6:6–7).

Whether Job now feels comfort, resolve, or regret is unclear. While a vision of God elicits this reversal, it is anchored to earthly reality. The NRSV translates the final phrase of this speech "in dust and ashes," but it might also be translated "concerning dust and ashes" (42:6). We remember that when Job learned of the death of his children, he fell earthward and prostrated himself (1:20). When sores infected his body, he sat amid a pile of ashes (2:8). When his friends saw his altered state, they flung dust upon their heads (2:12) then sat beside him upon the ground (2:13). In his speeches to his friends Job longed for burial (3:16, 21). He declared that his "flesh [was] clothed with worms and dirt" (7:5; cf. 9:31); he predicted that he soon would "lie in the earth" (7:21; cf. 16:15; 17:1). He reminded God, "Remember that you fashioned me like clay; and will you turn me to dust again?" (10:9; cf. 17:16). How does Job's reversal relate to the soil caked upon his skin and the earth to which he will one day return?

---

1. William Morrow's analysis of this verse argues for deliberate ambiguity. See "Consolation, Rejection, and Repentance in Job 42:6," *Journal of Biblical Literature* 105, no. 2 (1986): 211–25.

To Converse with God

In the first place, the soul learns to commune with God with more respect and reverence; always necessary in converse with the Most High. Now, in its prosperous days of sweetness and consolation, the soul was less observant of reverence, for the favours it then received, rendered the desire somewhat bold with God, and less reverent than it should have been. Thus it was with Moses, when he heard the voice of God; for carried away by the delight he felt, he was venturing without further consideration, to draw near, if God had not commanded him to stop, and put off his shoes, saying, "Come nigh hither; put off the shoes from thy feet." This teaches us how reverently and discreetly in spiritual detachment we are to converse with God. When Moses had become obedient to the voice, he remained so reverent and considerate, that not only did he not venture to draw near, but, in the words of Scripture, "durst not look at God." For having put off the shoes of desire and sweetness, he recognized profoundly his own wretchedness in the sight of God, for so it became him when about to listen to the words of God.

The condition to which God brought Job in order that he might converse with God, was not that of delight and bliss, of which he there speaks, and to which he had been accustomed. God left him in misery, naked on a dung-hill, abandoned and ever persecuted by his friends, filled with bitterness and grief, covered with worms: then it was that the Most High, Who lifteth up "the poor out of the dung-hill," was pleased to communicate Himself to Job in greater abundance and sweetness, revealing to him "the deep mysteries of His wisdom," as He had never done before in the days of Job's prosperity.

John of the Cross, *The Dark Night of the Soul,* trans. David Lewis (London: Thomas Baker, 1908), 52–53.

While dust, ash, and earth highlight mortality (of Job and his children), the book's concluding verses portray abounding life (42:12, 13, 16) and unexpected longevity (vv. 16–17), striking a chord many readers find dissonant with the earlier narrative and dialogues. Gold rings and beautiful women (vv. 11, 15) make for an enchanting fairytale ending, but "restored fortunes" (v. 10) do not resolve the questions and struggles at the book's heart. The ending sends us back to the beginning, and back to the middle as well, making the reader (and preacher) also a questioner, a debater, and a witness.

Jeremiah 31:7–9. The book of Jeremiah prepares and equips its audience to confront realities of disaster, loss, and death. Yet portions of the book also insist that through and beyond the ravages of siege warfare, displacement, and separation springs a future bursting with joy and new life. Jeremiah 30–33, commonly called the Book of Consolation, grounds this vision of future joy and security in the faithfulness and power of God and the enduring relationship between God and God's chosen people.

The oracle in Jeremiah 31:7–9 combines a wide array of sounds, emotions, images, and metaphors with speech-acts of supplication, praise, promise, and assurance, yielding a densely evocative scene that draws present grief into the confident expectation of future joy and relationship.

The poem's raucous soundscape includes shouting, neighing, and weeping. Jeremiah is a noisy book. Earlier in the book, the children of Israel were heard weeping and making supplication upon the heights (Jer. 3:21; cf. 7:29; 8:19; 9:19; 31:15). The prophet urged Judah and its people to lament and wail in the face of God's anger and coming destruction (4:8; 6:26; 9:10); even earth joined in lamentation (4:28; 12:4). War trumpets announced destruction (6:1, 17), and snorting war horses would be heard across the breadth of the land (8:16; cf. 10:22); "the roar of a great tempest" would come to consume Israel and Judah (11:16); God's own roaring, shouting, and clamor would echo to the ends of the earth (25:30–31).

For all this shouting, crying, and trumpeting, God had promised to banish the sounds of consolation and joy (16:7–9). God forbade the prophet's intercession and lament (11:14; 14:11; 16:5) and the communal practices of grieving that would make it possible for the people to comfort one another in the face of loss and begin the process of healing.

Now, in this promise of restoration, voices that weep, make supplication, and shout will no longer be silenced: the people are instructed to "make [others] hear" (*hashmiyu*, 31:7). Loss is not simply erased. Consolation now responds to grief (31:9). It is no longer the warhorses of the enemy who neigh, but God's people, whooping their confidence and excitement in the face of nations (31:7). New sounds are also heard: shouts of joy and songs of praise (31:7; cf. 31:12–13; 33:11). Jeremiah's promise of restoration and salvation moves God's people toward a future that holds the wounds of the past in trust, integrating trauma and sorrow into a life that also knows deep joy.

The theme of integration continues in the promise that God will gather together the scattered people and bring them "here" (31:8).

Among those who will return are people with impairments of sight and mobility and women whose bodies labor to bring forth their nation's future. No impairment will prevent *this* journey. The transformation of motor and sensory impairments is sometimes envisioned in prophetic texts (Isa. 29:18; 35:5–6) and is a hallmark of Jesus' ministry (Matt. 11:5; Luke 7:22), as attested in this week's Gospel reading (Mark 10:46–52). Jeremiah's oracle does not promise to remove or transform the physical conditions that produce blindness or lameness, but rather to ensure that these realities no longer function as an impediment to full inclusion and flourishing among God's people (for a similar vision, see Mic. 4:6–10; Zeph. 3:19). Women and children also receive the promise of full inclusion at the times of their greatest vulnerability (Jer. 31:8). The social world itself will be transformed. This radical vision grounds inclusion among God's people in the relationship between the people and God (31:9).

ANATHEA E. PORTIER-YOUNG

Commentary 2: Connecting the Reading with the World

Job bears his fair share of burdens. The weight on Job as he seeks out God leads him down a path of confusion, doubt, uncertainty, and despair. Job reaches out in his despair and cannot find God until God responds to Job's defiant questioning and seeking. In chapters 38–41, God makes his case to Job, and Job concedes to the wisdom in recognizing God's power and might. Job explains he has "heard of [God] by the hearing of the ear, but now my eye sees [God]" (Job 42:5).

Is the problem of Job's pain his lack of seeing God in these terms? Job seems to think so. He has experienced God's handiwork firsthand as he listens to God's retort. Job echoes God's opening response, "'Who is this that hides counsel without knowledge?' I have uttered what I did not understand" (42:3; see 38:2). What kind of "seeing" is it that Job is experiencing?

A number of new procedures are being developed to treat common causes of blindness.

Stem-cell therapy offers new hope for curing those who otherwise would have been subject to a life without sight. The procedure requires doctors to replace damaged cells with a group of stem cells. This technique, pioneered by the London Project to Cure Blindness, has been particularly helpful in cases where there is retinal damage.

Another group, the Himalayan Cataract Project (HCP), is facilitating cataract repair to people in places where it is not commonly an option. While cataract surgery has been present for years in the developed world, many around the globe do not have access to the procedure. The HCP has restored sight to hundreds of thousands of patients in multiple countries.

Imagine the excitement, elation, and perhaps even fear that people feel when they first see shapes, faces, and words that they have not seen in years or ever. How might this experience of restored physical sight speak life into this telling of Job's newly found "seeing"?

As we go further into Job 42, not only is Job's "seeing" restored, but we also see God's overwhelming return of abundance and joy to Job's life (vv. 10–17). God gives back Job's relationships with family. Job receives comfort and nourishment as he enjoys the companionship of brothers and sisters. He is returned to a state of wealth, well-being, and old age. Job is given children and is able to watch his family grow for four generations.

How might pastors invite congregants to ponder the depths of God's abundance, especially in the midst of a culture obsessed with scarcity, zero-sum political and business interactions, and prosperity gospels where wealth (or the lack thereof) is an indication of God's favor? They might invite members of the congregation to think about the gifts God has given them that have brought them abundance and joy, offering them a moment to write down the top three things. What would it mean for them to have this abundance taken away and then have it restored? Would it offer them a new way of understanding God?

Restoration and joyful abundance are two of God's primary hopes for God's people. The reader can discover similar themes in Jeremiah 31, couched in the story of Israel's homecoming from exile.

One of history's greatest announcements of a homecoming happened on September 2, 1945, the day that Japan surrendered, and American and Allied forces declared victory during World War II (V-J Day). It is hard to ignore the jubilant expressions on every face in photos of that day. Utter joy soaks those images.

In New York, seemingly every citizen that day crowded streets with a stream of people flowing to a river of the masses in Times Square. People danced on top of cars without any music playing. Each smile stretched wider and wider as the reality of the day settled in: the war was over. Tears of joy, ticker tape, and ecstatic celebrations were the ingredients of the day. Of course, there is the famous photo of Greta Zimmer Friedman and George Mendonsa—the sailor kissing the nurse in the middle of the multitudes.

Young people who were sent off to foreign lands to fight a war were coming home. Family members would return from a daily reality of violence and potential harm, from places where world powers fought for dominance, and from battles where atrocity and killing were everyday occurrences, to the safety, comfort, and peace of their hometowns and their families. An amazing sweetness must have run through the minds and hearts of each soldier. Finally, life as it should be was restored.

Another celebration that was unexpected and long-awaited came in 2016. The Chicago Cubs major league baseball team—otherwise called the "Lovable Losers" from the friendly confines of Wrigley Field—were once one of the most feared teams in baseball. At the turn of the twentieth century, the Cubs won back-to-back World Series in 1907 and 1908. Then the exile from baseball's greatest prize began. For 108 long, horrendous years, Cubs fans watched their beloved team lose, sometimes in spectacular fashion. Whole generations of Cubs fans and their families had come and gone without a victory. Prayers, rituals, and shrines were built to do away with "the curse," supposedly placed on Cubs by a disgruntled fan. In 2016, the Cubs found their way back to the top, beating a strong Cleveland Indians team. The return from exile was complete. The Cubs were the best again. People wept, smiled, laughed, embraced strangers, and called family members to share in the moment. Finally, "fandom" as it should be was restored.

The longing felt by God's people in exile must have been unbearable. Generations came and went without a return to the land promised to them by God. The temple was destroyed, and there was no guarantee of return to the place of their ancestors. The Lord's promise to the remnant would have been a bittersweet one. Imagine the day that the remnant received word that they would be able to return. What must that have been like? The words of the prophet Jeremiah probably only begin to grasp the depths and intensity of the psychological and emotional response of God's people: "With weeping they shall come, and with consolations I will lead them back" (Jer. 31:9a). God responds to the people's deepest yearnings: the restoration to their homeland. Finally, they will experience life where they know they belong.

A pastor might consider perusing videos and images from V-J Day or the celebration at Wrigley Field in 2016 to understand the range of experiences and discern the emotional impact of these days. If there is someone in your congregation who experienced World War II, you might consider asking them to tell their story about the end of the war. What special moments do they remember upon arriving home where family and friends greeted them? What memories of earlier days did they recall as they returned?

If you have a rabid Cubs fan in your midst, interview them about how they felt when Cubs fan Steve Bartman caught a foul ball in 2003—a potential catch for the Cubs outfielder—or when they saw team members Anthony Rizzo and Kyle Schwarber hoist the World Series trophy over their heads after their win in 2016. What was their experience? What did they feel?

As you engage in these conversations, you may begin to scratch the surface of the intensity of the emotional impact that the return from the exile would have had on the day the remnant entered Israel again.

BRADY BANKS

Proper 25 (Sunday between October 23 and October 29)

Psalm 34:1–8 (19–22)

[1]I will bless the LORD at all times;
   his praise shall continually be in my mouth.
[2]My soul makes its boast in the LORD;
   let the humble hear and be glad.
[3]O magnify the LORD with me,
   and let us exalt his name together.

[4]I sought the LORD, and he answered me,
   and delivered me from all my fears.
[5]Look to him, and be radiant;
   so your faces shall never be ashamed.
[6]This poor soul cried, and was heard by the LORD,
   and was saved from every trouble.
[7]The angel of the LORD encamps
   around those who fear him, and delivers them.
[8]O taste and see that the LORD is good;
   happy are those who take refuge in him.
. . . .
[19]Many are the afflictions of the righteous,
   but the LORD rescues them from them all.
[20]He keeps all their bones;
   not one of them will be broken.
[21]Evil brings death to the wicked,
   and those who hate the righteous will be condemned.
[22]The LORD redeems the life of his servants;
   none of those who take refuge in him will be condemned.

Psalm 126

[1]When the LORD restored the fortunes of Zion,
   we were like those who dream.
[2]Then our mouth was filled with laughter,
   and our tongue with shouts of joy;
then it was said among the nations,
   "The LORD has done great things for them."
[3]The LORD has done great things for us,
   and we rejoiced.

[4]Restore our fortunes, O LORD,
   like the watercourses in the Negeb.
[5]May those who sow in tears
   reap with shouts of joy.
[6]Those who go out weeping,
   bearing the seed for sowing,
shall come home with shouts of joy,
   carrying their sheaves.

Connecting the Psalm with Scripture and Worship

Psalm 34:1–8 (19–22). Psalm 34 is classified as a psalm of thanksgiving. It is certainly a song meant to exhort the people to praise, but it is also a piece of Wisdom literature with an aim to instruct. The psalm begins with an individual meditation, "I will bless the Lord at all times; his praise shall continually be in my mouth" (Ps. 34:1), but it quickly calls for others to join in, "O magnify the Lord with me, and let us exalt his name together" (v. 3). An initial statement of praise, "my soul makes its boast in the Lord" (v. 2), then offers an account of individual deliverance, "I sought the Lord, and he answered me, and delivered me from all my fears" (v. 4), and broadens to include "the poor soul" who "cried, and was heard by the Lord, and was saved from every trouble" (v. 6), and finally encompasses all "those who fear him," including those bruised and brokenhearted by life, around whom "an angel of the Lord encamps . . . and delivers them" (v. 7).

In response to God's saving acts, the psalmist "blesses" the Lord, by bending the knee and offering oneself, giving public witness, and inviting others to give thanks and praise. This psalm is part of a book that rejects the notion that a person's relationship with God is a private affair; instead, it reinforces the reality that individuals are related to God through a covenantal community. As Bernhard Anderson avows, "the individual praises God in concert with the worshiping community."[1] The psalmist starts with singing a solo of praise but is joined by a chorus singing a proclamation of hope to and for a congregation. The psalmist then expresses gratitude, inviting others to join: "O taste and see that the Lord is good; happy are those who take refuge in him" (v. 8).

The other readings speak of those who have found refuge and release from suffering in God. After many losses and laments, God answers Job's prayers and he is healed, his family and fortunes restored. In response, "he gave his daughters an inheritance, along with their brothers"

(Job 42:15). As Dale Andrews posits, "even our own experience of unjust suffering and restoration from beyond our own means redirects our attention."[2]

In response to divine deliverance, people can become a witness and a force for transforming suffering. In Hebrews, the great high priest Jesus offers intercession for believers who struggle. In Mark's Gospel, Bartimaeus, a blind beggar, calls out to Jesus, "Have mercy on me!" (Mark 10:47); the crowd does not help the beggar find Jesus but orders him to be quiet. In instructing them to "call him here" (v. 49), Jesus reminds them, as the psalmist does, to "let the humble hear and be glad" (Ps. 34:2), and "let us exalt [God's] name together" (v. 3).

Since the psalm is a call to worship, the liturgist can use it as such. Alternatively, it may be used as a responsive reading, with a sung refrain such as "Taste and see the goodness of the Lord." Hymns of thanksgiving that reflect Psalm 34 include "Great Is Thy Faithfulness," "God of Great and God of Small," and "Praise Ye the Lord, the Almighty."

Preachers may explore how the church might invite those whom we otherwise try to silence— the humble, or "the poor soul"—and how we can be a refuge for "those who fear him," so that together we become a chorus of thanksgiving, magnifying the Lord together.

Psalm 34 invites individuals and congregations alike to "taste and see that the Lord is good."

Psalm 126. Psalm 126 is from Book V of the Psalter, set in the postexilic era to address the ongoing theological crisis of people who are disappointed that the promised restoration (from Isa. 40–55) did not materialize, leaving them with no temple, no crops, and no peace. Still, their return to their homeland in Jerusalem was a source of hope: "When the Lord restored the fortunes of Zion, we were like those who dream" (Ps. 126:1).

---

1. Bernhard W. Anderson, *Out of the Depths: The Psalms Speak for Us Today* (Philadelphia: Westminster, 1983), 168.
2. Dale P. Andrews, "Homiletical Perspective on Job 42:1–6, 10–17," in *Feasting on the Word, Year B, Volume 4* (Louisville, KY: Westminster John Knox, 2009), 199.

Psalm 126 is one of fifteen psalms (Pss. 120–134) that share the superscript "A Song of Ascents." These songs were originally used by pilgrims going to Jerusalem as part of the festal celebration, and the word "ascent" refers to the temple steps.[3] Songs of Ascents were short and could be memorized and recited by the pilgrims as they walked. Throughout Psalm 126, the psalmist sounds a note of joy (vv. 2, 5, and 6), a fitting song to sing on the approach to the house of Yahweh: "Then our mouth was filled with laughter, and our tongue with shouts of joy" (v. 2).

Translation is an important question for Psalm 126. Some translations use all verbs in the past tense, making the psalm a song of thanksgiving: "The Lord has done great things for us, and we rejoiced" (v. 3). Others translate using the imperative, making the psalm a prayer of petition for Yahweh's help: "Restore our fortunes, O Lord" (v. 4). The New Revised Standard Version translates the first three verses in past tense and the last three verses in future tense, thus creating a tension between thankfully remembering what God has done and hopefully anticipating what God will do. Overall, there is a hopeful, even joyful sound: "May those who sow in tears reap with shouts of joy. Those who go out weeping . . . shall come home with shouts of joy" (vv. 5–6).

This hope that God will fully restore the chosen people to their homeland is reaffirmed in the other readings appointed for this day. Jeremiah speaks words of God's promise: "See, I am going to bring them from the land of the north, and gather them from the farthest parts of the earth, among them the blind and the lame . . . together . . . they shall return here" (Jer. 31:8). With the faith of his fathers, Bartimaeus cries out with hope for restoration, "Jesus, Son of David, have mercy on me!" (Mark 10:47).

Homiletically, the different verb tenses can be used to explore the tension between giving thanks for God's blessings, and still crying out in our grief. The preacher can teach about the kingdom of God as "already but not yet." That is, Jesus has inaugurated the kingdom on earth, but it has not been fully realized, and will not be until Jesus comes again to make all things new.

Liturgically, Psalm 126 can be read responsively, repeating the refrain: "The Lord has done great things for us, and we rejoiced." The spirit of joy can inspire a choral anthem like "Joy in the Morning" or the hymn "Joyful, Joyful, We Adore Thee." "Now Thank We All Our God" combines verbs of past and present tense to express gratitude for God's past deeds and for God's gracious activity in the present day.

Psalm 126 honors God's past faithfulness and anticipates God's full restoration, renewing our gratitude, strengthening our hope in the coming reign of justice and peace, and calling us to lift up our hearts with songs of joy.

DONNA GIVER-JOHNSTON

---

3. J. Clinton McCann Jr., "The Book of Psalms," in *The New Interpreter's Bible* (Nashville: Abingdon, 1996), 4:1176.

Hebrews 7:23–28

23Furthermore, the former priests were many in number, because they were prevented by death from continuing in office; 24but he holds his priesthood permanently, because he continues forever. 25Consequently he is able for all time to save those who approach God through him, since he always lives to make intercession for them.

26For it was fitting that we should have such a high priest, holy, blameless, undefiled, separated from sinners, and exalted above the heavens. 27Unlike the other high priests, he has no need to offer sacrifices day after day, first for his own sins, and then for those of the people; this he did once for all when he offered himself. 28For the law appoints as high priests those who are subject to weakness, but the word of the oath, which came later than the law, appoints a Son who has been made perfect forever.

Commentary 1: Connecting the Reading with Scripture

The writer of Hebrews wants to clarify that Jesus is our advocate; he hears our cries and responds with mercy. This is a common theme throughout the Scriptures, a common confession of people of faith. In Psalm 34, for example, the psalmist testifies, "I sought the Lord, and he answered me, and delivered me from all my fears. . . . This poor soul cried, and was heard by the Lord, and was saved from every trouble" (Ps. 34:4, 6). In Job 42, God responds to and restores an afflicted Job. In Mark 10, a blind man cries out relentlessly for mercy, and Jesus responds by informing him that his faith has made him well. In Jeremiah 31, God declares that "I will be their God and they will be my people." Together these passages remind us that when we seek the Lord, the Lord hears our cries, responds, and restores us. God promises to be with us and to work on our behalf. This is made clear even in Hebrews with the emphasis on Jesus as the high priest.

The writer of Hebrews continues the explanation of Jesus' priesthood in the seventh chapter. He begins by recalling the account of Abraham (then Abram) meeting King Melchizedek (see Gen. 14). A key feature of Jesus' priesthood highlighted in this text is its permanent nature. "Without father, without mother, without genealogy, having neither beginning of days

nor end of life, but resembling the Son of God, he remains a priest forever" (Heb. 7:3). While death prevents other priests from continuing in their office, Jesus' death does not stop his work. It simply transports it; that is, Jesus moves from earth to heaven. This is well established throughout the homily. Jesus' ascension results in his exalted state. In fact, Jesus' priesthood is described as unchangeable (*aparabaton*). The believer benefits from having Jesus as a priest because Jesus, an unchangeable and constant presence, is able to offer complete salvation for those who approach God through him.

Furthermore, Jesus' perpetual intercession benefits everyone. Not only does Jesus make intercession; he always *lives* to do so. That is, Jesus lives for the purpose of pleading for those who approach God through him; it is his delight. Christ's serving as an intercessor is attested in 1 John 2:1: "But if anyone does sin, we have an advocate with the Father, Jesus Christ the righteous." Jesus, described here as the righteous one, is an advocate for sinners. In Romans 8:34, Paul writes: "It is Christ Jesus, who died, yes, who was raised, who is at the right hand of God, who indeed intercedes for us."

Jesus' intercession did not begin with his ascension. Jesus' earthly ministry involved praying too. There are numerous examples of Jesus praying (Mark 1:35; Luke 5:16; 10:21; and John 17:20–21). In John 17:11, Jesus prays, "Holy Father, protect them in your name that you have given me, so that they may be one, as we are one." Jesus' prayer for unity and protection is an example of the intercession that Jesus had always, already provided on behalf of believers. As the risen Christ, Jesus continues to "stand in the gap" for all. This is the assurance of being a believer; one has an eternal advocate in Jesus.

Jesus' priesthood is also distinguished by his holiness. Jesus is described as "holy, innocent, undefiled, separated from sinners" (Heb. 7:26). He is similarly depicted in 1 Peter 1:19 and 2:22 as "a lamb without defect or blemish" who "committed no sin, and no deceit was found in his mouth." First Peter quotes Isaiah 53:9 to describe the servant and righteous one of God. Jesus is not like any other high priest or any other human. He is sinless. Holiness is an attribute of Jesus; in fact, all should aspire to be holy—consecrated or set apart for the work of God. The writer of Hebrews makes this explicit later in his homily when he admonishes them, "Pursue peace with everyone, and the *holiness* without which no one will see the Lord" (Heb. 12:14, italics mine). Jesus is described as a holy lamb; however, his sacrifice is unique.

As a high priest, Jesus offered a sacrifice for the people "once for all when he offered himself" (7:27). Other priests had to make sacrifices for their own sins daily and then sacrifices for the people. Jesus is the perfect sacrifice; there is no need for additional sacrifices. Paul describes Jesus' once-for-all (*ephapax*) act in Romans 6:10 thusly: "The death he died, he died to sin, once for all; but the life he lives, he lives to God." The once-for-all language is found again in Hebrews 9:12: "he entered once for all into the Holy Place, not with the blood of goats and calves, but with his own blood, thus obtaining eternal redemption." This emphasis is seen again in 10:10: "And it is by God's will that we have been sanctified through the offering of the body of Jesus Christ once for all." The believer's status is affirmed through the work of Christ. The writer emphasizes in Hebrews that Jesus' offering of himself was for all time a single sacrifice performed for all people. This sacrifice facilitated his entry into the Holy Place, the heavenly tabernacle. As such, Jesus' self-sacrifice not only redefines the priesthood; it also transforms sacrificial worship overall.

Jesus' high priesthood is distinctive because Jesus' status is assured by the word of the oath (*horkōmosias*). Echoes of Psalm 110:4 are heard in this text: "The Lord has *sworn* and will not change his mind. 'You are a priest forever, . . . according to the order of Melchizedek'" (Heb. 7:21, 17, italics mine). There are only a few oaths mentioned in the Bible (Gen. 22:16–17, 26:3; Exod. 32:13; 2 Sam. 3:9), and these oaths are associated with covenants. The Psalms often recall these oaths, as a reminder that God keeps God's promises (see Pss. 89:35; 105:9; and 132:11–12). Because there is no authority higher than God, God swearing an oath is a blessed assurance. It is a binding agreement upon which we can depend.

Finally, chapter 7 of Hebrews closes by portraying Jesus as a "Son who has been made perfect forever" (Heb. 7:28). Having established Jesus as a unique high priest, the writer of Hebrews goes on to show how Jesus presides over a new tabernacle. While sacrificial offerings may have ceased, worship persists, nonetheless. The heavens provide the ultimate example for how we are to approach God, for receiving grace and mercy. In doing so, we become inheritors of the promises given to Abraham. Much like the writer of James who declares: "and let endurance have its full effect, so that you may be mature and complete, lacking in nothing" (Jas. 1:4), believers are exhorted to stay the course with the promises of perfection, holiness, and rest awaiting them.

Within the homily of Hebrews, the writer develops a portrait of Jesus that establishes him as a heavenly king "who is seated at the right hand of the throne of the Majesty" (8:1), a high priest presiding over a heavenly tabernacle. He is continually making intercession for those who believe, offering eternal salvation to those who persevere in the faith. Believers are invited to find solace in this knowledge, even confidence in the assurance that the very Son of God is working on their behalf. They need only to approach the throne of grace boldly, and their cries will be heard and they, too, can be saved of their troubles.

JENNIFER T. KAALUND

Commentary 2: Connecting the Reading with the World

Identifying present-day connections to this text might be simple and straightforward if there were still a temple in Jerusalem with a priesthood that continued offering sacrifices. However, there has been no temple, and there have been no sacrifices, since the Roman armies destroyed the Second Temple in the year 70 CE. What of the priesthood? While it is still possible to trace priestly lineage, many of the elements described in the lectionary text concerning the ancient priesthood are no longer true for Jewish priests. The author of the Letter to the Hebrews notes, for instance, that day after day priests were required to offer sacrifices, first for their own sins and then for those of the people (Heb. 7:27). Nevertheless, one element does persist: their priesthood ends with their death. According to Hebrews, "former priests were many in number, because they were prevented by death from continuing in office" (v. 23). This limitation is not true of Jesus, who, in contrast, "holds his priesthood permanently, because he continues forever" and, in consequence, "is able for all time to save those who approach God through him" (vv. 24–25).

The author's affirmation—that Jesus "continues forever" and is "able for all time" to save— brings to light connections especially related to how Christians understand the work of God in Christ and their implication for our lives in the here and now. In our liturgies, for instance, we affirm through the Apostles' Creed or the Nicene Creed that "on the third day he rose again"! While the lectionary text does not speak of Jesus' resurrection, it nonetheless stresses the enduring fact that Jesus is now living and that his death did not interfere with his priesthood.

Thus, when we read this text, we do so from the long tradition of the faith passed down to us and in confidence of the power it holds. "He is risen indeed!" The risen Lord still accompanies and saves us. The author later echoes the importance of this in his affirmation that "Jesus Christ is the same yesterday and today and forever" (13:8). He is, as Lesslie Newbigin suggested, "our eternal contemporary." At whatever time in history, and in whatever part of the human family, Jesus is contemporary to that moment and place. He accompanies us here and now. For Newbigin that meant that the Jesus we follow and proclaim is "not a domesticated Jesus, not a Jesus who belongs to us, certainly not a Jesus who belongs to the past, not a character whom we have imprisoned in the religious and ecclesiastical categories of the past, but Jesus the crucified and risen Lord. . . . He is our living contemporary."[1]

Recognizing this connection also requires recognizing its flip side. Most people in our current world do not believe in Jesus or in his divinity or, least of all, that he has any saving power. God simply is not and cannot be like the one described in the lectionary text. Often, such belief in a risen Christ who saves may jar even his followers. If the text meets us and others with a potential disconnect, it also meets us with the prospect of bringing about a reconnect. The text invites and welcomes all its hearers into a fresh sense of the meaning and identity of Jesus, the divinely appointed high priest "who has been made perfect forever."

Talking about the priesthood inevitably means talking about sins, sacrifices, and salvation, as this text certainly does. Talk about sins and sacrifices gives way to notions of guilt and punishment, which people often resist. Most would rather not be told they are guilty of any wrongdoing. Life in our social order moves along nicely without reference to ourselves as sinners or to our actions as sins. There is often a kind of allergic reaction to any idea that someone would need absolution from a human priest, or pardon from a divine savior-priest.

Something else is also at play in the way many think that can be of value to the preacher. In a positive and almost universal way, people today resonate with a notion of redemption. In popular usage, in cinema and literature, in sport, business, and in governance, the idea of finding redemption for past failures or misdeeds has a great deal of play in our society. One of the authors in *The Oxford Handbook*

---

1. Lesslie Newbigin, *Christ Our Eternal Contemporary* (Madras: Christian Literature Society of India, 1968), 6.

of English Literature and Theology describes redemption as an important theme in English literature: "Redemption is a powerful and uplifting theme that acknowledges the human potential to succeed after failure."[2]

This general notion of redemption is not the same as theological understandings that accent a restored relationship with God, at God's initiative. The popular notion generally has to do with a person's effort to redeem themselves—not with what another person may do to grant it to them. It also has to do with a person's present life, rather than with what may follow in the afterlife. It may not have anything to do with divine action. Nonetheless, this human yearning for redemption may provide an important connection to this and to similar texts in Hebrews. The author describes Jesus as "able for all time to save those who approach God through him" (7:25). That points to a priestly companionship with human brokenness and renewal, fully within the context of life. When we wonder, "Is my life reclaimable?" the text answers with a resounding Yes!

Finally, when the text goes on to say that Jesus "always lives to make intercession for them" (v. 25), it signals a deep connection to the church's life of worship. Dietrich Bonhoeffer stresses the point that "the Psalter was the prayer book of Jesus Christ in the truest sense of the word."[3] It was true in his days on the earth, and it remains true today in his intercession.

Whenever we read, hear, or sing the Psalms, we are eavesdropping on what Jesus continues to pray on our behalf and on behalf of the world. It would certainly transform our worshipful use of the Psalms if we had an ever-present sense of who it is that was praying them long before us, prays them now, and will continue to do so long after we have ceased praying them.

The following insight from Bonhoeffer emphasizes another dimension of Christian worship that may provide the preacher with another lead: the use of the Lord's Prayer to guide and give voice to our own prayers. Along with others who preceded him, Bonhoeffer observes that there is a profound connection between the Lord's Prayer and the Psalter. He notes what other scholars have done to arrange the Psalter according to the seven petitions of the Lord's Prayer and concludes that "the whole sweep of the Book of Psalms was concerned with nothing more nor less than the brief petitions of the Lord's Prayer."[4]

Following Bonhoeffer, we may be confident that as Christians pray week by week and day by day, they are echoing on their lips what Jesus is praying. Likewise, when they read or sing the Psalms in their worship assemblies, they are uniting themselves to what Jesus is praying. Others who listen in are welcomed to hear Jesus' intercession for the world.

GEORGE R. HUNSBERGER

---

2. Daniel Boscaljon, "Possibilities of Redemption through the Novel," *The Oxford Handbook of English Literature and Theology*, ed. Andrew Hass, David Jasper, and Elisabeth Jay, 2009.

3. Dietrich Bonhoeffer, *Life Together* (New York: Harper & Row, 1954), 28.

4. Bonhoeffer, *Life Together*, 44–50.

Proper 25 (Sunday between October 23 and October 29)

Mark 10:46–52

⁴⁶They came to Jericho. As he and his disciples and a large crowd were leaving Jericho, Bartimaeus son of Timaeus, a blind beggar, was sitting by the roadside. ⁴⁷When he heard that it was Jesus of Nazareth, he began to shout out and say, "Jesus, Son of David, have mercy on me!" ⁴⁸Many sternly ordered him to be quiet, but he cried out even more loudly, "Son of David, have mercy on me!" ⁴⁹Jesus stood still and said, "Call him here." And they called the blind man, saying to him, "Take heart; get up, he is calling you." ⁵⁰So throwing off his cloak, he sprang up and came to Jesus. ⁵¹Then Jesus said to him, "What do you want me to do for you?" The blind man said to him, "My teacher, let me see again." ⁵²Jesus said to him, "Go; your faith has made you well." Immediately he regained his sight and followed him on the way.

Commentary 1: Connecting the Reading with Scripture

Mark 10:46–52 records Jesus' last stop before entering Jerusalem for the first time. A number of interpreters note the parallelism that exists between this scene and 8:22–26, when Jesus heals a blind man in Bethsaida. Given Mark's proclivity for *inclusio* (or "sandwich") structures, the bracketing of 8:22–10:52 seems intentional. Jesus' teaching about his identity, and especially his coming death and resurrection, is surrounded by episodes where blind men receive sight. Scholars highlight the similarities between the blind men's healings, particularly that of 8:22–26, and the disciples' persistent lack of understanding in 8:22–10:45.

Although misunderstanding Jesus is a consistent feature of Mark's characterization of the disciples, their confusion in 8:22–10:52 centers on the meaning of Jesus' identity. While they can confess the right words to Jesus—"You are the Messiah!" (8:29)—they cannot comprehend *how* this identity coheres with his threefold passion prediction (8:31–9:1; 9:30–32; 10:32–34). Like the blind man in 8:22–26, the disciples need repeated teachings and touches from Jesus in order to receive their sight.

By reiterating the motif of repeated touches and healings, Mark 10:46–52 offers hope that even the disciples will eventually be able to see

and joyously follow Jesus. The disciples, however, are not the lead characters in 10:46–52; if anything, they blend in with the "large crowd" and continue in their misguided prevention of people approaching Jesus. For the disciples, this blind beggar Bartimaeus is as annoying as the children being brought to Jesus for his blessing (10:13–16). The disciples need another lesson (see 9:33–37, 42–50)! In 10:46–52, Bartimaeus shines through as the one who approaches Jesus in humility, like the small child Jesus references in 9:36–37.

Bartimaeus is an example of one who is persistent in his calling for Jesus, despite the shouts for silence around him. Bartimaeus does not care about the crowd and the disciples' estimations of his worth; he is waiting to hear what Jesus, the Son of David, has to say. Although physically blind, he knows whose opinion matters and, like the hemorrhaging woman in 5:25–34, he knows where true power resides. In this respect, Bartimaeus is similar to James and John, who assume Jesus' authority in 10:35–40, but Bartimaeus's appeal to Jesus is very different. He does not try to trick Jesus into giving him what he wants; his is a call for help: "Jesus, Son of David, have mercy on me!" (10:47, 48).

Joel Marcus[1] notes the connection between Bartimaeus's cry and Jewish legends concerning another famous son of David, Solomon. Although Christians are more familiar with the royal and messianic overtones of the title "Son of David," Solomon was perhaps the most well-known son of David in first-century Judaism. According to a variety of extrabiblical materials, Solomon was an exorcist and healer (not entirely unlike his father before him; see 1 Sam. 16:14–23). Marcus writes, "Bartimaeus's invocation of Jesus as the 'Son of David,' therefore, exactly fits the remedy he seeks."[2] Bartimaeus persists in the face of "stern orders" or "rebukes" (*epitimaō*) from the crowd and disciples, resisting their demoniacal interference to keep him away from his Lord. This would not be the first time in Mark's Gospel that Satan works even through Jesus' own disciples to try to thwart God's plans (8:31–9:1; cf. 4:1–20).

Hearing his cries, Jesus calls for Bartimaeus to approach him. The eagerness of Bartimaeus's response mirrors the fervency of his previous petitions for mercy, as he throws down his cloak, springs up, and comes to Jesus (10:50). The act of discarding his cloak alongside the road is more than just an extravagant gesture; it is leaving behind a significant possession, a precious guard against the elements for one who is a blind beggar beside the road (v. 46). Leaving his old garment behind signals his trust and hope that Jesus will indeed have mercy upon him.

The Gospel audience should see parallels between Bartimaeus's actions and Jesus' instructions for his disciples in 8:34: "If any want to become my followers, let them deny themselves and take up their cross and follow me." Bartimaeus's sacrifice might also remind readers of Peter's comments in 10:28 that he and the other disciples had "left everything and followed you," as well as Jesus' promise that they will receive much more in return for their sacrifices (10:29–30).

When Bartimaeus and Jesus finally stand face to face, Jesus questions him: "What do you want me to do for you?" (v. 51). This is the same question that Jesus asks James and John in 10:36. Bartimaeus's answer, however, is different: he does not want a place above others; rather, he wants to see *again*. Moreover, Bartimaeus calls Jesus *rabbouni*, the Hebrew and Aramaic for "*My* teacher" (v. 51). The use of this term creates further contrast between James, John, and the wealthy man who came to Jesus (10:17), all of whom called Jesus by the Greek term *didaskale* ("Teacher").

Mark repeatedly includes Aramaic phrases at significant points in his Gospel: when Jesus raises Jairus's daughter from the dead (5:41) and when he calls out to God from the cross, quoting in Aramaic Psalm 22:2: "My God, my God, why have you forsaken me?" (15:34). Bartimaeus's mode of address, therefore, not only creates more intimacy between himself and Jesus; it also signals a significant episode for the Markan account. This is Jesus' last healing in the Gospel and his last action before entering Jerusalem for his passion.

Jesus answers Bartimaeus with another phrase that connects this story to the story of the woman who had long been suffering from hemorrhages (Mark 5). Just as he told the woman that her faith had made her well (v. 34), Jesus turns to Bartimaeus and says: "Go, your faith has made you well" (10:52). The comparison between the unnamed woman in Mark 5 and Bartimaeus in chapter 10 becomes richer when we remember that Jesus called her "daughter" and that Bartimaeus means "son of Timaeus." These designations in Mark's Gospel remind us that Jesus is creating a new family: "Whoever does the will of God is my brother and sister and mother" (3:35). The daughter in Mark 5 and this newly sighted son in Mark 10 join Jesus' family.

It is these—the least of society, so easily passed by and hindered by crowds pressing around Jesus—that shine as examples of faithfulness in Mark's Gospel. *They*—the ones who "hear the word and accept it and bear fruit"—are the "good soil" from Jesus' parable in Mark 4.

---

1. Joel Marcus, *Mark 8–16*, Anchor Yale Bible 27A (New Haven, CT: Yale University Press, 2009), 762–63.
2. Marcus, *Mark 8–16*, 762–63.

Notably, neither the woman nor Bartimaeus needs a cure for their bodily ailments in order to be faithful; they do not need to be socially acceptable before coming to their Lord. Instead, they embody faithfulness *before* being cured. Jesus publicly affirms the faith and trust that saves these two children of God. People do not need to be "fixed" or cohere with social expectations in order to access God. This is a human way of thinking (8:31–33). Instead, we need to remember our own brokenness and God's great graciousness. We need to learn in humility from those we would so quickly pass by, and we need to enable others to approach Jesus, instead of simply working to see how much *we* can get from our displays of seeming "faithfulness" (see Mark 12:38–44).

ALICIA D. MYERS

Commentary 2: Connecting the Reading with the World

In this Gospel reading, Jesus is continuing his journey to Jerusalem and to the cross. He has just told the disciples, for the third time, that he will be killed by the religious and political leaders. He also says, in no uncertain terms, that he will rise again after three days (Mark 10:34). When Jesus first discloses events to come (8:31–33), Peter tries to tell Jesus not to scare his followers with such premonitions. When Jesus speaks a second time to the disciples about what is to happen (9:31–32), they are too afraid to ask him what he means. After the third time (10:33–37), James and John ask Jesus to assure them places of honor when he inherits his kingdom. Those closest to him are unwilling or unable fully to hear Jesus' revelation about who he is and what he came to do. Then we have Bartimaeus who, though blind, seems to be one of the few who clearly sees who Jesus is.

In preparing for this Gospel reading, it is worthwhile to consider three different perspectives and how they work together. The first is that of the crowd that is accompanying Jesus and is determined to silence the blind beggar. In those days it was believed that a person with a disability or a disfiguration was being punished for their own sins or those of their parents. Bartimaeus is not simply seen as someone who is blind; he is seen as someone who is being punished by God and is therefore deserving of his status as an outcast. Bartimaeus asks Jesus to let him "see again" (v. 51), implying that he had been able to see at one point in his life.

Upon hearing this, the crowd may have suspected that his blindness was a consequence of his own sin, rather than the sins of his parents, which would have left him blind at birth. The crowd believes that by telling Bartimaeus to be quiet they are protecting Jesus from being bothered by an irredeemable sinner—someone who has no standing in the community and survives only through the charity of others. Such a person is not expected to speak, because he has nothing valuable to say.

It may be worthwhile to ask, Where and when is it that we behave like the crowd in this reading? When is it that we decide it is not worth listening to someone or some group, or that certain people's perspectives are not worthy of our attention because of who they are? A perfect example in our recent past is the debate over welfare reform. In our public discussions, we rarely heard from those who actually use the system. As a community, we seemed to treat those on welfare as outcasts who had nothing to add to the conversation about policies that critically impact their lives. Another example is the paucity of voices of everyday Palestinians in many of our conversations about Palestine-Israel relations. It seems those with the power to do so have decided that the position of people like those on welfare or Palestinians is illegitimate and that their voices do not belong in crucial policy-making discussions. Whose voices are being silenced in our churches, our politics, and our society? When are *we* the crowd that does not want to hear from those we have judged unworthy?

The second perspective is that of Bartimaeus himself. We know nothing about Bartimaeus except what we hear in this pericope. He is a blind man who has never seen Jesus and probably has had little exposure to him, since his blindness would likely have prevented him from traveling. Yet Bartimaeus is the one who is clear about who is passing by and what the Son of David can do for him. What is it about his life circumstance or his faith that makes him so sure that Jesus is indeed the Messiah, the one sent to deliver Israel? He calls Jesus "Son of David," one of the titles that Jews gave to the long-awaited Messiah who would deliver Israel. He does not simply call Jesus healer or miracle worker, titles he might have used if he had based his knowledge solely on Jesus' reputation. Not only is he clear about who Jesus is; he is determined not to be silenced by the crowd. He continues to call out, even in the face of the threats that most probably accompany the attempts to silence him.

It is possible to look at Bartimaeus and think he has nothing to lose in continuing to call out to Jesus. He has only his healing to gain. However, if Jesus had not stopped to listen to him, the crowd upon which he relied for alms could have taken it upon themselves physically to silence him or refuse to give him the scraps he counted on to survive. So, in fact, he has an awful lot to lose. What about his belief in the Messiah, in the goodness of God, allows him to insist on being heard, and at what possible price?

Is it possible that what we see in Bartimaeus is the kind of faith that has sustained Christians throughout history in the face of crowds and powers that would have them be silent or even denounce their faith? What does Bartimaeus have in common with those who have stood up for their faith in situations of oppression? Can we see in Bartimaeus's example the kind of faith that led Archbishop Oscar Arnulfo Romero to speak out against injustice in El Salvador, even in the face of attempts to silence him, which ultimately culminated in his assassination? It is true that Bartimaeus received the fruits of his faith immediately, but is there a larger lesson about faith and persistence that we can offer to our congregations?

The final perspective we can examine is that of Jesus. Throughout the Gospel of Mark, Jesus leads his disciples in a dance between healing, teaching, and challenging the power structures. He preaches, then explains the meaning of the lessons to his disciples. He challenges the law, then shows how much he respects it. He heals and connects the healing to the faith of those healed and the prayers of those around them. It is clear in the chapters and verses leading to this story that Jesus is preparing his followers for his final confrontation with the political and religious leaders who are threatened by his ministry and teachings.

The lack of faith and recognition of his identity as Lord and Messiah, the Son of God, by those who have been with him for three years, compared to the faith of the blind beggar, speaks to the power of Jesus' message and its resonance with the poor, the sick, the sinful. For Jesus, Bartimaeus's faith must have affirmed his mission, message, and presence to those on the margins, those whom the world rejected. Jesus is clear that he preaches, teaches, and heals as one on the margins himself, one who is constantly in conflict with the political rulers and religious elite, even as he shows himself to be well versed in the law. What is the dance that Jesus calls us to in this day and age? How is he leading the church to be those who challenge, teach, and heal?

NONTOMBI NAOMI TUTU

All Saints

Isaiah 25:6–9   Revelation 21:1–6a
Psalm 24   John 11:32–44

Isaiah 25:6–9

> [6]On this mountain the LORD of hosts will make for all peoples
>   a feast of rich food, a feast of well-aged wines,
>   of rich food filled with marrow, of well-aged wines strained clear.
> [7]And he will destroy on this mountain
>   the shroud that is cast over all peoples,
>   the sheet that is spread over all nations;
> [8]he will swallow up death forever.
> Then the Lord GOD will wipe away the tears from all faces,
>   and the disgrace of his people he will take away from all the earth,
>   for the LORD has spoken.
> [9]It will be said on that day,
>   Lo, this is our God; we have waited for him, so that he might save us.
>   This is the LORD for whom we have waited;
>   let us be glad and rejoice in his salvation.

Commentary 1: Connecting the Reading with Scripture

Isaiah 25:6–9 is part of a section scholars call the Isaianic Apocalypse (Isa. 24–27). It is situated within First Isaiah (chaps. 1–39), which is mostly dated before the fall of Jerusalem to Babylon in 587 BCE. Many scholars, however, think these four chapters were added much later, perhaps during the Persian era or even as late as the Hellenistic period.

Chapters 24–27 are placed in a longer section (chaps. 13–27) that mostly concerns the nations surrounding Judah, including Babylon, Assyria, Moab, Damascus, Egypt, and Tyre. The focus of these chapters expands to encompass the whole earth rather than particular locales. Their language displays elements scholars call protoapocalyptic: they are not the full-blown apocalypses written later in the Second Temple period and beyond, which include allegory, heavenly guides, stages of history, and other genre features present in Daniel, Revelation, and Jewish literature outside of Scripture. They tend toward the universalizing language we see in today's passage.

In soaring, lofty words, words too lofty for everyday reality, but nevertheless communicating hope, Isaiah 25:6–9 offers a portrait of celebration of divine faithfulness. A prophetic description in verses 6–8 of a universal banquet hosted by God "on this mountain"—that is, on Mount Zion, where the temple stood—is surrounded before and after by hymns of thanksgiving.

The chapter began in verses 1–5 with a communal hymn of thanksgiving for God's deliverance from tyrants. That hymn gathers themes and language well known from the rest of Isaiah, claiming that God's plans will come to fruition, a key theme in Isaiah.

The hymn also recalls the language of steadfast faithfulness that is found especially in prophecies surrounding the international crises faced in the eighth century BCE by Ahaz and Hezekiah. It repeats the term "tyrant" (NRSV "ruthless") three times in three verses, and it expresses hope for decisive deliverance from tyranny. The hymn goes on to praise God, as many psalms do, for acting as "shelter" and "refuge" for the poor and needy.

At the end of the previous chapter, in Isaiah 24:23, God is seen inaugurating divine reign on Mount Zion and in Jerusalem, attended by elders who see God's glory. That image harks back to the story in Exodus 24 in which seventy elders are invited with Moses, Aaron, and Aaron's sons to see the God of Israel on Mount Sinai, and to eat and drink in God's presence, just before the stone tablets containing the commandments are given to Moses. The only major element missing from Isaiah 24:23 is the meal.

However, in today's passage, following the hymn in verses 1–5, the meal that was missing from Isaiah 24:23 emerges in detailed glory, yet with some distinctive elements. It occurs not on Mount Sinai, but on "this mountain," Mount Zion. God prepares this banquet not only for the leaders, not only for Israel, but for "all peoples" (twice) and "all nations." "All faces" and "all the earth" are also mentioned, so that the word "all" is found five times in three verses. Here, God serves a very rich menu: choice wines, strained clear, and sumptuous meats.

Food is rarely described at length in Scripture. In fact, in the prophetic books especially, descriptions of foods and banquets often accompany covert or overt criticism of debauchery. In Isaiah 24, the wine had all dried up, along with mirth and joy. Here, food, drink, and delight return on God's terms, not as an occasion for social oppression, but in a spirit of celebration and harmony hosted by the creator of all foods. Mourning clothes are no longer necessary, since the people are comforted. As they eat, God "swallows" both their shrouds (25:7) and death itself (v. 8). Victorious over that most persistent foe, God wipes tears from all faces.

God's "swallowing" of death in this passage recalls the story of the Canaanite god Baal found in the Ras Shamra texts at Ugarit. There, the underworld god Mot ("death") either swallows Baal or threatens to swallow him—the text is unclear—but is defeated. Their battle recurs year after year in the seasonal alternation between drought and fertility. Distinct differences from the Baal story appear in this biblical poetry. Here, it is God who swallows death, rather than the reverse, and this victory is not subject to repetition, but stands forever.

Verses like this one do not yet reflect belief in physical, bodily resurrection, which will emerge centuries later. The apostle Paul nevertheless employs this image in his description of resurrection in 1 Corinthians 15:54: "Death has been swallowed up in victory." It is also paraphrased in Revelation 21:3–4, in which God "will wipe every tear from their eyes. Death will be no more; mourning and crying and pain will be no more, for the first things have passed away" (Rev. 21:4). The grateful hymn that follows in Isaiah 25:9 echoes the vocabulary of numerous psalms (see, e.g., Pss. 35:9; 130:5; and esp. 118:24).

The vision of an eschatological banquet hosted by God articulates some of Judah's most inclusive hopes and loftiest dreams of peace. It presents no program for realizing these hopes. Yet such attempts to imagine the future cultivate readers who embrace these dreams and seek their fulfillment. Such poetry deepens the human capacity to envision *shalom*, strengthening commitments to reduce barbarous acts of violence.

In a similar manner, and sometimes employing these very words, the service of Holy Communion invites Christians to experience themselves as participating in a banquet that is both part of Jesus' story in the past and part of God's eschatological story. Communion invites us for a few moments to set aside all that troubles us and to imagine ourselves, along with believers through the ages, seated with Christ as our host in a universal banquet of peace, a banquet undivided by geography, politics, and even doctrine. Taking time to imagine ourselves in communion with faithful God-seekers of all times and places helps us to remember that what unites humans runs far deeper than what divides us.

Such words that soar above reality can help fuel change. The picture of a banquet attended by all nations feeds the hope for peace among the earth's nations. It functions like the earlier, and similar, "swords into plowshares" passage in Isaiah 2:1–4.

Lofty visions such as these do matter. They may even change the world. The visionary words of the American Declaration of Independence,

"We hold these truths to be self-evident, that all men are created equal," have been reinterpreted several times to propose equalities that lay beyond the imagination of its original writers. They were invoked in 1848 by women's rights advocates, who paraphrased: "all men and women are created equal." They were invoked at Gettysburg by Abraham Lincoln shortly after he signed the Emancipation Proclamation, and again a century later by the Rev. Martin Luther King Jr., describing his dream that "one day this nation will rise up and live out the true meaning of its creed, that all are created equal."

The preacher who studies the broader literary context of the Isaiah lection will see that the banquet vision is followed by a far less generous vision, of Moab's violent demise: the Moabites will be "trodden down in their place as straw is trodden down in a dung-pit" (v. 10). Such triumphal wishes are discouraging and disturbing. Yet these verses serve as a sobering reminder of the bitter divisions that continue to fracture our world. Invoking the vision in verses 6–9, preachers can call their communities to a loftier dream: a dream of abundance, healing, and peace for all nations.

PATRICIA K. TULL

Commentary 2: Connecting the Reading with the World

"Death be not proud, though some have called thee mighty and dreadful, for thou art not so."[1] The British poet John Donne penned these words to open one of his most popular holy sonnets. Why adopt such a posture of bold defiance when death defies all our attempts to escape it? The apostle Paul describes it as "the last enemy to be destroyed" (1 Cor. 15:26). Yet Donne stares it down without flinching. He sings a hymn. His reason comes later in the sonnet, and it bears a striking resemblance to the good news that Isaiah 25:6–9 offers in the form of praise: not even death can stop God's plans to bring new life.

Isaiah 25:6–9 envisions the building of a new age that leads to life through the destruction of an old age that leads to death. This reordering of reality will come about in two ways: first, through the demise of enmity between peoples, and second, through the permanent removal of death's power over humanity. Verses 6–7 declare that God will bring about a radical new community for "all peoples." The God that the nation praises for defeating its enemies in Isaiah 25:2–3, 5, 10–12 is the same God who will prepare a lavish feast of the finest wines and meats for *all* peoples on Mount Zion (Isa. 25:6) and who, from that mountain, will remove the shroud that covers them (v. 7).

Later in Isaiah, the promise of hope for all peoples reminds those tempted toward ethnic exceptionalism—then and now—that the God of the nation is *also* the God of everyone else (56:6–7; 60:3; 66:18–24). The God who confronts foreign nations also confronts Israel. The God who rescues Israel also rescues other nations: "Are you not like the Ethiopians to me, O people of Israel? says the LORD. Did I not bring Israel up from the land of Egypt, and the Philistines from Caphtor and the Arameans from Kir?" (Amos 9:7). Wise preachers reject any brand of preaching that wraps the gospel in a flag or banner, that builds a citadel to separate "us" from "them," that embraces ethnic superiority instead of cultural humility. They remember that the same God who brought them up from captivity brings other people up as well.

Jesus adopts an all-people mind-set throughout his ministry, especially in the Gospel of Luke. In his inaugural sermon in the synagogue at Nazareth, he proclaims that the God who sent Elijah and Elisha to Israel also sent Elijah to the widow of Zarephath and Elisha to Naaman the Syrian (Luke 4:26–27; see 1 Kgs. 17:7–24; 2 Kgs. 5:1–27). Later in Luke, Jesus gives honorific titles to those that others consider outsiders. He calls a woman bent over for eighteen years a "daughter of Abraham" and Zacchaeus,

1. John Donne, "Holy Sonnet 6," in *John Donne: The Major Works,* ed. John Carey (New York: Oxford University Press, 2000), 175–76.

the tax collector, a "son of Abraham" (Luke 13:16; 19:9). Jesus confers status and worth on those that society sees as peripheral and, more importantly, on those that society thinks do not deserve it. In Luke, only outsiders receive the title of son or daughter of Abraham. With that in mind, consider what Jesus would say to today's religious insiders about his commitment to outsiders. What sorts of people does society cast as peripheral and undeserving of dignity and respect, and how might Jesus respond to them? Perhaps he would call them sons or daughters of Abraham.

Christian communities enact an all-people mind-set when they stretch their arms wider than their natural prejudices allow, when they decide that difference is an opportunity rather than a threat, when they conclude that culturally different others are divine image bearers instead of a danger to society. Ethnic superiority and cultural chauvinism cannot abide, especially when confronted with an Isaianic hymn that envisions God preparing a sacred gathering and lavish feast for all peoples. Neither can enmity.

Those that claim to be reconciled to Christ become reconcilers for Christ's sake because of the gospel (2 Cor. 5:16–21). They exchange xenophobia for xenophilia, estrangement from others for right relationships. Genuine neighbor-love requires a different way of seeing and being, indeed, a new commitment to expanding the circle of who gets to count as my neighbor. A prayer of C. S. Lewis in *A Grief Observed* comes to mind: "Not my idea of God but God . . . not my idea of my neighbor, but my neighbor."[2]

Isaiah 25:6–9 takes God's plan for humanity to another level, beyond that of a new community for all peoples. Indeed, God will not stop until death itself has been defeated. Most biblical scholars agree that death is the shroud cast over all peoples and the sheet spread over all nations (v. 7). What will happen to the shroud? What will become of the sheet? Notice the main verbs in verses 7 and 8. God will "destroy" the shroud and the sheet. God will "swallow up" death forever, in much the same way that a giant fish swallows up its helpless prey. God will "wipe away" tears from all faces

(Rev. 7:17; 21:4) and "take away" the disgrace of the nation. On that day, according to verse 9, those who are waiting will be delivered, and those who suffer will rejoice, for the shroud of death over all people will finally be removed. In a remarkable reversal, God will curse that which has cursed humanity. God will put death to death.

Herein lies the connection between Isaiah 25:6–9 and All Saints' Day, the day on which this lection is read and preached. Although All Saints' Day connects people to the past as they remember those who went behind them, it also connects them to the future as they await that which lies before them. In the Apostles' Creed, Christians confess: "We believe in the communion of saints," thus declaring that they are enrolled in a story much larger than their story, one that includes death but does not conclude with it. When they confess: "He was crucified, dead, and buried," they remember that Christ walked the *via dolorosa* in order to put death on notice that it could not abide forever. When they confess: "I believe in the resurrection of the body and the life everlasting," they proclaim the same truth that Isaiah 25 proclaims, that someday the grave will be emptied of its power, and death will be swallowed up by new life.

Although the apostle Paul is right when he says that death is the last enemy to be destroyed, he makes another claim in the same chapter that mitigates the first one: "Listen, I will tell you a mystery. We will not all die, but we will all be changed" (1 Cor. 15:51). In other words, death, which is our mortal enemy, cannot remain our enemy forever. Paul sings a hymn over death in much the same way that Donne does in his sonnet: "Death has been swallowed up in victory. Where, O death, is your victory? Where, O death, is your sting?" (1 Cor. 15:54b–55). How odd it is for one to talk to death that way, to speak with such bold defiance—unless, of course, one holds fast to a mystery much stronger than death! Donne names the mystery this way in the final line of his sonnet: "One short sleep past, we wake eternally. And death shall be no more; Death, thou shalt die."

JARED E. ALCÁNTARA

2. C. S. Lewis, *A Grief Observed* (New York: Harper One, 1994), 67.

Psalm 24

¹The earth is the LORD's and all that is in it,
    the world, and those who live in it;
²for he has founded it on the seas,
    and established it on the rivers.

³Who shall ascend the hill of the LORD?
    And who shall stand in his holy place?
⁴Those who have clean hands and pure hearts,
    who do not lift up their souls to what is false,
    and do not swear deceitfully.
⁵They will receive blessing from the LORD,
    and vindication from the God of their salvation.
⁶Such is the company of those who seek him,
    who seek the face of the God of Jacob.

⁷Lift up your heads, O gates!
    and be lifted up, O ancient doors!
    that the King of glory may come in.
⁸Who is the King of glory?
    The LORD, strong and mighty,
    the LORD, mighty in battle.
⁹Lift up your heads, O gates!
    and be lifted up, O ancient doors!
    that the King of glory may come in.
¹⁰Who is this King of glory?
    The LORD of hosts,
    he is the King of glory.

Connecting the Psalm with Scripture and Worship

Historically, Psalm 24 may have been used as liturgy to lead the congregation in a procession with the ark of the covenant into the temple. However, as J. Clinton McCann notes, "Whatever may have been its original setting and use, Psalm 24 in its current form is a powerful affirmation of the sovereignty of God, the identity of humankind, and the relationship between humanity and God."[1] Psalm 24 begins with a stirring declaration of God as sovereign Creator and Ruler of the earth that is reinforced by repetition: "The earth is the LORD's and all that is in it, the world, and those who live in it" (Ps. 24:1). The name "King of glory," unique to Psalm 24, is described as "strong and mighty, mighty in battle" (v. 8) and "the LORD of hosts" (v. 10).

In addition to affirming the sovereignty of God, the psalmist also confirms the identity of humankind, first by asking, "Who shall ascend the hill of the LORD? And who shall stand in his holy place?" (v. 3). The "hill of the LORD" refers to the temple on Mount Zion, which was believed to be God's earthly dwelling place. The psalmist offers access to God's holy presence to "those who have clean hands and pure hearts,

---

1. J. Clinton McCann Jr., "The Book of Psalms," in *The New Interpreter's Bible* (Nashville: Abingdon, 1996), 4:772.

who do not lift up their souls to what is false, and do not swear deceitfully" (v. 4). Those whose inner spirits motivate outward behavior that keeps covenant faithfulness are those who "will receive blessing from the Lord, and vindication from the God of their salvation" (v. 5). Psalm 24 celebrates the relationship between humanity and God as one of continual divine blessings for those who faithfully seek the face of God.

Those who with clean hands and pure hearts seek God's face are welcomed into the temple. In this antiphonal call and response, the psalmist cries, "Lift up your heads, O gates! and be lifted up, O ancient doors!" (vv. 7, 9), asking "that the King of glory may come in." "The intent is for the gates to be raised so high above the walls that they will never be shut again," asserts Michael Morgan, "and for the doors to be flung off their hinges, in order that the seekers and followers of the Lamb may follow him, redeemed and welcomed, into the courts of God."[2] The gates give access not only to the holy sanctuary of God, but also to God's eternal salvation.

Isaiah echoes this theme of the open gate by reminding those who suffer on this side of salvation of the promise that God "will swallow up death forever . . . will wipe away the tears from all faces" (Isa. 25:8). When that day comes, it will be said, "This is the Lord for whom we have waited; let us be glad and rejoice in his salvation" (v. 9). In the Gospel reading, Jesus is the one who opens the gates by taking away the stone that sealed the tomb of Lazarus and calling for him to come out—and Lazarus did! God's promise comes to ultimate fulfillment in the last days, as recorded in the book of Revelation, where there is "a new heaven and a new earth" (Rev. 21:1) and it is said, "See, the home of God is among mortals. He will dwell with them; they will be his peoples, and God himself will be with them" (v. 3) and "death will be no more" (v. 4). To reassure us that this is not just a promise made, but a promise kept, "then he said to me, 'It is done!'" (v. 6). So it is.

All Saints' Day is an occasion to witness to the truth that "It is done!"—not by any merit of ours, but by the gracious mercy of God, who by sacrificing Jesus on the cross opened the gates to heaven, that all may go in. Any of the biblical texts for the day provide rich material and real motivation to preach about the promise of resurrection to eternal life. On All Saints' Day, we are mindful that those who have kept the faith, finished their race, and now rest from their labors do so in the presence of God. The hymn "For All the Saints" recalls loved ones we have lost, but reminds us that "they in glory shine," even as we await our promised reunion with them and with all the saints in the heavenly realm. Other hymns with vivid imagery of gates are "Lift Up the Gates Eternal" and "Lift Up Your Heads, Ye Mighty Gates." Singing "Here in This Place" helps us to visualize the gates being opened as we wait for God to gather in all the lost and forsaken, all who suffer, that we might belong to God.

Liturgical options abound, including an antiphonal call to worship or a responsive reading of the psalm, a dramatic reading of the Gospel, and prayers with responses from Isaiah or Revelation. In words, songs, gestures, and rituals, the liturgist can affirm the sovereignty of God, confirm the identity of humankind, and celebrate the relationship between humanity and God. Liturgical dancers can creatively embody the opening of the gates, so that the congregation can experience the entrance of the King of glory. Rituals might include lighting candles for dearly departed saints of the congregation or a celebration of the Lord's Supper, which opens the gates and gives us a glimpse of the heavenly banquet that we will share with all the saints in glory.

Even while we wait on this side of the heavenly gate, Psalm 24 provides strength for today and bright and audacious hope for tomorrow, when death will be no more, and we will be in the presence of the Holy One and all the saints forevermore.

DONNA GIVER-JOHNSTON

---

2. Michael Morgan, "Pastoral Perspective of Psalm 24," in *Feasting on the Word, Year B, Volume 4* (Louisville, KY: Westminster John Knox, 2009), 228.

Revelation 21:1–6a

¹Then I saw a new heaven and a new earth; for the first heaven and the first earth had passed away, and the sea was no more. ²And I saw the holy city, the new Jerusalem, coming down out of heaven from God, prepared as a bride adorned for her husband. ³And I heard a loud voice from the throne saying,

"See, the home of God is among mortals.
He will dwell with them;
they will be his peoples,
and God himself will be with them;
⁴he will wipe every tear from their eyes.
Death will be no more;
mourning and crying and pain will be no more,
for the first things have passed away."

⁵And the one who was seated on the throne said, "See, I am making all things new." Also he said, "Write this, for these words are trustworthy and true." ⁶Then he said to me, "It is done! I am the Alpha and the Omega, the beginning and the end."

Commentary 1: Connecting the Reading with Scripture

Revelation 21:1–6a is the opening scene of John's final vision, the one toward which the one given to him on the island of Patmos has been moving since the very beginning.[1] Ironically, there is little in this vision that is new. John not only uses imagery, language, and ideas appearing in biblical prophets (esp. Isaiah and Ezekiel) and earlier Jewish and Christian apocalyptic writings (both in and beyond the canon) but also introduces them early in his own narrative. Still, 21:1–6a and its unfolding in 21:6b–22:7 constitute a dramatic, memorable climax to the Bible's last book, driving home its message that God controls what "must soon take place" (Rev. 1:1), using a variation of the phrase that appears repeatedly, "'I am the Alpha and the Omega,' says the Lord God, who is and who was and who is to come, the Almighty" (1:8; see also 4:8; 11:19; 19:6; and 21:6).

Following God's final victories over Satan and the forces of evil in 19:11–20:15 (which echo episodes in chaps. 5–18), 21:1–6a describes in vivid imagery the outcome of God's victory.[2] The first image is of "a new heaven and a new earth" (21:1), alluding to the opening lines of the creation poem in Genesis 1:1–2:4b. More directly, however, John's language is influenced by Isaiah 65:17 and 66:22, which use the image of "a new heaven and a new earth" to express the cosmic significance of God delivering the king and people of Judah from Babylonian captivity, restoring them to their homeland and calling the Persian king to set in motion the rebuilding of Jerusalem.

Isaiah's treatment of Jerusalem/Zion in the poetry of restoration has also influenced John's second image of the outcome of God's victory over the forces of evil: "the holy city, the new Jerusalem, coming down out of heaven

---

1. For an introduction to Revelation and apocalyptic works like it, see M. Eugene Boring, *Revelation* (Louisville, KY: Westminster John Knox, 2011). His thoughtful "Reflections" on important topics are excellent sources for sermon preparation.

2. Though Revelation appears to be a chronological account of God's victories, with one event following another, the fundamental theme of Revelation is that God's victory was already accomplished in the death and resurrection of Jesus. Revelation's kaleidoscopic format presents constantly changing visions of the one epoch-changing event, so that readers/hearers learn of God's victory in multiple forms over multiple enemies in multiple settings.

Let Forgiveness of Sins Come

Christ will come to your grave, and if He finds there weeping for you Martha the woman of good service, and Mary who carefully heard the Word of God, like holy Church which has chosen the best part, He will be moved with compassion, when at your death He shall see the tears of many and will say: "Where have you laid him?" that is to say, in what condition of guilt is he? In which rank of penitents? I would see him for whom you weep, that he himself may move Me with his tears. I will see if he is already dead to that sin for which forgiveness is entreated.

The people will say to Him, "Come and see." What is the meaning of "Come"? It means, Let forgiveness of sins come, let the life of the departed come, the resurrection of the dead, let Your kingdom come to this sinner also.

He will come and will command that the stone be taken away which his fall has laid on the shoulders of the sinner. He could have removed the stone by a word of command, for even inanimate nature is wont to obey the bidding of Christ. He could by the silent power of His working have removed the stone of the sepulchre, at Whose Passion the stones being suddenly removed many sepulchres of the dead were opened, but He bade men remove the stone, in very truth indeed, that the unbelieving might believe what they saw, and see the dead rising again, but in a type that He might give us the power of lightening the burden of sins, the heavy pressure as it were upon the guilty. Ours it is to remove the burdens, His to raise again, His to bring forth from the tombs those set free from their bands.

So the Lord Jesus, seeing the heavy burden of the sinner, weeps, for the Church alone He suffers not to weep. He has compassion with His beloved, and says to him that is dead, "Come forth," that is, "Those who liest in darkness of conscience, and in the squalor of thy sins, as in the prison-house of the guilty, come forth, declare your sins that thou mayest be justified. "For with the mouth confession is made unto salvation."

If you have confessed at the call of Christ the bars will be broken, and every chain loosed, even the stench of the bodily corruption be grievous. For he had been dead four days and his flesh stank in the tomb; but He Whose flesh saw no corruption was three days in the sepulchre, for He knew no evils of the flesh, which consists of the substances of the four elements. However great, then, the stench of the dead body may be, it is all done away so soon as the sacred ointment has shed its odour; and the dead rises again, and the command is given to loose his hands who till now was in sin; the covering is taken from his face which veiled the truth of the grace which he had received. But since he has received forgiveness, the command is given to uncover his face, to lay bare his features. For he whose sin is forgiven has nothing whereof to be ashamed.

Ambrose, "Concerning Repentance," in *Nicene and Post-Nicene Fathers*, second series, vol. 10, ed. Philip Schaff and Henry Wace (Buffalo, NY: Christian Literature Publishing, 1896), 352.

from God" (21:2, an image first appearing in 3:10–12). Compared to the highly wrought architectural features of the new Jerusalem that follow in 21:9–22:5 (which have precedent in Ezek. 40–48; Isa. 54:11–12; Tob. 13:16–17; and several important Jewish apocalyptic writings outside the canon), here John uses the more intimate imagery of Jerusalem as "a bride adorned for her husband."

Isaiah is influential here too, however, in 54:4–8, the poet takes up the marriage imagery of Hosea 1–2 but emphasizes the restored relationship between God and Judah: "with everlasting love I will have compassion on you, says the LORD, your Redeemer" (Isa. 54:8). For John, however, the marriage is not between God and Israel but between the church and the Lamb. He makes this point first in 19:7 and 9, identifying joyous celebration as the primary theme of the marriage, a theme that also appears in many early Christian allegorical readings of the Song of Solomon.

In 21:3–4, John draws out his first interpretation of "a new earth" and "the new Jerusalem, coming down out of heaven from God," with domestic, intimate language: (1) God's "dwelling" (NRSV "home") is among mortals and he "dwells" with them; "they will be his peoples, and God himself will be with them." Here, the repetition in the two couplets is used for emphasis, echoing the theme of Immanuel found in Isaiah 7:14 and 8:8 and Matthew 1:23; 18:20; and 28:20. (2) "Tears," "death," "mourning," "crying," and "pain" have no place in the new, heavenly, holy Jerusalem that serves as the dwelling place of God on earth. To use the words of Charles Wesley's hymn "Love Divine, All Loves Excelling," John's first interpretation of God's new Jerusalem is "joy of heaven to earth come down." By comparison, the second interpretation of the new Jerusalem, found in 21:9–22:5, is expressed in a different tone and with different imagery. Here, John focuses on the manifestation of God's glory as the light that defines "the holy city," not simply as an architectural wonder but as the site of "the throne of God and of the Lamb," where those who worship them will see God's face and be marked by God's own name, "and they will reign forever and ever" (Rev. 22:3–5).

In addition to these scriptural contexts, the language of 21:5–6a denotes another: Roman imperial politics. Verse 5 alludes to this theme with a reference to the words of the one seated *on the throne*: "I am making all things new"; "these words . . . are trustworthy and true"; "It is done! I am the Alpha and Omega, the beginning and the end." They point to the transcendent nature of God as "the Almighty" (*pantocrator*), a term used throughout (1:8; 4:8; 11:17; 15:3; 16:7; 19:6; 21:22) to contrast God's power and that of the Roman emperor, whose city is "Babylon," "the great whore" (Rev. 18), and whose name and "mark" link him to the beast, Satan, and the devil (Rev. 13). Again and again, John uses throne scenes like the one

in 21:5–7 to describe the joyful gathering of "saints," those "who conquer," those "who have come out of the great ordeal," and "those who had been beheaded for their testimony to Jesus" (1:4; 3:21; 4:1–11; 7:9–17; 19:4). For the first readers/hearers of Revelation, this was the living context. John exhorted them to be like such witnesses—faithful to the one who sits on the throne and to the Lamb.

Revelation 21:1–6a shares many terms, ideas, and concepts with the other readings for All Saints' Day in Year B of the Revised Common Lectionary, though there are some sharp differences also. Wisdom 3:1–9; Isaiah 25:6–9; and John 11:32–44 share with 21:1–6a a concern with death, but only Isaiah 25 and Revelation are apocalyptic/cosmic/political in their worldview. The Wisdom and John passages deal more with the individual. The references to "being disciplined," "tested," and "tried" in Wisdom 3:5–6 resonate with Revelation but lack its emphasis on persecution as the cause of the testing, as described, for example, in chapter 17. All express awareness of God's power/rule/glory, and at the same time refer to God's loving/watching over/blessing/saving.

The task of writing a sermon on these texts is to decide how to hold all these themes together, or how to decide which of them is most fitting for the moment or occasion. Some of them will be comforting, others more challenging. On first reading, 21:1–6a will likely seem comforting, with its description of the intimate joy of a wedding and of God's coming down to dwell among humans, wiping away the tears from their eyes. However, how will comfortable Christians deal with the challenges of Christians (and others) who face persecution because they are different from the norm—not in a foreign setting but in their own?

OLIVER LARRY YARBROUGH

Commentary 2: Connecting the Reading with the World

Revelation 21:1–6a promises salvation, liberation, and renewal for all humanity. This statement may come as a surprise to those who see Revelation as a "closed book," hard

to understand and consisting of intricate and bewildering visions. These literary features can make us forget that the aim of this sacred book is to give hope to oppressed peoples. Revelation was written not to instill fear, but to encourage its audience to persevere in the knowledge that God, the true ruler of the universe, will ultimately win the cosmic battle between the forces of life and the forces of death.

This triumphant, hopeful message is most clearly evident in the last two chapters of Revelation, which celebrate God's salvific acts and which envision a new universe. In the "great white throne" trial (Rev. 20:11–15), death itself is condemned to die in the lake of fire (20:14). This ushers in a new time in the history of salvation. In this new heaven and earth (21:1), God will be permanently present in the midst of God's people (21:3), liberating the people from death, grief, and pain (21:4). In this perfected new order, there will be no room for tears, pain, or suffering. Moreover, this new world was God's goal all along. This is God's finished project of salvation and liberation. Jesus, as the text proclaims, is the "Alpha and the Omega" (see Rev. 1:8, 17; 22:13). The reference to the first and last letters of the Greek alphabet affirms that Jesus is the beginning and the end of all, the point of the departure and the aim of the universe.

In reading Revelation 21:1–6a, I recall an important visit to my father when I was fourteen years old. My mother had died early in June after a two-year battle against cancer. My dad, who was practically a stranger to me, invited me to spend a few weeks with him and his new family in the US Virgin Islands. During the visit, early on the Fourth of July, my dad told me that we were all going to a "party." As one might imagine, the last thing I wanted was to attend a party. However, the "party" turned out to be very different from what I expected. Thousands of people landed, by ferryboats and planes, on the island of St. John, where the event was being held. Calypso bands, mounted in trucks equipped with public address systems energized by generators, filled the air with music. People danced in the streets to the different tunes that echoed from block to block. There were food and drink, music and laughter. The carnival ambiance was something I had never seen before. I also experienced something that was unexpected: joy.

When I read Revelation 21:1–6a, I imagine a similar cosmic carnival. I imagine people from every time and nation (see 7:9–17) singing praises to God and the Lamb as they dance, full of joy. This image leads me to ask, What are the myriad ways that joy is present in our worship services today? Indeed, not just in our services, what are the different ways that joy is present in our lives, as well? Relatedly, do we, as the church, behave in a way that exemplifies this divine joy? If not, how can we remind ourselves of this joy again?

Modernity, at times, privileges rational thought and as a result can undervalue emotions. However, displays of emotions are still evident in many of the worship traditions of certain denominations, such as Pentecostal groups. Given that emotions constitute an integral part of what it means to be human, how can we, the people of God, validate emotional expression—in all its myriad forms—in our churches and worship services? Indeed, it is worth pondering whether one's own church exemplifies and is open to expressions of joy, such as the ones described in Revelation 19:1–6b.

A wise preacher might reflect upon the ways in which their church is hindered by a mistrust of joy and other emotions. Perhaps a discussion about mental health issues, and how many of us feel ashamed or try to hide our emotional difficulties, especially in church, is also appropriate and, indeed, needed in our communities of faith.

Another way to emphasize joy in our worship services is to craft sermons on joy, celebrating not only what God has done but also what we hope God will do. Christian hope is based on our understanding of God's character. Our faith compels us to celebrate God and rejoice for God's past and future liberating acts. Our worship is thus prophetic, for it expresses our faith that our world can be different, transformed by the values of the kingdom of God. Indeed, just proclaiming and reminding our congregations that God will "wipe away every tear" (21:4), that through Christ the victory of life over the forces of death has been accomplished, might be enough to bring tears of joy to the eyes of those in the pews.

Moreover, quieter forms of joy should also be encouraged and welcomed. Immersion in the stories of Scripture, a focus on responding to the needs of others, and reflections on shining moments of love, compassion, solidarity, and unity in the life of the church should be affirmed as quieter ways to express joy. Relatedly, the other side of joy—disappointment and sadness—is also an important topic of discussion. How can we have joy in a world filled with constant bad news about diminishment, trauma, and loss? Indeed, affirmations of lament can be as helpful as affirmations of joy. It is important to remind ourselves and our worship communities that feeling grief or less than joyful is okay and not an expression of impiety. Disappointment and sadness are understandable responses, considering that we live in a world filled with suffering.

Speaking of suffering, another topic worthy of exploration is the complicated relationship between joy and pain. How can we talk about joy and hardships without resorting to the usual platitudes to be happy because God will correct everything in time? How, in other words, can we express joy when we are undergoing suffering and hardship?

Not just our own personal suffering but the suffering of others, especially those who are disenfranchised and powerless, should also be pondered. What can the Christian community do to transform the world into the image of God? Revelation 21:1–6a, exercising "prophetic imagination," pictures a world renewed by the Holy Spirit, free of the grip of death and its consequences. Where do we see the power of death at work currently in our world? Who is crying? Who is in pain? Who is being persecuted? Who are "the least of these"? (Matt. 25:40, 45).

What specific actions can we, the church, do, as a corporate body and as individual believers, to help transform this world? A social-justice sermon based on this text would be poignant and fitting. All Saints' Day gives us an opportunity to reflect on God's awesome power (Isa. 25:6–9 and Ps. 24); to explain the meaning of eternal life and the doctrine of resurrection (John 11:32–44); and to imagine a world transformed and renewed by the power of God (Rev. 21:1–6a). The lectionary thus suggests several different homiletic strategies to preach on this high and holy day. However, whatever sermon one crafts for this Sunday, the most important thing to remember, and to stress to our congregations, is that this promise of liberation is for all.

PABLO A. JIMENEZ

John 11:32–44

³²When Mary came where Jesus was and saw him, she knelt at his feet and said to him, "Lord, if you had been here, my brother would not have died." ³³When Jesus saw her weeping, and the Jews who came with her also weeping, he was greatly disturbed in spirit and deeply moved. ³⁴He said, "Where have you laid him?" They said to him, "Lord, come and see." ³⁵Jesus began to weep. ³⁶So the Jews said, "See how he loved him!" ³⁷But some of them said, "Could not he who opened the eyes of the blind man have kept this man from dying?"

³⁸Then Jesus, again greatly disturbed, came to the tomb. It was a cave, and a stone was lying against it. ³⁹Jesus said, "Take away the stone." Martha, the sister of the dead man, said to him, "Lord, already there is a stench because he has been dead four days." ⁴⁰Jesus said to her, "Did I not tell you that if you believed, you would see the glory of God?" ⁴¹So they took away the stone. And Jesus looked upward and said, "Father, I thank you for having heard me. ⁴²I know that you always hear me, but I have said this for the sake of the crowd standing here, so that they may believe that you sent me." ⁴³When he had said this, he cried with a loud voice, "Lazarus, come out!" ⁴⁴The dead man came out, his hands and feet bound with strips of cloth, and his face wrapped in a cloth. Jesus said to them, "Unbind him, and let him go."

Commentary 1: Connecting the Reading with Scripture

John 11:32–44 is integrally connected to 11:1–12:11 and narrates the raising of Lazarus, the culminating "sign" of John 1–12, that exemplifies Jesus' life-giving power over death. As Jesus says to Martha in 11:25–26: "Those who believe in me, even though they die, will live, and everyone who lives and believes in me will never die" (cf. John 3:16). Believing these words is not always easy. They are impossible to verify empirically and are challenged any time we are confronted with the reality of death, especially the death of a loved one as close to us as Lazarus to his sisters.

The ignorance and doubt displayed by Lazarus's sisters reflect the tension inherent in believing the Christian claim that Jesus grants eternal life to the believer. Mary approaches Jesus (11:32) ignorant of Jesus' earlier conversation with the disciples (vv. 1–16). Unaware that Jesus' delay was deliberate (v. 6) and that Lazarus will not die from illness (v. 4), because Jesus will awaken him (v. 11), she repeats Martha's guarded criticism of Jesus from 11:21.

Given Jesus' reputation as a healer (5:1–15; 6:2; 9:1–11), Mary could expect Jesus to save Lazarus, had he arrived sooner. Now it is too late. Likewise overwhelmed by the grim reality of Lazarus's death is Martha, whose reluctance to have the stone removed (11:39) suggests she has not fully grasped the implications of Jesus' words in 11:25–26, despite her confession in 11:27. Preachers may draw from the sisters' sadness and skepticism to remind their audiences of the challenges posed by the Christian proclamation of life when death is all around us.

Because new life for the believer springs from the death and resurrection of Jesus (10:10–11), connections to Jesus' death and resurrection are woven into the Lazarus narrative. In 11:32, Mary kneels at Jesus' feet, the feet she will soon anoint in an extravagant gesture that displays gratitude for Jesus' raising of Lazarus and anticipates Jesus' own death (12:1–8). John 11:32 is the second instance in 11:1–12:11 that anticipates Jesus' anointing, the first being Mary's initial introduction in 11:2. These proleptic references to the anointing serve John's theme of connecting the new life Jesus gives Lazarus—and to all believers—to Jesus' own death and resurrection. Indeed, the raising of Lazarus is the tipping point that leads the Jewish religious authorities to seek Jesus' execution (11:45–53).

Connections between Lazarus's revivification and Jesus' death and resurrection extend to the end of the Gospel. As the stone from Lazarus's tomb is removed (11:41), so does Mary Magdalene find the stone removed from Jesus' tomb (20:1). Peter and the beloved disciple find Jesus' burial clothes left in his tomb (20:5–7), recalling Jesus' order to unbind Lazarus from his burial clothes (11:44). Jesus left behind death and all its trappings, and in the wake of Jesus' resurrection so may all believers, whom the Johannine Jesus considers to be—as Lazarus was—his friends (15:15). For his friends, Jesus dies as an expression of his love for them (15:13), presenting preachers with an opportunity to reflect on Jesus' solidarity with us. Willingly experiencing the human condition of death, Jesus takes no shortcuts to make resurrected life available.

John's Gospel calls Jesus' miracles "signs" (*sēmeia*) because, from John's perspective, what ultimately matters is not the miracle itself but the truth that it signals. In line with this theme, 11:32–44 is replete with the language of "seeing," indicating the importance John's narration places on looking beyond the miracle to perceive it as a sign that reveals God's activity. In 11:32–33, Mary "saw" Jesus and Jesus "saw" her weeping. Jesus is told to "come and see" where Lazarus is buried (v. 34). The Jews' responses to Jesus' weeping refer to seeing (v. 36) and eyesight (v. 37). Jesus' words to Martha in 11:40 affirm the importance of seeing Lazarus's raising as a revelation of God's glory, and Jesus embodies this challenge to seek God's activity through his raising of Lazarus in 11:41, which literally states that Jesus "lifted his eyes upward" (my trans.) during the prayer that precedes the miracle.

Stating that the purpose of the prayer and the miracle is for the crowd to believe that he is sent by God (v. 42), Jesus challenges the witnesses of this sign to see God's life-giving presence in the world as a presence more powerful than death,

even if death remains part of the human experience. Preachers may extend this challenge to their audiences. Not all who see the raising will understand it as displaying God's glory (vv. 45–46), but those who accept Jesus' revelation can expect the life-giving work of God to operate in their lives as it has in Lazarus's. This sign—which shows Lazarus coming out of his tomb upon hearing Jesus' command (vv. 43–44)—visually reminds us that hearing Jesus' voice and following it lead to life (5:24–29; 10:27–28).

Among the Gospels, John most explicitly depicts Jesus as divine (1:1; 5:17–23; 10:30; 20:28). Yet, here, Jesus displays rather human emotions, described vividly with terms typically associated with anger. While scholars debate whether Jesus is grieving or upset (some suggest, at the lack of faith of Lazarus's sisters and the Jews), grief and anger are not mutually exclusive emotions, as many of us know if we have been troubled by or angry at the death of loved ones. Since he reacts upon witnessing the sorrow of Mary and the Jews (11:33–35) and arriving at his friend's tomb (v. 38), it seems—again in genuine solidarity with the human experience—Jesus expresses grief that includes anger at death's presence in the world.

His emotions contribute to rather than contradict John's depiction of Jesus as divine.[1] The Hebrew Scriptures hardly depict God as unemotionally involved in Israel's plight, and John insists that Jesus' presence in the world extends from God's love for it (3:16). Indeed, some at the scene understand Jesus' tears as a sign of his love for Lazarus (11:36). Preachers may note that Jesus' emotions remind us that the biblical God is not an abstract being aloof in the heavens. God is emotionally invested in our well-being.

The lectionary readings for All Saints' Day stubbornly proclaim God's victory over death. In Isaiah 25:6–9, we hear that the Lord "will swallow up death forever" and "wipe away the tears from all faces" (Isa. 25:8) of those who mourn. Revelation 21:1–6a echoes Isaiah's language. John 11:32–44 gives narrative expression to these eschatological expectations, but with a twist. For John, abundant, eternal life is available now for believers and not just

---

1. See Jo-Ann A. Brant, *John* (Grand Rapids: Baker Academic, 2011), 181–82.

as a future reality, as Martha appears to believe (John 11:24), in line with Isaiah, Revelation, and authors of other NT texts (e.g., 1 Thess. 4:13–17). This Gospel's "realized eschatology" insists that the "swallowing up" of death spoken of by Isaiah and Revelation is a present reality (e.g., John 3:36; 5:24), symbolized here by Jesus' command to unbind Lazarus of his burial clothes (11:44). When Jesus says, "Unbind him," the word used (*lysate*) can be translated as "release," and so conveys the notion that Lazarus be released from the constraints of death. John's Gospel thus joins other NT texts (e.g., Eph. 2:1–10; cf. 1:3; Col. 1:13; 2:9–14; 3:1; cf. Luke 4:21; 19:9; 23:43) that claim that the eternal life promised by God is realized in the present moment through the saving work of Jesus.

Taking their cue from the Gospel's insistence on the present availability of life, preachers may challenge their community to manifest God's life-giving work in the world today. At one point in the Gospel, Jesus tells his disciples that they will do greater works than his (John 14:12). In what ways do our actions signal and realize God's life-giving power?

GILBERTO A. RUIZ

Commentary 2: Connecting the Reading with the World

Unlike the mystical hush of Christmas, or the brassy pomp of Easter, All Saints' Day is, thankfully, comparatively quiet and unadorned. It sneaks in near the end of the Christian year, as days shorten, the weather gets cooler, and, as Presbyterian pastor Jon Maxwell Walton has put it, "our mortality presses its nose to the window, looks in against the evening chill, and watches us through the glass."[2]

That same mortality seems to dominate in this text. Jesus' friend Lazarus has died, and though Jesus takes his time deciding to go to Bethany, he eventually gets there four days later. Lazarus's sisters, Martha and Mary, both get their licks in immediately: "Lord, if you had been here," each of them says privately, "my brother would not have died." The scene—a weeping Jesus, two grieving sisters nursing bitter incrimination because of his long absence, their questions about his friendship, their caution of a "stench" if Jesus persists in rolling the stone from the entrance to the tomb—is all so intimately painful that a part of us wants to look away in embarrassment. The drama of this text—the pain, the pathos, the tears—seems to overwhelm the text.

Fred Craddock warns us that this story "is not about a family crisis in Bethany as much as it is about the crisis of the world caught in death and sin, not so much about resuscitating a corpse as it is about giving life to the world."[3] In this sense, it is important that the preacher keeps her eyes on Jesus, for ultimately in this text, Jesus is addressing a larger audience. He is addressing the church; in these days, he is addressing us. We are the "saints," and All Saints is a day that celebrates not only the "rock stars" of the faith, or the holiest of the holy, but also all believers—all of us. All of us are companioned and empowered by the one who announces in Bethany that he is "the resurrection and the life."

This is ultimately a sign story: a story intended to say, not just to this small group of family and friends in Bethany, but also to us, something very important about what the glory and presence of God in the world really mean. The point is that—through the life, death, and resurrection of Jesus Christ our Lord—the world is finally not a place where we need to revisit endlessly the losses in our lives that make us weep. The world is rather the arena in which all of that is being gathered up into something bigger. We are forever being given the opportunity to step out of sorrows that would otherwise bind us, and to be embraced by what the story points to: an upending, life-giving resurrection joy.

This sign story is not for people who have never wept, never lost; but it is a most appropriate text

---

2. Jon Maxwell Walton, "If You Had Been Here," sermon preached on November 5, 2000, at Westminster Presbyterian Church, Wilmington, DE.
3. Fred B. Craddock et al., *Preaching through the Christian Year (Year A)* (Philadelphia: Trinity Press International, 1992), 178.

for those who, like Lazarus, are being called by Jesus to get back up again—to honor and thank God for what has been, but also to step into a life that still begs to be lived and that invites them forward into a hope-filled future.

This text is certainly appropriate for a funeral, but is useful on many other occasions as well. I once used it at a wedding. I was presiding at the service of marriage for two dear friends, both of whom had lived well into their adulthood, then had lost their spouses to death, and later had discovered one another. On the day of their wedding, eyebrows were raised throughout the congregation as I read this complicated Gospel so closely associated with sadness. Then in my homily, I said to my two friends standing before me that this was a text for them, also. I told them that it was our job in that happy-sad setting to be like those who joined Jesus at the grave of Lazarus. After all, when Lazarus stepped out of that grave wrapped in grave cloths, Jesus told those people to unwrap Lazarus and let him go—to do what they could to help him remove the bonds of sorrow and sorrow's power in the world, and to point him forward toward the rest of his life yet to be lived. That was, I said, their job, and everybody else's job at that wedding, on that particular day.

I said to that bride and groom that their job on that day and the days ahead was to cheer each other on as they discovered, moment by moment, the deep dimensions of another hope entirely that had been returned to them. For, in very truth, the bonds of sorrow in each of their lives had been laid down, and they were reminded yet again of how the world is finally a marvelous arena of the resurrection activity of God. It is an activity that always, always ends in joy.

On All Saints' Day, the greatest gift of this text from John is the irreducibly communal nature of resurrection joy as, from that open tomb in Bethany, it prefigures Jesus' own empty tomb. Then, as Jesus was loosed into the world through the incarnation, that resurrection joy is loosed into the whole world, and back and forth through time, as it inhabits the saints of God in every generation. This joy is not intended to be a private thing; rather, it is intended to be shared.

A few years ago, my family and I went to Zambia, where we were struck by what was for us a new word, "Ubuntu." This southern African word, generally speaking, describes those who are generous, hospitable, friendly, caring, and compassionate. We witnessed that mutuality being acted out wherever we traveled in Zambia. In the dominant tribal language spoken in the area in which we spent most of our time, there was a particular greeting that embodied Ubuntu. Someone would meet someone else on the street, and would say, "Mooli bwanji?" ("How are you?"). The other would respond, "Endeeli bweeno, kaya eenu" ("I am fine—if you are"). It was an exchange that said, "My humanity is inextricably bound up in yours. My joy is expanded by your joy." This exchange was a by-product of resurrection.

It is even bigger than just that. Ultimately, it is a redemptive, even subversive, upending joy big enough for the whole world. Embodied by the saints of God, it is a joy that marches resolutely through every square inch of our human life that is still bound by some sad something not yet redeemed. It is a joy, embodied by the saints, who, even though they seek nothing for themselves, yet live to proclaim resurrection.

This poem written by Paul Hooker expresses something of that same joy:

> Who sees a wildflower in a field of weeds
> and rejoices just because it grows there,
> who hears a laughing child
> and is glad of happiness, even though in
>   sorrow,
> who witnesses beauty
> and does not yearn to grasp it with soiled
>   hands,
> who speaks a quiet truth
> and has no need of congratulation—
> these are the saints.
> The ones who leave no trace.[4]

THEODORE J. WARDLAW

---

4. Paul K. Hooker, *Days and Times: Poems from the Liturgy of Living* (Eugene, OR: Resource Publications, 2018), 40.

Proper 26 (Sunday between October 30 and November 5)

Ruth 1:1–18 and Deuteronomy 6:1–9   Hebrews 9:11–14
Psalm 146 and Psalm 119:1–8   Mark 12:28–34

Ruth 1:1–18

[1]In the days when the judges ruled, there was a famine in the land, and a certain man of Bethlehem in Judah went to live in the country of Moab, he and his wife and two sons. [2]The name of the man was Elimelech and the name of his wife Naomi, and the names of his two sons were Mahlon and Chilion; they were Ephrathites from Bethlehem in Judah. They went into the country of Moab and remained there. [3]But Elimelech, the husband of Naomi, died, and she was left with her two sons. [4]These took Moabite wives; the name of the one was Orpah and the name of the other Ruth. When they had lived there about ten years, [5]both Mahlon and Chilion also died, so that the woman was left without her two sons and her husband.

[6]Then she started to return with her daughters-in-law from the country of Moab, for she had heard in the country of Moab that the LORD had considered his people and given them food. [7]So she set out from the place where she had been living, she and her two daughters-in-law, and they went on their way to go back to the land of Judah. [8]But Naomi said to her two daughters-in-law, "Go back each of you to your mother's house. May the LORD deal kindly with you, as you have dealt with the dead and with me. [9]The LORD grant that you may find security, each of you in the house of your husband." Then she kissed them, and they wept aloud. [10]They said to her, "No, we will return with you to your people." [11]But Naomi said, "Turn back, my daughters, why will you go with me? Do I still have sons in my womb that they may become your husbands? [12]Turn back, my daughters, go your way, for I am too old to have a husband. Even if I thought there was hope for me, even if I should have a husband tonight and bear sons, [13]would you then wait until they were grown? Would you then refrain from marrying? No, my daughters, it has been far more bitter for me than for you, because the hand of the LORD has turned against me." [14]Then they wept aloud again. Orpah kissed her mother-in-law, but Ruth clung to her.

[15]So she said, "See, your sister-in-law has gone back to her people and to her gods; return after your sister-in-law." [16]But Ruth said,

"Do not press me to leave you
    or to turn back from following you!
Where you go, I will go;
    where you lodge, I will lodge;
our people shall be my people,
    and your God my God.
[17]Where you die, I will die—
    there will I be buried.
May the LORD do thus and so to me,
    and more as well,
if even death parts me from you!"

[18]When Naomi saw that she was determined to go with her, she said no more to her.

Deuteronomy 6:1–9

¹Now this is the commandment—the statutes and the ordinances—that the LORD your God charged me to teach you to observe in the land that you are about to cross into and occupy, ²so that you and your children and your children's children may fear the LORD your God all the days of your life, and keep all his decrees and his commandments that I am commanding you, so that your days may be long. ³Hear therefore, O Israel, and observe them diligently, so that it may go well with you, and so that you may multiply greatly in a land flowing with milk and honey, as the LORD, the God of your ancestors, has promised you.

⁴Hear, O Israel: The LORD is our God, the LORD alone. ⁵You shall love the LORD your God with all your heart, and with all your soul, and with all your might. ⁶Keep these words that I am commanding you today in your heart. ⁷Recite them to your children and talk about them when you are at home and when you are away, when you lie down and when you rise. ⁸Bind them as a sign on your hand, fix them as an emblem on your forehead, ⁹and write them on the doorposts of your house and on your gates.

Commentary 1: Connecting the Reading with Scripture

Passages from Ruth and Deuteronomy appear as alternatives for a harvest-season week late in the lectionary year. Ruth continues the following week, while the complementary lectionary jumps to a passage from 1 Kings. Today's semicontinuous reading from Ruth encompasses everything from the story's opening up to Naomi and Ruth's departure from Moab to return to Naomi's homeland, Israel. Set during Israel's early years, the story begins with one Israelite family's tragedies. During a famine, Elimelech and Naomi and their two sons leave their home in Bethlehem (ironically, *beyt-lehem,* the "house of bread") and seek refuge in Moab, east of the Dead Sea. Elimelech dies; the sons, appropriately and tragically named Mahlon ("sickness") and Chilion ("wasting away"), marry Moabite women, then die before their wives bear them any children. A household consisting of a woman and her three men has now become a family of three childless widows. In a society in which men provided security, this household's prospects have plummeted. Things have become dire indeed.

We do not know and never find out what caused the tragedies. We see only reflections of mutual kindness in Naomi's gentle words, and Ruth's and Orpah's tears. Naomi believes the young widows will fare better leaving to start over, but Ruth, at least, prefers to stay and become a foreigner herself.

Ruth's clinging to her mother-in-law when she is urged to abandon her is a gift of grace that Naomi cannot at first see. Naomi says God has turned against her (Ruth 1:13), and she later will say, "The Almighty has dealt bitterly with me . . . brought me back empty . . . dealt harshly with me, and the Almighty has brought calamity upon me" (vv. 20–21). Like so many of us when we are undergoing suffering, this is all she can see.

The narrator, though, sees things differently, attributing none of Naomi's tragedies to God, not even the famine. Rather, God has given the people food (v. 6). This point is underscored when Naomi's and Ruth's arrival in Bethlehem coincides with the barley harvest. Near the book's end, neighbors will articulate to Naomi what has been clear all along, that Ruth's love is worth more than seven sons (4:15). Grace is walking right beside Naomi, unseen, refusing to leave her.

Ruth holds a thoroughly action-oriented, pragmatic view. She does not argue with Naomi's perceptions, nor does she assert her own. She simply communicates presence. She refuses to leave. Ruth will worship the God that Naomi believes abandoned her. She swears to do what four other people—Elimelech, Mahlon, Chilion, and Orpah—could not do: stay. Not even death, their household's ubiquitous unwelcome guest, can stop her. In so doing, this foreign woman offers a model of biblical friendship and piety that wise preachers would do well to ponder alongside their congregations.

Naomi and Ruth's dialogue in this chapter is unique in Scripture: it is the only conversation between two women that concerns not a man—father, husband, or son—but each other's welfare. Ancient Israelite women presumably had such conversations daily, but Scripture, composed primarily by men, usually overlooks them. This caring exchange between in-laws stands in for dozens of missing portrayals of Israelite sisters, mothers, daughters, and friends.

The chain of coincidences that will bring Ruth to Boaz's field in chapter 2 offers more subtle reminders of divine favor. Boaz already knows who she is and retells her story as if it were Abraham's. Throughout the chapter, Boaz keeps giving her seed—to glean, to eat, to take home, and to return for every day of the harvest. Life-giving seed is as plentiful now as barrenness had been before. As readers we see the interactions among the three characters and watch in suspense, for this is only the story's beginning.

The book of Deuteronomy, from which today's complementary reading comes, reiterates speeches as given by Moses to the second generation of Israelites, most of them born in the wilderness between Egypt and the promised land. Chapter 6 follows the restatement of the Decalogue in Deuteronomy 5:6–21 and Moses' exhortations to "follow exactly the path . . . so that you may live . . . long in the land you are to possess" (Deut. 5:33). Deuteronomy 6:1–9, part of Moses' final introductory instructions (Deut. 6–11), is a well-known passage in which Moses meticulously reminds the Israelites to observe God's wishes and teach them to their children. This speech effectively instructs not only those in Moab but also those reading Deuteronomy many generations hence.

Moses begins with reminders that keeping God's commands will lead to life and prosperity. The foundational statement of Jewish faith, the Shema (named after its first word, "Hear"),

follows in verse 4: *Shema Yisra'el* ("Hear, Israel"), *Adonai Eloheinu Adonai ehad.* This seemingly simple four-word sentence translates word for word to "the LORD our God the LORD one/alone." Since Hebrew has no verb "is," readers must supply it. The ambiguity over where exactly the verb should stand and whether one chooses "one" or "alone" as the final word's meaning allows for a range of readings, or all of them together. NRSV captures four possible translations. Its text states, "Hear, O Israel: The LORD is our God, the LORD alone." Then the NRSV textual note offers, "The LORD our God is one LORD," "The LORD our God, the LORD is one," and "The LORD is our God, the LORD is one."

In other words, this creed may assert divine unity ("the LORD is one"), or religious exclusivity ("the LORD alone"), or it may represent both together. Mark Biddle notes that if it refers to divine unity, it means that God is not limited to one locality (as is implied in the name El-bethel, "God of Bethel" in Gen. 35:8, or "Baal of Peor" in Deut. 4:3) but is available as the same single God to worshipers everywhere they go.

The other implication of the Shema's ambiguous wording is that the Lord alone is God. Not only is God present everywhere, but this God is sufficient for all needs. There is no need to appeal to another fertility god, because the Lord provides bounty; no reason to beseech any other ancestral god, because the Creator has been present from all generations and will continue forever. No other deity need apply.

Westerners are so accustomed to monotheism that the idea of appealing to various gods may seem strange. We may struggle to understand Hindu conceptions of God as a unity of many divine personalities, or even Catholic prayers to Mary and other saints. Our challenge today is not the temptation to turn to different deities, but rather to turn to no deity at all, nor trust in material wealth, luck, or personal talent.

Every week for the past two millennia, Jewish worshipers have recited God's command to absolute loyalty by repeating the Shema and the several verses that follow. The first portion is familiar to Christians, since it is quoted by Jesus with minor variations in the Synoptic Gospels (Matt. 22:37; Mark 12:30; Luke 10:27): loving the Lord with all one's being. What follows in Deuteronomy

6:6–9 offers further instructions for remembering: recite the words to children wherever you are going and whatever you are doing; put them on your hand and forehead; write them on your doorposts. The many imperative verbs in this passage (hear, observe, love, recite, bind, fix, write) reinforce one another to communicate the urgency of remembering the Creator in every moment of our lives.

PATRICIA K. TULL

Commentary 2: Connecting the Reading with the World

The book of Ruth begins the same way that the book of Job does, with a happy family that is intact and healthy. Elimelech and Naomi are married. They have two sons of marriageable age, Mahlon and Chilion, in a culture that celebrates sons. Granted, Job has ten children and more wealth. His prosperous family lives in Uz, and Elimelech's family has to leave Bethlehem for Moab because of "a famine in the land" (Ruth 1:1). At least two similarities bind their stories together. Both of the main characters lose their families, and both come close to losing hope.

Think of Naomi's story as a Job story wrapped in different clothing. When she arrives in Moab, she comes with her family of four. By a few verses later, she has lost nearly everything. The demise of her family takes much longer than Job's family—ten years—but the narrator makes Naomi's plight known by verse 5: she is "left without her two sons and her husband." Suddenly, Naomi lives as a poor widow in a foreign land in a patriarchal society during a time when widows were vulnerable to exploitation, attack, and sexual violence.

Thankfully, Naomi is not completely alone. She has Ruth and Orpah, her Moabite daughters-in-law. She believes, however, that if they remain with her, a poor widow, they will jettison their futures. She gives them a way out, instructing them to go back to their families, reunite with their people, marry new husbands, and worship their gods (v. 15). Life has become bitter for her; they would do better without her (v. 13). Like Job, Naomi wrestles with why such an awful thing has happened. It seems as if nothing but a dreadful future awaits. Like Job, she blames God for abandoning her. "The hand of the LORD has turned against me," she says (Ruth 1:13; cf. Job 6:9; 10:8; 13:21; 19:21; 23:2; 30:21). Whenever preachers label laypeople who blame God for their suffering as "those of little faith," they would do well to remember that two paragons of faith, Job and Naomi, believed in a God big enough to handle their unresolved anger.

Too often, Christian leaders do not know what to do with the Naomis who sit in their pews, because they do not know what to do with lament. Their theologies make room for praise and celebration, but not for suffering and sorrow; lying in green pastures, but not walking "through the darkest valley" (Ps. 23:4). Some argue that the problem is cultural. In his book *Prophetic Lament*, Soong-Chan Rah observes, "The American church avoids lament. The power of lament is minimized and the underlying narrative of suffering that requires lament is lost."[1]

Naomis need pastors to create space for them to grieve and to wrestle through their doubt. Those who have endured unimaginable suffering struggle to find light as they make their way through darkness. Their doubt verges on disbelief, and their inner turmoil leaves them hollow. As they stand on the brink of despair, they need someone to stand with them, to weep with them, perhaps even to believe for them when they struggle to believe for themselves.

In Ruth, Naomi finds someone who will love her through the darkness, who will hold onto her as she struggles to hold onto God. Orpah functions as a foil in the story. She kisses Naomi goodbye, but Ruth "clings" to Naomi (v. 14). Orpah returns home, but Ruth refuses to leave. With an oath, Ruth pledges to be there for Naomi in a way that Job's friends were never there for him. The God whom Naomi worships will be her

---

1. Soong-Chan Rah, *Prophetic Lament: A Call for Justice in Troubled Times* (Downers Grove, IL: IVP Press, 2015), 22.

God (v. 16), Ruth says; only death will prevent her from keeping her promise. True depth in relationship refuses the superficiality of shallow promise making. It insists on radical truth-telling, the hard way of commitment instead of the easy way of involvement, pressing forward instead of shrinking back, no matter what the cost.

Ruth's decision to follow Naomi's God sounds more radical when it is placed in dialogue with the second lection, Deuteronomy 6:1–9, in particular with the command in verse 4: "Hear, O Israel: The LORD is our God, the LORD alone." God calls Israel to embrace radical monotheism in a radically polytheistic world, to love *one* God instead of many gods. The command in verse 4 also functions as a prayer known as the Shema, a prayer that observant Jews pray several times a day (see Mark 12:29–30).

How can a chosen people observe Torah on their way to the promised land? At least three emphases emerge in Deuteronomy 6. The first emphasis is to make Torah intergenerational: ensure that your children and your children's children fear the Lord (Deut. 6:2, 7). Second, make Torah personal. Love is deeply existential, a matter of the heart. Put that which God is "commanding you today in your heart," the writer says (see Jer. 31:33). Make it your own at both the cognitive and emotional levels. Third, make Torah habitual: recite God's commands at home and away from home, when lying down and getting up, as a sign on your hand, your forehead, and your doorposts. Do not choose between church and home, worship or work. Walk with God at church *and* at home, at worship *and* at work. The command "observe" can also be translated as "do." Torah is not just what people believe cognitively or what they assent to on particular occasions. God calls people to *embody* Torah, to do it, wherever they go.

So how does a person embody Torah? Two examples will suffice. Before becoming famous in movies, actor Hugh Jackman won acclaim on the stage in Australia and England. As his career took off, Jackman found himself longing to return to musical performance and accepted an offer to play Jean Valjean in the screen adaptation of Victor Hugo's *Les Misérables*. In an interview published shortly before the movie debut, Jackman said that his father inspired his portrayal of Jean Valjean, and he saw his performance as a way to honor him. Jackman's mother left the family when he was eight years old. His father, who had become a Christian at a Billy Graham Crusade, was his rock. "The church was a big part of our lives," Jackman said. "[Dad] was just one of those quietly religious people who believed that actions spoke louder than words." When reflecting on a line from the final song, "To love another person is to touch the face of God," Jackman commented, "This is the example I got from my father."[2]

Another illustration of embodying Torah comes by way of a Moabite refugee who lived in the promised land hundreds of years after Israel entered it. Her mother-in-law introduced her to Israel's God, so she took seriously the command to love *one* God with all her heart, soul, and might. In Ruth 3:11, Boaz calls her a woman of noble character (*eshet hayil*). Imagine Ruth, long after she gave birth to Obed, walking down the road with him, telling him about Torah. Perhaps she lived long enough to talk about it with her grandchild Jesse, the future father of King David, who became a man after God's own heart (1 Sam. 13:14). God is a God of surprises. How else could a foreign widow outside of the covenant community, who had never heard of Torah, instruct God's people on how to keep it?

JARED F. ALCÁNTARA

---

2. Jesse Dorris, "They Dreamed a Dream," *Time* 180, no. 25 (Dec. 17, 2012): 62–64.

Psalm 146

¹Praise the LORD!
Praise the LORD, O my soul!
²I will praise the LORD as long as I live;
    I will sing praises to my God all my life long.

³Do not put your trust in princes,
    in mortals, in whom there is no help.
⁴When their breath departs, they return to the earth;
    on that very day their plans perish.

⁵Happy are those whose help is the God of Jacob,
    whose hope is in the LORD their God,
⁶who made heaven and earth,
    the sea, and all that is in them;
who keeps faith forever;
    ⁷who executes justice for the oppressed;
    who gives food to the hungry.

The LORD sets the prisoners free;
    ⁸the LORD opens the eyes of the blind.
The LORD lifts up those who are bowed down;
    the LORD loves the righteous.
⁹The LORD watches over the strangers;
    he upholds the orphan and the widow,
    but the way of the wicked he brings to ruin.

¹⁰The LORD will reign forever,
    your God, O Zion, for all generations.
Praise the LORD!

Psalm 119:1–8

¹Happy are those whose way is blameless,
    who walk in the law of the LORD.
²Happy are those who keep his decrees,
    who seek him with their whole heart,
³who also do no wrong,
    but walk in his ways.
⁴You have commanded your precepts
    to be kept diligently.
⁵O that my ways may be steadfast
    in keeping your statutes!
⁶Then I shall not be put to shame,
    having my eyes fixed on all your commandments.

⁷I will praise you with an upright heart,
    when I learn your righteous ordinances.
⁸I will observe your statutes;
    do not utterly forsake me.

Connecting the Psalm with Scripture and Worship

Psalm 146. The Psalter concludes with a series of five "Hallelujah Psalms," so named because each opens and closes with an imperative phrase of *halal* and *YHWH*, translated as "Praise the LORD" (Ps. 146:1, 10) and the source of the word "hallelujah." Psalm 146 is the first of this final collection and it adds the verb *zmr*, meaning "sing praise" (v. 2b), to further emphasize our call to praise God.

Gloriously theocentric, the psalm spends refreshingly few words talking about human beings. There is the double vow to "praise God as long as I live; I will sing praises to my God all my life long" (v. 2); even there, although the phrases' subject is the psalmist, their focus is God. Furthermore, when compared with God's eternal existence extending over "all generations" (v. 10), the psalmist's one finite lifetime itself shows how much greater is God than humankind.

The psalm proceeds to offer a warning against relying upon humans: their inevitable death will put an end to their endeavors (vv. 3–4). Here we get our first close connection with today's passage from the book of Ruth. As that Hebrew Bible story tells us, Elimelech and Naomi and their sons journeyed from Bethlehem to Moab to escape famine—a disaster that Judah's human leaders could not prevent. In ensuing years, Naomi's husband and then her sons die and with them dies Naomi's security (Ruth 1:1–5); the family's plans indeed "perish" (Ps. 146:4).

The latter half of the psalm reads like a résumé for the Almighty, listing a dozen of God's achievements, from creating "heaven and earth, the sea, and all that is in them" (v. 6a) to "keep[ing] faith forever" (v. 6b), from meeting human needs such as "justice for the oppressed . . . . food to the hungry" (v. 7) to "lov[ing] the righteous" (v. 8). This list of actions that reveal the sovereign power and benevolent character of God also includes two other points of connection between Psalm 146 and the saga of Ruth: "The LORD watches over the strangers; [God] upholds the orphan and the widow" (v. 9). Naomi came as a "stranger" to Moab, Ruth will be a "stranger" in Judah, and both women endure the challenges of being widows. In other words, although grief-stricken Naomi asserts, "The hand of the LORD has turned against me" (Ruth 1:13b), the psalmist insists that YHWH is particularly attentive to anyone enduring circumstances such as hers.

Considered together, the texts from Ruth and Psalm 146 offer a fruitful direction for preaching. The book of Ruth is often regarded as a story of God covertly working through human beings. A preacher might lift up the psalm's claims about God's compassionate actions and then explore how Ruth is an instrument of God's will, vital in rescuing Naomi and rescuing Israel. A sermon could proceed to consider how we—as individuals and as a church—can be open to God working through us.

The book of Ruth is also known for its daring claim that foreigners are a godsend and not a threat, a provocative message that is particularly germane to the state of today's world. The psalm's assertion of God's particular care for strangers (Ps. 146:9) could reinforce a faithful sermonic exploration of this timely topic.

Of the musical settings of this exuberantly confident psalm, "I'll Praise My Maker" may be the most well-known. "God, Whose Giving Knows No Ending" is another apt option and has the added benefit of supporting the stewardship season in which many congregations are engaged at this time of year. Another fitting choice would be "When the Poor Ones," which aligns with the book of Ruth's theme of human actions as reminders of God's presence with us.

Psalm 146 is a lively expression of praise and well-suited for use as opening sentences as well as for reading or singing in its entirety. For an intercessory prayer designed with Psalm 146 as its template, see Proper 27 (p. 463).

Psalm 119:1–8. Psalm 119 is known for its exhaustive emphasis on God's law and the benefits of following it. Here, the first eight verses of the psalm respond to the foundational commandment of the Shema (Deut. 6:4–5), heard in the first reading and quoted by Jesus in the Gospel reading.

Over the course of this psalm, by far the longest in the Psalter, eight different words for the law are used. In these opening verses, six of those terms can be found: "law" (Ps. 119:1), "decrees" (v. 2), "precepts" (v. 4), "statutes" (vv. 5, 8), "commandments" (v. 6), and "ordinances" (v. 7). Additionally, a corresponding term, "way," appears repeatedly (vv. 1, 3, 5).

While Psalm 119's famous acrostic construction (because today's pericope is the first of the psalm's twenty-two sections, one for each letter of the Hebrew alphabet, each of the eight verses read today begins with *aleph*, the first letter of the Hebrew alphabet) may not be a sermon subject, it is indicative of the care that went into the construction of this lengthy poem. The psalmist takes God's law seriously, but not joylessly, framing obedience to the law in a thoroughly positive light. The poem even launches with a pair of beatitudes that explain how obeying the law will make us "blessed" or "happy" (vv. 1, 2).

After these beatitudes, the psalm's voice pivots to address God directly. This prayer section begins with a line that sounds a strong echo of the appointed passage from Deuteronomy, which does indeed command that God's "precepts . . . be kept diligently" (v. 4). The psalmist next expresses personal passion for adhering to God's way and asserts that remaining attentive to God's commandments will prevent the psalmist from being "put to shame" (v. 6).

The sense of God's "righteous ordinances" as something the faithful need to "learn" (v. 7) is now introduced. This is another point of connection with the Shema, which emphasizes the duty of God's people not only to internalize the law for themselves, but also to ensure that rising generations are equally well taught and steadfastly obedient (Deut. 6:2, 7).

The readings from Deuteronomy and Psalm 119 both contribute to the day's liturgy. For example, one may invite the people to a time of corporate confession by saying,

> Happy are those who keep God's decrees, the
>   psalmist declares.
> Moses urges the people to keep God's
>   commandments.
> Yet daily we fall short of such obedience.
> Knowing that God forgives us and wants
>   what is best for us,
> let us confess our sin before God and one
>   another.

A prayer of confession could also reflect the psalm as well as reference the Shema, as in the following example:

> Loving God, You have commanded us to
>   keep your laws,
> to be steadfast in following your ways.
> Yet we fail again and again to love you
> with all our heart, with all our soul, and with
>   all our might.
> Forgive us, O God, and set us on the right
>   path,
> that we may live in joy and praise.

One might also construct a prayer using a refrain such as, "Let me follow your ways, O Lord."

There are, unsurprisingly, many musical interpretations of this rich and lengthy text. A twenty-first-century setting that sounds suitably traditional without being at all archaic is "The Lord Is God." For churches focused on stewardship season, "Lord of All Good" can be helpful. A less obvious, but fruitful, choice would be "Jesu, Jesu, Fill Us with Your Love."

LEIGH CAMPBELL-TAYLOR

Hebrews 9:11–14

[11]But when Christ came as a high priest of the good things that have come, then through the greater and perfect tent (not made with hands, that is, not of this creation), [12]he entered once for all into the Holy Place, not with the blood of goats and calves, but with his own blood, thus obtaining eternal redemption. [13]For if the blood of goats and bulls, with the sprinkling of the ashes of a heifer, sanctifies those who have been defiled so that their flesh is purified, [14]how much more will the blood of Christ, who through the eternal Spirit offered himself without blemish to God, purify our conscience from dead works to worship the living God!

Commentary 1: Connecting the Reading with Scripture

Hebrews 9:11–14 is part of Hebrews' treatment of Jesus as high priest, a densely argued exegesis drawing on ancient Jewish texts (both canonical and later) and very early Christian liturgies. It is foreshadowed in Hebrews 1:3; 2:17; and 3:1; and it becomes the main theme in 4:14–10:18. The structure of the argument follows an interpretive pattern that contrasts what is inferior to what is superior, the first examples being angels as servants and Jesus as God's Son (Heb. 1:3–14); Moses as servant in God's household and Jesus as Son (3:1–19); and the promised rest in its earthly and heavenly forms (4:1–13).

With regard to Hebrews' treatment of Jesus as high priest, the author contrasts (1) high priests "chosen from among mortals" and Jesus the Son as "a priest forever according to the order of Melchizedek" (4:14–7:28) and (2) the priestly ministry of the earthly sanctuary and that of the heavenly sanctuary (8:1–7). In 8:8–12, the author of Hebrews takes up Jeremiah's prophecy of a new covenant (Jer. 31:31–34) as an overarching framework for these contrasts, and in chapters 9–10, he explores Jesus' sacrificial role as high priest in light of it.

Hebrews 9:1–10 provides the immediate context for Jesus' role as high priest in verses 11–14, by describing the "regulations for worship and an earthly sanctuary" outlined in "the first covenant" (Heb. 9:1). It is not a complete account of the commandments for worship, as the author admits in verse 5b, but one that focuses on the sacrifice for the Day of Atonement. The principal actor in this sacrifice is the high priest, who entered the Holy of Holies once a year, taking "the blood that he offers for himself and for the sins committed unintentionally by the people" (v. 7).[1] Significantly for the argument that follows, the earthly sanctuary in 9:1–10 is not the temple in Jerusalem but "the first one," the one God commanded Moses to make as a meeting place during the wilderness wanderings of Exodus, for which God provided the plans when giving Moses the Torah on Sinai (Exod. 25:1–31:11 and 36:1–40:38).

Having stripped the descriptions of both the worship and sanctuary in Exodus and Leviticus to their bare essentials, the author uses them for his exposition of Jesus as high priest in 9:11–14.[2] Two closely related points stand out in the interpretation at this stage of the argument: (1) Jesus' sacrifice involves his *own* blood and not the blood of goats and bulls as stipulated in Leviticus 16 (Heb. 9:12); and (2) while in Leviticus the blood of goats and bulls sanctifies/purifies the *flesh* (v. 13), Jesus offered himself

---

1. The description of the sacrifice for the Day of Atonement in Hebrews differs from the account in Lev. 16, most notably in saying that it covers only the "unintentional" sins of the people. In the Gospels, Paul's writings, and 1 Peter, Passover rather than the Day of Atonement provides the model for interpreting Jesus' death as a sacrifice.

2. Many of the terms and scriptural references appearing in 9:11–14 are repeated in 9:24–28, but to different effect. This commentary focuses on what is emphasized in 9:11–14. The commentary on Proper 27 will treat what is emphasized in 9:24–28.

as a sacrifice "through the eternal Spirit" and "without blemish," so that his blood "[purifies] our *conscience* from dead works to worship the living God" (v. 14).

With regard to the first point, the author of Hebrews gives another example of the contrast between what is inferior and what is superior: "For *if* the blood of goats and bulls . . . *how much more* will the blood of Christ . . ." Here, the superiority is measured by the offering's taking place in "the greater and [more] perfect tent" (9:11, described in v. 24 as "heaven itself"), its taking place "once for all" (v. 12), and the reference to "the eternal Spirit," through which the offering is made (v. 14). Most importantly, however, in verse 14 the author equates "entering with his own blood" (v. 12) to "[offering] himself," a sharp contrast to the high priest's "taking the blood that he offers for himself and for the sins committed unintentionally by the people" (v. 7).

The second point (concerning the "[purifying] of our conscience") derives from the author's use of Jeremiah's prophecy regarding "a new covenant" (Heb. 8:8–12=Jer. 31:31–34). Here, the author's focus is on God's words defining this new covenant, "I will put my laws *in their minds*, and write them *on their hearts*" (Jer. 31:33=Heb. 8:10). Applying them to the "eternal redemption" obtained through Jesus' offering of his blood/himself, the author translates Jeremiah's "mind" and "heart" into "conscience," concluding that it inaugurates the new covenant that can accomplish what the first covenant could not—the transformation of the inner life and worship of the living God (v. 14).[3]

Hebrews 9:11–14 illustrates many of the challenges of reading the book of Hebrews. In the first instance, it assumes familiarity with the sacrificial systems that were part and parcel of ancient Mediterranean culture. Almost every society that belonged to it performed sacrifices, not only on special days in the year's calendar but also on a daily basis. Officials sacrificed; individuals sacrificed. Sacrifices could take place in public temples, at major crossroads, in homes, or in fields. They served many functions, not only in relation to the gods, but also in relation to society at large.

Second, Hebrews makes reference to a particular system of sacrifice, the one practiced in ancient Israel. It, too, was a complex system, with many rules and regulations that changed over time, especially after the destruction of the temple in Jerusalem (70 CE). Not unlike the author of Hebrews (and about the same time), Jews for whom sacrifice was at the core of their worship of God sought new ways to understand it when sacrifice in the temple was no longer possible. Jeremiah 31 and similar texts were important to them also in their search for new meaning. It was, and remains, part of the Jewish Scriptures.

Because a sacrificial system is not part of common or private life for most of us, it takes considerable effort to appreciate its place in the ancient world, and to explore ways texts like Hebrews can still speak to us. Reflecting on the author's emphasis on the transformation of the inner life and worship of the living God is a good place to start. It allows a foreign (and ancient) worldview to speak to our own and so, too, do the exhortations the author draws out of his theological reflections on Jesus' sacrifice. In 10:19–25, for example, he speaks of "the new and living way" it opens for his readers, encouraging them to "hold fast to the confession of our hope without wavering," "to provoke one another to love and good deeds," and "to [encourage] one another." In 13:15–16, he reenvisions sacrifice as an offering of praise to God, adding that doing good to one another and sharing what you have are sacrifices that are pleasing to God.

There are pastoral dimensions that grow out of Hebrews' treatment of Jesus' role as high priest also. In spite of Jesus being "a great high priest who has passed through the heavens, the Son of God," the author reflects that he is able "to sympathize with our weaknesses," allowing us to "approach the throne of grace with boldness" (4:14–16).

OLIVER LARRY YARBROUGH

---

3. Jer. 31:33–34 appears again in Heb. 10:16–17 as part of a summary of the central argument, confirming its significance.

Commentary 2: Connecting the Reading with the World

Hebrews 9:11–14 bases its main argument on a practice that is alien to many of us: animal sacrifice. It is fair to say that most of us have never participated in a religious ceremony where blood is shed. Therefore, how can we explain the meaning of this text to a culture where most people have never seen an animal ritually slaughtered and butchered? To understand Hebrews 9 and the ideas presented there, it might be helpful for preachers to explain to their congregations the liturgical meaning of animal sacrifices as practiced in ancient Israel and the importance of the Day of Purification or Atonement, on which the high priest entered into the Holy of Holies to present a sacrifice for the sins of the people (Lev. 16). Indeed, it might be worthwhile for the preacher to watch some videos of animal sacrifices to gain a deeper understanding of the power, horror, and terror conveyed by this ritual. In so doing, the preacher might be better able to convey to their congregation the intertwined power, terror, and meaning at the heart of Jesus' sacrifice.

A close reading will reveal that the writer of Hebrews refers to the tabernacle in the wilderness, not to the temple of Jerusalem. The text mentions the "tent," not the temple. This is one of the many clues that leads scholars to think that Hebrews was written not by a Jewish author, but by a Gentile whose knowledge of Jewish ritual was based more on Scripture than on personal experience. Considering this, our passage presents a good opportunity to talk about cultural difference or the inadvertent cultural stereotypes or assumptions that we all have, which keep us from seeing people and groups as they truly are. Perhaps this text and the thorny question of its authorship might even allow the sensitive preacher to broach the problematic history of anti-Semitism and racism in the church. These are difficult topics, to be sure, and they must be handled with care. However, these are important problems concerning which the church needs reflection and healing.

That being said, great care should be taken with this text. The text affirms that Jesus offered the "perfect" sacrifice "once and for all," for the salvation of humanity. If we are careless, we might convey the false impression that Jewish people and their sacrificial system are inferior to Christians and our liturgies. That would be a big mistake, for Hebrews 1 affirms that the revelation of the Gospel through Jesus is the culmination of the long journey of faith that includes the history of Israel. To say this clearly: if we have a "new" covenant mediated by Jesus Christ, it is because there was an earlier covenant with the people of Israel (see Jer. 31:31–34). Any anti-Semitic reading of the New Testament in general, and of the Epistle to the Hebrews in particular, violates the text.

In addition to Jewish rituals, this text also refers to ideas from Greek philosophy. The reference to a "perfect" tent points to the metaphysical underpinnings of the text. Hebrews assumes a Neoplatonic cosmology, where the "perfect" archetypes are in the cosmic "world of ideas," which implies that everything we see in this world is a "copy" of one of those "perfect ideas." Without turning the sermon into a lesson on Greek philosophy, the preacher can use Plato's "Allegory of the Cave" to explain this point, perhaps projecting on a screen a video of one of the many animated explanations available on the internet.

Hebrews' cosmological point of view explains why the author affirms that Jesus' spiritual high priesthood is superior to the traditional role of human priests. It also explains how Jesus came to be the perfect priest, the perfect liturgist, and the perfect sacrificial victim. From a Neoplatonist point of view, these ideas make excellent sense: the "perfect" sacrifice that redeems humanity from sin "once for all" was consummated when Jesus ascended to heaven, in the cosmic presence of God. The tabernacle in the wilderness, the temple of Jerusalem, and the sacrificial system as a whole are only "imperfect copies" of the "perfect" cosmic liturgies that Jesus performs in the true Holy of Holies, which is the presence of the one and only true God.

As stated before, the argument and ideas that we find in this text are alien to our contemporary culture. This text, after all, focuses on the murder/sacrifice of an innocent victim. However, there is another way of conceiving Jesus' death that might be more familiar: Jesus was executed by a foreign colonial power in collusion with local colonial authorities. If we think about Jesus' death as occurring in the midst of empire, that is, in and as part of a system of exploitation and death, this event becomes more understandable.

It also heightens the radicalness of the message conveyed in Scripture. The New Testament describes Jesus' death as the cosmic event that kills "death," understood as a spiritual force. The death of Jesus of Nazareth ends the rule of death, disarms the negative principalities and powers, and liberates humanity from the fear of death. Even though people of faith will eventually die physically, they will live forever spiritually in communion with God, thanks to the sacrifice of Jesus, in the power of the Holy Spirit. Therefore it is only logical that neither the message of the gospel nor the proclamation of Jesus' death should be used to justify murder, exploitation, or abuse.

Yet this is precisely how the Christian faith has been utilized by some, both in the past and, unfortunately, in the present. Not only do we need to be willing to confront the bad parts of the church's history, but it is necessary to reaffirm our stance as worshipers of a life-giving God. To enable the dehumanization of others is heretical. If Jesus has truly defeated death as a spiritual power, Christians cannot condone, enable, or disregard the exploitation of "the other." The colonial system and its corollaries—such as classism, racism, and other forms of discrimination—are social expressions of the power of death. People of faith cannot condone such exploitations; remaining passive in the face of social manifestations of sin could negate the value and meaning of Jesus' sacrificial death.

Resisting exploitation is much more easily said than done. In this complex world, which is dependent on cheap goods made oftentimes by underpaid or exploited workers across the globe, how do we, as the people of God, abstain from participation in systems of colonization, exploitation, and death? If dehumanization is sinful, yet we live in a world where we are forced to participate in this dehumanization of others, what should we do? How do we make decisions that affirm life and the life-giving God at the center of our faith?

There are no conclusive answers to these difficult questions. However, despite the lack of easy answers, the questions are still worth sitting with and contemplating, both as individuals and as groups. Perhaps this has come to give us life, abundant life (John 10:10), and lead us to explore the ways in which we can become faithful messengers of our life-giving God.

PABLO A. JIMENEZ

Proper 26 (Sunday between October 30 and November 5)

Mark 12:28–34

28One of the scribes came near and heard them disputing with one another, and seeing that he answered them well, he asked him, "Which commandment is the first of all?" 29Jesus answered, "The first is, 'Hear, O Israel: the Lord our God, the Lord is one; 30you shall love the Lord your God with all your heart, and with all your soul, and with all your mind, and with all your strength.' 31The second is this, 'You shall love your neighbor as yourself.' There is no other commandment greater than these." 32Then the scribe said to him, "You are right, Teacher; you have truly said that 'he is one, and besides him there is no other'; 33and 'to love him with all the heart, and with all the understanding, and with all the strength,' and 'to love one's neighbor as oneself,'—this is much more important than all whole burnt offerings and sacrifices." 34When Jesus saw that he answered wisely, he said to him, "You are not far from the kingdom of God." After that no one dared to ask him any question.

Commentary 1: Connecting the Reading with Scripture

Escalating tension between Jesus and his opponents characterizes Jesus' Jerusalem ministry in Mark 11:1–13:37. Indeed, shortly after Jesus arrives in Jerusalem, the chief priests and scribes plot to kill him (Mark 11:18; see 3:6). For his part, Jesus charges the temple leadership with corrupting the temple (11:15–17), bests various authorities in debate (11:27–33; 12:13–27), tells a parable that indicts the priests, scribes, and elders as murderers of God's prophets (12:1–12), and challenges the scriptural interpretation of the Sadducees (12:24–27).

In this conflict-ridden context, Mark 12:28–34 stands out for its positive depiction of the scribe and the agreeable nature of his interaction with Jesus. Unlike Jesus' previous interlocutors (12:13, 15), this scribe does not seek to trap Jesus. He is an earnest questioner who, impressed by Jesus, asks a question posed to respected teachers (v. 28). The question seeks to know which among the commandments of the Torah (613 according to rabbinic tradition) is most important.

In Jesus' day (about forty years before Mark's Gospel), neither the scribe's question nor Jesus' response would have been intended to diminish the importance of the Law's other commands. The question sought a guiding principle for

keeping them all. Jesus responds by identifying two commandments: the "first" or foundational one is Deuteronomy 6:4–5, and the "second" commandment is Leviticus 19:18. For Jesus, love of God and love of neighbor are inextricably linked.

The scribe, by definition a scholar of the Law, affirms Jesus' response and repeats Jesus' teaching almost verbatim (vv. 32–33), meaning he has accepted it. He then builds on it to draw a conclusion that renders him near the kingdom of God (vv. 33–34). In a Gospel that portrays so many learned religious leaders, especially chief priests and scribes, as opposed to Jesus and his message (3:6; 11:18; 14:1), and even his own disciples as failing to grasp his message (e.g., 8:31–35; 9:30–37; 10:32–45), this is high praise indeed. This encounter should prevent us from pigeonholing all the religious authorities in Mark as antagonistic to Jesus. A sermon based on it may challenge us to recognize our own tendencies to lump persons together as if they were of a single mind-set or shared perspective, a move that hinders mutual understanding and constructive dialogue.

Only in Mark, written around 70 CE, does the scribe articulate what is from Mark's perspective a correct implication of Jesus' teaching: to

The Happiness for Which We Were Made

True religion is right tempers towards God and man. It is, in two words, gratitude and benevolence; gratitude to our Creator and supreme Benefactor, and benevolence to our fellow creatures. In other words, it is the loving God with all our heart, and our neighbour as ourselves.

It is in consequence of our knowing God loves us, that we love him, and love our neighbour as ourselves. Gratitude towards our Creator cannot but produce benevolence to our fellow creatures. The love of Christ constrains us, not only to be harmless, to do no ill to our neighbour, but to be useful, to be "zealous of good works;" "as we have time, to do good unto all men;" and to be patterns to all of true, genuine morality; of justice, mercy, and truth. This is religion, and this is happiness; the happiness for which we were made. This begins when we begin to know God, by the teaching of his own Spirit. As soon as the Father of spirits reveals his Son in our hearts, and the Son reveals his Father, the love of God is shed abroad in our hearts; then, and not till then, we are happy. We are happy, first, in the consciousness of his favour, which indeed is better than life itself; next, in the constant communion with the Father, and with his Son Jesus Christ; then, in all the heavenly tempers which he hath wrought in us by his Spirit; again, in the testimony of his Spirit, that all our works please him; and, lastly, in the testimony of our own spirits, that "in simplicity and godly sincerity we have had our conversation in the world." Standing fast in this liberty from sin and sorrow, wherewith Christ hath made them free, real Christians "rejoice evermore, pray without ceasing, and in everything give thanks." And their happiness still increases as they "grow up into the measure of the stature of the fullness of Christ."

John Wesley, "The Unity of the Divine Being," in *The Works of John Wesley,* vol. 7 (London: Wesleyan Conference Office, 1872), 286–94.

love God and neighbor is "much more important" than any cultic sacrifice (12:33; cf. Matt. 22:34–40; Luke 10:25–28). To Gentile converts, so accustomed to the cultic worship of many gods, this message asserted sole devotion to God and love of neighbor as the essence of their new religiosity. To Mark's Jewish readers, who after 70 CE could no longer offer sacrifice to God because of the temple's destruction by the Romans (cf. Mark 13:1–2), this point echoed teachings from their own Scriptures on the primacy of right action over sacrifice (e.g., 1 Sam. 15:22; Pss. 40:6; 51:16–17; Isa. 1:11–17; Jer. 7:22–23; Hos. 6:6). The next step for the scribe and for Mark's readers (including ourselves), left unstated in the text but certainly something the preacher could express from the pulpit, is to enact the love command so that we may not just remain near the kingdom of God but actually enter it and manifest its presence.

Mark's view that devotion to God is better carried out through means other than sacrificial worship resonates with the second reading in the lectionary, Hebrews 9:11–14. Hebrews joins Mark in proclaiming the superiority of Jesus' self-sacrifice to the cultic sacrifices of the temple, with Jesus' crucifixion being the defining event that forever alters the temple's place in the realization of God's purposes (Mark 15:37–38). The disciple, too, can practice a religiosity that, from Mark's perspective, is superior to temple sacrifice by following Jesus' double love command.

With a Gospel as critical of the first-century Jewish religious context as is Mark, preachers should recognize that Mark and his first audiences were in the early stages of developing their identity as believers in Jesus, which meant separating themselves from their Jewish roots in certain ways and upholding these roots in others. Long past this stage today, we ought not denigrate the Jewish traditions and institutions of the first century, or of our Jewish neighbors today, when challenging audiences to love God and neighbor. Otherwise, we might find that the scribe in 12:28–34 is closer to the kingdom of God than we are.

Jesus' response to the scribe in 12:29–31 introduces two important texts from the Old

Testament: Deuteronomy 6:4–5 and Leviticus 19:18. Contained in Deuteronomy 6:1–9, the alternate Old Testament text, Deuteronomy 6:4–5 is part of the Shema, a cornerstone of Jewish faith that pious Jews recite twice daily. The Shema affirms the unity and centrality of Israel's God, who alone merits the devotion of the whole person. Leviticus 19:18 commands love of neighbor, which originally designated a fellow member of the Israelite community.

By joining these commandments, Jesus places himself within the rich tradition of the biblical prophets, who stressed that love of God and neighbor are of a piece, with "love" signifying not sentiment or disposition but embodied action. For Jesus, as for the great prophets of Israel (e.g., Isa. 1:11–17; Amos 5:21–24), embodied devotion to God and just social relationships with members of the community go hand in hand. To lack one is to undermine or nullify the other.

Ruth 1:1–18, the lectionary reading from the Hebrew Scriptures, helps us understand Mark's love command. First, Ruth embodies the allegiance to God that she professes in 1:16. These are not mere words. Though she could have chosen to return home, she radically reorients her life by attaching herself to Naomi (Ruth 1:14–18). This comes at great cost to Ruth, who leaves behind her cultural roots and is put into some rather dangerous situations by Naomi (3:1–5).

Second, Ruth is a Moabite, not an Israelite. Even as a foreigner, she becomes memorialized as the great-grandmother of Israel's most famous king, David (Ruth 4:17–22; Matt. 1:5–6). Perhaps the biblical tradition's incorporation of this foreigner into its salvation history may inspire us to apply Jesus' love-of-neighbor teaching beyond those we are predisposed to favor because they belong to our own clan, nation, or group.

In this vein, Mark expands the notion of "neighbor" to include persons outside the Israelite community. In Mark 11:17, Jesus cites Isaiah 56:7 to designate the temple as a house of prayer for all "nations" or "Gentiles" (*ethnē*), thus declaring God's presence as open to non-Israelites. At Jesus' crucifixion, the tearing of the temple veil (15:38), together with the Roman centurion's identification of Jesus as God's Son (15:39), underscores this point.

Whereas John seemingly restricts the love command to fellow disciples (John 13:34–35), the other Synoptic Gospels follow Mark's trajectory of expanding the notion of neighbor. For Matthew, Jesus' love command extends even to one's enemies (Matt. 5:43–48), and Luke inserts the good Samaritan parable into this passage to indicate that the "neighbor" could certainly include the ethnic and religious "other," even a despised one (Luke 10:25–37).

Today, our world is more interconnected than ever. We can know almost in real time what happens to our neighbors across the globe, and we have a keener sense of the global impact of our actions. In light of these realities, the preacher may dwell on the expansion of who counts as "neighbor" that we find in the Synoptic Gospels. Beginning with Mark, these Gospel traditions challenge us to think broadly about whom we are to love as our neighbor, if we seek, like the scribe, to be near God's kingdom.

GILBERTO A. RUIZ

Commentary 2: Connecting the Reading with the World

In most of the twelfth chapter of Mark, Jesus is involved in verbal combat with temple authorities—Pharisees, Herodians, Sadducees armed with trick questions and open hostility. However, astonishingly, in this particular text, it is as if the setting there in Jerusalem, probably steps away from the temple, becomes still for a moment. It is just long enough for Jesus to have this profound conversation with a scribe.

Soon, beyond this oasis of seven verses, Jesus will denounce the scribes to his followers; but just now we encounter some razor-sharp irony. The scribe's demeanor is not combative, even if it is not necessarily polite, either. He does not address Jesus with any customary title of respect (such as "rabbi" or "teacher"), but it appears that this conversation is at a certain level of earnestness, devoid of conflict and suffused with holiness, that we do not experience in the verses on either side of this text.

"Which commandment is the first of all?" asks the scribe. Jesus quotes from Deuteronomy 6:4–5—the Shema, a central tenet of the liturgy of his day—and then, for good measure, adds words from Leviticus 19:18 regarding obligation to neighbor: "The first," says Jesus to the scribe, is "'Hear, O Israel: the Lord our God, the Lord is one; you shall love the Lord your God with all your heart, and with all your soul, and with all your mind, and with all your strength.' The second is this, 'You shall love your neighbor as yourself.' There is no other commandment greater than these" (Mark 12:29–31). The scribe gets two commands for the price of one.

In this rare and pleasant moment—a moment in Mark's Gospel when a scribe, of all people, appears to understand something rightly—there is theological agreement between Jesus and the scribe. Still, the scribe is lacking something—something other than intellectual assent to a theological assertion. So Jesus says to him, "You are not far from the kingdom of God." Even though the scribe's orthodoxy is in order, and even though his understanding of what is important is impeccable, it is not a given that all of that intellectual assent has yet been transformed into a different way of living day by day. "Though 'wiser' than his colleagues," say Brian Blount and Gary Charles, "the scribe is not 'wise' enough to recognize that he is standing in a building that is about to crumble upon him (13:1–2), for the building houses a system that does not liberate 'neighbors' but oppresses them."[1]

In fact, for this scribe who asks for one commandment and gets two, it is probably the second commandment that is vexing him most. In Leviticus, after all, "loving your neighbor as yourself" means not exploiting the less powerful or the stranger. It means feeding those who are hungry, protecting those who are vulnerable, caring for those who are not privileged. Ultimately, it means opening our eyes to the signs of need all around us, signs of need that are just begging us to connect our liturgy with our faithful living.

This is what keeps that scribe stuck—that one who is "not far" but "far enough" from the kingdom. He is stuck on the wrong side of that gap between his liturgy and his faithfulness. Many of us, for sure, are similarly stuck. We feel more comfortable being in general agreement with Jesus than we do following him to at least some of the addresses toward which he might be prone to lead us. We would rather, for example, talk theology with him over a latte than spend the evening massaging his blistered feet in a night shelter. We might prefer to write him a check than to cook for him in a soup kitchen. We would gladly have all the right instincts about "The Homeless" or "The Immigrants" or "Those in Prison," than know any of their names or hear any of their stories.

So perhaps we, too, are "not far from the kingdom of God." Perhaps we, too, need to be reminded by that ironic oasis of conversation between Jesus and that scribe, that being "not far from the kingdom of God" is not so much a judgment as it is an invitation. It is the invitation to take the next logical step, from agreeing with Jesus amiably to witnessing his love incarnationally, from having a safe relationship with him at a distance to following him on the Way.

There is a story told of an old rabbi who was teaching two of his brightest students. The students asked him, "How do we know that the night is over and that the dawn is coming?" The rabbi replied, "What do you think?" The first student said, "When it is light enough to tell the difference between a dog and a sheep?" The old rabbi shook his head and said, "No." The second student said, "When you can distinguish between a grapevine and a sycamore tree?" The old man shook his head again. Finally, after they petitioned him again and again, he said, "Here is how you tell when the night is over and the dawn is coming: It is when you can look into the face of a stranger and see a member of your own family. At that moment, it is the dawn that is coming."[2]

In Barbara Brown Taylor's seminal book *Leaving Church: A Memoir of Faith*, she explored what it meant to serve as an Episcopal priest for

---

1. Brian K. Blount and Gary W. Charles, *Preaching Mark in Two Voices* (Louisville, KY: Westminster John Knox, 2002), 197.
2. Agnes W. Norfleet, "From Text to Sermon," *Interpretation* (October 1997): 406.

twenty-some-odd years of parish ministry, and then to leave that life. Her book chronicled the conflicts inherent in this work in ways that all of us who have also spent time in the parish could understand. She wrote of the difference between *ink* and *blood*, and about what happens when people try to solve their conflicts with one another by hurling Bible verses back and forth until their sense of shared kinship, the one that the rabbi describes above, is destroyed by their defense of God: "If I am not careful," she writes,

> I can begin to mistake the words on the page for the realities they describe. I can begin to love the dried ink marks on the page more than I love the encounters that gave rise to them. If I am not careful, I can decide that I am really much happier reading my Bible than I am entering into what God is doing in my own time and place, since shutting the book to go outside will involve the very great risk of taking part in stories that are still taking shape. Neither I nor anyone else knows how these stories will turn out, since at this point they involve more blood than ink. The whole purpose of the Bible, it seems to me, is to convince people to set the written words down in order to become living words in the world for God's sake.[3]

It is not really liturgy, and it is certainly not incarnational love, until the ink becomes blood. It is not right doctrine until it is right relationship, until we are not just experts in the written word but are living words in the world for God's sake. Whenever this happens, the night is over and the dawn comes; and the church succeeds at who and what we are meant to be.

THEODORE J. WARDLAW

---

3. Barbara Brown Taylor, *Leaving Church: A Memoir of Faith* (New York: HarperCollins, 2007), 107.

Proper 27 (Sunday between November 6 and November 12)

Ruth 3:1–5; 4:13–17 and 1 Kings 17:8–16   Hebrews 9:24–28
Psalm 127 and Psalm 146   Mark 12:38–44

Ruth 3:1–5; 4:13–17

3:1Naomi her mother-in-law said to her, "My daughter, I need to seek some security for you, so that it may be well with you. 2Now here is our kinsman Boaz, with whose young women you have been working. See, he is winnowing barley tonight at the threshing floor. 3Now wash and anoint yourself, and put on your best clothes and go down to the threshing floor; but do not make yourself known to the man until he has finished eating and drinking. 4When he lies down, observe the place where he lies; then, go and uncover his feet and lie down; and he will tell you what to do." 5She said to her, "All that you tell me I will do." . . .

4:13So Boaz took Ruth and she became his wife. When they came together, the LORD made her conceive, and she bore a son. 14Then the women said to Naomi, "Blessed be the LORD, who has not left you this day without next-of-kin; and may his name be renowned in Israel! 15He shall be to you a restorer of life and a nourisher of your old age; for your daughter-in-law who loves you, who is more to you than seven sons, has borne him." 16Then Naomi took the child and laid him in her bosom, and became his nurse. 17The women of the neighborhood gave him a name, saying, "A son has been born to Naomi." They named him Obed; he became the father of Jesse, the father of David.

1 Kings 17:8–16

8Then the word of the LORD came to him, saying, 9"Go now to Zarephath, which belongs to Sidon, and live there; for I have commanded a widow there to feed you." 10So he set out and went to Zarephath. When he came to the gate of the town, a widow was there gathering sticks; he called to her and said, "Bring me a little water in a vessel, so that I may drink." 11As she was going to bring it, he called to her and said, "Bring me a morsel of bread in your hand." 12But she said, "As the LORD your God lives, I have nothing baked, only a handful of meal in a jar, and a little oil in a jug; I am now gathering a couple of sticks, so that I may go home and prepare it for myself and my son, that we may eat it, and die." 13Elijah said to her, "Do not be afraid; go and do as you have said; but first make me a little cake of it and bring it to me, and afterwards make something for yourself and your son. 14For thus says the LORD the God of Israel: The jar of meal will not be emptied and the jug of oil will not fail until the day that the LORD sends rain on the earth." 15She went and did as Elijah said, so that she as well as he and her household ate for many days. 16The jar of meal was not emptied, neither did the jug of oil fail, according to the word of the LORD that he spoke by Elijah.

Commentary 1: Connecting the Reading with Scripture

The first of two alternate readings concludes the book of Ruth from last week. The second reading from 1 Kings 17 relates another story of trust in the midst of dire circumstances. Since Ruth's prescribed passages hit only the highlights, preachers must fill in the gaps. Before returning to Bethlehem in chapter 1, Naomi had expressed concern for Ruth's economic security, saying she had no other sons to offer in marriage and no hope of offspring (Ruth 1:11–13). Beneath Naomi's words lies a mysterious Israelite custom, the levirate marriage, which dictated that a childless widow's brother-in-law must produce an heir for the deceased "so that his name might not be blotted out" (Deut. 25:5–6). As a more distant relative, Boaz is not obliged to marry Ruth, but he seems to respect her and treats her with kindness. Naomi views him as an attractive prospect. So she initiates a plan, telling Ruth to dress up and find Boaz at the threshing floor where he has been winnowing barley. She is to wait until he is asleep, slip into his bed, and do whatever he wants.

Until now, both Boaz and Naomi have protected Ruth from male harassment (Ruth 2:8–9, 21–22). Now Naomi's plan gambles on Boaz's honor, exposing her daughter-in-law to humiliation or even rape. Why does Naomi not just talk to Boaz? For one thing, this plot twist, dangling on the edge of morality and custom, makes a more intriguing story. Perhaps Naomi perceives that Boaz needs his initiative jump-started. It is a gamble, but Ruth concurs. "All that you tell me I will do," she replies (3:5).

When Boaz goes off script, Ruth improvises. He is too soundly asleep to notice her approach, and when he awakens at midnight, he seems too startled to play the part Naomi has assigned him. "Who are you?" he demands in surprise. Ruth identifies herself but does not wait for his instructions. "Spread your cloak over your servant, for you are next-of-kin," she says. In one of the least romantic proposals imaginable, she asks him to redeem her dead husband's inheritance.

Boaz considers her request neither crass nor unseemly, but generous. Like Naomi (2:2, 22; 3:1), he has called Ruth "my daughter" before (2:8) and continues to do so in this speech (3:10, 11), hinting at his own age. He believes that had she not been loyal to Naomi, she would have married a younger man. Boaz then offers another surprising detail: there is a nearer relative. Since this one has not stepped forward before, readers are not excited about him now. Balancing honor and desire, Boaz promises to sort things out. Before dawn he sends her home, giving her yet more food to take with her and the assurance that everyone knows she is a person of worth (*eshet hayil*; cf. the parallel description of Boaz in 2:1, *ish gibbor hayil*).

Just as Ruth improved on Naomi's instructions, Boaz improves on Ruth's request. He finds the other relative and, before witnesses, invites him to buy a field from Naomi. How he knows of this field is left unsaid. The man agrees, but the next revelation causes him to backpedal: Ruth comes with it; her first son will be Mahlon's heir; and her new husband will eventually lose the land he bought. He declines.

Complexities in the story's unfolding and gaps in our knowledge make it difficult to follow exactly what is transpiring, but we see the result. Publicly dismissing all other claims, Boaz clears the way both to enrich Naomi and to marry Ruth. Like a Greek chorus, the witnesses bless Ruth, not as a Moabite, but as the spiritual successor of fruitful and formidable, if unorthodox, ancestors—Rachel, Leah, and Tamar.

As soon as they are married, having given her all kinds of seed to eat, Boaz now gives her human seed. (The Hebrew word is the same.) She bears a son who, in the story's punchline, becomes the ancestor of the Davidic kings.

Like all fine narratives, the story is filled with gaps inviting reader participation. One value that communicates distinctly is loyalty (1:8; 2:20; 3:10). Ruth's loyalty to Naomi is reciprocated by Naomi and Boaz. The result is security for two widows, an heir for Mahlon and a son for Boaz, delight for the whole community, and a dynasty that will rule Judah, offering relative stability for four centuries.

First Kings 17:8–16 likewise concerns a drought, a powerful Israelite man, a foreign

Written in Love and Loyalty

There is a long and honored tradition of viewing the story of Ruth and Naomi as a book about women working to re-establish the line of their dead husbands. . . . Yet coupled with the scroll's concern for husbands and sons is a story of love between women that is not only the love of friends but also the love of mother and daughter. The narrative of the scroll of Ruth may provide insight into the situation of foreign women and childless women among the Israelites. It may say something about women and economic pragmatism and the family. It does say a lot about the relationship between God and his people and about the collective life of a nation. But embedded in all of that is a story of a particular relationship between two women—which closes with the strongest articulation of the love of a daughter for her mother and of a mother for her daughter that appears in the Bible [Ruth 4:15]. . . . This is a very direct observation on the love between Ruth and Naomi, and one that harks back to their initial condition— before Naomi's sons died, before Ruth married Boaz, for it must be noted that Ruth's second marriage does not officially make Naomi either her mother or her mother-in-law but rather a relative by marriage. It indirectly suggests that their initial relationship has become fixed, as if it were written in blood, in love and loyalty.

Leila Leah Bronner, "The Invisible Relation Made Visible: Biblical Mothers and Daughters," in *Ruth and Esther: A Feminist Companion to the Bible,* ed. Athalya Brenner (Sheffield: Sheffield Academic Press, 1999), 185–86.

outside Israel's borders but on behalf of a foreign family.

This passage is the complementary Old Testament reading accompanying a neighboring theme in Mark 12:38–44. There, Jesus condemns arrogant male leaders who display public piety while secretly preying on poor widows. He then spotlights contrasting behavior. Watching as various people offer money to the temple treasury, he points out a widow whom he sees offering only a penny's worth, which he reports is all she had, contributing out of her poverty more than all those who made donations from their wealth.

Both Old Testament passages, and the Mark passage, commend the generosity of those who are living on the economic edge. None of them demands that others do the same. Rather, they highlight a reality that is commonly seen to this day: generosity is more often born not of recognizing that one has plenty to spare, but of the opposite: of compassion nurtured by having known want oneself. One widow, a Moabite who had nothing to give but loyalty and love, offered what she had. Another widow, a Sidonian who believed she was facing starvation herself, provided for another in the same predicament. Both of these stories commend the noble deeds of foreign women.

Such stories become especially crucial in our era of xenophobia and ethnocentrism—when those in power attempt to limit others' access not only to equal protection but even to safety and health; when refugees at our own borders are derided and harshly treated; when the working poor are denied a living wage; when those affected by natural catastrophes struggle with lack of disaster assistance; and when health insurance and medical service for those who need it most continue to be inadequately available. These biblical stories indicate that saving

widow, danger, trust, and prosperity, but its plot is entirely different. In many ways it seems to illustrate elements of last week's reading from Deuteronomy 6, the Shema ("Hear, O Israel") in particular. Here, God participates explicitly rather than implicitly. The backstory begins with the Israelite king Ahab worshiping Baal, the god of his Sidonian wife Jezebel (1 Kgs. 16:29–33). Defying him, the prophet Elijah bursts on the scene with a warning that Israel's God will produce a drought, and then flees eastward (1 Kgs. 17:1–7). When the drought reaches Elijah's location, he, too, must move in search of food, going at God's direction to Sidon, north of Israel, Baal's and Jezebel's land. Therefore, the person whom he meets and who agrees to feed him, who trusts his promise of survival, who saves his life and is saved by his presence, is a foreign widow. The story demonstrates the power of Israel's God, not only the lives of the most vulnerable promotes the prosperity of the whole community. Preachers must take care not to suggest that grace should be extended only to the "deserving poor," as if humans were capable of such judgments, nor to idealize poverty itself, but rather to emphasize God's concern for and support of those who live on society's margins.

PATRICIA K. TULL

Commentary 2: Connecting the Reading with the World

Assemblage artists create beautiful art. Instead of using the best materials, they use everyday objects, usually the junk that others discard. Imagine the items that do not qualify for the give-away pile, the shards of glass swept into the dust pan, or the rusty bicycle with a bent frame. Line these items up on a curb, and most people see worthless junk. Assemblage artists look at the same items and imagine a beautiful future for them.

Now imagine two women in a contest for their survival. Residing in Bethlehem, Naomi and Ruth live as widows without sons or family in a patriarchal context, which means they lack economic security, physical protection, and a stable future. Ruth resides there as a foreigner, and Naomi is past childbearing age. Many in the ancient world would see them as worthless. We are not so different. Whom, in our context, do we dismiss and discard?

Ruth 3:1–5 catalogues Naomi's dangerous plan to secure a path to survival. Her idea, she claims, will lead to "some security" so that "it may be well" with Ruth (Ruth 3:1). These idioms usually mean prosperity, marital happiness, children, or long life (Gen. 12:13; Deut. 4:40; 5:16, 33; 6:3; Jer. 40:9; 42:6). Naomi's strategy makes most modern readers squirm, and for good reasons. She instructs Ruth to bathe, to anoint herself (the oil for which was rare among those living in poverty), to wear beautiful clothes, and to go to the threshing floor alone at night, a venue associated with sexual infidelity (Hos. 9:1). Then, she tells her to "uncover Boaz's feet," lie down, and wait for him to tell her what to do (Ruth 3:4). Elsewhere, the verb "uncover" describes sexually illicit situations (e.g., Lev. 18:6–19; Deut. 22:30), and the noun "feet" is a euphemism for sexual organs (Exod. 4:25; Deut. 28:57; Judg. 3:24; 1 Sam. 24:3; Ezek. 16:25).

Although commentators disagree on how to interpret the scene, this much remains clear: the narrator has put Ruth into a high-stakes situation. If the plan succeeds, the stable future will become a reality. If it fails, both women will fall into disrepute or perhaps something worse.

Naomi's strategy, though it may seem peculiar, parallels modern situations. Engaged in a battle for survival, millions of women around the world likely resonate with this tale. They, too, live in a patriarchal context; they must marry and have children to secure a future. Those who do not marry put themselves in peril, and those who do must develop innovative strategies for survival. A wise preacher could explore the ways in which people of God can respond with compassion and empathy, not judgment and condemnation, to those who are compelled to use such strategies to survive.

Ruth 4:13–17 discloses the remarkable result of Naomi's unconventional plan. Ruth and Boaz get married, and her status changes from a Moabite refugee to a member of the covenant community. God enables Ruth to bear a son, only the second time that the narrator mentions God's direct intervention (cf. Ruth 1:6). They present him to Naomi, and the women in the community celebrate God's grace in Naomi's life. Through a grandson, God has given her "next-of-kin," a "restorer of life," a "nourisher" in her old age (4:14–15). They praise Naomi on account of Ruth, whose loyalty, resilience, and love make her worth more than seven sons, a startling claim in a society that favored sons and saw seven as a number of perfection.

The narrator leaves room for one last twist. After "the women of the neighborhood" (v. 17) name the child "Obed" (a peculiar detail, since parents normally name their children), we discover that Obed became the father of Jesse, who became the father of David. Who else besides God could raise up a child from a Moabite mother, a wealthy father whose name should have been lost to history, and a mother-in-law who had almost lost hope, and graft that child into the royal line of Israel? God injects hope into impossible situations.

The final lection, 1 Kings 17:8–16, presents another seemingly impossible situation. God takes Elijah, a prophet miraculously fed by ravens, and sends him to Zarephath, the heart of Baal territory, so that he might rely on a foreigner for basic needs (1 Kgs. 17:8–9). As in Ruth 3–4, a widow serves as the central character in the narrative; like Naomi, she is tempted to abandon hope. Elijah finds her at the town gate, and after he asks her for food and drink, she tells him that she intends to go home and cook a meal for her son. After that, she expects they both will die. All she has left is some "meal in a jar" and "oil in a jug" (see 2 Kgs. 4:1–7). Elijah tells her not to fear. The meal will not run out and the oil will not fail until "the LORD sends rain on the earth" (1 Kgs. 17:14). But he also makes a dangerous request. Will she make *him* a meal before she makes herself a meal?

Here we see how the widow of Zarephath most resembles Ruth. As a foreigner, she must decide whether to choose faith over fear, hope over despair, the God of Israel or the gods of her native land. Can God be trusted? Even if most people cannot understand the depth of desperation this woman faced, they do resemble her in other ways. Like her, they must decide whether to choose faith over fear when faced with a stage-4 cancer diagnosis, hope over despair at the graveside of a loved one, the God of Israel or the gods that are easier to follow in a crisis. Like her, they ask, Can God be trusted? Verse 15 makes

the widow's choice clear. She bets her life on a God of the impossible. In doing so, she discovers that the God who brings hope to the hopeless is also the God who honors courageous faith.

Taken together, these two stories remind us of who God is and what God does. God works through ordinary people who trust God with what they have, even if the "what" is some meal in a jar, oil in a jug, or five loaves and two fish (Matt. 14:17; Mark 6:38; Luke 9:13; John 6:9). Ordinary people do not need the influence of Boaz or the gifts of Elijah for God to work through them. Although God's faithfulness does come through Boazes and Elijahs, it also comes through ordinary people with limited resources and deep faith. God knows the names of the leaders who put their homes up as collateral so that the sanctuary can be built. God remembers the sacrifice of Sunday school teachers who stay long enough to teach the children and the children's children. God hears the prayers of refugees whose worldly possessions can fit into a small backpack. God honors the copper coins dropped in the offering plate and knows how much they cost the one who gives them (Luke 21:1–4).

Perhaps Jesus draws attention to the widow of Zarephath's story in his inaugural sermon in order to remind religious people that God sees things differently (Luke 4:25–26). Too often, high-status people look on people they deem "low status" and predetermine their worth. Sometimes, pastors look at some of their parishioners that way. All they see is glass shards, broken pieces, or irreparable damage. God does not see it the same way. God is a great assemblage artist. God looks at those we are ready to discard and imagines a beautiful future for them.

JARED E. ALCÁNTARA

Psalm 127

[1]Unless the LORD builds the house,
 those who build it labor in vain.
Unless the LORD guards the city,
 the guard keeps watch in vain.
[2]It is in vain that you rise up early
 and go late to rest,
eating the bread of anxious toil;
 for he gives sleep to his beloved.

[3]Sons are indeed a heritage from the LORD,
 the fruit of the womb a reward.
[4]Like arrows in the hand of a warrior
 are the sons of one's youth.
[5]Happy is the man who has
 his quiver full of them.
He shall not be put to shame
 when he speaks with his enemies in the gate.

Psalm 146

[1]Praise the LORD!
Praise the LORD, O my soul!
[2]I will praise the LORD as long as I live;
 I will sing praises to my God all my life long.

[3]Do not put your trust in princes,
 in mortals, in whom there is no help.
[4]When their breath departs, they return to the earth;
 on that very day their plans perish.

[5]Happy are those whose help is the God of Jacob,
 whose hope is in the LORD their God,
[6]who made heaven and earth,
 the sea, and all that is in them;
who keeps faith forever;
 [7]who executes justice for the oppressed;
who gives food to the hungry.

The LORD sets the prisoners free;
 [8]the LORD opens the eyes of the blind.
The LORD lifts up those who are bowed down;
 the LORD loves the righteous.
[9]The LORD watches over the strangers;
 he upholds the orphan and the widow,
 but the way of the wicked he brings to ruin.

¹⁰The LORD will reign forever,
  your God, O Zion, for all generations.
Praise the LORD!

Connecting the Psalm with Scripture and Worship

Psalm 127. Like the seven psalms immediately before it and the seven psalms immediately after it, Psalm 127 is a Song of Ascents, thought to have been composed for use by pilgrims ascending to Jerusalem. Although this psalm's focus on matters of hearth and home may initially seem at odds with the very idea of a pilgrim journey, it is not difficult to imagine pilgrims carrying with them petitions and/or thanksgiving for their work life and family life. In fact, this psalm is all about the care and providence of God, which was believed to flow from the pilgrimage site of Jerusalem, and which is a major theme in the book of Ruth.

The psalm begins with three assertions of the futility of any efforts that are not wed to the purposes of YHWH: without God, it is useless to build (Ps. 127:1a), to watch over (v. 1b), or to expend long "anxious" hours (v. 2a). The brief psalm then closes with proverbial sayings (vv. 3–4) and a beatitude (v. 5a), all of them extolling the lasting gift of children.

This makes Psalm 127 a provocative response to the book of Ruth, which is filled with cause-and-effect relationships between having children and having security. Although the story starts with Naomi seemingly secure as the mother of two married sons, when both of these young men die without fathering children, her anticipated security evaporates (Ruth 1:1–5). The widowed and now-childless Naomi and her widowed and still-childless daughter-in-law Ruth then journey to Bethlehem (1:22). The two widows collaborate on a risky plan (3:1–5) that succeeds spectacularly: Ruth marries Boaz and bears a child (4:13). Thus a story that began with famine, death, and despair concludes with harvest and hope and Naomi rocking her grandbaby, who will one day have his own grandbaby, a shepherd boy who will become King David (4:16–17).

The conception of Ruth and Boaz's child (4:13) is one of only two (see 1:6) overt mentions of YHWH's involvement in the events of the story. Yet Christians can see in this story that, to paraphrase the opening line of Psalm 127, the Lord did indeed build this house: the bloodline of Ruth's child continues through King David to Joseph, the husband of Mary. So, Jesus the Messiah is a descendant of Ruth the Moabite.

A fruitful sermon approach for the Ruth pericope could explore how God's providence can be realized through the work of individuals: Naomi's plans, Ruth's labors, Boaz's actions, as well as the endeavors of members of your congregation. Psalm 127 could then serve as an important corrective, reminding everyone that the success of all these undertakings lies not with human effort but with God's gracious providing. The church in particular must always be reminded that whatever we undertake must be done in prayerful, humble harmony with the purposes of God.

A final note: interestingly, the term *bēn*, which does specifically mean "son," has often been translated, even in the King James Version, as the nongendered term "children." While the NRSV is accurate to translate it as meaning male children—and we know that sons were highly prized in ancient Israel—a pastor would do well to adhere to the more inclusive translations, doing your part to ensure that any girls who hear your words know that they, too, are "a heritage from the LORD, . . . a reward" (Ps. 127:3).

Congregational singing can underscore several theological themes. "Unless the Lord the House Shall Build" is a classic and straightforward setting of Psalm 127, while "Let Us Build a House" offers a more modern and expansive interpretation. "Guide Me, O Thou Great Jehovah" highlights the importance of God's hand in all that we do, while "How Clear Is Our Vocation, Lord" reminds us that we are called to participate in God's work.

Psalm 146. This ardently confident song of praise to YHWH is the first entry in the Psalter's collection of Hallelujah psalms, thus named because each one opens and closes with an imperative phrase of *halal* and *YHWH*, translated as "Praise the Lord" (Ps. 146:1, 10) and the source of our word "hallelujah."

The initial double exhortation to praise (v. 1a, b) is immediately answered by a double vow to praise (v. 2a, b). This vow is soon lived out as the psalmist proceeds with praise *of* God (vv. 5–10a), culminating in a final burst of praise *to* God (v. 10b).

First, the psalm offers a statement of cautionary antithesis: "Do not put your trust . . . in mortals. . . . When their breath departs, they return to the earth" (vv. 3–4). This warning regarding the frailty of human life is evocative of today's passage from 1 Kings, wherein we meet a poor widow whose household teeters on the brink of nonexistence (1 Kgs. 17:12) until it is miraculously rescued "according to the word of the Lord that [God] spoke by Elijah" (v. 16). As if to underscore the experience of the widow—not to mention that of Elijah himself—the psalmist offers an elaborate beatitude regarding those who trust in "the Lord their God" (Ps. 146:5–7a) instead of trusting in mortals.

This beatitude describes YHWH as the one "who made heaven and earth, the sea, and all that is in them; who keeps faith forever; who executes justice for the oppressed; who gives food to the hungry" (vv. 6–7a). Especially, though not exclusively, that last item speaks to the widow's divinely averted starvation.

The psalmist continues cataloging God's defining works of compassion and power (vv. 7b–10a). Again, while the entire list could harmonize with the widow's circumstances, one part is most directly applicable to the story of the stranger, Elijah, and the widow's plight: "The Lord watches over the strangers; [God] upholds the orphan and the widow" (v. 9a,

b). (In the fuller story of Elijah, note that the psalm's subsequent phrase is borne out in the fate of the prophet's nemesis, Jezebel [2 Kgs. 9:30–37].)

Although the widow of Zarephath is never seen to heed the psalmist's exhortation to offer praise to YHWH, her story is clarified by considering the priorities of Psalm 146. It is vital to think of her rescue not as the work of Elijah, but as the work of God through Elijah. That is also an important reminder in our self-focused world with its emphasis on self-reliance.

Perhaps the most well-known musical setting of this psalm is "I'll Praise My Maker." "Holy God, We Praise Your Name" is another traditional hymn well suited to the day's texts. Of course, Psalm 146 and the rest of the Hallelujah psalms could be seen as our earliest praise songs!

Liturgically, consider designing your intercessory prayers around the template of Psalm 146, as in this example:

> Almighty God, who made heaven and earth, and who keep faith forever, hear us as we pray.
> To the oppressed, O God, bring justice; we especially lift to You . . .
> To the hungry, O God, give food; we especially lift to You . . .
> To the wrongly imprisoned, O God, send liberty; we especially lift to You . . .
> For those who are differently abled, O God, ensure dignity and fulfillment; we especially lift to You . . .
> For those who are strangers, O God, grant hospitality; we especially lift to You . . .
> For those who are grieving, O God, be present to comfort; we especially lift to You . . .
> Guide us away from the wicked and fortify us in righteousness
> that we may serve you, O God, who reigns forever. Amen.

LEIGH CAMPBELL-TAYLOR

Hebrews 9:24–28

24For Christ did not enter a sanctuary made by human hands, a mere copy of the true one, but he entered into heaven itself, now to appear in the presence of God on our behalf. 25Nor was it to offer himself again and again, as the high priest enters the Holy Place year after year with blood that is not his own; 26for then he would have had to suffer again and again since the foundation of the world. But as it is, he has appeared once for all at the end of the age to remove sin by the sacrifice of himself. 27And just as it is appointed for mortals to die once, and after that the judgment, 28so Christ, having been offered once to bear the sins of many, will appear a second time, not to deal with sin, but to save those who are eagerly waiting for him.

Commentary 1: Connecting the Reading with Scripture

The key sentence of Hebrews 9:24–28 expresses one of the main themes, not only of this passage but of the book of Hebrews as a whole: "[Jesus] has appeared once for all at the end of the age to remove sin by the sacrifice of himself" (v. 26b). This confessional statement places the passage and the book squarely in the earliest proclamation of the gospel reflected in the Passion Narratives of the four Gospels, Paul's epistles, 1 Peter, and Revelation. It also fits into the interpretive practice of using Jewish Scriptures to define, defend, and promote the gospel. The quotation, the passage, and the broader context in which they appear in Hebrews show that its author draws on a different model of Jewish sacrifice than the one used in the other works.

While the Gospels, Paul, and the authors of 1 Peter and Revelation work from the traditions that focused on Passover as the starting point for interpreting Jesus' death, the author of Hebrews looks to traditions that focused on the sacrifice prescribed for the Day of Atonement, the main actor in which was the high priest. Consequently, to interpret the meaning of Jesus' death, Hebrews, uniquely among the writings of the New Testament, proposes a role for him as high priest, making it a central theme of the book.

The exegesis and application of the sacrifice for the Day of Atonement described in Leviticus 16 are intricately woven throughout Hebrews. They do not cover every aspect of it, as the author admits in 9:5b, but focus on the ones that support the claim that as high priest, Jesus simultaneously performs, and is, the sacrifice of atonement. The argument in 9:24–28 uses many of the terms and themes found in 9:11–14 (and in earlier passages) but stays closer to the language of Leviticus by focusing on the removal of sin rather than purification of conscience. Its central premise derives from the conclusion to the argument made in 9:15–21 regarding Moses' sprinkling "the blood of the covenant" on the scroll, the people, the tent, and the vessels used in worship to ratify the covenant God had ordained on Sinai: "Indeed, under the law almost everything is purified with blood, and with the shedding of blood there is no forgiveness of sins" (Heb. 9:22). For the author of Hebrews, the sacrifices Moses and the high priests performed were not sufficient, since "the heavenly things themselves need better sacrifices than these" (v. 23). Verses 24–28 address this necessity.

In keeping with 9:11–14, verses 24–28 distinguish Jesus' high-priestly sacrifice from the sacrifices prescribed in Leviticus 16 by arguing that (1) Jesus enters a holy place "not made with hands" to make the sacrifice of atonement; (2) Jesus offers his own blood and not the blood of goats and calves; and (3) he does this only once.

Elsewhere, the author makes clear that Jesus' unique and exalted status also make his sacrifice superior. Supplementing the author's exegesis in 9:11–14, the reading in 9:24–28 makes explicit that the place of Jesus' "true" sacrifice is in heaven (v. 24), emphasizes even more its taking place once and for all (mentioning twice more), and distinguishes between bearing the sins of many and appearing a second time "to save those who are eagerly waiting for him" (v. 28). The reference to Jesus' "appear[ing] in the presence of God on our behalf" (v. 24) adds an intercessory dimension to the priestly role he plays.

Jesus is explicitly referred to as high priest in Hebrews 2:17; 3:1; 4:14–15; 5:5, 10; 6:20; 7:26; 8:1; and 9:11. Working from the epistle for the day, there are at least three ways to explore ways to write a sermon using the image of Jesus as high priest: exalted, accessible, and exemplary.

In 9:24–28, Jesus as *exalted* high priest is implied in the contrast made between the earthly setting for the sacrifices high priests in the tent/temple perform and the heavenly setting for Jesus' sacrifice. They make sacrifices in a high place made with hands; Jesus sacrifices in a high place not made with hands, and in heaven—the one a mere copy of the other. The distinction reflects the Platonic framework for distinguishing the real from the shadow, used broadly in the Greco-Roman world of the period, including by Jewish writers such as Philo of Alexandria. Jesus' exalted status is also reflected in his accomplishing atonement as the result of one sacrifice, in contrast to the repeated sacrifices performed in the tent/temple. Beyond 9:24–28, the references to Jesus' exalted status are explicit and frequent.

The two most prominent themes giving expression to this are Jesus as Son of God and as "a priest forever according to the order of Melchizedek," sometimes treated separately, sometimes together. Hebrews 5:5–10 is the best example of the two titles used together (with citations of Pss. 2:7 and 110:4); chapter 7 offers the most extensive exegesis of Genesis 14:17–20 and Psalm 110:4, the two passages from the Hebrew Scriptures that refer to Melchizedek.

The first four verses of Hebrews are a highly rhetorical introduction to the major themes in Hebrews, using titles drawn both from Scripture and philosophy that bespeak Jesus' exalted status. Verse 4 leads immediately into a long chain of quotations that establish Jesus' exalted status in comparison to angels, and a comparison of Moses and Jesus that concludes, "[Jesus] is worthy of more glory" (3:3). As background for 9:24–28, these references to Jesus' exalted status confirm his worthiness to be called "a great high priest," whose sacrifice accomplishes what priests in the earthly tent could not.

At the same time, Jesus is an *accessible* high priest, one who "did not glorify himself" in fulfilling the role but was appointed to it (5:5). More pointedly, it was through his "reverent submission," demonstrated in his offering up "prayers and supplications with loud cries and tears" that "he learned obedience" and was "made perfect," so that he might become "the source of eternal salvation for all who obey him" (5:7–9). His being "tested" through suffering means that "we do not have a high priest unable to sympathize with our weaknesses" and may "approach the throne of grace with boldness, so that we may receive mercy and find grace to help in time of need" (4:15–16).

In his conclusion to Hebrews, the author refers to it as "a word of exhortation" (13:22), linking his own sermon to a genre commonly used by moralists in the Greco-Roman world who wrote to encourage their disciples to live the good life. Citing *exemplary* lives was a common feature of such works. Hebrews 11 goes through a list of examples drawn from Israel's history that is equivalent to the lives of philosophers the moralists counted as exemplary. It concludes with an exhortation to "run with perseverance the race that is set before us, looking to Jesus the pioneer and perfecter of our faith, who for the sake of the joy that was set before him endured the cross, disregarding its shame, and has taken his seat at the right hand of the throne of God" (12:1b–2). The author of Hebrews has prepared us to see Jesus as the exalted Son of God and the high priest who sacrifices himself, while also showing him to be an example of obedient faith and perseverance. A good preacher will do the same.

OLIVER LARRY YARBROUGH

Commentary 2: Connecting the Reading with the World

Hebrews 9:24–28 is found in a difficult section of Hebrews. Hebrews 7:1–10:18 argues that Jesus Christ is the high priest of the order of Melchizedek, who has offered "once for all" the "perfect" sacrifice for human sin. In a cosmic liturgy that began in heaven, was developed on earth, and ended in heaven, Jesus was both the liturgist and the sacrificial lamb. Jesus was the perfect high priest, who offered the perfect sacrifice that finally liberated humanity from sin and its consequences.

If the larger section is difficult to understand, Hebrews 9:24–28 may be the most challenging section within it. The author assumes a Neoplatonic cosmology, where the "perfect" archetypes are understood to reside in the cosmic "world of ideas," and the earthly realm is populated with "copies" of those "perfect ideas." Hebrews 9:24 affirms that Jesus entered heaven, the "true sanctuary," not a copy. This implies that the Israelites' tabernacle in the wilderness and the Jerusalem temple (in its different forms) were mere "copies" of the divine Holy of Holies. As the perfect high priest, Jesus presented his effective sacrifice "once for all" (Heb. 9:26). This also explains why Jesus died once, in sacrifice, on behalf of humanity (v. 26). Just as humans die once (v. 27), Jesus dies once to take away the sins of the world (v. 28). However, his death is not permanent, for the church expects Jesus' triumphant return (v. 28).

Hebrews 9:24–28 is one of the best-known sections of this epistle, given its role in evangelism. Hebrews 9:26–28 is a key biblical text for the exposition of the Four Spiritual Laws, a method used to present the plan of salvation through personal evangelism. This method of personal evangelism is popular in Latin America, in the Caribbean, and among Hispanic Americans. This method summarizes the message of the Gospel in a four-point "plan," namely: "(1) God loves you and offers a wonderful plan for your life (John 3:16; 10:10). (2) [Humanity] is sinful and separated from God. Thus [we] cannot know and experience God's love and plan for [our] life

(Rom. 3:23; 6:23). (3) Jesus Christ is God's only provision for [humanity's] sin. Through him [we] can know and experience God's love and plan for [our] life (John 14:6; Rom. 5:8; 1 Cor. 15:3–6). (4) We must individually receive Jesus Christ as Savior and Lord; then we can know and experience God's love and plan for our lives (John 1:12; 3:1–8; Eph. 2:8–9; Rev. 3:20)."[1]

Why is Hebrews 9:26–28 the key text that undergirds the Four Spiritual Laws? The answer is that, for many, Hebrews 9:26–28 summarizes the "plan of salvation," as it has been traditionally understood by evangelicals. Verse 26 proclaims that Jesus presented his life in sacrifice, "once and for all," for the sins of humanity. Verse 27 is key, for it reminds us that all humans will die and then face God's judgment. This verse supports the second spiritual law. Verse 28 emphasizes the importance of Jesus' sacrifice and the divine offer of salvation by grace. In addition, it adds an eschatological note to the process, as it speaks of the second coming of Jesus Christ and, therefore, of the end times.

The laudable goal of this evangelistic method is to bring people to faith in Jesus Christ as Lord and Savior, and the method has doubtless borne fruit. However, we should also sound a cautionary note. This plan—like many evangelistic exercises—reduces the message of the Gospel to bullet points. Instead of proclaiming the entire Christian message, it focuses on four "laws." In addition, the system uses biblical verses as proof texts, which can be misleading and yield results that are not well founded exegetically. The system also emphasizes the personal aspect of salvation, ignoring the social implications of the gospel of Jesus Christ. Finally, the greatest danger of this and any other system that reduces the gospel to "laws" or "canons" is its rigidity. Proponents of such systems may fall into the error of presenting the Christian life as an area of reduced freedom, where in order to conform to expected theological or ecclesiological norms, the believer has to wear the equivalent of an ideological or spiritual straitjacket.

---

1. R. K. Johnston, "Four Spiritual Laws, The," in the *Evangelical Dictionary of Theology,* ed. Walter A. Ewell (Grand Rapids: Baker Academic, 2001), 465.

Any of these concerns—reductionism, proof-texting, overemphasis on the personal, and religious rigidity—would be worthy of exploration from the pulpit. Perhaps the most important of these is the overemphasis on the personal. A wise preacher would do well to explain that salvation is not merely personal, but social. Hebrews 2:10 affirms that Jesus died to lead "many sons and daughters to glory," that is, to the presence of God: we are called in community. Hebrews also transcends individualism when it affirms that Jesus is not ashamed of calling us "brothers and sisters" (2:11). Hence, a sermon lifting up salvation as not just an internal, personal aspect but something that requires social engagement and responsibility would serve as a helpful reminder to congregations and deepen their understanding of salvation.

Another common way of understanding this text is through the metaphor of the bridge. Sin created a chasm between the fallen humanity and the holy God. No sinful human being can find a way to reach God through their own efforts. By the same token, no spiritual being can reach humanity to grant them redemption from sin. It would take a unique being, 100 percent human and 100 percent divine, to live without sin, opening a way of salvation.

Hebrews affirms that Jesus is that unique being, fully human and fully divine. His sinless life (4:15) gave him access to God. His dual role as high priest and as sacrificial lamb allowed him to present the perfect sacrifice for the redemption of humanity. Therefore, the cross of Jesus Christ is the "bridge" over the chasm that formerly separated humanity and God. Jesus is the "theo-anthropos" (God-human being),

the divine and human being who opened a "new and living way" (Heb. 10:20) to salvation through his death (cf. Heb. 2:10–18).

As most congregations have projection systems, it would be interesting to begin a sermon showing images of bridges, exploring their function. Such an introduction can lead the preacher to use the metaphor of the bridge to explain how the gospel leads us into a meaningful spiritual relationship with God and into better relationships with others. Seen from this point of view, Jesus is the way (cf. John 14:6) to both salvation and to human reconciliation (see Eph. 2:11–22). Indeed, the implications of reconciliation both between humanity and God and, by extension, among humans might serve as a worthy topic of a sermon.

Finally, Hebrews affirms that the forgiveness granted by God through the sacrifice of Jesus Christ is definitive (Heb. 10:18). Jesus died "once and for all," so that humanity can enjoy forgiveness of sins and salvation through an ever deeper relationship with God. The theological affirmation that "God's forgiveness is definitive" is truly "good news" for all peoples, for each one of us has hurt others and hurt ourselves, offending God in the process. Even in a world where sin is increasingly becoming a dated concept, the fact remains that humans have an enormous capacity to hurt and destroy others, the environment, and even ourselves. Therefore, we are all in need of forgiveness and reconciliation. Craft a sermon that affirms God's forgiveness for all and God's forgiveness "once and for all." Celebrate God's definitive forgiveness, which liberates us from guilt.

PABLO A. JIMENEZ

Proper 27 (Sunday between November 6 and November 12)

Mark 12:38–44

[38]As he taught, he said, "Beware of the scribes, who like to walk around in long robes, and to be greeted with respect in the marketplaces, [39]and to have the best seats in the synagogues and places of honor at banquets! [40]They devour widows' houses and for the sake of appearance say long prayers. They will receive the greater condemnation."

[41]He sat down opposite the treasury, and watched the crowd putting money into the treasury. Many rich people put in large sums. [42]A poor widow came and put in two small copper coins, which are worth a penny. [43]Then he called his disciples and said to them, "Truly I tell you, this poor widow has put in more than all those who are contributing to the treasury. [44]For all of them have contributed out of their abundance; but she out of her poverty has put in everything she had, all she had to live on."

Commentary 1: Connecting the Reading with Scripture

Mark 12:38–44 shares its immediate literary context with the previous lectionary reading in 12:28–34. Jesus' positive exchange with the scribe in verses 28–34 silences the interlocutors who have been approaching him (Mark 12:34). Jesus then offers two successive critiques against scribes (vv. 35–40) before praising a widow (vv. 41–44). Jesus' positive assessments of the scribe in verses 28–34 and the widow in verses 41–44 thus bracket the criticisms he levels at the scribes in verses 35–37 over their messianic expectations and in verses 38–40 over their preoccupation with status and appearance.

This sequence shows that even though during his Jerusalem ministry (11:1–13:37) Jesus is highly critical of the religious establishment, Jesus deems certain elements of the Jerusalem religious context worth admiring, including a scribe (12:34) and a woman of little social standing (12:43–44). Taking a cue from Mark's Jesus, the preacher may ask, how often do we look for and affirm the good in persons and places that we are disposed to evaluate negatively?

While scribes are featured in 12:28–34; 12:35–37; and 12:38–40, the passages in verses 38–40 and verses 41–44 are connected by the term "widow." One interpretative tradition argues

that the widow who donates to the temple treasury in 12:42 exemplifies how the scribes allegedly "devour widows' houses" (v. 40). Rather than extol the woman for her generosity, Jesus laments her enduring religious and economic exploitation at the hands of a religious system, promoted by the scribes, that demands contributions from even those who have minimal resources.

However, difficulties with this interpretation emerge when the passage is read with close attention to its literary context. If Mark's aim here were to indict the religious leaders for economic oppression, we would expect him to depict Jesus doing so directly, since throughout this section of Mark's Gospel Jesus criticizes scribes and other authorities publicly (11:15–19; 12:1–12, 18–27, 35–40). Instead, 12:41–44 is cast as Jesus' private instruction to his disciples (12:43). That Jesus calls his disciples aside to discuss the widow's contribution suggests that this passage functions primarily as an instruction on the nature of discipleship.

Indeed, when read in light of the Gospel's larger literary and thematic context, the whole of 12:38–44 reflects key aspects of Mark's understanding of discipleship.[1] The scribes are criticized for seeking recognition in public settings and

---

1. On the multiple ways this passage connects with its narrative context, see Elizabeth Struthers Malbon, *In the Company of Jesus: Characters in Mark's Gospel* (Louisville, KY: Westminster John Knox, 2000), 166–88.

at banquets. In a social context in which one's honor and status held immense cachet, respected religious leaders like the scribes would have considerable social capital that, from their perspective and that of many others, was worthy of recognition. For Mark, however, Jesus' disciples should eschew any desire for high social standing or influence, as Jesus often reminds them (e.g., 8:34–38; 9:33–37; 10:23–31, 35–45).

Such reminders tend to follow Jesus' passion predictions (8:31; 9:31; 10:32–34), because discipleship for Mark means forgoing glory and honor to instead take up the suffering and shame of the cross (8:34; cf. 1 Cor. 1:18–25). Unlike the scribes who seek literally the "<u>first</u> seats" (Mark 12:39) in synagogues (*prōtokathedrias*) and at banquet tables (*prōtoklisias*), disciples must have a "whoever wants to be first must be last of all and servant of all" mentality (9:35; 10:31, 43–44).

In this thematic context, the widow serves as a contrast to the scribes, because they inhabit opposite ends of the social spectrum. As if to make this clear, Jesus identifies her as a "poor" widow (12:42, 43). The scribes enjoy honor and status, and they continually seek those things. Lacking these, the widow devotes herself to God; in this, she is a model for Jesus' disciples. While not a precise analogue to the ancient Mediterranean, our own social context values wealth, prestige, and celebrity too. Mark's criticism of the scribes and shifting of our gaze to this widow provides an opportunity for pastors to form sermons that recapture the countercultural bent of the gospel.

Another valued component of discipleship in Mark is complete devotion to the kingdom of God, even at the expense of familial relations, social status, and economic livelihood. When Jesus summons them, Simon, Andrew, James, and John abandon their fishing posts, and in the case of the latter two, also their father (1:16–20). In his own teaching, Jesus elevates kinship among disciples over biological familial relationships (3:31–35; 10:28–30). The rich man, in contrast, cannot abandon his wealth and security to become a disciple (10:17–22; cf. 10:28). Even the scribe in 12:28–34 is only near the kingdom of God (12:34); to enter it, he must give himself fully to the gospel of the kingdom of God that Jesus proclaims (1:14–15).

Described in language that emphasizes the degree to which she gives, literally, "her whole life" (12:44, my trans.), this poor widow exemplifies the Markan virtue of giving over one's entire life, as Jesus himself did (10:45). While the rich give more money, her contribution is worth more in the eyes of Mark's Jesus, because it represents a total self-sacrifice on her part that Jesus wants his disciples—and Mark his readers—to emulate. Even so, preaching on the widow's self-sacrifice must be done with care, since Mark's challenge to take up our cross and give ourselves fully to the gospel (8:34–35) may inadvertently encourage the passive acceptance of suffering, poverty, violence, or injustice as one's cross to bear.

The Bible uses "widows and orphans" as shorthand for the most vulnerable members of society. The alternate psalm reading in the lectionary, for example, uses this cipher to praise God for caring for the most vulnerable (Ps. 146:9). First Kings 17:8–16, the alternate first reading, is a narrative demonstration of God's care for widows and specifies that the miracle by which the widow does not run out of food is God's doing (1 Kgs. 17:14). This tradition of articulating God's care for widows—and, by extension, all the vulnerable—adds context to Jesus' criticism of the scribes. To be aligned with the purposes of God, who "upholds the orphan and the widow" (Ps. 146:9), they should abandon their concern with status and serve even the lowliest, as should we. Instead, Mark depicts the scribes as so antagonistic toward God's purposes that they are alleged to "devour widows' houses" (12:40).

The lectionary text from the Hebrew Scriptures excerpts the book of Ruth, in which the widow Ruth manages to get Naomi's kinsman Boaz to marry her and thus be obliged to care for both her and her mother-in-law Naomi (another widow). Ruth bears a child, who is also lauded as a male who will care for them (Ruth 4:13–15). As necessary as Boaz and this child are to Naomi's survival, Ruth is said to be worth more to Naomi "than seven sons" (4:15). Like the widow in Mark 12:41–44, even in her dire circumstances Ruth commends herself to Naomi and her God (Ruth 1:15–18). Just as the women of Bethlehem extol Ruth because of her love for Naomi (4:15), Jesus extols the deep piety of the widow in contrast to the superficial piety of the scribes.

Both Ruth and the widow in Mark are validated for their actions despite their vulnerability. This detail should caution preachers to avoid reducing the poor and marginalized to objects of our well-intentioned charity. They are active agents, capable of their own transformation. Indeed, in many ways they are capable of transforming us, who might be like the rich in this passage, able to give of ourselves from a place of security.

GILBERTO A. RUIZ

Commentary 2: Connecting the Reading with the World

The traditional take on this text is that it is a little morality play showing the contrast between the negative example of the scribes and the positive example of the poor widow. In this approach, the widow becomes a sort of Madonna figure—a model for all disciples, and an eloquent warning against self-aggrandizing forms of religious professionalism. The scribes, on the other hand, are self-aggrandizing religious professionals prancing around in their robes and liturgical bling who cannot avoid stopping to admire themselves at any full-length mirror.

However, there is perhaps something too neat about this traditional take on this text. What if there are things we need to forget in order to engage the text more deeply? With respect to the scribes, we should not overinterpret them as paragons of self-indulgent hypocrisy. Some of them are city clerks (Acts 19:35), some of them are learned intellectuals (1 Cor. 1:20), some are experts in the interpretation of Jewish law. The preacher may wish to treat them with more nuance, and to check extreme negative rhetoric at the door.

Nevertheless, it is clear that the scribes Jesus has in his crosshairs are behaving dishonorably. Cloaked in ostentatious religiosity, they offer fraught public supplications for those in need (like widows), and then they use their profession and status to defraud those widows of their husbands' estates—widows who have very little power, very little recourse, even in a court of law.

A second thing the preacher needs to forget in order to approach the text faithfully is the notion that the widow's primary role in this text is to set up her piety as an example to be followed. For sure, the widow's gift—less than seven-tenths of one percent of a denarius, the normal daily wage for an unskilled laborer—is as generous as it possibly can be, coming from her, since it is not just a carefully figured portion of ample resources but literally all she has left. From this angle, what she gives is more meaningful than the calculated contributions of rich people, because she gives not according to her means but beyond her means. Her generosity constitutes the starkest possible contrast to the despicable greed of prominent religious leaders who feather their own nests at the expense of vulnerable women. From another angle, why do we interpret her gift as a demonstration of moral self-sacrifice, when the case here is in fact that the very institution to which the sacrifice is made is hopelessly corrupt?

This text is not so much a commentary on her extravagant piety as on what is at the center of Jesus' attention from the moment that he arrives in Jerusalem: the temple. Unlike our culture's assumptions about contemporary houses of worship. which tend to separate the sacred from the secular, first-century readers of Mark would accept the ethos of commerce as an ordinary aspect of the temple's life. It was the center of Palestine's redistribution economy, in which goods and services were expected to be collected and then fairly redistributed to those who needed them—but the system was rigged.

So Mark gives us a fitting analysis of temple practices when he includes the story of the fruitlessness of the fig tree (11:12–14), just before Jesus' entry into Jerusalem and his cleansing of the temple. Just as the fig tree is barren, so is the temple. At its heart is a crooked system in which its leaders are unfairly redistributing goods and resources. Those most penalized by it are the poorest peasants, such as the widow. Her gift of her last two copper coins is not finally an illustration of her piety, but of the horrific consequences of the economics of the temple.

In preparing to preach this text, the preacher needs to consider the multivalent layers of symbolism in it. The widow is a victim, but she is also a symbol of sacrifice. Jesus sits down, writes Mark, "opposite the treasury" (12:41), but that is not just a geographical location; it is also a theological and political location. Ultimately, from that location, Jesus sees everything clearly.

One question arising from this text, though, is, How clearly do these people with their offerings see things? Do they know how corrupt the temple is, or how close it is to being destroyed? Probably not. Jesus, as he watches their comings and goings, sees it all, and preaches against the excesses of the temple and its scribes. As this text zooms up close to show us this one widow, Jesus knows that there are thousands more people just as desperate as she is. We cannot know whether her house is one of the ones devoured by those duplicitous temple officials, but we do know she is down to her last coins. Her husband is dead; she has no voice in that culture, no income, nothing. She is totally vulnerable.

What does she do in the face of that kind of danger? She puts her last coins into the treasury. She gives everything at her disposal to a soon-to-be-defunct institution. Here is faith being practiced in a context that makes a mockery of it. Here is a woman who, in the midst of all the things that are not quite right, chooses nonetheless to give and be faithful to a vision of something bigger than what she can now see. What sense does that make? On the face of it, the only reasonable outcome would be for someone to step onto the scene and intervene on her behalf, to reach down into that alms box and fish out the coins, and to give back to her, maybe more than she put in. That would be justice.

That does not happen. Instead, Jesus says to his disciples, "Truly I tell you, this poor widow has put in more than all those who are contributing to the treasury. For all of them have contributed out of their abundance; but she out of her poverty has put in everything she had, all she had to live on" (12:43–44).

What does it mean to give your whole life for people who, for all of your trouble, may not even notice what you have done? What does it mean to care enough about an institution, however human it is, that you stubbornly decide not to abandon it and instead dedicate yourself to a vision of what it might be at its best, rather than what it is at its worst? What does it mean for you to come to church—week after week and year after year—with your cans for the homeless and your socks for the night shelter and your willingness to sign up for this or that task force focused on this or that justice issue, when what we clergy often worry about is how well the endowment is doing or how many security problems we have?

We preachers probably do not know what it all means, to be perfectly frank. This poor widow continues to do her job if she leaves us the gift of a handful of questions like these.

As much as we may love the notion that God remains busy setting up a new kingdom on earth, chances are that we do not support that kingdom as she does. Chances are that we do not give as she does—not to the temple, and not to any temple.

The fact is that there is only one other person we are likely to know who ever gives like that. That person is Jesus Christ our Lord.

THEODORE J. WARDLAW

Proper 28 (Sunday between November 13 and November 19)

1 Samuel 1:4–20 and Daniel 12:1–3   Hebrews 10:11–14 (15–18), 19–25
1 Samuel 2:1–10 and Psalm 16   Mark 13:1–8

1 Samuel 1:4–20

⁴On the day when Elkanah sacrificed, he would give portions to his wife Peninnah and to all her sons and daughters; ⁵but to Hannah he gave a double portion, because he loved her, though the LORD had closed her womb. ⁶Her rival used to provoke her severely, to irritate her, because the LORD had closed her womb. ⁷So it went on year by year; as often as she went up to the house of the LORD, she used to provoke her. Therefore Hannah wept and would not eat. ⁸Her husband Elkanah said to her, "Hannah, why do you weep? Why do you not eat? Why is your heart sad? Am I not more to you than ten sons?"

⁹After they had eaten and drunk at Shiloh, Hannah rose and presented herself before the LORD. Now Eli the priest was sitting on the seat beside the doorpost of the temple of the LORD. ¹⁰She was deeply distressed and prayed to the LORD, and wept bitterly. ¹¹She made this vow: "O LORD of hosts, if only you will look on the misery of your servant, and remember me, and not forget your servant, but will give to your servant a male child, then I will set him before you as a nazirite until the day of his death. He shall drink neither wine nor intoxicants, and no razor shall touch his head."

¹²As she continued praying before the LORD, Eli observed her mouth. ¹³Hannah was praying silently; only her lips moved, but her voice was not heard; therefore Eli thought she was drunk. ¹⁴So Eli said to her, "How long will you make a drunken spectacle of yourself? Put away your wine." ¹⁵But Hannah answered, "No, my lord, I am a woman deeply troubled; I have drunk neither wine nor strong drink, but I have been pouring out my soul before the LORD. ¹⁶Do not regard your servant as a worthless woman, for I have been speaking out of my great anxiety and vexation all this time." ¹⁷Then Eli answered, "Go in peace; the God of Israel grant the petition you have made to him." ¹⁸And she said, "Let your servant find favor in your sight." Then the woman went to her quarters, ate and drank with her husband, and her countenance was sad no longer.

¹⁹They rose early in the morning and worshiped before the LORD; then they went back to their house at Ramah. Elkanah knew his wife Hannah, and the LORD remembered her. ²⁰In due time Hannah conceived and bore a son. She named him Samuel, for she said, "I have asked him of the LORD."

Daniel 12:1–3

¹"At that time Michael, the great prince, the protector of your people, shall arise. There shall be a time of anguish, such as has never occurred since nations first came into existence. But at that time your people shall be delivered, everyone who is found written in the book. ²Many of those who sleep in the dust of the

earth shall awake, some to everlasting life, and some to shame and everlasting contempt. [3]Those who are wise shall shine like the brightness of the sky, and those who lead many to righteousness, like the stars forever and ever."

Commentary 1: Connecting the Reading with Scripture

Hannah, along with her son Samuel, marks an important transition within Israelite history from the period of judges to the monarchical period. Samuel, who embodies the offices of judge (1 Sam. 7:15), priest (1 Sam. 3), prophet/seer (1 Sam. 3, 9), and kingmaker (1 Sam. 10, 12, 15, 16), is the pivotal character. The story of Samuel, and so also of Israelite monarchy, begins with the story of Hannah, which recounts the dramatic transitions Hannah herself needs to undergo to connect the past and future with themes that resonate with traditions, old and new.

At the beginning of the story, Hannah is barren because "the LORD . . . closed her womb" (1 Sam. 1:5, 6). Her story is in part about the miraculous movement from childlessness to motherhood. Hannah's barrenness, her antagonistic relationship with Peninnah, and her eventual birthing of Samuel, make Hannah comparable to other biblical mothers of heroic sons: Sarah, Rachel, Moses' mother, and Samson's mother. Their similarities and differences warrant consideration for what they say about God, mothers, female relationships, and the agents of redemption. This deep tradition of mothers who give birth to heroic sons under duress informs the Lukan narrative of Jesus' birth (Luke 1–2).[1]

Hannah's story is also about the movement from distressed silence to exalted words. Hannah is initially passive. She is acted on but does not herself act. Elkanah loves her; God shuts her womb; Peninnah irritates her; and Eli misunderstands her. Hannah is also silent. Even when Elkanah asks her four direct questions (1 Sam. 1:8), Hannah remains silent. She also prays silently to God—all because of her "great anxiety and vexation" (1:16). As the story progresses, Hannah begins to speak and,

at the end, utters the famed words in 1 Samuel 2:1–10, the basis of Mary's Magnificat in Luke 1. How does Hannah move from silence to words? She prays and finds that prayer, offered in silent distress year after year, and her faith that she has finally found favor in God's eyes, are effective bulwarks against despair and are capable of moving God. The preacher could use this moment in Hannah's story to show that prayer can move the Mover of all things. That is reason for praise.

Hannah also moves from mournful fasting to joyful feasting. Hannah initially does not eat the double portion her husband lovingly gives her at the Lord's house (1:5). Her refusal to eat is an act of ritual fasting and is a protest against the real host of the meal, the Lord. Hannah recognizes that it is not Peninnah who is responsible for her sorrow, nor Elkanah, who can comfort her. It is God who has closed her womb and, she believes, can give her a child. Her fasting is thus a faithful protest and a prayer of lament that calls upon God to see, hear, and respond to her plight. It is incidentally also a foolproof defense against the judgmental eyes of Eli: "How long will you make a drunken spectacle of yourself?" (v. 14). When Hannah corrects Eli, he pronounces a blessing in response: "Go in peace; the God of Israel grant the petition you have made to him" (v. 17). With uncommon faith, Hannah chooses to understand Eli's generic words as divine response to her specific situation. She trusts that God has taken note of her fasting and will grant her wishes. Thus consoled, she partakes of the feast at the house of the Lord in recognition of God's gracious kingship (v. 18). Indeed, God is gracious to Hannah, whose name means "grace" (vv. 19–20).

---

1. Athalya Brenner, "Female Social Behaviour: Two Descriptive Patterns within the 'Birth of the Hero' Paradigm," *Vetus Testamentum* 36 (1986): 257–73.

Hannah's movement from childlessness to motherhood bridges the failed period of judges to the monarchical period. If the failure of the judges was written with the cloven body of a Levite's concubine (Judg. 19) and the abducted virgin women of Jabesh-gilead (Judg. 21), Hannah stands at the beginning of Israelite monarchy in protest and in contrast to history written on the traumatized bodies of women. She stands as a woman who speaks and takes bold actions to move God, who moves history.[2]

Daniel 12:1–3 speaks into a dire historical situation, described in the preceding passages in symbolic and mythological language (Dan. 7–11), and speaks of protection in the midst of religious persecution and of resurrection against the reality of death. A text fraught with background, the passage develops past traditions to encourage present faithfulness and future hope and, in so doing, sows the seeds for revolutionary developments in religious thought.

The details of the historical background remain a mystery. What is certain is that Antiochus IV Epiphanes ("God Manifest"), a Seleucid king, persecuted Jews in Judah beginning in 169 BCE by desecrating the Jerusalem temple, forbidding religious practices, and even putting people to death. Jewish response to the persecution was diverse and included cooperation and military resistance. The authors of Daniel chose to respond in nonviolent resistance: a program of fasting, praying, teaching, and preaching in courageous faithfulness to the God of Israel.[3]

Faith that God and God's agents fight and will ultimately triumph over evil inspired nonviolent resistance. The authors of Daniel 7–12 used mythological language taken from earlier biblical and nonbiblical sources to describe the eschatological battle between God and the chaos monsters, most memorably in Daniel 7. Michael (Dan. 12:1) represents God's heavenly forces that will defeat the enemy "at that time."

Resistance, even nonviolent resistance, meant persecution and death. Against this reality, the Danielic authors borrow language from Isaiah 26:19 to proclaim for the first time in biblical literature a belief in individual resurrection, "some to everlasting life, and some to shame and everlasting contempt" (v. 2). Resurrection means just reward for the faithful who have already died a martyr's death and punishment for their persecutors. It also calls the living faithful to continued endurance and commitment to nonviolence through "a time of anguish" (v. 1).

The preacher might hold up "those who are wise" and "lead many to righteousness" (v. 3) as models for the faithful. The wise, likely the authors of Daniel, appear to have understood themselves as disciples of the Suffering Servant in Isaiah 53, who also is said to have made "many righteous" and demonstrated a willingness to die (Isa. 53:11). This tradition concerning martyrdom and resurrection will enrich later Jewish and Christian thought, which for Christians culminates in the New Testament portrayals of Jesus Christ and the church (1 Cor. 15).

This wondrous passage is, however, riddled with hermeneutical pitfalls. One is the temptation to generalize the starkly binary understanding of good versus evil, us against them, that often characterizes apocalyptic thought. Another is the mistake of interpreting specific historical persons, especially those with whom we disagree, as fully representative of cosmic evil, even if we affirm with the entire Christian Bible that evil and sin are cosmic forces.

The Samuel and Daniel passages have to do with periods of transition, full of opportunity and danger, and dramatize the role that God and human beings play in such times. Both affirm divine agency and safeguard significant space for human participation in the form of prayerful resistance and faithful protest against personal suffering and world-historical evil. The struggle, taken up by individual saints together or apart, the passages seem to say, may have historical and cosmic consequences far beyond the reach of any single life.

PAUL K.-K. CHO

2. Gale A. Yee, "The Silenced Speak: Hannah, Mary, and Global Poverty," *Feminist Theology* 21 (2012): 40–57.
3. Anathea Portier-Young, *Apocalypse against Empire: Theologies of Resistance in Early Judaism* (Grand Rapids: Eerdmans, 2011), 229.

Commentary 2: Connecting the Reading with the World

On this next to last Sunday of Ordinary Time before we remind ourselves that Christ is our true king, we look to texts pointing to important transitional moments in Israel's history. During this season, we read narratives in Samuel and Kings and selections from Proverbs and Job. Characters such as Naaman, Esther, the woman poet in Song of Songs, and Ruth were also highlighted in the lections. These texts helped us focus on what it means to seek God's wisdom and live faithfully in the midst of suffering. They moved us to consider what it means to be leaders of God's people. This week's readings about Hannah, Eli, and Elkanah, and Daniel's final vision (see chaps. 10–12) continue these themes. Both texts bear upon the need for faithfulness to God in the midst of suffering and for wisdom and diligence in our search for godly leaders.

Hannah is a good example of what it means to persevere. Despite ridicule from others (1 Sam. 1:6–7, 12–14), she repeatedly seeks God in order to receive an answer to her prayer. As we think about her situation, we might consider the sociocultural systems that have kept her distressed over her inability to bear a child. Why is her worth tied to how many sons she can bear for Elkanah? Why is his apparent love, emphasized through the "double portions" with which Elkanah favors Hannah (v. 5), not enough? As the gathered people of God who seek to dismantle destructive systems, we may want to consider what kinds of institutional values keep people in places of pain and suffering. Preachers may invite audiences to pay attention to injustices that dehumanize our neighbors. They may also want to highlight Hannah's prayer as pointing to a theme of reversal in which God raises the lowly and brings down those in high places (1 Sam. 2), a theme that will be taken up in Mary's Magnificat (Luke 1:46–55). We should be encouraged to join in work that helps "reverse" structures that keep people from flourishing.

The work of reversing structures that cause suffering is not easy. Our two texts attest to that. Eli, a priest and judge, is unable to see the unjust practices of his sons. Daniel receives apocalyptic visions of reversals of fortunes because, in his suffering, he sees no possibility of changing Persian imperial practices. Both texts highlight the authors' hope that a different type of leader will emerge and order their world according to God's values. The reading in 1 Samuel looks forward to a king who will rule with justice for the people of Israel. Although each text looks in a different direction for help, they both encourage their readers to live according to values that reflect God's covenants. This hope gives readers reasons to be faithful and ways to live out their values in difficult times. Thus, as we think about our own lives, preachers can take cues from both texts about how we might live when life is not easy.

Being faithful through perseverance, despite our suffering, is an important Christian witness in the world. In light of these texts, the preacher may consider the way we participate in and/or enable institutions and systems that dehumanize us and others by alleging that our only value is in what we produce. Like Hannah and the Israelites of Daniel's day, we are often told that our value is in what we produce for society. The push to produce and to compete for the highest spot in the production line robs us of those characteristics that keep us grounded in the work of God in the world. Instead of showing humility, grace, and mercy, we destroy, steal, and kill in order to be the last person standing. Instead of listening, observing, and being peacemakers, we often choose to shout above those asking to be heard, close our eyes to the issues at hand, and, in the process, oppress others to ensure our self-preservation. Living out our calling and values means intentionally choosing to let God's love fill us and motivate us to persevere, even as we work for change.

Two contemporary examples offer opportunities to think about what it means to persevere and live faithfully in the midst of suffering while working to dismantle destructive systems. The first is the 2018 movie *Beautiful Boy*. It is the story of a father coping with his son's drug addiction. Throughout the movie, the father and the son struggle to find a way forward toward healing.

The Virtues of the Living God

Now a vow also is, to speak properly, a dedication, since he who makes a vow is said to offer up, as a gift to God, not only his own possessions, but himself likewise, who is the owner of them; for says the scripture, "the man is holy who nourishes the locks of the hair of his head; who has vowed a vow." But if he is holy he is undoubtedly an offering to God, no longer meddling with anything unholy or profane; and there is an evidence in favour of my argument, in the conduct of the prophetess, and mother of a prophet, Hannah, whose name being translated, signifies grace; for she says that she gives her son, "Samuel, as a gift to the Holy One," not dedicating him more as a human being, than as a disposition full of inspiration, and possessed by a divinely sent impulse; and the name Samuel being interpreted means, "appointed to God."

Why then, O my soul, do you any longer waste yourself in vain speculations and labours? and why do you not go as a pupil to the practiser of virtue, taking up arms against the passions, and against vain opinion, to learn from him the way to wrestle with them? For as soon as you have learnt this art, you will become the leader of a flock, not of one which is destitute of marks, and of reason, and of docility, but of one which is well approved, and rational, and beautiful, of which, if you become the leader, you will pity the miserable race of mankind, and will not cease to reverence the Deity; and you will never be weary of blessing God, and moreover you will engrave hymns suited to your sacred subject upon pillars, that you may not only speak fluently, but may also sing musically the virtues of the living God; for by these means you will be able to return to your father's house, being delivered from a long and profitless wandering in a foreign land.

Philo of Alexandria, "A Treatise on the Doctrine That Dreams Are Sent by God," in *The Works of Philo Judaeus,* vol. 2, trans. C. D. Yonge (London: Henry G. Bohn, 1854), 343–44.

Of many poignant moments in the movie, one of the most important comes after the son has relapsed. Up to that point, the father had worked diligently to help his son give up drugs. After the son's relapse, the father makes the difficult choice to stop helping his son. It is painful to watch. While the father continues to be in relationship with his son, he no longer tries to help his son make a change. The moment of change comes when his son, in the course of events, finds himself hitting bottom. The son makes a choice to change. At this point the father begins a new part of the journey with his son.

I find compelling the father's struggles to figure out how to lean into relationship with his son in the hope of offering an opportunity for a different choice. The story is primarily one of perseverance and compassion. As a parent, I recognize that no journey with a child (or family member, friend, or parishioner) who is making destructive choices is ever easy. This movie portrays the humanity of love in ways that are moving and persuasive, encouraging us to hope. It offers us an opportunity to think about what values we want to embody as the people of God. As the church, commissioned to be about works of mercy and healing, we are called to persevere in our journey with people who are caught in destructive cycles and to find ways to offer compassion and mercy as we hope for something better in this world.

A second contemporary example that should stir us to compassion comes from a particularly haunting piece of artwork by artist Ammar Salim. His paintings depict the destruction wrought by war and the dehumanization of countless persons created in the image of God.[4] These horrific visions of pain remind us that there are sisters and brothers suffering greatly around the world. For them, the hope of an intervention or reversal of fortune is not

4. Study of artist Ammar Salim; https://www.aljazeera.com/blogs/middleeast/2015/04/remembering-yazidi-suffering-art-150424162910046.html.

abstract. Though we may not have victims of war in our parishes, we may find that our listeners have experienced tragedy and carry with them wounds that leave them in need of hope.

We can continue to confess the hope of the resurrection, as we do regularly through the recitation of the creeds and the liturgy of the Eucharist. We may also offer hope by pointing to a vision advocated and to leaders, inspired by God, who intervene on behalf of the oppressed and the wounded in the political realities of daily life. The preacher may provide points of connection for people by inviting them to consider places and situations where others are vulnerable and in need of someone to step into the gap as Michael (an angelic being or patron-angel) does in the vision of Daniel (Dan. 10:13). These examples may provide a grounding as we seek to work together to bind up the wounds and heal the broken; they help us remember that our work is a part of the ongoing ordinary work of the church until Christ's rule is complete in our lives and in the world.

STEPHEN P. RILEY

1 Samuel 2:1–10

¹Hannah prayed and said,

> "My heart exults in the LORD;
>   my strength is exalted in my God.
> My mouth derides my enemies,
>   because I rejoice in my victory.

> ²"There is no Holy One like the LORD,
>   no one besides you;
>   there is no Rock like our God.
> ³Talk no more so very proudly,
>   let not arrogance come from your mouth;
> for the LORD is a God of knowledge,
>   and by him actions are weighed.
> ⁴The bows of the mighty are broken,
>   but the feeble gird on strength.
> ⁵Those who were full have hired themselves out for bread,
>   but those who were hungry are fat with spoil.
> The barren has borne seven,
>   but she who has many children is forlorn.
> ⁶The LORD kills and brings to life;
>   he brings down to Sheol and raises up.
> ⁷The LORD makes poor and makes rich;
>   he brings low, he also exalts.
> ⁸He raises up the poor from the dust;
>   he lifts the needy from the ash heap,
> to make them sit with princes
>   and inherit a seat of honor.
> For the pillars of the earth are the LORD's,
>   and on them he has set the world.

> ⁹"He will guard the feet of his faithful ones,
>   but the wicked shall be cut off in darkness;
>   for not by might does one prevail.
> ¹⁰The LORD! His adversaries shall be shattered;
>   the Most High will thunder in heaven.
> The LORD will judge the ends of the earth;
>   he will give strength to his king,
>   and exalt the power of his anointed."

Psalm 16

¹Protect me, O God, for in you I take refuge.
²I say to the LORD, "You are my Lord;
    I have no good apart from you."

³As for the holy ones in the land, they are the noble,
   in whom is all my delight.

⁴Those who choose another god multiply their sorrows;
   their drink offerings of blood I will not pour out
   or take their names upon my lips.

⁵The LORD is my chosen portion and my cup;
   you hold my lot.
⁶The boundary lines have fallen for me in pleasant places;
   I have a goodly heritage.

⁷I bless the LORD who gives me counsel;
   in the night also my heart instructs me.
⁸I keep the LORD always before me;
   because he is at my right hand, I shall not be moved.

⁹Therefore my heart is glad, and my soul rejoices;
   my body also rests secure.
¹⁰For you do not give me up to Sheol,
   or let your faithful one see the Pit.

¹¹You show me the path of life.
   In your presence there is fullness of joy;
   in your right hand are pleasures forevermore.

Connecting the Psalm with Scripture and Worship

1 Samuel 2:1–10. A psalm prayer illuminates the first reading, which tells the intimate story of Hannah and her overwhelming desire to bear a child (1 Sam. 1:5, 11). Her husband Elkanah, his other wife Peninnah, the priest Eli, and even the eventual child Samuel are, at this point, merely supporting characters in Hannah's personal trajectory. Whereas today's passage from 1 Samuel 1 encompasses all these characters, the accompanying passage from the second chapter focuses exclusively on Hannah and her God, thereby providing deeper theological insight. Furthermore, the earlier passage includes an assortment of devotional activities and roles—pilgrimage and sacrifice, traditional ritual and impromptu intercession, priests and supplicants—while the later passage presents the unalloyed prayer of one specific faithful individual.

Many twenty-first-century Christians are lacking in exposure to sizable swaths of Scripture, and since church is often the only place our parishioners encounter the Bible, we need to look for opportunities to address that lack. Make the most, therefore, of Hannah's high-stakes story by using both of today's texts to give your congregation a heaping helping of Scripture. Because these texts are not short, you might do well to recruit a quartet of strong readers as lectors to present the two pericopes back to back, in "readers theater" style, with one person serving as a narrator, and others speaking the words of Elkanah, Hannah, and Eli. Even without staging, costumes, and set, hearing the story thus delivered can actively engage parishioners.

This pair of texts—Hannah's story and Hannah's prayer—invites a sermon centered on Hannah. Consider creating a first-person reflection on this woman whose faith story sets the stage for the great saga of Israel's monarchy. In the voice of Hannah, draw upon this wonderfully rich source material to explore a faith in God that was vigorously expressed in prayers ranging from lament and entreaty to praise and thanksgiving (1:11; 2:1–10).

Whatever form your sermon takes and however you present the readings, be careful not to limit the meaning of these texts to the individual lives mentioned therein. This story is much bigger. Although it provides the opportunity for us to be captivated by the personal, this text is intended to highlight YHWH's vital, transformative role in the unfolding history of the people of Israel.

With Advent approaching, you can lay some beneficial groundwork by helping your congregation hear Hannah's prayer as an Old Testament precursor to the New Testament prayer of Mary that we know as the Magnificat (Luke 1:46–55). A brief explanation of the connection between Hannah's prayer and Mary's song might highlight how both texts express confidence in God's intention to end oppression and raise up the poor. Congregational singing could include a version of the Magnificat, such as "My Soul Cries Out with a Joyful Shout" or the Taizé chant "Sing Out, My Soul." The hymn "Great Is Thy Faithfulness" extols the steadfast love and provision of the God to whom both Hannah and Mary pray.

When dealing with any of the Bible's texts about barrenness, it is important to be sensitive to the fact that your congregation may well include folks who share Hannah's struggle to become a parent. While acknowledging the biblical writers' view of barrenness, we can also be aware of the scientific and cultural issues surrounding infertility. Although God's graciousness can be experienced in specific gifts like a long longed-for pregnancy, we cannot presume to tell God how to respond to prayer.

Psalm 16. The complementary track of the Revised Common Lectionary offers Psalm 16 as the response to the apocalyptic pericope from the book of Daniel. Because the psalm is relatively short, it is included unabridged, giving us the opportunity to deal with the psalmist's prayer in its entirety.

Psalm 16 is often identified as a psalm of trust. It opens with a direct plea to God for protection (Ps. 16:1a), but no desperation is heard in this cry, because there immediately follows a succinct, humble rationale for such protection. The formula phrase, "in you I take refuge" (v. 1b), is one of the Psalter's favorite expressions for the devotional decision to entrust one's life

to God's care. This sets the tone for the entire psalm, including the amplifying sentiment, "I have no good apart from you" (v. 2b).

The bulk of the psalm is addressed to an unspecified audience to whom the psalmist explains the good life that is found only in faithful relationship with YHWH. The psalm is saturated with joy and gratitude, so much so that the psalmist feels no need to dwell upon any unrighteous people, barely mentioning the "sorrows" (v. 4) that come from their faithless choices.

The nouns translated in the NRSV as "portion," "cup," "lot," boundary lines," "places," and "heritage" (vv. 5–6) connote material well-being, but the thrust of Psalm 16 transcends such concerns. YHWH is identified as the one who "gives me counsel" (v. 7); is immediately and efficaciously present (v. 8); is the reason "my heart is glad, and my soul rejoices; my body also rests secure" (v. 9); shields the psalmist from Sheol (v. 10); and shows the psalmist even "the path of life" (v. 11).

The psalm's quality of serene trust and glad reliance differs sharply from the unnerving imagery presented by the book of Daniel. As noted, although the psalmist launches this prayer by asking God's protection (v. 1), there is no hint of any menacing circumstances driving this call for refuge. By contrast, the Old Testament passage warns of a fearsome time to come: "a time of anguish, such as has never occurred since nations first came into existence" (Dan. 12:1b). How are we possibly to endure even contemplating so dreadful a time, much less undergoing it? Only by trusting God as fully as the psalmist does. Who knows? Such deep-seated dependence upon God for well-being could qualify believers as the wise ones who "shall shine like the brightness of the sky" (v. 3a). Further, as we remember that the church is commissioned to "lead many to righteousness" (v. 3b), perhaps we can see emulating the psalmist's sure trust in God as part of how we do that.

If your congregation, like many, is living with an undercurrent of anxiety—whether they are disconcerted by personal losses, by the vitriol of modern discourse, by the decline of the church—Psalm 16 offers a restorative prescription, suffused as it is with the calm joy of resting in God's provision. Contemplating that in companionship with the apocalyptic vision of Daniel may provide a tacit pastoral response to our cultural sense of dread.

As if suggesting that our anxiety is nothing new, several older hymns harmonize especially well with these texts, including "Amazing Grace," "Give to the Winds Thy Fears," "God Moves in a Mysterious Way," "It Is Well with My Soul," "Leaning on the Everlasting Arms," "O Worship the King, All Glorious Above,"

"Soon and Very Soon," and "Who Are These Like Stars Appearing."

With the exception of verse 3 (its translation is uncertain), Psalm 16 is easily mined for liturgy. For example, one might speak Psalm 16:2, 7–8 as opening sentences or create a call to worship from those same verses. Verses 9–11 may be adapted for use as words of pardon following a prayer of confession. With holy words such as these, we do indeed have "a goodly heritage" (Ps. 16:6).

LEIGH CAMPBELL-TAYLOR

Hebrews 10:11–14 (15–18), 19–25

[11]And every priest stands day after day at his service, offering again and again the same sacrifices that can never take away sins. [12]But when Christ had offered for all time a single sacrifice for sins, "he sat down at the right hand of God," [13]and since then has been waiting "until his enemies would be made a footstool for his feet." [14]For by a single offering he has perfected for all time those who are sanctified. [15]And the Holy Spirit also testifies to us, for after saying,

> [16]"This is the covenant that I will make with them
> after those days, says the Lord:
> I will put my laws in their hearts,
> and I will write them on their minds,"

[17]he also adds,

> "I will remember their sins and their lawless deeds no more."

[18]Where there is forgiveness of these, there is no longer any offering for sin.

[19]Therefore, my friends, since we have confidence to enter the sanctuary by the blood of Jesus, [20]by the new and living way that he opened for us through the curtain (that is, through his flesh), [21]and since we have a great priest over the house of God, [22]let us approach with a true heart in full assurance of faith, with our hearts sprinkled clean from an evil conscience and our bodies washed with pure water. [23]Let us hold fast to the confession of our hope without wavering, for he who has promised is faithful. [24]And let us consider how to provoke one another to love and good deeds, [25]not neglecting to meet together, as is the habit of some, but encouraging one another, and all the more as you see the Day approaching.

Commentary 1: Connecting the Reading with Scripture

This Sunday's reading is the last of seven Revised Common Lectionary readings from Hebrews in Year B. The congregation will not hear the rest of this story until next summer, when four more selections from the final chapters begin. A long sermon about the high priesthood of Jesus, the book of Hebrews is the only epistle that describes Jesus as a priest.

The entire sermon addresses a particular congregation's exhaustion. Like many congregations today, they have become so busy with the business of the church that they lose a sense of passionate spirituality about who Jesus is and what Jesus has done for us. We do not know the author of the letter, but many scholars and pastors refer to the author of Hebrews as the Preacher. The Preacher knows this congregation and is separated from them but intends to return. He addresses their fatigue by pointing to Christ.[1] Their problem and solution are identified in this passage through the Preacher's reference to the repeated—"day after day"—offering of the "same sacrifices that can never take away sins" (Heb. 10:11) and Christ's new way of offering "for all time a single sacrifice for sins" (v. 12). Christ completed the old way of sacrifices that required doing the same thing over and over without inner change to the

---

1. Thomas G. Long, *Hebrews*, Interpretation (Louisville, KY: John Knox, 1997), 3.

worshipers. The old way also required the priest to go through a heavy curtain to an inner sanctuary where the congregation was not allowed to follow. With Christ, the congregation no longer experiences such separation from holiness.

Verses 12 and 13 guide the reader to Psalm 110:1, where the Lord says, "Sit at my right hand until I make your enemies your footstool." This colorful image of Jesus as a priest sitting down contrasts with the image of priests standing day after day offering futile, never-ending sacrifices (10:11). Having perfected the sacrifice, such offerings are no longer needed. They are now complete, and Christ as the priest is now seated instead of standing. This image of being seated additionally serves to soothe the exhausted worshipers, who need rest and are being invited to find it in their great heavenly high priest. If their heavenly high priest embraces rest, surely they can as well.

Verses 15 through 18 are optional in the Revised Common Lectionary. In these four verses, the Holy Spirit testifies using language found in Jeremiah 31:33–34, also quoted earlier in this Hebrews sermon (8:10–12). Drawing from that prophetic book helps listeners absorb the enormity of Christ's completed sacrifice, which brings about this new, perfected covenant. While these verses are optional according to the Revised Common Lectionary, including them helps to avoid a temptation to denigrate Judaism at the expense of Christianity. Including these "optional" verses helps show how the Hebrew Scriptures tie into Christ, rather than being made invisible by him.

The final section in this pericope, verses 19 through 25, contain what Thomas Long refers to as the "so what" of the sermon. How should the people respond to all they have heard about the priesthood of Christ? We might have thought the proper response would be simply to give thanks,[2] but the Preacher takes his congregation further by pointing them into worship where they can now enter the sanctuary with "confidence," through the heavy curtain into that area that was formerly set aside only for the priest. Through Christ our great priest, we can all enter (v. 19). The exhausted congregation

could become tempted to neglect worship, as the Preacher explicitly warns by referencing those who "fail to meet together" (10:25).

The preacher addresses a congregation's weariness by pointing them back to Christ and reminding them of the reason they need to continue to gather to worship. Not only does he point them to Christ; he further implores them to encourage one another (v. 25) and provoke one another to good deeds (v. 24). Worship is a communal experience, so worshipers need one another. The community of the faithful is the church, not the building in which that community worships. Driving home this point can resonate with worshipers on this particular Sunday, when the Gospel reading (Mark 13:1–8) includes Jesus' telling his disciples that all the stones from the temple will be thrown down.

This entire section, according to Long, sums up a sermon-within-a-sermon, while emphasizing the assurance of forgiveness. This reminder of forgiveness can strengthen the bone-tired congregation into perseverance. In the lectionary, this pericope falls toward the end of the season after Pentecost, a time when our own congregations may need a call to persevere before the church year renews in Advent.

This pericope contains the fourth and fifth sections on the high priesthood of Jesus, each of which follow a formula contrasting an old way with a new way in Christ. One danger in preaching on this passage and highlighting this structure of the "old" way—that is, the priest offering the same sacrifice day after day (v. 11)—versus the "new" way through Christ's offering of a single sacrifice for all time (v. 12), is that it lends itself to misuse by promoting an anti-Semitic theology of supersessionism: that is, believing that the New Testament and Jesus replace the Old Testament and Judaism. Jesus himself was a Jew. Love and good deeds (v. 24), as well as regular worship and encouragement in a community (v. 25), were hallmarks of Judaism, not innovations of Jesus. Preachers today need to avoid disparaging the Hebrew Scriptures and Jewish practices in an attempt to lift up Jesus Christ.

The latter part of the fifth section on the high priesthood of Jesus (10:26–39) is excluded from

2. Craig R. Koester, *Hebrews: A New Translation with Introduction and Commentary* (New York: Doubleday, 2001), 448.

the Revised Common Lectionary but might be fruitful for today's preacher to explore. The section studied here provides encouragement, but the omitted section contains some harsh warnings about judgment and a fire of fury (v. 27). In addition to warnings, the omitted section also contains encouragement, reminding the listeners of their confidence and assuring them that they are not among the ones that "shrink back" and are lost (v. 39).

In addition, the excluded section contains an explicit memory about how the congregation interacted compassionately with those in prison, an especially significant memory to neglect, given guidance elsewhere in the Bible about the way faithful people are called to care for prisoners. Why erase such an important mention? Why are the warnings and judgment left out? Reflecting on why we avoid listening to biblical warnings and judgment in worship could be constructive ground for today's preacher to excavate, especially when reflecting on a passage in which a long-ago preacher attempted to comfort his congregation, without shying away from warnings and judgment, by pointing to Christ.

This church year's treatment of Hebrews draws to a close with this pericope. The following Sunday, Reign of Christ, will jump to Revelation, so this will be the last time for a while people hear from the Letter to the Hebrews. Given this, today's preacher may want to include some summary of the book to wrap up the autumn weeks devoted to this letter. The theme of Jesus' priesthood will be easy to tackle in a sermon, since it is the focus of this section, but previous chapters also focused on Christ's uniqueness and superiority in relation to angels and certain Old Testament figures. Tying this together can help avoid temptations to preach supersessionism.

ELIZABETH FELICETTI

Commentary 2: Connecting the Reading with the World

Writing to a community struggling under persecution that was perhaps feeling inadequate in the struggle, the author to the Hebrews offers a powerful reminder that shame is not a gift of the Holy Spirit. While shame as a psychological term would be anachronistic for the letter's original recipients, the author's theological insight echoes enduringly: life in God is not primarily about consciousness of sin and its expiation. Instead, Jesus offers us a profound assurance of reconciliation that we are called to do—as a community—through the work of the Spirit by living into the fullness of faith, hope, and love. Christ's life, death, and resurrection bring us wholly into God's care, liberating us to respond together as we practice world-changing, loving emancipation. We are freed for love.

The text opens by plunging its audience back into monotonous priestly sacrificial rituals that do not seem to disrupt the cycle of sin or comfort the community. Day after day, sacrifice follows confession of sin in hopes of reconciliation—yet nothing seems to change. Personal failings continue and social iniquities abide within and around them. A more thorough accounting of our brokenness and punctilious repentance will not get to the heart of the matter; rather, we require a transformative relationship with God to repattern our lives.

For the author of Hebrews, Jesus offers that fundamental reshaping: a christological (as in messianic) reset that recenters God in the ontology and psychology—mind, body, and soul—of a believing community and revives their capacity to act. By encountering the depth and breadth of the powers of sin and breaking their hold on humanity, Jesus the Christ has destroyed the monotonous persistence of division, hate, scorn, and selfishness in our lives.

Mary Oliver's poem "Wild Geese" opens with a stark repudiation of endless cycles of guilt: "You do not have to walk on your knees for a hundred miles through the desert, repenting."[3] Oliver and the writer of Hebrews seem to know all too well

---

3. Mary Oliver, "Wild Geese," in *Devotions: The Selected Poems of Mary Oliver* (New York: Random House, 2017), 347.

the distortions that come from dwelling so long on guilt that it turns into shame and permeates our identity. We become our guilt and act only in reaction to our shame. Contemporary moral psychology teaches us that while guilt can be a prosocial emotion that calls us to truthfulness, accountability, and repair, shame often leads to avoidance, isolation, and inaction.

Shame traps us in a loop of revisiting what is wrong, not imagining what could be. Not being a "good enough" friend or daughter becomes a deeply rooted identity that forestalls reparative phone calls and relational risks. For example, although white people should experience profound moral grief over their complicity in racist structures, antiracist educators warn against centering on a navel-gazing "white guilt" that stymies action rather than foregrounding the insights of people of color and seeking necessary structural changes. Guilt calcifies into shame and leads to moral paralysis, constraining our vision of what is possible and forestalling the spiritual risks necessary to achieve it.

Jesus' decisive, final sacrifice frees us from a spiral toward shame and enables us to dream and reach for another world. Jesus' work finalizes the victory over sin, symbolized by his seat at the right hand of God. Notice that Jesus remains "waiting" for his enemies' defeat (Heb. 10:13). Might Jesus' anticipation connect with the call placed upon God's community in verses 19–25? We play a role ushering in the victory that Christ has already achieved. Christ's work writes the law of love on our hearts and minds. Our task is to claim and substantiate the reality that no other forces can shape our will more powerfully than God, allowing us to reject cycles of shame and initiate patterns of communal care.

Preachers may wish to reflect on how we might live as if nothing—not money, greed, or fear—but the transformative love of God has a final say over our lives. Would we be willing to earn less return on our retirement investments if it ensured that companies served the good of the whole community? Might we be more honest and open to growth in our relationships if we were not governed by fear of abandonment?

The resultant shifts in our life of faith could be extraordinary. Jesus' divine work assures us that we can confidently enter the inner sanctuary of worship and be remade, purified, and perhaps baptized, allowing us to move through the curtain that separates us from God's presence to the heart of holiness. We are not relegated to watching holier others enter into transformative fellowship with God as we remain in our stagnant cycle. Instead, we can confess an eternal hope that all are freed from the power of evil and death-dealing sin.

Many baptismal vows follow this pattern of rejecting evil and claiming Christ's freedom. For example, the United Methodist Church asks the baptizand, "Do you renounce the spiritual forces of wickedness, reject the evil powers of this world, and repent of your sin?" After the affirmative answer, the vows continue: "Do you accept the freedom and power God gives you to resist evil, injustice, and oppression in whatever forms they present themselves?"[4] Our rejection of sin initiates the freedom granted through Christ. As the sacrament unfolds, the entire congregation vows to nurture the newly baptized in their shared faith.

Instead of undertaking a radically individualized journey, we move toward the promise of God with mutual encouragement and even provocation toward love and good deeds (v. 24). In this ecclesial vision, the synagogue/church is not a polite gathering, a lifestyle enclave, or even a liturgical affinity group; believers require a community of holy honesty, sacred risk, and audacious love.

Craig Koester reminds us why Hebrews became a vital book for the Confessing Church in Germany as its members sought, in the midst of dire and demoralizing circumstances, to resist the Nazi takeover of their faith and the persecution of Jews, the disabled, and queer persons.[5] Their regular meetings helped them refuse the formations of Germany's dominant culture and remember that the ultimate hope and victory of

---

4. United Methodist Church; http://gbod.org.s3.amazonaws.com/legacy/kintera/entry_186/19/BAPTISMAL-RITUAL-REVISED.PDF.

5. Craig Koester, "The Interplay of Word and World: Biblical and Experiential Reflections," *Word & World* 36, no. 4 (September 2016): 337–45.

their faith compelled them to action. In what ways might our own gathered church pursue the call found in Christ's freedom? Might we require tough conversations about the distorting impact of winner-take-all economies, gun-fueled cultures, and xenophobia, followed by disruptive, love-based action? Persisting in a world with pain and rupture and living beyond the current social vision require communal support. Rather than radical individualism or even individual redemption from sin, faith in Christ is sustained in and practiced for community.

It is fitting that this lectionary selection comes at the end of Ordinary Time, a liturgical season focused on the formation of the Christian community. Before preachers turn to Advent's anticipation, these passages remind us that the birth, death, and resurrection of Christ anchor our identity as reconciled children of God, who must live into the fullness of love. No longer trapped in shame but freed for transformative community, we may find spiritual resonance in the end of Oliver's poem, which speaks of the wild geese continuously proclaiming our inclusion in the kinship of creation. Jesus announces and embodies a spiritual and social world where we belong so profoundly that love reshapes our vision of ourselves, our place among God's family, and our lives of holy connectedness.

C. MELISSA SNARR

Mark 13:1–8

¹As he came out of the temple, one of his disciples said to him, "Look, Teacher, what large stones and what large buildings!" ²Then Jesus asked him, "Do you see these great buildings? Not one stone will be left here upon another; all will be thrown down."

³When he was sitting on the Mount of Olives opposite the temple, Peter, James, John, and Andrew asked him privately, ⁴"Tell us, when will this be, and what will be the sign that all these things are about to be accomplished?" ⁵Then Jesus began to say to them, "Beware that no one leads you astray. ⁶Many will come in my name and say, 'I am he!' and they will lead many astray. ⁷When you hear of wars and rumors of wars, do not be alarmed; this must take place, but the end is still to come. ⁸For nation will rise against nation, and kingdom against kingdom; there will be earthquakes in various places; there will be famines. This is but the beginning of the birth pangs."

Commentary 1: Connecting the Reading with Scripture

Mark 13:1–8 is part of the so-called Little Apocalypse of the Synoptic tradition. These verses can be divided into two subsections. Verses 1–2 contain a reference to the grandeur of the temple, followed by Jesus' prediction that the temple shall be destroyed, while verses 3–8 discuss the signs of the end of the age. Neither prediction provides an exact date as to when these things shall occur. The ancient implied reader of Mark's Gospel may know of the destruction of the temple by the Romans at the end of the Jewish War (66–70 CE), depending upon when Mark's Gospel was written. The reader who knows of the temple's destruction probably would take the prediction in verses 3–8 seriously. In this way, both predictions become connected and have become eschatological signs.

Mark 13:1 relates the degree to which Jesus' disciples were in awe of the size and the beauty of the temple. While they were impressed, Jesus was clearly not. Jesus responded that the entire temple would be leveled to the ground (Mark 13:2). There is nothing inherently eschatological or apocalyptic about these verses. Prophecy can be accurate and meaningful without referring to the end of time. These two verses are no different.

Mark 13:3–8 causes Mark's original readers to think of the preceding two verses as eschatological prophecy. Since modern readers know that the temple was destroyed in 70 CE, they also tend to think of verses 1–2 as an eschatological prophecy. Peter, James, John, and Andrew come to Jesus privately and ask when the destruction of the temple will occur (vv. 3–4). Peter, James, and John comprise an inner circle of the Twelve (see 9:2 and 10:35–40). By sitting to respond, Jesus gives the context a rabbinical dimension. This type of question has a home in apocalyptic literature (e.g., Rev. 6:10; *2 Bar.* 26; *4 Ezra* 4:33–37). People who suffer innocently, without having committed a malevolent act, understandably want to know when their suffering will end.

Jesus responds with two statements very much at home in an apocalyptic context. He first predicts that false messiahs will come and lead astray many of the faithful (Mark 13:6). The expectation of a messiah is an apocalyptic element that was pervasive within Palestinian Judaism in the first century. It spoke to a longing for political and religious freedom from Roman imperialism. Josephus refers to messianic pretenders in *Jewish War* (e.g., 2.19.2; 2.22.2 and 4.9.4–11). There are similar New Testament witnesses (e.g., 2 Thess. 2:3–12; 1 John 2:18; 2 John 7; Rev. 13:11–18). False messiahs with grandiose political aspirations would have appealed to the hopes and fears of the Jewish people.

Jesus also predicts "wars and rumors of wars" (Mark 13:7). This is also the type of imprecise statement at home in apocalyptic literature that leaves itself open to various misinterpretations. Jesus gives no hint as to when "these things" shall occur. The fact that every century has wars and rumors of wars does not clarify things. Indeed, wars between nations, earthquakes, and famines recur throughout history (v. 8). Jesus' words are not revelatory as much as they sustain hope among his followers in the post-Easter church. Moreover, these signs are only the beginning of the end. Christians must live by faith. Indeed, Mark 13:32 stands close at hand; the exact time is not something humans should know! Predicting the end says more about the needs of the predictor than the intentions of the evangelist or Jesus.

The reference to labor pains conveys that the end times will bring unavoidable trials and tribulations for Christians. The clear implication here is that Christians will not be "raptured" from trying times. Christians must endure the final days. Similarly, the Revelation to John does not include the rapture. One finds similar words in *4 Ezra* 13:31: "And they shall plan to make war against one another, city against city, place against place, people against people, and kingdom against kingdom" (RSV).

Verses 7–8 in Mark 13 also convey that eschatological woes are a necessary evil. Jesus predicts both natural catastrophes (earthquakes, famines) and human-made disasters (war and the negative social consequences that accompany them). In other words, some eschatological events will be acts of God; others will be acts of human beings. One finds similar traditions in other apocalypses. For example, *2 Baruch* 27 and 70, written sometime after the destruction of the temple, mention natural disasters and poor human decisions. First-century Christians might understandably perceive the civil wars among Roman leaders from 66 to 70 CE (which destroyed the Pax Romana) as the eschatological signs depicted in contemporary apocalypses and apocalyptic passages such as Mark 13.

Mark 13 is an apocalyptic discourse or an eschatological prophecy with apocalyptic overtones. A true apocalypse has a heavenly guide, usually an angel, and also a human seer. Examples from this period of Christian apocalypses within other genres include the *Testament of Levi* 2–5 and the *Ascension of Isaiah* 6–11.

Within the Gospel of Mark, chapter 13 is unique. The eschatological and apocalyptic features are robust. The four apostles ask when the end will come. This is an apocalyptic concern from a community under duress, wondering when it will end. Palestinian Judaism experienced foreign occupation for the better part of five centuries. Jews of this time naturally wanted foreign imperialism to end soon. Mark 13:14 might describe foreign rulers as inherently impure and inappropriately seeking divine honors. One finds similar accusations in LXX Daniel 12:11; *4 Ezra* 11–12; and Revelation 17:7–14. Most importantly, Mark 13 is messianic in tone. It looks for a Son of Man who shall close the present age and usher in a new paradise replete with blessings and exemption from woes. One finds similar hopes in *2 Baruch* 83; *4 Ezra* 13; and Revelation 19:11–21.

The reference to a woman in labor (Mark 13:17) also has apocalyptic, eschatological overtones, but its roots are in the prophetic tradition. Isaiah 26:17–18; 66:7–9 and Micah 4:10 provide some good examples (see also Isa. 13:8; 21:3; 42:14; Jer. 4:31; 6:24; 13:21; 30:6; 50:43; Ps. 48:6). Isaiah 26:17–18 relates how, without God, Israel writhed in pain helplessly like a woman in labor before its enemies, but a gracious God promises to restore the nation. In Isaiah 66:7–9, God promises miraculously to restore Jerusalem to its former splendor. Micah 4:6–13 prophesies that Judah shall be exiled but ultimately will be restored by God. All three passages connote periods of transition, the common denominator they share with Mark 13:8.

Mark 13:8 connects with other apocalyptic texts. A similar passage is found among the thanksgiving hymns and prayers discovered at Cave 1 in Qumran (1QH 3:7–12). Both passages refer to a messiah and to a birth. Again, *4 Ezra* is instructive: "He answered and said to me, 'Go and ask a woman who is with child if her womb can keep the child inside her any longer when her nine months have come to an end" (*4 Ezra* 4:40 RSV). This passage speaks of the unavoidable coming of a new age of painful change (cf. *4 Ezra* 4:41–42 and 5:46–49). Finally, Revelation 12:2–6 echoes the Qumran text and *4 Ezra* 4:40. As with the prophetic tradition, labor pains symbolize a stressful transition from one era to the next.

Mark 13:1–8 tells us that the end will come, but it will bring some hard times, and Christians should prepare themselves. Moreover, the imprecision of the prophecies may serve as a warning that our attempts to predict the Parousia are a wasteful and unbiblical exercise.

THOMAS B. SLATER

Commentary 2: Connecting the Reading with the World

Countless "wars and rumors of wars" (Mark 13:7) have broken out throughout the two millennia since Mark penned this Gospel. There have also been "earthquakes in various places" and "famines" (v. 8). Yet the day of Christ's return has not come. This apocalyptic chapter in Mark's Gospel is full of images and signs of what the disciples should look for in anticipating the end times. Christians throughout history have tried to decode the language to point to particular events in current history that signal the impending apocalypse. Persons purporting to serve as prophets have declared the "end times" as coming near, creating hysteria among their followers.

In recent memory, the Y2K scare around the turn of the millennium led many to stock their houses full of emergency gear, food, and water, in the event that the changing over of all computers to the year "00" would create instability on such a global scale that chaos and destruction would prevail. Hollywood entertains viewers by producing movies and television series around apocalyptic visions, such as the recent Netflix series *The Umbrella Academy*, where a time traveler sibling tries to enlist the help of his superpowered brothers and sisters to prevent the impending apocalypse. Perhaps humans are fascinated by this image of utter destruction and desolation, or perhaps, we are terrified and these kinds of shows provide us a catharsis for our fears.

How can preachers be faithful to this text in Mark by preaching a message that does not stir up unnecessary fears, but that also addresses the concerns that listeners may harbor about the end of the world?

One way to do this is to preach in a way that names the fears that listeners may be harboring,

and to present the good news of the gospel as giving us hope and promising new life amid these fears. The fear of our own death or the death of loved ones, the fear of the death of our churches, the fear of political crises and world disasters—all contribute in various ways to the palpable anxiety often encountered in churches. Jesus, in this passage, seems to stoke the fires of fear. In response to the disciples' awe of the temple's architecture, Jesus says: "Do you see these great buildings? Not one stone will be left here upon another; all will be thrown down" (v. 2).

Whatever in our listeners' lives that can count as "great" is also at risk. Persons who pride themselves on their career may lose their jobs. Persons running marathons at the peak of their physical fitness may discover they have cancer. Others who revel in their status as married to a successful person with a seemingly perfect family life may learn their partner is having an affair. Everything we prize and build our lives upon can be "thrown down" by life circumstances.

Metaphorically, these crises become personal apocalypses, the end of time for that individual, even if the world around them seems to keep going just fine. Perhaps the church itself is fast approaching its eschaton, running out of money and losing its remaining members through funerals. Preachers can turn the fear-inducing language of apocalypse into an opportunity to acknowledge the painful realities persons may be facing, and to point them to the cross. Jesus makes these comments in Mark just shortly before his crucifixion. What seemed like the end was only the beginning, and God raised Jesus from the dead. Preaching with pastoral sensitivity to the fears people may face can help them name their own "apocalyptic visions" and entrust their fears to the God who goes with us into death and raises us into new life.

Another way to connect this reading to the world is to address the ecological crisis. Climate change and rising ocean temperatures threaten the well-being of the entire planet. Robert Macfarlane writes about this in his book *Underland: A Deep Time Journey*, where he looks deep below the surface of the earth. What he discovers is haunting. In the northern parts of the world, where the ice has entombed the remnants of the dead buried for millennia, the permafrost is melting and revealing a history that also foretells a future. The crisis of global warming and its effects are already being felt around the world, and the emerging reminders of our mortality as individuals and as a species lead some to denial, others to inertia, and still others to action. Preachers can allow this text in Mark to speak to these realities, not simply as signs of the Parousia of Christ, but awakening in listeners the call to care for the earth as if our lives depended upon it—because they do.

In reflecting on what he has learned from his studies of what he found deep in the earth, Macfarlane writes:

> What does human behaviour matter when *Homo sapiens* will have disappeared from Earth in the blink of a geological eye? Viewed from the perspective of deserts or oceans, morality looks absurd, crushed to irrelevance. A flat ontology entices: all life is equally insignificant in the face of eventual ruin. We should resist such inertial thinking; indeed, we should urge its opposite— deep time as a radical perspective, provoking action not apathy. The shock of the Anthropocene requires a new time literacy, a rethinking of what the geologist Marcia Bjornerud calls 'our place in time.' This is already happening. Deep time is the catalysing context of intergenerational justice; it is what frames the inspiring activism of Greta Thunberg and the school climate-strikers,

and the Sunrise campaigners pushing for a Green New Deal in America. A deep-time perspective requires us to consider not only how we will imagine the future, but how the future will imagine us. It asks a version of Jonas Salk's arresting question: 'Are we being good ancestors?'"[1]

Preachers can also benefit from reading the work of homileticians who have studied ecology, such as Leah Schade, whose book *Creation-Crisis Preaching* can help provide further resources for preaching on this theme. For instance, Schade recommends that preachers lift up the question "Who is my neighbor?" to see beyond the human for an answer, and also to foster discussion in the community about which ecological issues have been most impactful and how local organizations are trying to address environmental sustainability. Schade offers suggestions such as preaching from the perspective of the earth or natural elements, such as Balaam's donkey or mountains or valleys, inviting listeners to share with the congregation the ways nature helps them experience God, and preaching about the way Jesus incorporates nature into his parables.[2] To preach this way from Mark's reading, preachers could try imagining the sermon from the perspective of the earth in "birth pangs" (v. 8). What might the earth be saying to humans who marvel at our own "large buildings" (v. 1), while we continue to harm the rest of creation?

Another way preachers could connect this text to the world is to focus on those that try to "lead many astray" (v. 6). This might include climate-change deniers or persons who focus on particular jobs and industries as taking precedence over the environment. It may be that in our haste to blame some for our climate problems, we are ignoring our own complicity. Empower listeners to proceed with humility as well as wisdom and discernment in listening for Christ's voice in the earth's "birth pangs" today.

CAROLYN BROWNING HELSEL

1. Robert Macfarlane, "What Lies Beneath," *Guardian*, April 20, 2019; https://www.theguardian.com/books/2019/apr/20/what-lies-beneath-robert-macfarlane?smid=nytcore-ios-share.

2. Leah D. Schade, *Creation-Crisis Preaching: Ecology, Theology, and the Pulpit* (St. Louis: Chalice, 2015).

Proper 29 (Reign of Christ)

2 Samuel 23:1–7 and
  Daniel 7:9–10, 13–14
Psalm 132:1–12 (13–18) and Psalm 93

Revelation 1:4b–8
John 18:33–37

2 Samuel 23:1–7

[1]Now these are the last words of David:

The oracle of David, son of Jesse,
    the oracle of the man whom God exalted,
the anointed of the God of Jacob,
    the favorite of the Strong One of Israel:

[2]The spirit of the LORD speaks through me,
    his word is upon my tongue.
[3]The God of Israel has spoken,
    the Rock of Israel has said to me:
One who rules over people justly,
    ruling in the fear of God,
[4]is like the light of morning,
    like the sun rising on a cloudless morning,
    gleaming from the rain on the grassy land.

[5]Is not my house like this with God?
    For he has made with me an everlasting covenant,
    ordered in all things and secure.
Will he not cause to prosper
    all my help and my desire?
[6]But the godless are all like thorns that are thrown away;
    for they cannot be picked up with the hand;
[7]to touch them one uses an iron bar
    or the shaft of a spear.
    And they are entirely consumed in fire on the spot.

Daniel 7:9–10, 13–14

[9]As I watched,

thrones were set in place,
    and an Ancient One took his throne,
his clothing was white as snow,
    and the hair of his head like pure wool;
is throne was fiery flames,
    and its wheels were burning fire.
[10]A stream of fire issued
    and flowed out from his presence.
A thousand thousands served him,
    and ten thousand times ten thousand stood attending him.

> The court sat in judgment,
>   and the books were opened.
>   . . . .
>
> [13]As I watched in the night visions,
>
> I saw one like a human being
>   coming with the clouds of heaven.
> And he came to the Ancient One
>   and was presented before him.
> [14]To him was given dominion
>   and glory and kingship,
> that all peoples, nations, and languages
>   should serve him.
> His dominion is an everlasting dominion
>   that shall not pass away,
> and his kingship is one
>   that shall never be destroyed.

Commentary 1: Connecting the Reading with Scripture

2 Samuel 23:1–7. David's so-called "last words" provide complex theological commentary about kingship and deal with such questions as the relationship between divine authority and human rule, the nature of the Davidic covenant, and the persistent threat of human evil. The difficult passage draws from diverse traditions to articulate a theological justification for, and the ethical function of, the Davidic monarchy that will inform later traditions.

The passage begins with repeated attempts to identify David, who, one might presume, requires no introduction at this point in the narrative (2 Sam. 23:1–3a). The reintroduction is necessary so as to recast David, not only as a king, but also as a prophetic figure who speaks divine words. David is said to speak an "oracle." The oracle, it should be remembered, is almost always ascribed to God in prophetic literature, as in "an oracle of the LORD." Thus, as a prophetic figure, David speaks not only for God but, the passage asserts, as God would speak. The epithets "the man whom God exalted" and "the anointed of God" underline the close relationship between David and God. Furthermore, 23:2–3a almost nervously repeats that God speaks through David and that David

speaks God's words. The repetition makes clear that what follows is important, and that it may be controversial.

What does David say? First, David borrows from prophetic, wisdom, and other traditions to describe the ideal ruler (vv. 3b–4). The emphasis on justice echoes prophetic as well as Deuteronomic traditions; the theme of "the fear of God" links to wisdom tradition (e.g., Proverbs); and the imagery of the sun and rain resonates with language used to describe the ideal king in the Psalter (e.g., Ps. 72) and elsewhere (e.g., Job 29:23–25). A just and pious ruler, it turns out, embodies the virtues of all of Israel's traditions.

Next comes the bold claim in 23:5. David claims that he and his descendants are, and shall be, the ideal just and pious rulers described. At the foundation of this confidence is the "everlasting covenant" God made with David and his household, the details of which we find in 2 Samuel 7 and Psalm 89. There, as here, God's covenant with David is a grant in which God, the master, unilaterally promises the servant David the gift of eternal kingship. That is, the Davidic covenant is different from the Sinaitic covenant, a treaty that places obligations on the servant, Israel, toward the master, God.[1]

---

1. Jon D. Levenson, "The Davidic Covenant and Its Modern Interpreters," *Catholic Biblical Quarterly* 41 (1979): 205–19.

The nature of the Davidic covenant and its relation to the Sinaitic covenant have interested ancient and modern interpreters. Within the Christian tradition, the messianic connection has inspired a wide range of interpretations, including supersessionism and its close cousin, anti-Semitism. For example, Martin Luther writes of this passage that Jesus inherits and fulfills the Davidic covenant, thus making "a nation . . . or kingdom of Israel unnecessary."[2] All that is to say that while Jesus' connection to David is canonical and important for Christians, preachers do well to be mindful of the pitfalls, especially of anti-Semitism.

David frames the statement about the eternal covenant with rhetorical questions: "Is not my house like this with God? . . . Will he not cause to prosper all my help and my desire?" (2 Sam. 23:5). The implied answer is "yes." However, the possibility the answer may be "no" cautions against cheapening God's grace. It is important to remember that the Deuteronomistic History details the failures of David and his household and that Psalm 89 acknowledges the reality of God's withdrawing divine protection (Ps. 89:39–52). It is not a given that David's house is "like this" and that God will always cause it to prosper. God's grace is not to be taken for granted.

In this light, the description of the fate of the godless in 2 Samuel 23:6–7 is double-edged. On the one hand, the judgment describes David's duty to join God in eradicating human evil. On the other, it warns that David and his household, should they prove godless and evil, will face God's wrath. The passage seems to say that human rulers—even the Davidic monarch—rule at the pleasure of God and must choose to rule justly and in the fear of God, lest they be "entirely consumed in fire on the spot" (v. 7).

Daniel 7:9–10, 13–14. The apocalyptic vision participates in Daniel's rich interpretation of the historical crisis of the 160s BCE under the reign of Antiochus IV and announces the ultimate victory of the God of Israel over cosmic monsters. Written in Aramaic, like Daniel

2–6, but an apocalypse genre like Daniel 8–12, Daniel 7 bridges the court tales of Daniel 1–6 and the apocalypse of Daniel 8–12. In this way, Daniel 7 connects earthly realities and heavenly events. The passage, in sum, borrows from ancient traditions to treat present issues and informs future traditions, not least concerning the identity of Jesus.

The vision reaches back to older Canaanite and Israelite traditions. The relationship between the two divine beings, the "Ancient One" and the "one like a human being" (lit. "one like a son of man"), reflects the relationship between El and Baal in Canaanite traditions, as well as God and David in Psalm 89.[3] The humanlike one appears to be a warrior, like Baal and David, who defeats the four monstrous beasts (Dan. 7:3) and, as a reward, receives everlasting dominion from the Ancient One. The humanlike one adapts older traditions for a new historical period and, in turn, informs later Christian understanding of the identify of Christ.

The presumed battle is between heavenly beings but has direct this-worldly consequences. The monstrous beasts (v. 3) represent world empires. Most significantly, the fourth beast represents the Greek empire and "the little horn" (v. 8) Antiochus IV Epiphanes, who desecrated the Jerusalem temple and persecuted Jews. The vision proclaims that the present historical crisis has its source in cosmic reality. This means that the resolution to the earthly crisis must have a heavenly dimension: the victory of the humanlike one over the monsters is the defeat of human evil.

The identity of the victorious humanlike one remains a matter of debate. For Christians, the humanlike one is rightly seen as a figure of Jesus, who identified himself as the "Son of Man" about eighty times (Matt. 8:20; 12:8; 20:18; Mark 14:61–62, and so on). The redemptive role the figure plays in Daniel and the later infusion of messianic hope powerfully resonate with and add depth to a Christian understanding of Jesus Christ. At the same time, the Danielic passage welcomes and rewards further consideration.

2. John T. Slotemaker, "The Trinitarian House of David: Martin Luther's Anti-Jewish Exegesis of 2 Samuel 23:1–7," *Harvard Theological Review* 104 (2011): 233–54, here 247.
3. Paul G. Mosca, "Ugarit and Daniel 7: A Missing Link," *Biblica* 67 (1986): 496–517.

One important arena for further reflection concerns the relationship between the humanlike one and the "holy ones" who (along with the humanlike one) receive "kingship and dominion" (v. 27). The identity of the holy ones, whether they are angelic or human, is unclear. What is clear is that not the humanlike one alone, but a community of beings shares the divinely given authority to rule. The expectation is that the humanlike one and the holy ones will rule in a manner diametrically opposed to the monstrous rule of the beasts. If the beasts enacted cosmic and historical evil, the humanlike one and the holy ones shall rule justly and in the fear of God, manifesting God's gracious kingship on earth as in heaven by defeating evil and establishing order and vitality.

PAUL K.-K. CHO

Commentary 2: Connecting the Reading with the World

Belief that God's reign can effect change in the realm of human politics is reflected in the selection of texts for Christ the King Sunday, the last Sunday before Advent. On this Sunday, the church concludes the church year with a reminder that our ultimate allegiance is to Jesus Christ and the reign of God. Interestingly, this celebration is one of the newest to the church calendar, having been established in 1925 by Pope Pius XI in the aftermath of World War I, in a context of growing secularism and nationalism. In his encyclical *Quas Primas*, the pope stated that he hoped the Sunday would remind celebrants that as long as persons and nations reject the reign of God, there would be no chance for lasting peace.

Our texts are set up to be read in light of this focus of returning us to live out the reign of God so the peace of Christ can extend in and through the church in the world. It is fitting that this Sunday falls right before the beginning of Advent, where we celebrate the first and second coming of Christ. Both the Samuel and Daniel texts take on an already-but-not-yet quality. We can see ways that God's reign has broken into our world, but we also notice multiple places where Christ's vision of the world is not fully present.

Pondering David's final words, the preacher might consider with their congregation what we hope for in our leaders and systems. Although human endeavors often fall short of the ideal— David is one example of this—we should not give up on aspiring to something more than the status quo. Neither should we give in to the temptation to believe that the only place we can accept real peace is in heaven. The church's vocation is to follow the leading of Jesus Christ through the fragile structures of which we are a part and bring about a world that looks more like the wholeness envisioned by God.

We can also take hope in Daniel's vision that the Ancient of Days has provided a model ruler who has been given dominion over every nation and tribe (Dan. 7:13–14). These texts provide us with a vision of wholeness that includes leaders who rule justly for all people. The tension then becomes how we live out this vision while also acknowledging the brokenness we see in the world.

There are many examples of how the church has attempted to wield power to bring about God's vision of wholeness and justice in the world. In their book *Saving Paradise*, Rita Nakashima Brock and Rebecca Ann Parker chronicle Christianity's struggle to heed Christ's call to engage with this world amid the dangers and allures of empire.[4] They highlight two ways in which we are especially tempted. On the one hand, we are tempted to strive to achieve a paradise on earth through political endeavors. As John Milton illustrated in his works *Paradise Lost* and *Paradise Regained*, there are dangers in attempting to bring about paradise through political means. On the other hand, we are tempted to flee from this world and avoid

---

4. Rita Nakashima Brock and Rebecca Ann Parker, *Saving Paradise: How Christianity Traded Love of This World for Crucifixion and Empire* (Boston: Beacon, 2008).

involvement in its structures. Apocalyptic movements proclaiming that the end is near fall into this category. Often, they interpret texts, such as the visions we find in Daniel 7:13–14, in this way, because their experiences have taught them to give up on human institutions. They believe that all structures will come to a violent end. The vision of God's reign is often anticipated only in a future time or an otherworldly existence.

Recent work on apocalypticism and its psychology has helped us understand the despair and fear that motivate such doomsday predictions.[5] When people feel as if there is no reason to engage in this world, they often live in ways that are at best unhelpful and at worst destructive. What we desperately need are reminders of how the church is called to bear witness to the work of God in this world in a compassionate and just way.

For the church engaged in the ongoing work of God, these two texts offer a wonderful counterbalance to the above-mentioned temptations. We are reminded that God has always chosen to work through fragile, flawed humans and institutions to bring about a world where humans and creation can experience the wholeness God created us for. We are also reminded that God is far greater than our human institutions and that our hope does not rest only in our own power to bring about change. Therefore, when we see failure and brokenness, we should not lose heart and remove ourselves from the work of living out God's reign.

Rather, we should be reminded that the work toward God's vision is always an already-but-not-yet process. As David reminds us in his prayer, "One who rules over people justly, ruling in the fear of God, is like the light of morning, like the sun rising on a cloudless morning, gleaming from the rain on the grassy land" (2 Sam. 23:3–4). When we work with God in partnership for justice and the well-being of our world, people are able to flourish.

It is always helpful for the preacher to consider embodied examples of this type of living into the already-but-not-yet of Christ's reign. A first impulse is to think about noteworthy exemplars, those people like Dorothy Day and Nelson Mandela, who made a significant impact through their work for justice on a nationwide scale. While their example is worth remembering and aspiring to, for most of us, the work of living into Christ's reign will take place at a local level. I have been inspired, for instance, by the work of Bryan Stevenson and the Equal Justice Initiative.[6] The Initiative's work of advocating for marginalized populations who have been wrongly incarcerated and for justice reform in the United States illustrates what it looks like to stand in the gap and seek to rule with justice for others.

I have also seen it in the work of a parishioner who is a social worker and serves at the Family Justice Center, in my hometown in western Idaho. Her work on the local scale—daily showing up for victims of domestic abuse to help break the cycle of violence—is something that helps me believe that Christ as King is making a difference in the lives of people through the mission of the church.

My friend's work is not flashy. Her multiple cases include helping women and men get out of broken domestic situations and working with children affected by domestic abuse through a camp that teaches positive personal skills. At our church, she has helped organize volunteers to work with the Family Justice Center to help women make it to court dates and to help purchase basic supplies for families in transition. I know that her work is tireless and frustrating and that not every story has a happy ending. However, she continues to show up and make an impact in the lives of those she encounters. This is the type of work that is the already-but-not-yet work of Christ the King in our daily lives and in the world.

STEPHEN P. RILEY

---

5. See, for instance, Charles B. Strozier and Katherine Boyd, "The Psychology of Apocalypticism," *Journal of Psychohistory* 37, no. 4 (2010): 76–295.

6. See the web page of the Equal Justice Initiative, https://eji.org/, and Bryan Stevenson, *Just Mercy: A Story of Justice and Redemption* (New York: Spiegel & Grau, 2015).

Proper 29 (Reign of Christ)

Psalm 132:1–12 (13–18)

¹O LORD, remember in David's favor
    all the hardships he endured;
²how he swore to the LORD
    and vowed to the Mighty One of Jacob,
³"I will not enter my house
    or get into my bed;
⁴I will not give sleep to my eyes
    or slumber to my eyelids,
⁵until I find a place for the LORD,
    a dwelling place for the Mighty One of Jacob."

⁶We heard of it in Ephrathah;
    we found it in the fields of Jaar.
⁷"Let us go to his dwelling place;
    let us worship at his footstool."

⁸Rise up, O LORD, and go to your resting place,
    you and the ark of your might.
⁹Let your priests be clothed with righteousness,
    and let your faithful shout for joy.
¹⁰For your servant David's sake
    do not turn away the face of your anointed one.

¹¹The LORD swore to David a sure oath
    from which he will not turn back:
"One of the sons of your body
    I will set on your throne.
¹²If your sons keep my covenant
    and my decrees that I shall teach them,
their sons also, forevermore,
    shall sit on your throne."

¹³For the LORD has chosen Zion;
    he has desired it for his habitation:
¹⁴"This is my resting place forever;
    here I will reside, for I have desired it.
¹⁵I will abundantly bless its provisions;
    I will satisfy its poor with bread.
¹⁶Its priests I will clothe with salvation,
    and its faithful will shout for joy.
¹⁷There I will cause a horn to sprout up for David;
    I have prepared a lamp for my anointed one.
¹⁸His enemies I will clothe with disgrace,
    but on him, his crown will gleam."

Psalm 93

¹The LORD is king, he is robed in majesty;
   the LORD is robed, he is girded with strength.
He has established the world; it shall never be moved;
   ²your throne is established from of old;
   you are from everlasting.

³The floods have lifted up, O LORD,
   the floods have lifted up their voice;
   the floods lift up their roaring.
⁴More majestic than the thunders of mighty waters,
   more majestic than the waves of the sea,
   majestic on high is the LORD!

⁵Your decrees are very sure;
   holiness befits your house,
   O LORD, forevermore.

Connecting the Psalm with Scripture and Worship

Psalm 132:1–12 (13–18). On this feast day known as Reign of Christ Sunday, it may seem odd to preach from texts about King David, but it is David whom we encounter as the Revised Common Lectionary's semicontinuous track finishes its brief foray into the books of Samuel and offers Psalm 132 as today's accompanying prayer. Together, these two texts lay a foundation for the Davidic fulfillment that is Jesus Christ.

Psalm 132 is by far the longest of the Songs of Ascents, a psalm collection believed to have been composed for pilgrims on their way to Jerusalem, or Zion, as the psalmist names it here (Ps. 132:13). With its emphatic extolling of David's single-minded devotion to God (vv. 2–5), this psalm could certainly have inspired weary pilgrims, given that God has been entreated to "remember . . . all the hardships [David] endured" (v. 1), the hardships of their own journey might have seemed less burdensome. Moreover, the psalmist's direct exhortation, "Let us go to [God's] dwelling place" (v. 7a), surely provided additional motivation for faithful travelers.

For a service on Reign of Christ Sunday, however, the most salient verses are probably those in which the psalmist references the

dynastic lineage that will one day culminate in Jesus of Nazareth: "The LORD swore to David a sure oath from which [God] will not turn back: 'One of the sons of your body I will set on your throne. If your sons keep my covenant and my decrees that I shall teach them, their sons also, forevermore, shall sit on your throne'" (vv. 11–12). Christians understand Jesus as the incarnate keeping of God's "sure oath" (v. 11) to David. In fact, this is why Jesus will, as related in today's Gospel passage, be tried as "the King of the Jews" (John 18:33).

The passage from 2 Samuel is a psalmlike poem. It emphasizes God's actions in making David a ruler: David is "the man whom God exalted, the anointed of the God of Jacob, the favorite of the Strong One of Israel" (2 Sam. 23:1b). Further, David is depicted as God's instrument: "The spirit of the LORD speaks through me, [God's] word is upon my tongue" (v. 2). The text then proceeds to describe a good ruler thusly: "One who rules over people justly, ruling in the fear of God, is like the light of morning, like the sun rising on a cloudless morning, gleaming from the rain on the grassy land" (vv. 3b–4), and then declares that this is the very sort of dynasty with which God has made "an everlasting covenant, ordered in all things and secure" (v. 5b). For Christians, the "sun rising on a cloudless morning" (v. 4) is, of course, the risen Son.

Psalm 132 is best sung or read on this day, rather than adapted for liturgical use. The appointed reading from Revelation, however, offers language that may be used for opening sentences that point to the eternal reign of the cosmic Christ.

Reader One:	Grace to you and peace from God who is and who was and who is to come, and from the seven spirits who are before God's throne, and from Jesus Christ, the faithful witness, the firstborn of the dead, and the ruler of the kings of the Earth.
Reader Two:	To him who loves us and freed us from our sins by his blood, and made us to be a kingdom, priests serving His God and Father, to Him be glory and dominion forever and ever.
Reader One:	Look! He is coming with the clouds.
Reader Two:	Every eye will see him, even those who pierced him.
Reader One:	The Lord God says, "I am the Alpha and the Omega."
Reader Two:	The Lord God is the Almighty, who is and who was and who is to come.

Psalm 93. Here on the eve of Advent, Reign of Christ Sunday dares us to proclaim Christ's glorious rule over all creation, but to do so in a way that respects the born-in-a-barn nature of Jesus. Given that we, despite our efforts to the contrary, still prize earthly power, we must be careful to honor the radical quality of Jesus' reign rather than attempting to reduce him to human standards of power.

The text from Daniel helps with this challenge, presenting one of Daniel's dreams in which "an Ancient One took his throne" (Dan. 7:9a) amid "ten thousand times ten thousand" (v. 10) attendants. Into this scene, Daniel sees "one like a human being coming with the clouds of heaven" (v. 13). To this one, who is like us and yet also infinitely beyond us, "was given dominion and glory and kingship, that all peoples, nations, and languages should serve

him. His dominion is an everlasting dominion that shall not pass away, and his kingship is one that shall never be destroyed" (v. 14).

Psalm 93 serves as a response to Daniel's vision by providing augmentations. The psalmist describes the Lord as clad not in mere velvet and ermine but in "majesty" and "strength" (Ps. 93:1). The Lord's dominion is over all space— "He has established the world" (v. 1b)—and over all time: "You are from everlasting" (v. 2). In addition to the "peoples, nations, and languages" (Dan. 7:14), the natural world also pays homage: "O LORD, the floods have lifted up their voice" (Ps. 93:3). God's "decrees," the 'edot God uses to order and govern all life, "are very sure" (v. 5a) and for all time, God's house—whether a Bethlehem stall or a heavenly abode—is a place of "holiness" (v. 5b).

In worship, Psalm 93 could serve as a scriptural affirmation of faith. It is also easily adapted for use as opening sentences, read responsively, as illustrated here:

Reader One:	The Lord is king; God is robed in majesty.
Reader Two:	The Lord is robed; God is girded with strength.
Reader One:	God has established the world; it shall never be moved.
Reader Two:	Your throne, O God, is established from of old; you are from everlasting. Let us worship God!

The psalm also invites a more creative treatment involving multiple voices, perhaps featuring children, and including ad hoc percussion. Consider this:

One voice:	The Lord is king;
Two voices:	God is robed in majesty.
Three voices:	The Lord is robed;
Four voices:	God is girded with strength.
Two voices:	God has established the world; it shall never be moved.
Four voices:	Your throne, O God, is established from of old.
One voice:	You are from everlasting.
One voice (percussion begins):	The floods have lifted up, O Lord;
Two voices (percussion builds):	the floods have lifted up their voice;
Three voices (percussion builds):	the floods lift up their roaring.

Two voices (percussion sustains):
>> More majestic than the thunders
>> of mighty waters,

Three voices (percussion builds):
>> more majestic than the waves of
>> the sea,

Four voices (percussion crescendos):
>> majestic on high is the Lord!

Four voices (in postpercussion stillness):
>> Your decrees are very sure;

One voice (in postpercussion stillness):
>> holiness befits your house, O
>> Lord, forevermore.

"O Worship the King, All Glorious Above!" is well suited to echo this image from Daniel's vision. In addition to the triumphant music often offered on this holy day—"Crown Him with Many Crowns," "He Is King of Kings," "Rejoice, the Lord Is King," and other rousing hymns—consider the more subtle "How Can I Keep from Singing" or the more complex "Christus Paradox," each of which is published both as an anthem and as a hymn.

LEIGH CAMPBELL-TAYLOR

Revelation 1:4b–8

[4]Grace to you and peace from him who is and who was and who is to come, and from the seven spirits who are before his throne, [5]and from Jesus Christ, the faithful witness, the firstborn of the dead, and the ruler of the kings of the earth.

To him who loves us and freed us from our sins by his blood, [6]and made us to be a kingdom, priests serving his God and Father, to him be glory and dominion forever and ever. Amen.

[7]Look! He is coming with the clouds;
    every eye will see him,
even those who pierced him;
    and on his account all the tribes of the earth will wail.

So it is to be. Amen.
[8]"I am the Alpha and the Omega," says the Lord God, who is and who was and who is to come, the Almighty.

Commentary 1: Connecting the Reading with Scripture

On this last day of the church year, we turn to the opening of one of the most mystifying books in the Bible: the Revelation to John of Patmos. The Revised Common Lectionary omits the first three verses, which explain that this is a revelation of Jesus Christ made known by God's angel to his servant John, who testified to what he saw (Rev. 1:1–2), and that all who hear and keep the words of the prophet are blessed (v. 3). Reflecting on the liturgical place of this book, which, like other epistles, was intended to be read aloud, may help confused listeners understand how this book was absorbed by its first hearers, and why it was included in the biblical canon.

The lectionary reading opens with a salutation, making this letter sound like just another epistle. The opening verses appear more innocuous than John's wild vision of the "great whore" or the "the beast" that come later (chaps. 13, 17). John of Patmos wrote to seven churches (1:4), and the number seven in the Bible signifies completion: God rested on the seventh day when creation was complete. Sabbatical years took place every seventh year, and a jubilee year

after seven times seven years. Jesus continued the practice of seven indicating completion when he advocated that we forgive those who have wronged us not just seven times, but "seventy times seven" (Matt. 18:21–22). Given the significance of the number seven as indicating completion, the writer likely intended it to be read at *all* the churches in that particular region, not just the seven to which it was addressed.

Brian Blount writes that this opening section establishes John's key theme of witnessing, including the faithful witness of Christ himself in verse 5.[1] By naming Christ as a faithful witness and king, John encouraged others to resist oppressive empires. The reference to Christ not only as king but the ruler of the kings on earth (Rev. 1:5) makes this reading particularly relevant on a Sunday focusing on Christ's kingship or reign.

While the salutation in this passage evokes other epistles, John of Patmos took traditional formulas further. The threefold pronouncement of God as "who is and who was and who is to come" was normative for deities, but John took

---

1. Brian K. Blount, *Revelation: A Commentary* (Louisville, KY: Westminster John Knox, 2009), 27.

this pronouncement even further by adding that *this* God was *coming* (v. 7). By further identifying God as Alpha and Omega, the opening and closing letters of the Greek alphabet, John claimed that God controls everything that occurs in human time. Emphasizing this point can help today's listeners absorb the significance of the use of the Greek letters.

The book of Revelation is one of only two books in the Bible that are true apocalypses. "Apocalypse" comes from the Greek word *apokalyptein*, meaning "uncover" or "reveal." Definitions of this type of literature from the early twentieth century include supernatural visions revealing an unearthly sphere. Revelation and the book of Daniel, also included in this week's lectionary readings, are both apocalypses by this definition. Some interpreters and preachers are tempted to diminish Revelation by reducing it to a political tract against Rome. Stephen Cook[2] rightly inveighs against this, encouraging Christians to engage not only in political struggles but also economic and cultural ones, and to recognize God's new creation breaking into the world. Reading Revelation through a purely historical lens diminishes the power the book has to speak to us today.

While the book of Revelation is an apocalypse, it also has a lot in common with biblical writings of the prophets, as in John's description of his commissioning by God (vv. 9–20). Lengthening this week's reading to show how John's call mimics calls to prophets in the Old Testament may help the preacher avoid the danger of supersessionism, the fallacy that the new covenant replaces the old, thereby making the Hebrew Scriptures irrelevant. Other ways this book evokes prophetic writings include John's writing in his own name while serving as a mouthpiece for the Divine. Emphasizing similarities between Revelation and the books of the Hebrew prophets can help listeners feel connected to a text that may seem alien.

The Revised Common Lectionary features only six sections from the twenty-two chapters of the book of Revelation, reflecting a possible discomfort with the baffling visions in the letter.

In the Easter season of Year C, some of the readings are sequential, but even sequentially, giant sections of the book are omitted. This particular reading appears on Christ the King Sunday without any other Revelation readings following it. The sequential track features King David's last words (2 Sam. 23:1–7), which are appropriate for looking at the last things, as the book of Revelation also does. The Gospel reading from John (18:33–37) includes dialogue between Jesus and Pilate, especially focusing on Pilate's question to Jesus as to whether he is king of the Jews. Jesus responds that his kingdom is not of this world.

The underrepresentation from Revelation in the Revised Common Lectionary seems to reflect a discomfort with its contents. While other short pieces of what Cook calls "apocalyptic literature" appear in the New Testament (e.g., 1 Thess. 4:15–5:11; 1 Cor. 15; and the so-called little apocalypses that appear in Matthew 24, Mark 13, and Luke 21), the book of Revelation appears, from its scant appearances, to be in tension with much of the rest of the canon as a whole. This is likely because of its distinct apocalyptic genre. Cook writes extensively about the danger of "domesticating" the book of Revelation through purely symbolic, futuristic, or historicized readings and through "overly credulous or overly suspicious" lenses.

On the Sunday in which we reflect on what the reign of Christ will look like, some talk of heaven can be appropriate. Sometimes preachers remind their listeners that Christians can be tempted to imagine the kingdom of God as some faraway, otherworldly heaven where we will be assigned harps and lounge on clouds. Such visions fail to bring about justice for and compassion toward the world in which we live. Revelation has much to teach us about heaven.

Michael Battle, for instance, describes Revelation as a vision of an inseparable heaven and earth joined together like two overlapping circles that form an almond shape or *mandorla* in the middle (*mandorla* is Italian for "almond"). The image of joined circles can serve preachers well when studying this passage with its powerful, overlapping images depicting Jesus as witness,

---

2. Stephen L. Cook, *The Apocalyptic Literature* (Nashville: Abingdon, 2003), 40, 44, 53.

firstborn of the dead, ruler of kings, Alpha and Omega. Jesus makes clear in the Gospel reading of the day from John (John 18:33–37) that his kingdom is not "from here." Countering those Christians who apparently did not believe in heaven, the book of Revelation describes God's presence and tells us who gets to be in that presence. Battle writes, "We read Revelation through our own eyes and interest groups. . . .Those in economic and political power tend to read Revelation in a more relaxed, 'objective' way in which there can be a wide girth of interpretations. . . . Those without such power and resources are less inclined to such objectivity and instead embrace apocalyptic and literal tone. . . . A good theology of Revelation is one in which we do not need to wait for Heaven."[3]

ELIZABETH FELICETTI

Commentary 2: Connecting the Reading with the World

Apocalyptic texts are meant to puzzle the powerful while they interpret history for those most beaten down by its apparent victors. These texts of resistance emerge from crisis and seek to galvanize sufferers toward a radically different theological and political future. The preacher should ask, Who exactly were these sufferers to whom this text was addressed, and why was it written?

Suffering greatly for his faith and work for the kingdom of God, John of Patmos wrote as an outsider from an island far from his era's dominant power centers. He did not embody a religious, political, or economic status that aligned with imperial Roman supremacy. His marginality opened him to hear God's revelation of a different version of time, history, and political rule. He writes to outsiders, not to the powerful, to share this vision and declaration of God's loving liberation.

With this background in mind, we must resist the urge to tame this text or glibly transpose it into our own reality, especially if we hold positions of economic, political, racial, or religious power in this world. What might it mean, for instance, to preach this text in a refugee camp, an asylum detention center, or in the midst of the daily grind of extreme poverty and inadequate health care due to political machinations? While the less powerful need the divine assurance of this text's vision of history, those of us with more power need to wrestle with what this divine disruption might mean for our relatively comfortable lives.

For all listeners, the text begins with a salutation of encompassing *shalom* (or wholeness for every sphere of our lives) from the "one who is and who was and who is to come" (Rev. 1:4). This phrase is repeated twice in today's reading, thereby emphasizing God's presence both within and beyond our normal sense of time. God's eternal nature—always before, in, and beyond our finite sense of history—relativizes the political and historical "reality" of this moment and frees us from its final determination on our lives. God's infinite timeline instead focuses us on the simultaneous immediacy and futurity of humanity's *telos*, or end: the eternal love of God. It shatters finite evaluations of worth based on stock-market prices, wealth accumulation, national pride, or exclusivist identities.

With additional greetings from the manifold Spirit and, finally, from Jesus Christ as "faithful witness, firstborn of the dead, and the ruler of kings of the earth" (v. 5), the author marshals rich symbolic language to issue a potent challenge to the current theological and political order. Jesus embodies God's vision of the beloved community so fully that he endures martyrdom, breaking death's eternal hold on our lives; ultimately, Jesus reigns over all those who seem to rule our lives now.

This kind of freedom may call us to profound resistance, like that of Bishop Óscar Romero (and many unnamed Salvadorans), among those martyred at the hands of a brutal authoritarian

---

3. Michael Battle, *Heaven on Earth: God's Call to Community in the Book of Revelation* (Louisville, KY: Westminster John Knox, 2017), 179, 181.

regime for working against government repression and human-rights violations. As Romero noted presciently: "As a Christian, I do not believe in death without resurrection. If they kill me, I will rise again in the people of El Salvador."[4] For a minority community in the ancient world (and even today), to know that God transcends and conquers their greatest uncertainties—life, death, and the whims of political control—is tremendously comforting and empowering.

However interpreted, this opening greeting serves as a reminder of the otherworldly and yet present majesty of God and evokes the doxological praise and ecclesial declaration beginning in verse 5b. Some scholars imagine these words of adoration as the worship response of a community who knows that God's active love and reconciliation render it a kingdom of priests who serve God. For contemporary hearers, the monarchical language describing communal transformation could prove challenging. Recognizing the purpose for which we are made a "kingdom" of priests may allow the words' import to hold greater resonance: the freedom we have in Jesus and his love makes possible an all-embracing beloved community that enacts social, political, and cultural care and right relationship.

Latina theologian Ada María Isasi-Díaz imagined this as the "kin-dom" of God, where relationships of mutuality, both personally and structurally, undo violence, poverty, and all forms of alienation for the salvation or wholeness of all. Seeking this kin-dom is not a spiritualized individual journey of faith; rather, we are called to another kind of holistic community where no one suffers under domination. Pairing this understanding with the declaration that we are all priests regardless of gender, race, or other exclusions, makes kin-dom work everyone's work. It is not for the specially gifted.

We are *all* called to serve God and bring healing to our communities. This calling echoes Exodus 19:6, where the God-who-liberates tells Moses that the people will be consecrated as a priesthood. Thus, the "every member a minister"

theme invites us to claim our theological, social, and political role to seek out those suffering in our world and fashion, with God's help, a different kind of community.

The subsequent vision (v. 7) points us to a consummation in which all people, even those who have rejected God by causing grave suffering, see God for who God is. Perhaps the tribes wail in painful recollection of the terrible harm and from the separation from God's fullness caused by collective sin. The preacher may want to help us imagine how finally seeing the fullness of God might move those with more privilege to a kind of global mourning about our/their transgressions (perhaps related to prejudice, poverty, or environmental devastation).

Although this verse may point to the future, apocalyptic visions are not about the complete destruction of this world; they are about the new heaven and new earth (Rev. 21) that God births in history by undoing ungodly distortions and destructions. These subversive narratives ground transformative power for a suffering community and animate not only their survival but renewed work for holistic *shalom*.

The text concludes with a restatement of the divine identity and timeline. Echoing Exodus 3:14, "I am who I am," the Greek phrasing can hardly contain the wonder of the God who is intimately present with us while also beyond our sense of time. This divine timeline and identity were so vital for the early church that some Christians inscribed the Greek letters on their signet rings and engraved these markings in Roman catacombs. The Alpha and Omega, often intertwined with the cross, have adorned church windows, banners, and stoles across the centuries.

The symbol is meant to anchor us in God's ultimate political reality, beyond the domination and death-dealing systems of our day. Claiming God's infiniteness should not turn us toward escapism or the next life. This mystical yet profoundly immanent theological and political statement cannot be divorced from our call to be the kin-dom, the beloved community, and an ongoing witness—like Christ—to another

---

4. https://kellogg.nd.edu/archbishop-oscar-romero.

kind of world *now*. To borrow the poetic imagery of Arundhati Roy: "Another world is not only possible, she is on her way. On a quiet day, I can hear her breathing."[5]

As we read this text at the close of the church calendar, we are reminded that we are all responsible as God's ministers to care for the suffering in such a way that we embrace the kin-dom of God in and with the most marginalized. As we renew the liturgical cycle, in what ways shall we seek to hear the Christian story (birth, death, and resurrection of Jesus Christ) from the margins and claim our priestly call for the healing of the world and the inbreaking of the beloved community?

C. MELISSA SNARR

5. Arundhati Roy, "Confronting Empire," lecture at the World Social Forum in Porto Alegre, Brazil, January 27, 2003: https://www.outlookindia.com/website/story/confronting-empire/218738.

John 18:33–37

³³Then Pilate entered the headquarters again, summoned Jesus, and asked him, "Are you the King of the Jews?" ³⁴Jesus answered, "Do you ask this on your own, or did others tell you about me?" ³⁵Pilate replied, "I am not a Jew, am I? Your own nation and the chief priests have handed you over to me. What have you done?" ³⁶Jesus answered, "My kingdom is not from this world. If my kingdom were from this world, my followers would be fighting to keep me from being handed over to the Jews. But as it is, my kingdom is not from here." ³⁷Pilate asked him, "So you are a king?" Jesus answered, "You say that I am a king. For this I was born, and for this I came into the world, to testify to the truth. Everyone who belongs to the truth listens to my voice."

Commentary 1: Connecting the Reading with Scripture

The issues of destiny and truth are inseparable throughout this reading. The question of destiny recurs three times. It comes first in Pilate's question in verse 33: "Are you the King of the Jews?" Pilate may or may not know of first-century-CE messianic expectations, but as the commander of an occupying foreign army, he would have known of Jewish discontent and accompanying aspirations for freedom. Indeed, Pilate's question has strong political and religious overtones because these were also inseparable in Roman society.

Pilate is actually asking whether Jesus is leading a revolution. The Romans were suspicious of any new movements, lest they lead to an insurrection. If Jesus had answered, "Yes," Pilate would have had sufficient reason to execute him. Jesus' answer reveals that he understands the nature of the question. Jesus attempts to deflate the situation with his own question in verse 34: Is this Pilate's own question or someone else's? Jesus' question also reveals that he is not unaware of the political landscape. Indeed, both the Romans and the Jewish elites prospered financially and politically from the status quo. Neither wanted an insurrection that could change the social context to their detriment. Jesus' question is also an attempt to drive a wedge between those strange bedfellows.

However, Pilate is unmoved. He will not consider the possibility that he has been misled by his Jewish collaborators. He would rather trust the devil he knows than the one he does not know. Pilate wants to convey that since he is not a Jew, he is neutral (John 18:35). Rather, Jewish leaders brought Jesus to him. Thus, he asks the question, "What did you do?" A more objective person might have asked, "How did we get here?"

Secondly, Jesus himself speaks to his destiny. He states that his kingdom is not an earthly kingdom. As evidence of this, Jesus says that, if it were an earthly kingdom, his followers would have fought to stop him from being handed over to the Jews (v. 36). Such a reaction would have been normal then and today. In short, Jesus should not be considered a threat, because his destiny is different. In actuality, any type of kingdom would have been seen as a threat by the Romans.

The question of Jesus' destiny arises a third time. Pilate has tunnel vision and repeats the initial question: "So you are a king?" (v. 37). In responding to Pilate, Jesus initially turns Pilate's words on their head (v. 33) but moves swiftly to clarify the nature of his destiny: "For this I was born, and for this I came into the world, to testify to the truth" (v. 37b). The Greek verbs in this statement are in the perfect tense, implying, in this instance, that Jesus' destiny has been determined and cannot be changed.

We turn now to our second topic: truth. Both of Pilate's questions seek the truth, but Pilate is looking for a specific kind of truth. He

Death Is Christ's Servant

To all [the] principles of hell, or of this world—they are the same thing, and it matters nothing whether they are asserted or defended so long as they are acted upon—the Lord, the king, gives the direct lie. It is as if he said:—"I ought to know what I say, for I have been from all eternity the son of him from whom you issue, and whom you call your father, but whom you will not have your father: I know all he thinks and is; and I say this, that my perfect freedom, my pure individuality, rests on the fact that I have not another will than his. My will is all for his will, for his will is right. He is righteousness itself. His very being is love and equity and self-devotion, and he will have his children such as himself—creatures of love, of fairness, of self-devotion to him and their fellows. I was born to bear witness to the truth—in my own person to be the truth visible—the very likeness and manifestation of the God who is true. My very being is his witness. Every fact of me witnesses him. He is the truth, and I am the truth. Kill me, but while I live I say, Such as I am he is. If I said I did not know him, I should be a liar. I fear nothing you can do to me. Shall the king who comes to say what is true, turn his back for fear of men? My Father is like me; I know it, and I say it. You do not like to hear it because you are not like him. I am low in your eyes which measure things by their show; therefore you say I blaspheme. I should blaspheme if I said he was such as anything you are capable of imagining him, for you love show, and power, and the praise of men. I do not, and God is like me. I came into the world to show him. I am a king because he sent me to bear witness to his truth, and I bear it. Kill me, and I will rise again. You can kill me, but you cannot hold me dead. Death is my servant; you are the slaves of Death because you will not be true, and let the truth make you free. Bound, and in your hands, I am free as God, for God is my father. I know I shall suffer, suffer unto death, but if you knew my father, you would not wonder that I am ready; you would be ready too. He is my strength. My father is greater than I."

George MacDonald, "Kingship," in *Unspoken Sermons,* vol. 3 (London: Longmans, Green & Co, 1889), 101–4.

---

is looking for seditious activity, and he will not stop until he finds it. The first question seeks a confession. Pilate probably assumes Jesus is a religious fanatic with foolish messianic pretentions without a realistic chance of making it happen.

Jesus' indirect response does not satisfy Pilate. Pilate wants an explicit answer. He is an aspiring politician who wants a definite answer so that his decision might be clear cut and beyond reproach. Unsatisfied with Jesus' first response, Pilate seeks truth another way. He asks Jesus why he has been brought to him, hoping to corner Jesus into a confession by having him explain why he was seized in the first place.

At this point, Jesus speaks his own truth: "My kingdom is not from this world" (v. 36a). Pilate has heard enough. "My kingdom" is apparently all Pilate wants or needs to know. This is Pilate's truth. The rest of Jesus' statement has no effect upon him (v. 36b). Jesus' complete truth has no point of contact with Pilate's truth. That

is why Pilate responds, "So you are a king?" At this point, Jesus realizes the futility of any explanation, so he speaks truth to power. He has been born for this specific time to "testify to the truth. Everyone who belongs to the truth listens to my voice" (v. 37).

Jesus has judged Pilate without Pilate realizing it; Pilate has not listened to Jesus (cf. John 8:45–47 and 10:26–27). Truth has eluded Pilate. He has not seen the messiahship of Jesus, his ministry among the people, and his witness to God. He has not seen the Son of God before him. He has not seen the truth. In the Gospel of John, such persons condemn themselves (e.g., 3:31–36; 8:47).

This section of the Gospel of John resonates with other parts of the Gospel. For example, in the Nicodemus episode in John 3, we have a verbal exchange where Jesus speaks a truth that his conversation partner cannot grasp. Nicodemus is not an antagonist. He is a man seeking truth, but the complex answer he receives confuses him. Nicodemus hears "born again," but Jesus means "born from above." Another example is the Samaritan woman at the well in John 4. Jesus speaks a truth about "living water," but the woman hears "running water." The woman seeks truth but, as with Nicodemus, Jesus' answer confuses her. Again, truth goes unrecognized. In both instances, the Greek can be interpreted in more than one way. The difference with these instances in John 3 and John 4 is that Jesus' conversation partners are actually trying to understand Jesus, while Pilate is not.

The narratives in John 3 and John 4 are what one would expect of two persons trying to understand one another. They are not adversarial. However, John 18:33–37 is more debate than intellectual exchange. The two men are adversaries, and one of them (Pilate) has no interest in understanding the other.

There are at least two preaching possibilities. With regard to destiny, we often make assumptions based upon externals and not inner substance. Frequently, leaders with great potential are overlooked because of their origins, their ethnicity, their gender, or where they were educated. For example, in a country of more than 330 million persons, it is not unreasonable to think that someone with a law degree from a

public university, such as the University of Arizona, University of California, Berkeley, University of Michigan, University of North Carolina, University of Massachusetts, University of Texas, Austin, or Southern University, would make an outstanding member of the Supreme Court. Not all outstanding lawyers come from Ivy League universities. In such ways, one's destiny can be denied. Life teaches us, if we let it, that skill is an equal opportunity employer.

Too often we, like Pilate, close ourselves off to the whole truth, because it is unpleasant or simply unwanted. We do not want complex answers. We want simple answers that bring less stress and less reflection, ignoring the reality of nuance and inconsistency common to human existence. We want the truth that convinces us, not the truth that convicts us; the truth that affirms us, not the truth that challenges us. We want a truth in our own image, not in the image of God.

Christ challenges us to look for destiny and truth from unusual persons in unusual places and to accept them even when acceptance makes us uncomfortable and challenges our assumptions. He calls us to remember that destiny and truth did not reside with Pilate and Rome but with a carpenter from Nazareth.

THOMAS B. SLATER

Commentary 2: Connecting the Reading with the World

This Sunday is known as Christ the King or Reign of Christ Sunday, the day in the liturgical year when the Alpha finally reaches the Omega. The Word who was with God in the beginning (John 1:1) is now celebrated as having the last word, the final word in the eternal story of God's redemptive history. For the liturgical year that begins in Advent, this is the final Sunday of the year. For congregations, this may feel premature, since the calendar still has another month, Thanksgiving celebrations are quickly approaching or have just concluded, and students still have too many days until their winter vacation. Nevertheless, in the worship life of the church, this Sunday marks a special day of claiming the victory of God in Jesus Christ over the powers of evil and death, a day on which

preachers can point to the reign of Christ as truly having come *already*. It is not until the following Sunday, when we begin a new year with Advent, that we remember that Christ has come, and also has *not yet* come again to realize fully the vision of God's reign for the cosmos.

The already-and-not-yet of Christ's reign is perhaps most poignantly seen in this week's text from John. Jesus stands before Pilate in the headquarters of the Roman governor. Pilate questions Jesus about whether Jesus is a king, and Jesus speaks of his kingdom as "not from this world" (John 18:36), declaring before Pilate: "You say that I am a king. For this I was born, and for this I came into the world, to testify to the truth" (v. 37). Here is Jesus, declaring his kingship, announcing his kingdom, yet facing crucifixion. Already, Jesus is a king and reigns over a kingdom not of this world; this kingdom is not yet part of this earthly reality or recognized by earthly governments. Thus Jesus speaks of a kingdom that is present, but still not fully realized.

Cynthia Rigby writes about this "now and not yet" tension by describing the way Christians struggle to have hope for the kingdom of God even in the midst of difficult situations. She points to how we as Christians can have hope in this world and believe that the coming kingdom of Christ has relevance for bodies today and for the fears people have here and now. To illustrate this, Rigby shares an image of listening to her son's orchestra play a piece of music they had never played before on stage. The conductor gave them a piece of music that was new to the students at the end of a concert. He then proceeded to lead the students through the music without their instruments, conducting the students through the sheet music until the students could get inside the music enough to own it. After going through the music once with annotated conducting that was free of instruments, the conductor led the students through a second time, now with them fully participating in the music and inviting the listeners into the song themselves. Rigby reflects: "It reminded me that to be people of hope is to 'watch and pray' for the Kingdom of God to come, actively looking for it along the way. . . . What remains is to reflect on how we do even more than witness and imagine the Kingdom, which already takes energy and attention. How do we 'lean into it,' even making a contribution to it?"[6] One way for preachers to preach about Christ the King is to invite their congregations into this imaginative process, to help persons see how they might live differently as citizens of the kingdom where Christ reigns, and to encourage them to lean into that reality in the here and now.

Another way for preachers to connect this text to the world is to highlight the importance of working within current political systems that promote justice or injustice. In celebrating the reign of Christ, Christians do not ignore or separate themselves from the actual governing processes that influence the ways persons are treated in society. While it may be easier to assume Jesus is "above" politics and that persons of faith should stay out of politics, it is imperative that Christians hear in this text that Jesus speaks directly to the political leaders of the day. Jesus declares to Pilate, "For this I came into the world, to testify to the truth" (v. 37). Christians today need to be testifying to the truth in the political sphere so as to follow Christ's example.

Christians already doing this include the Rev. Dr. William Barber, who began a weekly protest in front of the North Carolina state legislature in 2013 after the state approved some of the most restrictive voter identification laws in the country, making it more difficult for the poor and people of color to vote in elections. Rather than stand by and tell persons affected, "Do not worry—you will get to vote in the kingdom of God!" Barber began to lead Christians and non-Christians in speaking out against these laws, testifying to the truth about what was preventing people from fully engaging in the political process.

In a speech he gave on the eve of the fiftieth anniversary of Martin Luther King Jr.'s famous "I Have a Dream" speech, Barber preached to a group gathered in North Carolina—one of thirteen rallies across the state in a campaign to "Take the Dream Home"—reiterating King's call to "go back" to our homes to make a difference in our communities. Barber declared:

> Once again we are being summoned by history, and this is the moment to tell folk about the dream. Tell the nation's enemies and friends about the dream. We are being called to never give up. We are being called to resist being drunk with the wine of the world and instead to see what God sees. We are being called to prophetic vision, vision that comes from revelation by God. Vision and dreams that are not afraid of the enemy, vision and dreams that do not know how to fail or how to give up. The kind of vision that makes you run on and see what the end will be. The kind of vision and dream that keeps us

6. Cynthia L. Rigby, *Holding Faith: A Practical Introduction to Christian Doctrine* (Nashville: Abingdon, 2018), 284.

from perishing, from letting go, from bowing down, from living in depression. . . . Prophetic dreaming is the kind of vision that comes in the midst of nightmares. Yes, there are some nightmares, but the dream of justice is greater! The dream of truth is greater![7]

Christians who are shy about declaring truth in the midst of complicated policies and political climates need to be reassured by preachers that they can and should use their voices to speak to those in authority. Preachers do not need to have a congregation of a single political party in order to proclaim this: whatever their political affiliations, Christians need to work together on behalf of the poor and oppressed. Political leaders need Christians to offer a moral compass, recalling Pilate's question: "What is truth?" (v. 38), which, interestingly, is not included in today's lection reading. Perhaps, that, too, is telling. Have we stopped asking about truth? Have Christians stopped insisting upon the truth from our politicians?

CAROLYN BROWNING HELSEL

---

7. From Barber's August 23, 2013, speech, "Taking the Dream Home," in William J. Barber II with Barbara Zelter, *Forward Together: A Moral Message for the Nation* (St. Louis: Chalice, 2014), 97.

Contributors

CHARLES L. AARON JR., Associate Director of the Intern Program, Perkins School of Theology, Southern Methodist University, Dallas, TX

JARED E. ALCÁNTARA, Associate Professor of Homiletics, Holder of the Paul W. Powell Endowed Chair in Preaching, George W. Truett Theological Seminary, Baylor University, Waco, TX

SAMMY G. ALFARO, Professor of Theology, Grand Canyon University, Phoenix, AZ

BRADY BANKS, Development Director, Center for Youth Ministry Training, Brentwood, TN

JOHN M. BUCHANAN, Retired Pastor, Fourth Presbyterian; Retired Editor and Publisher, *The Christian Century*, Chicago, IL

LEIGH CAMPBELL-TAYLOR, Pastor, Presbyterian Church (U.S.A.), Atlanta, GA

CLÁUDIO CARVALHAES, Associate Professor of Worship, Union Theological Seminary, New York, NY

PAUL K.-K. CHO, Associate Professor of Hebrew Bible, Wesley Theological Seminary, Washington, DC

L. JULIANA CLAASSENS, Professor of Old Testament and Head of Gender Unit, Faculty of Theology, Stellenbosch University, Stellenbosch, South Africa

ADAM J. COPELAND, Client Experience Researcher, Mayo Clinic, Rochester, MN

MAGREY R. DEVEGA, Senior Pastor, Hyde Park United Methodist Church, Tampa, FL

DAN R. DICK, Assistant to the Bishop, Wisconsin Conference, United Methodist Church, Sun Prairie, WI

JILL DUFFIELD, Editor, *The Presbyterian Outlook*, Richmond, VA

CURTIS FARR, Rector, St. Paul's Episcopal Church, Fairfield, CT

ELIZABETH FELICETTI, Rector, St. David's Episcopal Church, Richmond, VA

RENATA FURST, Associate Professor of Scripture and Spirituality; Associate Dean for Hispanic Engagement, Oblate School of Theology, San Antonio, TX

GARRETT GALVIN, Vice President for Academic Affairs, Franciscan School of Theology, Oceanside, CA

DONNA GIVER-JOHNSTON, Pastor, Community Presbyterian Church of Ben Avon, Pittsburgh, PA

WILLIAM GREENWAY, Professor of Philosophical Theology, Austin Presbyterian Theological Seminary, Austin, TX

LETICIA A. GUARDIOLA-SÁENZ, Assistant Professor of Christian Scriptures, Seattle Pacific University and Seminary, School of Theology, Seattle, WA

ANGELA DIENHART HANCOCK, Associate Professor of Homiletics and Worship, Pittsburgh Theological Seminary, Pittsburgh, PA

CAROLYN BROWNING HELSEL, Assistant Professor of Homiletics, Austin Presbyterian Theological Seminary, Austin, TX

LUCY LIND HOGAN, Hugh Latimer Elderdice Professor of Preaching and Worship, Wesley Theological Seminary, Washington, DC

LAURA SWEAT HOLMES, Associate Professor of New Testament; Associate Dean of Graduate Studies, Seattle Pacific University and Seminary, Seattle, WA

J. SCOTT HUDGINS, Director, Helping Pastors Thrive Program, Cooperative Baptist Fellowship of North Carolina, Winston-Salem, NC

GEORGE R. HUNSBERGER, Professor Emeritus of Missiology, Western Theological Seminary, Holland, MI

PABLO A. JIMENEZ, Associate Dean of Hispanic Ministries Program, Gordon Conwell Theological Seminary, South Hamilton, MA

DAVID W. JOHNSON, Associate Professor of Church History and Christian Spirituality, Austin Presbyterian Theological Seminary, Austin, TX

JENNIFER T. KAALUND, Assistant Professor of Religious Studies, Iona College, New Rochelle, NY

EUNJOO MARY KIM, Professor of Homiletics and Liturgics, Iliff School of Theology, Denver, CO

ERICA A. KNISELY, Director of Programs for Education Beyond the Walls, Austin Presbyterian Theological Seminary, Austin, TX

MAX J. LEE, Associate Professor of New Testament, North Park Theological Seminary, Chicago, IL

JOEL MARCUS LEMON, Associate Professor of Old Testament; Director of the Graduate Division of Religion, Candler School of Theology, Emory University, Atlanta, GA

MICHAEL LODAHL, Professor of Theology and World Religions, Point Loma Nazarene University, San Diego, CA

KIMBERLY BRACKEN LONG, Editor, *Call to Worship: Liturgy, Music, Preaching, and the Arts*, Presbyterian Church (U.S.A.), Louisville, KY

BARBARA K. LUNDBLAD, Joe R. Engle Professor of Preaching Emerita, Union Theological Seminary, New York, NY

BENJAMIN P. MASTERS, Pastor at First Presbyterian Church, Hector, NY and Lodi Presbyterian Church, Lodi, NY, Hector, NY

J. CLINTON MCCANN JR., Evangelical Professor of Biblical Interpretation, Eden Theological Seminary, St. Louis, MO

MARK MCENTIRE, Professor of Biblical Studies, Belmont University, Nashville, TN

SCOT MCKNIGHT, Professor of Preaching and Worship, Northern Seminary, Lombard, IL

TIM MEADOWCROFT, Senior Research Fellow, Laidlaw College, School of Theology, Auckland, New Zealand

MARTHA L. MOORE-KEISH, J. B. Green Professor of Theology, Columbia Theological Seminary, Decatur, GA

ALICIA D. MYERS, Associate Professor of New Testament and Greek, Campbell University Divinity School, Buies Creek, NC

SUSAN K. OLSON, Part-Time Settled Pastor at First Congregational Church, Lyme, CT; Associate Director of the Student Accessibility Services Office, Yale University, New Haven, CT

PETER J. PARIS, Elmer C. Homrighausen Professor of Social Ethics Emeritus, Princeton Theological Seminary, Princeton, NJ

SONG-MI SUZIE PARK, Associate Professor of Old Testament, Austin Presbyterian Theological Seminary, Austin, TX

ZAIDA MALDONADO PÉREZ, Professor Emeritus of Church History and Theology, Asbury Theological Seminary, Florida Dunnam campus, Orlando, FL

SANDRA HACK POLASKI, New Testament scholar and author, Richmond, VA

ANATHEA E. PORTIER-YOUNG, Associate Professor of Old Testament, Duke Divinity School, Duke University, Durham, NC

ROBERT A. RATCLIFF, Editor-in-Chief, Westminster John Knox Press, Franklin, TN

WYNDY CORBIN REUSCHLING, Professor of Ethics and Theology, Ashland Theological Seminary, Ashland, OH

STEPHEN P. RILEY, Associate Professor of Old Testament, School of Theology and Christian Ministry, Northwest Nazarene University, Nampa, ID

GILBERTO A. RUIZ, Assistant Professor of Theology, Saint Anselm College, Manchester, NH

DAVID J. SCHLAFER, independent consultant in preaching and Assisting Priest, The Episcopal Church of the Redeemer, Bethesda, MD

GLEN G. SCORGIE, Professor of Theology and Ethics, Bethel Seminary, St. Paul, MN

MATTHEW L. SKINNER, Professor of New Testament, Luther Seminary, St. Paul, MN

THOMAS B. SLATER, Professor Emeritus of New Testament, McAfee School of Theology, Mercer University, Atlanta, GA

DANIEL L. SMITH-CHRISTOPHER, Professor of Old Testament, Loyola Marymount University, Los Angeles, CA

C. MELISSA SNARR, Associate Professor of Ethics and Society, Vanderbilt Divinity School, Nashville, TN

DEBORAH SOKOLOVE, Professor Emerita of Art and Worship, Wesley Theological Seminary, Washington, DC

ANNA GEORGE TRAYNHAM, Pastor and Head of Staff, Shallowford Presbyterian Church, Atlanta, GA

PATRICIA K. TULL, A. B. Rhodes Professor Emerita of Old Testament, Louisville Presbyterian Theological Seminary, Louisville, KY

NONTOMBI NAOMI TUTU, Canon Missioner for Racial and Economic Equity, The Cathedral of All Souls, Asheville, NC

LEANNE VAN DYK, President and Professor of Theology, Columbia Theological Seminary, Decatur, GA

OSVALDO D. VENA, Professor Emeritus of New Testament Interpretation, Garrett-Evangelical Theological Seminary, Evanston, IL

RICHARD W. VOELZ, Assistant Professor of Preaching and Worship, Union Presbyterian Seminary, Richmond, VA

ROBERT W. WALL, Paul T. Walls Professor of Scripture and Wesleyan Studies, Seattle Pacific University and Seminary, Seattle, WA

THEODORE J. WARDLAW, President and Professor of Homiletics, Austin Presbyterian Theological Seminary, Austin, TX

REBECCA ABTS WRIGHT, C. K. Benedict Professor of Old Testament and Biblical Hebrew, The School of Theology, The University of the South, Sewanee, TN

OLIVER LARRY YARBROUGH, Tillinghast Professor Emeritus of Religion, Middlebury College, Department of Religion, Middlebury, VT

WILLIAM YOO, Assistant Professor of American Religious and Cultural History, Columbia Theological Seminary, Decatur, GA

Author Index

Abbreviations

C1	Commentary 1		NT	New Testament
C2	Commentary 2		OT	Old Testament
E	Epistle		PS	Psalm
G	Gospel			

Contributors and entries

Charles L. Aaron Jr.	Proper 14 E C2, Proper 15 E C2, Proper 16 E C2
Jared E. Alcántara	All Saints OT C2, Proper 26 OT C2, Proper 27 OT C2
Sammy G. Alfaro	Proper 11 E C1, Proper 12 E C1, Proper 13 E C1
Brady Banks	Proper 23 OT C2, Proper 24 OT C2, Proper 25 OT C2
John M. Buchanan	Proper 11 G C2, Proper 12 G C2, Proper 13 G C2
Leigh Campbell-Taylor	Proper 26 PS, Proper 27 PS, Proper 28 PS, Proper 29 PS
Cláudio Carvalhaes	Trinity Sunday E C2, Proper 3 E C2, Proper 4 E C2
Paul K.-K. Cho	Proper 28 OT C1, Proper 29 OT C1
L. Juliana Claassens	Proper 14 OT C1, Proper 15 OT C1, Proper 16 OT C1
Adam J. Copeland	Proper 14 E C1, Proper 15 E C1, Proper 16 E C1
Magrey R. deVega	Proper 14 G C1, Proper 15 G C1, Proper 16 G C1
Dan R. Dick	Proper 5 E C2, Proper 6 E C2, Proper 7 E C2
Jill Duffield	Proper 20 OT C2, Proper 21 OT C2, Proper 22 OT C2
Curtis Farr	Proper 11 OT C2, Proper 12 OT C2, Proper 13 OT C2
Elizabeth Felicetti	Proper 28 E C1, Proper 29 NT C1
Renata Furst	Trinity Sunday G C1, Proper 3 G C1, Proper 4 G C1
Garrett Galvin	Proper 11 OT C1, Proper 12 OT C1, Proper 13 OT C1
Donna Giver-Johnston	Proper 23 PS, Proper 24 PS, Proper 25 PS, All Saints PS
William Greenway	Proper 5 G C1, Proper 6 G C1, Proper 7 G C1
Leticia A. Guardiola-Sáenz	Proper 20 G C1, Proper 22 G C1
Angela Dienhart Hancock	Proper 14 PS, Proper 15 PS, Proper 16 PS
Carolyn Browning Helsel	Proper 28 G C2, Proper 29 G C2
Lucy Lind Hogan	Proper 11 E C2, Proper 12 E C2, Proper 13 E C2
Laura Sweat Holmes	Proper 17 E C2, Proper 18 E C2, Proper 19 E C2
J. Scott Hudgins	Proper 5 OT C2, Proper 6 OT C2, Proper 7 OT C2
George R. Hunsberger	Proper 23 E C2, Proper 24 E C2, Proper 25 E C2
Pablo A. Jimenez	All Saints NT C2, Proper 26 E C2, Proper 27 E C2
David W. Johnson	Proper 3 E C1, Proper 4 E C1

Jennifer T. Kaalund	Proper 23 E C1, Proper 24 E C1, Proper 25 E C1
Eunjoo Mary Kim	Proper 5 PS, Proper 6 PS, Proper 7 PS
Erica A. Knisely	Trinity Sunday E C1
Max J. Lee	Proper 11 G C1, Proper 12 G C1, Proper 13 G C1
Joel Marcus LeMon	Trinity Sunday PS, Proper 3 PS, Proper 4 PS
Michael Lodahl	Proper 20 E C2, Proper 21 E C2, Proper 22 E C2
Kimberly Bracken Long	Proper 20 PS, Proper 21 PS, Proper 22 PS
Barbara K. Lundblad	Proper 14 G C2, Proper 15 G C2, Proper 16 G C2
Benjamin P. Masters	Proper 21 G C1
J. Clinton McCann Jr.	Trinity Sunday OT C1, Proper 3 OT C1, Proper 4 OT C1
Mark McEntire	Proper 8 OT C1, Proper 9 OT C1, Proper 10 OT C1
Scot McKnight	Proper 5 E C1, Proper 6 E C1, Proper 7 E C1
Tim Meadowcroft	Proper 14 OT C2, Proper 15 OT C2, Proper 16 OT C2
Martha L. Moore-Keish	Proper 17 PS, Proper 18 PS, Proper 19 PS
Alicia D. Myers	Proper 23 G C1, Proper 24 G C1, Proper 25 G C1
Susan K. Olson	Trinity Sunday G C2, Proper 3 G C2, Proper 4 G C2
Peter J. Paris	Proper 20 G C2, Proper 21 G C2, Proper 22 G C2
Song-Mi Suzie Park	Proper 17 OT C1, Proper 18 OT C1, Proper 19 OT C1
Zaida Maldonado Pérez	Proper 8 E C1, Proper 9 E C1, Proper 10 E C1
Sandra Hack Polaski	Proper 17 G C1, Proper 18 G C1, Proper 19 G C1
Anathea E. Portier-Young	Proper 23 OT C1, Proper 24 OT C1, Proper 25 OT C1
Robert A. Ratcliff	Trinity Sunday OT C2, Proper 3 OT C2, Proper 4 OT C2
Wyndy Corbin Reuschling	Proper 8 OT C2, Proper 9 OT C2, Proper 10 OT C2
Stephen P. Riley	Proper 28 OT C2, Proper 29 OT C2
Gilberto A. Ruiz	All Saints G C1, Proper 26 G C1, Proper 27 G C1
David J. Schlafer	Proper 5 G C2, Proper 6 G C2, Proper 7 G C2
Glen G. Scorgie	Proper 17 OT C2, Proper 18 OT C2, Proper 19 OT C2
Matthew L. Skinner	Proper 8 G C1, Proper 9 G C1, Proper 10 G C1
Thomas B. Slater	Proper 28 0G C1, Proper 29 G C1
Daniel L. Smith-Christopher	Proper 5 OT C1, Proper 6 OT C1, Proper 7 OT C1
C. Melissa Snarr	Proper 28 E C2, Proper 29 NT C2
Deborah Sokolove	Proper 11 PS, Proper 12 PS, Proper 13 PS
Anna George Traynham	Proper 8 PS, Proper 9 PS, Proper 10 PS
Patricia K. Tull	All Saints OT C1, Proper 26 OT C1, Proper 27 OT C1
Nontombi Naomi Tutu	Proper 23 G C2, Proper 24 G C2, Proper 25 G C2
Leanne Van Dyk	Proper 17 G C2, Proper 18 G C2, Proper 19 G C2
Osvaldo D. Vena	Proper 20 E C1, Proper 21 E C1, Proper 22 E C1
Richard W. Voelz	Proper 8 G C2, Proper 9 G C2, Proper 10 G C2
Robert W. Wall	Proper 17 E C1, Proper 18 E C1, Proper 19 E C1
Theodore J. Wardlaw	All Saints G C2, Proper 26 G C2, Proper 27 G C2
Rebecca Abts Wright	Proper 20 OT C1, Proper 21 OT C1, Proper 22 OT C1
Oliver Larry Yarbrough	All Saints NT C1, Proper 26 E C1, Proper 27 E C1
William Yoo	Proper 8 E C2, Proper 9 E C2, Proper 10 E C2

Scripture Index

OLD TESTAMENT

Genesis

1	50, 313, 365
1:1–31	363
1:1–2:4a	430
1:2	55
1:3–4	313
1:8–31	153
1:26–27	312
1:28	354
2:1–4	38
2:2–3	43
2:7	345, 355
2:18–24	361, 367
2:24	267
2:25	382
3	63, 356
3:8–15	**54–58**, 60, 63
3:8–20	57
3:8–21	62
3:16	356
3:23	56
6:6–7	408
9:1–17	21
12	399
12:1–3	86
12:8	146
14	416
14:17–21	399
16:13	382
17	399
18	293
22:1–18	154
22:16–17	417
26:3	417
29	146
35:8	441
38	180
47:6	319

Exodus 447

3:5	409
3:14	193, 198, 314, 503
4:13	5
4:25	459
6:7	21
6:33	210
13:17	408
14	56, 227
14:17–20	465
14:21–15:19	176, 193
15	202
15:22–26	337
15:24	198
16	38, 120, 192, 206, 227
16:2–4	**196–200**, 202, 210
16:2–15	206
16:9–15	**196–200**, 202, 210
16:18	199
16:20	202
16:31	198
17:3	198
18:13–27	141
18:21	319
19:22	328
20:1–18	38
20:8–11	43
20:11	46
20:17	374
20:20	193
24	425
25:1–31:11	447
28–29	399
32–34	20
32:12	408
32:13	417
33:19	382
34:6–7	110
34:29–35	27
34:30	328
36:1–40:38	447

Leviticus 447

2:4	180
6:2	387
8–9	399
10:3	328
12:2	248
12:4–5	248
12:7–8	248
15:19–30	248
15:25–27	124
16	447n1, 449
18:6–19	459
18:16	158
19:13	387
19:18	291, 386, 451, 453–54
19:35	387
20:21	158
21:16–23	248
25:1–13	274
25:47–49	308

Numbers

6:5	476
11:4–6	**335–39**, 342, 350
11:4–9	192
11:10–16	**335–39**, 342, 350
11:16–30	141
11:24–29	**335–39**, 342, 350
12:7–8	392
14	73
17–18	399
22:22–35	489
27:17	176

Deuteronomy

1:26–38	399
4:1–2	**264–68**
4:2	271
4:3	441
4:6–9	**264–68**
4:40	459
5	43
5:6–21	441
5:12–15	**36–40**, 44, 46, 50
5:15	43
5:16	459

Deuteronomy (*continued*)
5:21	374
5:33	441, 459
6–11	441
6:1–9	**439–43**, 453
6:2	446
6:3	459
6:4	386, 458
6:4–5	386, 446, 451, 454
6:5	386
6:7	446
8:3	192, 211
8:16	192
10:18	232
15:11	320
17:14–15	58
18:15	192
19:15	141
22:30	459
23:1–3	232, 248
24:1–4	367
25:5–6	457
25:6	283
28:1–68	343
28:30–44	374
28:48–68	374
28:57	459
31:8	195
34:9	249

Joshua — 56, 145
1:2	392
1:7	392
2	293
2:8–14	294
5:12	192
6	145
8:3	319
10	145
23:1	249
24	247–48, 252
24:1–2	**246–50**
24:2	249
24:3–13	247
24:14–18	**246–50**
24:15	261

Judges — 56, 145
3:24	459
3:29	319
7	56
8:28	37

13:5	37
17–21	37
19	474
19–21	43
20:1	215n1
20:44	319
20:46	319
21	474

Ruth — 470, 475
1:1–5	445, 462
1:1–18	**439–43**, 453
1:6	459, 462
1:8	457
1:11–13	457
1:13	445
1:15–18	469
1:20–21	440
1:22	462
2	441
2:1	319
2:1–2	457
2:8–9	457
2:20–22	457
3–4	460
3:1–5	319, 453, **456–60**, 462
3:10–11	457
3:11	443
4:1–4	308
4:13	462
4:13–15	469
4:13–17	**456–60**
4:14–15	459
4:15	440, 458
4:16–17	462
4:17	459
4:17–22	453

1 Samuel — 56, 129, 145–46, 475
1	37
1–2	475
1:4–20	**472–77**
1:5	479
1:11	479
2:1–10	37, 473, **478–81**
2:11–17	43
2:26	37
3	37, 42, 473
3:1	43
3:1–20	**36–40**

3:4	43
3:10	304
3:19–4:1	38
3:20	215n1
4–7	145
4:1	37
7	56
7:15	473
8	73, 232
8–9	74
8:1–18	37
8:1–9:2	127
8:4–11	**54–58**
8:9–20	86
9	73
9–10	473
9:2	75
9:3–10:16	127
10:17–26	127
10:27	127
11:1–8	234
11:1–15	127
11:12	234
11:14–15	**53–58**
12	473
13:14	443
15	74
15–16	473
15:22	452
15:34–16:13	**72**, 80
16–31	110
16:1–13	127, 169
16:14–23	421
16:21–23	91
17	98
17:1	**89–95**
17:4–11	**89–95**
17:19–23	**89–95**
17:32–49	**89–95**
17:55–58	128
18:20	147
19:11–17	147
21:1–6	49
23	325
24:3	459
25:44	147
27–29	91
31	111, 129

2 Samuel — 56, 128–29, 146, 475
1:1	**108–12**, 115

1:14	130	24:2	215n1	**2 Kings**	56, 475	
1:17–27	**108–12**, 115	24:15	215n1	2:1–15	141	
1:26	118			4:1–7	180, 460	
2:1–7	127, 129	**1 Kings**	56, 475	4:38–41	180	
3	146	1:5–2:35	320	4:41	180	
3:10	215n1	2	233, 239, 242	**4:42–44**	**179–83**, 185,	
3:15–16	147	2–3	231, 236		193	
3:18	391	2:9	233	5:1–27	426	
3:21–23	180	**2:10–12**	**230–34**	9:7	392	
4	128	3	234	9:30–37	463	
5	128	**3:3–14**	**230–34**	17:13	392	
5:1–5	**127–31**, 134	3:5	242	19:34	391	
5:9–10	**127–31**, 134	3:12	239	20:6	391	
6	150	3:15	234	21:8	392	
6:1–5	**144–48**, 153	4:25	215n1			
6:6–11	145	4:31	170	**1 Chronicles**	128	
6:12–19	**144–48**, 153	**8:1**	**246–50**	16	110	
6:20	147	8:1–66	253	17	153	
6:20–23	146	8:5	248	17:4	391	
7	492–93	**8:6**	**246–50**	17:7	391	
7:1–14	**162–67**, 170,	**8:10–11**	**246–50**	20:5	91	
	172, 176	8:13	231, 248	21:2	215n1	
7:5	391	8:16	248	22:8	75	
7:8	391	**8:22–30**	**246–50**			
7:12–16	248	8:31–46	250	**2 Chronicles**		
7:15	165	**8:41–43**	**246–50**	1:7–12	326	
11–12	75	8:56	250	5	110	
11:1–15	**179–83**, 199	11:13	391	7	110	
11:26–12:13	**196–200**, 203	11:32	391	12:18	164	
12	163	11:34	391	12:40	164	
12:1–13	206	11:36	391	18:16	176	
13	218	11:38	391	30:5	215n1	
14:1	218	12	146			
15–18	75	14:8	391	**Ezra**		
17:11	215n1	16:29–33	458	9	55	
18	221	17:1–7	458	9:7	55	
18:5–9	**214–18**	17:7–24	426			
18:14–15	215, 218	**17:8–16**	**456–60**	**Nehemiah**		
18:15	**214–18**	17:12	463	9	55	
18:16–29	215	17:14	469	9:20	192	
18:19–23	218	17:16	463			
18:28–32	180	18	217	**Esther**	341, 475	
18:29–30	218	18:20–40	215	1:12–22	337	
18:31–33	**214–18**	18:46	215	1:15–22	320	
19	216	19:3	217	**7:1–6**	**335–39**, 349	
19:1–2	216	19:3–5	215	**7:9–10**	**335–39**, 349	
19:4	216	**19:4–8**	**214–18**	**9:20–22**	**335–39**, 349	
19:5	215	19:10	217			
19:5–8	218	19:12	217	**Job**	475	
21:19	91	19:18	217	1–2	7, 354	
23:1	497	19:21	217	**1:1**	**353–58**, 360	
23:1–7	**491–95**, 493n1, 501	22:17	176	1:8	93, 354, 392	

Job (*continued*)

1:20	408
1:22	354
2:1–10	**353–58**, 360
2:3	392
2:8	408
2:12–13	408
3–31	373
3:1	373
3:16	408
3:21	408
5:13	137
6:9	442
7:5	408
7:21	408
9:31	408
10:8	442
10:9	408
11:5–6	391
11:7	373
13:3	391
13:21	442
13:24	373
16:15	408
17:1	408
17:16	408
19:21	442
22	373
22:5–11	373
22:23	373
23	386
23:1–9	**372–77**, 404
23:2	442
23:3	379
23:3–5	391
23:8–9	379, 408
23:15	374
23:16–17	**372–77**, 404
24:9–10	374
24:12	374
24:21–23	374
25	373
28	373
28:21	373
28:28	326
29:12–16	373
29:23–25	492
30:21	442
31	373
31:35	391
31:40–32:1	373

35:14	373
37:23	373
38	92, 404
38–39	408
38–41	374, 410
38:1–7	**389–94**
38:1–11	**89–95**, 97
38:1–40:2	387, 391
38:1–42:6	408
38:2	410
38:2–3	408
38:8–11	391
38:12–13	391
38:18	391
38:19–20	391
38:19–24	373
38:21	391
38:31	393
38:33	391
38:34–41	**389–94**
39:1–2	391
39:17	391
39:26	391
40:3–5	386
40:3–41	408
40:4–5	391
40:6–41:34	408
40:7	408
42	416
42:1–6	**407–12**
42:7	391
42:7–8	374, 392
42:10–17	**407–12**
42:15	414

Psalms

1	**323–25**
1–2	289
2:7	399, 465
2:8–14	294
5:11	308
6:33	206
6:50–51	206
8	**359–61**, 365
8:4	365
8:4–6	363
9	98–99
9–10	98
9:9–20	**96–99**
9:11	137
14	**184–86**

14:2	187
15	**269–71**, 288
16	**478–81**
16:5	110
19	301, **306–9**
19:1–6	342
19:1–14	302
19:7	273
19:7–14	**340–42**
20	**78**
21:6	379
22	373–74, 379–80
22:1–15	**378–80**
22:2	421
23	**168–70**, 172
23:1–6	176
23:4	379, 442
23:6	253
24	**149–51**, 153, **428–29**, 434
24:4	153–54
26	**359–61**
29	7–9, 11
30	**113–16**, 298
30:5	118
30:11	118
31:23	308
34	220, 223, 249, 416
34:1–8	**219–21**, **413–15**
34:8–22	236
34:9	232
34:9–14	**235–37**
34:15–22	**251–53**
34:19–22	**413–15**
34:22	249
35:9	425
40:6	452
40:16	308
42	133
45	270
45:1–2	**269–71**
45:3–5	269
45:6–9	**269–71**
45:11	270
48	**132–34**
48:6	488
51	207
51:1	203
51:1–12	**219–21**
51:16–17	452
54	**323–25**, **331–32**
	356

54:4	331	104	396, 404	146:1–10	283
68:18	206	**104:1–9**	**395–97**	146:9	469
72	186, 492	104:7	107	150	147
72:4	232	104:10–23	396		
72:12–14	232	**104:24**	92, **395–97**	**Proverbs**	475
73:24–25	43	104:34	404	1	303, 308
73:26	110	**104:35**	**395–97**	1–9	301, 324, 326
76	134	105:9	417	1:7	302, 319
78	206	106	110	**1:20–33**	**300–305**
78:5	202	107	97, 110	1:33	302, 308
78:23–25	192	**107:1–3**	**96–99**	2	319
78:23–29	206, 210,	**107:23–32**	**96–99**	2:6–15	326
	219–21	107:29	104	2:7–8	302
78:30–31	203	110:1	399, 483	2:21	302
78:70–71	164	110:4	399, 417, 465	3:2	231
78:70–72	176	**111**	**235–37**	3:15	324
81	50	111:10	232, 326	3:16–18	231
81:1–10	**41–44**	113:7	409	3:18–20	324
82:1	7	**116:1–9**	**306–9**	3:23–26	302
84	134, 249, **251–53**	118	110	3:33	302
84:11–12	255	118:24	425	5–7	239
85:1–7	150	119	446	8:1–11	302
85:8	154	**119:1–8**	**444–46**	8:13	302
85:8–13	**149–51**, 153	119:57	110	8:15	231
85:10	48, 154	120–134	133, 288, 415	8:18	231
85:12	154	122	134	8:22–31	302, 363, 391
87	134	**123**	**132–34**	9	**233–34**
89	492–93	123:2	136	**9:1–6**	**230–34**, 236
89:3	392	**124**	**340–42**	9:6	231
89:6–7	7	**125**	283, **287–89**	9:10	236, 302, 326
89:20	392	**126**	**413–15**	9:13	319
89:20–37	**168–70**, 176	**127**	**461–63**	10:1–22:6	283
89:35	417	**130**	**59–61**, **113–16**,	10:27	302
89:39–52	493		**219–21**	10:29–30	302
90	380	130:1	218	11:4–5	302
90:12–17	**378–80**	130:1–2	118	11:19	343
91	397	130:5	425	11:21	302
91:9–16	**395–97**	130:6–7	218	13:13–23	343
92	79	**132:1–18**	**496–99**	14:1–3	240
92:1–4	**78**	132:11–12	417	14:27	302
92:5–11	79	**138**	**59–61**	15:33	302
92:12–15	**78**	**139:1–6**	**41–44**	16:22	326
93	**496–99**	**139:13–18**	**41–44**	16:31	231
95	383	139:14	12	19:13	319
95:8	399	139:19–20	42–43	21:9	319
100	110	142:5	110	21:19	319
103	20–21, 25–26	**145:10–18**	**184–86**	22	283
103:1–13	**24–26**	145:14	187	**22:1–2**	**282–86**, 288
103:14–18	25	**146**	**287–89**, **444–46**,	22:4	284, 302
103:21	7		**461–63**	**22:8–9**	**282–86**, 288
103:22	**24–26**	146–150	288	22:15	284, 319

Proverbs (*continued*)
22:22–23   **282–86**, 288
31:1–9   319
31:10–31   **318–22**,
324, 331–32

Song of Solomon   475
1:2   265
1:5   265
2:8–13   **264–68**
2:12–13   270
3:9   417

Isaiah   437
1–5   2
1–39   284, 424
1:1   315
1:10–17   67
1:11–17   452–53
1:17   119
2:1–4   425
4:4   349
5   146
6   128
6–39   2
6:1–8   **2–6**, 8–9, 39
6:1–13   7
6:3   8
6:3–4   11
6:6–7   349
6:8   15
6:9–10   4
6:9–13   2–4
7   3
7:14   432
8:8   432
10:1–2   387
11:10–12   404
11:18–20   **318–22**
13–27   424
13:8   488
13:14   176
20:3   392
21:3   488
24   425
24–27   424
24:1–5   425
24:23   425
25   432
25:1–5   424
25:1–9   169
25:2–3   426

25:5   426
25:6–7   426
25:6–9   **424–27**, 432, 434, 436
25:8–9   429
25:9   392
25:10–12   426
26:17–18   488
26:19   474
27:6   392
28:16   174
29:13   278
29:18   4, 410
32:3   4
35:2   285
35:4–7a   **282–86**
35:5   4, 289
35:5–6   297, 410
35:10   284
37:18   344
37:35   392
40–55   302, 414
40–66   2
40:3   278
41:8–9   392
42:1–4   302, 392
42:9   83
42:14   488
42:16   4
42:18–19   4
43:1–2   195
43:8   4
43:10   392
43:18–19   83
44:1–2   392
44:21   392
45:1   315
45:4   392
48:6   83
49   101
49:1–6   302, 392
49:3   392
50   303
50:4–7   392
50:4–9a   **300–305**
50:6–9   308
52–53   393–94
52:13   391
52:13–53:12   302, 392
53:4–12   **389–94**
53:9   417
53:11   474
54:4–8   328, 431

54:8   431
54:11–12   431
54:13   227
55:1–2   229
56:1   232
56:4–7   232
56:6–7   426
56:7   453
60:3   426
61:1–2   387
62:8–9   374
63:11   176
65:7   146
65:8–9   392
65:13–14   392
65:17   83, 430
66:7–9   488
66:18–24   426
66:22   430

Jeremiah
1:1   320
1:2   320
1:4–10   2
1:5   46
1:6   5
1:11–12   146
3:1–5   20
3:21   409
4:8   409
4:28   409
4:31   488
6:1   409
6:14   107
6:17   409
6:24   488
6:26   409
7:1–15   3
7:22–23   452
7:23   21
7:25   392
7:27   3
7:29   409
8:16   409
8:18   46
8:19   409
8:21   46
9:10   409
9:19   409
10:22   409
10:24   146
11–20   163

11:14	410	1:29	291	2:1–13	20–21, 23
11:16	409	**2:1–5**	**127–31**, 133,	2:2–6	25
11:18–20	325		137, 141	**2:14–20**	**19–23**, 25, 28, 39
11:18–12:6	4	2:10	130	3–14	20
11:20	331	3:20	283	4:1–3	21
11:21	320	8–10	128	5:4	20
12:4	409	11:19–20	28	6:6	452
13:21	488	12:1–8	110	9:1	459
14:11	410	16	20	11:8–9	20
15:10–21	4	16:1–17	328	14	23
16:5	410	16:25	459		
16:7–9	409	17	73	**Joel**	
17:14–18	4	**17:22–24**	**72**, 79, 86	2:30–31	349
18:18–23	4	23	20		
20:7–18	4	28:25	392	**Amos**	147
22:16	285	34:2–5	176	2:6–8	374
23:1–5	176	34:18–19	176	3:15	374
23:1–6	**162–67**, 169	34:23–24	392	5:1–17	374
23:5–8	404	36:26–27	28	5:6	380
25:30–31	409	36:28	21	**5:6–7**	**372–77**
26:5	392	37	128	**5:10–15**	**372–77**
29:19	392	37:25	392	5:11–13	386
30–33	46, 409	38:17	392	5:14–15	380
30:6	488	40–48	128, 146, 431	5:21–24	453
30:10	392			5:24	386
31	416	**Daniel**		6:4	374
31:7–9	**407–12**	2–6	493	7:1–6	146
31:8	415	7–12	474	7:1–8:3	4
31:12–13	410	7:3	493	**7:7–15**	**144–48**, 150
31:15	408–9	7:8	493	7:10–13	157
31:31–34	447–49	**7:9–10**	**491–95**, 498	7:14	147
31:33	28, 443	7:13	497	8:1–3	146
31:33–34	27, 448n3, 483	**7:13–14**	315, **491–95**	8:4–6	374
33:11	410	7:27	494	8:4–7	387
33:21–22	392	8–12	493	9:7	426
33:26	392	9	55		
35:15	392	10–12	475	**Jonah**	
40:9	459	10:13	477	1:1–3	5
42:6	459	11:33	392	3:10	408
44:4	392	11:35	392	4:2	408
46:27–28	392	12:1	480		
50:43	488	**12:1–3**	**472–77**	**Micah**	
		12:3	392, 480	2:1–5	4
Lamentations		12:11	488	2:6	4
3	109			3:11	4
3:1–21	110	**Hosea**		4:6–10	410
3:22–33	**108–12**, 114	1–2	22–23, 431	4:6–13	488
3:32	118	1–3	19	4:10	488
		1:2–11	20		
Ezekiel		1:6	19	**Zephaniah**	
1–2	128	1:9	19	1:13	374
1:13	349	2	19, 23, 25, 32, 328	3:19	410

Haggai
1:5–6	374
2:23	392

Zechariah
1:6	392
2:2	146
3:8	392
8:7–8	404
10:2	176

Malachi
3:1	278

NEW TESTAMENT

Matthew	447n1, 464
1:5–6	453
1:23	432
2:18–24	**353–58**
4:35–41	97
5:1–13	275
5:12	141
5:17–20	274
5:27–30	349
5:43–48	453
5:44	67
5:48	223
6:2–5	276
6:10	61, 136
6:13	183, 356
6:24	68
6:25–34	141
7:3–5	276
7:20	103
8:7	63
8:17	392
8:20	493
9:14–17	85
10:16	197
10:35–45	392
11:5	410
11:27	22
12:8	493
12:13	459
12:48–50	10
13	86
13:13–15	4
13:31–32	86
13:57	141

13:58	141
14:13–21	191
14:15	337
14:15–21	232
14:16	192
14:17	460
14:18–20	401
15:8	328
15:33	337
16:1–4	210
16:13–28	314
16:17	22
18:1–7	312
18:3–4	369
18:8–9	313
18:16	141
18:20	432
18:21–22	500
18:28	22
19:9	369
19:16–22	40
20:16	406
20:18	493
21:42	174
22:34–40	452
22:37	141, 441
22:37–39	153
23	276
23:8–9	393
24	501
25:31–40	119
25:31–46	68, 82, 104, 293
25:40	434
25:45	434
26:17–19	387
26:26–29	232
26:39	136
26:42–44	136
27:51	172
28	105
28:5–6	195
28:20	432

Mark	447n1, 464
1–5	122
1:1	314
1:1–8	160
1:2–3	278
1:4	159
1:10	140

1:11	314
1:14	105
1:14–15	469
1:16–20	387, 469
1:21	175
1:21–28	256
1:22	140n1
1:24	314
1:24–25	104
1:25	187, 315
1:27	140n1
1:28	175
1:32–33	295
1:34	85–86, 104, 123, 314–15
1:35	417
1:37	295
1:43–45	104
1:44	123
1:45	85, 295, 315
2:1–12	277, 297, 345
2:1–22	51
2:2	295
2:2–4	123
2:5	104
2:12	140n1
2:13	175
2:13–17	68
2:13–22	28, **31–35**
2:14	39
2:15–17	277
2:18–20	277
2:18–26	292
2:22	85
2:23–27	277
2:23–3:6	46, **49–53**
2:27	67
3:1–6	278
3:1–7	61
3:5	67
3:6	85, 105, 451
3:7–8	85
3:7–10	295
3:9	315
3:11	314
3:11–12	85, 104
3:12	104
3:14–15	141
3:19–35	123
3:20	295
3:20–22	104

3:20–35	60–62	6:7–11	159	8:31	308, 331, 348,
3:21	141n2	6:7–12	175		403, 469
3:21–22	141	6:7–13	157	8:31–33	332, 422
3:31–35	86, 104,	6:12	159	8:31–34	387
	141, 469	6:12–13	350	8:31–35	402, 451
3:32–35	10	6:14–15	315	8:31–9:1	420–21
3:35	421	**6:14–29**	**157–61**,	8:31–9:8	64
4	421		161n5, 368	8:33	210
4:1	175, 295	6:17–29	367	8:34	4, 157, 421, 469
4:1–20	421	6:30	157, 165	8:34–35	386, 469
4:10	85	**6:30–34**	**175–78**	8:34–38	469
4:11	85	6:30–44	160	8:35	4
4:12	4, 85	6:31	295	9	332, 349n2
4:13–20	85	6:33–34	295, 337	9:2	487
4:17	140, 349	6:34	165, 172, 192	9:2–10	332
4:18–19	105	6:35–44	175–76, 191, 232	9:9	104
4:21–22	123	6:35–52	176	9:17	368
4:22	297	6:37	192	9:23	123
4:23	86	6:38	460	9:24	123
4:26–34	79–80, **85**	6:41–42	192	9:30	349
4:27	344	6:42	296	9:30–32	420
4:35–41	98, **104–7**	6:45–52	104, 107, 176	**9:30–37**	328, **331–34**, 451
4:38	105	6:50	123	9:31	348, 469
4:40	141	**6:53–56**	165, **175–78**	9:31–32	422
4:40–41	123	6:54–56	295	9:32	123
5	421	6:51	140n1	9:33–35	387
5:1–20	68	7	279, 283, 299	9:33–37	420, 469
5:7	314	**7:1–8**	**277–81**	9:34	348
5:15	123	7:1–23	297	9:35	386, 403, 469
5:19	123, 315	7:9–13	277–78	9:36–37	348
5:20	140n1	**7:14–15**	**277–81**	9:37	368
5:21–24	68	7:17–20	277	**9:38–50**	342, **348–52**
5:21–43	118, **122–26**, 142	7:20–23	159	9:42	368
5:23	295, 368	**7:21–23**	**277–81**	9:42–50	420
5:24	295	**7:24–37**	**295–99**	9:43–47	311
5:25–34	420	7:25	368	9:49	349
5:26	345	7:28	289	10	385–87, 416
5:33	123	7:36	123	10:1–31	385
5:34	104, 110, 421	7:37	140n1	10:2–9	386
5:35–43	68	8–9	388	10:9	349
5:36	22, 110–11, 123	8–10	402	10:13–14	348
5:41	297, 421	8:11–12	210	10:13–16	385–86, 420
5:42	124, 140n1	8:22–26	385, 420	10:13–52	386
5:43	104	8:22–9:50	385	10:14	386
6:1–6	157	8:22–10:52	385, 420	10:17	374–75, 421
6:1–13	129, 137,	8:26	123	10:17–18	404
	140–43, 160	8:27–36	301	10:17–22	386, 469
6:2	175	**8:27–38**	**314–17**	**10:17–31**	**385–88**, 402, 404
6:3	161, 176	8:27–10:52	348	10:18	386, 403
6:6	140n1	8:29	420	10:19	386
6:6–30	123	8:30	104, 123	10:21	375, 379

Mark (*continued*)
10:23	380
10:23–31	386, 469
10:26	140n1
10:26–27	379
10:28	402, 469
10:28–30	421, 469
10:29–30	141, 402
10:31	469
10:32	140n1
10:32–34	332, 388, 402, 420, 469
10:32–45	385, 451
10:33–34	348
10:33–37	422
10:34	331, 385, 422
10:35–40	420, 487
10:35–45	348, 387, **402–6**, 469
10:36	421
10:38	397
10:42–45	142
10:43	396
10:43–44	386, 469
10:45	331, 469
10:46–52	385, 386, 410, **420–23**
10:47	414–15
10:48	123
10:49	386, 414
10:50–52	387
11:1–13:37	451, 468
11:10	105
11:12–14	470
11:12–24	123
11:15–19	468
11:17	140n1, 453
11:18	140n1, 451
12	386, 453
12:1–12	468
12:18–27	468
12:28–34	386, **451–55**, 468–69
12:29–30	443
12:29–31	452
12:30	441
12:30–33	153
12:31	386
12:35–44	468
12:38–44	422, 458, **468–71**
13	488, 501
13:1–2	452, 454
13:1–8	483, **487–90**
13:9–11	159
13:32	488
14:1	451
14:1–12	105
14:10–11	105
14:12–16	387
14:22–25	232
14:27	140, 349
14:29	140
14:32–41	136
14:36	403
14:43–45	105
14:61–62	493
15:5	140n1
15:9	403
15:12	403
15:22–27	403
15:34	379, 421
15:37–38	452
15:38–39	453
15:39	104
15:42–46	68
15:43	159n3
15:44	140n1
16	105
16:7	123
16:8	123, 140n1

Luke 447n1, 464
1	473
1–2	473
1:26–55	37
1:46–55	475, 480
2:10	195
2:12	194
2:52	37
4:1–13	383
4:14–21	387
4:21	437
4:24	141
4:25–26	460
4:26–27	426
5:1	191
5:16	417
5:17	68
5:33–39	85
6:6–8	67
6:6–11	67
6:23	141
6:27–36	67
6:36	21
6:58	261
7:22	410
8:9–10	4
8:20–21	10
9:10	175
9:10–17	191, 232
9:12–17	337
9:13	192, 460
9:18–27	314
9:49–50	350
9:51	304
10:21	417
10:25–28	452
10:25–37	68, 104, 453
10:27	441
10:28	22
11:16	210
12:13–21	180
13:16	427
13:18–19	86
13:31–33	158
13:33–34	141
14:4–14	291
16	464
18:1–8	291
18:11	187
18:13	187
19:1–10	387
19:9	427, 437
21	501
21:1–4	460
22:7–13	387
22:17–19	192
22:17–20	232
23:6–12	158
23:43	437
24	105

John 447n1, 464
1	226
1–12	435
1:1	192, 436, 507
1:1–5	363
1:1–14	364
1:4	192
1:12	210, 466
1:14	192, 381
2:14–21	16
3	11
3–4	507
3:1–8	11, 466

3:1–17	**14–18**	8:12	193	18:36–37	176		
3:4	242	8:17	141	18:38	242, 509		
3:5–6	11	8:31–33	325	19:7	228		
3:16	193, 210,	8:34	193	19:12	228		
	243, 399,	8:45–47	506	19:14–16	228		
	435–36, 466	8:47	506	19:38–42	15–16		
3:17	344	9:1–3	343	20	105		
3:20–35	**67–71**	9:1–11	435	20:1	436		
3:31–36	506	9:2	163	20:5–7	436		
3:36	437	9:2–3	354	20:28	436		
4:9–15	211	**10:2–16**	**367–71**	20:30	226		
4:11	242	10:7	193	20:30–31	194, 263		
4:14	243	10:10	450, 466	20:31	210		
4:44	141	10:10–11	435	21	263		
5:1–15	435	10:11	193				
5:1–47	191	10:11–16	176	**Acts**			
5:8	344	10:22–39	191	1:8–9	5		
5:17–23	436	10:26–27	506	2:3	349		
5:24	437	10:27–28	243, 436	2:4	239		
5:24–29	436	10:28–29	193	2:5	152		
6	226–27, 260	10:30	436	2:13	83		
6:1–21	180, **191–95**	11:1–16	435	2:15–19	152		
6:1–23	209	11:1–12:11	435	4:4	152		
6:2	435	11:21	435	5:36	210		
6:5–13	337	11:24	437	7:52	141		
6:5–15	232	11:25	193, 243	8:1–3	117		
6:9	460	11:25–26	435	8:32–33	392		
6:11	193	11:25–27	435	9:10–18	40		
6:13	346	11:32	435	10	279		
6:15	227	**11:32–44**	432, 434,	10:44–46	119		
6:20	211		**435–38**	11:17–18	119		
6:22–23	175	11:45–46	436	11:27–30	117		
6:24–35	**209–13**	11:45-53	436	12:1–4	117		
6:25–35	198	11:52	193	13:32–33	399		
6:25–59	206	12:1–8	435	15:7–11	272		
6:25–71	191–92	12:24	46	15:11	320		
6:26	198	12:31	256	15:20	272		
6:29	198	13:34–35	453	15:28–29	119		
6:31–35	192	14:6	193, 466–67	15:29	272		
6:33	198	15	259	19:1–7	337		
6:35	193, 198, 217,	15:1	193	19:35	470		
	226–29	15:1–8	349	21:25	272		
6:36–71	211	15:5	174	26:6	152		
6:41–51	**226–29**	15:13	436	27:20	344		
6:48	192	15:15	198, 436	27:22	343		
6:51	192	17:11	417	27:25	343		
6:51–58	**242–45**	17:12	193				
6:54	228	17:20–21	417	**Romans**	40		
6:56–58	250	17:21–22	193	1:16	22		
6:56–69	255, **259–73**	18:33	497	2:14–16	82		
7:1–52	191	**18:33–37**	501–2, **505–9**	2:15	22		
7:45–52	15–16	18:36	210	3:2	152		

Romans (*continued*)
3:5	137
3:7–9	137
3:8	135
3:9–20	313
3:20	22
3:22	291
3:23	466
3:23–24	153
4:1–3	293
4:9–12	293
4:15	22
5:8	466
6:3–5	82
6:3–11	46
6:10	417
6:11–14	68
6:23	68, 466
7:7–8	28
7:12	28
8	11, 135
8:1	10
8:6	136
8:12–17	**10–13**
8:18	136
8:20–22	153
8:26–27	136
8:27	381
8:28–29	136
8:29	100
8:31	136
8:34	416
8:38–39	106
11:1–2	27
12:1–2	82
12:2	48
12:4–8	206
13–14	101
13:11–14	255
13:14	239
14:10	82
14:18	82
15:25–27	120
15:26	117
16:3	100
16:9	100
16:21	100

1 Corinthians
1–4	100
1:18–25	118, 142, 327, 469
1:18–31	137
1:20	470
1:24	136, 232
1:30	303
2:5	84
3:1–17	329
3:9	100
3:10–15	82
3:13	349
3:18	84, 137
4:4–5	82
4:5	381
4:10	84
6:9–10	278
6:19–20	164
7:6	119
8–10	278
9:3–15	142
11:24	192–93
11:29–30	343
12:9	62
12:12–28	206
12:13	174
12:27	152
13:1–3	118
13:1–14:1	137
13:13	286
14:12	118
15	474, 501
15:1–28	63
15:3–6	466
15:14	101
15:15	344
15:25–28	365
15:26	426
15:35	135
15:40	84
15:45	365
15:50–54	135
15:50–57	176
15:51	427
15:54	425
15:54–55	427
15:58	101, 255
16:1–4	117
16:13	137, 255

2 Corinthians
1–7	64
1:8–9	45–46
1:12–2:13	100
1:12–7:16	117
1:19–20	46
2:3–4	136
2:11–7:16	62
2:12–7:16	64
2:15–16	27
2:17	27, 135
3	45
3:1–6	**27–30**
3:1–18	62
3:3	32
3:4–6	137
3:6	22
3:18	137
4–5	64
4:1	45, 62, 101, 137
4:2	137
4:5	136
4:5–12	**45–48**, 62
4:7	136
4:8	137, 274
4:10	274
4:13–5:1	**62–66**
4:15	101, 118
4:16–18	81
5	137
5:1	84
5:1–5	81
5:1–6	64
5:5	81
5:6	101
5:6–17	**81**
5:8	101
5:16–21	100–101, 427
5:18–19	82–83
5:19	45
5:20–21	100
6	101
6:1	101
6:1–13	**100–103**
7	137
7:2	102
7:2–16	100
7:6	62
7:16	81
8	119, 121, 180
8:2–4	117
8:5	118
8:6	117
8:7	118
8:7–15	**117–21**
8:23	100, 117
9:1–2	117

10–13	62, 64, 100, 117
10:1	81
10:10	135
10:12	135
10:12–17	137
11:2	135
11:6	135
11:13–14	135
11:19–20	135
11:21–30	135
11:23–27	45
11:23–33	101
11:24–27	47
12	137
12:1	135, 137
12:2–10	**135–39**
12:2–12	152
12:8–10	142
12:9–10	101, 382
12:11	138
12:12	137
12:14	137
12:19	137
12:20	135
13:1	141
13:4	136, 142

Galatians

1:15	46
2:9–10	117
3:1–5	101
3:6–9	293
3:22	291
3:24–25	28
3:26–29	152
3:28	118
4:7	11
5:14	291, 293
5:19–21	278
5:22–23	84, 86
5:22–26	11
6:2	274, 293
6:15	83
6:17	47

Ephesians

1–3	205, 222
1:3	153, 437
1:3–14	**152–56**, 171
1:8–10	208
1:13	187
1:15–23	171

1:17–19	152, 187
1:18	187
1:21	255
1:22–23	255
1:23	188
2:1–2	187
2:1–10	171, 437
2:4	224
2:6	188, 205, 255
2:8	153
2:8–9	466
2:9	240
2:11–12	153
2:11–13	152
2:11–14	152
2:11–22	**171–74**, 467
2:13	187
2:15	239
2:17	153
2:21–22	153, 188
3:6	153
3:10	153, 224, 240, 255
3:13	190
3:14–21	**187–90**, 192, 207
3:20	188
4	224
4–6	205, 222
4:1	153, 207
4:1–6	153
4:1–16	**205–8**
4:2	224
4:14	153
4:15–16	224
4:16	153
4:17–24	153
4:22–24	224
4:24	222
4:25–5:2	**222–25**
4:32–5:2	225
5:1–14	238
5:8–9	255
5:8–11	223
5:10	82
5:14	240
5:15	232
5:15–20	**238–41**
5:21	233
5:22	328
5:27	188
6	249
6:10–20	**254–58**
6:11–17	153

6:12	260
6:17	381

Philippians

1:19	346
2:1–8	142
2:4	118
2:5–11	223
2:6–8	118
2:6–11	291
3:6	28
4:10–20	118
4:18	82

Colossians

1:12	152
1:13	437
1:16	223
1:16–20	153
2:9–14	437
2:18	363
3:1	437
3:5–8	278
3:5–17	84
3:18	328

1 Thessalonians 27

1:6	117
2:3–12	142
2:4	381
2:14	117
2:15	141
4:13–17	437
4:15–5:11	501
5:4–5	223
5:6–8	255
5:21	268
5:23	210

2 Thessalonians 27

1:8	349
2:3–12	487

1 Timothy

1:1	119
2:11–15	58

2 Timothy

2:9	343
3:2–5	278
4:5	343

Titus
2:5 — 328

Hebrews — 449
1 — 449
1:1–4 — **362–66**
1:1–3:3 — 465
1:2–3 — 401
1:5 — 399
1:6–8 — 363
1:14 — 363
2:2 — 363
2:5–12 — **362–66**
2:6 — 361
2:9 — 361
2:10 — 399
2:10–11 — 467
2:10–18 — 467
2:14 — 363
2:17 — 382–83, 398, 465
2:18 — 362
3:1 — 382–83, 398, 465
4:7 — 399
4:12–16 — **381–84**
4:14–15 — 398, 465
4:14–16 — 448
4:15 — 467
4:15–16 — 465
4:16 — 379
5:1–10 — **398–401**
5:2 — 382
5:5 — 465
5:5–10 — 465
5:7–9 — 465
5:8–9 — 397
5:10 — 465
6:4–6 — 362
6:12 — 399
6:20 — 399, 465
7 — 465
7:1 — 399
7:1–10:18 — 466
7:3 — 416
7:10 — 399
7:11 — 399
7:15 — 399
7:17 — 417
7:19 — 328
7:21 — 417
7:23–28 — **416–19**
7:26 — 465
7:28 — 382, 399

8:1 — 399, 417, 465
8:8–12 — 448
8:10–12 — 483
9 — 362
9:4–5 — 153
9:5 — 464
9:11 — 399, 465
9:11–14 — 447n2, 452, 465
9:11–23 — 464
9:12 — 417
9:24–28 — 447n2, **464–67**
10:10 — 417
10:11–25 — **482–86**
10:14 — 382
10:16–17 — 448n3
10:18 — 467
10:19–25 — 448
10:20 — 467
10:26–39 — 483
10:27 — 484
10:32–34 — 362
10:35 — 362
10:39 — 484
11 — 154
11:8–19 — 293
11:34 — 382
11:38 — 105
12:1 — 154
12:1–2 — 465
12:2 — 365, 382, 400
12:14 — 417
12:25 — 362
13:2 — 293
13:6 — 81
13:8 — 418
13:15–16 — 448
13:22 — 362, 381, 465

James
1 — 293
1–2 — 312
1:1–2 — 272, 290
1:2 — 274, 311
1:4 — 272–74, 417
1:4–5 — 326
1:5 — 327, 329
1:5–6 — 343–44
1:5–8 — 312
1:6 — 326–27
1:6–8 — 327
1:8 — 291, 345
1:12–16 — 272

1:13 — 275
1:14–15 — 290
1:14–16 — 275
1:15 — 292
1:16 — 275
1:17 — 327, 329
1:17–27 — **272–76**
1:18 — 310, 312
1:18–19 — 293
1:19–20 — 310
1:19–21 — 346
1:21 — 310, 312
1:22 — 266, 271, 293
1:24–27 — 292
1:25 — 266, 290–91, 293
1:26 — 310, 312
1:27 — 272, 290, 310–11
2:1–7 — 231, 327
2:1–10 — 275, 289
2:1–13 — 346
2:1–17 — **290–94**
2:5–7 — 329
2:8 — 311
2:10 — 311
2:14–17 — 273, 275, 289, 310
2:15–16 — 328
2:17 — 283
2:18–20 — 273
2:18–26 — 293
2:19 — 86, 326
2:23 — 273, 311
2:26 — 345
3:1 — 329
3:1–12 — 301, **310–13**, 327
3:5 — 329
3:5–6 — 275
3:5–12 — 328
3:6 — 272
3:8–12 — 275
3:9 — 291
3:13 — 273, 312
3:13–16 — 310
3:13–4:3 — **326–30**, 333
3:14–16 — 346
3:17 — 310
3:17–18 — 313
4:1–2 — 275, 346
4:3 — 346
4:4 — 272, 328
4:5 — 328
4:6 — 187

4:7–8	333
4:7–8a	**326–30**
4:8	291, 328
4:10	187
4:11–12	346
5:1–6	275, 346
5:1–8	343
5:4–6	291
5:6	345
5:8–9	344
5:10	343
5:11	343
5:13–20	**343–47**, 350
5:14–15	293
5:20	273

1 Peter — 447n1, 464
1:19	417
2:9	401
2:21–25	392
2:22	417
3:1	328
5:5–6	187
5:13	105

1 John
2:1	416
2:9	223
2:18	487
3:18	243
4:1	40

2 John
7	487

Revelation — 437, 464, 484
1:1	430
1:1–4	500
1:3	447
1:3–14	447
1:4	432, 502
1:4–6	401
1:4b–8	**500–504**
1:8	430, 432–33
1:9–20	501
1:17	433
2:2–4	154
2:17	447
3:1	447
3:1–19	447
3:10–12	431
3:20	466

3:21	432
4:1–11	432
4:1–13	447
4:8	430, 432
4:14–7:28	447
4:14–10:18	447
5–18	430
5:4	272
6:10	487
7:9–17	432–33
7:17	176, 427
8:1–7	447
8:8–12	447
9–10	447–49
9:11–14	**447–50**
11:17	432
11:19	430
12:2–6	489
13	432, 500
13:11–18	487
15:3	432
16:7	432
17	432, 500
17:7–14	488
18	432
19:4	432
19:6	430, 432
19:7	431
19:9	431
19:11–20:15	430
19:11–21	488
20:10	349
20:11–15	433
21	503
21:1	429
21:1–6a	**430–34**, 436
21:3–4	425, 429
21:4	427
21:5–7	432
21:6	429
21:6–22:7	430
21:9–22:5	431–32
21:22	432
22:3–5	432
22:13	433

OT APOCRYPHA

Tobit
13:16–17	431

Additions to Esther — 336

Wisdom of Solomon
1:16–2:1	332
2:12–22	332
2:13	331
3:1–9	432
7:22	363
9:9	363
16:20	210

Sirach (Ecclesiasticus)
1:4	363
1:14	326

Baruch
1–2	55

OT PSEUDEPIGRAPHA

Ascension of Isaiah
6–11	488

2 Baruch
26	487
27	488
29:8	210
70	488
83	488

4 Ezra (2 Esdras)
4:33–37	487
4:40	488–89
4:41–42	489
5:46–49	489
11–12	488
13	488
13:31	488

Testament of Levi
2–5	488

DEAD SEA SCROLLS

Hodayot (Thanksgiving Hymns)
1QH 3.7–12	488

Serek Hayahad (Community Rule)
1QS 9.10–11	192

Comprehensive Scripture Index for Year B

Scripture citations that appear in boldface represent the assigned readings from the Revised Common Lectionary:

ABBREVIATIONS

B1   Year B, Volume 1
B2   Year B, Volume 2
B3   Year B, Volume 3

OLD TESTAMENT

Genesis   198 (B2)
1   180 (B1); 50, 313, 365 (B3)
1–11   25 (B2)
1:1–2   31 (B1)
1:1–2:4a   168–70 (B1); 25, 317 (B2); 430 (B3)
1:1–5   **168–71**, 172, 176 (B1)
1:1–31   363 (B3)
1:2   67 (B1); 271, 329 (B2); 55 (B3)
1:3–4   313 (B3)
1:4   185 (B1)
1:5   147 (B1)
1:6–8   3, 169 (B1)
1:8–31   152 (B3)
1:26–27   312 (B3)
1:28   354 (B3)
1:31   14 (B1)
2:1–3   305 (B1)
2:1–4   38 (B3)
2:2   60 (B2)
2:2–3   43 (B3)
2:4b–25   169 (B1)
2:5   169 (B1)
2:7   4 (B1); 215, 320, 329 (B2); 345, 355 (B3)
2:9   302 (B2)
2:18–24   361, 367 (B3)
2:23   330 (B2)
2:24   192 (B1); 267 (B3)

2:25   382 (B3)
3   171 (B1); 63, 356 (B3)
3:1–7   77 (B2)
3:8–15   **54–58**, 60, 63 (B3)
3:8–20   57 (B3)
3:8–21   62 (B3)
3:11–15   77 (B2)
3:16   356 (B3)
3:23   56 (B3)
4:9   240 (B2)
5:24   311 (B1)
6–9   25, 310 (B2)
6:6–7   408 (B3)
6:9   4 (B1)
8:8–12   199 (B1)
9:1–17   21 (B3)
9:15   296 (B1)
11:1–9   292 (B2)
11:6   221 (B2)
11:26   40 (B2)
12   399 (B3)
12–50   40 (B2)
12:1–2   210 (B1)
12:1–3   70 (B1); 143 (B2); 86 (B3)
12:3   232 (B1)
12:8   146 (B3)
12:10–20   41 (B2)
14   416 (B3)
14:1–20   168 (B2)
14:17–21   399 (B3)
14:19   143 (B2)
14:20   4 (B1)
15   40 (B2)
15:5   245 (B1)
15:13   144 (B2)
16:1–4   41 (B2)
16:10   245 (B1)
16:13   382 (B3)
17   399 (B3)

17:1–7   **39–43** (B2)
17:9–14   60 (B2)
17:15–16   **39–43** (B2)
17:16   45 (B2)
17:17   40–41 (B2)
18   47 (B2); 293 (B3)
18:10   40 (B2)
18:13   40 (B2)
20:1–3   41 (B2)
22:1–14   143 (B2)
22:1–18   154 (B3)
22:2   56 (B2)
22:12   56 (B2)
22:16   56 (B2)
22:16–17   417 (B3)
23   52 (B1)
25   70 (B1)
25:1–2   41 (B2)
26:3   417 (B3)
28:10–17   196 (B1); 143 (B2)
28:10–19   195 (B1)
28:15–17   197 (B1)
29   146 (B3)
31:39   246 (B2)
31:42   143 (B2)
32:22–28   143 (B2)
32:22–31   186 (B1)
32:28   196 (B1); 40 (B2)
33   274 (B1)
35:8   441 (B3)
38   180 (B3)
41:1–11   169 (B1)
47:6   319 (B3)
50   274 (B1)

Exodus   447 (B3)
2:23–24   144 (B2)
3   147 (B2)
3–4   210 (B1)
3:1   246 (B2)
3:5   409 (B3)

Exodus (*continued*)
3:6 — 230 (B2)
3:7 — 18 (B2)
3:13 — 143 (B2)
3:14 — 88, 309 (B2); 193, 198, 314, 503 (B3)
4:1–5 — 78 (B2)
4:13 — 5 (B3)
4:22–23 — 29 (B1)
4:25 — 459 (B3)
6:6 — 136 (B1)
6:7 — 21 (B3)
6:33 — 210 (B3)
7:8–13 — 78 (B2)
12 — 147–49 (B2)
12–15 — 154 (B2)
12:1–14 — **143–47** (B2)
12:1–29 — 72 (B2)
12:27 — 144 (B2)
12:29 — 146 (B2)
12:31–34 — 144 (B2)
12:40 — 144 (B2)
13:17 — 408 (B3)
13:21–22 — 314 (B1); 211 (B2)
14 — 56, 227 (B3)
14:15–31 — 30 (B1)
14:17–20 — 465 (B3)
14:21 — 310 (B1)
14:21–15:19 — 176, 193 (B3)
15 — 270 (B2); 202 (B3)
15:1–8 — 210 (B1)
15:11 — 8 (B1)
15:13 — 136 (B1)
15:14 — 8 (B1)
15:22–26 — 337 (B3)
15:24 — 198 (B3)
16 — 38, 120, 192, 206, 227 (B3)
16:2–4 — **196–200**, 202, 210 (B3)
16:2–8 — 120 (B2)
16:2–15 — 206 (B3)
16:9–15 — **196–200**, 202, 210 (B3)
16:10 — 55 (B2)
16:18 — 199 (B3)
16:20 — 202 (B3)
16:22–30 — 304 (B1)
16:31 — 198 (B3)
17:1–7 — 120 (B2)
17:3 — 198 (B3)

18:13–27 — 141 (B3)
18:21 — 319 (B3)
19 — 313 (B2)
19–24 — 26 (B2)
19:16–23 — 59 (B2)
19:18 — 314 (B1)
19:22 — 328 (B3)
19:24–25 — 60 (B2)
20 — 73 (B2)
20:1–11 — 66 (B2)
20:1–17 — **59–63**, 65 (B2)
20:1–18 — 38 (B3)
20:8 — 293 (B1)
20:8–11 — 294, 304, 307 (B1); 43 (B3)
20:11 — 305 (B1); 46 (B3)
20:12–17 — 66 (B2)
20:17 — 41 (B2); 374 (B3)
20:18 — 55–56 (B2)
20:18–21 — 60, 62 (B2)
20:19 — 55 (B2)
20:20 — 60 (B2); 193 (B3)
22:13 — 246 (B2)
23:16 — 313 (B2)
23:20 — 30 (B1)
24 — 425 (B3)
24:3–8 — 315 (B1)
24:4 — 92 (B2)
24:12 — 92 (B2)
25:1–31:11 — 447 (B3)
25:30 — 7 (B1)
26 — 52 (B1)
28–29 — 399 (B3)
31:14 — 293 (B1)
31:16 — 25 (B2)
31:18 — 92 (B2)
32–34 — 20 (B3)
32:12 — 408 (B3)
32:13 — 417 (B3)
32:15–16 — 92 (B2)
32:22–32 — 169 (B1)
33:11 — 323 (B1)
33:19 — 382 (B3)
34 — 300 (B1)
34:5–6 — 200 (B1)
34:6 — 278, 282 (B1); 3–4 (B2)
34:6–7 — 272 (B1); 110 (B3)
34:28 — 59 (B2)
34:29–30 — 56 (B2)
34:29–35 — 27 (B3)
34:30 — 328 (B3)

34:35 — 56 (B2)
34:40 — 56 (B2)
36 — 52 (B1)
36:1–40:38 — 447 (B3)
40:34 — 153 (B1)

Leviticus — 447 (B3)
2:4 — 180 (B3)
6:2 — 387 (B3)
8–9 — 399 (B3)
10:3 — 328 (B3)
11:6–11 — 193 (B1)
12:2 — 248 (B3)
12:2–6 — 130 (B1)
12:4–5 — 248 (B3)
12:7–8 — 248 (B3)
12:8 — 130 (B1)
13 — 258 (B1)
13:2–3 — 258 (B1)
13:27 — 258 (B1)
13:45 — 258 (B1)
14 — 258 (B1)
15:19–30 — 248 (B3)
15:25–27 — 124 (B3)
16 — 447n1, 449 (B3)
17–26 — 193 (B1)
17:11 — 108 (B1)
17:11–12 — 193 (B1)
18:6–19 — 459 (B3)
18:16 — 158 (B3)
18:22 — 193 (B1)
19:9–15 — 193 (B1)
19:13 — 387 (B3)
19:18 — 157 (B2); 291, 386, 451, 453–54 (B3)
19:19 — 193 (B1)
19:35 — 387 (B3)
20:21 — 158 (B3)
21:16–23 — 248 (B3)
25:1–13 — 274 (B3)
25:10 — 35 (B1)
25:47–49 — 308 (B3)
26:14–17 — 241 (B1)

Numbers
3:38 — 84 (B1)
6:5 — 476 (B3)
11–25 — 76 (B2)
11:1–3 — 76 (B2)
11:1–12:15 — 120 (B2)
11:4–6 — **335–39**, 342, 350 (B3)

11:4–9	192 (B3)	6–11	441 (B3)
11:10–16	**335–39**, 342,	**6:1–9**	**439–43**, 453 (B3)
	350 (B3)	6:2	446 (B3)
11:16–30	242 (B3)	6:3	459 (B3)
11:24–29	**335–39**, 342,	6:4	56(B2); 386,
	350 (B3)		458 (B3)
12:7–8	392 (B3)	6:4–5	386, 446, 451,
14	107 (B1); 76 (B2);		454 (B3)
	73 (B3)	6:4–6	221 (B1)
14:1–35	120 (B2)	6:5	294 (B1); 386 (B3)
14:10	55 (B2)	6:7	446 (B3)
16	76 (B2)	6:18	84 (B1)
16:1–35	120 (B2)	7:6	117 (B1)
16:41–50	120 (B2)	7:15	241 (B1)
17–18	399 (B3)	8:1	84 (B1)
18:1–7	210 (B1)	8:3	117 (B1); 192,
19:16–18	331 (B2)		211 (B3)
20:2–13	120 (B2)	8:15	78 (B2)
20:22–29	76 (B2)	8:16	192 (B3)
21	87 (B2)	9:5	84 (B1)
21:1–3	76 (B2)	9:26	136 (B1)
21:4–9	84, 88, 120,	10:4	59 (B2)
	76–80 (B2)	10:15	210 (B1)
22:22–35	489 (B3)	10:16	42 (B2)
27:17	246 (B2); 176 (B3)	10:18	232 (B3)
33:38	31 (B2)	11:9	84 (B1)
		11:21	84 (B1)
Deuteronomy	77 (B2)	12:11	52 (B1)
1:3	31 (B2)	13:7	85 (B1)
1:8	84 (B1)	14:2	117 (B1)
1:26–38	399 (B3)	15:9	296 (B1)
2:14	84 (B1)	15:11	320 (B3)
4:1–2	**264–68** (B3)	15:12–18	35 (B1)
4:2	271 (B3)	16:9–12	313 (B2)
4:3	441 (B3)	17:14–15	58 (B3)
4:6–9	**264–68** (B3)	18	215 (B1)
4:9	296 (B1)	18:14–15	214 (B1)
4:13	59 (B2)	18:15	217 (B1); 56 (B2);
4:40	459 (B3)		192 (B3)
5	296 (B1); 43 (B3)	**18:15–20**	**214–17**, 226 (B1)
5:6–21	294 (B1); 60,	18:15–22	47 (B1)
	61 (B2); 441 (B3)	18:22	216–17 (B1)
5:12	298 (B1)	19:15	141 (B3)
5:12–15	**293–96**, 307 (B1);	21:4–9	82 (B2)
	36–40, 44, 46,	21:15–17	310 (B1)
	50 (B3)	21:23	220 (B2)
5:14	298 (B1)	22:30	459 (B3)
5:15	299 (B1); 43 (B3)	23:1	250, 259 (B2)
5:16	459 (B3)	23:1–3	232, 248 (B3)
5:21	374 (B3)	23:3–6	245 (B1)
5:22–27	214 (B1)	24:1–4	367 (B3)
5:33	441, 459 (B3)	25:5–6	457 (B3)

25:6	283 (B3)
26:3	84 (B1)
28:1–68	343 (B3)
28:11	84 (B1)
28:20–22	241 (B1)
28:30–33	84 (B1)
28:30–44	374 (B3)
28:48–68	374 (B3)
28:49	85 (B1)
28:57	459 (B3)
30:20	84 (B1)
31:7	84 (B1)
31:8	195 (B3)
33:2	8 (B1)
34:5–7	56 (B2)
34:9	249 (B3)
34:10	215 (B1)
Joshua	60 (B2); 56,
	145 (B3)
1:2	392 (B3)
1:7	392 (B3)
2:1–24	246 (B1)
2:8–14	294 (B3)
3:1–17	30 (B1)
3:14–17	37 (B2)
5:6	84 (B1)
5:12	192 (B3)
6	145 (B3)
7:1–26	246 (B1)
8:3	319 (B3)
9:1–27	246 (B1)
9:9–10	246 (B1)
10	145 (B3)
23:1	249 (B3)
24	247–48, 252 (B3)
24:1–2	**246–50** (B3)
24:2	249 (B3)
24:3–13	247 (B3)
24:14–18	**246–50** (B3)
24:15	261 (B3)
Judges	60 (B2); 56,
	145 (B3)
2:15	84 (B1)
3:24	459 (B3)
3:29	319 (B3)
7	69 (B1); 56 (B3)
7:1–9	70 (B1)
7:20	70 (B1)
8:28	37 (B3)
11:12	225 (B1)

Judges (*continued*)
13:5 — 37 (B3)
14 — 119 (B1)
17–21 — 37 (B3)
19 — 474 (B3)
19–21 — 43 (B3)
20:1 — 215n1 (B3)
20:44 — 319 (B3)
20:46 — 319 (B3)
21 — 474 (B3)

Ruth — 176 (B1); 470, 745 (B3)
1:1–5 — 445, 462 (B3)
1:1–18 — **439–43**, 453 (B3)
1:6 — 459, 462 (B3)
1:8 — 457 (B3)
1:11–13 — 457 (B3)
1:13 — 445 (B3)
1:15–18 — 469 (B3)
1:20–21 — 440 (B3)
1:22 — 462 (B3)
2 — 441 (B3)
2:1 — 319 (B3)
2:1–2 — 457 (B3)
2:8–9 — 457 (B3)
2:20–22 — 457 (B3)
3–4 — 460 (B3)
3:1–5 — 319, 453, **456–60**, 462 (B3)
3:10–11 — 457 (B3)
3:11 — 443 (B3)
4:1–4 — 308 (B3)
4:11–12 — 245 (B1)
4:13 — 462 (B3)
4:13–15 — 469 (B3)
4:13–17 — **456–60** (B3)
4:14–15 — 459 (B3)
4:15 — 440, 458 (B3)
4:16–17 — 462 (B3)
4:17 — 459 (B3)
4:17–22 — 453 (B3)

1 Samuel — 184 (B1); 60 (B2); 56, 129, 145–46, 475 (B3)
1 — 185 (B1); 37 (B3)
1–2 — 475 (B3)
1:4–20 — **472–77** (B3)
1:5 — 310 (B1); 479 (B3)
1:9–19 — 189 (B1)

1:11 — 479 (B3)
2:1–10 — 41 (B1); 37, 473, **478–81** (B3)
2:11–17 — 43 (B3)
2:12–17 — 184 (B1)
2:22–25 — 184 (B1)
2:26 — 37 (B3)
3 — 185 (B1); 37, 42, 473 (B3)
3:1 — 189 (B1); 43 (B3)
3:1–20 — **183–87**, 192 (B1); **36–40** (B3)
3:4 — 43 (B3)
3:10 — 304 (B3)
3:10–11 — 189 (B1)
3:18–19 — 189 (B1)
3:19–4:1 — 38 (B3)
3:20 — 215n1 (B3)
4–7 — 145 (B3)
4:1 — 37 (B3)
5:9 — 241 (B1)
7 — 56 (B3)
7:1–11 — 62 (B1)
7:15 — 473 (B3)
7:16 — 62 (B1)
8 — 185 (B1); 73, 232 (B3)
8–9 — 74 (B3)
8:1–18 — 37 (B3)
8:1–9:2 — 127 (B3)
8:4–7 — 161 (B2)
8:4–11 — **54–58** (B3)
8:9–20 — 86 (B3)
9 — 73 (B3)
9–10 — 473 (B3)
9:2 — 75 (B3)
9:3–10:16 — 127 (B3)
10 — 185 (B1)
10:1 — 111 (B2)
10:17–26 — 127 (B3)
10:27 — 127 (B3)
11:1–8 — 234 (B3)
11:1–15 — 127 (B3)
11:12 — 234 (B3)
11:14–15 — **53–58** (B3)
12 — 185 (B1); 473 (B3)
13:14 — 443 (B3)
15 — 74 (B3)
15–16 — 473 (B3)
15:17 — 210 (B1)

15:22 — 452 (B3)
15:24–31 — 185 (B1)
15:34–16:13 — **72**, 80 (B3)
16 — 52, 185 (B1)
16–31 — 110 (B3)
16:1–13 — 127,169 (B3)
16:14–23 — 421 (B3)
16:21–23 — 91 (B3)
17 — 98 (B3)
17:1 — **89–95** (B3)
17:4–11 — **89–95** (B3)
17:19–23 — **89–95** (B3)
17:32–49 — **89–95** (B3)
17:34 — 246 (B2)
17:55–58 — 128 (B3)
18:20 — 147 (B3)
19:11–17 — 147 (B3)
21:1–6 — 49 (B3)
21:6 — 7 (B1)
23 — 325 (B3)
24:3 — 459 (B3)
25:44 — 147 (B3)
27–29 — 91 (B3)
31 — 111, 129 (B3)

2 Samuel — 184 (B1); 60 (B2); 56, 128–29, 146, 475 (B3)
1:1 — **108–12**, 115 (B3)
1:14 — 130 (B3)
1:17–27 — **108–12**, 115 (B3)
1:26 — 118 (B3)
2:1–7 — 127, 129 (B3)
3 — 146 (B3)
3:9 — 84 (B1)
3:10 — 215n1 (B3)
3:15–16 — 147 (B3)
3:18 — 391 (B3)
3:21–23 — 180 (B3)
4 — 128 (B3)
4:4 — 296 (B1)
5 — 128 (B3)
5:1–5 — **127–31**, 134 (B3)
5:2 — 246 (B2)
5:9–10 — **127–31**, 134 (B3)
6 — 150 (B3)
6:1–5 — **144–48**, 153 (B3)
6:1–15 — 51 (B1)
6:6–11 — 145 (B3)
6:12–19 — **144–48**, 153 (B3)
6:20 — 147 (B3)

6:20–23	146 (B3)	23:1	497 (B3)
7	52, 57–58, 67 (B1); 492–93 (B3)	**23:1–7**	**491–95**, 493n1, 501 (B3)
7:1–11	**51–55** (B1)	24:2	215n1 (B3)
7:1–14	**162–67**, 170, 172, 176 (B3)	24:15	215n1 (B3)
7:5	391 (B3)	**1 Kings**	184 (B1); 60 (B2); 56, 475 (B3)
7:8	391 (B3)	1:5–2:35	320 (B3)
7:9–11	57 (B1)	2	233, 239, 242 (B3)
7:12–16	248 (B3)	2–3	231, 236 (B3)
7:13–14	29 (B1)	2:9	233 (B3)
7:14	57 (B1)	**2:10–12**	**230–34** (B3)
7:14–16	57 (B1)	3	234 (B3)
7:15	165 (B3)	**3:3–14**	**230–34** (B3)
7:16	**51–55** (B1)	3:5	242 (B3)
9	274 (B1)	3:12	239 (B3)
11	52 (B1)	3:15	234 (B3)
11–12	75 (B3)	4:25	215n1 (B3)
11:1–15	**179–83**, 199 (B3)	4:31	170 (B3)
11:26–12:13	**196–200**, 203 (B3)	7:48	7 (B1)
12	163 (B3)	**8:1**	**246–50** (B3)
12–14	51 (B1)	8:1–66	253 (B3)
12:1–13	206 (B3)	8:5	248 (B3)
12:1–14	52 (B1)	**8:6**	**246–50** (B3)
12:1–23	198 (B1)	**8:10–11**	**246–50** (B3)
12:15	241 (B1)	8:12	186 (B1)
13	218 (B3)	8:13	231, 248 (B3)
14:1	218 (B3)	8:16	248 (B3)
15–18	75 (B3)	**8:22–30**	**246–50** (B3)
16	51 (B1)	8:31–46	250 (B3)
16:10	225 (B1)	**8:41–43**	**246–50** (B3)
17:11	215n1 (B3)	8:56	250 (B3)
18	221 (B3)	10:2	155 (B1)
18:5–9	**214–18** (B3)	11:13	391 (B3)
18:14–15	215, 218 (B3)	11:32	391 (B3)
18:15	**214–18** (B3)	11:34	391 (B3)
18:16–29	215 (B3)	11:36	391 (B3)
18:19–23	218 (B3)	11:38	391 (B3)
18:28–32	180 (B3)	12	146 (B3)
18:29–30	218 (B3)	12:4	69 (B1)
18:31–33	**214–18** (B3)	14:8	391 (B3)
19	216 (B3)	15:11	161 (B2)
19:1–2	216 (B3)	15:26	184 (B1); 161 (B2)
19:4	216 (B3)	15:34	184 (B1)
19:5	215 (B3)	16:7	184 (B1)
19:5–8	218 (B3)	16:25	184 (B1)
19:22	225 (B1)	16:29–33	458 (B3)
20:12–13	85 (B1)	16:30	184 (B1)
21:19	91 (B3)	17:1–6	310 (B1)
		17:1–7	458 (B3)

17:7–24	426 (B3)
17:8–16	**456–60** (B3)
17:12	463 (B3)
17:14	469 (B3)
17:16	463 (B3)
17:18	225 (B1)
18	217 (B3)
18:20–40	215 (B3)
18:46	215 (B3)
19	55 (B2)
19:3	217 (B3)
19:3–5	215 (B3)
19:4–8	**214–18** (B3)
19:10	217 (B3)
19:11	329 (B2)
19:12	324 (B1); 217 (B3)
19:18	217 (B3)
19:19	310 (B1)
19:21	217 (B3)
22	19 (B1)
22:3	84 (B1)
22:17	246 (B2); 176 (B3)
2 Kings	184 (B1); 60 (B2); 56, 475 (B3)
1:8	30, 179 (B1); 36 (B2)
1:17–18	309 (B1)
2	247 (B1)
2:1–12	**309–13**, 321, 323 (B1)
2:1–15	141 (B3)
2:1–8:15	244 (B1)
2:2	321 (B1)
2:3	84 (B1)
2:4	321 (B1)
2:4–15	30 (B1)
2:5	84 (B1)
2:6	321 (B1)
2:11	294 (B2)
2:11–12	56 (B2)
2:13–14	294 (B2)
3:1–3	310 (B1)
3:13	225 (B1)
4:1–7	180, 460 (B3)
4:38–41	180 (B3)
4:41	180 (B3)
4:42–44	**179–83**, 185, 193 (B3)
5	246 (B1)
5:1–14	**244–48**, 250 (B1)

2 Kings (*continued*)
5:1–27   426 (B3)
5:15   245 (B1)
5:15–19   245 (B1)
5:19–27   245 (B1)
6:5–6   245 (B1)
6:17   313 (B1)
7:9   84 (B1)
9:3   111 (B2)
9:7   392 (B3)
9:13   111 (B2)
9:30–37   463 (B3)
14:25   199 (B1)
17:13   392 (B3)
18:4   78 (B2)
18:13–37   19 (B1)
19:34   391 (B3)
19:35–37   19 (B1)
20:6   391 (B3)
21:8   392 (B3)

1 Chronicles   128 (B3)
16   110 (B3)
17   153 (B3)
17:4   391 (B3)
17:7   391 (B3)
20:5   91 (B3)
21:2   215n1 (B3)
22:8   75 (B3)
29:11   210 (B1)

2 Chronicles
1:7–12   326 (B3)
5   110 (B3)
7   110 (B3)
12:18   164 (B3)
12:40   164 (B3)
18:16   176 (B3)
30:5   215n1 (B3)
32:1–19   19 (B1)
35:21   225 (B1)

Ezra
5:14–17   2 (B1)
9   55 (B3)
9:7   55 (B3)

Nehemiah
8   165 (B1)
9   55 (B3)
9:20   192 (B3)

Esther   341, 475 (B3)
1:12–22   337 (B3)
1:15–22   320 (B3)
7:1–6   **335–39**, 349 (B3)
7:9–10   **335–39**, 349 (B3)
9:20–22   **335–39**, 349 (B3)

Job   118 (B1); 313 (B2);
                475 (B3)
1–2   7, 354 (B3)
1:1   **353–58**, 360 (B3)
1:8   93, 354, 392 (B3)
1:17   246 (B2)
1:20   408 (B3)
1:22   354 (B3)
2:1–10   **353–58**, 360 (B3)
2:3   392 (B3)
2:8   408 (B3)
2:10   116 (B1)
2:12–13   408 (B3)
3–31   373 (B3)
3:1   373 (B3)
3:16   408 (B3)
3:21   408 (B3)
4:14   230 (B2)
5:13   137 (B3)
5:17–18   241 (B1)
6:9   442 (B3)
7:5   408 (B3)
7:21   408 (B3)
9:31   408 (B3)
10:8   442 (B3)
10:9   408 (B3)
11:5–6   391 (B3)
11:7   373 (B3)
13:3   391 (B3)
13:21   442 (B3)
13:24   373 (B3)
16:15   408 (B3)
17:1   408 (B3)
17:16   408 (B3)
19:21   442 (B3)
22   373 (B3)
22:5–11   373 (B3)
22:23   373 (B3)
23   386 (B3)
23:1–9   **372–77**, 404 (B3)
23:2   442 (B3)
23:3   379 (B3)
23:3–5   391 (B3)
23:8–9   379, 408 (B3)

23:15   374 (B3)
23:16–17   **372–77**, 404 (B3)
24:9–10   374 (B3)
24:12   374 (B3)
24:21–23   374 (B3)
25   373 (B3)
28   373 (B3)
28:21   373 (B3)
28:28   326 (B3)
29:12–16   373 (B3)
29:23–25   492 (B3)
30:21   442 (B3)
31   373 (B3)
31:24   100 (B1)
31:35   391 (B3)
31:40–32:1   373 (B3)
33:31   118 (B1)
33:33   118 (B1)
35:14   373 (B3)
37:15   299, 317 (B1)
37:23   373 (B3)
38   92, 404 (B3)
38–39   317 (B2); 408 (B3)
38–41   374, 410 (B3)
38:1   310 (B1)
38:1–7   **389–94** (B3)
38:1–11   **89–95**, 97 (B3)
38:1–40:2   387, 391 (B3)
38:1–42:6   408 (B3)
38:2   410 (B3)
38:2–3   408 (B3)
38:8–11   391 (B3)
38:12–13   391 (B3)
38:17   101 (B1)
38:18   391 (B3)
38:19–20   391 (B3)
38:19–24   373 (B3)
38:21   391 (B3)
38:31   393 (B3)
38:33   391 (B3)
38:34–41   **389–94** (B3)
39:1–2   391 (B3)
39:17   391 (B3)
39:26   391 (B3)
40:3–5   386 (B3)
40:3–41   408 (B3)
40:4–5   391 (B3)
40:6–41:34   408 (B3)
40:7   408 (B3)
42   416 (B3)
42:1–6   **407–12** (B3)

42:7	391 (B3)	22:1	128, 139, 175 (B2)	38:3	241 (B1)
42:7–8	374,392 (B3)	**22:1–15**	**378–80** (B3)	40:5	180 (B2)
42:10–17	**407–12** (B3)	22:2	421 (B3)	40:6	452 (B3)
42:15	414 (B3)	22:17	176 (B2)	40:16	308 (B3)
		22:23–31	**44–45** (B2)	**41**	**265–66** (B1)
Psalms	170 (B1); 331 (B2);	**22:25–31**	**254–55** (B2)	41:1–4	241 (B1)
	356 (B3)	22:26	161, 253 (B2)	41:3	224 (B2)
1	**302–3** (B2);	22:27	45 (B2)	42	133 (B3)
	323–25 (B3)	22:31	251 (B2)	42:6–7	200 (B1)
1–2	289 (B3)	**23**	198, 235, 237,	45	118 (B1); 270 (B3)
1:2–3	305 (B2)		**238–39**, 246 (B2);	**45:1–2**	**269–71** (B3)
1:6	305 (B2)		**168–70**, 172 (B3)	45:3–5	269 (B3)
2:1–7	29 (B1)	23:1–6	176 (B3)	**45:6–9**	**269–71** (B3)
2:7	57 (B1); 99, 101 (B2);	23:4	379, 442 (B3)	45:11	270 (B3)
	399, 465 (B3)	23:6	253 (B3)	46:9	85 (B1)
2:8–14	294 (B3)	**24**	**149–51**, 153,	47	281, **285–88**, 290 (B2)
2:43–47	298 (B2)		**428–29**, 434 (B3)	47:1	289 (B2)
4	**223–25** (B2)	24:1	17 (B2)	47:4	290 (B2)
5:11	308 (B3)	24:4	153–54 (B3)	47:6–7	289 (B2)
6	96 (B2)	**25:1–10**	**28–30** (B2)	47:9	290 (B2)
6:2	330 (B2)	**26**	**359–61** (B3)	**48**	**132–34** (B3)
6:33	206 (B3)	27:1	147 (B1); 211 (B2)	48:6	488 (B3)
6:50–51	206 (B3)	27:5	186 (B1)	50	314 (B1)
8	**359–61**, 365 (B3)	**29**	**172–73**, 176,	**50:1–6**	**314–15** (B1)
8:4	365 (B3)		180–81 (B1);	50:2	8 (B1)
8:4–6	363 (B3)		**7–9**, 11 (B3)	50:21	118 (B1)
9	98–99 (B3)	**30**	**249–51** (B1);	51	210 (B1); 96,
9–10	98 (B3)		**113–16**, 298 (B3)		104 (B2); 207 (B3)
9:9–20	**96–99** (B3)	30:5	11 (B2); 118 (B3)	51:1	203 (B3)
9:11	137 (B3)	30:11	118 (B3)	**51:1–12**	**95–98** (B2);
13	40 (B1)	31:6	200 (B1)		**219–21** (B3)
13:1	15 (B1); 32 (B2)	31:7	200 (B1)	**51:1–17**	**7–9** (B2)
14	**184–86** (B3)	**31:9–16**	**123–24** (B2)	51:7	55 (B2)
14:2	187 (B3)	31:10	330 (B2)	51:16–17	452 (B3)
15	**269–71**, 288 (B3)	31:15	180 (B2)	51:17	4 (B2)
16	314 (B2); **478–81** (B3)	31:23	308 (B3)	**54**	**323–25**, 331–32 (B3)
16:5	110 (B3)	32	96 (B2)	54:4	331 (B3)
18:26	313 (B1)	32:3–5	241 (B1)	56:4	100 (B1)
19	**64–66**, 73 (B2); 301,	34	220, 223, 249,	61:2	85 (B1)
	306–9 (B3)		416 (B3)	62	203–4, 210 (B1)
19:1–6	342 (B3)	**34:1–8**	**219–21**,	62:5	204 (B1)
19:1–14	302 (B3)		**413–15** (B3)	**62:5–12**	**203–4** (B1)
19:4	173 (B1)	34:8–22	236 (B3)	63:2	55 (B2)
19:7	273 (B3)	34:9	232 (B3)	66:9	227 (B1)
19:7–14	**340–42** (B3)	**34:9–14**	**235–37** (B3)	68:18	206 (B3)
20	**78** (B3)	**34:15–22**	**251–53** (B3)	68:20	101 (B1)
20:4	91 (B2)	**34:19–22**	**413–15** (B3)	69:9	72 (B2)
21:6	379 (B3)	34:22	249 (B3)	69:25	298, 303 (B2)
22	44–45, 142, **164–66**,	35:9	425 (B3)	72	57–58 (B1); 186,
	170, 175, 254–55 (B2);	35:22	117 (B1)		492 (B3)
	373–74, 379–80 (B3)	38	96 (B2)	**72:1–7**	**157–58**, 160 (B1)

Psalms (*continued*)
72:2 — 160 (B1)
72:4 — 159 (B1); 232 (B3)
72:10 — 155 (B1)
72:10–14 — **157–58**, 160 (B1)
72:12–14 — 232 (B3)
73–89 — 7 (B1)
73:24–25 — 43 (B3)
73:26 — 110 (B3)
74 — 4 (B1)
74:12–15 — 169 (B1)
74:13–15 — 26 (B2)
76 — 134 (B3)
78 — 206 (B3)
78:5 — 202 (B3)
78:23–25 — 192 (B3)
78:23–29 — 206, 210, **219–21** (B3)
78:30–31 — 203 (B3)
78:35 — 143 (B2)
78:70–71 — 210 (B1); 164 (B3)
78:70–72 — 176 (B3)
80 — 23, 40 (B1)
80:1–7 — 3, **7–8**, 14 (B1)
80:2 — 246 (B2)
80:3 — 40 (B1)
80:7 — 7, 40 (B1)
80:8–11 — 260 (B2)
80:16 — 3 (B1)
80:17–19 — 3, **7–8**, 14 (B1)
80:19 — 3, 40 (B1)
81 — 50 (B3)
81:1–3 — 8 (B1)
81:1–10 — **297–98** (B1); **41–44** (B3)
81:5 — 150 (B1)
81:6–10 — 299 (B1)
81:13 — 8 (B1)
82:1 — 7 (B3)
83:1 — 117 (B1)
83:9 — 70 (B1)
84 — 134, 249, **251–53** (B3)
84:11–12 — 255 (B3)
85 — 40 (B1)
85:1–2 — **23–24**, 40 (B1)
85:1–7 — 150 (B3)
85:4 — 24, 40 (B1)
85:4–7 — 23 (B1)
85:8 — 154 (B3)

85:8–13 — **23–24**, 40 (B1); **149–51**, 153 (B3)
85:9 — 26 (B1)
85:10 — 48, 154 (B3)
85:12 — 154 (B3)
86:15 — 278 (B1); 4 (B2)
87 — 134 (B3)
89 — 57 (B1); 492–93 (B3)
89:1–4 — **56–59** (B1)
89:3 — 392 (B3)
89:6–7 — 7 (B3)
89:19–26 — **56–59** (B1)
89:20 — 392 (B3)
89:20–37 — **168–70**, 176 (B3)
89:35 — 417 (B3)
89:39–52 — 493 (B3)
90 — 20 (B1); 380 (B3)
90–106 — 20 (B1)
90:4 — 15, 26 (B1)
90:5–6 — 20 (B1)
90:12–17 — **378–80** (B3)
91 — 397 (B3)
91:9–16 — **395–97** (B3)
92 — 79 (B3)
92:1–4 — **78** (B3)
92:5–11 — 79 (B3)
92:12–15 — **78** (B3)
93 — **285–88** (B2); **496–99** (B3)
93:1 — 100 (B1)
94:17 — 117 (B1)
95 — 383 (B3)
95–99 — 73 (B1)
95:7 — 246 (B2)
95:8 — 399 (B3)
96 — 68–69, **73–74**, 88 (B1)
96–99 — 286 (B2)
96:10 — 100 (B1)
97 — 84, **88–89** (B1)
97:1 — 100 (B1)
97:5 — 85 (B1)
97:8 — 85 (B1)
98 — 88, **104–5** (B1); **270–71** (B2)
98:7–9 — 101 (B1)
98:9 — 267 (B2)
99:1 — 100 (B1)
100 — 110 (B3)
102 — 96 (B2)

102:3 — 330 (B2)
103 — 20–21, 25–26 (B3)
103:1–13 — **281–83** (B1); **24–26** (B3)
103:3 — 272 (B1)
103:5 — 282 (B1)
103:8 — 227, 278 (B1)
103:14–18 — 25 (B3)
103:15–18 — 20 (B1)
103:17 — 282 (B1)
103:19 — 210 (B1)
103:21 — 7 (B3)
103:22 — **281–83** (B1); **24–26** (B3)
104 — 165 (B1); 317–19 (B2); 396, 404 (B3)
104:1–9 — **395–97** (B3)
104:7 — 107 (B3)
104:10–23 — 396 (B3)
104:15 — 318 (B2)
104:24 — 92, **395–97** (B3)
104:24–34 — **317–19** (B2)
104:29–30 — 320 (B2)
104:34 — 404 (B3)
104:35 — 318 (B2); **395–97** (B3)
104:35b — **317–19** (B2)
105 — 318 (B2)
105:9 — 417 (B3)
106 — 110 (B3)
107 — 82, 88 (B2); 97, 110 (B3)
107:1–3 — **81–82** (B2); **96–99** (B3)
107:2 — 85 (B1)
107:10–16 — 81 (B2)
107:17–18 — 81 (B2)
107:17–22 — **81–82** (B2)
107:23–32 — **96–99** (B3)
107:29 — 104 (B3)
107:33–42 — 81 (B2)
107:43 — 81 (B2)
109:8 — 298, 303 (B2)
110 — 314 (B2)
110:1 — 107 (B1); 399, 483 (B3)
110:4 — 99, 101, 168 (B2); 399, 417, 465 (B3)
111 — **218–19** (B1); **235–37** (B3)

111:5	227 (B1)	**133**	**208–9** (B2)
111:10	228 (B1); 232,	133:1	204 (B2)
	326 (B3)	137	230 (B1)
113–118	148 (B2)	**138**	**59–61** (B3)
113:5–9	41 (B1)	**139:1–6**	**188–89**, 192 (B1);
113:7	409 (B3)		**41–44** (B3)
116:1–2	**148–49** (B2)	139:7	188 (B1)
116:1–9	**306–9** (B3)	139:12	186 (B1)
116:3–11	149 (B2)	**139:13–18**	**188–89**,
116:12–19	**148–49** (B2)		192 (B1);
118	115, 183 (B2);		**41–44** (B3)
	110 (B3)	139:14	12 (B3)
118:1–2	**107–9**, **183–84** (B2)	139:19–20	42–43 (B3)
118:3–18	109 (B2)	139:24	108 (B2)
118:14–24	**183–84** (B2)	142:5	110 (B3)
118:19–29	**107–9**, 184 (B2)	143	96 (B2)
118:22	235 (B2)	145	4 (B2)
118:24	425 (B3)	145:8	278 (B1)
118:25–26	111 (B2)	**145:10–18**	**184–86** (B3)
118:26	115 (B2)	145:14	187 (B3)
118:28	180 (B2)	**146**	**287–89**, **444–46**,
119	200 (B1); 97–98 (B2);		**461–63** (B3)
	446 (B3)	146–50	234 (B1);
119:1–8	**444–46** (B3)		288 (B3)
119:9–16	**95–98**, 104 (B2)	146:1–10	283 (B3)
119:57	110 (B3)	146:3	100 (B1)
119:105	117 (B1); 211 (B2)	146:9	469 (B3)
119:130	117 (B1)	147	234 (B1)
119:176	246 (B2)	147:1	139 (B1)
120–134	133, 288, 415 (B3)	**147:1–11**	**234–35** (B1)
121:6	180 (B2)	**147:12–20**	**139–41**, 148 (B1)
122	134 (B3)	147:20	143 (B1)
123	**132–34** (B3)	**147:20c**	**234–35** (B1)
123:2	136 (B3)	**148**	**121–23**,
124	**340–42** (B3)		129–30 (B1)
125	283, **287–89** (B3)	148:12–13	125 (B1)
125:2	111 (B2)	148:14	122 (B1)
126	36, **39–41** (B1);	150	147 (B3)
	413–15 (B3)		
126:5	36, 40 (B1)	**Proverbs**	475 (B3)
127	**461–63** (B3)	1	303, 308 (B3)
129:8	76 (B1)	1–9	301, 324, 326 (B3)
130	96 (B2); **59–61**,	1:7	302, 319 (B3)
	113–16, **219–21** (B3)	**1:20–33**	**300–305** (B3)
130:1	218 (B3)	1:33	302, 308 (B3)
130:1–2	118 (B3)	2	319 (B3)
130:5	425 (B3)	2:6–15	326 (B3)
130:6–7	218 (B3)	2:7–8	302 (B3)
130:8	76 (B1)	2:21	302 (B3)
132:1–18	**496–99** (B3)	3:2	231 (B3)
132:11–12	417 (B3)	3:15	324 (B3)
3:16–18	231 (B3)		
3:18–20	324 (B3)		
3:23–26	302 (B3)		
3:33	302 (B3)		
4:11	312 (B1)		
5–7	239 (B3)		
8:1–11	302 (B3)		
8:13	302 (B3)		
8:15	231 (B3)		
8:18	231 (B3)		
8:22–31	302, 363, 391 (B3)		
9	233–34 (B3)		
9:1–6	**230–34**, 236 (B3)		
9:6	312 (B1); 231 (B3)		
9:10	236, 302, 326 (B3)		
9:13	319 (B3)		
10:1–22:6	283 (B3)		
10:27	302 (B3)		
10:29–30	302 (B3)		
11:4–5	302 (B3)		
11:19	343 (B3)		
11:21	302 (B3)		
13:13–23	343 (B3)		
14:1–3	240 (B3)		
14:27	302 (B3)		
15:33	302 (B3)		
16:22	326 (B3)		
16:31	231 (B3)		
19:13	319 (B3)		
21:9	319 (B3)		
21:19	319 (B3)		
22	283 (B3)		
22:1–2	**282–86**, 288 (B3)		
22:4	284, 302 (B3)		
22:8–9	**282–86**, 288 (B3)		
22:15	284, 319 (B3)		
22:22–23	**282–86**, 288 (B3)		
31:1–9	319 (B3)		
31:10–31	**318–22**, 324,		
	331–32 (B3)		

Ecclesiastes
3 295 (B1)

Song of Solomon 475 (B3)
1:2 265 (B3)
1:5 265 (B3)
2:8–13 **264–68** (B3)
2:12–13 270 (B3)
3:9 417 (B3)
3:11 118 (B1)

Isaiah   437 (B3)
1–5   2 (B3)
1–39   19 (B1); 119, 160, 179 (B2); 284, 424 (B3)
1:1   315 (B3)
1:7–9   19 (B1)
1:8   84 (B1)
1:10–17   67 (B3)
1:10–20   20 (B2)
1:11–17   452–53 (B3)
1:17   119 (B3)
1:18   55 (B2)
1:21–23   19 (B1)
1:29–30   209 (B1)
2:1–4   425 (B3)
2:1–5   19 (B1)
2:6–22   19 (B1)
2:12   35 (B1)
3:1–12   19 (B1)
3:13–15   19 (B1)
4:1–6   19 (B1)
4:4   349 (B3)
5   231 (B1); 146 (B3)
5:1–7   19, 184 (B1); 260 (B2)
5:1–10   260 (B2)
5:2   85 (B1)
5:16   101 (B1)
5:24–30   19 (B1)
5:26   85 (B1)
5:37   209 (B1)
6   20 (B1); 128 (B3)
6:1–3   19 (B1)
6:1–6   180 (B2)
6:1–7   78 (B2)
6:1–8   184, 210 (B1); **2–6, 8–9, 39 (B3)**
6:1–13   7 (B3)
6:3   8 (B3)
6:3–4   11 (B3)
6:5   230 (B2)
6:6–7   349 (B3)
6:8   21 (B2); 15 (B3)
6:9–10   4 (B3)
6:9–13   2–4 (B3)
7   3 (B3)
7:7   119 (B2)
7:14   180 (B2); 432 (B3)
8:8   432 (B3)
9:1–7   68, 117 (B1)
9:2   152, 185, 317 (B1)

9:2–7   **68–72**, 74 (B1)
9:4   329 (B2)
9:6   231 (B2)
10:1–2   387 (B3)
10:5   70 (B1)
10:12–19   24 (B1)
10:15   70 (B1)
10:17   69 (B1)
10:24   70 (B1)
10:26   70 (B1)
10:27   70 (B1)
11:1   70 (B1); 180 (B2)
11:1–3   117 (B1)
11:1–9   196 (B2)
11:4   70 (B1)
11:6–9   278 (B1)
11:10–12   404 (B3)
11:12   85 (B1)
11:18–20   **318–22** (B3)
12:37–41   149 (B1)
13–23   180 (B2)
13–27   424 (B3)
13:2   85 (B1)
13:8   488 (B3)
13:10   69 (B1)
13:14   176 (B3)
14:29   70 (B1)
18:4   69 (B1)
20:3   392 (B3)
21:3   488 (B3)
21:11–12   84 (B1)
24   425 (B3)
24–25   180 (B2)
24–27   424 (B3)
24:1–5   425 (B3)
24:11   180 (B2)
24:23   425 (B3)
25   182–83 (B2); 432 (B3)
25:1–2   180 (B2); 424 (B3)
25:1–9   169 (B3)
25:2   180 (B2)
25:2–3   426 (B3)
25:4–5   180 (B2)
25:5   426 (B3)
25:6–7   426 (B3)
25:6–9   179–82 (B2); **424–27**, 432, 434, 435 (B3)
25:6–10   181 (B2)
25:8   119 (B2)
25:8–9   429 (B3)
25:9   392 (B3)
25:10   182 (B2)

25:10–12   426 (B3)
26:1–2   19 (B1)
26:17–18   488 (B3)
26:19   474 (B3)
27:6   392 (B3)
28:16   119 (B2); 174 (B3)
29:1–4   19 (B1)
29:6   329 (B2)
29:13   278 (B3)
29:18   4, 410 (B3)
30:15   119 (B2)
30:19–26   19 (B1)
30:26   69 (B1); 211 (B2)
30:31   70 (B1)
31:4   246 (B2)
32:3   4 (B3)
34:8   35 (B1)
35   19, 135 (B1)
35:1–7   48 (B1)
35:1–8   30 (B1)
35:1–10   278 (B1)
35:2   285 (B3)
35:4–7a   **282–86** (B3)
35:5   4, 289 (B3)
35:5–6   100 (B1); 297, 410 (B3)
35:10   284 (B3)
36–39   19 (B1)
36:1–39:8   24 (B1)
37:18   344 (B3)
37:35   392 (B3)
37:36–38   19 (B1)
38:17   272 (B1)
39:1–8   19 (B1)
39:6   153 (B1)
40   26, 153 (B1)
40–55   2, 7, 19–20, 35, 101, 116, 260 (B1); 118–19, 160, 179 (B2); 302, 414 (B3)
40–59   20 (B2)
40–66   2 (B3)
40:1   100, 136, 153 (B1)
40:1–11   **18–22**, 23–24 (B1)
40:3   30, 85, 179 (B1); 278 (B3)
40:3–5   135 (B1)
40:9   209 (B1)
40:10   119 (B2)
40:11   135 (B1); 246 (B2)
40:18   232 (B1)
40:21–31   **229–33** (B1)

40:26	234 (B1)	45:18	261 (B1)
40:27	24 (B1)	45:21–22	100 (B1)
40:28–31	242 (B1)	45:22	261 (B1)
40:29	242 (B1)	46	221 (B1)
41:1	135 (B1)	46:9	261 (B1)
41:4	261 (B1)	47:15	100 (B1)
41:8–9	392 (B3)	48:1	261 (B1)
41:18	21 (B2)	48:1–7	261 (B1)
41:18–19	30 (B1)	48:1–8	261 (B1)
41:29	221 (B1)	48:3	261 (B1)
42:1–4	118, 179 (B2);	48:4–8	261 (B1)
	302, 392 (B3)	48:5	261 (B1)
42:1–10	261 (B1)	48:6	83 (B3)
42:1–17	261 (B1)	48:7	261 (B1)
42:3	118 (B2)	48:12	261 (B1)
42:4	119 (B2)	48:16–18	119 (B2)
42:6	69, 136, 261 (B1);	48:20–21	135 (B1)
	21, 119 (B2)	49	101 (B3)
42:8	261 (B1)	49:1	135 (B1);
42:9	261 (B1); 83 (B3)		118–19 (B2)
42:10	85 (B1); 118 (B2)	49:1–6	118, 179 (B2);
42:11–17	261 (B1)		302, 392 (B3)
42:14	488 (B3)	49:3	231 (B1); 392 (B3)
42:16	69, 185 (B1); 4 (B3)	49:4	119 (B2)
42:18–19	4 (B3)	49:5	119 (B2)
43	266 (B1)	49:6	69, 85, 231 (B1);
43:1–2	195 (B3)		21, 119, 180 (B2)
43:1–17	261–62 (B1)	49:13	100 (B1)
43:3	100 (B1)	49:22	119 (B2)
43:3–5	262 (B1)	50	120 (B2); 303 (B3)
43:6	85 (B1)	50:4–7	392 (B3)
43:8	4 (B3)	**50:4–9**	**118–22**, 179 (B2)
43:10	262 (B1); 392 (B3)	**50:4–9a**	**300–305** (B3)
43:16–17	230 (B1)	50:6–9	308 (B3)
43:18–19	266 (B1); 83 (B3)	51:1–3	99 (B1)
43:18–25	**260–64** (B1)	51:1–52:12	99 (B1)
43:19	266 (B1)	51:3	30 (B1)
43:19–20	262 (B1)	51:4	119 (B2)
43:22–24	261 (B1)	51:7	100 (B1)
43:22–25	266 (B1)	51:8	99 (B1)
43:25	266 (B1)	51:10	99 (B1)
44	4 (B1)	51:12	100 (B1)
44:1–2	392 (B3)	51:15	261 (B1)
44:1–9	262 (B1)	52	104 (B1)
44:6	261 (B1)	52–53	120, 162–63,
44:9–17	221 (B1)		175 (B2); 393–94 (B3)
44:21	392 (B3)	52:4	119 (B2)
45:1	135, 230 (B1);	52:7	24 (B1); 110 (B2)
	315 (B3)	**52:7–10**	88, **99–103** (B1)
45:1–7	29 (B1)	52:8	84 (B1)
45:4	392 (B3)	52:10	104–5, 136 (B1)
45:5–6	261 (B1)	52:13	391 (B3)
52:13–53:12	118, **159–63**,	58:1–12	
	179, 220 (B2);		
	302, 392 (B3)		
53:2–4	259 (B2)		
53:3	119 (B2)		
53:4–12	**389–94** (B3)		
53:5	119 (B2)		
53:6	246 (B2)		
53:7–8	250, 254 (B2)		
53:8	119, 175, 259 (B2)		
53:8–11	259 (B2)		
53:9	417 (B3)		
53:10	135 (B2)		
53:11	474 (B3)		
53:11–12	119 (B2)		
53:12	135 (B2)		
53:12–13	88 (B2)		
54:1–8	278 (B1)		
54:4–8	328, 431 (B3)		
54:8	431 (B3)		
54:11	100 (B1)		
54:11–12	431 (B3)		
54:13	119 (B2); 227 (B3)		
55:1–2	84 (B1); 229 (B3)		
55:10–12	135 (B1)		
55:12–13	101 (B1)		
56–59	20 (B2)		
56–66	7, 35, 116, 118,		
	152 (B1); 20, 160,		
	179 (B2)		
56:1	153 (B1); 232 (B3)		
56:1–2	40 (B1)		
56:3	250–51 (B2)		
56:4–7	232 (B3)		
56:5–7	250 (B2)		
56:6–7	426 (B3)		
56:7	13 (B1); 453 (B3)		
56:10	84 (B1)		
57:1–13	153 (B1)		
57:11	84 (B1)		
57:14	85, 153 (B1)		
57:14–21	153 (B1)		
58:1–12	**19–23** (B2)		
58:2–5	153(B1)		
58:5–10	4 (B2)		
58:6–14	153 (B1)		
59:1–15	153 (B1)		
59:9	211 (B2)		
59:15–20	153 (B1)		
59:21	153–54 (B1)		
60	157, 165 (B1)		
60–61	84 (B1)		

Isaiah (*continued*)

60–62	36, 116 (B1)
60:1	69, 116 (B1); 21 (B2)
60:1–6	**152–56**, 160 (B1)
60:2	159 (B1)
60:3	426 (B3)
60:3–5	160 (B1)
60:6–9	36 (B1)
60:9	153 (B1)
60:10	36 (B1))
60:10–13	153 (B1)
60:11	153 (B1)
60:13	153 (B1)
60:16	153 (B1)
60:18	117 (B1)
60:19	153 (B1)
60:19–20	153 (B1)
60:21	116 (B1)
61	35–36, 40–41 (B1)
61–62	130 (B1)
61:1	41, 43, 100, 117 (B1)
61:1–2	387 (B3)
61:1–4	**34–38** (B1)
61:2	117 (B1)
61:5–7	153 (B1)
61:6	153 (B1)
61:7	116–17 (B1)
61:8	116–17 (B1)
61:8–11	**34–38**, 130 (B1)
61:9	41 (B1)
61:10–11	36 (B1)
61:10–62:3	**116–20**, 122, 129 (B1)
62	84, 89 (B1)
62:1	3, 117 (B1)
62:1–2	117, 153 (B1)
62:1–5	84 (B1)
62:2	125 (B1)
62:4	36 (B1)
62:4–5	118 (B1)
62:6–12	**83–87**, 88 (B1)
62:8–9	374 (B3)
62:11	3 (B1)
62:12	36, 89, 116 (B1)
63:1–6	3 (B1)
63:7	2 (B1)
63:7–14	2, 14 (B1)
63:7–64:12	3 (B1)
63:11	176 (B3)
63:11–13	3 (B1)

63:15	3 (B1)
63:16	4 (B1)
64:1	8 (B1)
64:1–2	3 (B1)
64:1–3	8, 10 (B1)
64:1–9	**2–6**, 8, 14, 23 (B1)
64:1–11	7 (B1)
64:3	8 (B1)
64:5	8 (B1)
64:6–7	7 (B1)
64:7	3 (B1)
64:9	8 (B1)
64:11	3 (B1)
64:12	84 (B1)
65:6	117 (B1)
65:7	146 (B3)
65:8–9	392 (B3)
65:13–14	392 (B3)
65:17	8 (B1); 83, 430 (B3)
65:17–25	14, 84 (B1)
66:1–2	296 (B1)
66:7–9	488 (B3)
66:18–24	426 (B3)
66:22	430 (B3)

Jeremiah 136 (B1); 328 (B2)

1	210 (B1)
1:1	320 (B3)
1:2	320 (B3)
1:4–10	184 (B1); 2 (B3)
1:5	46 (B3)
1:6	5 (B3)
1:11–12	146 (B3)
2:31	148 (B1)
3:1–5	20 (B3)
3:21	409 (B3)
4:3–4	91 (B2)
4:8	409 (B3)
4:28	409 (B3)
4:31	488 (B3)
5:3	210 (B1)
6:1	409 (B3)
6:14	107 (B3)
6:17	84 (B1); 409 (B3)
6:24	488 (B3)
6:26	409 (B3)
7:1–15	184 (B1); 3 (B3)
7:22–23	452 (B3)
7:23	21 (B3)
7:25	392 (B3)
7:27	3 (B3)
7:29	409 (B3)

8:16	409 (B3)
8:18	46 (B3)
8:19	409 (B3)
8:21	46 (B3)
9:10	409 (B3)
9:19	409 (B3)
9:25–26	42 (B2)
10:19	237 (B1)
10:22	409 (B3)
10:24	146 (B3)
11–20	163 (B3)
11:14	410 (B3)
11:16	409 (B3)
11:18–29	325 (B3)
11:18–12:6	120 (B2); 4 (B3)
11:20	331 (B3)
11:21	320 (B3)
12:4	409 (B3)
13:16	148 (B1)
13:21	488 (B3)
14:11	410 (B3)
15:10	237 (B1)
15:10–21	120 (B2); 4 (B3)
16:5	410 (B3)
16:7–9	409 (B3)
17:10	91 (B2)
17:14–18	120 (B2); 4 (B3)
18:18–23	120 (B2); 4 (B3)
20:1–18	120 (B2)
20:7–9	237 (B1)
20:7–18	4 (B3)
22:16	285 (B3)
23:1–5	176 (B3)
23:1–6	**162–67**, 169 (B3)
23:5–8	404 (B3)
25:30–31	409 (B3)
26:5	392 (B3)
27:1–11	69 (B1)
28	215 (B1)
28:1	117 (B1)
28:14–16	215 (B1)
29:19	392 (B3)
30–33	91 (B2); 46, 409 (B3)
30:6	488 (B3)
30:10	100 (B1); 392 (B3)
31	136 (B1); 98, 104 (B2); 416 (B3)
31:7	140 (B1)
31:7–9	88 (B2); **407–12** (B3)
31:7–14	**134–38**, 148 (B1)

31:8	415 (B3)	1:1–3:16	184 (B1)	37:13	320 (B2)
31:9	140 (B1)	1:13	349 (B3)	37:23	76 (B1)
31:10	136 (B1)	1:29	291 (B3)	37:25	392 (B3)
31:10–11	143 (B1)	2:1	52 (B2)	38:17	392 (B3)
31:12	21 (B2)	**2:1–5**	**127–31**, 133,	39:15–16	331 (B2)
31:12–13	410 (B3)		137, 141 (B3)	40–48	128, 146,
31:13	140 (B1)	2:10	130 (B3)		431 (B3)
31:15	408–9 (B3)	3:17	84 (B1)	43:1–2	111 (B2)
31:27–30	91, 94 (B2)	3:20	283 (B3)	43:1–4	153 (B1)
31:31	135, 153 (B1)	4	328 (B2)	47:1–12	278 (B1)
31:31–34	**91–94**, 96–97 (B2);	7:27	330 (B2)		
	447–49 (B3)	8–10	153 (B1); 128 (B3)	**Daniel**	
31:31–36	94 (B2)	11:10	330 (B2)	1:8	179 (B1)
31:33	100 (B1); 28,	11:17–24	153 (B1)	2–6	493 (B3)
	443 (B3)	11:19	100 (B1)	3:29	100 (B1)
31:33–34	27, 448n3,	11:19–20	28 (B3)	7	282 (B2)
	483 (B3)	11:23	111 (B2)	7–12	474 (B3)
31:34	91 (B2)	12:1–8	110 (B3)	7:3	493 (B3)
31:34–37	91 (B2)	13:23	330 (B2)	7:8	493 (B3)
31:38–40	91, 94 (B2)	14:6	210 (B1)	**7:9–10**	**491–95**, 498 (B3)
32:37	88 (B2)	16	20 (B3)	7:13	14 (B1); 52 (B2);
32:38–40	91 (B2)	16:1–17	328 (B3)		497 (B3)
33:11	410 (B3)	16:25	459 (B3)	**7:13–14**	3 (B1); 315,
33:21–22	392 (B3)	17	73 (B3)		**491–95** (B3)
33:26	392 (B3)	**17:22–24**	**72**, 79, 86 (B3)	7:14	14 (B1)
34:8–22	35 (B1)	18	328 (B2)	7:23–27	14 (B1)
35:15	392 (B3)	18:1–32	184 (B1)	7:27	494 (B3)
38:1–13	120 (B2)	18:30	210 (B1)	8–12	493 (B3)
40:9	459 (B3)	20:34	135 (B1)	9	55 (B3)
42:6	459 (B3)	20:44	330 (B2)	10–12	475 (B3)
42:15–43:7	120 (B2)	23	20 (B3)	10:13	477 (B3)
44:4	392 (B3)	28:25	392 (B3)	11:33	392 (B3)
46:27–28	392 (B3)	33:2	84 (B1)	11:35	392 (B3)
47:3	329 (B2)	33:6–7	84 (B1)	12:1	480 (B3)
50:43	488 (B3)	33:11	210 (B1)	**12:1–3**	**472–77** (B3)
51:12	84 (B1)	34	246 (B2)	12:3	392, 480 (B3)
		34:2–5	176 (B3)	12:11	488 (B3)
Lamentations	137 (B1)	34:11–14	242 (B2)		
2:1	84 (B1)	34:15	246 (B2)	**Hosea**	328 (B2)
2:8	84 (B1)	34:18–19	176 (B3)	1–2	22–23, 431 (B3)
2:10	84 (B1)	34:23–24	392 (B3)	1–3	19 (B3)
2:13	84 (B1)	34:25	100 (B1)	1:2–8	278 (B1)
2:18	84 (B1)	36	328 (B2)	1:2–11	20 (B3)
3	109 (B3)	36:25	76 (B1)	1:6	19 (B3)
3:1–21	110 (B3)	36:25–28	91 (B1)	1:9	19 (B3)
3:22–33	**108–12**, 114 (B3)	36:26–27	28 (B3)	1:10	117 (B1)
3:32	118 (B3)	36:28	76 (B1); 21 (B3)	2	19, 23, 25, 32,
		37	320 (B2); 128 (B3)		328 (B3)
Ezekiel	119 (B2)	**37:1–14**	318, **328–32** (B2)	2:1–13	20–21, 23 (B3)
1	310 (B1)	37:5	320 (B2)	2:2–6	25 (B3)
1–2	128 (B3)	37:9	215 (B2)	2:2–13	276 (B1)
1–3	210 (B1)	37:11	321 (B2)	2:14–15	281 (B1)

Hosea (*continued*)
2:14–20   **276–80** (B1);
              19–23, 25, 28,
              39 (B3)
2:15   282 (B1)
2:16   282 (B1)
2:18   282 (B1)
2:18–20   282 (B1)
2:19   282 (B1)
2:21–23   277 (B1)
3–14   20 (B3)
3:1–5   278 (B1)
4:1–3   21 (B3)
5:4   20 (B3)
5:13–15   277 (B1)
6:6   452 (B3)
7:11–16   277 (B1)
9:1   459 (B3)
9:7   120 (B2)
9:8   84 (B1)
10:1–2   260 (B2)
10:13   100 (B1)
11:1–8   136 (B1)
11:8–9   278 (B1); 20 (B3)
13:14   136 (B1)
14   23 (B3)
14:4   278 (B1)

Joel
1:3–11   3 (B2)
1:4   3 (B2)
1:6   3 (B2)
1:8   3 (B2)
1:13   3 (B2)
1:16   3 (B2)
2   314 (B2)
2:1   35 (B1)
2:1–2   **2–6**, 8 (B2)
2:12–17   **2–6** (B2)
2:13   278 (B1); 8 (B2)
2:16   8 (B2)
2:17–29   4 (B2)
2:18–25   3 (B2)
2:28–32   91 (B1)
2:30–31   349 (B3)
2:32   314 (B2)
3:16–18   278 (B1)

Amos   147 (B3)
2:6–8   374 (B3)
3:12   246 (B2)
3:15   374 (B3)

5   231 (B1)
5:1–17   374 (B3)
5:6   380 (B3)
5:6–7   **372–77** (B3)
5:10–15   **372–77** (B3)
5:11–13   386 (B3)
5:14–15   380 (B3)
5:18–20   35 (B1)
5:21–24   184 (B1);
              453 (B3)
5:24   386 (B3)
6:1   135 (B1)
6:4   374 (B3)
7:1–6   146 (B3)
7:1–8:3   4 (B3)
7:7–15   **144–48**, 150 (B3)
7:10–13   157 (B3)
7:10–17   120 (B2)
7:14   147 (B3)
7:15   210 (B1)
8:1–3   146 (B3)
8:4–6   374 (B3)
8:4–7   387 (B3)
9:7   426 (B3)
9:14–15   278 (B1)

Jonah
1:1–2   203 (B1)
1:1–3   199, 204 (B1);
              5 (B3)
1:6   199 (B1)
1:8–9   199 (B1)
1:10–12   200 (B1)
2:1–6   26 (B2)
2:1–10   204 (B1)
2:10   200, 203 (B1)
3:1–5   **199–202**, 203,
              211 (B1)
3:3   204 (B1)
3:10   **199–202**, 203 (B1);
              408 (B3)
4:1   204 (B1)
4:2   200, 201, 278 (B1);
              4 (B2); 408 (B3)
4:8   200 (B1)
4:11   200 (B1)

Micah
2:1–5   4 (B3)
2:6   120 (B2); 4 (B3)
3:11   4 (B3)
4:1–4   101 (B1)

4:6–10   410 (B3)
4:6–13   488 (B3)
4:10   488 (B3)
5:2   51 (B1)
6:8   167 (B1); 41 (B2)
7:4   84 (B1)

Nahum
1:3   278 (B1)
3:2   329 (B2)

Habakkuk
1:1–15   53 (B1)
1:13–14   118 (B1)
3:3–5   241 (B1)

Zephaniah
1:7   118 (B1)
1:13   374 (B3)
3:13   100 (B1)
3:15–16   115 (B2)
3:15–17   117 (B1)
3:19   410 (B3)

Haggai
1:1–11   2 (B1)
1:5–6   374 (B3)
2:23   117 (B1); 392 (B3)

Zechariah
1:6   392 (B3)
2:2   146 (B3)
2:13   118 (B1)
3:8   392 (B3)
8:7–8   404 (B3)
8:16–17   100 (B1)
8:22   136 (B1)
9:9   113, 116 (B2)
9:13–14   25 (B2)
10:2   176 (B3)
10:8–10   135 (B1)
11:16   246 (B2)
13:7   246 (B2)
14:4–5   111 (B2)
14:5   329 (B2)

Malachi
3:1   179 (B1); 35n1,
              36 (B2); 278 (B3)
3:1–2   47 (B2)
3:1–3   30 (B2)
4:5–6   30, 47, 311 (B2)

NEW TESTAMENT

Matthew	114, 164–65, 257 (B1); 169, 274 (B2); 447n1, 464 (B3)
1:1	29, 51 (B1)
1:5–6	453 (B3)
1:6	164 (B1)
1:11	173 (B1)
1:20	164 (B1)
1:23	432 (B3)
1:25	163 (B1)
2	166 (B1)
2:1–12	154, 160–61, **163–67** (B1)
2:7–12	160 (B1)
2:10	159 (B1)
2:18–24	**353–58** (B3)
3:1–3	20 (B1)
3:9	42 (B2)
3:11	47 (B1)
3:13–16	178 (B1)
3:13–17	176 (B1)
3:14	36 (B2)
4:1–11	31 (B2)
4:4	117 (B1)
4:16	69 (B1)
4:23–25	225 (B1)
4:35–41	97 (B3)
5–7	226 (B1); 60 (B2)
5:1–13	275 (B3)
5:3	302 (B2)
5:3–12	16 (B2)
5:4	296 (B1)
5:12	141 (B3)
5:14–16	69 (B1)
5:17	61 (B2)
5:17–20	274 (B3)
5:20–26	61 (B2)
5:23–24	12 (B2)
5:27–30	61 (B2); 349 (B3)
5:33–37	61 (B2)
5:39	121 (B2)
5:43–48	453 (B3)
5:44	67 (B3)
5:48	223 (B3)
6:1–6	**15–18** (B2)
6:2–5	276 (B3)
6:4	8 (B2)
6:5	8, 25 (B2)
6:7	18 (B2)
6:7–15	15 (B2)
6:9–10	267 (B2)
6:10	61, 136 (B3)
6:11	171 (B1)
6:13	183, 356 (B3)
6:16–21	**15–18** (B2)
6:18	8 (B2)
6:20	8 (B2)
6:24	68 (B3)
6:25–34	141 (B3)
7:3–5	276 (B3)
7:20	103 (B3)
7:21	17 (B2)
8:1	25 (B2)
8:1–4	256 (B1)
8:1–11	166 (B1)
8:2	24 (B2)
8:5–13	246 (B1)
8:7	63 (B3)
8:17	392 (B3)
8:18–22	24 (B2)
8:20	493 (B3)
8:21	25 (B2)
8:26	51 (B2)
9:1	25 (B2)
9:1–7	24 (B2)
9:7	25 (B2)
9:8–17	**24–27**, 28 (B2)
9:14–17	85 (B3)
10:16	197 (B3)
10:20	324 (B2)
10:24	155 (B2)
10:35–45	392 (B3)
11:5	410 (B3)
11:11–13	46 (B1)
11:27	22 (B3)
11:28	296 (B1)
11:29–30	70 (B1)
12:1–3	26, 39 (B2)
12:1–14	305 (B1)
12:8	493 (B3)
12:9–14	219 (B2)
12:13	459 (B3)
12:42	156 (B1)
12:48–50	10 (B3)
13	86 (B3)
13:13–15	4 (B3)
13:31–32	86 (B3)
13:52	164 (B1)
13:57	141 (B3)
13:58	141 (B3)
14:13–21	191 (B3)
14:15	337 (B3)
14:15–21	232 (B3)
14:16	192 (B3)
14:17	460 (B3)
14:18–20	401 (B3)
15:8	328 (B3)
15:12–21	169 (B1)
15:33	337 (B3)
16:1–4	210 (B3)
16:10–13	18 (B2)
16:13–28	314 (B3)
16:17	22 (B3)
16:20–23	155 (B2)
16:23	222 (B2)
16:24–26	120 (B2)
17	40 (B2)
17:1–8	215, 321 (B1)
17:4	45 (B2)
17:8–14	39 (B2)
18:1–7	312 (B3)
18:3–4	369 (B3)
18:8–9	313 (B3)
18:16	141 (B3)
18:19–20	44 (B1)
18:20	432 (B3)
18:21–22	500 (B3)
18:28	22 (B3)
19:9	369 (B3)
19:16	226 (B1)
19:16–22	61 (B2); 40 (B3)
20:16	406 (B3)
20:18	493 (B3)
20:27	299 (B1)
20:28	76 (B1)
21:2	111, 114 (B2)
21:7	114 (B2)
21:7–8	111 (B2)
21:8	114 (B2)
21:10	112, 115 (B2)
21:42	174 (B3)
22:34–40	452 (B3)
22:37	141, 441 (B3)
22:37–38	156 (B2)
22:37–39	153 (B3)
23	276 (B3)
23:1–24	141 (B2)
23:8–9	393 (B3)
24	501 (B3)
24:4	222 (B1)
25:1–12	171 (B1)
25:31–40	119 (B3)

Matthew (*continued*)
25:31–46   23, 296, 307 (B2);
            68, 82, 104, 293 (B3)
25:37–40   17 (B2)
25:40   434 (B3)
25:45   434 (B3)
26:6–13   111 (B2)
26:12   111 (B2)
26:17–19   387 (B3)
26:17–29   144 (B2)
26:17–30   154 (B2)
26:23–25   169 (B1)
26:26–29   232 (B3)
26:27–28   92 (B2)
26:39   48 (B2); 136 (B3)
26:40–41   175 (B2)
26:42–44   136 B3)
27:5   298 (B2)
27:11–24   141 (B2)
27:32   114 (B2)
27:46   44, 48, 101, 165,
             175, 313 (B2)
27:51   172 (B3)
28   105 (B3)
28:5–6   195 (B3)
28:9   232 (B2)
28:10–17   169 (B1)
28:16–20   200, 230 (B2)
28:17   231 (B2)
28:18–20   312 (B1);
                     200n2 (B2)
28:19   176, 182 (B1);
                       48 (B2)
28:20   432 (B3)

Mark   114, 257 (B1);
              274 (B2); 447n1,
                      464 (B3)
1   257 (B1)
1–5   122 (B3)
1:1   209, 257 (B1); 53,
             133, 136, 139 (B2):
                      314 (B3)
1:1–3   20, 61 (B1)
1:1–8   **29–33**, 256 (B1);
               35 (B2); 160 (B3)
1:1–11   209 (B1)
1:1–13   180 (B1)
1:1–8:29   139 (B2)
1:2–3   278 (B3)
1:3   180 (B1)
1:3–4   180 (B1)

1:4   209, 240(B1);
             36 (B2); 159 (B3)
1:4–11   170, 176, **179–82**,
                      185 (B1)
1:4–13   179 (B1)
1:6   47 (B1)
1:7   47, 211, 225 (B1);
                      134 (B2)
1:7–8   26 (B1)
1:8–11   176 (B1)
1:9–13   135 (B2)
1:9–15   29, **35–38** (B2)
1:10   171, 225 (B1);
                      140 (B3)
1:10–11   321 (B1)
1:11   29 (B1); 56,
             139 (B2); 314 (B3)
1:12   240 (B1)
1:12–13   180, 243 (B1);
                       31 (B2)
1:13   226, 240 (B1);
                       53 (B2)
1:14   61, 180, 209 (B1);
                      105 (B3)
1:14–15   241 (B1); 53 (B2);
                      469 (B3)
1:14–20   206, **209–13** (B1)
1:15   14, 29, 225, 241,
              257 (B1); 133,
                      201 (B2)
1:15–20   206 (B1)
1:16–20   241 (B1); 53,
             134 (B2); 387,
                      469 (B3)
1:17   289 (B1)
1:20   291 (B1)
1:21   175 (B3)
1:21–28   219, **225–28**, 242,
             305 (B1); 134 (B2);
                      245 (B3)
1:21–39   225 (B1)
1:22   140n1 (B3)
1:24   225 (B1); 314 (B3)
1:24–25   104 (B3)
1:24–26   241 (B1)
1:25   258–59 (B1); 187,
                      315 (B3)
1:26   180 (B1)
1:27   140n1 (B3)
1:28   258 (B1); 175 (B3)
1:29–39   **240–43** (B1)
1:32–33   295 (B3)

1:32–34   241 (B1)
1:33   257 (B1)
1:34   241, 259 (B1);
             113 (B2); 85–86, 104,
             123, 314–15 (B3)
1:35   180, 241 (B1);
                      417 (B3)
1:36   258 (B1)
1:37   295 (B3)
1:39   226, 241 (B1)
1:40   241, 256 (B1)
1:40–42   241 (B1)
1:40–45   250, **256–59**,
                  271–72 (B1)
1:41   240 (B1)
1:43–45   104 (B3)
1:44   113 (B2); 123 (B3)
1:45   180, 226 (B1);
             134 (B2); 85, 295,
                      315 (B3)
2:1   241 (B1)
2:1–2   226 (B1)
2:1–5   241 (B1)
2:1–12   241, 262, **271–75**,
                  289 (B1); 277,
                  297, 345 (B3)
2:1–22   51 (B3)
2:1–3:6   271–88 (B1)
2:2   295 (B3)
2:2–4   123 (B3)
2:4   226 (B1)
2:5   134 (B2); 104 (B3)
2:1   14 (B1)
2:11   258 (B1)
2:12   140n1 (B3)
2:12–13   226 (B1)
2:13   258 (B1); 175 (B3)
2:13–14   134 (B2)
2:13–17   271, 289 (B1);
                       68 (B3)
2:13–22   **288–92** (B1); 28,
                  31–35 (B3)
2:14   39 (B3)
2:15–17   277 (B3)
2:16   271 (B1)
2:18–20   277 (B3)
2:18–22   271 (B1)
2:18–24   271 (B1)
2:18–26   292 (B3)
2:22   85 (B3)
2:23–27   277 (B3)
2:23–28   271, 289 (B1)

2:23–3:6	**304–8** (B1); 46, **49–53** (B3)	4:22	297 (B3)	6:7–12	175 (B3)
2:27	295 (B1); 67 (B3)	4:23	86 (B3)	6:7–13	157 (B3)
2:28	14, 226 (B1)	4:26	209 (B1)	6:12	159 (B3)
3	257 (B1)	**4:26–34**	79–80, **85** (B3)	6:12–13	350 (B3)
3:1	226 (B1)	4:27	344 (B3)	6:14–15	315 (B3)
3:1–6	240, 271, 289, 301 (B1); 278 (B3)	4:30	209 (B1)	**6:14–29**	209 (B1); **157–61**, 161n5 (B3)
3:1–7	61 (B3)	**4:35–41**	134 (B2); 98, **104–7** (B3)	6:15	226 (B1)
3:2	271 (B1)	4:38	226 (B1); 105 (B3)	6:17–29	367 (B3)
3:2–4	226 (B1)	4:40	200 (B2); 141 (B3)	6:30	157, 165 (B3)
3:5	256 (B1); 67 (B3)	4:40–41	123 (B3)	6:30–32	241 (B1)
3:6	226, 271, 291 (B1); 53 (B2); 85, 105, 451 (B3)	4:41	226 (B1); 139 (B2)	**6:30–34**	**175–78** (B3)
		5	257 (B1); 421 (B3)	6:30–44	160 (B3)
		5:1–13	134 (B2)	6:31	295 (B3)
		5:1–20	68 (B3)	6:31–32	180, 258 (B1)
3:7	226 (B1); 53 (B2)	5:7	226 (B1); 314 (B3)	6:33–34	295, 337 (B3)
3:7–8	85 (B3)	5:15	123 (B3)	6:34	165, 172, 192 (B3)
3:7–10	295 (B3)	5:19	123, 315 (B3)	6:35	180 (B1)
3:9	315 (B3)	5:20	226 (B1); 140n1 (B3)	6:35–44	175–76, 191, 232 (B3)
3:10	240 (B1)	5:21–24	68 (B3)		
3:11	226 (B1); 314 (B3)	**5:21–43**	118, **122–26**, 142 (B3)	6:35–52	176 (B3)
3:11–12	85, 104 (B3)			6:37	192 (B3)
3:12	259 (B1); 104 (B3)	5:23	241 (B1); 295, 368 (B3)	6:38	460 (B3)
3:13	258, 320 (B1)			6:41–42	192 (B3)
3:14–15	141 (B3)	5:24	295 (B3)	6:42	296 (B3)
3:19	209 (B1)	5:24–34	272 (B1)	6:45–52	104, 107, 176 (B3)
3:19–35	123 (B3)	5:25–34	420 (B3)	6:46	241 (B1)
3:19b	241 (B1)	5:26	345 (B3)	6:50	123 (B3)
3:20	295 (B3)	5:27	240 (B1)	6:51	226 (B1); 140n1 (B3)
3:20–22	104 (B3)	5:31	272 (B1)		
3:20–35	60–62 (B3)	5:33	123 (B3)	**6:53–56**	165, **175–78** (B3)
3:21	141n2 (B3)	5:34	272 (B1); 200 (B2); 104, 110, 421 (B3)	6:54–56	295 (B3)
3:21–22	141 (B3)			6:56	226, 240 (B1)
3:22–27	226 (B1); 134 (B2)	5:35–43	68 (B3)	7	257 (B1); 279, 283, 299 (B3)
3:31–35	86, 104, 141, 469 (B3)	5:36	200 (B2); 22, 110–11, 123 (B3)		
				7:1–8	**277–81** (B3)
3:32–35	10 (B3)	5:37	320 (B1)	7:1–23	297 (B3)
3:35	421 (B3)	5:41	240 (B1); 297, 421 (B3)	7:9–13	277–78 (B3)
4	421 (B3)			7:14	226 (B1)
4:1	175, 295 (B3)	5:42	124, 140n1 (B3)	**7:14–15**	**277–81** (B3)
4:1–20	421 (B3)	5:43	257 (B1); 104 (B3)	7:17	226, 241 (B1)
4:10	226 (B1); 85 (B3)	6:1–6	157 (B3)	7:17–20	277 (B3)
4:10–12	226 (B1); 180 (B2)	**6:1–13**	129, 137, **140–43**, 160 (B3)	7:20–23	159 (B3)
4:11	61, 257 (B1); 85 (B3)			**7:21–23**	**277–81** (B3)
		6:2	226 (B1); 175 (B3)	7:24	241 (B1)
4:11–12	257 (B1)	6:3	161, 176 (B3)	**7:24–37**	**295–99** (B3)
4:12	175, 199 (B2); 4, 85 (B3)	6:5	240 (B1)	7:25	368 (B3)
		6:5–6	199 (B2)	7:26	241 (B1)
4:13–20	85 (B3)	6:6	200 (B2); 140n1 (B3)	7:28	289 (B3)
4:17	140, 349 (B3)	6:6–30	123 (B3)	7:32	241 (B1)
4:18–19	105 (B3)	6:7	111 (B2)	7:32–33	240 (B1)
4:21–22	123 (B3)	6:7–11	159 (B3)	7:36	257 (B1); 123 (B3)

Mark (*continued*)

7:37	226 (B1); 140n1 (B3)
8	113 (B2)
8–9	388 (B3)
8–10	402 (B3)
8:11–12	210 (B3)
8:22–26	240 (B1); 51, 199 (B2); 385, 420 (B3)
8:22–9:50	385 (B3)
8:22–10:52	385, 420 (B3)
8:26	123 (B3)
8:27	111 (B2)
8:27–30	257, 322 (B1); 111 (B2)
8:27–31	312 (B1)
8:27–36	301 (B3)
8:27–38	112 (B2); **314–17** (B3)
8:27–10:52	348 (B3)
8:29	210, 240 (B1); 41 (B2); 420 (B3)
8:29–33	155 (B2)
8:30	113 (B2); 104, 123 (B3)
8:30–16:8	139 (B2)
8:31	14 (B1); 45, 111, 139, 200 (B2); 308, 331, 348, 403, 469 (B3)
8:31–33	322 (B1); 332, 422 (B3)
8:31–34	387 (B3)
8:31–35	402, 451 (B3)
8:31–38	41, 48, **51–54** (B2)
8:31–9:1	56 (B2); 420–21 (B3)
8:31–9:8	64 (B3)
8:32	53 (B2)
8:33	320 (B1); 47, 113, 140 (B2); 210 (B3)
8:34	226, 291 (B1); 45, 134, 137 (B2); 4, 157, 421, 469 (B3)
8:34–35	386, 469 (B3)
8:34–37	120, 141 (B2)
8:34–38	140 (B2); 469 (B3)
8:35	209 (B1); 4 (B3)
8:38–9:1	14 (B1)
9	257 (B1); 332, 349n2 (B3)
9:1	209, 257 (B1)
9:2	487 (B3)

9:2–8	215 (B1)
9:2–9	311, **320–24** (B1); **55–58** (B2)
9:2–10	332 (B3)
9:2–13	210 (B1)
9:3	315 (B1)
9:5	241 (B1)
9:7	180 (B1)
9:7–8	315 (B1)
9:9	14, 259, 317 (B1); 200 (B2); 104 (B3)
9:11–12	47 (B1)
9:11–13	30 (B1)
9:12	14 (B1)
9:13	47 (B1)
9:17	368 (B3)
9:23	200 (B2); 123 (B3)
9:24	123 (B3)
9:28	241 (B1)
9:30	349 (B3)
9:30–32	322 (B1); 112 (B2); 420 (B3)
9:30–37	328, **331–34**, 451 (B3)
9:31	14, 209 (B1); 52, 111, 139, 200 (B2); 348, 469 (B3)
9:31–32	422 (B3)
9:32	123 (B3)
9:33	241 (B1)
9:33–34	111, 140 (B2)
9:33–35	226 (B1); 387 (B3)
9:33–37	420, 469 (B3)
9:34	348 (B3)
9:35	240 (B1); 141 (B2); 386, 403, 469 (B3)
9:35–37	140 (B2)
9:36–37	348 (B3)
9:37	368 (B3)
9:38–50	342, **348–52** (B3)
9:42	368 (B3)
9:42–50	420 (B3)
9:43–47	311 (B3)
9:47	209 (B1)
9:49	349 (B3)
10	385–87, 416 (B3)
10:1	226, 322 (B1)
10:1–31	385 (B3)
10:2–9	386 (B3)
10:9	349 (B3)
10:10	226, 241, (B1)
10:13–14	348 (B3)

10:13–16	385–86, 420 (B3)
10:13–52	386 (B3)
10:14	256 (B1); 386 (B3)
10:14–15	209 (B1)
10:17	374–75, 421 (B3)
10:17–18	404 (B3)
10:17–22	61 (B2); 386, 469 (B3)
10:17–31	**385–88**, 402, 404 (B3)
10:18	386, 403 (B3)
10:19	386 (B3)
10:21	291 (B1); 375, 379 (B3)
10:23	380 (B3)
10:23–25	209 (B1)
10:23–31	226 (B1); 386, 469 (B3)
10:26	140n1 (B3)
10:26–27	379 (B3)
10:28	402, 469 (B3)
10:28–30	421, 469 (B3)
10:29	209 (B1)
10:29–30	141, 402 (B3)
10:31	469 (B3)
10:32	111 (B2); 140n1 (B3)
10:32–34	322 (B1); 111–12 (B2); 332, 388, 420, 469 (B3)
10:32–45	140 (B2); 385, 451 (B3)
10:33–34	14 (B1); 52, 139 (B2); 348 (B3)
10:33–37	422 (B3)
10:34	200 (B2); 331, 385, 422 (B3)
10:35–37	320 (B1); 111 (B2)
10:35–40	210 (B1); 420, 487 (B3)
10:35–41	140 (B2)
10:35–45	141 (B2); 348, 387, **402–6**, 469 (B3)
10:36	421 (B3)
10:38	397 (B3)
10:39	180 (B1)
10:41	111 (B2)
10:42–45	142 (B3)
10:43	240 (B1); 396 (B3)
10:43–44	157 (B2); 386, 469 (B3)
10:44–45	299 (B1)

10:45	14, 76, 242 (B1); 134, 140 (B2); 331, 469 (B3)	13:3–37	210 (B1)	15:15	209 (B1)
		13:5	222 (B1)	15:18	180 (B1)
		13:5–23	14 (B1)	15:21	114 (B2)
10:46–52	385, 386, 410, **420–23** (B3)	13:9–11	159 (B3)	15:22–27	403 (B3)
10:47	111 (B2); 414–15 (B3)	13:10	209 (B1)	15:26	180 (B1)
10:48	123 (B3)	13:11	324 (B2)	15:32	180 (B1)
10:49	386, 414 (B3)	13:24–27	3 (B1)	15:34	180 (B1); 44, 101, 165, 175, 308 (B2); 379, 421 (B3)
10:47–52	241 (B1)	**13:24–37**	**13–17**, 23 (B1)		
10:50–52	111 (B2): 387 (B3)	13:26–27	14 (B1)	15:37	180 (B1)
11:1–2	114 (B2)	13:30	257 (B1)	15:37–38	452 (B3)
11:1–11	**110–13** (B2)	13:32	488 (B3)	15:38	180 (B1)
11:1–13:37	451, 468 (B3)	13:35	10 (B1)	15:38–39	453 (B3)
11:5	114 (B2)	14	113, 141 (B2)	15:39	180 (B1); 56, 175 (B2); 104 (B3)
11:7	108 (B2)	14–15	133, 140 (B2)		
11:8	114 (B2)	14:1	451 (B3)	15:40	200 (B2)
11:9	108 (B2)	14:1–12	105 (B3)	15:40–41	240 (B1); 201 (B2)
11:10	105 (B3)	**14:1–15:47**	**130–37** (B2)	15:42–46	68 (B3)
11:11	115 (B2)	14:3	110 (B2)	15:43	209 (B1); 159n3 (B3)
11:11–12	110 (B2)	14:3–9	111 (B2)	15:44	140n1 (B3)
11:12–14	226 (B1); 470 (B3)	14:8	111 (B2)	15:47	200 (B2)
11:12–24	123 (B3)	14:9	209 (B1)	16	256 (B1); 105 (B3)
11:13–17	226 (B1)	14:10	209 (B1)	16:1	240 (B1)
11:15–17	13, 185 (B1)	14:10–11	105 (B3)	**16:1–8**	**199–203** (B2)
11:15–19	71 (B2); 468 (B3)	14:12–16	387 (B3)	16:5–7	180 (B1)
11:17	140n1, 453 (B3)	14:12–25	144 (B2)	16:7	180 (B1); 123 (B3)
11:18	115 (B2); 140n1, 451 (B3)	14:12–26	154 (B2)	16:8	257 (B1); 52, 134n2 (B2); 123, 140n1 (B3)
		14:22–25	232 (B3)		
11:20–26	226 (B1)	14:24	92, 140 (B2)		
11:22–24	200 (B2)	14:25	209 (B1)	16:9–11	200n2 (B2)
11:27–12:44	13 (B1)	14:26–31	210 (B1)	16:9–15	201 (B2)
12	386, 453 (B3)	14:27	140, 349 (B3)	16:9–20	199–200 (B2)
12:1–12	468 (B3)	14:28	200 (B2)	16:12–13	200n2 (B2)
12:6	180 (B1)	14:29	140 (B3)	16:13–14	231 (B2)
12:18–27	468 (B3)	14:32	258 (B1)	16:14	200n2, 201 (B2)
12:28–34	386, **451–55**, 468–69 (B3)	14:32–36	104 (B2)	16:15	200n2 (B2)
		14:32–40	241 (B1)	16:16	176 (B1)
12:29–30	443 (B3)	14:32–41	320 (B1); 136 (B3)	16:17–18	200 (B2)
12:29–31	452 (B3)	14:33	210 (B1)	16:19	200n2 (B2)
12:30	294 (B1); 441 (B3)	14:36	128 (B1); 52 (B2); 403 (B3)		
12:30–33	153 (B3)	14:43–45	105 (B3)	**Luke**	59, 66, 100, 114, 257 (B1); 203, 274, 294 (B2); 447n1, 464 (B3)
12:31	386 (B3)	14:51	199, 202 (B2)		
12:34	209 (B1)	14:53–65	257 (B1)		
12:35–37	57–58 (B1)	14:61–62	493 (B3)	1	473 (B3)
12:35–44	468 (B3)	14:62	14 (B1)	1–2	473 (B3)
12:38–44	422, 458, **468–71** (B3)	14:66–72	210 (B1); 52 (B2)	1:1–2	30 (B1)
		15:1	209 (B1)	1:1–4	185 (B2)
13	488, 501 (B3)	**15:1–47**	**138–42** (B2)	1:4	131 (B1); 297, 299 (B2)
13:1–2	452, 454 (B3)	15:2	180 (B1)		
13:1–8	483, **487–90** (B3)	15:5	114 (B2); 140n1 (B3)	1:5–25	131 (B1)
13:1–37	13 (B1)	15:9	180 (B1); 403 (B3)	1:8–20	64 (B1)
13:2	136 (B2)	15:12	403 (B3)		

Luke (*continued*)
1:12 — 95 (B1)
1:15 — 64 (B1); 234 (B2)
1:16–17 — 47 (B1)
1:26–38 — 52, **64–67**, 131 (B1)
1:26–55 — 37 (B3)
1:27 — 58 (B1)
1:28 — 95 (B1)
1:29–30 — 95 (B1)
1:32 — 58 (B1)
1:32–33 — 281 (B2)
1:34 — 58 (B1)
1:39–56 — 166 (B1)
1:41 — 234 (B2)
1:42 — 41 (B1)
1:45 — 41 (B1)
1:46–55 — 36, **56–59**, 65 (B1); 475, 480 (B3)
1:46b–55 — **39–41**, 43 (B1)
1:47–55 — 36 (B1)
1:48 — 41, 95 (B1)
1:54 — 36 (B1)
1:57–80 — 131 (B1)
1:67 — 234 (B2)
2 — 78, 85, 89, 166 (B1)
2:1–7 — 131 (B1)
2:1–14 — 73 (B1)
2:1–20 — 74, **79–82**, **94–98** (B1)
2:4 — 51 (B1)
2:8–20 — 70 (B1)
2:8–38 — 131 (B1)
2:10 — 195 (B3)
2:12 — 194 (B3)
2:14 — 106 (B1)
2:19 — 114, 166 (B1)
2:22–40 — **129–33** (B1)
2:25–38 — 100 (B1)
2:30–32 — 136 (B1)
2:32 — 100 (B1)
2:35 — 65 (B1)
2:38 — 117 (B1)
2:41–50 — 185 (B1)
2:41–51 — 184 (B1)
2:49 — 233 (B2)
2:51 — 95, 166 (B1)
2:52 — 95 (B1); 37 (B3)
3:1–6 — 20 (B1)
3:1–23 — 186 (B2)
3:2–14 — 80 (B1)
3:3 — 187 (B2)

3:16 —
3:21–22 — 176 (B1)
4:1 — 234 (B2)
4:1–13 — 31 (B2); 383 (B3)
4:14–21 — 387 (B3)
4:16–21 — 186 (B2)
4:16–30 — 246 (B1)
4:16–37 — 225 (B1)
4:17 — 250 (B2)
4:18–19 — 234, 281 (B2)
4:21 — 437 (B3)
4:24 — 141 (B3)
4:25–26 — 460 (B3)
4:26–27 — 426 (B3)
5:1 — 191 (B3)
5:12–16 — 256 (B1)
5:16 — 417 (B3)
5:17 — 68 (B3)
5:33–39 — 85 (B3)
6:1–11 — 305 (B1)
6:6–8 — 67 (B3)
6:6–11 — 219 (B2); 67 (B3)
6:12–16 — 298 (B2)
6:17–49 — 226 (B1)
6:20 — 302 (B2)
6:23 — 141 (B3)
6:27–36 — 67 (B3)
6:36 — 21 (B3)
6:40 — 155 (B2)
6:58 — 261 (B3)
7 — 192 (B2)
7:2–9 — 246 (B1)
7:22 — 410 (B3)
7:28–30 — 46 (B1)
7:44 — 156 (B2)
8 — 191, 300 (B2)
8:2 — 298 (B2)
8:9–10 — 4 (B3)
8:20–21 — 10 (B3)
8:36 — 235 (B2)
8:48 — 235 (B2)
8:50 — 235 (B2)
9:1 — 298 (B2)
9:10 — 175 (B3)
9:10–17 — 231 (B2); 191, 232 (B3)
9:12–17 — 337 (B3)
9:13 — 192, 460 (B3)
9:18–27 — 314 (B3)
9:22 — 220 (B2)
9:23–25 — 120 (B2)
9:28–36 — 215, 321 (B1)

9:31 — 294 (B2)
9:38 — 226 (B1)
9:46–48 — 41 (B1)
9:49–50 — 350 (B3)
9:51 — 304 (B3)
9:62 — 221 (B2)
10 — 300 (B2)
10:21 — 417 (B3)
10:25–28 — 452 (B3)
10:25–37 — 198 (B1); 68, 104, 453 (B3)
10:27 — 441 (B3)
10:28 — 22 (B3)
11:16 — 210 (B3)
11:31 — 156 (B1)
12:11–12 — 237 (B2)
12:12 — 220, 324 (B2)
12:13–21 — 41 (B1); 180 (B3)
13:10–17 — 254 (B1); 186 (B2)
13:16 — 255 (B1); 427 (B3)
13:18–19 — 86 (B3)
13:31–33 — 158 (B3)
13:33–34 — 141 (B3)
14:4–14 — 291 (B3)
14:15–24 — 180, 231 (B2)
15:1–2 — 80 (B1)
15:1–7 — 231 (B2)
15:2 — 266 (B2)
15:11–32 — 198 (B1); 231 (B2)
16 — 464 (B3)
16:19–31 — 41 (B1)
17:7–10 — 236 (B1)
17:19 — 235 (B2)
17:25 — 220 (B2)
18:1–8 — 291 (B3)
18:9–14 — 211 (B2)
18:11 — 187 (B3)
18:13 — 187 (B3)
18:18–25 — 41 (B1); 61 (B2)
18:42 — 235 (B2)
19:1–10 — 80 (B1); 387 (B3)
19:5 — 233 (B2)
19:9 — 427, 437 (B3)
19:29–30 — 114 (B2)
19:30 — 111 (B2)
19:33 — 114 (B2)
19:35 — 114 (B2)
19:35–36 — 111 (B2)
19:36 — 114 (B2)
19:38 — 108 (B2)
19:39 — 112 (B2)
19:45 — 115 (B2)

19:45–46	185 (B1)	24:41	293–94 (B2)	1:27	47 (B1)
19:46	250 (B2)	**24:44–53**	290, **293–96**,	1:29	154 (B2)
20:17	235 (B2)		309 (B2)	1:29–31	48 (B1)
21	501 (B3)	24:47	186 (B2)	1:29–34	149, 176 (B1)
21:1–4	460 (B3)	24:49	281 (B2)	1:29–39	196 (B1)
21:8	222 (B1)	24:50–51	111, 200n2 (B2)	1:30	46 (B1)
22:1–23	144 (B2)			1:32–34	48 (B1)
22:1–38	154 (B2)	**John**	47, 257 (B1); 68,	1:33	36, 48 (B1)
22:3–6	297 (B2)		73, 212, 274, 277,	1:34	274 (B2)
22:7–13	387 (B3)		304 (B2); 447n1,	1:36	154 (B2)
22:14–20	231 (B2)		464 (B3)	1:38	226 (B1); 156 (B2)
22:17–19	192 (B3)	1	109 (B1); 226 (B3)	1:39	50, 195 (B1)
22:17–20	232 (B3)	1–12	435 (B3)	1:41–42	196 (B1)
22:19–20	76 (B1)	1:1	30 (B1); 177, 309 (B2);	1:43	189 (B1)
22:20	92 (B2)		192, 436, 507 (B3)	**1:43–51**	185, 192,
22:27	157 (B2)	1:1–5	46 (B1); 125 (B2);		**195–98** (B1)
22:28–30	298 (B2)		363 (B3)	1:44	103 (B2)
22:39–46	220 (B2)	**1:1–14**	88, 104,	1:45–46	189 (B1)
22:41–44	174 (B2)		**111–15** (B1);	1:47	192, 196 (B1)
22:42	31, 308 (B2)		364 (B3)	1:49	189 (B1); 115,
22:44	308 (B2)	1:1–15	110 (B2)		156, 274 (B2)
22:47–54	297 (B2)	**1:1–18**	105, 108, **147–51**,	1:50	189 (B1)
22:54–62	298 (B2)		195 (B1)	2:1–10	71 (B2)
23:6–12	158 (B3)	1:1–27	196 (B1)	2:1–11	119 (B1)
23:26	114 (B2)	1:4	192 (B3)	2:3–4	262 (B2)
23:34	220 (B2)	1:4–5	88 (B2)	2:4	104, 154 (B2)
23:43	437 (B3)	1:5	169, (B1); 88 (B2)	2:11	262 (B2)
23:49	298–99 (B2)	1:6	311 (B2)	2:13	103, 115 (B2)
23:55	298 (B2)	**1:6–8**	36, **46–50** (B1)	**2:13–22**	68, **71–75** (B2)
23:55–56	299 (B2)	1:8–9	46 (B1)	2:14–21	16 (B3)
24	280, 299, 325 (B2);	1:9	46, 48 (B1); 115 (B2)	2:15	115 (B2)
	105 (B3)	1:9–14	46 (B1)	2:17	115 (B2)
24:1–12	191 (B2)	1:10	117 (B2)	2:19	115 (B2)
24:7	220 (B2)	1:10–11	136 (B1); 309 (B2)	2:22	115 (B2)
24:10–11	298 (B2)	1:11	143 (B1)	2:23	103, 115 (B2)
24:11	65 (B1); 198 (B2)	1:12	274 (B2); 210,	3	175 (B2); 11 (B3)
24:13–27	312 (B1)		466 (B3)	3–4	507 (B3)
24:13–35	200n2 (B2)	1:13	274 (B2)	3:1	258 (B2)
24:16	232 (B2)	1:14	46, 58 (B1); 72, 117,	3:1–8	11, 466 (B3)
24:25–27	293 (B2)		126, 175–77, 257 (B2);	3:1–10	47 (B1)
24:26	220 (B2)		192, 381 (B3)	3:1–12	71 (B2)
24:30	231 (B2)	1:15	46 (B1); 110 (B2)	**3:1–17**	**14–18** (B3)
24:30–31	293 (B2)	1:16	311 (B2)	3:2	148 (B1); 156,
24:31–32	231, 293 (B2)	1:16–18	46 (B1)		175 (B2)
24:32	293 (B2)	1:17	140 (B1); 72 (B2)	3:3	87, 258, 274 (B2)
24:33	230 (B2)	1:17–18	46 (B1)	3:4	242 (B3)
24:35	293 (B2)	1:18	227, 257, 274,	3:5	87, 258, 274 (B2)
24:36–43	200n2 (B2)		309 (B2)	3:5–6	11 (B3)
24:36–53	280 (B2)	**1:19–28**	36, **46–50** (B1)	3:5–8	31 (B1)
24:36b–48	**230–33** (B2)	1:19–36	46 (B1)	3:7	274 (B2)
24:37	293–94 (B2)	1:21	47 (B1)	3:14–15	78 (B2)
24:39	293 (B2)	1:23	43 (B1)	**3:14–21**	**87–90**, 104 (B2)

John (*continued*)

3:16	52, 103, 117, 246, 277, 306, 309, 311 (B2); 193, 210, 243, 399, 435–36, 466 (B3)
3:16–17	115, 154, 257 (B2)
3:16–18	177 (B2)
3:17	116, 175, 309 (B2); 344 (B3)
3:18	257, 274 (B2)
3:18–24	156 (B2)
3:19	148 (B1)
3:19–21	88 (B2)
3:20	48 (B1)
3:20–35	**67–71 (B3)**
3:22–30	46 (B1)
3:30	47, 149 (B1)
3:31	112 (B1); 115 (B2)
3:31–36	506 (B3)
3:36	437 (B3)
4:1–41	191 (B2)
4:7–21	156 (B2)
4:7–42	177 (B2)
4:9–15	211 (B3)
4:11	242 (B3)
4:11–15	175 (B2)
4:14	88 (B2); 243 (B3)
4:16–30	40 (B1)
4:19	47 (B1)
4:21	104 (B2)
4:21–23	154 (B2)
4:22	176, 177 (B2)
4:23	104 (B2)
4:25	115 (B2)
4:39	47 (B1); 324 (B2)
4:42	103, 257 (B2)
4:44	141 (B3)
4:46–54	177 (B2)
5:1	115 (B2)
5:1–9	37 (B2)
5:1–15	435 (B3)
5:1–18	191 (B2)
5:1–47	191 (B3)
5:2–18	219 (B2)
5:8	344 (B3)
5:14	272 (B1)
5:17–23	436 (B3)
5:19	112 (B1)
5:20	112 (B1)
5:21–22	88 (B2)
5:24	88 (B2); 437 (B3)

5:24–29	436 (B3)
5:25	104 (B2)
5:26–27	88 (B2)
5:28	104 (B2)
5:29	88 (B2)
5:30	112 (B1)
5:32–33	47 (B1)
5:33	324 (B2)
5:33–39	304 (B2)
5:34	304 (B2)
5:36	149 (B1)
5:36–37	112 (B1)
5:37	324 (B2)
5:39	47, 149 (B1)
5:43	115 (B2)
5:46	149 (B1)
6	226–27, 260 (B3)
6:1–21	180, **191–95 (B3)**
6:1–23	209 (B3)
6:1–59	73 (B2)
6:2	435 (B3)
6:4	103, 115 (B2)
6:5–13	337 (B3)
6:5–15	232 (B3)
6:9	460 (B3)
6:11	193 (B3)
6:13	346 (B3)
6:14	47 (B1)
6:15	115 (B2); 227 (B3)
6:17–20	148 (B1)
6:20	211 (B3)
6:22–23	175 (B3)
6:24–35	**209–13 (B3)**
6:25–35	198 (B3)
6:25–59	206 (B3)
6:25–71	191–92 (B3)
6:26	198 (B3)
6:28–29	274 (B2)
6:29	198 (B3)
6:31–35	192 (B3)
6:33	198 (B3)
6:35	260, 309 (B2); 193, 198, 217, **226–29 (B3)**
6:35–40	88 (B2)
6:36–71	211 (B3)
6:38	112 (B1)
6:41–51	**226–29 (B3)**
6:42	112 (B1)
6:46	88 (B2)
6:48	260 (B2); 192 (B3)
6:51	88 (B2); 192 (B3)

6:51–58	**242–45 (B3)**
6:54	228 (B3)
6:56	260 (B2)
6:56–58	250 (B3)
6:56–69	255, **259–73 (B3)**
6:68	156 (B2)
7:1	72 (B2)
7:1–52	191 (B3)
7:6	104 (B2)
7:8	104 (B2)
7:10	115 (B2)
7:13	214 (B2)
7:16	112 (B1)
7:20	72 (B2)
7:25	72 (B2)
7:30	72, 104 (B2)
7:31	115 (B2)
7:32	72 (B2)
7:37–39	31 (B1)
7:40	47 (B1)
7:44–45	72 (B2)
7:45–52	47, 112 (B1); 15–16 (B3)
7:50–52	88 (B2)
8:4	156 (B2)
8:12	46, 185 (B1); 88, 175, 261, 309 (B2); 193 (B3)
8:12–13	148 (B1)
8:14	115 (B2)
8:17	141 (B3)
8:20	104 (B2)
8:23	88 (B2)
8:28	88 (B2)
8:31–33	325 (B3)
8:31–38	176 (B2)
8:32	104 (B2)
8:34	193 (B3)
8:39–59	149 (B1)
8:42	112 (B1); 88, 115 (B2)
8:44	175–76 (B2)
8:45–47	506 (B3)
8:47	506 (B3)
8:48	72 (B2)
8:48–52	112 (B1)
8:52	72 (B2)
8:56–58	47 (B1)
8:59	72 (B2)
9	196 (B1); 191, 325 (B2)
9–10	246 (B2)

9:1–3	246 (B2); 343 (B3)	11:3	156 (B2)	12:37–43	48 (B1)
9:1–11	435 (B3)	11:4	274 (B2)	12:45	112 (B1)
9:2	156 (B2); 163 (B3)	11:8	156 (B2)	12:46	88 (B2)
9:2–3	354 (B3)	11:12	156 (B2)	12:50	112 (B1)
9:4	147 (B1)	11:18	110 (B2)	13	144, 154, 276 (B2)
9:5	46 (B1); 261 (B2)	11:21	156 (B2); 435 (B3)	13–16	308 (B2)
9:13–34	47 (B1)	11:24	437 (B3)	13–17	260, 276, 324 (B2)
9:13–41	214 (B2)	11:25	193, 243 (B3)	13–20	276 (B2)
9:16	112 (B1); 72 (B2)	11:25–26	261 (B2); 435 (B3)	13:1	104, 117, 261 (B2)
9:17	47 (B1)	11:25-27	435 (B3)	13:1–7	276 (B2)
9:22	214, 261 (B2)	11:27	115, 274 (B2)	**13:1–17**	151, **154–58** (B2)
9:24	72 (B2)	11:32	156 (B2); 435 (B3)	13:8	116 (B2)
9:29	112 (B1)	**11:32–44**	432, 434,	13:14–17	175 (B2)
9:39–41	48 (B1)		**435–38** (B3)	13:15	277 (B2)
10	237, 246, 260 (B2)	11:33	104 (B2)	13:18–31	155 (B2)
10:2–16	**367–71** (B3)	11:34	156 (B2)	13:20	261 (B2)
10:7	261 (B2); 193 (B3)	11:41–42	308 (B2)	13:25	156 (B2)
10:10	115, 176 (B2); 450,	11:43–44	246 (B2)	13:27	261 (B2)
	466 (B3)	11:44	192 (B2)	**13:31b–35**	**154–58** (B2)
10:10–11	242 (B2);	11:45–46	436 (B3)	13:33	309 (B2)
	435 (B3)	11:45-53	436 (B3)	13:34	242, 258,
10:11	115, 175, 235, 240,	11:49–57	72 (B2)		276–77 (B2)
	261, 309 (B2);	11:52	193 (B3)	13:34–35	453 (B3)
	193 (B3)	11:53	111, 115 (B2)	13:37–38	240 (B2)
10:11–16	176 (B3)	11:55	103 (B2)	14	311 (B2)
10:11–18	242, **245–48** (B2)	11:57	115 (B2)	14–16	176 (B1)
10:12–13	235 (B2)	12	100, 104, 243 (B2)	14:1–2	274 (B2)
10:14	261 (B2)	12:1	103, 115 (B2)	14:3	115 (B2)
10:14–16	175 (B2)	12:1-8	435 (B3)	14:5–7	175 (B2)
10:15	115, 235, 240 (B2)	12:2–3	196 (B1)	14:6	116, 175, 261,
10:15–16	104 (B2)	12:7	196 (B1)		309 (B2); 193,
10:16	235, 246 (B2)	12:9	115 (B2)		466–67 (B3)
10:17	240 (B2)	12:10–11	111, 115 (B2)	14:7	112 (B1)
10:17–18	235, 242 (B2)	**12:12–16**	112, **114–17** (B2)	14:7–10	112 (B1)
10:18	115 (B2)	12:12–19	103 (B2)	14:10	112, 148 (B1)
10:20	72 (B2)	12:14	111 (B2)	14:10–12	88 (B2)
10:22	115 (B2)	12:16	115 (B2)	14:15	258, 276 (B2)
10:22–39	191 (B3)	12:17	115, 117 (B2)	14:16	324 (B2)
10:26–27	506 (B3)	12:19	112, 115 (B2)	14:18	309 (B2)
10:27–28	104 (B2); 243,	**12:20–33**	**103–6** (B2)	14:21–24	258 (B2)
	436 (B3)	12:23	103–4, 154 (B2)	14:22–25	73 (B2)
10:28	88 (B2)	12:23–24	87 (B2)	14:23	242 (B2)
10:28–29	193 (B3)	12:24	104 (B2); 46 (B3)	14:26	324 (B2)
10:30	436 (B3)	12:25–26	104 (B2)	15	260, 276 (B2);
10:31	72 (B2)	12:27	104 (B2)		259 (B3)
10:33	72 (B2)	12:27–28	242 (B2)	15:1	193 (B3)
10:39	72 (B2)	12:28	104, 154 (B2)	15:1–2	251 (B2)
10:42	246 (B2)	12:29–32	104 (B2)	15:1–7	242 (B2)
11	115 (B2)	12:31	256 (B3)	**15:1–8**	**260–64** (B2);
11:1–16	435 (B3)	12:32	88 (B2)		349 (B3)
11:1–44	110 (B2)	12:35	148 (B1); 88 (B2)	15:1–10	277 (B2)
11:1–12:11	435 (B3)	12:35–36	46 (B1)	15:2–3	261n1 (B2)

John (*continued*)

15:4–10	196 (B1)
15:5	174 (B3)
15:9–17	242, **276–79** (B2)
15:10	260 (B2)
15:12	242, 276 (B2)
15:12–17	156, 241 (B2)
15:13	245 (B2); 436 (B3)
15:13–14	267 (B2)
15:14–15	118 (B1)
15:15	198, 436 (B3)
15:16	196 (B1)
15:17	276 (B2)
15:26	149 (B1)
15:26–27	314, **324–27** (B2)
15:27	149 (B1)
16:1–2	310 (B2)
16:1–4	324 (B2)
16:4	115 (B2)
16:4–13	314 (B2)
16:4b–15	**324–27** (B2)
16:11	309 (B2)
16:20	216 (B2)
16:26–27	276 (B2)
16:28	115 (B2)
16:32	104 (B2)
17	116, 175, 276, 325 (B2)
17:1	104, 308 (B2)
17:3	308 (B2)
17:5	309 (B2)
17:6	303 (B2)
17:6–19	**308–11** (B2)
17:8	306 (B2)
17:11	104, 297 (B2); 417 (B3)
17:12	303 (B2); 193 (B3)
17:14	306 (B2)
17:17	303 (B2)
17:18	306 (B2)
17:18–20	216 (B2)
17:20–21	309 (B2); 417 (B3)
17:21	297 (B2)
17:21–22	193 (B3)
17:24	104 (B2)
18	246 (B2)
18:1–19:42	**172–78** (B2)
18:4	114 (B2)
18:6	309 (B2)
18:10–11	116 (B2)
18:15–27	116 (B2)

18:28	73, 156 (B2)
18:28–19:6	141 (B2)
18:28–19:16	72 (B2)
18:33	115, 161 (B2); 497 (B3)
18:33–37	501–2, **505–9** (B3)
18:33–38	185 (B1)
18:36	115, 161 (B2); 210 (B3)
18:36–37	114 (B2); 176 (B3)
18:37	324 (B2)
18:38	242, 509 (B3)
18:39	73, 115 (B2)
19:1	175 (B2)
19:3	115 (B2)
19:7	274 (B2); 228 (B3)
19:11	114, 161 (B2)
19:12	115, 277 (B2); 228 (B3)
19:14	73, 115 (B2)
19:14–16	228 (B3)
19:17	114 (B2)
19:19	115 (B2)
19:23–24	155 (B2)
19:30	87, 115, 126 (B2)
19:34–35	273, 307 (B2)
19:35	47 (B1)
19:38	214 (B2)
19:38–42	47 (B1); 88 (B2); 15–16 (B3)
20	192, 216, 306 (B2); 105 (B3)
20:1	436 (B3)
20:1–9	215 (B2)
20:1–18	**190–94** (B2)
20:5–7	436 (B3)
20:11–18	200n2 (B2)
20:17	232, 274 (B2)
20:19	214, 232 (B2)
20:19–23	204 (B2)
20:19–31	230, **214–18** (B2)
20:21	156, 246, 274 (B2)
20:25	231 (B2)
20:28	155 (B2); 436 (B3)
20:30	226 (B3)
20:30–31	196 (B1); 194, 263 (B3)
20:31	274, 305 (B2); 210 (B3)
21	175 (B2); 263 (B3)
21:2–14	196 (B1)

21:12	196 (B1)
21:15–19	277 (B2)
21:15–24	156 (B2)
21:18	155 (B2)
21:24–25	47 (B1)
Acts	59, 66, 100 (B1); 203, 274, 294 (B2)
1–7	281 (B2)
1:1	294 (B2)
1:1–5	219 (B2)
1:1–11	**280–84**, 286–87, 290–91 (B2)
1:3–9	290 (B2)
1:6–8	162 (B1)
1:8	95, 162 (B1); 185–86, 234, 250, 267, 294, 299, 305, 313 (B2)
1:8–9	5 (B3)
1:12–8:1	251 (B2)
1:13	298 (B2)
1:13–14	298 (B2)
1:14	66 (B1); 299–300 (B2)
1:14–17	297 (B2)
1:15–17	**297–301**, 302 (B2)
1:16	298, 303, 305 (B2)
1:18	298 (B2)
1:18–20	300 (B2)
1:20	298, 303 (B2)
1:21–22	305 (B2)
1:21–26	**297–301**, 302 (B2)
1:22	303 (B2)
1:25	297, 303 (B2)
2	217, 281, 326 (B2)
2:1–4	266 (B2)
2:1–13	219 (B2)
2:1–21	**312–16**, 318 (B2)
2:2	320 (B2)
2:3	349 (B3)
2:4	176 (B1); 234–35, 320 (B2); 239 (B3)
2:5	152 (B3)
2:6–13	320 (B2)
2:11	318 (B2)
2:13	83 (B3)
2:14	235 (B2)
2:15	171 (B1)
2:15–19	152 (B3)
2:17–21	91 (B1)
2:19–20	318 (B2)
2:21	235 (B2)
2:22	234 (B2)

2:22–35	290 (B2)	4:31	162 (B1); 205, 234–35 (B2)	9:40–41	265 (B2)
2:24	101 (B1)			10	251 (B2); 279 (B3)
2:25–31	314 (B2)	**4:32–35**	**203–7** (B2)	10:1–2	268 (B2)
2:29	235 (B2)	4:33	209 (B2)	10:1–33	185 (B2)
2:32	305 (B2)	4:36–37	204 (B2)	10:1–43	265–66 (B2)
2:33	281 (B2)	5:1–11	203–5, 316 (B2)	10:2	186 (B2)
2:34–35	314 (B2)	5:12	234 (B2)	10:4–6	268 (B2)
2:37	178 (B1)	5:18	205 (B2)	10:9	171 (B1)
2:38	91, 174, 210 (B1); 187 (B2)	5:27–32	215 (B2)	10:9–16	185 (B2)
		5:30–31	290 (B2)	10:15	187 (B2)
2:43	234, 234 (B2)	5:31	187 (B2)	10:17	186 (B2)
2:43–47	267 (B2)	5:32	305 (B2)	10:19	186 (B2)
2:44–47	203 (B2)	5:36	257 (B2); 210 (B3)	10:25–28	185 (B2)
2:47	219 (B2)	6–7	220 (B2)	10:26	164 (B1)
3:1	171 (B1)	6:1	251 (B2)	10:29	186 (B2)
3:1–10	203, 206, 219, 234 (B2)	6:1–7	249 (B2)	10:30	186 (B2)
		6:3	234 (B2)	10:30–33	186 (B2)
3:2	236 (B2)	6:5	234 (B2)	**10:34–43**	**185–89**, 191, 265 (B2)
3:4–10	205 (B2)	6:8	249 (B2)		
3:8	236 (B2)	7:37	47 (B1)	10:38	234 (B2)
3:10	219 (B2)	7:52	141 (B3)	10:39	305 (B2)
3:11–26	234–36 (B2)	7:54–60	250 (B2)	10:39–40	191 (B2)
3:12–19	**219–22**, 223 (B2)	7:55	234 (B2)	10:41	305 (B2)
3:15	235, 305 (B2)	8–12	281 (B2)	10:44	187 (B2)
3:17–26	220 (B2)	8:1–3	205 (B2); 117 (B3)	10:44–46	119 (B3)
3:18	250 (B2)	8:1–25	250–51 (B2)	**10:44–48**	**265–69** (B2)
3:19	210 (B1); 187 (B2)	8:6	249 (B2)	10:45	271 (B2)
3:19–22	47 (B1)	8:16–17	266 (B2)	10:46	176 (B1)
3:21	235, 250 (B2)	8:22	210 (B1)	10:47	271 (B2)
3:22	234 (B2)	8:26	255 (B2)	11:2–3	185 (B2)
3:26	234 (B2)	**8:26–40**	**249–53** (B2)	11:3	266 (B2)
4:1–4	236 (B2)	8:27	255 (B2)	11:17	266 (B2)
4:1–22	203, 205 (B2)	8:29	265 (B2)	11:17–18	187 (B2); 119 (B3)
4:3	206, 237 (B2)	8:31	255, 259 (B2)	11:19	250 (B2)
4:4	234 (B2); 152 (B3)	8:32–33	392 (B3)	11:22–24	205 (B2)
4:5–12	**234–37** (B2)	8:34	259 (B2)	11:24	234 (B2)
4:7–8	239 (B2)	8:35	254 (B2)	11:27–30	117 (B3)
4:8–12	235 (B2)	8:36	266 (B2)	12:1–4	117 (B3)
4:9	235 (B2)	8:36–39	178 (B1)	12:15	65 (B1)
4:10	238–39 (B2)	8:39	255 (B2)	12:20–23	164 (B1)
4:11	235 (B2)	9:1–19	210 (B1)	12:21–23	241 (B1)
4:12	239 (B2)	9:1–22	198 (B1)	13–28	196, 281 (B2)
4:13	162 (B1); 203, 220, 235, 237 (B2)	9:2	312 (B1)	13:1–14:28	174 (B1)
		9:3–6	265 (B2)	13:9	234 (B2)
4:14	220 (B2)	9:10–16	265 (B2)	13:31	305 (B2)
4:16	234, 234 (B2)	9:10–18	40 (B3)	13:32–33	399 (B3)
4:16–18	236 (B2)	9:17	234 (B2)	13:38	187 (B2)
4:22	234 (B2)	9:17–18	178 (B1)	13:40	222 (B1)
4:27–28	235 (B2)	9:27–28	235 (B2)	13:46	235, 306 (B2)
4:29	162 (B1); 203, 235 (B2)	9:32	185 (B2)	14:9	235 (B2)
		9:32–43	185 (B2)	14:15	164 (B1)
4:30	234–35 (B2)	9:34	265 (B2)	15	193 (B1)

Acts (*continued*)

15:1 — 46 (B2)
15:1–6 — 42 (B2)
15:7–9 — 187 (B2)
15:7–11 — 272 (B3)
15:9 — 187 (B2)
15:11 — 320 (B3)
15:20 — 272 (B3)
15:28–29 — 119 (B3)
15:29 — 272 (B3)
15:36–18:21 — 174 (B1)
16:14 — 103 (B2)
16:16–34 — 11 (B1)
16:33 — 178 (B1)
17:4 — 103 (B2)
17:6 — 59 (B1)
17:30 — 210 (B1)
18:1–28 — 195 (B2)
18:7 — 103 (B2)
18:15–20 — 219 (B1)
18:18–22 — 174 (B1)
18:21–22 — 215 (B1)
18:22–21:25 — 174 (B1)
18:23–19:41 — 159 (B1)
18:24–28 — 174 (B1)
19:1–7 — **174–78** (B1); 337 (B3)
19:6 — 176 (B1)
19:9 — 312 (B1)
19:10 — 195 (B2)
19:11–19 — 174 (B1)
19:35 — 470 (B3)
20:27 — 234 (B2)
20:31 — 174 (B1)
21:4 — 267 (B2)
21:10 — 267 (B2)
21:10–13 — 11 (B1)
21:25 — 272 (B3)
22:15 — 305 (B2)
22:16 — 187 (B2)
22:20 — 305 (B2)
23:8 — 234 (B2)
24:14 — 312 (B1)
24:22 — 312 (B1)
24:44–53 — 287 (B2)
26:2 — 237 (B2)
26:6 — 152 (B3)
26:16 — 305 (B2)
26:18 — 185 (B1); 187 (B2)
26:20 — 210 (B1)
27:20 — 235 (B2); 344 (B3)

27:22 — 343 (B3)
27:25 — 343 (B3)
27:31 — 235 (B2)
27:34 — 235 (B2)
28:12 — 267 (B2)
28:14 — 267 (B2)
28:31 — 235 (B2)

Romans

1–7 — 40 (B3)
1–7 — 320 (B2)
1:2 — 60 (B1)
1:4 — 60 (B1); 196 (B2)
1:5 — 60, 60n* (B1); 46 (B2)
1:9 — 60 (B1)
1:11 — 60 (B1)
1:13–14 — 60 (B1)
1:16 — 60 (B1); 47 (B2); 22 (B3)
1:16–17 — 61 (B1)
1:17 — 60 (B1); 48, 290 (B2)
1:19–21 — 47 (B2)
1:24–27 — 193 (B1)
1:29–31 — 193 (B1)
2:4 — 26 (B1)
2:14–15 — 92 (B2)
2:14–16 — 82 (B3)
2:15 — 22 (B3)
3:2 — 152 (B3)
3:5 — 137 (B3)
3:7–9 — 137 (B3)
3:8 — 135 (B3)
3:9–20 — 313 (B3)
3:20 — 22 (B3)
3:21–22 — 40 (B2)
3:22 — 291 (B3)
3:23 — 466 (B3)
3:23–24 — 153 (B3)
3:24 — 192 (B1)
3:29–30 — 60 (B1)
3:31 — 144 (B1)
4:1–3 — 293 (B3)
4:9–12 — 293 (B3)
4:13–25 — 40, 45, **46–50** (B2)
4:15 — 22 (B3)
4:18 — 45 (B2)
5–7 — 317 (B1)
5:1–5 — 257 (B2)
5:5 — 242 (B2)
5:5–11 — 101 (B1)
5:6 — 221 (B1)
5:8 — 466 (B3)

5:9–11 — 241, 257 (B2)
5:12–17 — 320 (B2)
6 — 91 (B1); 46 (B2)
6:1–2 — 211 (B2)
6:1–11 — 120 (B2)
6:3–5 — 82 (B3)
6:3–11 — 46 (B3)
6:4 — 178 (B1)
6:10 — 417 (B3)
6:11–14 — 68 (B3)
6:20–23 — 320 (B2)
6:23 — 68, 466 (B3)
7:7–8 — 28 (B3)
7:12 — 28 (B3)
7:24 — 320 (B2)
8 — 301 (B1); 321 (B2); 11, 135 (B3)
8:1 — 10 (B3)
8:1–17 — 241 (B2)
8:2 — 320 (B2)
8:4–6 — 320 (B2)
8:6 — 136 (B3)
8:10–11 — 320 (B2)
8:11 — 101 (B1)
8:12–17 — 242 (B2); **10–13** (B3)
8:13 — 320–21 (B2)
8:14 — 29 (B1)
8:15 — 125 (B1)
8:15–17 — 321 (B2)
8:17 — 29 (B1)
8:18 — 136 (B3)
8:19–23 — 136 (B1)
8:20–22 — 153 (B3)
8:21 — 321 (B2)
8:22 — 49 (B2)
8:22–27 — 314, **320–23** (B2)
8:23 — 125 (B1)
8:24–25 — 8 (B1)
8:26–27 — 44 (B1); 136 (B3)
8:27 — 381 (B3)
8:28 — 174 (B2)
8:28–29 — 136 (B3)
8:28–35 — 196 (B2)
8:29 — 100 (B3)
8:31 — 136 (B3)
8:34 — 416 (B3)
8:38–39 — 322 (B2); 106 B3)
8:39 — 213 (B2)
9 — 296 (B1)
9:1–5 — 47 (B2)

Reference	Pages
10:14	100 (B1)
10:17	216 (B2)
11:1–2	27 (B3)
11:18	47 (B2)
11:25	61 (B1)
11:33–36	60 (B1)
12:1–2	82 (B3)
12:2	206 (B1)
12:16	60 (B1)
13:1–7	62 (B2)
13:9	61 (B2)
13:11–12	26 (B1)
13:14	239 (B3)
14:2	221 (B1)
14:10	82 (B3)
14:15	289 (B2)
14:18	82 (B3)
14:23	61 (B1)
15:13	322 (B2)
15:22–23	46 (B2)
15:25–27	120 (B3)
15:26	117 (B3)
16:3	100 (B3)
16:9	100 (B3)
16:21	100 (B3)
16:23	61 (B1)
16:25–27	52, **60–63** (B1)
16:26	60n* (B1)
1 Corinthians	164, 222, 253 (B1); 69 (B2)
1	73, 150 (B2)
1–2	68 (B2)
1–4	67–68, 195 (B2); 100 (B3)
1:1–9	69 (B2)
1:1–4:20	190 (B1)
1:3–9	3, **9–12** (B1)
1:7	10 (B1)
1:10–17	69 (B2)
1:10–6:20	190 (B1)
1:10–16:4	190 (B1)
1:11	9, 205 (B1); 195n1 (B2)
1:12	198 (B2)
1:12–15	251 (B2)
1:17	9 (B1); 70–72 (B2)
1:18–25	**67–70** (B2); 118, 142, 327, 469 (B3)
1:18–31	137 (B3)
1:20	290 (B2); 470 (B3)
1:20–25	206 (B1)
1:21	240 (B1); 290 (B2)
1:23	238 (B1); 68 (B2)
1:24	290 (B2); 136, 232 (B3)
1:25	221 (B1)
1:26–28	68 (B2)
1:27	221 (B1)
1:30	290 (B2); 303 (B3)
2:1–5	221 (B1)
2:2	238 (B1); 69 (B2)
2:4	68 (B2)
2:5	84 (B3)
2:5–6	290 (B2)
2:7	290 (B2)
2:13	290 (B2)
3–4	236 (B1)
3:1–17	329 (B3)
3:9	100 (B3)
3:10–15	82 (B3)
3:13	349 (B3)
3:18	84, 137 (B3)
3:18–23	206 (B1)
3:19	290 (B2)
3:22	198 (B2)
4:4–5	82 (B3)
4:5	381 (B3)
4:10	221 (B1); 84 (B3)
5:1	205 (B1)
5:1–13	190 (B1)
5:1–7:40	205 (B1)
5:7	238 (B1)
6:1–8	190 (B1)
6:1–11	195 (B2)
6:6	317 (B1)
6:9–10	278 (B3)
6:12–20	**190–94** (B1)
6:19–20	164 (B3)
7	205, 208 (B1)
7:1	205 (B1)
7:1–16	205 (B1)
7:1–28	205 (B1)
7:1–40	190 (B1)
7:1–16:4	190 (B1)
7:5	205 (B1)
7:6	119 (B3)
7:7	205 (B1)
7:12–15	317 (B1)
7:17–25	205 (B1)
7:25	205 (B1)
7:25–28	205, 206, 208 (B1)
7:28	205 (B1)
7:29	211 (B1)
7:29–31	**205–8**, 211 (B1)
7:32–35	205–6 (B1)
7:36	205 (B1)
8	224, 236–37 (B1)
8–10	236 (B1); 195 (B2); 278 (B3)
8:1	9 (B1)
8:1–13	219, **220–24**, 227 (B1)
8:1–11:1	190 (B1)
8:12	222 (B1)
9	238–39 (B1); 150 (B2)
9:1	237–38 (B1)
9:1–15	236 (B1)
9:3–15	142 (B3)
9:5	198 (B2)
9:12	237 (B1)
9:16–23	**236–39**, 255 (B1)
9:18	243 (B1)
9:22	242 (B1)
9:24–27	250, **252–55** (B1)
10	221, 236 (B1)
10:14–11:1	237 (B1)
10:19–22	222 (B1)
10:23	190 (B1)
10:25–29	221 (B1)
10:27	317 (B1)
10:31–11:1	312 (B1)
10:33	237 (B1)
11	9 (B1)
11:1	238 (B1)
11:2	291 (B2)
11:2–16	190 (B1)
11:11	206 (B1)
11:17–19	150 (B2)
11:17–34	195 (B2)
11:20–22	150 (B2)
11:21–22	150 (B2)
11:23–25	76 (B1)
11:23–26	148, **150–53** (B2)
11:24	192–93 (B3)
11:25	92 (B2)
11:27–31	151 (B2)
11:29–30	343 (B3)
12	9, 43, 285 (B1); 150–51 (B2)
12:9	62 B3)
12:12–13	242 (B2)
12:12–28	206 (B3)

1 Corinthians (*continued*)
12:13 174 (B3)
12:27 152 (B3)
12:31 150 (B2)
13 150–51, 289 (B2)
13:1–3 118 (B3)
13:1–14:1 137 (B3)
13:12–13 151 (B2)
13:13 221 (B1); 136 (B2); 286 (B3)
14 221 (B1)
14:1–40 190 (B1)
14:6 290 (B2)
14:12 118 (B3)
14:22–23 317 (B1)
14:26 290 (B2)
14:34–35 190 (B1)
15 190, 301 (B1); 197 (B2); 474, 501 (B3)
15:1–11 **195–98** (B2)
15:1–28 63 (B3)
15:3–6 466 (B3)
15:12 195 (B2)
15:12–34 196 (B2)
15:14 101 (B3)
15:15 344 (B3)
15:20–28 290 (B2)
15:25–28 365 (B3)
15:26 426 (B3)
15:35 197 (B2); 135 (B3)
15:35–58 196 (B2)
15:40 84 (B3)
15:45 365 (B3)
15:50–54 135 (B3)
15:50–57 176 (B3)
15:51 427 (B3)
15:54 181 (B2); 425 (B3)
15:54–55 192 (B2); 427 (B3)
15:55 101 (B1)
15:58 101, 255 (B3)
16:1–4 117 (B3)
16:2–7 269 (B1)
16:10–12 284 (B1)
16:13 137, 255 (B3)
16:17 195n1 (B2)

2 Corinthians 318 (B1); 151 (B2)
1–7 64 (B3)
1:4 301 (B1)

1:4–5 316 (B1)
1:6 299 (B1)
1:8–9 45–46 (B3)
1:12 316 (B1)
1:12–2:13 100 (B3)
1:12–7:16 117 (B3)
1:14–17 269 (B1)
1:18–22 255, **267–70** (B1)
1:19–20 46 (B3)
1:22 300 (B1)
1:23–24 270 (B1)
2:3–4 136 (B3)
2:11–7:16 62 (B3)
2:12–7:16 64 (B3)
2:14 301 (B1)
2:15–16 27 (B3)
2:16–17 316 (B1)
2:17 27, 135 (B3)
3 45 (B3)
3:1 316 (B1)
3:1–6 **284–87** (B1); **27–30** (B3)
3:1–18 62 (B3)
3:3 300 (B1); 32 (B3)
3:4–6 137 (B3)
3:6 22 (B3)
3:7–11 300 (B1)
3:18 137 (B3)
4–5 64 (B3)
4:1 45, 62, 101, 137 (B3)
4:2 316 (B1); 137 (B3)
4:3–6 **316–19** (B1)
4:5 136 (B3)
4:5–12 **299–303** (B1); **45–48**, 62 (B3)
4:6 299 (B1)
4:7 298 (B1); 136 (B3)
4:8 300 (B1); 137, 274 (B3)
4:10 274 (B3)
4:10–11 300 (B1)
4:13–5:1 **62–66** (B3)
4:15 101, 118 (B3)
4:16 10 (B2)
4:16–18 81 (B3)
4:17 300 (B1)
5 137 (B3)
5:1 84 (B3)
5:1–5 316 (B1); 81 (B3)
5:1–6 64 (B3)
5:1–10 11 (B2)

5:5 81 (B3)
5:6 101 (B3)
5:6–17 **81** (B3)
5:8 101 (B3)
5:16 316 (B1)
5:16–21 100–101, 427 (B3)
5:17 68 (B2)
5:18 10 (B2)
5:18–19 82–83 (B3)
5:18–20 11 (B2)
5:19 45 (B3)
5:20 10 (B2)
5:20–21 100 (B3)
5:20b–6:10 **10–14** (B2)
6 101 (B3)
6:1 12 (B2); 101 (B3)
6:1–13 **100–103** (B3)
6:3–7 316 (B1)
6:8–10 8 (B2)
6:10 206 (B1)
6:11 300 (B1)
6:14–15 317 (B1)
6:16–17 11 (B2)
7 137 (B3)
7:1–2 316 (B1)
7:2 102 (B3)
7:2–16 100 (B3)
7:3 300 (B1)
7:6 62 (B3)
7:16 81 (B3)
8 119, 121, 180 (B3)
8:2–4 117 (B3)
8:5 118 (B3)
8:6 117 (B3)
8:7 118 (B3)
8:7–15 **117–21** (B3)
8:16 300 (B1)
8:23 100, 117 (B3)
9:1–2 117 (B3)
10–13 62, 64, 100, 117 (B3)
10:1 81 (B3)
10:10 135 (B3)
10:12 135 (B3)
10:12–17 137 (B3)
11:2 206 (B1); 135 (B3)
11:6 135 (B3)
11:13–14 135 (B3)
11:16–33 196 (B2)
11:19–20 135 (B3)
11:21–30 135 (B3)
11:23–27 45 (B3)

11:23–33	101 (B3)	5:14	291, 293
11:24–27	47 (B3)	5:15	222 (B1)
12	137 (B3)	5:19–21	278 (B3)
12:1	290 (B2); 135, 137 (B3)	5:22	26 (B1)
12:2–10	**135–39** (B3)	5:22–23	84, 86 (B3)
12:2–12	152 (B3)	5:22–26	11 (B3)
12:7	290 (B2)	6:2	274, 293 (B3)
12:8–10	142 (B3)	6:15	83 (B3)
12:9–10	101, 382 (B3)	6:17	47 (B3)
12:11	138 (B3)		
12:12	137 (B3)	**Ephesians**	164 (B1); 289n1 (B2)
12:14	137 (B3)	1	144, 146 (B1)
12:19	137 (B3)	1–3	205, 222 (B3)
12:20	135 (B3)	1:1	159 (B1)
13:1	141 (B3)	1:3	153, 437 (B3)
13:4	136, 142 (B3)	**1:3–14**	**142–46** (B1); 289 (B2); 152–56, 171 (B3)

Galatians		1:5	125 (B1)
1:4	76 (B1)	1:7–10	136 (B1)
1:12	290 (B2)	1:8–10	208 (B3)
1:15	46 (B3)	1:9	143, 160 (B1)
2:2	290 (B2)	1:13	174, 180 (B1); 187 (B3)
2:9–10	117 (B3)	**1:15–23**	84, 287, **289–92** (B2); 171 (B3)
2:19–20	120 (B2)		
2:20	63, 76 (B1); 290 (B2)	1:17–18	281 (B2)
3–4	317 (B1)	1:17–19	152, 187(B3)
3:1–5	125 (B1); 101 (B3)	1:18	187(B3)
3:2	174 (B1)	1:19	160 (B1)
3:2–3	125 (B1)	1:19–21	281 (B2)
3:5	125 (B1)	1:20	143 (B1)
3:6–9	293 (B3)	1:21	255 (B3)
3:6–14	124 (B1)	1:22–23	159 (B1); 255 (B3)
3:13	125, 192 (B1); 220 (B2)	1:23	188 (B3)
3:19–29	124 (B1)	2:1	88 (B2)
3:22	291 (B3)	2:1–2	187 (B3)
3:24–25	28 (B3)	**2:1–10**	**83–86** (B2); 171, 437 (B3)
3:26–28	160 (B1)		
3:26–29	152 (B3)	2:4	224 (B3)
3:27	155 (B2)	2:5	88 (B2)
3:28	124–25, 162 (B1); 118 (B3)	2:6	188, 205, 255 (B3)
4:4–7	**124–28** (B1)	2:8	153 (B3)
4:6	117 (B1)	2:8–9	466 (B3)
4:7	11 (B3)	2:9	240 (B3)
4:8–11	125 (B1)	2:11–12	153 (B3)
5	299 (B1)	2:11–13	152 (B3)
5:6	290 (B2)	2:11–14	152 (B3)
5:13	289 (B2)	**2:11–22**	**171–74**, 467 (B3)

2:11–23	290 (B2)
2:13	187 (B3)
2:14	161 (B1)
2:14–15	143 (B1)
2:15	239 (B3)
2:15–16	161 (B1)
2:17	153 (B3)
2:21–22	153, 188 (B3)
3:1–12	**159–62** (B1)
3:3–4	143 (B1)
3:5	290 (B2)
3:6	153 (B3)
3:8–9	143 (B1)
3:9	143 (B1)
3:10	153, 224, 240, 255 (B3)
3:12	166 (B1)
3:13	190 (B3)
3:14–21	**187–90**, 192, 207 (B3)
3:20	160 (B1); 188 (B3)
3:25–26	84 (B2)
4	224 (B3)
4–6	205, 222 (B3)
4:1	153, 207 (B3)
4:1–3	11 (B1)
4:1–6	153 (B3)
4:1–16	**205–8** (B3)
4:1–6:24	160 (B1)
4:2	289 (B2); 224 (B3)
4:5	273 (B2)
4:13	273 (B2)
4:14	153 (B3)
4:15–16	289 (B2); 224 (B3)
4:16	153 (B3)
4:17–24	153 (B3)
4:22–24	224 (B3)
4:24	222 (B3)
4:25–5:2	**222–25** (B3)
4:30	196 (B2)
4:32–5:2	225 (B3)
5:1–14	238 (B3)
5:2	76 (B1); 289 (B2)
5:8	185 (B1)
5:8–9	255 (B3)
5:8–11	223 (B3)
5:10	82 (B3)
5:14	240 (B3)
5:15	232 (B3)
5:15–20	**238–41** (B3)
5:21	233 (B3)
5:21–33	143, 206 (B1)

Ephesians (*continued*)
5:22 328 (B3)
5:27 188 (B3)
5:28–30 254 (B1)
5:32 143 (B1)
6 249 (B3)
6:10–20 161 (B1);
 254–58 (B3)
6:11–13 142 (B1)
6:11–17 153 (B3)
6:12 143, 317 (B1);
 260 (B3)
6:12–14 182 (B2)
6:17 381 (B3)
6:18–20 11 (B1)
6:19 143 (B1)
6:23 273 (B2)

Philippians
1:5 9 (B1)
1:19 346 (B3)
1:20 126 (B2)
2:1–8 142 (B3)
2:1–11 222, 312 (B1)
2:3–11 68 (B2)
2:4 118 (B3)
2:5 204 (B2)
2:5–11 299 (B1); **125–29** (B2);
 223 (B3)
2:6 117 (B1)
2:6–8 118 (B3)
2:6–11 291 (B3)
2:10–11 136 (B1)
3:6 28 (B3)
3:8 252 (B1)
3:12 252 (B1)
3:14 252 (B1); 221 (B2)
4:2–4 11 (B1)
4:8 136 (B2)
4:9 296 (B1)
4:10–20 118 (B3)
4:18 82 (B3)

Colossians
1:1–15 136 (B1)
1:12 152 (B3)
1:12–13 296 (B1)
1:13 437 (B3)
1:15 317 (B1)
1:15–20 117 (B1); 125 (B2)
1:16 223 (B3)

1:16–20 153 (B3)
1:23 273 (B2)
2:2 61 (B1)
2:8 222 (B1)
2:9–14 437 (B3)
2:18 363 (B3)
3:1 437 (B3)
3:5–8 278 (B3)
3:5–17 84 (B3)
3:11 237 (B1)
3:12 26 (B1)
3:14 289 (B2)
3:18 328 (B3)
4:10 11 (B1)

1 Thessalonians 27 (B3)
1:3 9 (B1); 290 (B2)
1:6 117 (B3)
2:3–12 142 (B3)
2:4 381 (B3)
2:13 43 (B1)
2:14 117 (B3)
2:15 141 (B3)
3:6 290 (B2)
3:12 289 (B2)
4:9–18 43 (B1)
4:13–17 437 (B3)
4:15–5:11 501 (B3)
5:1–11 43 (B1)
5:2 36 (B1)
5:4–5 223 (B3)
5:6–8 255 (B3)
5:8 290 (B2)
5:16–24 36, **42–43** (B1)
5:21 268 (B3)
5:23 210 (B3)

2 Thessalonians 27 (B3)
1:8 349 (B3)
2:3–12 487 (B3)
3:7–9 312 (B1)

1 Timothy
1:1 119 (B3)
2 206 (B1)
2:11–15 58 (B3)
5:8 317 (B1)
5:10 157 (B2)

2 Timothy
2:2 311 (B1)

2:9 343 (B3)
2:20 300, (B1)
2:22 312 (B1)
3:2–5 278 (B3)
4:5 343 (B3)
4:9–18 11 (B1)
4:18 143 (B1)

Titus
1:15 317 (B1)
2 206 (B1)
2:1–10 76, 90 (B1)
2:5 328 (B3)
2:11 91 (B1)
2:11–14 **75–78** (B1)
2:11–3:7 75, 90 (B1)
3 89 (B1)
3:4 75 (B1)
3:4–7 85, **90–93** (B1)
3:5–6 76 (B1)

Philemon
5 290 (B2)
13 11 (B1)

Hebrews 110 (B1); 449 (B3)
1 449 (B3)
1:1–3 117 (B1)
1:1–4 **362–66** (B3)
1:1–12 88, **106–10** (B1)
1:1–3:3 465 (B3)
1:2–3 401 (B3)
1:2–4 125 (B2)
1:3–4 168 (B2)
1:5 399 (B3)
1:5–14 107 (B1)
1:6–8 363 (B3)
1:10–12 100 (B1)
1:14 107 (B1); 363 (B3)
2:2 363 (B3)
2:5–12 **362–66** (B3)
2:6 361 (B3)
2:9 361 (B3)
2:10 399 (B3)
2:10–11 467 (B3)
2:10–18 467 (B3)
2:14 363 (B3)
2:17 382–83, 398,
 465 (B3)
2:17–18 100 (B2)
2:18 362 (B3)

Reference	Locator
3	107 (B1)
3:1	382–83, 398, 465 (B3)
3:8–9	107 (B1)
4:1	107 (B1)
4:7	399 (B3)
4:11–13	99 (B2)
4:12–16	**381–84** (B3)
4:14–15	398, 465 (B3)
4:14–16	99, **167–71** (B2); 448 (B3)
4:14–5:10	99 (B2)
4:15	36, 176 (B2); 467 (B3)
4:15–16	465 (B3)
4:16	379 (B3)
5	104 (B2)
5:1–4	99 (B2)
5:1–10	**398–401** (B3)
5:2	382 (B3)
5:5	465 (B3)
5:5–10	**99–102** (B2); 465 (B3)
5:6–7	168 (B2)
5:7–9	**167–71** (B2); 465 (B3)
5:8–9	397 (B3)
5:10	167 (B2); 465 (B3)
5:14	312 (B1)
6:4–6	362 (B3)
6:12	399 (B3)
6:20	399, 465 (B3)
6:20–7:17	167 (B2)
7	99 (B2); 465 (B3)
7:1	399 (B3)
7:1–10:18	99 (B2); 466 (B3)
7:3	416 (B3)
7:10	399 (B3)
7:11	399 (B3)
7:15	399 (B3)
7:17	417 (B3)
7:19	328 (B3)
7:21	417 (B3)
7:23–28	**416–19** (B3)
7:26	465 (B3)
7:28	382, 399 (B3)
8:1	290 (B2); 399, 417, 465 (B3)
8:1–6	92 (B2)
8:7	92 (B2)
8:8	107 (B1)
8:8–10	107 (B1)
8:8–12	92 (B2); 448 (B3)
8:10–12	483 (B3)
8:13	92 (B2)
9	362 (B3)
9–10	108 (B1)
9:4–5	153 (B3)
9:5	464 (B3)
9:11	399, 465 (B3)
9:11–14	447n2, 452, 465 (B3)
9:11–23	464 (B3)
9:12	108 (B1); 417 (B3)
9:15	92 (B2)
9:22	108 (B1)
9:24–28	447n2, **464–67** (B3)
9:26	108 (B1)
10	176 (B2)
10:10	417 (B3)
10:11–12	168 (B2)
10:11–16	92 (B2)
10:11–25	**482–86** (B3)
10:14	382 (B3)
10:16–17	448n3 (B3)
10:16–25	**167–71** (B2)
10:18	467 (B3)
10:19	176 (B2)
10:19–25	448 (B3)
10:20	161 (B2); 467 (B3)
10:26–39	483 (B3)
10:27	484 (B3)
10:32–34	362 (B3)
10:35	362 (B3)
10:39	484 (B3)
11	154 (B3)
11–12	168 (B2)
11:1	8 (B1)
11:8–19	293 (B3)
11:34	382 (B3)
11:38	105 (B3)
12:1	154 (B3)
12:1–2	29 (B1); 465 (B3)
12:2	40, 107 (B1); 221 (B2); 365, 382, 400 (B3)
12:14	417 (B3)
12:22	143 (B1)
12:25	222 (B1); 362 (B3)
13:2	293 (B3)
13:6	81 (B3)
13:8	418 (B3)
13:15–16	448 (B3)
13:22	362, 381, 465 (B3)
15	176 (B2)

James

Reference	Locator
1	293 (B3)
1–2	312 (B3)
1:1–2	272, 290 (B3)
1:2	274, 311 (B3)
1:4	272–74, 417 (B3)
1:4–5	326 (B3)
1:5	327, 329 (B3)
1:5–6	343–44 (B3)
1:5–8	312 (B3)
1:6	326–27 (B3)
1:6–8	327 (B3)
1:8	291, 345 (B3)
1:12–16	272 (B3)
1:13	275 (B3)
1:14–15	90 (B1); 290 (B3)
1:14–16	275 (B3)
1:15	292 (B3)
1:16	275 (B3)
1:17	327, 329 (B3)
1:17–27	**272–76** (B3)
1:18	310, 312 (B3)
1:18–19	293 (B3)
1:19–20	310 (B3)
1:19–21	346 (B3)
1:21	310, 312 (B3)
1:22	266, 271, 293 (B3)
1:24–27	292 (B3)
1:25	266, 290–91, 293 (B3)
1:26	310, 312 (B3)
1:27	272, 290, 310–11 (B3)
2:1–7	231, 327 (B3)
2:1–10	275, 289 (B3)
2:1–13	346 (B3)
2:1–17	**290–94** (B3)
2:5–7	329 (B3)
2:8	311 (B3)
2:10	311 (B3)
2:14–17	273, 275, 289, 310 (B3)
2:15–16	328 (B3)
2:17	283 (B3)
2:18–20	273 (B3)
2:18–26	293 (B3)
2:19	86, 326 (B3)
2:23	273, 311 (B3)

James (*continued*)

2:26	345 (B3)
3:1	329 (B3)
3:1–12	301, **310–13**, 327 (B3)
3:5	329 (B3)
3:5–6	275 (B3)
3:5–12	328 (B3)
3:6	272 (B3)
3:8–12	275 (B3)
3:9	291 (B3)
3:13	273, 312 (B3)
3:13–16	310 (B3)
3:13–4:3	**326–30**, 333 (B3)
3:14–16	346 (B3)
3:17	310 (B3)
3:17–18	313 (B3)
4:1–2	275, 346 (B3)
4:3	346 (B3)
4:4	272, 328 (B3)
4:5	328 (B3)
4:6	187 (B3)
4:7–8	333 (B3)
4:7–8a	**326–30** (B3)
4:8	291, 328 (B3)
4:10	187 (B3)
4:11–12	346 (B3)
5:1–6	275, 346 (B3)
5:1–8	343 (B3)
5:4–6	291 (B3)
5:6	345 (B3)
5:8–9	344 (B3)
5:10	343 (B3)
5:11	343 (B3)
5:13–20	**343–47**, 350 (B3)
5:14–15	293 (B3)
5:20	273 (B3)

1 Peter — 447n1, 464 (B3)

1:1	31 (B2)
1:3–5	32 (B2)
1:3–9	31 (B2)
1:6	31 (B2)
1:7–9	32 (B2)
1:10–11	61 (B1)
1:19	417 (B3)
1:20	32 (B2)
2:2	32 (B2)
2:9	185 (B1); 401 (B3)
2:10	135 (B1)
2:12	31 (B2)
2:13	32 (B2)
2:19–20	31 (B2)
2:21	312 (B1); 31 (B2)
2:21–24	31 (B2)
2:21–25	392 (B3)
2:22	417 (B3)
2:23	31 (B2)
3:1	328
3:9	42 (B1); 31–32 (B2)
3:14–17	31 (B2)
3:15–16	32 (B2)
3:17–18	31 (B2)
3:18–22	25, **31–34** (B2)
3:20	26 (B1)
3:22	290 (B2)
4:1	150 (B1); 31 (B2)
4:1–2	31 (B2)
4:2	32 (B2)
4:4	31 (B2)
4:7	32 (B2)
4:10	150 (B1); 31 (B2)
4:12–14	31 (B2)
4:12–19	31 (B2)
4:16	32 (B2)
5:4	246 (B2)
5:5–6	187 (B3)
5:9–10	31 (B2)
5:13	105 (B3)

2 Peter

1:1	25 (B1)
1:16–18	25 (B1)
1:16–21	25 (B1)
3	43 (B1)
3:3–4	26 (B1)
3:5–7	26 (B2)
3:8	15 (B1)
3:8–15	23–24, **25–28** (B1)
3:15–16	25 (B1)

1 John — 212–13, 274–75, 304 (B2)

1	210 (B2)
1:1	306 (B2)
1:1–2	197 (B1)
1:1–2:2	210–13 (B2)
1:2	256–57, 273 (B2)
1:2–3	304 (B2)
1:3–4	257 (B2)
1:5–7	226 (B2)
1:5–2:29	210, 225 (B2)
1:7	227 (B2)
1:8	228 (B2)
1:8–2:2	226 (B2)
2:1	416 (B3)
2:2	227 (B2)
2:3–11	210, 226 (B2)
2:4–5	257 (B2)
2:5	275 (B2)
2:6	241, 273 (B2)
2:7–8	257 (B2)
2:7–11	258 (B2)
2:8	273 (B2)
2:9	240 (B2); 223 (B3)
2:10	275 (B2)
2:11	185 (B1); 240 (B2)
2:12–14	210, 226 (B2)
2:13–14	240, 273 (B2)
2:14	257 (B2)
2:15–17	210, 226, 240 (B2)
2:17	273 (B2)
2:18	487 (B3)
2:18–28	258 (B2)
2:18–29	210, 226 (B2)
2:19	305 (B2)
2:24	257 (B2)
2:25	257 (B2)
2:27	257 (B2)
2:28	241, 257 (B2)
2:29	272, 274 (B2)
3	228, 242 (B2)
3:1–3	240, 273 (B2)
3:1–7	**226–29** (B2)
3:2–3	257 (B2)
3:4–10	226–27 (B2)
3:5	256 (B2)
3:9	257, 272–73 (B2)
3:10	240, 274–75 (B2)
3:11	275 (B2)
3:11–12	272 (B2)
3:11–24	226 (B2)
3:12	240–41 (B2)
3:13–18	240 (B2)
3:14–15	257 (B2)
3:14–24	240 (B2)
3:15	257 (B2)
3:16	235 (B2)
3:16–18	236, 275 (B2)
3:16–24	**240–44** (B2)

3:17	257 (B2)	**3 John**	210 (B2)
3:18	243 (B3)	7	305 (B2)
3:19–22	257 (B2)		
3:21	236, 257 (B2)	**Revelation**	323 (B2); 437,
3:23	257, 275 (B2)		464, 484 (B3)
3:23–24	258 (B2)	1:1	430 (B3)
3:24	257 (B2)	1:1–4	500 (B3)
4	43 (B1)	1:3	447 (B3)
4:1	241, 257, 273,	1:3–14	447 (B3)
	305 (B2); 40 (B3)	1:4	432, 502 (B3)
4:1–6	226, 242, 257 (B2)	1:4–6	401 (B3)
4:2	240 (B2)	**1:4b–8**	**500–504** (B3)
4:2–3	307 (B2)	1:8	430, 432–33 (B3)
4:2–5:4	226 (B2)	1:9–20	501 (B3)
4:4	273–74 (B2)	1:17	433 (B3)
4:6	256 (B2)	2:2–4	154 (B3)
4:7	272, 275 (B2)	2:5	210 (B1)
4:7–8	275 (B2)	2:16	210 (B1)
4:7–21	**256–59**, 272 (B2)	2:17	118 (B1); 447 (B3)
4:9	241 (B2)	2:21–22	210(B1)
4:11	241 (B2)	3:1	447 (B3)
4:12	227, 274 (B2)	3:1–19	447 (B3)
4:13	242 (B2)	3:3	210 (B1)
4:14	241, 251 (B2)	3:4–5	155 (B2)
4:15	253 (B2)	3:10–12	431 (B3)
4:16	243, 306 (B2)	3:20	466 (B3)
4:17–18	241 (B2)	3:21	432 (B3)
4:19	306 (B2)	4:1–11	432 (B3)
4:20	227, 251, 307 (B2)	4:1–13	447 (B3)
4:20–21	275 (B2)	4:8	430, 432 (B3)
5:1–5	258 (B2)	4:14–7:28	447 (B3)
5:1–6	267, **272–75** (B2)	4:14–10:18	447 (B3)
5:5–8	304 (B2)	5	145 (B1)
5:5–13	226 (B2)	5–18	430 (B3)
5:6	242, 307 (B2)	5:11–13	144 (B2)
5:6–7	273 (B2)	5:4	272 (B3)
5:6–8	257 (B2)	6:10	487 (B3)
5:9–13	303, **304–7** (B2)	7:9–17	432–33 (B3)
5:10–11	273 (B2)	7:17	176, 427 (B3)
5:11	273 (B2)	8:1–7	447 (B3)
5:11–13	257 (B2)	8:8–12	447 (B3)
5:13	211 (B2)	9–10	447–49 (B3)
5:14	241, 257 (B2)	**9:11–14**	**447–50** (B3)
5:19	240, 274 (B2)	10:7	61 (B1)
5:20	210 (B2)	11:15	216 (B2)
5:21	211 (B2)	11:17	432 (B3)
		11:19	430 (B3)
2 John	210 (B2)	12:2–6	489 (B3)
7	487 (B3)	13	432, 500 (B3)
8	222 (B1)	13:11–18	136 (B2); 487 (B3)

15:3	432 (B3)	
16:7	432 (B3)	
17	432, 500 (B3)	
17:5	136 (B2)	
17:7–14	488 (B3)	
18	432 (B3)	
19:4	432 (B3)	
19:6	430, 432 (B3)	
19:7	431 (B3)	
19:9	431 (B3)	
19:11–20:15	430 (B3)	
19:11–21	488 (B3)	
20:10	349 (B3)	
20:11–15	433 (B3)	
21	26 (B2); 503 (B3)	
21:1	25 (B2); 429 (B3)	
21:1–6a	**430–34**, 436 (B3)	
21:3–4	181 (B2); 425,	
	429 (B3)	
21:3–5	322 (B2)	
21:4	427 (B3)	
21:5–7	432 (B3)	
21:6	429 (B3)	
21:6–22:7	430 (B3)	
21:9–22:5	431–32 (B3)	
21:22	100 (B1); 73 (B2);	
	432 (B3)	
21:23–24	136 (B1)	
22	169 (B1)	
22:2	302 (B2)	
22:3	100 (B1)	
22:3–5	168 (B1);	
	432 (B3)	
22:13	433 (B3)	

OT APOCRYPHA

Tobit
13:16–17   431 (B3)

Additions to Esther 336 (B3)

Wisdom of Solomon
1:16–2:1	332 (B3)
2:12–22	332 (B3)
2:13	331 (B3)
3:1–9	432 (B3)
7:22	108 (B1); 363 (B3)
7:25–8:1	108 (B1)

Wisdom of Solomon
(*continued*)
9:9	363 (B3)
10:15	143 (B1)
10:18	135 (B1)
16:2	210 (B3)

Sirach (Ecclesiasticus)
1:4	363 (B3)
1:14	326 (B3)
24:6	135 (B1)
24:11	135 (B1)

Baruch
1–2	55 (B3)

OT PSEUDEPIGRAPHA

Ascension of Isaiah
6–11	488 (B3)

2 Baruch
26	487 (B3)
27	488 (B3)
29:8	210 (B3)
70	488 (B3)
83	488 (B3)

4 Ezra
4:33–37	487 (B3)
4:40	488–89 (B3)
4:41–42	489 (B3)
5:46–49	489 (B3)
11–12	488 (B3)
13	488 (B3)
13:31	488 (B3)

Jubilees
15:25–27	42 (B2)

Psalms of Solomon
17:4	29 (B1)
17:21–46	29 (B1)

Testament of Levi
2–5	488 (B3)

DEAD SEA SCROLLS

Hodayot (Thanksgiving Hymns)
1QH 3:7–12	488 (B3)

Serek Hayahad (Community Rule)
1QS 9:10–11	192 (B3)

NT APOCRYPHON

Acts of Peter	185–86 (B1)

APOSTOLIC FATHER

Epistle of Barnabas	185 (B1)